THE GOSPEL OF JOHN

COMMENTARY ON JOHN

Thomas Whitelaw

kregel PUBLICATIONS
Grand Rapids, MI 49501

Commentary on John by Thomas Whitelaw, © 1993 by Kregel Publications, a division of Kregel, Inc., P.O. Box 2607, Grand Rapids, MI 49501. All rights reserved.

Cover Design: Alan G. Hartman

Library of Congress Cataloging-in-Publication Data

Whitelaw, Thomas, 1840–1917
[Gospel of St. John]
Commentary on John / Thomas Whitelaw.
    p.   cm.
Originally published: Gospel of St. John. Scripture Truth Book Company.
    Includes index.
    1. Bible. N.T. John—Commentaries. I. Title.
BS2615.3.W48   1993   226.5'07—dc20   92-23991
                                                            CIP

ISBN 0-8254-3979-5 (paperback)
ISBN 0-8254-3984-1 (deluxe hardcover)

1 2 3 4 5 Printing/Year 97 96 95 94 93

Printed in the United States of America

CONTENTS

INTRODUCTION

THE Gospel of St. John has long enjoyed the double distinction of being "greatly spoken against" by unfriendly assailants and highly extolled by eager defenders. By both it has been subjected to microscopical analysis and searching criticism, conducted for the most part with unrivalled learning and skill. The most contradictory judgments have been pronounced on its intrinsic worth. It has been stigmatized as a myth (Strauss), a theological romance (Baur), a misty picture without reality (Weitzsäcker), a product of dotage and fancy (Gfrörer); it has been eulogized as "the chief gospel, unique, tender and true" (Luther), as an "echo of the older gospels in more exalted strains" (Herder), as "the heart of Christ" (Ernesti), as "the diamond among the gospels" (Lange). Whether the latter series of utterances contains the truth or not, it will be evident that the former departs considerably from the truth.

The scientific criticism of this gospel may be said to have begun with the present century. In 1792 Edward Evanson, minister of Ipswich, sounded the first note of suspicion against its apostolic origin and historic credibility, in a work entitled 'The dissonance of the four generally received evangelists'; but the assault was not seriously commenced until 1820 when Bretschneider published his 'Probabilia de evangelii et epistolarum Joannis apostoli, indole et origine.' The doubts raised by this volume were so successfully combated by Stein (1822), Usteri (1823), and others, that their author in a later publication declared them removed. After a pause of 20 years the task of demonstrating the untrustworthy character of this gospel was again resumed by Strauss, Lutzelberger, and Bruno Bauer. Along the line opened by Bretschneider the assault was advanced by Schwegler, Kostlin, and Baur, whose "critical investigations" (1844) marked a new stage in the controversy. These attacks have been followed since by efforts, conceived in the same spirit and tending in the same direction, from the pens of Zeller, Hilgenfeld, Volkmar, Keim, Hausrath, Honig, Thoma, Schenkel, Holtzmann, and others. At the same time the defence has been throughout conducted, with hardly less intrepidity and talent, by an array of Biblical scholars of acknowledged eminence—critics of the rank of Ebrard, Lücke, Tholuck, Reuss, Bleek, Beyschlag, Brückner, Meyer, Weiss, Ewald, Godet, Luthardt, Hengstenberg, Tischendorf, Alford, Sanday, Westcott, Salmon, and others—contending for both the apostolic origin and historic credibility (in whole or in part) of this simplest, yet sublimest of the gospels.

The topics falling to be discussed in connection with this gospel are principally these :—1. Its Authenticity, or the historic credibility of its contents ; 2. Its Authorship, or the writer from whom it emanated ; 3. Its Composition, or the biography of its author, with the place and date of its writing; 4. Its Purpose, or the specific aim contemplated in its preparation ; and 5. Its Plan, or the method by which that aim is sought to be carried out. Without attempting exhaustive treatment, the present essay will endeavour to furnish such a statement of each as will assist the reader to intelligently grasp what is usually styled **The Johannine Question.**

§ 1. THE AUTHENTICITY OF THE GOSPEL

The historic credibility of this gospel is disputed mainly on the following grounds :—(1) Its theological standpoint, as seen in the doctrine of the Word (Logos) with which it opens ; (2) Its artificial structure, of which a hint is given in xx. 30 ; (3) Its outline of Christ's ministry, which in a variety of ways diverges from that of the Synoptists ; (4) Its discourses of Jesus which are pronounced irreconcilable with those reported in the earlier narrations ; and (5) Its image of Christ, which, it is alleged, is wholly out of harmony with that presented in the first three gospels.

I. **The Theological Standpoint.**—The dogmatical views or speculative theories which constitute the prologue or exordium of this gospel— in particular, the doctrine of the Word or Logos, represented as a light shining in darkness, and afterwards becoming incarnate in Christ— has been pronounced absolutely fatal to the idea of its historic truthfulness. " Whoever sees a historian " says Keim (Jesus of Nazara, vol. i. p. 167) " begin with his philosophy, may with good reason feel convinced that he has before him a writer whose starting point and deepest sympathies consist in philosophic studies, whose study of history is a philosophy of history, and who in imparting it, may adapt that which actually happened, not always faithfully, to suit the points of view of his exalted contemplation of the universe." To a similar effect writes Holtzmann (Lehrbuch der historisch-kritischen Einleitung in das N. T. p. 454). Already Baur had propounded the theory that the Fourth Gospel is a freely projected religious poem (or work of the imagination) whose fundamental idea lies in the opposition between the godlike principle of light and life which appeared

in Christ and the contrary principle of darkness and death which was represented by Jewish unbelief ; that the development of the struggle between the
two principles aforesaid constitutes the leading aim of the Evangelist who for
this purpose culls, shapes, and arranges his materials in such a way as to
make them at each stage of the unfolding conflict uphold the view he has
adopted ; that from first to last the history is so dominated by the contained 'idea' that it is not so much the latter which looks out of the
former as the former which is made an appearance-form or external
clothing for the latter ; and that on this account it is idle to claim for the
fourth gospel the character of history (Kritische Untersuchungen uber die
kanonischen Evangelien (1847), pp. 80 ff.). To the objection thus stated
it seems pertinent to reply—(1) *The mere prefixing to a writing*, as is done
in this gospel, *of a doctrinal programme*, or speculative theorem, whether
philosophic or theological or both, *does not necessarily invalidate the contents
of that writing*, unless it can be shown that the author has deliberately
tampered with his materials in such a way as to make them do what otherwise they would be incapable of doing, viz., lend support to the prefixed
speculative views. That he has done so is the contention of Baur and his
school ; but it is certain that such a manipulation of facts as, on this
hypothesis, is assumed to have taken place, cannot be made out except by
imposing on the Evangelist's statements meanings they do not naturally
bear. (2) *The correspondence between 'idea' and 'history' exhibited in this
gospel is susceptible of explanation without resorting to the theory of either invention
or falsification.* Instead of the former being "only a disappearing moment
in a purely historical tendency," or the latter "merely the appearance-
form of the idea " (Baur), the true relation between both is rather that of
" equal importance, or much more of congruence, in virtue of which the
idea overheard (by the author) in the history becomes the legitimate leading star in the selection and treatment of his material " (Beyschlag, Zur
Johanneischen Frage, p. 7). In other words, if the gospel opens with
certain doctrinal views, or (so-called) theological speculations, that is not
because the author had previously imported these from Alexandrine
philosophy for the purpose of imposing them upon the history of
Jesus, but because with finer susceptibilities than those who had preceded
him in this domain possessed, he had detected as harmonious and harmonizing undertones running throughout that history, what had obviously
escaped their ears, the exalted views of Christ's person, which he places in
the forefront of his writing, which he purposes to use the facts of evangelical history at his command to illustrate, and which he firmly believes
these facts of history when properly regarded will amply bear out. This,
as all must perceive, is not writing history for a purpose, manufacturing
or modifying it to suit preconceived ideas, but setting it in such light as

will bring to visibility the ideas it contains. "It is thus that Sallust begins his history of Catiline with a philosophical dissertation," says Godet, "without anyone imagining on that account that the narrative of the conspiracy is merely a romance composed on that theme. It is not the fact which has come out of the idea; on the contrary, it is the idea which has proceeded from the contemplation of the fact" (Commentary on John's Gospel, vol. i. p. 99). (3) *It is conceivable that the speculative preface of this gospel might be erroneous and yet the history be true.* The possession of well-authenticated facts of history is not the same thing as the interpretation of their doctrinal significance; and one who showed himself incompetent as a theologian might still be capable of composing an accurate history. Hence it does not appear relevant to challenge the historic credibility of the gospel on this first mentioned ground.

II. **The Internal Structure.**—The objection here alluded to is derived from (1) the acknowledged principle of selection in accordance with which its materials were prepared (xx. 30, 31); and (2) the (alleged) manifest artificiality with which they have been arranged. " The Gospel of selection," affirms Keim, " is a one-sided gospel. Since it altogether omits many parts of the life of Jesus, and treats of another part with an almost exclusive tenacity, it gives in any case a one-sided picture of the life of Jesus, in which there is only half the truth." Again, " the artificial mysticism of the threefold form in which not only a few lesser scenes, but the whole life of Jesus is throughout woven, are another sign of the author's subjective freedom. . . . Who is responsible for the six feasts, the three passovers, for Galilee and Jerusalem with their threefold journeys and miracles? It is the author who has so smoothly polished the history of Jesus, in order that it might be called an ingenious work of ar; rather than the most solemn act of history. And who cannot see that the writer has not arranged his history in accordance with its strict reality, but at his desk, and in accordance with the fair order of his pages?" (Jesus of Nazara, vol. i. pp. 165-167). This *trinitarian* rhythm which, according to the author just cited, " is diffused with artistic skill, and, indeed, mysteriously into the most minute and delicate veins of the book " (vol. i. p. 157), is thus enlarged upon by Holtzmann, " All that the Logos does appears branched out and bounded by number arrangement. With 3 sentences begins the prologue, 3 days are distinguished in the preliminary stepping forth of Jesus in the neighbourhood of the Baptist, 3 times is Jesus in Galilee, 3 times He journeys to Judæa, 3 passovers and 3 other feasts fall within the time of His activity, 3 miracle sections fill out the Jewish and 3 the Galilean hemisphere, in 3 expressly distinguished scenes falls the discourse upon the last day of the feast of Tabernacles, in 3 utterances makes Jesus the betrayer known, 3 times is He condemned,

3 attempts to rescue Him Pilate undertakes, 3 words He speaks from the cross, after 3 days He rises, and 3 times He appears to His disciples " (Einleitung, p. 451). But with reference to this argument against the authenticity of the gospel, certain obvious reflections occur.

1. *The admission of a principle of selection in composition is not necessarily fatal to a claim of credibility on behalf of what is written.* If it were, not only would the world need to bid farewell to the delusion that it possesses authentic history of any sort, either sacred or profane, whether relating to individuals or bearing on specific times or countries ; but in particular the three Synoptical narrations whose reliability is vouched for by the above-named scholars, would have to be abandoned as equally unworthy of credit, inasmuch as they, no less than the Fourth Gospel, proceed upon a principle of selection. So universally is this recognized that demonstration of its correctness is not required. 2. *Just as little can artificial arrangement, in itself considered, be urged as a bar to historic truthfulness.* It depends entirely upon the limits within which such arrangement is exercised, and the design with which it is carried out. If cognate incidents are placed side by side for the purpose of shedding light upon some latent truth, principle, or doctrine, or of illustrating some important phase of character in the individual whose biography or history is being written, it is felt that the author who so deals with his materials cannot fairly be charged with presenting untrustworthy reports to his readers, or deprived on that account of all title to their confidence. But if, on the other hand, events are deliberately recorded out of place and out of time, with a view to uphold some preconceived theory which, in the absence of their assistance, would be left without support, then with equal readiness is it conceded that such manipulation of facts would be destructive of all claim to be regarded as authentic on the part of the document in which they were engrossed. Examples of the former kind of arrangement are of frequent occurrence in the Synoptists as, e.g. the parables of the Kingdom of Heaven in Matt. xiii. ; the series of miracles in Mark iv. 35—v. 43 ; the conversations with and about the Pharisees in Luke xiii. 22—xiv. 35. A clear illustration of the latter kind has never been produced from John. 3. *It is doubtful if too much is not made of the (so-called) threefold rhythm which is supposed to have governed the Evangelist in disposing of his materials.* Close inspection shows that this exists more in appearance than in reality. ' With three sentences begins the prologue,' but manifestly the prologue must begin somehow, and might as well commence with three clauses as with two or even one. ' Three days ' (Holtzmann), ' twice three days ' (Keim) Christ moves in the vicinity of the Baptist. But the second three are rather occupied in moving from the Baptist (i. 43, ii. 1), while of the first three it is only on the second (i. 29) that He first appears in His

forerunner's presence. Besides, it is not certain that not 6 but 7 days are included between i. 19 and ii. 1. (O. Holtzmann, Das Johannes-evangelium (1887), pp. 200, 204). 'Three times He visits Galilee, and three times He journeys to Jerusalem." In reality He presents Himself in the metropolis on *five* separate occasions (ii. 13 ; v. 1 ; vii. 10 ; x. 22 ; xii. 12). 'Three passovers and three other feasts fall within the time of His public ministry.' But this assumes that the feast of v. 1 was not a passover, which is, to say the least, doubtful (see Exposition). 'Three miracles occur in Judæa and three in Galilee.' In point of fact the Galilean miracles were four (ii. 1-11 ; iv. 46-54 ; vi. 1-14 ; 16-21), without counting xxi. 1-14. Then the discourse upon the last day of the feast of Tabernacles may as easily be divided into four scenes as into three ; and Pilate's attempts to rescue Jesus reckoned four as three (see Exposition). Hence the notion of a threefold rhythm can only be established by resorting to a little of that manipulation of which the Evangelist is believed to have been guilty. But, even if without this it could be established, the question would remain whether a claim might not also be advanced for the number seven, especially in connection with the miracles, since the number John reports in all is seven. At the seventh hour the nobleman's son begins to amend, in the miracle of feeding 5 barley loaves and 2 fishes $(5 + 2 = 7)$ constitute the starting point for the banquet, and seven disciples go a-fishing on the Galilean lake. Then seven apostles only are named in this gospel, and seven women are alluded to. Seven times Christ is depicted as delivering continuous discourses. Perhaps, too, it may be permissible to suggest that the other evangelists are not entirely free from the subtle domination of this mysterious spirit of arithmetic. Matthew in particular, no less than the fourth Evangelist, evinces an unmistakeable partiality for three and seven. Not only does he know of three temptations and three favoured disciples, but he speaks of three measures of meal, three tabernacles, three days and nights in the bowels of the earth, three prayers in Gethsemane, three mockings, three hours of darkness during the crucifixion, and three women at the cross. He distributes his material round three principal discourses, and arranges Christ's genealogical tree into three main divisions. There is only room to suspect that he displays a like fondness for the number seven, since he writes of twice seven generations between Adam and Christ, of seven beatitudes, seven petitions in the Lord's prayer, seven loaves and seven baskets, seven brethren, seventy times seven acts of forgiveness, and seven woes. In short, nothing is easier than to play tricks with numbers ; and to urge against the authenticity of this gospel the recurrence with greater or lesser frequency of any number (three or seven) does not strike one as powerfully convincing argument.

III. **The Outline of Christ's Ministry.** This deviates, it is said, from that furnished by the Synoptists in such a manner and to such an extent, that if the latter be accepted as authentic (which it usually is by Tübingen critics) the former must be rejected as non-authentic.

A. Alleged geographical discrepancies between this gospel and the Synoptists.

Under this head the main difficulty relates to the theatre of Christ's Messianic activity. Whereas in John's gospel this is chiefly found in Judæa, and in particular in Jerusalem, with three visits to Galilee of a longer or shorter duration, in the Synoptists' Christ's labours are confined almost exclusively to Galilee with only one journey to Jerusalem at their close. The two accounts, it is urged, are mutually destructive; and since the Synoptists are by the supposition accurate, the present Evangelist must be in error. Before however this can be assented to, the following facts must be considered.

1. *The Synoptists agree in representing Christ's Galilean ministry as having commenced shortly after the Baptist's imprisonment* (Matt. iv. 12 ; Mark i. xiv ; Luke iii. 20) which occurred at least six months, if not a year after Christ's baptism. Unless therefore it can be supposed either that during this period there was no Messianic activity on the part of Christ, or that if there was, the Synoptists were not aware of it, it must be held that they tacitly assume Christ to have been working elsewhere before He established His headquarters at Capernaum. And indeed Mark's language— " Jesus, preaching the gospel of God, went into Galilee "—seems to countenance the idea that already Christ had been proclaiming the advent of God's kingdom, when, according to Matthew, in consequence of becoming apprised of His forerunner's incarceration He withdrew (from Judæa) into Galilee. Luke (iv. 23) also appears to have been aware of a miraculous activity of Jesus in Capernaum prior to the formal commencement of His ministry in Galilee by preaching in the synagogue ; and to what, it may be asked, can this early miraculous activity refer more appropriately than to the work of healing on the nobleman's son (with perhaps other wonders), which according to John (iv. 54), " Jesus did, having come out of Judæa into Galilee ? "

2. *Certain incidents recorded by the Synoptists in connection with Christ's Galilean ministry are more easily explained on the theory of an antecedent and contemporaneous Judæan ministry such as John describes.* (1) The instantaneous obedience of Andrew, Peter, and the sons of Zebedee, when Christ in Galilee called them to follow Him (Matt. iv. 19-22 ; Mark i. 16-20). Though not impossible that this might have happened on first meeting with their future Master (cf. i. 43), there is more probability in John's story that they had previously been introduced to Christ, while attending

the ministrations of the Baptist in Judæa. (2) The flocking of crowds from Jerusalem and Judæa (as from Galilee and Decapolis) to Christ's ministry almost as soon as it opened (Matt. iv. 25). To say the least this is easier to understand if an antecedent activity in the southern parts of the country is presupposed. (3) The readiness of the owners of the colt to lend it to Jesus (Matt. xxi. 3; Mark xi. 3; Luke xix. 33, 34), and of the goodman to give his upper room in the city for the celebration of the paschal meal (Matt. xxvi.17-19; Mark xiv. 14; Luke xxii. 11, 12). It is difficult to read of these services without the thought intruding that the men who rendered them were disciples Christ had gained on former visits to the metropolis. (4) The welcome accorded by the Jerusalemites to Jesus on the day of His triumphal entry into their capital (Matt. xxi. 8-11; Mark xi. 8-10; Luke xix. 36-40). On the supposition that Christ had never before been in their midst, the extraordinary enthusiasm displayed on His arrival is nearly inexplicable, more especially as He only brought with Him the reputation of a not very successful Galilean prophet. That the multitude are represented as asking "Who is this?" does not imply that they had never seen Christ before. As Lange remarks, "Jerusalem knew the person of Jesus sufficiently to have spared the question, had it wished" (Com. on Matt. xxi. 11). (5) The rapid development of the final catastrophe (Matt. xxvi. 3-5). How is this to be accounted for if Jesus had never before been in Jerusalem? The triumphal entry and the purging of the temple, with the controversies of the following days, it is answered, hastened Christ's overthrow (Keim, vol. 1, p. 176). It is even urged against John's narrative that it does not sufficiently explain why the first sojourn of Jesus in the metropolis was not also the last, seeing He so powerfully excited the hostility of the Pharisaic party by His temple purging (Strauss, Das Leben Jesu, i. pp. 316, 317; 4th ed. 1877). But according to John's report of Christ's behaviour on His first visit to the metropolis nothing occurred of a nature fitted to precipitate His death—that which first started His adversaries on the path of murder was, according to this Evangelist (v. 18) the same thing as in the Synoptists (Matt. xii. 14), a case of healing on the Sabbath— and even critics of the school of Strauss admit that John's account of Christ's earlier visits to the capital must be presupposed to render the rapid denouement, traced in the Synoptists, at all credible, Weizsacker recognizing that in the latter narratives, Christ's fate falls on Him without preparation, and Renan pronouncing the account in John's gospel much more probable than that of the Synoptists. (6) The forwardness of Joseph of Arimathea in connection with Christ's burial (Matt. xxvii. 57; Mark xv. 43; Luke xxiii. 50). Does not this suggest that Joseph had already been acquainted with Christ and in fact become His disciple (in secret) in consequence of having listened to His teaching in Jerusalem ?

3. *The Synoptists directly and indirectly allude to earlier visits made by Christ to the capital.* In proof let the following be noted. (1) Matt. xxiii. 37 ; Luke xiii. 34, 35—"O Jerusalem, Jerusalem, how often would I have gathered thy children together!" It is not self-evident that 'thy children,' as in Gal. iv. 25, should be explained of the Jewish people generally without restriction to the inhabitants of the metropolis to whom the words were addressed (Baur, Holtzmann); while the hypothesis (Strauss) that the whole utterance has been taken from an imaginary prophetic writing belonging to the times of the Jewish wars has been well styled "an evidence of extremest perplexity" (Beyschlag, Zur Johanneischen Frage, p. 72). (2) Luke xix. 42—"If thou hadst known in this thy day, etc." How could Christ have so spoken concerning the city, and why should He have so bewailed the obdurate insensibility of its people, if He was now entering the former for the first time and the latter had never yet beheld Him ? (3) Matt. xi. 25—"I thank Thee, O Father, that Thou didst hide these things from the wise and prudent." By the 'wise and prudent' did Christ refer exclusively to the representatives of the Pharisaic party in Galilee ? or, did He not also, and perhaps principally, point to the masters in Israel who resided in Jerusalem ? (4) Matt. xxvi. 55—"I sat daily in the temple." Must this sitting in the temple be restricted to the passion week?—in which case 'daily' would signify 'thrice'—or, should it not rather be regarded as containing an allusion to what had been His practice during earlier visits ? (5) Matt. xxvi. 61— "This man said, I am able to destroy the temple of God and build it in three days." There is no evidence that Christ ever made this remark in Galilee, while the only words resembling it, those addressed to the disciples two days before on quitting the temple for the last time (Matt. xxiv. 2 ; Mark xiii. 2 ; Luke xxi. 6), were distinctly different. John reports the utterance as having fallen from Christ's lips on the occasion of His first visit to the temple. (6) Luke x. 38-42—"A certain woman named Martha received Him into her house." Unless this Martha was another Martha than the one mentioned by John (xi. 1)—a supposition in the highest degree improbable—Christ must have been at Bethany, and therefore in Judæa once at least before the visit at the time of the last passover (Matt. xxvi 6).

4. If Christ's ministry was confined exclusively to Galilee and He had never been in Jerusalem until He entered it to be crucified, *it is, to say the least, surprising that exactly there the first Christian community should have not only sprung up, but succeeded in maintaining itself against the opposition of the unbelieving hierarchy.* Peter's sermon on the day of Pentecost, addressed specially to the "men of Judæa and dwellers at Jerusalem," notices the

fact, that Jesus of Nazareth had been "approved of God unto them by mighty works and wonders and signs, which God did by Him in their midst," as they themselves knew. Now as Christ wrought no miracles in either Judæa or Jerusalem on His last visit, the inference is that there must been earlier visits on which He did so; and that this accounts for the speedy establishment of a Christian community in the metropolis —Peter's preaching having fallen upon hearts that had previously been favourably disposed to the Saviour.

5. *If Christ never laboured in Jerusalem and Judæa, an explanation is required for the reception by the Church of the second century of a writing so persistently affirming that He did.* Unless on this point the views of John had been universally recognized as compatible with those of the Synoptists, it is difficult to see how it could have been so soon admitted into the N. T. canon.

B. Seeming chronological differences between this gospel and the Synoptists.

1. *The duration of Christ's ministry.* Whereas according to this gospel the ministry of Jesus extended over two or three years (according as the feast in v. 1 is regarded as that of Purim or as a pass-over), "the other gospels apparently allow space for only one year of teaching" (Keim), more correctly for a year and a half; the former placing within that ministry three passovers (ii. 13; vi. 4; xii. 1), or four, if v. 1 be added, the latter speaking of only one, the last. But (1) the Synoptists agree in describing only the Galilean activity of Christ, the commencement of which they are also unanimous in dating from a point soon after the Baptist's imprisonment. (2) As this occurred shortly before the feast of v. 1 (see ver. 35), if this feast was a passover, a period of 12 or 15 months must have passed since Christ was baptized; and it is barely credible that all these months were spent by Christ in absolute inactivity. Of course if the feast in v. 1 was Purim in March then the Baptist's imprisonment must have taken place almost immediately after Christ's baptism. But the difficulties connected with this hypothesis are too formidable to be readily admitted (see Exposition on v. 1). (3) Taken either way, the date furnished by the Synoptists for the commencement of Christ's Galilean activity in no way conflicts with John's statement that Christ had carried on a Judæan ministry prior to the period of the Baptist's incarceration. (4) Dating the Galilean ministry from the Baptist's arrestment, the Synoptical accounts will harmonize with that of John, if it can be shown that they find room for one passover (to correspond with vi. 4) or at most two (if v. 1 was a passover and the Galilean ministry was already begun); and this will be the case if, as is generally allowed, the incident of ear-rubbing mentioned by all the Synoptists (Matt. xii. 1; Mark ii. 23; Luke

vi. 1) pointed to a season closely following on a passover (possibly the pass-over of v. 1), and the payment of the temple-tax recorded only by the first (Matt. xvii. 24), due between the 15th and 25th of Adar or Feb-Mar. (Jos. Ant. xviii. 9, 1), also indicated the proximity of a paschal feast (perhaps that of vi. 4). 2. *The date of the Bethany Supper.* Whereas in the Synoptists (Matt. xxvi. 2, 6 ; Mark xiv. 1, 3) this is said to have been given to the Saviour two days before the passover, in this gospel (xii. 1, 2) it is declared to have been six days before that event. But an examina-tion of the earlier accounts renders it apparent that the nexus which binds their paragraphs together at this point is not chronological but logical, and that the aim which both writers contemplated in introducing just here the story of the feast in Simon's house was not to fix the time of its occurrence but to show how Judas and the chief priests had been brought together in the nefarious plot which was on the eve of being carried out. 3. *The day of Our Lord's death.* This according to the Synoptists, it is said, and correctly, was the day after the legal celebration of the passover ; whereas according to John it was the day on which the legal passover was observed. The questions relating to this supposed discrepancy are discussed in the commentary (see Expos. xiii. 2, note), and nothing more need be stated here than that in our judgment no such discrepancy exists.

C. So-called historical inconsistencies between this gospel and the Synoptists.

In respect of what the former adds to and takes from the latter, it shows such deviations from the previously accepted story of Christ's life, that it cannot possibly be regarded as authentic history.

1. *Additions to the Synoptists.* The Fourth Gospel describes scenes, as e.g. the meeting of Andrew and John with Jesus (i. 35-42), the feet-washing in the upper room (xiii. 1-11), Christ's interview with His disciples beside the Galilean lake after the resurrection (xxi. 15-23) ; introduces persons, as Nicodemus (iii. 1), the Samaritan woman (iv. 7), Annas (xviii. 13), Malchus (xviii. 11) ; reports conversations, for instance, of the Baptist with the Sanhedrists (i. 19), of Jesus with His disciples (i. 43-51), with Nicodemus (iii. 2 ff.), with the Samaritan woman (iv. 7 ff.), with the Jews (viii. 12-20), with Pilate (xviii. 33-37 ; xix. 9-11) ; narrates events such as the attempt of the Galileans to make Christ a king (vi. 15) and the coming of the bailiffs to apprehend Him (vii. 32, 45) ; records miracles as of turning water into wine at Cana (ii. 11), and curing the nobleman's son at Capernaum (iv. 46-54), healing the lame man at Bethesda (v. 1) and the blind man in the street (ix. 6), and raising Lazarus from the grave (xi. 43, 44) ; and rehearses discourses, on the New Birth (iii. 3 ff.), Christ's divine Son-ship (v. 19 ff.), the Bread of Life (vi. 26 ff.), with the farewell discourses in the supper room (xiv.-xvii.) ;—of all of which the Synoptists know nothing.

It is not necessary to impugn the accuracy of this statement; it suffices to call attention to the unreasonableness of basing on it any conclusion as to the validity or non-validity of the gospel itself. (1) If John describes scenes, introduces persons, reports conversations, etc., unknown to the Synoptists, any one can see that such of them as belong to the Judæan ministry did not fall within the circle of vision of the Synoptists who deliberately limited their efforts to preserving a record of Christ's Galilean ministry; while (2) those which he selects from the Galilean ministry may have been omitted by the Synoptists for sufficient reasons, some of which are not hard to discover, while others can with a high degree of probability be surmised.

2. *Omissions from the Synoptists.* The Fourth Gospel is silent concerning incidents of moment related by the earlier biographers, as e.g. the Baptism (Matt. iii. 13-17), the Temptation (Matt. iv. 1-11), the Transfiguration (Matt. xvii. 1-8), the Agony in Gethsemane (Matt. xxvi. 36-46); the Ascension (Mark xvi. 19); omits the institution of Baptism (Matt. xxviii. 29) and of the Lord's Supper (Matt. xxvi. 26-29), says nothing about the Sermon on the Mount (Matt. v. vi. vii.), the Parables of the Kingdom (Matt. xiii.), the Instructions to the Twelve (Matt. x.); knows nothing of publicans and sinners (Luke xv. 1), and has no cures of either lepers (Mark i. 40-45) or demoniacs (Matt. xii. 22). But here again (1) If on account of sundry omissions John is to be pronounced unhistorical, then, by parity of reasoning, Matthew and Mark must also be unhistorical, seeing they omit Christ's early preaching in Nazareth, the anointing in Simon's house by the woman who was a sinner, the visit to Bethany, and the story of Zaccheus, with the parables of the Importunate friend, the Importunate widow, the Unjust steward, the Missing coin, and the Prodigal son, Dives and Lazarus, the Good Samaritan, the Pharisee and the Publican, the Farmer and the Ploughboy, with the miracles of 'The miraculous draught,' 'The raising of the widow's son,' 'The cleansing of the ten lepers,'—all of which are recorded in Luke; and Luke must be unhistorical since he says nothing about Christ's walking on the sea, healing the Syrophenician woman's daughter, feeding the four thousand, or cursing the fig-tree, nothing about the birthday celebration of Herod, the question of the Pharisees concerning divorce, the request of the sons of Zebedee, and the banquet at Bethany, nothing about the false-witnesses at Christ's trial, or Christ's cry of forsakenness upon the cross,—all of which are, conversely, mentioned by Matthew and Mark. (2) If John omits portions of the current synoptical tradition, he distinctly intimates that it had been his intention from the first to proceed upon a principle of selection. (3) With some of the incidents referred to in those omitted portions, the Evangelist shows himself to have been acquainted, as e.g. the Baptism (see i. 33), the

Agony in Gethsemane (see xii. 27 ; xviii. 11); while others are passed over for sufficient reasons,—'The Temptation,' because he begins his gospel at a point subsequent to that experience ; 'The Transfiguration' because that entered not directly into his design, which was to show how the glory of Jesus unfolded itself before the Jewish nation ; the Ascension (an omission he shares with Matthew) probably because he regarded it as implied in Christ's utterances regarding Himself (iii. 13 ; vi. 62) ; the institution of Baptism and of the Lord's Supper because already these were well known and in their spiritual significance had been distinctly involved in Christ's teaching (iii. 3 ; vi. 53) ; the Sermon on the Mount and the Parables of the Kingdom because these did not lie within his programme.   (4) That neither publicans nor sinners are introduced into his pages requires no further explanation than that it was not of our Lord's intercourse with them that he purposed to write, but of our Lord's presentation of Himself to the rulers and heads of his nation and people.   (5) The absence of 'healings of lepers' and 'castings out of devils,' so far as Christ's work in Jerusalem is concerned is doubtless accounted for by the fact that these forlorn creatures were not to be met with within the precincts of the Holy City, while with regard to His ministry in Galilee it is enough to say that no miracle of the sort referred to occurred in the part selected by the author for incorporation in his book.

IV. **The Discourses of Jesus.** In respect of form and contents these, as reported in this gospel, diverge so widely from those put into Christ's mouth by the Synoptists that, it is argued, both cannot be true ; and inasmuch as by Tübingen critics the latter in their naturalness and simplicity bear the stamp of historicity, the non-authenticity of the former follows.

1. *The form of our Lord's discourses.* With reference to this, these difficulties have been urged :—(1) The discourses reported by John are so dissimilar to those preserved by the Synoptists, that the inference is irresistible, " If Jesus spoke as Matthew represents, He could not have spoken as John relates " (Renan).   In particular, the discourses in the Fourth Gospel contain no parables or short proverbial utterances, but consist for the most part (Holtzmann, pp. 441, 442) of " long chains of testimonial and controversial speeches, delivered in a style which sweeps away beyond the comprehension of hearers, awakens in them movement only by their incessant misunderstandings of, and efforts to grasp, its dark, enigmatical words, and advances after the manner of far-going circles, which return again to their original starting point."   " Where the form and manner of expression of this Evangelist (John) bears the stamp of authenticity he has drawn it out of the Synoptists and other gospels then existing ; so far as on the other hand it is peculiar to himself, it has all the marks of

being manufactured and unhistorical" (Strauss, Das Leben Jesu, vol. i. p. 331). (2) The style of the Johannine discourses is the same as that of the Evangelist himself (i. 1-18), of the Baptist (iii. 27-36), of the author of the first epistle of John, and even of the man born blind (ix. 27, 30, 33), so that one can scarcely help concluding "The Evangelist has used one speech for all, his own speech and sphere of thought as an author" (Keim, vol. i. p. 166). "The discourses and dialogues of the Fourth Gospel are not genuine reports of the teaching of Jesus, but mere ideal compositions by the author" (Supernatural Religion, vol. ii. pp. 468, 9). (3) It is simply impossible that the writer, who must have composed his gospel at the soonest 50 years after Christ's death, "could have retained in his memory these long and even interminable utterances of Jesus" (Keim). It is useless to assert that these objections have no (seeming) ground to rest upon, or that they do not call for answer on the part of defenders of the gospel; only much may be adduced to considerably weaken, if not altogether, nullify their force.

(1) The Synoptists show that Jesus sometimes spoke as in John He is represented doing; in fact, the number of parallels between this and the earlier gospels with reference to utterances of Jesus is greater than would perhaps at first sight strike a superficial reader. The appended list should be carefully examined. Cf. with ii. 9, Matt. xxvi. 61; xxvii. 40; Mark xiv. 58; xv. 29; with iii. 18, Mark xvi. 16; with iv. 35, Matt. ix. 37; with iv. 44, Matt. xiii. 57; with v. 8, Matt ix. 6; Mark ii. 9; Luke v. 24; with vi. 20, Matt. xiv. 27, Mark vi. 50; with vi. 35, Matt. v. 6; Luke vi. 21; with vi. 37, Matt. xi. 28, 29; with vi. 46, and x. 15, Matt. xi. 27; with xii. 8, Matt. xxvi. 11, Mark xiv. 7; with xii. 25, Matt. x. 39, xvi. 25; Mark viii. 35, Luke ix. 24, xvii. 33; with xii. 27, Matt. xxvi. 38, Mark xiv. 34; with xiii. 3, Matt. xi. 27; with xiii. 16, Matt. x. 24; with xiii. 20, Matt. x. 40; with xiii. 21, Matt. xxvi. 21, Mark xiv. 18; with 38, Matt. xxvi. 34, Mark xiv. 30, Luke xxii. 34; with xiv. 18, 23, Matt. xxviii. 20; with xiv. 28, Mark xiii. 32; with xiv. 31, Matt. xxvi. 46; with xv. 20, Matt. x. 25; with xv. 21, Matt. x. 22; with xvi. 32, Matt. xxvi. 31; with xvii. 2, Matt. xxviii. 18; with xviii. 11, Matt. xxvi. 39, 42, 52; with xviii. 20, Matt. xxvi. 55; with xviii. 37, Matt. xxvii. 11; with xx. 23, Matt. xvi. 19, xviii. 18.

(2) If John contains no parables strictly so called it has similitudes or allegories as of the Good Shepherd (x.) and the True Vine (xv.), besides a rich supply of metaphorical expressions, which belong to the same category of thought and speech.

(3) It is not impossible that John's style (assuming him to have been the author) was framed upon the model of Christ's. Indeed a high degree of

probability attaches to this conjecture when it is borne in mind that between John and Jesus existed a near mental affinity and subsisted a close personal relationship (cf. Bleek's Introduction, vol. 1, § 77). Reuss reasons that if the Evangelist had acquired his peculiarities in writing and speaking from Christ's manner of thought and utterance, "this must have been a style so constant and so sharply defined as to exclude that borne witness to in the other gospels" (Geschichte der heiligen Schriften des N. T., § 219). But this proceeds on the hypothesis already cited in the words of Renan, that if Christ spoke as in Matthew, He could not have spoken as in John. The well-known example of Socrates however advises caution in deciding on what is palpably a recondite psychological problem. If the Socrates of Xenophon and the Socrates of Plato are not mutually destructive —and that they are not is now acknowledged—why should it be inconceivable that Christ should at one time have discoursed as in the Synoptists and at another time as in John? "If a wise man who was merely human like Socrates, could present such a manifoldness in unity that two of his pupils could give such contrasted yet true pictures of his teaching, surely the same is possible in the case of Christ—in the case of Him whose office and work was to be the Redeemer of men of all shades of character and life" (Bleek). Hence it is by no means inconceivable that Christ, at one time addressing the less cultured populations of the North should have adopted the simple, sententious, and parabolic style exhibited in the Synoptists, and at another time bearing witness of Himself before the educated classes, especially before the leaders of intellectual and religious society in the metropolis, or unfolding the sublime truths of religion to His disciples, should have selected that elevated and semi-mystical tone which appears in John. It may be answered that if this suggestion explains the resemblance of the Evangelist's speech to that of Christ, it does not account for the correspondence in style between the Baptist and the Evangelist, or for the fact that in the Synoptists the Baptist talks like himself while in the Fourth Gospel he discourses like the Evangelist who also orates after the pattern of Jesus. But the different dictions of the Baptist in John and in the Synoptists may have been rendered necessary by the different themes on which they were engaged—in the latter the necessity and duty of repentance, in the former the heavenly dignity and divine Sonship of Jesus. That the forerunner should have been capable of using two such divergent styles—that he who commenced his desert preaching with short, sharp, thunderclaps of rebuke and admonition should before it ended talk like one who "testified that which he had seen" will not be perplexing to one who recollects that between the two modes of utterance intervened the Baptism and the Voice from heaven. (cf. Oosterzee, John's Gospel, pp. 80. 81). The resemblance between John's speech and that of the blind man is more apparent than real.

(4) As to the objection that the Evangelist could not have retained in his memory the *ipsissima verba* of discourses so long, intricate, metaphysical, and spiritual as those recorded in this gospel, no further answer appears demanded than this of Reuss (Geschichte, etc., § 219), and Pressensé (Jesus Christ, His Times, etc., bk. i. ch. iv. iv.) that it is not at all requisite to assume the Evangelist only then for the first time wrote them down when he composed his book. If more be deemed necessary, the believing critic will remember that no one can tell how much may have been possible to a writer who enjoyed the help of the Paraclete (xiv. 26).

(5) At the same time the hypothesis that in John Christ's discourses have not been mechanically taken up and set down by the author, but, first believingly and freely absorbed by his own living personality, and afterwards as freely and lovingly reproduced under the guidance of the Holy Spirit, need not invalidate their claim to be regarded as historically true representations of the thoughts and words of Jesus. " As the evangelists were concerned, not about documentary literality, but about the thoughts and subject matter, such an assumption might be admitted without the slightest difficulty, and without impugning the credibility of John " (Ebrard, The Gospel History, E.T., p. 224).

2. *The contents of Our Lord's discourses.*   In this gospel, it is said, and with truth, the principal theme of Christ's discourses is the pre-existence and divine Sonship of His Own person, whom He sets before His audience, under a variety of metaphors, as The Bread of Life, The Water of Life, The Light of the World, The Good Shepherd, The True Vine, and faith in whom He declares to be the only means of obtaining eternal life : in the Synoptists Christ's teaching is mainly occupied with the doctrine of the Kingdom of Heaven—of its righteousness (Matt. v. vi. vii.), of its establishment and growth (Matt. xiii.), of its consummation at the final *parousia* (Matt. xxiv. xxv.).   But (1) if Christ chose, for reasons known to Himself, to make this distinction between the teaching presented to the Galileans and that unfolded before the Judæans, one fails to perceive how on that fact can be based an argument for the non-historicity of the latter. If it can, then the same reasoning will apply to the former, and both forms of teaching will equally require to be pronounced fictitious, since they were not each delivered to both classes of auditors, in the north and in the south of the land ; and thus by a simple stroke of the pen the entire gospel history will be deprived of every shred of credibility and consigned to the limbo of romance.   But no sensible person will admit the correctness of this conclusion.   Then (2) since, even were it the case that between the Johannine and the Synoptical teachings an impassable gulf stretched, it

would not be permissible to argue against the credibility of either, still less can it be permissible when a slight examination makes it clear that neither was the Christ of the Synoptists entirely unacquainted with the doctrine of His pre-existent Sonship (cf. Matt. xi. 25-27; xxii. 42; xxvi. 63, 64, with parallels), nor was the Johannine Christ wholly ignorant of the doctrine of the kingdom (see iii. 3; xviii. 36, 37).

V. The Image of Christ. Against the picture of Jesus presented in this gospel it is usual to bring a charge of unreality based upon an alleged absence of true human development or growth. " Of this there can be no doubt," writes Keim, " this image of Christ only corresponds to the requirements of a human being in the narrowest sense; it belies our own view of human nature, of its restrictions as a created thing, of its slow growth, its need of teaching, and its struggles, and it allies in an inconceivable manner the majesty of God and the limits of a man " (Jesus of Nazara, vol. i. p. 169). Whereas in the Synoptists Christ enters upon the theatre of mundane existence by the gateway of birth and passes through regular stages of development, not merely in infancy and youth (Luke ii. 40, 52), but also in manhood, being influenced like ordinary mortals by the circumstances of the times in which He lived, affected, as it is now expressed, by His environment, geographical, temporal, social, intellectual, religious;—in John He steps forth from a pre-existent state or condition at once and majestically as a heavenly and divine being who needs no development, who having no temptations to overcome has no inner struggle to maintain, who is always conscious of His higher nature, who from the first recognizes Himself, and is by others recognized, as the Son of God, who enters upon His public career with a clear foresight of His end, who has a perfect knowledge of men and things and requires not that any should instruct Him, who performs miracles with the creative ease and calm majesty of a God, and miracles in their character transcending anything reported in the earlier biographies. Accordingly John's picture of Jesus is marked by a complete absence of everything suggesting imperfection or in any degree troublesome to harmonize with the exalted portrait intended to be sketched. There is no birth at Bethlehem or boyhood at Nazareth, no baptism in Jordan, or temptation in the wilderness, no transfiguration upon Hermon or agony in the garden. There is nothing to hint defective knowledge or power. The Johannine Christ makes no mistakes and suffers no defeats; is not taken unawares by Judas whom He has known from the beginning; is not captured by the armed band in Gethsemane, so much as self-delivered into their hand; does not die by the hand of violence, but freely renders up His spirit. "In consequence of all which," writes Schenkel, "we are obliged to infer an essentially different background as to matters of fact between the

first three gospels and the fourth.   (Nay) if any conclusion be more
certain and well-grounded than another it is this :—If the Synoptical
representation of the evangelic history be the right one, then this of the
Fourth Gospel is the wrong one and conversely." (Das Characterbild Jesu,
p. 369).   Before endorsing this, however, it may be inquired whether as
regards this gospel the question has been accurately stated.   Is it the case
that the Evangelist has outlined a " Christ " so radically different from that
of the Synoptists ?   On the contrary the record shows that, though seemingly an inevitable, this is nevertheless not a perfectly correct deduction
from the premises.   For 1. *The Johannine Christ is as truly human as is that
of the Synoptists.*   If the Fourth Gospel has no Incarnation story, it nevertheless says " And the Word became flesh and dwelt amongst us,"—
yea, it introduces Christ as claiming to have been born (xviii. 37), which
the Synoptists never do ; it represents Him as having been possessed of
all the component parts of a true human nature—of a body
that could walk (x. 22), or ride (xii. 15), that could be wearied
(iv. 6), that could eat and drink (iv. 10, 31 ; xiii. 18), that could
be bound (xviii. 12), and flogged (xix. i), that could weep (xi. 35), that
could thirst (xix. 28), that could be crucified (xix. 18), die (xix. 30) and
be buried (xix. 42) ; of a mind that could know (ii. 24), learn by asking
(xi. 34), and express its thoughts in words (iii. 3) ; of a soul that could be
troubled (xii. 27), and a spirit that could be moved with indignation (xi. 33).
It depicts Him as undergoing experiences and performing actions of which
only a real man is capable as *e.g.* sitting at a marriage feast (ii. 1-10),
shedding tears at a friend's grave (xi. 35), accepting hospitality (xii. 2),
and doing the office of a menial (xiii. 5) ; conversing with a rabbi (iii. 3),
with a woman (iv. 7), with the people (vii. 28), with His disciples (xiv. 1),
with His captors (xviii. 4), with His judge (xviii. 34) ; preaching in the
temple (vii. 14), in a synagogue (vi. 59), in the street (ix. 2-6), and in the
house (xii. 8) ; exposing Himself to the close and constant scrutiny of
friends with whom He associated (xi. 1-5), as well as of enemies with whom
He reasoned (viii. 48 59).   In short, if John's Christ was not a *verus homo*,
it will be difficult to find one such on earth (cf. : " How is the Divinity of
Jesus depicted ?" by the Author: pp. 123, 124).   Then 2 : *The Synoptic
Christ is as perfect as is that of John.*   If the latter came forth from a pre-
existent state or condition, so did the former (Matt. i. 18-25 ; iii. 17;
viii. 29 ; Mark i. 11 ; Luke i. 32-36 ; iii. 22 ; ix. 35),—Keim's assertion
that " the older evangelists do not give a syllable from the mouth of Jesus
about His existence before the worlds " (Vol. i. p. 174) being distinctly
open to challenge (Matt. v. 17 ; x. 34, 35 ; xxii. 45 ; Mark i. 38 ; ii. 10 ;
xii. 37 ; Luke xx. 44).   If the latter was " perfectly developed " when He
entered on His public ministry, so also was the former, as His baptism

secured (Matt. iii. 16, 17) and the temptation attested (Matt. iv. 11). Was John's Christ on His first stepping forth saluted by Nathanael as the Son of God (i. 49)? So was Luke's at the opening of the Galilean ministry recognized by Peter as a supernatural and divine being (v. 8), and by demons as "The Holy One of God" (iv. 34). Had John's Christ a clear perception of His death, even from the outset of His career? The Jesus of the earlier evangelists had a similar outlook towards the end (Matt. ix. 15; Mark ii. 20; Luke v. 35). In the Fourth Gospel Jesus knew what was in man (i. 42; iv. 17; v. 6; vi. 61-64; xvi. 19): in the preceding gospels He did the same (Matt. xii. 15-25; Mark xii. 15; Luke vi. 3). But John's Christ never failed in any miracle He attempted to perform! Neither did the Christ of the Synoptists, Matthew's statement (xiii. 58) implying not that Christ ever attempted a miracle and failed, but that because of the absence of the necessary moral conditions there were instances in which He did not attempt. Nor were the miracles of John's Christ really greater than those of the Christ of the Synoptists, since all acts are equally easy to omnipotence; and every miracle that Christ wrought in John has its counterpart in those mentioned in the Synoptists. As for the assertion that the Christ of the earlier evangelists only gradually attained to a full consciousness of His Messianic calling and divine Sonship, whereas the Christ of John possessed that from the moment of His entering on His public career, it is doubtful if the former statement can be maintained. That there was order, succession, progress, development, growth in the presentation or revelation of Himself to the Galileans is conceded; but the like phenomena were observable in His unveilment of Himself to the Judæans. Matthew, Mark, and Luke represent Christ as acting under the constraint of the same divine imperative (Matt. xxvi. 54; Mark viii. 31; Luke ii. 49; iv. 43; xix. 5) which so frequently leads Him in John (iii. 14; iv. 4; ix. 4; x. 16). In this, as in those, the path He is to follow opens up before Him in successive steps. At every stage of His earthly progress He hears and learns from the Father, and when the goal is reached He can say, "I have finished the work which Thou gavest Me to do." Yet it is incorrect to assert that according to the Synoptists Christ did not know Himself to be the Israelitish Messiah or the Divine Son until towards the end of the Galilean ministry. If He did not, He might have done it, since it was authoritatively proclaimed to Him at the baptism (Matt. iii. 17). And the devils knew it (Matt. iv. 3-6; viii. 29). The Galileans, it is true, were not aware of it at the commencement of His ministry. Nor was it in accordance with Christ's plan that the exact truth as to His personality should be laid before them, except by degrees. Hence He forbade the unclean spirits to make Him known. Hence also it was not until He had laboured for a twelvemonth among the Galileans that He set before them with clear utterance the exalted doctrine of His Sonship. As it were when by preliminary labours He had brought the Galileans up to the standard of preparedness for hearing at which the Judæans were, He discoursed to those as He had done to these; alas! with a similar result, they turned from Him in unbelief and scorn. And this perhaps explains why the Evangelist out of all the Galilean ministry selected only this one scene. It was the scene in which the claims of Christ were placed before the Galileans in a manner similar to that in which they had been laid before the Judæans—the scene in which, so to speak, Galilee was brought to decision. And possibly if this be remembered it will satisfactorily account for the omission of this discourse by the Synoptists. Even had the authors of the earlier records been capable of reproducing the lofty and mystic utterances of Jesus concerning Himself, the circle of readers for which they wrote needed more the style of teaching of Christ's preparation time in Galilee. But in any case it seems impossible to establish such a wide distinction between the two portraits, the Synoptic and the Johannine, as to make of them two Christs instead of one.

So far then as this investigation has proceeded, the non-authenticity or unhistorical character of this gospel has not been made out.

§ 2. THE AUTHORSHIP OF THE GOSPEL

Under this section an inquiry will be conducted into (1) the Internal Evidence, or the testimony furnished by the gospel itself; and (2) the External Evidence, or the witness supplied by tradition, as to the person of the author.

I. **Internal Evidence** ; or, the testimony of the gospel as to its author. It was quite in accordance with literary practice among the Hebrews to publish an anonymous gospel, and if ever a case existed in which an author was justified in not obtruding his own personality before his readers, it was, this in which the theme to be described was the transcendent personality of Jesus. Yet a careful perusal of the gospel renders the following conclusions relative to its author, if not mathematically certain, at least in the highest degree probable.

1. *The Author must have been a Jew.* Not only does he show himself acquainted with (a) the early history of the Jewish people, with Abraham and the patriarchs (vii. 22, viii. 56) as well as Moses (i. 17, 45 ; v. 45), Isaiah (xii. 38, 39, 41), and the prophets (i, 45 ; viii. 53), with the institution of circumcision (vii. 22), and the giving of the law (i. 17), with the coming down of the manna (vi. 31), and the lifting up of the serpent (iii.

15), the smiting of the rock (vii. 37), and the leading of the pillar (viii. 12) in the wilderness, but (β) he manifests an intimacy with, as well as appreciation of, their sacred Scriptures which suggest that he himself must have been a Jew. For him the Old Testament was the inviolable and infallible word of God (xii. 38; xix. 24, 36, 37; xx. 9). Quoting from it, which he does 14 or 15 times (i. 23—Is. xl. 3; ii. 17—Ps. lxix. 9; vi. 31—Ps. lxxviii. 24; vi. 45—Is. liv. 13; vii. 38—no exact parallel; x. 34—Ps. lxxxii. 6; xii. 13—Ps. cxviii. 26; xii. 15—Zech. ix. 9; xii. 38—Is. liii. 1; xii. 40—Is. vi. 9, 10; xiii. 18—Ps. xli. 9; xv. 25—Ps. xxxv. 19; lxix. 4; xix. 24—Ps. xxii. 18; xix. 36—Ex. xii. 46; Ps. xxxiv. 20; xix. 37—Zech. xii. 10), he sometimes freely adapts its language (i. 23; vi. 31; vii. 38; xix. 36), sometimes differs from the Hebrew original and the Greek translation (lxx.) as well when these agree (ii. 17) as when they disagree (xii. 15, 40), and sometimes accords with both (x. 34; xii. 38; xv. 25; xix. 24); but in three instances he prefers the Hebrew to the LXX. (vi. 45; xiii. 18; xix. 37), while in not one does he select the Greek rather than the Hebrew. The picture of Christ sketched by him is also without question that of a Jew who regards the Scriptures as the indestructible word of God (x. 35; xiii. 18), which testifies of Him, the Christ (v. 39, 46), which points to Him by its oracles (vii. 42; xiii. 18), types (iii. 15; vi. 51; vii. 37; viii. 12), and allegories (x. 11; xv. 1), and which becomes a source of spiritual life to all who receive it into their hearts (v. 38). Then besides the history and the Scriptures of the Jewish people, the author (γ) exhibits a perfect knowledge of the Jewish temple (ii. 14), its original erection by Solomon (x. 23), its reconstruction by Herod (ii. 20),—condescending to the time occupied in the latter work, its porches (x. 23) and courts (viii. 20), the feasts of which it was the centre, as the Passover (ii. 13; vi. 4; xiii. 1), Tabernacles (vii. 2), and Dedication (x. 22), with the orders of its ministers, high priest (xi. 51), priests and levites (i. 19). He likewise (δ) discovers himself possessed of accurate information about the land and people in the first Christian century—about the classes that composed Jewish society, as, *e.g.* the Pharisees (i. 24), the chief priests (vii. 32), the rulers (vii. 48), the common people (vii. 49); about the Sanhedrim or council of the Jewish church and people (vii. 45; xi. 47); about the relations of Judæa to Rome (xviii. 31), no less than about ordinary Jewish manners and customs (ii. 6; iv. 9, 27; xi. 31; xiii. 29; xviii. 32, 39; xix. 31, 40);—with reference to this last see below. Add to this (ε) that while the language of this gospel is Greek, its thought and expression bear the clearest marks of being Hebrew (Ewald, Die Johanneischen Schriften vol. i. p. 44; Keim, Jesus of Nazara, vol. i. p. 157; Holtzmann, Einleitung, p. 468); and it will be well nigh impossible to resist the inference that whoever was the composer of the present gospel, he must have been a Jew.

The *objections* raised against this conclusion are certainly not devoid of countenance from great names, but are nevertheless capable of being satisfactorily answered. (1) A Jew, it is urged, would never have himself spoken of his own people as one not belonging to them, calling them " the Jews," their religious celebrations, " feasts of the Jews " (ii. 13 ; v. 1 ; vi. 4 ; vii. 2), their Sanhedrists, " rulers of the Jews " (iii. 1), or represented Christ as saying not " our law," like Nicodemus (vii. 51) and the Jews (xix. 7), but " your law " (viii. 17 ; x. 34), precisely as Pilate did (xviii. 31), or " their law " (xv. 25), as if he himself had no connection therewith. A detailed exposition of these passages will be found in the commentary ; here it may suffice to indicate the mode in which the difficulty to which they are supposed to point may be turned aside. So far as the Evangelist is concerned, his peculiar manner of writing may have been due to the circumstance that his work was intended for Gentile readers ; and even if it was not, the same style of speech occurs in Matt. xxvii. 11, 29, 37 ; xxviii. 15, Mark vii. 3, Luke vii. 3 ; xxiii. 51, and the Pauline Epistles— Rom. ix. 24, Gal. ii. 14, 2 Cor. xi. 24, 1 Thess, ii. 14. The pronouns ' your ' and ' their ' put into Christ's mouth with reference to the law were neither inappropriate nor strange, since in both Christ spoke either from the standpoint of His opponents, who regarded themselves as the only true keepers of the law, or from His own standpoint as above the law. (2) A Jew, it is contended, would never, as this Evangelist does, have placed himself in an attitude of uncompromising hostility towards his countrymen, invariably designating them, as above stated, " the Jews," depicting them as the unsleeping and embittered enemies of Christ, representing them as embodiments of the principle of darkness by which the light shining in Jesus was opposed (i. 5), character- izing them as ' of this world,' ' from beneath,' ' children of the devil ' (viii. 23, 44), whose leaders were ' thieves, robbers, and murderers ' (x. 8, 10), in contrast to Christ whom he calls, or permits to call Himself, ' not of this world,' ' from above,' ' the Son of God,' ' the Good Shepherd, who giveth His life for the sheep.' In this author, writes Holtzmann (Einleitung, etc., p. 468) " one traces nothing more of the sorrow laden plaint of Jesus over His own people (Luke xix, 41-44), nothing more of the sympathy of Paul for his ' brethren according to the flesh ' (Rom. ix. 3)." With him " Judaism has no future more. A definite irrevocable doom of rejection is uttered over it (xii. 38-40). No future conversion (as in Rom. xi. 25 is held up before the people, but only (the appalling sentence) ' Ye shall die in your sins ' (viii. 24)." Hence, the critic argues,

what the composer has before him is " the Judaism of the second century,"
—quoting with approbation in this connection the words of Zeller, "The
history of primitive Christianity is at an end, and that of Catholicism
begins" (Vorträge and Abhandlungen I., p. 256) ; the final inference being
that the composer was not a Jew. But the Judaism of which Christ
speaks was that not of the second but of the first century ; and if Christ, in
this gospel, animadverts with severity upon the spiritual obduracy of its
representatives and leaders in the metropolis, it is certain He does as
much in the earlier narrations (Matt. xxiii. 1, 39 ; Mark xii. 1-12 ; Luke
xix. 41-44 ; xx. 9-18), while in both cases the reason was, that His words
were justified by facts. If the Evangelist in turn, looking back to the same
period, recognizes in the Jewish authorities an embodiment of the principle of
darkness, the explanation of this also is that such in reality they were,
although perhaps it was not until after years of meditation under the
Spirit's guidance upon the appalling phenomenon of Christ's rejection by
those who should have welcomed and received Him that the full significance of their unbelief dawned upon the writer's soul. (3) A third
objection it is usual to derive from the "universalism" exhibited in
this gospel—a universalism "far transcending that of Paul"—which, it is
maintained, was not only highly improbable in any Jew, but was specially
incompatible with the strongly Judaistic John of the gospels (Mark ix. 38 ;
Luke ix. 54 ; Matt. xx. 20), and of the Jerusalem church (Gal. ii. 9). But
the universalism of this gospel (x. 16 ; xi. 52) was the universalism of Jesus
(Matt. viii. 11 ; xxi. 43 ; xxii. 10), and four things may have contributed to
John's perception of this when the time came for him to pen this gospel :—
(1) The complete abrogation of Judaism as a visible church by the destruction of Jerusalem ; (2) the rapid spread of Christianity among the Gentiles
which was then taking place ; (3) the "universalism of Paul" (Rom. i. 16 ;
Gal. iii. 28 ; Eph. i. 10 ; ii. 14-18) with which John had doubtless become
acquainted through the publication of the Pauline epistles ; and (4) the
teaching of the Holy Spirit which enabled him ever more deeply to sink
himself into the profound and far-reaching significance of Christ's
words.

2. *The Author must have been a Palestinian.* Otherwise it is impossible
to account for his accurate knowledge of the country in the time of Christ.
Not only is he informed concerning the main geographical divisions of the
land—Judæa, Galilee, Samaria, Peræa—but he understands the positions
of its more important localities—knows, for example, the Sea of Galilee,
can tell its breadth and name the towns upon its shores (vi.), can describe
the situations of well-known places like Capernaum and Bethany, depicting
the former as " down " from Cana of Galilee (ii. 12 ; iv. 47), and the latter
as " nigh unto Jerusalem, about fifteen furlongs off " (xi. 18). Others not

mentioned elsewhere he can set down, fixing their sites, and recording their distinctions with complete accuracy. Bethany beyond Jordan, as distinguished from Bethany nigh unto Jerusalem (i. 28); Cana of Galilee (ii. 1), so called probably to mark it off from another Cana in Asher (Josh. xix. 28); Ænon, near to Salim (iii. 23); Sychar, near to Jacob's Well (iv. 6); Bethesda (v. 2) in, and the Pool of Siloam (ix. 7) near, Jerusalem; Ephraim, near to the Wilderness (xi. 54); Tiberias, opposite the place where the people had eaten after the Lord had given thanks (vi. 23); Gethsemane, across the Kidron, close to Jerusalem (xviii. 1), are illustrations of the author's topographical exactitude. Then, with reference to the people, his information is so explicit and detailed, as well as confidently and accurately given, that it harmonizes more with the original knowledge of a born Jew than with the acquired learning of a foreign scholar. By one touch (xi. 48) he reveals that he knows of the political subjection of the Jewish people, and by another (xviii. 31) that he is aware of the curtailment of their powers with regard to the administration of justice, which had taken place shortly before. Especially does he show himself at home in matters concerning the religious life of the people. With a stroke of his pen he can sketch a life-sized portrait of the sensuous, sign-seeking, and miracle-loving Galilean (iv. 45-48; vi. 26), no less than of the ceremonious, arrogant, disputatious and hypocritical Judæan (vii. 48, 49). The Pharisee, with his ponderous legalism, dead literalism, oppressive Sabbatarianism, with his hairsplitting casuistry, unwearying controversy, insufferable vanity and nauseating sanctimony (iii., v., vii., ix.), was as familiar a personage to this Evangelist as to either of the Synoptists; but so also was the haughty and scornful, reckless and semi-infidel Sadducee, though not named, who formed the dominant faction in the hierarchical party of the day. Nor does he forget to emphasize, what a careful study of the First Three Gospels discovers to have been the case, that of the two classes, the latter (the Sadducees, of whom the chief priests were principally composed) were mainly responsible for the crucifixion, as even Pilate was able to perceive (xviii. 35). With the constitution of the Sanhedrim (vii. 45; xi. 47-57), with its functions and disabilities, he approves himself conversant. The anomalous condition into which at that time its presidency had fallen escapes not his notice (xi. 49-51; xviii. 13). He is acquainted, moreover, with the names of the acting high priest in that memorable year when Christ was crucified, Caiaphas (xi. 49), of an ex-high priest, Annas (xviii. 13), and of two councillors, Nicodemus (iii. 1) and Joseph of Arimathea (xix. 38). He mentions also individuals, not alluded to by the Synoptists, as at that time resident in Palestine; such as, in addition to Nicodemus, Lazarus of Bethany (xi. 1), and Malchus xviii. 10). When, therefore, the comparatively late origin of this gospel is considered

—at the earliest towards the end of the first century, when the entire
social and religious aspect of the country, and of the metropolis especially,
had been changed by the sacking of Jerusalem (A.D. 70), and when through
the lapse of years many of the old landmarks must have been removed
since Jesus was baptized at Bethany beyond Jordan, or sat on Jacob's
Well, or lived in retirement at Ephraim—when these things have been
weighed, it will be found a herculean labour to demonstrate that the Fourth
Evangelist was not a native born, but a foreign, perhaps an Alexandrian,
Jew. Yet this is the task attempted by Baur, Strauss, Schenkel, and
others, relying on alleged geographical and historical mistakes which the
author is believed to have committed, but chiefly on the theological
position he is supposed to occupy, as indicated by the (so called Alexandrian)
logos doctrine with which his gospel is introduced. But (1) with regard to
the (so-called) geographical blunders in transferring Bethany (i. 28) from
the Mount of Olives to Peræa, writing Sychar (iv. 5) for the celebrated
Sychem, making out of the Kidron brook a Cedar brook (xviii. 1), and
such like, it has not yet been proved that the author, in any of these
instances, has fallen into error (see Exposition); and till this is done it
seems unnecessary to offer further reply,—the more so, as Keim admits, the
" assumed errors are the less believed, because the author shows otherwise
a tolerable acquaintance with the country " (Jesus of Nazara, vol. i. p. 179),
and Holtzmann concedes that at least they have not been made good
(Einleitung, etc., p. 469). (2) The much emphasized historical inaccuracy
(xi. 49-51 ; xviii. 13), which, according to this school of criticism " always
in unbiassed minds, casts back the doubt whether the Fourth Evangelist
may not have bound up with this assertion the conception of a yearly
change of the high-priestly office " (Schenkel : Das Characterbild Jesu,
p. 375), and " rather looks as if the composer of a book written in pro-
consular Asia were thinking of there-existing relations," according to which
the high priesthood was a yearly appointment (Holtzmann : Einleitung,
p. 469)—even this may be allowed to drop. " The high priest of the year
of death," writes Keim, " is significant, and does not imply the belief that
there was an annual change." (3) The theological standpoint of the
author, supposed to be indicated by the Logos doctrine of the prologue—
the so-called philosophical or metaphysical terminology that runs through
the book, exhibiting itself in a series of contrasts between God and the
devil (viii. 44-47), the kingdom of God and the kingdom of the world
(viii. 23 ; xv. 19 ; xvii. 14-16), light and darkness (i. 4, 5-10 ; iii. 19-21 ;
xii. 35), the truth and the lie (viii. 44 ; xviii. 37), and the mysticism so
characteristic of this gospel, which, it is affirmed, makes, or appears to
make, the incarnation rather than the death of Christ the central point in
redemption, the judgment a present inner process rather than a future

external event, eternal life a state of existence beginning on this side of
the grave rather than on that, and the second advent a spiritual coming to
the souls of believers rather than a visible manifestation at the end of time
—all these would admittedly constitute a powerful argument against the
Palestinian authorship of this gospel, if it could be established that the
Logos doctrine of the prologue was derived from Alexandria (Baur), or that
the metaphysical terminology completely betrayed the approach of the age
of gnosticism (Holtzmann), or that the mysticism alluded to could have
grown up upon neither Jewish nor primitive Christian soil (Holtzmann).
But not one of these positions can be effectually maintained.   Rather, it
is easier to demonstrate that the doctrinal standpoint of this gospel is a
direct product of the Hebrew Scriptures and of the sayings of Jesus (see
note on i. 1 Exposition) ; that the metaphysical conceptions complained of
were thoroughly current and popular in Judaism (Reuss, Geschichte, etc.,
p. 214), and that the mystical presentation of truth it contains is in no
sense incompatible with, but is only the legitimate development of, views
propounded in the earlier gospels.   Hence a just consideration of the
points adverted to rather lends confirmation to the otherwise acquired
inference that the author of this gospel must have been a Palestinian
Jew.

3. *The Author must have been an eye-witness.*   This indeed is directly
claimed to have been the case, twice by the author himself (i. 14 ; xix. 35),
and once by either the author or the persons by whom the gospel was first
put in circulation (xxi. 24).   In various ways the force of these declarations has been attempted to be broken.   a. With regard to i. 14 it has been
urged (Baur, Keim, Schenkel, and others) that the verb " seen," ἐθεασάμεθα,
denotes a purely spiritual perception, a seeing in the spirit, and that the
unwritten "we" refers to the Christian consciousness generally, as
frequently in the First Epistle of John.   But while conceding that the
verb sometimes includes the notion of spiritual apprehension (1 John iv.
14), it is doubtful if it ever points to a spiritual apprehension not based
upon a preceding bodily perception, which latter is indeed the ordinary
acceptation of the word (cf. iv. 35 ; xi. 45 ; 1 John i. 1 ; iv. 14) ; and if
the author conjoins others with himself in saying " we beheld," that cannot
possibly be made to prove that though they had been eye-witnesses he
himself had not.   β. The second passage xix. 35 has been ingeniously
explained.   As everything is ἀληθινός which belongs to the spiritual
world, (i. 9 ; iv. 23 ; vi. 32 ; vii. 28 ; viii. 16 ; xv. 1 ; xvii. 3 ; cf. 1 John ii.
8 ; v. 20 ; Luke xvi. 11 ; Heb. viii. 2 ; ix. 24), so it is said (Holtzmann),
the ἀληθινὴ μαρτυρία or true testimony should also be spiritual.
The form of the sentence also, it is maintained (Weisse, Schweizer), proclaims the Evangelist a late writer who here distinguishes himself from 'the

disciple whom Jesus loved,' since no one would introduce his own witness by saying "he knoweth." If the Evangelist, it is contended (Holtzmann), had desired to represent himself as an eye-witness he would have written "And he testifying hath seen" ὁ μαρτυρῶν ἑώρακεν. But of the things specified in the cited texts, 'the true light' 'the true worshippers,' 'the true bread,' 'the true vine' at least, though belonging to the ἄνω κόσμος, were objects of external vision as well as of spiritual perception; while in speaking of himself in the third person the Evangelist was only following the example of Christ (ix. 37); and it is always hazardous to pronounce how an author under given circumstances would have expressed himself. γ. The third passage, xxi. 24, distinctly identifies 'the disciple whom Jesus loved' as the author of the foregoing gospel, and is not weakened but rather strengthened as a testimony, if it be regarded as an attestation proceeding from those into whose hands the writing was committed for publication. The well known hypothesis, that the composer of this gospel only wished to secure for it a kindly reception when he put it forth under the name of 'this disciple,' need not be considered. "Although the ideas of the time," writes Renan, "respecting literary honesty differed essentially from ours, there is no example in the apostolic world of a falsehood of this kind" (The Life of Jesus, p. 15). There is therefore no ground for questioning that the Book directly and indirectly claims to have been the work of an eye-witness; and that this claim is supported by the narrative, a brief examination renders clear. Not only does the dramatic presentation of such scenes as the visit of the embassy to the Baptist (i. 19-27), of the Cana wedding (ii. 1-11), of the cleansing of the Temple (ii. 13-22), of the walking on the Sea (vi. 16-21), of the controversies in Galilee (vi. 24-71) and in Jerusalem (vii. viii), of the arrest, trial and crucifixion of Jesus (xviii. xix.), suggest the report of a personal spectator, but minute characteristics reveal themselves which almost shut one up to this conclusion. The writer supplies *dates*, days and hours, of events in a manner that only an individual present at the time of their occurrence could have done. He remembers the day when the legation came to the Baptist (i. 28, 29), the day when the marriage took place in Cana (ii. 1), the day when the bailiffs were sent to apprehend Jesus (vii. 45), the day when Christ arrived at Bethany (xii. 1), the day of the crucifixion (xix. 31). He can tell the hour when Andrew and his companion (himself) first spoke to Jesus (i. 39), the hour when Christ reached Jacob's Well (iv. 6), the hour when the nobleman's son began to amend (iv. 52), the hour of the crucifixion (xix. 14). He gives *numbers* in cases where his sole reason for doing so can have been that he knew them. He states that in the wedding hall at Cana six waterpots were set (ii. 6), that at Bethesda the porches were five (v. 2), that the lad at Bethsaida had five barley

loaves and two fishes (vi. 9), that the persons fed were about five thousand
(vi. 10), and that the fragments filled twelve baskets (vi. 13), that the
mixture of myrrh and aloes brought by Nicodemus to the burial of Jesus
weighed 100 lbs. (xix. 39), and that the fish caught in the miraculous
draught numbered 153 (xxii. 11). He recalls *circumstances*, connected with the
scenes and occurrences he reports, that are not recorded elsewhere and
that only an actual observer could have reproduced.   He mentions, for
instance, that the water-pots at Cana were filled to the brim (ii. 7), that
Christ made a scourge of small cords to drive out the cattle from the
temple (ii. 15), that the woman left her water-pot when she departed from
the well (iv. 28), that there was much grass in the place where the people
sat down (vi. 10), that the disciples had rowed about five-and-twenty
furlongs when Christ appeared to them on the sea (vi. 19), that the Jews
who came with Mary were also weeping (xi. 33), that a stone lay against
the cave in which Lazarus was buried (xi. 38), and that when Lazarus
came forth his face was bound about with a napkin (xi. 44), that it was
night when Judas left the supper room (xiii. 30), that the captors of Jesus
carried lanterns and torches as well as weapons (xviii. 3), that Christ was
taken first to Annas (xviii 13), that the servants and the officers in the
high priest's palace-court had kindled a fire (xviii. 18), and that Peter stood
among them warming himself, because the night air was chill (xviii. 18, 25),
that Pilate pronounced judgment from a *bema* or raised platform outside
the palace (xix. 13), that Christ's legs were not broken after crucifixion,
but that His side was pierced, while a stream of blood and water issued
from the wound (xix. 33, 34), and that the net with its multitude of great
fishes was not rent (xxi. 11).   And finally the Evangelist *locates incidents*
in a way that a spectator alone could or would have attempted.   The
Baptist, he says, was at Bethany beyond Jordan when approached by the
legation (i. 28), and at Ænon near to Salim when the dispute arose between
his disciples and a Jew (iii. 25); Christ was at Cana when He healed
the nobleman's son in Capernaum (iv. 46), and in Bethesda sanatorium
when He cured the cripple (v. 6); the discourse about the Bread of Life
was delivered in a synagogal assembly at Capernaum (vi. 59), that about
His person in the Treasury as He taught in the temple (viii. 20), and that
about His oneness with the Father in Solomon's porch (x. 23); Christ's
first examination took place before Annas, His second before Caiaphas,
and His third before Pilate (xviii. 12, 24-28); with reference to this
latter not only did the Jews not enter the prætorium but Pilate went back
and forward between them and his prisoner as the trial passed from stage to
stage (xviii. 28, 29; 33, 38; xix. 1, 4; 9, 13); Christ's condemnation was
pronounced at a place called Gabbatha (xix. 13), His crucifixion carried out
upon Golgotha (xix. 17), and His burial performed in Joseph's garden

tomb (xix. 42). It is doubtful if any writer ever furnished more conclusive evidence that he was an actual observer, a personal spectator, a direct eye and ear witness of the events he related.

4. *The Author must have been an apostle.* This follows from what has been already said. Only one of the twelve could have been an eye and ear witness of many of the transactions recorded and words reported in this gospel. In addition to the miracle of walking on the sea and the discourses in the upper room, incidents and conversations may be pointed out of which only an immediate attendant, in fact a member of the apostolic circle, could have been cognizant. Of the former the following may be taken as examples :—The visit of Nicodemus to Christ (iii. 1 ; cf. vii. 50 ; xix. 39), Christ speaking with the woman at the well, (iv. 27) ; the feet washing in the upper room (xiii. 5), the giving of the sop to Judas (xiii. 26), the appearance of the risen Lord to the disciples (xx. 19, 26). Of the latter, illustrations will suggest themselves :—The remarks addressed to Peter (i. 42), to Philip (i. 44), to Nathanael (1 47) ; the conversations with Nicodemus (iii. 3-20), with the disciples at the well in the absence of the woman (iv. 31-38), with the nobleman (iv. 48-50), with Philip and Andrew at the miracle of feeding (vi. 5-9), with the twelve in Peræa (xi. 7-16), the request of the Greeks (xii. 21), the communication of Mary (xx. 18). Then the reflection seems decisive that only one who had himself heard our Lord's discourses, and was familiar with His modes of thought and expression, who had largely felt the influence of His transcendent personality and had drunk deeply of His spirit, could have supplied the subjective psychological conditions requisite for reproducing, and of course much more for inventing, such discourses as in this gospel are placed in Christ's mouth. But if the author of this book was an apostle, the next steps in the argument are unavoidable.

5. *The Author must have been the disciple whom Jesus loved.* Explicitly asserted in the attestation (already referred to) appended to the work on its first publication by the elders of the church at Ephesus (xxi. 24), as much as this may be inferred from the writer's own statement (xix. 35). No impartial reader will doubt that the eye-witness of the spear thrust was 'the disciple whom Jesus loved,' to whom the dying Saviour, a moment before, had commended His mother (xix. 26).

6. *The Author must have been one of the inner circle of three.* Attempts have been made to prove that 'the disciple whom Jesus loved' was not an individual at all, but an ideal personage, a representative of the spiritualized Christianity of the Fourth Gospel (Scholten), or if a veritable human being and an apostle, then either Andrew (Lützelberger), or Nathanael (Späth); but the special tokens of favour that, according to the Synoptists, were bestowed on Peter, James, and John (Matt. xvii. 1 ; Mark v. 37 ; ix.

2 ; xiv. 33 ; Luke viii. 51 : ix. 28), ought to place it beyond contradiction that 'the disciple whom Jesus loved' was one or other of these. Hence the last step in this argumentative progress may be taken.

7. *The Author must have been John.* (1) All the foregoing marks of the required author meet in John. The younger son of Zebedee was a Jew— a Palestinian—an eye-witness—an apostle—one of the inner circle of three. The sole question that remains is : Was he the disciple whom Jesus loved ? (2) All the signs furnished by the gospel point to the conclusion that he was. (a) The disciple whom Jesus loved was not Peter from whom he is always distinguished (xiii. 24 ; xviii. 5 ; xx. 2), or James who died before this gospel was written (Acts xii. 2), and therefore must have been John. (β) The disciple whom Jesus loved was the intimate associate of Peter, and after the resurrection, in the church of Pentecost, the one who appears oftenest in Peter's company is John (Acts iii. 1, 11 ; iv. 13; viii. 14 ; Gal. ii. 9). (γ) The disciple whom Jesus loved must have been John, else there is no mention of, or allusion to, him at all in this gospel which is, to say the least, surprising, considering the prominence of John in the apostolate. (δ) The disciple whom Jesus loved was among the seven mentioned in xxi. 2, of whom the only one that answers all the requirements of the case is John (see Exposition on xxi. 24). (3) Several collateral considerations confirm the conclusion that John was the author. (a) The affinity between the 1st Epistle of John and this gospel in thought and expression is such that they must have proceeded from the same hand (see Reuss, Geschichte, etc.). But the Johannine authorship of the epistle is one of the recognized tenets of the best criticism of the day. Hence the Johannine authorship of the gospel can with difficulty be denied. (β) A similar deduction may be made from the correspondence in theological conceptions and linguistic phrases between this gospel and the Apocalypse. If the latter was the work of John, as it purports to have been (Rev. i. 9), as ecclesiastical tradition affirms it was (Justin Martyr, Irenaeus, Tertullian, Clement), and as many competent critics admit (Eichhorn, Ebrard, Hofmann, Hengstenberg, Oosterzee, Gebhardt, etc.), it is hard to see how the inference can be evaded that the same writer must have composed the former (cf. Alford's N. T., vol. iv. p. 226).

II. **External Evidence** ; or the witness of tradition to the author of the gospel.

The precise value of the testimony now to be adduced, it may be well to state. It is obvious that mere silence in any age concerning a book does not prove conclusively that the book in question was not then in existence. On the other hand the appearance in contemporaneous and succeeding literature of either direct or indirect reference to a book affords constructive evidence that the book must have been in circulation, though such references need not imply a judgment upon either its historic credibility or authorship. At the same time, in the present instance, should it turn out that this gospel was in use towards the close of the apostolic age, that circumstance will unquestionably have weight in determining the personality of its author; and in case it should happen that specific declarations can be culled from the first and second centuries with reference to this, these, it will be evident, must be looked upon as valuable contributions towards the settlement of this important problem.

For convenience the investigation will arrange itself in four divisions:— (1) The Apostolic Fathers (80-150 A.D.), (2) The Christian Apologists (150-175 A.D.), (3) The Second Century Canonists (175-200 A.D.), and (4) Writers of the period, outside the Church—whether apocryphists, heretics, or pagans.

A. THE APOSTOLIC FATHERS: 80-150 A.D.

1. **The Epistle of Clement.** Written to the Church of the Corinthians by Clement—whether Paul's companion mentioned in Phil. iv. 3 (Origen, Eusebius, Jerome) or not (Reuss) is uncertain—who was bishop of Rome from either 68-77 A.D. (Jerome) or 91-101 A.D. (Eusebius), this "precious relic of later apostolic times," exhibits points of contact with St. John's gospel, in word and phrase, which are both numerous and striking. "The true and only God" (xliii. 6) may be compared with John xvii. 3 (less appropriately with 1 John v. 20, and 1 Thess. i. 9); "to work a work" (xxxiii. 8) with John vi. 28; "to do the truth" (xxxi. 2) with John iii. 21, 1 John i. 6; "the flock of Christ" (xvi. 1), and "the sheep of His pasture" (lvii. 4), with John x. 1 ff. But inasmuch as this epistle cannot be dated later than 95-97 A.D., and may have been written earlier, nothing can be deduced from it concerning the gospel beyond the fact, that the forms of thought and expression characterizing the latter were already current towards the close of the first century. At the same time if Clement's epistle may not be cited as a witness for John's gospel, just as little can John's gospel be shown to have been dependent on Clement's epistle (cf. O. Holtzmann's Das Johannesevangelium, 1887, p. 179). A second letter bearing Clement's name discovers a closer approximation to the phraseology of the Fourth Gospel; but, being generally pronounced spurious, it may be passed without remark.

2. **The Epistle of Barnabas.** Whether a production of Paul's companion and fellow-traveller (Vossius, Rosenmuller, Bleek) or an apocryphal writing (Ménard, Ullmann, Neander, Winer), this epistle is believed from internal considerations to have been composed either in the closing decade of the first (see Reuss, Geschichte der heiligen Schriften, etc., p. 223; Tischendorf, 'When were our gospels written?' p. 93), or the begin-

ning of the second century (Hilgenfeld, Keim, Beyschlag, Westcott). Differ-
ing from the Fourth Gospel in its more frequent references to the O. T. it yet
reveals a correspondence with that gospel in terms and ideas. "The new
law of Our Lord Jesus Christ" (ii. 6) recalls John xiii. 34. The citation
of Is. liii. (v. 2) brings to recollection John i. 29. According to Barnabas
Christ behoved to be "manifested in the flesh" (v. 6) and of Him it is
taught that "The Son of God came in the flesh" (v. 10, 11), and was
"manifested in the flesh" (xii. 10)—language which echoes John i. 14, 31.
Again "They (the Jews) did not hear the voice of the Lord" (xii. 10)
suggests John x. 16 ; while the allusion to the brazen serpent as a
type of Jesus (xii. 5-7) connects directly with John iii. 14. Many
of these expressions, it is thought, may have been derived from the
First Johannine epistle, and the allusion to the serpent from the
Wisdom of Solomon, xvi. 5-12 (H. Holtzmann, Einleitung, p. 478,
and O. Holtzmann, Das Johannesevangelium, pp. 180, 181); and
this may have been the case, if the composition of Barnabas's
epistle synchronized with that of St. John's gospel; but if, as seems
indubitable, at the time when the epistle was composed Matthew, Mark
and Luke were already regarded as "canonical," or at least as "authoritative Scripture"—a quotation from Matt. xx. 16 or xxii. 14 being introduced by the formula "as it is written" (iv.), the presumption is that
John also was in the same sense 'canonical' or 'authoritative'—("The
gospel of John was in as early use as the Synoptic gospels," Keim, vol. i p.
184)—and was the true source of the above cited words and phrases (cf.
Tischendorf, "When were," etc., p. 94).

   3. **The Letters of Ignatius.** Purporting to have been written by the
bishop of Antioch when on his way to martyrdom at Rome (107-115 A.D.),
these letters have been transmitted to posterity in three forms, (1) in a
longer Greek recension generally regarded as spurious, (2) in a shorter Greek
form, discovered by Vossius about the middle of the seventeenth century, and
(3) in a still shorter Syriac dress, published by Cureton in 1845. Accepting
the third, the Curetonian, or Syriac epistles as the only genuine letters of
Ignatius (Bunsen, Ewald, Weiss, cf. Lightfoot, Cont. Rev. (1885) p. 355),
the following passage occurs, "I seek the bread of God which is the flesh
of Jesus Christ, and I seek His blood, a drink which is love incorruptible,"
(Ad Rom. vii.), which unmistakeably reechoes the language of Jesus in
John vi. If the Vossian or short Greek form of the epistles be admitted
(Uhlhorn, Petermann, Hefele, Zahn, cf. Lightfoot, Cont. Rev. (1885),
p. 357), the passage just cited will run thus :—"I desire the bread of God,
the heavenly bread, the bread of life, which is the flesh of Jesus Christ,
the Son of God . . . ; and I desire the drink of God which is incorruptible love and eternal life ; " while to it may be added these "He

(Christ) is the door of the Father " (Ad Phil. ix.), and "The Spirit, as being from God, is not deceived. For it knows both whence it comes and whither it goeth, and detects (ἐλέγχει) the secrets of the heart" (Ad Philad. vii.),—which may be compared, the first with John xiv. 6, and the second with John iii. 8, xvi. 8.

4. **The Epistle of Polycarp.** Dating from 107 A.D. (Gaussen) or 115 A.D. (Tischendorf, Westcott),—in any case proceeding from a point of time not far-removed from the martyrdom of Ignatius to which it alludes (chap. ix.), this brief letter contains more clear references to the N. T. Scriptures than any other work of the post-apostolic age. Its author, a pupil of St. John, had been associated with those who had seen the Lord and had been placed over the Church at Smyrna by the apostle himself (Iren. Haer. iii. 3, 4 ; Euseb. H.E. iv. 14). At his martyrdom about 167 A.D. (Neander, C.H. vol. i. p. 150), or, according to recent investigation, 155-6 A.D.(Lightfoot, Cont. Rev. (1875), p. 838), he had been 86 years a Christian. Hence his ministry at Smyrna must have been for some years contemporaneous with that of St. John at Ephesus. In this letter to the Church of the Philippians, which gives evidence of being acquainted with most of the N. T. books, there is no mention of the Fourth Gospel ; and this has been pronounced "the more surprising since the Fourth Gospel as a work of the Apostle John must have been for Polycarp of special value " (Schenkel, Das Characterbild Jesu, p. 370). But (1) the letter being short could not have contained everything its writer might have inserted, while (2) no more unsafe principle of reasoning exists than to argue *ex silentio* that what a writer omits allusion to he does not know, and (3) Polycarp may not have had occasion to cite from St. John's gospel, to which may be added (4) that the letter contains an almost direct citation from St. John's First Epistle—" Whosoever confesses not that Jesus Christ is come in the flesh is Antichrist " (vii., cf. i. John iv. 3). Unless therefore this verse was a popular maxim current in the Church which both the apostle and the Christian father borrowed (Baur, Scholten, and others, cf. Supernatural Religion, vol. ii. p. 269)—a pure hypothesis, or St. John quoted from Polycarp (Bretschneider, Lützelberger, Volkmar),—a theory which Bleek declares "utterly futile and unreasonable," and Tischendorf thinks "a man must have some courage to start," while Keim regards it as " not successful," drawing attention to the posteriority of the Polycarpian epistle implied in its use of " an Antichrist," instead of " the Antichrist," as in John (but see 1 John ii. 18)—the conclusion is inevitable that the former drew from the latter; and though certainly this cannot be held as guaranteeing the existence and canonicity of St. John's gospel in the time of Polycarp, it at least vouches for the Johannine authorship of the epistle and through that, also, indirectly of the gospel.

5. **The Writings of Papias.** Usually reckoned among the apostolic fathers, Papias, bishop of Hierapolis in Phrigia, died as a martyr at Pergamos in the reign of M. Aurelius, 161-180 A.D. He was probably born in the first century, since Irenaeus calls him "an ancient man" (ἀρχαῖον ἄνδρα), a companion (ἑταῖρον) of Polycarp, and a hearer of John (Haer. v. 33, 4; cf. Euseb. H.E. iii. 39), but whether of the apostle John (Lightfoot, Cont. Rev. (1875) vol. xxvi. p. 379), or of Presbyter John (Keim, Holtzmann) is debated. A work of five books called Expositions of the Oracles of the Lord, written by him perhaps about the middle of the second century, reports that he derived his information mostly from persons who had talked with the apostles. "If then" he says "any one who had attended on the elders (obviously the immediate disciples of the Lord) came, I asked minutely after their sayings—what Andrew or Peter said, or what was said by Philip, or by Thomas, or by James, or by John, or by Matthew, or by any other of the Lord's disciples : which things (or and what things) Aristion and the presbyter John, the disciples of the Lord say" (Fragments of Papias, I). In this book though other gospels (Matthew and Mark) and epistles (including 1 John) are mentioned, there is seeming silence preserved regarding the gospel of St. John ; and on this has been based an argument against the existence of the latter in the time of Papias. "What Papias has said," writes Strauss, we know indeed only "out of Eusebius ; but as it lies in the plan of his church history to collect the oldest testimonies for the N. T. writings, and as he cites Papias for the first Johannine epistle, so is his silence concerning the witness of Papias for the Johannine gospel much the same thing as the silence of Papias himself. And this silence of Papias concerning John as the composer of a gospel strikes one the more forcibly, since he not only expressly certifies that he had zealously inquired after traditions also of John, but as a bishop in Asia Minor, and an acquaintance of John's scholar, Polycarp, who spent his last years in Ephesus, he might have easily ascertained the exact truth" (Das Leben Jesu (1877), vol. i. p. 78). "Had Papias expressed any recognition of the Fourth Gospel, Eusebius would have mentioned the fact, and this silence of Papias is strong presumptive evidence against the Johannine gospel" (Supernatural Religion, vol. ii. p. 322). In reply, however, it is reasonably urged :—(1) That Eusebius's object did not require him to mention the 'acknowledged' books of Scripture unless there was something of special interest to communicate regarding them. Hence, however frequently Papias may have quoted from or referred to John's gospel, Eusebius may have felt absolved from the necessity of noticing it, by the plan he had adopted ; and thus, so far from Eusebius's silence being an argument against this gospel, it is rather an indirect proof that this gospel was already amongst the universally acknowledged books of Scrip-

ture (cf. Westcott, On the N. T. Canon, pp. 61, 65; Lightfoot, Cont. Rev. (1875) vol. xxv. p. 183, vol. xxvi. p. 828 ; Godet, vol. i. pp. 233, 234).   (2) That not even Papias proposed to present a catalogue of the sacred books, but merely " Expositions " of Our Lord's sayings,—the notices Eusebius (H. E. iii. 39) quotes from Papias concerning Matthew and Mark (Fragments of Papias vi.) having been introduced not to prove that these were the authors of the gospels then existing under their names, but for the sake of the particular details that Papias supplied.   (3) That the fact of Eusebius's reminiscences of Papias being fragmentary, renders it impossible to affirm there was no reference to John's gospel in any part of Papias's work.   (4) That, as Papias makes no mention of Luke's gospel, it would be requisite to argue that in the days of Papias this also had not been composed—a proposition to which few, if any, will commit themselves.   (5) That Eusebius does not always record all he might concerning those books of which he treats, as e.g. when he states that Polycarp's letter contains passages from the first epistle of Peter but omits to say that the same letter is also full of quotations from Paul (Tischendorf: ' When were,' etc., pp. 110, 111 ; Lightfoot, Cont. Rev. vol. xxv. p. 177). (6) That Papias distinctly declares he drew his materials not from apostolical writings but from oral tradition (cf. Ebrard, The Gospel History, § 127, 4).   (7) That a Latin MS. of the gospels, dating from the ninth century, in its preface assigns to Papias an account of the composition of the Gospel by John (cf. Luthardt, The Gospel of John, vol. i. p. 221; Westcott, The Gospel of St. John, Introd., p. xxxi). (8) That, like Polycarp, Papias made use of John's first epistle (Euseb.: H. E. iii. 39)—from which it may be argued, at least he was acquainted with John's writings.   (9) That it is too hastily assumed no trace of the Fourth Gospel can be detected in Papias's fragments.   a. The expression " The commandments given to the faith by the Lord and which come to us from the truth itself " (Frag. I.) reminds one more readily of John xiv. 6, than of 3 John 12 (Holtzmann). β. Papias's list of the apostles places Andrew at the head, then Peter, Philip, and Thomas, next James, John, and Matthew "—an order more likely to have been learnt from John (cf. i. 40-47; xxi. 2), than from Matt. (iv. 18 ; x. 2), or Mark (i. 16 ; iii. 17). γ. Irenaeus reports an explanation of John xiv. 2, given by the elders or presbyters of Asia Minor to which circle Papias belonged (Haer. v. 36), and an opinion entertained by them, manifestly based on John viii. 56, that Jesus lived till the age of 50 (Haer. ii. 22). If these reported facts are authentic history the deduction from them is good logic, that Papias must have been acquainted with the Fourth Gospel.   Nor is the soundness of this conclusion affected, even if Irenaeus is not quoting from Papias (Super. Rel. ii. 324 ff.); while, on the other hand, if he is as Lightfoot believes (Cont. Rev. xxvi. p. 841), that conclusion is considerably strengthened.

6. The Shepherd of Hermas.—Regarded by Muratori's canon as the production of one Hermas, the brother of Pius I., bishop of Rome, 140-150 A.D., this writing was considered by Eusebius, Origen, and Jerome as a genuine composition of the Hermas of Rom. xvi. 14, and therefore as written about the end of the first century. The points of contact between it and John's gospel are numerous as well as striking, and occur in each of its three divisions, 'The Visions,' 'The Similitudes,' 'The Commandments'; so much so that while H. Holtzmann thinks 'nothing hinders the priority from being assigned to the Shepherd' (Einleitung, p. 479), and O. Holtzmann deems it "hazardous to ground upon passing similarities conclusions as to the origin of the gospel" (Das Johannesevangelium, p. 182), Keim is of opinion that Hermas "was evidently acquainted with the first epistle, while his whole terminology often reminds us of the gospel of John" (Jesus of Nazara, vol. i. p. 192).

7. The Teaching of the Twelve Apostles.—Διδαχὴ Κυρίου διὰ τῶν δώδεκα ἀποστόλων. Presenting an occasional echo of Johannine thought and expression, it is doubtful if closer connection can be established between this recently discovered and seemingly ancient monument (belonging in all probability to the first half of the second century) and the Fourth Gospel than exists between this and the letters of Clement of Rome and of Barnabas.

B. CHRISTIAN APOLOGISTS : 150-175 A.D.

1. Justin Martyr.—Born at Shechem in Samaria about 103 A.D., converted from Greek philosophy about 133-140 A.D., and martyred about 167 A.D. Amongst other works now lost, Justin left behind him two apologies (one addressed to Antoninus in 139, another to Marcus Aurelius in 163) and a dialogue with Trypho the Jew. These writings, still extant, it has been customary to assert, betray an acquaintance only, or principally, with the Synoptists, the Johannine Apocalypse, and the Gospel of Peter ; hardly, if at all, with the Fourth Gospel (Reuss, §294). This position, however, can scarcely be maintained. It may be open to challenge whether the statement made by Justin, that "the Memoirs of the Apostles (ἀπομνημονεύματα τῶν ἀποστόλων) or the writings of the prophets are read, as far as time permits," (Apol. i. 67) every Lord's day in the assemblies of the Christians, amounts to a demonstration of the canonicity of St. John's gospel (Tischendorf). This is usually supposed to be made out by citing the following extract :—" For that He was the only begotten of the Father of all, in peculiar wise begotten of Him as Word and Power, and afterwards became man through the Virgin, as we have learnt from the Memoirs, I have already stated" (Dial. c. 105)—which, it is assumed, must have been derived from the Fourth Gospel. But, inasmuch as the birth of Jesus may have been learnt from Luke, and the phrase "only begotten of the Father" drawn, though not likely, from Matt. xi. 27 (Holtzmann), this need not be pressed. Apart from this, the correspondences between Justin's writings and St. John's gospel are too explicit to be overlooked. Prominent among these is the doctrine of the Word or Logos, who, in Justin as in John, was "with God, and begotten by God, when at the beginning He created all things by Him" (Apol. ii. 6), was "begotten by the Father and before all creatures with the Father" (Dial. c. 62), who "took flesh and blood" (Apol. i. 66), and "became man for the race of man" (Apol. ii. 6, 13 ; Dial. c. 127). So unmistakeable is this resemblance that the author of Supernatural Religion labours to demonstrate that Justin borrowed his conceptions from the Alexandrine Philo rather than from the Palestinian John (vol. ii. pp. 273 ff.). This explanation, however, one feels, must be abandoned when not only Dorner (Doct. of the Person of Christ, div. 1, vol. i. pp. 264 ff.) calls it in question, but even Strauss (Das Leben Jesu, vol. i. p. 82) admits the closest parallel between the two, though maintaining that the Logos of Justin was only John's Logos coloured through Philonian philosophy, and Keim writes "It is quite impossible not to admit that the ideas of Justin are, on the whole, far more advanced, and at the same time derived from those of John" (Jesus of Nazara, vol. i. p. 187). Then as to particular passages in Justin revealing acquaintance with John, these may be specified :—(1) Dial. c. 63, "His blood did not spring from the seed of man, but from the will of God"—an echo of John i. 13 ; (2) Dial. c. 88, "I am not the Christ, but the voice of one crying"—a literal citation of John i. 20-23 ; (3) Apol. i. 61, "Christ has said, Except ye are born again ye cannot enter into the kingdom of God ; now that it is impossible that those who are once born should enter into their mother's womb is clear to every one"—which recalls the language of Christ to Nicodemus (John iii. 3-5). On the ground that the first part of this verse is to be found in the Clementine Homilies, with similar deviations from Christ's words in John, and that the second may have been derived from Matt. xviii. 3, Strauss (Das Leben Jesu [.1877], vol. i. p. 63) thinks both Justin and John may have borrowed from the Gospel to the Hebrews, which contains, it is said, an analogous expression to that in Matt. xviii. 3 ; but, besides being purely conjectural, this hypothesis shatters itself against the fact that Justin in the latter part of his statement does not quote from the words of Christ, but comments upon the objection of Nicodemus. (4) Apol. i. 63, "They knew neither the Father nor the Son"—reminding one of John viii. 19; xvi. 3. (5) Apol. i.

22 ; Dial. c. 69, Jesus healed "the blind from birth"—an allusion to John ix. 1. (6) Apol. i. 52. Here the text Zech. xii. 10 is cited exactly as in John xix. 37. (7) In other places, as in John, Christ is designated 'Light,' 'The Water of Life,' 'a Fountain of Living Water,' etc. Now, as it is impossible to believe that "the original and spiritual author of the gospel was the scholar of Justin Martyr, who was notoriously a man whose powers of mind were moderate, dependent upon what he gleaned from others, and ineloquent" (Keim, Jesus of Nazara, vol. i. p. 187), and as the suggestion of a community of sources (Holtzmann, Einleitung, p. 480) at the best wears the look of an evasion, the natural conclusion is that Justin drew his information in these several passages from John. It need scarcely be added that if this was so, the further deduction follows that the Memoirs of the Apostles of which he speaks must have included this gospel.

2. **Tatian.**—A scholar of the preceding Justin, by whom he was ostensibly converted to Christianity,—about 150-160 A.D. (Holtzmann)‚ about 170 A.D. (Bleek, Tischendorf)—from which, however, he eventually declined. He, prior to his apostasy, composed an apology styled "An address to the Greeks," and a harmony or *diatessaron*, i.e. a gospel according to four,—the former still extant and the latter known through the writings of Eusebius and Theodoret in the fourth and fifth centuries. The apology John expressly cites the Johannine prologue as 'already authoritative' (e.g. John i. 1 in chap. v.; i. 3 in chap. xix.; i. 5 in chap. xiii.; and iv. 24 in chap. iv.); and the diatessaron, though not naming the authors of the gospels, and exercising considerable freedom with the gospels themselves, yet leaves no doubt that these were the gospels of Matthew, Mark, Luke, and John.

3. **Theophilus of Antioch.**—Contemporary with Tatian, about 170 A.D. (Tischendorf, Bleek), about 180 (Reuss, Holtzmann). With Theophilus commence positive testimonies to St. John as the author of the Fourth Gospel. Converted to Christianity by reading the Scriptures, he, according to Jerome, wrote a book combining the sayings of the four evangelists into one work, *quatuor evangelistarum in unum opus compingens* (Ep. 151 ad Algasiam)—which four evangelists Jerome takes for granted were our canonical gospels. In another treatise still extant 'Ad Autolycum,' not only are the books of the O. and N. Testaments placed on an equal footing as regards canonical worth, but the evangelists are declared to be not less 'borne by the Spirit' πνευματοφόροι, than the prophets (ii. 9, 22 ; iii. 12), one of those evangelists being expressly named John—" Of whom John says, In the beginning, etc." (ii. 22). Theophilus also speaks of the "Word through whom God made all things," and calls Him God's Son (ibid.).

4. **Apollinaris of Hierapolis.** Writing (170 A.D.) against the observance of the Christian passover on the 14th Nisan because, according to Matthew's gospel, Christ on that evening celebrated the paschal feast, dying on the 15th, Apollinaris remarks that in that case "the gospels would seem to contradict one another" (Chron. Pasch. 1-14). But the gospels thus referred to could only have been John and Matthew. Hence whatever opinion may be entertained of Apollinaris's judgment on the passover controversy, it is clear that he recognized the four gospels as in his day "already a solid whole" *ein solidarisches Ganzes* (Holtzmann, Einleitung, p. 130).

5. **Athenagoras**, an Athenian philosopher who embraced Christianity, composed an apology, or 'embassy' (πρεσβεία), for the Christians, which was presented to the Emperors Aurelius and Commodus about 177 A.D. Not only does he speak in this of God as "having made all things by the Word (Logos) which is from Him" (chap iv., vi.), but he also designates that Word (Logos) "The Son of God," "by whom all things were made, the Father and the Son being one," "The Son being in the Father and the Father in the Son," adding "He (the Son) is the first product of the Father, not as having been brought into existence, for from the beginning God, who is the eternal mind, had the Logos in Himself" (chap. x.). It is impossible to doubt that the source of these ideas was the prologue of the Fourth Gospel.

6. **The Epistle to Diognetus.** Neither author nor date of this eloquent and interesting letter can be ascertained, though from its recognition of the equal position of 'the law and the prophets' on the one hand, and of 'the gospels and apostles' on the other (see chap. xi.), it should probably be assigned to the latter half of the second century. In any case the author shows himself acquainted with the Fourth Gospel, by using expressions that could certainly be more easily derived thence than from any other source, not only calling Christ "The Truth," "The holy and incomprehensible Word," "The very Creator and Fashioner of all things," "God's only begotten Son," who "was manifested" and "sent not to judge" but to save men (see chaps. v. and x.), but also depicting Christians as "not of the world" (chap. vi. ; cf. John xvii. 11, 14, 16).

C.   WRITERS ON THE CANON : 170-200 A.D.

1. **The Canon of Muratori.** Discovered by A. Muratori, librarian of the Ambrosian College at Milan, in 1694-1700 A.D., and dating from about 170 A.D. (Tischendorf, Westcott, Holtzmann), this fragment contains a catalogue of the books of the New Testament, prepared probably in Rome, and places at the head of the list our canonical gospels, mentioning "in barbarous and often meaningless Latin the gospels of Luke and

John, the Acts, thirteen letters of Paul, a letter of Jude and two of John, the Apocalypses of John and of Peter, the last, however, with mention of a contradiction (Reuss, § 310). The absence of Matthew and Mark is accounted for by the fact that the first lines have mostly perished. Explaining how the gospels were given the writer says:—"The Fourth Gospel is that of John, one of the disciples," adding that he wrote "at the request of his fellow-disciples and bishops, in obedience to a revelation given to the apostle Andrew, aided by the revision of all" . . . and that in all he wrote he professed himself "not only an eye-witness, but also a hearer, and, moreover, a historian of all the wonderful works of our Lord."

2. **Irenaeus.** Born in Asia Minor about 120 A.D., *i.e.* 17 years after the death of St. John, educated in Greek culture and in Christian learning, admitted in early life to frequent intercourse with Polycarp, to which in later years he alluded in a letter to one Florinus (Euseb. H.E. v. 19, 20), in 178 A.D., he was appointed Bishop of Lyons, where he was subsequently martyred in 197 or 202 A.D. Though not a canonist in the sense of furnishing a list of the New Testament books, the number of quotations made by him from these enables a judgment to be formed as to the Scriptures currently accepted as canonical in the latter half of the second century by the Gallican Churches over which he presided. Not only are the gospels (New Testament) and the prophets (Old Testament) for him the entire Scriptures, *universae Scripturae*, of equal credibility and authority —the former proceeding from the apostles exactly as the latter did from the prophets, by inspiration, (Haer. II. 27, 2), but "that which the prophets proclaimed, the Lord taught and the apostles handed down" (I. 8, 1) is the truth. Not only does he know of the existence of four gospels under the names of Matthew, Mark, Luke, and John—of the last saying, "Afterwards John, the disciple of the Lord, who also had leaned upon His breast, did himself publish a gospel during his residence in Ephesus, in Asia" (iii. 1, 1)—but he endeavours to demonstrate the necessity of the gospels being four in number, and no more—"the gospel under four aspects, but bound together by one spirit"—from there being four regions of the earth, four winds, and four cherubim (III. xi. 7). Then while the quotations in all amount to about 400, those taken directly from John exceed 80.

3. **Tertullian.** Born about 50 years after St. John's death, converted to Christianity at the age of 35, this presbyter of Carthage, who lapsed into Montanism 199 A.D., and died about 223 A.D., is in like manner a witness to the views on canonical Scripture entertained about the end of the second century by the churches of North Africa. In his writings he appears to have employed a Latin translation of the New Testament, in which already the books were thus divided. 1. The *instrumentum evangelicum*, or body of

the four gospels; 2. the *instrumenta apostolica,* including (1) the *instru-mentum actorum* (Acts), (2) the *instrumentum Pauli* (13 Epistles), (3) the *instru-mentum Johannis* (1 John and Revelation), (4) another group of Antilego-mena containing 1 Peter, Jude, Hebrews, and James. Prefixed to the whole was a similar translation of the Old Testament. Of the two thus bound together Tertullian speaks as one, calling it *totum instrumentum utriusque testamenti* (Adv. Prax. 20), and naming both testaments *sacramenta* as com-prehending all the ordinances and commandments of God (Apol. 47). Not only does he recognize the canonicity and Johannine authorship of John, saying—"John and Matthew first instil faith into us; while of apostolic men, Luke and Mark renew it afterwards" (c. Mar. iv. 2); and again calling the gospels of John and Matthew (perhaps also of Mark and Luke, as indirectly those of Peter and Paul) "the work of apostles" (c. Mar. iv., v.), but "his numerous writings contain several hundreds of pages taken from the gospels—two hundred of these at least from John" (Tischendorf, "When were" etc., p. 49).—**Note.** In this connection mention may be made of the Syriac Peschito (i.e. *simple, literal* version), probably an earlier translation than the old Latin version above alluded to (West-cott), certainly in existence about the middle or end of the second century (Tischendorf)—which also contained the Four Gospels, and in fact the whole of our Canon except the Apocalypse, with the four small epistles of Jude, 2 Peter, 2 and 3 John.

4. **Clement.** A celebrated Christian teacher in Alexandria, and the master of Origen, this voluminous and gifted writer, who also flourished towards the end of the second century (A.D. 189-220), may be cited to attest the faith of the Churches of the East with regard to the canon. Like Irenaeus and Tertullian, he also knows of other inspired writings besides the Old Testament, naming them, equally with these latter, Scripture γραφή (Strom. ii. 6, 29), considering the gospel and the apostles along with the prophets as co-ordinate sources of truth (Strom. vii. 16, 95), and in particular distin-guishing our canonical gospels from the gospel of the Egyptians (Strom. iii. 13, 93), though this is questioned by H. Holtzmann (Einleitung, p. 155). Clement also furnishes this account of the origin of the Fourth Gospel:— "John received the first three gospels, and observing that they comprized the external facts in the life of the Lord, he, at the instance of eminent men in the church, wrote a spiritual gospel" (Euseb. H.E. vi. 14). From this gospel also he makes numerous citations.

D. WRITERS OUTSIDE THE CHURCH

1. **Apocryphal.** (1) *The Acts of Pilate.* Whether the original of these now incorporated in the gospel of Nicodemus was a forgery (Bleek), or a genuine writing of the Roman procurator (Tischendorf), it is certain that

the Acts of Pilate were cited as an authority by Justin (Apol. i. 35-48), and contain traces of having drawn their information from the Fourth Gospel, as when they introduce the lame man of Bethesda and the man born blind as witnesses who speak to the Governor for Christ (Gosp. of Nicod. vi.), and describe Pilate's going back and forward between the Jews without and Jesus within the Praetorium exactly as John does (G. of N. iii., iv.). (2) *The Clementine Homilies.* Attributed to Clement of Rome, but in reality an apocryphal writing of the second or third (Neander) —about the middle of the second (Holtzmann)—century, these also exhibit indications of a literary dependence on the Fourth Gospel, which are too striking to be overlooked. (*a*) H.C. iii. 52 :—" Wherefore He, being the true prophet, hath said, I am the gate of life ; he coming in through Me, cometh in unto life " : cf. John x. 3-9. (*β*). H.C. iii. 52 :—" My sheep hear My voice " : cf. John x. 27. (*γ*). H.C. xix. 22 :—" Wherefore also our Teacher, to those who inquired concerning the man blind from his birth whose sight was restored, whether this man sinned or his parents that he should be born blind, answered—Neither hath this man sinned in any respect or his parents, but that through him the power of God might be manifest, curing the sins of ignorance : cf. John ix. 1-3. Scholten, followed by the author of Supernatural Religion, thinks that John and the author of the Clementines may have alike borrowed from some source now lost, or that John may even have copied from the author of the Clementines ; but when Hilgenfeld declares himself satisfied by the third of the above instances that " John's gospel is made use of without scruple by the author of the Clementines," it may be assumed that further opposition to the earlier existence of John's gospel is unavailing.

2. **Heretical.** (1) *Basilides, a gnostic,* in Alexandria (117-138 A.D.), wrote a work in explanation of the gospels, and used at least two sentences, preserved by Hippolytus (Originis Philosophoumena, vii. 22, 27), which must have been derived from the Fourth Gospel, viz., "That was the true light which lighteth every man that cometh into the world " (John i. 9), and "Mine hour is not yet come " (ii. 4). (2) *Valentinus, another gnostic,* (presumably) of Alexandria, who settled in Rome about 135-139 A.D., and spent there the last years of his life, propounded a gnosis compounded of Jewish theology, N. T. history, Greek philosophy, and Oriental theosophy, for information concerning which we are indebted to Irenaeus and Tertullian. In that system occur terms and phrases to be found in the Fourth Gospel, as *e.g.* The Word, The Only begotten, Life, Light, Truth, Fulness, Grace, The Saviour, The Comforter ; while according to Irenaeus (i. 3, 6 ; iii. 11, 7) the Valentinians generally defended their opinions by appealing to the writings of the evangelists and apostles, and specially by making copious use of the Gospel according to John. Now, as it is pre-

posterous to suppose that the Evangelist borrowed his ideas from Valentinus (Bretschneider, Baur), we must conclude that Valentinus was indebted for his to the Evangelist ; and this appears to be borne out by the following facts :—(α) Hippolytus, already referred to, reports in his Originis Philosophoumena (vi. 35) a sentence from Valentinus, in which Christ is introduced as saying, "All that ever came before Me were thieves and robbers" (John x. 8). (β) Ptolemæus, a disciple of Valentinus (150 A.D.), quotes John xii. 27 (Iren. Haer. i. 8, 2), claims John as a fellow-disciple on the ground of the views propounded in the prologue (Haer. i. 8, 5), and cites John i. 3 in a letter to one Flora (Epiphan. Haer. xxxiii. 3). (γ) Heracleon, another Valentinian (150 A.D.) composed a commentary on John's gospel which Origen refuted, giving extracts from it in his own exposition of the same gospel. (3) *Marcion, a third heretic of this century,* "one of the most remarkable and influential men of the period" (Volkmar), born at Sinope, on the Black Sea, but from 140 to 170 A.D. the head of a dualistic school at Rome, endeavoured "to break the link which connected Christianity with Judaism" (Tischendorf), and for this purpose prepared a canon of Scripture adapted to his own views. The only gospel which found a place in this canon was a mutilated Luke (Tert. c. Mar. iv. 2) from which it has been argued that Marcion cannot have been acquainted with the Fourth Gospel. But (α) according to Irenaeus (Haer. i. 27, 4) and Tertullian (c. Mar. iv. 3) Marcion did not dispute the authority of those books he rejected, or deny that they were composed by the authors to whom at the time they were currently assigned ; simply he excluded them from his collection as unfavourable to his notions, while such books as he admitted he curtailed and purged to bring them into harmony with the same. (β) Marcion and his followers appear to have acknowledged there were other Scriptures besides those they had shortened (Iren. Haer. iii. 12, 2). (γ) Tertullian mentions an earlier letter of Marcion's in which he made use of all the four gospels, and that to suit his own purposes he afterwards rejected all but that of Luke (c. Mar. i. 1 ; iv. 4).

3. **Pagan.** *Celsus,* the first known writer who opposed Christianity, composed a work (176-180 A.D.) entitled "The True Discourse," in which he attempted to refute Christianity by "the writings of the disciples of Jesus" themselves—by which Origen, who wrote against him, understood "the narratives of our gospels" (Contra Celsum ii. 74). In this work, long since perished, of which fragments have been preserved by Origen, Celsus accused the Christians of having "corrupted the gospel from its original integrity to a threefold, and fourfold, and manifold degree, and have remodelled it, so that they might be able to answer objections" (C. Celsum ii. 27), from which, it is apparent, that Celsus knew the Christians

possessed a threefold, yea a fourfold, gospel; while the facts taken from them by him show that these must have been our canonical gospels. Besides, he expressly cites the gospel of St. John, as, e.g. when he charges Christians with sophistical reasoning in saying, The Son of God is the Word himself (C. C. ii. 31), when he recalls that Jesus was asked by the Jews in the temple "to exhibit some unmistakeable sign that He was the Son of God" (C. C. i. 67), when he mockingly alludes to the fact that blood and water issued from the pierced side of Jesus (ii. 36), and when he endeavours to establish a contradiction between those gospels (Matthew and Mark) which speak of one angel at the tomb of Jesus, and those (Luke and John) which mention two (C. C. v. 56); from all which it follows that Celsus was acquainted with the gospel of St. John, and regarded it as authoritative Scripture among Christians of the second century.

The result of this historical investigation may now be stated. (1) During the latter half of the second century the gospel of St. John was universally recognized by Christians, heretics, and heathen opponents in Alexandria, Carthage, and Lyons, i.e. in east, south, and west, as forming a part of canonical Scripture, and as having proceeded from the pen of St. John, the apostle of Jesus, and the son of Zebedee—being, indeed, expressly ascribed to him by Theophilus, Irenæus, Tertullian, Clement, and the author of Muratori's Canon. That it was not ascribed directly to St. John at an earlier date may be satisfactorily explained by supposing that during the first half of the century it was generally known to be his, and that the fact of his authorship did not require special mention until a generation rose who were not acquainted with, or began to challenge, its apostolic origin. (2) During the earlier half of the century all the signs tend in the direction of supporting the belief that a book similar to St. John's gospel, most probably John's gospel itself, and regarded as authoritative Scripture, was then in existence and silently influencing the current of contemporaneous and succeeding literature. (3) Hence the strong presumption is—if the preceding evidence from the gospel itself be conjoined with this just concluded, the moral certainty is—that the author of the book was St. John, the apostle of Jesus.

§ 3. THE COMPOSITION OF THE GOSPEL

1. *The History of the Author.* Originally a young Galilean fisherman, St. John belonged in all probability to the town of Bethsaida, the city of Andrew and Peter (John i. 44; cf. Luke v. 10), or to its vicinity. His father, Zebedee, also a fisherman, appears to have been well-to-do, since, in addition to boats and nets, he had hired servants (Mark i. 20). John's

mother, Salome, seemingly the sister of our Lord's mother (cf. Matt. xxvii. 56 ; Mark xv. 40, xvi. 1 ; John xix. 25) was one of those Galilean women who early cast in their lot with Jesus and the Twelve, to whom they ministered of their substance (Luke viii. 3). Whether John himself had a house in Jerusalem (John xix. 27) cannot be determined. That he was known to the high priest (xviii. 15) may be held as indicating the good social standing of his family. Of his eldest brother, James, little is recorded. A fisherman like his father and brother, by the latter brought to Jesus (i. 41), eventually called into the apostolate, and even into the inner circle of the Three, he was early cut off by martyrdom (Acts xii. 2).

Brought up in a pious home, and possessed of a deeply religious spirit, no doubt early and earnestly fostered by his mother (Matt. xx. 20), himself also (as James, too, appears to have been) a young man of electric energy that usually slumbered peacefully within his bosom, but was liable at times to sudden and even violent eruptions of passionate zeal (Luke ix. 54), John speedily felt the inspiration of the Baptist's trumpet-call in the Judæan wilderness, and was found in the company of the forerunner when Jesus entered on His public ministry (John i. 35). From the servant the son of Zebedee appears to have passed over to the Master without inward struggle or convulsion. Recognizing in Jesus the Messiah (i. 41), he, along with his brother and companions, attached himself to the person of the new prophet, in whose train he also returned to Galilee, first to Cana, then to Nazareth, and eventually to Capernaum. There, as Christ seemingly was not prepared to initiate a movement alongside of that being carried on by the Baptist, he resumed his accustomed occupation on the Lake. When the Baptist's imprisonment a year later determined Jesus to begin the work of preaching in Galilee, John, with his brother and two comrades, were invited to become permanent followers (Matt. iv. 18-22). All four found a place among the Twelve, having been selected soon after to be apostles (Matt. x. 1-2; Mark iii. 16-19; Luke vi. 14-16). In all the lists furnished by the Synoptists, Simon Peter occupies the first place ; in Matthew's and Luke's, Andrew, James, and John follow ; in Mark's, James and John stand second and third, with Andrew as a fourth. Along with Simon and James, John was one of the Three who formed an inner circle of intimates whom Jesus favoured above the rest, at least on three occasions—in the house of Jairus (Mark v. 37), on the Mount of Transfiguration (Matt. xvii. 1), and in the garden of Gethsemane (Matt. xxvi. 37). To John and Peter was entrusted the task of making ready the passover in the upper room (Luke xxii. 8). John and Peter were the first to recover from their flight in the garden, and to follow Christ when He was led to the palace of the high priest--John entering in and Peter standing without (John xviii.

15-16). John alone of Christ's apostles stood by the Cross (xix. 26), and beheld the dying agonies of Jesus, most likely assisting at His interment. John alone was honoured to receive Christ's dying charge concerning His mother (John xix. 26-27). On the resurrection morning John was the first to reach the tomb (xx. 4), and the first to believe that Christ was alive (xx. 9). In the Galilean manifestation, he was the first to recognize the risen Lord (xxi. 7), who, in the subsequent interview, uttered concerning him words which afterwards gave rise within the Church to a legend, in correcting which, he brings his gospel to a close. After the Ascension he continued in Jerusalem at least for a time. Among "the brethren" at the election of Matthias (Acts i. 13), and on the day of pentecost (Acts ii. 14), he accompanied Peter to the Temple, when the lame man was healed at the gate Beautiful (Acts iii. 1). Later in the day he was apprehended along with Peter, and sent to prison for his boldness in preaching and working miracles in the name of Jesus (Acts iv. 3), and on the morrow the two stood together before the Sanhedrim, when called to account for the good deed done (Acts iv. 13). With Peter he was afterwards despatched on a mission to Samaria, which had received the word of God (Acts viii. 14), returning on its expiry to Jerusalem. It is probable that soon after he withdrew from the metropolis, and retired to Galilee with the Virgin, induced to do so, it may be supposed, by the dislike of the latter to remain in the city where her Lord (as well as Son) had been crucified, and by the increasing hostility of the Jews against the Church (Acts viii. 1). If this was so, it will explain how three years after, on the occasion of Paul's first visit to the city after his conversion, he did not meet with John (Gal. i. 18), whom he only first saw fourteen years later, on his second visit, at the Council called to settle how much liberty should be granted to the Gentile Churches (Gal. ii. 9). John, it is believed, had by this time (A.D. 50) returned to the headquarters of the Church in Jerusalem, in consequence of the Virgin's death in 48 A.D. (Godet). There, having immediately resumed his natural position of influence and authority among the brethren, along with James and Cephas, he was recognized by Paul as one of the "pillars" of the Church. How long he abode in Jerusalem is not certain. His final departure probably took place before the war broke out against the Romans ; perhaps he accompanied the Jewish Christian Church when it migrated to Peræa about 67 A.D. In later years, though not till after Paul's death, possibly not till the deaths of Timothy and Titus had deprived the Churches in Asia Minor of everything like apostolic guidance, according to well authenticated tradition, he settled in Ephesus. Irenaeus gives authority for saying that many were "conversant in Asia with John, the disciple of the Lord," who "remained among them up to the times of Trajan" (Haer. ii. 22-5), and that "the Church in Ephesus, founded by Paul, and having John remaining among them permanently until the times of Trajan, was a true witness of the tradition of the apostles" (Haer. iii. 3-4). The reign of Trajan commenced in 98 A.D. Irenaeus also states that "John, the disciple of the Lord, who also had leaned upon His breast, did himself publish a gospel during his residence at Ephesus in Asia" (Haer. iii. 11), and reports a saying handed down from Polycarp "that John, the disciple of the Lord, going to bathe at Ephesus, and perceiving Cerinthus within, rushed out of the bath-house without bathing, exclaiming, "Let us fly, lest even the bath-house fall down, because Cerinthus, the enemy of the truth, is within" (Haer. iii. 3-4); while in a letter to Florinus, a former co-disciple with him of Polycarp, he says—" I could still show thee the place where he (Polycarp) sat when he taught and gave an account of his relations *with John and with the others who had seen the Lord*" (Euseb. v. 24). According to Eusebius (v. 28) Apollonius, an anti-Montanist writer, "relates that a dead man had been brought to life again at Ephesus by John"; while Polycrates, the Bishop of Ephesus, about 190 A.D., describes "John, who rested on the bosom of the Lord" as "the high priest wearing the plate of gold," and as being "buried at Ephesus" (v. 24, 3). Clement, too, about the same time (190 A.D.) wrote that John "after the tyrant (Domitian) was dead returned from Patmos to Ephesus, and there visited the surrounding countries in order to establish bishops, and to organize the churches" (Quis divus salv. ? c. 42). And, finally, on the authority of Jerome (Com. in Gal. vi. 10) it is reported that "when John had tarried at Ephesus to extreme old age, and could only with difficulty be carried to the church in the arms of his disciples, and was unable to give utterance to many words, he used to say no more at their several meetings than this, "Little children, love one another." Doubtless, there is not a little connected with these traditional reminiscences that partakes of the character of legend, but through them all gleams the fact that John spent the closing years of his life at Ephesus. Following in the wake of Lützelberger, Keim and Holtzmann have revived the insinuation that this whole traditional story of John's residence in Asia is a mistake, in fact, a hallucination, founded mainly on a blunder of Irenæus, who confounded the two Johns, the son of Zebedee, and the friend of Aristion, thinking that Polycarp referred to the former when in reality he spoke of the latter. But the proof alleged in support of this assertion is inadequate, while in the absence of clear evidence to the contrary, it will be prudent to believe that Polycarp understood whom he was talking of, and Irenaeus was not so dull as not to recognize the difference between John, the Apostle of our Lord, and John, the Presbyter of Ephesus.

2. *The Place of Publication.* (1) The gospel, as much in the preceding

pages has already shown, bears internal evidence of having been prepared
beyond the bounds of the holy land, explanations being inserted in its
narratives for the benefit apparently of readers uɪ.acquainted with its
localities, customs, and people ; and (2) ecclesiastical tradition, as just
rehearsed, may be said to be unanimous in asserting that John composed his
gospel at Ephesus.   Even those who deny the Ephesian residence of the
apostle are nevertheless constrained to admit that from that region in Asia
Minor this gospel must have emanated.   And certainly a more appropriate
birthplace it could not have had.   Since the fall of Jerusalem Ephesus,
the brilliant and busy metropolis of Asia Minor, had become the church's
centre.   There men of all nationalities had been accustomed to meet, and
the fantastic speculations of the east to blend with the severer thoughts of
the west.   In Ephesus accordingly had heresy obtained a most congenial
soil ; and though not directly written to oppose false systems, this gospel
nevertheless bears decided impress of having issued from a region in which
these existed and indeed abounded.

3. *The Time of Writing.*   This may also be said to follow from what has
been advanced.   If the gospel was written at Ephesus it could only have
been in the closing years of the apostle's life.   Now as John lived till the
times of Trajan 98-117 A.D. (Iren. Haer. ii. 22),—according to Jerome (Ep.
to Gal. vi. 10) dying 68 years after our Lord's passion, i.e. in 98 A.D.—it
may well be, as Epiphanius asserts, that he composed his gospel when 90
years of age (Haer. ii. 12).   Supposing him to have been 23 at the time of
Our Lord's death, 68 years additional would make him 91.   Hence it may
be safely concluded that the gospel was prepared and given to the church
somewhere between 80-100 A.D.   The only passage that seems to speak
against this—v. 1, "Now there *is* at Jerusalem"—is susceptible of easy
explanation without assuming that it was written either in Palestine or
before the destruction of Jerusalem.

§ 4. THE PURPOSE OF THE GOSPEL

Among the theories that have been put forward to account for the
peculiar structure and complexion of this gospel, the following are the
chief and may call for a word in passing.

1. *The Supplemental Theory*—according to which St. John having before him
the three Synoptical gospels, and observing that they had not given a complete account of the Saviour's life, desired to prepare another ' Life ' which
might supplement the earlier biographies where these were defective.
Originally propounded by Eusebius (iii. 24) who asserted that he did so on
the testimony of the ancients, it was afterwards adopted by Theodore of
Mopsuestia and Jerome in the fourth century, and has always commanded

a considerable degree of support (Ewald, Die Johanneischen Schriften, vol. 1. pp. i. ff.), on the ground that, whether intending to do so or not, the Fourth Gospel in point of fact does supply numerous details with reference to Christ's life which the Synoptists omit. But (1) it is not absolutely certain that John wrote with the other three gospels before him, although Clement of Alexandria states that he knew of their existence and was acquainted with their contents (Euseb. Haer. vi. 14), and Eusebius testifies that before John wrote Matthew, Mark, and Luke had each published their gospels and that these had come into John's hands (Haer. iii. 24). (2) The unity of the gospel shows that it is no mere patchwork such as this hypothesis would make of it. (3) Some things are repeated in this gospel which are to be found in the other three, as e.g. the miraculous feeding (vi. 1-12), the walking on the sea (vi. 15-21), the supper at Bethany (xii. 2-8), the denials of Peter (xviii. 15-18; 25-27), the burial of Jesus (xix. 38-42). (4) Some (at least apparent) contradictions exist between this and the Synoptical accounts, as e.g. in regard to the dates of the Passover and of the Crucifixion. (5) No attempt is made to harmonize seemingly conflicting statements in the Synoptists themselves, as e.g. that according to Matthew (xx. 29, 30) Christ cured *two* blind men on the way *out* of Jericho, while according to Mark (xi. 46) he cured *one*, and according to Luke (xviii. 35) as He was going *in*. And these arguments are, in our judgment, sufficient to set aside this idea of supplementing and correcting the other evangelists as an unsatisfactory explanation of the author's aim.

2. *The Polemical Hypothesis*—of which there are varieties, as for instance that John in preparing his work was governed by a distinct controversial purpose;—to refute

(1) The Cerinthians who "represented Jesus as the son of Joseph and Mary according to the course of human generation, while He nevertheless was more righteous, prudent and wise than other men," who taught that "after His baptism Christ descended upon Him (Jesus) in the form of a dove from the Supreme Ruler, after which He proclaimed the unknown Father, and performed miracles"; and who also asserted that "Christ departed from Jesus who then suffered and rose again, while Christ remained impassible, inasmuch as He was a spiritual being" (Iren. Haer. i. 26, 1). Irenaeus advocated this view of the Gospel writer's purpose (Haer. iii. 11, 1).

(2) The Ebionites, a sect of Judaizing Christians who, with respect to the person of Christ, held similar views to the Cerinthians, rejected all the gospels but Matthew, repudiated Paul, practised circumcision, and generally were so Judaic in their style of living that they even adored Jerusalem as if it were the house of God (Iren. Haer. i. xxvi. 2). This idea of John's

aim was maintained by Epiphanius (Haer. li. 12) and by Jerome (de vir. illust. ix.).

(3) The Docetæ, who taught that Christ was not possessed of a true human nature, had not actually come "in the flesh" but wore the mere semblance of a body (Iren. Haer. i. 7, 2). This opinion of the Evangelist's design has frequently been upheld, as by Semler, Schneckenburger, Ebrard and others.

(4) The disciples of John who preferred to be called by the name of the Baptist without passing over into the school of Christ, of whom Paul found a number in the city of Ephesus about the year 55 A.D. (see Acts xix. 1-7), and who, in the years following the destruction of Jerusalem, formed themselves into a distinct church community, maintaining that the Baptist had never acknowledged Christ as the 'Sent of God' (Ewald, Die Johanneischen Schriften, vol. i., p. 13). This belief as to the author's object has been put forward by Grotius and others.

Now, it is undeniable that expressions may be culled from this gospel which are capable of being employed against every one of these heresies, but the number altogether is so small that one can hardly suppose John in using them had any such polemical design as is here ascribed to him. Besides, as Bleek observes, speaking of the supposed intention to controvert Cerinthus, there are passages, as e.g. i. 31, 51, 'which the Cerinthians might with some plausibility have used in favour of their views; while in answer to the notion that John composed his gospel against Docetism it is sufficient to remark that "Baur considered Docetism to be the doctrine of the Evangelist himself" (Introd. to the N. T., vol. i. § 117).

3. *The Personal Design.*   (1) As regards Christ—to exhibit the inner and more spiritual aspect of the Saviour's character. This, as Tholuck remarks, is a view of the Evangelist's purpose which "readily occurs to him who has been attracted by the wonderfully sublime simplicity and the heavenly gentleness, which pervade this whole work, as well as by the many expressions to be found in it with regard to the higher nature of Christ." Clement of Alexandria is an instance from the early fathers of one who embraced this idea :—" But John, last of all perceiving that what had reference to the *bodily* was sufficiently retailed in the gospels (meaning the Synoptists) encouraged by his friends and divinely incited by the Spirit, composed a *spiritual* gospel" (Euseb. H.E. l. 6, 14). Of modern authors Pressensé may be taken as a sample :—" His great design is to give us the highest and deepest revelations of the Master concerning Himself" (Jesus Christ, His Times, etc., bk. I., ch. iv. v.). And to this extent the view must be recognized as correct that, more than any of the three earlier biographies, this gospel affords a glimpse into the higher nature of Jesus and into the

more spiritual aspects of His character; but this arises, it may be noticed, quite as much from the theme of the gospel as from the subjective intention of the author. (2) As regards John—to establish his equality with, if not superiority to, Peter in the Apostolical college. Following in the wake of Hilgenfield, Weizsäcker, and Baur, Renan writes :—" We are tempted to believe that John in his old age having read the gospel narratives, on the one hand remarked their various inaccuracies, on the other was hurt at seeing that there was not accorded to himself a sufficiently high place in the history of Christ; that then he commenced to dictate a number of things which he knew better than the rest with the intention of showing that in many instances in which Peter only was spoken of, he had figured with him and even before him" (The Life of Jesus, p. 15). Not to insist upon the fact that a spirit of petty jealousy is here ascribed to John, for which nothing in his character as presented by the Synoptists affords foundation, the passages usually relied on to support this contention only do so when their obvious sense is perverted by ingenious exegesis, while other texts can just as readily be adduced to show, on the same principles of interpretation, that they must have been dictated by a desire to exalt Peter above John.

These various conjectures as to the Evangelist's design then may be set aside. The *true purpose* of his writing he himself declares, first generally in xx. 30, 31, and second specifically in i. 11, 12.

I. The Author's General Design. This was threefold: To prove (1) that Jesus was the Christ, (2) that He was the Son of God, and (3) that believers enjoy eternal life in Him, xx. 30, 31.

1. *The first of these subordinate ideas clearly runs through the gospel.* The writer manifestly wishes to impress upon his readers that Jesus of Nazareth was none other than the Jewish Messiah. Accordingly he draws attention to the following facts—(1) that Jesus was distinctly pointed out by the Baptist as Israel's Messiah (i. 19-34) ; (2) that in Him all Messianic Scripture was fulfilled—its types, inasmuch as He was the true tabernacle (i. 14) and the true temple (ii. 19), the antitype of the brazen serpent (iii. 14), of the manna (vi. 35), of the smitten rock (vii. 37), of the pillar of fire (viii. 12), of the paschal lamb (i. 29 ; xix. 36) ;—its emblems, He having been the True Shepherd of Israel (x. 11) and the True Vine of which Israel was a figure (xv. 1) ;—its oracles, since in Him numerous O.T. predictions conspicuously met (i. 45 ; ii. 17 ; vi. 31; xii. 13, 35; xiii. 18 ; xv. 25 ; xix. 24, 36, 37); and (3) that He was frequently recognized as such, as e.g. by the Baptist (i. 34), by Andrew (i. 41), by Philip (i. 45), by the woman of Samaria (iv. 29), by the citizens of Sychar (iv. 42 A.V.), by the Galileans (vi. 14), by the men of Jerusalem (xii. 13), and even by Pilate (xix. 19). 2. *The second notion of the Divine Sonship of*

Jesus equally pervades the book. In the prologue the pre-existence of Christ occupies the foreground, his relation to the Deity being set forth under names (The Word, The Only begotten, The Son) which expressly involve essential equality with, and yet filial dependence on the Father. In the body of the book this claim is supported by showing that Jesus Christ in His earthly appearing, not only avowed Himself to have come from the Father and to have been the Father's Son in the lofty sense just explained (v. 17; vi. 32; vii. 29; viii. 42; x. 30), but demonstrated the truth of that amazing assertion by doing the Father's works (v. 17, 19, 20; x. 32, 37; xiv. 10), and speaking the Father's words (viii. 26, 28; xii. 49),—in particular by rising from the dead (xx. 17). In the epilogue the same conception of the exalted dignity and divine nature of Jesus is maintained (xxi. 17), though the term Son of God is not formally employed. 3. *The third part of his design the author carries out* by exhibiting Christ's death upon the Cross as the only source of legal and moral cleansing for the world at large (xix. 34), and by recording his own personal experience in conjunction with that of others, fellow Christians, that life had come to him and them through believing in His name (i. 14, 16).

It is however obvious that the general purpose thus described may be said to have been also, more or less, the purpose of the Synoptists. In particular, the first part of this design John's gospel may be said to share with Matthew's, which undoubtedly has for an aim to show that Jesus of Nazareth was Israel's Messiah, and this it does pretty much in the way that it is done in John by calling attention to the fulfilment in Jesus of Messianic Scripture. The second it has in common with the gospel of Mark, which significantly points to its object in the opening sentence— "The beginning of the gospel of Jesus Christ, the Son of God;" and this also is carried out by Mark in a fashion not remote from that of John by reciting the 'works' which convinced devils (Mark i. 24; iii. 11; v. 7), and ought to have convinced men (ii. 7; vi. 52), that Christ was the Son of God, as well as reporting the 'words' which everywhere left upon ingenuous minds the impression of His superhuman greatness (vi. 2). The third it possesses hardly more than Luke's gospel which in its introductory pages lays special emphasis upon the fact that Christ was a Saviour not to Israel alone but to mankind at large (i. 50; ii. 10, 14), "a light for revelation to the Gentiles" as well as "the glory of God's people Israel" (ii. 32), and in its ensuing narrative incorporates examples of persons beyond the pale of the Hebrew church, who obtained temporal and spiritual healing from Jesus solely on the exercise of faith (cf. vii. 2, 9; x. 33; xvii. 16; xxiii. 33, 43). Hence it has been widely felt that something more specific must be found to explain the peculiar form and complexion of this latest of the gospels.

II. The Author's Specific Purpose. This was fourfold: (1) To show how the Pre-existent Word of God who became incarnate in Jesus of Nazareth "came unto His own" (the Jewish people), unfolding before them His glory as "the glory of an only-begotten from a father"; (2) how that glory was either not discerned by "His own," the Jewish people, through inward moral and spiritual blindness, or if perceived (as one can hardly help thinking it was by the ecclesiastical leaders) was deliberately rejected, because "they loved the darkness rather than the light"; (3) how, notwithstanding, this glory of the incarnate Son was recognized and received by another "own," the spiritually born, who were inwardly drawn of God to believe upon His name; and (4) how by further revelations of His glory in dying for them on the cross and rising again to a superterrestrial form of existence He gave to these latter the right and the power to become the sons of God (i. 11, 12). As this fourfold purpose is fully opened up in the commentary (see pp. 24, 25), it is not necessary to do more in this place than call attention to it. Nor need it be surprising that John in old age should have deemed it proper to compose another gospel with this specific aim. For nearly a generation had the Christian Church and the Jewish Synagogue parted company. For the former, Judaism dead, unspiritual, letter-bound, and hostile, had dropped back into line with ordinary heathen religions. Moreover its original antagonism to Christianity had not been mellowed by passing years, but rather accentuated by the evident vitality and progress of that gospel it had not been able to kill though the Founder thereof it had crucified. Finding itself powerless to initiate measures of violence against professors of the hated faith, it could insinuate suspicions against their characters and raise such questions concerning their doctrine as might bring them and the Master they served into discredit among the heathen. They could ask how it came to pass that Jesus, living amongst His own people, had found so little acceptance at their hands, that only a few fisher-folk— "only ten sailors and tax-gatherers" (Celsus)—from Galilee had become His disciples, while the men of 'light and leading' of the age had pronounced against Him. And more than likely ordinary Christian people had begun to feel perplexed, because they were not always able to furnish replies to these undoubtedly true allegations, and could even derive little or no direction on the subject from the then existing gospels—rather discovered in these gospels some things which seemed to countenance the enemies of the faith in their objections. Possibly John himself in late life had come to see that this was a view of Christ's historical appearing which, the further that transcendent 'manifestation' receded into the past, would more readily present itself to critical inquirers, a view moreover which, besides being natural, was fitted to occasion stumbling in such as had be-

lieved, as well as to hinder faith altogether in them who were unfavourably
disposed towards the Christian system, and a view which had not been
sufficiently considered, or, indeed, at all dealt with by preceding writers.
John therefore, having recognized the situation, resolved, as one might
suppose, and as all the internal signs suggest, to prepare a new history of
Jesus in which this phase of it should be duly weighed, and the difficulties
springing from it fairly answered. He would study so to set forth the
details of Christ's life and passion as on the one hand to confirm the faith
of the Church that Jesus was not only Israel's Messiah but God's
Son and the Author of eternal life in them that believe, and on
the other hand to break the force of such objections as might
be drawn from the apparent failure of Christ's mission, by showing
that while He had come unto His own, and His own had received
Him not, neither had He failed to find acceptance from another
and better "own" than Israel after the flesh, nor had His mission been
without success, since for them had He acquired the right as well as conferred on them the power of becoming sons of God. Thus the two purposes
suggested by the book itself—the general and the specific, the didactic and
the apologetic—are harmoniously united, and the key found for the understanding of its exalted contents (cf. Ewald, Die Johanneischen Schriften,
vol. i. p. 11).

§ 5. THE PLAN OF THE GOSPEL

Nothing can be further from the truth than the assertion (Weisse) that
the Fourth Gospel is "utterly devoid of plan," and that the uniform
character of its discourses as well as the particular selection of events
it narrates may be perfectly accounted for by assuming that just "these
and no other words and occurrences came to the author's recollection," and
that their connection with the subject in hand was a pure accident. It
requires only slight examination to perceive that more than any of its predecessors this gospel is an organic unity, dominated by a subjective design
or leading idea on the part of its author, in accordance with which both
its form is draughted and its contents are filled up. That purpose, object, or
aim has been explained in the preceding section. To carry it out the author
has arranged his work in three main divisions—a prologue or exordium
(i. 1-18), a history or record of the life and death of Jesus (i. 19—xx. 31),
and an epilogue or conclusion (xxi.). Through these he distributes the
materials he has drawn principally from the rich storehouse of his own
reminiscences. In the *prologue* the personal subject of the ensuing history
is introduced :—His pre-existent glory described (i. 1-5), His coming into
the world heralded (i. 6-13), His actual incarnation announced (i. 14-18),
and the specific purpose of the author declared (i. 11, 12). In the *history*

two sub-divisions present themselves—a history of Christ's life and a history of Christ's passion.   (1) In the former (i. 19—xii. 50), after showing in a series of introductory paragraphs how the glory of the Incarnate Word was perceived by the Baptist (i. 19-34), by the Baptist's disciples (i. 35-51), and by Christ's newly gained followers (ii. 1-11), he records how in five successive presentations of Himself before His own (the Jews) Christ unfolded to them His glory, always with the result above described, that " His own " according to the flesh rejected Him, while " His own " according to the Spirit received Him.   (2) In the latter he continues his self-elected task of exhibiting the glory of the Incarnate Word or Son as it unveiled itself before the second " own " which had stepped into the place of the first, in stooping on their behalf as far as to death, even the death of the cross, and rising again on the morning of the third day in order to be able to bestow upon them power to become sons of God.   In the *epilogue* he sets forth the post-resurrection glory of the exalted Word or Son, who continues to manifest His gracious presence in the midst of His believing Church till the close of time, directing her in all her efforts to ingather sons into His kingdom, and preparing for His faithful servants a rich reward when He and they shall meet upon the shores of bliss.   The details of this plan are fully exhibited in the commentary and need not further be enlarged on, although it may be useful to present a tabular view of the contents of the entire gospel as arranged in accordance with the view taken of its ground-work or plan.

Subject—The Gospel of the Glory of the Word or Son of God.

I. THE PROLOGUE

1. The Subject of the history introduced.

   (1) The Pre-existent Word : i. 1-5.
   (2) The Coming Light : i. 6-13.
   (3) The Incarnate Son : i. 14-18.

2. The purpose of the author declared : i. 11, 12.

   To show how the Glory of the Word was
   (1) Revealed to 'His own' (the Jews).
   (2) Rejected by ' His own' (the Jews).
   (3) Received by ' His own' (Believers).
   (4) Reflected in 'His own' (Believers).

II. THE HISTORY

PART I. THE HISTORY OF CHRIST'S LIFE: i. 19—xii. 50.

Subject: The Glory of the Word revealed to His own (the Jewish people) :—" He came unto His own, and His own received Him not." i. 11.

A. The Dawning of the Glory of the Incarnate Word or Son: i. 19—ii. 11.
    1. Recognized and attested by the Baptist: i. 19-36.
    2. Discovered and acknowledged by John's Followers: i. 37-51.
    3. Discerned and accepted by Christ's Disciples: ii. 1-11.

B. The Glory of the Incarnate Word or Son presented to His own (the Jewish people): ii. 12—xii. 20.

Section First.—Christ's *First Presentation* of Himself in the first year of His ministry: ii. 12—iv. 54.

I. In Jerusalem; at the Passover.
    1. To the Rulers—first national rejection: ii. 13-22.
    2. To the Inhabitants—first beginnings of faith: ii. 23-25.
    3. To Nicodemus—first approach of inquiry: iii. 1-21.

II. In Judæa, at Ænon—the Baptist's last testimony to Christ: iii. 22-26.

III. In Samaria.
    1. To the Woman at the Well—Christ recognized: iv. 1-26.
    2. To the Citizens of Sychar—Christ confessed: iv. 27-42.

IV. In Galilee.
    1. To the Galileans—Christ welcomed: iv. 43-45.
    2. To the Nobleman—Christ believed: iv. 46-54.

Section Second.—Christ's *Second Presentation* of Himself in the second year of His ministry: v. 1—vi. 71.

I. In Jerusalem at a feast (the Passover): v. 1-47.
    1. The Miracle of Bethesda: v. 1-9.
    2. The Hostility of the Jews: v. 10-18.
    3. The Reply of Vindication: v. 19-47.

II. In Galilee before the following Passover: vi. 1-71.
    1. The Miracle of the Loaves: vi. 1-14.

2. The Sign upon the Sea : vi. 15-21.
3. The Meeting in Capernaum : vi. 22-59.
4. The Turning of the Tide : vi. 60-71.

Section Third.—Christ's *Third Presentation* of Himself in the third year of His ministry, at the feast of Tabernacles : vii. 1—x. 21.

I. The Beginning of the Feast—from Galilee to Jerusalem : vii. 1-13.

II. The Middle of the Feast—Christ teaches in the Temple : vii. 14-36.

III. The Last Day of the Feast.
    1. Teaching in the Temple : vii. 37-44.
    2. A Meeting of the Sanhedrim : vii. 45-52.
    (3. The Woman taken in Adultery) : vii. 53—viii. 1-11.
    4. Teaching in the Temple : viii. 12-59.

IV. After the feast.
    1. The Healing of a Man born blind : ix. 1-41.
    2. The Parables of the Good Shepherd : x. 1-21.

Section Fourth.—Christ's *Fourth Presentation* of Himself in the third and fourth years of His ministry : x. 22—xii. 11.
    1. In Jerusalem—at the Feast of Dedication : x. 22-39.
    2. In Peroea—with the Mountaineers : x. 40-42.
    3. In Bethany—amongst His Friends.
        (1) The Raising of Lazarus : xi. 1-57.
        (2) The Supper in Simon's House : xii. 1-11

Section Fifth.—Christ's *Fifth Presentation* of Himself on the day of the triumphal entry : xii. 12-50.
    1. The Entry into the City : xii. 12-19.
    2. The Inquiring Greeks : xii. 20-28.
    3. The Address to the Multitude : xii. 29-36.
    4. The Final Departure : xii. 37-43.
    5. The Last Words : xii. 44-50.

PART II. THE HISTORY OF CHRIST'S PASSION : xiii. 1—xx. 31.

Subject : The Glory of Christ unveiled to His own (believers):—" As many as received Him to them gave He right (and power) to become sons of God." i. 12.

THE GOSPEL OF JOHN

THE PROLOGUE.

CHAP. I. VER. 1-18.

1. The *Extent* of the Prologue, as the opening verses of this Gospel have been styled, has by expositors been fixed with almost perfect unanimity. The limit to which it reaches, they are agreed, is the close, not of ver. 5 (Reuss), or of ver. 14 (Bengel), but of ver. 18; this being demanded by the internal structure of the passage, as well as by the feeling of incompleteness which arises in the reader's mind through pausing at any point short of this goal. 2. The *Object* of the Prologue is to furnish neither a history of the Logos (Olshausen), nor the programme of a theologian (Reuss), but a suitable exordium or preface to the ensuing narration; to introduce the exalted personage who is to form its theme, to set forth the heavenly origin and Divine dignity of Him whose earthly history is to be traced in its pages, and to indicate the end or purpose at which the author aims in its composition. With the soaring flight of a sanctified imagination the author transports himself to the initial boundary of time, and travelling backwards through the measureless spaces of eternity, deposits himself in thought before the throne of the Supreme. With a daring genius he makes the ineffable nature of the Deity the object of his contemplation. In the one essence of the Godhead he distinguishes a twofold personality, whom he names God and the Word or Logos, and subsequently designates the Father and the Son. Depicting the relations of this latter to the former, of the Word or Son to the Godhead, to the universe, to the world of mankind, and to the nation of the Jews, he concludes by announcing the sublime fact of the incarnation of that Word in the person of Jesus of Nazareth, whose glory had been beheld, shining through the veil of His humanity, as the glory of an only-begotten from a Father, full of grace and truth, and the story of whose earthly appearing he is about to rehearse. At the same time he by no means obscurely intimates the specific purpose he has in view in afresh recording

the life of Jesus, which is to prepare a gospel of the glory of the Son of God, to show (1) how that glory unveiled itself before Israel, the people whom God through centuries of special discipline, by type and symbol, priest and sacrifice, king and prophet, had been training that they might apprehend and rejoice in that glory when it began to shine; (2) how, nevertheless, they had failed through unbelief to receive or even so much as perceive it—" He came unto His own, and His own received Him not" (ver. 11); (3) how in their room and stead He gradually acquired another " own," a spiritual Israel, who did discern His glory, and opened their hearts to admit its gracious beams; and (4) how these received in turn from Him power to become sons of God—" But as many as received Him to them gave He the right to become children of God, even to them that believe upon His name : which were born not of blood, nor of the will of the flesh, nor of the will of man, but of God" (ver. 12, 13). 3. The *Subdivision* of the Prologue has been variously attempted ; some inter-preters arranging its contents into two, and others, the majority, into three sections. As an example of the twofold division, may be studied the arrangement of Lücke—I. The primordial existence of the Logos (ver. 1-5); II. The historical appearance of the Logos (ver. 6-18): as specimens of the threefold division, the arrangement of Olshausen--I. The primordial activity of the Word or Logos (ver. 1-5); II. His activity under the Old Testament (ver. 6-13); III. His Incarnation and activity in the Church of the New Testament (ver. 14-18) : that of Ewald—I. The premundane history of the Logos (ver. 1-3) ; The history of His first purely spiritual working up to the time of His Incarnation (ver. 4-13); III. The history of His human manifestation and ministry (ver. 14-18): that of Meyer—The Logos (I.) as creator (ver. 1-4a) ; II. As the source of light (ver. 4b-13) ; III. As the manifestation of the God Man (ver. 14-18) : that of Luthardt and Hengstenberg, who repre-sent the three different paragraphs as " three periods," not continuous and progressive, but co-ordinate and parallel, all beginning from the same point, but the second going beyond the first and the third advancing higher than the second—I. The primordial activity of Christ, His coming into the world, and the general ill success of His ministry (ver. 1-5); II. The same thoughts, with added mention of the Forerunner, of the unbelief of the Jewish people, of the blessedness of those who received Him (ver. 6-13) ; III. The same commencement as before, and the same progress of ideas, but this time terminating in the fulness of the Blessing of Divine Sonship (ver. 14-18) ;—the culminating points in the different sections being unbelief, unbelief and belief, the blessedness of belief: that of Godet—I. The Word (ver. 1-4); II. Unbelief (ver. 5-11); III. Faith (ver. 12-18): that of Westcott, which combines the twofold and threefold divisions by first setting apart the opening verse as a distinct paragraph, and then dividing the remaining verses into three groups, as thus—I. The Word in His Absolute Eternal Being (ver. 1); II. The Word in relation to creation (ver. 2-18), 1. The essential facts (ver. 2-5), 2. The historic manifestation of the Word generally (ver. 6-13), 3. The Incarnation as apprehended by personal experience (ver. 14-18). In the main all agree that the paragraphs are three, the dividing lines being at the ends of ver. 4 (or 5), and of ver. 11 (or 13). The present work adopts the latter as the more correct, and expresses the contents of each section as under :—

§ 1. The Pre-existent Word, ver. 1-5.
   2. The True Light, ver. 6-13.
   3. The Incarnate Son, ver. 14-18.

SECTION I.—THE PRE-EXISTENT WORD
CHAP. I. VER. 1-5

EXPOSITION

Chap. i. ver. 1. **In the beginning** Ἐν ἀρχῇ, *in principio* (Vulgate); not of the gospel dispensation as in Mark i. 1, Acts xi. 15 (Socinus), or of human history as in viii. 44, 1 John iii. 8; Matt. xix. 4, where the phrase ἀπ᾽ ἀρχῆς is used, but of creation as in Gen. i. 1, *bereshith*, in the beginning, ἐν ἀρχῇ (LXX.); equivalent to *in initio rerum*, in the beginning of things, if indeed the thought, rising to the conception of anteriority to time or of pre-creaturely existence, does not necessarily involve or at least suggest the notion of eternity (xvii. 5; 1 John i. 1; Eph. i. 4; 1 Peter i. 20; Prov. viii. 23). That the *Arche* was neither the Everlasting Father (Cyril of Alexandria), nor the Divine Wisdom (Origen), nor a distinct hypostasis between the Father and the Son (Valentinians), requires no demonstration. **was** i.e. *existed*, ἦν, as opposed to *became*, ἐγένετο, which is afterwards used of the universe (ver. 3), of John the Baptist (ver. 6), and of the Word when He assumed flesh (ver. 14), though not to *only begotten*, μονογενής (ver. 14). "*Non dicit* est, *ne putes verbum tunc cœpisse; nec* fuit *ne intelligeres verbum postea esse desiisse; sed quod inter illa medium est,* erat, *quod etiam opponit verbo Mosaico* creavit; q.d. *non tunc creavit, sed tunc erat verbum*" (Lucas Brugensis). That the verb implies "the eternal

generation of the Son" (Beza) may be doubtful; taken in connection with the preceding clause it involves the notion and presupposes the fact of eternal existence, since "*qui erat cum omnia fierent, ex eorum numero non fuisse, et antequam aliquid factum esset, existisse credendus est*" (Lampe), and "*qui in principio erat, intra se concludit omne principium*" (Augustine). **the Word** or Logos, ὁ λόγος; *verbum* (Vulgate), *sermo* (Calvin); neither a personification, sc. of the Divine Wisdom as in Prov. viii. 23 (Bauer); nor an emanation from the Divine substance (Valentinus); nor a principle grounded in the Divine essence (Beyschlag); but a Divine intelligence, essentially one with, and yet personally distinct from, God, since to the Word or Logos is ascribed life (ver. 4), while He is represented as the Author of creation (ver. 3), and declared to be God, i.e. in the highest sense divine (ver. 1). As to the *import* of this designation of the Second Person of the Godhead, it has been interpreted as signifying — 1. *The Promised One*, as if synonymous with ὁ λεγόμενος, or ἐπαγγελλόμενος, as elsewhere (vi. 14; xi. 27; Matt. xi. 3) Christ is styled The Coming One, ὁ ἐρχόμενος (Beza, Ernesti, Tittmann); 2. *The Speaking One*, as if equivalent to ὁ λέγων (Eckermann, Justi, and others), a sense in support of which it is usual to cite Origen, who characterizes the Logos or Word as one whose office it is "to announce the secret things of the Father," τὸ ἀπαγγέλλειν τὰ κρύφια τοῦ πατρὸς (Com. in Joan. § 42), and Epiphanius who introduces two Semi-Arians as saying, "The Son is named the Word or Logos because He is the Interpreter of the counsels of God," ἑρμηνεὺς τῶν τοῦ θεοῦ βουλημάτων (Haeres. lxxiii. 12) ; and 3. *The Objective Word of God*, the Gospel preached to the world, imperfectly, partially, and mediately through the prophets, perfectly, fully, immediately, and finally through Christ, who in His own person was the essential substance and entire contents of the Divine evangelic revelation (Hofmann, Luthardt). Had the first been the sense John intended to convey, he would probably have chosen ὁ λεγόμενος or ὁ ἐπαγγελλόμενος instead of ὁ λόγος ; the only form in which the second can be entertained is that which understands it to exhibit Christ as "The revealing principle for the mysterious essence of God" (Neander's Planting of Christianity, vol. ii. p. 35, Bohn) ; that the third was not the author's meaning may be inferred from the impossibility of supposing he could have wished to say, "The Gospel message was God and afterwards became flesh." So far as Biblical usage can determine the signification of this term, the word λόγος would seem, when employed impersonally, never to bear the sense of *ratio*, reason, thought, the λόγος ἐνδιάθετος of Greek philosophy, but of *oratio*, speech, the λόγος προφορικός of Greek philosophy (cf. Matt. viii. 8 ; xiii. 20 ; xxiv. 35 ; John v. 24 ; xii. 48 ; xvii. 20 ; 1 John ii. 7 ; iii. 18 ; Rev. i. 2, 3 ; xii. 11 ; xxii. 18) ; but, as John departs from common usage in employing the term personally, and as the Objective Word according as it is written or spoken is an embodiment to the eye or ear of the Subjective Thought, the term, it may be fairly contended, should be here understood as bearing the fullest possible significance, and therefore as including the Divine Thought and the Divine Word. Hence the definition is by no means inappropriate which makes the Logos equivalent to the Eternal Revealer of the Divine Being (Neander), as in pre-incarnate times the Maleach Jehovah was the Visible Revealer of the Invisible God; meaning thereby "an Intelligence in whom the Divine Thought and Speech both find personal realization and through whom they are both communicated outwards to the universe,—an intelligence existing eternally over against God as His Image or εἰκὼν (2 Cor. iv. 4; Col. i. 15),—His *alter ego* or other self in whom He beholds Himself perfectly reflected, and with whom He eternally dwells in the most absolute intercommunion of love" ("How is the Divinity of Jesus depicted ?" by the Author, p. 31). On the probable source of the term Word, see note at the close of this section. **And the Word was with God.** This expression, which repeats itself again in Scripture (1 John i. 2), is entirely absent from Philo's description of the Logos. The exact force of the preposition πρός is not brought out by translating *with*, *apud* (Vulgate), *neben*, *bei* (Luther), as if it were equivalent to παρὰ (xvii. 5), and imported nothing more than co-existence or closeness of fellowship (De Wette, Brückner, Lücke, and others), a sense which πρὸς with the accusative sometimes has (Matt. xiii. 56; Mark vi. 3 ; ix. 19 ; 1 Cor. xvi. 6, 7 ; Gal. i. 18), though along with that sense, in every one of the instances cited, it combines the idea of annexation (Winer's Grammar of the N.T. Diction, § 49, h.). Its full significance can be obtained only by adhering to what appears its literal meaning in both classical and Hellenistic Greek, viz., motion towards, as if the writer's object were to say that while the Logos or Word as the Divine Absolute Self-Revelation eternally proceeded forth from God, He yet eternally returned to God, as it were in order to receive that Infinite Fulness of which He was the complete personal Bearer and Manifestation (cf. Haupt on 1 John i. 2). So to speak the thought here expressed is the complement of that going before, and depicts not only "the personal distinction of the Son from the Father" (Calvin), but also as it were " the perpetual tendency of the Son towards the Father in the unity of Essence" (Bengel), as well as that eternal relationship of love towards the Father in which the personal subsistence of the Son is realized (Luthardt, Godet, Meyer, Westcott, and others). **And the Word was God.** That "God" is the predicate and not the subject (cf. iv. 24), though not determined by the absence of the article (Olshausen, Luthardt), which is conjoined to the predicate much more frequently than is commonly supposed, not only by Greek authors (Xen. M. 3, 10, 1 ; Plato, Phaedr. 64), but by N. T. writers as well (Matt. xxvi. 26, 28 ; Mark xii. 7 ; 1 Cor. x. 4), and in particular by John, as e.g. i. 4, 8, 50 ; iii. 10 ; iv. 29, 37 ; v. 35, 39 (Winer's Grammar § 18, 7), is yet decided by the context. To have said 'God was the Word' would have contradicted the preceding declaration that the Word was *with*, and therefore personally distinct from, God. For the same reason the omission of the article before 'God' was required, since its presence would have intimated that the Word contained the whole Godhead (Swedenborg), which according to the previous assertion He did not. Nor would it have sufficed to write θεῖος, which might have suggested the idea that the Word was an inferior divinity, like the δεύτερος θεός of Philo. The sentence as it stands affirms the true and supreme divinity of the Word, not alone in His Self-revelation outward (Beyschlag), but in the inmost essence of His Being.

2. **The same** lit., *this* Word or Logos so described, **was in the beginning with God.** The first two clauses of the preceding verse are repeated— if indeed the third clause is not also reproduced in the οὗτος (Brückner)— not simply as a fresh starting point, the first verse being regarded, like Gen. i. 1, as a general heading (Westcott), but in order to emphasize His relationship to God before proceeding to treat of His relationship to the universe (Meyer, Godet) ; perhaps also with an eye to the contrast introduced in ver. 14 (Gess).

3. **All things** Different from the "all things," τὰ πάντα, of Paul (1 Cor. viii. 6; 2 Cor. v. 18 ; Col. i. 16) which denotes a special and determined totality (Godet), the whole of what actually exists (Meyer), the all as a unity (Luthardt), and from "The World," ὁ κόσμος of ver. 10, which suggests the notion of an ordered and beautified realm, the "all things" here mentioned mean not the moral universe alone (Socinus), but the totality of created things considered singly and separately (Luthardt), in their individuality which precedes their combination into a whole (Milligan and Moulton). " *Grande verbum, quo mundus,* i.e. *universitas rerum factarum denotatur*" (Bengel). **were made** lit., *began to be,* or come into existence, in antithesis to the "was" of ver. 1 ; declaring the non-eternity of matter or of any such primitive ὕλη as heathen philosophy imagined to be the *arche* or beginning of things. **by Him** δι' αὐτοῦ i.e. through or by the instrumentality of the Logos as distinguished from God, whose relation to the universe is commonly expressed either directly (Acts xiv. 15 ; Eph. iii. 9 ; Heb. iii. 4) or by the preposition "of," ἐκ, (1 Cor. viii. 6 ; xi. 12 ; 2 Cor. v. 18 ; Rom. xi. 36), although διὰ with the gen. is also used of the Father (Rom. xi. 36). According to Philo, God was the cause of the World, the Logos His instrumentality or οργανον, and the four elements the primordial ὕλη out of which it was mixed (De Cherub. i. 162). **and without Him** lit., *apart from Him,* either as to agency or end ; *absque eo* (Vulgate), *sine ipso* (Lampe). **was not anything made that hath been made** lit., *came into existence not any one thing which has come into existence.* Not a mere Hebrew parallelism of which this Gospel affords examples, as i. 20 ; x. 28 (Grotius); but an emphatic reassertion, in negative form, of the previous declaration, and as such an express denial of the existence of anything outside of His creative activity ; though not necessarily designed as a polemic against the Plato-Philonic doctrine of a ὕλη (Lücke, Olshausen, Frommann, Lange, Alford, and others). A different punctuation of the present verses places the period after ἓν and connects ὃ γέγονεν with what follows (C* D L, Clem. Alex., Origen, Latin Fathers, Augustine, Erasmus, Griesbach, Wetstein, Lachmann, Weisse, Hilgenfeld, Westcott and Hort, Milligan and Moulton). But 1. this punctuation is not adopted by the later MSS. C*** E G** H K M U X Λ etc. (see Tischendorf's Synopsis, p. 1), the Syriac, Arabic and Italic versions, or the early fathers Ignatius and Chrys-

ostom ; and 2. it is rejected by competent modern exegetes (Calvin, Lücke, Meyer, Godet, Luthardt, Brückner, Lange, and others) on the grounds chiefly (1) of grammar which would require after "that which has been made" not "was" but "is," (2) of linguistic usage, John never employing γενέσθαι ἐν for to be made by, and (3) of doctrinal interpretation, since thereby the creature rather than the creator would be represented as the light of men; while 3. it is as probable that the punctuation here objected to was preferred by the early fathers in order to avoid what seemed like a redundancy when δ γέγονεν was connected with the antecedent words, as that the accepted punctuation was introduced through dogmatic interest to preclude the hypothesis for instance that the Holy Ghost was created by Christ, which was altogether unnecessary, since the Holy Ghost did not become but was (Alford).

4. In Him was life. Neither 'that which had been made by' or originated in 'Him was life,' nor 'that which had come into being was life in Him,' but *in Him*, the Word or Logos, through whose creative energy all things, collectively and individually, had sprung into existence, *was*,—not is, ἐστί (א D and MSS. of Origen), which is manifestly a correction—*life;* the Evangelist, after defining His relation to the universe at large, passing on to exhibit His relation to men, and in preparation for so doing introducing Him as the absolute possessor of life (cf. Philo's πηγὴ ζωῆς, which occurs also in the LXX.'s rendering of Ps. xxxvi. 10), not of physical life merely, such as appears in the preservation of the universe (Chrysostom, Calvin, B. Crusius, Westcott), nor of spiritual life only, the ζωὴ αἰώνιος of xvii. 2, 3 (Origen, Lampe, Kuinoel, Hengstenberg, Luthardt, Weiss); but of life in its widest and highest conception, life without limitation, "in its full state of prosperity, in its normal expansion," in and for Himself (v. 26 ; 1 John v. 11), but also for His creatures. **and the life was the light of men.** Like "life" the term "light," φῶς, must be taken in its most comprehensive signification as equivalent to that which imparts illumination, mental (Calvin), moral (Luthardt), and

spiritual (Hengstenberg). According to Scripture φῶς when subjectively considered, as a state of being, describes the intellectual atmosphere of truth and the moral atmosphere of purity in which such being normally exists. Hence God is spoken of as 'Light' (1 John i. 5), and Christians are represented as Light in the Lord (Eph. v. 8). But in the present instance "light" must be taken objectively as that which communicates to man such inward illumination ; and in this sense John ascribes the light-giving agency not to the Truth (Meyer) which is not yet spoken of, but to the 'Life,' which already has been declared an absolute and eternal possession of the Word, meaning thereby that only then is man inwardly 'Light' when he is filled with the Life which proceeds from the Word. As it were the True Light-Bringer, φωσφόρος (2 Pet. i. 19) not to the Jews only between the Fall and the Incarnation (Luthardt), but to men as men on the platform of creation, or while yet in paradisaiacal innocence (Meyer, Godet, Lange and others) is the Logos or Word who also when incarnate exhibits Himself as 'the Light of the World," τὸ φῶς τοῦ κόσμου (viii. 12); only the dispensation of this 'Light' is not direct but indirect, through impartation of the 'Life,' for, "as bodily sight is one of the functions of physical life, so, in the normal state, spiritual light is an emanation from moral life" (Godet).

5. And the Light. The outwardly manifested Life rather than the inward principle of the Life (Lücke, **shineth** φαίνει ; not appeareth, φαίνεται ; expressive of continous activity, from the beginning to the present time (Meyer, Lange, Westcott) ; and therefore to be restricted neither to the operations of the Pre-incarnate Logos, λόγος ἄσαρκος, under the O. T. through the medium of the prophets (De Wette), nor to those of the Incarnate Logos, λόγος ἔνσαρκος, through the historical appearing of Jesus Christ (Hengstenberg, Godet), but extended to both. **in the darkness.** Another peculiarly Johannine expression (viii. 12; xii. 35, 46; 1 John i. 5; ii. 8, 9, 11), signifying not an eternal principle lying over against the Light (Baur, Hilgenfeld), or the Jews in their opposition to Christ (Lampe, Hengstenberg), but humanity as turned away from the light; implying an alteration of the primitive condition of mankind through the intervention of a Fall (Olshausen, Meyer, Godet, and others). **and the darkness apprehended it not** either 1. *did not overcome*, in the sense of extinguish, *it;* cf. xii. 35, where the image is supposed to be that of darkness following in pursuit so as to enwrap and overwhelm men, vi. 17 (Codex Sinaiticus) κατέλαβεν δὲ αὐτοὺς ἡ σκοτία, "but the darkness had fallen on them," and Mark ix. 18, where the same sense of the verb will apply (Origen, Chrysostom, Theophylact, Lange, Westcott, Milligan and Moulton); or 2. and, better, *did not apprehend*, in the sense of intellectually grasping, *it*, a meaning the verb commonly has in the Middle Voice in the N. T. (cf. Acts iv. 13; x. 34; xxv. 25; Eph. iii. 18), which is not opposed to the radical idea contained in vi. 17; xii. 35; Mark ix. 18, as above explained (in these passages the verb might fairly enough be rendered grasp, take, seize, as in Rom. ix. 30), and seems at least equally well suited to the parallels in ver. 10, 11 (Bengel, Lampe, Calvin, Olshausen, Luthardt, Godet, Meyer, Brückner, Tholuck, and others).

Note. *Whence did John derive his Doctrine of the Logos?*
The claims of Philo, to be regarded as the source whence the Author of the Fourth Gospel, directly or indirectly, drew his doctrine of the Logos have been largely advocated by modern exegetes (De Wette, Lücke, Gfrörer, Dähne, Lutterbeck, Ewald, Brückner, and others). But I. *It is not certain that John was acquainted with Philo's writings or even with the Alexandrine Gnosis.* The evidence relied on to show that he was is at best fragmentary and indirect. 1. It is argued that the inter-relations of a commercial sort which existed in the first and second centuries between Ephesus from which this Gospel is supposed to have proceeded, and Alexandria, rendered it at least possible for its author, whoever he was, to attain to a knowledge of the philosophico-religious speculations of the day which had that Egyptian city as their headquarters. 2. It is assumed that Apollos

the eloquent Jew who assisted largely in building up the Ephesian Church (Acts xviii. 24), having been an Alexandrian by birth, could not fail to carry over into Asia a knowledge of the doctrines of Philo. 3. The statement of Theodoret (Haer. fab. ii. 3) that Cerinthus received his first impulse from the theology of the Alexandrian Jews, and drew from them the germs of his doctrine before appearing in Asia Minor (Neander's Church History, ii. 42, Bohn's edition), is regarded as pointing to another channel through which the tenets in question might have found their way to the Christian circles in Asia Minor. And 4. the circumstance that at the time the tenets of the Neo-Platonic Philosophy to which Philonism was closely allied were widely spread amongst the Hellenistic Jews and Jewish Christians for whom this Gospel was written, is supposed to lend probability to the belief that John would not neglect to avail himself of the opportunity of enlisting the sympathies of his readers by presenting the new wine of his Life-giving Gospel in the old bottles of a familiar and favourite philosophic terminology. The most however that these considerations can be used to prove is the unlikelihood that John had no acquaintance with either Philo or his writings : they cannot be regarded as establishing that John had either perused the works or informed himself as to the opinions of the Platonizing Jew of Alexandria. Still, should both of these be conceded, it may be urged—II. *That, with the exception of the term Logos, the Fourth Gospel contains not a trace of Philonism*, which is, to say the least, remarkable if John began its composition under the influence of that celebrated master. The number of parallels between the Alexandrian philosopher and the Christian Evangelist that can be made good is four, and these are confined exclusively to the Prologue. With ver. 1 in John have been compared the words of Philo, τῆς ἀιδίου εἰκόνος αὐτοῦ, λόγου τοῦ ἱερωτάτου, de Conf. Ling. 28, p. 427 ; καλεῖ δὲ θεὸν τὸν πρεσβύτατον αὐτοῦ νυνὶ λόγον, de Somn. i. 39, p. 655 ; πρὸς τὸν δεύτερον θεὸν ὅς ἐστιν ἐκείνου λόγος, Fragm. p. 625 ; —with ver. 3 the words λόγος δὲ ἐστιν εἰκιὸν θεοῦ, δι' οὖ σύμπας ὁ κόσμος ἐδημιουρ-γεῖτο, de Monarch. ii. 5, p. 225 ;—with ver. 4 the statement καὶ ταύτης εἰκόνα τὸ νοητὸν φῶς ἐκεῖνο, ὁ θείου λόγου γέγονεν εἰκιὼν τοῦ διερμηνεύσαντος τὴν γένεσιν αὐτοῦ, de Mundi Opif. 8, p. 6 ;—and with ver. 18 the language οὐ περὶ τῆς φύσεως αὐτοῦ διαγνῶναι δύναται ἀλλ' ἀγαπητὸν, ἐὰν τοῦ ὀνόματος αὐτοῦ δυνηθῶμεν, ὅπερ ἦν, τοῦ ἑρμηνέως λόγου, Legis Alleg. iii. 73, p. 128. Other parallels, as between John iv. 10 and de Prof. 18, p. 560, and John vi. 32 and Legis Alleg. ii. 21 ; iii. 56, 59, are questionable. But even had the similarities in respect of language been more numerous and striking than they are, it is indubitable—III. *That the Logos of Philo is essentially different from that of John.* For 1. it is impossible to determine whether the Philonian Logos is a Person, or only an attribute, or at most a Personification, while the Logos of John is distinctly personal. Notwithstanding that the terms 'archangel,' 'second god,' 'image of God,' 'chief priest,' 'first begotten son,' applied by Philo to the Logos, appear to involve his real hypostatical subsistence (Grossmann, Gfrörer, Lücke), other designations employed as certainly suggest his non-personality, as for instance, 'Idea of Ideas,' 'Shadow of God,' 'Seal of the World,' 'Place of the World of Ideas.' Indeed it is problematical whether Philo had made up his mind on the Personality or non-Personality of the Logos, or whether he only "sometimes thought of a personal Logos but never believed in one" (Liddon's Divinity of Christ, chap. ii. p. 67). 2. It is certain that the Philonian Logos is not divine in the same exalted sense as is the Logos of John. If the former be styled δεύτερος θεὸς, it is yet unquestionable that the passage in which this occurs "alludes to a less perfect divine element which is capable of coming into contact with the World, whereas the highest divine element cannot do so." That which is highest in the divine nature, according to Philo's conception of it, is incommunicable and does not admit of personal distinctions. Hence, although the Logos may sometimes be represented as the ideal-world-forming God, and therefore as divine, it is only in the sense that the mind of God is divine, or, if the Logos be conceived as a hypostasis, in a sense altogether subordinate to that in which God is divine. "The Divine Logos (of Philo)" says Dorner, "is as little God *per se*, as he is a hypostasis." "Philo only metaphorically gives the name of δεύτερος θεὸς to the Logos ; but John calls Him θεὸς in the strictest didatic sense" (Schmid). 3. The Logos of Philo is essentially a metaphysical conception, whereas the Johannine Logos is an object of religious contemplation. The former is required to fill the gulf which, in the theory of Philo, yawns between the transcendent deity and the external world, to stand midway between that which is abstract and impersonal on the one side, and definite and personal on the other, and is accordingly described in language which "wavers between the two conceptions without succeeding in combining them": the latter is the only begotten Son who is eternally in the bosom of the Father, who declares Him to men and conducts men to Him. 4. Philo's Logos has no real connection with human history and salvation such as John's has. The divine energies of the former are concerned purely with the creation and preservation of the sensible world; and since with the Alexandrian Platonist matter is the Principle of Evil, an Incarnation of the Logos must for ever be impossible. "In real, human appearing, Philo could not make the Logos thinkable to himself : the human, the earthly is only a symbol and instrument of the Logos : a true man-becoming of the same is to him a completely strange thought" (Lücke). Of John's Logos on the other hand it is announced that "He became flesh" and entered into human history in order to effect the salvation of men. In short, to use the words of Gess, "So totally different are the writings of John and the thoughts of Philo that he who allows the former, especially with regard to the Logos, to grow out of the latter, understands nothing either of John or of Philo."—IV. *It was unnecessary for John to have recourse to Philo for this peculiar expression*, since it was open to him to derive it from other sources, from some of which Philo himself may have drawn his speculations. 1. In the Hebrew Scriptures, which must have largely contributed to the religious education of the Author of the Fourth

Gospel, it is not difficult to trace the germs at least of a Logos doctrine. (1) In the Mosaic Account of creation (Gen. i.) the various works of the six successive days in which the Divine Formative Energy laboured in the arrangement of the present Cosmos are exhibited as the immediate result of as many separate voices or spoken words proceeding from the mouth of Elohim. What if the Evangelist simply purposed to represent the uncreated Logos as the personal Being by whom these creative voices were uttered? (2) The doctrine of the Maleach Jehovah who in former times had appeared to the patriarchs and others as God's Messenger, who announced His will sometimes by an audible word (Gen. xv. 1), and who, if occasionally distinguished from God (Gen. xvi. 11), was also frequently identified with Him (Gen. xvi. 13; xix. 16; xxxii. 30, etc.), would unquestionably prepare the way for the conception of a divine Personal Logos such as John here presents. "Indeed that John's doctrine of the Logos is related to the O. T. doctrine of the Angel of the Lord can be the less doubted, since the Apostle himself elsewhere refers frequently and unquestionably to this doctrine," as e.g. when he characterizes Christ as *sent* by God, by which appellation "is everywhere intimated the personal identity of Christ with the O. T. angel or messenger of the Lord," and again "when he designates (ver. 11) the covenant people as the property of Christ," and yet again, "when in xii. 41 he says without further explanation that Isaiah saw the glory of Christ, while it is the glory of Jehovah that is spoken of" (Hengstenberg). (3.) The Creative Activity assigned to the Word of Jehovah in the Book of Psalms (xxxiii. 6, 9) would likewise tend to foster the notion of a distinct divine hypostasis to whom the name of Logos might with propriety be assigned. (4.) The poetical personification of Wisdom in the Book of Proverbs (viii. 22-31) would further serve to develop the idea, and all the more effectively that the personification approximates so closely to the portraiture of a real hypostasis (Meyer). 2. In the Chokmah writings of the Post-Exilian Period, which carried on and perfected the tendency already begun in the Old Testament theology,

the Fourth Evangelist would find another contributory source to the Logos doctrine which was taking shape in his mind. In those writings the transition from an impersonal to a personal Sophia appears as an accomplished fact. (1) In the Wisdom of Sirach, dating probably from the latter half of the 2nd century before Christ, Sophia or Wisdom is described as having existed "beside the Lord and with Him for ever" (i. 1), and "before all things" (i. 4), as having proceeded "from the mouth of the highest" (xxiv. 3), as having been fashioned "before the World from the beginning" (xxiv. 9). (2) In the Wisdom of Solomon (100 B.C.) she is depicted as "the breath of the power of God, and a pure influence flowing from the Glory of the Almighty" (vii. 25), as "the brightness of the everlasting light, the unspotted mirror of the power of God, and the image of His goodness" (ver. 26), as "the Maker of all things" in whom is "an understanding spirit, holy, only begotten, manifold" (ver. 22), with many other epithets designed apparently to set her forth as "a real and independent principle revealing God in the World (especially in Israel) and mediating between it and Him after it has, as His organ, created the World" (Meyer). (3) The Chaldee Targumists, the oldest of whose works (Onkelos and Jonathan) go back in their earliest forms at least to apostolic (Godet), if not to prechristian (Olshausen) times and certainly embody interpretations which had been current at a much earlier period (Westcott), substitute in their translations for Elohim or Jehovah the words Memra-da-Yeya, by which they meant a personal being who served as the permanent agent or representative of God in the sensible world, and who was likewise identified in their theology with the Schekinah and the Person of the Messiah (Weber, System der Altsynagogalen Palästinischen Theologie, § 38). Hence so far from John requiring to go to Philo for a Logos doctrine it is probable that Philo went to the same sources as John himself, and that in Philo we behold Philosophy labouring ingeniously at a problem which John saw resolved for him and mankind generally in the Person of Christ. 3. Nor should it be overlooked that a third source was open to the Christian Apostle which was not accessible to the Jewish Philosopher, viz., the sayings of Jesus. It is true that Christ never employed this term "Word" or "Logos" as a designation of Himself ; but a careful examination of His utterances concerning His Person will render it apparent that these might easily have suggested to John the propriety of using it. Without alluding to individual expressions such as those recorded in chaps. v. 38 ; xiv. 24 ; xvii. 14 of this Gospel, the aspect in which Christ's Person, character, and work are here contemplated is so prominently that of One who has come to men with Divine words of Truth and Life that, apart altogether from the current of O.T. history and tradition, the transition must have seemed both natural and easy to pass from thinking of Christ as the speaker of God's words to writing

of Him as God's Spoken Word itself. If therefore it may be supposed that John had recourse to all these different sources which have been mentioned, it will not excite surprise that, without borrowing from Philo, he should have represented Christ as the Divine Logos, or the Personal Self-Revelation of God (Dorner on the Person of Christ, vol. i. pp. 24-45 with Note A. (C. F. T. L.) ; Lücke, Commentar über das Evangelium des Johannes, pp. 233-251 ; Gess, Christi Person und Werk, vol. ii. pp. 634-646 ; Weiss, der Johanneische Lehrbegriff, pp. 239-251 ; Frommann's Johanneische Lehrbegriff, pp. 115-117 ; Schmid, Bib. Theol. of N. T., part ii. div. 2, § 92 ; Godet's Commentary on John, vol. i. pp. 174-180, 388-390 (C. F. T. L.); Prof. Mansel in Kitto's Bib. Cyclopædia, art. Philosophy).

HOMILETICS

VER. 1-5.—THE GLORY OF THE WORD.
I. **His Essential Dignity.** 1. *His Eternal Existence.* "In the beginning was the Word." The proposition predicates of the Word a premundane and pre-creaturely existence, anterior to time and the origin of things. The Word never began to be, but always was, not simply from, but at, in, and before the beginning ; which teaches that the true sphere of His subsistence was not Time, but Eternity. 2. *His Personal Intelligence.* The theme of the evangelist's discourse was not a metaphysical abstraction, or a poetical personification, but a veritable person. Implied in the application to him of the personal pronoun and the ascription to him of works competent only to intelligence, this is likewise involved in the import of the appellation Word which marks him out as the absolute self-revelation of the Supreme. Inasmuch as intelligence alone can fully image forth intelligence, and only a person can adequately manifest a person, the eternal self-revelation of the personal God can only realize itself in and through the medium of a personal intelligence. 3. *His Absolute Divinity.* "And the Word was God." The language is selected with deliberate precision. The Word was not godlike merely, since in that case He might have been an insubstantial abstraction, an impersonal attribute, a rhetorical phrase, an elegant prosopopeia ; nor again was He 'The God,' since this might have fostered the delusion that the entire Godhead was summed up in Him ; but He was God, i.e. an eternally existing, absolutely self-centred, Divine person.
II. **His Manifold Relationship.** 1. *To God.* "And the Word was with God" : "the same was in the beginning with God." The clauses intimate that the Word as a Divine Person is (1) a distinct hypostasis from the Father—otherwise he could not be described as *with* God, (2) an absolute self-revelation of the Father—otherwise He could not properly be designated "The Word," (3) one in essence and fellowship with the Father—otherwise he could not be represented as eternally moving towards the Father, and (4) possessed of true equality with the Father—otherwise He could not be spoken of as eternally co-existing with the Father as His absolute image, counterpart, self-revelation, *alter ego.* 2. *To the Universe.* "All things were made by Him ; and without Him was not any one thing made that has come into existence." The state-

ments exhibit the Word as (1) The Personal Divine Agent through whose creative energy the universe in its vast totality and in its infinitude of individual details was summoned into being, i.e. as the First Cause of all Things, and (2) as the Personal Divine Being with reference to whom every minute particle within the circle of creation subsists, for whose end and glory each and all, separately and conjointly, have been commanded from the formless womb of non-existence—i.e. as the Last Cause of All Things. 3. *To Man.* " In Him was life, and the Life was the Light of men." Besides possessing in Himself life, original and underived, He was (1) and immediately the Life of Men, the sole fountain whence humanity derived its life, physical, intellectual, moral, and spiritual, and (2), but mediately, the Light of Men, through the free communication of that life which when embraced by the human spirit becomes in turn a light of life, irradiating and illuminating the being in whom it shines, in every department, from centre to circumference, from base to summit.
III. **His Pre-incarnate Activity.** 1. *Shining in the darkness.* The term darkness points with melancholy emphasis to the doctrine of a Fall. Had the organic bond wherewith Humanity and the Logos were at first united continued unbroken, the Life of the Unbeginning Word would have streamed forth with ever-increasing radiance round the souls of men, encompassing them with a light which would have been the finite projection of the Light Inaccessible and full of Glory, in which He himself dwelt, inspiring their minds with the clear illumination of unmixed and Eternal Truth, and arraying their moral natures in the lustrous garment of celestial purity. But contrary to Heaven's purpose that link of connection between the Creature and his Creator was by the free act of the former severed. Turning from the light man elected for himself a sphere and a development outside the light, amid intellectual and moral darkness. Nevertheless, the light continued shining, mercifully penetrating with its radiant beams the dark atmosphere of ignorance and sin man was gradually thickening around himself. 2. *Rejected by the darkness.* Though the light kept on shining before men in general through the teachings of nature, and the moral intuitions of conscience, and before the Jews in particular through the sacrificial system of Moses and the witness of the prophets, yet men laid not hold of that light partly because they did not fully understand it, and partly because they did not see it, but chiefly because they did not want it, because they neither loved nor desired but hated and rejected it.
Lessons. 1. The doctrine of our Lord's Supreme Divinity. 2. The plurality of Persons in the Godhead. 3. The doctrine of Creation ; Evolution may be, Dualism, Pantheism, Atheism, Materialism cannot be compatible, with Scripture. 4. The True Source of Happiness for Man, being filled with the Life that is in the Word. 5. The intimate connection between the different dispensations that have been set up in the past history of the World. 6. The Mercy of God in keeping the Light of Life burning through centuries of darkness. 7. The natural repugnance of the fallen heart against that which is good.

SECTION II.—THE TRUE LIGHT

CHAP. I. VER. 6-13

EXPOSITION

Ver. 6. **There came** lit., *began to be,* arose, ἐγένετο in antithesis to the Word who was (ver. 1). Denoting a historical appearance, the verb is to be connected not with " sent " (Chrysostom, Hengstenberg), but with 'man.' a **man** perhaps undesignedly contrasting with what in ver. 1 is predicated of the Word (Olshausen, Luthardt, Godet, and others) ; possibly also containing an allusion to the mystery disclosed in ver. 14 (Westcott) : compare Luke i. 5, and contrast John iii. 1. **sent from God** *definitio prophetae* (Bengel) ; cf. Mal. iii. 1 ; Matt. xi. 10 ; John iii. 28 ; alluding to the Baptist's divine commission. **whose name was** lit., *the name to him was ;* cf. iii. 1 ; 1

Sam. i. 1 (LXX.); otherwise (Luke i. 27; ii. 25). **John** Ἰωάννης יוֹחָנָן (Heb.) = God shows grace ; significant of the era about to open (Godet) ; the son of Zacharias and Elizabeth the kinswoman of Mary, and therefore the kinsman of Jesus (Luke i. 36, 57, 61). That he is not styled "The Baptist," his traditional name (Jos. Ant. xviii. 5, 2), as well as his customary appellation, with the Synoptists (Matt. iii. 1 ; Mark vi. 14 ; Luke vii. 20) has been supposed to indicate that the author of this Gospel was John (Meyer, Godet) ; seeming, as it does, to show that the writer must have known the Baptist before that official title was conferred upon him, and probably avoided a designation well-known in the Church as distinguishing the two Johns, in order the better to preserve his incognito (Credner). Introduced not so much in his private as in his official capacity, as the greatest of O. T. prophets, the Baptist may be regarded as their representative, and his testimony as a summing up and crowning of theirs (Olshausen, Lange).

7. **The same** *This man* just referred to : cf. οὗτος in ver. 2, which looks back to ver. 1, and contrast ἐκεῖνος in ver. 8. **came** not ἐγένετο which described his historical appearance, but ἦλθε, the complement of ἀπεσταλμένος, 'sent' (ver. 6), marking his entrance on official activity : cf. Matt. xi. 18. **for witness** i.e. for the purpose of witness-bearing generally, of making known by personal testimony what was prophetically and by Divine Revelation communicated to him concerning another : the specific character of the Witness-bearing being next declared. **that** ἵνα, in order that, expressive of design as well as sequence, a favourite conjunction with the Author. "It gives the relation of aiming at, whether that be a specially designed or an essential and hence internally necessary relation" (Luthardt). **he might bear witness of**—better, 'concerning,' περί,—**the Light**. Not simply foretell its coming, in which sense the entire succession of O. T. prophets were witnesses to the Light (Olshausen), but point it out when it had come (ver. 31), a function in which both the Mission and

the Testimony of the Baptist transcended those of his predecessors (Lange, Westcott). Witness - bearing, a conception peculiar to, and frequently occurring in, the Johannine Scriptures—nearly 50 times in this Gospel and 30 or 40 times in the Epistles and Apocalypse—is designed to provide a basis for faith. **that** may be connected either with 'bear witness,' as its immediate purpose, or with 'came,' as its final end. **all** not of John's hearers only (Piscator, Lücke), or of those besides to whom his testimony might be reported (Bengel, Lampe), but all mankind, whether Jews or Gentiles. **might believe.** For the first time mentioned, this great word 'believe,' one of the key-notes of this Gospel, and occurring no fewer than 90 times, always signifies the soul's trustful reception of (1) the Divine Testimony concerning Christ (ver. 37 ; cf. 1 John v. 9), whether delivered by the O. T. Scriptures (v. 39), by the Baptist (v. 33), or by Christ Himself (iii. 11, 32), and (2) of the Saviour's Person (ii. 11 ; iii. 16, 18 ; vi. 29). **through him** not on him, the Baptist, since he was not the Light (ver. 8); or on God through Him, Christ (Grotius, Lampe, Semler); but on the Light, sc. Christ, through him, the Baptist.

8. **He was not the Light,**—better than 'He was not that Light' (A. V.), the emphasis resting either on 'he' as thus, 'Not that person, ἐκεῖνος, but another, to be introduced (ver. 9), was the Light' (Luthardt, Godet), 'or on 'was,' in which case the antithesis lies between John's personality and John's Mission (Meyer, Brückner), or on 'The Light,' the sense being 'That man was not the Light,' but only 'The Lamp' for the Light, v. 35 (Westcott). Though not certainly demonstrable that the Evangelist had a polemical design against the followers of the Baptist who continued unbelievers, Acts xix. 3, 4 (Olshausen, Godet, and others), it is impossible dogmatically to affirm that he had not (Hengstenberg, Meyer), while he may have desired to indicate that he knew of their existence (Tholuck, Westcott), and his language requires no straining to enable one to find in it an allusion to the popular sentiment entertained

concerning John at the time of his appearing (Bengel, Lampe, Meyer). **but came,** ἦλθεν being supplied (Meyer, Westcott), or ἐγένετο (Tholuck), or, better than either, ἦν, was (Lücke, Godet, Lange, and others), or the ἵνα may stand absolutely as in ix. 3 ; xiii. 18 ; xv. 25 (Luthardt, Brückner), the supplement γέγονε τοῦτο, 'this happened,' or something similar, being mentally supplied : Winer's Grammar of the N. T. Diction, § 43, 5. **that he might bear witness of the Light.** The introduction of the Baptist's witness into the Prologue was due not to the fact that with it the subsequent history (ver. 9) should begin (De Wette), or that the Baptist was in himself " an illustrious exception " to the darkness already mentioned (Ewald), or that his witness was designed to be ideally regarded as the first means of mediating between the Light and the Darkness (Baur), or that it was needful to prepare the way for the non-recognition and rejection alluded to in ver. 11 (Meyer, Godet), or to set forth the greatness of Christ in comparison with the Baptist, the greatest of O. T. prophets (Hengstenberg) ; but to the desire of attesting the reality of the Word's entrance into the world as The True Light (Brückner).

9. **There was** Not 'that' (A. V.), or 'The Word' (Kuinoel), or 'The Light' testified to by John, *lux ipsa* (Bengel, Grotius, Godet) was, but 'The True Light' was, or as it here stands, There was—**the True Light.** Not "the true" as opposed to the false light, which the Baptist was not (v. 35), but the Original Light as opposed to the derived (Calvin, Olshausen, Lücke, Alford) ; the essential as distinguished from the shadowy or phenomenal (Hengstenberg, Godet, Lange) ; the archetypal in which the reality corresponds with the idea in antithesis to the imperfect and incomplete (Tholuck, Meyer, Luthardt); the permanent in opposition to the transitory (Westcott): cf. iv. 23; vi. 32; xv. i.;—*even the light* **which lighteth every man.** The clause describes the active efficiency of the True Light, 1. intensively as light giving —φωτίζει, it lighteth, i.e. objectively giveth light to (Rev. xviii. 1 ; xxi. 23 ; xxii. 5; cf. Luke xi. 36; 1 Cor. iv. 5 ; 2 Tim. i. 10) or subjectively illuminateth

(Heb. vi. 4 ; x. 32); and 2. extensively as all-embracing—πάντα ἄνθρωπον, meaning all mankind, if the former be the sense of the verb, but, if the latter, all who are illuminated. In both respects Christ as the True Light surpassed His predecessor who simply pointed to the Light (ver. 29-36 ; iii. 28-36), and to that extent shined (v. 35), but himself imparted none. **coming into the world** ἐρχόμενον has been connected 1. with ἄνθρωπον, man (Syriac, Chrysostom, Augustine, Luther, Calvin, Meyer, Godet). But against this may be urged (1) that the *solemn redundance* or *epic fulness of the words* (Meyer), implied in defining every man by the superadded phrase 'that cometh into the world' adds nothing to the conception of humanity and as little to the progress of thought ; (2) that so explained the sentiment is incorrect except in the sense of the inner light of conscience which every man brings with him into the world as a birth gift from Christ, which is not the subject of the Evangelist's discourse, and (3) that the phrase "coming into the world" appears to be set apart by the writer of this Gospel to express the historical advent of Christ (i. 15 ; 27, 30 ; iii. 31 ; vi. 14 ; xi. 27 ; xii. 46 ; xvi. 28 ; xviii. 37). 2. With ἦν, was, either as a purely historical Imperfect, equivalent to " came " (Bengel, Bleek, Baumgarten-Crusius, Lange, Hengstenberg), or as a future, the present participle indicating that the expected event was on the eve of happening (Lampe, Olshausen, Tholuck, Luthardt: cf. Winer's Grammar, § xlv. 1, d, b), or as a continuous present, representing a state of things still going on, " it was (in the act of) coming into the world " (Hilgenfeld, Brückner). If the wide separation between ἦν and ἐρχόμενον cannot be urged as fatal to this construction, it may be contended that the supposed interchange of tenses is a purely arbitrary device of expositors and not at all demanded by competent exegesis (Winer's Grammar, § xl. 1). 3. With τὸ φῶς, as a qualifying clause descriptive of the state or condition of the True Light at the time of John's testimony (Lange, Westcott, Milligan and Moulton). Taken thus, the clause asserts that at the time of John's appearing the True Light existed, not however in Incarnate form, but as " coming into the world."

He had been "coming into the world" from the first, "advancing towards His Incarnation by preparatory revelations" (Westcott), and was not fully come till made manifest to Israel by the Baptismal Act of John. The world into which He was coming was man's moral world considered as an organized whole (iii. 16), existing outside of the light in moral and spiritual darkness (iii. 19), actively opposed to God (1 John ii. 15) and therefore liable to pass away and perish beneath sentence of condemnation (1 John ii. 17). "Only rarely does ὁ κόσμος stand for the universe (xvii. 5-24 ; xxi. 25), or for the earthly world (xvi. 21 ; I. iii. 17), which in most cases is more closely designated as ὁ κόσμος οὗτος (ix. 39 ; xi. 9 ; xii. 25 ; xiii. 1 ; xviii. 36) ... ὁ κόσμος is a technical term for the world of men as a whole" (Weiss, Bib. Theol. of the N. T. § 153, a, note 1).

10. He rather 'it,' the True Light, **was** not merely at the time when the Baptist was bearing witness, in the Person of Christ (Meyer, Hengstenberg, De Wette), but always had been from the beginning, so that practically ἦν has the force of an Imperfect. **in the world** i.e. the material and moral world generally, and not simply the latter (Weiss). **and the world** not the former alone (Lange), but both as before. **was made by Him** or came into existence, not δι' αὐτόν (א) on account of Him, but δι' αὐτοῦ, through Him (ver. 3 ; Colos. i. 16 ; Heb. i. 2) ; a preparation by way of climax for the mournful announcement next made. **and** with the force of a 'but'; "The very semblance of indifference that lies in καί makes the contrast the more impressive and really startling" (Luthardt). **the world.** Again the same world but viewed as summed up in humanity, its intelligent and moral head. **knew** i.e. recognized, apprehended so as to understand ; cf. i. 48 ; ii. 24, 25 ; v. 42 ; x. 15. **Him** Whereas αὐτοῦ was neuter, αὐτὸν is masculine, and suggests the personal character of the Light. **not.** Although for the twofold reason alleged in the preceding clauses it ought to have done so.

11. **He came.** Referring to His personal historical manifestation as distinguished from His spiritual invisible presence alluded to in ver. 10. **unto**

His own τὰ ἴδια ; not the World or Mankind generally (Maldonatus, Kuinoel, Tholuck, Reuss), but the things that pertained to Messiah, as the Temple, the City, the Land of Israel (Bengel), his own home as in xvi. 32 ; xix. 27 (Godet), hi. own land (Westcott), or His own possession as in Acts iv. 32 (Lampe) ; all however practically signifying the same thing, viz., the Theocratic Nation. **and His own** οἱ ἴδιοι, His own people, i.e. the Jews, who were Messiah's kinsmen (Rom. i. 4), and Messiah's possession as they had previously been Jehovah's (Ex. xix. 5 ; Deut. vii. 6 ; Ps. cxxxv. 4 ; Is. xxxi. 9). **received Him not** into their hearts ; the verb παραλαμβάνειν conveying the ideas of accepting what has been offered by another, 1 Cor. xi. 23 (Bengel, Westcott), of according welcome to one's house, Matt. i. 20, 24 (Godet, Brückner), of assuming to oneself as a friend or companion, John xiv. 3 (Lücke, Alford). Corresponding to these senses of the verb, Christ was presented to Israel, (1) as the Messiah promised through the prophets, and held out for acceptance by John, (2) as the Bridegroom of the Church advancing to claim his bride (iii. 29), (3) as the Heavenly Friend who sought to bless sinful man with His love (xv. 15) (4) as the Master of the House returning to His home (Matt. xxv. 50 ; Luke xii. 43). It is not needful to see in the use of παρέλαβον instead of ἔγνω an allusion to the greater guilt of Israel in rejecting Christ relatively to that of mankind, who simply did not know Him (Meyer), though the substitution of παραλαμβάνειν for καταλαμβάνειν (ver. 5) may be due to the circumstance that while the object of the former is a person, that of the latter is a principle (Godet, Lange).

12. But as many of the Jews who were His own and as a body rejected Him, though not excusing others *qui antea non fuerant* ἴδιοι (Bengel). **as received Him** lit., *took Him*, ἔλαβον, not equivalent to παρέλαβον (Alford, Brückner), but expressive of the act by which the reception was completed (Westcott), not *vice versa* (Milligan and Moulton) ; emphasizing the willingness of the action even more than the compound (Luthardt) ; perhaps also in contrast to the compound pointing to the indi-

vidual character of this act (Godet, Lange), which is further defined in the last clause as a "believing on His name" : cf. iii. 32 ; v. 43 ; xiii. 20 ; xvii. 8 ; 1 John v. 9 ; in which the moral act of faith is expressed by λαμβάνεν. **to them** individually **gave He the right** ἐξουσίαν ; not merely honour, privilege, prerogative (Chrysostom, Erasmus, Kuinoel, Bengel), possibility (De Wette), capability (Hengstenberg, Brückner), or right, authority (Calvin, Westcott, Milligan and Moulton), but power in the fullest sense, involving everything needful for the realization of sonship (Lücke, Meyer, Alford), and thus implying a new standing, Paul's υἱοθεσία (Godet), a new title (Meyer), a new power (Luthardt, Tholuck, Olshausen, and others). **to become.** The verb may suggest the gradual character of that process by which complete sonship is attained. **children of God.** The noun τέκνα, from τίκτειν to beget, points to the actual communication of the life of God, while υἱός rather intimates the notion of Sonship by Adoption : cf. Matt. ii. 18 ; vii. 11 ; Luke vii. 35 ; xx. 1 ; John viii. 39 ; xi. 52 ; Rom. viii. 10 ; Eph. ii. 3 ; 1 John iii. 1, 2, 10, in which τέκνον is used with Matt. v. 9, 45 ; xvii. 25, 26 ; John iv. 12 ; xii. 36 ; Rev. ii. 14 ; vii. 4 ; xx. 1, 7, 12, in which υἱός is employed. This distinction is also Pauline (Gal. vi. 6). Yet by the Evangelist τέκνον θεοῦ is never applied to Christ. When the idea of paternity is to be conveyed, μονογενής, or μονογενής υἱός (i. 14, 18 ; iii. 16, 18 ; 1 John iv. 9), or simply υἱός is employed (iii. 35, 36 ; v. 23, 25 ; xvii. 1 ; xx. 31); the reason probably being in the ambiguity of τέκνον which may refer to maternal as well as to paternal origin. Even **to them that believe** lit., *to them believing*, the participle denoting an enduring habit rather than an isolated act, which would have demanded πιστεύσασιν. **on His Name.** Not one particular name to the exclusion of others, as that of Word (Godet, Olshausen), or The Only Begotten (Bengel), or The Christ the Son of God (Westcott), Jesus (Alford), Jesus Christ, the historically manifested Logos (Meyer), but all of these together, *tota excellentia ejus divina, omnesque perfectiones quas tum in reliquis operibus, tum praecipue in opere gratiae revelabit*

(Lampe), or "the concentrated expression of His Nature in His Gospel in which truth and personal fact are one" (Lange). If πιστεύειν εἰς τὸ ὄνομα αὐτοῦ differs from π. εἰς αὐτόν (cf. iii. 16 and 18), which is doubtful, it is only in the sense of more fully characterizing the act of faith as an outward expression, since the *uttered* name contains the whole confession of faith (Meyer), or of serving as a prelude to what must ever constitute the fundamental basis and inmost essence of faith, viz., a resting on the Person whom the Name reveals (Milligan and Moulton) : cf. Weiss, der Johanneische Lehrbegriff, § 3.

13. which οἵ, who, not ὅς or the Word (Irenaeus, Tertullian), but believers, the antecedent being τοῖς πιστεύουσιν, though by *constructio ad sensum* (2 John 1 ; Gal. iv. 19 ; cf. Eurip. Suppl. 12 ; Aristoph. Plut. 292 ; Winer's Grammar, § 21, 2), it may also be τέκνα θεοῦ; in which case the verse is substantially a development of the idea of "children of God." But as on this assumption faith would be excluded from the ἐξουσία of ver. 12, being antecedent to it, the first interpretation is to be preferred. **were born** lit., *were begotten*, ἐγεννήθησαν. What Paul describes as a New Creation (2 Cor. v. 17), and a Moral Resurrection (Rom. vi. 4), is here defined as a Spiritual Palingenesia or Regeneration (iii. 3 ; 1 John ii. 29 ; iii. 9 ; iv. 7 ; v. 1, 4, 18). **not of blood** lit., *bloods;* not of the sexes (Augustine, Lücke, Ewald), but of man, the plural for the singular denoting not the multiplicity of the children of God (Baumgarten-Crusius) or the successive orders of propagations (Hœlemann), or the ethical distinction of bloods (Lange), or the variety of origins (Bengel), but the constituent elements of which the blood consists (Meyer, Luthardt, Godet, Westcott and others). Cf. ἄλλων τραφεὶς ἀφ' αἱμάτων (Euripides, *Ion* 693). "The blood is here considered as the original material and, as it were, the chaos from which the whole human organism proceeds" ; and as such is denied to be the origin of the spiritual life. See Delitzsch, Biblical Psychology, § 11, p. 290, C. F. T. L. **nor of the will of the flesh nor of the will of man.** Not epexegetic of the preceding clause, so that σάρξ refers to the woman and ἀνήρ to the man (Augustine, Erasmus, Olshausen, Lücke), since the conjunctions οὔτε ... οὔτε would then have been employed as indicating two parallel clauses (v. 37), whereas οὐδέ ... οὐδέ introduce a gradation (Winer's Grammar, § lv. 6); but containing a further definition of the Theocratic Birth in its antithesis to purely physical generation which proceeds from the factor of the will as determined on the one side by the animal nature, and on the other side by the personality of man (Tholuck, Luthardt, Godet, Meyer, Westcott). " In

this passage οὐκ ἐξ αἱμάτων denies the material basis : οὐδὲ ἐκ θελήματος σαρκός the causality of the fleshly, therefore unspiritual unsanctified will ; οὐδε ἐκ θελήματος ἀνδρός the causality of man's and therefore of created will"(Delitzsch, Bib. Psych, § xi.). but of God. The words ἐκ θεοῦ contain the antithesis to each of the preceding clauses. The spiritual birth has its primal source and originating cause in God. *Naturali hominum generationi opponitur generatio ex Deo* (Bengel).

HOMILETICS

VER. 6-13.—THE COMING OF THE LIGHT.
I. **The Witness of the Light**, ver. 7. 1. *His Appearance.* "There came" or arose ; suggesting ideas of origination, commencement, dependence, mutability, and decay, in opposition to the Word whose creature he was (ver. 3), whose existence began not but always was (ver. 1), whose power was the Source of all things (ver. 3), and whose underived life was the light of men (ver. 4). 2. *His Nature*—"A Man." Parted as a creature by an infinite gulf from the Word, who was God (ver. 1), he was yet, in virtue of "the image and glory of God" (1 Cor. xi. 7) which adorned him, but a short remove from divinity (Ps. viii. 5), besides being "crowned with glory and honour" through the near relationship in which he stood to the Word as His Instrument and Minister, His Herald and Forerunner. 3. *His Name*—"John" or "Jehovah is gracious" ; a fitting designation of one whose birth was a gift of grace (Luke i. 13), whose manhood was the flower and fruit of grace (Luke i. 80), and whose life-work was to be a publisher of grace (Luke i. 76). 4. *His Mission*—which was (1) in its character prophetic, he being "sent from God" as the last of the O. T. prophets, again in contrast to the Word who was eternally in the bosom of the Father (i. 18), and who, while He was "sent" by (ver. 36, 57 ; viii. 42), also came out from, the Father (xvi. 28) ; (2) in its authority divine, he being an ambassador despatched upon the business of Jehovah ; (3) in its work or occupation witness-bearing, he having been appointed to announce the coming, declare the rising, and indicate the shining of the True Light ; and (4) in its object saving, that all men, whether Jew or Gentile, belonging to the then present or to future ages, might through him be led to faith in Christ, and as a consequence to the attainment of Eternal Life. 5. *His Relation to the Light*, which is described (1) negatively : "He was not the Light," and (2) positively : "He came that he might bear witness of the Light."
II. **The Arrival of the Light**, ver. 9. 1. *Its Nature;* "The True Light," not the genuine as opposed to the false, but the substantial, the essential, the original, the permanent as distinguished from the shadowy, the phenomenal, the derived, the transitory. (See Exposition.) 2. *Its Influence;* set forth (1) intensively, as light-giving—"it lighteth," and (2) extensively, as reaching to every man, i.e. to all mankind in the sense that its light exists for all, and to some degree shines on all, and to all souls that inwardly admit its light-giving beams. 3. *Its Condition;* described as (1) "coming into the world," i.e. in process of passing from a Divine and Eternal into a human and temporal mode of existence, and (2) coming into His own, i.e. as unfolding His Glory before the Theocratic People.
III. **The Rejection of the Light**. 1. *Generally and prior to His Incarnation, by the World:* "The world knew Him not" (ver. 10) ; which was (1) inexcusable, since He had been in the world for centuries shining even in the darkness, so that the world's inhabitants ought to have recognized Him (Rom. i. 20),

(2) unnatural, since "the world had been made by Him," and the dependent creature, in particular, the organized community of mankind, living, moving, and having its being in Him ought to have discerned and understood its Creator (Ps. ciii. 22); (3) heinous, since the non-recognition of which complaint is made was less intellectual than moral (Rom. i. 21), arising not from failure to discern, but from the absence of inward affinity to the light (John iii. 19; Eph. iv. 18; Job xxiv. 13); and (4) prophetic, since it ominously foreshadowed Christ's reception when as the Incarnate Word He should present Himself before Israel, with an outlook towards which it is here introduced. 2. *Particularly and during the period of His Incarnation, by His Own*, i.e. by the Jews, whose rejection of Him, besides sharing the criminality incurred by the world, displayed (1) monstrous ingratitude, the Jewish People having for no peculiar excellence or merit of its own been selected by the Word as His special treasure and possession, and been subjected to centuries of gracious teaching and discipline to enable them to recognize and embrace Him when He became Incarnate (Isa. i. 2); (2) shamefaced robbery, Christ having presented Himself before the Israelitish Hierarchy in the character of an Heir claiming his inheritance (Matt. xxi. 38), and of a Master returning to His house (Matt. xxv. 14) only to find His possessions forcibly withheld from Him, and Himself rudely debarred from His own dwelling, yea even violently cast forth and killed; (3) Incorrigible wickedness, since whatever may have been the ignorance of the unthinking populace, and whatever apology Paul may have afterwards felt disposed to offer for the conduct of the Rulers of this World (1 Cor. ii. 8), the Ecclesiastical Authorities in Jerusalem were more or less aware that the prophetic signs of Messiahship had met in Christ; and (4) dire infatuation, inasmuch as through rejecting Him they not only thrust from themselves the kingdom of God, but missed the vocation they might otherwise have enjoyed of occupying the position, afterwards conferred upon the Apostles, of being the foundation-stones of the New Temple of the Christian Church.

IV. **The Reception of the Light**, ver. 12, 13. 1. *The Parties who received the Light*—the Divinely Born or spiritually regenerated. The truth here formulated that faith in Christ or a believing reception of the truth presupposes an inward soul-renewal by God (or the Holy Spirit), corresponds with the teaching of Christ (vi. 44, 45; viii. 47; x. 26), of Paul (1 Cor. ii. 14), and of the Johannine Epistles (1 John i. 20; v. 20). 2. *The Mode in which the Light was received*—by believing on Christ's name, by accepting and trusting in the revealed character of God in Christ. This also harmonizes with Scripture teaching generally, that Salvation, or the Eternal Life in Christ, can only pass into the human spirit by the gateway of faith. 3. *The blessing which the Light conferred*—Power to become children of God, implying (1) the standing (Eph. ii. 19; Gal. iii. 26), (2) the character (Rom. viii. 14; Phil. ii. 15; 1 John iii. 10), and (3) the privileges (Heb. xii. 6, 7; Gal. iv. 6, 7) of a son in God's family.

Lessons.—1. The Mercy of God; (1) in causing the Light to shine at all in a dark world, (2) in sending it into the world in the form of an Incarnation, (3) in taking steps that men should be able to recognize it, (4) in arranging that, though the world in general might reject it, it should still be accepted by some, and (5) in conferring on these the privilege and power, rank and character, of sons of God. 2. The Depravity of Man, attested by the following facts: (1) That the world did not recognize the light of the Pre-incarnate Word, (2) that all God's efforts failed to make the Jews see the Light of the Incarnate Word, and (3) that those who did eventually recognize the latter required previously to have the eyes of their understandings opened. 3. The Mystery of Regeneration, concerning which it is declared (1) in what Regeneration consists, viz., in such a change of heart and disposition as enables one previously blind to apprehend and embrace the light, (2) by what it is produced, viz., not by human birth, natural development, or educational influence, but by Divine Power, (3) how it operates, viz., by leading men to believe in the name of Christ, and (4) to what it conducts, viz., to moral and spiritual sonship in God's redeemed family.

SECTION III.—THE INCARNATE SON

CHAP. I. VER. 14-18

EXPOSITION

Ver. 14. **And** καὶ, not equivalent to *for* (Augustine, Chrysostom, Grotius, Lampe, Godet), or *therefore* (Bleek), but simply carrying forward the discourse, doubtless with a latent emphasis indicating the writer's thought to be on the eve of culmination (cf. Heb. iii. 19; Winer's Grammar, § liii. 3); hence connecting not with ver. 4 (Maldonatus), ver. 9 (De Wette), ver. 11 (Lücke, Lange), or ver. 13 (Meyer), but with ver. 1 (Westcott, Milligan, and Moulton). **the Word.** See on ver. 1. **became** not was transformed into or made (A. V.), *factum est* (Vulgate), or took into union with himself (Calvin), but began to be—ἐγένετο in contrast to ἦν (ver. 1)—yet "in such a manner that He still continued to be what He was" (Calvin); i.e. He who from Eternity had existed in a Divine condition began to appear in a finite and human condition, but whether at the cost of renouncing (Godet, Luthardt), as Paul seems to imply (Phil. ii. 7), or still retaining (Calvin, Reuss, Meyer, and others) His divine form of existence, cannot be determined from the verb, which, while it signifies to become what one was not before (ii. 9; ix. 39), does not necessarily imply that one has ceased to be what he formerly was (v. 14; 1 Cor. xv. 20). **flesh** σάρξ; not σῶμα, which might have existed without σάρξ (1 Cor. xv. 40, 44), and would not have included the ψυχή, but σάρξ, meaning not the appearance only, the *simulacrum*, of a human body (Docetae), or a veritable human body without the soul or spirit, the place of this being filled by the Word or Logos (Apollinaris), or simply the visibility or corporeality of Jesus as opposed to Docetism (De Wette, Reuss), or human nature in its weakness and poverty (Olshausen, Tholuck, Hengstenberg), but human nature in its totality, as consisting of a true body and a reasonable soul (Godet, Luthardt, Meyer, Westcott, Alford, and others). "The word σάρξ describes the whole man, as he consists of body and soul, as

a sensuous, earthly being, in antithesis to God, the Spiritual and Eternal and Heavenly"; in this sense "the Logos who was with God has appeared in the Flesh" (Frommann, Der Johanneische Lehrbegriff, pp. 312, 313). That this is the signification attached by John to the word the following passages will show (iii. 6; vi. 51; xvii. 2; I. iv. 2, 3; II. 7); that Paul employed it in the same sense may be inferred from his epistles (Rom. i. 3; iii. 20; vii. 18; 1 Cor. i. 26; x. 18; Gal. ii. 16; v. 17; Eph. ii. 3, etc.). "The Flesh is nothing else than the sensuous, animal nature of man, to which, on the ground of nature, must be reckoned not the mere corporeality, but also the physical life principle, and the manifold susceptibilities, impulses, desires, arising out of it" (Julius Muller, on the Doctrine of Sin, vol. i. 435; cf. Cremer, Lexicon of the New Testament, pp. 517, 521). That the phrase "to become flesh" is not synonymous with ἄνθρωπος ἐγένετο (Luthardt, Meyer) is apparent, since in that case the Incarnate Word would have been described as "a determinate human personality," whereas what the Word took into union with Himself was humanity in its widest conception, the Humanity of the Race. **and dwelt** lit., *tabernacled*, ἐσκήνωσεν, *habitavit* (Vulgate), יִשְׁכֹּן (Heb.); with allusion to the transitory character of Christ's residence on earth (Calvin, Tholuck, Godet), the pilgrim condition of His life (Maldonatus), or, more probably, the Tabernacle in the Wilderness (Ex. xxv. 8; xxix. 45; Lev. xxvi. 11), or the Temple in Jerusalem (1 Kings vi. 13; Isa. viii. 18; Ezek. xliii. 7, 9; Joel iii. 21), in which the glorious presence of Jehovah resided—as if to indicate that all the O. T. promises of God's dwelling with His people had at last obtained fulfilment in the Incarnation of the Word, who abode in human nature as in a tent (cf. Rev. vii. 15), and whose Glory shone through the veil of His flesh as the sublime

antitype of the material splendour—
called the Shechinah by the Targumists (Weber, System der Altsynagogalen Palästinischen Theologie, § 39),
which burned between the cherubim
(Bengel, Tholuck, Olshausen, Meyer,
and others), though it is not necessary
to hold that the Evangelist was
actually thinking of this Shechinah
(Reuss, Lücke, B. Crusius, De Wette).
among us Not the Christian consciousness (Hilgenfeld, Keim, or the
Twelve as such (Tholuck), but first
the immediate circle of Christ's disciples
who like John were eye-witnesses of
His glory (Calvin, Lampe, Luthardt,
Godet, Westcott), then the "as many
as received Him" of ver. 12 (Meyer,
Lücke), and finally mankind as a whole
(Bengel, Lange, Alford). **and** Usually
regarded as parenthetical (Bengel,
Lampe, Lücke, De Wette, Godet); the
clause introduced by this conjunction
is better taken as an integral part of
the verse (Tholuck, Brückner, Meyer,
and others; Winer's Grammar, § 62, 1).
we amongst whom He dwelt; in particular the apostles, Peter, James and
John (Bengel): cf. Luke ix. 32 ; Matt.
xvii. 1-9 ; 2 Pet. i. 16-18. **beheld by**
spiritual contemplation (Baur, Keim)
certainly, but also by actual personal
observation (1 John i. 1-3); the inward vision being based upon, and
rising out of, the outward bodily
sight. **His glory** δόξα, from δοκεῖν,
in the sense of φαίνεσθαι, signifies
"the external form in any way per-
ceivable, in which the life and nature
of a personal or real subject comes to
its actual manifestation, represents
itself by itself" (Delitzsch, Bib. Psych.
part i. § iii. note 3). As distinguished
from כָּבוֹד of which it is the translation
(LXX.), and which points rather to the
impression produced by the majesty of
God, it describes the ineffable splendour
or beauty of the Divine Nature. Applied to the Deity in general it denotes
"the glorious appearance of the absolutely holy nature of God" (Ex. xxxiii.
18 ; Deut. v. 24 ; Ps. xxix. 9 ; Isa. xlviii.
11); from which it passes over to the
light inaccessible in which God eternally dwells (1 Tim. i. 16), and the
luminous cloud by which He made
known His presence to Israel (Exod.
xvi. 10 ; xxiv. 16 ; xl. 34, 35 ; Num.
xx. 6, etc.). Used of the Pre-incarnate

Word the term designates the god-like
effulgence of His divinity (xii. 41; xvii. 5),
being equivalent to the μορφὴ θεοῦ of Paul
(Phil. ii. 6), and the δόξα ὡς μονογενοῦς of
the succeeding clause. Ascribed to the
Incarnate Word it imports the outward
radiation of this essential majesty,
perfection, or glory through the veil of
His humanity (ii. 11 ; Luke ix. 32);
which, as it implies a reduction, so to
speak, of that ineffable glory upon
which mortal vision cannot look (i. 18 ;
cf. Exod. xxxiii. 20 ; 1 Tim. i. 16) to
the dimensions of a human personality,
may be held to accord with the κενώσις
(Phil. ii. 7), or laying aside of the absolute form of divinity in which He
originally was. **Glory as of the** (or an)
only begotten from the (a) Father. 1.
The conjunction "as," ὡς, is not *declara-
tive* (Bengel, Lampe, Kuinoel, Calvin),
equivalent to ὄντως καὶ ἀληθῶς (Chrysostom) or כְּ veritatis in Hebrew (Olshausen), a use of ὡς, which is imaginary,
the examples usually quoted (Rom. ix,
32 ; 1 Cor. iv. 1 ; 2 Cor. ii. 17 ; Phil. ii.
12 ; Philem. 9 ; 1 Pet. i. 19 ; 2 Pet. i.
3) requiring no such device for their
interpretation ; but *comparative* like
quippe (Meyer), setting forth the correspondence of the reality with the idea
(Lücke, Godet, Lange, Westcott, and
others: cf. Winer's Grammar, § lxv. 9),
and thus practically harmonizing with
Chrysostom's definition: δόξαν οἵαν ἔπρεπε
καὶ εἰκὸς ἔχειν μονογενῆ καὶ γνήσιον υἱὸν ἔντα
τῶν πάντων βασιλέως θεοῦ, a glory such as
it was becoming and reasonable that an
only begotten and true Son of God the
King of all should have. 2. The term
μονογενής, only-begotten (Luke vii. 12 ;
viii. 42 ; ix. 38) applied to Christ (i. 18;
iii. 16, 18; 1 John iv. 9) is without the
article not because there is no other only
begotten of the Father, but to emphasize
the uniqueness of Christ's relationship
to the Father who has other children
or sons indeed, but none in the way
that He is (Luthardt, Brückner). "The
thought centres in the abstract relation
of Father and Son, though in the actual
connexion this abstract relation passes
necessarily into the relation of the Son
to the Father" (Westcott). The designation of Christ as "only born" refers
not to His human birth (Hofmann), or
to the "wholly unique and incomparable descent of the Man Jesus from
God," corresponding to the Johannine

phrases 'from above,' 'from heaven,' 'from God' (Beyschlag), but to His eternal generation (Luther, Calvin, Bengel, Godet, Meyer, Tholuck, Gess, and others), rather than to the historical relation of communion with God in which Christ lived when on earth (Luthardt), which falls below the elevation of thought contained in the δόξα μονογενοῦς. Though the Synoptists employ not this appellation, they also ascribe aloneness to Christ's Sonship (Matt. iii. 17 ; xvii. 5 ; xxvii. 43). Cf. Paul's expression πρωτότοκος (Col. i. 15). 3. The phrase "from the Father," παρὰ πατρὸς, has been connected with δόξα as in v. 44 (Theophylact, Grotius, Hofmann), but should be conjoined with μονογενοῦς, not however as expressive of the *generatio aeterna*, already implied in the latter, for which the preposition ἐκ (viii. 42, 47) or perhaps the simple genitive or dative might have been employed (Winer's Grammar, § 47), but as intimating that the Only-begotten had come forth from the Father's vicinity : cf. i. 6 (Beza, Lampe, Bengel, Kuinoel, Meyer, Godet, and others). **full** πλήρης ; not to be construed with Ἰωάννης, John, as the editorial "we" (Erasmus), or with δόξαν, "glory," reading πλήρη as in Cod. D (Olshausen), or with "only-begotten," μονογενοῦς. taking πλήρης by enallage for πληροῦς (Grotius, Tittmann, Tholuck), but either with λόγος, The Word, if the clause from καὶ to πατρός be parenthetically regarded (Calvin, Bengel, Lampe, Kuinoel, Godet, Lücke, Westcott, and others), or, if the clauses be read continuously, with αὐτοῦ, πλήρης being put in the nominative absolute as in Luke xx. 27 ; Eph. iii. 17 ; Rev. i. 5 (Alford, Luthardt, Meyer, Hengstenberg ; Winer's Grammar, § 29) **of grace and truth.** The two nouns, which are not to be explained as a hendiadys for χάριτος ἀληθινῆς, true grace (Cyril of Alexandria, Kuinoel), depict the two essential elements in the Divine Manifestation, which were χάρις, Grace, or Love towards the undeserving, corresponding to the nature of the Word as 'Life,' and ἀλήθεια, Truth, or the Revealed Thought of God, which harmonizes with the nature of the Word as 'Light.'

15. John i.e. the Baptist (ver. 6) **beareth witness.** The present tense is used for solemnity ; as if the fore-runner's testimony were still sounding when the Evangelist wrote, which in a sense it was, as in the same sense it still is, having from the first been designed as a witness for all succeeding ages. **of Him,** viz., The Incarnate Word. **and crieth** lit., *cried*, or *hath cried* (A. V.), the perfect being employed as a present (Bengel, Alford, Meyer, Tholuck, and others ; cf. Buttmann's Larger Greek Grammar, p. 240, 3rd ed. ; Winer's Grammar, § 40), or, perhaps more correctly, the perfect pointing backwards to what constituted the Baptist's continually sounding witness, viz., the voice uttered when he cried. *Clamat Johannes cum fiducia et gaudio, uti magnum praeconem decet* (Bengel). **saying** λέγων, omitted in ℵ* D. The summarized testimony which follows is manifestly that delivered by the Baptist after Christ's return to Jordan subsequent to the Temptation (ver. 30), in which he alludes to an earlier occasion, viz., before Christ's baptism when he gave utterance to the remarkable language here recorded ; cf. Matt. iii. 11 ; Mark i. 7 ; Luke iii. 16. **This was he.** The presence of ἦν, was, instead of ἐστὶ, is (ver. 30), is not sufficiently accounted for by saying that the Baptist referred to his testimony as something already past (Lücke, Meyer), having been delivered before the Baptism (Lange, Westcott), or desired to emphasize the testimony previously given, as thus—"This whom ye saw was he of whom I spake" (Luthardt), or "This was the person I meant" (Tholuck, Godet, Brückner), but must be explained either as a corruption of the text, or as an instance of *oratio obliqua*. **He that cometh after me is become before me : for he was before me** lit., *he coming after me* not so much in age (Augustine) as in official manifestation (Calvin), *has become before me*, not was before me in time, i.e. in respect of his pre-incarnate manifestation (Godet, Lange), or in His Divine and Eternal condition (Origen, Luther), or as having come forth from God prior to all time (Meyer), or as having preceded the Forerunner in the sense of having sent him (Hengstenberg), but has become before me in honour or official dignity (Chrysostom, Calvin, Bengel, Lampe), *for he was my first,* i.e. existed absolutely before me (Luther, Clericus, Bengel, Lücke, Godet, Meyer, Westcott), not was superior to me in rank (Chrysostom, Calvin, Beza, Hofmann, Luthardt). 16. For ὅτι, as in ℵ BC* D LX, etc. (Griesbach, Tischendorf, Westcott, Meyer), instead of καὶ as in A E F G H T Δ Λ II and some ancient versions (Bengel, Lampe, Hengstenberg, Godet); introducing the language not of the Baptist (Origen, Augustine, Erasmus, Luther, Calvin, Lange), but as the phrase " all we " shows of the Evangelist (Bengel, Lampe, etc.); connecting with ver. 14 ; confirming the Baptist's testimony, parenthetically interposed because of its precedence both in time and thought ; and supplying proof for the sublime mystery of the Incarnation already announced. of ἐκ, out of as a source or fountain. His fulness i.e. the fulness of which He was full, viz., grace and truth (ver. 14); πλήρωμα being here employed passively (Col. i. 19 ; ii. 9) rather than actively (Eph. i. 23 ; iii. 19 ; iv. 13), and quite unconnected with Valentinian Gnosticism (Schwegler, Hilgenfeld), the occasion of its introduction lying in the preceding πλήρης (ver. 14). we Not O. T. saints (Lange) as if the Baptist were the speaker, but Christian believers all without exception : *non omnes viderunt,* (*sed*) *omnes acceperunt* (Bengel). received Not ' have received ' (A. V.), but simply 'received,' the verb standing absolutely, without reference to time ; the relation of believers to Christ is one of receiving. and Epexegetic of the proceeding (Winer, § 53, 3), explaining and laying special stress on what was received, rather than defining the mode of its reception (Godet). grace for grace χάριν ἀντὶ χάριτος, i.e. *the grace neither* of the N. instead of that of the O. Test. (Chrysostom, Theophylact, Erasmus), nor of life Eternal for that of faith (Augustine), nor of God's favour toward us on account of His favour towards His Son (Camerarius), nor of restoration for the grace lost in paradise (Starke, Calovius), but one new grace coming in the room of that which has gone before (Bengel, Kuinoel, Hengstenberg, Meyer, Luthardt, and others), not however as its legal reward (Godet),

or spiritual recompense (Westcott, Milligan and Moulton) ; merely as its constant successor, the idea being that of grace uninterruptedly and unceasingly renewed (cf. Winer, § 47, 5, a). It is not probable that the writer's thought refers to the Charisms of the early Church, 1 Cor. xii...xiv (Ewald). 17. For ὅτι, introducing not a parallel (Westcott) but a subordinate clause to ver. 16, and adducing the reason for the foregoing statement. the Law ὁ νόμος, neither the decalogue alone (Kuenen, Robertson Smith), nor the ceremonial institute, by itself, but both together as forming one whole (i. 45 ; vii. 19 ; viii. 17 ; x. 34 ; xii. 34), which is here contrasted with Christianity (cf. Rom. iv. 15 ; x. 4 ; Gal. iii. 10). was given ἐδόθη, was sent forth as something external (Godet), as a lifeless statute (Lange), as something definite and circumscribed (Alford), with boundaries not stretching out into the infinite (Milligan and Moulton), and for a special purpose (Westcott). by Moses i.e. through his instrumentality, so that the Law was something distinct from the human Lawgiver ; which was not the case with Christ. *Mosis non sua est lex, Christi sua est gratia et veritas* (Bengel). grace and truth As opposed to Mosaism which was law, *iram parans* (Bengel), Christianity was grace or free favour ; as distinguished from that which possessed the Gospel in type and symbol, *umbram habens* (Bengel), it was Truth. came historically appeared (i. 14), in contrast to 'was given'; by As above, through the instrumentality of Jesus Christ Ἰησοῦς Χριστὸς (xvii. 3 ; cf. Matt. i. 1 ; Mark i. 1 ; Rom. i. 1 ; 1 John i. 3 ; ii. 1 ; iv. 2). The historical designation of the Word Made Flesh now for the first time announced, synonymous with Joshua (" Jehovah is Salvation," Num. xi. 28) Messiah (" Anointed," Dan. ix. 25), and pointing out the man whose name it was—the reputed son of Joseph and Mary of Nazareth (Luke ii. 4, 5 ; Matt. i. 25)— as " the complete concrete embodiment of the manifestation of the Logos," who in the writings of this Evangelist is never so named after the mention of the Incarnation : cf. 1 John i. 1-3. 18. No man hath seen God at any time lit., *God no man hath seen ever yet,* or at any time up to this time ; the emphatic position assigned to 'God' showing the thought to be that the coming of Grace and Truth to men through Jesus Christ presupposed such a knowledge—not bodily vision, but direct spiritual intuition—of God as no mere man, not even Moses, enjoyed ; since, though inspired persons might hear God, and even behold Him in visions, Theophanies, and such like (Gen. xxxii. 30 ; xvi. 13 ; Exod. xxxiii. 9 ; xxxiv. 6, 28 ; xxiv. 10 ; Judg. xiii. 22 ; Isa. vi. 1-5), to see Him in the sense of knowing and understanding His essential name and nature clearly transcended finite faculties (Ex. xxxiii. 20 ; Job xxxvi. 26 ; xxxvii. 23 ; 1 Cor. ii. 11 ; xiii. 12 ; 1 Tim. vi. 16 ; 1 John iv. 12). Hence the verse connects not with ver. 16 as a parallel exposition of the ἀλήθεια, or 'Truth,' contained in the 'Fulness' of the Incarnate Logos (B. Crusius, Godet, Hengstenberg), but with ver. 17 as the reason why Grace and Truth came by Jesus Christ (Luthardt, Meyer), and is to be regarded as the language, not of the Baptist (Lange), but of the Evangelist, who in using πώποτε, ever yet, appears to anticipate the open vision reserved for believers : cf. 1 John iii. 2 ; Matt. v. 8 (Westcott). **The only begotten Son** ὁ μονογενὴς υἱός (A X, secondary uncials, all cursives except 33, the Lt. vt., Syr. Hcl. and Hier., Vulg. Arm. ; T. R., Lücke, Alford, Meyer, Godet, Luthardt, Tholuck, Brückner) ; μονογενὴς θεός, only begotten God (א B C* L, Peshito, Syr., Basil, Clement, Origen, Tischendorf, Lachmann, Tregelles, Westcott and Hort). 1. In favour of the latter are urged (1) that it is best attested by ancient authority, (2) that it harmonizes better with the structure of the prologue, gathering up as it were in a final clause the two ideas of sonship and deity which have already been predicated of the Word, (3) that the expression "Son" is more likely to have been substituted for "God" than *vice versa*, being in fact suggested by the term "Father," which occurs in the verse, and (4) that it more satisfactorily accounts for the absence of the article in the phrase μονογενὴς θεός to suppose it stood so originally than to regard θεός as having been by a later hand

substituted for υἱός. 2. Yet considerations as strong and numerous support the Received Reading, as that μονογενὴς θεός (1) betrays the touch of later dogmatics, (2) introduces a new and harsh term into Scripture, (3) is less likely to have been written by the Evangelist than ὁ μονογενὴς υἱός, which corresponds more appropriately to ὁ ὢν εἰς τὸν κόλπον τοῦ πατρὸς, and (4) harmonizes more exactly with the aim of the Prologue, which is to introduce the leading *momenta* of the subsequent discourse amongst which the Sonship of Christ occupies a prominent position. 3. The evenly balanced arguments on either side render it impossible to decide dogmatically which reading stood in the original text ; and to do so there is the less need since the two readings are substantially of equal import, The Only Begotten God implying the Eternal Sonship of Christ, and the Sonship as necessarily involving the Supreme Divinity of the Word. **which is** ὁ ὤν, omitted in א, not referring to Christ's present state of Exaltation (Hofmann, Meyer, Luthardt), or to His condition while on earth (Beyschlag), or to His prehuman state, as if the participle were equivalent to an imperfect (Bengel), but taken as a timeless present (cf. iii. 13), indicating the absolute, permanent, and indestructible relation between the Father and the Son (De Wette, Brückner, Lücke, Tholuck, and others : see Winer's Gram. § 45, 1). **in the bosom of the Father** lit., *into*, εἰς, never interchangeable with ἐν (Grotius, Bengel, Olshausen, Hengstenberg : cf. Glass. Phil. Tract. p. 484) ; pointing out the *terminum ad quem*, not of Christ's ascension (Hofmann, Meyer, Luthardt), but of the Eternal 'with God' alluded to in ver. 1 ; depicting the Son's complete fellowship in love with the Father, the image being borrowed from that of a guest reclining at table by the side of his friend, as in xiii. 23 (Lange), or more probably of a Son resting on his father's bosom, as in Luke xvi. 22 (Lücke, Brückner, Meyer, Godet, Westcott, and others : cf. Winer, § l. 4) ; and thus representing the infinite love of the Father as the home and rest into which the Son eternally returns, as assuredly it was the unbeginning source whence He proceeded (Milligan and Moulton). **he** ἐκεῖνος, that one, strongly emphatic; yet not as pointing heavenward (Meyer), but as alluding to the ineffable majesty of the Son (Bengel, Lange), and certainly as excluding every other, he and he alone (Godet). **hath declared** him lit., *declared*, i.e. once for all, *et verbis suis et conspectu sui* (Bengel). The verb ἐξηγήσατο (whence the Athenian ἐξηγήται and the modern *exegete*), *enarravit* (Vulgate), occurs only here, being employed, not after classical writers (Plato, Pol. iv. p. 427; Xen. Cyr. viii. 3, 11; Soph. El. 417), as a technical expression for the interpretation of Divine Matters (Meyer, Lange, Luthardt), but in its ordinary acceptation (Lücke, Godet, Alford), to set forth the thought that Christ alone is the authoritative and complete Expositor of the Father's mind. The object of the verb may be either the Grace and Truth seen by the former in God (Kuinoel, Lücke, Olshausen), the substance of His intuition in God (Meyer), or the truth concerning God as a Father (Westcott), perhaps more simply God (Godet, Alford); though the verb might be taken absolutely as setting forth Christ in the character of the Divine Interpreter.

HOMILETICS

VER. 14-18.—THE INCARNATION OF THE SON.

I. **A Transcendent Mystery**—"And the Word was made, or became flesh" (ver. 14). 1. *The Meaning.* Neither (1) that the Word was changed into flesh, or became human so that He ceased to be divine, which was impossible; nor (2) assumed merely a corporeal existence, a body as distinguished from a soul (Apollinarianism); nor (3) because *a* man, since in that case Christ, though the greatest and best of men, would have been only an individual member of the race, incapable of representing any outside of Himself, far less humanity as a whole; nor (4) simply adopted human nature into formal alliance with His divinity, so that one part of His being remained distinctively and essentially divine, while the other part continued intrinsically and exclusively human (Nestorianism), the connection between the two being effected by a mysterious and wholly inexplicable *communicatio idiomatum;* but (5) that the Word, who was in the beginning with God and was God (ver. 1), became man in such a way that, from having previously existed in a Divine Form, He began to be or to manifest Himself in a human form (Phil. ii. 6). 2. *The Mystery.* (1) The phenomenon it announces is such as the human mind could not have conceived without a revelation. The Greeks never soared beyond the notion of an apotheosis of human heroes (Homer, Iliad xx. 232), or of a descent of Olympian divinities to Earth (Acts xiv. 11); the Jews were so little prepared for an Incarnation that they put Christ to death because He made Himself equal with God (v. 18; x. 36; xix. 7). (2) Even when discovered by revelation, the phenomenon so transcends mortal faculties by reason of its sublimity, that in every age the mind of man has found itself baffled to propose any satisfactory theory on the subject. The number of suggestions that have been advanced, Ebionism, Docetism, Apollinarianism, Nestorianism, Eutychianism, The Chalcedonian Formula, The Lutheran and Reformed Christologies, with the Modern Kenotic Theories, is proof sufficient that "such knowledge is too wonderful for us," that "it is high, and we cannot attain unto it" (Ps. cxxxix. 6).

II. **An Unchallengeable Certainty**, ver. 14-16. Resting on 1. *Apostolic Witness.* "We," Apostles, and in particular Peter, James, and John, "have seen His glory," and avow it to have been "Glory as of an only-begotten from a Father, full of grace and truth" (cf. Matt. xviii. 1-8; Mark ix. 2-8; Luke ix. 28-36; 2 Pet. i. 16-18). Of such an eye-witness the present Gospel is the work, and contains the deposition. 2. *Prophetic Testimony.* "John beareth witness of Him"; began to do so when He cried to the multitudes in the Wilderness before Christ's baptism (Matt. iii. 11); a second time did so after that event (ver. 30); continues doing so through the preservation and diffusion of his testimony in the Written Gospel. The Baptist gathered up and expressed in a great representative utterance all the voices of the preceding prophets who testified of Christ (1 Pet. i. 11 ; Rev. xix. 10). 3. *Christian Experience,* ver. 16, the argument contained in which stands thus—(1) We Christians have received what we did not possess before, inexhaustible supplies of grace ; but (2) no mere man could have authoritatively imparted or even declared such grace to us, since all that Moses, the greatest of men, could communicate was not Grace, but Law; hence (3) Christ from whom we have derived that Grace must be more than man, can be no other than the Only-Begotten Son of God.

III. **A Blessed Evangel,** ver. 18, concerning 1. *The Character of God,* whom it declares to be not an abstraction but a Person, not a Supreme Intelligence merely but an Infinite Heart as well, not a Divinity enthroned in the serene altitudes of His own measureless perfections, but a Father taking an interest in the affairs, and even providing help for the necessities, of His children, yea, coming near to them in gracious condescension, and in the person of His own Son who became flesh, that men might be able to look upon Him, and that He might be able to say to them, "He that hath seen Me hath seen the Father"(xiv. 9). 2. *The Destiny of Man,* by establishing the inherent dignity of human nature since it was capable of being taken into union with divinity, by revealing its lofty possibilities when so allied, and so discovering that Man must have a future before Him that is not bounded by the contracted horizon of time. The first prediction of Man's essential nobility and ultimate immortality was his creation in God's Image (Gen. i. 27) ; the second was The Word's Incarnation in his Image (Heb. ii. 14). 3. *The Substance of the Gospel,* which it announces to be Grace and Truth, two things without which neither could the Nature of God be revealed nor the destiny of Man attained.

Lessons. 1. Do we believe in the sublime mystery of the Incarnation ? Our answer to this discloses the inner quality of our souls (1 John iv. 2, 3). 2. Have we accepted the cheering Gospel it brings? This also is a heart-searching, character-revealing, and destiny-fixing inquiry (iii. 33, 36 ; 1 John v. 10). 3. Can we confirm from personal experience the constantly accumulating testimony in behalf of the Incarnation ? If so, our faith will be invincible, if not unassailable, by modern doubt.

Ver. 16. The Fulness of Christ. 1. A Divine, 2. a Delegated, 3. a Gracious, 4. a Communicable, 5. an Inexhaustible Fulness.

Ver. 17. Moses and Christ. I. A Comparison. 1. Both men. 2. Both Messengers from God. 3. Both bearers of a Revelation. II. A Contrast. 1. Moses, only a man ; Christ, The Son of God. 2. Moses raised up by God ; Christ sent forth from God. 3. Moses, the bearer of a Revelation outside of himself ; Christ the Bringer of a Revelation in Himself. 4. Moses, a Law-Giver ; Christ a Grace and Truth declarer.

THE HISTORY

CHAP. I. 19—XX. 31

IN the preceding prologue the Author has briefly introduced the exalted personage who is to form the subject of his contemplated history, viz., the Incarnate Word or Son of God, and with some degree of clearness indicated the specific purpose aimed at in its composition. That purpose is twofold. I. To show (1) how, after shining for centuries in the midst of earth's darkness, unrecognized and unaccepted by those before whom His Glory was displayed, the Pre-existent Eternal and Divine Word, having become incarnate, unfolded the effulgent radiance of that same glory before the Covenant-People, the Jews, whom He regarded as "His own"; (2) how the reception accorded to the Glory of the Incarnate Word at the hands of the Theocratic Nation was nothing different from, but the same as, that which had been given to the Glory of the Pre-incarnate Word, inasmuch as, though He came unto His own, His own received Him not; and (3) how, nevertheless, alongside of this national blindness and obduracy, there were not a few, designated The Divinely Born, by whom as individuals His Glory was both apprehended and believed in; and II. To demonstrate how, by a further exhibition of the Glory of His Godhead in stooping to a cross, "becoming obedient unto death" on their behalf, He gave to such as had believed upon His Name and thereby had become "His own" in a sense never true of Israel after the Flesh, power to become Sons of God, i.e. everything needful to constitute them, not in name simply, but in reality members of God's spiritual family. Accordingly the ensuing narrative divides itself into two main portions—The History of Christ's Life" (i. 19—xii. 50), at the head of which, as at once a summary of its contents and an explanation of its purpose, may appropriately be placed the Superscription:— " He came unto His own and His own received Him not" (ver. 11); and— The History of Christ's Passion (xiii. 1—xx. 31), above which may also stand inscribed as its befitting title—" But as many as received Him, to them gave He the right (power) to become sons of God, even to them that believe on His name" (ver. 12). Neither of these divisions is complete in the sense of reciting all that might have been recorded under each concerning the Life or Death of Him who is its theme; both will be found sufficient for the purposes aimed at in their construction.

Part I.—The History of Christ's Life
(i. 19—xii. 50)

Subject:—The Glory of the Incarnate Word or Son unveiled before His own People (the Jewish Nation)—" He came unto His own and His own received Him not" (i. 11).

The specific object of the Evangelist in this division of His work having been as above explained, it was manifestly not required that he should narrate every incident that formed an integral part of Christ's mundane history, but simply that, out of the materials lying ready to his hand in the Memoirs of the Synoptists or in the Repositories of his own Recollection, he should select such scenes and events as appeared to him best adapted for the purpose he had in view. Accordingly, first establishing in a brief series of preliminary paragraphs, three in number, that the Glory of the Incarnate Word was actually shining in such a way that it could be apprehended by willing and ingenuous souls, he advances to the chief theme of his discourse which he executes by furnishing narrations of five successive presentations of Himself which Christ made before the Jewish Nation; in each case carefully bringing out the three points above alluded to—The Shining of the Glory of the Incarnate Son; the Rejection of that Glory, and of the Son whose glory it was, by the Jewish People; the Acceptance of that Glory, and of that Son, by the divinely-born, the second "Own" who should dispossess Israel at once of her inheritance and her mission. The appended table will afford a bird's-eye view of this portion of the Evangelist's work.

I. The Dawning of the Glory of the Incarnate Word or Son: i. 19—ii. 11.
1. Perceived and attested by John the Baptist: i. 19-36.
2. Discovered and acknowledged by John's disciples: i. 37-51.
3. Discerned and accepted by the disciples of Christ Himself: ii. 1-11.
II. The Glory of the Incarnate Word or Son presented to His own (the Jewish Nation): ii. 12—xii. 20.
1. During the *First* year of Ministry; in Jerusalem, Judæa, Samaria, and Galilee; extending from the Passover in March or April till December or January, a period of 8 or 9 months: ii. 13—iv. 54.
2. During the *Second* year of Ministry; in Jerusalem and in Galilee; embracing a period of 12 or 7 months according as its starting point, the unnamed Feast of v. 1, is pronounced a Passover or a Feast of Tabernacles: v. 1—vi. 71.
3. During the *Third* year of Ministry; in Jerusalem; at the Feast of Tabernacles in Oct.; covering a space of at least 8 days: vii. 1—x. 21.
4. During the *Third* and *Fourth* years of Ministry; in Jerusalem, Perœa, and Bethany; beginning at the Feast of Dedication in December and closing 6 days before the Passover in April, a term of 4 months: x. 22—xii. 11.
5. During the *Fourth* year of Ministry; in Jerusalem; on the Day of Triumphal Entry: xii. 12-50.

I. THE DAWNING OF THE GLORY OF THE INCARNATE WORD OR SON.
(i. 19—ii. 11)

SECTION I.—THE GLORY OF JESUS PERCEIVED AND ATTESTED BY THE BAPTIST

CHAP. I. VER. 19-36

As the Baptist delivered three testimonies on three successive days, the present section cannot close at ver. 34 (De Wette, Brückner, Lücke, B. Crusius, Hengstenberg, Lange, Westcott), but must be continued, if not to ver. 40 (Luthardt, Olshausen, Alford), to ver. 37 (Godet), or better, to ver. 36 (Baur). The subdivisions of the section are 1. John's First Witness to Christ—to the Sanhedristic Embassy (i. 19-28) ; 2. John's Second Witness to Christ—to the Multitudes around (i. 29-34) ; 3. John's Third Witness to Christ—to Two of His disciples (i. 35-37).

1. JOHN'S FIRST WITNESS OF JESUS—TO THE SANHEDRISTIC EMBASSY

CHAP. I. VER. 19-28

EXPOSITION

Ver. 19. **And** In the closest possible way the narrative ensuing is conjoined with that preceding,—"striking its roots, as it were, in the prologue" (Godet), with which it has a twofold connection, through the subject of which it treats ; the Glory of the Incarnate Word and the Testimony borne thereto by the Baptist. **this** viz., which I am going to relate ; the demonstrative pronoun being here, as always in John, the predicate of identification (Alford). **is the witness** not the witness already referred to in the prologue and now only detailed as to its circumstances (Olshausen, Tholuck, Meyer, Godet), but the substance or tenor of John's testimony on this particular occasion (Lange). That the Author should commence his narration with the testimony of the Baptist accords with the style of the Synoptists (Mark i. 1 ; cf. Acts x. 36, 37 ; xiii. 23-25), with his own design to set forth the first recognitions of the Saviour's Glory, and with the fact that his acquaintance with Jesus was brought about by a witness of the Baptist. **of John** see on i. 6. **when** commencing not a new sentence (Origen) but one subordinate to the preceding ; indicating the time of John's testimony, which was not before (Olshausen, B. Crusius, Ewald, Hengstenberg and others) but after (Bengel, Ebrard, Luthardt, Godet, Meyer, Lücke, etc.) the Baptism, since immediately thereafter ensued the 40 days of the Temptation history, which can neither be thrust in between verses 28 and 29 (Brückner), nor thrust forward to iii. 22 (Hengstenberg). 1. Against this the following objections have been urged. (1) If Christ had already been baptized, John would not

have spoken concerning Him so indistinctly as He does to the priestly legation. (2) The question which occupies the mind of the deputation relates not to Christ but to John, which would hardly have been the case had the former been already pointed out to the nation. (3) The words of John to the embassy (verses 26, 27) resemble those put into his mouth by Matt. (iii. 11) before the baptism. (4) The phrase "coming unto him" (ver. 29), which closely corresponds with that in Matt. (iii. 13), appears to point to the Saviour's approach to John for baptism. 2. All these difficulties vanish before the considerations (1) that the Sanhedrim may not have heard about the baptism, (2) that John discerning the captious spirit of his interlocutors may have deemed it prudent to answer them curtly, (3) that the narrative, as already stated, seems to imply that the Baptism had taken place. **the Jews** οἱ Ἰουδαῖοι ; originally the members of the tribes of Judah and Benjamin after the separation of the kingdoms (2 Kings xvi. 6 ; xxv. 25 ; 2 Chron. xxxii. 18) ; subsequent to the return from captivity, the whole body of the people (Ezra iv. 12 ; v. 1 ; vi. 14 ; Neh. i. 2 ; ii. 16 ; Esth. iii. 6, 10, 13 ; iv. 3) ; in the Synoptists where the term occurs 16 times, also the community of the twelve tribes at large (Matt. ii. 2 ; xxvii. 11 ; Mark vii. 3 ; xv. 2 ; Luke vii. 3 ; xxiii. 3, 37, 38, 51) ; in the Fourth Gospel, where the expression is characteristic and employed more than 60 times, it denotes not the Jews as distinguished from John's Gentile readers (Bengel, Ebrard), but either the leaders of the people, their ecclesiastical and civil representatives (Alford, Westcott, Milligan and

Moulton, Olshausen, Tholuck), or, the entire theocratic community as summed up in its official heads and as historically fixed in an attitude of hostility to Christ and the Christian Church (Lampe, Kuinoel, Luthardt, Meyer, Godet : cf. Andrew's Life of our Lord, p. 112, ed. 1863). The use of this expression has been supposed (Fischer, Hilgenfeld, Bretschneider, Baur) to prove that the Author of the Gospel could not have been a Jew ; against which may be studied Bleek (Introduction to the N. T. vol. i. p. 233, C. F. T. L). **sent unto him** an official deputation from the Sanhedrim, alluded to by Christ, v. 33. The High Court of Jerusalem, though of considerable antiquity, was not of Mosaic origin, or called Sanhedrim, τὸ συνέδριον, until the days of Antipater and Herod (Josephus, Antiq. xiv. 9, 4). In the time of Christ it was composed of 71 members, chosen from 1. The Chief Priests, ἀρχιερεῖς, and their families, the officiating High Priest being president, 2. The Elders, πρεσβύτεροι, amongst which were included both priests and laymen, and 3. The Scribes, γραμματεῖς, i.e. professional jurists or experts in law. If the Priestly members were mostly Sadducees, the Scribes adhered chiefly to the party of the Pharisees. The court resembled that mentioned as existing in the days of Jehosaphat (2 Chron. xix. 8-11). For the jurisdiction of the court see below. **from Jerusalem** ἐξ Ἰεροσολύμων ; the plural form Ἰεροσόλυμα, 'the Possession of peace,' being employed here, as generally in the later books, probably in allusion to the two parts of the city, the upper, ἡ ἄνω, and the lower, ἡ κάτω ; Ἱεροσόλυμα occurring only twice in the earlier books (Matt. ii. 3 ; iii. 5), which prefer the indeclinable Ἱερουσαλήμ (Matt. xxiii. 37 ; Mark xi. 1 ; Luke ii. 25) ; in Hebrew *Jeruschalem*, in the Assyrian Inscriptions *Ursalimmu*. Originally a Jebusite fortress (Judg. xix. 10, 11) ; from the date of its conquest by David (2 Sam. v. 6-9) the capital of his kingdom ; in the time of Christ the Metropolis of Palestine, and the Theocratic centre of Israel, "the high watchtower from which all phenomena of the religious life in the country were beheld and watched over" (Hengstenberg). It stood chiefly upon three hills : Sion on S., the highest, containing the citadel, the palace and the upper city ; Moriah, the site of the Temple, a lower hill towards the N.E., separated from the preceding by a ravine ; and Acra, N. of Zion, covered by the lower city. At the present day Jerusalem is the chief town of the Jerusalem Paschalik, and contains 24,000 inhabitants, of whom the half are Mohammedans, about a third are Christians, and a sixth are Jews (Warren's 'Underground Jerusalem,' chap. iii. pp. 40-58 ; Riehm's Handwörterbuch des Biblischen Altertums : art. *Jerusalem*). **priests and Levites.** The former, descendants of Aaron, employed in the religious services of which the Temple was the centre (Matt. viii. 4 ; xii. 4 ; Mark i. 44 ; Luke i. 5 ; v. 14; Acts vi. 7 ; Heb. ix. 6) ; the latter, pertaining to the tribe of Levi, appointed for the menial offices connected with the same (Luke x. 32 ; Acts iv. 36 ; cf. Num. i. 50). It is not likely the latter were conjoined with the former in the present instance as a convoy or police to apprehend the Baptist if deemed desirable (Lange) but as sharing to some extent in the priestly function of teaching, Deut. xxxiii. 10 ; 2 Chr. xxxv. 3 ; Neh. viii. 7 (Ewald, Hengstenberg, Meyer), perhaps also to lend additional dignity to the mission (Godet). The use of "priests and Levites" instead of the more familiar "Scribes and Pharisees" of the Synoptics is no reason for doubting the genuineness of the Gospel (Weisse), but rather an example of the Evangelist's precision of statement (Meyer) and a touch of historical accuracy (Lange), since at the time when the Fourth Gospel was composed the Synoptical combination had become strange and out of date. **to ask him** Not necessarily in a malicious or captious spirit (Chrysostom, Alford) were these emissaries sent by the Sanhedrim, but in the exercise of its judicial authority (Deut. xviii. 21) to inquire into his credentials as a prophet. The Tribunal of the Seventy possessed "the power of judging a Tribe, a false prophet, and a chief priest" (Mishna. Sanh. i. 5). The Sanhedrim was not so much "a theological court to whose jurisdiction belonged all offences against the Theocratic principles of the State" (Hausrath, N. T. Times, vol. i. p. 81), as "the supreme native tribunal of Judea to which all matters were referred that could not be dealt with in inferior courts or that were not reserved by the Procurator" (Schürer, The Jewish People in the Time of Christ, div. ii. vol. i. p. 185, C. F. T. L; Keil, Handbuch der Biblischen Archäologie, § 151 ; Riehm, Handwörterbuch, art. *Synhedrium*. **Who art thou** More correctly, "Thou, who art thou?" What uncommon (Luthardt), what expected (Godet) person art Thou? Alluding to the popular anticipations current respecting the Baptist, Luke iii. 15 (Alford, Godet, and others) ; perhaps also implying that he himself had put forward such pretensions (Meyer, Tholuck) ; and hence having this further question in the background, Art Thou the Christ? (Hengstenberg).

20. **And he confessed and denied not** i.e. he confessed and took not back his confession. Dependent on ὅτε, when, (ver. 19), the clause signifies "this was John's witness when he confessed," etc. ; the first term marking the spontaneity and openness (ix. 22 ; xii. 42 ; 1 John i. 9 ; iv. 2, 3, 15) ; the second the completeness and finality of his witness. **and he confessed** a repetition for the sake of emphasis, meaning 'And this was the substance of his confession,' **I am not the Christ** The best authorities (א A B C * L X Δ etc., Tischendorf, Meyer, Westcott and Hort) assign precedence to the pronoun "I," ἐγώ, thus making John reply, "Not I am the Christ but another!" which is more striking than to answer with both Authorized and Revised Texts, "*I am not* the Christ !" Οὐκ εἰμι ἐγὼ ὁ Χριστός.

21. **And they** The Legates of the Jews **asked him** on that same occasion **what then?** Not 'What art thou then?' (Beza), but 'What then is the case?' i.e. if thou art not the Christ **art thou Elijah?** Alluding to Mal. iv. 5, which was supposed to promise the appearance not of an antitypical, but of the real, Elijah. **and he saith** responding to the sense in which their question was put. **I am not** i.e. Not the literal flesh and blood Elijah ; for he must have been aware he was the spiritual Elijah who had been promised (Luke i. 27). **Art thou the prophet?** ὁ προφήτης ; The article signify-

ing 'the well-known prophet, i.e. the prophet like unto Moses, Deut. xviii. 15 (Chrysostom, Bengel, Meyer, Godet, Westcott) and commonly distinguished from Christ, rather than Jeremias (Grotius, Kuinoel, Olshausen, Hengstenberg, Lange, and others), spoken of in Matt. xvi. 14 ; and the noun (the equivalent in the LXX. of נָבִיא, one to and through whom God speaks : Numb. xii. 2) meaning 'one who speaks openly before one,' hence the interpreter of a Divine Message, one who receives and imparts to others Divine Communications (1 Pet. i. 12 ; Eph. iii. 5 ; 1 Cor. xiv. 3). See Cremer, Biblical Lexicon, pp. 568, 569. **and he answered, No.** According to him the nameless prophet of Deut. xviii. was Christ : cf. Acts iii. 22 ; vii. 37.

22. **They said therefore** because of their perplexity and bewilderment **unto Him** devolving the business of accounting for himself upon the one best able to do so, 1 Cor. ii. 11, **Who art thou?** A question impossible to meet with a bare negative. **that we may give an answer to them that sent us** i.e. to the Sanhedrim ; see above, ver. 19. **What sayest Thou?** Having exhausted all the wonderful personages their theology enabled them to think of, they were content to hear his own description of himself, of his whence and whither, of his origin and errand.

23. **He said**, perhaps with an infusion of gratified feeling on beholding their discomfiture, **I am the** lit., *a*, **voice of one crying in the wilderness**, i.e. of Judea (Matt. iii. 1) between the Dead Sea and the Hebron Mountains, in O. T. Scripture called Jeshimon or "Solitude" (1 Sam. xxiii. 19). "It is a plateau of white chalk, 2,000 feet lower than the watershed, and terminated on the East by cliffs which rise vertically from the Dead Sea shore to about 2,000 feet. The scenery is barren and wild beyond all description. The chalky ridges are scored by innumerable torrents, and their narrow crests are separated by broad flat valleys. Peaks and knolls of fantastic forms rise suddenly from the swelling downs, and magnificent precipices of ruddy limestone stand up like fortress walls above the sea. Not a tree or a spring is visible in the waste ; and only the

desert partridge and the ibex are found ranging the solitude" (Conder, Handbook to the Bible, pp. 213, 214). According to Josephus, the unfruitful limestone mountains of Judea were more hospitable then than now; but while even in the earliest times mention was made of the cedars of Lebanon, of the oaks of Bashan, of the forest-crowned heights of Samaria, no similar description of scenic beauty, taken from Judea, ever became proverbial. Strabo found the country about Jerusalem so unfruitful, barren, and stony "that no one would risk a serious engagement on its account" (Geogr. 16, 2, p. 761; cf. Hausrath, N. T. Times, vol. i. p. 28). **Make straight the way of the Lord.** Quoted from Is. xl. 3 (LXX.), with the substitution of εὐθύνατε for ἐτοιμάσατε, the words are put into the Baptist's mouth by the Evangelist, as they subsequently are by the Synoptists : Mark iii. 3; Mark i. 2; Luke iii. 4. **as said Isaiah the prophet** the language of the Baptist rather than of the Evangelist.

24. **And they had been sent** So the best authorities (א* A* C* L, etc., Tischendorf, Westcott and Hort), instead of 'they who had been sent were' (Meyer, Godet). **from the Pharisees.** Not a new deputation (Origen, B. Crusius), but the class of whom the first embassy consisted ; who are here introduced in accordance with the usual manner of the Evangelist (Bengel), not to explain their hostility (Lücke, and others), but to elucidate the point of their subsequent inquiry about baptism (Brückner, Meyer, Luthardt, and others). The Pharisees, as a party in the Jewish State, represented the Judaism of the Post-Exilian Era. Originally purists as well as legalists, they "strove to carry out in practice the ideal of a legal life set up by the Scribes." Hence they were denominated Perushim, Pharisees, or Separatists. First mentioned by Josephus (Antiq. xiii. 5, 9; 10, 6), under Jonathan and Hyrcanus, High Priests, about B.C. 145-130, in the time of Christ they had so far degenerated from their primitive piety as to make the essence of religion lie in ceremonial observance ; an apostasy which drew down upon them the exposures, rebukes, and denunciations of Jesus

(Matt. v. 20; xii. 2; xix. 3; xxiii. 13). They were the "ultra-conservatives" in Israel, the champions of orthodox literalism, *qui magni facerent baptismum Judaicum* (Bengel), and who accordingly "watched everywhere with inquisitorial severity to see that the Theocratic order was preserved intact, not merely as to ritual, but also with respect to the competence of office and doctrine, ix. 13; vii. 47, 48; xii. 42" (Hengstenberg). Cf. Hausrath, vol. i. pp. 135-153; Schürer, The Jewish People in the Time of Christ, § 26, 1; Keil, Handbuch der Biblischen Archäologie, § 133.

25. **And they** i.e. The Commissioners of the Pharisees **asked Him** or, questioned him. The clause is omitted in Codex א **and said unto him, Why then baptizest thou, if thou art not the Christ, neither Elijah, neither the prophet?** The Messiah and his two forerunners, they conceded, would inaugurate their respective missions by instituting water-baptism; but if John was none of these personages, it seemed to them self-evident that he had no title to baptize.

26. **John answered them, saying, I baptize with water** or, in water, ἐν ὕδατι; signifying not 'My baptism is only a water-baptism' as if to depreciate the rite he practised in comparison with the Spirit-baptism to be afterwards administered by Christ (Calvin, Meyer, Hengstenberg, Westcott), but without such antithesis, 'I am baptizing with' or 'in water,' and if you wish to know the reason, it lies in this (Godet, Milligan and Moulton). **in the midst of you standeth one** not as if Christ were then present, but alluding to the fact that Christ was already entered on his public career ; a fact which had been revealed to the speaker on the occasion of Christ's baptism (ver. 33). **whom ye** 1. legates of the Sanhedrim ; 2. expectant multitudes around **know not.** The words imply that John was by this time acquainted with the person of the Messiah; from which it is an easy inference that already the Baptism had taken place. Even **He that cometh after Me** lit., *He coming after Me*, ver. 15, **the latchet of whose shoe,** "shoes," Matt. iii. 11; Luke iii. 16. **I am not worthy** ἄξιος; ἱκανὸς, Matt. iii. 11; Mark

i. 7 ; Luke iii. 16. **to unloose** " To bear " (Matt.) ; " having stooped down to unloose " (Mark). To untie the shoe string was the work of a menial or slave. The double genitive οὖ and αὐτοῦ, "an imitation of the Hebrew construction" (Baümlein), is of frequent occurrence in the N. T. : cf. Mark vii. 25 ; Rev. iii. 8 ; vii. 2, 9 ; xx. 8 ; and in the LXX. Ex. iv. 17 ; Lev. xi. 32, 34 ; xiii. 52 ; Num. xvii. 5, etc. See Winer's Grammar, § 22, 4. On ἄξιος with ἵνα instead of inf. as in Classical Greek Prose, and in Luke iii. 16, see ibid. § 44, 8.

28. **These things** relating to the Embassy from the Sanhedrim and the Witness of the Baptist **were done** ' came to pass,' ' happened,' ' took place,' ἐγένετο **in Bethany** ἐν Βηθανίᾳ, 'The House of the Boat,' from *beth*, a house, and *onijah*, a boat (Hug) ; not the well-known village on the Mount of Olives (xi. 1, 18 ; xii. 1 ; Matt. xxi. 17 ; xxvi. 6 ; Mark xi. 1, 11 ; xiv. 3 ; Luke xix. 29 ; xxiv. 50) ; or a place between Lake Merom and the Sea of Galilee (Lightfoot) ; but a locality on the East bank of the Jordan in the district of Peræa, probably situated at one of the fords near Jericho (Andrew's Life of Christ, p. 128; Tristram, The Land of Israel, p. 522) by which according to tradition the Israelites crossed under Joshua at the conquest, and near which a mediæval authority (Arculf) reports that in his day, 700 A.D., a wooden crucifix in the river marked the spot of Our Lord's Baptism. The reading ἐν Βηθαβαρᾶ (Origen, Vulgate, Textus Receptus, and some minor codices),

adopted by Origen probably because of his inability to find a Bethany East of the Jordan, while he had discovered a Bethabarah or 'The House of the Ford,' connected by tradition with the Baptist and his ministry, is not without advocates in recent times ; Bethabara being located at a ford near Succoth by which Jacob crossed the river from Mahanaim (Stanley, Sinai and Palestine, p. 310), in the province of Batanea (Bethania), extending from Pella to Galilee, at a spot named Abârah, near one of the fords of the Jordan, a little north of Beisân (Palestine Exploration Map; Conder's Handbook to the Bible, pp. 319, 320). **beyond Jordan** added to distinguish it from Bethany in Judea to be afterwards mentioned ; not because the Author wished to represent Christ as both commencing and closing his ministry at Bethany (Baur), since it is not Christ's ministry but John's to which the Author alludes. The ' Jordan,' " the only stream in Palestine deserving the name of ' river,' " rises in the Antilibanus out of three chief sources, passes over 27 rapids in its course of 200 miles, pours its waters first into the Sea of Galilee, then flows directly south between long and deep ravines, and finally debouches into the Dead Sea 1316 feet below the level of the Mediterranean. **where John was, baptizing.** Not, ' was baptizing,' as an imperfect ; but ' was,' i.e. was located, being then engaged ' baptizing.' For similar construction, cf. v. 39, 45 ; viii. 18 ; xi. 1 ; xviii. 18, 25 ; and see Winer's Grammar, § 45, 5.

HOMILETICS

VER. 19-28.—THE FORERUNNER'S CONFESSION.
I. From whom it proceeded :—John. This on the double testimony of the Evangelist (ver. 19) and of the Baptist himself (ver. 23). 1. *The Evangelist's estimate of John was high :* A Divinely commissioned prophet (ver. 6), and a witness of the Light (ver. 7). These proclaimed the dignity of his person, the nobility of his character, the elevation of his calling. "Let another praise thee and not thine own mouth" (Prov. xxxii. 2). 2. *The Baptist's estimate of himself was low :* "A voice crying in the wilderness" (ver. 23), an obscure desert preacher, an unheeded echo sounding through the moral solitudes and unspiritual wastes of a degenerate people, the insignificant forerunner of a Greater One who was already in their midst, and the latchet of whose shoe he was not worthy to unloose (ver. 23, 27) ; a feeble reformer, a water baptizer (ver. 26), who could only call men to outward amendment, but could not touch the springs of their interior life. The language revealed the essential humility of John's nature (iii. 30 : cf. Phil. ii. 3), the felt loneliness of his position (iii. 26 ;

cf. 1 Kings xix. 10), the conscious feebleness of his strength (iii. 27 ; cf. 2 Cor. xii. 9, 10), the expected fruitlessness of his mission (v. 35).

II. **In what region it sounded** :—The wilderness. 1. *Locally :* (1) Generally, the wilderness of Judea (Matt. iii. 1). (2) Particularly, Bethany beyond Jordan: see Exposition. 2. *Metaphorically :* in the moral desert of Judea. When John appeared Israel was indeed a wilderness and Zion a desolation. The Hope of Israel survived only in the breasts of a few (Luke i. 25). Corruption of the deepest dye and hypocrisy of the basest sort reigned amongst the priesthood (Matt. xxiii. 13, 39). John's language discloses the depths of moral and social degradation into which the common orders had sunk (Matt. iii. 8 ; Luke vii. 7, 8, 14). Amongst the intellectual classes scepticism stalked abroad without attempting to veil her features (Matt. xxii. 23 ; Acts xxiii. 8). In every possible sense John was a Voice crying in the wilderness. But prophet's voices are neither unsuitable for, nor undemanded by, the moral and spiritual wastes of society ; rather it is there they should cry aloud and spare not (Is. lviii. 1).

III. **When it was delivered** :—On the occasion of the embassy (ver. 19) ; i.e. after the Baptism : see Exposition. It was 1. *timely :* given at the moment when required, when his priestly visitors demanded to know who he was. So should one "be ready always to give answer to every man that asketh him a reason concerning the hope that is in him" (1 Pet. iii. 15). 2. *prompt :* delivered without hesitation or reluctance, knowing he had nothing to conceal or be ashamed of. So should Christians not be ashamed of the testimony of the Lord (2 Tim. i. 8). 3. *consistent :* not one thing one moment and another the next ; one thing to the legates from Jerusalem, and a different thing to the vulgar throng. So should the followers of Jesus always speak the same thing, letting their yea be yea and their nay nay (Matt. v. 37 ; 2 Cor. i. 18). 4. *final :* he confessed and resiled not from his avowal. So believers are exhorted to hold fast the confession of their hope that it waver not (Heb. x. 23), its boldness and glorying firm unto the end (Heb. iii. 6).

IV. **To whom it was addressed** :—The Deputation from Jerusalem, ver. 19. 1. *Composed* of Priests and Levites (see Exposition) who would doubtless keep each other in countenance in the delicate mission they had undertaken, and perhaps better overawe the desert prophet by the spectacle of their combined greatness. 2. *Prompted* by growing excitement, if not apprehension, amongst the Temple Authorities on account of John's preaching. Perhaps hastened by the report of Christ's Baptism. They who enter upon evil courses are easily alarmed (Job xviii. 7-11). Rulers governing by force and fraud are always afraid of democratic commotions. 3. *Instructed* to ask who the Baptist was. Prophets and those occupying public positions must lay their accounts with being observed, criticized, and questioned not always in a friendly spirit, sometimes out of jealousy, often out of fear, occasionally even out of hate.

V. **Of what it consisted** :—Of John's Testimony concerning himself. 1. *Negative ;* stating who he was not : (1) Not the Christ, concerning whom at first he volunteers no information—"there is a time to keep silence" (Eccles. iii. 7). (2) Not Elijah ; i.e. in the sense they meant, though he was Elijah in the sense of Malachi (iv. 5), and of Christ (Matt. xi. 14). "A fool uttereth all his mind, but a wise man keepeth it till afterwards" (Prov. xxix. 11). (3) Not *the* prophet ; neither Moses nor Jeremiah. Dead men return not again to life, even though they have been prophets (Job. x. 21 ; Zech. i. 5). 2. *Positive ;* declaring who he was : (1) a voice in the wilderness, (2) a herald of Jehovah, (3) a baptizer with water, (4) a servant of the Christ. On these see above.

Learn : 1. The best qualifications for a witness of Christ—humility and courage. 2. The secret of success in one's earthly calling—To know who oneself is not, as well as to know who oneself is. 3. The inferiority of all Christ's servants to Himself—they being voices in the wilderness, baptizers with water, nothing more ; He, the Lord of Glory, the Prince of Life, the King of Saints.

Ver. 23.—A Voice in the Wilderness : 1. Lonely, 2. Authoritative, 3. Prophetic. 4. Directive, 5. Arrestive.

2. JOHN'S SECOND WITNESS OF JESUS—TO THE MULTITUDE

Chap. I. Ver. 29-34

Exposition

Ver. 29. **On the morrow** i.e. the day after he had been interviewed by the Jerusalem deputies **he** John, although the ὁ Ἰωάννης of the T. R. is spurious. **seeth** βλέπει, perceiveth with the bodily organ of vision (v. 19 ; ix. 7, 15, 19, 21 ; xi. 9 ; xx. 1 ; xxi. 9), as distinguished from soul apprehension which is usually expressed by θεάομαι (i. 14, 32, 38 ; vi. 40, 62 ; xiv. 17, 19) **Jesus** see on ver. 17. **coming unto him** Not to take farewell of the Baptist before withdrawing to the desert (Kuinoel), which ver. 35 disproves ; or to receive the rite of baptism (Ewald, Hengstenberg), already obtained (ver. 19) ; or to hear the Baptist (B. Crusius), but to begin His work as Redeemer (Godet), to be pointed out to the nation (Lange), and to draw towards Himself disciples (Lücke) ; although the Evangelist emphasizes not the motive which led Christ to return, but the testimony the Baptist gave Him when returned (Meyer). **and saith** to his hearers generally, rather than to any one in particular, and certainly not to Jesus **Behold** See ! here he is, a characteristic expression with the Evangelist : ver. 36, 47 ; xix. 5, 14 ; cf. Matt. x. 16, and contrast Luke xxiv. 39. **the Lamb of God** The article refers to "a definite" Lamb, characterized as "of God," which may signify chosen (Lange), consecrated (Brückner), furnished or provided by (Bengel, Hofmann, Westcott), pleasing (Tholuck), or belonging to (Meyer) God ; and which was probably the Lamb of Is. liii. 7 (Meyer, Lücke, Tholuck, Brückner, Alford), or the Paschal Lamb of Exodus xii. 3 (Luther, Grotius, Bengel, Lampe, Olshausen, Luthardt, Hofmann, Hengstenberg), or the Lamb of the daily morning and evening sacrifice, Lev. iv. 32 (B. Crusius), or all of them together, since there is no reason why the Evangelist's allusion should be restricted to one of these, more especially as all were alike fitted to afford a basis for the designation given to Christ (Godet). **which taketh away** Not

'patiently endureth' (Gabler), but either (1) taketh upon himself in order to expiate (Lücke, B. Crusius, De Wette, Brückner, Hengstenberg, Tholuck, and others), or (2) taketh away in the sense of removing and destroying (Kuinoel, Luthardt). In favour of the latter meaning it is usual to urge (1) that the term נָשָׂא used in Isa. liii. 4 to express the idea of expiation, is never translated in the LXX. by αἴρειν, but always by φέρειν, while on the other hand the notion of removing is expressed by αἴρειν as in 1 Sam. xv. 25 ; xxv. 28 ; and (2) that in 1ˢᵗ John iii. 5 the word αἴρειν has the latter signification of removing or destroying. But against these considerations in so far as they exclude the idea of expiation, and in favour of the former import of the verb without abandoning the latter, it is enough to state (1) that in Isa. liii. the suffering servant of Jehovah bears, i.e. expiates, the guilt of our iniquities in order that by His stripes we might be healed, i.e. takes them upon Himself that He might take them away, and (2) that in 1 John iii. 5 the effectual removal of our sins presupposes and is based upon an expiation of their guilt (1 John ii. 2), i.e. Christ takes away our sins by taking them upon Himself ; so that both conceptions of the word may justly be included in the writer's thought (Melancthon, Baümlein, Meyer, Godet, Westcott, and others). **the sin** Not the particular sins as in 1 John iii. 5, but the sin as a collective unity : *una pestis quae omnes corrumpit* (Bengel) **of the world** of humanity at large. Cf. the Baptist's use of the term κόσμος to designate an organized confederacy of evil existing over against God, with that of the Evangelist (i. 10 ; I. v. 19) and that of Paul (Eph. ii. 23). That the view of Christ's work here put into the Baptist's mouth could not have been entertained by him, has been maintained on insufficient grounds. 1. The Pre-christian Times, it is alleged, were not acquainted with the idea of a suffering Saviour. *Answer.*

This idea is not foreign to the O. T. with which the Baptist may be presumed to have possessed some acquaintance. 2. The Disciples of Jesus themselves were incapable of understanding this idea (Matt. xvi. 22). *Answer.* Though not understood by, the idea cannot be shown to have been strange to, the disciples ; while, even if it was, that would not prove it to have been strange to John who had been reared as a prophet. 3. The idea which was only at a later period in the Christian Church fully developed could hardly have been anticipated by individual reflection. *Answer.* The Baptist refers to Divine Inspiration as the source of his knowledge (ver. 33). 4. The Baptist expected a Theocratic and not a suffering Messiah (Matt. xi. 3). *Answer.* John's doubt while in prison was occasioned not by our Saviour's sufferings, but by His delay, as it seemed, in asserting His Messianic dignity. Besides, it is not safe to argue from the thoughts of one shut up in prison to the views of the same individual at liberty. There does not therefore appear sufficient ground for impeaching the trustworthiness of this portion of the Evangelist's narrative.

30. **This** The Person pointed out as 'The Lamb of God.' **is he of whom I said** To his hearers generally before the baptism (ver. 15 ; cf. Matt. iii. 11), and to the deputation of priests and Levites after it (ver. 26, 27), though of this latter the people now addressed may not have been aware. **After me cometh a man** The definite term ἀνήρ, "man," probably occasioned by the visible presence of Jesus, was more dignified and becoming than the indefinite adjective "one" or the generic noun ἄνθρωπος. **which is become before me** Having in virtue of His higher dignity and calling stepped into a place and office transcending and preceding mine in importance ; see on ver. 15.

31. **And I knew Him not** i.e. as Messiah, or as the Lamb of God, a statement perfectly consistent with Matt. iii. 14 ; since, although before the Baptism John may have been acquainted with Jesus, it is not likely he knew him to be Messiah until that event occurred, when the fact was revealed to him in the manner about to be described. **but that He should be**

made manifest to Israel Not a subjective purpose on the part of the Baptist, but an objective aim on the part of God by whom the Baptist was sent. **for this cause came I** i.e. entered upon my official activity. **baptizing with** (or in) **water** The phrase includes John's whole work. All that John understood on commencing his ministry was that through his instrumentality the Messiah should be pointed out to Israel, which implied that in due time Messiah would be pointed out to him.

32. **And John bare witness** then and there, to the multitudes, as he beheld Christ approaching, **saying**—giving an account of what occurred at the baptism, **I have beheld** τεθέαμαι ; I have calmly and steadily gazed upon what I am now to mention, and the impression then made upon me by the sight remains. Whether this look was performed by the bodily organ or by the eye of the soul, see below. **the Spirit** τὸ πνεῦμα ;—τὸ πνεῦμα τοῦ θεοῦ (Matt. iii. 16); τὸ πνεῦμα τὸ Ἅγιον (Luke iii. 22);— here for the first time introduced, signifies the Divine Personality afterwards frequently alluded to (ver. 33 ; iii. 5, 6, 8, 34 ; iv. 23, 24 ; vi. 63 ; vii. 39 ; xiv. 17 ; xv. 26 ; xvi. 13) as the Author of Life and Salvation in believers and as the bond of union between them and Christ. That the Baptist could speak of the Spirit shows the doctrine was recognized by him as contained in the O. T. Scriptures: Gen. i. 2 ; vi. 3 ; Neh. ix. 20 ; Job xxxiii. 4 ; Ps. li. 12 ; Is. lxiii. 10. **descending as a dove** The Baptist beheld not "the sudden downward flight of a bird" (Ewald), but an external figure shaped like a dove, which an inward illumination at the moment taught him was the outward emblem or visible symbol of the Spirit. **out of heaven** Not merely from the upper regions of the air but from the opened firmament : cf. ver. 51. The origin here assigned by the Baptist to the Spirit, Christ afterwards claims for himself : iii. 13. **and it abode upon Him** This implies more than the 'coming' or 'descending upon Him' of the earlier Evangelists, and points to the continuance for a time of the celestial dove over—not upon, as if it had lighted on His head or shoulder, which would have required ἐπ' αὐτοῦ (cf. xix.

31); but directed towards as if hovering over and overshadowing His person (cf. Luke i. 35). The action and attitude of the dove were designed to symbolize the impartation to the baptized Christ of the fulness of the Spirit's influences which were requisite to fit His humanity to be the instrument or organ of His higher nature. The importance of this may have suggested the change of style from the participle "descending" to the finite verb "it abode." Neither the Baptist nor the Evangelist mentions whether the sight beheld by the former was observed by the multitude or even by Jesus, though this latter is, according to some authorities, implied in Matt. and in Mark, while Luke leaves it undetermined. The two Johns also omit allusion to the voice which according to Luke was addressed to Jesus—"Thou art my beloved Son!" but according to Matt. and Mark was directed to another, most probably to the Baptist—"This is My beloved Son!" There is no reason to suppose that either the sight was beheld or the voice heard by the people generally, or, if they were, that they were understood : cf. xii. 29.

33. **And I knew Him not** An emphatic repetition : see ver. 31. **but He that sent me** God: i. 6. The Baptist claims to have been conscious of a divine commission. **to baptize with** (or, in) **water** see on ver. 26, 31. **He** ἐκεῖνος, that one, God, in antithesis to οὗτος, this one, Christ : cf. ver. 7, 9. **said unto me** Not necessarily in audible tones ; possibly by inward impressions. **upon whomsoever thou shalt see** lit., *may'st have seen;* equivalent to a future : cf. 1 John iv. 15 ; see Winer's Grammar, § xlii. 3, 6. When, how, or where this sight was to be vouchsafed is not specified, although John may have naturally enough connected it with the baptism he had been sent to administer. The indefiniteness of the information was perhaps intended to excite the Baptist's attention, quicken his expectation and test his faith. **the Spirit descending** "As a dove," being no part of the real sign, is omitted. **and abiding upon Him** see on ver. 32. The essential mark of Messiahship was not the external phenomenon, but the inward possession and outward manifestation by Christ of the fulness of the Spirit's power ; cf.

iii. 33 ; Luke iv. 14, 17. **the same** οὗτος; this person: see above **is he that baptizeth with** (or, in) **the Holy Ghost** i.e. that communicateth to believers the Holy Spirit—so called to indicate His essential character (Acts v. 3 ; Eph. iv. 30 ; 2 Cor. xiii. 14) and distinctive work (xvi. 8; Eph. v. 9 ; Gal. v. 16); the impartation of His influences being set forth under the image of a baptism partly because already O. T. Scripture (Joel ii. 28 ; cf. Acts ii. 33) had employed for the same purpose the figure of outpouring, and partly because of its connection with the baptism of John. The two phrases 'baptizing with (or, in) water' and 'baptizing with (or, in) the Holy Spirit' indicate the characters respectively of John's Baptism and of Christ's ; John's, a symbol of repentance, μετάνοια, had for its object the preparation of souls for the Messianic salvation ; Christ's was and is the introduction of a soul so prepared into the enjoyment of salvation by the impartation of a new principle of life.

34. **And I** I, on my part ; corresponding to the "and I" of ver. 31, 33. **have seen** beheld, not alone as an inward vision, but also as an outward occurrence ; and what I then learnt by seeing I still have before my mind as a completed fact. **and have borne witness** Not 'will have borne witness' e.g. when my testimony is completed (De Wette, Brückner, Tholuck, and others), but 'have borne witness,' ever since I beheld that sight, as e.g. now when I point you to Him as the Lamb of God. **that this is the Son of God** Codex ℵ reads 'The chosen of God, ὁ ἐκλέκτος τοῦ θεοῦ. The phrase ὁ υἱὸς τοῦ θεοῦ may in the first instance signify the Messiah as the personal representative of God (cf. 2 Sam. vii. 14 ; Ps. ii. 6 ; lxxxix. 28 ; Dan. iii. 25), in which sense angels (Job i. 6) and Kings (Ps. lxxxii. 6) are in the O. T. designated God's sons ; but that in the Baptist's mouth the phrase pointed to Christ's higher or Divine nature is a necessary inference from ver. 30, as well as from the fact that in using it he simply re-echoed the testimony God Himself had given at the Baptism : cf. on ver. 49. See "How is the Divinity of Jesus depicted ?" (Whitelaw), p. 55.

HOMILETICS

VER. 29-34.—ISRAEL'S MESSIAH.

I. **John's Proclamation of Messiah.** 1. *His Person identified:* ver. 30 ; Jesus, at the moment returning towards Bethany, where the Baptist was carrying on his ministry, after the Temptation, to begin His Messianic career. 2. *His calling declared:* ver. 29. (1) Divine in its appointment. He was the Lamb chosen, provided, and sent by God ; the Lamb consecrated and belonging to God. (2) Saving in its character—He was come to take away sin, to realize towards, and fulfil for, the world all that had been foreshadowed in the Paschal Lamb, the Lamb of the Burnt Offering, and the suffering Servant of Jehovah, likened by Isaiah to a lamb (see Exposition). (3) World-wide in its destination ; He was set forth as a Saviour, not for Israel alone, or believers simply, but for Humanity at large, for the world as a whole, for all the families of the Earth (iii. 16 ; xii. 32 ; 1 John ii. 2 ; 1 Tim. ii. 6 ; iv. 10). Whether this affords support to the doctrine of Universal Salvation may be questioned ; it unmistakeably involves that of Universal Redemption, in the sense that by Christ has been rendered a true and all-sufficient expiation for the sins of men, upon the ground of which there is in the Gospel extended to every individual in the race a *bona-fide* offer of redemption through His blood, even the forgiveness of sins (Eph. i. 7). 3. *His dignity announced;* (1) His higher being—"He was before me" —a clear acknowledgment of Christ's pre-existence (ver. 15); (2) His loftier calling—"He has become before me" ; John was Messiah's Forerunner, Christ was Messiah ; John a witness to the Light, He the Light ; John a preacher of Salvation, He the bringer and bestower of Salvation ; (3) His nobler name ; John a servant, Christ the Son of God.

II. **John's Knowledge of Messiah.** 1. *When it originated.* At the Baptism, ver. 33. Prior to this John may have had surmises, hopes, expectations concerning Jesus ; certain knowledge, infallible assurance that his relative was indeed the Messiah he could not have had. Neither could we be sure of Christ's Messiahship to-day without the Father's testimony, to which also Christ (v. 37), John (I. v. 9, 11), and Peter (II. i. 16, 17) appeal. 2. *Whence it proceeded.* From the Spirit. It was no deduction of natural reason, or conclusion arrived at by his own unassisted faculties, after reflecting on the situation, comparing O. T. predictions with appearances in the character and history of Jesus. It was a direct supernatural impartation which he traced to God. From the same source proceedeth all spiritual understanding either of Christ or of His Truth (xiv. 26 ; xvi. 13, 14, 15 ; I. ii. 20, 27 ; v. 20 ; cf. 1 Cor. ii. 14). 3. *On what it rested.* (1) An opened Heaven. As in ancient times to Jacob (xxviii. 12), to Isaiah (vi. 1), to Ezekiel (i. 1), to Daniel (x. 5, 6), and in after times to Stephen (Acts vii. 5, 6), to Paul (2 Cor. xii. 4), and to John (Rev. iv. 1), so now to the Baptist the Heavens opened, when Christ ascended from baptism to the river bank. It was a symbolic representation of what had taken place. The Heavens had opened that God's Son might come forth, and that Christ's believing brethren might enter in. This is the first pillar of the Christian's faith in Christ. In Him Heaven has been opened for the outflow of Grace to men, and for the entrance of men to Glory. (2) A descended Spirit. Of this the dove was an emblem. Believing apprehension of what the symbol signified, viz., the permanent endowment of the Divine-Human Personality of Jesus with the fulness of the Spirit convinced the Baptist of Christ's Messiahship and Divine Sonship ; recognition of this fulness of the Spirit in Christ to-day, as proved by the constant impartation of the same to His disciples and followers, forms the second pillar of a Christian's faith in Him, as the Son of God and the Saviour of men.

Lessons.—(1) The twofold character of Christ's Salvation :—The removal of sin, its guilt and power, and the implantation of a new life by the Holy Spirit. (2) The twofold condition of receiving Christ's Salvation:—repentance, symbolized by John's water-baptism ; and faith, implied in beholding the

Lamb of God. (3) The twofold qualification for preaching Christ's Salvation :—
a knowledge of Christ and an acquaintance with self. (4) The twofold evidence
that Christ is the Son of God :—He can open heaven by removing sin, and He
can qualify for heaven by imparting the Spirit.

3. JOHN'S THIRD WITNESS OF JESUS—TO ANDREW AND JOHN

CHAP. I. VER. 35-37

EXPOSITION

Ver. 35. Again on the morrow
Hence the second day after the deputation : cf. ver. 29. **John was standing**
cf. vii. 37 ; xviii. 5, 16, 18 ; xix. 25 ;
xx. 11: "The picture is one of silent
waiting. The hearts of all were full of
some great change" (Westcott). The
scene is still laid at Bethany. **and two
of his disciples** Andrew and John :
ver. 40. The preposition ἐκ, 'of,' 'from
amongst,' intimates that already the
Baptist had secured a number of adherents.
36. **And he** i.e. the Baptist **looked
upon** with fixed attention and penetrating glance. Cf. ver. 42: the only
other place in John where the verb
occurs, though it is frequent in the
Synoptists: Mark x. 21, 27 ; xiv. 67 ;
Luke xx. 17 ; xxii. 61. **Jesus** whose
higher nature and loftier mission the
Baptist now recognized: ver. 34. **as
He walked** at a distance from him on
the river bank, sunk in meditation,
rather than conversing with people
(Brückner); obviously no longer coming

to (De Wette), but departing from
(Luthardt) the Baptist. **and said**—
renewing his testimony of the previous
day, possibly with a view of indirectly
urging his disciples to transfer themselves to Jesus (Luthardt, Hengstenberg, Brückner, Godet). **Behold the
Lamb of God!** Repeated not because
Andrew and John had been absent on
the previous day (De Wette, Ewald) ;
the abbreviated form of the testimony
rather suggesting that they had already
listened to a more extended statement
(Meyer).
37. **And the two disciples heard him
speak** The Baptist had not specially
addressed them, but spoken either to
himself in soliloquy or to his disciples
generally. **and they followed Jesus**
To make further acquaintance with
Him. Though this following was not
perhaps, in intention, the decisive com-
mitment of themselves to Christ as
disciples, yet in practical effect it was
so: *primae origines ecclesiae Christianae*
(Bengel).

HOMILETICS

VER. 35-37.—THE LAMB OF GOD.
I. **Seen.** 1. *By whom?*—The Baptist. The Forerunner, who had been preparing the way of the Lord, was at length privileged to behold Him, as all will,
first here in spirit and afterwards in the body, first by faith and afterwards by
sight, who by penitence, humility, and reformation, faith, hope, and desire, make
themselves ready for His coming (Matt. v. 8 ; John xvi. 16 ; 1 John iii. 2). 2.
When?—On the morrow, the day after the preceding vision. Christ seldom
puts His servants and followers off with one sight of Himself ; here and now, as
well as there and then, view follows upon view. The oftener also one sees
Christ the more is he qualified for seeing Him, the more does he desire to see
Him, the more is he actually privileged to see Him. Men are likeliest to see
what they look for, as John probably was on the outlook for Christ when he
perceived Him. 3. *Where?*—As He walked, on the river bank, it may be
assumed, at a short distance from the Baptist, but this time not coming towards,
rather departing from His servant—more than likely proceeding to separate
Himself from the Baptist in order to commence His own work. So Christ is
best seen when viewed at a distance from His servants, and best understood
when contemplated directly in His own Person, Character, Mission, and Work.

4. *Why ?* for what purpose ?—to be pointed out. For this reason Christ again came within the range of the Baptist's vision. For the same reason still Christ reveals Himself to men that having recognized Him as the Son of God and Saviour of the World, they might cry—Behold the Lamb of God !

II. **Pointed out.** 1. *In what character ?*—As the Lamb of God. Suggestive of (1) the personal innocence or sinlessness of Jesus ; (2) the meek and unresisting patience with which He should carry out His work; and (3) the propitiatory character of His mission; all of which should find a place in every witness borne of the Saviour to the world, whether by the Church in her collective capacity, or by ministers in their official teaching, or by believers in their private relations. 2. *In what manner ?*—With a " Behold ! " to indicate (1) the importance of the announcement made, and no message of higher moment can be communicated to mankind than that which directs them to the Lamb of God ; (2) the earnestness of those who make such announcement, and nothing is of greater consequence for the success of the Gospel Message, from a human point of view, than sincerity in those who preach it ; and (3) the liveliness of mind with which an announcement of so much significance should be welcomed by those to whom it is addressed. 3. *With what intention ?*—To send men to Christ. In the highest degree probable that such was the Baptist's intention in a second time proclaiming—" Behold, the Lamb of God ! " Without controversy nothing short of this should be the aim of all who assume or have laid upon them by a divine calling the responsibility of speaking to their fellow men about Christ. 4. *With what result?*—Two of his disciples followed Jesus. So need none who faithfully testify of Christ fear lest their ministries should be unproductive. Under the Gospel dispensation as under the Mosaic, God's word shall not return unto Him void (Is. lv. 11).

III. **Followed.** 1. *Promptly.* Without hesitation, or further parley, Andrew and John obeyed the implied injunction of their Master and went over to the New Teacher. The momentous character of the communication made by John, as well as the tremendous issues involved in its acceptance or rejection, rendered delay on their part imprudent as well as dangerous. If Christ was the Messiah and the Lamb of God they could not too soon become His disciples ; if He was not, the quicker He was found out and exposed the better would it be for them and the world. Hence they followed instantly. 2. *Inquiringly.* Without at once and finally committing themselves to Christ, they were willing to inquire ; and this is all Christ demands of any in the first instance. He is agreeable that men should look into His claims, being satisfied these will bear examination, and ultimately lead sincere inquirers to Himself. The chief complaint Christ has against the world is that it rejects Him without taking trouble to examine His credentials. 3. *Finally.* Having entered on the path which led to Christ, honestly and sincerely, with no inward reservation or disingenuous stipulations, they rested not until they fully and finally became His disciples. So will all find Christ who seek Him with a whole heart (Ps. cxix. 2) ; so will all who make the experiment of following Christ in earnest follow Him to the end. 4. *Exemplarily.* The first of John's disciples who went over to John's successor, they led the way in what soon became a larger movement. They were the first fruits of the faith, the earliest disciples of the Saviour, the first members of the Christian Church, the first subjects of the kingdom of heaven, the first participants of the new life or Messianic salvation Christ had come to bestow, the first to experience the heavenly baptism of the Holy Spirit.

Learn 1. The proper business of the Christian ministry—to point out Christ to the world and the world to Christ. 2. The necessary qualification for the Christian ministry—to behold Christ, to have a personal insight into the character and work of the Saviour. 3. The encouraging reward of the Christian ministry—to behold disciples going over to and following after Christ.

Section II.—THE GLORY OF JESUS DISCOVERED AND ACKNOW-
LEDGED BY JOHN'S DISCIPLES

Chap. I. Ver. 37-51

Exposition

Ver. 37. **And the two disciples** Andrew and John, referred to (ver. 35) and named, the one directly, the other indirectly (ver. 40), **heard him** John, being at the moment by His side or within earshot. Some codices read "His disciples," connecting αὐτοῦ with μαθηταί (C* L T B X etc.). **speak** lit., *speaking*, in an extended discourse with his followers (Lücke, Tholuck); pointing out Christ to the multitude (Meyer); more probably soliloquizing (Godet, Lange), the words uttered being those of ver. 36. **and they** convinced by what they heard from John, as well as attracted by what they saw in Christ, **followed Him** Christ. If not once for all as disciples (Westcott), or in a sense profoundly symbolic (Godet), at least sincerely and inquiringly (Augustine), humbly and respectfully.

38. **And Jesus turned** lit., *but Jesus having turned;* scarcely by accident, but through having heard their footsteps behind (Kuinoel, Meyer, Godet), though at the same time *per omniscientiam suam non ignarus et* quod *sequerentur et* cur (Lampe); the particle δὲ conveying the suggestion that had Christ not turned the two might have continued following in silence and unperceived (Westcott) without finding courage to address Him. **and beheld** lit., *having beheld*, with that inward look which enabled Him to know what was in man (ii. 25); θεασάμενος as distinguished from ὁρωμενὸς, pointing rather to mental and spiritual contemplation than to purely external and visible perception (i. 14, 18, 32, 34). **them** following, and saith (lit., *saith*) **unto them** Neither as soliciting information, since He knew they sought Him, nor in consequence of perceiving them to be shy and modest (Euthymius), but because He understood their desires (Hengstenberg, Meyer) and wished to assist them in their embarrassment (Luthardt), above all, because having already by His presence in their midst invited them to come to Him, He could not now reject them when they did come (Calvin), and because it is ever the part of Divine grace to meet seeking souls, Is. lxiv. 5 (Grotius). **What seek ye?** The first public utterance of Christ ; Matt. iii. 15 having been spoken prior to His baptism, and Mark i. 15 at the commencement of His Galilean Ministry. If not shaped to try their faith by suggesting that one who was ignorant of what they sought could not in the highest sense be the Son of God (Lampe), the question showed He had so far discerned their spirits as to apprehend they sought something (Bengel), and was willing to accord them an opportunity of preferring their request. The invitation extended to Andrew and John now belongs to all (Calvin). **And** lit., *but.* The adversative force of δὲ, which should seldom be overlooked, in this instance signifies that the disciples were solicitous of no material gift from the Saviour, but merely of permission to make His acquaintance. **they said unto Him, Rabbi** Ῥαββί, from רַב, great, equivalent to *vir amplissime,* hence, *doctor,* teacher, master ; a title of honour in Jewish schools (ver. 50 ; iii. 2, 26 ; iv. 31 ; vi. 25 ; ix. 2 ; xi. 8 ; cf. Matt. xxiii. 7, 8 ; xxvi. 25, 49 ; Mark ix. 5 ; xi. 21 ; xiv. 45. which is **to say being interpreted** for John's Greek readers **Teacher** διδάσκαλος, with reference to usage, rather than signification ; otherwise explained as καθηγητής, leader (Matt. xxiii. 8, T. R.). **where abidest Thou?** The inquiry shows they were still in the open air (Luthardt), regarded Christ as a travelling Rabbi lodging in the neighbourhood in the house of some friend (Meyer), and modestly desired to speak with Him in private (Godet).

39. **He saith unto them, Come and ye shall see** ἔρχεσθε καὶ ὄψεσθε (B C* L Tᵇ, etc., Tischendorf, Meyer, Westcott and

Hort); cf. ver. 47; iv. 29 ; xi. 34 ; Ps. xlvi. 8 ; lxvi. 5. Our Lord's second utterance ; neither an allusion to the Rabbinical formula בֹּא וּרְאֵה (Buxtorf, Lightfoot, Lange, Stier), which is improbable ; nor a gentle hint of His deity (Hengstenberg) ; but a gracious invitation to accompany Him at once instead of deferring their visit to a later period as perhaps they designed (Meyer). The reading ἴδετε for ὄψεσθε (א) is followed by authorities of weight (Vulgate, T. R., Godet, Hengstenberg) ; but the words εἶδαν (ver. 40) and ἴδε (ver. 47) render it likelier that a transcriber would substitute ἴδετε for ὄψεσθαι than *vice versa*. **They came therefore and saw where He abode.** The quiet reduplication on Christ's words reveals the simplicity of the narrative as well as the sincerity and earnestness of the men. **and they abode with Him** If in His humble dwelling *quae erat simplex, tranquilla, munda, silens, frugalis, sine egeno vasorum et librorum apparatu* (Bengel), they discerned not the signs of Messiahship, from Himself there can be small doubt they received such instructions as led them afterwards to devote themselves entirely to His service (Calvin) : cf. Luke xxiv. 29. **that day :** Not from that day onward (Credner), but during the remainder of that day. **it was about the tenth hour** i.e. about 4 P.M. (Jewish), or 10 A.M. (Roman). In favour of the latter (Ebrard, Ewald, Tholuck, Westcott, and others) it is urged that it (1) harmonizes better with the expression 'that day,' (2) affords more space for the incidents which occurred after meeting with the Saviour, and (3) agrees with the other notes of time in this Gospel (iv. 6 ; iv. 52 ; xix. 14) which appear to point to the Western mode of calculating hours as that employed by John. But against this and in support of the former or Jewish horology, it is contended that (1) the Greeks of Asia Minor no less than the Jews, Babylonians, and Romans reckoned their day from sunrise to sunset or from 6 A.M. to 6 P.M. (Herod. ii. 109 ; cf. Keil, Handbuch der Biblischen Archäologie, § 74), (2) the above cited passages admit of satisfactory explanation in accordance with the Jewish mode of reckoning, and (3) that even of a late part of the day it might be said in popular speech 'they abode with Him that day.' The mention of the day, *O felix dies!* (Bengel), and hour reveals the deep impression made upon the Evangelist's heart by his first meeting with Christ.

40. One of the two that heard John speak and followed John lit., hearing of, or by, John and following Him, i.e. Christ. **was Andrew** A Galilean, born at Bethsaida (ver. 45), whose name signified 'courageous.' **Simon Peter's** See on ver. 42. **brother** The other was the Evangelist himself who with fine modesty, and no small tact, does not once name himself throughout this Gospel.

41. He lit., *this one*, Andrew ; not both (Bengel, Tholuck, Hengstenberg, etc.). **findeth** The same day, not the next (De Wette, Baur). **first** πρῶτον (א᷄ A B M T᷸ X, etc.), probably the correct reading (Vulgate, Origen, Brückner, Lachmann, Westcott and Hort), implies that Peter afterwards found others ; but πρῶτος (א), by many authorities preferred (Tischendorf, Meyer, Godet) not unsuitably suggests that while Andrew and John both went in search of Peter, the former was the first to find him (Bengel), or that each going for his own brother Andrew was first successful (Meyer, Godet, Luthardt). **his own brother** τὸν ἴδιον, occasionally employed where a possessive pronoun might have been expected (Matt. xxii. 5 ; Eph. v. 22 ; Tit. ii. 5), and generally importing more than the bare notion of possession, points to the antithesis between what belongs to self and what pertains to another (v. 18 ; x. 3 ; Matt. xxv. 15): cf. Winer, § xxii. 7. **Simon** 'Hearing with Acceptance' (Gesenius), the Hebrew name of Peter : a popular cognomen in the time of Christ, being borne by nine different persons in the Gospels and the Acts : (1) Peter, Matt. xiii. 55 ; (2) Zelotes, Luke vi. 15 ; (3) Brother of James the Less, Mark vi. 3 ; (4) Father of Judas Iscariot, John vi. 71 ; (5) The Pharisee, Luke vii. 40 ; (6) The Leper, Mark xiv. 3 ; (7) The Cyrenian, Matt. xxvii. 32 ; (8) The Sorcerer, Acts viii. 9 ; (9) The Tanner, Acts ix. 43. **and saith unto him, We have found** The position of the verb indicates the result of a long continued search (Meyer, Westcott); the plural expresses the joint conviction of the two disciples. **the Messiah** i.e. The Anointed, from *mashach*, to anoint ; a current title of the coming Deliverer, used again only in iv. 35. **which is, being interpreted, Christ,** The Anointed. The designation Χριστός given in the O. T. to Kings (1 Sam. xii. 3, 5 ; xvi. 6 ; 2 Sam. i. 14 ; Ps. xviii. 51) is in the N. T. carried over to Jesus Christ commonly as an appellative (Mark xv. 32 ; Acts ii. 36 ; John i. 20, 25), but frequently also as a cognomen or proper name (Rom. v. 6 ; viii. 10 ; 1 Cor. i. 12 ; iii. 23 ; Gal. i. 6).

42. He brought him unto Jesus i.e. by persuasion Andrew induced Simon to accompany him to the lodging where Christ resided. **Jesus looked upon him** lit., *having looked upon him* with that penetrating glance which searched the heart (ii. 24), **said ;** first addressing him by his customary name in order to impart solemnity to the scene as well as mark the importance of the change to be effected. **Thou art Simon, the Son of John.** Not of Jonas (T. R.) which is probably a correction from Matt. xvi. 17, where Ἰωνᾶ can only be an abbreviation of Ἰωάννου (Godet, Meyer, Westcott). **Thou shalt be called Cephas** i.e. Rock ; hence 'Man of Rock' : cf. 1 Cor. i. 12 ; iii. 22 ; ix. 5 ; xv. 5 ; Gal. ii. 9. **which is by interpretation Peter** Πέτρος, from πέτρα a rock ; cf. Matt. xvi. 18 ; xxvi. 33 ; Acts xv. 7. The change in Peter's name was intended to foreshadow a change in Peter's character and position in life : cf. Gen. xvii. 5 ; xxxii. 28. Peter was henceforth, i.e. in virtue of his connection with Jesus, to undergo such a transformation as would fit him to become the foundation (Matt. xvi. 18 ; Eph. ii. 20), and one of the pillars (Gal. ii. 9) of the N. T. Church. The present narrative offers no contradiction to that of Matt. xvi. 18 (Hilgenfeld, Baur, Scholten) or even of Mark iii. 16 (Meyer), since in the former it is presupposed (Lücke), while in the latter it is not denied.

43. On the morrow i.e. the day after this interview with the two pairs of brothers. **He** Jesus ; some texts without sufficient authority insert ὁ Ἰησοῦς **was minded** desired, wished, purposed, was about to, was on the eve of : vi. 21 ; vii. 17 ; 1 Cor. x. 27 ; see Robin-

son's Lexicon of N. T. sub voce ; and cf. Winer's Grammar, § lxv. 7. **to go forth** out of the tent where He lodged, out of Bethany where He then was, and out of the immediate neighbour‑ hood of John (with whom He appears never again to have come in contact) ; partly through a desire to leave His Forerunner free to carry forward his own mission, and partly to prevent His own work from being supposed to be merely a development of John's. **into Galilee** Galilee, meaning a 'circuit' or 'ring,'—first mentioned by Joshua (xx. 7) as a district in Mount Naphtali ; afterwards by the writer of the Books of Kings (II. xv. 29) as co-terminous with all the Land of Naphtali ; in the time of Christ by the Synoptists (Matt. iv. 12-16 ; Luke iii. 1) as a large province, about 50 miles in length by 25 in breadth, embracing the whole of Northern Palestine, bounded on the E. by the Jordan, on the W. by Phoenicia, on the S. by Samaria, its northern limit being uncertain ; forming the tetrarchy of Herod Antipas who received it from his father Herod the Great, and occupied by a numerous population, largely heathen, residing in 204 villages and cities, the smallest of which contained 15,000 in-habitants, and consisting of a soil uni-versally rich and productive (Josephus, Wars, ii. 6, 3 ; iii. 3, 1, 3) : cf. Haus-rath, N. T. Times, vol. i. pp. 1-13 ; Schürer, The Jewish People in the Time of Christ, vol. i. p. 3 ; Merril, 'Galilee in the Time of Christ,' pp. 15-19 ; Stanley, Sinai and Palestine, pp. 361 ff. **and He findeth** whether before (Meyer, Godet, Luthardt, and others) or after (Lücke, Tholuck) his depar-ture, cannot be determined, though the former is the more probable ; it seems unquestionable the finding was not ac-cidental but designed on the part of Christ, who knew both where to seek and whom (vi. 37 ; xvii. 6). **Philip** It has been supposed (Alford) that Christ was previously acquainted with Philip, and now beheld him conversing with Andrew and Peter (Godet), per-haps also preparing to start for home (Lange) ; but the only points certain are that he formed one of the circle of the Baptist's followers (Luthardt) and that Christ in virtue of His mysterious insight into human character recognized his readiness to welcome the Messiah. **and Jesus saith unto him** The T. R. after F H M omits ὁ Ἰησοῦς and with sanction of F G H, Syr. inserts it before ἠθέλησεν ; but the best authorities, ℵ A B E G etc., Vulgate, Origen, Lachmann, Tischendorf, Westcott and Hort reverse this. **follow Me.** This was not a call to join the travelling company homewards (Lücke, Hengstenberg, Godet) or an invitation to apostleship which came after (Matt. x. 3 ; Mark iii. 18 ; Luke vi. 14), but a summons to discipleship, which of course implied external following. Pronounced here for the first time the words were frequently repeated afterwards (Matt. viii. 22 ; ix. 9 ; xix. 21 ; Mark ii. 14 ; Luke v. 27 ; John xxi. 19-22. That they were now promptly obeyed is tacitly assumed.

44. Now Philip was from Bethsaida Bethsaida of Galilee (xii. 21), "The House of the Fishing," was situated not on the shore of Gennezareth between Capernaum and Magdala (Robinson, Biblical Researches, iii. 294) or at Ain Tabighah, N. of Capernaum (Tristram, The Land of Israel, p. 444), but most probably at the mouth of the Jordan as it falls into Lake Tiberias, on the western side of the river (Josephus, Wars iii. 10, 7), that part of the city which lay upon its Eastern bank being distinguished as Bethsaida Julias, Luke ix. 10 (Thomson, The Land and the Book, p. 360; Stanley, Sinai and Palestine, p. 375; Warren, The Recovery of Jerusalem, pp. 342, 375 ff. ; Conder, Handbook of the Bible, p. 320 ; Merril, Galilee in the Time of Christ, p. 51). **of the city of Andrew and Peter.** This, it may be supposed, was inserted to hint that Philip had been made acquainted with the Messianic claims of Jesus through his fellow-townsmen (Meyer, Godet, Westcott), and perhaps assisted in his determination to follow by perceiving them in Christ's train (Luthardt); though John, it has likewise been surmised (Milligan and Moulton) may have desired to emphasize the fact that Philip and the rest of his fellow apostles, with the exception of Judas Iscariot, were Galileans.

45. Philip findeth At the close of the journey, in Cana of Galilee to which Nathanael belonged, xxi. 2 (Ewald);

but more probably on the way thither, though whether going to (Godet, Luthardt) or returning from (Hengstenberg, Lange) John's baptism can only be conjectured. Note that Philip, like Andrew and John, no sooner finds or is found by Christ than he seeks to make Christ known, *Philippus vocatus statim lucrifacit* (Bengel). **Nathanael** Nethaneel (Num. i. 8 ; 1 Chron. ii. 14), equivalent to θεόδωρος, "Gift of God" ; mentioned only here and in xxi. 2 ; generally identified with Bartholomew the Apostle because (1) his calling is circumstantially narrated as are those of Andrew and Peter, James and John, who all were apostles ; (2) in the Apostolic lists Bartholomew is commonly associated with Philip as Nathanael here is ; (3) while the Synoptists make no mention of Nathanael, the Fourth Evangelist is equally silent about Bartholomew ; and (4) in xxi. 2 Nathanael appears to be distinguished, as the apostles there named are from the two ordinary disciples who were present. If therefore this hypothesis be correct, Nathanael will be his proper name and Bartholomew (i.e. the son of Tolmai), like Barjonah (Matt. xvi. 17) and Barjesus (Acts xiii. 6), a patronymic. Other conjectures, as that Nathanael was Matthew or Matthias (Hilgenfeld), or John himself under a symbolic name (Spaeth) require no refutation. **and saith unto him,** *voce magna et hi'ari* (Bengel). **We have found** The plural implies that Andrew and John with their brothers, as well as Philip, were now accompanying Christ. **Him of whom Moses in the Law and the prophets did write.** The position of this clause before the verb "seems to imply that Philip and Nathanael had often dwelt on the O. T. portraiture of Christ" (Westcott). The introduction of the name of Moses in connection with the Law certifies that at least in the judgment of Christ's contemporaries the Pentateuch proceeded from his pen, and was not a late compilation on the lines of the primitive Torah (Kuenen, Wellhausen, Graff, Smith). The Scriptures referred to were probably Gen. xvii. 7; xlix. 10 ; Deut. xviii. 15 ; and the Messianic predictions generally. **Jesus of Nazareth, the Son of Joseph.** lit., *the Son of Joseph*, the (sc. prophet) *from*

Nazareth (E F G H K M U etc.), *Nazaret* (א A B L X), *Nazarath* (Δ), or *Nazara* (e); in which designation of the Saviour is to be seen not the view of the Evangelist (Strauss, De Wette), but either the imperfect information of Philip (Meyer, Godet, Luthardt), or the popular characterization of the Saviour, which was all that required to be stated (Olshausen), certainly not the smallness of Philip's faith (Lampe, Calvin). Not mentioned in Josephus or in the O. T., in the N. T. Nazareth (now En-Nāzirah) is invariably spoken of as a city (Matt. ii. 23 ; Luke ii. 4), while its site is "a lovely little spot shut in on all sides by dreary and unprofitable hills" (Warren, The Recovery of Jerusalem, p. 455). Generally believed to have been in Christ's time a place of mean reputation, chiefly on account of Nathanael's exclamation, ver. 46 (see Warren, ibid. p. 455 ; Delitzsch, Jesus and Hillel, p. 13 ; Schaff, Person of Christ, p. 34 ; Stanley, Sinai and Palestine, p. 358),—an opinion which is controverted (Merril, Galilee in the Time of Christ, chap. xviii.) ; it appears to have been a town of 15 or 20,000 inhabitants. The name has been variously understood as meaning "consecrated" or "devoted to God" (Bengel, Calvin), "the sprout" or "shoot" (Hengstenberg), "the watched or guarded one" or "the one watching or guarding" (Merril). **46. And Nathanael said unto Him,** Neither disdainfully (Calvin), disparagingly, nor prejudicially, but doubtfully (Meyer, Westcott), as failing to discern probability in Philip's statement. **Can any good thing come out of Nazareth ?** lit., *out of Nazareth can any good thing be*,—anything so eminent, noteworthy, illustrious, as this Messiah of Israel ; implying that such was impossible, not because of the general contempt in which Galilee was held among the Jews (Luther, Ebrard), since Nathanael was a Galilean, or because of the meanness and insignificance of the town (Lücke, De Wette, Ewald, Brückner, and others), which is doubtful (see above) ; or because of the immoral character of its inhabitants (Bengel, Hengstenberg, Meyer), for which there is no historical proof ; but probably because of the silence of prophecy as to Galilee, and much more as

to Nazareth, having anything to do with Messiah, vii. 53 (Godet, Luthardt, Westcott). **Philip saith unto him, Come and see.** Unnecessary to find in these words an allusion to the well-known formula of the Rabbis, or to the words of Christ to Andrew and John (ver. 39), it is permissible to regard them as the best remedy against preconceived opinions (Bengel), the simplest and profoundest apologetics (Godet), the essence of the true solution of religious doubts (Westcott), the shortest and easiest method of arriving at truth (iv. 29) ; a valuable and memorable watchword of Christianity (Lange). **47. Jesus saw** with the same glance with which He had previously beheld Peter (ver. 42). Codex א reads ἰδών, seeing. **him** i.e. Nathanael **coming unto Him** Christ ; having accepted Philip's challenge. **and saith of him** presumably to those beside Himself, but still in tones that were audible to Nathanael **Behold, an Israelite indeed** Either, *Behold truly*, or *behold, tru'y an Israelite*, i.e. not merely a descendant of Israel according to the flesh, but one whose inner character corresponds to the ideal conception of the name (Tholuck, Meyer, Godet, and others), and therefore a true branch or member of the people of God (Hengstenberg), which every one was not who belonged to the visible Theocracy (Ps. xv. 1 ; xxiv. 6 ; lxxiii. 1 ; Is. lxxvii. 4 ; Rom. ii. 29 ; ix. 6 ; Gal. vi. 16. **in whom is no guile** The clause contains an allusion to those Scriptures which depict the ideal Israelite as one distinguished by the absence of duplicity (Num. xxiii. 10 ; Ps. xxxii. 1), and in particular to the fact that the original name Jacob ('Supplanter') for which Israel was substituted symbolized a spirit of deception which was henceforth to become foreign to both himself and his spiritual descendants (Godet, Westcott). **48. Nathanael** (who had heard the lofty commendation of himself as he approached the Saviour) **saith unto Him** in astonishment (Meyer, Alford), though as yet without recognizing in Christ's words anything supernatural **whence knowest Thou me ?** — The question has been regarded as a proof of Nathanael's want of modesty, but was rather a sign of his genuine sincerity and even humility (Meyer); since had he not been conscious of the correctness of Christ's remarks he would either have repudiated it as an honest, or exulted in it as a deceitful man. But, being of a guileless disposition, and knowing Christ's utterance to be true, he could not with false modesty affect to disbelieve or depreciate it. It is also doubtful whether Nathanael was not thinking less of the laudatory verdict on himself than of the amazing fact that Christ had been able to read his interior character, and of the manner in which that had been done. **Jesus answered and said unto him, Before Philip called thee, when thou wast under the fig tree I saw thee.** Whether Nathanael was under the fig-tree (*ficus Carica*, a well known plant in Palestine (Num. xiii. 24; Deut. viii. 8) indigenous to Eastern Asia but now spread abroad through the whole of Southern Europe), when Philip called him (Greek fathers, B. Crusius, Luthardt, Lange) or, as is more probable, when Christ saw him (Godet, Meyer, Alford), the sense is that Christ had read his secret thoughts on some specific occasion which instantly recurred to his recollection. The verb 'saw' points to a supernatural searching of Nathanael's soul, and not merely to a miraculous vision of his person (Meyer), or first sight discernment of his character (Lücke). The particular occasion was in all likelihood connected with a season of devotion, when having retired to a fig-tree, perhaps near his own house (henceforth to him 'the fig-tree') and sat down beneath its shade (the exact force of ὄντα ὑπό), he read, meditated and prayed concerning the great hope of Israel, the Coming of Messiah. According to the Talmud, Rabbis were wont to pursue their studies beneath the shade of fig-trees; while in O. T. times to sit beneath the shade and eat the fruit of one's own fig-tree represented the highest degree of material prosperity (1 Kings iv. 25; 2 Kings xviii. 31; Mic. iv. 4; Zach. iii. 10). Cf. Riehm's Handwörterbuch des Biblischen Altertums, art. *Feigenbaum*.

49. **Nathanael** convinced by this astonishing display of supernatural knowledge **answered Him** Codex ℵ adds "and said"; other codices insert "and saith unto" between 'answered'

and 'Him' **Rabbi** wanting in Nathanael's first address (ver. 48); its presence here an indication of growing reverence for Christ's person occasioned by the impression Christ's words had made upon his heart. **Thou art the Son of God, Thou art King of Israel.** The two designations have been explained as equivalent, the second defining the sense in which the first was intended to be applied, and both together characterizing Christ as Israel's expected Messiah (Lücke, Tholuck, Meyer, Alford); but the phrase "Son of God" (see on ver. 34) was not commonly regarded as synonymous with Messiah (x. 36) and can be satisfactorily explained, not as an echo of the Baptist's teaching (Olshausen) but only as a recognition, dim and imperfect but still real, of the Divine Sonship of Jesus (Godet, Luthardt, Hengstenberg, Westcott, and others), whilst the appellation "King of Israel" evidently points to His human sovereignty over all guileless hearts (cf. Bruce, The Training of the Twelve, p. 10).

50. **Jesus answered and said unto him, Because I said unto thee** The best codices (ℵ A B G L etc.) insert ὅτι, 'that.' **I saw thee underneath the fig-tree** (see on ver. 48) **believest thou?** An interrogation (Chrysostom, Bengel, Lücke, Meyer, etc.), uttered not in censure of Nathanael's imperfect faith which did not yet fully believe in Christ's Godhead (Theophylact); or in disapproval of his faith as based on insufficient grounds (De Wette, Brückner); or even in surprise at its unexpected rise (Meyer); but in joyful admiration of its hearty and spontaneous character. With much the same purport the words may be understood as an affirmation (Luther, Hengstenberg, Godet, Lange, etc.). **thou shalt see greater things than these** i.e. behold proofs of My Sonship and Messiahship more startling and convincing than even the revelation of thy secret thoughts which presently forms the basis of thy faith.

51. **And he saith unto him, Verily, verily** Ἀμὴν, ἀμὴν, אָמֵן from אָמֵן, to prop or support, a verbal adjective signifying firm, hence faithful, is frequently employed as an adverb meaning 'truly,' more especially in confirmation of a declaration or expression of a wish; like *fiat, ita sit*, and γένοιτο: cf

Num. v. 22 ; Deut. xxvii. 15 ; 1 Kings i. 36 ; Ps. cvi. 48 ; Jer. xi. 5 ; Matt. v. 18 ; xvi. 28. Its double repetition, characteristic of the Fourth Gospel in which it occurs 25 times, the Synoptists never using more than one Amen, indicatés the solemnity of Him who speaks and the certainty of that which is spoken, perhaps also the existence of doubt in the mind of the hearer (Godet) ; and, while generally marking an advance in Christ's words to a higher stage (Milligan and Moulton), appears to intimate that He speaks with Divine authority (Lampe), as in fact one who is Himself the Truth (xiv. 6) and the Faithful and True Witness (Rev. iii. 14). **I say unto you** i.e. to Philip, Simon, Andrew, James, and John as well as to Nathanael, the pronoun being plural. **ye** And, by implication, all who like you shall believe. **shall see** ὄψεσθε, emphatic ; implying that such had never before been beheld, the vision however being not literal but figurative, not external and corporeal, but internal and mental. **the heaven opened** An allusion to Jacob's vision at Bethel (Gen. xxviii. 12, 13) ; the opened heaven symbolizing the establishment of free intercourse between earth and heaven (Lampe), and the perfect participle indicating that what was about to be established should be rendered permanent (Bengel). **and the angels of God** Neither the divine perfections (Reuss), the personal forces of the Divine Spirit (Hofmann, Luthardt), nor personified divine powers (De Wette), but veritable spiritual intelligences (Bengel, Calvin, Lampe, Meyer, Brückner, Godet, Westcott) ; Ps. viii. 5 ; lxviii. 17 ; civ. 4 ; Isa. vi. 2 ; Matt. xiii. 39 ; xviii. 10 ; xxiv. 31 ; Rev. x. 1 ; xiv. 10. **ascending and descending.** The 'ascending' is placed first not because Christ having ascended far above all principalities and powers the angels first ascend to Him and then descend (Lampe), but perhaps as a reminiscence of Jacob's dream (Meyer, Hengstenberg), or because the angels are already on the earth although we see them not (Bengel), or because they first bear our supplications upwards before returning downwards with God's

answers (Luther), or because as Christ's servants they wait upon His bidding, from whom having received their commission, they first ascend to heaven for power and then descend to earth to execute their tasks (Godet), or what seems preferable, because in the Incarnate Logos the whole world of spirit was potentially upon the earth, so that the flowing and ebbing of such life was continually from and to Him (Olshausen). The phenomenon described alludes not to individual appearances of angels in the subsequent history of Christ (Chrysostom, Grotius), or to the miraculous energies Christ was soon to put forth(Godet,Olshausen), but to the fact that in and through the Incarnation of the Word the entire spiritual world has been brought into direct and immediate contact with earth and man (Calvin, Meyer, Westcott, and others). **upon the Son of Man.** A designation of Christ occurring in the Synoptists (Matt. xi. 19 ; xii. 8 ; xvi. 27 ; Mark xiv. 21 ; xiv. 62 ; Luke vi. 5 ; ix. 56 ; xviii. 8) as well as in John (iii. 13, 14 ; vi. 53, 62 ; xii. 34, etc). Selected by Christ Himself in contrast to appellations given Him by others, as e.g. The Successor of the Baptist (ver. 26), The Lamb of God (ver. 29, 36), The Son of God (ver. 34, 49), The Messiah (ver. 41, 45), The King of Israel (ver. 49). Containing an allusion to the woman's Seed of Gen. iii. 15 (Gess, Godet), the glory crowned Son of Man of Ps. viii. 4-6 (Schmid, Keim), and the One like unto a Son of Man of Dan. vii. 13, 14 (Weiss, Beyschlag, Lücke, Bleek, Ewald, Renan, Strauss, Meyer, Tholuck, and others). Yet essentially emanating from the inner depths of His own divine-human consciousness, with reference however not to the earthly weakness of his humanity (De Wette, Tholuck), or to the godlike majesty in which it was enshrined (Gess, Schmid), but to His ideal and representative character, as the Son not of a man but of humanity, and thus as the Second Adam of the race, as the personal goal of its history (Calvin, Bengel, Lampe, Neander, Ebrard, Beyschlag, Gess, Godet, Weiss, and others).

HOMILETICS

VER. 37-51.—THE FIRST DISCIPLES ; OR SONS OF THE LIGHT.
    I. **Andrew and John :**—Attracted towards the Light.   1. *Discerning the Light.*
Galilean fishermen, of deeply religious susceptibilities, in all probability belonging to the pious few throughout the land who waited for the Consolation of
Israel, as they plied their arduous callings upon the lake, they heard, and their
souls responded to the trumpet tones of the Baptist's preaching in the distant
Judean Desert.   Leaving their boats and nets they hurried to the great
national rendezvous on the Jordan, submitted to the rite of Baptism, attached
themselves to the circle of the Forerunner's scholars, and waited for the future
development of events.   Accordingly when Christ was pointed out by their
Master as the Lamb of God, and therefore by implication as the long-expected
Messianic King, they felt themselves shut up by personal consistency, by
intellectual conviction, by spiritual aspiration, to seek His further acquaintance ;
and so will the Light still be discerned by all who, like them, prepare for its
coming by penitence and faith (Is. lxvi. 2 ; Zech. i. 3 ; Mal. iii. 7 ; Matt. iv. 17 ;
Acts xx. 21 ; 1 John v. 9-12).   Faith is the organ by which Christ's glory
is discerned (xi. 40 ; xii. 36) ; Repentance is the tear-drop that keeps the soul's
eye pure and clean.   2. *Following the Light.*   Many discern the Light who
neither rejoice in it (iii. 19) nor walk after it (1 Thes. v. 5).   Not so these
Bethsaida fishermen, who no sooner beheld than they followed (1) promptly as
men who realized their need (2 Kings vii. 3), knew the value of their discovery
(Matt. xiii. 44-46), and recognized the danger of delay (2 Cor. vi. 2 ; Heb. iv.
7) ; (2) humbly, walking respectfully at a distance behind, so exemplifying that
spirit of lowliness which should characterize suppliants at heaven's gate (Gen.
xviii. 27 ; Job. ix. 14 ; xl. 4 ; Ps. cxxxi. 1) ; (3) sincerely, with unaffected simplicity, replying to Christ's question, as persons who had nothing to conceal,
again teaching that openness and frankness of disposition which in religion is
the opposite of guile, and is indispensable to success in prayer (Ps. xxxii. 2 ;
lxvi. 18) ; and (4) earnestly, embracing Christ's invitation at once, since the
King's business requires haste (1 Sam. xxi. 8), and Christ's kingdom brooks no
delay (Luke xix. 44 ; Heb. iii. 7, 15 ; iv. 7), and becoming so absorbed in the
conversation that ensued, that they heeded not the lapse of time, but lingered
listening to their New Teacher, till the falling twilight deepened into night—
once more a picture of earnestness in religion (1 Sam. xii. 24 ; Prov. ii. 3 ;
Eccles. ix. 10 ; Luke xiii. 24 ; Phil. iii. 14).   3. *Finding the Light.*   Their
judgments were convinced that Christ was the Messiah ; and so will all who
turn towards the Light as they did be conducted to a right decision (viii. 12 ;
cf. Hoz. vi. 3).   Only 'following' must precede 'finding' (vii. 17 ; xii. 36).   In
the order of nature seeing goes before believing ; in the realm of grace a soul
believes to see (xi. 40 ; Ps. xxvii. 13).
    II. **Simon and James.**   Conducted to the Light.   1. *Sought out by brotherly
affection.*   If Andrew was the first evangelist and home missionary, John was
the second.   In both behold the true genius of Christianity, which at once and
of necessity impels to self-propagation, in ways and by methods wholly reasonable, beginning with those nearest and passing outwards in ever widening
circles to the home, the city, the country, the world !   Cf. Luke xxiv. 47.   2.
Constrained by intelligent persuasion.   Improbable that Simon and James were
forcibly compelled or moved by curiosity to accompany their brothers.   So
neither can men be dragooned into piety, nor long preserved in it by mere love
of novelty.   The narrative implies that each received from his brother such
intelligence about Christ as convinced him that Christ was Messiah.   Unless
men can be persuaded of the perfect reasonableness of Christ's claims they will
not either largely or permanently be induced to attach themselves to His cause.
3. *Presented by grateful adoration.*   Is it too much to see in the triumphant
emotion of Andrew and John as they introduce their brothers to the Saviour a
picture of the joy with which earnest workers for the Saviour lay their trophies

at His feet ?   4. *Accepted by gracious condescension.*   Brought before the Saviour they were kindly welcomed, as all comers are (vi. 37). Though not faultless, Christ was able to make allowance for their imperfections, think charitably of their infirmities, even discern beneath the surface of their natures qualities which when transformed and glorified by grace would prove noble and enduring. So Christ still puts the best construction on the characters and lives of men (Heb. iv. 14, 16 ; v. 1, 2). Of all men grace ever brings the best uppermost, and makes the best. They whom grace transforms obtain a new name (Rev. ii. 17 ; iii. 12), corresponding with the new nature they have received.

III. **Philip and Nathanael :**—Invited by the Light.   1. *Philip.* (1) Prepared for the Light. John's mission had in his case been successful. (2) Waiting for the light. Characteristically slow and deliberate (vi. 7 ; xiv. 9), perhaps at first hesitating to cast in his lot with Christ until he has beheld a Simon and Andrew in Christ's train, he yet figures as an earnest inquirer who, having thoroughly searched out the truth, has arrived at a decision, but is prevented by a constitutional shyness from taking the initiative, though ready, should Christ call him, to rise and follow. (3) Obedient to the Light. Immediately the summons comes he is up and moving, as afterwards Levi (Matt. ix. 9) and Saul (Acts ix. 8). (4) Speaking for the Light. Forthwith like Andrew and John, Philip becomes a witness for Christ, as subsequently the woman of Samaria (iv. 29), the Apostles (Acts iv. 20), and Paul (Acts ix. 22) did, and as all believers should do (Matt. v. 16 ; Phil. ii. 15), as far as possible also imitating Philip's promptitude, assiduity, intelligence, kindliness, patience, and tact in dealing with Nathanael. 2. *Nathanael.* (1) Searched by the Light. Approaching Christ's presence, He was examined as Peter previously had been (ver. 42), as doubtless also the others were (ii. 24) although it is not so recorded, and as every soul still is that comes before His footstool (Heb. iv. 12, 13 ; Rev. i. 14 ; ii. 23 ; 1 Chron. xxviii. 9 ; Ps. vii. 9). (2) Approved by the Light : ver. 47. Not every one whom Christ judges wins His commendation ; as for instance the Pharisees (Matt. xxiii. 27) and Judas (vi. 70). Even the eulogium pronounced on Peter had regard to the potentialities rather than the actualities of his character ; while what in Nathanael elicits Christ's approbation is not the complete absence of moral imperfection, nowhere to be found in man (Ps. xiv. 3 ; Rom. iii. 10), but the presence of spiritual sincerity. (3) Illumined by the Light : ver. 48. That which doth make manifest is light (Eph. v. 13). Already has Christ illumined him as to his own character. Referring to an incident in his spiritual history, Christ exhibits a higher knowledge which no longer permits him, Nathanael, to doubt he stands before Israel's King and God's Son. So is Christ always the best witness to His own Divinity : iv. 42. (4) Instructed by the Light : ver. 51. It is ever Christ's way to impart grace and truth where these are welcome, and further light to meek souls that cheerfully and humbly improve what they have (xv. 15 ; Luke xxiv. 32 ; 1 Cor. i. 30 ; Ps. xxv. 9 ; xxxvi. 9). Pleased with the frankness and heartiness of Nathanael's confession, Christ informs him he shall yet have greater cause for trusting in Him than simple astonishment at His superhuman knowledge, shall yet behold the whole angelic world doing service to Him whom men count the Nazarene, but who calls Himself the Son of Man. This sight the saints enjoy here and now, on earth and by faith (Heb. ii. 9 ; 1 Pet. iii. 22), and will enjoy hereafter in heaven in immediateness and by sight (Rev. xxii. 4).

Lessons. (1) The greatest discovery a soul can make—" The Messiah, Christ." (2) The purest felicity a soul can enjoy—fellowship with Christ—" they abode with Him that day." (3) The noblest life a soul can lead—following Christ. (4) The loftiest calling a soul can pursue—commending Christ to others. (5) The grandest philanthropy a soul can practice—bringing men to Christ. (6) The sweetest commendation a soul can receive—to be called an Israelite in deed. (7) The sublimest spectacle a soul can see—The Son of Man enthroned in an opened heaven.

Ver. 39. A Memorable Day. I. For Jesus—the first fruits of His redeeming work. II. For John—the beginning of a new life. III. For the Church—

the day of its foundation. IV. For the World—a promise of its regeneration. Lesson—the importance of little things.

Ver. 42. A True Missionary. I. His *Qualifications*. 1. A man of earnest spirit, typified by his name Andrew. 2. A person of religious inclinations, shown by his connection with the Baptist. 3. A soul who had been with Christ. II. His *Message*. 1. A blessed gospel, a proclamation of Christ. 2. A personal experience, "we have found." 3. A conjoint testimony—"we" have found. The true preacher never separates himself from the fellowship of the faithful. III. His *Sphere*. 1. Those at hand, as in the home, the city, the country. 2. Those afar off, dwellers amidst heathen darkness. IV. His *Aim*. 1. To inform their understandings concerning Christ. 2. To inflame their desires after Christ. 3. To conduct their souls to Christ.

Ver. 46. Nathanael's Question. I. A good man's surprise. II. An incorrect judgment. III. A popular prejudice. IV. A falsified proverb.

Ver. 48. Christ's Knowledge of His People. I. Their characters He understands. II. Their conduct He observes. III. Their thoughts He discerns.

Ver. 51. Heaven opened. 1. *A certain fact :* Christ has come forth. 2. *A blessed gospel :* Christ's appearing a manifestation of Divine Grace. 3. *A joyous hope :* Christ's coming forth suggests the possibility of Man's going in. 4. *A glorious prediction :* the re-institution of fellowship between earth and heaven tacitly predicts the assimilation of the former to the latter.

Ver. 51. The Names of Jesus. I. Proclaim His Personal Dignity. 1. *The Word*—The Revealer of Deity. 2. *The Son of God*—the Equal of the Father. 3. *The Son of Man*—The Representative of Humanity. 4. *The Lord*—The Supreme Sovereign of the Universe. II. Declare His Redeeming Work. 1. *Jesus*—The Saviour. 2. *The Lamb of God*—His Atoning Sacrifice. 3. *The True Light*—His Impartation of Life. III. Announce His Mediatorial Relations. 1. *Messiah*—His relation to Israel. 2. *King of Israel*—Monarch in His N. T. Church.

SECTION III.—THE GLORY OF JESUS DISCERNED AND ACCEPTED BY CHRIST'S OWN DISCIPLES

CHAP. II. VER. 1-11

EXPOSITION

Chap. ii. ver. 1. **And the third day** Not from the coming of the deputation (ver. 19), and therefore to be identified with the day mentioned in ver. 43 (Grotius, Lisco, Lange), or from the arrival of Christ in Cana (Ewald), an event not yet alluded to ; but either from the calling of Nathanael or the giving of the promise in i. 52 (Bengel, Lampe, Hengstenberg, Trench), or from the departure of Christ into Galilee, i. 43 (Origen, Beza, Meyer, Brückner, Godet, Luthardt, Tholuck), supposing this to have taken place the day before the calling of Nathanael ; so that, reckoning from the day of the official deputation, it is either the sixth (Meyer, Godet) or the seventh (Hengstenberg, Luthardt) that is meant, according as the day of Nathanael's calling is included in, or excluded from, the reckoning as a separate item. **there was a marriage** A wedding festival usually lasted seven days (Gen. xxix. 27 ; Judg. xiv. 14 ; Tobit ix. 12 ; x. 1) ; in this instance it was probably some days advanced when Christ arrived upon the scene. **in Cana** " A Place of Reeds " ; identified with *Kana-el-Jelil,* 8 or 9 miles N. of Nazareth (Robinson, Biblical Researches, ii. 347 ; iii. 108 ; Thomson, The Land and the Book, p. 426 ; Conder, Hand-book of the Bible, p. 321), or *Kefr Kana,* 4½ miles N.E. of Nazareth (De Saulcy, ii. 376), with which since the eighth century it has been traditionally identified (Hengstenberg, Godet, Milligan and Moulton), if indeed it is not to be sought in *Katana,* 4 miles N. of Nazareth (Westcott). **of Galilee** Added probably to distinguish this Cana from another in the tribe of Asher (Josh. xix. 28). **and the mother of Jesus** Mary, the wife of Joseph, the carpenter of Nazareth (Matt. i. 16 ; Luke ii. 7). **was there** Not because she now resided there, having by this time removed from Nazareth (Ewald, Renan), but probably because she was a friend of the family ; her husband's presence not being mentioned it is supposed because he was already dead (Lampe, Hengstenberg, Westcott), although vi. 42 renders this doubtful, and her own name being omitted either as traditionally well known (Bengel, Lücke, Hengstenberg), or because it is as the mother of Jesus she is about to play the important part assigned her in the present narrative (Godet), or what seems as likely, because the writer felt he could describe her by no more tender appellation than this which he employs (Lampe), 'the Mother of Jesus,' which she ever afterwards became to him in consequence of Christ's words upon the Cross (xix. 26, 27).

2. **And Jesus also was bidden** Not ' had been bidden ' before His baptism (Schleiermacher) or before setting out for Galilee, but was bidden on arriving at Nazareth (Luthardt, Lange) or on reaching Cana (Meyer, Godet). **and His disciples** Andrew and Simon, James and John, Philip and Nathanael, who could not have been invited earlier and were now invited only for His sake. **to the marriage** i.e. to the not yet terminated festivities.

3. **And when the wine failed** lit., *and the wine failing*, through the unexpected arrival of six or seven additional guests (Godet, Luthardt, Meyer, Westcott) rather than because the supply had been limited in consequence of the poverty of the family (Lampe, Tholuck), or since it was towards the end of the feast (Calvin). The reading "And they had no wine because the wine of the marriage was finished" (א, Tischendorf) is only a diluted paraphrase of the text. **the mother of Jesus saith unto Him, They have no wine** lit., *there is no wine ;* i.e. the wine is done ; hinting thereby not that the company should depart (Bengel, Paulus) or that Christ should deliver some pious exhortation (Calvin), in some natural

way interpose by furnishing more wine (Meyer), or merely in some extraordinary, i.e. miraculous, fashion render help (Lücke), but specifically that He should now embrace the opportunity afforded for the public assumption of His Messianic dignity by the performance of a miracle (Olshausen, Tholuck, Godet, etc.) ; not however because she had already seen him work miracles in the narrower circle of His private life (Tholuck), or because He had previously informed her He would there initiate His miraculous deeds (Olshausen, Alford), but most probably because by her recollection of the wonderful circumstances connected with His birth, by conversation she may have had with Him before He left Nazareth for the Jordan, by the report of what had taken place at His baptism, by the promise he had made to Nathanael of which doubtless she would also hear, and perhaps by the elevated aspect of His countenance which she had learnt to interpret, she had been led to expect that the moment had arrived for His showing unto Israel (Chrysostom, Theophylact, Lücke, Hengstenberg, Godet, Westcott, and others).

4. **And Jesus saith unto her, Woman** γύναι, not a term of disrespect (cf. xix. 26, and xx. 15, where it is only possible to think of mingled pity and affection ; and see Iliad xxiv. 300 ; Odys. xix. 21 ; Xen. Cyr. vii. 3, 4), but a courteous and gentle reminder that in the higher sphere of His Messianic calling she could no longer stand to Him in the relation of 'mother' (He being in this truly ἀμήτωρ, Heb. vii. 3), but only of woman. That Christ designed to convey a warning against Mariolatry (Beza, Calvin, Hengstenberg) is improbable, though the passage certainly tells against such worship (Meyer). **What have I to do with thee ?** lit., *What to me and to thee ?* Cf. Matt. vii. 29 ; xxvii. 19 ; Mark i. 24 ; Luke viii. 28 ; corresponding to the Hebrew phrase, מַה־לִּי וָלָךְ, Judg. xi. 12 ; 2 Sam. xvi. 10 ; 1 Kings xvii. 18 ; 2 Kings iii. 13, and usually implying the rejection of another's proposal. **Mine hour** ἡ ὥρα, characteristic of John (vii. 30 ; viii. 20 ; xii. 23 ; xiii. 1 ; xvii. 1); referring not always to the hour of His death (Bauer), but almost invari-

ably to the pre-ordained season or moment for some specific movement or operation in connection with His Messianic calling, that movement or operation being determined by the context. Accordingly the hour here intended was not that of His withdrawing from the feast (Bengel), or of His emancipation from His mother's authority (Gregory Nazianzen), or of His interposing with assistance (Calvin, Meyer, Lange, Hengstenberg), but either of the manifestation of His glory by working miracles (Lücke, Brückner, Westcott, and others), or, better, of the public entering on His Messianic career (Godet, Tholuck, Luthardt). **is not yet come** i.e. if the former interpretation be adopted, my time for working this miracle you expect has not yet arrived, not because the wine is not yet done (Grotius, Trench), but because the spiritual conditions for its performance are yet awanting (Westcott); or if the latter be preferred, the precise time has not arrived for my stepping out before Israel in the character of Messiah (Tholuck, Godet, Luthardt). As events showed, this was not to happen till the Passover season brought Him to Jerusalem (ii. 13). Hence Christ's declinature of Mary's request did not imply a refusal to extend help in the emergency that had arisen; and it is obvious that Mary did not so understand it.

5. **His mother** anticipating that He would in some extraordinary fashion interpose to relieve the present embarrassment, **saith unto the servants** διακόνοις (whence deacons), those waiting at the table (x. 40; xii. 37; xxii. 27; Acts vi. 1; Jos. Antiq. vi. 4; Xen. Mem. 1. 5. 2): cf. xii. 26, where the term is applied to Christ's followers. **Whatsoever He saith unto you do it.** Mary neither failed to understand Christ's reply (Luthardt), nor meant that Christ would require their services to fetch wine (Meyer), but expected that Christ would do something unusual (Trench, Godet, Alford, and others); only what, she left with perfect confidence in the hands of her Divine Son (Westcott), reserving to Him perfect liberty of action (Godet), casting all her care upon Him (Bengel) —thus furnishing a beautiful example

of faith and humility, which supplied the moral conditions necessary for His working (Westcott), and so hastened the coming of His hour (Besser, Stier). Cf. Pharaoh's words to the Egyptians, Gen. xli. 55 ; to which however it is unnecessary to see an allusion (Hengstenberg).

6. **Now there were six water pots of stone set there** lit., *but there were there*, whether in the banqueting chamber or in the vestibule is not stated, and therefore uncertain, though the latter was probably their station ; *stone water pots*, i.e. jars for carrying (iv. 28) or holding water, which circumstance (of their use) is here specified to obviate the notion that the vessels may have contained some dregs of wine (Chrysostom, Beza, Lampe) ; *six*, the number being told not as possessing any symbolic significance, as e.g. of poverty (Lange), or as more certainly attesting the reality of the miracle (Calvin), but as contributing to the picturesqueness of the narrative (Meyer), which is manifestly that of an eyewitness (Olshausen) ; *set*, κείμεναι, indicating not necessarily that they were broader than deep, *latiores quam altiores* (Bengel), but merely that they were arranged in an orderly manner ; cf. xix. 29. **after the Jews' manner of purifying** lit., *for the sake of*, with a view to (Meyer) ; or, *according to* (Godet), the purification of the Jews, i.e. in conformity with the custom of cleansing practised among the Jews, which extended to the washing of hands and vessels both before and after meals : Matt. xv. 2 ; Mark vii. 3 ; Luke xi. 39 : cf. Keil, Handbuch der Biblischen Archäologie, § 100. **containing two or three firkins apiece** lit., *having room for two or three metretes ;* i.e. not in all (Paulus), but each, ἀνά being distributive: Luke ix. 3; x. 1; Mark vi. 40; Rev. iv. 8 ; xxi. 21 : see Winer's Grammar, § xlix. b ; Glass. Phil. Sac., p. 504. The metretes (Attic), equal to 1 bath (Jewish), 1½ amphorae (Roman), or 72 sextaries (Joseph. Antiq. viii. 2, 9), contained 8⅞ gallons ; so that the entire quantity (assuming the water was transformed into wine within the vessels ; but see below) must have been between 106½ and 159¾ gallons ; which has seemed incompatible with historic credibility (Schweizer, Strauss, De

John 2:6–10 51

Wette), but is perfectly analogous with the known methods of Christ in providence and grace, afterwards symbolized in the miraculous Feedings (Meyer, Alford), not to say that it was specially appropriate as Christ's wedding present to the married pair (Godet, Luthardt).

7. Jesus saith unto them i.e. the servants: ver. 5. **Fill the water pots with water** First emptying them of what they originally contained, if indeed that had not been already wholly consumed, and then refilling them. **and they filled them up to the brim** ἕως ἄνω: denoting the eagerness with which Christ's command was implemented by the domestics (Godet), and probably recorded only to note the abundance of the wine Christ produced (Meyer), but see below ; though it likewise precludes all thoughts of mixing (Lange).

8. And He saith unto them The miracle is commonly believed to have been performed at this point (Lücke, Godet, Meyer, Tholuck, Hengstenberg, and others); but this is purely conjectural as the water may have been transformed into wine in the drawing forth (Milligan and Moulton). **draw out now** i.e. out of the stone vessels just filled, the contrast lying between "draw" and "fill" (ver. 7); rather than out of the well from which the jars had been replenished (Westcott), as if the antithesis were between 'now' and an imaginary 'then.' **and bear unto the ruler of the feast** The *Architriclinos*, in classical usage, the president or master of the Triclinium, a dining room with three couches, was in the present instance either the *symposiarch* of the Greeks, συμποσίαρχης, the *modimperator bibendi, magister convivii* of the Romans, who was commonly selected by the guests themselves from amongst their own number (Xen. Anab. vi. 1-30 ; Hor. Od. i. 4, 18 ; ii. 7, 25), or the table master or superintendent of the servants whose duty it was to arrange the details of the banquet as well as taste the meats and drinks furnished to the guests (Ecclus. xxxii. 1, 2). **and they bare it** lit. *and they bare*, sc. what they had drawn forth.

9. And when the ruler of the feast tasted the water now become wine Not the wine which had been water

(Luther), but the water which had become wine (Meyer, Westcott) ; the words in the original describing a miraculous transformation of the substance of the water (Godet), and the want of a τὸ before οἶνον indicating that the entire contents of the water pots had been so changed (Meyer). This latter inference, however, is doubtful : see above, ver. 8, and below. **and knew not** He had not been present at the drawing, which circumstance lends support to the view that he was one of the guests rather than a hired official. **whence it was** lit. *whence it is*, πόθεν ἐστίν as in i. 40; an example of the intermingling of direct and indirect narration characteristic of N. T. writers : see Winer, § lxiii. ii. 2. **but the servants who had drawn the water** This appears to favour the idea that the stone jars contained only water, and that the miracle occurred either in the drawing or in the goblets. **knew** sc. *whence it was*. It is not necessary to assume they were unaware that what they drew forth and bore to the Architriclinos was wine (Meyer). *Ignorantia architriclini comprobat bonitatem vini: scientia ministrorum veritatem miraculi* (Bengel). **the ruler of the feast calleth the bridegroom** Not necessarily a proof that the ruler was not one of the guests (Lampe), since the bridegroom, in whose house the banquet was held, may at that particular moment have been outside (Nonnus), or reclining at the table (Maldonatus), or employed in the chamber (Meyer). **and saith unto him** rallying him on account of the pleasant surprise he had prepared for his guests, **every man setteth on first the good wine** Though of this popular custom no trace can be detected, its credibility or existence need not on that account be challenged. **and when men have drunk freely** i.e. *to intoxication* (Godet, Meyer, Westcott, and others), *cum inebriati fuerint* (Vulgate), and not simply *enough* (Beza, Tholuck, De Wette, and others), an unnecessary softening of the expression which implies neither that the guests had exceeded the limits of moderation nor that Christ extended His sanction to inebriation, the table master merely quoting a familiar proverb with reference to a common practice at social banquets. **then** omitted by ℵ B L Tᵗ and some other MSS. **that which is worse** lit. *the smaller*, i.e. the weaker and poorer, in contrast to *the good*, i.e. the rich and well-flavoured. **thou hast kept the good wine until now** Not merely held it back but watched the proper time for its introduction, although ἔως ἄρτι, which simply contrasts the later with the earlier stage of the banquet, must not be pressed to signify that the guests were now incapacitated for appreciating the generosity of their host.

11. **This beginning** Not 'the beginning' the τὴν before ἀρχήν (א) being rejected on the authority of the best MSS. (A B L T\u1d47 etc.) and critics (Tischendorf, Lachmann, Meyer, Lücke, Westcott and Hort), but this 'a beginning.' **of His signs** lit. *of the signs*, which He wrought; thus excluding the wonders of the Infancy narrated in the Apocryphal Gospels. The miracles of Jesus were not mere *powers*, δυνάμεις (Matt. vii. 22; xi. 20; Mark vi. 2, 5, 14; ix. 39; Luke x. 13), or *prodigies* exciting wonder, τέρατα (Matt. xxiv. 24; John iv. 48); or *works*, i.e. deeds or performances, ἔργα (v. 36; vii. 21; x. 32; xiv. 10, 11, 12; xv. 24), they were likewise *signs*, σημεῖα (ii. 23; iii. 2; iv. 54; vi. 2, 14, 26; vii. 31 etc.), constituting "visible emblems of what He was and

had come to do" (Godet), "images raying forth from the permanent miracle of Christ's manifestation" (Reuss), symbolic representations of His character and work, in short material reflections of His indwelling glory. **did Jesus in Cana of Galilee** It is not meant that this was the first of Christ's Galilean wonders (Paulus), but that Galilee, and in particular Cana, was the scene of His first miraculous operations (Lücke, De Wette, Meyer, etc.), though the one interpretation excludes not the other. **and manifested** φανερόω, to render apparent, to make visible; a peculiarly Johannine term which commonly implies the pre-existence in a higher sphere and form of that which is disclosed on earth and in time (cf. xvii. 6; xxi. 1, 14; 1 John i. 2), and involves the subjective illumination of those to whom it appears (see Cremer's Biblical Lexicon, p. 566). **His glory** See on i. 14. **and His disciples** As yet only those who had accompanied Him to the wedding; not His brethren (vii. 5), who were also spectators of the miracle. **believed on Him** i.e. had their already awakened (i. 41, 45, 49) faith in His Messiahship and divine Sonship established and conformed: *crediderunt amplius* (Bengel).

HOMILETICS

VER. 1-11.—THE MARRIAGE AT CANA.

I. The Wedding Feast. 1. *Attended by Christ's friends.* At the banquet were those connected with Him through ties of blood and those united to Him by bonds of grace. It is wrong for neither saint nor sinner to take part in such rejoicings as accompany weddings. Marriage though not a Christian Sacrament is yet a religious ordinance (Gen. ii. 24; Matt. xix. 5; Mark x. 7; Eph. v. 31), and is not only honourable in all (Heb. xiii. 4), but where the partners are well mated and bound together by reciprocal affection as well as by a common religious hope, is specially a matter for congratulation. Ordained for the happiness of the individual no less than for the onward development of the race, it is pre-eminently calculated, when entered into "solemnly, advisedly, and in the fear of the Lord," to promote the physical and moral welfare, and enhance the comfort and usefulness of both husband and wife, not to speak of securing in the shelter of a home advantages for the godly upbringing of children that could not otherwise be enjoyed (Mal. ii. 15). 2. *Graced by Christ's Presence.* The first wedding on earth attended by God (Gen. ii. 25). If not the first Christian marriage in the strict sense of that expression, this Cana wedding was the first marriage Christ honoured with His presence after entering on His high career as Israel's Messiah and the world's Saviour. Nor was it strange that Christ should have thus set a mark of honour on the institution His Father had appointed (Luke ii. 49), while it was peculiarly appropriate that He should inaugurate His mission of Redemption by, as it were, placing His hand upon the springs of

Humanity; lifting up this holy ordinance which perhaps had suffered more than any other through the fall,—men having by polygamy, concubinage, divorce, adultery, and fornication departed from its original idea—and restoring it to its pristine dignity and beauty.

II. **The Anxious Mother.** 1. *The Solicitude she felt.* While it becomes all, but especially the friends and followers of Christ, to be careful for nothing (Phil. iv. 6), and to take no thought for to-morrow or even for to-day, saying, 'What shall we eat and what shall we drink?' (Matt. vi. 31), and least of all to be careful and troubled about many things (Luke x. 41), the distress of Mary on account of the failure in the wine was (1) natural, seeing it had likely been occasioned by the arrival of her Son with His six companions, (2) beautiful, inasmuch as it was sympathy for others rather than concern about herself, and (3) permissible, for the reason that Christ enjoins us to cultivate the habit of feeling for our fellow-men and interesting ourselves in all that relates to them (Mark xii. 31; Luke vi. 31; x. 36; John xv. 17; Rom. xii. 10; Phil. ii. 4). 2. *The Request she expressed.* That Christ should embrace the opportunity that had arisen to establish His Messiahship by working a miracle in order to supply the lack of wine. (1) In so far as Mary turned to Christ in her emergency she acted with combined wisdom and propriety; teaching us who now have greater ground than she had to cherish expectations of Christ's ability to help where to go with our cares and troubles as they successively arise (Heb. iv. 15; 1 Pet. v. 7). (2) In so far as she indirectly prescribed to Christ the manner in which His help should be given her example must be carefully eschewed, Christ still as then regulating all His movements in the realm of grace by the higher will of His Father (Eph. i. 11). (3) In so far as she failed to grasp the character of Christ's mission she remains a standing witness to the natural dulness and incapacity of the human heart to understand the things of God (1 Cor. ii. 14). 3. *The Reproof she received.* (1) Inconceivable that the least flavour of contempt could have been conveyed by Christ's response to his mother (1 John iii. 5; 1 Pet. ii. 22); let Christ in this be our exemplar (Eph. vi. 2). (2) Impossible to avoid seeing that He designed respectfully to remind her that henceforth He had passed beyond the precincts of His earthly home and entered upon the engagements of another sphere in which the will of His Father was supreme (iv. 34; vi. 38); let this instruct us that those whom Christ loves He does not hesitate to reprove when they go astray (Heb. xii. 6; Rev. iii. 19), that there are higher obligations than those due to parents (Acts iv. 19), and that in all matters connected with religion and conscience "One only is the Law-Giver and the Judge" (Jas. iv. 12). 4. *The Comfort she obtained.* Distinctly repelling the suggestion that He should utilize the occasion for a public demonstration, He yet by some unexplained sign gave His mother to understand that so far as the present emergency was concerned His assistance would not be wanting. So it ever was His custom when on earth like His Father (Ps. ci. 1) to mingle mercy with judgment. 5. *The Trust she displayed.* With quiet confidence she directed the servants to hold themselves in readiness to execute whatever instructions He might be pleased to issue; so symbolizing that faith which is ever ready to interpret and cling to Christ's hints of favour, however imperfect and slight, whether detected in His Word or discerned in the ordinary movements of His Providence.

III. **The Unexpected Miracle.** 1. *Supernatural in its character.* A miracle not against but above nature. So far from violating or opposing nature, the power which operates a miracle begins by inserting itself in and working along the lines of nature as far as these go, after which it sweeps out into the region beyond and executes results of which nature by itself is wholly incapable. 2. *Unostentatious in its execution.* So little open to a charge of vulgar display was Christ on this occasion that no one now can, as probably no one then could, tell at what point exactly the miracle was wrought. Like the kingdom of God (Luke xvii. 20), of which it was an emblem and for which it was a preparation, it came without observation. In this Christ followed the silent methods of working adopted by His Father in nature (Eccl. iii. 11); by this He calls His followers to do their righteousness in secret, before their Father in heaven rather than before the gaze of men (Matt. vi. 1).   3. *Beneficent in its design.*   He who refrained from employing His divine power to relieve His own necessities in the wilderness (Matt. iv. 4) could not remain deaf to the appeal made to His loving heart to supply the wants of others.   So Christ ever pleased not Himself (Rom. xv. 3), but sought His Father's glory (vii. 18; viii. 50) and the good of man (Matt. xi. 4-6; Acts x. 38).   Nor were the miracles of the cursing of the fig-tree (Matt. xxi. 19) and the destruction of the swine (Matt. viii. 32) exceptions if we include in the good of man His higher spiritual as well as lower material interests.   4. *Symbolic in its significance.*   (1) In reference to Christ's person, it was a manifestation of His glory.   (2) In relation to Christ's disciples it was a picture of the joyous life to which they were called in contrast to the asceticism practised and enjoined by His Forerunner (Matt. xi. 18, 19; Mark ii. 18, 19; John xvi. 22; 1 Thess. v. 16).   (3) As regards Christ's work, it was a reminder that He had come not to condemn but to save, not to diminish but to increase the sum of human happiness, not to abstract a single blessing from the lot of man, but to transform even common mercies into gifts of celestial love, and to suffuse the happiness of earth with the felicities of heaven.

IV.   **The Astonished Table-Master.**   1. *The Wrong Interpretation of his words.* (1) Reflects upon the good behaviour of the company.   While drunkenness, revelling and such like are to be condemned in all (Gal. v. 21), and Christ's followers in particular should study temperance in eating and drinking (Rom. xiii. 14; Phil. iv. 5; Tit. ii. 12; 1 Pet. iv. 7), and on no account let their good be evil spoken of (Rom. xiv. 16), it is no less dutiful and becoming to avoid taking up an evil report against one's fellow-men and much more against one's Christian brethren (Ps. xv. 3; cxl. 11; Eph. iv. 31; Tit. iii. 2; Jas. iv. 11), especially when, as in the present instance, that report rests on no substantial foundation.   Charity taketh not account of evil, but believeth all things and hopeth all things (1 Cor. xiii. 5).   (2) Puts a stain upon the good name of Christ.   Though Christ was no ascetic, He was neither a glutton nor a wine bibber, and it is simply inconceivable that He would have either furnished more wine to persons already drunk, or countenanced intoxication by His presence. Had He done either no further proof would have been required that He was not the Son of God or Saviour of the world, however willing Israel may have been to accept Him as Messiah.   2. *The Right Interpretation of His words.*   (1) Attests the reality of the miracle, showing it to have been no mere *simulacrum* of a miracle, but a veritable wonder.   (2) Proclaims the generosity of Christ, who not merely gave His friends wine, but gave it of the best quality and in ample abundance.   So in nature God giveth to all liberally (Jas. i. 5), and in grace Christ exceeds His people's loftiest imaginings (Eph. iii. 20).

Lessons.   1. The sanctity of marriage.   2. The best guest at a wedding feast.   3. The lawfulness of mirth, when innocent.   4. The loveliness of sympathy.   5. The limits of parental authority.   6. The lordship of Christ over nature.   7. The riches of Christ's liberality.   8. The glory of giving.

II. The Glory of the Incarnate Word or Son presented to His Own (the Jewish Nation)

(ii. 12—xii. 50)

The public Self-Manifestations of Jesus were five in number, each beginning in Jerusalem, the centre of the ancient Theocratic kingdom, and some of them extending outwards to remote districts of the land.   So to speak the Light of His Glory, which in every instance commenced to unveil its splendour in the Metropolis, the first and second times travelled northwards as far as Samaria and Galilee, the third time concentrated its illumination in and on the capital, the fourth time flashed out again beyond the city to Peræa, and the fifth time with intensified brilliance directed its beams upon Jerusalem. Always, by means of prophetic word and symbolic act, He made a solemn and deliberate proffer of Himself to " His own," being moved thereto by the pre-determinations of His Father's will, which alone guided Him in all matters connected with the development of His Messianic calling. The method followed by the Author in the compilation of this portion of his Gospel is in the first place to depict with sufficient clearness the manner in which these presentations or proffers of Himself were made by Christ ; then to emphasize the melancholy fact that with the Jews, i.e. the official heads and representatives of the people, the result was invariably rejection ; and finally to show how nevertheless and notwithstanding with individuals here and there He was slowly making His way into the favour of the Spiritually-born.

SECTION FIRST.—CHRIST'S FIRST PRESENTATION OF HIMSELF TO HIS OWN (THE JEWISH PEOPLE) IN THE 1ST YEAR OF HIS MINISTRY.
CHAP. II. 12—IV. 54.

I. In Jerusalem, at the Passover ;—

1. To the Rulers ;—first national Rejection : ii. 13-22.
2. To the Inhabitants ;—first beginnings of Faith : ii. 23-25.
3. To Nicodemus ;—first approach of Inquiry : iii. 1-21.

II. In Judea, at Aenon ;—the Baptist's last testimony to Christ : iii. 22-36.

III. In Samaria ;—

1. To the Woman at the Well ;—Christ recognized : iv. 1-26.
2. To the Citizens of Sychar ;—Christ confessed : iv. 27-42.

IV. In Galilee ;—

1. To the Galileans ;—Christ welcomed : iv. 43-45.
2. To the Nobleman; —Christ believed : 46-54.

I. IN JERUSALEM, CHRIST REVEALS HIS GLORY AS THE INCARNATE SON ;—1. TO THE RULERS IN THE TEMPLE

CHAP. II. VER. 12-22

EXPOSITION

Ver. 12. **After this** Clearly, after the wedding feast at Cana, though not necessarily immediately ; the preposition conveying merely the idea of posteriority : cf. iv. 43 ; v. 1 ; vi. 1. **He** i.e. Christ, whose glory had been manifested in the preceding miracle. **went down** From Cana (Bengel, Olshausen,

Tholuck, and others), if immediately after the wedding; if not, then probably from Nazareth where Christ yet resided and whither doubtless he proceeded on leaving Cana (Meyer, Hengstenberg, Ebrard, Godet, Luthardt). In either case the expression 'down' is used because the point of departure Nazareth or Cana was on the highlands, and Christ's journey was towards the sea (Luke iv. 31); while the verb is in the singular to denote that Christ was the leader of the train (Lange). **to Capernaum** Καπερναούμ; "Nahum's village," though whether or how connected with the Hebrew prophet of that name is unknown. Styled Κεφαρνώμη, Cepharnome, by Josephus (Life § 92), who also mentions (Wars iii. 10. 8) Καφαρναούμ as the name of a fountain which watered the Land of Gennesaret or El-Ghuweir, in Christ's time it was a thriving and populous city with a 'seat of custom' (Mark ii. 14), and a 'military garrison' (iv. 46; Luke vii. 2), in or near the Land of Gennezaret which lay upon the western shore of Lake Tiberias (Matt. xiv. 34; Mark vi. 53; John vi. 17), was formed by a recession of the hills from the water-margin in the shape of a segment of a circle, 30 furlongs in length and 20 in breadth, and was remarkable both for fertility and beauty. At the present day it has been variously identified with (1) *Tell Hum,* near Bethsaida, at the head of the Lake (Thomson, The Land and The Book, pp. 352-356; Wilson, Our Work in Palestine, pp. 187 f.; The Recovery of Jerusalem, pp. 375 ff.; Andrew's Life of Our Lord, pp. 181-195; Wolff in Riehm's Handwörterbuch, art. Capernaum); (2) *Khan Miniyeh,* an hour's journey to the south of Tell Hum (Robinson, Biblical Researches, vol. iii. 293; Stanley, Sinai and Palestine, p. 384; Conder, Handbook of the Bible, pp. 325, 326); (3) *A in Mudawarah,* a spring in the centre of the plain of Gennezaret, about half a league to the west of Khan Miniyeh (Tristram, The Land of Israel, p. 442). The first of these is probably correct. That this removal to Capernaum was not identical with that recorded in Matt. iv. 13 and Luke iv. 16-30 (Godet, Tholuck, Brückner, and others) is proved by the circumstance that that did not take place till after the imprisonment of John. In all probability this was due either to Christ's having been invited thither by Peter and Andrew who appear to have resided there (Matt. viii. 14; Mark i. 29) although Bethsaida was their birth-place (i. 44), or to His wish to join some party of pilgrims going up to Jerusalem (Lange), while John's reason for alluding to it may have been purely a personal one, because he himself was "from Capernaum," and Christ during his stay in the city "put up at the house of (Zebedee) his father"! (Hengstenberg). **He and his Mother** (see on ver. 1) **and His Brethren** James, Joses, Simon, and Judah (Matt. xiii. 55), who were either 1. *The cousins of Jesus,* i.e. the children of Alpheus and Mary (Jerome, Augustine, Bengel, Hengstenberg, Lange, and others). In support of this view it is usual to advert to (1) the customary practice among the Jews of employing the term brother in a loose sense as equivalent to near kinsman, (2) the circumstance that Christ when dying commended His mother to John (xix. 26) which, it is thought, He would hardly have done, had she possessed other children besides Jesus, (3) the Scripture statement that Alpheus or Cleopas and Mary had two sons named James and Joses (Mark xv. 40), if not a third called Judas (Acts i. 13), and (4) the appearance of individuals bearing the names of James, Simon, and Judas in the circle of the Apostles who are not the brethren of Our Lord but the sons of Alpheus (Matt. x. 3; Mark iii. 8). Against this however are commonly adduced, and with force, (1) the fact, remarkable though not decisive, that they are never styled Christ's cousins, but always His brethren, (2) the circumstance, scarcely less noteworthy, that they always appear associated not with the wife of Cleopas but with the mother of Jesus, (3) the uncertainty as to whether the Mary named as the mother of James and Joses was really the sister of Our Lord's mother (see on xix. 25), and (4) the certainty that Our Lord's brethren were not even among His disciples till towards the close of His ministry (vii. 5), whereas the two sons of Alpheus and Mary were among the Apostles from the first; 2. *The half-brothers of Our Lord,* i.e. the sons of Joseph by a former marriage (Origen, Westcott, Milligan and Moulton ; cf. Lightfoot on Galatians, Essay II. ; Morison on Matt. xiii. 55, 56) an interpretation which though not in itself improbable, rests solely on traditional authority (Gospel of James, chap. ix.); or 3. *The children of Mary herself by her husband Joseph* (Calvin, Lücke, Meyer, Luthardt, Godet, Alford, and others ; cf. Weiss, Life of Christ, vol. i. p. 281, C.F.T.L. ; Andrews' Life of Our Lord, pp. 98-108 ; Farrar, Life of Christ, chap. vii.), which may fairly claim in its support (1) that it is the simplest and most natural hypothesis, (2) that Our Lord's brethren are always designated brothers, never cousins, (3) that they are never said to be sons of Joseph but always spoken of as brethren of Jesus, and (4) that they always appear to be under Mary's care. **And His disciples** i.e. Andrew and Simon, John and James, Philip and Nathaniel, who had not yet returned to their former avocations, as they subsequently did (Matt. iv. 18-22). This clause is wanting in א. **and there they abode not many days** Not because of misconstruction and hostility (Ewald), but either because the Passover was at hand (Bengel, Meyer, Brückner) or because they only now intended a passing visit, not a permanent location (Luthardt, Westcott). The calling of the disciples narrated by the Synoptists belongs to a later period.

13. **And the Passover** τὸ πάσχα, the annual Jewish festival commemorative of the Exodus from Egypt, appointed to be held on the 14th day of the 1st month, Nisan (Exod. xii. 18), and this year falling on April 9th (Greswell) or 11th (Friedlieb). **of the Jews** cf. vi. 4 ; xi. 55. Appended because John wrote for Gentile readers (Godet), or what was originally the Lord's passover had become degraded into a purely human institution (Origen), or John had completely broken with the institutions of his countrymen (Milligan and Moulton), or the Evangelist designed to imply the existence at the time when he wrote of a Christian Passover (Westcott). **was at hand** Showing that Christ commenced His Ministry in the spring of the year 779 or 780 A.U.C. **And Jesus went up** This visit, not recorded by the

Synoptists, whose memoirs commence with the Galilean Ministry, appears to have been made (1) to fulfil all righteousness in accordance with both His baptism and His circumcision (Lampe), (2) to observe the exercises of religion along with His people (Calvin), (3) to secure the greatest publicity for His teaching (Lampe, Calvin), (4) and chiefly to inaugurate His Ministry in accordance with Mal. iii. 1-3. **to Jerusalem**—the metropolis of the country, and the centre of the Theocracy ; which explains the phraseology of the writer (see on i. 19).

14. **And He found in the Temple** ἱερόν, that which stands in any connection with God, that which is holy, sacred, reverend, as being consecrated to the Divine service ; hence the Temple as a whole with all its courts and appurtenances (vi. 14 ; viii. 20 ; x. 23 ; xviii. 20 ; Matt. xii. 6 ; xxi. 12 ; Mark xi. 15 ; xiii. 1 ; Luke ii. 27 ; xviii. 10 ; 1 Cor. ix. 13 : cf. Josephus, Antiq. xv. 11 ; Wars, v. 5) ; the term ναός standing for the sacred edifice, or Temple proper (ver. 19, 20, 21 ; Matt. xxiii. 16, 17 ; xxvi. 61 ; xxvii. 51 ; Mark xiv. 58 ; Luke i. 9, 21, 22 ; xxiii. 45 ; 1 Cor. iii. 16). According to Josephus the Temple consisted of three parts. (1) The first enclosure, which surrounded the whole building, and was open for all, contained the porches and piazzas in which the people assembled, the animals for sacrifice were bought and sold, and the money-changers' tables placed. This was the outer court, or court of the Gentiles. (2) The second enclosure, which was 10 steps higher, was divided into the court of the women and the court of the priests ; was the place where the sacrifices were prepared and offered, and could only be entered by such as were clean. (3) The inner edifice, the Temple proper, into which alone the priests could enter, consisted of the Sanctuary or Holy Place, and the Holy of Holies. The ἱερόν is never put for the ναός alone ; it is mostly applied to the whole building (Cremer, Biblical Lexicon, p. 293), though, as in the present instance, it may sometimes refer to a portion of it. **those that sold** lit., *those selling*, being engaged in traffic at the time of Christ's visit. **oxen, sheep, and doves** the animals required for oblations : Deut. xiv. 24-

26. **and the changers of money** The κερματισταί, from κέρμα, a piece of money, were changers of large into small coins, whereas the κολλυβισταί (ver. 15) were those who changed foreign money into home, charging as their fee a κόλλυβος or small coin. In this case the two were the same individuals, who had abundance of occupution, since no foreign money could be accepted for the temple capitation-tax of half a shekel (Ex. xxx. 13), which though it might be paid elsewhere (Matt. xvii. 24), was usually paid in Jerusalem. **sitting** as if they were leisurely going about a legitimate business, which they were not, at least as to its place or the manner of its carrying on.

15. **And He made a scourge of small cords** lit., *having made a whip of bulrushes ;* these having probably been littered down for the cattle to lie on ; so that the scourge, or whip, could only have been designed as an emblem of authority—ein göttliche Straffsymbol (Tholuck). **and cast** lit., *he cast,* i.e. forcibly expelled, not however by the scourge which was manifestly insufficient, but either by an authoritative gesture (Origen, Tholuck, Godet), or by the power of His holy personality (Luthardt): cf. xviii. 6. **all** The masculine adjective suggests that the persons are included, though the following clause points only to the animals. If however the former be included it will not be necessary to suppose that Christ ejected them in any other fashion than by driving out their beasts. *Neque dicitur hominibus ictum inflixisse, terrore rem perfecit* (Bengel). **out of the temple** i.e. the forecourt as above explained (ver 14). **both the sheep and the oxen**, epexegetic of the "all," if these were only the animals (Meyer); if the sellers were included (Godet), then the clause depicts the completeness of the expulsion—'the sellers,' not forgetting their beasts, 'both the sheep and the oxen.' **and He poured out** with His own hand **the changers' money** On the word here used for "changers" see ver. 14. **and overthrew their tables** lit., *the tables,* sc. at which they sat, though we can hardly think of Him as "dashing upon the tables hither and thither, and then overturning them" (Lange).

16. **And to them that sold doves he said** Not dealing more mildly with them because the doves were purchased by the poor (De Wette, Brückner), or because He beheld in them the emblem of the Holy Ghost (Stier), but acting with equal severity towards all. **Take these things hence** Being in cages or baskets the pigeons could not be driven, and were not set free because Christ did not contemplate any injury to property. **Make not** Addressed equally to the cattle-dealers, money-changers, and pigeon-sellers. **My Father's House** A clear assertion of His Divine Sonship : cf. v. 17 ; vi. 32 ; x. 29, 36, 37 ; xii. 27, 28 ; the first dawnings of which within the sphere of His consciousness had occurred 18 years before within the same Temple (Luke ii. 49), and the first recognition of which by others had been lately made by Nathanael (i. 49). On the ground of that sublime fact, thus indirectly presented to the minds of His People, Christ claimed to be accepted as Messiah, who, as a Son in His Father's house, had perfect right to vindicate the honour and restore the purity of the desecrated temple. That Christ does not say "Our," but " My" Father, attests His consciousness of being more than a prophet ; that on leaving it for the last time (Matt. xxiii. 38) He calls it 'your house,' draws attention to the fact that it was thenceforth abandoned by the Father and as such given over to desolation. **a house of merchandize** In the Synoptists (Matt. xxi. 13 ; Mark xi. 17) the desecrated Sanctuary is likened to 'a den of robbers' ; as yet it is only styled 'a place of marketing,' *negotiationis* (Vulgate).

17. **His disciples** Those then present (ver. 12) **remembered** Not afterwards at the resurrection (Calvin, Bengel, Olshausen, Tholuck), which would have been mentioned as in ver. 22 (Lücke), but already at the time of the occurrence. **that it was written** lit., *is written*, stands recorded on the page of Scripture, e.g. in Ps. lxix. 10, which, whether composed by David as the Inscription asserts (Tholuck), by Jeremiah (Hitzig, Perowne), or by a writer during the Exile (Meyer), depicts a Theocratic sufferer whose experiences are frequently quoted in the N. T. as typical of those of Messiah (xv. 25 ;

xix. 28 ; Matt. xxvii. 27-30, 34 ; Rom.
xv. 3). **The zeal of thine House** i.e.
the burning or consuming jealousy
which the good man feels for the glory
of God and the holiness of His worship : cf. Rom. x. 2 ; 2 Cor. xi. 2.
shall eat me up Not alluding to
Christ's death (Bengel, Luther, Olshausen, Tholuck), of which the disciples
then had no idea, but to the intensity
of Christ's fervour for His Father's
honour (Calvin, Meyer, Godet, Luthardt, and others).
18. **The Jews** οἱ Ἰουδαῖοι : see on i.
19. **therefore answered** The verb
always conveys the sense of replying
to a question either expressed or implied, the question in this instance
being practically involved in Christ's
action : cf. v. 17 ; xix. 7 ; Matt. xi. 25 ;
xvii. 4 ; xxviii. 5 ; Mark x. 51. **and
said unto Him** disclosing by their
demand "the whole abyss of their
opposing will" (Luthardt). **What
sign** On the word for "sign" see ii.
11. **showest Thou unto us** The
Theocratic propriety of Christ's action
had commended itself to their consciences ; they could not deny that the
Temple stood in need of "purging";
what they wanted to know was
whether He was the proper party to
do it. Altogether ignorant of the
significance of the action itself which
was offered to, and should have been
accepted by them as a sign, they demanded a visible and miraculous token
that He was acting with prophetical
authority : cf. the demand of the
Galileans (vi. 30). **seeing that Thou
doest these things.** i.e. takest upon
Thee this great work of ecclesiastical
reform ; the present tense intimating
that the speakers viewed the act in
question not as an isolated deed, but
as the commencement of a mission.
19. **Jesus answered and said unto
them, Destroy** 1. Either permissive
and hypothetical, meaning, ' If ye shall
destroy' (Bengel, Lücke, B. Crusius,
De Wette, Lange, Tholuck, and others),
*imperativus interdum permissive ex-
ponendus*, as in Matt. viii. 32 ; Luke
viii. 32 (Glass, Phil. Sac. p. 406), which
however is more than doubtful (Winer,
Grammar, § 43, 2). Or 2. imperative,
' Break down ' (Meyer, Godet, Luthardt,
and others), signifying ' Go on as you
are doing and end by breaking down ' ;

which is better, though in point of
fact the difference between the two is
imperceptible. **this temple** This sacred
edifice, this shrine (ναὸν, see ver. 14) ;
alluding not to the material structure
alone, as the Jews mistakenly imagined (Matt. xxvi. 61 ; Mark xiv. 57,
58 ; Acts vi. 14) ; or, even to this as a
symbol of the Jewish religion (Lücke,
De Wette, Reuss, Neander, Olshausen,
and others) ; but rather, as the Evangelist explains, to this as the type and
figure of His body (Calvin, Kuinoel,
Tholuck, Meyer, Luthardt, Godet, and
others), to which however it is unnecessary to suppose that He points,
nutu gestuve, Judaeis non observato
(Bengel). **and in three days** Not
merely ' soon,' ' in a short time,' as in
Hoz. vi. 2, or Luke xiii. 32 ; but in
three literal days. **I will raise it up**
i.e. first the Temple of My Body ;
secondly, with it the Old Jewish Religion, but as much transformed as my
body will be. That the resurrection
of Christ is here ascribed to Himself
does not contradict those passages in
which it is exhibited as the work of the
Father (Matt. xvi. 21 ; Acts ii. 24 ; iv.
10 ; x. 40 ; Rom. iv. 24 ; Eph. i. 20),
since Christ speaks (x. 18) of the
Father's power having been committed
to Him for the purpose of enabling
Him to resume His life ; while it harmonizes with those texts in which He
claims to be the author of His own
resurrection (Matt. xx. 19 ; xxvi. 32 ;
Luke xxvi. 46).
20. **The Jews therefore said** putting
a literal construction on His words.
**Forty and six years was this temple in
building** The renovation and enlargement of the Post-Exilian temple of
Zerubbabel, commenced in the 18th
year of the reign of Herod the Great,
i.e. 20 or 21 B.C., was completed under
Agrippa II. A.D. 64 (Josephus, Antiq.
xv. 11, 1 ; xx. 9, 7). If the forty-six
years, reckoning backwards, date from
the present Passover, i.e. if the work of
reconstruction had suffered no inter-
mission, and was still proceeding, then,
as the 18th year of Herod was from
Nisan 734 to Nisan 735, the present
passover must have fallen in Nisan 780
(Lardner, Friedlieb, Luthardt, Beyschlag) or 781 (Wieseler, Lange, Godet,
Schürer), rather than 782 (Meyer) ;
though, if the building had been some

time stopped, it will be impossible to use this chronological datum, at all events by itself, for the determination of Our Lord's Birth, or even to fix the year of the present Passover (Westcott). **and wilt thou raise it up in three days?** The idea seemed incredible to those literalists who must have sadly forgotten the past history of their people before they could discern an impossibility in the literal resurrection of a material building at the word of one of God's prophets : Hag. i. 14.

21. **But He** In contrast to the Jews who were thinking of something different, and even to His disciples who at the time failed to understand. **spake** i.e. alluded to in what He spake. **of the temple of His body** lit., the temple (ναὸς), His body, the genitive being that of apposition as in xi. 13 ; Rom. iv. 11 ; 2 Cor. v. 5 ; cf. Winer, § 59. 8. That the Evangelist in so saying misinterpreted our Lord's meaning (Herder, Lücke, De Wette, Ewald, and others) is untenable.

22. **When therefore He was raised from the dead** (cf. xx. 1 ; Matt. xxviii. 1 ; Mark xvi. 1 ; Luke xxiv. 1 ; see on ver. 19) **His disciples** i.e. those of them who heard His words. **remembered** Having previously forgotten what had not at the moment of utterance been understood. It is doubtful whether they would know till afterwards that the false witnesses at Christ's trial had not forgotten Christ's declaration (Matt. xxvi. 61). **that He spake this** Concerning the temple, with significant outlook to His own resurrection, and the resuscitation of the new spiritual temple or the Christian Church. **and they believed** " Faith and memory are mutually helpful " : *fides et memoria mutuam opem prestant* (Bengel). **the Scripture** τῇ γραφῇ, the Writing, the O. T. reve-

lation, whose numerous predictions were rendered lucid by the event of Christ's resurrection : cf. Ps. ii. 7 ; xvi. 10 ; lxviii. 18 ; Is. xxvi. 19 ; liii. 7 ; Jonah i. 17 ; all of which are referred to in the N. T. as having testified beforehand of Christ's resurrection : see Matt. xii. 10 ; Acts ii. 27 ; xiii. 5 ; viii. 35 ; 1 Cor. xv. 4 ; Eph. iv. 8 ; 1 Pet. iii. 19. **and the word which Jesus had said** That is, they came more fully to understand its import. *Note :* That the incident here recorded is not the same as that detailed by the Synoptists (Matt. xxi. 12-16 ; Mark xi. 15-19 ; Luke xix. 45, 48) will appear, if it be noticed (1) That the two purgations are represented as having taken place at different times ; this at the first, that at the last passover of Our Lord's Ministry ; (2) That in the two actions many of the details were dissimilar ; in particular, the Synoptists making no mention of a scourge ; (3) That the language employed by Christ to the traders on the second occasion was much more severe than that used in the first instance ; (4) That the second time Christ makes no mention of the breaking down and building up of the temple ; but replies to those who demand to know His authority by a question concerning the baptism of John ; (5) That the design of the two purgations was not the same ; that of the first being to advance His own Messianic pretensions ; of the second to pronounce the condemnation of those by whom these pretensions had been rejected. If more be needed to confirm the correctness of this conclusion, it may be found in the uncertainty of those who identify the two whether it should be placed as in the Fourth Gospel at the commencement (Lücke, De Wette, Ewald, Beyschlag), or as in the Synoptists at the close (Keim) of Christ's Ministry.

HOMILETICS

VER. 12-22—THE PURGING OF THE TEMPLE.

I. **The Symbolic Action** : He "cast all out of the temple," ver. 15. 1. *Appropriate.* Suitable to (1) the place where it was performed, Jerusalem, the Metropolis of the country, the centre of the Theocracy, and the predicted theatre of Messiah's self-revelation (Zech. ii. 10, 11 ; ix. 9) ; (2) the time when it occurred, at the Passover, when the Paschal Lamb of which He was the Antitype and fulfilment was about to be offered, and when the Israelitish people were assembled in large numbers within the Holy City, thus affording a favourable opportunity for impressing the national mind and conscience ; (3) the condition of the temple, whose forecourt which had been wont to be reserved for the sacrificial offerings and other religious exercises of heathen proselytes had been transformed into a common cattle market and pigeon fair, under pretence of religion,—a melancholy because faithful picture of the secularization which under the *régime* of the Pharisees had overtaken that religion of which the temple was the seat and sign ; (4) the character of Him by whom it was carried through. The Messiah, who in all that He did claimed to act as His Father's Son and to be inspired with holy zeal for His Father's house : ver. 16. 2. *Supernatural.* Though not usually reckoned among Christ's miracles, the expulsion of the traders was as much the effect of Christ's superhuman character as the transformation of the wine was of His superhuman power. The manifest insufficiency of the means employed leaves no room for doubt that the occurrence belonged to the same category as the incident which happened in Gethsemane (xviii. 6). At the same time the suddenness of Christ's action may have surprised, and an inward consciousness of guilt paralyzed, the traders, thus rendering their ejection from the sanctuary the combined result of causes both natural and supernatural. 3. *Significant.* Designed to be a revelation to the Ecclesiastical Authorities of the day as to who He was and what He had come to do (Ps. lxix. 9 ; Mal. iii. 2, 6), it was a practical proclamation of His Messiahship. Nor does it militate against this to say that "it could not be so understood by the people" (Weiss, Life of Christ, vol. ii. p. 5, C.F.T.L.), since it was not addressed directly to them but to their rulers. 4. *Suggestive.* Recalling to the minds of the disciples the words of the Psalmist, it confirmed the views they already entertained concerning Christ's Messiahship. If they did not require to deduce this from either His action (ver. 15) or His utterance (ver. 16), because they already knew it (Weiss), it would at least help to verify the correctness of their belief to perceive that both Christ's deed and word were foreshadowed in the language of ancient Scripture. 5. *Alarming.* It startled the Sanhedrim, who recognized perfectly the Messianic character of the action, but wanted to know whether He was the Messianic King for whom they were looking. Secretly they must have dreaded that He was. But because He was wholly another sort of Messiah than they had been expecting, they declined to receive Him, at least without investigation. They trifled with their consciences by asking "a sign." They temporized, they delayed, they refused to go forward, they drew back. They saw the Light, dimly it is true ; but they preferred the darkness ; they beheld the glory of the Incarnate Word, but did not care to believe.

II. **The Mysterious Sign :** "Destroy this temple, etc.," ver. 19. A word 1. *Enigmatical ;* conveying one thing to the ear and understanding of reason and unbelief, another thing to the insight of faith. Under the figure of a destroyed and rebuilded temple Christ announced that his Death, brought about by them, and His Resurrection, effected by Himself, would be to them an adequate legitimation of His present action and an ample demonstration of who He was. The same sign he subsequently gave them in Galilee, calling it the sign of the prophet Jonas (Matt. xii. 40). 2. *Misunderstood.* (1) By the Pharisees ; through slavish adherence to the letter of Scripture (2 Cor. iii. 6), spiritual blindness occasioned by hypocrisy (Mark iii. 25 ; Rom. xi. 25), and positive aversion arising from inward moral corruption (iii. 20 ; viii. 43, 44. (2) By the disciples ; through imperfect knowledge, and immature faith ; for though already they had begun to see the Light, like men whose eyes have just been opened, they were as yet unable accurately to discern the objects the light revealed (Mark viii. 24). 3. *Memorable.* Hid away in the storehouse of their recollections, this word never dropped entirely out of view of the disciples. It recurred to them after Christ's resurrection, when it suddenly became illuminated by the stupendous fact to which it pointed, and thus finally helped to seal their faith in the crucified and risen Jesus as The Messiah of Israel, The Son of God and The Saviour of Mankind (Acts iv. 10 ; xxvi. 23 ; Rom. i. 4 ; iv. 25 ; 1 Pet. i. 3).

Lessons. The duty and privilege of observing the ordinances of religion—Christ at the Passover. 2. The need of purity and order in all matters connected with God's sanctuary—Christ purging the temple court. 3. The danger of a worldly spirit intruding into the domain of religion—the traders in the sacred edifice. 4. The propriety of being zealously affected in the Divine service—the example of Christ. 5. The complete ability of Christ to justify all His ways before God and man—Christ's readiness to furnish a " Sign." 6. The irrefragable certainty of Christ's death and resurrection—attested by the knowledge and experience of His disciples. 7. The veiled secret of Holy Scripture—the testimony of Jesus Christ. The incomparable blindness of unbelief—seen in the Pharisees. 9. The blessedness of faith which rejoices in the Light and advances in the power of seeing.

2. TO THE INHABITANTS OF THE CITY

CHAP. II. VER. 23-25

EXPOSITION

Ver. 23. **Now** δὲ: introducing a contrast to the preceding narrative of Christ's rejection, as well as forming a transition to the next recorded interview with Nicodemus. **when He was in Jerusalem** if not in the temple, at least in the Holy City ; ἐν in this place being *local*. **at the Passover** i.e. during the Holy Week as distinguished from the preceding day : cf. ver. 13 ; vi. 4 ; xi. 55 ; xii. 1 ; xiii. 1 ; a note of time, ἐν now being *temporal*. **during the feast** lit., *in the feast;* while engaged in its celebration ; a note of the surrounding circumstances, with special reference to either (1) Christ Himself as having been so occupied (Meyer, Lange), (2) the Nation as then at the height of its jubilation (Westcott), (3) the City as at such a season the theatre on which the whole nation assembled (Godet), or the particular moment which may thus be more closely defined (Luthardt), as the very night of the Paschal Supper (Milligan and Moulton). **many** individuals as opposed to the collective body of the nation ; private persons as distinguished from the representative authorities of Judaism ; comprising non-Judean and especially Galilean visitors to the Holy City (iv. 45), but not excluding the inhabitants of Jerusalem. **believed on His Name** see on i. 12. Unlike the Rulers who rejected Christ's Messianic pretensions, these accepted them not at first decisively or even firmly, perhaps doubtfully and hesitatingly, but still honestly

and sincerely. If ' milk faith ' (Luther) it was still faith ; imperfect or immature faith (Westcott) ; hardly to be characterized as " unbelief in the form of belief " (Luthardt), or as " faith not really of the essence of faith " (Godet). **beholding** marking that to which their incipient belief was attributable (Westcott), if not proclaiming it to have as little duration as the sight (Godet)—an inference the words do not justify. **His signs** see ii. 11 ; and compare iii. 2. The miracles of this period are unrecorded. **which He did** ἃ ἐποίει, which He kept on doing from time to time; ὅσα ἐποίησεν (iv. 45) regards these same miracles as historically completed.

24. **But Jesus** Another antithesis. While the many believed, He on His part, which is the force of αὐτὸς, did **not trust Himself to them** The repetition of πιστεύειν is neither a play on the word (Lücke, De Wette, Brückner), nor a mere coincidence in sound (B. Crusius), but either an intentional antithesis (Meyer) or an illustration of the simplicity of John's style (Alford). The import of the word is that Christ did not respond to the upward movement of the popular faith by trusting, not His doctrine (Chrysostom, Bengel, Kuinoel) or His work (Ebrard), but Himself to them ; meaning not that He did not offer Himself to them as Messiah (Lange), but that He refrained from closer personal intercourse with them (Lampe, Meyer), did not treat

them as disciples (Alford, Godet). for that stating the reason of this singular reserve. **He** emphatic. He, Himself and of Himself. **knew** i. 42, 48. **all men** of both sexes, and of all ages and conditions. **and because He needed not that** negative expression of preceding thought; construction same as in i. 27 : cf. xvi. 30 ; 1 John ii. 27. **any one should bear witness concerning man** lit., *the man ;* not Christ Himself (Ewald), but the person with whom Christ had to do. **for He Himself knew what was in man** His knowledge of the individual was original, intuitive, penetrating, complete. It embraced the circuit of his goings ; it reached to the centre of his thinkings.

HOMILETICS

VER. 23-25.—THE FIRST JERUSALEM BELIEVERS.

I. **The Object of their Faith**—*The Name* of Christ : ver. 23. The name of anything being that by which it is known in whole or in part, the name of Christ presented in Scripture as the object of faith can only signify that revelation of the Saviour which at any time is proposed for faith's acceptance. Hence faith may vary in its clearness at different ages of the world, in different persons belonging to the same age, and even in the same individual at different times, according as the object to which it looks is fully unveiled or distinctly apprehended. Faith can never travel beyond the bounds of the testimony to which it looks and on which it rests. What was offered as an object of faith to Abraham was a Saviour to come (viii. 56); to his descendants a Saviour come ; to John's disciples Christ as the Lamb of God (i. 29); to Nathanael Christ as the King of Israel and the Son of God (i. 49) ; to the rulers in the Temple and the people in the city Christ had as yet presented Himself only in the character of Messiah. As such He had been rejected by the former and was now accepted by the latter. The same name of Christ, now completely unveiled, is still faith's object (Acts iii. 16 ; iv. 12).

II. **The Ground of their Faith**—*The Miracles* of Christ : ver. 23. Called "signs," they were visible pictures of the work Christ as Messiah had come to accomplish (see on ii. 11), as well as attestations of the Divine mission of their Worker (iii. 2 ; Acts x. 38). In this sense the Cana miracle, the temple cleansing, and the wonders performed at the feast were signs. In the same manner still the miracles of Jesus are helps to faith in the name of Jesus. They operate as obstacles to faith only when considered as à priori impossibilities. That miracles are not now continued is because they are no longer necessary, having been superseded on the one hand by a complete historical revelation of the Incarnate Son, and on the other hand by a conscious Indwelling of the Holy Ghost in the hearts of believers.

III. **The Character of their Faith**—1. *Sincere :* so far as it went. At least the contrary cannot be inferred from the words of the Evangelist. If afterwards those Jews who took up stones to kill Jesus (viii. 59) are said to have believed Him (viii. 31), the meaning is that inwardly they were persuaded of His Messiahship, which constituted the damning character of their crime. Besides some who now believed in Christ's name at a subsequent period attached themselves to Christ's person as disciples (iv. 45). 2. *Incomplete :* inasmuch as it went not far enough. Resting satisfied with intellectual acknowledgement of Christ's Messiahship, it passed not on to moral and spiritual surrender of the being to His authority and sway. It had taken the preliminary step of believing on Christ's name ; it wanted that additional of trusting in His person. 3. *Superficial :* in that it was occasioned chiefly by the impression made upon their hearts by His miracles, and was liable in consequence to disappear when that impression faded.

IV. **The Treatment of their Faith**—1. *The Nature of it :* Reserve : ver. 24. He did not trust Himself to them, enter into close spiritual relations with them, unite them to Himself as disciples, give Himself over to them in the capacity of Master, Teacher, Saviour, Friend. When Christ puts Himself into the hands of a believing soul, the result is Salvation and Eternal Life (vi. 50-54). 2. *The Reason of it:* Insight : ver. 24, 25. He knew what was in them, saw they had not fully surrendered themselves to Him, had not put themselves into His hand. When a soul does so, the act of faith is complete. Christ's knowledge of the human heart was the deepest ground of the different treatment accorded to the Baptist's disciples (i. 38-51) and the Jerusalem believers ; and that knowledge was (1) immediate, instantaneous, intuitive—"He knew" at a glance, without long observation or careful ratiocination (vi. 64 ; xiii. 1 ; Luke vi. 8 ; Acts i. 24 ; Heb. iv. 13) ; (2) original, underived, of Himself and in virtue of His own power —"He Himself knew" (Col. ii. 13 ; Rev. ii. 18); (3) universal, extending to all men.—"He knew all" (xvi. 30 ; xviii. 4 ; xxi. 17) ; (4) particular, descending to individuals, "He needed not that any one should bear witness concerning *the* man" (iv. 29 ; v. 42 ; xiii. 11 ; xx. 27); and (5) complete, embracing all that was in man, "He Himself knew what was in man" (i. 48 ; vi. 64 ; Rev. ii. 23 ; Luke v. 22).

Lessons. 1. Christ commonly obtains a readier welcome from lowly people than from the dignitaries of either church or state. 2. No faith is of the right sort that does not look to the right object. 3. Faith may sometimes look to the right object and yet be exceedingly defective. 4. The soul that would fully enjoy Christ's fellowship must study to have perfect faith. 5. All faith is incomplete that stops short of trusting in Christ's person. 6. Christ knows precisely the quality and quantity of every man's faith. 7. He who would have Christ trust Himself to him must first trust himself to Christ.

3. TO NICODEMUS : CONVERSATION ON THE NEW BIRTH

Chap. III. Ver. 1-21

Exposition

Chap. iii. ver. 1. **Now** The following narrative connects with the preceding as supplying not a type of outwardly believing yet inwardly unbelieving Judaism (Baur), but an example of the beginnings of faith described in the foregoing section (Tholuck), an instance of Christ's higher knowledge of the human heart (Lücke), or both ; perhaps also as marking a transition from Christ's dealings with the multitude to His treatment of an individual (Luthardt), and furnishing an exception to the general rule of reserve maintained towards the former (Westcott). **there was a man** Pointing back to ii. 25, and presenting Nicodemus as a specimen of that human race (ἄνθρωπος) which Christ knew. **of the Pharisees** see on i. 24 ; and cf. Acts xxv. 5. **named Nicodemus** cf. vii. 50 ; xix. 39 ; a name of Greek origin frequent among the Jews. The Talmud mentions a *Nakedimon ben Gorion* who survived the destruction of Jerusalem, was recognized as a disciple of Christ, and traditionally identified as Christ's nocturnal visitor. That this

was he, though possible, is still uncertain. **a ruler of the Jews** ἄρχων, one who holds the first place, hence a chief person, or ruler ; here applied to individuals of weight and influence among the Pharisees (and other sects at Jerusalem) who were also members of the Sanhedrim (vii. 26, 48 ; xii. 42 ; Acts iii. 17 ; iv. 5, 8 ; xiii. 37). On the Sanhedrim, see i. 19.

2. **The same** οὗτος ; not, 'this one', a Pharisee and ruler of the Jews' (Stier), but merely "a repetition in hastening to what follows" (Luthardt): cf. i. 7, 33 ; iii. 36 ; vii. 18. **came** Presumably alone, though it is doubtful whether Christ was alone during the interview (De Wette), and not rather attended by His disciples (Meyer, Luthardt). Without sufficient reason this narrative has been pronounced 'a poetical, free and highly spiritualized reproduction" (De Wette), representing the believing and yet really unbelieving Judaism (Baur), showing how Christianity essentially distinguished itself from Judaism (Hilgenfeld), exhibiting

the power of Christianity to triumph over the slowness of the heart and the prejudices of the learned (Scholten), and designed to refute the idea that Christianity prevailed only among the common people (Strauss). **unto Him** viz., *Jesus;* the Textus Receptus, after Griesbach, reading " unto Jesus," πρὸς τὸν Ἰησοῦν. **by night** " A characteristic memorial of the state of Nicodemus's heart at the time " (?) (Hengstenberg) ; perhaps only a sign of timidity and caution on the part of one who was both afraid of his colleagues and unwilling to accord more authority to the young teacher than he yet possessed (Godet) ; certainly not an evidence that Nicodemus was a hypocrite who affected simplicity in order to entrap the Saviour (Koppe). **and said unto Him** " the learned talking with the unlearned " (Luthardt), " an educated man of age sitting as pupil to a young, untitled Rabbi " (Lange). **Rabbi** A mark of respect and sincerity on the part of Nicodemus, who thereby acknowledged Christ's dignity : see on i. 38. **We know** With perhaps a touch of official pride he alludes, it may be supposed, to persons of a like mind with himself, *ego et mei similes* (Bengel), amongst his colleagues (Godet) or amongst those who believed because they saw His miracles (Hengstenberg), though Nicodemus, being a ruler of the Jews, was hardly likely to appear as their representative (Alford). **that thou art a teacher come from God** lit., *that from God thou art come a teacher;* the first clause, ἀπὸ θεοῦ (cf. i. 6, παρὰ θεοῦ) recognizing Christ's authority as that of one divinely commissioned in contrast to those who emanated from the schools of the Rabbis, holding the regularly granted doctor's diploma ; the second, ἐλήλυθας (cf. i. 15 ; vii. 42), covertly adverting to the pretensions of Christ as 'The Coming One ' (vi. 14 ; xi. 27; Matt. xi. 3 ; xxi. 9 ; Luke vii. 19, 20), a quasi-admission of, and half-belief in, Christ's Messiahship ; and the third, διδάσκαλος (xi. 28 ; xiii. 13, 14), betraying a secret uneasiness lest he should have gone too far with his concessions, and a desire to neutralize their force by explaining that all he meant was merely a recognition of Christ's prophetic, as distinguished from his Messianic, character. After

this the language of Nicodemus dwindles down into feebleness. **for no man can do these signs** (see ii. 11) **that Thou doest** A valuable testimony to the reality of Christ's miracles. **except God be with him** A truism (see Num. xiv. 22 ; Deut. xi. 3 ; Judg. vi. 13 ; John xv. 5 ; Acts xix. 11 ; 1 Cor. xii. 10) which hardly required statement in the circumstances. Still it showed the signs Christ supplied in His miracles were, in part at least, correctly understood by Nicodemus, and the miracles accepted by him as irrefragable proofs of Christ's heavenly commission.

3. **Jesus answered** Replying either (1) to his *words*, in an unreported conversation (Kuinoel) or in the statement just narrated ; wishing to convince Nicodemus who imagined he had made a great confession in his first words that he had not yet so much as entered the porticoes of true knowledge (Chrysostom), or to lead him on from faith in miracles to faith which works a moral change (Augustine), or to intimate that He, Christ, was more than a teacher, even a moral reformer (Cyril, Theophylact), or to explain that He was much more than come from God, since even the man who would see the kingdom of God must be born from above (Lange) ; or (2) to his *thoughts*, which were palpably directed towards the Messianic kingdom, the opening of which he may have fancied he had witnessed in the miracles Christ had wrought (Lightfoot, Lücke, Luthardt) ; perhaps desiring to know whether that kingdom were as near as it seemed (Godet) and what were the terms of its membership (Meyer) ; or (3) to his *disposition*, which was that not alone of timid hesitation conjoined with secret anxiety to learn, but also of supercilious haughtiness combined with a flavour of duplicity, rendering him, though half convinced, unwilling to make open confession of his convictions. **and said unto him**—without according him the title Rabbi !— (Matt. xxiii. 8). **Verily, verily** See i. 51. Here twice repeated to arrest attention and foreshadow the importance of what was on the eve of being proclaimed. **I say** A majestic antithesis to the Rabbi's " we know " (Lange). **unto thee** who art a Master

in Israel : ver. 10. **except a man** τις, any one. **be born anew** ἄνωθεν ; either (1) *from above* (ver. 31 ; xix. 11, 23 ; Matt. xxvii. 51 ; Mark xv. 38 ; Jas. i. 17 ; iii. 15), the opposite of κάτωθεν, and the equivalent of ἐκ τῶν ἄνω (viii. 23), ἐκ τοῦ θεοῦ (1 John ii. 29 ; iii. 9 ; iv. 7 ; v. 1), with reference to the supernatural origin of regeneration (Origen, Cyril, Bengel, Lücke, De Wette, Meyer, and others) ; or (2) what seems demanded by the reply of Nicodemus, *from the beginning* (Luke i. 3 ; Acts xxvi. 5 ; Gal. iv. 9) with allusion to the completeness of the moral transformation implied in the new birth (Vulgate, Augustine, Luther, Calvin, Tholuck, Luthardt, Godet, Westcott, and others). **he cannot** Not because of physical defect or external constraint, but because of the moral characteristics of the individual (ver. 6, 19 ; viii. 44). **see,** enjoy, participate in, understand, have any conception of (1 Cor. ii. 14) ; all of which ideas are included in the 'entering,' εἰσελθεῖν (ver. 5), with which this 'seeing,' ἰδεῖν, is synonymous. **the kingdom of God** An expression occurring only elsewhere in ver. 5,—an indirect proof of the historicity of the narrative (Godet, Meyer); though frequently appearing in the Synoptists (Matt. vi. 33 ; Mark i. 15 ; Luke xiii. 18), the first of whom also employs the corresponding phrase 'The kingdom of heaven' (Matt. iii. 2 ; iv. 17 ; xi. 12). Both expressions point to a reign of God in, through, and over men ; the former indicating its source and end (xviii. 36), the latter its nature and character (Matt. v. 3) ; the one contrasting it with the kingdom of the devil (Matt. xii. 26), the other opposing it to the kingdom of the world (Rev. xi. 15).

4. **Nicodemus saith unto Him** Neither desiring to entangle Jesus in His talk (Luther), nor purposely ridiculing Christ's statement by accepting it in a literal sense in order to expose its absurdity (Riggenbach), nor stupidly misunderstanding Christ's words (Reuss), nor speaking ironically (Godet), or under excitement (Bengel), certainly not wittily (Lange) ; but with perfect sincerity, as one in grave perplexity (Meyer), giving expression to his amazement (Milligan and Moulton), and his overwhelming sense of the impossi-

bility of complying with Christ's demand (Westcott). **How can a man be born when he is old ?** It can hardly be that Nicodemus misapprehended Our Lord's meaning (Meyer, Brückner), or intended to emphasize the incomprehensibility of Our Lord's saying, as thus—"If the repetition of corporeal birth be so utterly impossible, how am I to understand thy saying about the new birth?" (Lücke), or suggested that what Christ demanded was as impossible as for an old man to be a second time born (Tholuck, Hengstenberg) ; it may be that he desired to express his conviction that such a moral and spiritual transformation as required a fresh start in life was impossible to one who was old (Luthardt, Lange, Westcott, and others). **can he enter a second time into his mother's womb and be born ?** According to Nicodemus such a change as Christ pointed to was possible only as the result of a second natural birth or was impossible because a second natural birth was impossible.

5. **Jesus answered** explaining more fully the import of the New Birth— **Verily, verily, I say unto thee** The repetition of this formula marks the calm confidence of Christ. **Except a man be born of water and of the Spirit** The two phrases are exegetical of ἄνωθεν. In the first, the term 'water' is not, directly at least, a symbol of the Holy Ghost, with allusion to its purifying influences (Calvin), or the element of the soul purified by true repentance (Olshausen), or a pointing to the symbolic meaning of the water of baptism (Lücke), but simply the water of baptism itself (Brückner, Meyer, Godet, Westcott, and others), with which Nicodemus was familiar, both in John's baptism and in the baptism of Jewish proselytes (see Schürer, The Jewish People in the Time of Christ, vol. ii. § 31 ; Riehm's Handwörterbuch des Biblischen Altertums, art. *Proselyten ;* Kitto's Biblical Cyclopaedia, art. *Proselyte*). In the second, the term 'Spirit' denotes the Holy Ghost with whom John said the Messiah was to baptize (i. 33), and who in Scripture is represented as the author of the soul's renewal and sanctification (Ezek. xxvi. 26, 27 ; Ps. li. 11 ; John vi. 63 ; Tit. iii. 5 ; 2 Thess. ii. 13 ; 1 Pet. i. 2). The first, 'water,'

is the *causa medians;* the second, 'Spirit,' the *causa efficiens,* of the palingenesia of the soul. The one symbolizes the soul's purification (1 John v. 6, 8); the other effects the soul's quickening (vi. 63); and the combination of the two perhaps points back to the primeval creation when the Spirit shaped a material cosmos out of the formless abyss of waters (Gen. i. 3). **he cannot enter into the kingdom of God** The word 'enter,' εἰσελθεῖν, substantially equivalent to 'see,' ἰδεῖν (ver. 3) fixes attention on the passage 'into' rather than the enjoyment of the kingdom, which is again defined as 'of God' rather than 'of heaven' (codex ℵ*),

6. That which is (or, has been) **born** The neuter, τὸ γεγεννημένον, indicates that, although relating to persons, it is the abstract product, not that product as individualized of which Christ speaks. **of the flesh** ἐκ τῆς σαρκὸς ; the preposition marking the source which is declared to be human nature, body, and soul, considered as fallen and influenced by moral impulses proceeding from sin : see on i. 13. **is flesh** i.e. partakes of the nature of that from which it springs ; in the sphere of the natural everything produces according to its kind (Gen. i. 24). The addition "because it is born of the flesh" found in some Western MSS. is to be rejected. **and that which is** (or, has been) **born of the Spirit** The spiritual production as such, that whose moral and spiritual nature has proceeded from the Holy Ghost, ἐκ τοῦ Πνεύματος. **is spirit** i.e. a being of spiritual nature and therefore permeated by the life as well as under the dominion of the Holy Ghost. The words "because God is spirit," "it is born of God," "because it is spirit," contained in some documents are, as above, to be rejected.

7. Marvel not that I said unto thee cf. v. 28. It is not necessary to suppose that Christ observed a look of astonishment depicted on the countenance of his listener, since such astonishment had already been expressed in that listener's words. **Ye must be born anew.** If the verb 'must' emphasizes the indispensable necessity of a new birth for every individual member of the race, with equal precision the pronoun 'ye' excludes Christ from the sweep of such necessity.

8. The wind τὸ πνεῦμα : not the Spirit (Origen, Augustine, Bengel), but the air, a frequent symbol of the Holy Ghost (Ezek. xxxvii. 9 ; Acts iv. 31 ; ii. 2). **bloweth** The evening wind may at the moment have been heard whispering outside the tent in which Christ and Nicodemus talked. **where it listeth** or, *wills;* scarcely accurate from a scientific point of view, the atmospheric ocean being as much under the dominion of law as any other portion of the universe. The language however implies nothing more than the impossibility, in each particular instance in which an air current is set in motion, of determining precisely the point at which the phenomenon is started or that at which it ends (Godet). **and thou hearest the voice thereof**—the sound of its soft movement : a beautiful prosopopoeia. **but knowest not whence it cometh** i.e. the first point of its departure. **and whither it goeth** Eccles. xi. 5 ; to be understood as above. **So is every one that is born of the Spirit.** Not 'of water and of the Spirit' (ℵ) ; "a good example of a natural corruption of the text by assimilation" (Westcott).

9. Nicodemus answered and said unto Him No longer in frivolity or pride (Olshausen), but in spiritual ignorance (Godet, Meyer), arising from imperfect credence of Christ's Testimony (ver. 12). **How can these things be** lit., *how can these things come to pass,* πῶς δύναται γενέσθαι, *fieri* (Vulgate), the emphasis lying rather on 'how' (Lange, Brückner, Milligan and Moulton), than on 'can' (Meyer, Lücke, Westcott), and suggesting that, while the speaker conceded the necessity of a new birth, he still failed to discern the manner in which it was to be realized or brought about (Luthardt).

10. Jesus answered and said unto him, manifesting in turn an astonishment more natural and just than that Nicodemus had displayed. **Art thou the teacher of Israel** ὁ διδάσκαλος ; the well-known and recognized teacher, "the representative of the Israelitish doctorate" (Godet), as Melancthon was styled *doctor Germaniae* (Brückner), the teacher by pre-eminence, *ille doctor cujus tam celebris est opinio* (Erasmus, Lücke), *doctor plurimorum auditorum veteranus, et ceteris, corruptissimis, ali-*

quantum melior (Bengel); though Christ may have intended nothing more than 'the teacher' as distinguished from 'the scholars' he taught, the article being rhetorical as in ὁ λύχνος, ver. 34 : cf. Winer's Grammar, § 18. 8. **and understandest not these things?** Without either irony in the article or indignation in the question (Meyer), the words expressed a degree of wonder that one whose professional studies had brought him into close contact with the Scriptures had not been able to recognize the truth of Christ's teaching. The doctrine of a new birth was according to Jesus exhibited in O. T. Scripture, though this has by some theologians (Pelagius, Socinus) and philosophers (Kant, Wegscheider) been denied. But (1) the doctrine of a fall implies it, especially when viewed in connection with the Divine purity or holiness as the only moral standard for humanity (Gen. xvii. 1 ; Ex. xxii. 31 ; Lev. xi. 44 ; Ps. xxiv. 3, 4 ; Is. xxxv. 8). (2) The O. T. Scriptures, as an indispensable qualification for serving God, required circumcision of the heart (Deut. x. 16 ; xxx. 6) which was symbolized then by circumcision (Rom. ii. 29), as in the Christian Church it is by Baptism (1 Pet. iii. 21). (3) It was prefigured in the change of heart conferred on Saul and David, when they ascended the Israelitish throne (1 Sam. x. 9 ; xvi. 13). (4) It was recognized in David's prayer for purity (Ps. li. 10). (5) It was expressly promised as a Messianic blessing (Ezek. xi. 19 ; xviii. 31 ; xxxvi. 26 ; Jer. iv. 4 ; xxxi. 33). (6) Even the term "Regeneration" was not unknown to Hebrew Scripture (Job. xi. 12 ; Ps. lxxxvii. 5).

11. **Verily, verily, I say unto thee** Repeated for the third time (see on i. 51), this formula introduces another sublime disclosure of truth on the part of Jesus, who now, in contrast to Nicodemus, quietly assumes the function, if not the designation already given Him (ver. 2), of Rabbi, though in doing so, He practically distinguishes Himself from His auditor as a teacher of another sort. **We** not Christ and John the Baptist (Weiss, Hofmann, Luthardt), or Christ and the prophets (Beza, Luther, Calvin, Tholuck), or Christ and God (Chrysostom), or Christ and the Holy Ghost (Bengel, Besser) ;

but either Christ and His disciples as representing a specifically new form of teaching (Hengstenberg, Godet, Westcott), or, what seems preferable, Christ Himself (De Wette, Brückner, Lücke, Ewald, Meyer), although the employment of the rhetorical "We," the *pluralis majestaticus,* is certainly unusual in the mouth of Christ. **speak that we do know, and bear witness of that we have seen.** The first verb refers to Christ's oral publication of truth (ver. 31, 34 ; vi. 63 ; vii. 18); the third to His attestation of truth as a personal experience (ver. 32 ; 1 John i. 2 ; Rev. i. 2). The second verb marks Christ's knowledge as certain and absolute (vii. 29 ; viii. 55 ; xxi. 17); the fourth as immediate and direct (viii. 38 ; 1 John i. 1, 3 ; Rev. i. 7). **and ye** Nicodemus first and behind him 'The Jews'; though these need not be supposed to have been amongst Christ's auditors (Olshausen). **receive not** cf. ver. 32 ; v. 34 ; xii. 48 ; xvii. 8 ; 1 John v. 9. **our witness** As John had witnessed of Christ (i. 7, 8), so Christ, as the Faithful and True Witness (Rev. iii. 14) testified of God, and in particular of God's kingdom ; of the condition of entrance into it—a new birth ; and of the means of attaining it, faith, or a believing reception of His testimony.

12. **If** = Since : cf. vii. 23 ; xiii. 17 ; Matt. vi. 30. **I** Not they, i.e. the prophets as if εἶπον had been a 3rd pers. plu. (Ewald), in which case "I," ἐγώ, would probably have stood in the apodosis (Matt. v. 22, 28, 32, 34); but Christ Himself. **told you** sc. in the words just spoken, **earthly things** Alluding neither to the parable of the wind (Beza), nor to the comparison of regeneration to a birth (Grotius), nor to doctrines easily understood as distinguished from such as are unsearchable and profound (Lücke, Reuss), nor to moral things in which man's faith is active, whereas in heavenly things it is passive (De Wette, B. Crusius) ; but to things that, having their seat and sphere of operation on the earth, can be verified by the human consciousness (as e.g. regeneration), "the shape and realization of the kingdom of God as it belongs to earth" (Luthardt). **and ye believe not** i.e. receive not my testimony concerning them (ver. 11);

faith being the moral and spiritual act in which the reception of Christ's testimony culminates. **how shall ye believe** Christ opposes His "How" to that of Nicodemus (ver. 4, 9). **if I tell you of heavenly things.** These were the higher mysteries of God's kingdom which, finding their appropriate origin and province in the heavenly world, cannot be excogitated by man, but must be brought down to him from above, such doctrines as Christ had come to promulgate and now proceeds to divulge.

13. And Either adversative, 'yet' (Olshausen, Godet), or demonstrative, 'for' (Beza, Tholuck, Luthardt), or concessive, 'indeed' (B. Crusius), or simply continuative, 'and' (Brückner, Meyer, Westcott); the sense in each case being practically the same. **no man hath ascended into heaven** Not alluding to the actual resurrection of Christ, which was yet future, as if the meaning were 'No man will ascend' (Augustine, Bengel, Stier); or to an ecclesiastical ascension, like the rapture of Paul, 2 Cor. xii. 2 (Socinus); or to a tropical ascension by means of spiritual perception so as to bring down and reveal truth : cf. Deut. xxx. 11, 12 ; Prov. xxx. 4 ; Rom. x. 6 ; Baruch iii. 29 (Grotius, Kuinoel, Lücke, Olshausen, De Wette, B. Crusius, Ewald); nor simply equivalent to 'No man was in heaven' (Meyer, Tholuck), but categorically stating that no man had ever ascended into celestial regions so as to be able to return with those heavenly things of which he had spoken (Godet, Luthardt, Westcott, and others). The intended inference is that he who could unfold such heavenly things must himself be a heavenly Being. **but he that descended out of heaven** Implying *pre-existence* in the heavenly world and an actual descent into the world of time by means of an *Incarnation* (ver. 31 ; vi. 33, 38, 42), but not a previous ascension ; εἰ μὴ not requiring another ἀναβέβηκε, of which ὁ καταβάς should be the subject. A better supplement would be ἐξηγήσατο (i. 18), "hath declared," *even* **the Son of Man** (see on i. 51) **who is in heaven.** Omitted (אּ B L T b); wanting (Eusebius, Nazianzen, and Origen); deleted (Tischendorf, Westcott and Hort, Luthardt), as an early gloss

designed to bring out the contrast between Christ's earthly life of humiliation and His perpetual divine abiding in heaven ; retained (Lücke, Meyer, Godet) on the ground that they might easily have been regarded as superfluous or objectionable, and so at an early date removed from the text ; explained not by changing "is" into "was" (Erasmus, Luthardt), but by understanding Christ to say that although He had descended out of (ἐκ) heaven, He had not locally left that eternal and supersensible sphere, but, while the Son of man upon the earth, was also ὁ ὢν ἐν τῷ οὐρανῷ : cf. i. 18.

14. And Variously interpreted as indicating an advance from (1) the mention to the actual communication of the heavenly things (Tholuck), which however is practically begun in the preceding verse ; (2) from the possibility to the necessity of imparting those heavenly things (Lücke), (3) from the ground to the blessedness of faith (Meyer), (4) from the descent to the exaltation of Christ (Luthardt), (5) from the Word to His manifestation (Olshausen), (6) from present want to future rise of faith (Jacobi), (7) from the work to the person of Christ (B. Crusius, Stier) ; but it manifestly points to a continuation of those heavenly things of which Christ has begun to speak (Godet, Lange, Hengstenberg, Alford, Westcott). **as Moses** cf. i. 17. "The first mention of Moses made by Christ" (Bengel). **lifted up the serpent in the wilderness** See Num. xxi. 8 ; Christ's words are an authentication of this part, and so far by implication of the whole, of the Mosaic narrative. **even so** καθὼς... οὕτως ; as...so ; indicating that Christ's elevation was to be after the manner not of Solomon's enthronization, but of the brazen serpent's impalement on the pole. **must** The resemblance between the two events was not a fortuitous but a necessary correspondence—necessary (1) typically to fulfil Scripture prophecy, (2) eternally to execute the divine decree of which the typical emblem was only a manifestation ; cf. Matt. xvi. 21 ; Luke xxiv. 26 ; and (3) ethically, "to satisfy the moral necessities known only to God of which this decree itself is the result" (Godet). **the Son of Man** See on i. 51. The selection of this name may have been designed to suggest that "it is on the complete homogeneousness of His nature with ours that the mysterious substitution proclaimed in the verse rests" (Godet). **be lifted up** ὑψωθῆναι, *exaltari* (Vulgate)—used of the passion (viii. 28 ; xii. 32, 34), and also of the subsequent ascension (Acts ii. 33 ; v. 31)—does not here mean the glorification of Christ either actually by His ascension (Bleek), or ideally in the thoughts of His people (Paulus), but His elevation on the cross (Meyer, Godet, Luthardt, and others), as the preliminary step to His assumption of the throne. **that**—introducing the purpose contemplated in Christ's 'lifting up'—**whosoever** Not of Israel alone, nor of the elect alone, but of humanity. **believeth** Faith, the moral act of which the look towards the serpent was the type. Hence the words 'in Him' or 'on Him' are usually connected with 'believeth.' **may in him** i.e. resting on, trusting in, identified with Him : vi. 56; x. 38; xv. 5; 1 John ii. 6; cf. 1 Cor. viii. 6 ; Eph. i. 4 ; Phil. iii. 9 ; Col. ii. 10. **have** as a present possession, not merely as a future inheritance : iii. 36; v. 24 ; vi. 47 ; xx. 31 ; 1 John v. 12, 13. **Eternal Life** ζωὴ αἰώνιος : Aeonian Life (ver. 16, 36 ; iv. 14, 36 ; v. 24, 39 ; vi. 27, 40, 47, 54, 68 ; x. 28 ; xii. 25, 50 ; xvii. 2, 3; 1 John i. 2 ; ii. 25 ; iii. 15 ; v. 11, 13, 20; cf. Matt. xix. 16, 29 ; xxv. 46 ; Mark x. 17, 30 ; Luke x. 25 ; xviii. 18, 30 ; Acts xiii. 46, 48 ; Rom. ii. 7 ; v. 21 ; vi. 22, 23), the Johannine synonym for salvation, meaning life belonging not to this transitory state, but to that permanent condition of existence which Christ, in whom it was original and underived (i. 3), has introduced to men, and which, according to Him, consists in the contemplative knowledge of God (xvii. 2). The clause "might not perish, but," μὴ ἀπόληται ἀλλ', wanting in best codices (א B L Tᵇ and others) is by eminent authorities (Tischendorf, Westcott, Meyer, Alford) retained.

16. **For** A continuation of Christ's discourse, introducing the third and greatest of the heavenly things, viz. the Love of God, as the primal fountain of man's salvation, although by many (Kuinoel, Paulus, Neander, Tholuck, Olshausen, Westcott, Milligan and Moulton) the conjunction is believed to commence a commentary on Christ's words ; chiefly on the grounds (1) of the past tenses ; (2) of certain supposed Johannine expressions, as e.g. "only begotten" (i. 14, 18 ; 1 John iv. 9), "believe on the name" (i. 12 ; ii. 23 ; 1 John v. 13), and "doing the truth" (1 John i. 6), and (3) of the cessation of the dialogue. But (1) the tenses could not have been other than preterite if Christ purposed to divulge the secrets of a past eternity ; while (2) if the phrases mentioned were Johannine the writer may have learnt them from Christ, and (3) on the assumption that Nicodemus had no more questions to ask, his silence was both natural and becoming. To these may be added (4) the unusualness of connecting a text with its commentary by 'for,' and (5) the abruptness it would give to Christ's discourse to terminate at ver. 15. "Who can believe that Christ dismissed Nicodemus dryly after ver. 15" (Godet). **God** whose son Christ was (i. 34), on whose embassy He had come (ver. 2), whose kingdom He was publishing (ver. 3-5), and of whose world Nicodemus was a member. **so** Perhaps an echo of the 'so' in ver. 14 (Lange). **loved** In eternity at the time of the 'giving'; setting forth the Divine Love as the original source of salvation, *salutis principium* (Calovius). **the world** = whosoever (ver. 15) ; i.e. of mankind at large ; not of the elect (Calvin), but the human world, considered as an organized whole existing apart from Him. **that** ὥστε with the finite verb, expressive of the result of the 'love' and measuring the intensity of the 'so' : see Winer, § 41, 5. **He gave**—although He could have retained (Rom. viii. 32)—"To death," εἰς θάνατον, though implied, need not be added (Olshausen) : cf. Rom. viii. 32. **His only-begotten Son** Occurring in Christ's speech only here, but not necessarily on that account unauthentic ; an allusion to Abraham's offering of Isaac (Gen. xxii. 2 ; Heb. xi. 17) ; an enhancement of the Divine love (1 John iv. 9), for which reason "Son of God" may have been substituted for Son of man (ver. 13, 14). **that** ἵνα with the subjunctive defining the purpose of God's gift. **whosoever** proclaiming the universality of the Gospel offer : see on ver. 15. **believeth in Him**

εἰς αὐτὸν (iv. 39 ; vi. 40 ; vii. 31 ; xii. 46, and elsewhere) instead of ἐν αὐτῷ (ver. 15 ; Tischendorf) occurring only once in this Gospel ; the former marking the direction in which faith moves and the object on which it rests ; the latter, the sphere in which faith abides. The clause announces the simplicity of the terms of salvation. **should not perish** The negative side of salvation, according to the Evangelist, is deliverance from that destruction, ἀπώλεια, which sin as death brings on the unbelieving world (x. 28 ; xi. 50 ; xvii. 12 ; Rev. xvii. 8, 11 ; Acts viii. 20 ; Rom. ix. 22 ; Phil. i. 28 ; 2 Pet. ii. 1, 3 ; iii. 7, 16). Cf. Weiss, Biblical Theology of N. T., § 148 ; der Johanneische Lehrbegriff, § 7. **but have everlasting life.** The positive side of salvation : see on ver. 15. Both together complete the Johannine conception of the Messianic blessing.

17. **For** A confirmation of the preceding statement (Meyer); a proof that the Son's mission proceeds from Divine love (Godet) ; more probably a caution against supposing the words just uttered contradicted the account of Messiah's mission given by Malachi (iii. iv.) and John (Matt. iii. 10) both of whom had represented it as a work of judgment on the Gentile nations (Lücke, Brückner, Lange). **God sent not** Christ's historical appearing, in itself a " descending out of heaven " (ver. 13), in its relation to Christ " a coming " (ver. 2 ; 31 ; x. 10), in its relation to God was a sending (ver. 36, 38 ; vi. 29 ; viii. 42 ; xvii. 3 ; cf. i. 6). **the Son** The first instance in which Christ styles Himself ' The Son ' absolutely (cf. ver. 19, 20, 21, 22, 23 : cf. Matt. xi. 27 ; Luke x. 22), though the expression is used by the Baptist (iii. 35) ; a clear assertion of Christ's Eternal Sonship, since prior to the sending He names Himself the Son (cf. x. 36). **into the world** Though the κόσμος (i.e. humanity as sinful) was the sphere into which the Son was sent, the Son, by entering the world, became partaker only of its humanity, not of its sin. **to judge the world** κρίνειν ; not directly to condemn (A.V.) which would probably have been expressed by κατακρίνειν (viii. 10 ; Matt. xxvii. 3 ; Luke xi. 32 ; Rom. ii. 1), but to divide, separate, make a distinction, come to a decision, judge, form a basis

for ultimate judicial procedure (Rev. vi. 10 ; xi. 18 ; xvi. 5 ; xvii j.8, 20 ; xix. 2, 11 ; xx. 12, 13 ; see Cremer, Biblical Lexicon, p. 371.) Indirectly Christ's appearance was a preliminary judgment of a moral sort upon mankind separating the evil from the good (ver 18, 19, 20 ; ix. 39), with the result moreover of condemnation to the world, since it lieth in the wicked one (1 John v. 19), and is already under condemnation (Rom. v. 18) ; the ultimate decision should not be given till His second coming in glory on the last day (ver. 27 ; vi. 39, 40, 44, 45 ; xi. 24 ; xii. 48 ; cf. Matt. xxv. 31 ff.). **but that the world** The threefold repetition of the term world, full of solemnity and significance, discovers at once the momentous interest with which it was invested in the mind of Christ and the universality of the sense in which it was now employed. **should be saved** The opposite of judged and destroyed, and the equivalent of eternal life (ver. 15, 16) **through Him.** The Son hereby proclaims Himself the sole medium of salvation for a perishing world ; cf. xiv. 6 ; Acts iv. 2 ; 1 Cor. iii. 11 ; 1 Tim. ii. 5.

18. **He that believeth on Him** (see on ver. 16) **is not judged** Equivalent to " is set free from the final judgment " (Godet) ; is not judged in the sense of being condemned as the unbelieving will be (Lücke, Brückner) ; is delivered from present condemnation (Meyer, Hengstenberg) ; or, better, is in a state or condition to which judgment belongs not (Westcott, Milligan and Moulton). Judgment passes not on him, either now or hereafter, because he is not " of " or " in " the world which will eventually be judged and condemned, but in virtue of his faith is separated from, and removed out of it into another sphere to which Christ's work of judging does not apply. **He that believeth not** The second of the two classes into which Christ's appearing divides men. **hath been judged already** The attitude assumed by the unbeliever towards Jesus indirectly delivers a preliminary verdict on his moral character, which the final judgment will only confirm. So far as the ultimate issue of such a state or condition is concerned there is no need for a second tribunal. The world, to which the unbeliever belongs,

has already been judged ; and he accordingly has been judged in the world. **because** not giving the external ground of the unbeliever's judgment (Chrysostom, Hengstenberg), as if that were his unbelief ; but furnishing the reason why as an unbeliever he is judged. **he hath not believed on the name of the only begotten Son of God** The fact that a soul does not believe in the revelation of Divine love given to the world in the person and work of the Only begotten Son of God is a declaration that that soul belongs to the world which already has been practically judged. On the phrase ' to believe on the name of ' which has been regarded by some authorities as peculiarly Johannine and therefore a proof that the present section contains not Christ's but John's words, see i. 12 ; and iii. 16. On "only begotten," see i. 18

19. And this is the judgement κρίσις, or judgment, in N. T. Greek invariably signifies a judicial process, sentence, or verdict, leading up to condemnation, it being characteristic of the Divine judgment that it is directed against the guilty (ver. 24, 29 ; xii. 31 ; xvi. 8, 11 ; 1 John iv. 17 : cf. Cremer, Biblical Lexicon, p. 371). **that** Αὕτη ... ὅτι, this ... that, characteristic of John (I. i. 5 ; v. 11, 14), was probably derived from Christ. **the Light** Christ and the saving illumination brought by Him (i. 4, 5, 7, 8, 9 ; viii. 12 ; ix. 5 ; xii. 35). Christ's use of this term to describe Himself will explain John's introduction of it in the prologue (cf. Gess, Christi Person und Werk, vol. ii., p. 649). **is come into the world** Christ implies that before He came the world was in darkness, σκοτία : cf. the language of the prologue (i. 5, 9) **and men loved the darkness** τὸ σκότος ; occurring here only and in 1 John i. 6 ; the usual term being σκοτία (i. 5 ; viii. 12 ; xii. 35, 46 ; 1 John i. 5 ; ii. 8, 9, 11) ; the former "darkness absolutely as opposed to the light" ; the latter "darkness realized as a state" (Westcott). **rather than the light** The words contain three ideas: (1) that men could escape from darkness only by a free choice of the light ; (2) that the world of humanity elected to remain in the darkness rather than to come forth into the light ; and (3) that the result of Christ's appeal to men to decide between the light and the darkness

was as good as settled in the attitude of Israel towards Himself, which was only a reflection of the inner character of humanity at large. This will explain Christ's use of the past tense (Godet, Luthardt, Meyer, etc.) without resorting to the hypothesis that the words are John's (Westcott). That the phrase ' rather than '—' a mournful meiosis ' (Meyer)—suggests the possession by even wicked men of some innate admiration of, and affection for, the truth (Bengel, Lücke, Brückner, Stier) shatters itself against ver. 20. **for their works** ἔργα ; the complete outward expression of their inner life in all its individual manifestations (viii. 41 ; Luke xi. 48 ; Rom. xiii. 12 ; Eph. v. 11). **were evil** πονηρά, burdensome, laborious ; hence bad in a moral sense (vii. 7); not simply in the sense in which all men's deeds are tainted with evil (Ps. xiv. 1 ; Rom. iii. 10), but in that of being wholly and solely, essentially and radically bad. The man who finally takes up a position against the light thereby demonstrates the fundamental baseness of his moral nature. The past tenses are explained by the circumstance that Christ contemplates men's evil deeds as the reason of men's love for the darkness, and both as preceding the advent to them of the light.

20. For The ensuing words shed illumination on the psychological ground or basis of wicked men's antagonism to the light. **every one that doeth ill** lit., *every one doing ill,* i.e. habitually practising poor, worthless, good-for-nothing actions, φαῦλα (v. 29 ; Rom. ix. 11 ; 2 Cor. v. 10) ; defined above as bad, repulsive, revolting, πονηρά. **hateth the light** Not of the natural day (Job. xxiv. 13-17), but of life (viii. 12), proceeding from Christ (i. 4). **and cometh not to the Light** makes no endeavour to move his intellectual and moral being in the direction of or towards (πρὸς with acccus., as in i. 1) the light. **lest his works should be reproved** lit., *in order that his works should not be* searched out with an unfriendly purpose : cf. viii. 46 ; xvi. 8) ; hence *convicted,* demonstrated to be of the evil character that they are, πονηρὰ καὶ φαῦλα, *talia esse qualia sunt* (Bengel) ; this demonstration or conviction taking place not before others, as it will in the final judgment (Matt. xxv. 45), but internally, before himself, in the court of conscience. 21. **But** Introducing an antithesis to the foregoing. **he that doeth** ποιῶν, as distinguished from πράσσων (ver. 20), suggesting the easy and peaceful character of virtuous living as opposed to the restless and laborious toil of wickedness, *malitia est irrequieta, est quidam operosius quam veritas* (Bengel) ; or, what is more probable, pointing to habitual action rather than to the perpetration of individual deeds (Alford, Stier, Tholuck), or to the permanent results achieved by the worker in contrast to the separate efforts put forth to accomplish deeds (Meyer, Godet, Westcott, Milligan, and Moulton). **the truth** Not excellent and serviceable actions, χρηστὰ, as distinguished from the wicked, πονηρὰ, and worthless, φαῦλα, deeds above mentioned, but that which is the vital principle of the former, τὴν ἀλήθειαν ; here not the truth spoken by Christ (viii. 47 ; xviii. 37), but the truth revealed to men by the inner light of conscience (xviii. 37 ; Rom. i. 25), or by the O. T. Scriptures (v. 39 ; Matt. xxii. 29 ; 2 Tim. iii. 15), both of which proceed however from Him who is the Truth (xiv. 6). For the phrase "doing the truth" cf. 1 John i. 6 ; Gen. xxiv. 49 ; xlvii. 29 ; Neh. ix. 33 ; Is. xxvi. 10. **cometh to the light** That which had come into the world (ver. 19); being drawn towards it through natural affinity (xviii. 37 ; Ps. l. 23), as

Nicodemus had been towards Christ who perhaps designed the phrase to convey a delicate allusion to his evening visit. **that** ἵνα, expressive of the truth-doer's purpose in coming to the light, as ἵνα μὴ (ver. 20) declared the reason why the evil-worker shunned it. **his works** These, above described as inspired by the truth, "include the sighs of the contrite publican, and of the penitent thief, as well as the noble aspirations of a John or a Nathanael" (Godet). **may be made manifest** φανερωθῇ, the opposite process to that described by ἐλεγχθῇ, might be rendered visible (ii. 11 ; xvii. 6 ; 1 John ii. 19), hence discovered in their true character, which could only be done by the light (Eph. v. 13). **that** ὅτι, expressive of a fact (Westcott, Godet, and others), or declaratory of a reason (Lücke, Brückner, Meyer, Milligan and Moulton). **they have been wrought in God** i.e. in fellowship with God, and therefore by His power (Is. xxvi. 12 ; Phil. ii. 13). According to the first translation of ὅτι, the sense is that the doer of the truth is secretly impelled by the truth within him to seek the light that the true character of his actions as 'wrought in God,' and therefore of himself, may be discovered; according to the second, the meaning is that because the works of the truth-doer have been wrought in him by God's grace and spirit, he by inward spiritual affinity draws toward the light of truth in Christ that by it the true character of his works may be rendered apparent.

HOMILETICS

VER. 1-3.—THE DISTINGUISHED VISITOR.
I. **The Dignity of His Person.** 1. *An old man.* This was doubtless a difficulty in the way of Nicodemus becoming a disciple of Jesus, notwithstanding the impression made upon his heart by Christ's miracles. No longer a boy, he could scarcely be expected to change his mind in a moment of enthusiasm. 2. *A learned Rabbi.* A doctor of the Law, his reputation would be sullied if he allowed himself to veer about by every wind of doctrine, or if it were noised abroad that he had gone to learn from one who held no diploma from Jerusalem University. 3. *A civic ruler.* A member of the Sanhedrim, one of the chosen representatives of the covenanted people ; for him to follow an excited and impressionable crowd would be to degrade his office and humiliate himself. 4. *A stainless Pharisee.* Pre-eminently good, pure in doctrine, zealous in worship, punctilious in obedience, he belonged to the favourites of Jehovah, who were sure of the first places in the future kingdom of Messiah, and to whom Messiah was certain to make Himself known when He appeared. It would therefore

ill become Him to be seen frequenting the levees of a youthful carpenter from Galilee.

II. **The Time of His Visit**—Night. Perhaps 1. *Symbolic of his spiritual state.* If not now in absolute darkness, since he had been attracted by the Light (i. 4), he was yet not standing as much in its illuminating beams as the disciples (ii. 11), or as the first Jerusalem believers (ii. 23) were. Certainly 2. *Indicative of his natural timidity.* Like Joseph of Arimathea (xix. 38), and other members of the Sanhedrim at a later period (xii. 42), he was afraid of openly espousing the cause of the new prophet lest he should be put out of the synagogue.

III. **The Purpose of His Coming.** I. *Not to play the hypocrite.* Such a notion is at variance with all we know of Nicodemus, but especially of Christ, who never failed to uncloak deception. 2. *Perhaps to patronize.* The human heart dearly loves to stand upon its dignity ; yet seldom hesitates to stoop when by doing so it can reflect a lustre upon its own greatness. 3. *Certainly to inquire.* Like an honest man he deemed it necessary to reconnoitre this new movement, to interview the youthful prophet, and investigate his credentials.

IV. **The Opening Address.** 1. *The courteous salutation*—Rabbi! Nicodemus thereby showed his politeness at least. 2. *The pompous admission*—" we know " ! Notwithstanding the concealed dignity it was a candid avowal that Christ was no impostor and had a claim to be heard. 3. *The hopeful confession*—" Thou art come from God " ! Whoever Jesus was, Nicodemus recognized His divine commission. 4. *The disappointing conclusion*—A Teacher ! Many who begin well end ill. Some who promise fair at the outset of their religious careers suddenly break off and pause in their onward course. 5. *The feeble argument*—" No man can do," etc. Of course not. Not even Elijah or Moses could have wrought miracles without divine assistance. A bald truism !

V. **The Startling Response.** 1. *Its abruptness.* This was due not to want of politeness on the part of Jesus, but to a desire of awakening His hearer's attention. 2. *Its fitness.* The connection though not evident is deep and true. (See Exposition.) Christ's words are always appropriate. 3. *Its certainty.* Guaranteed by an asseveration Christ afterwards appropriates to Himself as a name (Rev. iii. 14). In now using it Christ showed He talked neither as a philosopher nor as a theologian, but as the faithful and true witness. 4. *Its authority.* Christ required not to go beyond Himself for testimony to the validity of any utterance that fell from His lips, but always opposed His simple " I say " to the " we know's " of men. No more astonishing peculiarity of Christ's teaching than this of authoritativeness. When Christ spoke men's consciences listened. 5. *Its solemnity.* What Christ declared to Nicodemus imported four truths ; (1) that the kingdom of God was at hand ; (2) that no man was in that kingdom naturally ; (3) that before that kingdom could be discerned, much more entered, a radical transformation, called a new birth, must be passed upon the human heart ; and (4) that this new birth was indispensable not for one but for all.

Lessons. 1. The duty of inquiring into the claims of Christ. 2. The propriety of doing so with fearless boldness, if also with becoming caution. 3. The welcome Christ accords to all who propose to examine His credentials. 4. The certainty that man is a fallen creature. 5. The absurdity of glorying in earthly distinctions. 6. The blessedness of knowing that such a transformation as will fit man for God's kingdom is possible. 7. The tidings that it is so constitutes the Gospel.

VER. 4-8.—THE INCREDULOUS LISTENER.

I. **The Amazed Interrogation**—" How can a man be born when he is old ? " (ver. 4). 1. *Its origination :* astonishment and perplexity. Though the truth commends itself to every man's conscience in the sight of God (2 Cor. iv. 2), it does not in every instance achieve an instantaneous conquest over heart, will, and understanding. To one contemplating religious truth from the standpoint of natural reason it is not surprising that that truth should be involved in obscurity, occasion perplexity, and awaken incredulity (1 Cor. ii. 14). 2. *Its intention:* investigation and inquiry. A tribute to the power of conscience that in Nicodemus it was able to restrain the will from coming to a premature decision and the heart from instinctive resilience against Divine Truth, while the understanding searched and examined into the new and startling ideas with which it was confronted. A testimony to the inborn sincerity of Nicodemus's soul (viii. 47 ; xix. 37). A silent prophecy of the side to which victory would ultimately incline. 3. *Its explanation:* the new birth an impossibility. In the case at least of an old man whose habits were fixed, whose tendencies of thought, feeling, and action were crystallized, such a transformation of the interior structure of the soul was pretty nearly unthinkable. In the plastic period of youth a human spirit might be revolutionized in the manner indicated by this extraordinary Teacher. But to one like Nicodemus, already past middle life, there would need to be secured a fresh start in life, before any such reorganization of his moral and spiritual nature could be effected. So to speak he would need to be transported backwards to the days of boyhood, deposited a second time at the gateway of existence ; and this it seemed hopeless to expect. 4. *Its demonstration:* the presupposition of the new birth was itself an impossibility. The moral *palingenesia* might, if the physical could, be accomplished. The futility of such an ' if ' Nicodemus expressed by demanding—' can he enter, etc. ? '

II. **The Sublime Elucidation.** 1. *The exposition:* " Verily, verily, I say unto thee, etc.," (ver. 5); in which are noticeable—(1) that the former truth is repeated with the old solemnity, authority, particularity, universality, certainty ; Christ abating nothing in these respects from the lofty elevation and divine imperiousness of His preceding statement, conceding nothing to the rank, learning, virtue, seriousness of His interlocutor, softening down nothing either in thought or expression to propitiate the goodwill and avert the prejudices of one so influential and likely to be helpful ; in this supplying an example to all who in His name and with His authority proclaim the Gospel to their fellow-men ; and (2) that the hard truth is explained with much simplicity, fulness, kindness, and condescension, also furnishing a pattern for his followers in general and his official servants in particular. 2. *The argumentation:* " That which is born of the flesh is flesh, etc." (ver. 6). The law of propagation is one throughout the entire realm of animated existence—every creature after its kind. (1) In the sphere of matter, like produces like (Matt. vii. 16 ; Luke vi. 44). *Heterogenesia*, or the doctrine that one thing may produce another and wholly different thing from itself has not yet been established by modern science, and is not likely soon to be. (2) In the loftier domain of man, nature can never rise higher than itself. Nicodemus appeared to think it might with a fresh start. According to Christ a spiritual birth can be obtained only from a spiritual being. Hence the nature of man, which is flesh, must be born anew by the Holy Spirit before it can itself produce a spiritual birth.

III. **The Simple Illustration.** 1. *The natural phenomenon:* the wind ; selected as an emblem of the Spirit, probably because of (1) its ethereal character, the Greeks naming it ' breath,' and science declaring it to be, though ponderable, composed of a highly attenuated matter, (2) its free motion, which, though not scientifically accurate, is yet, popularly regarded, true, the atmospheric ocean being seemingly exempt from all control but its own, and (3) its inscrutable mystery, to the common understanding in Christ's day greater than it is in this, though even yet there are problems in meteorology which await solution. 2. *The spiritual interpretation:* " So is every one that is born of the Spirit " (ver. 8). The Spirit's grace is like the wind's blowing in respect of (1) its origin, coming from heaven ; (2) its sovereignty, blowing where it listeth : (3) its movement, going softly like the summer breeze ; (4) its influence, penetrating and quickening ; (5) its results, becoming sooner or later perceptible to those in whom, as well as to those before whom, it works.

Lessons.—1. The natural blindness of the understanding in the region of the spirit. 2. The hopefulness of those who bring their intellectual and moral difficulties to Christ. 3. The danger of reasoning that what is impossible in the sphere of nature must also be impossible in that of grace. 4. The moral impotence of human nature. 5. The necessity of regeneration.

VER. 9-12.—THE TWO TEACHERS.

I. **The Teacher of Israel :** Nicodemus. 1. *A wise man perplexed :* "How can these things be " (ver. 9). The difficulty felt by Nicodemus was not so much to comprehend the nature and necessity (at least in some cases) of a new birth, or discover the power by which alone it could be brought about, as to perceive how the required supernatural agency should be set in operation. God often hides from the wise and prudent what He graciously reveals to babes (Matt. xi. 25). 2. *A proud man humbled :* "Art thou the Teacher of Israel and knowest not these things ? " (ver. 10). The instructor of others should not himself be ignorant (Rom. ii. 21). Those who lead the blind should not themselves be blind (Matt. xv. 14). Above all teachers of religion should know their Bibles (Matt. ii. 7). When a nation's lights are extinguished, it is not surprising that the nation itself should be in darkness (Prov. xxix. 18 ; Hoz. iv. 6). 3. *An inquiring man directed :* "Verily, verily, I say unto thee," etc. (ver. 11). It was to the credit of Christ's pupil that he had both perceived and expressed his perplexity and ignorance. In so doing he had taken the first step towards true wisdom (Ps. xxv. 9). It was not less to his profit that he did so. Christ immediately directed him to one whose knowledge of Divine things, earthly and heavenly, was intuitive, direct, original, underived, and therefore clear, full, and adequate to answer the soul's deepest and most urgent questions. The attitude of learners in Christ's school should be that of lowly humility and meek receptivity : like that of Mary (Luke x. 39) : cf. Samuel (I. iii. 10). 4. *An erring man cautioned :* "If I told you," etc. (ver. 12). On the right path, he was still in danger of straying. He had inquired, confessed, listened ; he had not yet believed. Till the act of faith was definitely concluded, neither was Christ honoured (ver. 23, 38) nor was Nicodemus safe (viii. 24). The tendency of unbelief is never to diminish but always to increase. The heart that stumbles over the doctrine of a new birth is not likely to accept with readiness that of Christ's divinity or Christ's atoning work.

II. **The Teacher come from God.** Jesus. 1. *His character :* a Rabbi of a different order from Nicodemus : "We speak," etc., ver. 11. Christ talked not as a philosopher or student who slowly groped His way to conclusions and propounded them as 'theories,' 'views,' 'speculations,' but as one who looked directly upon truth (viii. 38), possessed it absolutely (xiv. 6), and announced it authoritatively (vii. 47). 2. *His themes :* earthly and heavenly things. (1) The earthly things were not worldly matters, pertaining to the present life, such as politics or civil affairs (Matt. xxii. 17 ; Luke xii. 13), or material things, such as atmospheric motion or physical birth,—Christ aspires not to teach men political economy or jurisprudence, meteorology or physiology ; they were Divine matters which had their seat and centre on earth, as e.g. truths about regeneration. (2) The heavenly things were doctrines that belonged to the region of faith rather than of consciousness, as e.g. the Divinity and Incarnation of Jesus Christ, the Atonement, God's eternal love and salvation by faith. 3. *His requirement :* faith. Christ demands not of His pupils lofty intellectual endowments, extensive erudition, or even intense application, but merely the capacity and disposition to receive. If Christ's witness be received, it will speak for itself (1 Thess. i. 5 ; ii. 13). 4. *His treatment :* unbelief. "If I told you of earthly things, and ye believe not" (ver. 12). Then Nicodemus had as yet not believed. Great as Christ was He had begun to experience the fate of all those heaven-sent ambassadors who had preceded Him (Is. liii. 1). When the world sends out teachers, men accord them a welcome (ver. 43), no matter how obscure their persons or worthless their doctrines ; e.g. Buddha, Confucius, Mohammed, Joseph Smith. When God commissions prophets to speak for Him, men reject, persecute, and kill them ; e.g. Noah, Abraham, Moses, Samuel, Isaiah, John, Christ, Paul.

Lessons—1. The incomprehensibility of a doctrine no argument against its truths. 2. The study of Scripture the first duty, the knowledge (believing) of Scripture the first requirement, of a religious teacher. 3. The position claimed by Christ as a religious teacher explicable only on the presupposition of His Divinity. 4. Unbelief the greatest hindrance to knowledge. 5. Faith the true pathway to wisdom.

VER. 13-16.—HEAVENLY THINGS.

I. **The Person of Christ** : ver. 13. 1. *His pre-existence* He who descended out of heaven must have been previously in heaven. This the testimony of Christ concerning Himself, in this gospel (vi. 38, 51, 62 ; viii. 38, 42, 58 ; ix. 39 ; xii. 46 ; xvi. 28 ; xvii. 5), and in the synoptists (Matt. v. 17 ; x. 34, 35 ; Mark i. 38 ; Luke xix. 10) ; of the evangelists (i. 1 ; iii. 31 ; xii. 41) ; of Paul (Phil. ii. 4, 5 ; Eph. iv. 8, 10 ; 1 Cor. viii. 6) ; of Peter (I. i. 11, 20) ; of the writer to the Hebrews (i. 1, 3, 6 ; ii. 14 ; x. 5). 2. *His incarnation.* If the pre-existent Son appeared in Jesus, then the doctrine of the Incarnation is true. This, though never alluded to by Christ Himself, except indirectly by the self-designation 'Son of man,' was the belief of Matthew (i. 23), Luke (i. 35), John (i. 14), Paul (Gal. iv. 4 ; Phil. ii. 7), Peter (I. i. 21), the writer to the Hebrews (ii. 14 ; x. 5). 3. *His heavenly existence* (in time). Though the Son of man clothed in a form of flesh He was still "in heaven" (v. 19, 20 ; x. 30 ; Matt. xi. 27 ; cf. John i. 18). Practically this is a claim of omnipresence and omniscience. 4. *His representative humanity.* Expressed in the appellation " Son of man," which is never applied to Christ by any Scripture writer, though frequently by Christ to Himself. First used to Nathanael (i. 51 ; see Exposition). 5. *His future ascension.* Suggested, though not directly alluded to, by Christ (see Exposition). That Christ ascended into heaven, not spiritually or metaphorically, not ecstatically or prophetically, but actually and visibly was the testimony of Christ Himself (vi. 62 ; viii. 21 ; xii. 23 ; xiii. 31 ; xiv. 4, 28 ; xvi. 7, 28 ; xx. 17 ; Matt. xxvi. 64 ; Luke xxiv. 26) ; and of His apostles (Acts i. 9, 22 ; xxii. 7, 10, 14 ; 1 Pet. iii. 22 ; Eph. i. 20 ; Phil. ii. 9 ; Heb. vii. 26, 28 ; Rev. i. 12-20).

II. **The Work of Atonement** : ver. 14, 15. Typified by the story of the brazen serpent (Num. xxi. 8). 1. *The malady.* Poison in the veins, an emblem of sin, which like the ailment of Israel was (1) produced by a serpent's bite (Gen. iii. 1 ; Ps. lviii. 4 ; Rev. xii. 9), (2) wide-spreading in its influence (Gen. vi. 12 ; viii. 21 ; Ps. xiv. 3 ; cxliii. 2 ; Rom. iii. 23 ; Gal. iii. 22), (3) deadly in its character (Gen. ii. 17 ; Ps. xi. 6 ; cxlv. 20 ; Matt. xxv. 46 ; John v. 29 ; Rom. i. 18). 2. *The remedy.* A brazen serpent elevated on a pole, typical of Christ suspended on the cross. This, like the former, a remedy (1) provided by God (Gen. iii. 15 ; Is. liii. 6 ; Rom iii. 25), (2) closely allied to the disease (Rom. v. 19 ; 1 Cor. xv. 21 ; Gal. iv. 4, 5), from which (3) it was in itself entirely free (2 Cor. v. 21 ; Heb. iv. 15 ; 1 Pet. ii. 22 ; 1 John iii. 5), and the effects of which (4) it exhibited as overcome and destroyed (Rom. viii. 3 ; Col. ii. 15 ; Heb. ii. 14). 3. *The application.* By means of a look, suggestive of faith, which was represented in (1) the elevation of the brazen serpent on a pole, an emblem of Christ's exaltation on the cross, (2) the invitation of the wounded to look thereupon, a picture of the soul's glance towards Christ crucified (Is. xlv. 22 ; John vi. 40 ; Rom. x. 13). 4. *The result.* Healing which shadowed forth the soul's cure as (1) instantaneous (iii. 36 ; Acts xvi. 32 ; Rom. viii. 1), (2) universal (i. 12 ; v. 24 ; xi. 51 ; Acts x. 43 ; Rom. x. 13 ; Heb. vii. 25 ; 1 Tim. ii. 3 ; 1 John ii. 2), and (3) complete (vi. 35 ; x. 28 ; Acts xxvi. 18 ; Phil. i. 11 ; Col. ii. 10).

III. **The Love of God** : ver. 16. 1. *The unworthiness of its object.* The world. A creature, sinful and organized in opposition to Himself. Man's affection pitches on the good, the lovely, the meritorious ; God's love flows out in the direction of the undeserving, guilty and vile (Rom. v. 8 ; Eph. ii. 4, 5 ; 1 John iv. 10). It is love's essential characteristic and chief glory to be able to condescend. The loftier the fountain from which love's stream issues, the deeper can it run. The greatest being can stoop the lowest (Matt. xviii. 4 ; xx. 27 ; John xiii. 5 ; Luke xxii. 27). God's love limited by neither distance in time (Jer. xxxi. 3) or space (Rom. x. 12), nor moral condition (Mark iii. 28 ; Eph. i. 7 ; 1 John i. 9). 2. *The vastness of its sacrifice.* His only-begotten Son. Self-sacrifice the true test and sole measure of love. The greatest love evinced its sincerity and intensity by the immensity of its gift,—not a creature, not a universe, not an angel or battalions of angels, but a Son, an only-begotten, dearer to Him than Isaac was to Abraham (Rom. v. 8 ; 1 John iii. 16 ; iv. 9). 3. *The sublimity of its purpose.* The salvation of the world. True love can contemplate no ignoble design. A Godlike love and a Godlike gift must have a Godlike aim. Love ever seeks the welfare of its objects. The purest love desires the highest good of its beloved. This for a condemned and depraved world means redemption and rescue from its perilous position and degraded condition. To have continued in the former would have been to sink into moral corruption and everlasting destruction ; to have lingered in the latter would have been to be shut out and off from participation in eternal life. The love of God and the death of Christ proposed as their intention the averting from the world of the saddest possible calamity and the procuring for the world of the sweetest conceivable felicity (xii. 32 ; Rom. iii. 25 ; Gal. iv. 4, 5). 4. *The simplicity of its method.* Faith. By this the unspeakable gift was brought (1) within reach of the greatest number, even of all mankind, (2) on the easiest terms, viz., on the exercise of trust, and (3) with the greatest certainty, seeing it is not of works but of grace.

Lessons. 1. The value of the Scriptures. They contain Christ's revelation of heavenly things. 2. The importance of the doctrine of the Cross. Apart from it, salvation is impossible ; resting on it, salvation is sure. 3. The greatness of the love of God. Like the love of Christ it passeth knowledge.

VER. 18-21.—PRELIMINARY JUDGMENTS.

I. **The Startling Phenomenon.** The judicial separation of mankind into two classes, the believing and the unbelieving, the workers of evil and the doers of the truth : ver. 20, 21. 1. *When it occurred.* At the appearing of Christ : ver. 19. Before Christ's advent, the existence of two such classes among men was not unknown ; ever since it has been a recognized fact. 2. *How it was effected.* By the appearing of Christ, or the coming of the light into the world, the effects of which were :—(1) Illumination. As when the sun rises the hitherto indistinguishable surface of the earth is turned to it as a sheet of prepared clay is to a seal (Job xxxviii. 14), and form after form starts into visibility like figures rising upon a garment, so the dawning of the Sun of Righteousness upon the moral world, or the coming of the Lord Jesus Christ among men as the highest revelation of the Father, shed upon moral distinctions a light, which did not previously exist, and set forth in bold relief what was antecedently obscure that there are only two varieties of character in the human family, the good and the bad, the believing and the unbelieving, the truth-loving and the truth-hating, the right acting and the evil working (Mal. iv. 1, 2). (2) Separation. Not through direct influence exerted on them by Christ, but solely through the indirect action of the truth which operates in the moral sphere as the light of day does in the physical (Ps. civ. 20-23). In the loftier domain of man and man's movements there are those upon whom the light of day exercises a repellent influence, "rebels against the light, who know not the ways thereof, neither abide in the paths thereof, to whom the morning is as the shadow of death" (Job xxiv. 13) ; and those who have no need to shun but rather every cause to welcome its cheering beams, knowing as they do that their works and ways amongst their fellow-men will bear the closest scrutiny and the severest investigation. In the highest region of the spirit, the light of the Sun of Righteousness is the great discoverer of hearts and actions, laying open the wickedness of the wicked, and bringing to recognition the goodness of the good. As the former are repelled, though, like the Capernaumites, they may linger for a season in its neighbourhood (vi. 66), or like Judas may seem to rejoice in it up till the last moment (xiii. 30) ; so the latter are attracted, coming to the light and being gradually transformed into children of the light (xii. 36). (3) Arbitration The man who comes to the light judges himself, separates himself from the darkness, declares himself to be antagonistic to the darkness, and possessed of affinities with and for the light. Accordingly, by that very act he passes into a sphere to which judgment in its condemnatory form belongs not (Rom. viii. 1). The man who turns from the light equally pronounces judgment upon himself, declares himself to be against the light and in favour of the darkness (Acts xiii. 46). Thus by simply coming into the world as the Incarnate Son and coming before men in His gospel, Christ initiates a judicial process which will culminate in the disclosures of the great day (Mal. iii. 18 ; Matt. xxv. 46).

II. **The Solemn Explanation.** 1. *Of the behaviour of those who come not to the light.* (1) They love the darkness rather than the light—not 'more than they love the light' as if within their breasts lingered some traces of an inborn appreciation of the light, but 'rather than the light,' which they do not love at all (ver. 20), for reasons after specified. They love the darkness because it is congenial to the works in which they delight, here named "wicked and worthless deeds," elsewhere styled "works" (Eph. v. 11), and "ways" (Prov. ii. 13 ; cf. Ps. lxxxii. 5) "of darkness," and to the characters of themselves, the workers who are children of darkness (1 Thess. v. 5), i.e. persons of whose inner life 'darkness' or sin is the moving principle. (2) They hate the light as well as love the darkness. If possible an intensified degree of moral depravity is hereby indicated. The light not merely illuminates their minds on the subject of their evil deeds, but awakens their consciences which reprove them for their wickedness, exposing its criminality, insisting on their responsibility, and whispering of a future judgment. Hence they hate the light first for prophesying evil as Ahab hated Micaiah (2 Chron. xviii. 7), and then for suggesting good, as one may suppose Judas hated Jesus when he received the sop (xiii. 26, 27). Hence also when about to perpetrate deeds of wickedness they shun the light, like the murderer, the adulterer, and the robber (Job xxiv. 14-16), like Lady Macbeth when about to assassinate Duncan, "Come, thick night, and pall thee in the dunnest smoke of hell" (Macbeth, act i. sc. 5). Afterwards they drift along to roll iniquity under their mouths like a sweet morsel (Job xx. 12), to put sweet for bitter and bitter for sweet (Is. v. 20), to choose evil as their good, like Milton's Satan—"To do aught good never will be my task, but ever to do ill our sole delight" (Paradise Lost, book I. 159), to positively hate good like Aaron in Titus Andronicus (act iv. sc. 3), "If one good deed in all my life I did, I do repent it from my very soul." 2. *Of the conduct of those who come to the light.* (1) They have a natural affinity for the light. The principle of all their good deeds is truth ; and, as Christ is the truth, He and they mutually attract one another (xviii. 37). (2) They are not afraid of the light. Exactly as the light would condemn the wicked, they know it will acquit them (Eph. v. 8-13).

Lessons. (1) If a sinner is condemned, himself only, and neither God nor Christ, is to blame. (2) If a sinner refuses to believe the Gospel he must share in the judgment which will ultimately fall upon the world. (3) It is a sure sign of depravity when a soul turns from that which is good, and especially from Him who is God's highest revelation of truth and love. (4) The judgment Christ passes on the works of unbelievers ought to excite their alarms and give them pause. (5) The best preparation for receiving Christ is to be faithful to the truth so far as it is known. (6) When souls come to the light they universally acknowledge themselves to have been impelled thereto by prevenient grace. (7) The whole of Christ's truth is for doing.

II.—CHRIST'S GLORY UNVEILED IN JUDÆA, AND
RECOGNIZED BY THE BAPTIST

CHAP. III. VER. 22-36

EXPOSITION

Ver. 22. After these things viz., Christ's visit to the Passover, the incidents which then occurred, and in particular the interview with Nicodemus. The phrase need not imply immediate sequence (see v. 1), for which 'after this' (xi. 7, 11 ; xix. 28) is the usual expression. **came** rather, *went;* as subsequently appears, in a N.W. direction. **Jesus and His disciples** who had been gathered at John's baptism (ii. 2, 12). The same combination occurs in the earlier gospels (Matt. ix. 10; Mark ii. 15 ; viii. 27). "In each case there is a special force in the vivid representation of the Great Teacher and of the accompanying disciples as two distinct elements in the picture" (Westcott). **into the land of Judæa** lit., *into the Judæan land;* occurring only here, the country district of Judæa (Mark i. 5 ; Acts xxvi. 20), as distinguished from the metropolis : cf. Luke v. 17 ; vi. 17. **and there He tarried with them** Ver. 26 seems to indicate a stay of at least several weeks, perhaps months, over seven (Weiss, Life of Christ, vol. ii. p. 27), about nine (Geikie, The Life and Words of Christ, vol. i. chap. 31). **and baptized** the imperfect ἐβάπτιζεν signifying continuous activity (see Winer, § 40, 3) : "he went on baptizing"—not with His own hand, but through the instrumentality of His disciples (iv. 2). "The moral act belonged to Jesus ; the material operation was performed by His disciples" (Godet). On the ground that this early Judæan baptism is not mentioned by the Synoptists, its historicity has been challenged (Bauer); for reply see afterwards (ver. 24). On the relation of Christ's baptism to John's, see on iv. 2.

23. And John also was baptizing lit., *was* (in the locality to be mentioned) *baptizing,* ἦν δὲ . . . βαπτίζων, was still actively engaged in his calling. **in Aenon** Αἰνών ; either = יוֹן עֵין, meaning 'dove fountain' (Meyer) ; or, an intensified plural of עַיִן, a spring,

hence 'a place rich in springs' (Lücke, De Wette, Ewald, Brückner, Godet, Tholuck, and others). **near to Salim** Σαλείμ. The locality of Salim, and with it of Aenon, is not to be sought in Samaria, either in the valley of the Jordan, eight miles south of Scythopolis (Eusebius, Jerome), or in the vicinity of Shechem (Epiphanius), or on the heights lying east of the plain near Nablous, where Robinson (L. R. 333) found two villages named Salim (Judith iv. 4), and 'Ainûn,' with "two sources of living water, one in a cavern and the other in a fountain" (Conder, Handbook of the Bible, p. 320 ; Palestine Exploration Report, 1874, pp. 141 ff. ; 1876, p. 99); since "in Samaria the Baptist had nothing to do (Hengstenberg), and the Jews were little likely to have followed the Baptist into that province (iii. 22 ; iv. 3), but in Judæa, near the town of *Shilhim* (Σελεείμ, LXX.), which, with *Ain* and *Rimmon* (Josh. xv. 32) was situated in the southern desert (Wieseler, Ewald, Hengstenberg, and others): cf. Riehm's Handwörterbuch, art. *Aenon.* **because there was much water there** lit., *many waters,* springs, or fountains (cf. Mark ix. 22 ; Matt. xvii. 15); if required because John practised immersion (Olshausen), which is doubtful, also needful for the coming together of a large concourse of people in an arid region like the Judæan wilderness. **and they came and were baptized** lit., *were arriving and were getting baptized.* The continuance of John's baptism after the appearance of Jesus as little indicates a split in the Messianic party (Keim) as uncertainty on the part of John about the Messiahship of Jesus (Weizsäcker) ; it only proves either that John did not regard Christ's public inauguration as having been formally completed (Meyer), or that He awaited the Divine direction for discontinuing His work (Luthardt), or that he saw nothing incongruous in still preparing men for Christ by baptism, and afterwards sending away the more susceptible of them, as he had had already sent John and Andrew into the fellowship of Christ (Tholuck).

24. For John was not yet cast into prison. The Galilean ministry of which alone the Synoptists write (Matt. iv. 12 ; Mark i. 14 ; Luke iii. 19) was therefore not yet commenced. Hence their silence about this early Judæan ministry which was contemporaneous with that of John ; hence also perhaps the Evangelist's object in inserting this note was not to correct an inaccuracy in the Synoptist's statement (Meyer), but to obviate the appearance of discrepancy between his narrative and theirs (Luthardt, Godet, Tholuck, and others ; cf. Ebrard, Gospel History, § 26). Concerning the actual date of John's imprisonment this Evangelist is silent (see Matt. xiv. 1-12), permitting the Baptist to disappear from the history after the present testimony to Christ as Messiah, and only once again mentioning him in such a manner as to show that his great career was closed (v. 35).

25. There arose therefore or, *then ;* οὖν marking either simple sequence (iv. 5, 28 ; xiii. 6), or implied consequence (iv. 1, 9 ; ix. 7 ; xix. 24). If the former, the meaning is that the incident to be narrated took place at the time when John and Jesus were baptizing in the same locality ; if the latter, that it resulted from this contiguous and synchronous activity. **a questioning**—a disputation or controversy : cf. Acts xv. 2 ; 1 Tim. vi. 4 ; 2 Tim. ii. 23 ; Tit. iii. 9. **on the part of John's disciples** i.e. originating with, (ἐκ, proceeding from) those who adhered to the forerunner without going over, like Andrew and John, to the fellowship of Christ. Of these a party existed as late as the time of Paul (Acts xix. 4). **with a Jew** Not with the Jews (T. R.), but with an individual Jew ; scarcely a follower of Moses who had been baptized by Christ (Chrysostom, Euthymius, Semler, Ewald, Westcott) since in this case he would hardly have been still characterized as a Jew (Tholuck), and would probably have been more exactly designated (Meyer, Brückner) ; but in all likelihood a disciple of the

Pharisees (Hofmann, Tholuck, Luthardt, Alford), of distinctly hostile spirit, who hoped to sow dissension between the Baptist and Christ by stirring up the angry feelings of their respective adherents. **about purifying,** or, concerning that of which baptism was the symbol and the supposed instrument (1 Pet. iii. 21) ; hence concerning the efficacy to be ascribed to the rite as performed by the Forerunner and Christ respectively ; the disciples of the former perhaps exalting that of their Master as possessed of greater power to cleanse, and therefore as more indispensable, because of its priority and superiority, since even Christ submitted to it, while John had not been baptized by Christ ; and the Jew, on the other hand, assigning the palm to Christ's baptism on the ground that John's was merely preliminary and preparatory, while Christ's was that to which the Forerunner's pointed and was besides at the time the more popular of the two.

26. And they, John's disciples, **came unto John, and said to him,** with considerable excitement as their communication showed, yet not without becoming courtesy and respect, **Rabbi** a title of reverence addressed by scholars to their teachers (iii. 2). **he** It is doubtful whether jealous feeling was betrayed by the speaker's avoidance of the name of Jesus (Lange). **that was with thee beyond Jordan** i.e. at Bethany, the scene of Christ's baptism (i. 28). **to whom thou hast borne witness.** The words were presumably designed to suggest the idea of Christ's subordination to John from whom, it might be said, He had received His commission (Tholuck, Luthardt) ; perhaps also to extol John's generosity in first setting up a rival to himself (Godet), and then continuing to support His claims (Westcott). **behold,** marking the surprise, if not also the irritation and jealousy, of the speaker. **the same** οὗτος ; *this one* I am speaking of, **baptizeth**—hath started a rival, if not an antagonistic, movement. "Baptism was a special rite introduced by John, and distinguishing his ministry from every other. By appropriating it to Himself, Jesus seemed to be usurping the peculiar place of John" (Godet). **and all men,** not, all who wish to be baptized (Hengstenberg) ; but all men generally, either "as a popular generalization, like Matt. iii. 5" (Tholuck), or as a vehement exaggeration due to angry zeal (Westcott), excited feeling (Meyer), or even petty spite (Godet). **come to Him** "Passion speaks with exaggeration"; yet the exaggeration shows that Jesus had at this time a great throng of followers (Luthardt).

27. John answered and said. The Baptist's reply falls into two parts ; the first setting forth the relation between himself and Jesus (ver. 27-30), and the second unfolding the relation of Jesus to the world (ver. 31-36)—corresponding it has been aptly said (Godet) to the two expressions "I" and "He." **A man** the Baptist alone (Cyril, Beza, Bengel, Calvin, Lücke) ; Christ alone (Godet, De Wette, Olshausen); both (Kuinoel, Tholuck, Luthardt); best, man absolutely, i.e. any man (Brückner, Meyer, Westcott). **can receive nothing** lit., *is not able*, not through want of capacity, but because of Divine ordination ;—*to take*, in the sense either of arrogating to himself what does not belong to him (xix. 1 : cf. Heb. v. 4), or of accepting that which is given (xvi. 24); *anything*, lit., *nothing*, the two negatives, οὐ. . . . οὐδέν, rendering the negation more emphatic (cf. xv. 5 ; see Winer's Grammar, § lv. 9). **except it have been given** lit., *was given*, **him from heaven.** In order to a man's receiving anything, that which he receives, accepts, or takes must have been granted to him by a power, and must have proceeded from a source, outside of himself, that power and that source being the highest, viz. God : cf. 2 Cor. v. 18 ; Jas. i. 17.

28. Ye yourselves bear me witness. So Paul appealed to the Thessalonians (1 Thess. ii. 1 ; iii. 3 ; 2 Thess. iii. 7), even using the Baptist's reduplication (I. iv. 9). **that I said** furnishing the exact contents of that witness to which they had appealed (ver. 26). **I am not the Christ.** So the Baptist told the legates of the Jews (i. 20). **but** (I said) **that I am sent before Him**—"Him" referring to 'The Christ,' the nearest subject as in vii. 45 ; Acts iii. 13 (cf. Winer, § 23); rather than to Jesus, the subject of ver. 26 (Bengel, De

Wette, Brückner, Meyer, Luthardt, and others). This combination of direct and indirect narration in the same sentence is of frequent occurrence in N. T., e.g. in which the writer passes from direct to indirect (Matt. ix. 6 ; Mark ii. 10 ; Luke v. 24) from indirect to direct (Luke v. 14 ; Acts i. 4 ; xxiii. 22).

29. He that hath the bride is the bridegroom. Frequently employed in the O. T. (Is. liv. 5 ; Hos. ii. 18, 19 ; Ezek. xvi. 8 ; Mal. ii. 11), the image here selected depicts the relation of Christ to the Messianic community of believers. Used by Christ Himself for this purpose (Mark ii. 19, 20), it was subsequently adopted by the Epistle writers (Eph. v. 32 ; 2 Cor. xi. 2 ; Rev. xix. 7 ; xxi. 2, 9 ; xxii. 17). The allusion to Solomon's Song (Bengel, Hengstenberg, Olshausen), is doubtful (Luthardt), and cannot with certainty be presupposed (Meyer), since no quotation is made from that book by any N. T. writer. The fact to which John's disciples referred (ver. 26) was a sign to him that Jesus was the Bridegroom, νυμφίος, to whom belonged the Bride, νύμφη, and to whom accordingly precedence and superiority pertained. **but the friend of the bridegroom.** The chief of the companions of the bridegroom (Judges xiv. 11 ; 1 Macc. ix. 39); or of the sons of the bride chamber (Matt. ix. 15), styled by the Greeks the Paranymph, and by the Talmudists the *Schôschben*, to whom the special functions were assigned of first asking the bride's hand in marriage for his friend (2 Cor. xi. 2), then of acting as the medium of communication between the bride and bridegroom during the period of betrothal, and finally of arranging and presiding over the feast (ii. 9). See Riehm's Handwörterbuch des Biblischen Altertums : art. *Ehe*, § 5 ; Keil, Handbuch der Biblischen Archäologie, § 109. **who standeth** as a servant ready to execute the slightest wish of the bridegroom, *tanquam apparitor* (Bengel) ; **and heareth Him** not merely approaching, i.e. on His way to set up His spiritual kingdom (Luthardt), or issuing His commands which the friend delighted to fulfil (Meyer), but also conversing with the bride, *cum sponsa loquentem* (Bengel), not alone inside the chamber outside of which the friend stands (Olshausen), but at the wedding festival in which the friend bears his part. **rejoiceth greatly** lit., *with joy rejoiceth* (cf. Luke xxii. 15); a Hebraism expressive of fulness of pleasure : cf. "I will greatly rejoice," שׂוֹשׂ אָשִׂישׂ (Is. lxi. 10), translated εὐφροσύνη εὐφρανθήσονται, LXX., instead of εὐφρανθή-σομαι (see Winer, § liv. 3). **because of the bridegroom's voice,** as above indicated, conversing with the bride rather than with himself. **This, my joy, therefore** lit., *this, then, the joy which is mine,* which belongs to me as the friend of the bridegroom, the joy, viz., of bringing the bride and the bridegroom together. **is fulfilled** has reached its height, so that nothing is awanting to its completion (cf. xv. 11 ; xvi. 24 ; xvii. 13 ; 1 John i. 4). What consummated the Baptist's joy, the report brought by His disciples that the populace were flocking to Christ's baptism, was an indication that his work was done, or nearly so ; and that now he had little more to do than stand aside and contemplate with holy satisfaction the onward progress of Messiah's kingdom.

30. **He must increase, but I must decrease.** The necessity in both cases was of Divine ordination. There was no further need of a friend when the bridegroom had received his bride. John's mission therefore having been accomplished, it was thenceforward John's destiny to grow less, and ultimately disappear from the scene ; whereas the bridegroom having obtained his bride must proceed to build up through her a spiritual household of faith.

Ver. 31-36. This section has been regarded as the Evangelist's commentary on the Baptist's words, as ver. 16-21 were supposed to be on the Saviour's (Bengel, Kuinoel, Paulus, Olshausen, Lücke, Tholuck, Westcott, and others). The arguments adduced in support of this opinion are mostly these :—(1) That the section generally wears a Johannine complexion ; (2) that ver. 32 appears to contradict ver. 26 ; (3) that the aorists in ver. 33 describe the later experience of the Christian life ; (4) that the passage seemingly recites or alludes to well-known expressions of Christ first ut-

tered later ; (5) that the term "Son" indicates a theological standpoint too advanced for the Baptist ; and (6) that there is no further mention of the Baptist. But against these it is fairly urged that—(1) The Johannine colouring of the speech may be admitted without supposing that it did not in substance proceed from the Baptist (Lücke, De Wette, Brückner, Ewald, Meyer), may in fact be explained by regarding it as in its present form a Johannine translation (Godet). (2) The seeming contradiction between verses 32 and 26 may be removed by observing that the latter were the words of John's disciples with reference to Christ's temporary popularity, while the former, which fell from the Baptist's lips, looked towards the final result of that popularity. (3) The later Christian life in so far as it consisted in receiving Christ's testimony, was precisely that to which John had urged His disciples. (4) That the expressions in ver. 31, 32, 35, and 36 afterwards uttered by Christ (viii. 23 ; v. 34 ; v. 20 ; v. 24), should have been first uttered by the Baptist will not be surprising if both spoke under the guidance of the same spirit. (5) The theological standpoint indicated by the term 'Son' was given to the Baptist by the voice from heaven (i. 33, 34). (6) If the Baptist after this testimony to Jesus disappears from the Evangelist's page, the reason is that soon after this he disappeared into the Machaerus prison, from which he never again emerged to testify of Christ as the lamb of God (i. 29), and the bridegroom of His church (iii. 29).

31. **He that cometh from above** Equivalent to 'He that cometh from heaven' (cf. ver. 13 ; vi. 33 ; viii. 23), signifying Christ ; and containing a reference to the Divine origin not of Christ's mission in contrast to John's (B. Crusius, Luthardt), which was also from heaven (i. 6), but of Christ's person, as distinguished from John's which was not "from above" but "of the earth" (Godet, Meyer, Brückner), as well as an assertion of the preincarnate existence of Jesus and of His coming forth into earthly manifestation in the Incarnation (Meyer ; cf. Weiss, Bib. Theol. of N. T. vol. ii.

§ 144). If the phrase contains an echo of the words of Christ (iii. 13 ; vi. 33 ; viii. 23), it is still a phrase never used by the Evangelist himself when speaking of Christ's historical appearing (see 1 John v. 6). **is above all** : not merely all interpreters (Meyer), or servants (Godet) of God, or all belonging to the earth (Lücke, Luthardt, Lange), i.e. all men (Vulgate, Bengel), but all things absolutely (Westcott) : cf. iii. 35. **He that is of the earth** i.e. the person whose being takes its rise within the earth sphere (ἐκ τῆς γῆς) as distinguished from the celestial (cf. Matt. xi. 11), and has as its principle of existence that which is earthly and human rather than divine, **is of the earth** i.e. is possessed of a nature and character corresponding to his origin, **and of the earth he speaketh** deriving from it (ἐκ) his inspiration and utterance. The language does not exclude the idea of Divine revelation or prophetic illumination by and through which the Baptist and other teachers of the Old Dispensation spoke (2 Pet. i. 21), but signifies that none of these could trace their utterances, however divine as to contents, farther back than to the earth-sphere in which they were first found. **He that cometh from heaven is above all**—and therefore speaks in a manner wholly different.

32. **What He hath seen and heard** prior to His coming from heaven and during His pre-existence with God, **of that He beareth witness** having direct and perfect knowledge thereof : cf. i. 15, 18 ; iii. 11 ; viii. 38 ; **and no man receiveth his witness**—a hyperbole of deep sorrow (Meyer), of grief and indignation (Lange), on account of the smallness of the number who had been led through his testimony to adhere to Christ (cf. i. 11, 12)—at first to John's disciples 'all men' (ver. 26), now to John's better understanding, in comparison with the multitude of unbelievers, 'no one.'

33. **He that hath received** lit., *he having received ;* the aorist participle represents the act of faith as past and completed before the act described by the principal verb (see Winer, (§ 45, 1). **His witness** The pronoun indicates the transcendent importance of the testimony delivered by such a messenger, and the responsibility such a testifier lays upon the listener. **hath set his seal to** *this,* or, *hath sealed,* through his previous acceptance hath confirmed as true (cf. vi. 27 ; Rom. iii. 11 ; xv. 28 ; 1 Cor. ix. 2 ; 2 Cor. i. 22 ; Eph. i. 13) this which follows : **that God** who sent Christ (ver. 17, 34) and whose words Christ speaks (vii. 16), **is true** in the witness given not merely concerning (v. 36 ; viii. 18) or by (viii. 28), but also in Christ (1 John v. 20). "Belief is the Yea and Amen to God's Word" (Luthardt).

34. **For** furnishing the reason why acceptance of Christ's testimony practically amounts to an acknowledgment of the Divine veracity. **he whom God hath sent** lit., *sent ;* the aorist again contemplating Christ's mission as a definitely realized fact. The language in its highest import is applicable to Christ alone (iii. 17 ; v. 38 ; xi. 42 ; xviii. 3 ; xx. 21) ; not to the Baptist (Lange) ; prophets and other messengers being sent only in a secondary degree. "To be sent in the strict sense of the word, the messenger must be from above" (Godet). **speaketh** Not merely as an inspired prophet might utter Divine communications, but as one who possesses direct, personal, intuitive knowledge of that concerning which he testifies (ver. 32) ; and not alone in broken, isolated fragmentary sentences as might be done by ordinary human messengers (Heb. i. 1), but in complete, manifold, authoritative and final revelation (Heb. i. 2). **the words of God** the separate and detailed utterances of God (viii. 47 ; xiv. 10 ; xvii. 8), in their character and effect 'words of eternal life' (vi. 68), as distinguished from the personal Word of God, Christ Himself (i. 1) and the objective word considered as an abstract whole (x. 35 ; xiv. 24 ; xvii. 17). **for** explaining Christ's ability thus to speak, which is elsewhere (viii. 38) traced to His pre-existence with the Father. **he giveth not the Spirit by measure.** The words are susceptible of a threefold rendering. 1. *He,* (i.e. God, the immediate antecedent) *giveth not,* (to Christ, αὐτῷ, being supplied by some MSS.) *the Spirit by measure ;* the sense being that whereas God gives the Spirit to prophets in definite proportions He

bestoweth it on Christ not ἐκ μέτρου, by measure, but without measure, or in limitless fulness (Augustine, Bengel, Calvin, Hengstenberg, Lücke, Tholuck, Alford, and others); or, without supplying αὐτῷ, taking the words more generally, God giveth not the Spirit by measure, i.e. is not necessitated to communicate the Spirit only in definite proportions, but is at liberty to proceed in dispensing it without having respect to any *metron* or measure, and consequently can and does (δίδωσι expressing a continuous act, Olshausen) so confer it upon Christ (Meyer, Ewald, Luthardt, Westcott, Milligan and Moulton). 2. *He,* i.e. *Christ* (the subject of the verb, 'speaketh') *giveth not the Spirit by measure,* but dispenseth it in fulness, and thereby evinceth his true Messianic calling (Cyril, B. Crusius, Westcott)—an admissible interpretation whether the Baptist or the Evangelist be regarded as the speaker (xv. 26 : cf. Matt. iii. 11). 3. *He,* i.e. the *Spirit giveth not* (in this, as in every other case) *by measure;* meaning that Christ is able to speak the words of God because the Spirit imparts them to Him without measure (Godet). In favour of this interpretation can be urged that nothing is required to be added in supplement ; but in each case the practical effect is the same. According to the second by what He gives, according to the first and third by what He receives, He is declared to be the only authoritative and complete revealer of the Father. Nor if either of these latter be adopted does the statement involve a contradiction to Christ's testimony regarding Himself (ver. 11 ; viii. 38), according to which His higher knowledge was derived from his pre-existence with the Father, since "the Spirit was in Christ the principle whereby He communicated to men that which He had beheld with God " (Meyer), and the principle by which the knowledge possessed by His higher pre-existent nature was transmitted to the human consciousness of Christ (cf. Weiss, Bib. Theol. § 145, c. note 15).

35. The Father loveth the Son A further description of the dignity of the Son (Meyer), the clause also offers an explanation of the absolute com-munication to Him of the Spirit (Alford), as well as exhibits the ground on which the subsequent endowment of Messianic fulness of power is based (Lücke, Brückner); the 'Son' being not simply the historical Christ (Luthardt) but the pre-existent Being whom the Father had sent (ver. 34), and who was named 'Son' even then, not merely as the object of special love (Weiss), but as standing towards the Deity in a filial relation (cf. ver. 17). On the Baptist's knowledge of the Sonship see i. 34 ; Matt. iii. 17. **and hath given** not simply after the resurrection (Matt. xxviii. 18 ; Eph. i. 22), or at His incarnation, but in eternity and prior to His coming forth from the Father (xiii. 3 ; Matt. xi. 27). **all things** neither all the mysteries of the kingdom, *omnia mysteria regni* (Grotius), nor all parts of His doctrine, *omnes doctrinae suae partes* (Kuinoel), nor all things pertaining to the saving office of Christ (Luthardt), nor all power to quicken as in v. 21, xvii. 2 (Tholuck), but all things absolutely, as in the above cited texts, hence also the Spirit. **into His hand,** lit., *in His hand; a constructio pregnans,* signifying that all things have been placed into Christ's hands so that they are and remain there (Winer, § 66, 2).

36. He that believeth on the Son hath eternal life : cf. Christ's language to Nicodemus (iii. 15, 16), and to the Galileans (vi. 40). That the Baptist should have expressed Himself in terms corresponding with the utterances of Christ may be explained by supposing either (1) that the Evangelist has freely rendered the Baptist's and Christ's thoughts into His own style of speech (Godet, Luthardt, Beyschlag, Weiss, and others); or (2) that the Baptist learnt the ideas and expressions here employed from Christ through the medium of John (Hengstenberg) ; or (3) that the Baptist derived them as Christ did from the Holy Scriptures through the teaching of the Spirit. For the idea of the " Son," see Ps. ii. 11 ; Is. ix. 6 ; Dan. iii. 25 ; for that of " Faith" as the medium of salvation, see Gen. xv. 6 ; Ps. xxxvii. 40 ; Is. xxviii. 16 ; for that of eternal life, see Ps. xvi. 11 ; Dan. xii. 2. **but he that obeyeth not the Son** The verb ἀπειθέω, which forms the antithesis to πιστεύειν, describes unbelief as an act of disobedience (Acts xiv. 2 ; xix. 9 ; Rom. xi. 30 ; 1 Pet. iv. 17), as faith is sometimes represented as the highest form of obedience (1 John v. 20 ; Rom. i. 5). "Always in the N. T. the former denotes the behaviour of those who turn away from God's revealed will, and reject the offers of His grace " : see Cremer, Bib. Lexicon, p. 475. **shall not see** perceive, attain to, or enjoy either here or hereafter **life, but the wrath of God** cf. the wrath to come (Matt. iii. 7 ; Luke iii. 7); the outward manifestation of God's judi-

cial anger against sin (Rom. i. 18 ; Eph. ii. 3 ; v. 6 ; Col. iii. 6 ; 1 Thess. i. 10) : the opposite of eternal life, or salvation (1 Thess. v. 9), the equivalent of ' judgment ' (v. 30 ; 1 John iv. 17), ' destruction ' (iii. 16), ' death ' (viii. 51). **abideth** not ' cometh ' as if it were first awakened by unbelief (Godet), but 'abideth' (cf. i. 33), remaineth where already it is (iii. 18). **on Him** the unbeliever, who, disobeying Christ's command to believe, refuses to perform the one act by which escape from wrath and entrance into life can be effected (viii. 24).

HOMILETICS

VER. 30.—THE SERVANT AND THE SON.

I. **The Unconscious Greatness of the Servant.** 1. *His lofty contentment:* ver. 27. A maxim recognized by David (1 Chron. xxix. 14), Solomon (Ps. cxxix. 1, 2), Nebuchadnezzar (Dan. iv. 35), Paul (Acts xvii. 26) ; of universal application, in the realm of nature (Rom. xi. 36) and in the sphere of grace (1 Cor. iv. 7 ; xii. 6 ; Jas. i. 17); specially significant with reference to individual success whether in the ordinary callings of life (Ps. lvii. 2) or in the nobler ministries of the Church of God (2 Cor. iii. 5). So far from Christ's greater popularity exciting in the Baptist's mind either irritation or jealousy, it filled him with calm, holy peace. Recognizing it as a sovereign appointment of heaven, he was satisfied ; exhibiting the spirit afterwards exemplified by Christ (Matt. xi. 26 ; xxvi. 39) and by Paul (Acts xxi. 14), which also should be conspicuous in Christ's followers, " Whate'er my God ordains is right." 2. *His profound humility :* ver. 28. Consider how great this man must have been who required to say to his contemporaries, " I am not the Christ ! " That this was no assumption on the part of the Baptist was confirmed by the Evangelist, who deemed it needful to say of him, ' He was not that light ! ' (i. 8), and by Christ who acknowledged him to have been " a burning and a shining light " (v. 35), yea " the greatest among men born of woman " (Matt. xi. 11). Yet not only does this man who was in danger of being mistaken for Messiah repudiate all pretensions of, or claims to, greatness on the part of himself, but nothing can surpass the lowliness of the estimate he forms of his person and position. He is a voice crying in the wilderness (i. 23) ; a public herald announcing the approach of the King ; at most the friend of a happy bridegroom about to claim his bride. Wonderful humility ! amazing self-abnegation ! 3. *His absolute unselfishness:* ver. 29. Had the soul of the Baptist been inflamed with ambition, he could easily like another Theudas have boasted himself to be somebody (Acts v. 36), played the rôle of a pretender to the Messianic throne, and perhaps snatched the diadem of kingly honour from a fanatical people. Or, had he aspired to distinction as a religious teacher, he might have founded a school like Hillel or Gamaliel, or at least drawn around him an independent circle of followers. But, instead, the end of all his aspiration and effort was to proclaim the Messianic Kingship of Jesus, to do the humble, though honourable, office of espousing the nation to that Greater One as a chaste virgin to her affianced lover. Yea, in the successful realization of this ambition and prosperous completion of this labour, this magnanimous and heroic preacher of repentance found his sweetest satisfaction and purest felicity. Like that Greater One for whom he lived and laboured, John pleased not himself (Rom. xv. 2, 3) : as Christ's aftercomers should, so His distinguished forerunner did, denied himself and lived for the Lord (Matt. xvi. 24, 25 ; Luke xiv. 27 ; Rom. xiv. 7, 8 ; Phil. iii. 7, 8). 4. *His cheerful resignation :* ver.

30. So far from being annoyed at the popularity of Jesus, he was able to contemplate it with complacency and delight, to behold men falling away from himself, as it seemed, and going over, as he desired, to swell the train of the new prophet ; yea, to anticipate without a murmur the time when he should be left alone, deserted and perhaps despised, while Jesus was exulting in ever augmenting prosperity and steadily moving forward amid the acclamations of an admiring populace towards the splendid goal of His glorious career. It was such an outlook as only a veritable great heart could have endured with composure. But the friend of the bridegroom was without a pang of jealousy, without a spark of envy, without an ache of disappointment, without a touch of dispeace. With the clearest sincerity, he could have taken on his lips the words—

" Nay, then, farewell !
I have touched the highest point of all my greatness;
And from that full meridian of my glory,
I haste now to my setting : I shall fall
Like a bright exhalation in the evening,
And no man see me more."—(King Henry VIII. act iii. sc. 2.)

II. **The Transcendent Glory of the Son** : ver. 31-36. 1. *His pre-existent being.* The Baptist describes Him as " He that cometh from above," and " He that cometh from heaven." The same celestial and pre-creaturely existence is everywhere throughout the N. T. Scriptures claimed for Jesus, by the Evangelist (i. 1 ; xii. 41), by the Synoptists (Matt. i. 18-25), by Christ Himself (viii. 58), by the Epistle Writers (Phil. ii. 6 ; Heb. i. 2). The certainty that Christ's historical appearing cannot be explained on purely natural principles, but must be regarded as proceeding from a different source than this temporal earth-sphere, marks Him off from every other son of mother Eve and infallibly proclaims His supreme Divinity. 2. *His universal sovereignty.* The desert prophet represents Him as " above all," all prophets, all persons, all things, not alone in the dignity of His person, the elevation of His character, the splendour of His fame, the vastness of His power, but also in the absoluteness of the authority or sway He exercises over them. They are His creatures, for He made them (i. 3, 10; 1 Cor. viii. 6; Eph.iii. 9; Col.i. 16, 17; Heb.i. 2); His property, for "the Father hath put them all into His hand" (ver. 35); His subjects, for all have been placed beneath His rule (Ps. viii. 6 ; 1 Cor. xv. 24-28 ; Eph. i. 22 ; Heb. ii. 8). Belonging to Him from eternity as an inherent right in virtue of His Godhead, in eternity also this universal lordship was by the free act of the Father conveyed over to and deposited with Him the Son, in the character of Mediator (Heb. ii. 9). That it was so was distinctly asserted by Christ Himself before His death (Matt. xi. 27 ; John xiii. 3). After His death it was signally attested by His resurrection and ascension which constituted as it were His formal enthronization in sight of angels and of men (Matt. xxviii. 18 ; Acts x. 36 ; Rom. xiv. 9 ; Eph. iv. 10 ; 1 Pet. iii. 22). 3. *His authoritative testimony.* John exhibits this as resting upon three things which again mark Him off from the category of ordinary witness-bearers. (1) A direct vision of the truth : ver. 32. The Son who is always in the bosom of the Father sinks Himself eternally into the infinite depths of the divine mind, beholding there with open countenance the thoughts, counsels, purposes, desires, commandments of the ineffable Supreme, and receiving such communications as the Father may will to express through the Son in whom He delights ; and coming forth in the fulness of the times into this world-sphere, in the likeness of sinful flesh, that Son publishes abroad, testifies, witnesses to what in His pre-existent state He had seen and heard with the Father. (2) A special commission to reveal the truth : ver. 34. In a sense impossible to be affirmed of any besides Himself, He was sent forth from heaven by God ; He was sent from a pre-existent state or condition ; He was charged to be a speaker of the " words," or utterances, "of God." (3) A complete impartation to Him of the truth : ver. 34. The Holy Ghost the mediating divine personality through whom the Father conveys to the Son and the Son receives from the Father the words the Son is to speak and the truth He is to reveal ; also through whom the Son communicates to men that which He reveals. Only to men, whether prophets, apostles, or private believers, the truth is never imparted in more than broken fragments, side lights, relative aspects ; to the Son it is communicated in its fulness, so that He not only has, but is, the Truth (xiv. 6). 4. *His supreme divinity.* Implied in His pre-existent being, His universal dominion, His authoritative revelation, it is further involved in His sonship, since if the Father be God so also must the Son be God. 5. *His twofold work.* (1) Salvation; the essence of which is eternal life, and the condition believing on the Son. (2) Condemnation, the import of which is leaving men to reap the fruit of their own doings (Gal. vi. 8), to fall beneath that cloud and stroke of wrath from which they seek no escape ; and the ground or basis of which is their disobedience of the Son who desires and commands them to believe (Rom. ii. 8; 2 Thess. i. 8).

Lessons. (1) The secret of true greatness—humility before Christ. (2) The insignificance of human glory—compared with that of Christ. (3) The dignity of ministerial service—that of acting as Christ's friend. (4) The pathway to ever-during renown—to efface oneself for the sake of Christ.

III.—IN SAMARIA : CHRIST REVEALS HIS GLORY AS THE INCARNATE SON. 1. TO THE WOMAN AT THE WELL

Chap. IV. Ver. 1-38

Exposition

Ver. 1. **When therefore the Lord** ὁ κύριος; a title rarely given to Jesus during His earthly life and always in circumstances suggestive of His divinity; see vi. 34, 68 ; ix. 36, 38 ; xi. 3, 12, 21, 27 ; xiii. 6, 37 ; xiv. 8, 22 ; xx. 28; xxi. 17 ; Matt. vii. 21 ; viii. 2, 21, 25 ; xii. 8 ; xiv. 30; xviii. 21 ; Mark v. 19 ; xi. 3 ; Luke ii. 11 ; v. 12 ; xxii. 33. Whether the designation as applied to Christ is ever equivalent to the use of κύριος for which in the LXX. it usually stands (Olshausen), or only to Adonai which also it translates (Cremer, Bib. Lexicon, p. 382), it clearly points to the notion of supreme authority and kingship, such as the Baptist, in the preceding chapter (ver. 35), ascribed to the Saviour. **knew** Not necessarily by the exercise of supernatural discernment as in ii. 24 ; xvi. 19 (Lange, Milligan and Moulton), though this may be favoured by the use of κύριος, instead of 'Ιησοῦς (א D Λ, Tischendorf), since in all probability αὐτός would have been inserted (see Winer, § xxii. 2) ; but either by information having reached him (Brückner, Westcott), or "*nemine nunciante*" (Bengel) by natural deduction from the crowds flocking to His ministry (Meyer) as well as from the event recorded in iii. 25, 26 (Luthardt). To this latter source of information the conjunction 'therefore'

points. **how that the Pharisees** See on i. 24. **had heard** most likely through the disputatious Jew mentioned above (iii. 25), who may have been commissioned by the Sanhedrim to watch the new movement. **that Jesus was making and baptizing** lit., *is making and baptizing;* an instance of transition from indirect to direct narration, frequently occurring with N. T. writers (Luke v. 14 ; Acts i. 4 ; xxiii. 22) : see Winer, § lx. 9. **more disciples than John** sc. 'is making' (Milligan and Moulton) rather than 'had made' (Hengstenberg, Olshausen, Westcott), as if John had by this time been cast into prison (Matt. iv. 12 ; Mark i. 14 ; Luke iii. 20), which is not stated and cannot certainly be inferred from the narrative.

2. **Although Jesus Himself baptized not, but His disciples.** Not because Christ thought baptism, as less important than preaching, might be entrusted to others as was afterwards done by Paul, 1 Cor. i. 17 (De Wette, Tholuck), or because He must needs in that case have baptized unto Himself (Tertullian), or because He would not obscure the truth that "He it is who baptizes all even to the present day" (Hengstenberg), or because "He would testify to all ages that baptism loses nothing of its value when administered

by a mortal man" (Calvin), but because the work of baptizing was more suited to the servants than to the Lord of the Messianic kingdom (Lücke), and because He as such baptized with the Spirit (Bengel, Meyer, Godet, Luthardt, Brückner, Westcott, and others). **3. He left Judea** Not because the Baptist had by this time been imprisoned (Tischendorf, Ebrard, Olshausen, Hengstenberg, Godet, Farrar, Westcott), which is doubtful (cf. Andrew's Life of Our Lord, p. 147 ; Weiss, The Life of Christ, vol. ii. p. 51); but probably because He feared the hostility of the Pharisees, who had greater reason to be incensed against Him than against John on account of His freer address as seen in His more public appearance in Jerusalem, His stronger influence exemplified in His purification of the Temple, His higher authority evinced by His miracles, as well as by the attestation given Him by John ; or "because the moral conditions for the successful prosecution of His baptismal labours were awanting" (Andrews), the dissensions sown between His disciples and those of John rendering the opportunity unfavourable for the prosecution of His work—to which perhaps there is a reference in the term ἀφίημι, 'to let go,' or 'give up,' which may mean either that for a time He abandoned Judea, "leaving it to its own wishes, ways, fate" (Westcott), or that He discontinued the work He had begun. **and departed again** πάλιν, in some MSS. omitted, is probably authentic. **into Galilee** On Galilee see i. 43 ; in which mention is made of Christ's first journey into that northern province ; the object of this second visit being not to commence His Galilean ministry (Neander, Ebrard, Hengstenberg, Westcott), but to seek retirement for a season (Meyer, Luthardt, Andrews) ; and its date falling in all probability in December four months from the beginning of harvest on 16th Nisan or 1st April.

4. And He must needs pass through Samaria i.e. if He would follow the direct route commonly observed by pilgrims from Galilee attending the feasts (Jos. Ant. xx. 6, 1), and by such travellers as had occasion to study speed, the journey through Samaria being accomplished in three days (Jos.

Life, § 52). (Scrupulous Jews ordinarily made a detour through Peræa lest they should come in contact with any of the hated nation; a prejudice against which Christ set Himself not only now, but also on a later occasion : Luke ix. 52.) At the same time the frequency with which the term 'must,' δεῖ, falls from Christ's lips with reference to His earthly movements (iii. 14 ; ix. 4 ; x. 16 ; xx. 9 ; Matt. xvi. 21 ; Luke ii. 49 ; iv. 43 ; xiii. 33) renders it probable that the 'necessity' to which He now alluded arose from the inner constraint of His Father's leading. **5. So He cometh** or, 'He cometh then,' i.e. for the reason above given. **to** εἰς ; not 'into,' but 'to the vicinity of' : ver. 28 ; xi. 38, 41 ; xx. 1, 11. **a city of Samaria** The kingdom of Samaria called after its chief city (Samaria, in Hebrew *Schomeron,* 'watch-mountain,' in Aramaic *Schamerâjin* (Ezra iv. 10, 17), whence the Assyrian *Samîrina*), the modern *Sebaste,* lay between Judea and Galilee, began at a village in the great plain Ginea (En-gannim) and ended at the Acrabbene toparchy, south of Gerizim and north of Shiloh. Like Judea, Samaria was made up of hills and valleys, moist enough for agriculture, and extremely fruitful, possessed abundance of trees, both wild and cultivated, as well as grew excellent grass, causing its cattle to yield more milk than those of other places. In Christ's day it supported a large population consisting of the descendants of those Assyrian colonists whom Ezarhaddon had settled in the land, of the Jewish remnant who adhered to the deserted territory after the captivity, and of the exiled Judæans who from time to time were driven from Jerusalem through its long party contests ; all of whom coalesced to form a separate Mosaic community (2 Kings xvii. 29 ff. ; Jos., Wars, iii. 3, 4 ; Hausrath, N. T. Times, vol. i. p. 14 ; Riehm's Handwörterbuch des Biblischen Altertums, art. *Samaria*). **called Sychar** Συχάρ ; commonly regarded as another reading for Sichem, Shechem, *Neapolis, Nablous* (Acts vii. 16), either by voluntary alteration of the liquid *m* into *r,* effected by the Evangelist himself (Hengstenberg), which is far from probable, or by the Jews (Reland, Lightfoot) to express their contempt for the inhabitants, Sychar signifying 'the city of drunkards' with allusion to Is. xxviii. 1, 7 (Reland) or 'the city of liars' after Hab. ii. 18 (Lighfoot); or by involuntary change of the liquids as in *Beliar* instead of Belial (Tholuck, Olshausen) which is less satisfactory as an explanation. Now more generally believed to mark a distinct town from Sychem though in its immediate vicinity, most likely a suburb of the same (Hug, Lichtenstein, Ewald, Godet, Luthardt, Brückner, Meyer, Weiss, Westcott); Eusebius in his Onomasticon stating that it lay " in front of Neapolis"; the Talmud making mention of a place and a spring called Sychar, and a modern town *El Askar* still existing in the neighbourhood of *Nablous* so like the Sychar of the present narrative that Thomson (The Land and the Book, p. 472) feels inclined to adopt it. Once considered an error and evidence of late authorship (Schenkel), this distinction of Sychar from Sichem rather constitutes a proof of the directness and exactitude of the Evangelist's knowledge (Luthardt). **near to the parcel of ground that Jacob gave to his son Joseph.** Neither an inaccuracy resting on a mistranslation of Gen. xlviii. 22 by the LXX. (De Wette, Brückner); nor a traditional development of Gen. xxxiii. 19 ; xlviii. 22 ; Josh. xxiv. 32 (Lücke, Tholuck) ; but a correct interpretation of the just cited passages (Godet, Luthardt, Hengstenberg, and others), which say (1) that Jacob bought a parcel of ground (χωρίον) at the hand of the children of Hamor, Shechem's father, for an hundred pieces of money, (2) that Jacob on his death-bed bequeathed to Joseph one portion (lit., one shoulder, ridge, or elevated tract of land, *shechem*) above his brethren, intending probably by the use of this word to convey a hint that the tract to be in future assigned to Joseph's descendants would be the district round about the ancient city of Shechem (see Pulpit Commentary on Genesis, p. 521), and (3) that this parcel of ground in which subsequently the bones of Joseph were deposited in due course became " the inheritance of the children of Joseph."

6. **And Jacob's well** or, spring (πηγὴ) as in ver. 14, though in ver. 11, 12 a

different term, φρέαρ, is employed. **was there.** Though the writer of Genesis makes no mention of Jacob having dug a well at Shechem, and the Evangelist's narrative implies not necessarily more than that tradition ascribed the construction of the then existing well to the patriarch, yet the fact may have been as tradition said. It was the custom of Abraham and Isaac to dig wells (Gen. xxi., xxvi.), and Jacob may have felt himself impelled to follow their example either (1) because of a scarcity of water in the neighbourhood, the springs at present plentiful in the region (The Land and the Book, p. 473) having begun to flow at a later period, or (2) because the springs, if they then existed, were in the hands of disobliging neighbours "who were unwilling to share the water with him " (Andrews), or (3) because being separated from the inhabitants of the country he wished to have his own supply, and at the same time to establish his right in the soil, of which the well would be a monument (Hengstenberg, Godet). If the modern identification be correct which discovers the remains of the ancient structure in the modern *Bir-Jakoub*, or *Ain Jakoub*, 1½ or 2 miles distant from Shechem, seven minutes' walk from the traditional grave of Joseph, it was situated " on the end of a low spur or swell running out from the northeastern base of Gerizim, and is still 15 or 20 feet above the level of the plain below." It is dug out of the solid rock to the depth of 75 or 80 feet, although in ancient times it may have been much, as in 1838 it was 30 feet, deeper. Its diameter is 9 feet. Its sides are smooth hewn stones, and perfectly round as well as regular. Two centuries ago it contained · 15 feet of water ; in 1842 it was nearly, in 1866 quite dry (Robinson's Biblical Researches, vol. iii. 109 ; Thomson, The Land and the Book, p. 473 ; Lieut. Anderson, 'The Survey of Palestine' in Warren's Recovery of Jerusalem, p. 465 ; Riehm, Handwörterbuch des Biblischen Altertums, art. *Jakob's-brunnen*. **Jesus therefore, being wearied with His journey,**—a tender reminder of the true humanity of the Saviour, wholly inconsistent with the notion of a doketic Christ—**sat** lit., *was sitting,* at the time when the woman came; the picture being transferred to the author's page exactly as he recalled it to his imagination. **thus** οὕτως; *as he was*, i.e. wearied (Erasmus, Beza, Hengstenberg : cf. Winer, § lxv. 9), although in this sense οὕτως commonly stands before the verb (Acts vii. 8 ; xx. 11 ; xxvii. 17); hence preference should perhaps be given to the sense ἀπλῶς ὡς ἔτυχεν, *just as it happened* (Chrysostom, Lücke, Meyer, Brückner), i.e. without more ado. **by the well** ἐπὶ τῇ πηγῇ ; not necessarily upon the spring, i.e. on the stone wall or parapet ; at or by the spring (cf. v. 2 ; Rev. xxi. 12 ; Acts iii. 10 ; v. 9) will equally satisfy the demands of grammar. **It was about the sixth hour** 1. According to Jewish reckoning, noon; 2. according to Roman computation 6 a.m. or 6 p.m. The customary objections to the former, such as that noon was an unfit time to travel in (Ebrard, Ewald), and an unusual hour for drawing water (Rettig, Schweitzer), are disposed of by considering that the journey fell, in all probability, in December (see on ver. 4, 35), and that the exceptional character of the time explained the circumstance that the woman visited the well alone. The difficulties attending the latter are too formidable to be easily removed, as e.g. (1) that 6 a.m. would have required a start the night before so as to arrive at the well at the breakfast hour, (2) that 6 p.m. would leave too little time for the occurrences narrated in ver. 28-30, and (3) that the author would hardly have left it undetermined whether he meant the morning or evening. The mention of the hour supplies another indication that the fourth gospel is the work of an eye-witness.

7. **There cometh** on her way home from the fields where she worked (Godet) ; more probably out from the city, being attracted either by reverence for the name of Jacob, or by the excellence of the water in the well, **a woman of Samaria** not of the city 2 hours distant, but of the country of Samaria ; her place of abode being Sychar (ver. 28), and the phrase γυνὴ ἐκ τῆς Σαμαρείας being equivalent to Σαμαρεῖτις, a Samaritan woman. If in some degree possessed of a representative character (Hengstenberg), her

strongly individualized personality refutes the ideas that she symbolized the religious attitude of her people to Jehovah (Strauss, Weisse, Hausrath), and that the narrative was invented to explain Acts viii. 5 (Baur). **to draw water** No longer as in patriarchal times (Gen. xxiv. 15 ; xxix. 9 ; Exod. ii. 6) the work of women of station, the woman's purpose was an indication of her poverty (Westcott) : cf. Tristram, The Land of Israel, p. 25 ff. **Jesus saith unto her** "Another refutation of the theory that assigns an Alexandrian origin to this gospel. A man trained in that school would have been as little disposed as a Jewish theologian of Palestine to represent Jesus as conversing with a poor woman" (Neander, Life of Christ, § 121). **Give me to drink** Spoken first literally and designed so to be understood by the woman : *Jesus was thirsty*. That it was also intended to express the notion of a spiritual thirst, similar to the spiritual hunger of ver. 32 (Hengstenberg), is by no means impossible : *Jesus desired the spiritual refreshment of saving this woman's soul.* He purposed to awaken in her a thirst for the living water.

8. **For His disciples** All of them : there is no ground for supposing (Hengstenberg, Godet, Westcott) that John remained behind ; this hypothesis being unnecessary to ensure an accurate report of the occurrence, which the Evangelist might have derived from Christ Himself, rather than from the woman (Luthardt). **were gone away into the city** carrying with them, it is conjectured, the only vessel (ἀντλημα, ver. 11) wherewith He might have drawn for Himself, and so obliging Him to crave the assistance of the woman (Lücke, Meyer, Godet, and others) ; though it is possible the disciples may have been purposely sent away that Christ might be alone when conversing with the woman (Hengstenberg). **to buy food** lit., *things that nourish ;* hence, meat, victuals ; the word in the plural occurring here only, the singular being commonly employed (Matt. iii. 4 ; vi. 25 ; Luke xii. 23). Neander (Life of Christ, § 121) thinks Our Lord may have despatched His disciples to purchase provisions, "not without the intention to elevate them above the Jewish prejudice which re-

garded the Samaritans as unclean": see on ver. 9.

9. **The Samaritan woman therefore saith unto Him, How is it** πῶς ; expressive of wonder, occasioned perhaps partly "by the presentiment that one is standing before her who is exalted above the common type of Jew" (Hengstenberg, Lange), but chiefly by her knowledge of the national estrangement existing between the Jews and the Samaritans. It is not necessary to charge her with either pertness (Tholuck, Meyer) or conscious superiority (Lange). **that thou** lit., *how dost thou?* **being a Jew** i.e. since, or because, thou art a Jew, the participial clause expressing the latent ground of her surprise : cf. x. 33. That Christ was a Jew she might recognize by His dress (Lücke), or by His speech (Brückner), "the Samaritan dialect standing between the Hebrew and the Aramaic" (Tholuck), and the Hebrew for "Give me to drink," תְּנִי לִשְׁתּוֹת containing the letter שׁ whose pronunciation (Judg. xii. 6) distinguished the Jews from the Samaritans (Stier). **askest drink of me** The straitened relations existing between the two peoples formed her first cause of astonishment. **which am a Samaritan woman?** Her second ground of surprise was that so distinguished a stranger should condescend to converse with a woman—a circumstance at which even the disciples marvelled (ver. 27). **For Jews have no dealings with Samaritans.** The clause, omitted in some MSS. (א² D it³), may be put into the woman's mouth (Calvin, Lange, Milligan and Moulton), in which case it will express her contemptuous and disdainful feelings ; but is better assigned to the Evangelist (Bengel, Lücke, Brückner, Godet, Meyer, Luthardt, Westcott), who thereby explains to his readers the source of the woman's wonder. That the Jews did not absolutely avoid intercourse of a commercial nature with the Samaritans was proved by the mission of the disciples (ver. 8), and by the recognized trade carried on in eggs and fruit (Hausrath, New Testament Times, vol. i. p. 26) ; but that such dealings were generally regarded as unlawful may be inferred from the statements of the Talmud : "He who takes bread of a Samaritan is like unto him who eats the flesh of swine" (Pirq. R. El. c. 38) ; "It is unlawful to eat the flesh or drink the wine of a Samaritan" (Rasche ad Sota, p. 515). This estrangement appears to have survived till the present day. "On asking drink from a woman (near Nablous) who was filling her pitcher, we were angrily and churlishly refused :—'The Christian dogs might get it for themselves,'" Tristram, The Land of Israel, p. 134.

10. **Jesus answered**—" leaving His own want in abeyance" (Meyer), probably without having been supplied with what He sought (Jacobus), though it has been suggested, the honour done to her caused her to make haste (Tholuck)—**and said unto her, If thou knewest** If her answer showed she had recognized Him as a Jew, His reply reminded her that as yet she was unacquainted with His true character and mission. **the gift of God** The gracious opportunity then afforded to the woman of conversing with Jesus (Grotius, B. Crusius, De Wette, Lücke, Brückner, Meyer, Tholuck, and others) ; the person of Christ Himself (Erasmus, Calvin, Ebrard, Hengstenberg, Godet [1]) ; all that is freely offered in the Son (Westcott) ; best, the living water Christ should give, which is afterwards explained to be the Holy Spirit (Augustine, Bengel, Alford, Luthardt, Godet[2], Gess, Milligan and Moulton). **and who it is that saith to thee, Give Me to drink** The 'and' is not epexegetic (Calvin, Tholuck, Lange) as if Christ were unfolding the nature and contents of the 'gift,' but continuative (Luthardt, Meyer, Godet), Christ distinguishing Himself as the Giver from the living water, His gift, which can only be obtained through knowledge of and application to Himself. **thou wouldest have asked of Him** as He has now asked of thee ; thou, and not He, wouldst have been the petitioner. **and He would have given to thee** as thou hast given to Him, if she had already granted His request ; or if that was still delayed, though thou hast not yet given to Him. **living water** ὕδωρ ζῶν ; מַיִם חַיִּים, i.e. fresh, spring water as opposed to the stagnant water of a pool or cistern (Gen. xxvi. 19 ; Lev. xiv. 5 ; Jer. ii. 13), in which sense it was understood by the

woman (ver. 11). Employed by Christ as an emblem of the spiritual blessing of salvation or eternal life (ver. 13, 14: cf. Rev. vii. 17 ; xxi. 16 ; xxii. 1, 17) ; not of the waters of baptism in which it is symbolized (Justin, Cyril), or of the evangelic doctrine through which it is proclaimed (Grotius, Brückner), or of the grace of justification by which it is conditioned (Tarnovius), or of the faith by which it is received (Lücke), but of that in which it consists, God's grace and truth as in i. 14 (Meyer), or of the indwelling of the Holy Spirit, as in vii. 38 ; xi. 26 (Hofmann, Gess, Luthardt, Godet, and others).

11. **The woman saith unto Him** failing to apprehend the spiritual import of Christ's language—an indirect evidence that the present colloquy is no invention (cf. Weiss, The Life of Christ, vol. ii. p. 35) ; yet not without respect and reverence, as the appellation she employs indicates. **Sir** κύριε, a title of honour then in vogue : cf. v. 7 ; vi. 34 ; xii. 21 ; xx. 15. **Thou hast nothing to draw with** She was manifestly thinking of the fresh spring that supplied the well, for the drawing of which He had neither a bucket or vessel provided with a long rope to draw with (ἄντλημα, occurring here only, but cf. ii. 8, 9). **and** meaning 'even though thou hadst thou couldst not reach it': cf. 3 John 10 ; see Winer, § lv. 7. **the well is deep** This rendered it impossible to obtain water without a bucket. The term φρέαρ, signifying a pit dug in the ground, suggests the idea of deepness, πηγὴ (ver. 6) the notion of a structure erected round the spring. **from whence then hast Thou that living water?** A question resembling those in ii. 20 and iii. 4 in its total failure to grasp the spiritual import of Christ's words ; if not distinguished by malevolence like the former, perhaps sharing in the wonder of the latter. A question of incredulity rather than of pertness.

12. **Art Thou greater**—more distinguished as in viii. 3, of more exalted rank and therefore of larger ability ; the position of 'thou' indicating the woman's surprise that He should pretend to be so—**than our father Jacob** The Samaritans claimed though falsely to be descended from this patriarch (Jos. Ant. vii. 7, 3). **who gave us the**

well The woman follows the traditional belief : see ver. 6. **and drank thereof** What was good enough for him should suffice for thee. **himself and his sons and his cattle?** i.e. his entire household, for though τὰ θρέμματα, things reared, hence sheep and goats (Jos. Ant. vii. 7, 3 ; Xen. Oec. xx. 23), can only signify the patriarch's flocks and herds, *pecora* (Vulgate), *boves et oves* (Bengel), rather than his slaves, these latter included in the household so designated by the Evangelist.

13. **Jesus** ὁ Ἰησοῦς (the art. being omitted by some authorities, א A B C D etc., Chrysostom, Cyril, Griesbach, Lachmann, Tischendorf). **answered and said unto her,** replying to her thoughts rather than her words, **Every one that drinketh,** lit. *every one drinking ;* the adj. describing a universal experience : the part. a habitual act. **of this water** primarily of that contained in the well, to which He may have pointed as he spoke ; secondarily of every material and temporal gratification of which the water was an emblem. **shall thirst again** because of its inability to either permanently quench the appetite to which it ministers or periodically reproduce itself so as to renew its satisfactions.

14. **But**—introducing the great antithesis to which He has been leading up—**whosoever drinketh** or, *may drink,* ἂν with the subjunctive, rather than the participle, directing attention to the simple act (see Winer, § xlii. 3). **of the water that I shall give him shall never thirst** lit., *shall not thirst, for ever :* cf. viii. 51, 52 ; x. 28 ; xi. 26 ; xiii. 8 ; 1 Cor. viii. 13 ; meaning not shall never again be conscious of a desire after this living water, since "believers to the very end of life burn with desire for more abundant grace" (Calvin), and Wisdom saith, "They that eat me shall yet be hungry, and they that drink me shall yet be thirsty" (Eccles. xxiv. 20); but signifying, "shall never feel the pain of an unsatisfied want" (Westcott), " shall never have to go away and be exhausted and come again to be filled" (Alford). **but the water that I shall give him shall become in him** i.e. shall not pass away but abide and transform itself into **a well of water springing up,** a fountain of water leaping up ; " pouring forth in rich abundance" (Tholuck);

which it seldom does in Oriental springs. **unto eternal life** More than a mere strengthening of the notion of 'living water' (De Wette, B. Crusius, Lücke), or a statement of that for which the well suffices (Luthardt), the clause points to the ocean towards which this fountain of springing water flows and in which it finds its terminus—the Messianic eternal life, which believers first experience here, which maintains within them "a heavenly eternity during this mortal and perishing life" (Calvin), and which attains to its fullest measure and completest realization in the future life of endless felicity and of perfected fellowship with God. The idea of the water returning to its source,—"The eternal flows back to the eternal" (Stier); "the eternal rests not till it comes to the eternal" (Olshausen); *omnia ex Deo in Deum* (Bengel); "the life comes from the Source of Life and ascends to Him again" (Westcott)—though beautiful, does not appear to be contained in the words.

15. The woman saith unto Him If not in irony (Lightfoot, Lücke), frivolity (Godet), superstition (Maier), or curiosity (Lampe), still less in contemptuous unbelief (Calvin), but sincerely (Hengstenberg, Meyer), though still with much dimness of understanding as to the true import of Our Lord's words. **Sir, give me** The woman and Christ have changed places : see ver. 7. **this water** which neither needs a bucket to draw with, nor fails to satisfy the thirst of those who drink. **that I thirst not** It is as likely she had a glimmering of what Christ alluded to as that she only dreamt of a miraculous beverage. Even she could appreciate the happiness depicted in the language of her mysterious monitor. **neither come hither** not 'pass by this way' (Godet), but 'come across the intervening plain' (Westcott). **to draw** as I am now purposing to do.

16. Jesus saith unto her Apparently paying no heed to her request, in reality He commences to prepare the way for bestowing the living water. **Go, call thy husband** i.e. her so-called husband, since Christ knew the relations in which she stood towards the man with whom she lived. **and come hither.** Even if the woman fancied her husband's presence

was required to enable her to carry home the water (Bengel), Christ's reason for directing her to fetch him was not because it was improper to converse alone with a woman (Grotius), or because the female mind was incapable of understanding what was about to be said (Cyril), or because Christ did not wish her to act without the knowledge of her husband (Lange), but either because Christ desired to make him a partaker of the gift of life (Chrysostom, Lücke, Westcott), or because He wished by the sign of His prophetic knowledge to secure her confidence for higher things (Cyril, Chrysostom), or because it was necessary as a first step to awaken in her the sense of sin (Calvin, Bengel, Neander, Stier, Luthardt, Tholuck, and others).

17. The woman answered and said unto Him not "openly and frankly" (Milligan and Moulton), but "half sadly and half apologetically" (Westcott) acknowledging her sin ; with a sensitive shrinking from the touch of our Lord's words (Ebrard) ; perhaps with a secret desire to dissemble and conceal her exact position (Jacobus) ; replying in words which were half true and half false (Alford), true when taken literally, but false as being designed to convey an erroneous impression (Lange), **I have no husband** lit., *I have not a husband :* or, *a husband I have not* (א) ; which, besides agreeing with the order of the words as repeated by Christ, would tend to save the woman's credit, by making her thereby delicately hint at her sinful relations towards the man with whom she was united. Whether the woman's remark was the first thing that awakened Christ's prophetic insight into her antecedents (Godet), cannot be determined, as "we are not acquainted with the laws under which the beams of supernatural knowledge broke forth from the soul of Christ, nor with the relation between external *occasions* and the internal development of His higher knowledge" (Neander). **Jesus saith unto her** with a touch of caustic irony (Lücke, Godet) ; rather with serious solemnity, **Thou saidst well** The reading "thou sayest" has the authority of א B*. The translation of ὅτι is omitted in English as unnecessary. **I have no husband** ἄνδρα οὐκ ἔχω ; *a husband I have not.* If

Christ changed the order of the woman's words His intention may have been to convince her that her mental reservation was detected and her secret history known (Meyer, Godet, Lange, Alford, Westcott) ; if Christ repeated the woman's words as she gave them (see above), His purpose, conjecturally, was to emphasize her confession in such a manner as to make her feel its full force (Luthardt).

18. For thou hast had five husbands lit., *five husbands*, not paramours (Chrysostom), but lawful spouses (Euthymius), whom Christ distinguishes from her present partner—*thou hadst*, in contrast to 'thou hast' used of the latter. These five successive marriages were probably an indication of the woman's sensuality (Luthardt) ; yet it must not be assumed either that in themselves they were sinful alliances (Hengstenberg), or that some of them were dissolved by divorce on account of the woman's wantonness (Tholuck), even if it should be improbable (Luthardt) that all her five husbands had been removed by death. **and he whom thou now hast is not thy husband** The position of 'thy' before 'husband' has been thought (Godet) to suggest that the woman's partner was the husband of another ; but this is making the worst of the woman's case. **this hast thou said truly** lit., *this, a true thing, thou hast spoken*, whatever falsehoods otherwise or at other times, thou mayest have uttered. See Winer, § liv. 2. This remark of Christ's by anticipation disposes of the hypothesis (Strauss, Bauer, Weizsäcker) that the five husbands of the woman were the five heathen deities introduced into Samaria from Assyria (2 Kings xvii. 24, 33 ; Jos. Ant. ix. 14, 3), and that Jehovah was the sixth, since, not to mention that the five nations brought with them seven divinities which were not successively but contemporaneously adored, it is inconceivable that even a second century romancist would depict Christ as calling Jehovah Samaria's unlawful spouse and Jehovah's service whoredom, whilst He characterized the worship of heathen idols as lawful marriages. The notion that our Lord intended to supply an allegorical picture of the nation in its relations to Jehovah (Hengstenberg) has no foundation.

19. The woman saith unto Him desiring with woman's cleverness to turn the conversation from an unacceptable theme (De Wette, Ebrard, Tholuck, Meyer) ; more likely impelled by the conscious awakening of a better life (Godet, Brückner, Weiss) which, however, may not then have amounted to an earnest longing after salvation (Stier, Besser, Luthardt) ; perhaps also wishing to test the new prophet before committing herself further to Him (Hengstenberg), or to evince the interest in religion which had been kindled in her mind by Christ's words (Chrysostom, Calvin, Neander, Godet), **Sir, I perceive** This the knowledge of her past life Christ's words revealed (ver. 29) may have helped her to do—a knowledge not derived from others (Paulus) or from the woman by observing in her manner and mien the traces of her past wickedness (Lange), but by direct supernatural insight (ii. 24). **that thou art a prophet** not *the* prophet, the Messiah whom she afterwards said (ver. 25) she expected, but *a* prophet, having now arrived at the position occupied by Nicodemus at the commencement of this interview with Christ (iii. 2). On the meaning of the term ' prophet,' see i. 21.

20. Our fathers not the progenitors of Israel, either in patriarchal (Chrysostom, Calvin, Bengel, Kuinoel, Westcott) or post-Mosaic (Godet) times, but the Samaritan forefathers from the Separation downwards· (Meyer, Luthardt, Brückner, Tholuck, and others), **worshipped in this mountain ;** *Gerizim,* the southern—Ebal being the northern —of the two hills overlooking the plain of Shechem in which Sychar was situated ; the mountain from which Moses directed the blessings for obedience to be spoken (Deut. xi. 29 ; xxvii. 12), an instruction which was faithfully carried out (Josh. viii. 33). On the summit of Gerizim, according to Samaritan tradition, Abraham had erected his first altar, held his interview with Melchizedek, and offered up Isaac ; Jacob had enjoyed his vision of the mystic ladder; Moses had burned the ancient sacred vessels (Jos. Ant. xviii. 4, 1), and Joshua had reared his first altar on entering the land. Here for 200 years the Samaritans had possessed a temple resembling that of the Jews on Mount

Moriah in Jerusalem. Whether built in the time of Nehemiah (xiii. 28), or a century later in the days of Alexander (Jos. Ant. xi. 8, 2-4), cannot be ascertained with exactitude ; though it was certainly destroyed in B.C. 129 by John Hyrcánus (Ant. xiii. 9, 1), and its site long afterwards regarded as holy (Ant. xviii. 4, 1). There is no evidence that it was ever rebuilt. From the well where Jesus sat the ruins on the hill top would be visible (Porter, in Kitto's Cyclopædia, article *Gerizim*). As to worship the Samaritans accepted the five books of Moses with the religious prescriptions contained therein ; although in order to support their contention that Gerizim and not Jerusalem was the true place for worship they changed the reading " will choose " in Deut. xii. 14 ; xviii. 6, into " hath chosen " ; substituted " Gerizim " for " Ebal " in Deut. xvii. 4 ; and inserted after Exod. xx. 17 and Deut. v. 22 a command to erect an altar on Gerizim. **and ye say** i.e. ye Jewish people in opposition to our Samaritan fathers, **that in Jerusalem** the metropolis of the kingdom with its one temple, **is the place** Though not mentioned in the Pentateuch, it was clearly pointed out in the later books (Ps. ix. 11 ; cxxii. 4, 5 ; cxxxii. 13 ; Is. xxviii. 16 ; li. 11 ; Joel iii. 17) which the Jews accepted, but the Samaritans rejected. **where men ought to worship** lit., *where it is necessary to worship*, the δεῖ pointing not so much to the divine obligation of worship in the abstract as to the imperative requirement of connecting it with some heaven-appointed locality or centre (Deut. xii. 5).

21. **Jesus saith unto her**, understanding her to ask his decision on the litigated question, **Woman** A solemn and elevated manner of address corresponding to the transcendent revelation about to be made : cf. ii. 4. **believe Me** Thus He advances a claim to prophetic insight and authority : cf. xiv. 11. **the hour cometh** Not an old prophetic (B. Crusius), but a strictly Johannine expression (cf. ver. 23 ; v. 25, 28 ; xvi. 32) indicating the arrival of a new epoch in the development of the Messianic kingdom. The words "and now is" are not added because ' local ' worship had not yet begun to give way to ' spiritual.' **when neither**

in this mountain Gerizim, with its traditional sanctity : see above. **nor in Jerusalem** with its temple of Herod still gleaming in magnificence. **shall ye** not Samaritans alone (Meyer), but Jews and Samaritans together (Bengel), or mankind generally. **worship** Used indefinitely by the woman, but by Christ connected with its proper complement, the personal Divine Being, towards whom all genuine adoration must be directed, viz., **the Father** τῷ πατρί ; a familiar Johannine term (see throughout), here selected, it has been thought (Calvin), not without a latent antithetical allusion to the οἱ πατέρες ἡμῶν (ver. 20) of the woman. Though under the O. T. dispensation Jehovah was represented as standing in a fatherly relation to Israel (Exod. iv. 22 ; Deut. xiv. 1 ; Ps. lxxxix. 26 ; Is. lxiv. 8 ; Jer. xxxi. 9 ; Mal. i. 6), and the idea might not be unfamiliar to the Samaritans who claimed to be descendants of Jacob, yet the fatherhood of God as here announced—a fatherhood not for Israel or Samaria alone, but for humanity at large—even if dimly foreshadowed by the Hebrew prophets (Mal. ii. 10) was substantially a NEW REVELATION to afford which had been the object of the Incarnation (xiv. 9.)

22. **Ye** i.e. you Samaritans as distinguished from us Jews. **worship** Christ now pronounces a verdict on the popular controversy submitted to Him for decision. **that which** ὅ instead of ' whom,' ὅν, not because God was imperfectly known by the Samaritans (Olshausen, Lücke, Lange), since ὅν is also used to designate the object of Jewish worship, or because Christ referred to the act of worship as one of ignorance rather than to the object of worship as a person unknown (De Wette, Ebrard), or because the point in question was not so much the personality of God as the circumstance that He was the God of redemption and salvation (Luthardt), or because God is defined as to His nature and essence (Meyer), but because it is the abstract conception of Deity which is exhibited as the object of worship (Tholuck, Alford, Westcott). **ye know not** Their ignorance was not absolute since they possessed the Pentateuch, but relative inasmuch as they were without that further revelation of the name of God

which had been furnished to Israel in the prophets they rejected : cf. Weiss, Bib. Theol. § 152 ; Der Johanneische Lehrbegriff, § 6, p. 60. **we** i.e. **we** Jews, in contrast to you Samaritans; not **we** Christians as distinguished from you both (Hilgenfeld). In this solitary instance Christ places Himself in the same category with the Jews, not because He desired to free the woman from the untruth of her nationality (Luthardt), or to emphasize the corruption of the Samaritan life (B. Crusius), but because He was a Jew, having been born amongst the Jews (Brückner), and as such only was as yet known to the woman (Bengel). To discover in this a contradiction to Christ's usual behaviour explicable only by ascribing it to the error of a copyist (M. D'Eichthal), or of the Evangelist (Renan), is mere arbitrariness. **worship that which** instead of ' whom ' for the reason above specified. **we know** i.e. in comparison with you Samaritans. **for salvation** lit., *the salvation*, signifying neither " all the benefits of salvation " (Chrysostom, Theophylact), nor the Saviour (Olshausen, Tholuck) alone, but both, i.e. the Messianic salvation. **is of the Jews** i.e. proceeds from, ἐκ, finds its source in, the Jews ; i.e. is the culmination of those gracious revelations they received ; so that inasmuch as with all its imperfections Jewish worship has kept itself within the line of those revelations it has thereby declared itself to be the true worship : cf. Is. ii. 3 ; Zech. xiv. 8. 23. **But** In antithesis to that just affirmed concerning the superiority of Jewish over Samaritan worship. **the hour cometh and now is** The new dispensation which was to abolish all distinctions of time and place was even then in existence, inasmuch as He, the originator of it, was already there, and true worshippers, represented by His disciples, had already begun to call upon the Father. **when the true worshippers** i.e. those in whom the true idea of worship is recognized. On ἀληθινοί see i. 9. **shall worship the Father** Christ alludes not to pre-Christian worshippers who under the O. T. dispensation might have attained to some degree of spirituality (Deut. xxx. 11-14 ; Is. i. 10-20 ; xxix. 13 ; lxvi. 2 ; Ps. l. 13, 14 ; Mic. vi. 6-8), but

to worshippers under the N. T. dispensation to whom the Father as the object of adoration should be clearly revealed. **in spirit and truth** " This is the spaceless place of prayer in distinction from Gerizim and Jerusalem " (Lange) ; to be interpreted not as a *hendiadys* for " in a true spirit " (Tittmann), or adverbially as equivalent to " spiritually and truly " (Winer, § li. 1), but as a complex phrase descriptive of the sphere in which alone true devotion can exist and be performed, viz., (1) in spirit, ἐν πνεύματι, not in the divine spirit (Athanasius, Bengel, Besser), but the inner spirit of man, 1 Thess. v. 23 (Calvin, Meyer, Godet, Luthardt, and others), and (2) in truth, ἐν ἀληθείᾳ, which again is not ' the Son ' (Athanasius, Bengel, Besser), or ' sincerely ' (Vatablus), but marks the correspondence between the worship offered and the true ideal of worship as presented to God, hence the true as opposed to the false, the limited, the imperfect, the Christian service as opposed to the ritual of Judaism no less than to the erroneous adorations of the Samaritans. **for** καὶ γάρ, *nam et* (Vulgate), assigning the reason why the true worshippers worship the Father in spirit and in truth : Winer, § iii. 8. **such** viz., those who worship in this manner. **doth the Father** not ' the Father also,' i.e. as well as the Son (Besser), but ' the Father on His part ' as distinguished from the ' worshippers ' (Meyer, Westcott). **seek to be his worshippers.** The emphasis lies not on ' seeketh ' alone (Tholuck), or upon ' the Father' alone (Meyer), but upon the whole fact here stated, that corresponding to the human side of true worship there is a divine side which is the secret cause and inspiration of the former, viz., the seeking of the Father. "He seeketh for Himself such worshippers : these worshippers seek for themselves such a God " (Lange).

24. **God is a Spirit** or, ' Spirit is God,' πνεῦμα ὁ θεός ; the term 'spirit' defining the nature and essence of God as that which is incorporeal,—' spirit ' being in the O. T. (Is. xxxi. 3), no less than in the N. (1 Cor. vi. 20), opposed to body, flesh, that which discovers itself to the senses—though not therefore impersonal (Ps. xxxiv. 19 ; li. 19 ; Is. lxi. 3 ; lxvi. 2 ; Rom. i. 9 ; viii. 16). " That

God is spirit proves certainly more than that He is incorporeal. He is absolutely free—personality operative in itself, and the absolute opposite of blind necessity,—life essentially revolving on itself, indivisible and having nothing external to itself" (Delitzsch, Bib. Psychology, p. 1, § iii.). The proposition, though not occurring in the O. T., was easily deducible therefrom (cf. Ex. xx. 4; Deut. xvi. 22; Is. xxxi. 3; 1 Kings viii. 27; Ps. cxxxix. 7), and was with propriety addressed to the woman of Samaria, the theologians of her country having "altered a number of passages in the Pentateuch which seemed to speak of God in language properly applicable to man, and to ascribe to Him human form and feeling" (Watkin). **and they that worship Him must worship in spirit and truth** See on ver. 23; and contrast with the 'must,' δεῖ of ver. 20, the present 'must,' which substitutes the inner sphere of man's spirit for external localization, whether at Jerusalem or Gerizim, as the absolutely divine requirement of all true worship.

25. **The woman** Our Lord's sublime communication had passed beyond her capacity to understand. **saith unto Him** Hardly in a spirit of dissatisfaction because Christ had not decided the controversy in her favour (Lücke), or with a view to put Him off because disinclined to discuss matters so high (De Wette, Tholuck), or under a presentiment that Christ was Messiah (B. Crusius, Luthardt); but in a spirit of docility (Godet), conscious of requiring further illumination (Meyer), filled with a longing for the inner life (Lange), perhaps also with a desire for the coming of Messiah (Hengstenberg). **I know** Not 'I believe,' because with the fact to be stated she was already acquainted prior to, and independently of Christ's appearance before her. **that Messiah** The woman, not the Evangelist (Tholuck), uses the Jewish name 'Messiah' which had probably come into vogue amongst the Samaritans as well as the Jews, though the customary designation for Messiah amongst the former was *Hasshaheb* or *Hattaheb*, signifying 'the converter' (Gesenius, Ewald) or "the returning one' (Hengstenberg, Meyer, Tholuck), the present appellation being *El-Muhdy*, 'the guide'

(Robinson, iii. 100). "Six thousand years after the creation of the world will the *Taheb* or Messiah appear, to find upon Mount Gerizim the law of Moses, the holy vessels and the manna, and to bring all peoples to the true faith. As they do not consider the *Taheb* will be greater than another Moses, they ascribe to him only a life duration of 110 years; after which he will die and be buried beside Gerizim. At the end of the seventh thousand year the final judgment will take place," Dr. Kautzsch in Riehm's Handwörterbuch, art. *Samaritaner.* **cometh** If as yet she suspected that Christ was the Messiah, she manifestly believed Messiah's advent was at hand. **which is called Christ** Though this clause (cf. i. 4) probably belongs to the Evangelist (Godet), nothing prevents it from having been uttered by the woman (Alford), who might as easily have known the import of the one name as the other. **when He is come, He will declare** ἀναγγελλεῖ, *adnunciabit* (Vulgate), will report, announce, proclaim, as one who brings a message (cf. xvi. 13, 14, 15; 1 John i. 5); in which respect it differs from ἀπαγγελεῖ, to publish something that has happened, been experienced, heard (cf. xvi. 25; 1 John i. 3). See Cremer, Bib. Lexicon, pp. 25, 26. **unto us all things** The woman (1) comprehends that the doctrine of the law was not absolutely perfect, and that nothing more than first principles was delivered in it, else she would not have said "all" things; (2) declares that she expects such a Christ as will be the Interpreter of His Father and the Instructor of all the godly; (3) expresses her belief that we ought not to desire anything better or more perfect than His doctrine (Calvin).

26. **Jesus saith unto her** That Christ now imparts to her a revelation He had not yet made to any of His countrymen, and for some time longer forbade such as discovered it to make known (Matt. viii. 4; xvi. 20) involves no contradiction (De Wette), but is sufficiently explained by (1) the greater freedom of the Samaritan Messianic hope from political elements, and (2) the preparedness of the woman's heart to receive the sublime communication. **I that speak unto thee am He**, lit., *I*

am (sc. The Messiah), *He speaking to thee ;* the first clause, being the great 'I am' which runs throughout John's gospel (vi. 35 ; viii. 12, 58 ; xii. 26 ; xvii. 24) ; the ellipsis being readily supplied from the context ; and the second clause fixing the woman's attention on the fact that He was now doing to her what she expected of Messiah. "The seventh and last word of Jesus" (Hengstenberg).

HOMILETICS

VER. 1.—THE RITE OF BAPTISM.

I. **As practised by John** : i. 25, 26, 28, 33 ; iii. 23 ; cf. Matt. iii. 5, 12 ; Mark i. 4, 8 ; Luke iii. 3, 20. 1. *Its nature*—water baptism. Whether by immersion, pouring, or sprinkling cannot be deduced from the meaning of the word, which signifies to apply either an object to water or water to an object, hence either to dip, to immerse (2 Kings v. 14), or to wash (Mark vii. 4 ; Luke xi. 38). Against the notion that John's baptism was performed by immersion stand (1) the multitudes that gathered to it, (2) the impromptu and public manner in which it was dispensed, and (3) the fact that it was practised in all seasons. In favour of the idea that the son of Zacharias baptized by pouring may be quoted the contraposition of "with water" and "with the Holy Spirit" (i. 33) by which the two baptisms are distinguished. As the believer is not immersed in the Holy Ghost, but the Holy Ghost descends upon the believer, so arises the probability at least that John's baptism was, and that Christian baptism may be administered by pouring or sprinkling. 2. *Its import*—purification. This, though of a moral sort, was purely external, being equivalent to reformation rather than regeneration. It symbolized the cleansing of the life from open wickedness and immorality ; and, where that was sincere, of necessity also a change of mind or renovation of heart and will. But what it mainly represented was the reconstruction of the conduct rather than the recreation of the spirit. 3. *Its design*—preparation for Messiah. It was intended to rouse the nation from lethargy, purge it from corruption, and so put it in a state of readiness to welcome and accept the Messiah whensoever He should be revealed. 4. *Its obligation*—faith. It took the individual who received it bound to believe in and go over to Messiah immediately on His appearing.

II. **As celebrated by Christ** (through His disciples) : iii. 22, 26. 1. *Its resemblance to John's baptism.* It was (1) performed in the same way, being externally, like that of His forerunner, a water baptism ; (2) possessed the same symbolic significance, repentance and reformation ; and (3) looked towards the same end, the preparation of the people as a nation for the setting up of the Messianic kingdom of salvation. 2. *Its difference from John's baptism.* It was administered (1) by Christ's express authority, which John's was not, (2) to such as professed their faith, not in a 'coming,' but in a 'come' Messiah, (3) with the view of admitting to the circle of Christ's disciples, and (4) as an acknowledgment that the person baptized took himself bound to further instruction and obedience.

III. **As administered by the Apostles** : Matt. xxviii. 19 ; Mark xvi. 16 ; Acts ii. 38, 41 ; viii. 13, 36 ; ix. 18, etc. 1. *How far it agreed with the preceding.* (1) In form, it was a baptism with water. (2) In authority, it rested on the personal commandment of Christ. (3) In significance, it was a symbol of purification and a seal of faith in the Messiah. (4) In effect, it evidenced introduction into the Messianic Church. (5) In design, it bound the recipient of it to accept the teaching and obey the rule of Christ. 2. *How far it went beyond the preceding.* It (1) rested on the authority of the risen Christ, and not merely of the incarnate Son ; (2) symbolized the putting away not merely of the filth of the flesh but the inward renewal of the conscience by the descent and indwelling (or the spiritual and heavenly baptism) of the Holy Ghost ; (3) was administered on a profession of faith not simply in the Messiah, but in the Father, Son, and Holy Spirit ; (4) was not restricted to the Jewish people but extended to all nations ; (5) was not provisional and temporary, but permanent, in its intended duration.

Lessons. 1. The value of Christian baptism as an emblematic picture of the gospel. 2. The power of Christian baptism in stimulating to a holy life. 3. The continuance of Christian baptism a testimony to Christ's resurrection and therefore to His divinity.

VER. 6.—JACOB'S WELL.

I. **An Ancient History revived** : ver. 5, 6, 12. 1. *The digging of the well.* (1) By whom ? Jacob. Neither patriarch nor prince should be ashamed of work. He who will not dig for water when he wants it and it cannot otherwise be obtained is not likely either to have a well opened for him as Samson had (Judg. xv. 19) or shown to him as was done to Hagar (Gen. xxi. 19), or waiting for him as Israel found (Exod. xv. 27). If a man will not work neither should he eat nor drink (2 Thess. iii. 10). It is God's custom to give wells to those who dig for them (Num. xxi. 17, 18). (2) When ? On returning from Padan-aram, laden with the wealth he had acquired in exile, with numerous flocks and an extensive household. After all, God's commonest gifts are the least dispensable. Without water Jacob's flocks would soon have been "minished and brought low" and Jacob's servants cut off. (3) Where ? In the vale of Shechem, in the parcel of ground Jacob purchased from Hamor for a hundred pieces of money, on or near which afterwards rose the town of Sychar. Though Jacob was a rich man and the heir of the soil he would not seem to appropriate without paying for it what at common law was not his own. God's children and Christ's followers should provide things honest in the sight of all men (Rom. xii. 17 ; 2 Cor. viii. 21). (4) Why ? Probably to avoid the risk of quarrelling with his neighbours. Having but a little before been surnamed a Prince of Elohim and reconciled with Esau, he would not on the first opportunity begin to wrangle with the Shechemites. So should the saints follow peace with all men (Heb. xii. 14 ; 2 Tim. ii. 22). 2. *The using of the well.* "Jacob drank thereof, and his sons, and his cattle." (1) A testimony to the patriarch's independence. Though the Israelites on Moab's plains were promised that in Canaan they should drink of wells they had not dug (Deut. vi. 11), the royal preacher's counsel is a safer maxim to follow in ordinary life, "Drink water out of thine own cisterns" (Prov. v. 15). (2) A token of the patriarch's humility. He sought not a special and select spring for himself, but shared the one well with his children, dependents, and beasts. The class distinctions of modern society had not then arisen, as they have not yet been removed by Christianity (Rom. xii. 16). 3. *The bequeathing of the well.* "Our father Jacob gave us this well," said the woman ; perhaps meaning only it was believed to be the well Jacob dug. If Jacob bequeathed it to any, it was to Joseph and his descendants (Gen. xlviii. 22). 4. *The preservation of the well.* Its existence in the days of Christ was an indirect attestation of the historicity of the ancient records which testified that Jacob had once resided near Shechem and that it was customary for the patriarchs to dig wells. On the present appearance of the well, see Exposition.

II. **A Memorable Interview described** : ver. 6, 7, 8. 1. *Memorable to Jesus.* (1) For the place where it occurred—Jacob's well, a scene of material beauty, the vale of Shechem being distinguished for its loveliness and fertility (Stanley, Sinai and Palestine, pp. 236, 237), marred only by the presence in it of a city of liars or drunkards, as anciently the Jordan circle had been by the towns of Sodom and Gomorrah (Gen. xiii. 10-13) ; a spot consecrated by sacred memories (see Exposition). (2) For the time when it happened—at noon in midwinter, an unusual season of the year and hour of the day for such an interview to take place ; at the close of a long journey through Samaria, undertaken in obedience to the inward constraint of His Father's will ; at a moment when He sat upon the well's brink wearied with travel, alone, His disciples having gone into Sychar to purchase food,—perhaps saddened by the thought that He had been obliged to retire from Judæa,—almost certainly waiting to catch the next indication of His Father's leading. 2. *Memorable to the woman.* Because of (1) the person she met—seemingly a fatigued traveller, a member of the hated nation of the Jews, yet in reality God's Son incarnate, the Messiah of Israel and the Saviour of the world. How little men know the characters of those they encounter on the highways of life ! Even those esteemed enemies are not unfrequently truest friends (Heb. xiii. 2). (2) The truths to which she listened, —about the living water, the spirituality of true worship, the essential character of God (see next Homiletics). (3) The discoveries she made—concerning the vanity of earthly gratifications, the need of a higher principle of being than she had up to that moment possessed, the wickedness of her past life, the guiltiness and pollution of her conscience and heart, the one thing by which alone these could be met, the water of eternal life. (4) The treasures she found—herself, Christ, God, Salvation. 3. *Memorable to the Evangelist.* On account of (1) the insight it afforded into Christ's character, His meek humility, freedom from prejudice, devotion to the will of God, burning enthusiasm for souls (ver. 27-34). (2) The light it cast upon the work in which he and his fellow-apostles had been, and were to be, engaged (ver. 38). (3) The prospect it opened up of the ultimate triumph of the kingdom of heaven upon earth (ver. 35).

III. **A Profitable Conversation opened :** ver. 7, 11. 1. *A simple request preferred.* "Give me to drink," ver. 7. A request natural, Christ was thirsty (Judg. iv. 19); moderate, only a drink (1 Kings xvii. 10); courteous, considering from whose lips it fell (Ps. xlv. 2 ; Luke iv. 22); condescending, He who thus asked to be served by another was Himself the Lord of all (Matt. xi. 27) ; honouring, the woman afterwards would see this when she came to know who the speaker was (ver. 26 ; gracious, since He asked less to satisfy His own bodily necessity than to find a way to give her the living water. 2. *An astonished answer returned.* "How is it that thou," etc., ver. 9. A small thing needed to excite wonder ! Persons of narrow intelligence and meagre culture not unfrequently surprised to find others capable of rising superior to limitations of age and country, and throwing off the fetters of prejudice, ignorance, and superstition ! As Christ here by His behaviour caused the woman and even His disciples to marvel, so afterwards Paul by his free communion amongst the Gentiles produced consternation in the breasts of the 'pillars' in the church (Acts xv. 1, 2 ; xxi. 22 ; Gal. ii. 11, 14). The Spirit Christ exemplified at the well it is the mission of His religion to diffuse throughout the world (Gal. v. 6 ; vi. 15 ; Rom. ii. 28 ; Eph. ii. 14). 3. *An important truth announced.* "If thou knewest," etc., ver. 10. What more than any other thing keeps men from becoming Christians is ignorance (Eph. iv. 18)—(1) of God's unspeakable gift to men—the Holy Spirit (vii. 39 ; Acts ii. 38) ; (2) of the person and character of Him through whose mediation that gift is offered to mankind (viii. 19 ; 1 Cor. ii. 8), viz. Christ, the Son of God ; (3) of the terms upon which it can be secured, simply by asking (Matt. vii. 7 ; James iv. 3), without money and without price (Is. lv. 1), than which none can be easier ; (4) of the certain success of every application, Christ denying none that ask (vi. 37 ; Rev. xxi. 6) ; and (5) of the value of such a gift to the soul, importing as it does the impartation of eternal life (vii. 38, 39 ; Rom. viii. 2 ; 2 Cor. iii. 6 ; Gal. vi. 18).

Lessons—1. A glimpse into the true humanity of Christ—sitting on the well, asking to drink. 2. An illustration of Christ's diligence in the work of salvation—embracing every opportunity that arises. 3. A reminder of the need of diffusing abroad the Scriptures, seeing they alone can remove ignorance and make wise unto salvation.

VER. 14.—THE LIVING WATER.

I. **The Fountain**—*God.* The woman fancied Christ spoke of the fresh spring water bubbling up out of the soil at the bottom of Jacob's well, and on that account conceived it impossible Christ without a bucket could draw forth better water than she herself could obtain (ver. 11). As yet she had no conception either of the spiritual character of the water Christ alluded to or of the heavenly location of the well in which it was contained. But Christ had already set in the foreground with her (ver. 10), as earlier with Nicodemus (ver. 16), that the heart of God is a spring larger, deeper, fuller (Job xi. 7, 9 ; Eph. iii. 18) fresher than any cistern that man can hew, or well he can sink, in the hope of procuring happiness (Jer. ii. 13 ; xvii. 13). No doctrine more conspicuous in revelation than that God is the author of salvation (Ex. xv. 2 ; Job xxxiii. 29, 30 ; Ps. iii. 8 ; lxii. 1 ; Is. lv. 21 ; Jon. ii. 9 ; Luke i. 68 ; John iii. 16 ; Rom. vi. 23 ; 2 Cor. v. 18 ; Tit. i. 2, etc.).

II. **The Dispenser**—*Christ.* Leaving no uncertainty as to whence the living water shall proceed, Christ equally emphasizes that He Himself is the sole water drawer for a perishing world. He alone was possessed of ability to fetch that water up out of the infinite depths of the Divine nature. Hence He alone could give it to any. How He fetched it up and brought it forth by His incarnation, suffering, death, and resurrection is the burden of the N. T. Scriptures ; how He offers it now to men from the throne of His heavenly glory is the substance of His gospel message.

III. **The Water**—*The Holy Spirit* (see preceding Homiletics). 1. *Its satisfying character.* Whosoever drinketh of it shall never thirst after lower satisfactions. 2. *Its self-renewing power.* Material water and earthly gratifications can appease appetite only for a brief period, having no ability to prevent its recurrence ; the living water Christ bestows never loses its capacity to yield satisfaction to the soul that receives it, transforming itself into a perennial fountain, that constantly renews its supplies of spiritual refreshment as the soul's appetite for the same arises. 3. *Its ultimate destination.* If like a well it satisfies, like a river it bears the soul along towards the ocean of eternal life, which with Christ and John always signifies more than unending existence, even existence in a blessed fellowship, of knowledge, love, and joy with God.

IV. **The Recipients**—Whosoever. 1. *All in the widest sense, possible recipients.* The living water is adapted for all, provided for all, offered to all (i. 7 ; iii. 16, 17 ; Mark xvi. 15). 2. *All who comply with the prescribed conditions, actual recipients.* These conditions are (1) asking (ver. 10), as the woman did (ver. 15), without which preceding, receiving will not follow ; (2) acknowledging one's need of the living water, as the woman did when she owned her wicked life (ver. 17).

Lessons —(1) Gratitude to God ; (2) application to Christ, for the living water.

VER. 20-24.—THE TRUE WORSHIP OF GOD.

I. **Is not restricted to definite localities,** ver. 20, 21. 1. *Prior to the Advent of Christ it was.* The controversy to which the woman's language pointed circled round the claims of Jerusalem and Gerizim respectively to be the proper place for worshipping Jehovah. The Pentateuch, acknowledged by both Jews and Samaritans, without condescending on any particular locality, enunciated the general principle, that the worship of Jehovah to be acceptable must be rendered in one place, to be pointed out and commanded by Him (Ex. xx. 24 ; Deut. xii. 5, 11 ; xvi. 6 ; xxvi. 2 ; xxxi. 11). In selecting Jerusalem as the spot on which alone acceptable homage could be offered, the Jews believed they were following the guidance of Jehovah Himself, who had manifestly chosen that city by establishing there first the tabernacle and afterwards the temple. This belief first found utterance for itself in the later poetical and prophetical books (Ps. cxxxii. 13 ; 2 Chron. vii. 17 ; Is. lvi. 7 ; Zech. xiv. 17) and gradually diffused itself throughout the community. On the other hand, the Samaritans, finding no mention of Jerusalem in the Pentateuch, but observing the prominence assigned to Gerizim (Deut. xi. 29 ; xxvii. 12), recalling that in Joshua's day the blessings were recited from Gerizim (viii. 33), while in Nehemiah's time or 100 years later (see Exposition) a temple similar to Solomon's was erected on its summit where the ruined edifice was even then visible, were at no loss to make out a claim for Gerizim. Christ, however, waived the controversy and declared that a new era was about to dawn when the spirit of worship should be set free from the trammels of place, time, and form in which it had till then been confined, and when the momentous problem propounded by the woman would no longer require to be answered, but would answer itself by becoming obsolete and dropping out of sight. That era has dawned. 2. *Since the day of Pentecost it has not been, and never again can be, so restricted.* It is true that men, not always excepting the followers of Christ, have sometimes refused to be emancipated from the bondage of consecrated places and times, like the Jews who clung to the temple in Jerusalem, even after its vail had been rent in twain, till Jehovah was constrained to lay it in ruins as already He had overthrown the edifice on Gerizim ; but that of course is not the fault of Christ or of Christianity. The prophet Isaiah (lxvi. 1), 700 B.C., had a glimpse of the absurdity of localizing Deity, had attained to the sublime discovery that God might be worshipped anywhere ; but not even he could set this latter truth in the clear light in which it has stood since Christ spake to the woman at the well, and afterwards to His disciples, "Where two or three are gathered together in My name there am I" (Matt. xviii. 20), "Lo ! I am with you always" (Matt. xxviii. 20). What in these words was promised became possible on and after Pentecost (Acts ii. 17). The emancipation of religious worship from all external limitations is one thing the church owes to Jesus of Nazareth.

II. **Lies in the line of God's gracious revelations** : ver. 32. 1. *It had been so with the Jews.* By adhering to the Pentateuch and accepting the later prophets the Jews had a clearer, fuller, and more accurate idea of God the supreme object of worship than the Samaritans possessed who only received the five books of Moses and mingled the service of Jehovah with idolatries presented to heathen divinities. The gracious purpose of God towards Israel and through them to mankind had developed itself along the line of Jewish history. Hence the Jewish worship was superior to that performed on Gerizim. It had clearer light, was more in accordance with Divine prescription, and was inspired with an outlook of hope towards the glorious horizon of the future. To this extent Christ decided the controversy of the day in favour of the Jews. 2. *It must continue to be so with the Christian.* Had God not revealed Himself in a way of grace, it might have been possible to worship acceptably in what is called the temple of nature (Ps. xix. 1 ; Rom. i. 20). But, having manifested His name in the person of His Son, any worship presented to Him which ignores that is and must be unacceptable, what Paul styles " will worship " (Col. ii. 23), self-devised adoration. Nay, whatever worship professes to be based upon the revelation of the Divine nature furnished in and through the historical appearing of the Son, without advancing to accept the higher revelations of the Spirit as expressed in the developed teaching of the Apostolic Church, is to that extent defective, in the same manner relatively as was the worship of the Samaritans through rejecting the post-Mosaic books of the Hebrew Scriptures.

III. **Accords with the being and essence of God Himself** : ver. 23, 24. 1. *Spiritual, since God is Spirit.* Not *a* spirit, as if He were one among many, but *spirit*, signifying that as to essence He is not flesh or corporeity, or even matter in its most ethereal form, but pure spirit. Not impersonal, because the article is wanting, any more than when it is written God is light (1 John i. 5) and God is love (1 John iv. 16). But absolute being, personality, life, infinitely removed from those imperfections that adhere to created things, beings, or intelligences. Hence no worship can be acceptable that has not regard to this, that finds not its source and seat in, that does not emerge and ascend from, the innermost being, personality, life of the spirit that worships. 2. *True, since God is the Truth*, the only legitimate object of worship for a human soul. It must correspond to the ideal of worship, and be such as is worthy to be offered to Him and as He can worthily receive. 3. *Filial, since God is the Father.* Pious Israelites had already known that God regarded them with fatherly compassion ; but not till Christ spoke was ' the fatherhood of God ' exhibited in its true light (Matt. v. 45 ; vi. 9). The supreme being Christ called men to adore was the absolute Father, father of the spirits of all flesh, of His believing people, of the only-begotten Son. As such the only worship He could worthily receive behoved to be filial, in a spirit of adoption (Rom. vii. 15 ; Gal. iv. 6), a spirit of dependence and love.

Lessons. 1. Great controversies upon which much heat is expended mostly answer themselves when left to time. 2. Questions concerning the externals of Christian worship do not belong to its essence. 3. Christian freedom is not the same thing as will worship. 4. The characteristics of Christian worship here enunciated fit it to become universal. 5. In these lie the prophecy and promise of its ultimate triumph. 6. The Founder of such worship requires no surer witness to His supreme divinity.

2. TO THE CITIZENS OF SYCHAR

Chap. IV. Ver. 27-42

Exposition

Ver. 27. **And upon this** ἐπὶ τούτῳ, i.e. when Christ had so spoken, rather than ἐν τούτῳ (ℵ* D), whilst the conversation was going on (see Winer, § 48, c). **came His disciples** back from the town (ver. 8); **and they marvelled** lit., *kept on marvelling*, though the reading 'marvelled' is not without sanction, **that He was speaking**—they had obviously arrived within seeing, if not hearing, distance before the conversation ended—**with a woman**—not with *this* woman in particular (Kuinoel), or with a woman of Samaria (Hengstenberg), but with a woman at all, rabbinical theology having declared it unlawful to converse on the street with women, even with one's own wife, and asserted that the female sex was incapable of receiving rabbinical instruction (Lightfoot, Schöttgen, Wetstein); **yet no man said** The reticence of the disciples was doubtless dictated by reverence as much as by astonishment, **What seekest Thou?** τί ζητεῖς, what service dost thou ask of her? is it food or drink? or generally, what service of any kind art thou craving? (cf. i. 38), **or, Why speakest thou with her?** lit., *why talkest thou with her.* Both questions were addressed to Christ, rather than the former to the woman and the latter to Christ (Alford).

28. **So** οὖν, accordingly, therefore, then; not so much because the arrival of the disciples had interrupted her interview with Christ (Meyer), as because Christ's communication had filled her with joy (Luthardt). **the woman left her waterpot** The leaving of the waterpot (ii. 6, 7) by the woman may be regarded as an indication that she purposed to return and that her heart was meanwhile aglow with ardent zeal, which caused her through exuberance of joy to forget her business at the well as the Lord had forgotten His necessities (Tholuck), to set aside her

errand as the Lord had set aside His want (Westcott); the mention by the Evangelist of the waterpot and in particular of the woman's leaving it a proof that the author was an eye witness at least of this part of the scene. **and went away into the city** Sychar, about 2 miles distant (ver. 2), **and saith to the men** i.e. to those she first met within the gates, thus becoming like Andrew and John (i. 41) a herald of Messiah in the hour of her conversion, and attaining to the honour of being the first female missionary of Christ; in remarkable contrast to Nicodemus who went away "contemplative but silent" (Luthardt).

29. **Come, see a man** (cf. i. 39, 46) **who told me all that ever I did** lit., *all things which,* πάντα ἅ (ℵ B C*, Tischendorf, Westcott), rather than πάντα ὅσα (T. R), all things as many as, since ὅσα is included in the πάντα. The exaggeration lying in the use of "all" indicates an awakened conscience on the part of the woman. **can this be the Christ?** μήτι οὗτός ἐστιν ὁ Χριστός; this is not the Christ, is he? Surely not! The particle μὴ (cf. viii. 22; xviii. 35; Matt. xii. 23; xxvi. 22, 25) suggests that she expected not an affirmative (Lücke, Brückner), but a negative answer (see Buttmann's Larger Greek Grammar, § 148, 5; Winer, § lvii. 3); though this was not because of uncertainty in her own mind, but because, like the women after the resurrection, she hardly believed for joy (Luke xxiv. 41).

30. **They** i.e. the townspeople to whom she had imparted her tidings (ver. 28), **went out of the city** under the impulse of wonder and excitement, **and were coming to Him.** The Evangelist depicts the scene as he remembers to have seen it:—they were hurrying across the intervening plain towards the well.

31. **In the meanwhile** i.e. after the departure of the woman and before the arrival of the Sycharites, **the disciples prayed Him,** asked Him entreatingly : cf. ver. 40, 47 ; xii. 21 ; Matt. xv. 23 ; Luke xiv. 18, 19, **saying, Rabbi** (see iii. 2 ; 26), **eat.** The disciples were probably thinking of their own hunger as well as His, and of the trouble they had in securing provisions.

32. **But He said unto them** in words as enigmatical to them as those about the Living Water had been to the woman, ver. 10, **I have meat to eat that ye know not** lit., *I*, as distinguished from you with your provided victuals ; *an eating,*—βρῶσις, always with Paul the act of eating, *actio edendi* (Rom. xiv. 17 ; 1 Cor. viii. 4 ; 2 Cor. ix. 10 ; Heb. xii. 6), though with John frequently equivalent to βρῶμα, food (vi. 27, 55) ;—*have,* or possess, *to eat,*—φαγεῖν, which disposes of the idea that Christ meant He had drunk of the woman's waterpot in her absence, since in that case he would have said 'to drink,' πιεῖν ;—*which ye know not,* of which ye have as yet no experience, understanding neither its nature nor power, — not words of rebuke or blame (cf. ver. 10), but a most sweet riddle, *dulcissimum enigma* (Bengel).

33. **The disciples therefore** as preplexed as the woman had been, ver. 11, "*Quid mirum, si mulier non intelligat aquam, ceu discipuli non intelligebant escam ?*" (Augustine), **said one to another** if in undertone, yet sufficiently loud to be overheard by Christ : cf. xvi. 7, **Hath any man brought Him aught to eat ?** lit., *no one surely hath brought Him to eat,* the particle μή, as above explained, ver. 29, suggesting that no one had.

34. **Jesus saith unto them** having either overheard their words or read their thoughts : cf. ii 24, 25 ; Matt. ix. 4 ; xii. 25 ; Luke v. 22 ; **My meat** βρῶμα, that which constitutes for me a βρῶσις or 'eating,' **is to do** ἵνα ποιήσω, (B C D K L Tᵇ H etc., Origen, Lachmann, Westcott and Hort), *that I should do,* or according to the better reading, ἵνα ποιῶ (א A E G M S U V Γ Δ A etc., Tischendorf, Meyer, Brückner, Alford, Lange, Godet), *that I may do,* for which ποιήσω was probably substituted to make it correspond with τελειώσω. In both cases ἵνα is expressive of

the purpose in which Christ declares His meat to consist (see Winer, § xl. 8, c, a), viz. the doing of the will of God ; the aorist of the verb representing this doing as a 'completed,' the present as a 'continuous' process. **the will of Him that sent me** The first allusion in the hearing of the disciples to the fact of His pre-existence and coming forth from the Father, unless it be held that they were present during the colloquy with Nicodemus (iii. 17) ; after this the clause frequently recurs in the teaching of Jesus ; v. 30 ; vi. 38 ; vii. 18 ; viii. 50 ; ix. 4 ; xii. 49, 50 ; xiv. 31 ; xv. 10 ; xvii. 4 : cf. Job xxiii. 13. **and to accomplish** lit., *that I should perfect,* or bring to a complete and final consummation, this being the characteristic Johannine sense of the verb τελειόω : xvii. 4, 23. **His work,** i.e. the work assigned Christ by God who had sent Him, which work was pointed out from time to time by particular expressions of the Divine Will (θέλημα) and was carried forward step by step towards its ultimate realization by the constant, joyous, regular, and unwearied ' doing ' of Christ.

35. **Say not ye** The following clause has been variously understood. 1. As *a proverbial expression* for the interval between seed-time and harvest (Lightfoot, Grotius, Tittmann, Lücke, De Wette, Tholuck, and others),—against which press the facts (1) that no trace of such a proverb can be found, (2) that the usual interval between seedtime and harvest was not four months but six (though the Talmud mentions four), (3) that the so-called proverb contains no allusion to seed-time, and (4) that, if it was such, it would hardly have been put into the mouth of the disciples as distinguished from Himself. 2. As *an incidental allusion* to an observation that had that day fallen from the lips of the disciples as they passed through the cornfields (Hengstenberg, Godet, Milligan and Moulton) ; which is plausible enough, though not hinted at in the text. 3. As *a colloquial description* at the time uttered of the then appearance of the country (Lampe, Meyer, Luthardt, Brückner, Westcott). **There are yet four months** lit., *that yet,* i.e., from this time on, *an interval of four months it is.* **and then cometh the harvest** lit., *and*

the reaping cometh. As the reaping began about the middle of April, the 16th Nisan (Lev. xxiii. 10 ; Deut. xvi. 9 : cf. Tristram, The Land of Israel, pp. 583 f ; Keil, Bib. Archäologie, § 118), the conversation must have taken place in December (Hengstenberg, Godet, Meyer, Luthardt and others), or, if a leap year (Wieseler), with a month intercalated in March, in January (Westcott, Watkin), so that our Lord's first visit to Jerusalem and Judæa must have extended over a period of eight months. See on ver. 3. **behold I say unto you** soliciting attention to, and claiming authority for, the communication about to be made, **lift up your eyes** cf. Is. xlix. 18 ; lx. 4. The words render it not unlikely that Christ pointed to the approaching Samaritans. **and look on the fields that they are white already unto the harvest** or, *white unto the harvest already.* Taken literally, the words seem to imply that the time then present was the season immediately preceding harvest (Greswell, Townsend, Farrar) ; but it is better to regard them metaphorically as referring not to the material harvest, then four months distant, but to the spiritual harvest of which Christ at the moment beheld the promise in the flocking of the Sycharites towards the well (Godet, Luthardt, Meyer, Westcott) and contrasting the celerity with which seed sown in the spiritual domain sprang up with the long interval of waiting that in the natural sphere preceded the time of reaping (Olshausen). That our Lord's prophetic glance was directed in the first instance to the conversion of the Samaritans (Godet, Lange) need not prevent it from being true that the same glance looked beyond to the conversion of the heathen world generally (Baur, Stier, Luthardt, Meyer, Tholuck and others). The position of ἤδη at the end of the verse (cf. 1 John iv. 3) forms a rhetorical counterpart to ἔτι at its commencement.

36. **He that reapeth** The ἤδη of the preceding verse is sometimes joined with ὁ θερίζων, in accordance with what seems Johannine usage, see ver. 51 ; vii. 14 ; ix. 22 ; xi. 39 ; xv. 3 (A C* D E L ℵ, Schulz, Tischendorf, Ewald, Ebrard, Lücke, Godet, Westcott and Hort, Milligan and Moulton), as if the meaning were " already he that reap-

eth " ; but it was scarcely correct to say that the reaping had commenced in Samaria. The words rather enunciate a general principle as to the recompense awaiting both sower and reaper in the spiritual, no less than in the natural, kingdom ; the sower in the former being not the O. T. prophets (Chrysostom, Lange), or at least not these alone, or chiefly, but Christ Himself (cf. Matt. xiii. 37), and the reapers being the Apostles, whom he encourages to enter on the labour of gathering in Samaria's harvest, perhaps manifesting an undertone of sadness that He will not live to see them reaping in Samaria's fields, yet rejoicing in spirit that all the same their joy would be His. **receiveth wages** not merely hereafter in heaven (Calovius), but also here upon the earth, **and** The καί is expletive and more particularly defines that in which the wages consists, viz., the joy of gathering souls into the kingdom. **gathereth fruit unto life eternal** The image seems to be that the souls of converted men are the harvest sheaves reaped by the labours of the Apostles, while the words " unto eternal life " may suggest the local idea of the heavenly granary (cf. Matt. iii. 12 ; xiii. 30) into which they are ultimately brought (De Wette, Brückner, Meyer, Lange), or the character of the fruit they gather, which is spiritual and imperishable, enduring unto life eternal (Luthardt, Westcott). **that** ἵνα ; expressive of the Divine purpose in making the reapers partakers of the reward of harvest. **he that soweth** viz. *Jesus.* The word "both" here omitted (B C L Tᵇ U etc., Origen, Westcott and Hort) should perhaps be retained (ℵ, Tischendorf, Godet, Meyer, Luthardt) as better bringing out the simultaneousness of the joy experienced by both classes of labourers. **and he that reapeth** i.e. the Apostles **may rejoice together** lit., *that he who soweth may rejoice,* ὁμοῦ, not as really as (B. Crusius, Luthardt), but *at the same time* (cf. xx. 4), *and he that reapeth.*

37. **For herein** i.e. either in this sphere of the kingdom of God (Westcott) or in this matter of sowing and reaping (Brückner, Meyer, Godet), **is the saying true** not ' says the truth' (Lücke, De Wette), but ' holds good,' has its proper significance, finds its essential realization, its ideal (ἀληθινὸς)

fulfilment (Meyer, Tholuck, Godet, and others) ; or, retaining the article before ' true ' (א, Tischendorf, Tholuck, Meyer, Alford), " is that which corresponds to its thought" (Luthardt). That the writer has not followed his usual practice in joining ὁ λόγος ὁ ἀληθινός (i. 9 ; xv. 1), forbids the rendering ' and herein the true saying applies ' (Bengel, Hengstenberg, Alford, Stier). **one soweth and another reapeth** lit., *one is he who sows and another is he who reaps ;* i.e. they are not always or even commonly the same individuals. The maxim applied in the case of Christ and His disciples. 38. **I** So emphatically He designates Himself as the sower. **sent you** The aorist is here employed not as a prophetic future (Kuinoel, De Wette, Tholuck, Alford),—" It is only in appearance that the aorist is ever used for a future " (Winer, § xl. 5, b) ; or because their sending virtually dated from their calling (Lampe, Lücke, Meyer, B. Crusius, Stier, Ewald, and others) ; but either because He had just invited them to accord a welcome to the Samaritans (Godet), or because He had already employed them in spiritual harvesting in Judea (Bengel, Westcott). **to reap** This, and not sowing, was specifically the work entrusted to them. **that whereon ye have not laboured** Hitherto, so far as the disciples were concerned, in Judea and in Samaria, the spiritual harvests they had been, or were about to be, privileged to gather in had not been prepared by them, but by others ; and this was the relation in which throughout the future they should stand to the harvest work in which they should be summoned to engage. **others have laboured, and ye are entered into their labour.** Though an illustration of these " others " was afterwards found in Philip the Evangelist (Acts viii. 15) to whom Peter and John served as reapers (Baur), and in Paul who was followed on the harvest field by the Twelve (Hilgenfeld), yet it is clear Christ now alludes either to Moses and the Prophets of the O. T. dispensation (Luthardt, Lange), or to John the Baptist and Himself (Godet), or to Himself and the Samaritan women (Godet, Watkin), or most probably to Himself alone (Lücke, Hengsten-

berg, Meyer, Tholuck), though it is by no means improbable He selected the plural expressly for the purpose of associating with Himself all whose labours had in any way contributed towards the preparation of His kingdom (Westcott, Milligan and Moulton). 39. **And**—resuming the historical narration interrupted at ver. 31—**from that city** Sychar into which the woman went (ver. 28), and from which the men came (ver. 30), **many of the Samaritans believed on Him** cf. iii. 16. This friendly reception by the Sycharites a contrast to that Christ met in Jerusalem (ii. 18, 24)—**because of the word of the woman who testified** A specific testimony the requisite basis of faith : i. 7. **He told me all things that ever I did.** See on ver. 29. Though the woman in all likelihood would rehearse with as much accuracy as she could the declarations of Christ about the living water and the spirituality of true worship, that which seems to have carried conviction to their minds was Christ's power of reading the woman's heart and knowing the woman's life : cf. i. 48 ; ii. 24. 40. **So when the Samaritans came unto Him** as He still rested at the well, **they besought Him** with earnest entreaty : cf. ver. 31, **to abide with them** : cf. Luke xxiv. 29, and contrast Luke viii. 37, **and He abode there two days.** How these days were employed though not stated, may be easily imagined : see ver. 34, 41 ; ix. 4, 5. 41. **And many more** i.e. others besides those mentioned in ver. 39, **believed** sc. on Him, as in ver. 39, **because of His Word** ; not as distinguished from His miracles, but in contrast to the woman's word, ver. 39 ; **and they said to the woman** whose report they had at first either credited or been inclined to credit, **Now we believe not because of thy speaking**—more correctly, *no longer because of thy speaking we believe ;* conveying no idea of contempt (Meyer, Brückner), since the woman's communication styled by the Evangelist a λόγος (ver. 39) had been to them full of significance (Tholuck), but distinguishing it as ' talk,' λαλιά (corresponding to the verb used in ver. 26, 27), from the word of Jesus which they designate as λόγος. Elsewhere Christ describes His own discourse as a 'speaking' (viii. 43). **for we have heard for ourselves** lit., *we ourselves have heard ;* i.e. have ourselves become listeners, viz. to Him or His Word, so that we are no longer dependent on thy 'report'; or, connecting both verbs with the subordinate clause, "we ourselves have heard that this is," etc., the source whence this 'hearing' was derived being the 'Word' of Christ Himself. Compare Rom. x. 17. **and know** From faith which at first rested on indirect testimony (ver. 39), they had progressed to faith based on direct personal knowledge. " *Primo per famam : postea per presentiam* " (Augustine). **that this is indeed the Saviour of the world.** ὁ σωτὴρ τοῦ κόσμου, *Salvator Mundi* (Vulgate); occurring elsewhere only once (1 John iv. 14), is not on that account to be suspected as put into the mouth of the people by the Evangelist (Lücke, Tholuck), since the fact that the Messiah was to be the Saviour of the world

could have been learnt from the Samaritan Pentateuch (Gen. xii. 1 ; xlix. 10), even if it was not, more probably, unfolded to them by Christ Himself in the two days' teaching He gave them ; and in point of fact was more likely to be inferred by them seeing they were not hampered by the feeling of national exclusiveness which so frequently veiled the significance of Scripture to the Jewish mind (Meyer, Lange); while Jesus could only have presented Himself to these Samaritans as the Saviour of the world, since "He entirely rejected their pretensions to have a part in the covenant" of God with Israel (Hengstenberg). The absence from the text of ὁ Χριστος in accordance with the best authorities (א B C, Origen, Vulgate, Lachmann, Tischendorf, Meyer, Westcott and Hort), renders it less justifiable to regard the above expression as a Johannine addition.

HOMILETICS

VER. 38, 39.—THE FIRST FEMALE MISSIONARY.
I. **Her Previous Character :** ver. 7, 17. 1. *Of dissolute morals.* Antecedent wickedness, even of the grossest type, no barrier to the reception of Divine grace, provided repentance and faith supervene (Is. i. 18 ; lv. 7, 8, 9 ; Mic. vii. 18 ; Matt. xii. 31 ; 1 John i. 7, 9); examples—Manasseh (2 Kings xxi. 16 ; 2 Chron. xxxiii. 12, 13); Saul of Tarsus (Acts ix. 1-18); the Philippian jailor (Acts xvi. 34); and no disqualification for being afterwards employed in the service of God or Jesus Christ. 2. *Of lively understanding.* A quick-witted woman, she had a tolerable acquaintance with the traditions of her country as well as with the outstanding religious controversy of the day. Christ is certainly not dependent for the ultimate success of His Gospel on the intelligence of those who proclaim it, but just as little does He regard high mental endowments in His servants as a misfortune. If He now had in His train unlettered fishermen like Andrew and Peter, He afterwards possessed a Paul and a Luke amongst His missionary agents. 3. *Of religious inclinations.* She was expecting the advent of Messiah and hoping to be guided by His revelations to a perfect knowledge of the true mode of worship. Thus Divine grace often keeps alive in souls that seem going downwards to perdition a small, oftentimes imperceptible spark of goodness that only waits the Spirit's breath to fan it into a flame of true spiritual life.
II. **Her Inspiring Motive.** 1. *Not mere excitement.* To ascribe this woman's behaviour to love of novelty and adventure is wholly unsatisfactory, since she grounds her invitation to her countrymen upon a basis entirely moral and spiritual (ver. 29). 2. *Not conscious peace.* As little plausible is the notion that she was already rejoicing in the assurance of salvation. This were to assign to her newly awakened religious life an introspectiveness and maturity, to say the least uncommon, if not also unnatural. But, 3. *simple faith.* She believed Christ to be the long-expected Messiah, and having made this discovery felt it impossible to be silent, acting in like this like David (Ps. lxvi. 16 ; cxvi. 10), like the Apostles (Acts iv. 20), like Paul (2 Cor. iv. 13), like the leper (Mark i. 45).

III. **Her Glowing Zeal** : ver. 28. 1. *The trivial action.* " She left her water-pot." Note the bearing of this on the credibility of the narrative (see Exposition). As a straw sometimes shows how a stream flows, so a word or deed may reveal how the inner current of thought and feeling runs (Prov. xxiii. 7). 2. *The important revelation.* The woman's behaviour on leaving the well evinced (1) an intention to return, as otherwise she would have carried off her vessel ; (2) the greatness of her zeal, which caused her errand to be forgotten through eagerness to proclaim her new found joy (cf. Christ, ver. 34) ; (3) the importance she attached to her discovery of one who could answer all the questions of her time and, better, satisfy all the aspirations of her soul (Matt. xiii. 44-46) : (4) the estimate in which she held things spiritual and Divine in comparison with the lesser matters of time and sense, since she had listened to the Saviour's talk about the living water ; and (5) the desire she felt that others should be acquainted with the good news which had been told to her, in which respect her conduct contrasted with that of Nicodemus (iii. 1), while it closely resembled that of Andrew and Philip (i. 41, 45).

IV. **Her Gladsome Message**: ver. 29. 1. *The startling announcement:*—" He told me all things that ever I did." The language of exaggeration, it nevertheless contained a truth. Christ had not merely shown Himself acquainted with the details of her personal history, as He had been with those of Nathanael's (i. 48), and with the quality of her spirit as He had been with that of Peter's (i. 42) ; but He had discovered her to herself in such a fashion as to enable her to realize her guiltiness before God, as He afterwards did to Peter (Luke v. 8), and her need of that living water of which He spake, and of which she ultimately drank. The inshining of that light upon her soul was the first symptom of the entrance into it of that life which He alone could communicate (i. 4). So can no soul ever see or come to know itself except in the light Christ imparts (Ps. xxxvi. 9). 2. *The joyous question:*—" Can this be the Christ ? " An interrogation not of doubt or unbelief, but of faith, certainty, and joy. It was a settled conviction in her own mind, though she spoke as if she believed not for joy (Luke xxiv. 41); and certainly no more powerful evidence exists for the individual of the high claims of Jesus to be the Messiah of Israel, the Son of God, and the Saviour of the world than just this power which belongs to Him of revealing the human heart to itself. Yet in the woman's words appears an adroitness by no means unworthy of imitation by those who would win men for Christ. 3. *The eager invitation:*—' Come and see !' Compare Christ's address to Andrew and John (i. 39). It was a summons to her countrymen to make trial of the stranger for themselves, to interview Him as she had done, listen to his teaching and judge for themselves. It is the attitude religion ever takes in its approaches to the soul of man (Ps. xxxiv. 8 ; John vii. 17).

V, **Her Wonderful Success** : ver. 30, 39, 41. 1. *The extent of it.* (1) She produced a commotion in the city. The gospel usually did so when preached in a Gentile city ; e.g. in Samaria (Acts viii. 8), Antioch (Acts xiii. 44), Thessalonica (Acts xvii. 5) ; commonly does so to-day when proclaimed with the freshness and power of a heaven-born enthusiasm. (2) She enkindled faith in the hearts of many citizens. These, crediting her testimony, recognized the stranger at the well as Messiah, and accorded a welcome to the teaching He offered. 3. *The reason of it.* That the townspeople so readily accepted the words of a light woman was probably due to two causes. (1) A persuasion of the woman's sincerity and of the substantial accuracy of her report, both of which they may have held as guaranteed by the humiliating confession of her past wicked life ; and (2) a feeling of the self-evidencing power of the truth concerning the living water, the fatherhood of God, and the spiritual nature of worship, even when reported to them at second hand (2 Cor. iv. 2 ; 1 Thess. i. 5 ; ii. 13).

Lessons. 1. The duty of those who know the truth to publish it to others : xvii. 18 ; xx. 21 ; Matt. v. 16 ; x. 8 ; Acts v. 20 ; Rom. x. 14, 15. 2. The place and power of female agency in the church : e.g. Mary, Luke i. 26-38 ; Elizabeth Luke i. 6 ; Anna, Luke ii. 37 ; Dorcas, Acts ix. 36 ; Lydia, Acts xvi. 14 ; Priscilla, Acts xviii. 26, etc. 3. The adaptation of the gospel to the highest needs of man : Is. lii. 7 ; Ezek. xlvii. 8 ; Luke i. 78, 79 ; John viii. 32 ; xii. 50 ; Rom. i. 16, etc.　4. The certainty that all nations will yet be obedient to the faith : Ps. ii. 8 ; lxxii. 8 ; Is. xi. 9 ; Dan. ii. 35 ; Matt. xxviii. 18 ; Rom. i. 5 ; Phil. ii. 11 ; Rev. xi. 15.

Ver. 32-34. The zeal of Christ.　I. For His Father's house (ii. 17)—purity of worship.　II. For His Father's will (ix. 4)—the salvation of men.　III. For His Father's children (xvii. 9)—the sanctification of His church.

Ver. 32. The food of Christ.　I. Heavenly in origin ; II. Spiritual in character ; III. Sustaining in quality ; IV. Sufficient in supply.

VER. 35-38.—SOWERS AND REAPERS.

I. **The different Spheres occupied and Works performed by Christ and His disciples** in transforming the wilderness of earth into a rich and ripe harvest field for God.　1. *He, the sower ; they, the reapers.* The maxim " one soweth and another reapeth " has its application in the kingdom of grace no less than in that of nature (Mark xiii. 34 ; 1 Cor. xii. 11).　The place of sower Christ reserves for Himself (Matt. xiii. 37). This He filled visibly in the days of His flesh by preaching and teaching in synagogues, by waysides, and on mountain slopes ; and fills yet in the days of His exaltation, though invisibly, as really as at any time before, more really perhaps Christ would say, since now in the person of His Spirit He has permanently established Himself upon the earth.　Apostles, evangelists, pastors, teachers are merely instruments He employs in sowing, which is not effected when the word is simply poured into the ear or understanding, but only when it is deposited in the deeper furrows of the heart.　At the most their connection with the harvest is that of gathering it in ; they are bearers of the sheaves Christ by his word and Spirit has sown and ripened in the soul of humanity.　2. *He, the master ; they, the servants.*　" I sent you to reap," says Christ, depicting Himself as the lord of the harvest for whom the spiritual grain was ripening, while they, the disciples, He had invited to accord a welcome to the approaching Samaritans, were His servants to whom He deputed corresponding tasks.　A truth requiring to be emphasized, that, as in the realm of nature (i. 3), so in the kingdom of grace, Christ is the sole head, master, lord, king (xiii. 13 ; xviii. 37 ; Matt. xxiii. 10 ; Eph. i. 23 ; iv. 5, 16 ; Col. i. 18) and therefore the exclusive fountain of law and authority within the Church (xv. 12 ; 1 John iii. 23) ; that whatever diversities of talent or of toil may be assigned to officials or private members therein, all are equally under law to Him (Rom. xiv. 4) ; that no man is called into the church to carry out theories, schemes, purposes of his own, but solely to do his Master's will (xv. 14).　3. *He, the pioneer ; they, the aftercomers.*　" Others have laboured ; and ye have entered into their labours."　As in all departments of life and industry, so within the kingdom of heaven upon earth there must be pioneers who go before, do the hard work of reclaiming the waste land, digging and trenching, draining and subsoiling, plowing and sowing, before others can come after to discharge the easy task of reaping.　Such pioneers have been in the field of doctrine, the Calvins, Augustines, and Athanasiuses ; in the field of missionary enterprise, the Careys, Williamses, Moffats, and Livingstones.　Such pioneers were the prophets of the old dispensation with the Baptist at their head.　But the chief pioneer was Christ Himself who in eternity commenced to labour for a harvest of souls upon the earth, and in the fulness of the times descended from a God-equal condition, taking upon Him the form of a servant, and becoming obedient as far as to death, even the death of the cross.　In comparison with Him all human workers were and are but aftercomers who carry on the enterprise which He began, and mow down the stalks which His hand sowed.

II. **The different kinds of Joy experienced and Recompense received by Christ and His disciples**, for their respective labours.　1. *His, that of the sower ; theirs, that of the reaper.*　His, that of a husbandman who witnesses the toil of preceding months crowned with success : theirs, that of a mower who rejoices in being privileged to gather up precious and necessary fruit.　He sees of the travail of His soul and is satisfied (Is. liii. 11) ; they have the gratification of beholding the outcome of their efforts in converted souls which even here are " fruit unto eternal life," and will eventually be collected into heaven's granary. 2. *His, that of the master ; theirs, that of the servant.* His, that of wealth augmented ; theirs, that of wages received. His, that of an empire enlarged by every soul added to His kingdom ; theirs, that of exulting with exceeding joy when He repays them for their service ;—here with inward comforts, there with outward glories. 3. *His, that of the pioneer ; theirs, that of the aftercomer.* His, that of one who lives and labours for posterity, like the joy of a Moses or a Paul ; theirs, that of those who complete the tasks of the daring and heroic spirits that have gone before, like that of a Joshua or a Timothy.

Lessons.—A suggestion of dignity—the Christian a fellow-labourer with Christ (2 Cor. vi. 1). 2. A call to humility—the Christian only a servant (Rom. xii. 3). 3. A summons to activity—the hard work has already been done by Christ (Is. lxiii.). 4. A support in despondency—success will eventually crown the Christian's labours (Ps. cxxvi. 6). 5. An encouragement to fidelity—the Christian will yet partake of his Master's joy (Matt. xxv. 23 ; Rom. ii. 10).

VER. 42.—THE PROGRESS OF FAITH.

I. **Its Awakening.** *Through indirect testimony concerning Christ.* As in this case through the 'speaking' of the woman, so in other cases through the witness borne of and to Christ by parents to children, by ministers to congregations, by teachers to scholars, by believers generally to the word, as well as by the word of Scripture to readers.

II. **Its Confirmation.** *By the direct testimony of Christ Himself.* As in the present instance through Christ's conversation with the Samaritans, so in other instances through the word of Christ carried home to the individual heart and conscience by the Spirit of Christ.

III. **Its Illumination.** *In the attainment of a true knowledge of Christ's person and work.* As with the Samaritans, hearing led to believing and believing to knowing that Jesus was the Saviour of the world, so with all in whom the ear and eye of faith are opened, the taking up of Christ's word, and through that of Christ Himself, into the heart leads to that higher knowledge of Christ in which consists salvation or eternal life (xvii. 2).

Lessons.—1. The value of Christian instruction. 2. The indispensableness of Christ's own teaching. 3. The insight of faith.

IV.—IN GALILEE, CHRIST REVEALS HIS GLORY AS THE INCARNATE SON. 1. TO THE GALILEANS

CHAP. IV. VER. 43-45

EXPOSITION

Ver. 43. **And after the two days** a ready mentioned, ver. 40, **He went forth from thence** The words καὶ ἀπῆλθεν (T. R.) are omitted on the authority of א B C D Tᵇ etc. **into Galilee,** the original destination of his journey, ver. 3.

44. **For Jesus**—not merely others, but Himself testified Whether then, at the time of quitting Samaria (Meyer), or previously (Tholuck, Godet, Luthardt), cannot and need not be determined, since Christ appears to have more than once made the like observation (Matt. xiii. 57 ; Mark vi. 4 ; Luke iv. 24) ; and, without explicitly asserting that

Christ repeated it at this particular moment, the Evangelist may have simply wished to indicate what was the latent motive for his journey. **that a prophet** The use of this expression (ver. 19) does not warrant the inference that hitherto Christ had not regarded Himself as Messiah(Schenkel). **hath no honour in His own country.** 1. If Christ's own country was *Judæa,* either because it contained Bethlehem, his birthplace (Lücke, Ebrard, West-cott, Milligan and Moulton), or because it was the land of His vocation and activity (Baur), or because it was the home of the prophets (Origen, B. Crusius), then the Evangelist's meaning can only be that Christ, when rejected in Jerusalem, turned northwards to Galilee where an altogether different reception awaited Him (ver. 45). But against this interpretation stand the facts—(1) that Christ though born in Judæa was brought up in Nazareth and was familiarly known as the prophet of Galilee (i. 45 ; vii. 41, 52) ; (2) that Christ on more than one occasion (Luke iv. 23 ; Mark vi. 4 ; Matt. xiii. 57) used the term ' country ' (πατρίς) of Nazareth in Galilee ; (3) that Jesus had actually found considerable acceptance in Judæa (ii. 23 ; iii. 26 ; iv. 1) though not by the ecclesiastical authorities in Jerusalem ; and (4) that the reason of His leaving Judæa has already been represented as something different from this supposed want of acceptance (iv. 1-3). 2. If Christ's own country was *Galilee* as opposed to Judæa (Kuinoel, De Wette, Brückner, Hofmann, Luthardt, Godet, Meyer, Tholuck, and others), then the explanation is that Christ went into Galilee, because He hoped there to find retirement in consequence of the operation of this proverbial maxim (Luthardt, Hofmann), or contrariwise, to be well received, on account of the fame He had already acquired in Judæa, the proverb on this assumption teaching that without renown achieved in foreign parts no prophet could expect to be esteemed in His native place (Meyer, Godet). But the former of these explanations shatters itself against the double circumstance (1) that the Saviour did not obtain in Galilee the retirement He sought and therefore must have been disappointed—in which case what comes of his prophetic insight?—and (2) that the Evangelist writes "then," οὖν, instead of " but," δὲ or ἀλλὰ, which would naturally have been employed had Christ's experience in Galilee been contrary to His expectations. The latter explanation is exposed to the obvious objections (1) that it is extremely forced, (2) that even if true that a prophet must bring honour to, rather than expect honour from, his own country, that does not appear a self-evident reason why Christ should have proposed to go to Galilee, and (3) if it was the reason for Christ's northward journey it would have much

more appropriately found a place in the narrative at ver. 1. 3. If Christ's own country is *Nazareth* as opposed to Galilee in general (Calvin, Bengel, Olshausen, Hengstenberg) or Lower Galilee, to which Nazareth belonged, as distinguished from Upper, i.e. Galilee proper, in which Capernaum was situated (Lange), then the sense of the passage is that Christ in returning into Galilee did not make His head-quarters in His own country of Lower Galilee or His own city of Nazareth, but turned aside into other parts and in particular into Cana and afterwards to Capernaum ; and in favour of this, perhaps the most satisfactory explanation of the narrator's language, it may be contended (1) that it gives to πατρίς the meaning John's readers must have known it bore in the Synoptists (see above) ; (2) that it accounts for the use of " then " instead of " but " in the verse which follows ; (3) that it harmonizes with the statement of the Synoptists that when Christ opened His Galilean ministry He found a most unfavourable reception in Nazareth (Luke iv. 23, 24) ; and (4) that a similar antithesis between town and country has already been made by the Evangelist (iii. 22). The suggestion that ' for,' γὰρ, should be connected not with what precedes but with what follows (De Wette, Lücke, Tholuck,) as a preliminary explanation of the fact that on this occasion the Galileans received Jesus well, not out of sincere goodwill towards Him, which would have contradicted the proverb, but because of the miracles they had witnessed at Jerusalem, does not commend itself as being in harmony with that simplicity of construction which prevails in this gospel, while the practice of placing γὰρ before rather than after that to which it refers is wholly foreign to the N. T. (Brückner, Meyer : cf. Winer, § liii. 8, c).

45. So when He came into Galilee i.e. the province of that name,—in particular, Upper Galilee, as above explained—**the Galileans received Him** ἐδέξαντο ; occurring here only in this Gospel ; not simply accorded to him a welcome as in Col. iv. 10 (Brückner), but extended to Him faith, Matt. x. 14, 40 ; Mark ix. 37 ; Acts viii. 14 (Meyer) : cf. Luke iv. 14, 15). **having**

seen Resting on sight, their faith differed from that of the Samaritans, ver. 39. **all things** i.e. miracles (iii. 2), **that He did** lit., *as many as he did*, ὅσα being here supported by the best authorities (A B C L etc., Lachmann, Meyer). **in Jerusalem at the feast**—a double use of ἐν, first local and second temporal : cf. ii. 23-25 ; **for they also went unto the feast** i.e. the passover which had been celebrated in the preceding March or April.

Homiletics

VER. 43-45.—A TWICE VERIFIED PROVERB.

I. **Negatively**—" A prophet hath no honour in his own country " : ver. 44.
1. *Regarded.* Christ had an eye to this maxim when He avoided settling in Nazareth ; which showed (1) Christ's intimate acquaintance with human nature, (2) His ability to read the signs of the times, and (3) His wisdom in selecting always the most advantageous spheres of labour ;—all of which qualities are more or less indispensable for those who would play the role of prophet, preacher, or teacher in the N. T. church (1 Chron. xii. 32 ; Matt. xvi. 3 : 1 Cor. xvi. 9). 2. *Exemplified.* The fear of an unfavourable reception which presently deterred Christ from visiting His own city was afterwards verified. When a little later, after the Baptist's imprisonment, He entered on His Galilean ministry proper, He encountered such hostility in Nazareth that His life was endangered (Luke iv. 29), and met with so cold a reception that He could there do no mighty works because of their unbelief (Matt. xiii. 58). So Christ's official servants and people generally often find that the circles most difficult to impress are those of one's own household and city. The servant is not greater than his master (Luke vi. 40). It is enough that a disciple be as His teacher (Matt. x. 25). 3. *Explained.* The cause of Christ's non-acceptance in Nazareth lay in three things—(1) Envy. His fellow townsmen were amazed at His superior wisdom and manifest supernatural gifts. " Whence hath He this wisdom and these mighty works ? " (Matt. xiii. 54). It was hardly in unsanctified human nature not to begrudge an old neighbour such eminence. (2) Pride. It is more than likely they resented the falsely-imagined air of arrogance with which they supposed He looked down upon them. A large proportion of the ' injuries ' men receive are of their own fancying. If Christ became an innocent occasion of offence to His countrymen, it need not surprise His people, who have not His innocence, to find that they too are at times accused of crimes they do not commit. (3) Familiarity. The men of Nazareth had known Christ since he was a boy, were acquainted with His (so-called) father, Joseph the carpenter, with His mother who bore the exceedingly common name of Mary, with His brothers and sisters, had played with Him perhaps in the village streets, had seen Him working at the bench with His tools ; and that was enough. A person about whom they knew so much could never be to them a prophet. A prophet must be something of a mystery-man, if He would make His way in the world (vii. 27). Familiarity breeds contempt.
II. **Positively.** " A prophet is not without honour save in His own country, and in His own house " : Matt. xiii. 57. 1. *Illustrated.* As in Judea (ii. 23 ; iv. 1), and Samaria (ver. 39, 41), so now in Galilee, the inhabitants accorded Him a joyous welcome. The instincts of the masses are always truer than those of the classes, and the judgments of strangers more to be relied on than those of friends. As it now fared with Christ so fared it subsequently with His apostles who obtained for themselves and their gospel a heartier reception amongst the Gentiles than amongst the Jews (Acts xiii. 46 ; xv. 3, 7, 12 ; xviii. 6). 2. *Justified.* The behaviour of the Galileans was not an unreasoning enthusiasm. They had witnessed the miracles Christ had nine months before performed at Jerusalem (ii. 23), and had apparently then arrived at Nicodemus' conclusion (iii. 2). It was therefore in the highest degree becoming, prudent, and right, that they should meet Him with acclamation, treat Him with defer-

ence, and extend to Him a hearing. So already has the gospel of Christ effected such marvels, wrought such cures, accomplished such transformations, and generally performed such mighty works upon individuals and communities that it has a right to expect from all to whom these things are known a favourable and even cordial reception.

Lessons. 1. The power of prejudice. 2. The advantage derived by the gospel from publicity. 3. The ultimate triumph of Christ's kingdom.

2. TO THE NOBLEMAN FROM CAPERNAUM

CHAP. IV. VER. 46-54

EXPOSITION

Ver. 46. **He came therefore** i.e. in His wanderings through Galilee, and perhaps also in consequence of the favourable reception accorded to Him on a previous occasion (ii. 1), although it cannot be deduced from the particle οὖν that, as on that earlier occasion, He had first visited Nazareth (Lange), **again into Cana of Galilee** (see on ii. 1) **where He made the water wine.** Doubtless He expected there to find the soil in some degree prepared for His teaching, by the miracle He had formerly wrought. **And there was a certain nobleman** βασιλίκος, a regal personage, not a member of the royal family, but employed in the service of the king (Jos. Ant. xv. 8, 4; Wars, vii. 5, 2),—the king referred to being Herod Antipas, who though officially only a tetrarch was yet popularly known as king (Matt. xiv. 9; Mark vi. 14); and the nobleman, it has been conjectured (Lightfoot), Chuza, Herod's steward (Luke viii. 3) or Manaen, his foster-brother (Acts xiii. 1), though as good a case for identification might be made out for the centurion of Matt. viii. 5 (Irenæus, Strauss, B. Crusius)—**whose son**, a little boy, or child (ver. 49); perhaps the only one, **was sick** of fever (ver. 52) **at Capernaum.** These words should be connected with was—"there was at," etc. On Capernaum, see ii. 12.

47. **When he heard**—which he might easily have done, Cana being only 3 geographical miles distant from Capernaum—**that Jesus was come out of Judæa into Galilee** (see on ver. 45) **He went unto Him** from Capernaum to Cana, **and besought** *Him:* cf. ver. 31, 40. The pronoun, wanting in best

manuscripts (ℵ B C D L Tᵇ etc.) is probably a supplement. **that He would come down** lit., *in order that He might*, the subject of entreaty being expressed by its purpose. On καταβῇ, see ii. 12. **and heal his son** The petitioner by this request indicates the reality and extent of his faith, since he is satisfied the healing of his child is within the Saviour's power; but also its feebleness and defect inasmuch as He regards Christ's presence as necessary for the performance of the miracle. **for he was at the point of death** lit., *he was about to die, incipiebat mori* (Vulgate); compare xii. 33; Luke vii. 2; contrast Matt. viii. 6.

48. **Jesus therefore** discerning both the strength and weakness of the man's faith **said unto him** as the representative of the Galileans generally, **Except ye see** The emphasis lies not on 'see,' ἴδητε, (which would then have stood first), as if Christ charged the petitioner with a desire to see with his own eyes the working of the cure, but on 'signs and wonders' to which Christ points as the exciting cause of the faith of the Galileans. Though there is no reason to suppose this 'nobleman' had witnessed any of Christ's miraculous works as the Galileans generally had done (Kuinoel), he may yet have heard of the wonders both at Jerusalem and at Cana, while his faith so far resembled that of the Galileans that it rested on, and largely consisted in, a persuasion of Christ's ability to work miracles. **signs and wonders** The combination occurs so in the synoptists (Matt. xxiv. 24; Mark xiii. 22), in the Acts (iv. 30; xiv. 3), and in the Epistles (Rom. xv. 19; 2 Cor. xii. 12; Heb. ii. 4); in the reverse order in the

Acts (ii. 19, 22, 43 ; vii. 36). On the import of the words, see ii. 11, 23. **ye will in no wise believe** or, *will ye in no wise believe ?* (Westcott): cf. xviii. 11 ; Luke xviii. 7. Either way the words contain a rebuke, the double negative (cf. Heb. xiii. 5) intimating in the strongest manner that, unlike the Samaritans, without a sign, and perhaps even with a sign (vi. 26) the Galileans would not believe (1 Cor. i. 22). Possibly also faith would have failed in this king's man, had the miracle not followed ; yet from the first his faith went before the sign ; from which, however, it required to be detached.

49. **The nobleman** not understanding Christ's words as either a rejection of his petition, or a condemnation of himself, **saith unto Him** with increased urgency and gathering confidence, though still with a faith defective in its enlightenment, **Sir Lord !** (cf. iv. 11, 19) **come down** He still regards Christ's presence as essential to the performance of the desired miracle : contrast the language of the centurion (Matt. viii. 8). **ere my child** παιδίον, little boy, a term of endearment (cf. θυγατρίον, little daughter, Mark v. 23), extremely natural on a father's lips, the Evangelist and Christ using ' son ' (ver. 47, 50), and the servants of the nobleman ' boy ' (ver. 51). **die.** In the father's judgment the case was too critical for delay (cf. Mark v. 23). Unlike Abraham (Rom. iv. 17 ; Heb. xi. 19), he had no conception of a power that could raise the dead.

50. **Jesus saith unto him** granting his request, not to get rid of him (De Wette), but to prove and educate his faith,—**Go thy way : thy son liveth.** The man's faith was invited before he had beheld the 'sign.' The wonder was wrought without Christ's going to Capernaum. The cure was not a case of medical prognostication (Paulus), of magnetic healing (Olshausen), or of supernatural knowledge (Lücke), but of miraculous working. By an act of will Christ arrested the disease (v. 53). **The man believed the word that Jesus spake unto him** "The miracle was a double one—on the body of the absent child ; on the heart of the present father ; one cured of his sickness, the other of his unbelief" (Trench). **and**

he went his way. His obedience proved at once the reality, the intensity, and the enlightenment of his faith. Without seeing and without requiring Christ's presence at Capernaum he believed.

51. **And as he was now going down** lit., *but already he descending*, i.e. when by this time he was on his homeward way ; conveying the idea of haste, *festinabat ergo* (Bengel), rather than of leisurely procedure (Lampe, Trench, Farrar)—**his servants** slaves or bondservants employed chiefly in domestic service, **met him** having hastened probably both to acquaint their master with the good news and to prevent Christ's coming since that was no longer necessary—**saying, that his son lived.** They use the term ' boy,' παῖς, perhaps as being neither so familiar as ' little boy,' παιδίον, nor so dignified as ' son,' υἱός.

52. **So he inquired of them the hour when he** (the sick child) **began to amend** lit., *in which he began to do more finely.* The phrase κομψῶς ἔχειν, occurring only here in the N. T. though in perfect accordance with the mode of speech of the time (see Arrian, Epict. iii. 10), corresponds exactly with the modern expression used of a patient, ' to do well, or nicely ' ; the opposite phrase being to do badly, κακῶς ἔχειν. **They said therefore unto him,** Yesterday at the **seventh hour,** ὥραν ἑβδόμην. The accusative which usually denotes duration, here indicates the point, of time (see Winer, § xxxii. 6); i.e. according to the Jewish mode of reckoning 1 p.m. (Meyer, Godet, Luthardt, Hengstenberg, Brückner, Weiss, Farrar, and others) ; according to the Romans 7 a.m. or more probably 7 p.m. (Ewald, Westcott, Milligan and Moulton). If the former be adopted, and the Galilean servants would most likely employ their own customary system of counting, then, since a new Jewish day would commence at 6 p.m., they might easily enough speak of the cure as having been wrought yesterday, if it was after that hour when they met their master ; if the latter be followed it only requires the by no means violent supposition that the father and the servants started on their respective journeys as soon as possible after 7, but only met after midnight. **the**

fever left him—not merely reached its turning point from which it began to abate, but actually and totally disappeared : cf. Luke iv. 39.

53. **So the father knew that** *it was* **at that hour in which Jesus said unto him, Thy son liveth.** Thus his faith which rested on the naked word of Christ was eventually confirmed by an undeniable miracle. **and himself believed** not 'that his son lived,' but on Jesus Christ. **and his whole house.** Not 'the miracle-child' only, but all his dependents. The first believing household mentioned in the N. T.: cf. Acts xvi. 14, 15 ; xviii. 8.

54. **This is again the second sign that Jesus did** better, *this again the second sign did Jesus ;* not the second absolutely, but only the second in Cana, the first having been the turning of water into wine (ii. 1)—**having come out of Judæa into Galilee.** It was this circumstance that in the Evangelist's mind connected these miracles as first and second. They were both wrought in Cana, both after he had come from Judæa, and both shortly after His arrival.

Note. *Is this miracle the same as that recorded in the Synoptists* (Matt. viii. 5 and Luke vii. 2)?

1. The affirmative has been maintained (Irenæus, Semler, De Wette, Baur, Ewald, Weiss, and others) chiefly on the grounds that according to both narratives (1) the person in whose behalf the miracle is wrought belongs to, or resides in, Capernaum, (2) the invalid for whom he intercedes is called

'the boy,' ὁ παῖς, (3) the malady is pictured as extremely dangerous, (4) the cure is wrought at a distance, and (5) a mission or embassy of servants or friends occurs in each. But 2. the differences between the two narratives are too numerous and important to admit of the identification of the two incidents. (1) The Synoptists place the incident in the course of the Galilean ministry ; in the fourth gospel the Galilean ministry proper is not yet begun. (2) The former say the miracle was wrought at Capernaum ; the latter at Cana. (3) With Matthew and Luke the applicant is a centurion or captain of a hundred, a heathen ; with John, a member of the king's household and probably a Jew. (4) Those describe a master interceding for his servant ; this, a father pleading for his son. (5) The centurion employs the mediation of the Jewish elders : the king's man goes in person to the Saviour. (6) That one deprecates the entering of Christ beneath his roof : this one will, at first, be satisfied with nothing less. (7) The Gentile officer is commended for his faith : the Jewish nobleman is reproved for his unbelief. (8) The malady in Matthew is palsy : in John, a fever. (9) The embassy in Luke is of friends who are sent to the Saviour: in John it is the nobleman's domestics who meet him. With such an array of discrepancies between the two accounts it is idle to persist in maintaining that we have only a threefold report of one and the same event.

HOMILETICS

VER. 53.—THE FAITH OF A NOBLEMAN.
I. **Its Imperfect Character.** 1. *Not settled on the best foundation.* It had been excited by the report of Christ's miracles in Jerusalem and at Cana. That a faith resting on miracles is not spurious Christ showed at a later period by claiming exactly on that ground the confidence of His countrymen in general (v. 36 ; x. 37, 38), and of His disciples in particular (xiv. 11). Only Christ never esteemed this as faith's highest form, but always regarded it as rude and elementary, though valuable as leading up to that more advanced and spiritual form which reposed on His bare word. The faith of this Jewish nobleman was sincere, as the event showed, but wanted the element of permanence, upheld as it was mainly by miracle props and therefore likely to stagger and give way when these were withdrawn. Even so is it doubtful if faith is rightly grounded when it rests exclusively on the external transaction of the cross, detached from the living person of the glorified Redeemer. The ultimate support and lowest foundation for faith to-day, as then, is the word of Him who has proclaimed

Himself the faithful and true witness (Rev. iii. 14). 2. *Not free from ingredients of ignorance and superstition.* It imagined Christ's presence indispensable to the working of a miracle. The nobleman had no idea that Christ's power was limited by neither time nor place, was able to work without means as easily as with them, could reach to the boundaries of life or time and beyond them ; no conception that Christ Himself was the resurrection and the life (xi. 25), who, even if death carried off his child, could follow after the retreating conqueror as Abraham pursued the kings of the East, and compel it to disgorge its prey as Abraham recovered Lot ; no conviction to sustain him in the trying moment to which he had come like the father of the faithful when he stood on Mount Moriah (Heb. xi. 19). Difficult to say how much information concerning Jesus was possessed by this courtly suppliant ; it is clear he had still much to learn.

II. **Its Gracious Education.** 1. *Its radical defect was pointed out:* ver. 48. The faith possessed by the nobleman, like that of the Galileans generally, was the product more of temporary excitement than of deep-rooted conviction. These welcomed Christ chiefly as a thaumaturgist, and followed Him for the unwonted sensation of beholding His spectacular displays. By and by they degenerated even from that and went after Him, like a troop of children or paupers, for the good things He distributed (vi. 26). As yet however they were in the first stage of believing through wonder (iv. 45) ; and like them the nobleman had been stirred to faith, if not by sight, at least by report, of Christ's miracles. It was doubtful also if his faith, any more than theirs, would continue if Christ should cease to excite it by means of 'wonders.' This faith has its modern counterpart in that belief which is born of excitement and rests on feeling rather than on understanding and conviction. 2. *Its inward sincerity was tried :* ver. 48. Instead of going with the man, as might have been expected from the extreme urgency of the case, Christ seemingly paid no attention to his entreaty, but proceeded to pass judgment on, and find fault with, himself—the man ! And the king's man underwent the ordeal with success. Instead of ruffling his composure, offending his dignity, or exciting his displeasure, Christ's remark only served to augment his importunity (ver. 49). In similar fashion Christ dealt with the Syrophenician woman (Matt. xv. 23) ; and often deals with such as come to Him yet. 3. *Its formal request was denied.* Christ declined to go to Capernaum. Had He done so, He might have confirmed the ruler's first belief, that His presence was indispensable for doing any work of healing ; had He done so at once he might have fostered the notion that His power was of no avail beyond death. So He frequently denies His people's urgent entreaties and tearful supplications, because they know not what they ask (Matt. xx. 22), and because to grant them in the form asked would be to inflict upon them spiritual injury, perhaps confirm them in some erroneous view of truth or duty, possibly leave them at a lower level in the Christian life than they ought to occupy. 4. *Its essential petition was granted :* ver. 50. Not in the way expected, but in a larger and better way. The nobleman himself was cured of unbelief as well as his boy of fever. So Christ's time and modes of answering His people's prayers are always the best, while the answers themselves not unfrequently surpass their grandest imaginings (Eph. iii. 29).

III. **Its Complete Development.** The nobleman believed 1. *without a miracle.* The miracle was wrought indeed, but all the evidence he had for it was Christ's word. By and by he obtained the additional testimony of his domestics ; and on reaching home had the clear and irrefragable assurance of sight. But in Capernaum with nothing except the naked utterance of Christ to rest upon he believed. That is faith in its purest essence. Of that sort was the faith of Abraham (Gen. xv. 6 ; Rom. iv. 3, 20), of the centurion (Matt. xiii. 13), of the Syrophenician mother (Matt. xv. 28 ; Mark vii. 30), of the blind man (John ix. 11) ; and of such sort must be the faith of all who seek Christ for salvation. 2. *Without delay.* "Go thy way ! " said Christ ; and the nobleman went. Prompt obedience one of the truest and most reliable marks of faith. Examples : Noah (Gen. vi. 9, 22 ; Heb. xi. 7) ; Abraham (Gen. xii. 1 ; Heb. xi. 8) ; Peter (Luke v. 5) ; Paul (Acts xxvi. 19). According to one of its simplest definitions faith is doing as Christ directs (xv. 14 ; Rom. vi. 17). 3. *Without after-regrets.* He was not disappointed with his experiment of trusting Christ ; and neither will any have cause to repent who enter on a life of faith. Nor did he abandon his religious profession after securing the benefit he had craved, as persons have been known to do, after God has raised them or their children from a sick bed. But after his boy's recovery as before he believed. Constancy, steadfastness, perseverance, are qualities of faith that is lofty and pure (viii. 31 ; xv. 4 ; Acts xi. 23 ; xiv. 22 ; Rom. ii. 7 ; 1 Cor. xv. 58). 4. *Without being left to stand alone.* Doubtless had he been so left he would not have wanted courage to adhere to Christ. But wherever faith arises it becomes contagious ; and he was soon joined by his entire household, by the boy who had been sick but was cured, by the servants who had nursed the invalid, by all the inmates who would not fail to hear the details of the wondrous story.

Learn 1. The ability and willingness of Christ to save the diseased and dying souls of men. 2. The eagerness and zeal Christian parents should display to bring the cases of their children before that heavenly physician. 3. The nature and the excellence of faith which is simply taking Christ at His word. 4. The value and efficiency of prayer which enables the soul's requests to be laid before the glorified Redeemer. 5. The possibility and certainty that miracles may be wrought without any dislocation of nature's laws. 6. The increasing and brightening evidence faith obtains the longer it continues to believe. 7. The beauty and advantage of household religion.

SECTION SECOND.—CHRIST'S SECOND PRESENTATION OF HIMSELF TO HIS OWN (THE JEWISH PEOPLE); IN THE SECOND YEAR OF HIS MINISTRY

CHAP. V. 1—VI. 71

The second exhibition of the glory of the Incarnate Word commenced like the first in the metropolis and terminated in the provinces. In Jerusalem, as on the previous occasion, Christ encountered hostility and rejection : in Galilee He was welcomed with enthusiasm by the populace, and gathered numerous disciples until "The Jews," i.e. the representatives and rulers of the people, who belonged principally to the Pharisaic party, began to put forth their influence against Him, and ultimately succeeded in securing His rejection in the North as in the South of the land. The section may be arranged thus :—

I. Christ's manifestation of Himself in Jerusalem : v. 1-47 ; including—

1. The Miracle of Bethesda : ver. 1-9.
2. The Hostility of the Jews: ver. 10-18.
3. The Reply of Vindication : ver. 19-47.

II. Christ's manifestation of Himself in Galilee : vi. 1-71 ; including—

1. The Miracle of the Loaves : ver. 1-14.
2. The Sign upon the Sea: ver. 15-21.
3. The Meeting in Capernaum : ver. 22-59.
4. The Turning of the Tide : ver. 60-71.

Between those Jerusalem and Galilean incidents lie the commencement and progress of the Galilean ministry which the Evangelist omits, perhaps on the ground that these were sufficiently known from the Synoptical narrations, but chiefly for the reason that they were not required for the object he had in view, which was to show the character and issue of Christ's second presentation of Himself to His own. For this purpose it was enough to give its opening scene in Jerusalem, the result of which directly led to the projecting and commencing of a Galilean ministry, and its closing scene in Capernaum, in which the Galilean ministry may be said to have culminated.

I. CHRIST'S MANIFESTATION OF HIMSELF IN JERUSALEM

1. THE MIRACLE AT BETHESDA

CHAP. V. VER. 1-9

EXPOSITION

Chap. v. ver. 1. **After these things** How long after cannot be inferred from the phrase (cf. iii. 22 ; v. 14 ; vi. 1 ; vii. 1), and will depend on the exegesis of the next clause. **there was a feast of the Jews** ἑορτὴ, without the art. (A B D G K U V Γ Λ etc., Origen, T. R., Westcott and Hort) ; or ἡ ἑορτὴ with the art. 'the' feast (ℵ C E F H I etc., Tischendorf). If the latter reading be adopted then the feast was in all probability the passover, the principal Jewish festival styled elsewhere ἡ ἑορτὴ τῶν Ἰουδαίων (vi. 4 : cf. iv. 45, with ii. 13 ; and xi. 56, with xi. 55 ; xii. 12, with xii. 1) ; although this perhaps is not absolutely certain since ἑορτὴ is also applied to the feast of tabernacles (cf. vii. 10, 14, 37 ; with vii. 2), which according to Browne, "Ordo Saeclorum," p. 87 (quoted by Westcott, p. 93), was 'the feast of the Jews' by pre-eminence. If the former reading be preferred the passover cannot be excluded from consideration, as it equally with the others the designation suits. Hence the solution of the question raised must be sought independently of the phrase used by the author. Seeing it was now December or January the feast referred to may have been that of Dedication in December, of Purim in March, of the Passover in April, of Pentecost in May, or of Tabernacles in October.

The first may be discarded as too near, if not already past. 1. In favour of *Purim* (Olshausen, Wieseler, Meyer, Godet, Lange, Gess, and others), it is urged (1) that this was the feast next in order, (2) that it was one of the post-exilic, i.e. minor feasts, which sufficiently accounts for the omission of its name, and (3) that it fell between the time then present and the passover fast approaching (vi. 4), i.e. supposing this to be the passover of that spring. The objections to this solution of the problem are (1) the unlikelihood that Christ would repair to Jerusalem in order to observe a non-Mosaic ordinance of so unspiritual a character as that of Purim, which besides might as easily and legitimately have been celebrated in any part of the provinces ;—though the feast of dedication (x. 22) which Christ afterwards attended was also of post-exilic origin, and therefore destitute of Divine authority ; and (2) the impossibility of inserting Christ's Galilean ministry between chap. v., after which according to one view it began, or between the previous December from which, according to another view, it should be reckoned, and chap. vi. when it culminated. 2. In support of the *Passover* (Irenæus, Luther, Grotius, Lampe, Kuinoel, B. Crusius, Hengstenberg, and others), speak the facts (1) that the Passover was the greatest of all the Jewish feasts, of a decidedly religious character, one which would naturally have attraction for Jesus, and one moreover it was His duty as a pious Jew to attend, (2) that the Passover is the only feast mentioned in the preceding narrative (iv. 45), which naturally suggests the inference that the author is still thinking of the same, and (3) that otherwise the ministry of Christ will be reduced to $2\frac{1}{2}$ years, which seems to contradict the teaching of Luke xiii. 6-9. Against it stand as difficulties — (1) the omission of the article before 'feast' ἑορτὴ; though the insertion of the article would not necessarily prove it to have been the Passover (see above); (2) the non-designation of the feast by its customary name, as in vi. 4; which however may, in this instance, have been deemed unnecessary, if the writer was thinking of iv. 45; (3) the occurrence of an interval of twelve months, between chap. v. and chap. vi., concerning which the Evangelist relates nothing;—which again, admits of explanation from the purpose and plan of his gospel; (4) the absence of Christ from the next Passover (vi. 4), if, as the hypothesis assumes, He was present at this; a difference sufficiently accounted for by the hostility of the Jews which originated at the one feast and culminated at the other. 3. *Pentecost* which occurred in May, though favoured by some interpreters (Cyril, Chrysostom, Erasmus, Beza, Bengel, Calvin) does not appear possessed of advantages superior to the Passover, while it is difficult to understand why Christ should have gone to the later festival and avoided the earlier. 4. *Tabernacles* in October (Ebrard, Ewald, Hilgenfeld) derives support from observing (1) that, next to the Passover, this festival was attended by the greatest numbers of the people, (2) that Christ visited Jerusalem at the feast of Tabernacles after the Passover in vi. 4, (3) that the events in chap. v. and vi. are thus brought considerably nearer, and (4) that the shorter interval renders Christ's language in vii. 23 of easier explanation. 5. *Dedication* (Keppler, Petavius) need hardly be taken into reckoning. With such a conflict of opinion it is obvious

the question must be left undecided, though it need not be assumed either that such was the Evangelist's intention (Lücke, De Wette, Brückner, Tholuck, Luthardt) or that the particular festival had escaped his memory (Schweitzer) We decide for the Passover. **and Jesus went up to Jerusalem.** In obedience to legal prescription, and to renew His presentation of Himself to the Jewish people in the persons of their religious heads and representatives : cf. ii. 13. That Christ was unattended by His disciples seems to indicate that the Galilean ministry was not yet begun.

Ver. 2. **Now there is** The present tense proves, not that the Gospel must have been composed after the destruction of Jerusalem, although it almost certainly was so, but only either that the pool was not destroyed on account of its beneficent character (Ewald), or that the writer mentally transposed himself into the past and viewed it as present (Brückner). **in Jerusalem** See on ii. 13. **by** ἐπί, in the vicinity of, rather than ἐν, 'in,' favoured by some authorities (אᶜ A D G L etc.): cf. iv. 6. **the sheep** *gate* τῇ προβατικῇ, sc. πύλῃ (gate) or ἀγορᾷ (market): Neh. iii. 1, 32; xii. 39. Probably so styled because through the former the sheep for sacrifice were brought into the city, or in the latter were bought and sold. It appears to have been in the east wall, at its northern corner and near the temple. **a pool** or plunging-bath, κολυμβήθρα; not κολυμβήθρᾳ in the dative, meaning 'sheep pool' (Hammond, Paulus, Meyer), a reading purely conjectural. **which is called in Hebrew** Not in old Hebrew, but in Aramaic (Acts xxii. 2), the popular speech of the country after the exile. **Bethesda** βηθεσδά, בֵּית חַסְדָּא, *domus benignitatis*, 'house of mercy' (Meyer, Godet, Luthardt, Brückner), less probably בֵּית אָסְטִין, οἶκος στοῆς, 'house of the portico' (Delitzsch), or בֵּית אֲשֵׁדָא, *domus effusionis*, 'house of outpouring' (Michaelis). If the reading βηθζαθά (א) shortened into βηζαθά (Eusebius) be adopted (Tischendorf, Westcott and Hort) the signification may be 'house of the olive' (Westcott). Mentioned neither in the O. T. nor in Josephus, the Bethesda has been identified (1) with the *Fountain of the Virgin* in the Kidron valley, an intermittent spring bubbling up sometimes two or three times a day, sometimes only once or oftener in two or three days (Robinson, Bib. Researches, i. 342 ; iii. 249 ; Porter, Handbook for Syria and Palestine, i. 115) ; (2) with *Birket Israel*, the double pool recently discovered at the N.W. angle of the Noble Sanctuary, near the present gate of St. Stephen's, which appears to be that mentioned by Eusebius as "a pool at Jerusalem, which is the *piscina probatica*, and had formerly five porches, and now is pointed out as the twin pools there, of which one is filled by the rains of the year, but the other exhibits its waters tinged in an extraordinary manner with red, retaining a trace it is said of the victims that were formerly cleansed in it" (Warren, The Recovery of Jerusalem, pp. 196 ff.) ; (3) with a pool somewhat north of the preceding, near the Church of St. Anne, mentioned by old writers as *piscina interior* and distinguished at the time of the Crusades from Birket Israel (Riehm, Handworterbuch des Biblischen Altertums, art. *Bethesda*). **having five porches** i.e. cloisters, covered spaces, pillar halls, for the reception of its invalid visitors.

3. **In these lay a multitude** The addition of 'great,' πολύ (T. R.), is rejected on the authority of א B C D L (Tischendorf, Westcott and Hort). **of them that were sick, blind, halt, and withered.** The withered were such as had a limb affected with atrophy or wasting : Matt. xii. 10 ; Luke vi. 6, 8. "The enumeration by four, when meant to be exhaustive, is a favourite one in Scripture : cf. Ezek. xiv. 21 ; Matt. xv. 31 ; Rev. vi. 8" (Trench). The clause "waiting for the moving of the water" (A.V.) is to be rejected (א A* B C* L etc.), as also is ver. 4 of the T. R. (א B C* D etc.).

5. **And a certain man was there** Whether one of the "withered" cannot be determined. **which had been thirty and eight years in his infirmity.** Not lying all that time in the Porch or in Jerusalem, but having passed thirty-eight years under his trouble ; the construction of ἔχων with ἔτη, rather than with ἐν τῇ ἀσθενίᾳ, being favoured by ver. 6. The number of years is stated probably to indicate the inveteracy of the disease or to magnify the

power and compassion of Christ, not to remind readers of the death sentence pronounced upon Israel in the wilderness (B. Crusius, Ebrard, Hengstenberg).

6. **When Jesus saw him lying, and knew** from information imparted by bystanders (Brückner, Meyer) or from His own intuitive and supernatural discernment (ii. 24), **that he had been now a long time** *in that case*, suffering from his malady and visiting the pool, **He saith unto him, Wouldest thou be made whole?** lit., *dost thou will*, or wish, *to be made whole?* A question designed not to detect an impostor (Paulus), or simply open up a conversation (De Wette), but (1) to excite the man's attention, desire, and expectation (Meyer, Tholuck, Brückner, and others), (2) to stimulate the flagging energies of his feeble will which perhaps had begun to passively acquiesce in his hopeless condition (Lange, Westcott), and (3) to set him in connection with the person of Jesus who was to be to him a true Bethesda (B. Crusius, Godet).

7. **The sick man answered Him** if with pointless feebleness (Lange) and a certain tone of resignation (Luthardt), yet not without respect and reverence, **Sir** or, Lord (see on iv. 11) **I have no man** The delay in reaching a cure had been occasioned by want not of will but of ability on the part of the sufferer. **when the water is troubled** The pool was no doubt periodically agitated by an intermittent spring : see ver. 1. **to put me into the pool** The use of the aorist βάλῃ, instead of βάλλῃ (T. R.), may express the idea that the action needed only to be once performed (Brückner), if not also quickly done (Meyer, Luthardt). **but while I am coming** His paralyzed or withered limbs necessarily rendered his movements difficult and his progress slow. **another steppeth down before me.** The pool was probably approached by a descending flight of steps. That only one could be healed as the apocryphal ver. 4 says may have been suggested by, but it is not necessarily implied in the man's answer, which requires for its explanation the hypothesis neither of a narrow staircase that would admit of only one bather at a time (Lange), nor of an

ebullition of the pool at only one point on its surface (Meyer), but merely of the intermittent action of the spring (Godet).

8. Jesus saith unto him, Arise, take up thy bed and walk. Compare Matt. ix. 6, where the first and third of these verbs are employed ; Mark ii. 9, where the three occur exactly as here ; and Mark ii. 11, where the first and second appear, with a variation for the third. If the first verb was used because the invalid had lain down (ver. 6), the third was perhaps selected because he had hitherto been unable to walk, while the second was of necessity chosen because the couch, no longer wanted, would require to be removed.

9. And straightway εὐθέως appears in this gospel only here and in vi. 21, though in the Synoptists, in Mark especially, it is of frequent occurrence. **the man was made** (lit., *became*) **whole, and took up his bed** The bed, κράβ-βατος, *grabbatus* (Vulgate)—a word said to be of Macedonian origin and to occur only in very late writers—was a small couch which might easily be carried about : Mark ii. 4, 9, 11, 12; vi. 55 ; Acts v. 15 ; ix. 33 ; see Stapfer's Palestine in the Time of Christ, p. 179. **and walked.** Thus he evinced the com-

pleteness of his cure. That the preceding narrative in some respects resembling those furnished by Matthew (ix. 1-8) and Mark (ii. 1-12) of the healing of the palsied man was no compilation by a later writer from these earlier materials (Baur, Strauss, Hilgenfeld, Weisse) but an independent composition becomes apparent when it is observed (1) that the locality of this miracle was Jerusalem while the scene of that was Capernaum, (2) that the circumstances generally in which this was wrought were different from those that attended the earlier, (3) that while in that Christ was solicited to extend His aid, in this His help was spontaneously proffered, (4) that this calls attention to the long duration of the sufferer's malady while that makes no allusion to the length of time the invalid had been palsied, (5) that this emphasizes the loneliness of the patient whereas that sets in the foreground the kindness of his friends, (6) that this was wrought in the absence of the Jewish authorities, that in their presence, and (7) that whereas that led to an extension of Christ's fame this excited against Him a hostility never afterwards allayed.

HOMILETICS

VER. 2-9.—AN OLD JERUSALEM INFIRMARY.
I. **The Hospital** : ver. 2, 3. 1. *Its Site.* In Jerusalem ; near the sheep gate ; not far from the temple. No better ornament can a large and populous city have than a house of refuge for the sick and infirm. On grounds of humanity, not to speak of religion, such buildings should be provided by every considerable community. Much more, wherever God has a temple His worshippers should found an hospital (Is. lvii. 7 ; Matt. xxv. 35-40). 2. *Its form.* Five stone porches hewn out of the rock round a pool whose waters were periodically agitated by eruptions from an underlying intermittent spring. It was not the porches of man's construction that contained the healing, but the water of God's providing. Yet the former were of service to enable invalids to take advantage of the latter. Thus in nature and in grace God permits man to be His fellow-worker, while in both He claims to be the prime agent (Deut. viii. 3 ; viii. 18 ; Ps. xxiii. 1 ; lxvii. 6 ; Hos. ii. 21 ; 2 Cor. vi. 1 ; Phil. ii. 13). In particular in both He is *Jehovah Rophi*—"The Lord that healeth thee" (Exod. xv. 26 ; Deut. xxxii. 39 ; Ps. ciii. 3). 3. *Its name.* Bethesda, house of grace ; than which no more appropriate designation could have been devised for an institution whose origin was love, pity, kindness, and whose end was healing, help, and hope. The fitness of the name became trebly conspicuous after the visit and the miracle here recorded. The truest glory either places or persons can possess is that reflected on them by and from Christ (Ezek. xvi. 14). 4. *Its inmates.* A multitude of sick, blind, halt, withered ; specimens of the poor diseased creatures that still crowd the world's infirmaries and appeal to the sympathies of humane

and Christian people ; emblems of the sadder invalids, the spiritually feeble, sightless, lame, and shrivelled who throng the vast lazar-house of this fallen world, and attract the compassion and help of Christ.

II. **The Patient** : ver. 5. 1. *A great sufferer.* Whatever the specific form of his ailment, it had been his constant companion for 38 years—half a life-time ! How meek and uncomplaining should those be whose "light afflictions," in comparison, are as it were "but for a moment" (2 Cor. iv. 17). 2. *A friendless outcast.* "He had no one to put him into the pool, when the water was troubled." Surely he has touched the lowest deep of wretchedness who in the season of adversity has no relative, neighbour, or acquaintance to whom he can look for a smile of sympathy, a word of cheer, or a hand of succour ! Yet many such are in the vast lazar-house of humanity ; and many more who as regards their spiritual condition might with justice exclaim—"I looked on my right hand, and beheld, but there was no man that would know me : refuge failed me : no man cared for my soul" (Ps. cxlii. 4). 3. *A disappointed seeker.* Often during these eight and thirty years had he attempted to reach the pool while its waters were agitated by the medicinal spring ; but always another nimbler or less feeble than himself had stepped in before him, and prevented him from getting to the water while its virtue lasted. Poor fellow ! One wonders that his heart was not broken (Prov. xiii. 12), that his spirit was not crushed (Prov. xviii. 14).' "But "hope springs eternal in the human breast" ; "we are saved (preserved, or kept alive) by hope" (Rom. viii. 24); and "all things come to him who waits." What a comfort there are no such disappointed seekers after spiritual health (Is. xlv. 19) Nothing and no one can prevent him who seeks aright from finding (Matt. vii. 7, 8). In the fountain of Emmanuel's blood (Zech. xiii. 1) and in the laver of regeneration (Tit. iii. 5) there is room for all, while both are at every moment accessible to all.

III. **The Physician** : ver. 6. 1. *His quick observation.* No sooner had Christ entered the sanatorium than His discerning eye lighted on the thirty-eight years' cripple. Instinctively He recognized that a fit object for His compassion and a proper subject for His assistance lay before Him. So Christ daily walked amongst men inquiring after patients upon whom to exercise His healing power and saving skill (Matt. xviii. 11). So Christ's people who would play the part of 'good physician' to their fellow-men should cultivate the 'seeing eye.' There is no lack of opportunities for doing good to such as seek and care to find them (Eccles. ix. 10 ; Heb. xiii. 6). 2. *His perfect diagnosis.* Immediately Christ's glance rested upon His patient He comprehended the case—discerned the nature, the cause, and the duration of the old man's trouble, was cognizant of his painstaking and repeated though unsuccessful efforts to recover health, understood his present mood of mind and disposition. So Christ apprehends both the man and the malady in every instance that is brought before Him or that He in His grace seeks to cure (1 Chron. xxviii. 9 ; Ps. vii. 9 ; cxix. 168 ; cxxxix. 1-4 ; Prov. xv. 11 ; John i. 48 ; ii. 24, 25 ; iv. 29 ; Rev. ii. 23). 3. *His tender compassion.* This, if not expressed, is implied. Christ's sympathy, at first excited by His knowledge that the sufferer "had been a long time in that case," was not subsequently repelled by the further perception that the patient's malady had been occasioned by previous profligacy. Christ distinguished between the sinner and his sin ; and, whilst He could not but condemn the latter (ver. 14), He felt equally constrained to commiserate the former. So "the Father maketh His sun to rise on the evil and the good" (Matt. v. 45); and so should Christian philanthropy embrace even the criminal classes within its care (Gal. vi. 10). 4. *His hopeful inquiry.* "Wilt thou be made whole ?" "The simple putting of such a question would serve to rouse the man's attention, shake off the stupor from his spirit, stimulate his feeble will, and draw forth his hopes and expectations. It was not likely a benevolent stranger such as Jesus appeared to be would mock his misery by such an interrogation—'Art thou willing to be made whole ?' The Bethesda cripple may have reasoned there was hope in the question ; and so may sin-sick souls argue to-day, when in similar fashion Christ asks them, if they are willing to be healed. 5. *His ex-*

traordinary prescription. "Arise, take up thy bed, and walk." Marvellous pharmacy!—to bid a paralytic rise, a palsied man shoulder his couch, a person with withered limbs go erect (cf. Mark iii. 5). So Christ commands those dead in trespasses and sins to awake and arise (Eph. v. 14), and souls without strength to repent and believe (Mark i. 15). So Christian duty always transcends natural ability. But as in this case, so in that of every willing soul, what Christ commands Christ is willing to supply (i. 12).

IV. **The Cure** : ver. 9. 1. *Instantaneous.* "Straightway the man was made whole." As in nature so in grace Christ speaks and it is done, commands and it standeth fast. Examples of Christ's power in the former were the leper (Mark i. 42), the deaf mute (Mark vii. 35), the dead youth (Luke vii. 14), etc. So in the latter when Christ says to any, "Neither do I condemn thee" (viii. 11), immediately "there is no condemnation" (Rom. viii. 1); when He pronounces the verdict, "Son, thy sins are forgiven" (Mark ii. 5), forthwith ensues "the redemption through His blood even the forgiveness of sins" (Eph. i. 7). 2. *Complete.* "The man took up his bed and walked." This supplied evidence that his restoration was perfect. What had first been proposed as the condition of his cure is now cited as its consequence and demonstration. So Christ demands that sinful souls shall repent, believe, and obey if they would be saved : that they do so is a sign that they have passed from death to life.

Application. 1. Wilt thou be made whole? 2. Art thou ready to obey the gospel?

Ver. 6. The Good Physician's question. I. Assumes that they to whom it is addressed are not whole. II. Suggests that nevertheless they may be made whole. III. Implies that it depends upon their own wills whether or not they shall be made whole. IV. Proffers the needed wholeness to all who are willing to receive it.

2. THE HOSTILITY OF THE JEWS

CHAP. V. VER. 10-18

EXPOSITION

Ver. 10. **Now it was the Sabbath on that day.** Lit., *but it was Sabbath,* i.e. the weekly Sabbath rather than a day of rest other than the seventh (Westcott), the article being omitted because the context (ver. 18 ; cf. vii. 23 ; ix. 14, 16) leaves it unambiguous what day of rest is intended : see Winer's Grammar, § xix. 1. The Sabbath, τὸ σάββατον (Mark ii. 27 ; Luke vi. 5 ; John xix. 31), σάββατον (Matt. xii. 2 ; Mark vi. 2 ; Luke vi. 1 ; John v. 16), τὰ σάββατα (Mark ii. 23 ; Luke iv. 31 ; vi. 2 ; xiii. 10), *Shabbath* (Heb.), rest, as a Jewish institution dated from the giving of the law on Sinai (Exod. xx. 8, 10 ; Lev. xxiii. 3 ; Deut. v. 14, 15), though traces are not wanting of its observance in pre-Mosaic times amongst the Hebrews (Ex. xvi. 23, 25, 26, 29 ; Gen. xix. 27, 28 ; viii. 6, 12 ; iv. 3), the Babylonians (see Records of the Past, vol. ix. p. 117 ; vii. p. 160), Egyptians

(Wilkinson, Ancient Egyptians, vol. ii. p. 320), and other peoples of antiquity. Grounded on divine example (Ex. ii. 2), it enjoined upon the followers of Moses absolute cessation from labour, except in such cases as were prescribed by necessity and mercy (Ex. xx. 8, 10 ; xxxi. 14 ; xxxv. 2 ; Lev. xxiv. 8 ; Num. xv. 32 ; xxviii. 19), and the observance of holy convocations (Lev. xxiii. 3, 4, 7, 8). **So the Jews,** who were probably Sanhedrists and Pharisees (ver. 33 ; see i. 19), **said unto him that was,** or had been **cured** by the supernatural word and power of Christ (ver. 8), **It is the Sabbath,** or Sabbath it is! *interpellatio intempestiva* (Bengel), **and** omitted in some MSS. **it is not lawful for thee to take up thy bed.** The divine law which the prophets afterwards interpreted as prohibiting the bearing of burdens (Jer. xvii. 21 ; Neh. xiii. 19) and the prosecution of trade (Amos viii. 5), was regarded by rabbinical theology as interdicting 39 different kinds of work amongst which was the carrying of a load from one place to another. Mishnah, "Shabbath," vii. 2 ; see Hausrath, N. T. Times, vol. i. p. 101 ; Stapfer, Palestine in the Time of Christ, p. 350.

11. **But he answered them,** with ready wit and resistless logic, **He that made me whole,** Christ being as yet to the healed man a stranger, **the same said unto me,** or, with emphasis on 'the same,' ἐκεῖνος (cf. i. 18, 33 ; ix. 37 ; x. 1 ; xii. 48 ; xiv. 21, 26 ; Mark vii. 20), *that person to me said,* as he had perfect right and authority to do, having wrought such a miracle upon me, **Take up thy bed and walk.** In the man's judgment the Being who could by a word restore a 38-year-long cripple to health could not possibly be other than one who had power to abrogate such a Sabbath ordinance as they referred to.

12. **They asked him,** with scornful indignation, passing over the miracle of healing which should rather have arrested their attention, **Who is the man**—the man ! so marking the contempt they felt for such an irreligious person, **that saith unto thee** opposing his authority to that of the divine law, **Take up** thy bed **and walk,** or more expressively, '*take up and walk,*' i.e. take up, not thy bed alone, but take up anything, the sin consisting not in the circumstance that the man bore his couch, but in the fact that he carried at all.

13. **But he that was healed,** ὁ ἰαθείς, rather than ὁ ἀσθενῶν (D. Tischendorf), the sick man ; meaning he, when he had been healed, as distinguished from ὁ τεθεραπευμένος (ver. 10), the healed man as an objective fact, **wist not who it was,** not because intent upon carrying his couch and distracted by the interpellation of the Jews, *grabbato ferendo intentus et Judaica interpellatione districtus* (Bengel), but because Jesus had appeared to him as a stranger and he had not yet been able to learn who Jesus was either from others or from Christ Himself ; **for Jesus had conveyed Himself away,** or turned aside silently and secretly, i.e. privately withdrew ; ἐξένευσεν, found nowhere else in the N. T.,

being the aorist of a verb signifying to avoid by inclining the head or body ; the reason of this hasty exit from Bethesda having been in all likelihood that He wished to escape the noise and confusion that would almost certainly ensue upon the crowds in the sanatorium getting acquainted with the miracle (cf. vi. 15 ; Matt. xii. 16),— hardly because already He beheld the man entangled with the Jews (Meyer). **a multitude being in the place.** The presence of the crowd, while rendering desirable, would also facilitate His departure (Hengstenberg).

14. **Afterward,** lit., *after these things ;* i.e. probably at a later hour on the same day, though this cannot certainly be inferred, **Jesus findeth** (cf. i. 43 ; ix. 35) **him,** who had been healed, **in the temple,** i.e. in the temple court (see on ii. 14), having gone there, it may be supposed, to present a thank-offering (cf. Is. xxxviii. 20 ; Luke xvii. 15 ; Acts iii. 7, 8), though Christ's address to him, it has been said (Lange), does not indicate a man thoroughly possessed by gratitude ; **and said unto him,** bringing out its spiritual lesson without which the miracle of healing would have been incomplete (Westcott), **Behold,** arresting and fixing the man's attention upon the special act of mercy of which he had been the subject, **thou art made whole** The miracle was undeniable and was consciously acknowledged by the man. **Sin no more** The admonition (cf. viii. 11) implies more than a general connection between sin and suffering (Irenæus, Calvin, Neander, Hengstenberg) ; it distinctly suggests the inference (cf. Luke v. 20, 24) that the man's ailment had been produced by his previous wickedness (Chrysostom, Bengel, Godet, Meyer, Tholuck, and others), though it must not be deduced from this instance that in every case suffering is the consequence and punishment of some particular sin. The acquaintance with the healed man's antecedent history which this showed (cf. iv. 17) could not fail to make a deep impression on his mind. **lest a worse thing,** worse even than a malady of 38 years' standing, a greater and heavier physical infirmity, a sorer and sadder spiritual infliction, even the loss of salvation and the suffering of damnation, **befall**

thee, lit., *happen to thee*, not by chance or accident, but arise to thee out of thy continued wickedness.

15. **The man went away and told the Jews** neither out of gratitude, being desirous to get Christ acknowledged among the Jews (Cyril, Chrysostom, Grotius, Hengstenberg), nor out of malice in order to entangle Christ with the authorities (Schleiermacher, Paulus), nor in obedience to the rulers who had a right to be informed (Bengel, Lücke, De Wette, Brückner, Luthardt, Westcott), nor through stupidity (Stier, Tholuck) or fear (Lange), nor in conscious defiance as proclaiming to the Sanhedrim an authority higher than theirs (Meyer), but simply to vindicate himself (Ewald, Godet, and others), by answering the question (ver. 12) to which he had previously been unable to reply—that **it was Jesus who had made him whole.** The authorities wished to know who had directed him to violate the Sabbath : the man informed them who it was that had made him whole. " All this shows the mood of both " (Luthardt).

16. **And for this cause did the Jews persecute Jesus,** not as yet by a judicial process (Lampe, Kuinoel) say by arraignment before the little Sanhedrim (Lange), but in a general way by continued and repeated manifestations of hostility, as the imperfect, *were persecuting,* shows ; **because He did these things,** lit., *was doing,* was in the habit of doing, *these things,* such as the healing of the paralytic—the expression pointing to a settled principle of action as already adopted by Christ—**on the Sabbath.** See on ver. 10. The clause " and sought to slay him " (T. R.), obviously borrowed from ver. 18, must be omitted in accordance with B C D L (Tischendorf, Meyer, Godet, Westcott and Hort, and others).

17. **But Jesus answered them** ἀπεκρίνατο, occurring only here (ver. 19) and in xii. 23 (cf. Matt. xvii. 12 ; Acts iii. 12), presupposes accusation and hostile observation, though not necessarily judicial examination. **My Father** A second clear assertion of divine sonship on the part of Christ : see on ii. 16. **worketh even until now** or, preserving the order of the original, *until now worketh,* or is working. In so saying

Christ refers to the ceaseless activity of God in providence and in grace, in upholding the universe (Deut. xxxiii. 26 ; Job ix. 4-10 ; Ps. cxv. 3 ; Is. xlvi. 10) and in seeking the salvation of men (Is. l. 2 ; Mic. vii. 18 ; Ezek. xxxvi. 25 ; Luke i. 50 ; Acts xvii. 30 ; Rom. x. 12, 13), which is perfectly consistent with His resting from the creating and world-building operations of which Moses speaks (Gen. ii. 2). **and I work** or, *am working,* in cooperation with the Father in the activities He carries on in both spheres (Heb. i. 3 ; Matt. xviii. 11) ; the relation of Christ's working to that of the Father being not that of imitation (Grotius, Ewald) merely, but of perfect equality in will and procedure (Meyer).

18. **For this cause therefore the Jews** (i. 19) **sought the more to kill Him** The force of ' more ' is not that they lately were satisfied with persecution but now contemplated murder, *modo persequebantur, nunc amplius quaerunt occidere* (Bengel, B. Crusius, Lange), which may be said to have already existed in latent form in the ' persecution,' but that they redoubled their efforts to carry out what from the first had been their secret purpose, viz., to kill the object of their hostile demonstrations (cf. vii. 1, 19, 25 ; viii. 37, 40). **because He not only brake the Sabbath** lit., *was breaking,* or loosening, *the Sabbath,* not merely violating a Sabbatic precept, but undermining the Sabbatic institution—by healing on that sacred day, is what they meant. This was the doctrine of the Shammaite Pharisees, to whom probably belonged Our Lord's opponents, who " expressly forbade the instruction of children, the care of the sick, the succour of the afflicted and almsgiving" on the Sabbath day (Stapfer, Palestine in the Time of Christ, p. 354, 355). " Medical assistance was allowed only on the assumption that life was in danger " (Schürer, The Jewish People in the Time of Jesus Christ, § 28, II.). This interpretation of the Sabbath law however Christ repudiated and condemned (vii. 23 ; Matt. xii. 12). **but also called God His own Father** ἴδιος, His own in a peculiar sense (cf. i. 41), for so they rightly translated the possessive pronoun " My " : for the correlative idea

" His own Son," see Rom. viii. 32. **making Himself equal with God.** The clause may be regarded as an inference from (Lücke), or a presupposition for (B. Crusius), the preceding ; but is better taken as a declaration of the sense in which they understood the placing of His own working on a level

with the Father's (Meyer, Godet, Westcott, and others). This the Jews discerned to be tantamount to a claim of absolute and essential equality with God : cf. Phil. ii. 6. *Ecce intelligunt Judæi quod non intelligunt Ariani* (Augustine).

Homiletics

VER. 10-18.—THE ARREST OF A (SO-CALLED) SABBATH-BREAKER.
I. **An Accusation preferred :** ver. 10. 1. *Certainly strange.* The Jewish authorities, paragons of virtue, might have been expected to congratulate the poor man whom they met on the recovery of his health, and to compliment his benefactor, on having proved himself so skilful a physician. But, alas ! (such is the blinding power of literalism), they were so scandalized at the profanity of a recovered invalid carrying home his bed from the hospital on the day of rest that they quite forgot their manners, and left the benevolent stranger who had performed so great a marvel to go without recognition. Nay, so inflamed were their pious bosoms with indignation at the appalling wickedness of making a man whole on the Sabbath that they determined to persecute Jesus, in fact to kill Him if they could, and so put Him out of the way. 2. *Seemingly just.* The indictment had an appearance of being well-founded. The man's action was in flagrant violation of Rabbinical prescription and the letter at least of Scriptural injunction. Neither of these however was or is the ultimate standard of right and wrong. An action may contravene the literal sense of Holy Writ, and yet be in exact accordance with its spirit (Matt. xii. 4, 5), as, on the other hand, a deed may adhere closely to the former while deviating widely from the latter (Matt. xv. 3-6). So man-made law may pronounce that a crime and a sin which in Heaven's sight is blameless and even praiseworthy, as contrariwise it may approve and reward for virtue what in reality should be condemned as vice. 3. *Essentially false.* The validity of that Pharisaic ordinance which forbade a convalescent to carry home his bed Christ repudiated. The interpretation of Scripture precept in such a fashion as to render the man's action criminal Christ challenged. The former He expressly abrogated or set aside, if it ever had validity ; which He denied : the latter He declared an incorrect exposition of the ordinance of Heaven.
II. **An Explanation offered :** ver. 11. 1. *Transparently simple.* Without evasion, attempted concealment, or sophistical argument, the man gave a simple recitation of the facts of the case. So should all, but especially Christ's followers, speak the truth each one with his neighbour (Eph. iv. 25 ; Col. iii. 9), letting their yea be yea and their nay, nay (Matt. v. 37 ; Jas. v. 12) ; in particular remembering that the best vindication one can offer of his acts and words is to show them done and spoken in obedience to Christ. 2. *Perfectly natural.* To the unsophisticated mind of the couch-bearer, it seemed obvious that one who with a word could restore another to health had a right to bid that other take up his bed and walk. Even had the health-restorer been a mere man and the prohibitory statute of Divine appointment, the logic was good which reasoned that, if the former had received from God power to work such a miracle (iii. 2), he might also have obtained authority to suspend such a statute. And of course the reasoning was better when the physician was Divine and the ordinance was human. 3. *Wholly insufficient.* In the eyes of the inquisitors the man's defence was an aggravation of his original transgression. He had acted in obedience to one who was himself a law-despiser and a Sabbath-breaker. The man's physician was a more abominable sinner than himself. So men who from good motives at the outset begin to deviate from the laws of Heaven, by adding to them no less than by taking from them, not

unfrequently end by confounding moral distinctions and turning vice and virtue upside down (Matt. xvi. 12).

III. **A Vindication given :** ver. 17. The (so-called) Sabbath-breaker's explanation practically transferred the case to Christ. Against Christ therefore as the original and greater sinner, the impeachment of Sabbath-breaking was directed ; and by Christ accordingly the man's defence as well as His own was undertaken. That defence was—1. *Startingly bold.* Christ based His authority to heal on the Sabbath as on other days on the three following facts,—(1) that God the Supreme Lawgiver ceased not from activity upon the Sabbath, but continued His providential and gracious operations on behalf of men, (2) that He, Christ, stood towards that Supreme Sabbath-worker in the relation of Son, and (3) that as such He was a co-worker with God in all that God did. Hence whatever He as the Father's Son did was not only in perfect harmony with the Father's working, but was that very Father's working itself ; and from this the deduction was legitimate that He, like the Father, could heal on the Sabbath-day and be blameless. 2. *Completely unanswerable.* The Pharisees were shrewd enough to see that if they yielded the postulate they could not escape the conclusion. Hence they resorted to the only device open to them. Like baffled disputationists in general, they denied their opponent's premiss. They declined to recognize Him as the Father's Son. They determined to affix on Him the gravest charge of which a Jew or indeed a man could be guilty. They directly accused Him of blasphemously pretending to be God. Thus early the leaders of the people discerned where lay the *crucial* point in the awakening controversy. It was not whether Christ was a good man or a deceiver, a true Messiah or a false, but whether or not He was God's Son and God's equal. 3. *Fatally decisive.* It kindled against Christ the religious bigotry, purblind fanaticism, personal hostility, persecuting malignity of the Jewish authorities. It suggested to them from the outset the conviction that as they could not answer Christ they would need to kill Him ;—it is often easier to commit a murder than to make a syllogism, to take a man's life than to refute his teaching. Only as the would-be assassins were good (!) men, they must go about their work with prudence and with piety, but above all with circumspection ;—which also they did.

Learn 1. That the best way of sanctifying the Sabbath is to spend it in doing good to the bodies and souls of men. 2. That the most efficient way of helping Christ's cause is to tell what great things He hath done for one's soul and body. 3. That people do not always know who their best benefactors are. 4. That there is no more appropriate place for one whom Christ has healed to visit and be found in than the temple or the Christian sanctuary. 5. That the best prophylactic against physical disease is to fear God and keep His commandments. 6. That the cause which professedly good men persecute is not always a bad one. 7. That Christ is perfectly able at all times to vindicate His words and ways before men.

3. THE REPLY OF VINDICATION—DISCOURSE UPON THE BREAD OF LIFE

CHAP. V. VER. 19-47

The present section in which Christ replies to the veiled accusation of blasphemy preferred against Him by the Jewish authorities because of His saying—" My Father worketh hitherto and I work " (ver. 17), naturally falls into three subdivisions. In the first (ver. 19-29) Christ develops, amplifies, and elucidates the sublime claim to be regarded as the Divine Son which they recognize and He admits in that saying to be advanced. In the second (ver. 30-37) He directs the attention of His hearers to the threefold witness they themselves possessed of His Sonship. In the third (ver. 38-47) He warns them of the fact and of the inexcusable character of their unbelief in and rejection of Him, God's Son so clearly and sufficiently attested.

EXPOSITION

Ver. 19. Jesus therefore, i.e. because His opponents, besides condemning Him as a Sabbath-breaker (cf. vii. 23), stumbled at His assertion of Divine Sonship (ver. 18), and practically charged Him on that account with blasphemy (cf. x. 36), **answered,** not by denying the truth of their imputation, or by explaining His language in such a fashion as to evade the charge of blasphemy, but by unfolding the significance of the Sonship He claimed, **and said unto them,** the Jews (ver. 18), **Verily, verily, I say unto you** (see on i. 51 ; iii. 3, 5, 11)—**The Son,** i.e. the Son absolutely, in His pre-existent being and in His historical appearing (iii. 17), the whole divine-human subject (Meyer, Brückner, Luthardt), and not merely the Son in His human manifestation (Weiss, De Wette), **can do nothing,** lit., *is not able to do anything,*—this inability arising not from external but from internal necessity (Luthardt), consisting not of a physical but of a moral impossibility (Godet), grounded on a oneness of essence with the Father (Lücke)—**of Himself** ἀφ' ἑαυτοῦ, not merely of His own knowledge (xviii. 34), but of His own impulse, as acting by an absolutely independent and self-contained life. In this way the Son cannot act because of His oneness with the Father (x. 30) ; **but He,** *the Son, can do,* though not of Himself,—ἐὰν μὴ connecting not with ἀφ' ἑαυτοῦ but with ποιεῖν —**what he seeth** — βλέπειν, like ὁρᾶν (iii. 32), being used of external contemplation — **the Father doing,** the image being that of a child directing its admiring and loving glance upon its parent's movements ; **for,**—furnishing a reason why the Son cannot act independently of the Father,—**what things so ever He,** ἐκεῖνος, that one, the Father, **doeth, these the Son also doeth,** His

activity being co-extensive with that of the Father, **in like manner,** not by way of imitation merely (Ewald), but as performing the same things, "in virtue of His sameness of nature" (Westcott). The Father's acts therefore the Son claims as His acts.

20. **For**—explaining the basis and presupposition upon which this identity of working rests—**the Father loveth the Son,** the term φιλεῖν pointing to the tenderness of that affection of which the latter was the object (cf. xvi. 27 ; xxi. 17), as distinguished from the love of approbation ἀγαπᾶν (iii. 35 ; xv. 9 ; xvii. 24), which also was extended to Him by the former, **and sheweth Him,** as a father to his son, the shewing being the antecedent condition, ground, or basis of the seeing, and the seeing on the other hand the cause and motive of continued and greater shewing on the part of the Father, **all things**—love having no secrets : *qui amat, nil celat* (Bengel)—**that Himself doeth.** The Father constitutes the Son the personal depositary of His eternally-proceeding and infinitude-filling self-revelation, thus exalting Him above all prophets to whom He reveals not all, but only part of what He doeth (Gess) ; **and greater works** ἔργα, products or achievements of the Messianic activity (ver. 36 ; vii. 3, 21 ; xiv. 10 ; xv. 24 ; cf. Matt. xi. 2 ; see on ii. 11)—Our Lord here refers to the works about to be mentioned, of quickening and judging.—**than these,** the healing of the cripple and such like, as already they had witnessed (ii. 23), **will he,** the Father, **show him,** the Son. The knowledge the Son (Incarnate) possessed of the Father was progressive. "The Father shows Him everything He does, but not everything at the same time ; and the greater (thing) stands still in the

front. Jesus's knowledge of God is from face to face, and it possesses clearness of vision ; but it spreads itself abroad only by degrees over the wide territory of divine realities, and advances from stage to stage " (Gess, Christi Person und Werk, 1 Ab. pp. 30, 31). that, indicative of the Divine purpose in granting this disclosure to the Son, **ye,** unbelieving Jews who now hear Me, **may marvel.** The effect of Christ's miracles on such as beheld them had chiefly been surprise and amazement. Accordingly Christ now announces that wonder and astonishment of a different sort will result from the greater works of quickening and judging He shall afterwards perform. The former will awaken a surprise that may terminate in faith or complete submission to the Son (ver. 23), as in the conversion of Israel through observing the work of the Gospel among the Gentiles (Rom. xi. 23) ; the latter will overwhelm the finally impenitent and unbelieving with dismay (Rev. vi. 16) as they gaze upon their Judge whom they recognize as the rejected Son. 21. **For,** offering a specimen of those greater works alluded to, **as the Father raiseth the dead and quickeneth them,** not the literally and corporeally dead alone as in Rom. iv. 17 ; viii. 11 ; 1 Cor. vi. 14 ; 1 Tim. vi. 13, referring to the general resurrection (Tertullian, Chrysostom, Erasmus, Beza, Grotius, Bengel, Kuinoel, Ewald, and others), or, the spiritually dead alone, as in Eph. ii. 5 ; Col. ii. 13 (Calvin, Lampe, Lücke, Tholuck, Meyer, De Wette), but both, or the whole work of quickening as it is performed by the Father and " in like manner also " by the Son (Godet, Luthardt, Hengstenberg, Brückner, Westcott) ; **even so the Son also quickeneth whom He will.** The ' quickening ' in this case is not to be restricted to the impartation of spiritual life (Reuss), but must be viewed as including the raising of the body, as the last result of the former (Tholuck). The emphasis rests neither on ' whom ' as if the thought were that only ' the elect ' were quickened (Calvin), nor on ' He '—the pronoun being omitted in the Greek— as if the Son's work of quickening were meant to be distinguished from the Father's work of raising (Reuss),

but on 'will ' to mark the absolute efficiency of the Son's power (Luthardt, Godet). *Nunquam ejus voluntatem destituit effectus* (Bengel). The proper subject of ' will ' is not God (Ewald) but Christ ; though the Son is to be thought of as the organ through whom the Father works—only not in a dependent manner, since the Son quickens whom He wills. " The will of the Father and that of the Son go hand in hand " (Gess, Christi Person und Werk, 1 Ab. p. 31).

22. **For,** setting forth the reason why the work of quickening has been entrusted to the Son (Tholuck, Luthardt, Hengstenberg, Godet, Brückner, and others) rather than why the Son quickens ' whom He will ' (Lücke, De Wette, Stier), **neither,** *and not* (cf. vii. 5 ; viii. 42 ; xxi. 25), adding an additional factor to the preceding **work** of ' quickening ' of which also the new element supplies an explanation, **doth the Father,** to whom the work of judging primarily and essentially belongs (Ps. l. 4 ; lviii. 11 ; Ezek. xviii. 30 ; Ecc. xi. 9 ; Dan. vii. 10 ; John viii. 50 ; Rom. ii. 16 ; 2 Tim. iv. 1 ; Heb. x. 30), **judge,** cf. on iii. 17, 18, **any man,** i.e. directly ; **but He hath given,** not in time but in eternity, δέδωκε being frequently employed to describe the privileges and offices of the Son (ver. 36 ; iii. 35 ; vi. 37, 39 ; x. 29 ; xvii. 2, 4), **all judgment,** the whole judicial function in all its parts and sorts, embracing therefore present moral and future legal judgments upon men, **unto the Son;** because the work of quickening with which also He has been entrusted requires such work of judging at one time as its presupposition, at another time as its consequence.

23. **That**—declaring the ultimate purpose contemplated by the Father in this arrangement—**all,** i.e. men, **may,** — not *should,* as if the realization of this end were hypothetical, but *may,* since either in joy or in sadness, in quickening or judging, it will be translated into fact—**honour,** not necessarily accord believing adoration to, but recognize as the supreme object of a creature's homage, **the Son even as,** καθώς not because (Baümlein), but in the same manner as **they honour the Father.** "The manner of honouring

corresponds with the sort of benefit and dependence. Humanity shall recognize that their eternal salvation or damnation proceeds from the hand of the Son as from that of the Father. Therefore honour they not the Son as one honours a human benefactor who gives only small and momentary help, but as one honours the Father in whom the whole of salvation and its opposite rests" (Gess, Christi Person und Werk, 1 Ab. p. 32). **He that honoureth not the Son,** by recognizing Him and treating Him as such, i.e. as the Father's equal, **honoureth not the Father who sent Him** : see on iii. 17. To truly worship, love, and serve God while denying the Supreme Divinity and Eternal Sonship of Christ is impossible.

24. **Verily, verily,** guaranteeing the certainty of that about to be announced (see on i. 51), **I say unto you,** proclaiming its authority, **He that heareth,** not with the bodily ears alone, but with the understanding and the heart (ver. 30; viii. 38, 43, 47; Matt. xiii. 43), **My Word,** i.e. the announcement, proclamation, message, of which I am the bearer, which proceeds from me, and belongs to me, and of which I am the Substance (viii. 31, 37, 43), **and believeth Him that sent Me,** i.e. the Father (iii. 17, 34; v. 38; vii. 28, 29; viii. 29, 42; 1 John iv. 14) —πιστεύειν with the dative as in iv. 21, 50; v. 38, 46; x. 37; xiv. 11—**hath,** is presently possessed of **eternal life** (see on iii. 15), **and cometh not into judgment** the negative side of salvation : see on iii. 18, **but hath passed out of death into life,** the positive aspect of salvation ; the transition of a soul out of the sphere and condition of spiritual death, here and now, into the state and realm of spiritual life : cf. 1 John iii. 14.

25. **Verily, verily, I say unto you, The hour cometh and now is** (see iv. 23)—the latter clause proves the quickening spoken of to be spiritual—**when the dead,** those entombed in the sepulchres of sin (Matt. viii. 22; Rom. vii. 8; Eph. ii. 1; Rev. iii. 1), **shall hear the voice of the Son of God** addressed to them in His Word (ver. 24); shall hear, in the sense that this voice shall audibly be spoken to them, though the next clause proves it will

not be heard by all in the sense of being intelligently received and responded to ; **and they that hear,** lit., *those having heard,* **shall live,** through having been made alive.

26. **For** — discovering the primal source of this quickening power which Christ declares to reside in His Word—**as the Father hath life in Himself,** originally, absolutely, eternally : cf. vi. 57 ; **even so,** marking the fact not the degree, **gave He to the Son also**—ἔδωκε denoting a bestowment not in time (Meyer, Luthardt) but in eternity (Godet, Gess, Westcott)—**to have life in Himself,** exactly as the Father hath, originally, absolutely, eternally (cf. i. 3). Hence the Son can impart life to others.

27. **And He,** the Father, **gave also** in eternity **Him,** the Son, **authority** ἐξουσίαν, right, power, every qualification necessary (cf. i. 12) **to execute judgment,** which pertains as above mentioned (ver. 22) to the quickening faculty, **because He is the Son of man.** υἱὸς ἀνθρώπου, without the articles cannot signify 'The Son of man,' ὁ υἱὸς τοῦ ἀνθρώπου, i. 51 ; iii. 13, 14 ; vi. 27, 52, 62 ; viii. 28 ; xii. 23, 34 ; xiii. 31 (Grotius, Lampe, Kuinoel, Olshausen, Lücke, Ewald, Tholuck), but 'a Son of man ' (Meyer, Luthardt, Godet, Brückner, Westcott). Hence a new thought is introduced, that the Son of God has been appointed judge because He is also a son of man, i.e. partaker of the nature of the judged ; and this appointment of the Son of God as 'a son of man' to be judge has been made, it has been thought, because the judge must be visible since the judgment is to take place with human publicity (Luther, De Wette), because as man the Son of God carries out the whole work of redemption (Meyer), because man should be judged by the lowliest and most loving of men (Stier), because the power of judging is the reward of the Son's incarnation (Hengstenberg), because Jesus as incarnate is the Redeemer and along with this is given the judgment (Tholuck), because only as man could Christ enter into that sphere in which the judicial office moves, or have the compassion which a judge of men should possess (Baur), though perhaps better than either of the above, be-

cause the judge must share the nature of those who are brought before him (Westcott), or because the judgment of humanity, partaking of the nature of a homage rendered to the holiness of God, a reparation for the outrage of sin, the act must go forth from the bosom of humanity itself (Godet), or because the judgments the Son of God executes and shall execute are just those which have begun and completed themselves through His appearing as a Son of man (Weiss).

28. Marvel not at this : cf. iii. 7 ; v. 20. The combination of this with the preceding clause on the authority of some inferior texts (Chrysostom, Theophylact) is objectionable as not in keeping with the context or with the position of 'this,' which obviously points to the whole of the previous assertion. **for,** ὅτι ; not *that* (Ewald), since Christ declared (ver. 20) that such a miracle as the resurrection would excite wonder, unless the sentence be regarded as elliptical, as thus —'Marvel not at this,' since I must more say, viz. *that* (Brückner) ; hence practically equivalent to *because,* and meaning that a greater ground for wonder would be found in the fact to be next stated, that **the hour cometh**—the absence of 'and now is' shows the future resurrection to be the subject of remark—**in which all that are in the tombs,** the literally dead, as shown by the more specific description than that given in ver. 25, **shall hear His voice,** i.e. the voice of the Son of God, **and shall come forth ;**—another indication that Christ speaks of a physical and not merely of a spiritual resurrection ; **they that have done good,** lit., *those having done the good things,* of hearing His word, believing on His name, keeping His sayings, doing His will: cf. iii. 21 ; **unto the resurrection of life,** the resurrection which proceeds from (xi. 25, 26), and culminates in (Luke xx. 36) life, the Messianic salvation (Luthardt, Tholuck, Lange, Weiss), rather than the resurrection of which the necessary result is life (Lücke, De Wette, Meyer, and others) ; **and they that have done ill,** lit., *those having done the ill,* absolutely, essentially, and generically the things that are worthless,—such things as those do who hate the light : cf. iii. 20 ; **unto the**

resurrection of judgment, the resurrection that springs out of, pertains to, follows on that preliminary moral judgment Christ pronounces in and through His word, and that eventually issues in the final decision and condemnation of the last day. It is thus apparent that John knows of a future judgment no less than the Synoptists, and that the idea of flagrant contradiction existing between them on this point (Reuss, Scholten, Hilgenfeld, Frommann, Koestlin, and others) is a pure invention of the critical imagination.

30. I can of Myself do nothing : cf. ver. 19. With this declaration Christ advances to the second branch of His discourse. Having exhibited Himself as a Divine co-worker with the Father He proceeds to show how that relation in which He stood to the Father of necessity involved that His acting should not be either in-self originated ἀπ' ἐμαυτοῦ), or by-self regulated (τὸ θέλημα τὸ ἐμὸν), or to-self directed (οὐ ζητῶ τὸ θέλημα τὸ ἐμὸν), but that it should be strictly in the character of one who served as the Father's ambassador and whose prime duty it was to faithfully execute the Father's trust or commission. That His acting and speaking were of this character He appeals to the threefold witness of John, His own miracles and the Father's voice. **As I hear,** sc. from the Father, corresponding to the seeing of ver. 19, **I judge,** both now and afterwards, the characters and destinies of men ; **and my judgment,** whether I acquit or condemn, **is righteous,** is in accordance with the requirements of absolute law and justice ; **because I seek not Mine own will, but the will of Him that sent Me :** cf. vi. 38. This explained the righteousness of Christ's judgments : they were in no case pronounced until they were seen reflected in the Father's mind and heard resounding from the Father's lips, and they were never given forth as utterances of His own but as declarations of His Father's will.

31. If I, "I," by myself, alone, **bear witness of Myself** (iii. 11), offer testimony concerning (περὶ) myself, as the Jews afterwards asserted He did (viii. 13), **My witness is not true,** i.e. formally, or in the sense of being legally valid ;

the customary rule in courts of justice having been then (Num. xxxv. 30 ; John viii. 17) as now that no one's testimony about himself, if unsupported by others, could be accepted. Subsequently (viii. 14) Christ claimed to stand superior to this law.

32. It is another that beareth witness of Me—that other being not the Baptist (Chrysostom, Theophylact, Grotius, B. Crusius, De Wette, Ewald), although, if it is not, the continuity of Christ's thought appears to be broken ; but God (Cyril, Augustine, Bengel, Kuinoel, Lücke, Tholuck, Meyer, Godet, Luthardt, Westcott and others), to whose testimony Christ in the context attaches the principal, indeed supreme importance, alluding to John not so much as one of His witnesses as one of theirs ; **and I** not 'ye' (א Tischendorf) **know,** absolutely, in the inner depths of my consciousness (iii. 11 ; vii. 29 ; viii. 55), and not merely have learnt from experience (ver. 42), **that the witness which He witnesseth of Me is true.** Not 'feeble' as being an unnecessary certificate of the Divine veracity (De Wette) ; rather a joyful expression of Christ's confidence in the same (Meyer); certainly not an accidental utterance, cf. vii. 28, 29 ; and probably far too solemn to be applied to the Baptist (Meyer).

33. Ye have sent unto John and he hath borne witness (see i. 19, 27)—the perfects indicating the abiding character of the results that proceeded from that early embassy—**unto the truth,** better, *in favour of the truth* (cf. iii. 26 ; xviii. 37 ; 3 John 3, 6), i.e. truth concerning and represented by me.

34. But the witness which I receive is not from man ; or, better, *But I,* on my part, as distinguished from you for whom John's testimony was valid and ought to have been successful, *not from man,* or any one whosoever he may be, *the witness,* which is requisite to substantiate my claim and legitimate my mission, *receive,* not strive after or lay hold of (Lücke, B. Crusius, De Wette), but accept, rely upon, appeal to, invoke ; **howbeit I say these things** not concerning my Sonship (Ewald), but concerning John's witness **that ye** cn **your side may be saved,** by believing it and through faith in it becoming partakers in the Messianic redemption.

35. He, John the Baptist, **was,**—his imprisonment (Matt. iv. 12 ; xiv. 3) or death (Matt. xiv. 10) having by this time intervened,—**the lamp,** not τὸ φῶς, the light of day (cf. i. 8), but ὁ λύχνος, the article being rhetorical as in iii. 10 ; an allusion neither to the Mosaic symbol of a candlestick for the Church of God (Hengstenberg, Lange), nor to the words of the son of Sirach (xlviii. 1) concerning Elias, " And his word burned as a torch," ὡς λαμπὰς ἐκαίετο (Bengel, Lücke, Stier), nor to the torchbearer in a bridal procession (Luthardt), but to the torch in the dwelling (Mark iv. 21 ; Luke xi. 36), of which there was never more than one (Godet, Westcott). Such a lamp the Baptist had been in the house of the Israelitish nation—one **that burneth and shineth** lit., *the burning and shining one,* not with reference to the splendour of his illumination, as David was called ' the light of Israel,' 2 Sam. xxi. 17 (Ewald), or to the fiery zeal and glowing eloquence by which John was distinguished (Bengel, Olshausen, Lange), but to the twofold fact that a lamp *shines by burning* and *burns in shining,* iu contradistinction from the sun which wastes not while it rays forth its beams ; **and ye were willing,** or, *but ye willed*(this was all you ever seriously contemplated) **to rejoice** to leap, dance, make sport of, like gnats in the twilight, like flies round a lamp, like dancers at a wedding (Lange) ; hence to be pleased with (cf. Matt xi. 16, Luke vii. 24, 32) **for a season,** meaning either ye willed for a season (Bengel, Westcott), or to rejoice for a season (Brückner, Godet), lit., *for an hour* (cf. Gal. ii. 5 ; Philemon 15) the phrase marking not the briefness of the Baptist's career (Ewald), but either the short-lived character of their favourable mood towards him or the celerity with which their satisfaction **in his light,** i.e. in the radiance emitted by him, turned into disgust.

36. But the witness which I have is, lit. *but I have the witness* which is requisite, **greater than** that of **John,** μείζω τοῦ Ἰωάννου, a condensed form of comparison (cf. Matt. v. 20) ; though *greater than John,* sc. was, is also admissible : (cf. 1 Cor. i. 25. See Winer, § xxxv. 5). Greater, Christ meant, as to dignity, authority, permanence (cf. 1 John v. 9) ; **for,** introducing the greater witness just spoken of, the **works** ἔργα, not His teaching activity (Eichhorn) or His ordinary actions (Paulus), or His miracles only (Kuinoel, Olshausen), but His whole Messianic activity (Lücke, Tholuck, Meyer, etc. : see on ver. 20), **which the Father hath given Me**, not gave (T. R., Godet), **to accomplish**, lit., *that I should finish them* (iv. 34 ; xvii. 4), **the very works**, the same works, or the works themselves **that I do, bear witness of Me** (see xiv. 11) **that the Father hath sent Me :** cf. iii. 34.

37. **And the Father which sent Me,** a solemn repetition of His Divine Sonship and pre-existence, **He,** ἐκεῖνος, 'that one,' rather than αὐτός, himself, (T. R., Godet); that One, the Sender, whose works I, the Sent, perform, **hath borne witness of me,** through the preceding works (Augustine, Grotius, Olshausen, Lücke, Neander, Stier), through the Baptist and the works (Ewald), through the Baptist, the works, and O.T. prophecy (Hengstenberg), through the voice at the Baptism (Chrysostom, Bengel, Lampe, Godet), through the inner witness of the Spirit (De Wette, Brückner, B. Crusius, Tholuck),—best, through the Holy Scriptures (Cyril, Theophylact, Calvin, Kuinoel, Luthardt, Meyer, Lange). **Ye have neither heard His voice at any time, nor seen His form.** Neither an allusion to the voice and the shape at Christ's baptism, Matt. iv. 16 ; Luke iii. 22 (Godet), to the Angel of the Lord whose manifestations through a voice and in an outward form the ancient Hebrew Church enjoyed (Gen. xxxii. 30 ; Exod. xx. 19; xxiv. 10; Deut. iv. 12) although they did not obey (Hengstenberg), to the revealing voice heard in the O. T. prophets (De Wette) ; nor to be understood as a declaration of man's natural inability to know God as Christ did, i. 18 (Godet), as a concession to the Jews of something for which they could not be blamed (Ewald, Tholuck), as an intimation that they had not accepted Christ (Westcott) ; but to be regarded as a rebuke of the utter insensibility of the Jewish people to the voice of God speaking to them and the appearance of God disclosing itself to them in the O. T. Scriptures (Meyer, Brückner, Luthardt, Lange.)

38. **And,** a progression,—' what is even worse,' **ye have not His word,** delivered to you in the Scriptures, cf. xvii. 6 ; 1 John ii. 14, not implanted in the conscience (Frommann, Olshausen), **abiding in you**—either, with emphasis on the verb, 'ye have it in you indeed, but not abiding' (Meyer) ; or, with emphasis on the prepositional clause, 'ye have it abiding with you' as an external possession, ' but not in you' as a spiritual experience (Luthardt) : **for whom He, the Father, sent, Him ye believe not.** Of the three antecedent charges this was the proof, they neither accepted nor recognized Christ of whom the Father spake.

39. **Ye search the Scriptures** The unbelief of the Jewish hierarchy arose not from a formal neglect of the sacred oracles, which they explored, dissected, and explained with laborious minuteness and unweariable diligence. Hence it is better to understand ἐρευνᾶτε as an indicative (Bengel, Kuinoel, Lücke, Olshausen, Brückner, Luthardt, Godet, Westcott, and others) rather than as an imperative (Chrysostom, Augustine, Luther, Calvin, Tholuck, B. Crusius, Ewald, Hengstenberg, and others), which would probably have been followed by ' ye have ' instead of ' ye think ye have.' **because ye think that in them ye have eternal life** The words indicate the popular belief amongst the Jews (ὑμεῖς, ye, on your part, think !) rather than the admission of Christ that mere external possession of or literal acquaintance with Scripture constituted a passport to the Messianic salvation : see on iii. 15. **and these are they that testify of Me.** That is their character, purpose, and constant function.

40. **And,** with the force of ' and yet ' **ye will not,** better than ' will ye not ?' (Ewald), marking the voluntary side of faith, which must ever be an expression of the individual's free will : cf. ver. 6 ; vi. 67 ; vii. 17 ; Mark viii. 34 ; Luke ix. 23 ; Rev. iii. 20. **come to Me** A common Scriptural metaphor for faith, or the believing acceptance of Christ : iii. 20 ; vi. 35, 37, 44, 45 ; xiv. 6 ; Matt. xi. 28 ; Luke xiv. 17, 26, 27. **that ye may have life,** not in seeming but in reality (cf. x. 10, 28), the adjective ' eternal ' being omitted perhaps to convey the idea that without this they could not have any life at all (Lange).

41. **I receive not glory from men,** i.e. I reject, as in ver. 34 (Meyer), or, simply

announcing a fact, I do not obtain from men δόξαν, glory,—not 'honour' merely, but the glory belonging to Him as Son of God (i. 14 ; ii. 11 ; xii. 41), the glory of absolute communion and fellowship with the Father (xiii. 31, 32 ; xvii. 1, 5), the glory of believing recognition of His Sonship (xi. 4 ; xvii. 10). The verse has been explained as a repudiation of selfish motives on the part of Jesus in complaining of Jewish unbelief. He had not addressed them as He had done because they had withheld from Him honour ; since honour, or ' glory ' in the sense of mere human recognition and approbation, as such, was a thing He did not seek and could not accept (Ewald, Meyer, Brückner, Luthardt, Godet). But the verse may also be regarded as a solemn and mournful announcement of the fact that even if He did accept glory from men, men in general, and they in particular had not accorded that to Him, had not extended to Him that recognition of His glory which they should have given and He had a right to expect,— that He had come unto His own and His own had received Him not : cf. i. 12.

42. But, introducing a strong antithesis, **I know you,** although you have not known me (cf. viii. 19), and accorded to me that reception which would have been to me a glory, **that ye have not the love of God in yourselves ;** otherwise ye would have received Me. The absence of this love of God, —not of God's love to you (Stier) but of your love to God, which is the root of all moral excellence, explains your rejection of me.

43. I am come in My Father's name, i.e. as the Father's representative (xiv. 9) and ambassador (ver. 37, 38) in order to accomplish His gracious will (vi. 38), and do His works (x. 25), **and ye receive Me not:** This explains the import of ver. 41. Their receiving of Christ would have been on His side a receiving of glory from them. But this Christ obtained not. **if another,** i.e. a false Christ, **shall come** Christ expected such deceivers to come (Matt. xxiv. 5, 24), and 64 are said to have appeared since the days of Christ (Bengel). **in his own name,** representing himself and prosecuting his own selfish ends : cf. vii. 18. On

" own " see i. 14. **him ye will receive,** ye will take to your bosoms and cover with your approbation, because he satisfies your self-love.

44. How can ye believe on me who accepting no glory from man give none —ye ! i.e. people such as you, **which receive** lit., *receiving* **glory one of another,** i.e. giving and taking to and from each other what is supposed to be agreeable to self-love and advantageous to self-interest, **and the glory that cometh from** not God only (Grotius, Lücke, De Wette, Godet), but **the only God,** as in xvii. 3 ; 1 John v. 20 ; 1 Tim. vi. 15 (B. Crusius, Meyer, Tholuck, Luthardt, Brückner, Westcott), the exclusive bearer of that title and therefore the sole dispenser of such honour as man should aspire to win and wear, **ye seek not ?** The transition from the participle to the finite verb adds to the impressiveness of Christ's words. Habitually seeking the lesser glory, ye never seek the higher.

45. Think not that I will accuse you to the Father The language assumes that Christ's preceding denunciations either had occasioned or might occasion the thought that He intended to impeach them at heaven's tribunal for rejecting His personal testimony. Such a proceeding on His part however Christ declares to be unnecessary, adducing to their surprise as a reason that the office of *public prosecutor* would in their case be discharged by another. **there is one that accuseth you** Better, *there is who accuseth you ;* already he exists and will not only first appear at the last day. *even* **Moses** As the representative of the law (i. 17), not of the whole O. T. (Ewald). **in whom ye have set your hope,** for salvation : cf. 2 Cor. i. 10 ; 1 Tim. iv. 10 ; v. 5.

46. For if ye believed Moses, ye would believe Me Their unbelief in Christ showed them to be no true disciples of Moses. **for he wrote of Me :** cf. i. 45. This indirect announcement of Christ's Messiahship which seems " at variance with His usual policy of concealment" is nevertheless in perfect harmony with His plain avowal that He was the Messiah (iv. 26), and need not be regarded as put into His mouth by the Evangelist

(Paley, The Gospel of St. John, p. 39).

47. **But if ye believe not his writings, how shall ye believe My words?** The contrast lies not between writings and words as if the former were easier of belief (Brückner), but between 'His' and 'My.'

HOMILETICS

VER. 19-23.—THE SON A CO-WORKER WITH THE FATHER.

I. **The Ground of this Co-working.** 1. *The Son's equality with the Father.* Implied in Christ's assertion that God was His Father (ver. 17), this is no less involved in the claim advanced by Christ to be possessed of equal knowledge (ver. 20), power (ver. 21), and honour (ver. 23) with the Father. 2. *The Father's love for the Son.* This again rests on the facts that the Son is the Father's only-begotten (i. 18), perfect image (Col. i. 15), supreme delight (iii. 35), and absolute interpreter (x. 15 ; Matt. xi. 27).

II. **The Manner of this Co-working.** 1. *The Father's showing to the Son.* As from Abraham His friend Jehovah hid not His purpose concerning Sodom (Gen. xviii. 17), so from the Word His Son the Infinite Father has no conceal-ments. The whole fulness of the uncreated life eternally residing in and welling up from the depths of the Godhead pours itself forth into the equally unbeginning and immeasurable being of the Son. The entire contents of the Supreme Father's mind unfolds itself before the Son's gaze perpetually, clearly, unreservedly, as an object of contemplation, apprehension, admiration, appro-priation. 2. *The Son's beholding of the Father.* Deriving His subsistence from the Father, the Son ever gravitates in the centre of His Being towards the Father (i. 1). Eternally surrounded by the Father's love as by a vital atmo-sphere, the Son ever turns to Him reciprocally with corresponding affection. Ever directing His gaze into the pure depths of the Father's bosom the Son sees the thoughts ineffable, acts immeasurable, and purposes unfathomable that therein find their primal source and native habitation. As the Word, it belongs to Him to interpret those thoughts, perform those acts, and execute those pur-poses. 3. *The conjoint action of both.* In the same manner as the Father works so works also the Son. The Father and the Son work not simultaneously merely, as two artificers co-operating with one another at different departments of the same work, or as a pupil copying his master, or as an ambassador repre-senting his sovereign ; but the Father and the Son work equally, identically, (*samely*, if one might coin an expression), so that the Son does what the Father doeth and *vice versa* the Father executes what the Son accomplishes.

III. **The Extent of this Co-working.** 1. *Generally.* It embraces everything the Father doeth, in nature and in grace, in creation, in providence, in redemp-tion, in the realm of matter and in the domain of spirit, in heaven above as well as on earth beneath. 2. *Particularly.* It included the miracles of healing and such like that Christ had performed in Jerusalem. Christ declared it would likewise comprehend in its sweep the greater marvels of quickening and judging which were to be, and already were, the specific ends of His mission. See next Homiletics.

IV. **The Purpose of this Co-working.** 1. *As regards the Son.* To set Him forth as the supreme object of worship, honour, love, obedience for man, and to secure that all men should ultimately be brought, willingly or unwillingly, in sorrow and shame, if not in joy and satisfaction, to a recognition of this sublime truth. 2. *As regards the Father.* To impart clearness, fulness, and reality to that homage men on grounds of nature or pre-Christian revelation might be disposed to render to the Father. (1) Clearness ; since apart from the Son neither could the nature of the Father nor the character of His working be correctly understood (xiv. 6). (2) Fulness ; since to acknowledge the Father without the Son is of necessity to worship a mutilated Godhead (x. 30 ; 1 John ii. 23). (3) Sincerity ; since "he that honoureth not the Son honoureth not the Father which sent Him " (ver. 23).

Lessons—1. The duty of seeing the Son as well as the Father in all things. 2. The gratitude due to the Father for discovering Himself to men in and through the Son. 3. The certainty that they who in faith contemplate the Son shall attain to a knowledge of the Father.

VER. 24-29.—THE GREATER WORKS OF THE SON.

I. **The Work of Quickening.** 1. *The spiritual awakening:* ver. 25. (1) The time of it. Now, during the currency of this Christian dispensation, at any and every moment thereof (2 Cor. vi. 2 ; Heb. iii. 7 ; iv. 7). (2) The subjects of it. The dead in trespasses and sins (Eph. ii. 1) generically viewed are the class or category to which the spiritually awakened originally belong and out of which they are called. (3) The manner of it. The vitalizing of a dead soul results from an infusion into it of life by the Son of God (ver. 21)—not directly, immediately and independently of any instrumentality ; but indirectly, mediately and dependently through the agency of the word which the Son speaks (ver. 24). (4) The condition of it. Not all the spiritually dead are quickened, or even all to whom the word of Christ is externally addressed, but only those who hear and believe (ver. 24, 25 : cf. Is. lv. 3). (5) The ground of it. That which renders such a spiritual quickening possible is the fact that the Son is possessed of life in Himself as an original, underived, and inexhaustible fountain, even as it exists in the Father (ver. 26). (6) The end of it. The soul whom Christ quickens and who awakens in answer to His energizing word 'lives' in the fullest and highest sense of that expression. 2. *The physical resurrection:* ver. 28. (1) Who shall be raised ? All that are in their tombs, i.e. the corporeally lifeless, those who shall have previously returned to the dust, a doom under which all have fallen in the past except two (Gen. v. 24 ; 2 Kings ii. 11), and all shall fall in the future except those who shall be alive at Christ's coming (1 Cor. xv. 51 ; 1 Thess. iv. 15). (2) When shall they be raised ? At a date which Christ designates as "a coming hour," but afterwards calls "the last day" (vi. 39, 54), the closing day of this present age, æon, or dispensation, when the affairs of time shall be wound up (Rev. x. 6) by a second advent of the Son of Man (Matt. xxv. 31) and the institution of a general judgment (Acts xvii. 31). (3) How shall they be raised ? By the voice of the Son of God (1 Thess. iv. 16), that voice which said to the young man at Nain, Rise ! (Luke vii. 14), and to Lazarus at Bethany, Come forth ! (xi. 43). (4) To what shall they be raised ? To diverse experiences ; "they that have done good unto the resurrection of life, and they that have done ill unto the resurrection of judgment" (ver. 29). Of the former the work of healing on the cripple was an emblem ; of the latter Christ's judgment of the Pharisees was a foretaste.

II. **The Work of Judgment.** 1. *Its specific character ;* a judgment concerning the characters and destinies of the wicked ; hence a judgment of condemnation. In this respect to be distinguished from the general assize of which other Scriptures speak, at which the world (Acts xvii. 31 ; 1 Cor. vi. 2), all nations (Matt. xxv. 32), every man (Matt. xvi. 27 ; Rom. ii. 6 ; 2 Cor. v. 10), small and great (Rev. xx. 12), shall appear, and from which they shall depart in two separate companies, the righteous and the wicked (Matt. xiii. 41, 43 ; xxv. 46), into everlasting abodes of happiness and misery. It is the bearing upon the unbelieving and impenitent of the final decisions of that momentous tribunal of the skies that Christ more particularly alludes to as His work of judgment, although the phrase as employed in this discourse (ver. 22) may be held as including both the preliminary moral verdicts that are passed upon men's characters by His word (iii. 18 ; ix. 39), and the sentences of acquittal that before heaven's bar will be pronounced in favour of the faithful followers of Christ (Matt. xxv. 21, 23, 40 ; 2 Tim. iv. 8). 2. *Its divine authority ;* being undertaken and performed by the Son not of Himself (ver. 19), but in virtue of an express commission received from the Father because of His assumption of human nature. The truth here insisted on is recognized in other Scriptures (Matt. xvi. 27 ; xxvi. 64 ; Acts x. 42 ; xvii. 31 ; Rom. ii. 16). 3. *Its successful execution.* Besides being designated to the office of judge by the Father the Son has been furnished with every qualification (the right and the power) requisite to carry such a vast and momentous undertaking to a prosperous termination ; and to this thought perhaps there is a significant outlook in the observation that the delegation of every kind of judgment to the Son has its perfect warranty and complete vindication in the fact that He, the Son, is also a son of man. See Exposition. 4. *Its ultimate aim.* That all men should honour the Son in the same measure and manner, with the same soul and spirit, as they honour the Father (ver. 23). See above.

Lessons. 1. The bearing of belief in these greater works of the Son on the credibility of His lesser works, the miracles of Scripture. 2. The necessity of a prior spiritual awakening for him who would attain to a future resurrection of life. 3. The certainty of final retribution for every one who doeth ill.

VER. 24.—A SHORT SERMON ON A GREAT TEXT.

I. **The Preacher.** 1. *The dignity of His person.* (1) The Son of God. (2) The ambassador of the Father. (3) The faithful witness. 2. *The solemnity of His manner.* As became one who spoke with (1) full knowledge, (2) absolute authority, (3) tender sympathy, (4) personal directness.

II. **The Discourse.** 1. *The meaning of salvation.* (1) Eternal life. (2) No condemnation. (3) Fulness of existence. 2. *The way of salvation.* (1) Hearing Christ's word. (2) Believing Christ's Father.

III. **The Audience.** 1. Their *persons*—men. 2. Their *characters*—dead. 3. Their *numbers*—whosoever. 4. Their *responsibilities*—involved in their ability to hear and believe.

Lesson. Take heed how ye hear !

VER. 31-40.—THE THREE WITNESSES OF THE SON.

I. **A Great Witness :** *His forerunner.* John the Baptist as a witness of Christ was 1. *Human.* As John previously acknowledged himself to be " of the earth " (iii. 31), so Christ now distinguishes him as belonging to the category ' man ' (ver. 34). 2. *Brilliant.* While he lasted he was like a lamp that burned and shone, giving light to all the household of the Jewish people. So should every Christian in his place, parent in his family, master in his workshop, teacher in his class, citizen in his city, be a blazing torch, or at least a useful lamp, emitting light to guide others to Jesus Christ (Matt. v. 16 ; Phil. ii. 15). 3. *Acceptable.* For a season the Jewish nation, leaders and populace alike, buzzed around the desert preacher like moths around a flame, sunning themselves in his prophetic radiance, musing in their hearts whether or not he were Messiah (Luke iii. 15). John was thus, it may be said, a witness of their own selection : hence a witness that might be supposed to be impartial. 4. *Transient.* Their early enthusiasm which had been quickly excited was as quickly allayed. Their admiration of him had been like the passing of a summer's cloud ; while his opportunity of addressing them had been brief. So Christ's human witnesses can seldom count on protracted popularity ; and even though they could are not suffered to continue by reason of death (Heb. vii. 23). 5. *Permanent.* Nevertheless Christ speaks of John's witness as having been possessed of an abiding character (ver. 33). A true word truly spoken for Christ never dies.

II. **A Greater Witness :** *His works.* These, though impersonal, in comparison with John's witness or John himself, provided Christ with a testimony, 1. *More exalted in its origin.* " He that is of the earth speaketh of the earth," said the Baptist himself (iii. 31). Hence the witness he gave Christ could characterize as " from man " (ver. 34). It originated in the earth or human sphere to which the forerunner belonged. But the testimony of the works proceeded from the higher heavenly and divine sphere in which the Father and the Son worked. 2. *More direct in its expression.* If in a manner John's testimony or witness bearing was also from the Father (i. 6), yet it came to mankind through the medium or channel of ' a man.' But, the works Christ did being the Father's works, the testimony they gave was immediate, and proceeded straight from them without passing round through any subsidiary messenger such as the son of Zacharias. 3. *More conclusive in its significance.* After all, the Baptist being human and therefore fallible, his witness could not escape the taint of imperfection. But in the case of Christ's works no deduction whatever required to be made from the binding force of that logic with which they appealed to the minds and hearts of spectators. If these works were such as the Father only could do (iii. 2 ; xiv. 10, 11), if Christ had received these works from the Father to accomplish (ver. 36), and if moreover Christ did these works in the same manner as the Father did them (ver. 19), then the inference was unavoidable, that Christ was the Son of God.

III. **The Greatest Witness :** *His Father.* 1. *The Scriptures the medium of the Father's testimony.* "These are they which bear witness of Me" (ver. 39), says Christ ; and again "Moses wrote of Me" (ver. 46). This accorded with Philip's faith (i. 45) as declared to Nathanael, with Peter's as recorded in his First Epistle (i. 11), and with John's as preserved in the Apocalypse (xix. 10). And, inasmuch as "no prophecy ever came by the will of man, but men spake from God, being moved by the Holy Ghost" (2 Pet. i. 21), the Scriptures of the O. T. were in Christ's day the Father's testimony regarding His Son, as in this day are these with the Gospels and Epistles of the N. T. Church. 2. *The Scriptures the Father's testimony par excellence.* Inasmuch as they were and are the special production of the Holy Spirit they constitute the highest witness the Father can give or the Son receive. So to speak, in them the Father speaks in and by the Holy Ghost. Hence to reject the witness of God in behalf of Jesus Christ contained in the Scriptures of the Old and New Testaments is to reject the last and highest form of evidence God can give.

Lessons. 1. The relatively subordinate position of the official ministry in the Christian Church. 2. The evidential value of Christ's miracles in attesting His divinity. 3. The supreme importance of Holy Scripture as a witness for Christ.

Ver. 39, 40.—THE WRONG AND THE RIGHT USE OF SCRIPTURE.

I. **The Wrong Use.** To suppose that either 1. the *having*, 2. the *knowing*, or 3. the *loving*, of the Scriptures merely as a book will confer eternal life.

II. **The Right Use.** To treat it as a witness for Christ—1. *divine*, 2. *authoritative*, 3. *full*, 4. *clear*, 5. *final*.

Lesson. Search the Scriptures diligently, sincerely, prayerfully, believingly.

VER. 37-47.—THE SON'S COMPLAINT AGAINST "HIS OWN."

I. **A Grave Indictment.** 1. *Non-acceptance of His Father's ambassador:*— "whom He sent, Him ye believe not" (ver. 38). Though the Son had offered Himself unto 'His own' as Jehovah's Messenger, they had not opened their hearts to receive Him, had not accorded Him that glory which was His due, had not admitted Him to their confidence or love. 2. *Unwillingness to partake of His salvation:*—"ye will not come to me that ye may have life" (ver. 40). Thirsting for eternal life they sought it everywhere except from Him. Hewing out for themselves broken cisterns they forsook Him who was the only fountain of life. They would scarcely enter upon serious inquiry concerning Him as to whether or not he could bestow salvation upon any. Simply they ignored Him, stood aloof from Him, came not to close quarters with Him, and eventually drifted into hostility against Him. 3. *Rejection of His gracious message :*—They believed not "His words" (ver. 47). They listened not to His teaching except to despise it and, if possible, extract from it grounds of accusation against Him. They turned the truth of God into a lie, wrested the utterances of the Holy One to their own destruction, perverted the speech of the Eternal Son into a weapon wherewith to accomplish His death.

II. **A Sufficient Proof.** 1. *They entirely misconceived the nature and use of the Bible* (ver. 39). What God had given them as a revelation from which His voice should at all times have been heard sounding forth (Ex. xxiv. 4 ; 2 Chron. xxxiii. 18 ; Ps. lxxviii. 1 ; 2 Tim. iii. 16) as a mirror in which His form should have always been beheld (2 Cor. iii. 18), as a schoolmaster to prepare them for and to conduct them to Christ (Gal. iii. 24), they had absolutely failed to understand. They saw not in it God's face, heard not from it God's voice, received not from it God's word (ver. 37). Merely they beheld in it a superior sort of talisman that endowed them with eternal life. They never dreamt of searching it for light to lead them to the Son. N.B. It is possible for even a Christian to make a Saviour of the Scriptures rather than of Christ. 2. *They were perfectly devoid of any true love of God within their hearts* (ver. 42). They had much profession of knowledge and zeal for God's law, but absolutely no sincere regard for the Divine Lawgiver Himself. This was evinced by the fact that though they possessed His word amongst them, they had it not within them; or if they ever had it in them it was only as a temporary visitor, not as a permanent occupier (ver. 38). 3. *They were wholly out of sympathy with a Saviour such as Christ professed to be* (ver. 43). Had Christ presented Himself as an earthly and ambitious monarch, dazzling them with the splendour of His projects, kindling in their bosoms the fires of revolution, promising to lead them to victory against the power of Rome and offering to reinstate fallen Israel in her pristine ascendancy as the foremost of nations, they would have listened to Him and rallied to His standard. Had He arrived amongst them as an adventurous charlatan who hoped to use them as a stepping stone to greatness for Himself, they would have welcomed Him with plaudits, woven chaplets for His brow, poured out their wealth at His feet, and made ballads in His praise. But because He came in His Father's name, with His Father's image in His person, His Father's love in His heart, His Father's words upon His lips, His Father's work in His hands, His Father's glory in His eye, neither seeking nor accepting praise from men, but craving only the approbation of Him in whose name He had appeared, they could not recognize Him, or if they recognized Him they determined to have none of Him. What a melancholy tale for the Son of God to be obliged to recite concerning the people He had originally chosen for Himself ! What an appalling revelation of the depravity of the human heart in Israel in Christ's day ! Are there not those in our day who are equally offended at the Saviour with these haughty Pharisees, and offended for the same or similar reasons ? 4. *They were completely absorbed in their own personal ambitions* (ver. 44). As such they were incapable of appreciating or desiring that glory which God alone or the only God could give. As such they were precluded by an inward moral blindness from either discerning the Father or beholding the Son. 5. *They were thoroughly steeped in scepticism even with regard to Moses* (ver. 46, 47). Hence their unbelief in Him of whom Moses wrote, though not excusable, was not surprising.

III. **A Fearful Fate.** 1. *To be accused to the Father* (ver. 45)—to be impeached before the high tribunal of heaven, as those who had dishonoured the Father's majesty in despising His Son. 2. *To be prosecuted by Moses,*—to have the very lawgiver in whom they trusted rise up against them in judgment, and condemn them because they believed not. 3. *To be deserted by the Son.* Christ notes that so convincing will be the evidence of Moses that nothing will require to be added by Him ; but alas ! His words no less imply that so great will be their guilt and so merited their doom that not even He, the Son, will be moved to interpose. Appalling retribution !

Lessons. 1. A call to self-examination. 2. A note of warning.

II. CHRIST'S MANIFESTATION OF HIMSELF IN GALILEE

1. THE MIRACLE OF THE LOAVES

CHAP. VI. VER. 1-14

EXPOSITION

Chap. vi. ver. 1. **After these things** —a few weeks after if the feast in v. 1 was Purim ; a twelvemonth after if it was the second Passover in Christ's ministry and that of vi. 4 was the third ; seven months after if the former was the feast of Tabernacles and the latter the Passover following (see on v. 1)—**Jesus** accompanied by His disciples (showing that the Galilean ministry was begun) **went away** from Jerusalem, no doubt (B. Crusius, Meyer) in relation to the preceding narrative, though, viewed in connection with what follows, His immediate point of departure was some place in Galilee (Brückner, Hengstenberg, Godet, Luthardt, and others),—more likely Capernaum (Matt. xiv. 13 ; Mark vi. 32; Luke ix. 10), than Tiberias (Paulus) which ver. 33 suggests,—since He *departed* in a boat, **to the other side of the sea of Galilee,**—i.e. to the eastern shore, "to a city called Bethsaida" (Luke ix. 10 ; Mark vi. 45), in all probability Bethsaida Julias at the mouth of the Jordan and on its eastern bank, Bethsaida, the city of Andrew and Peter, being on its western (see on i. 44)—**which is** *the* **sea of Tiberias :** cf. xxi. 1. Neither implying that Tiberias (see on ver. 23) was Christ's point of departure (Paulus), nor suggesting that the spot to which Christ proceeded was on the south-east shore of the lake, exactly opposite Tiberias on the west (Meyer), but simply appending the name current among foreigners (Ewald, Lücke, Brückner, Hengstenberg, Godet, and others), as the designation 'Sea of Galilee' was popularly used by Galileans (Matt. iv. 18 ; Mark i. 16). On the site of Tiberias see ver. 23. The Sea of Galilee or Tiberias is pear-shaped, the broad end being towards the north. Its greatest width from Mejdel, "Magdala," to Khersa, "Gergesa," about one third of the way down, is six and three quarter miles ; its extreme length twelve and a quarter. The Jordan enters it a muddy stream and emerges from it pure and bright. Its water is clear, in fact greyish blue like that of Lake Neuchatel which it resembles. Its shores, now desolate, were in the first century fertile and populous. Lying 600 or 700 feet below the level of the Mediterranean, in summer it is warm, though not oppressive, as there is usually a morning and evening breeze. Surrounded on three sides by hills it is exposed to storms such as that mentioned in ver. 18. At the present day as in Christ's time it is well stocked with fish (see Josephus, Wars of the Jews, iii. 10, 7 ; Wilson's The Sea of Galilee, in Warren's Recovery of Jerusalem, pp. 337-341 ; Stapfer, Pal-

estine in the Time of Christ, pp. 39, 40 ; Conder, Handbook to the Bible, pp. 213, 214).

2. And a great multitude out of the cities of Capernaum, Chorazin, and Bethsaida (Matt. xiv. 13 ; Mark vi. 33) **followed Him** on foot, travelling round the head of the lake, a distance of 10 or 12 miles, **because**—not necessarily implying that Christ's miracles were wrought immediately before crossing the lake, but only that they were the cause of His popularity—**they beheld** ἐθεώρουν (א B D L etc., Lachmann, Tischendorf, Westcott and Hort) rather than ἐθεώρων (A) or ἑώρων (Griesbach, Meyer, Godet), i.e. beheld, were watching, with wonder and partial appreciation (ii. 23 : cf. v. 19), rather than merely looked upon as spectacular displays, **the signs which He did,** ἐποίει, *faciebat* (Vulgate), was continuously doing, not merely upon the way (Meyer), but during His ministry in Galilee, **on them that were sick,** lit., *upon the sick* brought to (Matt. iv. 23, 24 ; Mark i. 32 ; ii. 3) or met by (Mark i. 40 ; iii. 1-5) Him.

3. And Jesus went up into the mountain, i.e. the mountain in that locality (Matt. xiv. 23), as in Matt. v. 1 (Meyer), or the mountainous district as opposed to the seashore (Godet) ; **and there He sat,** lit., *was sitting,* with **His disciples,** doubtless engaged in conversation with them, and probably unaware as yet that the people had arrived upon the scene : cf. Matt. xiii. 1 ; xv. 29.

4. Now the Passover (see on ii. 13 ; xi. 55) **the feast of the Jews**—applied also and specifically to the feast of Tabernacles (vii. 2)—**was at hand,** not already past (Paulus) but fast approaching. The proximity of the Passover, it has been supposed, is mentioned as a chronological datum (B. Crusius, Ewald, Brückner), as an intimation that the multitude mentioned in ver. 5 consisted of feast pilgrims from the north, whereas that spoken of in ver. 2 was composed of the dwellers in the cities round the lake (Meyer), but was probably intended as an explanation of the crowds that now flocked towards Christ (Bengel, De Wette, Tholuck) and possibly also as a hint that Christ's miracle and discourse were suggested by the approaching festival (Lampe, Bruno Bauer, Baur, Hengstenberg, Luthardt, Godet, Westcott, Milligan and Moulton). That Christ attended this Passover has been asserted (Lücke), and considered doubtful (Luthardt), but is commonly denied.

5. **Jesus therefore lifting up His eyes** lit., *having lifted up His eyes:* see on iv. 35 and cf. xvii. 1 ; Matt. xvii. 8 ; Luke vi. 20 ; **and seeing**, lit., *having seen* (cf. i. 38) **that a great multitude**—not a new crowd distinct from (Meyer), but the same as (Luthardt) that mentioned in ver. 2, since there was no occasion for travellers to Jerusalem, if such the new crowd were, selecting a route through Decapolis (Godet), while one at least of the Synoptists (Mark vi. 33) states that the crowd from the western shore outwent Christ and His disciples, and arrived upon the scene before them. At the same time this does not prevent it from having been also true that the crowd gradually became swollen by absorbing groups of pilgrims encountered in the cities through which it passed. **cometh unto Him** lit., *is in the act of coming towards Him*, not to be fed (Bruno Bauer), but to be healed (ver. 2 : cf. Matt. xiv. 14). Though the multitude was first at Bethsaida, the travellers might not all at once light upon the spot where Christ was sitting with His disciples. **saith unto Philip** Not because Philip managed the *res alimentaria* (Bengel), which he did not, that department falling properly to Judas ; or because Philip's temperament was specially thoughtful and reflective (Luthardt) ; or because naïveté formed the predominant feature in Philip's character (Godet) ; but probably because Philip happened to be standing beside Christ at the moment (Ebrard), or perhaps had already suggested (cf. Matt. xiv. 15) that the multitude should be dispersed (Lange). **Whence are we** The pronoun indirectly points to the feeling of compassion adverted to by the Synoptists (Matt. xiv. 14 ; Mark vi. 34). **to buy bread** lit., *loaves:* cf. xxi. 9, 13 ; Matt. iv. 3, 4 ; vii. 9 ; xiv. 17, 19 ; xv. 34, 36 ; **that these may eat?** That Christ here takes the initiative seemingly on the first approach of the

crowd, is not contradicted by the synoptical accounts which state that the banquet was prepared towards evening at the close of a day of preaching and healing. The apparent—not real (Meyer, Brückner)—discrepancy will be removed by supposing not that the Evangelist abridges the earlier narratives (Lücke, Neander, Hengstenberg, Lange), or desires to call attention to the spiritual character of the miracle (Baur), but either that Christ's question to Philip had not been heard by the other disciples, who accordingly at nightfall approached the Saviour with a request that the people should be dismissed (Westcott, Milligan and Moulton), or that it was not spoken until after He had said to the disciples, 'Give ye them to eat' (Godet, Luthardt). On the one hand, John's narrative does not state that Christ's question was put to Philip in the morning, but only when He saw that a multitude kept on coming, as they had been doing all day ; while, on the other hand, the silence of the Synoptists as to the question addressed to Philip does not demonstrate that it never took place.

6. **And this He said to prove him** lit., *proving him*, trying not whether he could suggest any way out of the difficulty (Meyer, Tholuck, Godet, Westcott), which was plainly ridiculous, but whether he had faith that Christ could (Luthardt, Hengstenberg, Lange, Brückner). The notion that John's language is a consequence of the glorification in which Christ's earthly history had long spread itself out before his gaze (Ewald) is to suppose the Evangelist himself felt at liberty to write down subjective impressions as objective facts. **for He Himself knew**, without the assistance of any counsellor (cf. Is. xl. 13) from his own absolute, internal knowledge,—the force of εἰδέναι (ver. 61, 64 ; viii. 37, 55 ; xi. 42 ; xiii. 11) as distinguished from γινώσκειν which points to knowledge derived from experience), ii. 25 ; iv. 1 ; v. 42 ; x. 27 ; xvi. 19)—**what He would do** lit., *was about to do*.

7. **Philip answered Him**, failing to catch the spirit and purpose of Christ's question and supposing Christ intended him to recommend an expedient—a proof of Philip's natural dulness, perhaps also

an evidence of the feebleness of his faith (De Wette): **Two hundred pennyworth of bread** lit., *loaves of two hundred denarii* in value ; the *denarius* being the tribute coin of Tiberius Cæsar (Matt. xxii. 17) struck in the 17th year of his tribunate—a silver coin of the value of 8d. or 8½d. in English money ; so that the sum calculated by Philip as barely sufficient would be about seven pounds (£7). How Philip arrived at this computation cannot be known. That the amount represented the total contents of the Apostolic purse (Grotius) is conjecture and improbable. **is not sufficient for them** lit., *will not suffice for them.* The disciples are represented in Mark (vi. 37) as mentioning the like sum, but thinking it might do ; which is no contradiction, but only another way of expressing the same thought, that a large quantity of bread would be required. **that every one may take a little.** As 200 denarii amongst 5,000 men, not counting women or children, would admit of no more than 8d. worth of bread to 25 persons, Philip might well cherish doubts of its sufficiency to give more than a morsel to each.

8. **One of His disciples**—not a gloss (Wassenbach), but inserted as a more accurate description of Andrew, as Philip himself is afterwards (xii. 21) more minutely characterized (Ewald) ; perhaps also to call attention to the circumstance that after all relief came, indirectly, from the circle of the disciples (Meyer), through the remark of **Andrew,** who elsewhere (i. 44, 45 ; xii. 22) appears associated with Philip, and whom the Evangelist introduces as **Simon Peter's brother,** because at the time when he wrote either Peter was better known or more influential than Andrew or because Andrew was already dead (Bengel). If the former supposition is correct then the hypothesis that this gospel was composed with an anti-Petrine aim (Baur) will require to stand on its defence. This individual so introduced **saith unto Him,** Christ, with much of the natural blindness displayed by Philip—

9. **There is a lad here** lit., *a little boy,* παιδάριον (א B D L etc., Tischendorf, Westcott and Hort), though the ἓν of the T. R. is by some authorities retained as more accurately expressing

the meagreness of the supply—" one single lad, a mere boy, who can carry little enough ! " (Meyer), " only one who has anything to suggest and that one how little " (Godet). But it is doubtful if John ever uses " one " as an indefinite article (Winer, § xviii. 9). **which hath** Most likely for sale, the lad being " a bread vendor or sutler accompanying some caravan " (Lange), though of this the text says nothing ; in which case the disciples could easily have said " we have " (Matt. xiv. 17). **five barley loaves** Barley was the food of the poorer classes : cf. Judg. vii. 13 ; 2 Kings iv. 42. The mention of the kind of loaves another hint that the author of this gospel had been an eye-witness of the scene. **and two fishes** ὀψάριον, occurring only here and in xxi. 9, 13, signifies any little thing, but chiefly fish, cooked, and eaten with bread as a relish. **but what are these among so many?** Though equally with Philip unable to perceive that what in their hands would not suffice for distribution amongst so great a multitude, might nevertheless avail in the hands of Him who had turned the water into wine at Cana, Andrew was not behind Philip in recognizing the impossibility of coping with the problem, how to feed so large a crowd in a desert.

10. **Jesus said, Make the people,** τοὺς ἀνθρώπους, the entire company, including women and children (Matt. xiv. 21) as distinguished from the men, **sit down** or, recline, ἀναπεσεῖν, cf. xiii. 12 ; xxi. 20 ; Matt. xv. 35 ; Mark vi. 40. "The fifth word of Jesus upon this occasion " (Stier), the carrying out of which must have consumed a considerable space of time, since according to Mark they sat down in ranks and by companies of hundreds and fifties. **Now there was much grass in the place.** Another note from an eye-witness. Mark's statement that the grass was green, χλωρὸς (vi. 39), must also have proceeded from a spectator. **So the men** οἱ ἄνδρες, the men as distinguished from the women and children who were probably grouped around the former, as far as possible in families, **sat down** —not the men only but the different companies of which they were the centres—**in number about five thousand.** As this number appears in all the four

Evangelists, it may be accepted as correct. A hundred companies of fifty persons each (or thereabout) composed the assembly. With the women and children added the aggregate might reach 10,000 souls.

11. Jesus therefore, i.e. after the arrangements had been completed, **took the loaves** having first said, "Bring them hither to me" (Matt. xiv. 18). By the act of 'taking' Christ brought the loaves into visible connection with Himself as the source of that power which was immediately to operate in their multiplication : cf. xxi. 13 ; Matt. xiv. 19; xv. 36; xxvi. 26; Mark vi. 41; viii. 6; xiv. 22; Luke ix. 16; xxii. 19. It is noticeable that He did not take the cup into his hands when He changed the water into wine at Cana. The different actions, it is likely, rose from the different characters and aims of the miracles. See Homiletics. **and having given thanks** As the father of the family Christ offers grace before meat (cf. Luke xxiv. 30), the word εὐ- χαριστεῖν, which occurs again in this gospel only once (xi. 41), referring to the gratitude due to God for His temporal bounties (Godet), perhaps designed to impart a semi-paschal character to the banquet, since, in that religious festival 'thanksgiving' was conspicuously prominent (Milligan and Moulton), and containing an acknow- ledgment on Christ's part of the revela- tion of the Father's will in accordance with which the miracle was wrought (Westcott), as well as a supplication with regard to the miracle about to be performed (Luthardt, Godet, Tholuck, and others). The term εὐλογεῖν em- ployed by the Synoptists, while largely synonymous with εὐχαριστεῖν (cf. Matt. xxvi. 26, 27; Mark xiv. 22, 23; Luke xxii. 19; also 1 Cor. x. 16; xi. 24), may point more to the external form of the prayer than to its inward contents which seem specially alluded to in the latter (Lücke). **He distributed** i.e. through the instrumentality of the dis- ciples, Matt. xiv. 19; Mark vi. 41; Luke ix. 16, giving the bread first to these, and through these **to them that were set down** lit., *to those reclining* or *lying back* (on the grass). The words "to the disciples" (T. R.) are to be omitted in accordance with the best MSS. **like- wise also of the fishes as much as they**

would. Not *as He would* (Luther). The desire of everyone was appeased before the creative energy of the giver ceased : cf. Ps. cxlv. 16.

12. And when they were filled The satisfaction of the multitude guarantees the reality of the miracle. **He saith** The command following, though not preserved by the Synoptists, is not thereby contradicted. **Gather up the broken pieces which remain over** That out of five barley loaves and two small fishes anything remained furnished an- other indication of the presence of supernatural power : cf. 2 Kings iv. 42, 44. **that nothing be lost.** The fragments were to be collected, not alone as a memorial of the miracle, like the manna in the wilderness (Exod. xvi. 33), or to prevent the people from taking relics of it with them (Stier), but because "a gift so obtained was not to be squandered" (Godet), because frugality is a result and sign of grati- tude (Hengstenberg), and because God would thereby afford them a picture of that beautiful economy He Himself observes in nature (Stier, Olshausen) and desires in His creatures.

13. So they gathered them up, and filled twelve baskets—presumably each apostle taking one basket, κόφινος, which, if a 'travelling wallet' (Luthardt, Meyer), and he did not himself possess one, may have been obtained from some person in the company, while if a larger basket (Westcott) or 'hamper' be in- tended, this may also have been pro- cured from a neighbouring hamlet— **with broken pieces,** not left by the satiated eaters, but still undistributed, **from the five barley loaves,** not from these alone (Meyer), but also from the fishes (Mark vi. 43), **which remained over unto them that had eaten,** i.e. which had not been required to satisfy their necessities.

14. When therefore the people, as in ver. 10, **saw the sign** The miracle is here characterized as a 'sign,' σημεῖον, from the standpoint not simply of its worker, or of its reporter, but also of its observers, to whom the supernatural occurrence was a 'sign,' though not in the sense meant by Christ. **which He did** The reading 'signs which He did' (A) is adopted by Westcott and Hort. **they said** to one another, **This is of a truth the prophet** So far the people's interpretation of the 'sign' was correct. It led them like Nicodemus (iii. 3) to think of Christ as a prophet. It even raised an expectation that he might be the prophet, ὁ προφήτης, the well-known and expected prophet spoken of by Moses (Deut. xviii. 15). **that cometh into the world.** The usual designation for Messiah. See on i. 21, 25 ; vii. 40.

HOMILETICS

VER. 1-14.—THE BETHSAIDA BANQUET.
I. The Historical Setting. 1. *The place.* Galilee as distinguished from Jerusalem ; the eastern side of Lake Tiberias ; near the city of Bethsaida-Julias ; in a desert place, probably the plain of *Butaiha.* 2. *The time.* The third year of Our Lord's ministry ; about a twelvemonth after the Bethesda miracle (v. 1); when His Galilean ministry was approaching its culmination ; shortly after the death of His forerunner and the return of the seventy (Matt. xiv. 13 ; Mark vi. 30) ; in the afternoon of a day spent in teaching and healing. 3. *The company.* The inhabitants of Capernaum, the dwellers in Chorazin, Bethsaida, and other cities or villages by the sea, with such southward-moving pilgrims as were met and absorbed by the main body of the throng which surged northwards round the head of the lake. 4. *The occasion.* The worn-out and exhausted condition of the people who had hung upon His lips and drawn upon His healing powers all day long from early morn till afternoon. 5. *The motive.* The tender compassion which their presence excited in Christ's bosom.
II. The Miraculous Sign. 1. *The preparation.* (1) The question put to Philip—" Whence are we to buy bread," etc., ver. 5 ; serving to show that Christ recognized it as a part of His mission and of His people's duty to care for the physical necessities and temporal wants of men ; to convince Philip and his fellow-apostles of the utter inadequacy of ordinary means to provide such a banquet as He contemplated ; and to arrest the attention as well as excite the expectation of His disciples, that, being on the outlook for some sort of divine or supernatural interposition, they might the more easily understand the forthcoming ' sign.' (2) The observation made by Andrew—" There is a lad here," etc., ver. 9. It was needful if Christ was to claim for His impending action the dignity and value of a miracle that the entire absence of natural resources should be emphasized. This was done by the double testimony of Philip and Andrew, that as it were in the mouth of two witnesses the truth might be established. It was also requisite, if Christ's disciples were to think of a divine interposition, that they should cease to look for succour through purely human aid. That they had done so Andrew's question, no less than Philip's remark, showed. (3) The direction given about the crowd—" Make the people sit down," ver. 10. Order is heaven's first law, in that which is supernatural, spiritual, and eternal, as in that which is natural, material, and temporal. In the unseen universe equally with the seen, in the kingdom of grace as in the realm of nature, God is not a God of confusion but of peace (1 Cor. xiv. 33), and both Himself does and requires His servants to do " all things decently and in order " (1 Cor. xiv. 40). 2. *The performance.* (1) The taking of the loaves, ver. 11 ; thus visibly connecting the external means with Himself, without whose power no means, however splendid, would have availed (Ps. cxxvii. 1, 2), and imparting to the feast a semi-sacramental character it would otherwise have wanted (1 Cor. xi. 23). (2) The giving of thanks, ver. 11, in which doubtless was included supplication concerning the wonder about to be performed, Our Lord in both furnishing to His followers and to all men an example of that gratitude which should be exhibited by those who possess nothing that they have not received (iii. 27 ; Rom. xiv. 6 ; 1 Cor. iv. 7) and of that dependence on divine power without which the best conceived projects of men come to nought (Ps. cxxvii. 1 ; John xv. 5). (3) The distribution of the bread, ver. 11. This was done, as the Synoptists say, through the medium of the disciples, Christ thereby showing how in grace as in nature He invites the co-operation of His

people (2 Cor. vi. 1) ; to them that were set down and submissively waiting on His bounty, as the Lord ever is good unto them that wait for Him (Lam. iii. 25), and hath promised that the meek shall eat and be satisfied (Ps. xxii. 26) ; to all that were present, overlooking the necessities of none, as He neglects none either in the common ministries of His providence (Ps. civ. 14, 15, 27, 28 ; cvii. 35-38 ; cxxxvi. 25 ; cxlv. 15, 16 ; Matt. v. 45) or in the higher dispensations of His grace (Ps. cxv. 12, 13 ; Isa. lxi. 9 ; Acts iv. 33) ; and to the complete satisfaction of their wants, as He still engages to satisfy Zion's poor ones with bread (Ps. cxxxii. 15 ; John iv. 14 ; vi. 35). (4) The collection of the fragments, ver. 12, which was done to teach a lesson of economy and prudence, since if God's Son was frugal God's children should not be prodigal (Prov. x. 4 ; xxvii. 23 ; xxxi. 27) ; to serve as a memorial of the divine goodness, as the pot of manna was laid up in the ark (Exod. xvi. 33), and as God's people should still thankfully recall His benefits and blessings (Ps. ciii. 1, 2 ; 1 Thess. v. 17) ; and perhaps also to furnish a proof of the reality of the miracle, it being inconceivable that 5000 persons besides women and children gathered fortuitously in a desert should be found possessed of as many loaves and fishes as would furnish an extempore banquet at which every guest should be satisfied and ten baskets of broken pieces remain unconsumed.   3. *The purpose.* (1) To accredit His commission.   As Moses (Exod. xvi. 4), Elijah (1 Kings xvii. 14), and Elisha (2 Kings iv. 42) had each in turn performed miracles in attestation of his calling, so did Christ.   Not that Christ could not have been a prophet without working miracles, since the Baptist did no miracle (x. 41), but He could not have wrought miracles without being a prophet (iii. 2).   (2) To manifest His glory.   Like the miracle at Cana (ii. 11) it was a forth-flashing of the glory of the Incarnate Son, and, if rightly pondered, should have led those beholding it to perceive He was more than " that prophet that cometh into the world," should have conducted them to faith in His Divinity and Messiahship together.   (3) To illustrate His work.   As that day He had supplied their physical, so had He appeared to provide for their spiritual necessities.   As by a power proceeding from above He had furnished them with 'bread that perisheth,' so by a like power was He able to bestow upon their souls the 'bread of life.' The banquet at Bethsaida was a picture of the truths afterwards symbolized by the Lord's Supper, which, like it, represents the Lord Jesus Christ as the only source of spiritual sustenance for souls.   (4) To educate His disciples.   Having determined after John's death to withdraw Himself into the inner circle of His disciples in order to perfect their ministerial education in anticipation of the time when His own death would devolve on them exclusively the work of the kingdom, this Bethsaida banquet may be said to have been the first lesson He submitted for their study.   As such it was fitted to remind them that Christ alone could furnish souls with the bread of life, that all they could do was to prepare these souls for its reception, or at most pass it round for participation.   So of pastors and teachers in the Church to-day ; if they cannot make the bread of life, they can distribute what Christ has made and themselves have received from Him, or at least can assist in making souls ready for what Christ bestows.

III. **The Popular Effect.** 1. *Incipient faith:* ver. 14.   The imagination of the multitude was dazzled, the judgment half convinced. Christ was the prophet that was coming into the world.   So far it was a sound conclusion.   It contained the dawnings of faith.   Had they put themselves into His hands to be instructed concerning Heaven's will it might have shot up into meridian light.   But though they had begun well they quickly turned aside, as many still do in the Christian way (Gal. v. 7).   2. *Mistaken enthusiasm:* ver. 15.   Swarming round His person they acclaimed Him King ! and would have crowned Him on the spot, or marched with Him at their head to Jerusalem and carried through the ceremony in the capital amid the high solemnities and splendid gaieties of the Paschal season, as men still have no objections to accept Christ as King so long as they conceive His kingship to be after their own carnal notions and expectations. But the only throne Christ condescends to receive at men's hands is the throne of their believing and obedient hearts.

Lessons. 1. The unwearied activity of Christ in doing good. 2. The infinite compassion of Christ for human misery. The inexhaustible ability of Christ to supply His people's wants. 4. The gracious condescension of Christ in accepting His people's assistance in carrying on His works. 5. The beautiful economy of Christ even in the midst of profusion. 6. The sublime self-renunciation of Christ in rejecting the offer of a temporal crown.

2. THE SIGN UPON THE SEA

CHAP. VI. VER. 15-21

EXPOSITION

Ver. 15. **Jesus therefore perceiving,** by the enthusiasm of the multitude, by the words they had just uttered, perhaps chiefly by the gestures with which they gathered round Him, **that they were about to come and take Him by force,** ἁρπάζειν : cf. Acts viii. 39 ; 2 Cor. xii. 2 ; 1 Thess. iv. 17 ; **to make Him King** whether on the spot or at Jerusalem (Luthardt, Meyer) cannot be determined and is not of importance to know. The substitution of 'to show' (ℵ) for 'that they might make' is to be rejected (A B L). **withdrew** It was His Father's business, not theirs, to make Him king,—*regem eum facere patris erat, non populi ; neque adhuc tempus erat* (Bengel) ; hence He could not accept a crown at their hands any more than at Satan's (Matt. iv. 8, 9). **again** He had at first withdrawn to the mountains as the crowds approached (ver. 3) ; from this He had afterwards emerged to teach, heal, and feed the people ; now a second time He seeks the retirement of the hills. **into the mountain** (see on ver. 3) **Himself alone,** unaccompanied by His disciples, whom according to the Synoptists He had sent away ; and, as these also mention, for prayer (Matt. xiv. 22, 23 ; Mark vi. 45, 46), whereas the first time His object was to teach His disciples.

16. **And when evening** ὀψία, i.e. the second evening, from sunset till dark (ver. 17 ; cf. Matt. xiv. 15, 23), **came, His disciples went down unto the sea** in obedience to instructions, to go before Christ unto the other side (Matt. xiv. 22 ; Mark vi. 45).

17. **And they entered into** lit., *having entered into* **a boat,** εἰς πλοῖον (ℵ B L Δ etc., Tischendorf, Westcott and Hort), most likely that which had conveyed

them thither—which would be expressly implied were the article retained τὸ πλοῖον (Meyer)—**and were going** the imperfect, ἤρχοντο, denoting an unfinished action — they were on the passage across, **over the sea unto Capernaum.** The first clause states their general, the second their particular, destination. As, according to Mark, Bethsaida was the point towards which they were directed to shape their course, it is probable that Christ had expressed His intention of embarking with them, after He had dispersed the multitudes, and for this purpose had instructed them to proceed along the coast northwards towards Bethsaida Julias before crossing to Capernaum (Godet, Lange, Westcott, and others). If this not unnatural hypothesis be correct there is not even an immaterial discrepancy (Meyer) between this and the Synoptical narration. **And it was now dark** The reading κατέλαβεν δὲ αὐτοὺς ἡ σκοτία (ℵ D), 'but the darkness overtook them,' is less expressive than καὶ σκοτία ἤδη ἐγεγόνει, 'and darkness had already become present,' while the pluperfect ἐγεγόνει harmonizes better with the following ἐληλύθει. The time might be at, or after, 9 o'clock, when they finally started for the other shore, **and Jesus had not yet come to them.** They had probably been expecting to take Christ on board at some point on the coast near Bethsaida. Hence the 'not yet' is not to be dropped (Origen, Vulgate), as a gloss (Meyer), but retained (ℵ B D L etc., Lachmann, Tischendorf, Westcott and Hort).

18. **And the sea was rising by reason of a great wind that blew** lit., *a great wind blowing ;* descending

through the funnels of the northern hills. Thomson thus describes one of these sudden squalls :—" The wind howled down every wady from the NE. and E. with such fury that no efforts of rowers could have brought a boat to shore at any point along that coast. In a wind like that (which we experienced) the disciples must have been driven quite across to Gennesaret. . . . The whole lake, as we had it, was lashed into a fury" (The Land and the Book, p. 374). The violence of the storm having destroyed all hopes of reaching the eastern beach so as to take in Christ, the disciples determined to make for Capernaum.

19. **When therefore they had rowed,** lit., *having then gone,* **about five and twenty furlongs** They were therefore about half way across, μέσον τῆς θαλάσσης (Matt. xiv. 24), the lake being about 40 stadia or 2 leagues wide (Jos. Wars, iii. 10, 7). The *stadium,* one fortieth part of a geographical, or a little less than one eighth of an English, mile, is here properly translated furlong. The distance traversed was thus a little over 3 miles. The accuracy of this detail again bespeaks the hand of an eye-witness. **they behold** The present tense marks the dramatic liveliness of the situation. The time was in (Matt. xiv. 25) or about (Mark vi. 48) the fourth watch ; i.e. between 3 and 6 o'clock in the morning. **Jesus** whom they had left upon the eastern side of the lake, and certainly did not now expect, **walking** not swimming, as a ship is said (Gen. vii. 18) to go upon the face of the waters (Bolten), **on the sea,** not upon the beach as in xxi. 1 (B. Crusius), or towards the lake (Paulus), but over the sea, ἐπὶ τὴν θάλασσαν (Matt. xiv. 25), and on the sea, ἐπὶ τῆς θαλάσσης, as the context shows—" As they themselves are on the sea, it is self-evident that ἐπὶ τῆς θαλάσσης can only mean ' on the sea' " (Ewald)—though it is this last idea of Christ's being supported in a walking posture, ἐπὶ, upon and above (see Winer's Grammar, § xlvii. 5, g) the sea that is represented as arresting their attention. **and drawing nigh** lit. *becoming near* **unto the boat** That the Evangelist designed to depict a supernatural occurrence and not to indite an allegory (Weisse) or clothe

a natural event in a symbolical dress (Hase, De Wette), or favour Docetism (Baur, Hilgenfeld), or narrate a mythical legend of the sea (Strauss), or merely to imitate Hebrew poetry (Job ix. 8) or Roman mythology (Virg. Æn. vii. 810), is confirmed by the appended clause. **and they were afraid** (Matt. xiv. 26 ; Mark vi. 49 : cf. Luke xxiv. 37). Why should they have been alarmed if no such event as this happened, or if Christ had only been beheld upon the shore? On man's dread of the supernatural see Job iv. 12-16.

20. **But He saith unto them, It is I** (cf. iv. 26 ; viii. 24, 28, 58 ; xiii. 19 ; xviii. 5, 6, 8 ; Mark xiii. 6 ; Luke xxi. 8) ; **be not afraid.** The words, preserved by all the three Evangelists who report the event, show how deep an impression it must have made upon the hearts of the disciples. Matthew and Mark prefix θαρσεῖτε, be of good cheer. The former also at this stage inserts the incident of Peter's walking on the sea, which John omits as not immediately bearing on his theme, viz., The Glory of Jesus.

21. **They were willing therefore to receive Him into the boat** The significance of ἤθελον, not ἦλθον (א, J. D. Michaelis), has been conjectured to be that while they desired to take Christ on board this was now unnecessary because straightway the boat touched the land (De Wette, Ewald, Luthardt, Meyer), but more probably is that whereas, before they recognized Him and while yet they accounted Him a phantom, they had been alarmed at His approaching the boat's side, they were now full of eagerness to have Him in their midst (Hengstenberg, Ebrard, Tholuck, Godet, Westcott, and others) and, as stated by Matthew and Mark, actually did receive Him on board : *locutio concisa: subaudiendum,* et acceperunt (Bengel). **and straightway,** i.e. immediately on Christ's stepping on board, and while yet the disciples were conscious only of the joy with which they welcomed Him. On εὐθέως, see v. 9. **the boat was at the land,** more than moving in the direction of the land, actually landed, **whither they were going.** That the Evangelist alludes to another miraculous phenomenon can scarcely be

doubted. Not only was Christ's embarkation the signal for the instantaneous lulling of the storm (Matt. xiv. 32 ; Mark vi. 51), it effected as well a miraculous acceleration of the speed and a seemingly instantaneous landing of the boat.

HOMILETICS

VER. 15-21.—THREE VIEWS OF CHRIST.
I. **Amid the Mountains** : ver. 15. 1. *A Couch of Repose.* The physical exhaustion consequent on a day spent as Christ's had been could not fail to render rest desirable and needful ; and nowhere was this more likely to be obtained than amongst the hills. Rest and invigoration for His wearied frame were in their cooler and more bracing air ; soothing and refreshment for His agitated mind in their stillness and peace ; support and encouragement for His spirit in the fellowship with His Father there enjoyed. 2. *A Temple of Prayer* (Matt. xiv. 23 ; Mark vi. 46). Beneath the troubled sky, for the night was coming on tempestuous, His bowed head wrapt in mist, Christ poured out His soul in supplication to His Father. (1) For Himself, that He might be assisted to crush the temptation from which He had just escaped, as formerly He had crushed it in the wilderness (Matt. iv. 8-10), and supplied with strength for the miracle He was that night to perform. (2) For the people whose miseries He had pitied and whose needs He had relieved, who, like sheep without a shepherd (Mark vi. 34), were prone to err, and perhaps never more stood in need of counsel and protection than just then when the grand question of their acceptance or rejection of Him was on the eve of being decided. (3) For the disciples, gone before, who were already toiling in rowing through a troubled sea. 3. *A Tower of Observation.* From His watch among the hills, Christ perceived the distressed situation of His friends upon the deep (Mark vi. 48), as to-day from His post of observation beyond the stars, " He looketh to the end of the earth and seeth under the whole heaven" (Job xxviii. 24), noteth every voyager across life's ocean (Job xxxiv. 21), and especially considereth the anxieties and fears, dangers, and difficulties of His people (2 Tim. ii. 19 ; Heb. iv. 13 ; Rev. iii. 10).
II. **Upon the Sea** : ver. 19, 20. 1. *The Mysterious Apparition.* (1) What it was. No ingenuity can evade the plain import of what three Evangelists assert, viz., that Jesus appeared upon the sea walking—not metaphorically as when it is said of Jehovah,." He treadeth upon the waves of the sea " (Job ix. 8), or as if the meaning were that Christ swam to His disciples ; nor seemingly as if the sense ran that the disciples, while they rowed through the storm, observed Jesus walking on the high land along the shore ; but in sober reality. How this was done,—whether by the power of His indwelling Divinity sustaining His humanity, or by a temporary raying outward of that glory which belonged to the Incarnate Son of God, afterwards disclosed in transient vision upon the mount of transfiguration, and in permanent form at the resurrection —cannot be determined and need not be minutely inquired into. The Being who could feed 10,000 persons with five barley loaves and a few small fishes could have had no difficulty in supporting Himself against gravitation, even upon the liquid surface of the deep. Nor, if Jesus was the Son of God in human form, should there be the smallest difficulty in believing He could perform those wonders. (2) Why it came ! In walking on the sea as in multiplying the loaves, Christ proclaimed Himself the Lord of nature. This was specially significant for the Apostles, who, though they had witnessed, had not yet considered the miracle of the loaves (Mark vi. 52), and who perhaps in their secret hearts were astonished that their Master had not accepted the crown the populace would yesterday have thrust upon Him. (3) When it appeared. Between 3 and 6 o'clock in the morning, when the toiling rowers were at their wit's end (Ps. cvii. 27). So Christ interposes with His heavenly succour just when His people's need is greatest (Matt. xiv. 31). Man's ex-

tremity is ever God's opportunity; and when the latter comes it is usual for souls to see that the darkness is past and morning begun to dawn (Amos v. 8). (4) How it was regarded. The disciples were afraid (ver. 19)—"Of Him in whom was laid up all their comfort" (Trapp). So are Christ's people not unfrequently alarmed at unusual providences, mistaking Christ's approaches because He presents Himself at unexpected times and in unaccustomed ways. 2. *The Familiar Voice.* (1) What it said—"It is I, be not afraid" (ver. 20). The words contained a note of assurance; weird as the seeming phantom appeared bearing down upon them through the morning mist, it was the form of their Master and Friend. So the follower of Jesus may know that however dark and tempestuous the clouds rest upon the ocean of his life, and however fiercely and angrily the waves of tribulation career around or dash upon the frail skiff of his soul, the spirit of Jesus is in the storm and on the sea. The words also wafted to the trembling seamen a message of cheer, bidding them dismiss apprehension, since He was there; and to every distressed Christian they still proclaim, "O, thou afflicted, tossed with tempest and not comforted, fear not; when thou passest through the waters, I will be with thee" (Is. xliii. 2; liv. 11). (2) How it acted. It dispelled their alarms; whereas they had been terrified they now rejoiced at the thought of His "drawing nigh unto the boat." So powerfully the voice of Jesus allays the inner tempests of the soul! So welcome sounds that voice to those who can call Him Saviour and Friend. III. **In the Boat** : ver. 21. 1. *The wind was hushed* (Matt. xiv. 32). "As if it had been weary of blowing so big, and now desired rest after hard labour" (Trapp), it lay down in silence at its Master's feet. So lull the soul's hurricanes when Christ steps within (xiv. 27). 2. *The disciples were amazed* (Mark vi. 51). Not terrified, but overawed, they felt constrained to worship Him, saying, 'Of a truth Thou art the Son of God' (Matt. xiv. 33). Christ's supremacy over nature unmistakably betokened His Divinity. 3. *The voyage was completed* (ver. 21). The mysterious acceleration of the boat's speed can only be explained as another miracle. Perhaps it is legitimate to view it as an earnest of that glorification of the powers of nature which shall take place on the day of the manifestation of the sons of God (Rom. viii. 19-22).

Learn 1. The dependence Jesus ever felt on prayer. 2. The notice Christ continues to take of His people. 3. The ability Christ possesses to help in time of need. 4. The glory Christ shall yet bring to His people and even to this material world. 5. The object of all Christ's manifestations of Himself, to lead men to recognize His Divinity.

Ver. 17. A night upon the deep. I. Of disappointed hope. II. Of unsuccessful effort. III. Of deepening alarm. IV. Of divine manifestation. V. Of supernatural deliverance.

Ver. 29. The Lord's voice to His people. I. Proclaiming His presence. 1. In unexpected places. 2. At unwonted times. 3. In unfamiliar forms. II. Dispelling fear. 1. Of danger. 2. Of death. 3. Of evil.

3. THE MEETING IN CAPERNAUM—SERMON ON THE BREAD OF LIFE

Chap. VI. Ver. 22-59

This discourse was spoken in the synagogue to the multitude who had been fed on the preceding day (ver. 26), with whom also were now mingled emissaries from Jerusalem (ver. 41, 52). After a brief historical introduction (ver. 22-25), it divides itself into three parts. In the first (ver. 26-40), directed to His auditors in general, Christ reproves them for the unworthiness of their motives in seeking Him (ver. 26), exhorts them to labour for the meat that abideth unto eternal life (ver. 27), and declares that He Himself is that abiding meat, 'the true bread' (ver. 32), 'the bread of God' (ver. 33), 'the bread out of heaven' (ver. 32), 'the bread of life' (ver. 35). In the second (ver. 41-51) addressed more immediately to the Jewish emissaries, He replies to certain whispered objections these had taken to His description of Himself as having come down out of heaven (ver. 41-43), affirms the impossibility without divine illumination of understanding His doctrine (ver. 44-46), reiterates His claim to be the bread of life (ver. 47, 48), and asserts the necessity of eating that bread if they would live for ever (ver. 50, 51). In the third, still intended for the same listeners, the crowd in general, and the Jerusalem spies in particular (ver. 52-58), in response to an objection taken by these latter (ver. 52), He first amplifies His preceding testimony about Himself as the bread of life (ver. 53), explains the way in which that bread is to be eaten (ver. 54), and emphasizes the results that will infallibly ensue thereupon (ver. 56-58). The discourse opens at a moment when His fame in Galilee seems to have attained to meridian splendour; when it closes He has already begun to discern the beginning of the end, to perceive the prognostications, and experience the foretastes, of His final rejection.

EXPOSITION

Ver. 22-25. Historical Introduction.

Ver. 22. **On the morrow,** i.e. the day after the miraculous feeding, **the multitude which stood on the other side of the sea,** that portion of the crowd which had lingered on the eastern shore after Christ had dispersed the would-be king-makers, who were most probably feast pilgrims travelling towards Jerusalem, **saw** εἶδον (A B, Chrysostom, Lachmann, Westcott and Hort), the historical aorist with the force of a pluperfect (see Winer, § xl. 5), meaning, perceived as they had done the preceding evening ; hence pretty nearly equivalent to ἰδών (T. R., Tischendorf, Meyer, Godet, Brückner), having seen, i.e. the night before—**that there was none other boat,** lit., *little boat* (see ver. 23 ; xxi. 8 ; Mark iii. 9 ; iv. 36), **there, save one,** viz. the craft which had conveyed Jesus and His disciples across the lake and in which these latter had departed, **and that Jesus entered not with His disciples into the boat, but that His disciples went away alone.**

This, which they had witnessed the night before, is now introduced to explain (1) their lingering overnight upon the east shore and (2) their searching for Christ next morning on that side of the lake.

23. **Howbeit,** or, 'but,'—ἀλλά, a strong adversative, explaining the action of the principal verb (ver. 24) which would otherwise have been impossible, —**there came boats** πλοιάρια, little boats (resembling that belonging to the disciples) which had been either driven across the lake by the contrary wind, Matt. xiv. 24 (Westcott), or sent across in expectation of finding passengers (Luthardt, Godet), or perhaps rowed across in search of Jesus (Hengstenberg). **from Tiberias** Tiberias, then a town lately built by Herod Antipas, A.D. 27, in honour of the Emperor Tiberius, was situated in a beautiful and fertile district in the neighbourhood of celebrated warm springs, and occupied, according to the Talmud, the site of the ancient Rakkath (Josh. xix. 35), which, as its name "Shore" im-

ports, in all probability stood upon the margin of the lake. There the murderer of the Baptist had erected magnificent colonnades, Roman gates, splendid public buildings, regal palaces, marble statues, and "the finest synagogue in all the north." The population of that renowned city was a genuine *colluvies hominum*, composed of Greek and Roman rather than of Jewish settlers. It is not mentioned that Christ ever visited Tiberias. With orthodox Jews He may have deemed the city unclean, standing as it did upon the site of an old burying ground ; or He may have purposely avoided meeting Antipas. The present-day town *Tabar*îya contains little of note beyond the probable remains of a theatre and stadium with a small Franciscan chapel dating from the time of the Crusades (Jos. Ant. xviii. 2, 3 ; Wars ii. 9, 1 ; Schürer, The Jewish People in the Time of Christ, div. ii. vol. i. § 23 ; Riehm's Handwörterbuch, art. *Tiberias ;* Warren, The Recovery of Jerusalem, p. 360 ; Conder, Handbook of the Bible, p. 324). **nigh unto the place,** the plain of *Butaiha*, in the vicinity of Bethsaida (vi. 1), **where they ate the bread** τὸν ἄρτον, the bread provided for them in so miraculous a manner, **after the Lord had given thanks,** lit., *the Lord having given thanks ;* not ' through the thanksgiving of the Lord,' *durch des Herrn Danksagung* (Luther), as if the participial clause expressed antecedence not merely in time, but in causality as well. "The mention of Christ's thanksgiving recalls the vivid impression made by this solemn moment upon the spectators, and the great importance attached by them to this action " (Godet). The insertion of this clause about the boats was obviously designed to explain how the multitudes obtained means of transportation across the lake.

24. **When the multitude therefore saw** The course of thought, begun by ὁ ὄχλος in ver. 22 and interrupted by the interjection of two subordinate clauses as above, is now resumed, and the exact situation described as it stood on the morning after the banquet. What they had at that point ascertained is summed up in two brief statements. **that Jesus was not** (lit.,

is not) **there.** At least they had not been able to find Him. **neither His disciples** The crowd had witnessed overnight the departure of the boat containing these, and it had not returned. **they themselves** Not the entire multitude of 5000 persons, but that portion of it which had lingered near the scene of the miracle after the rest had been dispersed. **got into the boats,** the *ploiaria* or small vessels which had arrived from Tiberias, ver. 23, **and came,** went, or proceeded, **to Capernaum.** This city they knew to be Christ's headquarters, and to it doubtless themselves principally belonged. That they did not try Tiberias may be explained by supposing that the boatmen from that town informed them Christ had not gone thither. **seeking Jesus.** That they expected to find Him in Capernaum clearly presupposes their acquaintance with a Galilean activity on the part of Our Lord.

25. **And when they found Him on the other side of the sea,**—in the synagogue as it appears (ver. 59), though that which surprised them was His presence on the western side of the lake—**they said unto Him, Rabbi** (see i. 49), **when camest Thou hither?** They do not say " How ?" πῶς ; but that is really included in the " When ?" πότε. *Quaestio de tempore includit quaestionem de modo* (Bengel). "The time is to them inexplicable because the manner is " (Luthardt). They may even have had " a dim presentiment of something miraculous "(Meyer).

Ver. 26-40. The first part of Our Lord's discourse.

26. **Jesus answered them,** replying as usual (ii. 4 ; iii. 3) to their state of mind rather than to their interrogation, **and said** Though the Synoptists have no account of this conversation, its historicity is not thereby impeached. **Verily, verily, I say unto you** (see on i. 51), **Ye seek Me not because ye saw signs** σημεῖα, as in ii. 11 ; referring to Christ's miraculous works in general and to the miraculous feeding in particular ; which Christ here declares to have been of His higher Messianic activity ' signs ' which the people had failed to comprehend. Their crowding after Him was not because in those healings or in this feeding they had

discerned the forth-radiations of His indwelling glory, the manifestations of His higher nature, or the credentials of His heavenly embassy, which they had not. The antithesis is not comparative, as if the sense were 'not so much because ... as because' (Kuinoel), but absolute. They had seen the feeding : they understood not the 'sign' of the loaves. **but because ye ate of the loaves and were filled.** The verb means ' were satisfied as a beast is with fodder '—*saturati estis* (Vulgate). They had been drawn to Christ solely by their animal appetites. They believed Him to be a person capable of gratifying their fleshly inclinations. This the context shows to be its import here, though the same verb is elsewhere used of spiritual satisfactions (Matt. v. 6 ; Luke vi. 21).

27. **Work not** There may lie in the expression (ἐργάζεσθαι, to work for a reward, to labour for a recompense, to earn by active service, 2 John 8) an allusion to the toil they had undergone and the effort they had made in pursuing Christ during the past days. The like activity, energy, perseverance was demanded in the higher moral and spiritual sphere. It was only out of place when misdirected towards lower objects of carnal desire or earthly ambition. Hence they were not to set their powers of soul and body into laborious, exhaustive exercise **for the meat which perisheth,** for the food, τὴν βρῶσιν (see iv. 32) that is not permanent either in its power to satisfy (cf. iv. 13) or in its nature (Matt. xv. 17 ; 1 Cor. vi. 13 ; Col. ii. 22), **but for the meat which abideth unto eternal life,** neither changing in itself nor losing its soul-satisfying properties (ver. 35 ; cf. iv. 14. On 'eternal life' see iii. 15), **which the Son of Man** (see i. 51) **shall give unto you,** who must therefore direct your energies and efforts towards Him ; **for Him the Father,** *even* **God hath sealed,** or, better, *for this* person viz., the Son of Man, *the Father,* the designation being used absolutely as in iii. 35, *hath sealed* (cf. iii. 33), in the clearest fashion, by those 'signs' you have failed to understand, attested as His commissioner and representative, and therefore as the sole depositary and dispenser of that 'abiding food' ; even

God, the divine name standing last as a solemn and emphatic pointing to Him as the absolute first source of such authority as the Son of Man wields and such meat as the Son of man gives.

28. **They said therefore unto Him,** perceiving He alluded to some moral and spiritual requirement, **What must we do that,** by performing them, **we may work the works of God,** i.e. such works as God requires, accepts, and recompenses ?

29. **Jesus answered and said unto them, This is the work of God,** the work which is His by pre-eminence, **that ye believe,** lit., *that ye may believe,* ἵνα with the subjunctive indicating this as the end and aim of their working— "a working that ye may believe" **on Him whom He,** ἐκεῖνος, that one, God, **hath sent,** or, *sent,* the aorist depicting Christ's mission as an accomplished fact : cf. iii. 34.

30. **They said therefore unto Him, What then doest Thou**—Thou, on thy part—**for a sign** (see ii. 18), **that,** in order that **we may see,** recognize its significance as such (ver. 26), **and believe Thee ?** They perfectly understood Christ to signify Himself when He spoke of 'whom the Father sent.' **What workest Thou ?** What kind of a thing is it that Thou workest ?

31. **Our fathers** (cf. iv. 20) **ate the manna,** the well-known food from heaven, **in the wilderness** of Sinai (Exod. xvi. 4) ; **as it is written** (Ps. lxxviii. 24 ; cv. 40), **He,** God, **gave them bread out of heaven to eat.** Our Lord's interlocutors furnish Him with a specimen of the kind of 'sign' they required, at the same time indirectly hinting that if He claimed to be another Moses He must establish His right to such a name and position by performing if not identical at least similar deeds of supernatural power and authority. According to the Rabbis, Messiah would repeat the miracle of Moses. *Qualis fuit redemptor primus* (Moses), *talis erit redemptor ultimus* (Messias), and *Redemptor prior descendere fecit pro iis manna, sic et redemptor posterior descendere faciet manna:* Midras Coheleth 86. 4 (Lightfoot, Wetstein, Schöttgen ; quoted by Lücke).

32. **Jesus therefore said unto them,**

correcting two misapprehensions under which they laboured, first as to the giver and second as to the nature of the manna : **Verily, verily, I say unto you** (see i. 51), **It was not Moses that gave**, lit., *not Moses*, but another to be mentioned presently, *gave*. Moses merely was the medium of transmission. What he imparted he had himself to receive. **you** The people are identified with their progenitors. Christ recognizes the solidarity of nations : the Bible throughout assumes the solidarity of the race. **the bread out of heaven** The manna in the desert Jehovah claimed as His gift (Ex. xvi. 4). **but** — introducing the double contrast already specified—**My Father** (cf. v. 17)—not Moses—**giveth you**, not simply *gave* your fathers that manna, but still *giveth* you that which the manna was not, viz., **the true bread** τὸν ἄρτον τὸν ἀληθινόν, the bread which corresponds to its idea (cf. the true light, i. 9 ; the true vine, xv. 1) **out of heaven**—not descending from the upper reaches of the atmosphere, but proceeding from the unseen heavenlies whence the Son of Man Himself hath proceeded (iii. 31).

33. For the bread of God, i.e. given by God (ver. 32), **is that which cometh down** lit., *that descending* out of heaven (see above) **and giveth** life, lit., *and giving* life, ζωήν, the Messianic life of salvation, **unto the world.** By two specific properties the bread the Father gives is declared to be the *true* bread. It comes from heaven in the highest sense ; it imparts life to the widest extent.

34. They said therefore unto Him, —if not yet with even a dim presentiment of the spiritual character of that bread of which Christ spake (Lücke, B. Crusius), certainly not in irony (Calvin, Bengel, Lampe), but in perfect earnest as understanding Christ to allude to a superior kind of manna (Ewald, Hengstenberg, Luthardt, Meyer, etc.), perhaps "a magical food or means of life from heaven" (Tholuck) : cf. the Samaritan woman, iv. 10—**Lord** mingling a degree of reverence with their address, κύριε, elsewhere (iv. 15, 19, 49) translated ' Sir,' **evermore** πάντοτε, always and not occasionally only, **give us this bread**, "that we may always have it to eat" (Luthardt).

35. Jesus said unto them, I am the bread of life. Placing " I " in the foreground, He emphasizes the thought that the bread of life, i.e. the life giving (ver. 33), and not merely life having (ver. 51), bread, was not anything distinctly apart from, but was wholly identical with Himself (cf. the tree of life : Gen. ii. 9 ; iii. 22, 24 ; Prov. iii. 18 ; xi. 30 ; xiii. 12 ; xv. 4 ; Rev. ii. 7 ; xxii. 2 ; the water of life : Rev. xxi. 6 ; xxii. 1 ; and the word of life : 1 John i. 1). **He that cometh to Me**, i.e. appropriates Me as his soul's food ; equivalent to the parallel phrase "he that believeth on Me" (cf. v. 40), **shall not hunger**, shall be perfectly satisfied, **and He that believeth on Me** If ' coming ' represents the active and outward character of the soul's Christward movement, perhaps ' believing ' describes its inward and restful aspect (Westcott). But the two phrases allude to the same act of which they depict distinct but mutually complimentary phases. **shall never thirst.** The addition of this clause emphasizes the certainty, fulness, and permanence of the satisfaction Christ gives. The two images of ' eating ' and ' drinking ' were probably derived from the idea of the Paschal feast which was at hand. The double parallel was an indication of Christ's mental elevation. See Winer's Grammar, § lxviii. 3.

36. But I said unto you See above, ver. 26 (Grotius, Bengel, B. Crusius, Luthardt, Godet, and others) ; though with less probability, Christ may have referred to some unreported saying (Euthymius Zigabenus), to an utterance recorded in a lost fragment (Ewald), or to the general tenor of His teaching (Brückner). The translation ' I will have said unto you ' (Meyer) is unnatural ; while the conjecture that He was thinking of v. 37-44 (Lücke, De Wette) is inapposite, since it was spoken in Jerusalem. **that ye have seen Me** Of those ' signs ' they had witnessed Christ was Himself the greatest. **and yet believe not.** Although you profess to believe Moses whom you never saw. The two conjunctions καὶ . . . καὶ rather intensify than diminish the contrast. ' Ye have both seen Me and ye believe not ' ; see Winer's Grammar, § liii. 4.

37. All that which the Father giveth Me shall come unto Me. If at this point Christ's speech (Brückner) paused not, unquestionably His thought did. The Jews who listened neither believed on, nor came to, Him. Nevertheless there were who should come to Him, such, viz., as the Father gave Him, who are here represented as a totality or unified mass—πᾶν ὅ (ver. 39 ; xvii. 2). The Father's giving (x. 29 ; xvii. 2, 6 ; cf. Is. viii. 18), which eventuates in the believer's 'coming,' cannot be restricted to that 'drawing' in time and through grace by which the 'coming' is originated and set up (Bengel, Lücke, Luthardt, Godet, etc.), whether granted to all as a *gratia generalis* (Arminius) or specifically to those in whom faith follows (Calvin),— and still less to that natural piety which is supposed to be inherent in man (Socinus) or that overruling Providence which presides over occasions and opportunities for faith (Brückner), but must be held to include the notion of a donation in eternity (Augustine, Calvin, Hengstenberg, Lange, and others), though not necessarily of such sort as to override the free action of the human will or be inconsiderate of human character. Hence it is added **and him that cometh to Me I will in no wise cast out**, out of my house and fellowship (Ewald), out of the kingdom of God I have come to establish (Lücke), out of the eternal life I bestow (Luthardt). The clause first individualizes the abstract whole of the antecedent member, next describes the faith of those the Father gives as a free moral volition, and finally declares their certain acceptance by Christ : cf. ver. 39, 40 ; ix. 34 ; xii. 31 ; xv. 6 ; Matt. viii. 12 ; xxii. 13.

38. For—stating the reason why Christ will not cast out such as come to Him—**I am come down from heaven** ἀπὸ οὐρανοῦ expressing ideas of local transition, divine commission, self-renunciation ; ἐκ οὐρανοῦ (iii. 13) the conception of heavenly origin and therefore of supreme divinity—**not to do Mine own will**, i.e. to act independently and carry out a scheme or purpose of my own contriving, **but the will of Him that sent Me**. Cf. iv. 34; v. 30 ; Heb. x. 7.

39. And this is the will of Him that sent Me, that of all that which He hath given Me πᾶν ὅ ... a nominative absolute : cf. vii. 38 ; xv. 2 ; xvii. 2 ; Matt. xii. 36. **I should lose nothing** The verb which is used not in the active sense of 'destroy,' but in the intransitive of permitting to become lost (cf. xvii. 2 ; xviii. 9), expresses the direct negative to that eternal life which constitutes salvation (iii. 16). **but should raise it up at the last day.** I.e. of the Messianic æon or world-period (ver. 40, 44, 54 ; xi. 24 ; xii. 48), ἐν τῇ συντελείᾳ τοῦ αἰῶνος, at the consummation of the 'age' (Matt. xiii. 40), when according to the Evangelist "they that have done good," corresponding to πᾶν ὅ δέδωκέ μοι, "shall come forth unto the resurrection of life " (v. 29).

40. For, amplifying, explaining, and minutely defining the foregoing, **this is the will of My Father** (see v. 17), **that** ἵνα, pointing out the end or aim towards which the Father's will is directed. **every one that beholdeth the Son**—with inward soul contemplation (see on i. 32 ; and cf. xii. 45 ; xiv. 19 ; xvi. 10), as distinguished from outward bodily vision (ver. 36) such as the Jews had enjoyed without being thereby conducted to faith—**and believeth on Him** See on ii. 15. The clauses more fully characterize on the one hand those whom the Father gives, and on the other hand those who come, to Christ. **should have eternal life** See iii. 15. **and I will raise him up** Taking ἀναστήσω as an independent future (Vulgate, Luther, Luthardt, Hengstenberg, Godet, Westcott)—'I, the Son, on My part will complete and crown the Father's will by raising up him who believes to the possession and full enjoyment of eternal life '; or placing ἀναστήσω along with ἐχῇ under the regimen of ἵνα (Beza, Brückner, Meyer),—'This is the will of My Father that ... and that I should raise him up." **at the last day**, not of the believer's earthly life (Reuss), but of the Messianic age, as above, ver. 39.

Ver. 41-51. The second part of Our Lord's discourse.

41. The Jews οἱ Ἰουδαῖοι (see i. 19), the emissaries and representatives of the Sanhedrim who according to the Synoptists had by this time followed Christ into Galilee (Matt. xv. 1 ; Mark vii. 1), and may have been amongst the crowd in the synagogue from the first, though only now do they venture to break silence (B. Crusius, Ewald, Lange, Meyer, Westcott, etc.). Some however regard the appellation as given to the Galilean multitude because of its community in unbelief with the leaders of the people (De Wette, Tholuck, Brückner, Godet, Hengstenberg, and others). **therefore,** i.e. after listening to the preceding discourse, **murmured concerning Him** Not merely whispered and jeered amongst themselves, because the presence of those favourably inclined did not permit them to give open expression to their dissatisfaction (Ewald, De Wette), but muttered angrily against Him (Meyer, Godet, Tholuck, and others). **because He said, I am the bread which came down out of heaven.** The ground of their complaint was that in so saying Christ claimed to be a being of distinctly supernatural origin, which to them appeared absurd as well as monstrous, if not openly blasphemous, considering that they were well acquainted with His earthly parentage. The exact words that Christ used are not repeated but summarized and curtailed, all allusion to the kind of bread Christ claimed to be as well as to the purpose of His coming (ver. 33, 35) being perhaps designedly omitted, and the one point of His pretension to heavenly origin being fastened on : cf. v. 12.

42. **And they said** amongst themselves **Is not this Jesus,** with no doubt a touch of contempt in their tones as they emphasized the pronoun *this,* **the son of Joseph** Such according to the Synoptists (Matt. xiii. 55 ; Mark vi. 3 ; Luke iii. 23 ; iv. 22) was the popular belief. **whose father and mother we know?** Added not because of the recognized understanding that the Messiah must be of unknown descent (vii. 27), must be ἀπάτωρ ἀμήτωρ without father and without mother, Heb. vii. 3 (Lücke), but to emphasize the impossibility of harmonizing earthly parentage and heavenly origin in one and the same individual. The phrase 'we know' does not necessarily imply that the speakers were either Galileans (Godet) or personally acquainted with Joseph and Mary ; but only that the human parentage of Jesus was a matter

of public notoriety. For the same reason it need not be inferred that Joseph was still living (Meyer). **how doth he**—'this man,' οὗτος (א), may have been dropped from the text to avoid repetition—**now** either temporarily, "*now*, at last, when for so long he has lived as one of ourselves" (Westcott) ; or logically, *now*, this being so that He is Joseph's son, how doth he **say, I am come down out of heaven?** See on ver. 38.

43. **Jesus answered and said unto them**—their murmurings having either been overheard by Himself or reported to Him by others—**Murmur not among yourselves.** Instead of clearing up the difficulty they felt or pretended to feel in His assertion of divine descent, Christ simply called attention to the fact that the real reason of their objection to His teaching concerning Himself was not its incomprehensibility or irrationality, but their want of spiritual affinity with Him.

44. **No man** οὐδείς, the antithesis of 'all,' πᾶν, ver. 37, **can**—is able to—**come to Me,** or towards Me, πρός με, so as to arrive at and rest upon Me, in the way of self-surrendering faith (cf. v. 40), **except the Father which sent Me** (see on v. 36, 37 ; vi. 57 ; viii. 18 ; xii. 49 ; xiv. 24 ; 1 John iv. 14) **draw him** i.e. with such gracious and divine influence as on the one hand furnishes the soul with 'power to come' of which it would otherwise remain destitute, and on the other hand preserves intact the soul's moral freedom, without which its approach towards the Saviour might be a 'dragging,' but could not be a 'coming'—the nature and manner of this drawing being explained in the next verse : cf. Jer. xxxi. 3 ; **and I will raise him up in the last day,** thus completing the work which the drawing of the Father begins : see ver. 39, 40.

45. **It is written in the prophets,** i.e. in the book of the Prophets (Acts vii. 42) ; the citation being freely drawn from Is. liv. 13, and its substantial contents also found in Jer. xxxi. 33, 34 ; and Joel iii. 1 ff.—**And they shall be all taught of God,** διδακτοί τοῦ θεοῦ, i.e. instructed by God, *docibiles dei* (Vulgate), *docti a Deo* (Bengel), this divine teaching being the human side of the Father's drawing. **Every one**

that hath heard from the Father, and hath learned, lit., *every one having heard from the Father,* παρὰ τοῦ πατρὸς (cf. i. 40 ; vii. 52 ; viii. 26), *and having learned*—The Father's drawing, which as to its nature is a teaching, completes itself on the side of the individual in a voluntary 'hearing' and 'learning'; which again issues in a free movement towards Christ—**cometh unto Me**, to accept My teaching, receive my person, enjoy my salvation : see v. 40.

46. Not that any man hath seen the Father (cf. i. 18) **save He which is from God** παρὰ τοῦ θεοῦ, descriptive of Christ's origin, not as to essence, which is expressed by ἐκ (viii. 42, 47), but as to locality (vii. 29 ; xvi. 28); hence also suggestive of His divine commission (xvi. 27 ; xvii. 8 : cf. i. 6). **He hath seen the Father**, hath looked upon Him (cf. v. 19) in that pre-existent state where He was 'with God' (i. 1) before He came forth into the world. Hence the conclusion to which this conducted was that he who would hear from and learn of the Father, and so be taught by God, must believingly accept the teaching of the Son.

47. Verily, verily, I say unto you With much fitness this solemn and impressive formula (see on i. 51) introduces the sublime declaration in which Christ's train of reasoning culminates. **He that believeth** The verb stands absolutely as in i. 7, according to the best authorities (א B L T etc., Tischendorf, Westcott and Hort), signifying 'he that believeth' not simply 'on Me' εἰς ἐμὲ (T. R.), or 'on my words,' but according to the true idea of belief which of course has for its object Christ in His person, teaching, and work. **hath** in the present, through and in the act of believing, **eternal life.** See on iii. 15.

48-51. Having as it were by a divine logic shut up His hearers to the indispensable necessity of believing on Himself if they would learn of the Father, He renews His already uttered testimony concerning His person, His mission, His salvation, and the means of attaining it.

48. I am the bread of life, i.e. the bread that truly giveth and supporteth life (see on ver. 35),—which the manna was not.

49. Your fathers By this expression Christ differentiates Himself from His hearers. Their fathers were the desert pilgrims. His Father was God. *Vestri, inquit, non nostri : quo ipso ostendit se altiorem habere ortum quam ille putarant,* ver. 42 (Bengel). **did eat the manna in the wilderness** exactly as you said they did (ver. 31), is what Christ means ; and so far from being kept alive in consequence thereof, **they died.** This showed that the manna of which you boast was no true bread of life.

50. This is the bread which cometh down out of heaven, that—meaning either 'of such a character, power, or nature is the bread . . . that' (Brückner, Meyer, Tholuck, Luthardt, etc.), or 'This' (bread), i.e. the true manna, 'is the bread which cometh down . . . that' (Westcott), or better, taking ὁ ἐκ τοῦ οὐρανοῦ καταβαίνων as a qualifying clause descriptive of the heavenly manna or bread of life (ver. 33), 'This is the bread which cometh down out of heaven,' i.e. the true bread of life, which cometh down 'that' . . . the habit of reduplicating in thought on the clause immediately preceding ἵνα being peculiar to John : cf. ver. 29, 40; xvii. 3 ; 1 John iii. 11 ; **a man** τις, any one, **may eat thereof and not die.** Both verbs stand beneath the regimen of ἵνα, and announce the purpose of the 'coming down out of heaven' of the true bread. The 'not dying' declared to result from 'eating this bread' need not be restricted to moral and spiritual death (Bengel, Meyer), but in order to complete the antithesis should be viewed as embracing also exemption from physical death, which to the believer is a totally different thing from what it is to the unbeliever (viii. 51 ; xi. 26) ; just as the 'dying' of the Israelitish fathers (ver. 49) may have been designed to suggest the thought of that moral and spiritual death, 'in unbelief,' which preceded their corporeal dissolution (Godet, Luthardt, Hengstenberg, and others).

51. I am the living bread ὁ ζῶν, not the same as ὁ ζωοποιῶν, the life-giving, though this notion cannot be excluded (ver. 33), but 'the living or possessing life' (v. 26 : cf. 'living water,' iv. 10 ; vii. 38) ; hence able also to impart life to others (ver. 37 ; xiv. 19). **which**

came down out of heaven: see ver. 38, 41, 58 ; and cf. iii. 13 : **if any man eat of this bread**, not ἐκ τοῦ ἐμοῦ ἄρτου (אֲ), of my bread, or of the bread which I give, **he shall live for ever** : ver. 58 ; cf. iii. 15. The threefold advance of the present as compared with the preceding verse deserves attention. 1. 'The living bread' instead of simply 'bread' ; 2. 'Which came down out of heaven' in the historical personality of Christ, rather than the general formula 'which cometh down out of heaven' ; and 3. 'Shall live for ever' which goes beyond 'may not die' (Meyer, Brückner). **yea and the bread** The particles καὶ, *and*, and δὲ, *but*, in the same clause—occurring elsewhere in the N. T. (viii. 17 ; xv. 27 ; 1 John i. 3 ; Matt. xvi. 18 ; Acts xxii. 29 ; 2 Pet. i. 5), as also in classical authors (see Winer's Grammar, § liii. 7, b),—commonly serve to introduce something important, as thus :—'and also,' 'and in point of fact.' **which I**—I, on My part, as distinguished from Moses on his part—**will give**, in full and free communication when My mission is realized and My work accomplished, **is My flesh** ἡ σάρξ μου, My human nature (see on i. 14) ;—though whether as then existing before His hearers, or as suspended on the cross, or as exalted in resurrection glory does not yet appear. Possibly all three should be included ; the first since Christ says 'I am the bread of life' (ver. 41) ; the second because the verb 'give' already contains a hint of the giving up to sacrificial death, which is afterwards developed in the double phrase 'flesh and blood' ; and the third as Christ by using the future 'I will give' clearly points to His glorified humanity as the proper nourishment of souls. **for the life of the world.** Not instead of, as if the notion of substitution were intended, but for the advantage or benefit of, this being the specific import of ὑπὲρ, leaving undetermined the mode in which this advantage or benefit is, or may be, brought about (Winer, § xlvii. 5, 1). The contemplated idea is that of support, nourishment, food, rather than that of propitiation, atonement, expiation. The second 'which I will give' (T. R.), wanting in the best codices (א B C D L T etc.), is rejected by eminent authorities

(Lachmann, Ewald, Tischendorf, Westcott and Hort) and is not required to furnish an intelligible meaning. On the other hand such an abbreviated style of composition as its omission occasions is unusual with John (De Wette, Meyer, Tholuck, Godet), while its insertion in no way obscures the sense, and the clause "for the life of the world," detached and standing by itself, seems awkward and sounds harsh. Chiefly on this last ground the reading "the bread which I shall give for the life of the world is My flesh" (א) is by some preferred (Tischendorf), though it greatly resembles "a correction to make the passage easier" (Luthardt).

Ver. 52–59. The third part of Our Lord's discourse.

Ver. 52. **The Jews therefore strove one with another**, lit., *fought against each other*, i.e. with words (cf. 2 Tim. ii. 24 ; Jas. iv. 2)—**saying, How can this man give us His flesh to eat ?** The question shows Christ was understood by His listeners as having promised to give His flesh for the support of, rather than instead of, the world. The "how" reveals that Christ had passed beyond the comprehension of His hearers.

53. **Jesus therefore said unto them**, leaving their "how" unanswered, and concentrating their thoughts upon the necessity of personally appropriating His gift, **Verily, verily, I say unto you**, see on i. 51, **except ye eat** with your souls, as with your bodies you eat bread, **the flesh**, i.e. the humanity of **the Son of Man** See on i. 51. Here introduced to show that Christ is speaking of His human nature. **and drink His blood** The addition of this clause and in particular of the term 'blood' brings into prominence the idea of death as the mode in which Christ's humanity should be given as bread. **ye have not life in yourselves**, as an inherent and permanent possession : cf. v. 26.

54. **He that eateth My flesh and drinketh My blood** The corporeal and external actions of eating and drinking are visible symbols of spiritual and inward acts by which the soul appropriates and uses the flesh and blood, i.e. the complete humanity of Christ (crucified and

glorified) as its support and sustenance. "Faith throws the believer
upon and into its object ; this spiritual
eating and drinking brings the object
of faith into the believer" (Westcott).
hath eternal life hath now as the
inward, essential, and abiding principle of His soul's being,—life, true,
spiritual, and eternal (cf. iii. 15), **and
I will raise him up at the last day.** See
ver. 39, 40, 44. The frequency with
which Christ mentions the raising up
of the believer points to the desire of
both obviating a difficulty—'If the believer has eternal life now, why should
his body die ?' and emphasizing the
thought that the eternal life He alludes
to is not merely spiritual existence in a
disembodied state, but corporeal existence in a future world.

**55. For My flesh is meat indeed and
My blood is drink indeed** lit., *a true
eating and a true drinking*, rather than
truly an eating and truly a drinking,
although the sense is the same. Christ
designed to say that His flesh and
blood were an eating and drinking
truly worthy of the name inasmuch as
they imparted life genuine and abiding. The reading ἀληθής (B C Fᵃ K L T
etc.) is adopted by the majority of
scholars (Lachmann, Tischendorf, Luthardt, Alford, Westcott and Hort),
although ἀληθῶς (ℵ) has the support of
critics of eminence (Lücke, Godet).

**56. He that eateth My flesh and
drinketh My blood** (see on ver. 54)
abideth in Me and I in Him. A peculiarly Johannine phrase (xv. 4 ; xvii.
23 ; 1 John iii. 24 ; iv. 16), presenting
the eternal life (ver. 54) for which it is
an equivalent, as a permanent inward
spiritual fellowship between the believer and Christ based upon the new
life the former receives through eating
Christ's flesh and drinking Christ's
blood : cf. Weiss, der Johanneische
Lehrbegriff, p. 72.

Note. Did Christ in the use of the
peculiar phraseology of this verse
allude to the Lord's Supper ? and if so,
in what sense ? 1. *It has been maintained that He did* (Chrysostom, Cyril,
the principal Fathers and Catholic
expositors, Calixtus, Scheibel, Olshausen, Stier, Kling, Bretschneider,
Strauss, Baur), chiefly on the following
grounds :—(1) That the terms 'flesh'
and blood,' 'eating and drinking,' cor-

respond with those used by Christ in
the institution of the Supper. (2) That
as already Christian baptism had been
referred to in the conversation with
Nicodemus, so now it is natural to
suppose Christ intended an allusion to
the Lord's Supper. (3) That otherwise
John betrays no acquaintance with the
institution of the Supper. 2. *Against
this however it has been contended*
(Calvin, Luther, Meyer, Luthardt,
Brückner, Godet, and others) — (1)
That the term 'flesh' employed in this
discourse is not the same as that of
'body' which occurs in the institution
formula of the Lord's Supper. (2)
That the 'eating and drinking' spoken
of in this discourse describe not isolated and external acts, but inward
and continuous spiritual processes. (3)
That, according to ver. 53, on this assumption eternal life would be made
to depend on a corporeal operation and
ceremonial observance rather than on
faith, which throughout this sermon
and Scripture generally is represented
as the sole condition of a sinner's
justification and salvation. (4) That a
direct reference at this stage to the
Lord's Supper must have been devoid
of meaning to even the apostles, and
therefore much more to the Jews. 3.
The truth seems to be that *the idea
here expressed of inward, believing,
spiritual fellowship with the crucified
and risen Christ was afterwards embodied by our Lord in the Holy Supper*,
but whether at the time of announcing
it He had before His mind the institution of that supper (Bengel, Hofmann, Luthardt, Hengstenberg, Godet,
Tholuck, and others), or whether this
was an after-thought, 'the product of
the hour of the supper itself' (Meyer,
Brückner), cannot be determined.

57. As the Living Father (see v. 26 :
cf. 'the living God,' Matt. xvi. 16 ; 2
Cor. vi. 16 ; Heb. vii. 25) **sent Me**, not
hath sent Me, now in time after My
birth as John was a man sent from
God (i. 6), but *sent* Me in eternity
out from My pre-existent state, (iii. 17,
34 ; v. 38 ; vi. 33, 38, 39 ; xiv. 24), as
His representative and ambassador,
and I live because of the Father, διὰ τὸν
πατέρα, not by or through (De Wette),
but on account of the Father (Winer's
Grammar, § xlix. c) ; i.e. because the
Father lives (v. 26), and My life has

in His life not its originating cause—"The will of the supreme works here not creatively" (Ewald)—but its absolute ground or reason **so he that eateth Me, he also shall live because of Me,** or on account of Me, receiving into himself My life as I receive of the Father's life. The word 'so' institutes a parallel between the relation existing on the one hand between the Father and the Son, and that existing between the Son and the believer. The life that is in the Son has its uncreated source, eternal spring and absolute ground in the life that is in the Father; so the life imparted to the believer through eating Christ's flesh and drinking His blood has its primal fountain and essential basis in the life that is in Christ. It is Christ's life reproducing itself in the believer that constitutes the life of the latter.

58. **This,** viz., My flesh and blood, **is the bread which came down out of heaven,** of which the earthly manna was but a type: **not as the fathers** of whom already mention has been made (ver. 31, 49), and who in what they did acted as their nation's heads and representatives (Westcott), **did eat**—the word 'manna' (T. R.) omitted in the best MSS. (‫א‬ B C D L T etc.), being unnecessary, as the things contrasted are not the earthly and heavenly breads, but the corporeal and spiritual eatings—**and died** This was the issue of the former of those eatings. **he that eateth this bread shall live for ever.** Such will be the result of the latter of those eatings : cf. ver. 51.

59. **These things,** the contents of the preceding discourse, not from ver. 40 (Ewald) merely but from ver. 26,

said He in the synagogue ἐν συναγωγῇ without the art. as in xviii. 20, may signify 'in synagogal assembly.' Synagogues were prayer houses, προσευχαί (Acts xvi. 13 ; Jos. Ant. xiv. 10, 23) or places of worship among the Jews, the precise origin of which cannot be ascertained, though they probably took their rise in post-exilic times. In Christ's day they were found in all towns of Palestine as well as in foreign cities wherever Jews were settled (Acts xv. 21), while "teaching in the synagogue on the Sabbath day" was already an established and naturalized institution: Mark i. 21 ; vi. 2 ; Luke iv. 16, 31 ; vi. 6 ; xiii. 10 ; Acts xiii. 14, 27, 42 ; xvi. 13 ; xvii. 2 ; xviii. 4 (see Keil, Handbuch der Biblischen Archäologie, § 30 ; Schürer, The Jewish People in the Time of Jesus Christ, vol. ii. § 27 S). The synagogue in Capernaum had been erected by the Roman centurion who came to Christ (Luke vii. 4, 5). If *Tel Hum* be Capernaum, then the white synagogue whose ruins have been brought to light by recent excavations was probably the edifice in which Christ's discourse was delivered. If it was so, it must have been a conspicuous object, standing out from the dark basaltic background, and constructed entirely of white limestone. The original building was 74 ft. 9 in. long, by 56 ft. 9 in. wide. On turning over a large block the excavators found "the pot of manna engraved on its face" (see Warren, The Recovery of Jerusalem, pp. 343, 345). **as He taught** lit., *teaching,* as was His wont in the synagogues of the country. **in Capernaum** : see on ii. 12.

HOMILETICS

VER. 26-29.—THE SERMON OF THE LOAVES.
I. **A Solemn Reproof** : ver. 26. 1. *To whom addressed?* The inhabitants of Capernaum who the day before had beheld His miracle, partaken of His bounty, demonstrated in His favour, had He then permitted, would have summarily proclaimed Him King, and now crowded round Him in the synagogue. But excitement and noise are not religion, and those who to-day cry, Hallelujah ! may to-morrow shout, Crucify ! Many who seem to be fervid religionists as much merit rebuke as the sensation-loving Galileans. 2. *By whom spoken?* By One who had just shown Himself to be the Son of God, and therefore possessed of right to judge, as well as competent to search the hearts and try the reins of

those on whom He looked. By One who on the previous day had pitied and healed, taught and fed His auditors ; hence by One whose smitings was a kindness, and whose reproof was an excellent oil (Ps. cxli. 5). 3. *For what given?* Not for seeking Christ, which was what He desired ; or witnessing His miracle, for that also He intended ; or partaking of His bounty, since that He freely furnished ; but for the motive which impelled them to follow in His train, which was (1) sensational—they loved to gaze upon the wonders He performed while they beheld not the 'signs' He gave—they saw the phenomenon, they were blind to its significance ; and (2) sensual—they were gratified with the banquet they had got, delighted with the bodily provision they had enjoyed—they followed Him for the loaves as the ox follows a farmer for a bunch of hay.

II. **An Earnest Exhortation** : ver. 27. 1. *A labour discommended.* "Work not for the meat which perisheth." (1) The import. Christ meant not to deny the necessity, affirm the impropriety, challenge the expediency, or discourage the practice of toiling for daily bread. So long as man's primeval doom is unrevoked (Gen. iii. 19), and apostolic teaching speaks as it does (2 Thess. iii. 10), so long will it be impossible to hold Christ intended to foster the delusion that a believer should trust for daily bread to prayer rather than to toil. What Christ discommended was the spirit that attached supreme importance to earthly things, deemed it the chief end of man's existence to provide things needful for the body, lavished energy and thought on meat and drink, dress and houses, pictures and pleasures, out of all proportion to the intrinsic value of these commodities (Matt. vi. 25). (2) The reason. These commodities were perishing ; which signified that besides being composed of perishable materials, they both themselves perished in the using (Col. ii. 22) and at best contributed to the upkeep of a system constantly decaying and destined to fall beneath the stroke of death (1 John ii. 16, 17 ; 2 Pet. iii. 11). 2. *A labour enjoined :*—"Work for the meat which abideth unto eternal life." A precept (1) admitting the perfect legitimacy of human effort. Man was not made for sloth (Gen. ii. 15), and Christ never counselled idleness, either in His teaching (Luke xiii. 24 ; xvi. 16) or by His example (John ix. 4). The rightness or wrongness of man's exertions depends on the character of that towards which they are directed. Hence (2) prescribing the proper object of human effort. The one thing worthy of such devotion and energy as men accorded to the acquisition of meat for the body was food for the soul,—spiritual in character, vivifying in effect, and permanent in duration (Matt. vi. 20). And still further (3) declaring by implication the absolute necessity of such effort to attain such object (Matt. vii. 13 ; Luke xiii. 24 ; Phil. ii. 12 ; iii. 14 ; Heb. iv. 11 ; xi. 6).

III. **A Clear Direction** : ver. 27-29. 1. *Whence the abiding meat must be sought.* From "the Son of Man, whom the Father, even God, hath sealed"—language intimating (1) the accessibility of the source, since application was directed to be made to a son of man, (2) the sufficiency of the supply, inasmuch as the holder and dispenser of this meat was not *a* but *the* Son of Man, and (3) the authority of the giver, the Divine Father having commissioned and empowered the Son of Man for such a purpose. 2. *How the abiding meat may be got.* (1) As a gift. The Son of Man must bestow what no one by wisdom or strength of his own can procure. It is not of works but of faith ; not of merit but of grace (Rom. iv. 4-6 ; xi. 6 ; Gal. ii. 16 ; Eph. ii. 8, 9). (2) Through the medium of faith. The only labour admissible in connection with salvation is that of believing. Of necessity excluding work and merit as a ground of justification and acceptance before God (Job ix. 2, 3 ; Ps. cxliii. 2 ; Is. lvii. 12 ; Acts xiii. 3, 9 ; Rom. iii. 20 ; Gal. iii. 11), this denies not that faith and salvation must result in, and approve themselves by 'works' (Rom. ii. 13 ; iii. 31 ; vi. 16 ; Eph. ii. 10 ; Tit. ii. 14 ; Jas. ii. 20-26).

Lessons. 1. Christ's power of reading the heart of man. 2. The supreme importance attached by Christ to motive in religion. 3. The transcendant value in Christ's eyes of the salvation of the soul. 4. Christ's clear conviction that faith in Himself would lead to eternal life.

Ver. 30-35.—The Mistakes of the Galileans.

I. The Secondary for the Primary : ver. 31. Confounding the instrument with the agent who wielded it, they ascribed to the creature what was due to the Creator. Citing the ancient hymn concerning manna (Ps. lxxviii. 24, 25), they thought rather of Moses than of Jehovah as the giver. Upon the head of one who was a creature, a servant, an instrument, they put the crown which belonged to the Creator, the Master, the Prime Actor. This is one of the commonest errors of the present day. The man of science falls into this mistake when he talks about the forces and laws of nature as the all and in all, overlooking the fact that those forces and laws are only expressions of the Divine power and will. The Christian repeats the blunder when he ascribes the conversion of a sinner to the eloquence of a preacher, or the power of the truth, instead of to the quickening influence of the Spirit (Zech. iv. 6 ; John vi. 63 ; Eph. ii. 1). Every person similarly errs who forgets that every good and perfect gift is from above, coming down from the Father of lights (Jas. i. 17). Christ corrected this error on the part of the Galileans (ver. 32).

II. The Shadowy for the Substantial : ver. 33. The persons Christ addressed had no idea of heavenly bread other than that which had fallen from the skies in the desert. They perceived not that strictly speaking manna was not bread out of heaven at all, but merely bread out of the surrounding atmosphere. Though produced by the fiat of Elohim, it had been fashioned out of earthly elements, and could be called bread of God only in a sense figurative or typical. It was a material representation of this bread, but not this bread itself. The bread of God proceeded not from the terrestrial firmament but from the unseen habitation of the Eternal, came not through the medium of Moses but by the hand of the Son, and imparted life not for a few years on earth to a section of the race, but for evermore to mankind as a whole. The tendency to mistake the typical for the real, the shadowy for the substantial, had clung to the Jewish people all along their career. For a Saviour they were satisfied with Moses without anticipating Him whom Jehovah was to raise up like unto Moses (Deut. xviii. 17). For a salvation they were pleased with the prospect of national ascendancy (Ps. xlviii. 4) without aspiring after moral purity (Is. lviii. 1, 2 ; lxiv. 7). For a worship they wanted nothing better than the ritual of the Tabernacle and latterly of the Temple, cumbersome and oppressive as it was (Acts xv. 10), without troubling to reach the nobler service of the broken and the contrite heart (Ps. li. 17 ; Is. lvii. 15 ; lxvi. 2 ; John iv. 24 ; Rom. xii. 1). Nor is it certain that something of a like sort does not happen with ourselves, as e.g. when it is supposed true religion consists of forms and ceremonies instead of the desires and emotions of the heart (Rom. xiv. 17), salvation arises from connection with the visible church instead of from regeneration of the heart and mind (iii. 3), and heaven can be secured through acquaintance with the truth without a personal knowledge of Him who is the Truth.

III. The Impersonal for the Personal: ver. 35. Christ's auditors imagined the bread of life to be only a better sort of manna, as the woman of Samaria conjectured Christ intended by the living water merely a liquid of fresher and finer quality than Jacob's well could furnish (iv. 15). As in that case however the water, so in this the bread, of life was personal ; in that the Holy Spirit, in this Christ the Son of God who had come from above to give life to a dying world. Yet the Saviour's listeners could not follow Him into regions so ethereal. Plainly as He indicated the bread of life to be a *person*, they continued thinking of a *thing*. Though with seeming earnestness they cried—" Lord ! evermore give us this bread," it is doubtful if they entertained a higher notion than of a superior kind of manna. Among the Jews the expectation was common that when Messiah came He would provide all manner of delicacies and among them manna, wine, and spicy oil. " The hope of Israel is this," says Rabbi My Yemen, " that the Messiah shall come and raise the dead ; and they shall be gathered together in the Garden of Eden, and shall eat and drink and satiate themselves all the days of the world. Then the houses shall be builded with precious stones, the beds shall be made of silk, and the rivers shall flow with wine and spicy oil. So shall it be in the days of Messiah." So do many still suppose the bread of life for man is something different from Christ, is scientific education, moral culture, social refinement, political advancement. But now as then the bread of God and bread of life is Christ Himself.

IV. **The Transient for the Eternal :** ver. 49. The manna of the Israelitish fathers was after all but a temporary gift—in its continuance and its effects. The desert pilgrims ate of it until they came to the borders of the Promised Land, after which it disappeared. And even while they ate of it they died. It kept them alive for a season, but eventually one and all succumbed beneath the stroke of dissolution. The bread of life will not thus terminate either in itself or in its effects. It will endure unto everlasting life (ver. 27), it will satisfy every want of the soul (ver. 35).

Lessons. 1. The men who err most in life and in religion are those who walk by sight rather than by faith. 2. Christ Himself is a greater sign to the world than any of His miracles. 3. Christ's best recommendation to the soul is the perfect satisfaction He is able to impart. 4. Men may have some degree of ardent desire after Christ and yet be without true faith. 5. None who come to Christ in sincerity will depart from Him in sorrow.

VER. 36-40.—ACCUSATIONS AND CONSOLATIONS.

I. **Accusations.** 1. *Christ seen and yet not believed:* ver. 36. The Galileans had boastfully proclaimed themselves Moses's disciples and yet they had never seen Moses. They had however beheld Christ, not merely in the ordinary sense of gazing on His countenance, but in the higher sense of observing Him in the exercise of His divine calling, as for instance in the miracle of the loaves ; and yet they extended not towards Him credence. Nor could want of evidence be urged in extenuation of their reluctance to believe. Had it even been true, as they alleged, that Christ's miracles were inferior to those of Moses, that was no sufficient ground for withholding their confidence, since Moses was an earth-born mortal who, just on that account, required stronger credentials that he was sent of God ; whereas He, Christ, had descended out of heaven, while that was in His person which was not discernible in Moses—the glory as of an only-begotten from a father (i. 14),—which should have supplemented any supposed deficiency they found in His credentials. But such deficiency did not exist, the works of Christ being as much greater than those of Moses as Christ's person was superior to the person of Moses. Hence if they believed in the servant they ought to have believed in the Son. 2. *The Father's drawings resisted:* ver. 37. These drawings by which souls are inwardly persuaded and enabled to come to Christ are explained to be of a moral and spiritual kind (ver. 45). Yet Christ speaks of those thus drawn or brought to Him as given by the Father. This they are *in time* when the Father by His word and spirit allures them to Christ, and perhaps it is this thought which occupies the foreground in Christ's mind in ver. 36 ; but it is equally apparent that the Father's drawing which begins to operate upon the individual in the time-sphere cannot be dissociated from the eternal sphere in which the Father dwells. Hence the Father's giving to the Son may be also viewed as an act begun and completed in eternity (xvii. 6). Still it is as realizing itself in time that Christ thinks of this 'giving' of the Father ; and He says that His hearers proved they did not belong to that gracious " all " which the Father was then engaged in drawing towards Him. All who opened their hearts to these drawings would come to Him. They were not coming. The reason was they were not being given in the sense of being drawn, and they were not being drawn because they were not hearing and learning of the Father. 3. *Christ's welcome refused.* 'Coming' was all that was needful to prove a soul one whom the Father was bringing. Every one who sought Christ's face and favour with such a mark upon his front might confidently reckon on a welcome. This made their unbelief the less excusable. Had Christ ever rejected any their standing aloof in doubt and hesitation might have been defended. But Christ cast out none. Nay He even assured His hearers that He never would avert His smile from an approaching suppliant, but rather extend to him the freest and most cordial reception.

II. **Consolations.** Christ had come—1. *To prosecute no selfish interest.* This Christ had already declared in the private circle of His disciples (iv. 34) as well as in the hearing of the Jerusalem Pharisees (v. 30). A third time he repeats it to the Galilean crowd. Whatever be thought of Christ's testimony concerning the entire disinterestedness of Himself and His work on earth, its rare and unwavering consistency cannot be challenged. 2. *To execute His Father's will.* (1) In preserving all whom the Father by His gracious drawings put into His hand, so that none of them should fall into final destruction—the negative aspect of salvation. (2) In bestowing eternal life upon all who should come to Him in faith—the positive aspect of salvation. (3) In raising up at the last day every one whom the Father gave and who himself came to Him—the completed aspect of salvation.

Learn 1. The primal cause of any man's salvation is the grace or free favour of God. 2. The salvation of those who have been given by the Father to the Son is assured. 3. There is no way of ascertaining whether one has been 'given' by the Father except by 'coming' to the Son. 4. The anxious sinner has the greatest encouragement to come.

VER. 37.—COMERS WELCOMED.

I. **Grounds on which they fear Rejection.** 1. *Supposed omission from the number of the 'given'*;—in which case they deem it hopeless to come. 2. *Greatness of guilt*—they are too bad to be received. 3. *Absence of merit*—they are not good enough to be accepted. 4. *Lateness of repenting*—they are too old to be welcomed. 5. *Defects in believing*—their faith is too feeble or it is not of the right sort.

II. **Reasons why they are sure of a Welcome.** Christ will not cast out comers. 1. *For their sakes;*—He knows the value of the soul, the greatness of its peril, the blessedness of salvation. 2. *For His Father's sake;*—to do so would be to place dishonour on the Father whose will He had been sent to perform. 3. *For His own sake;*—since every sinner saved is an increase to His glory, a triumph of His grace, a trophy of His power, a subject added to His empire. 4. *For the world's sake;*—as how ever would the gospel prevail, if it got noised abroad that any were rejected?

Lessons. 1. Despair for none. 2. Hope for all.

VER. 41-51.—FOUR ENIGMAS RESOLVED.

I. **The Enigma of Christ's heavenly Origin:** ver. 41-43. 1. *The Mystery propounded.* The difficulty felt by Christ's auditors was not that a mysterious origin should be claimed for Messiah. The book of Daniel (vii. 13) had familiarized the Hebrew mind with the idea of a Messiah who should come upon the clouds of heaven; and this was commonly interpreted as signifying that something unusual would be connected with His earthly appearing. The popular opinion, e.g. was that when the Christ came no one should know whence He was (vii. 27). But the Jews supposed they knew exactly whence Jesus was; and it was simply absurd that He, a man like his fellows, should talk about having come down from heaven. 2. *The mystery resolved.* (1) One wonders that to the Pharisees this difficulty did not immediately suggest its own solution, as it does to us, viz., that Christ having descended out of heaven could not have ascended out of earth, having come from above could not also and in the same sense have come from beneath, having God as His Father could not really, however seemingly, be of the parentage of man. Only it is forgotten that what to us who live after the resurrection is a natural and easy deduction could not have been either natural or easy for those who beheld Christ in the flesh, and "in fashion as a man." (2) Almost equally is one at first surprised that Christ did not cut the Gordian knot of their dilemma by announcing that He was not "the son of Joseph" as they assumed. But He did not. What to the learned Scripturists of His day was a puzzle He left a puzzle. Concerning the mystery of Bethlehem He preserved silence, partly, it may be credited, to shield the fair fame of Mary which would only thereby have been endangered, but chiefly for the reason that His cause would in no degree thereby have been advanced,—men would simply have rejected His pretensions with scorn; and because He preferred they should arrive at the perception of His higher nature through being convinced of its godlike glory than by resting on unproved assertions. So the true method of faith still is to reason not that Christ is divine because the story of Bethlehem's manger is authentic, but that Christ having been powerfully declared the Son of God by His resurrection from the dead (Rom. i. 4), the account given by the earlier Evangelists (Matt. i. 18 ; Luke i. 35) of His supernatural conception must be correct.

II. **The Enigma of Man's Responsibility :** ver. 43-45. 1. *The difficulty set forth.* Christ blamed His hearers for their unbelief (ver. 36) and yet affirmed "no man could come unto Him except He was drawn by the Father" (ver. 44). It is the old puzzle of how to harmonize Divine sovereignty and human responsibility ; a problem on which the intellect of centuries has reflected without being perceptibly nearer its solution. 2. *The difficulty set aside.* (1) Not by denying the fact of man's responsibility. This which Christ repeatedly emphasizes (v. 40 ; vi. 36) and Scripture often declares (Rom. i. 18 ; vi. 23 ; Eph. v. 6 ; 1 Pet. iii. 12) conscience universally confirms. (2) Not by explaining away the alleged necessity of divine grace. Though His hearers are staggered at the doctrine (ver. 37), He does not take it back, soften, or qualify it in any way so as to render it less offensive, if not more palatable, but on the contrary reasserts it in stronger form, alleging not only that no man *does*, but that no man *can*, come to Him without a gracious drawing on the part of His Father (ver. 44). Nay, He even appealed to O. T. Scripture in support of His teaching (ver. 45). But (3) by showing that the Father's drawing interferes not with human freedom. Both in naming it a 'drawing' and defining it as a 'teaching,' Christ practically says it partakes wholly and exclusively of the nature of moral suasion. If a sinner comes to Him at all, he does so freely, and of his own accord ; nevertheless what makes him willing is the Father's speaking and teaching without which neither would his mind have been enlightened, nor his heart changed, nor his will renewed ; while that speaking and teaching of the Father is of such sort that when honestly and humbly received, it so illuminates the understanding and moves the affections, quickens the conscience, and stimulates the will that the soul forthwith casts itself in faith upon the Saviour; so that if one refuses to believe it can only be because, as Christ affirms, he has deliberately declined to hear and learn of the Father.

III. **The Enigma of Saving Faith :** ver. 46, 47. 1. *The perplexity stated.* If, as just announced by Christ, no one could come to Him without first hearing and learning of the Father, then it was obvious no one could ever come to Him, since no one could converse with God in the manner indicated (Exod. xxxiii. 20; 1 Tim. vi. 16). This, though not expressed, it was clear was the thought Christ's words had called up in His hearers' minds. 2. *The perplexity recognized.* Christ conceded that on their understanding of His language there was a difficulty. Yet He had not affirmed it was either necessary or possible for any one to talk with the Father in the fashion they supposed. He admitted no one had ever seen the Father. 3. *The perplexity removed.* He, the Son, had seen the Father (v. 19), having been from eternity in His bosom (i. 18), and having come forth from His presence (xvi. 28), to declare Him to men. Hence to hear and learn of the Father, nothing more was required than to hear and learn of Him whom the Father had sent. Nor was this reasoning in a circle, as at first may be thought. What Christ announced was one of those antinomies that contain the profoundest truth. The soul that would come to Him so as to receive eternal life must be inwardly drawn by the teaching of the Father ; while he that would hear and learn of the Father must first become a pupil in the school of Christ. That is to say, a twofold coming to the Saviour is both possible and requisite ; first a coming to be instructed and drawn, to hear and learn, and after that a coming in the way of intelligent, believing, and voluntary self-surrender (xli. 47 ; Rev. iii. 20).

IV. **The Enigma of Eternal Life :** ver. 47-51. 1. *The riddle proposed.* The manna which was 'bread from heaven' had not been able to do more than support physical or corporeal life for a few years. The fathers who had partaken of it were in their graves, and had even died while they were eating it. Like the woman of Samaria (iv. 12) the Jews were at a loss to comprehend how Christ could do more for them than Moses had done for the early progenitors of the nation, how any bread He could bring from above would obviate the necessity of their succumbing to the power of dissolution as their predecessors had done. 2. *The riddle read.* (1) The bread of life to which Christ alluded was not a dead material thing, but a living spiritual person, was Himself (ver. 48). (2) It was not only capable of sustaining life when that existed, but was in itself 'living' and 'life-giving,' possessed of, and able to impart what it possessed, viz., a principle of true, undying, eternal being. (3) This bread when it was eaten by the soul, i.e. when appropriated and assimilated by faith, communicated to the eating soul the life itself contained. (4) The soul thus vivified could no more die than the bread of life, Himself, could die.

Lessons. 1. Preconceived judgments as to what the truth should be are a powerful obstacle to its believing reception. 2. That may be divine truth which transcends the grasp of natural reason. 3. Saving faith has its first cause in the gracious drawing of the Father. 4. Knowledge may exist without faith, but not faith without knowledge. 5. That soul is dead which has not begun to believe in Christ. 6. Immortality for man commences on this side of the grave. 7. For the Christian believer death is abolished.

VER. 52-58.—EATING CHRIST'S FLESH AND DRINKING CHRIST'S BLOOD.

I. **The Quality of the Food** :—Christ's flesh and Christ's blood. 1. *A gradation observable in Christ's language.* (1) He, the Son of Man, shall give the bread of life (ver. 27) ; (2) He, the Son of Man Himself, is the bread of life (ver. 35, 48, 51) ; (3) the bread of life which He, the Son of Man, shall give is His flesh (ver. 51); and (4) it is His flesh and blood (ver. 53-56). 2. *A distinction perceptible in Christ's meaning.* (1) According to the first the bread which truly imparted and sustained the soul's life could be conferred by Him alone, and from Him alone must in consequence be sought. Of true spiritual life, of life for souls as well as for bodies, Christ is pre-eminently the giver, (xvii. 2 ; 2 Pet. i. 3). (2) According to the second such bread of life was not anything impersonal or material outside of Himself, as His doctrine, His example, or even His death considered in themselves and apart from their vital connection with His person, and far less any celestial ambrosia or exhilarating nectar like that which heathen divinities were fabled to feed upon ; but was Himself in His divine-human personality (Col. iii. 4). (3) According to the third the bread of life was more immediately identified with His human nature as that from, through, and in which souls were to find their true subsistence. (4) According to the fourth the bread of life was in some mysterious manner to be connected with the separation of Christ's human nature into its constituent elements of flesh and blood. 3. *An inference deducible from Christ's thought.* That which constitutes the soul's food is the divine-human personality of Christ, which being appropriated by, and received into, the understanding and the heart becomes therein a principle of true spiritual life (Eph. iii. 17; Col. i. 27). 4. *An explanation desirable of Christ's speech.* To what does He refer when He calls His human nature the bread of life ? (1) His human nature in its then condition of temporal humiliation cannot be excluded, since He said to His hearers—" I *am* the bread of life" (ver. 35, 48). Yet that cannot be regarded as exhausting Christ's idea, inasmuch as the bread of life was not merely that which He was then giving but that which He was afterwards to give (ver. 51). (2) His human nature as resolved by death into its constituent elements of flesh and blood cannot be excluded from Christ's thought, seeing that on the eating of His flesh and the drinking of His blood, as two separate parts of one momentous transaction, special emphasis is laid. Yet it will equally be impossible to restrict the significance of Christ's language to His sacrificial death for the reason that He refers to the giving of His flesh as having for its object not the expiation of the soul's guilt, but the nourishment of the world's life. Hence (3) His human nature in its present glorified form to which it has attained and into which it has passed, after having first appeared on earth " in fashion as a man," and been "made perfect through suffering," must be viewed as that which in accordance with Christ's language, at least when interpreted in its most exalted sense, constitutes the bread of life. It is Himself the glorified Son of Man who was delivered for our offences and raised again for our justification (Rom. iv. 25) that He gives to the soul as its true meat and true drink (ver. 55).

II. **The Mode of Participation** :—Eating and drinking. Terms—1. *Symbolic.* Under the name of physical processes they describe spiritual transactions of which souls alone are capable. Corresponding to the body's manducation of bread or flesh and absorption of liquid whether water, wine, or blood, the soul must appropriate and assimilate the manifested, crucified, and glorified Christ who offers Himself to it as the bread of life, His flesh and blood as its meat and drink, if it would derive from Him nourishment and strength. 2. *Suggestive.* The soul's appropriation of Christ as the bread of life must be (1) personal, since no man can eat or drink for his neighbour but only for himself, (2) free, as no man can be made to eat or drink against his will, (3) constant, not once for all, but day by day as the body needs and receives its daily bread, (4) complete, not taking this and leaving that which Christ offers, accepting for instance His historical personality with its teaching and example, and rejecting His sacrificial death, or, laying hold of this and neglecting that, or, appropriating Christ upon the cross but not also Christ upon the throne, as the body to be well nourished must not eat or drink alone, but accepting and embracing Christ in all His parts, His flesh and blood, His life with its teaching and example, His death with its sacrifice and expiation, His resurrection with its glory and intercession, as the body to be adequately fed must both eat and drink.

III. **The Nature of the Benefit** :—Eternal life. 1. *Its source.* Not earthly but heavenly (ver. 58), not human but divine (ver. 53), not the soul itself but Christ, the maker and renewer of the soul (ver. 57). 2. *Its basis.* The indwelling within the soul of Christ's life, yea in a sense of Christ Himself. As the life of the Father reproduces itself eternally in the Son, so the life of the Son reproduces itself, temporally, in the believer (ver. 57 ; xiv. 19). 3. *Its character.* A life of closest personal fellowship with Christ, He abiding in the soul, and the soul abiding in Him, He ever imparting to the believer the life that is in Himself, the believer constantly deriving from Him the requisite support of that life by eating His flesh and drinking His blood, through absorbed contemplation, individual appropriation, spiritual assimilation (xv. 4, 7 ; 1 John ii. 6 ; iii. 24). 4. *Its duration.* Not for few years or many on this material globe, but to the end of one's earthly pilgrimage and beyond it, even for ever and ever (xi. 25 ; 1 John ii. 17). 5. *Its culmination.* On the last day the believer whose soul has been made partaker of eternal life will be re-united with his risen body, which will then die no more but be co-partner with himself of a blessed immortality (xi. 23 ; Luke xx. 36 ; Rom. viii. 23 ; 1 Cor. xv. 42-44, 53).

Lessons. 1. Gratitude for the bread of life. 2. Self-examination as to whether one is truly eating the flesh and drinking the blood of Christ. 3. The proper dignity of the Christian as one who lives in Christ and has Christ living in him. 4. The magnificent destiny of the body, to be raised up at the last day. 5. The melancholy state of both soul and body apart from Jesus Christ.

4. THE TURNING OF THE TIDE

Chap. VI. Ver. 60-71

Exposition

Ver. 60. **Many therefore of His disciples,** i.e. of His adherents or followers, the term 'disciple' being used in the wider sense as distinguished from the twelve (ver. 67), **when they heard** *this,* the preceding teaching about eating Christ's flesh and drinking Christ's blood, **said, This is a hard**

saying, or *hard is this saying.* The emphatic position is assigned to σκλη- ρὸς which signifies, hard, tough, the opposite of 'soft,' μαλακός, whether used of persons (Matt. xxv. 24), of things (Jas. iii. 4), or of speeches (Jude 15), and here refers not so much to the obscurity or darkness of Christ's utterance (Augustine, Chrysostom, Grotius, Tittmann, Olshausen, and others), as to its offensiveness or distastefulness to the heart, the ground or reason of this again being supposed to have lain either in the allusion to a suffering Messiah which was not then in their thoughts, Matt. xvi. 23 (Kuinoel, De Wette, B. Crusius, Meyer, etc.), in the presumption of ascribing to Himself a heavenly origin (Lampe), of insisting that eternal life could only be obtained by eating His flesh and drinking His blood (Tholuck, Luthardt), of demanding that He should be all and they nothing (Hengstenberg), or in the impossibility of doing what He required (Ewald, Brückner), though perhaps it should be found in them all together. **Who can hear,** lit., *who is able to hear,* in the sense of listen to, accept as credible, believe with the intention of acting in accordance therewith; as in vii. 40; x. 20; xii. 47; xviii. 37; **it** the saying or speech, rather than Him.

61. **But Jesus knowing** (cf. ii. 24; Matt. xii. 25), **in Himself** Not a superfluous addition (Kuinoel), but intimating that He knew if not without any external sign (Bengel), at least without any communication from others, as the result of His own higher knowledge. **that His disciples murmured at this,** as the Jews had done when He called Himself the bread of life (ver. 41), **said unto them,** in the hope of assisting them to believe, as they were not hostilely disposed Jews, but favourably inclined disciples: **Doth this,** i.e. this saying, utterance, or speech, as above, **cause you to stumble**—in a moral sense to take offence or become displeased so as to prevent your acceptance of the same and even lead to your withdrawal from My side? cf. xvi. 1.

62. *What* **then if ye should behold** lit., *if then ye shall behold.* The principal member of the sentence, suppressed through strong emotion (see Winer, § lxiv. II.), requires to be supplemented from the context, as thus :—What will ye say then if ye behold? (Euthymius, Kuinoel, and others), meaning either 'how much more will ye be offended' if ye shall behold (Meyer, De Wette, Lücke, and others), or 'ye will not then be offended, will ye,' if ye behold" (Ebrard, Hofmann, Hengstenberg, Ewald, Brückner, Godet, and others); the former implying that their present offence would be accentuated, the latter that it would be removed, by what they should see. Which interpretation is the more correct will depend on what the event was Christ affirmed they should behold: **the Son of Man** (see on i. 51) **ascending where He was before.** If this referred to Christ's death, then the former interpretation of the verse should be preferred; if to Christ's ascension (xx. 17), the latter. If Christ's hearers were scandalized at His talking about the eating of His flesh and drinking of His blood, it is certain they would much more be offended when asked, as they soon would be, to accept as Messiah Him whom they should see upon the cross. But, on the other hand, their offence would cease when they perceived Him no longer dead, but alive again and visibly ascending to His native skies. Both statements are and were correct. The cross deepened, while the ascension lightened, the offence Christ's disciples presently felt. Yet the latter is perhaps the thought Christ designed to set before His followers, since it is doubtful if 'ascending' can be taken as equivalent to 'dying on the cross,' least of all when followed by the words 'where He was before' which obviously point to a returning to that heavenly sphere out of which He descended at the Incarnation.

63. **It is the Spirit that quickeneth; the flesh profiteth nothing.** The truth thus generally stated that not flesh but spirit, not corporeal but pneumatical nature is the source of life had its bearing on the theme Christ was seeking to illustrate. The eternal life concerning which He had spoken could not come from His external and corporeal organization considered as such, however exalted that might be, but

from the nature of the case could proceed only from the life-giving spirit it
enshrined. Hence nothing in what He
had said should have given them offence. He did not mean, and could not
have meant, that they should literally
eat His flesh and drink His blood,
since dead matter and merely corporeal
actions could impart life to none. Nor
though He should die need it stagger
them as the life-giving power was not
in His body but in His spirit, the holy
and eternal spirit which had been
given to Him without measure (iii.
34), through which He should offer
Himself without spot unto God (Heb.
ix. 14), by which He should be quickened (1 Pet. iii. 18), and which He
should outpour upon His church on
the day of Pentecost (Acts ii. 33). **The
words that I have spoken unto you are
spirit and are life.** So He adds, furnishing an illustration of the life-
giving power of the spirit. The *utterances*, ῥήματα as distinguished from
λόγος, ver. 60), *which I*, and not a mere
earthly teacher like Moses, *have spoken
to you* both now and heretofore, *are
spirit*, having their primal source in
the Spirit who is within Me ; *and* for
the same reason they *are life*, to such
as hear and receive them with the
spirit.

64. **But,** instead of thus accepting
them and deriving from them the life
of which they are the bearers, **there
are some of you** who now follow Me
externally listening to my teaching
that believe not οἱ οὐ πιστεύουσιν, *who* as
a matter of fact *believe not*, and in
consequence are scandalized. Such a
style of remark was adopted, the
Evangelist adds, **for Jesus knew from
the beginning** (cf. xvi. 4)—not of all
things (Theophylact), or of His acquaintance with each individual (De
Wette, B. Crusius, Tholuck, Luthardt,
and others), or of the murmuring
(Bengel), or of the germ of unbelief
(Lange), but of His gathering of disciples, to which ver. 70 refers (Meyer,
Godet, Westcott) –**who they were that
believed not,** lit., *who are the not believing*, according to the supposition, οἱ
μὴ πιστεύοντες (cf. iii. 18 ; and see Winer,
§ lxv. 1); i.e. in every instance the 'not
believing' were under His observing
gaze (Heb. iv. 14), **and who it was that
should betray Him,** lit., *who is he about*

to betray Him ; Christ discerned from
the first that the one who should deliver Him up was Judas.

65. **And He said, For this cause,** διὰ
τοῦτο, with reference to this unbelief,
have I said unto you, ver. 44, **that no
man can come unto Me, except it be
given unto him of the Father.** Of this
the clear and sufficient evidence was
their want of sincere faith in Him and
consequent non-acceptance of His
words.

66. **Upon this** ἐκ τούτου, either *on this
account*, i.e. because of these words
(Meyer, Luthardt), or *from that time*
(De Wette, Lücke, Godet, and others),
or both ideas may be included as in
xix. 12 (Westcott). **many of His disciples** in the wider sense **went back,**
lit., *into the behind parts*, cf. xviii. 6 ;
xx. 14, **and walked no more with Him,**
as His followers or adherents : cf. vii.
1 ; xi. 54 ; Rev. iii. 4.

67. **Jesus said therefore unto the
twelve,** i.e. the apostles (ver. 71 ; xx.
24 ; Matt. xxvi. 20, 47 ; Mark xiv. 10,
17 ; Luke xxii. 14, 47), whose election
to the apostolate, though not previously recorded, is now implied in
accordance with the synoptical accounts (Matt. x. 1, 2 ; Mark iii. 14 ;
Luke vi. 13): **Would ye also go away?**
lit., *ye also do not wish to go away, do
you?* the conjunction μὴ, while suggestive of a fear, yet anticipative of a
negative reply : cf. iv. 29 ; vii. 26, 35 ;
and see Winer, § lvii. 3.

68. **Simon Peter** (see i. 40-42) **answered Him,** in the name of his co-
disciples and himself (cf. Matt. xvi.
16), **Lord, to whom shall we go?** or
depart (from thee)? **Thou hast the
words,** or, words, **of eternal life,** utterances (ῥήματα, an echo of ver. 63) that
relate to eternal life, or that have
eternal life as their contents and produce eternal life as their effect.

69. **And we have believed and know**
Here faith, final and conclusive, once
for all, πεπιστεύκαμεν, is represented as
conducting to knowledge ; elsewhere
knowledge is declared to precede faith
(xvii. 8 ; 1 John iv. 16). Both views
are correct. **that thou art the Holy
One of God.** So the best authorities
(א B C* D L etc., Griesbach, Lachmann, Tischendorf, Westcott and
Hort), rather than 'that Christ, the
Son of the living God' (T. R.), which

appears to have been taken from Matt. xvi. 16 ; the sense probably being that Peter and his co-disciples had attained to a clear, definite, and permanent conviction that Jesus was the one consecrated by and for God, as Messiah (x. 36 ; 1 John ii. 20), and therefore the absolutely pure and sinless one : cf. Acts ii. 27 ; iii. 14 ; iv. 27, 30 ; 1 Pet. i. 19 ; ii. 21 ; iii. 18. 70. **Jesus answered them** in justification of the question put in ver. 67 (Brückner), perhaps to shame the overconfidence of Peter, as in xiii. 37, 38 (Hengstenberg), or to vindicate Himself from a charge of want of discernment in admitting Judas to the apostolic circle (Godet), though probably only with a sorrowful outlook to the tragic issue He foresaw (Meyer, Ewald) : **Did not I choose you the twelve,** or, *did not I,* whom you have just designated as God's Holy One, *you* who have now proclaimed your faith in Me as such, *the twelve,* with allusion not so much to their number as to their representative character as the heads of God's spiritual Israel, the N. T. Church, *choose* for Myself, this being the force of the middle voice, ἐξελεξάμην, and to be admitted to My society and friendship ? **and one of you is a devil,** or, *and of you,* thus chosen and honoured, *one is a devil,* διάβολος which can hardly be softened down to

mean *informer* (De Wette), opponent (Lücke), but must be taken as in viii. 44 ; 1 John iii. 8, 10, to signify one who is of diabolic nature and disposition (Meyer, Brückner, Godet, and others).

71. **Now He spake of Judas,** *the son of* **Simon Iscariot,** or, 'man of Kerioth,' commonly believed to have been a town in the tribe of Judah (Josh xv. 25) now called *Kureitein,* or 'two fortresses,' south of Hebron, and 4½ miles north of Arad, though the claims of Kerioth, a town of Moab (Amos ii. 2 ; Jer. xlviii. 24, 41) have also been advocated. The genitive Ἰσκαριώτου (BCGL etc., Tischendorf, Westcott and Hort) intimates that already the surname belonged to Simon the father ; the reading Ἰσκαριώτην (T. R., Meyer), would assign the appellative to Judas the son, who appears also to have borne it (xiv. 22). **for he,** Judas, **it was that should betray Him,** lit., *that was about to betray him,* the language not necessarily implying that already Judas had formed the design, but simply intimating the fact that to Judas it was to fall to perpetrate the deed, *being* **one of the twelve**—directing attention to the monstrous, yea, diabolic wickedness involved in the commission of such a crime by one occupying such a position.

Homiletics

VER. 66.—THE DEFECTION OF THE DISCIPLES.

I. **Occasioned by a hard saying** : ver. 60. The saying (ver. 51, 53, 57) was unquestionably hard. 1. *Difficult to understand,* even for Christians who possess a complete gospel and an unction from the Holy One (xiv. 17, 26 ; 1 John ii. 20, 27), but especially for unbelievers (1 Cor. ii. 14). 2. *Difficult to receive,* demanding from all humility, self-abnegation (Matt. xvi. 24), whole-hearted surrender of one's being to Christ (Rom. xiii. 14 ; Eph. iv. 22 ; Col. iii. 8), none of which are easy for the unrenewed. 3. *Difficult to practise,* by such as would sincerely and lovingly render it obedience hardly less than by those who only pay it formal and forced respect.

II. **Arrested by a high saying** : ver. 62. 1. *Retrospective.* Directing the minds of His hearers to His pre-existent condition out of which He had descended (iii. 13 ; vi. 38, 51 ; vii. 29 ; viii. 38). 2. *Predictive.* Foretelling the future fact of His ascension to heaven, with His human nature, and in the sight of men (vii. 33, 34 ; viii. 28, 54 ; xii. 23 ; xiv. 2, 3 ; xvii. 5, 24 ; Mark xvi. 19 ; Luke xxiv. 50, 51). 3. *Anticipative.* Cherishing a hope that when His future exaltation was an accomplished fact, beheld by the eye or perceived by the mind, the difficulties felt at present by His followers would disappear, which in the case of many they did (Matt. xxviii. 17).

III. **Instructed by a deep saying** : ver. 63. 1. *The announcement of a truth.*

Only spirit can impart life, since life in its highest sense pertains to the domain of spirit. 2. *The removal of an error.* That which belonged to the unspiritual realm of flesh was not capable as they supposed of communicating true existence. Hence they erred in thinking He could mean a literal eating of His flesh or drinking of His blood. 3. *The illustration of a principle.* The words He had spoken, if taken literally, might cause stumbling ; if rightly understood, the inner life of which they were the bearers would impart itself to the souls receiving them.

IV. **Warned by a sharp saying :** ver. 64. 1. *Discriminating.* Christ distinguished between those amongst His auditors who believed and those who believed not, as He still does, walking in the midst of the golden candlesticks (Rev. ii. 1, 18, 23). 2. *Informing.* Christ announced to His hearers that He was perfectly acquainted with their characters and dispositions, as He still knows the works and ways (Rev. ii. 2, 9, 13, 19 ; iii. 1, 8, 15) of His professed followers on earth. 3. *Reproving.* Not purely as an item of information Christ made this communication, or as an exhibition of His skill in psychological analysis, or thought and character reading, but as representing to his hearers the guilt under which they lay. Christ never regarded unbelief as an accident, misfortune, or disease (unless of the heart and will !), but always as a sin. 4. *Sorrowing.* With sadness in His heart, if not also in His tones, He made the proclamation. Christ felt for and sympathized with the miseries of men. He was grieved for their hardness of heart (Mark iii. 5), and marvelled at their unbelief (Mark vi. 6).

V. **Explained by a dark saying :** ver. 65. 1. *A rebuke to their self-sufficiency.* They deemed themselves competent to pronounce judgment on Christ, to gauge His profound utterances with the plummet of their understanding, to estimate the value of His teaching, and to determine His position in God's kingdom ; Christ assures them that none of these things could they do without Divine assistance. 2. *A declaration of their irreligion.* The Father had not extended to them that gracious influence without which they could not come to Him. They were therefore yet in their natural and unrenewed condition, and as such incapable of receiving the truth in the love of it that they might be saved.

Learn 1. The sin of stumbling at Christ's words. 2. The best way to resolve difficulties in religion is to wait for further light. 3. The danger of literalism in interpreting the Spirit's revelations. 4. The propriety of self-examination as to whether one truly believes. 5. The possibility of repeating the sin of Judas. 6. The need of daily prayer for Divine grace.

VER. 67-70.—THE WAVERING OF THE TWELVE.

I. **A Searching Question :**—" Would ye also go away ?" ver. 67. 1. *An appeal to their sympathy.* While Christ could not be other than grieved over the defection of those who had long companied with Him, His anguish must have been intense when He saw His hitherto faithful twelve beginning to be affected with the humour of the crowd. " Ye also will not go away, will ye ?"—like the cry of a stricken heart, bowed beneath a burden of woe, and ready to break if another drop be added to its load ; as if He purposed to say, 'I can bear the apostasy of these fair-weather followers, and 'trencher friends' who have sought Me for the loaves I gave them ; but how shall I endure, if ye, my chosen companions and much-prized intimates, desert Me ?' 2. *A test of their sincerity.* Without holding that Christ meant to say, 'Ye also can go if ye desire,' the question was no doubt aimed at proving the quality of their devotion, of bringing to light that they were not mere *ephemerœ*, summer flies that sported in the sunshine and dropped into the dust at eventide, but were attached to Him in genuine faith and with hearty love. 3. *A call for their constancy.* The question is so shaped as to show that Christ expected a negative reply. Ye will not go away, will ye ? You, Andrew, the first to follow Me ; you, Nathanael, the first to confess Me ; you, Peter, the first to be brought to Me ; you, John, the first to appreciate Me ! Ye will not now forsake Me, stumbling at My doctrine, rejecting My salvation ! Christ knew they believed and would not now abandon

Him. The manner in which He spoke to them would help to steady their determination.

II. A Serious Answer:—"Lord! to whom shall we go?" etc., ver. 68. 1. *A reverential address.* Although on the lips of others (iv. 15, 49), the term 'Lord' may have been equivalent to 'Sir' on those of Peter, who had witnessed the miracle of the loaves and the 'sign' upon the sea, who, with his co-disciples had already worshipped Him as the Son of God (Matt. xiv. 33), and who in the present instance spoke for these co-disciples as well as for himself, it imported more than a courteous salutation, it testified to an inward recognition of Christ's divinity (ix. 38). 2. *A significant inquiry.* It was a strong way of asserting not alone that they intended to adhere to Him, but that they reckoned Him the only Teacher, Messiah, Saviour to whom they could adhere. If He was not the 'Sent of God,' the Christ, they could not hope to discover another with better credentials; if He could not assist them with heaven's grace or enrich them with eternal life, it was useless to dream that one different from Him could. If therefore they left Him they could turn to no other quarter in search of what they most required, light for the path of duty, life for the dying soul, grace in the present, glory in the future. Not back again to Judaism or out to Gentilism could they go. They could only abandon themselves to despair. 3. *A confident avowal.* If there was none but He to whom they could direct their steps, they were satisfied that none but He was needed. The words He spoke might be involved in obscurity to the natural understanding, or occasion resilience in the unrenewed heart, but they were words of eternal life. They concerned the highest theme a teacher could descant on, the deepest need a soul could feel, the greatest blessing heaven could bestow. And what they published they could impart. They possessed a power of which other teachers' words were destitute. They could recommend themselves to sincere souls, explain themselves to docile understandings, justify themselves to pure hearts. They could awaken in bosoms previously cold, despairing, lifeless, pulsations of life, hope, love. They could animate spirits before dead with visions, expectations, foretastes of a blessed immortality.

III. A Simple Confession:—"We have believed and know," etc., ver. 69. 1. *An antecedent faith.* The disciples commenced their investigations into the engrossing theme of Christ's personality, not by practising unlimited credulity as opposed to sober inquiry, not by superstitiously and blindly committing themselves to extravagant and baseless conceptions as to the rank which belonged to Him in the scale of being, but by accepting honestly and trustfully the evidence placed before them, before their intellects, hearts, imaginations, consciences, wills, in the character, wisdom, works of Jesus, allowing these to plead their case in the inner court of the mind, without let or hindrance, partiality or prejudice, connivance on the one hand or contradiction on the other, and then forming the conclusion to which these led. 2. *A consequent knowledge.* The result was that they arrived at a clear, definite, intelligent, and deliberate judgment as to who Christ was. He was the Holy One of God. The glory of the Incarnate Son having shined into their souls, the light it imparted enabled these to recognize the glory of God in the face of Jesus Christ (2 Cor. iv. 6). As the light streaming forth from the sun into the eye gives it power to behold the sun and all things on which the sun's light falls, so the glory of Jesus beaming down upon and receiving admission into the soul causes it to perceive and know Him to whom the glory belongs as the Holy One of God.

IV. A Solemn Warning:—'Did not I choose you the twelve,' etc., ver. 70. 1. *For the twelve.* Peter had spoken in the name of his co-disciples as well as of himself; Christ replies that there is nevertheless ground for self-examination. The distinguished honour and exalted position they enjoyed as His apostles and (possibly) the future heads of the church of God was no infallible guarantee of their sincerity. Nay, it was certain one among them was a hypocrite, a deceiver, a liar, a potential traitor, a devil. There was therefore room for heart-searching, each with himself and before God. 2. *For Judas.* How Christ came to elect Judas as an apostle knowing him to be what he was, and his destiny to be what it eventually proved, presents no more insuperable problem than that which constantly recurs in connection with every attempt to harmonize the action of Divine sovereignty and human freedom in providence or in grace. Why should God to whom the issues of all men's lives no less than the characters of all men's hearts are known, call into His church those whom He perfectly discerns shall (visibly) turn His grace into lasciviousness, aggravate thereby their guilt, and plunge themselves into irremediable destruction? In this case, as in that of Judas, the answer is that divine grace does not regulate its operations in and on the hearts of men by *a priori* knowledge of whether it shall be humbly used or wickedly abused. God and Christ deal with men as free agents, and often extend to those whom they know from the beginning will be sunk into deeper condemnation thereby opportunities that if improved would exalt them to heaven and enrich them with eternal life. If Christ elected Judas, it was probably because (1) He recognized that to be His Father's will, (2) He would rescue if He could a soul as black and perfidious even as that of Judas, (3) He would not have it said that nothing had been done, or that anything had been left undone, to avert the fate of that unhappy man; and (4) He would make it clear that Judas was self-destroyed. The present warning was manifestly dropped for the sake of Judas to discover to him, what probably he was not yet aware of, that already he was standing on the edge of a precipice at whose base moaned the dark waters of eternal death.

Lessons. 1. A frequent cause of apostasy—stumbling at Christ's words. 2. The highest ground of a saint's attachment to Christ—the consciousness that Christ has words of eternal life. 3. An admirable model for a church's creed—the confession of Peter. 4. The danger of a merely nominal and external connection with Christ—seen in the case of Judas. 5. The ultimate responsibility of every man for his own destruction.

SECTION THIRD.—CHRIST'S THIRD PRESENTATION OF HIMSELF TO HIS OWN (THE JEWISH PEOPLE); IN THE THIRD YEAR OF HIS MINISTRY

CHAP. VII. 1—X. 21

An interval of six months elapsed between Our Lord's rejection in Galilee and His appearance in Jerusalem at the feast of Tabernacles in October to present Himself a third time before the official heads and representatives of His nation. Of His journeyings, works, and teachings during this period details are given in the Synoptists (Matt. xvi., xvii., xviii.; Mark vii., viii., ix.; Luke ix.), from which it is evident that, after the Galilean crisis described in the preceding chapter, Our Lord withdrew Himself largely into the inner circle of the Twelve, with a view to instruct and prepare them for taking up the work of the Kingdom when He should be compelled by a violent death to lay it down. At the end of this space, the third of the great national celebrations approaching, He is urged by His brethren to transfer the theatre of His activity from the province to the capital, which He at first declines to do, but afterwards when the gaieties and solemnities of the festal season are at their height He seemingly changes His determination and hastens towards the Metropolis. There, first in the Temple by a series of conversations and afterwards in the streets by a miracle and the incidents to which it gives rise, He once more with conspicuous fulness, clearness, earnestness, and solemnity brings Himself and His claims under the notice of the chief priests and Pharisees, the ecclesiastical dignitaries and authorities of the day, but only to have Himself rejected and them spurned. Beginning in the middle of the festal week, and continuing probably one or two days beyond its close, the entire duration of this appeal to the nation may be set down as covering at least eight days. The contents of the section may be thus arranged : —

I. The Beginning of the Feast :—
From Galilee to Jerusalem : vii. 1-13.

II. The Middle of the Feast :—
Christ teaches in the Temple : ver. 14-36.

III. The Last Day of the Feast :—
1. Teaching in the Temple resumed : ver. 37-44.
2. A Meeting of the Sanhedrim convened : ver. 45-52.
(3. The Woman taken in Adultery : vii. 53 ; viii. 1-11.)
4. Teaching in the Temple continued : ver. 12-59.

IV. After the Feast :—
1. The Healing of a Man born blind : ix. 1-41.
2. The Parables of the Good Shepherd : x. 1-?1.

IN JERUSALEM ON THE OCCASION OF THE FEAST OF TABERNA-
CLES CHRIST REVEALS HIS GLORY AS THE INCARNATE SON.
I. THE BEGINNING OF THE FEAST—FROM GALILEE TO
JERUSALEM

CHAP. VII. VER. 1-13

EXPOSITION

Chap. vii. ver. 1. **And after these things** recorded in the preceding chapter **Jesus walked** prosecuted His Messianic labours, the verb depicting its constantly shifting scene and the tense its continuous character (cf. vi. 66), **in Galilee** (see on ii. 11) : **for He would not walk in Judæa**—to avoid provoking a premature conflict with the national authorities—**because the Jews,** the hierarchical party in the state, as in i. 19, **sought to kill him.** They had come to this decision immediately after the Bethesda miracle eighteen months before (v. 18) ; and

the sudden cropping up of hostility against Him in Galilee eighteen months after at the instigation of their emissaries (vi. 66) gave unmistakable indication that His Jerusalem adversaries had not departed from their murderous designs, and that accordingly a return to either the metropolis or its vicinity would not be safe.

2. **Now**—better 'but,' marking an antithesis and introducing that which ultimately led to His change of purpose—**the feast of the Jews** ἡ ἑορτὴ τῶν Ἰουδαίων, the feast of the Jews by pre-

eminence, which in some respects the under-mentioned was. Josephus names it 'far the holiest and greatest feast' (Ant. viii. 4, 1), and "the feast most commonly observed" (xv. 3, 3); Philo calls it "the greatest of the feasts" (II. p. 286); the Rabbis on account of the immense number of offerings it witnessed style it "the day of multiplication," though the correctness of this assertion is by some disputed (Ginsburg); and Plutarch for the extravagance of the rejoicings in which its celebrants in later times indulged describes it as a feast of Bacchus (see Keil, Handbuch der Biblischen Archäologie, § 85): cf. v. 1. **the feast of tabernacles** ἡ σκηνοπηγία, *the booth or tent pitching,* the third great annual festival of the Jews in which all the males were required to appear before Jehovah at the tabernacle or temple, the other two being the Passover and Pentecost (Lev. xxiii. 34-36, 39-43; Deut. xvi. 13-15). The feast was so entitled because of the booths (*succoth*) of boughs and leaves in which the people dwelt during its continuance, to commemorate the days when Jehovah "made the children of Israel to dwell in booths." From the season of the year when it occurred it was likewise known as the feast of ingathering (Ex. xxiii. 16). **was at hand**. It commenced on the 15th of Tishri (September—October) and continued 7 days, after which on the 8th followed a holy convocation (Lev. xxiii. 36; Neh. viii. 18). 3. **His brethren** (see on ii. 12) **therefore,** because of the proximity of the feast which they perhaps supposed Christ would attend, seeing He had not visited Jerusalem at either of the two preceding festivals, **said unto Him** in unbelieving opposition (Hengstenberg), out of a desire to give Him friendly counsel (Lange, Westcott), or because they were puzzled by the claims of their brother (Godet), and wished to bring the truth or falsehood of these claims as quickly as possible to a decision (Meyer):—**Depart hence,** lit., *make change from this place* (to another), **and go into Judæa,** and more particularly into *Jerusalem,* the capital being in their estimation the true sphere of Messianic activity, **that thy disciples also**—not His Galilean followers since these had witnessed His miracles, but

either His adherents in Judæa and Jerusalem (De Wette, Tholuck, Ewald, Godet), or His disciples generally who would then be collected in Jerusalem from all parts of the country (Lücke, Meyer, Westcott)—**may behold thy works** (see v. 20) **which thou doest.** They question not that He had wrought miracles (B. Crusius), but complain of the obscurity in which He had performed them. 4. **For no man doeth anything in secret, and himself seeketh to be known openly,** lit., *to be in freespokenness;* perhaps here suggesting the idea of openness (ver. 13, 26; x. 24; xi. 14, 54; xvi. 25, 29) rather than of boldness (Acts iv. 13; 2 Cor. iii. 12). He who would secure public recognition for himself (αὐτὸς) must not perform in secret the acts on which he grounds his expectations, but must step forth into the 'open' and work his marvels in the full blaze of public criticism. The construction for which classical Greek would have read—"No man does ... seeking," is characteristic of N. T. writers. See Winer, § lxvi. 7. **If thou doest these things,** i.e. such miracles, not as we hear of thee doing (Brückner), but as in point of fact thou doest,—Christ's brethren contested not the reality of Christ's miracles, but simply challenged their value as credentials and urged that the question should be brought to a decision by His stepping forth and doing them on such a theatre as would secure their examination and appreciation.—**manifest thyself** make thyself known to be what thou art (cf. i. 31; iii. 21; ix. 3) **to the world.** To the Jewish mind Jerusalem was the world, the ὀμφαλὸς τῆς γῆς; and certainly, if at any time it merited this designation, it was on the occasion of its great national feasts: xii. 19; cf. Acts ii. 5. 5. **For even his brethren did not believe on him** as Messiah any more than others did. With them faith was not merely weak, imperfect, contending with unbelief, wanting in complete self-surrender (Hengstenberg, Lange, Westcott); it was as conspicuously absent as in the case of the Galileans or Judæans (Meyer, Godet, Luthardt). 6. **Jesus therefore saith unto them,** explaining the reason of His procedure, **My time** not for suffering—the hour of My passion (Chrysostom, Lampe, Ebrard, B. Crusius) ; or, for going up to the feast (Luther) ; but for showing Myself to the world (De Wette, Lücke, Meyer, Godet, Luthardt, Tholuck, and others),—the seasonable moment (καιρός occurring only here in this gospel) for taking the step you indicate. The term 'hour,' ὥρα (viii. 20), marks that 'time' or seasonable moment as one fixed and ordained by God for Him "as distinguished from the hours arbitrarily chosen by men for themselves" (Lange).—**is not yet come,** though doubtless it will arrive when the Father shows it to the Son (v. 19, 30) ; **but your time** for showing yourselves to the world **is alway ready** and requires no waiting ; a statement for which the reason is next given.

7. **The world cannot hate you,** who belong to it through your unbelief, are in sympathy with it and loved by it (xv. 19) ; the "inability" here arising from moral affinity between the subject and the object (cf. v. 19), as elsewhere and in other relations it proceeds from the absence of such affinity (cf. ver. 34, 36 ; viii. 21; xiv. 17); **but Me it hateth, because I testify of it that its works are evil,** and so discover My inner moral and spiritual antagonism to it : see on iii. 19.

8. **Go ye up unto the feast** and let the world see what *you* are : I, on My part, **go not up yet unto this feast** Whether 'not yet' (T. R., Meyer, Westcott) or 'not' (אDKM etc., Tischendorf) be adopted as the true reading, the utterance in view of ver. 10 is not to be explained as an indication of fickleness on the part of Christ (Porphyry), or of honest purpose subsequently changed (Meyer), or of intentional evasion as if He wished to leave His counsellors uncertain how He meant to act (Hengstenberg), or signified that though He was really going to Jerusalem He was not going just yet,—with the mental substitution of a 'now' (Chrysostom, Lücke, Olshausen, Tholuck), or with the public caravans and feast trains (Bengel, Ewald, Westcott), or to attend the feast in a legally prescribed manner (Lange, Ebrard). The sense Christ desired His words to bear was probably that He was not yet (though afterwards He would), or not (absolutely, for the present) going up

to the metropolis to manifest Himself to the world (Godet) ; if He went up, it would not yet be for any such purpose as they contemplated. **because my time is not yet fulfilled.** The seasonable moment, when He would 'manifest Himself to the world,' was not to arrive till the next Passover.

9. **And having said these things unto them He abode** *still* **in Galilee,** waiting the signal from His Father which determined all His earthly movements : cf. xi. 6.

10. **But when His brethren were gone up unto the feast** The clause 'unto the feast,' omitted in the T. R., is adopted by the best MSS. (אBKLTH II etc.) and critics (Tischendorf, Westcott and Hort). The aorist does not require to be taken as a pluperfect (Lücke, Meyer, Winer), but represents the departure of Christ's brethren as a past event. **then,** at the time thus defined, **went He also up** "To the feast" (T. R.) should here be omitted. **not publicly** οὐ φανερῶς, not openly as His brethren desired (ver. 4), **but as it were in secret**—in a concealed manner, as a private person, *incognito*, not in a mysterious fashion allied to Docetism (Baur, Hilgenfeld). Whether or not Christ travelled through Samaria, so avoiding the ordinary path (Wieseler, Hengstenberg), He did not accompany any of the public caravans, but selected a solitary route. The "in secret" shows that this was neither the journey mentioned in Luke ix. 51 (Wieseler), nor the final departure from Galilee, Matt. xix. 1, 2 (Meyer), both of which took place in public. Though Christ's journey to the city was "in secret" it is not said His visit to the feast was.

11. **The Jews,** the Sanhedrists or hostile hierarchy (ver. 1, 13 ; cf. i. 19 ; v. 10, 15), rather than the common people (Hengstenberg), **therefore** because of the expectation that as a devout Jew He would not absent Himself from the festival ; perhaps also because they saw His brethren had come, **sought Him at the feast** before He arrived and with a hostile intention as in ver. 1, 19 ; v. 18 (De Wette, Lücke, Meyer, Brückner) and not simply out of curiosity (Luthardt), **and said, Where is he?** *that one!* that

celebrated (Hengstenberg), well-known, but absent (Meyer, Tholuck) one ; perhaps with a flavour of contempt in their tones (Luthardt), 'that boastful miracle doer who now fears to show himself.' **12. And there was much murmuring among the multitudes concerning Him** (cf. vi. 41, 61): **some said, He is a good man,** ἀγαθός, a sincere, honest, upright man who will not deceive others (Matt. v. 45 ; xii. 35 ; Mark x. 17 ; Acts xi. 24) ; **others said, Not so,** or, simply, *No,* **but he leadeth the multitude astray,** *seducit* (Vulgate), *causeth them to*

err, in judgment as to His person : Matt. xxvii. 63. **13. Howbeit no man** of those favourably (Augustine, De Wette, Lücke, Ewald, and others), but perhaps also of those unfavourably (B. Crusius, Brückner, Meyer, Tholuck, Westcott, and others) disposed towards Him, **spake openly of Him,** i.e. with perfect freedom, **for fear of the Jews.** Until they knew the attitude towards Him which would be taken by the authorities it was perilous, they perceived, to commit themselves to a decided opinion on the one side or the other.

HOMILETICS

VER. 1-13.—THE SITUATION SURVEYED.

I. The Scene in Galilee : the attitude of Christ's brethren. 1. *The counsel they offered.* That Christ instead of dallying in the provinces should repair to the centre of the theocratic kingdom and put forth His Messianic claims where they could be competently examined (ver. 3). Doubtless perfectly unanimous, ostensibly friendly, pressingly urgent, seemingly good, it was yet wholly mistaken, and if not openly hostile, at least essentially insincere. 2. *The argument they used.* That as one could not possibly acquire fame by living in obscurity, if He really aspired to the Messianic throne He must come into the clear light of day and flash forth the splendour of His miracles not before a crowd of Galilean rustics but in presence of the leading people of the metropolis (ver. 4). A reasonable proposition, an indisputable maxim, a forceful contention, it was also a doubtful recommendation, if not a perilous temptation which already He had twice encountered (Matt. iv. 9 ; John vi. 15). 3. *The spirit they cherished.* They did not believe in His Messianic pretensions, though they could not deny the reality of His miracles. They were impatient to have His true character settled and His true position fixed. If He was Messiah, they wanted to see Him crowned ; if He was not, they desired to have the bubble burst. 4. *The reply they received.* Christ was not going up to the feast at Jerusalem for any such purpose as they suggested (1) because the hour for His doing what they desired had not arrived—there being, as for every purpose under heaven (Eccles. iii. 1), so much more for the work in which He was engaged and for every detail of it a seasonable moment ; and (2) because to go before that seasonable time would not secure what they desired—the great world of Jerusalem was not as ready to accord a welcome to Him as to them (ver. 7). It would hate and reject Him while embracing and loving them. Hence while any time would do for them to exhibit who and what they were in the capital, His time was not yet.

II. The Scene in Jerusalem : the hierarchy and the populace. 1. *The bloodthirsty Sanhedrists.* These searched for their intended victim among the crowds that thronged the city (1) with unsleeping hostility, which they had now nursed for 18 months, (2) with murderous intent, distinctly purposing to apprehend Him, (3) with eager inquiry, asking all they met if they had seen Him, (4) with contemptuous scorn, calling Him "that celebrated person who has been dazzling you with his wonders !" 2. *The whispering multitudes.* These were (1) divided in their judgments concerning Him as Simeon predicted at His birth (Luke ii. 34), and Christ Himself afterwards affirmed men would be (Matt. x. 34, 35), and as history proves they have ever been ; and (2) afraid to speak openly about Him, which as much betokened their insincerity as their cowardice, indicating they were quite prepared, suppressing their opinions, to think and speak as their leaders bade them. Miserable crew !

Learn 1. It is not only not wrong but in all respects becoming and right to walk with circumspection and prudence among men. Christ did so. 2. In matters pertaining to the religious life the wisdom of this world is almost always wrong. It was so with Christ's brethren. 3. A man's friends are frequently the last to believe in either his greatness or his goodness. It was so with Christ. 4. The more a man resembles Christ the more will he be hated by the world. 5. The best of men may be evil spoken of. Christ was.

II.—THE MIDDLE OF THE FEAST—CHRIST TEACHES IN THE TEMPLE

Chap. VII. Ver. 14-36

Exposition

Ver. 14. **But when it was now the midst of the feast** lit., *but already the feast being at its middle point:* cf. Ex. xii. 29 (LXX.) ; probably on the fourth day of the festival—**Jesus went up into the temple** having, it has been thought (Meyer) arrived earlier in the city, **and taught.** The first mention of Christ as a teacher in Jerusalem (ver. 28 ; viii. 20), although teaching had been his customary occupation in Galilee (vi. 59 ; Matt. iv. 23 ; Luke iv. 15).

15. **The Jews,** the hierarchical opposition mentioned in ver. 11, **therefore,** because of the excellence of His teaching, the power of His word (Matt. vii. 29), and the depth of His insight (ii. 25 ; v. 42), **marvelled,** expressed to one another their astonishment (Matt. xxii. 22 ; Luke iv. 22), **saying, How knoweth this man letters,** not the O. T. Scriptures (Luther, Grotius, Kuinoel), but theological learning which however mostly consisted in knowledge of the former (cf. Acts xxvi. 24), **having never learned,**—having never studied at any rabbinical school as Paul had done (Acts xxii. 3) ?—an important biographical notice showing that Christ was popularly recognized as one who had received no formal academical training, being regarded by the Jewish doctorate as an ἰδιώτης, or private person, an unlettered plebeian (Acts iv. 13), who knew not the law (ver. 49) ; hence also proving the impossibilty of tracing back Christ's doctrine to purely human sources (Meyer). The mention of this circumstance that Christ had never ' learnt ' reveals a change in the tactics

of Christ's assailants. On the former occasion (chap. v.) they had accused Him of law-breaking ; on this they charge Him with defective education.

16. **Jesus therefore,** having either overheard their remarks or divined their thoughts, **answered them, and said,** solving the enigma of His wisdom without having learned (Meyer), **My teaching,** the teaching which I propound and which is distinctively Mine, i.e. Mine as contrasted with yours, **is not Mine,** does not belong to Me, as something I have excogitated and created, hence is not from Me as its source (ἐμὴ = ἀπ' ἐμαυτοῦ, ver. 17 : cf. v. 19, 30), **but is His that sent Me,** is the property of God whose messenger I am and who hath given Me the message I bring (iii. 34 ; viii. 28 ; xii. 49), a message welling up in and proceeding forth from the infinite and eternal fountain of pure truth.

17. **If any man willeth to do His will,** not exclusively that revealed in O. T. Scripture (Bengel, Hengstenberg, Weiss, Tholuck, and others), or written on the conscience (Godet), or contained in Christ's demand that men should believe (Augustine, Lampe, Luther, Tittmann, etc.), but, including these and every other form, if such there be, that in which the will of God is made known to man (Grotius, Meyer, Brückner, Westcott), **he shall know of the teaching**—the moral attitude of preparedness to do the Divine will (the emphasis lying on θέλῃ, ' willeth ') putting him into such inner harmony with Christ's teaching that its true nature discovers itself first to his heart, and

through this to his understanding (1 Cor. iii. 14; 2 Cor. iv. 2; v. 11; 1 Thess. i. 5) **whether it be of God** as to its source (ἐκ), or *whether* **I speak from Myself**, with self-devised words and self-assumed authority: cf. v. 30,

18. **He that speaketh from himself** in the sense just explained **seeketh his own glory**, i.e. *the glory which properly belongs to himself* (ἰδίαν, see on i. 41) *he seeketh*, necessarily does so, since what he speaks originates with himself: but **he that seeketh the glory of Him that sent him** (see on v. 30, 41) **the same is true**, which he could not be if he claimed to speak 'from God' and yet sought not God's glory but his own; **and no unrighteousness is in him**, the term ἀδικία, unrighteousness, not being restricted to overt acts of wrong-doing, such as Sabbath-breaking, with which Christ had been charged, v. 18 (Beza, Godet), or lying and deception, for which He was now blamed, ver. 12 (Grotius, Kuinoel), but extended to unrighteousness in general, and in particular to ' self-seeking,' which constitutes the 'inner moral basis' (Meyer) and source (Brückner) of the untruth or lie.

19. **Did not Moses give you the law** —not the law against Sabbath-breaking merely (Kuinoel, Godet) or forbidding murder (Paulus), but the law in general (Meyer, Brückner, and others), moral and ceremonial, which had come by Moses (i. 17), whom therefore their sacred books styled The Lawgiver (Num. xxi. 18; Deut. xxxiii. 21), although a later prophet recognized that the appellation properly belonged to God (Is. xxxiii. 22); **and yet none of you doeth the law?** (cf. Lev. xx. 22; Gal. v. 3)—not the Sabbath law, of breaking which all were rendered guilty by practising circumcision on the Sabbath (Godet), but the law in general, which they violated not simply as all alike sin and come short of its requirements, but in the special sense that they were all alike, leaders and people, desirous of accomplishing His death (Meyer, Luthardt, Brückner). The sudden turn which at this point the Saviour's language takes requires not for its explanation any unrecorded word (Kuinoel) or act (Olshausen) of the Jews, but arises naturally from the situation (ver. i. 13), and is on Christ's part a carrying of the war

into His assailants' camp. **Why seek ye to kill me?** as ye are now doing.

20. **The multitude**, not the Jews(Chrysostom), but the mixed crowd of Judæan and Galilean worshippers, 'the masses,' **answered**, if not maliciously (Hengstenberg), at least unsympathetically, certainly not compassionately (Lange), or only in amazement (Meyer), **Thou hast a devil**, a *demon*, or evil spirit, such as had been earlier attributed to the Baptist (Matt. xi. 18; Luke vii. 33); by which probably was meant that He was the victim of a diseased mind: **who seeketh to kill thee?** The people as yet were hardly conscious of the fixity of that hostile purpose which Christ already discerned was impelling them to compass His destruction; while some amongst them may have been uninformed as to the murderous designs of the rulers.

21. **Jesus answered and said unto them**, to the multitude (Meyer, Luthardt), to the Jews (Ebrardt, Brückner, Tholuck, Godet); why not to both? **I did one work**, the Sabbath healing of v. 8, **and ye all marvel.** Christ's language in vindication of the miracle assumed that this had been the effect of that 'sign' upon their minds: see v. 20.

22. **For this cause** διὰ τοῦτο—not closing the preceding (Lücke, Tholuck, Ewald, Brückner, Hengstenberg, and others) but commencing a new sentence (Meyer, Godet, Luthardt, Westcott), since this harmonizes better with the style of the Evangelist (v. 16, 18; vi. 65; viii. 47; x. 17); not to be connected with 'not that' (Bengel, Meyer, Luthardt), as if the meaning were, 'Moses gave you circumcision for this reason that it is not of Moses but of the fathers,' which is nonsensical; or conjoined with ver. 24 as if the import were 'It is exactly for this reason to teach you not to judge as you do' (Godet), which was not the lawgiver's intention at all; but to be construed with the ἵνα of ver. 23, as in i. 31; ix. 22, 23; xii. 39; where that to which διὰ τοῦτο refers is introduced by ἵνα and at a distance from διὰ (see below) —**hath Moses given you circumcision**, Lev. xii. 3 (**not that it is of Moses**, i.e. of his origination or even first proclamation, **but of the fathers**, having been first enjoined upon Abraham, Gen. xvii. 10, 12); **and on the** (or, a) **sabbath**, should that happen to be the eighth or

legally appointed day, **ye circumcise a man.** Here the fact is simply stated, without any suggestion of such behaviour being wrong—which it was not, in Christ's eyes any more than in theirs.

23. **If a man receiveth circumcision on the (a) sabbath that the law of Moses may not be broken;** which in point of fact was the ultimate end the lawgiver had in view in engrossing the statute of circumcision in his legal code—it was to prevent the previously existing ordinance from being habitually violated as it had been prior to the days of Moses and that even by Moses himself (Ex. iv. 24-26). Our Lord is conducting an argument whose premiss has for its central idea the sanctity of the law. For this cause, that ye may keep the law (ver. 19) in the matter of circumcision,—in other words ' that the law may not be broken,' Moses hath given you circumcision, and for the same reason ' that the law may not be broken ye circumcise a man on the Sabbath.' Well, then the reasoning proceeds :—" if a man receiveth circumcision on the Sabbath that the law may not be broken ; **are ye wroth with Me,** the verb occurring here only in the N. T., **because I made a man every whit whole on the sabbath?** lit., *an entire man sound,* ὅλον ἄνθρωπον ὑγιῆ, *totum hominem sanum* (Vulgate), in contrast to the one member which as it were, and indeed ceremonially and symbolically, was rendered pure and healthy by the rite of circumcision.

24. **Judge not,** either actions or men, **according to appearance,** as ye manifestly have been doing : cf. κατὰ τὴν σάρκα viii. 15 ; **but judge righteous judgment,** or *the righteous judgment,* the one true verdict which every deed or person both admits and demands.

25. **Some therefore of them of Jerusalem.** (see Mark i. 5), who were better acquainted with the plans of the rulers than the mixed multitude who had last spoken (ver. 20), **said,** when they listened to the fearless speech and crushing logic of the Saviour, **Is not this he whom they,** the sacerdotal authorities, **seek to kill?** (see ver. 1, 19) ; meaning, ' of course it is !'

26. **And lo ! he speaketh openly** (cf. ver. 4), **and they say nothing unto him,**

although it is well known they wish to destroy him. **Can it be that the rulers indeed** or truly **know that this is the Christ?** The second ἀληθῶς, ' very,' before Christ (T. R.) is ungenuine and was probably inserted to make the clause resemble those in iv. 42; vi. 14; vii. 40. The people felt it difficult to explain the inaction of the hierarchical party except on the hypothesis that these had positively ascertained that Jesus whose death they had been striving to compass was after all the Messiah.

27. **Howbeit**—meaning, if that is the belief now restraining them they must be wrong, since **we know** and everybody knows **this man whence he is,** exactly as the Galileans said they knew (vi. 42) ; understanding not merely the birth-place, Nazareth as they supposed, since they also were acquainted with the birthplace of Messiah (ver. 42), but also the parentage (vi. 42), the father, the mother, the family (Matt. xiii. 55) : **but when the Christ cometh, no one knoweth whence He is,** i.e. none will be acquainted with His lineage and descent, though the place of His nativity will be known (ver. 42). The popular belief here mentioned, though incapable of historical verification, is perfectly credible, and may have been suggested by such passages of the O. T. as pointed to a mysterious and heavenly origin for Messiah (Ps. cx. 4 ; Is. liii. 2, 8 ; Dan. vii. 13 ; Mic. v. 2 ; Heb. vii. 3). Justin Martyr states that according to Jewish opinion the Messiah should be unknown to Himself no less than to others until Elias should anoint Him (Dial. with Trypho, p. 226); and a Jewish saying runs that " three things come wholly unexpected —Messiah, a Godsend, and a scorpion" (Sanhedr. 97 a). " In the Targum on Micah iv. 8, it is assumed that He is already present, but *still concealed,* and that because of the sins of the people.. In later writers is found the view that He would proceed from Rome"(Schürer, The Jewish People in the time of Christ, div. II. vol. ii. § 29).

28. **Jesus therefore,** responding to their exclamation, **cried in the temple,** as the Baptist had done in the wilderness (i. 15),—the verb (occurring only here and in ver. 37 ; i. 15 ; xii. 44) in-

dicating intensity, earnestness, and elevation of manner, *clamores quos edidit magnas habuere causas* (Bengel) ; and the clause 'in the temple' perhaps pointing to a different part of the edifice from that in which the former words were spoken,—teaching and saying, not interrogatively (Grotius, Lampe, Kuinoel, Luthardt, Ewald), but categorically, and not in irony (Calvin, Tholuck, Olshausen, Lücke, B. Crusius, Godet), since it is doubtful if Christ ever employed this manner of speech, *Ironia nunquam usum invenias dominum* (Bengel), but in simple earnest (Brückner, Lange, Meyer, Westcott, and others) : Ye both know Me, and know whence I am, so far as outward appearance, earthly history, or corporeal nature is concerned ; and with the force of 'and yet,' meaning, 'notwithstanding this human origin which ye correctly enough, so far as appearances go, assign to me, there is something ye do not know,'—viz., that I am not come of Myself, the words alluding to His mission which He declares had not been self-assumed (see on v. 30, and cf. viii. 42), rather than to His higher nature, although the verb assumes the fact of His pre-existence, as also does the clause following ; but He that sent Me (see on iii. 17) is true, not veracious (Lampe, Luther, B. Crusius, Stier, Ewald): but real, corresponding to the idea of a sender : cf. i. 9 ; iv. 23 ; vi. 32 (Meyer, Brückner, Luthardt, Westcott), i.e. my *true* sending is from another whom ye know not : see on iv. 22, and cf. viii. 19. "The real living God who had sent the real living Christ they knew not" (Lange).

29. I, ἐγώ, as opposed to you, ὑμεῖς, know Him (see viii. 55); because not 'that' (De Wette) I am from Him, My being takes its point of departure, derives its origin from Him : see xvi. 27 ; xvii. 8 ; and cf. viii. 42 ; xvi. 28, (where ἐκ is used), and He sent Me. My mission rests on My antecedent community of essence with Him. To assert that here the Evangelist "has introduced his own view of Jesus' heavenly origin" (Weiss) is misleading, since the Evangelist's view was not different from that of Jesus.

30. They, the Jews (ver. 1), the rulers (ver. 26), who doubtless formed part of the 'some of them of Jerusalem' mentioned as forming Christ's audience (ver. 25), and to whom it is probable the last words were chiefly directed, sought therefore because He had so unmistakably and emphatically asserted His Divine origin and mission, to take Him (cf. ver. 32, 44 ; viii. 20 ; x. 39 ; xi. 57) : and no man laid his hand on Him lit., *and* (yet), as in ver. 28, *no man laid upon Him the hand*, being restrained by conscience (Hengstenberg, Godet), by fear of the people (Luthardt), but principally and primarily by the overruling providence of God, because His hour, the moment fore-appointed by God for such an experience (see on ii. 4 ; viii. 20 ; xiii. 1 ; and cf. vii. 6), was not yet come. See on ver. 6.

31. But, in contrast to the Jerusalemites or leaders of the people above-mentioned, of the multitude (ver. 20) many believed on Him not simply as a prophet (Tholuck) or messenger of God (Grotius), but as the Messiah (Meyer), although as yet their faith was mainly grounded on His miracles ; and they said, *kept on saying*, if not openly, at least to and amongst themselves, When the Christ shall come, i.e. if this be not He, will He do more signs, σημεῖα (see on ii. 11), than those which this man hath done ? lit., *did*, ἐποίησεν, rather than 'doeth,' ποιεῖ (א* D, Tischendorf), the miracles of Jesus, wrought in Jerusalem and in Galilee, being regarded from the standpoint of the future Messiah and accordingly represented as past events. The question implies that no one could do in their estimation more miracles than Christ did ; hence that they believed Him to be Messiah.

32. The Pharisees (see on i. 24) heard, being present in the temple (Meyer), or passing near it, on the way to their accustomed place of meeting (Godet), the multitude murmuring whispering, talking in suppressed tones, whether unfavourably (ver. 41), or, as here, favourably (ver. 12), these things concerning Him, about the probability of His being indeed the Christ (ver. 31) ; and the chief priests and the Pharisees, as the best authorities read (אBDGKLTUX etc., Tischendorf, Westcott and Hort), i.e. the Sanhedrim in its constituent

elements (Matt. xxi. 45 ; xxvii. 62 ; see on i. 19)—although the order ' Pharisees and chief priests ' (T. R.) is by some (Meyer, Brückner) preferred, on the ground that the Pharisees having been "the first to moot the matter" naturally fell to be mentioned first—**sent officers** ὑπηρέτας, primarily ' under rowers' or seamen as distinguished from ' shipmasters'; hence generally 'agents' or 'attendants' serving under the direction of another ; here the beadles of the Sanhedrim (ver. 45, 46 ; xviii. 3, 12, 18, 22 ; xix. 6 ; Matt. xxvi. 58 ; Mark xiv. 54, 65 ; Acts v. 22, 26), **to take** Him, as already they themselves had wished to do (ver. 30).

33. Jesus therefore, either because He knew in Himself what had taken place (cf. ii. 24 ; vi. 61 ; xvi. 19 ; Matt. xii. 25), or because it had been reported to Him by one friendly to His cause, or because He observed the council constables in the audience in the temple and divined the reason of their coming, **said** (1) to the officers, though 'to them,' αὐτοῖς (T.R.), should be be omitted ; (2) to the Sanhedrim, their masters ; and (3) to the assembled multitude ; **Yet a little while am I with you**—afterwards spoken to the Twelve (xiii. 33), with allusion to His then impending death, which however was still six months distant—**and I go** ὑπάγω, I lead (myself) *away, under cover,* out of sight, the idea being that of a still and stealthy withdrawal, without noise or notice (viii. 14, 21 ; xiii. 3, 33, 36 ; xiv. 4, 28 ; xvi. 5, 10, 16 ; cf. vi. 67 ; xii. 11), as distinguished from πορεύομαι, I pass from place to place, I proceed upon a journey, with the notion perhaps of accomplishing a mission (ver. 35 ; xiv. 3, 12, 28 ; xvi. 7, 28), and from ἀπέρχομαι, which brings into prominence the point of departure or the place left (vi. 68 ; xvi. 7) ; see Robinson's Lexicon of the N. T. *sub vocibus,* and compare Westcott *in loco ;* **unto Him that sent Me.** Regarded as a Johannine addition (Paulus, Meyer) on the ground that they both deprive Christ's utterance of its enigmatical character and the question of ver. 35, 36 of its occasion, since it is thought, if Christ had actually so spoken, His enemies could not have failed to understand whither He purposed to withdraw, the words of this clause are nevertheless to be viewed as forming an original part of Christ's speech, as the Jews did not know "Him that sent Christ" (ver. 28), and therefore failed to understand His allusion.

34. Ye Jewish people, rulers and ruled alike, **shall seek me,**—spoken not of a *hostile* seeking (Origen), since Christ says the same thing of His disciples (xiii. 33), or a *penitential* seeking, after Christ's resurrection (Augustine), which does not harmonize with the clause 'and shall not find Me,' but of a *real literal* seeking, not however of Jesus as the Messiah they had rejected (Lampe, Kuinoel, Neander, Tholuck), but of Jesus as one they had persecuted and driven from them, but now wished to return in their time of need (Meyer, Luthardt, Ewald, Brückner, Hengstenberg), the time of need thus tacitly alluded to being that which should overtake the nation in the impending destruction of Jerusalem (Luke xix. 42-44) ;—**and shall not find Me,** or, some authorities omitting ' Me,' *shall not find,* Him whom ye will then wish to see amongst you (cf. Luke xvii. 22, and contrast Matt. vii. 7)—the appalling significance of which 'not finding' in the case of the unbelieving Jews He afterwards explains as a 'dying in their sins ' (viii. 21) : **and where I am,** not 'where I go' (Bengel), as if the verb were εἶμι (= ὑπάγω, viii. 21), which is not used in the N. T., but 'where I am ' (in My heavenly glory (xiv. 3) as I shall be when ye will be seeking Me), **ye cannot come** in order to find Me and obtain My help—a clause again twice repeated, to the Jews (viii. 21), and to the disciples (xiii. 33).

35. The Jews therefore failing to grasp the true significance of Christ's words, **said among** (or *to,* πρὸς), **themselves,** with mocking and scornful irony, **Whither will this man go,** upon what embassy is this pretender (ver. 25) about to proceed (μέλλει), **that** ὅτι (supplying the reason for the question : cf. ii. 18), seeing that, as He asserts, **we shall not find Him? will He go**—asking with μὴ to mark their sense of the absurdity of the suggestion—' He is not about to go, is he ?' **unto the Dispersion among the Greeks,** lit., *the dispersion of the Greeks,* not the Greek-speaking Jews scattered abroad (Lightfoot, B. Crusius), since in the N. T. (xii. 20 ; Acts xiv. 1 ; xviii. 4) Greeks are constantly opposed to the Jews, but the Jews dispersed among the Greeks (see Winer, § xxx. 2) in the various Roman provinces, the representatives of the Gentile world ; **and teach the Greeks ?** either withdrawing Himself from further teaching among the Jewish brethren and confining His efforts to make disciples among the Greeks (Paley), or through the former seeking to ingratiate Himself with the latter (Meyer).

36. What is this word that He said, lit., *what is this, the word which He spake,* **Ye shall seek Me and shall not find Me, and where I am ye cannot come?** "They cannot get away from this saying. They seem to feel the dark, fearful mystery in the words, but are inclined to persuade themselves that it is sheer nonsense" (Lange).

HOMILETICS

VER. 16.—THE TEACHING OF CHRIST.
I. **Its Contents declared.** 1. *Concerning God.* (1) His nature—spirit (iv. 24) ; (2) His character—love (iii. 16); (3) His purpose—salvation (iii. 17); (4) His requirement—faith (vi. 29). 2. *Concerning Himself.* (1) His heavenly origin—from above (vi. 38); (2) His higher being—the Son of the Father (v. 17); (3) His Divine commission—sent by God (v. 37); (4) His gracious errand—to give life to the world (v. 21 ; vi. 51); (5) His future glory—to raise the dead (v. 28). 3. *Concerning man.* (1) Apart from Him, Christ—dead (v. 24) and perishing (iii. 16); (2) in Him possessed of eternal life (v. 24). 4. *Concerning salvation.* (1) Its substance—eternal life (v. 24); (2) its condition—hearing Christ's word (v. 24), believing in God (v. 24), coming to Christ (v. 40).
II. **Its Divinity asserted.** Three sources possible for Christ's teaching. 1. *Others.* Christ might have acquired it by education. But this Christ's contemporaries negatived. He had never studied at a rabbinical school (ver. 15). 2. *Himself.* He might have evolved it from the depths of His individual religious consciousness. But this Christ Himself repudiated (ver. 16). 3. *God.* He might have received it from God. This He expressly claimed, and that not merely as prophets before Him had obtained communications it from the skies, but in a way that was unique (v. 19, 20; viii. 28; xii. 49), as one who had "been in eternity" with God (i. 1), in the Father's bosom (i. 18), who had personally seen in the Divine mind that which He revealed (iii. 11), and been shown that which He declared.
III. **Its Credentials exhibited.** Christ based the claim of His teaching to a supernatural origin on three things. 1. *Its self-verifying character.* It was of such sort that it would infallibly produce in the mind of every sincere and honest person who desired to do the Divine will, and much more of him who for this purpose studiously cleansed his vision by avoiding sin and following holiness, and most of all of that individual who was willing to embrace it and so put it to the test of experience, a clear and immovable conviction of its Divinity (ver. 17). 2. *Its God-glorifying aim.* Had Christ's teaching been an exclusively human and wholly individual creation, it would have inevitably followed the law of all such developments. The bearer and publisher of it would certainly, and quite unconsciously on his part, have exhibited a tendency to glorify himself in its propagation. But the entire absence of this in Christ's case was a phenomenon He invited His contemporaries to observe. Not only did He not pursue the bubble reputation for Himself ; there was not a sentence or syllable in all His teaching that could be suspected of even an infinitesimally small tendency to the glorification of Him the Teacher. The complete absorption of both the messenger and the message in the Divine glory was proof that both belonged to a different category from human messengers and messages. 3. *Its sinless bearer.* This followed as an obvious deduction from the preceding. A messenger whose devotion to Him that sent him was perfect as Christ's was could not be other than sinless. But if the messenger was sinless there could

be no unveracity either in His message or in what he said concerning it. Hence if such a messenger affirmed of his message that it was divine as to its origin and contents, that affirmation must be true.

Lessons. 1. The marvellous in Christianity. 2. The insight of obedience. 3. The danger of high intellectual endowments. 4. The connection between truth and righteousness. 5. The sinlessness of Jesus an argument for His divinity.

VER. 19-24.—THE ASSAILANTS ASSAILED.

I. **A Fourfold Fact premised.** 1. *Moses gave the Jews the law*—moral and ceremonial, with its statute against murder, with its enactment about the Sabbath, with its prescription of circumcision. 2. Moses incorporated circumcision in his statute book *to prevent the law, in this item, from being broken,* as it had often been prior to the days of Moses. 3. *The Jews were accustomed to administer the rite upon a Sabbath* if that was the legal day. 4. *They did so that the law might not be broken,* as it would have been had the ceremonial observance been delayed beyond the legally prescribed time.

II. **A Simple Argument conducted.** 1. *The Jews were not wrong in their procedure with regard to circumcision.* Christ does not say they were guilty of law transgression in suspending the Sabbath ordinance in favour of that of circumcision. Christ taught that the Sabbath was made for man, not man for the Sabbath (Mark ii. 27, 28)—a saying which the Talmudists have echoed :—"The Sabbath was given to thee : thou wast not given to the Sabbath" (Stapfer, p. 357). 2. *Christ a fortiori could not have been wrong in His work on the Bethesda cripple.* Did He suspend the Sabbath law on that occasion ? They themselves often did. Had they a good reason for so doing every time they circumcised a man ? He had a better when He performed the miracle at the pool. Circumcision made a member of the body sound and clean, did they assert ? His action had made an entire man, with all his members, clean. 3. *The leaders of the people were wrong in seeking to kill Christ.* This was obvious since He had proved that in healing the man He had broken neither the Sabbath nor the law.

III. **A Necessary Lesson taught.** 1. *Not to judge according to appearance.* Neither men nor deeds can be safely estimated by their purely external aspects. As it is the man's interior that constitutes the man (Prov. xxiii. 7), so it is the motive therein enshrined that forms the act. Appearances are frequently deceptive : cf. Hannah (1 Sam. i. 15) and Paul (Acts xxvi. 25). 2. *To judge according to the truth.* In every instance there is a judgment, of man or deed, which corresponds with truth and justice. This always is the character of the divine (Ps. lxvii. 4; xcvi. 13; 1 Sam. xvi. 7; John v. 30; 1 Pet. ii. 23), and ever should be of human (Lev. xix. 15 ; Deut. i. 16 ; Prov. xxxi. 9 ; Phil. iv. 8) judgments concerning either.

Learn 1. Pretenders to the greatest reverence for divine law are sometimes its most flagrant transgressors. 2. A man may meditate murder in his heart and yet think himself a saint. 3. It is easier to keep the law in the letter than in the spirit, to circumcise the body than to circumcise the heart. 4. The Sabbath was made for man, not man for the Sabbath. 5. Nothing more attests depravity than to hate Christ and Christianity for their practical beneficence. 6. The only physician who can work a cure upon the whole man is Christ. 7. The propriety of sitting in judgment on the judgments we form on the persons and lives of others.

VER. 25-30.—THE ORIGIN OF JESUS.

I. **The Cogitations of the Jerusalemites.** 1. *Wonder.* (1) The fearless publicity with which Christ taught in the temple (ver. 26) startled them— considering that He was already a marked man whom the authorities had determined to remove (ver. 25). Being themselves destitute of moral courage (ver. 13), they had no idea of such fortitude as innocence and truth inspire, knew not that "thrice is he armed whose cause is just" (Henry VI. pt. 2, act iii. sc. 2), and that 'whom God shields' is invulnerable (Is. liv. 17) until his work is done (Deut. xxxiii. 25) and his hour is come (ix. 4 ; Heb.

ix. 27). (2) The manifest timidity of the rulers in not even breathing forth a word against Christ (ver. 26) puzzled them. They had as little comprehension of the essential cowardice of wickedness (Prov. xxviii. 1 ; Job xviii. 7-21), as of the moral majesty of goodness, which often causes base men to tremble in its presence, holds back their hands when these would strike, and makes them "afeard to be the same in act and valour as in desire" (Macbeth, act i. sc. 7). 2. *Suspicion.* Ruminating on the strange inaction of the city potentates, they began to whisper to themselves that something had occurred to change the tactics of these would-be-murderers, that perhaps these had obtained information which convinced them that this courageous preacher they wished to assassinate was in reality the Messiah for whom the nation was looking (ver. 26). The idea however was barely called up when they dismissed it, as one that would not stand examination—little guessing that truth oftentimes presents itself to the mind in such momentary visitations and seemingly involuntary suggestions. 3. *Decision.* The question of who Jesus was they could settle in a moment. (1) When Messiah came no one would be able to tell whence He was, of what lineage He came, from what parentage He sprang (ver. 27), though His birthplace, Bethlehem, would be known (ver. 42). (2) Concerning this man everybody knew not the birthplace alone, Nazareth, but the lineage and parentage as well. Hence (3) this man could not be Messiah, but must only be 'a man' like his fellows. Good logic, it is obvious, is not the same thing as sound divinity.

II. **The Declarations of Jesus.** 1. *A Concession.* Their knowledge of His origin was (1) ostensibly complete—what they knew about His human and historical birthplace, lineage, parentage, family, relations was correct ; yet (2) essentially defective, since they had no acquaintance with His higher nature. 2. *A Proclamation.* (1) Concerning Himself ;—His divine mission :—"I am not come of Myself ": "He sent Me " ; His divine knowledge—" I know Him who is the true sender of Me the sent " ; His divine essence—" I am from Him." (2) Concerning them ; their ignorance of God—" Whom ye know not " ; and as a consequence their non-recognition of Him—" Ye know Me outwardly as to My human personality ; ye do not know Me inwardly as to My heavenly mission and divine nature."

Lessons. 1. The true humanity of Jesus. 2. To know Christ after the flesh only is to be ignorant of Him in reality. 3. No one knows Christ who recognizes not His divine origin and mission. 4. A knowledge of Christ's Father necessary to a true acquaintance with Christ Himself (Matt. xi. 27). 5. It is not possible for wicked men to do all they wish except God wills.

VER. 31-36. THE COMING OF THE BAILIFFS.

I. **A Hostile Embassy.** Its *occasion ;*—the favourable impression made upon the multitude by Christ's appearance and address, (ver. 31). 2. Its *promoters ;*—the chief priests and Pharisees who at the instigation of the latter resolved to take a forward step by despatching a number of their constables to the temple (ver. 32). 3. Its *object ;*—to mingle with the crowd that surrounded the Saviour's person, listen to His teaching with as much show of favour as possible, so as to throw Christ and the crowd off their guard, embrace the first opportunity that presented of detaching Him from them, or them from Him, make Him their prisoner and fetch Him to the council chamber.

II. **An Unexpected Greeting.** Having probably observed the presence of the officers in the crowd and correctly interpreted the significance of their appearance, Our Lord replied to this forward movement on the part of the Sanhedrim by announcing the fact of His approaching departure from the earth, in particular intimating concerning it four things. 1. *It would be soon.* "Yet a little while am I with you" (ver. 33). The increasing hostility of the rulers as well as the fickle and inconstant character of the populace rendered it apparent that the final collision between Himself and those could not be long delayed. The bailiffs in the temple brought the end perceptibly near. 2. *It would be voluntary.* The successful carrying out of their designs on the part of the rulers might indeed in the providence of God be a link in the chain of events that would lead to His departure, it would in no sense be a cause of that departure itself (x. 18), which on His part would be a voluntary going from, as His incarnation had been a voluntary coming to the earth. "Yet a little while and I go" (ver. 33). 3. *It would be a home-going.* Though He foresaw that a death of shame lay before Him (Luke ix. 31) He was not dismayed, but with eyes fixed upon the life beyond, He spoke about His dying as a going home to Him that sent Him (ver. 33). As He never volunteered statements as to how He had come, so neither did He now enlighten His hearers as to how He should go. Simply He would return to the place where He had been before (vi. 62), going back like an ambassador to report the success or failure of His mission, or like a son to the presence of a much loved parent from whom he has been long absent (xiv. 2), though the term 'Father,' afterwards introduced (viii. 16), is here omitted presumably in order to avoid giving undue offence. 4. *It would terminate their day of grace.* His appearance in their midst had been to them a 'day of salvation,' a 'time of visitation,' a gracious opportunity of attending to the things that belonged to their peace (Luke xix. 42). When He should have departed, that season of mercy, for the nation at least, would be for ever closed. When the hour of their calamity approached, as after His withdrawal it inevitably would, they would wish, but wish in vain, to have Him back amongst them, they would seek for Him but should not be able to find Him (ver. 34; Luke xvii. 22). 5. *It would place an impassable gulf between Him and them.* Where He would then be they should not be able to come (ver. 34). Without foreclosing heaven's gate upon the crowd that was listening in the temple, many of whom were probably after His resurrection converted (Acts ii. 41), or upon the individual members of the Sanhedrim, some of whom became obedient to the faith (xix. 38, 39; Acts vi. 7), the words announced that, when Christ ascended to the skies, the day of grace for Israel as a nation would be over, and that for many an individual before Him His departure would inaugurate an eternal separation.

III. **A Melancholy Result.** 1. *Perplexity.* They failed to understand the Saviour's meaning or at least pretended to do so (ver. 36). Considering that the apostles at the supper table were at a loss to comprehend a somewhat analogous expression (xvi. 17), the Jewish hierarchs may have been stating the truth when they declared themselves at a loss to apprehend the Saviour's intention. Yet the language of Christ was plain. But the rulers did not wish Christ's words to have the sense they conveyed to the ear, and accordingly pronounced them nonsensical. 2. *Ridicule.* They endeavoured to make sport of both Him and His words. To-morrow, when He repeats the latter, they will ask if He purposes to commit suicide (viii. 12), to-day they inquire if He contemplates playing at Messiah among the Greeks (ver. 35). 3. *Rejection.* The true reason why they could not understand Christ's words was that already in their hearts they had rejected Him and them.

Lessons. 1. The day of grace to all is of limited duration. 2. Who improves that 'day' so as to find Christ will eventually be conducted to where Christ is. 3. To such as find Christ on earth, departing from the world is 'going home.' 4. They who reject Christ here will not be able to accept Him hereafter. 5. The sayings of Jesus are enigmas to those who do not wish to understand them. 6. Scoffing at good men marks the last stage of depravity.

III. THE LAST DAY OF THE FEAST. 1. TEACHING IN THE TEMPLE RESUMED

Chap. VII. Ver. 37-44

Exposition

Ver. 37. **Now on the last day, the great** *day* **of the feast,** the seventh (Bengel), or more probably the eighth (Meyer, Brückner, Godet, Westcott, and others) day of the feast, although (1) the feast is spoken of in Scripture as extending over seven days (Lex. xxiii. 34 ; Deut. xvi. 13) ; (2) it cannot be shown that the Jews ever designated the eighth day as John here does, the expression which occurs in the Talmud *the last and good day of the feast* (Succah iv. 8) signifying only the last feast day, טוֹב יוֹם ; and (3) it is not absolutely certain that the ceremony of water-drawing to which Christ's language contains an allusion continued longer than the seventh day. On the other hand it may be urged that (1) the books of Moses speak of an eighth day on which a holy assembly should be held (Lev. xxiii. 26 ; Num. xxix. 35); (2) the later times were acquainted with an eight days' feast of tabernacles (Neh. viii. 18 ; 2 Macc. x. 6 ; Jos., Ant. iii. 10, 4) ; (3) in the Talmud the rite of water-drawing is stated to have been practised also on the eighth day (Succah iv. 9). Though not of divine institution this ceremony was of old standing, and had probably lost its original significance, which, it has been thought, commemorated the water-giving in the desert (Exod. xvii. 6 ; Num. xx. 7 ; 1 Cor. x. 4), or was a survival of the old 'water libation' mentioned both in Scripture (1 Sam. vii. 6) and in classical literature (Odyss. xii. 363 ; Œd. Col. v. 482), although the Rabbis based it on Is. xii. 3, and found in it a symbol of the giving of the Holy Spirit (Succah f. 55 c. 1). Fetching water in a golden vessel from the pool of Siloam, situated then as now at the foot of Mount Moriah on the other side of the Temple, a priest bore it up through a throng of spectators towards the forecourt of the Temple. Entering the sacred enclosure by the water-gate he moved slowly up towards the altar, when, mixing the clear water with ruddy wine he poured it out into two cups upon the altar, each of which possessed an opening through which the stream ran away. Then the Levites clanged their cymbals and sounded trumpets ; while the people sang " With joy therefore shall ye draw water out of the wells of salvation." So great was the rejoicing that the Rabbis were accustomed to say, " He who hath not seen these festivities knows not what rejoicing means." The characterization of the last day as *the great day* of the feast may have referred to the peculiar solemnity and exuberant emotion with which this ceremony was performed on this day, if it was then performed, which is doubtful (see above) ; or may have sprung from the circumstance that that day closed the feast and with it the festal season of the year, being kept as a Sabbath with a special sacrificial ritual (Lev. xxiii. 36), and perhaps also, as the day when the people left their booths and returned to their dwellings, designed to commemorate the entrance of Israel into Canaan (Lange). **Jesus stood,** His customary practice having been to sit while He taught (viii. 2 ; Matt. xxvi. 55 ; Luke iv. 20 ; v. 3), **and cried,**— employing a louder tone of voice than usual (ver. 28) ; the two verbs marking the solemnity of Christ's manner and the importance of His communication ; **saying** If the ceremony of water-drawing was not observed on the eighth day, then the moment in which Christ broke silence may have been while the people passed up from their booths into the temple court (Westcott) ; if it was, then it may have been the instant when the water was being poured from the golden pitcher into the altar cups, or, what is more likely, when the shout of jubilation had ceased and a lull had ensued. **If any man thirst,** with true spiritual longing after that which will satisfy his soul's needs and desires, and be to him a veritable water of life (cf. iv. 13, 14), **let him come unto Me** or 'let him come.' The omission of 'unto Me' (א D) makes no difference in the sense, since, if they stand not in the text, they must be supplied in the thought. Christ compares Himself to the rock in the wilderness (1 Cor. x. 4), as already He had likened Himself to the brazen serpent (iii. 14, 15). As the people in the desert flocked towards the smitten rock and drank, so Christ invites men to come towards (πρὸς) Him (vi. 35) **and drink,** the water of life which flows from Him (cf. Rev. xxii. 17). The construction which connects πινέτω, 'drink,' with 'he that believeth,' ver. 38 (Stier), is to be rejected as harsh (Bengel) ; but *see below.*

38. **He that believeth on Me**—best taken as a nom. absol. (vi. 39), and understood as defining what is meant by 'coming' (vi. 36, 37) ; **as the Scripture hath said**—to be conjoined not

with the antecedent clause, as if the sense were 'he that believeth truly' or 'in accordance with Scripture' (Chrysostom) — an unusual expression; but with the succeeding clause in which the Scripture saying is particularized. Though not occurring in any part of O. T. Scripture as presently known, the quotation is not to be sought for in a lost writing either apocryphal or canonical (Ewald), but viewed as a free rendering of the spirit of different passages (Meyer, Brückner, Luthardt, Godet, and others), as e.g. Is. xii. 3; xliv. 3; lviii. 11; Joel iv. 18; Zech. xiv. 8: Ezek. xlvii. 1, 12—**Out of his,** not Christ's (Bengel, Stier, Gess), but the believer's (yet *see note* at the end of the verse) **belly**—κοιλία, used in the LXX. (Job xv. 35; Prov. xx. 27) and in the Apocrypha (Sir. xix. 12; li. 21) for the interior of man, 'the inner man,' the heart, having obviously in this place the same significance—**shall flow forth,** as from the smitten rock (Ex. xvii. 6; Num. xx. 11), as from the golden pitcher in the ceremony of the water-drawing, and as from the temple out of which the poured-out liquid was carried by a conduit or pipe, **rivers**—conveying an idea of abundance in contrast to the small quantity, 3 logs, or 2 pints of water that were fetched from the fountain of Siloam—**of living water,** of gracious spiritual influences proceeding from the Holy Spirit. The notion is that the living water bestowed by Christ upon the believer should not only be in him, the believer, a well of water springing up unto eternal life (iv. 14), but should issue forth from him and upon others in a stream of gracious spiritual and quickening influences—a notion which was realized generally in the Pentecostal church when the Spirit had been poured out upon it by the glorified Jesus (Acts ii. 17, 47), and is still being realized particularly in the individual believer who, himself a partaker of eternal life, becomes a means of transmitting it to others (Matt. v. 16: Phil. ii. 15). The peculiar metaphor of 'water flowing forth from the belly,' supposed to have been suggested by the belly of the temple-hill (Gieseler) or the body of the golden pitcher (Bengel, Lange), appears to have been known to Oriental

symbolism outside the sacred Scripture. A recently-recovered Babylonian seal, believed to depict the disembodied soul as brought up for judgment in the lower world, exhibits the deity before whom the soul (represented by a figure half-man and half-bird) is conducted as " distinguished by streams flowing from his abdomen, while near them are several fishes to indicate that it is water which is delineated." Though in the seal it is the reins of the god from which the water flows, while in Christ's metaphor it is the κοιλία of the believer, yet the correspondence between the two makes it clear that in speaking as He did Christ was making use of "symbolism with which not only the Jews, but other Orientals also were familiar" (see The Babylonian and Oriental Record, vol. i. pp. 55, 68). N.B. The above-given exposition of this verse is that followed by the majority of interpreters, and presents thoughts at once Scriptural and true; but it may be doubted if sufficient consideration has been given to the view (Bengel, Stier, Gess) commonly set aside, which regards the flowing fountain not as the believer but as Christ, and which reads : " And let him who believeth on Me drink, as the Scripture hath said, 'Rivers from His (Christ's) belly shall flow,'" i.e. that believers may drink. Against this interpretation stands as a solitary difficulty the order of the words καὶ πινέτω ὁ πιστεύων εἰς ἐμέ ; while in favour of it much may be urged. 1. It harmonizes with Paul's interpretation of the Smitten Rock in the desert as a symbol of Christ (1 Cor. xi. 4). 2. It corresponds with the passages from O. T. Scripture usually cited, not one of which speaks of the living water of salvation as flowing from the individual who drinks, but either from Jehovah or Messiah or the temple. 3. It agrees with the exposition furnished in the next verse by the Evangelist who represents the Glorified Jesus as the fountain whence the Spirit or the Living Water should flow, and the believer as one who should receive or 'drink.' 4. It derives a measure of support from the fact that in the Babylonian seal above referred to the streams of water are exhibited as proceeding from the reins of the god. 5. As regards the antecedent clause, should it

John 7:38–42

be rendered—'and let him believing on Me drink,' it is not unusual for a verb to be placed before its nominative, or, should καὶ πινέτω be connected with ἐρχέσθω πρός με, for a nom. absol. to stand at the end of a sentence as thus, 'let him come unto Me and let him drink—the man believing on Me' (see Winer, § xxix. 1).

39. But this spake He of the Spirit τὸ πνεῦμα i.e. the Holy Spirit, i. 32, which —οῦ, in the genitive by attraction— they that believed on Him, οἱ πιστεύσαντες (B L T etc., Lachmann, Westcott and Hort), or they that believe on Him, οἱ πιστεύοντες (ℵ,Tischendorf, Meyer),the former describing the faith of the believing as a completed act, the latter representing it as then existing at the moment of their endowment with the Spirit, were to (or, about to) receive, after His return to the Father, xiv. 16, 26; xvi. 7, 13 ; for the Spirit—still the personal spirit, since the art. before πνεῦμα is not indispensable (see Winer, § xix.); and the adjective holy (T. R.) being omitted in accordance with ℵ K T (Tischendorf, Godet, Westcott and Hort)—was not yet given; δεδομένον (B, Lachmann), though not necessary, accurately expressing the sense. The Spirit in its full, final and permanent operation, influence, and efficiency, was not then present when Christ spoke, because it had not then been dispensed, poured out, or given; or, if a distinction be made between πνεῦμα with and without the art., for spirit was not yet, i.e. an operation, manifestation or gift of the Spirit (Godet, Westcott, Milligan and Moulton) had not yet come into existence (than which no better proof could be desired that the personal Spirit had not been then given); because Jesus was not yet glorified, ἐδοξάσθη, publicly exhibited or set forth in His essentially glorious character as the Son of God, declared and incontestably proved to be the possessor of a glory such as was befitting 'an only-begotten from a Father' (i. 14). According to this Evangelist that was done in a preliminary and anticipatory manner by Christ's miracles (ii. 11), an opinion Christ Himself advanced (xi. 4). According to the former it was done in the completest and most convincing fashion when Christ was received up into the glory of the Father from whom

He came (xii. 16); and with this teaching also Christ agreed (xvii. 5). But inasmuch as the cross was the way along which, and the gate through which, Christ passed to His ascension glory, the hour of His death or crucifixion is sometimes represented as that of His glorification (xii. 23 ; xvii. 1). Yet was it not the death of Christ as such that constituted His glorification, but the death of Christ as conducting to His resurrection and ascension. Hence the true connection between the glorification of Christ and the giving of the Spirit lay not in the fact that Christ's atoning death rendered such a giving of the Spirit possible (Hengstenberg), but in this that the exaltation of the Risen Christ furnished all the requisite conditions for the permanent establishment of a Dispensation of the Spirit upon the earth and amongst believers, by (1) attesting Christ to be the Son of God and therefore One who both had the Spirit to give and the authority as well as power to give it, (2.) setting Christ's humanity free from those limitations of time and sense which operated as a barrier and restraint to the free communication of the Spirit (Lücke); and (3) completing the personal consummation (τελείωσις) of Jesus, without which the Spirit's work of "causing Christ to live in the heart of the believer" (Godet) could not have been perfectly accomplished.

40. Some of the multitude therefore when they heard, lit., having heard, these words, i.e. the sayings of Christ at the feast, and not merely this last utterance, said, or, kept saying, This is of a truth the prophet mentioned by Moses (Deut. xviii. 15). See on i. 21.

41. Others said, or were saying, This is the Christ, and not merely the prophet who should precede His coming. But some said, or were saying, What, doth the Christ come out of Galilee? lit., not surely out of Galilee cometh the Christ? meaning 'that cannot be; for (preserving the original force of γὰρ) out of Galilee cometh the Christ?—no, certainly !' cf. ix. 30; Matt. xxvii. 23. On Galilee see i. 43.

42. Hath not the Scripture said that the Christ cometh out of the seed of David, cf. Is. xi. 1 ; Jer. xxiii. 5 ; and from Bethlehem 'The house of bread,' not the town belonging to Zabulon

(Jos. xix. 15), which still survives in the modern hamlet *Beit-lahm*, in the vicinity of Nazareth, but that pertaining to Judah about six miles south of Jerusalem, and situated on a rocky eminence 300 feet above the city. First named Ephratah in connection with the death of Rachel (Gen. xxxv. 16, 19), it afterwards became the ancestral seat of the house of David (Ruth i. 1, 2 ; iv. 17). In the days of the later prophets it was remarkable chiefly for its insignificance (Micah v. 2). It is not mentioned among the towns of Judah in the Hebrew text of Josh. xv., or in Neh. xi. 25. At the present day it is a small town situated upon a saddle ridge connecting two hills, and surrounded by gardens and fruitful corn fields. "It consists of about 100 indifferent dwellings partly cut out in the rock, and contains 600 inhabitants capable of bearing arms, partly Turks and partly Christians" (Robinson, Biblical Researches, vol. i. p. 472). **the village where David was,** i.e. where David was born and spent his youth ? (1 Sam. xvi. 1 ; xvii. 12). That the Evangelist does not rectify the popular misunderstanding as to the place of Christ's birth by expressly stating that it occurred not at Nazareth but at Bethlehem is no indication that he either did not know or denied the whole story of the Bethlehem nativity and Davidic descent (De Wette), but only that he regarded the truth as already sufficiently known from the Synoptical narrations, or that he intended to confine himself to a purely objective representation of the views expressed by the multitude (Brückner, Meyer).

43. **So there arose a division in the multitude because of Him,** i.e. a split occurred amongst those who were more or less favourable inclined, as subsequently happened with those who were out and out hostilely disposed (x. 19) towards Him.

44. **And some of them,** not the officers (ver. 32), but those of the populace who held the last mentioned view concerning Him (ver. 41), **would have taken Him** as at an earlier stage the Jerusalemites would have done (ver. 30) ; **but no man,** not even the officers, **laid hands on Him,** being like the others deterred by His personal majesty, their own fear, and God's hand. See on ver. 30.

HOMILETICS

Ver. 37-39.—THE FOUNTAIN OF LIFE.

I. **A Spiritual Condition described :**—" If any man thirst " (ver. 37). The language presupposes in the soul, whose inner state is thus portrayed, three things. 1. *The existence of an appetite.* Not some souls only, but all have this appetite, as a fundamental and integral part of their being. There is something as necessary for the soul's healthful and happy existence as water is for the body, which something is here declared by Christ to be 'living water,' and by John to be the 'Holy Ghost' (ver. 39). 2. *The perception of a want.* The soul's thirst arises from the lack of spiritual, as the body's from the absence of material, water. As with the body so with the soul the sensation of need may for a season be appeased by a substitute for that which constitutes its true requirement. With souls also as with bodies a state of numbness and insensibility may be superinduced in which the want of living water is not felt (Ps. lxxxii. 5 ; Is. vi. 10 ; xliv. 19 ; Eph. iv. 19 ; Rev. iii. 17). The recognition of this want lies at the foundation of religion in the soul (Matt. v. 3). 3. *The forth-going of a desire.* In addition to the conscious realization of its dangerous and dying condition, Christ ever demands in the soul that would enjoy that 'living water' He bestows, the existence of a definite wish, longing, yearning (iv. 14 ; Rev. xxi. 6 ; xxii. 17 ; cf. Is. lv. 1).

II. **A Gracious Invitation issued :** ver. 37, 38. Accepting the second rendering of the words as at least justifiable, they exhibit Christ as a Fountain of Living Water. 1. *Hidden.* The living water has its primal source in His interior divine nature as the Word of God in whom was life (i. 4). 2. *Flowing.* Besides springing up within the inner divine nature of Christ the living water issues forth from Him as from the Smitten Rock in the desert, that thirsty souls may drink (1 Cor. x. 4). 3. *Full.* The supplies of living water contained in and pouring themselves forth from Christ are inexhaustible. Not brooklets but rivers broad, deep, ever flowing, never resting, is the image Christ employs to set forth the fulness that resides in Him (Ps. xxxvi. 8; Is. xxxiii. 21; Col. i. 19; ii. 9). 4. *Accessible.* The way to Christ is barred by no obstruction, else Christ would never have invited men without restriction to come to Him. Nor is Christ less accessible because of His removal from the earth, since the 'coming' to which Christ summons men is not a physical, but a spiritual, approach, to be performed by the heart and mind through the exercise of faith (Rom. x. 10). 5. *Free.* Christ's invitation is conjoined with no embarrassing conditions or limitations. The thirsty one who repairs to Him is not required to pay for the privilege of drinking at a fountain so glorious or of water so refreshing. Simply he is invited to drink without money and without price (Is. lv. 1; Rev. xxii. 17).

III. **An Encouraging Promise given**: ver. 37, 38. As usually rendered, the words depict not Christ, but the believer as the fountain, whence rivers of living water should proceed. The 'living water' Christ should bestow, and he should receive, would possess at least three distinctive properties. 1. *It would satisfy the soul's thirst.* Otherwise it could not be described as, and would not be, a living water (iv. 14). But this it would do because it should consist of an impartation to the soul of the Holy Spirit, the original, underived, and eternal spring and source of life in the material creation (Gen. i. 2; Ps. civ. 30) and in the kingdom of man (Gen. xli. 38; Ex. xxxi. 3), in the body (Job xxxiii. 4), in the mind (xiv. 7), in the heart (vi. 63). 2. *It would transform the soul into a fountain.* The 'living water' of the Holy Spirit received from Christ would become within the soul "a well of water springing up unto eternal life" (iv. 14). The soul would then and ever afterwards possess in its interior depths a permanent and constantly operating principle of holy being, which would appease its inextinguishable appetite for felicity. 2. *It would cause the soul to overflow in rivers of living water for the refreshment of others.* The truth here stated is frequently insisted on in Scripture (Job vi. 10; Ps. li. 13; Matt. v. 13-16; Acts v. 42; Phil. ii. 15), and was conspicuously exemplified in the wondrous effusion of the Holy Spirit at Pentecost (Acts ii. 4, 41; iv. 33).

Lessons. 1. The freeness of the Gospel. 2. The sufficiency of Christ. 3. The dignity of the Christian. 4. The power of the Spirit. 5. The significance of Christ's exaltation.

VER. 39.—CHRIST AND THE SPIRIT.
I. **The Spirit's Equality with Christ.** Both 1. Divine persons. 2. Eternally existent. 3. Manifested in time. 4. Sources of salvation.
II. **The Spirit's Subordination to Christ.** 1. Dispensed by Christ. 2. After Christ's glorification. 3. Because of Christ's work. 4. To Christ's believing people.

VER. 40-44.—A DIVISION IN THE MULTITUDE.
I. **The Friends of Jesus.** 1. *Convinced in their minds.* They feel persuaded that Christ was at least a prophet; some regarding Him as the prophet who should precede Messiah, others pronouncing Him to be Messiah Himself. Yet 2. *not converted in their hearts.* This, it is feared, is the inevitable inference from the effect produced upon them by the subsequent disclosures Christ gave them (viii. 31-59).
II. **The Foes of Jesus.** 1. *Confident in their opinions.* They had no doubt that Christ was an impostor, and that they had Scripture on their side in treating Him as such (ver. 42). Yet 2. *not courageous in their actions.* They wanted to apprehend Him, but were afraid—showing either that they were secretly not so sure of their position as they pretended, or that inwardly they were cowards, however much they talked like heroes.
Lessons. 1. Conviction is not conversion. 2. Confidence is not the same thing as courage.

2. A MEETING OF THE SANHEDRIM

Chap. VII. Ver. 45-52

Exposition

Ver. 45. **The officers therefore, be-cause they felt it impossible to carry out their mission, came to the chief priests and Pharisees,** or proceeded to the Sanhedrim—the absence of the article before 'Pharisees' probably suggesting that the united body is meant rather than its constituent elements. Though the day was a Sabbath the rulers had manifestly assembled to await the return of their commissioners and, assuming that these could not fail to be successful, to deal with their prisoner ; **and they said unto them,** the hierarchical authorities to the bailiffs ; ἐκεῖνοι, contrary to general usage, referring not to the remote subject ' the officers,' but to the nearest ' the chief priests and Pharisees ' who were the remotest in thought, being those who stood behind the officers and impelled them into activity (Winer, § xxiii. 1): **Why did ye not bring him?** meaning ' why did ye not take him and bring him ?'

46. **The officers answered** with simplicity and sincerity, **Never man so spake !** the clause 'as this man ' (T. R., Tischendorf, Meyer), or 'as this man speaketh' (אּ* D), being omitted in accordance with the best texts (אּᶜBLT, Lachmann, Westcott and Hort).

47. **The Pharisees,** standing forth as the more zealous and active members in the council, **therefore,** listening to the officers' defence, **answered them, Are ye also led astray?** or, *even you* —you ! our menials, whose business it is not to think but to act as we think and command—an expression of surprise at their presumption ; or you ! ' the officers' of this supreme spiritual college' (Lange), indicating astonishment at their being deceived, *are not caused to wander* in your judgments and actions, *are you?* the particle μὴ conveying that they hoped not.

48. **Hath any of the rulers,** the official representatives of law and order (see on iii. 1), **believed on him?** (For a reply to this see xii. 42.) **or of the Pharisees ?** the patterns of orthodoxy and morality. The case of Nicodemus to be presently mentioned shows they erred in this no less than in that assertion.

49. **But this multitude**—spoken with contempt, *this crowd here,* from which you have just come, though perhaps exclusive of the officers themselves—**which knoweth not the law,** lit., *the* (mob) *knowing not the law*—the supplement ' believeth ' (Paulus, Kuinoel) being unnecessary—**are accursed,** not by the law of God which pronounced wrath only against the transgressors of its precepts (Deut. xxvii. 26 ; Gal. iii. 10), but in the estimation of the Pharisees, who do not now impel the Sanhedrim to emit a decree of excommunication against the people (Kuinoel, Luthardt), or declare their conviction that because the people were disposed to follow Christ they were cursed (Ewald, Hengstenberg), but merely splutter forth the scorn they cherished for a rabble who were ignorant of sacred learning, whom they were accustomed to call *Am-haarez,* 'people of the earth,' as distinguished from themselves who were the *chaberim,* 'neighbours,' 'fellow-countrymen,' or educated persons who composed the true community of Israel (Schürer, The Jewish People in the Time of Christ, div. II. vol. ii. § 26).

50. **Nicodemus** (see on iii. 1) **saith unto them,** calling their attention to an instance of their violation of that very law of which they were the custodians, and in the knowledge of which they so highly prided themselves—**(he that came** by night (T. R., with E G H M S etc.) being omitted in accordance with אּ B L T etc. (Tischendorf, Westcott and Hort) **to Him,** Christ, **before** omitted (אּ Tischendorf), **being one of them)** to be connected not with ' came' as if the sense were ' came though he was one of them ' (Meyer), but with

'saith,' meaning 'he, one of themselves saith'—

51. Doth our law judge a man lit., *our law* personified in the judge *does not judge the man* brought before it in each particular instance, *does it?* the answer being 'No' (see Exod. xxiii. 1 ; Deut i. 16, 17 ; xix. 15), **except it first hear from himself,** by sending an embassy to him as they had already done in the case of the Baptist (i. 19), or by bringing him before them as they afterwards did with the blind man (ix. 13, 24), **and know** by listening to his own deposition **what he doeth?** what the true character of his action or conduct is.

52. They answered and said unto him, Art thou also of Galilee? or ' *Thou also of Galilee art not, art thou?* (expecting a rejoinder in the negative)— thou art not a Galilean art thou? They could not imagine a Judæan adhering to a Galilean prophet. **Search**—'the Scriptures,' they mean—**and see that,** or *for, ὅτι* being capable of either rendering, **out of Galilee ariseth no prophet,** or, *a prophet ariseth not,* laying down as a general principle that Galilee is not the home of prophets.

HOMILETICS

Ver. 45-52—THE RETURN OF THE BAILIFFS.

I. **The Majesty of Jesus confessed :**—"Never man so spake" (ver. 47). One almost wishes the officers had indicated what it was in Christ's teaching which arrested them, placed an embargo on their movements, fixed them spell-bound to the temple floor, and whispered to them thoughts of His superhuman greatness and godlike dignity. Perhaps it was the same qualities that from the first had affected Christ's listeners wherever they waited on His ministry. 1. *Openness.* The people of Jerusalem were amazed at the fearless courage and unshrinking publicity with which He confronted high dignitaries of both church and state (vii. 26). No greatness overshadowed Him, no criticism staggered Him, no danger daunted Him. In the presence of the hierarchs (xviii. 20), before a hostile mob (xviii. 5), at the bar of Pilate (xviii. 33), He was ever the same resolute and outspoken preacher of the truth. 2. *Authority.* When the preacher from the hills of Nazareth stood forth to proclaim the acceptable year of the Lord (Luke iv. 16), or to talk about the water of life (vii. 37), men felt they were listening to one who was profoundly in earnest, whose words not merely thrilled with emotion and glowed with love, but were 'winged' and 'living,' were charged with a resistless might, were vehicles of a power that was hardly less than divine. Nor did there appear to be a solitary realm in which and over which that gentle voice (Matt. xii. 19) did not reign supreme ; neither the kingdom of nature (Matt. viii. 26 ; xiv. 32), nor the world of humanity (Matt. viii. 8); neither the empire of devils (Mark i. 27 ; Luke iv. 36), nor the dark Hadean region of the dead (Matt. ix. 25 ; Luke vii. 15 ; John xi. 44). Even the innermost domain of conscience owned His sway (John viii. 9). (See Whitelaw, "How is the Divinity of Jesus depicted?" p. 187.) 3. *Graciousness.* The utterances of Jesus were pre-eminently "words of grace" (Luke iv. 22), which dried the tears from weeping eyes, brought serenity to furrowed brows, infused hope into desponding hearts, and breathed peace upon penitent souls ; and no doubt it was this quality even more than the two preceding that charmed the bailiffs.

II. **The Friends of Jesus silenced.** 1. *The bailiffs rebuked :* ver. 47-49. The brave men were reminded they were only menials who had no right to think and whose business it solely was to carry out the bidding of their lords ;—worthless vermin who belonged to the ignorant and accursed rabble out of doors who had no acquaintance as they 'the great and the good,' the rulers and the Pharisees, had with the law ;—hearing all which we cannot doubt the crestfallen officers slunk away abashed ;—let us hope also rejoicing that they had been counted worthy to suffer for His name (Acts v. 41), and resolving to follow up the favourable impressions they had that day received by learning more of Himself and His mission. 2. *Nicodemus put down :* ver. 50-52. The Sanhedrists indeed could not frown on him as a menial or rail at him as one who had less acquaintance with the law than they—the sequel proved he had more (ver. 51); but they could sneer at his sympathy with the Galilean preacher. In vain did he remind his colleagues that the law under whose sanction they believed themselves to be acting declined to condemn any one unheard, perhaps recalling to their memories that they had acted differently in dealing with the Baptist. They stopped his mouth by delicately hinting he was growing old and did not know his Bible so accurately as he should (ver. 52). Exactly so have Christ's champions in all ages been treated. Attempting to raise a voice in His behalf before kings and counsellors, before magistrates and governors, before philosophers and scientists, before public assemblies and private meetings, they have been met with opprobrium and calumny, with reproaches and sneers, with false accusations and baseless insinuations, when they have not been subjected to imprisonment and death.

III. **The Enemies of Christ hardened.** The Jewish hierarchs having already inwardly determined, if they can, to effect Christ's removal, are from this time forward impervious to everything advanced in His favour, by Himself or others, by one of themselves no less than by one of their officials. If the light that was in them was not by this time darkness, all darkness, only darkness, it would soon be. If not already beyond the reach of Christ's power to save, they were fast drifting towards that appalling condition.

Lessons. 1. The power of Christ's words over honest and sincere hearts. 2. The doctrine of Christ an argument for His divinity. 3. The superior religious instincts of the masses as distinguished from the classes. 4. The certainty that Christ and His cause will never lack defenders. 5. The downward course of those who wilfully oppose Christ.

(3. THE WOMAN TAKEN IN ADULTERY)

CHAP. VII. 53—VIII. 11

EXPOSITION

[Chap. vii. 53. **And they went every man** of the Sanhedrists, if the verse is a continuation of ver. 52 (Lange); but, more probably, of the feast pilgrims in the temple (Luthardt and others), if the paragraph is either as genuine to be connected with ver. 44, or pronounced an interpolation by a later hand (see note at end of section), **unto his own house.** εἰς τὸν οἶκον αὐτοῦ is certainly un-Johannine (cf. xix. 27) and more in accordance with Synoptic usage (cf. Luke i. 23, 56; v. 25; viii. 39; Matt. ix. 8; Mark ii. 11).

Chap. viii. 1. **But Jesus went unto the mount of Olives,** to find there His night quarters as He subsequently did during Passion Week (Luke xxi. 37). The Mount of Olives, *the Har ham-mischah,* of the *Ta'muds* (not elsewhere mentioned in this Gospel), lay upon the east of Jerusalem, from which it was separated by the brook Kedron (xviii. 1). Five furlongs distant and rising to a gentle eminence, it commanded a charming view of the city. Its slopes were well wooded and studded with gardens.

2. **And early in the morning** ὄρθρου δὲ (cf. Luke xxi. 38; xxiv. 1); πρωΐ being the term usual in this Gospel (xviii. 28; xx. 1); **He came again into the temple** (see on ii. 14), **and all the people,** πᾶς ὁ λαὸς (cf. Matt. iv. 23; xv. 8; Mark xi. 32; xiv. 2; Luke i. 10; viii. 47; ix. 13; John xi. 50; xviii. 14), the word ὄχλος being in this Gospel of commoner occurrence (vi. 22, 24; vii. 12, 20, 31, 32, 40, 43, 49; xi. 42; xii. 9, 12, 17, 18, 29, 34) **came unto Him; and He sat down and taught them,** lit., *and having sat down He taught them,* the expression being Synoptical (Matt. xiii. 48; Mark ix. 35; xii. 41; Luke v. 3) rather than Johannine (vii. 28; xviii. 20).

3-5. **And the scribes and the Pharisees** See on i. 24. The former, not elsewhere mentioned in John, are frequently referred to by the earlier narrators (Matt. v. 20 ; vii. 29 ; Mark ii. 6 ; iii. 22 ; Luke v. 30), who employ the combination ' Scribes and Pharisee' to designate Christ's opponents, called by John ' The Jews.' The scribes, οἱ γραμματεῖς (corresponding to the Hebrew *sopherim*, i.e. those occupied with books, *homines literati*), were persons professionally skilled in the Jewish law, to whom was committed the task of transcribing the sacred Scriptures, of interpreting difficult passages, and of deciding cases arising out of ceremonial observance. Many of them were members of the Sanhedrim (Schürer, The Jewish People in the Time of Christ, vol. i. § 25). **bring**, or lead into His presence, **a woman taken in adultery**, her partner in wickedness having probably fled ; **and having set her in the midst**, ἐν μεσῷ (cf. Matt. xviii. 2) ; εἰς τὸ μέσον (xx. 19), **they say unto Him**—whether speaking as zealots who would have executed summary justice upon the faithless wife (Num. xxv. 8), or as witnesses who should cast the first stone at her (ver. 7), or as accusers who preferred an indictment against her (ver. 10), need not be curiously inquired—**Master**, or *Teacher* (i. 38 ; xi. 28 ; xiii. 13 ; cf. Matt. viii. 19 ; Mark iv. 38 ; Luke iii. 12), **this woman hath been taken in adultery, in the very act.** ἐπαυτοφώρῳ, used of any crime (Jos. Ant. xvi. 7, 5 ; Thucy. vi. 38), is here specifically employed of a breach of the seventh commandment. Whether the story mentioned by Papias as found by him in the Gospel to the Hebrews (Eusebius, H. E. iii. 39), of a woman brought before Our Lord " for many sins " was the present narrative or that of Luke vii. 36, 50, or a blending of the two, cannot be determined.

5. **Now in the law Moses commanded us to stone such.** See Lev. xx. 10, and Deut. xxii. 22, in which ' death,' and Deut. xxii. 23, 24, in which ' stoning' is mentioned as the penalty of this sin, the former for adulterers in general, the latter for a betrothed maiden who had become unchaste and for her partner in wickedness. Either therefore in the present instance the woman was one who had proved unfaithful to her vows of betrothal (Meyer, Westcott, Luthardt), or the death penalty which the law left indefinite was understood

to mean, or permit, stoning: cf. Ex. xxxi. 14, and xxxv. 2 with Num. xv. 32-34 (Tholuck, Godet, Ewald) ; although, according to the Talmud, not ' stoning' but ' strangulation' was the customary mode of inflicting sentence. In any case the narrative cannot be set aside as unhistoric (Paulus, Lücke, Baur, De Wette). **What then sayest thou of her ?** or, *thou, then* as distinguished from our lawgiver, *what sayest thou concerning her ?*—this being the state of the case according to the legal code of the country, what judgment hast thou to give, or what opinion hast thou to offer ?

6. **And this they said, tempting, or** *trying,* **Him** (cf. Matt. xvi. 1 ; xix. 3 ; xxii. 35), **that they might have** *whereof* **to accuse Him.** Their action was not a good-natured questioning (Olshausen), but a malicious and hostile catechizing. The insidiousness of the interrogation lay in this that if He decided for ' stoning' He would be open to impeachment as counselling resistance to the Roman law which in Judæa as in other subject countries had reserved to itself the power of the sword (xviii. 31), or as being less mild and gentle than He seemed to be ; while if He recommended leniency He could be charged with traversing the statute of Moses. **But Jesus stooped down, and,** lit., *having stooped down,* **with His finger wrote on the ground.** Whether He wrote the contents of ver. 7, the first clause at the first, and the second at the second, stooping (Ewald, Godet), or not, His object in writing can hardly have been to signify His indifference to the whole matter (Luthardt), His occupation with His own thoughts (Brückner) and consequent inattention to their question (Meyer), or only to hint that He did not desire to give while they did not deserve to receive an answer (Luthardt), or to suggest that He would not intrude into the judicial sphere (Meyer), but was probably designed (1) to arrest their attention by its strangeness, (2) to touch their consciences by its stillness, and (3) to symbolize the judgment He was about to pronounce.

7. **But when they continued asking Him, He lifted up Himself** that He might speak with freedom, directness, and boldness, **and said unto them, He that is without sin among you** The

word ἀναμάρτητος, *faultless,* occurring here only in the N. T., being taken not in its widest sense of absolute purity (Calvin, Baur, Luthardt, and others) since that is not indispensable to a judge, or in its narrowest sense as freedom from actual violations of the marriage law since Christ could not have intended to accuse the whole Sanhedrim of adultery, but in the sense of being not chargeable with the sin of unchastity at least in thought (Meyer, Tholuck, Brückner, Westcott) : cf. ἁμαρτωλός (Luke vii. 37). let him first cast a stone at her, i.e. *let him* take the place of the witnesses and be the *first* to *cast a stone,* or, according to some MSS., *the stone* required by the law *upon her* (Deut. xvii. 7).

8. **And again He stooped down, and with His finger wrote on the ground.** To indicate that He had nothing further to do with the case (Meyer) and was unwilling to speak more (Westcott), or because the accusers neither needed nor deserved further advice (Luthardt); perhaps better, to put these to shame, to allow His shaft time to reach their consciences, and to afford them opportunity to withdraw.

9. **And they, when they heard it,** lit., *having heard it,* the clause "being convicted by their own conscience" (T. R., Tischendorf) being omitted on the authority of A D M U etc., **went out one by one** (cf. Mark xiv. 19) **beginning from the eldest,** or, *the elders,* the senior in years (Meyer, Tholuck, Godet, Westcott) rather than in office (Lücke, Brückner, Lange), *even* **unto the last,** not the youngest, but the *last who went out,* rather than the last or lowest in station, viz., the servants : **and Jesus was left alone,** so far as the company of Scribes and Pharisees were concerned, **and the woman, where she was, in the midst,** lit., *being,* according to some authorities (T. R., Tischendorf) standing, *in the midst,* of the wider circle of the disciples and people.

10. **And Jesus lifted up Himself, and said unto her, Woman** (see on ii. 4), **where are they?** 'thine accusers' being understood, and in some texts inserted (T. R., Tischendorf) : **did no man condemn thee?** *did no one,* just a moment ago, *pronounce thee guilty,* treat thee as such by executing sentence upon thee ? cf. Rom. viii. 3, 34 ;

1 Cor. xi. 32 ; 2 Pet. ii. 6 ; see Cremer, Biblical Lexicon, p. 377.

11. **And she said, No man, Lord.** This was quite true since they refused to cast at her a stone. **And Jesus said, Neither do I condemn thee,** in the sense of adjudging thee to punishment : **go thy way: from henceforth** ἀπὸ τοῦ νῦν (cf. Luke i. 52 ; v. 10 ; xii. 52)— contrast ἀπ᾽ ἄρτι (Rev. xiv. 13 ; Matt. xxiii. 39 ; xxvi. 29)—**sin no more.** This sentence has been pronounced too mild (De Wette), but Christ came not to condemn (iii. 17), His object being to awaken penitence on account of, rather than inflict punishment for sin.]

Note. 1. *Of the preceding section the genuineness has been maintained* (Lampe, Bengel, Kuinoel, Ebrard, Lange, Stier, and others) on the following grounds :—(1) It is found in codices D F G H K M U, which of D dates in all probability from the 5th or 6th century, though its text is characterized by apocryphal additions, as well as in the general body of later cursive MSS. proceeding from the 9th century downwards. (2) It is contained in the Apostolic Constitutions, though whether these cite it as a part of the Fourth Gospel or as a fragment of Apostolic tradition cannot be determined. (3) It occurs in the Vulgate and most Latin copies ; in the Syriac, Ethiopic, and other translations. (4) It is supported by many Church fathers, such as Jerome, Ambrose, Augustine, Euthymius. (5) The incident in itself is by no means incredible. (6) It seems necessary to explain Christ's words in viii. 15. (7) Its removal from the text may be accounted for on the ground mentioned by Augustine that it was deemed prejudicial to morality. 2. On the other hand *its genuineness is contested* (Erasmus, Beza, Grotius, Wetstein, Griesbach, Paulus, Lücke, Meyer, Godet, Westcott and Hort, and modern critics generally) for the appended reasons :—(1) It is wanting in codices ℵ (A) B (C) L T X Δ ; A and C, though defective MSS., yet showing by the extent of their *lacunæ* that they could not have contained this section, while L and T, the former belonging to the 8th, the latter to the 9th century, have empty spaces where it occurs. (2) It is absent from 60 other MSS. of later date, as well as from 30 versions, amongst these the Peschito and the Nestorian. (3) It is not mentioned by Origen, Appollinaris, Theodore of Mopsuestia, Cyril of Alexandria, Chrysostom, Basil, and other fathers. It is marked by asterisks suggestive of suspicion in many MSS. which contain it. (5) It is inserted in different parts of the gospel, as e.g. at the end by 11 MSS., after vii. 36 by 225, or in a different gospel, e.g. Luke after xxi., by 4 MSS. (6) The introduction of the section where it stands in the Fourth Gospel interrupts the continuity of Christ's discourse as reported by the Evangelist. See Exposition, ver. 12. (7) The language and structure of the section are non-Johannine and correspond strikingly with those of the Synoptical narrations, especially of Luke. See Exposition.

3. *The conclusion most warranted* by the facts of the case *seems to be* that the paragraph did not originally form part of John's Gospel, but was inserted by a later hand, after the middle of the 4th century ; having been drawn not from an oral Johannine source (Luthardt), but probably, though not certainly, either from the Gospel to the Hebrews (Lücke, Bleek) or from Papias' Expositions of the Lord's Oracles (Lightfoot, Westcott and Hort), or from an independent oral tradition (Brückner) ; and its introduction just at this point being explained by its relating an abortive attempt to entangle Christ similar to the unsuccessful effort made by the Sanhedrim (Meyer) or by the desire of its interpolator to place it as near as possible to viii. 15 as the best elucidation of that short word (Ewald).

HOMILETICS

VER. 1-11. THE TRIBUNAL OF THE HOLY ONE.
I. **The Judgment of Hypocrites** : ver. 1-9. 1. *The crafty question :*—" Moses commanded us to stone such," etc., ver. 5. The dilemma prepared for Christ by the Scribes and Pharisees was undoubtedly a dexterous contrivance. He must either pronounce Himself against the woman or intercede in her behalf ; while His taking either course would equally suit their design (see Exposition). 3. *The significant action.* " But Jesus stooped down," etc., ver. 6 (see Exposition). (1) Discovering the purity of the Holy One who for very shame, as it were, was obliged to hide the crimson flush that mantled His brow in presence of such wickedness as now thrust itself before His vision. (2) Proclaiming the true character of His mission, which was not to judge men in the sense His tempters desired (iii. 17), but in that loftier spiritual sense of which already He had spoken (iii. 17 ; v. 22). (3) Symbolizing and foreshadowing the verdict He was about to deliver on the case as it stood before Him. (4) Inviting their attention to and consideration of the answer He was now to give. 3. *The solemn verdict.* " He that is without sin among you," etc., ver. 7. (1) The crime was proved. Though Christ was not at all required to assume this and the woman's accusers were quite equal to the task of trumping up a fictitious story and setting forth a deliberate untruth, yet the appearance of the woman and much more her silence furnished proof sufficient that her guilt was real. (2) The law was correctly interpreted. Whatever defect existed in the private morals of her accusers, there was not much wrong with their legal acumen, at least in this instance. If not remarkable for piety, they were distinguished for knowledge of the Scriptures. If bad men, they were good jurists. (3) The judges were disqualified. They wanted the first requisite for playing the part of prosecutors against a fallen woman (Rom. ii. 22). He that would condemn others for a crime ought himself to be free from the crime he condemns.

" Thieves for their robbery have authority
When judges steal themselves,"
(Measure for Measure, act ii. sc. 2)—

and

" He who the sword of heaven will bear
Should be as holy as severe," etc.
(ibid. act iii. sc. 2)—

4. *The baffled tempters.* Stooping again upon the ground Christ gave His words time to reach the understandings and consciences of His hearers ; who, taking advantage of the moment when they saw His eye averted, swiftly withdrew from His presence (1) with conscious guilt in their hearts, "being convicted in their own consciences," and (2) with pride upon their brows, as indicated by the orderly manner of their retirement, "beginning from the eldest even unto the last." Detected, convicted, exposed, ashamed, they are hypocrites still.

II. **The Judgment of a Sinner.** 1. *The guilty woman.* (1) A great transgressor, she had not merely turned aside from the paths of virtue, but perpetrated such a wickedness as God himself pronounces "abominable" (Jer. vii. 9), and man has ever regarded as "a heinous crime, yea, an iniquity to be punished by the judges" (Job xxxi. 11), such a deed as not merely evinces want of understanding on the part of those who commit it (Prov. vi. 32), but also like a fire "consumes to destruction," and roots out health from the body (1 Cor. vi. 18), life from the soul (Prov. vi. 32), substance from the barn (Job xxxi. 12 ; Prov. xxix. 3) and happiness from the home (Prov. ix. 18)—a melancholy exhibition of the frailty and wickedness of the human heart (Matt. xv. 19) ; a profitable warning to all, even to those "whose blood is very snow-broth" to consider themselves lest they also should be tempted (Gal. vi. 1). (2) She now made a candid confession, neither denying nor extenuating her offence, but tacitly acknowledging she had no right to expect a remission of the penalty. Christ asked her, 'Did no man condemn thee ? or cast a stone at thee ?' 'No man, Lord,' (ver. 10) ; which, if it was not penitence in its full flower and fruit, was at least that grace in its presupposition and beginning. 2. *The compassionate Redeemer.* (1) He assumes the reality and greatness of the woman's guilt. The Holy One never makes light of sin, which to purity must ever appear loathsome and heinous (Job xxiv. 5, 6 ; Hab. i. 13 ; Jer. xliv. 4). (2) He conveys to her by implication that He had power to inflict upon her the legal penalty. If her accusers possessed not the quality of heart and life that entitled them to execute the sentence against her evil deed, He did ; if they were not without sin, He was (viii. 46). And the same authority does Christ possess still to judge men's hearts and lives as well as to vindicate upon offenders the majesty of the broken law. (3) He assures her of His willingness not to press against her this power which resided with Him. Though He might have cast a stone at her He would not. A beautiful act of clemency, symbolic of that remission which He was ready then to extend to her soul, on hearing her exclaim, 'I have sinned,' and is ready still to grant to ours on a like condition (1 John i. 8). (4) He adds a solemn exhortation to holiness of living (ver. 11) which it should henceforth be her duty as a recipient of Christ's mercy and forgiveness to carry out, as it is still required of those whom grace pardons (2 Cor. vii. 1).

Lessons. 1. The perpetual obligation of the Seventh Commandment. 2. The depth of human depravity. 3. The power of conscience over sinners. 4. The tenderness of Jesus in dealing with penitents.

4. TEACHING IN THE TEMPLE—(Continued)

CHAP. VIII. VER. 5-9

Ver. 12. **Again** The day after the feast, if the preceding paragraph be genuine (Ebrard, Lange) ; if it be spurious then the last and great day of feast (Ewald, Luthardt, Godet), though this is by no means certain (Lücke, Meyer, Westcott). **therefore** Because 'no man had laid hands on him' (vii. 44), and the failure of the plan to apprehend Him left Him still at liberty (vii. 45). **Jesus spake** with less elevation and intensity than in His former utterance

(vii. 37) **unto them**, the multitude (vii. 43) or the people (viii. 2), among whom the Pharisees mingled (viii. 13), **saying, I am the light of the world** (cf. i. 4). An allusion either (1) to the two golden candelabra which were lighted on the first day (Talmuds) of the feast (whether on the other days (Maimonides) is uncertain) in the forecourt of the women where also the treasury (ver. 20) was situated (Wetstein, Hug, Olshausen, Lange, Brückner, and others), and of which the radiance was so brillant that it illumined all Jerusalem, or (2) to the Fiery Pillar which guided the Israelites in the desert as the Rock furnished them with drink (Godet, Westcott); other and less satisfactory explanations being (3) that the language was suggested by the reading in the temple of O. T. passages speaking of Christ as the light of the Gentiles, such as Is. ix. 1, 2; xlii. 6; xlix. 6 (Lücke)—such reading of Scripture lessons in the temple being an improved hypothesis, although it was customary in the synagogue (Luke iv. 17; Acts xiii. 15), (4) that it was based upon the Biblical conception of God as 'light,' Ps. xxxvi. 9 (Luthardt), and (5) that it pointed to the setting (Paulus) or rising (Stier) sun. **He that followeth Me** in faith, love, and obedience (cf. i. 38) **shall not walk in the darkness of** intellectual and moral error (see on i. 5; and cf. 1 John i. 6; ii. 11); **but shall have the light of life**, the light proceeding from, consisting of and conducting to life: cf. 'the bread of life' (vi. 48), 'the water of life' (Rev. xxi. 6), 'the tree of life' (Rev. xxii. 14). The juxtaposition of the two conceptions 'life' and 'light' in Christ's discourses at this feast accounts for their similar position in the Evangelist's prologue (i. 4); not *vice versa* (Ewald).

13. The Pharisees therefore, having heard this declaration, **said unto Him,** in accordance with a well-known legal maxim, that "no man can give witness for himself" (Mishnah, 'Kethub' II. 9), **Thou bearest witness of,** or concerning (περί), **Thyself; Thy witness is not true,** is not valid in respect of form, and accordingly cannot be accepted as a true basis for judgment.

14. Jesus answered and said unto them, Even if I bear witness of Myself, My witness is true (cf. v. 31), the rule which applies to ordinary human testi-

mony not holding good for me; **for I know** (as in vii. 29) **whence I came, and whether I go**—referring not to His official calling (Grotius) but to His personality, and implying that He possessed a consciousness of both His origin, or heavenly pre-existence, and His destination, or post-temporal return to the Father (xvi. 17). The fact that such self-knowledge belonged to Christ both differentiated His being from that of ordinary men and lifted His 'witness of Himself' out of the sphere to which the current maxims of jurisprudence applied. A self-consciousness like that of Christ's owned the knowledge requisite to enable one to testify to 'self,' and as such could only speak the truth. **But ye know not,** though ye also might have known, **whence I come** ἔρχομαι instead of ἦλθον, because their knowledge of His heavenly origin could only date from the then present moment, whereas His took its rise in eternity, being co-eternal with the act expressed in ἦλθον. The seeming contradiction between this statement and that of vii. 28 admits of easy explanation; this pointing to Christ's heavenly, that to His earthly origin. **or**—ἤ (B D K T U X Λ etc.) rather than 'and' (T. R.) which appears to have been introduced into the text for the sake of uniformity —**whither I go.** See above.

15. **Ye judge after the flesh** (cf. 2 Cor. v. 16), or according to appearance (vii. 24); i.e. ye form your estimate of Me, as of men generally, by having regard to My external sensuous nature, and therefore ye decide against My claim to be of a higher nature and heavenly origin. **I judge no man** either in this way 'after the flesh' (Cyril), according to mere outward appearance as you judge Me (Lücke), or *now*, though at a future time (Augustine, Chrysostom, Westcott), or *alone* (Godet); or indeed in any way, that not being the end or aim of my 'coming," iii. 17; xii. 47 (Tholuck, Meyer, Luthardt, Westcott, and others).

16. **Yea and if I judge** lit., *and if I also judge,* i.e. if My 'coming' and 'witnessing of Myself' in any case be a 'judging,' as in your case it is through unbelief (iii. 18, 19), **My judgment,** i.e. the judgment which proceeds

from Me (cf. 'my doctrine,' vii. 16), is true, ἀληθής, not only as to contents but as to legal validity (ver. 13), or ἀλη- θινή (B D L T X), genuine, corresponding to what a real judgment should be, and not simply a judgment in name or according to appearance ; **for I am not alone** in judging (v. 30), **but I and the Father that sent Me,** are one in every judgment we offer (v. 32, 37)— the figure of speech being perhaps borrowed from the πάρεδρος or assessor who took part in giving judicial sentences (Paley).

17. **Yea and in your law**—*the law which is yours,* which you possess (vii. 49) and in which you boast (cf. v. 45) ; a peculiarly Johannine expression (x. 34 ; xv. 25) never occurring in the Synoptists, which has been regarded as disclosing the Gentile or Christian attitude (De Wette, Tholuck), or hostile and anti-Judaic spirit (Reuss, Baur) of the Evangelist, but which should rather be viewed as spoken by Christ either from the standpoint of His opponents who considered themselves the only true keepers of the law of which they pronounced Him a violator (Meyer, Luthardt), or from His own standpoint as one who knew Himself to be exalted in His higher nature above the law (Godet)—**it is written** (see Deut. xvii. 6 ; xix. 15, which are here freely rendered)—**that the witness of two men is true,** is accepted as establishing the truth—the emphasis being placed upon the word 'men' in order to supply a point of transition to the ensuing argument.

18. **I am He that beareth witness of myself,** *I,* not as a human knower of Myself (Paulus) or as the Son of God (Olshausen), but as an individual, in consciousness of my divine origin and sending (Brückner), *am the* (one) *bearing witness of myself;* **and the Father that sent Me beareth witness of Me ;** *in and through me,* giving to every one who receives my testimony an inward confirmation of its truth.

19. **They said therefore unto Him**— not, Who is thy Father ? since Christ had declared to them that His Father was God (v. 18) but—**where is thy Father ?** as if to indicate that though he claimed to be accredited by the witness of God, of this witness they could discern no trace. **Jesus answered,**

Ye know neither Me, nor my Father (cf. vii. 28), and as a consequence ye cannot recognize in Me the Father's testimony concerning Me (v. 38) : **if ye knew Me, ye would know My Father also,** since in and through Me alone can the Father be understood : cf. xiv. 9 ; xvi. 3.

20. **These words spake He in the treasury,** or the place containing the treasure, one of the courts of the temple (Neh. x. 37, 38 ; xiii. 4-8)—according to the Talmudists the court of women, the most public part of the sacred edifice, where stood 13 chests called from their shape 'rams' horns,' *shopharoth,* into which the worshippers cast their offerings (Mark xii. 41 ; Luke xxi. 1. See Stapfer, Palestine in the Time of Christ, p. 411)—**as He taught** (lit., *teaching*) **in the temple,** the particular locality being specified because of the remark which follows : **and no man took Him,** although some desired to do so (vii. 44); **because His hour was not yet come.** See on vii. 30.

21. **He said therefore again unto them,** whether on the same (Origen, Lange, Godet) or a following (Meyer, Ewald) day and in the same or a different part of the temple, cannot be determined—**I go away and ye shall seek Me** (see on vii. 33, 34) **and shall die,** not on account of (Hengstenberg) but **in your sin,** in your state of condemnation and internal depravity which shall not have been removed through believing upon Me (ix. 41 ; cf. iii. 18) ; ἀμαρτία, 'sin,' being here used in the singular to indicate not the one root sin of unbelief (Lampe, Kuinoel), but the collective idea of sin as an essential unity (cf. i. 29 ; ix. 41) notwithstanding its manifoldness of form and expression (ver. 24) : **whither I go ye cannot come.** Cf. vii. 34. Here the 'cannot' is absolute ; applied to the disciples (xiii. 36 ; xiv. 3), as the context shows, it is only for a season.

22. **The Jews therefore said,** not in concern and fear for Him (Ewald) but in impious and sarcastic mockery at Him, **Will he kill himself?** i.e. commit suicide and so depart "to the darkest place in Hades" (Jos. Wars, iii. 8, 5), **that he saith, Whither I go ye cannot come?** The substitution of ὑπάγω for εἰμί (vii. 34) may have lent countenance in their eyes to the notion of self-

murder. If this supposition was correct He was also correct in adding, 'Ye cannot come,' as they would certainly never think of exchanging Abraham's bosom (Luke xvi. 26) for fellowship with Him in Gehenna.

23. **And He said unto them,** without noticing their impertinence and scorn, simply calling their attention to the infinite chasm of a moral and spiritual kind which already parted them from Him, **Ye are from beneath; I am from above :** ἐκ τῶν κάτω, *from the things below,* and ἐκ τῶν ἄνω, *from the things above,* placing in contrast the lower, earthly, sensuous, not necessarily diabolic (Lange), realm from which they derive the principles of their being, and the upper, heavenly and spiritual, region from which He proceeds (cf. iii. 31 ; Col. iii. 1, 2 ; Phil. iii. 14). **Ye are of this world ; I am not of this world.** The same antithesis presented in another form. They had their roots in, and drew their life from, the present transitory and sinful order of things : He did not. Thus in negative terms He asserted His super-terrestrial, heavenly and divine, origin and essence : cf. xviii. 36.

24. **I said therefore unto you, that ye shall die in your sins :** the emphasis laid upon 'sin' in ver. 21 being here transferred to 'die' as if to accentuate the inevitable issue of such a quality of being as they possessed ; **for except ye believe that I am** *he,* or *that I am,* (cf. ver. 28, 58), not merely the Messiah, iv. 26 (Ewald, Meyer, Brückner, Godet), but the personage I have represented myself to be, the Son of the Father (v. 18 ; viii. 19), the fountain of life (vii. 38), the light of the world (viii. 12), "in short, the entire full salvation which formed the contents of all God's promises, the hope and the belief of Israel from the very beginning" (Luthardt), **ye shall die in your sins**—faith in Me being the only way of escaping from condemnation and death (iii. 18, 36).

25. **They said therefore unto Him,** pertly and contemptuously (Meyer, Luthardt), though perhaps also craftily and slyly (Lange), desiring an explanation of the elliptical 'I am,' **Who art thou?** or, *Thou, who art* thou ? a depreciatory interrogation, in reply to which **Jesus said unto them, Even that which**

I have also spoken unto you from the beginning. A *crux interpretum.* 1. Regarded as a *question* the words have been translated :—(1) How, or why, is it that I even speak to you at all ? (Chrysostom, Lücke, Ewald, Westcott) ; or (2) what I from the very beginning also say to you, do you ask ? (Meyer, Hilgenfeld). 2. Viewed as *a declaration,* they have been explained as meaning :—(1) 'The beginning,' i.e. Me, the Word, believe, because I also speak to you (Augustine, Vulgate, Lampe) ; (2) what I said to you from the beginning, as in Herod. i. 9, 1 (Calvin, Grotius, B. Crusius, Tholuck); (3) to begin with, the chief thing, first of all I am that which I am saying to you (De Wette, Brückner, Luthardt) ; (4) absolutely, essentially, wholly I am what I even speak to you (Winer, Godet). 3. Connected with the ensuing clause they have been interpreted as saying—"In the first place, since I speak to you, I have many things to speak," etc. (Bengel, Olshausen, Hofmann) ; but as this interpretation makes Christ leave His interlocutors without a reply to their question it may be set aside. The choice seems to lie between the first and second methods of exposition. Of the two examples given of the former method that marked (1) is perhaps to be preferred to that marked (2), as less complicated besides leaving ἀρχὴν in its right place, though it is doubtful if ἀρχὴν ever signifies 'at all' when not followed by a negative (see Liddell and Scott's Greek Lexicon, *sub* ἀρχή). But the context scarcely requires, even if it admits, a departure from the positive form of expression (see Winer, § liv. 1) ; and of the four proposed renderings under this method preference must be given to (4), since (1) is artificial, (2) besides being inaccurate as to fact would most likely have demanded a different place for ἀρχὴν and a different tense of the verb, e.g. λελάληκα, and (3) would have required a different verb, λέγω instead of λαλῶ. (See Buttmann's Larger Greek Grammar, § 115, 4 ; Robinson's Lexicon of the N. T. *sub voce;* Cremer's Lexicon of N. T. Greek, p. 114.)

26. **I have many things to speak and to judge concerning you,** which however I refrain from speaking and

judging, restricting myself to my more immediate task of communicating to the world what I have heard from the Father (Meyer) ; or, which nevertheless I must speak and judge at all costs (Godet, Westcott) ; or, so that I cannot go on to the final decisive declaration concerning myself (Lange): **howbeit He that sent Me is true** (see iii. 33) ; **and the things which I heard from Him** (see iii. 32 ; v. 30), **these speak I unto the world** not *to* (the .dative), but *into* the world (εἰς with the accusative : cf. Mark i. 39) ; the world being not merely the recipient of Christ's speech, but the subject to which it refers, and the object on which it terminates : see Winer, § xlix. c.

27. **They perceived not that He spake to them of the Father.** This seemingly improbable (De Wette) statement is to be explained not by supposing it addressed to a different section of hearers (Meyer), to the crowd as distinguished from the priests and rulers (Godet), but by holding that clear as Christ's declarations (viii. 16, 18, 19) had been, His hearers had after all not really risen to the grand idea that the personage Christ had been talking of was the absolute Father (Milligan and Moulton).

28. **Jesus therefore said,** because of their failure to understand, **When ye have lifted up,** by crucifixion (iii. 14) to His throne (vi. 62), the **Son of man** (see on i. 51), **then shall ye know,** or perceive, as in ver. 27, **that I am** *he*, lit., *that I am* not simply the Messiah, but the Father's Son, or *that I am* (without any supplement), meaning that I exist, am one whose being transcends all finite limitations (cf. ver. 24), **and** *that* **I do,** if the clause is under the regimen of the preceding 'that' (Meyer) ; or, *and I do*, if the clause is independent (Lampe), **nothing of Myself** (see v. 30 ; vii. 16, 17 ; and cf. xv. 4) ; **but as the Father taught Me** (see v. 19, 20), **I speak these things,** i.e. my speaking is in exact accordance with His teaching.

29. **And He that sent Me is with Me** (cf. ver. 16, 18) ; **He hath not left Me,** or better, *left Me not* **alone**—a negative expression of the previous thought that the inner fellowship between Father and Son which had antecedently and eternally rested on community of es-

sence was not interrupted by His, the Son's mission, but was and had been maintained up to the moment when He spoke ; **for** furnishing the reason (Meyer, Brückner) or setting forth the evidence (Olshausen) of His non-forsakenness by the Father, **I do always the things that are pleasing to Him.** The completeness of the Son's obedience (v. 30 ; vii. 18) was first the indispensable presupposition of His fellowship with the Father in eternity and in time, and second the clear signal that such fellowship was a reality.

30. **As He spake these things,** lit., *He speaking these things,* **many** of His hearers, amongst whom were not a few belonging to the hierarchical party, and probably some of the rulers (xii. 42), **believed on Him** : if not yet in the fullest sense (Westcott) at least in the sense of becoming disciples (ver. 31), with a faith which, though better than that of the citizens on the occasion of Christ's first visit (ii. 11), since that was based on His miracles but this upon His word, was still superficial like that of the Galileans (vi. 66), and required confirmation.

31, 32. **Jesus therefore said,** or *went on to say* (imperfect), opening a new section of His discourse, though whether on the same (Meyer) or on the following (Godet) day is uncertain ; **to those Jews which had believed Him,** or *to those who had trusted Him, Jews*, i.e. persons belonging to the hierarchical party, who were probably included in the 'many' of ver. 30, and who seemingly went so far as to avow their confidence in Him as Messiah ; **If ye abide in My word,** in believing reception thereof, loving obedience thereto, and faithful continuance therein, as the source and sustenance, the guide and rule of your spiritual life (cf. v. 38 ; xv. 7 ; 2 John 9), **then are ye truly My disciples,** and not merely in appearance or by profession ; **and,** on this condition, **ye shall know,** become acquainted with, from personal experience ascertain, understand and appreciate, **the truth** which I announce (i. 17, 18), which I possess (ver. 28), which I am (xiv. 6)—its excellence and divine origin (vii. 17)—" the full revelation of the true nature of things, that is to say, of the sacred character of the relations between God and man as a moral being, and consequently of salvation" (Godet); **and the truth shall make you free,** from the bondage of error, from the slavery of sin (ver. 34), from the necessity of death (ver. 21).

33. They, i.e. the Jews who had just professed to believe upon Him (Bengel, Olshausen, Lücke, Godet, Meyer, and expositors generally), rather than other Jews from the unbelieving crowd (Augustine, Calvin, Lampe, De Wette, Brückner, Tholuck, Luthardt), **answered unto Him,** being offended at the insinuation His words conveyed, **We be Abraham's seed,** of no servile origin like the sons of Canaan (Gen. ix. 25, 26), but of princely descent (Rom. ix. 7), a people to whom belongs the sovereignty of the world (Gen. xvii. 16; xxii. 17), **and have never yet been in bondage to any man** — either through pride forgetting the captivities of Egypt and Babylon as well as the conquests of Syria and Rome (Brückner, Ewald, Meyer); or deeming these as "mere transitory accidents not touching the real life of the people, who had never accepted the dominion of their conquerors or coalesced with them" (Westcott); or thinking of the civil liberty which under Roman rule they at the moment enjoyed (Grotius, Lücke, Godet); or distinguishing between dominion *de facto* and *de jure,* and denying only the latter (Lange, Tholuck): **how sayest thou**—*thou,* "a solitary, if a great teacher, against the voice of the national consciousness?" (Westcott), **Ye shall be made** or *become free.*

34. Jesus answered them, with special solemnity, because of the greatness of their misunderstanding, and the momentous significance of His communication, **Verily, verily, I say unto you** (see on i. 51), **Every one that committeth sin,** lit., *doing the sin* (cf. 1 John iii. 4); i.e. this or that particular sin, or perhaps better, sin in the abstract, 'the sin' being viewed as an antithesis to 'the truth': contrast 'doing the truth' (iii. 21; 1 John i. 6), and 'doing righteousness' (1 John ii. 29; iii. 7), **is the bondservant of sin,** of *the* sin which he commits, or of sin *in general.* The clause 'of sin,' omitted by some codices, and by some authorities rejected (Westcott and Hort, Godet, B. Crusius), should in accordance with preponderating evidence be retained (Tischendorf, Meyer, Brückner, and others).

35. And the bondservant—not a reference to Ishmael (Ebrard) or to Moses (Chrysostom), but to slaves generally—**abideth not in the house for ever,** has no permanent footing in the family, but is liable, as a slave, to be sold and ejected therefrom: in contradistinction from whom, **the son,** not Christ in the first instance (Godet), although the abstract conception has its highest realization in, and ultimately passes over to Him, but the son generally, as distinguished from the slave, **abideth for ever,** is not similarly subject to removal. The general principle thus stated Christ takes to illustrate the respective relations of 'him who does the sin' and 'him who does the truth' to the Household of God. The former, if in the family at all as the Jews were, has only the position of a bondservant; the latter has the standing of a son.

36. If therefore the Son shall make you free—an allusion to the Roman practice of manumitting slaves, making them *liberti,* i.e. really and legally free; which was sometimes done *per testamentum,* the master of the house commanding or requesting the heir, his son, to emancipate the slave (see Adams' Roman Antiquities, p. 33, note 13). The propriety of Christ adopting such an image will appear if it be borne in mind that He was the Father's Son *par excellence,* and that He had come to earth to carry out that Father's will (vi. 38) :—**ye shall be free indeed,** lit., *really,* ἔντως, occurring here only in John, i.e. essentially *free,* and not merely free in appearance (ver. 33): equivalent to ἀληθῶς (ver. 31), from which however it perhaps differs in suggesting the inwardness of this freedom rather than its visible correspondence with the idea of freedom.

37. I know that ye are Abraham's seed—a new turn in Christ's thought, taking its rise from the proud claim of Abrahamic origin advanced by His hearers (ver. 33); **yet ye seek to kill Me,** who also am Abraham's seed (Gal. iii. 16) ;—which is surely a contradiction, proving that you want the moral and spiritual qualities of Abraham's true children, and are only His children in appearance, after the flesh (1 Cor. x.

18), but not after the spirit (Rom. ix. 7, 8) ; as is also shown by the fact, to which your murderous thoughts must be traced back, that or **because My word** (see on v. 24) **hath not free course in you** ; the verb χωρεῖν signifying to give place or room, hence (in N. T.) to go forward or make progress, and here expressing the idea that though they had received Christ's word into their understandings, they were not willing to accord it free scope to operate upon or within their hearts (Lampe, Meyer, Brückner, Godet, Westcott, and others), rather than the notion that it had not found entrance into them (Grotius, Kuinoel, Rosenmüller, Luthardt), or had not obtained room, an abiding place, within them (A. V., B. Crusius), or among them (Lücke, Hengstenberg).

38. **I speak the things which I have seen with *My* Father**, lit., *what I have seen with the Father, I speak* (cf. iii. 11 ; v. 19 ; viii. 28) ; **and ye also do the things which ye heard from** *your* **father** or, *and ye then what things ye have heard from the father do ;* meaning (if 'do' be indicative) that, as Christ by His words revealed His paternity, they by their actions discovered theirs ; —the father in Christ's case being 'God' (Meyer, Luthardt), but in their case 'the devil' (ver. 44) ; against which however it is urged that this latter thought is not yet introduced ; or (if 'do' be imperative) that as Christ spoke what He had seen with His Father (God) so should they do what they had heard from their father (Abraham), i.e. follow the teaching of Abraham, whose children they professed to be ; or from *the* Father (God), i.e. follow the teaching of God in whom they boasted (Westcott). At the same time the phrases παρὰ τῷ πατρί (with the father) and παρὰ τοῦ πατρός (from the father) may be taken figuratively, and the clauses regarded as slightly varying expressions of the popular maxim that each individual carries a certificate of his moral parentage in his words and works (Lücke, Godet).

39. **They answered and said unto Him** with indignation—according to the first interpretation of the preceding verse, repelling the suggestion of diabolic or Satanic paternity which it secretly conveyed ; according to the

second, resenting the insinuated doubt of their paternity implied in His exhortation—**Our father is Abraham.** This was true in the sense attached by them to the idea of paternity which was purely physical, but not in that meant by Christ, which was wholly ethical. **Jesus saith unto them, If ye were Abraham's children,** τέκνα, better than σπέρμα (seed), expressing the idea of moral descent, **ye would do the works of Abraham.** The varying texts of this verse admit of three different renderings. 1. As above, *if ye were,* ἦτε (13 uncials) ... *ye would,* ἐποιεῖτε (א B D L T[5] etc.) or with the unnecessary addition of ἀν (Stephen's and Griesbach's texts) ; 2. *if ye are,* ἐστε (א B D L T etc., Griesbach, Lachmann, Tischendorf, Westcott and Hort) ... *do ye,* ποιεῖτε (Origen, Vulgate, Westcott and Hort, Paley) ; 3. *if ye are,* ἐστε, *ye would do,* ἐποιεῖτε (Tischendorf, Meyer, Luthardt, Paley). The *third* reading is hardly Greek (Paley) ; the *second* is probably the correct reading (Paley, Westcott) ; the *first,* though intelligible, is of doubtful validity.

40. **But now** as things are **ye seek to kill Me** (vii. 1, 19, 25), **a man**— ἄνθρωπον, nowhere else used by Christ of Himself, distinguishing Him from God, asserting the truth of His humanity, though not to the prejudice of His divinity (Beyschlag), *absque praejudicio deitatis* (Lampe), and perhaps suggesting the claim He had on their sympathy rather than on their hate (Westcott)—**that hath told you the truth,** or *who have spoken to you the truth,* **which I heard from God** in my pre-existent state ; cf. ver. 28 : **this did not Abraham :** i.e. Abraham did not seek to kill those who came to him as messengers from heaven, or bearers of God's truth, but on the contrary ever accorded them a friendly welcome (Gen. xviii.).

41. **Ye do,** or *are doing,* **the works of your father.** This mention of another father for them than the patriarch suggested the answer they returned. **They said unto Him, We were not born of fornication.** These words have been explained as signifying that the Jews were not descended like Ishmael from any secondary marriage like that of the patriarch with Hagar (Euthymius, Wetstein, Tittmann)—which however

could scarcely be called 'fornication'—
or from Sarah through another man
than her lawful husband (Meyer, Luthardt); but are probably to be understood as asserting that their pure
Abrahamic descent had been corrupted
by no admixture of heathen blood,
"the children of such marriages being
regarded after the return from the
Babylonian captivity as illegitimate,
as belonging through one parent to the
family of Satan, the god of the heathen"
(Godet), or, better, that their relation
of sonship to Jehovah had not been
rendered impure by the worship of
false gods, in which case they had been
"children of whoredom" (Hos. ii. 4),
but that, as they were physically Abraham's seed, so were they spiritually
God's children (Lampe, Kuinoel,
Lücke, Tholuck, Westcott, and others).
This interpretation seems to be demanded by the next words : **We have
one Father** *even* **God.** By this they
signified not that 'God alone' in
opposition to heathen divinities was
their father (De Wette, Brückner), but
that, spiritually as well as corporeally,
they traced their descent back to one
parentage, as in the latter case to
Abraham, so in the former case to God
(Mal. ii. 10).

42. **Jesus said unto them,** repudiating
their claim to be spiritually descended
from God, **If God were your Father,** as
ye allege, **ye would love Me,** or "be
devotedly attached to Me" (Paley);
**for I came forth and am come from
God,** or ἐκ τοῦ θεοῦ ἐξῆλθον—*ex deo
processi* (Vulgate), *I from God came
forth* (cf. xiii. 3, ἀπὸ θεοῦ ἐξῆλθε ; xvi. 27,
ἐξῆλθον ἐκ (or παρὰ) τοῦ πατρός ; 30,
ἀπὸ θεοῦ ἐξῆλθες ; xvii. 5, παρὰ σοῦ
ἐξῆλθον) ;—alluding not to His divine
sending (Grotius, Kuinoel) which,
besides scarcely harmonizing with the
context whose dominant idea is the
fatherhood of God, is directly referred
to in the clause following ; but to His
coming forth at the incarnation from
His pre-existent state of fellowship
with God (xvii. 5), which seems borne
out by the above-cited passages
(Meyer, Godet, and others) ; if indeed
the use of ἐκ, the Johannine Christo-
logy (i. 13 ; iii. 16), and the argument
of Christ do not point to the notion of
a metaphysical coming forth of the
Divine Son from the Father (Brückner,

Westcott), the incarnation being suggested by the next words, *and am
come* (sc. into the world) or (without
any supplement) *and am here ;* **for
neither have I come of Myself,** ἀπ'
ἐμαυτοῦ, of My own independent and
self-originated action (cf. v. 30 ; vii.
28), **but He,** ἐκεῖνος, 'that' one, God,
sent Me. See on iii. 17 ; v. 36 ; vii. 29.

43. **Why do ye not understand My
speech?** lit., *on account of what do ye
not know,* or acquaint yourselves with,
this talk of Mine, and so recognize it
to be what it is, that of one who has
come from God ? *even* **because ye
cannot hear My word,** i.e. because
through moral and spiritual incapacity
ye are unable to hear, so as to penetrate to the significance of, my discourse, λόγος, which is the kernel or
inner content of my talk, λαλιά : cf.
xviii. 37.

44. **Ye,** who claim to have God for a
father, **are of,** derive your moral being
from, **your father,** lit., *the father*
(according to some texts, *a father*)
whom ye have, or who is **the devil**—τοῦ
διαβόλου (xiii. 2 ; 1 John iii. 8 ; Rev. xii.
9) standing in apposition to, and not
under the regimen of, τοῦ πατρός, as if
the spiritual parent of the Jews were
declared to be 'the father of the devil'
(Hilgenfeld, Volkmar), a personage not
known to Scripture, and never having
had an existence outside the imagination of an early sect of Gnostics (the
Ophites) who "called Jaldabaoth (the
Creator of the world and the God of
the Jews) the father of the serpent"
(Godet, vol. ii. p. 344 ; cf. Neander's
Church History, vol. ii. p. 108) ; **and
the lusts of your father it is your will to
do,** ye *are resolved and inclined to do*
(Winer) or ye *desire to go on doing*
(Paley) : cf. 1 John iii. 8. **He was a
murderer,** a manslayer, **from the beginning,** ἀπ' ἀρχῆς ; either 'from the
first' as a general description (B. Crusius, Brückner); or, better, from the
beginning of human history (Meyer),
with special reference to the seduction
of Adam (Origen, Chrysostom, and expositors generally), rather than to the
murder of Abel by Cain (Cyril, Lücke,
De Wette, Reuss, Paley); **and stood
not in the truth** οὐκ ἔστηκεν (‫א‬ B* D L X
etc., Westcott and Hort) ; *he was
not standing in the truth,* then when
he showed himself a manslayer—

ἕστηκεν being the imperfect of a late-formed verb στήκω (i. 26 ; Mark xi. 25 ; Rom. xiv. 4 ; 1 Cor. xvi. 13 ; 1 Thess. iii. 8 ; cf. Buttmann's Larger Greek Grammar, § cvii. 11, 2 note) ; rather than οὐχ ἕστηκεν (Griesbach, Meyer) or οὐκ ἕστηκεν (Tischendorf), the perfect of ἵστημι, meaning *he stands not in the truth* (Brückner, Meyer, Paley), the perfect being taken with a present signification as in classical Greek (cf. Buttmann, § cvii. 11, 1) ;—not, *he did not continue in the truth* (Augustine, Vulgate, Luther, etc.) as if the allusion were to the fall of the angels (2 Pet. ii. 4 ; Jude 6), or *he did not place himself in the truth*, when God offered him the opportunity (Godet), the truth being some self-revelation of God (cf. Candlish, The Fatherhood of God, p. 170) ; **because there is no truth in him**, or *because truth is not in him*, and was not in him at the beginning when he became a murderer. **When he**, the devil, **speaketh a lie**, τὸ ψεῦδος, 'the falsehood,' as opposed to 'the truth,' **he speaketh of his own**, draws forth his utterances from (ἐκ, out of) those things which are peculiarly his own, and constitute the innermost essence of his being (cf. Matt. xii. 34) : **for he is a liar, and the father thereof.** αὐτοῦ may signify *of it*, the lie (Origen, Winer, Ewald, and others), or *of him*, the liar (Bengel, Meyer, Luthardt, Godet, etc.) ; although the whole clause should perhaps be translated thus :— *When one utters that which is a falsehood he is speaking from his own, because he is a liar and* (so is) *his father*, the devil (Paley), or *because a liar is also his father*, the devil (Westcott).

45. **But because I say the truth**, lit., *but I*, in opposition to the devil, or the liar, *because the truth*, as distinguished from the lie, *I speak*, find a different reception from him : **ye believe Me not**, or *ye do not believe Me ;* meaning that they the Jews, who were of their father, the devil, would have believed Him (Christ) had He spoken to them 'the lie.'

46. **Which of you convicteth Me of sin**—not of *untruth*, *error* (Origen, Calvin, Bengel, Kuinoel, and of others), but of *moral defalcation?* **If I say truth**, ἀλήθειαν, not *the* truth as a whole abstract conception, but that which is true—an assumption Our Lord here

regards as indisputably proved by the preceding fact of His sinlessness which also could not be gainsaid—**why do ye not believe Me?** That they did not believe He had already noticed (ver. 45): now He demands to know the reason : in the next verse He will furnish the answer.

47. **He that is of God**, as to his moral origin and nature (ver. 42 ; 1 John iv. 6), **heareth the words of God**, from whom he is descended (cf. ver. 43 ; xii. 47) : **for this cause ye hear** *them* **not, because ye are not of God :** cf. ix. 16.

48. **The Jews answered and said unto Him, Say we not well**—the phrase obviously pointing to a current reproach—**that thou art a Samaritan**, *that a Samaritan art thou*, for all thy pretended holiness and heavenly dignity—by which they meant not to retort upon Christ for His assertion that they were not genuine sons of Abraham (Lücke, De Wette), to accuse Him of law-breaking (Euthymius), or to reprove Him for His intolerable assumption, that being "the special quality of the Samaritan" (Luthardt), but to characterize Him as an enemy of their race (Godet, Westcott), perhaps as a heretical antagonist of the pure people of God (Meyer, Brückner, Tholuck, Hengstenberg) ; **and hast a devil** —*a demon?* So crazed as well as absurd did Christ's utterances seem that the Jews could account for them only by supposing Him to be possessed : cf. vii. 20 ; x. 20.

49. **Jesus answered, I have not a devil**, or, I am not possessed ; **but I honour My Father**, through the proclamation of His word and the performance of His will generally, as in vii. 18 (Bengel, Lücke), and more particularly by speaking as I now do (Meyer, Godet, Luthardt, etc.) ; **and ye dishonour Me** by your unbelief.

50. **But I seek not Mine own glory:** or, *but* (it is) *not I* (that) *seek my glory*, the glory of being welcomed, believed in, and honoured by you ; i.e. the quest is not on my part (cf. vii. 18) ; **there is one that seeketh and judgeth ;** that one being the Father (ver. 54), who seeks that all men should honour the Son (v. 23), and who judges those who refuse to do so (iii. 18).

51. **Verily, verily, I say unto you** (cf.

i. 51), **If a man keep,** *watch attentively*
(τηρεῖν : cf. xv. 20), so as to fulfil by
obedience (Meyer) and not simply preserve in the heart (Tholuck), **My word,**
as a whole (xiv. 33), including its
several parts or commandments, ἐντολαί
(xiv. 15 ; xv. 10), **he shall never see
death,** lit., *he shall not behold* (so as to
know and experience : cf. iii. 16) *death*
(the opposite of ' life,' the great Messianic blessing) *for ever;* i.e. he shall
never die (cf. v. 24 ; vi. 50). " There is
that in the believer which never dies,
even though he seems to die ; and conversely Adam died at the moment of
his disobedience though he seemed to
live " (Westcott).
52. **The Jews said unto Him, Now
we know,** lit., *have known,* and still
know, from personal observation and
experience, the perfect being used for
a present (Buttmann's Larger Greek
Grammar, § cxiii. 7 ; Winer's Grammar
of N. T. Diction, § xl. 4, a), **that thou
hast a devil,** or *demon.* See ver. 48.
Abraham is dead (Gen. xxv. 8) **and the
prophets** (Zech. i. 5) ; **and thou**—an
obscure and unlettered teacher !—
sayest, If a man lit., *any one* keep **My
word** (see on ver. 51) **he shall never
taste of death.** The substitution of
' taste ' (א A C D K L M S U X Δ) for
' see ' (B), though probably without
any conscious design, had nevertheless
the effect of altering the sense of Our
Lord's saying ; the believer (Matt.
xvi. 28), and even in a special sense
Christ (Heb. ii. 9), ' tasting ' but not
' seeing ' death. The two terms are
not substantially the same (Luthardt) ;
the former—an image borrowed it has
been thought from the death-cup given
to a condemned man (Lücke)—pointing
to the objective act, the latter to the
inward experience, of death.
53. **Art thou greater than our father
Abraham who is dead?** Cf. iv. 12 :
and the prophets are dead: whom
what sort of a person **makest thou
thyself?** cf. v. 18 ; x. 33 ; xix. 7, 12.
54. **Jesus answered,** replying to the
second question first, **If I,** acting from
my own impulse and moved by pure
self-love or vanity, **glorify Myself,** set
myself forth as one greater than I
really am, as one entitled to your
honour, when I am in reality not so,
My glory, even supposing I should
obtain your admiration and applause,

is **nothing,** is no reality but a sham :
cf. v. 30, 31 ; vii. 18 ; Prov. xxv. 27 :
it is My Father that glorifieth Me, lit.,
is the one glorifying me, habitually,
continuously, by the works He em-
powers me to do, by the testimonies
He commissions me to utter, by the
exaltation to which He is conducting
me forward. Hence not only are the
claims I advance true as being practically the Father's testimonies concerning me (viii. 18), but for the same
reason you should have recognized
them as such, since they are the witness
of one **of whom ye say that He is your
God.**
55. **And (yet) ye have not known
Him** become experimentally acquainted
with Him (ἐγνώκατε), as ye might have
done by listening to His voice in the
Scriptures and now in the Son ; **but I
know Him,** immediately, absolutely,
essentially (οἶδα) ; **and if I should say I**
(lit., *that I*) **know Him not** in this
sense, **I shall be like unto you, a liar** :—
alluding to ver. 44 ; **but I know Him
and keep His word,** exactly as I invite
you to keep mine (ver. 51). " By the
last words Jesus asserts that in His
faithfulness to His Father's instructions, He possesses the same guarantee
of victory over death as that which
shall be possessed by His people,
through their persevering obedience
to His word " (Godet).
56. **Your father Abraham,** in whom
ye boast (ver. 39)—answering now the
first of the two questions above propounded (ver. 53)—**rejoiced** put himself
into a state of delight or exultation,
not *in paradise* but on earth, when he
received the promises, Gen. xv. 6 ; xvii.
17 ; xviii. 10 (Grotius, Kuinoel, Lücke,
Meyer, Godet, and others), **to see** ἵνα
ἴδῃ, not because he saw, or when he
saw, or in order to see, but that he
should see (Winer, Luthardt, Brückner), or better *that he might see* (Meyer,
Godet, Lange, Westcott, etc.), the exultation of his spirit having as its purpose and goal that he might see—**My
day** the day not of Isaac's birth
(Hofmann, Luthardt), or of Christ's
crucifixion (Chrysostom), Parousia
(Bengel), or Incarnation (Schleusner),
but of Christ's historical appearing or
earthly manifestation generally (cf.
Luke xvii. 22, 26) ; **and he saw it** not
figuratively when Isaac was born

(Hofmann, Luthardt), but either ecstatically and spiritually, when at some period in his earthly career (as e.g. at the sacrifice of Isaac) his soul realized the certainty of the future appearing of the Greater Seed in whom all the families of the earth should be blessed (Luther, Calvin, Olshausen, Westcott, and others), or actually, through announcement made or sight granted to him in paradise, of the fact of the Incarnation (Origen, Lampe, Lücke, De Wette, Meyer, Godet, and others). In favour of the former view stand (1) its agreement with the tense of the verb, (2) its possibility (cf. Job's vision, xix. 25), and (3) its sufficiency as an explanation, since the soul's discerning is as real a beholding as the body's seeing ; while against it can be urged only that the fact of such a vision is not mentioned in O. T. Scripture. The latter view may claim in its support that it also is (1) neither impossible, since obviously Moses and Elias in glory had become acquainted with Christ's day (Matt. xvii. 3), nor (2) insufficient, but against it can be pressed the fact that it does not so well accord with the tense, which should rather have been present 'he sees' than past 'he saw'—**and was glad.** The sight filled him, on the first hypothesis, with that joy and peace which spring from believing ; on the second assumption, with holy satisfaction in the fulfilment of Jehovah's promise.

57. The Jews therefore said unto Him, imagining that Christ meant He had lived in the days of the patriarch, **Thou art not yet fifty years old,** the number fifty, not forty (Δ, 3 codd. Chrysostom, Ebrard), being selected as that of completed manhood (Num. iv. 3, 39 ; viii. 24), the period of full age, rather than because Jesus looked (Lampe), or was taken to be (Euthy. Zigabenus), or was (the Presbyters of Asia Minor : see Iræneus II. 22. 5) so old ; **and hast thou seen Abraham?** What Christ said was that Abraham had seen Him (or His day).

58. Jesus said unto them, Verily, verily, I say unto you, Before Abraham was, lit., *began to be* or *was born,* rather than 'was' (Tholuck, De Wette, Ewald), γενέσθαι denoting the transition from non-existence to existence, **I am:**— the verb being a timeless present, and pointing to absolute existence, being *per se,* and not to a mere ideal pre-existence (De Wette), in the divine counsel as Messiah (Grotius, Paulus, B. Crusius), or in the divine essence as an impersonal principle (Beyschlag).

59. They took up stones therefore to cast at Him; because they distinctly interpreted His language to imply a claim of absolute equality with God, and as such to be blasphemous. The stones were probably building stones lying in the temple fore-court (Lightfoot). Stoning was prescribed by the law as the punishment for a false teacher (Deut. xiii. 1). Regarding Christ as such, the Jews would have executed on Him summary justice ; **but Jesus hid himself,** or *was hidden;* in the former case the act, which was His own, being performed not by miraculously rendering Himself invisible (Bengel), for which the phrase ἄφαντος ἐγένετο (Luke xxiv. 31) would probably have been used, but by losing Himself in the crowd which His personality had overawed (Meyer, Godet, etc.); in the latter case, the act, which was God's, can only be explained as a supernatural concealment, perhaps by the holding of their eyes (xx. 14 ; Luke xxiv. 16; cf. 2 Kings vi. 18) ; **and went out of the temple.** The addition "going through the midst of them, and so passed by" (T. R.) must be omitted in accordance with the best authorities.

HOMILETICS

VER. 12-20.—THE LIGHT OF THE WORLD.
I. **A Startling Pretension,** ver. 12. Christ claims to be for men a source of enlightenment, a guiding light. 1. *Personal.* As distinguished (1) from the column of cloud and smoke which went before the Church in the Wilderness (Ex. xiii. 21, 22), (2) from the Hebrew Scriptures, of which it is written, 'Thy word is a lamp unto my feet and a light unto my path' (Ps. cxix. 105), and even

(3) from 'My' doctrine which, though light-giving (xii. 36 ; 1 John i. 7), is nevertheless not the source but the medium of that illumination it imparts—" I " am the light of the world. 2. *Spiritual.* The light I afford is not material but spiritual, and not simply mental but also, and principally, moral and religious, being light for the soul and spirit rather than for the body, "light of life" rather than "light of day." 3. *Exclusive.* Nor am I merely one among many lights equally accessible and efficient, but "the" light, the one peerless orb in the moral firmament overarching humanity, shedding light upon the soul's path no other prophet, teacher, or heaven's messenger has ever done or will do, rather myself constituting the central sun from which all who have preceded me have drawn, as all who may come after me will draw, whatever genuine radiance they have had or may have to distribute (xiv. 6 ; Acts iv. 12). 4. *Universal.* I am the light, not of the Jews only, or of the Gentiles exclusively, but of both simultaneously (Luke ii. 32), of the vast world of humanity, and not alone of one hemisphere at a time or of one continent after another, but of both hemispheres and continents at once, with all their varieties of peoples, tongues, and tribes, of races, nationalities, and clans, of ranks and classes and grades. 5. *Sufficient.* The light I communicate will answer every question the soul can need to know with reference to God, Sin, Salvation, Duty, Time, Eternity ; so that 'he who followeth Me shall not walk in the darkness' and shall not stumble in the path he pursues under my guidance and in obedience to my direction (xii. 46). 6. *Certain.* It will conduct him without fail to life—" the inheritance of the saints in light" (Col. i. 1).

II. **A Plausible Objection**, ver. 13. 1. *The true statement.* That Christ in advancing the above claim was bearing testimony concerning Himself, and asking credence for it seemingly on His own authority, was undeniable. 2. *The erroneous inference.* That Christ's witness was not true, or valid as legal evidence, and that as a consequence His astounding pretension was incredible, might have been a legitimate deduction had Christ been an ordinary man—although at times persons are met with, whose moral honesty is so conspicuous and whose spiritual integrity is so unassailable that their naked word affords as strong a foundation for confidence as any further multiplication of witnesses could give ; but as Christ was not an ordinary man—and this His interlocutors well knew, since otherwise they would simply have laughed at His assertions as the ravings of a madman—the ordinary maxim of jurisprudence did not in His case apply.

III. **A Triumphant Refutation**, ver. 14-19. Christ grounded the truth of His utterances concerning Himself upon two things. 1. *His own perfect knowledge of Himself.* The reason why in ordinary circumstances a man's testimony concerning himself is not admissible is that through metaphysical and moral imperfection he has not that complete acquaintance with himself, i.e. with his essential being, which either enables him to pronounce an absolutely true verdict concerning it, or warrants others to accept his judgments upon and concerning himself as unassailably correct. The same absence of complete acquaintance with Him, Christ, on the part of His hearers, the Pharisees, disqualified them from sitting in judgment upon Christ's witness concerning Himself ;—they knew not whence He came or whither He went. But Christ knew both the source and the goal of His being and His mission ; and therefore was in a position to deliver a true testimony concerning Himself. 2. *The concurrent witness of His Father.* If they insisted in His case upon a formally valid testimony—though they were not themselves always careful to arrive at the truth in their judgments, being usually satisfied to judge their fellow-men 'after the flesh' or according to outward appearance (vii. 24), a principle of procedure never acted on by Him ;—still, if they insisted upon the supporting evidence of another witness besides Himself, even that He could furnish, since the witness He offered them was not His own isolated, individual, independent witness, but the witness also of His Father who testified through Him ; and, if they objected that they could not see or hear His Father unless that Father should show Himself, He had to answer that that Father was already present, that, if they had known Him, they would have known His Father, and that just because they did not really know Him, so neither did they know His Father.

Lessons. 1. The pretensions put forth by Jesus Christ inexplicable except on the presupposition of their truth. 2. Objections to these pretensions proceeding from the natural reason discredited by the incompetence of the natural reason to perfectly understand that to which it objects. 3. The adaptation of Christ to the universal needs of humanity a powerful argument for His divinity. 4. The twofold certainty, that out of Christ the world is in darkness and death, and that from Christ it may receive light and life. 5. The impossibility of knowing God in any other way than by studying Jesus Christ.

VER. 21-30.—THINGS OLD AND NEW.

I. **Old Truths rehearsed.** 1. *Concerning Himself.* (1) His impending departure :—"I go away," ver. 21. (2) His heavenly origin :—"I am from above"; "I am not of this world," ver. 23. (3) His absolute existence :—"I am," ver. 24, 28. (4) His divine Sonship :—Exactly as He had ever told them He was the Father's Son, ver. 25, 27, 28. (5) His representative humanity :—He was "the Son of man," ver. 28. (6) His heavenly mission :—He had been sent by the Father, ver. 26, 29. (7) His filial dependence :—"I do nothing of myself," ver. 28. 2. *Concerning His hearers.* (1) A future awakening. They would yet realize their present folly in rejecting Him—"Ye shall seek Me," ver. 21. (2) An eternal separation. They would never be able to come into the land or state and condition of existence into which He was withdrawing, ver. 21. (3) A character description. They were inwardly and essentially different from Him, being "from beneath," and "of this world," ver. 23—a description amply justified by the reception of mockery they had just accorded to the announcement of His departure, ver. 22. (4) A solemn requisition. The only hope of betterment and salvation lay in faith—"Except ye believe," ver. 24.

II. **New Thoughts advanced.** 1. *Concerning them.* (1) Apart from Him they were already in a sinful and perishing condition, ver. 21. This had practically the force of a new truth to them who "as touching the righteousness which was in the law" were in their own estimation "blameless" (Phil. iii. 6). (2) Out of that condition they could not be taken except by believing on Him, ver. 24. To them who sought life by the way of legal obedience Christ taught that a fleckless observance of religious ordinances and even of moral statutes, if only external and superficial, left a man where it found him—"in sin" (Gal. ii. 16). (3) That the inevitable outcome and issue of such a state and condition would be death. "Ye shall die in your sin" (ver. 21), or "in your sins" (ver. 24). "The soul that sinneth it shall die" (Ezek. xviii. 4 ; Prov. v. 22 ; Rom. vi. 23). 2. *Concerning Himself.* (1) His sinlessness—"I do always the things that are pleasing to Him"—the Father, ver. 28 ; cf. Matt. iii. 17 ; xvii. 5, with parallels. (2) His exaltation, which would be by way of a cross (iii. 14) and would be brought about by them—"when ye have lifted up the Son of man," ver. 28. This is the first mention to His enemies of His future glorification. (3) His vindication. Then would they understand who He had been and was, viz., God's Son, ver. 28 : cf. Rom. i. 4.

Learn 1. That old truths stand in need of constant repetition. 2. That old truths received prepare a way for the understanding of those that are new. 3. That new truths can never contradict truths that are old, however much they may seem to do so. 4. That new truths should be only gradually and slowly presented to the mind. 5. That old truths and new mutually supplement and illustrate one another. 6. That both sorts of truth proceed from the Father and the Son as their source. 7. That both have the world and its salvation as their end.

VER. 31-45.—THE TRUE (REAL) DISCIPLES OF CHRIST.

I. **Their Designations.** 1. *Christ's freemen* (ver. 36 : cf. 1 Cor. vii. 22). (1) Their original condition :—slaves of sin (ver. 34). Sin personified as a power by whom the soul is captured and deprived of its original liberty to obey the will of God, to love the truth, do the right, and choose the good. Even renewed hearts are conscious of the existence and operation within them of this hostile force ever striving to lead them back into captivity (Rom. vii. 23). Hence much more in hearts that are unrenewed are the presence and power of sin as an enslaving principle, terrible realities (Rom. vi. 16 ; 2 Pet. ii. 19). (2) Their spiritual emancipation ;—" Ye shall be free indeed" (ver. 36). Brought about by Christ (Gal. v. 1) who, in manumitting those who in His Father's house occupy the inferior position of slaves, only carries out His Father's will (Is. lxi. 1 ; Luke iv. 18), it is effected by the truth, which He at first in His own person proclaimed and still through the gospel disseminates (1 John iv. 14; Gal. iii. 13; Rom. viii. 2). 2. *Abraham's seed* (ver. 37 : cf. Gal. iii. 29). (1) Not physically. At least not necessarily so. In this sense the Jews were lineal descendants of the patriarch. But to belong to the seed of Abraham in the sense intended by Christ one needs not have any external connection with the ancestor of the Hebrews (Rom. ii. 28 ; ix. 6). (2) But spiritually. The real bond of union between the father of the faithful and his true seed is the possession of a like faith in Jesus Christ (Rom. iv. 12), to whose day he looked forward in believing anticipation (ver. 56), and they look back with trustful retrospection (1 John v. 1). 3. *God's sons* (ver. 35 ; 1 John iii. 1). (1) Through adoption. In civil life a slave might be liberated without being admitted to a place within the household of his late master ; but in the life of grace the attainment of freedom is ever followed by introduction into the position of a son (Rom. viii. 15 : Gal. iii. 26 ; iv. 5-7 ; Eph. i. 5 ; ii. 19). (2) Through regeneration. Besides being received into the family of God, believers are renewed in the Divine image (Col. iii. 10), being born of God (i. 13 ; 1 John iii. 9 ; v. 1, 4, 18), by the Spirit (iii. 5, 6, 8 ; vi. 63 ; Rom. viii. 9 ; 2 Thess. ii. 13 ; 1 Pet. i. 2, 22), and through the truth (Jas. i. 18 ; 1 Pet. ii. 23).

II. **Their Characters.** 1. *They abide in the truth of Christ* (ver. 31). (1) As Christ's freemen they value it as the instrument of their manumission (ver. 32), as the emancipating word of the Son who set them free (ver. 37), and as the means of conferring on them larger measures of moral and religious liberty. (2) In so doing they distinguish themselves from the devil who stood not in the truth (ver. 44), and from his children who delight to do the lusts of their moral parent, and, so far from loving the truth, make lies and speak them. 2. *They do the works of Abraham* (ver. 41). (1) To every heavenly embassy the patriarch gave joyous welcome (Gen. xviii. 1). Jehovah's voice was no sooner uttered than it was recognized, believed, and obeyed (Gen. xii. 1 ; xv. 6 ; xxii. 3 ; Heb. xi. 8). So, as Abraham's spiritual seed, do believers "walk in his steps " (Rom. iv. 12), according humble, trustful, loving, and prompt submission to the word of Jesus, the truth which He heard from God and made known to them. (2) In this they differentiate themselves from the seed of Abraham after the flesh —from the unbelieving Jews in Christ's day who not only rejected God's message through His Son (ver. 40), but actually sought to kill the messenger, that Son Himself, and from all who have inherited their moral and spiritual antagonism to the truth as it is in Jesus, who hate the light and disobey the Son. 3. *They love the Father's Son.* This they do as God's children. (1) Discerning in Christ the tokens of a heavenly origin and mission, they embrace Him with confiding affection as one to whom they feel themselves inwardly related (ver. 42), knowing that "the Father loveth the Son" (iii. 35), they also, as the Father's children, love that Son. (2) So doing they contrast with the children of the wicked one. These also imitate their moral parent, who was a murderer from the beginning, and was incited thereto by deep-rooted hatred first to the Son and subsequently to the woman's seed. Like the devil, the Jews sought to kill Christ through hatred of the truth (ver. 40) ; and like the devil sinful men still "crucify the Son of God afresh" (Heb. vi. 6).

III. **Their Privileges.** 1. *Knowledge of the Truth.* Through believing reception of, obedient submission to, and steadfast continuance in the truth, they attain to fuller, clearer, more assured acquaintance with the truth (ver. 37). Following on they come to know by personal experience its heavenly origin, divine purity, and ineffable graciousness, its adaptedness to the soul's wants, its irresistible might to liberate from sin, to sanctify, to enlighten, to strengthen and protect, to comfort and sustain (Hos. vi. 3 ; Heb. vi. 1 ; 2 Pet. iii. 18). 2. *Complete emancipation* (ver. 36). From the first the liberation of believers is complete in the sense that they are freed from sin's condemning (Rom. viii. 1, 34), and enslaving (Rom. vi. 14) power, as also renewed in the spirit of their minds (Rom. vii. 22), and furnished in Christ with all that is needful to perfect their salvation (Col. ii. 10) ; but it is not yet complete in the sense that they are entirely delivered from the assaults (Rom. vii. 23), or the acts (Rom. vii. 19) of sin. The attainment of this is a gradual process which is carried on through the operation of the truth. 3. *Permanent establishment in God's house* (ver. 35). As a slave may be sold and so removed from his master's house, so will the unbeliever, who, though in a sense in God's house, is a slave, be ultimately ejected from the family of the redeemed (Matt. xiii. 42, 49 ; Rev. xx. 15) ; as a son abides ever in his father's house, the object of his care and love, so will the believer never be removed from the household of God (Rev. iii. 12).

Lessons. 1. The dignity of Christ's disciples. 2. The progressive character of the religious life. 3. The safety of believers—the perseverance of the saints.

VER. 46-50.—THE SINLESSNESS OF JESUS.

I. **A Fearless Challenge** :—" Which of you convicteth me of sin ? " 1. *The extraordinary claim.* Obvious that Christ meant this to be an assertion not merely of His freedom from civil offences or from flagrant transgressions of the divine law, but of His exemption from anything and everything that the most religiously pure, morally correct, intellectually penetrating, closely observing, severely criticizing, inwardly hating of his adversaries could bring under the category of sin. It is conceivable that Christ might have been guilty of moral defalcations which were not observable by His contemporaries, or which, though they had been observed, and though in God's sight regarded as sins, would not have been so considered by them. Hence it may seem as if Christ's language did not necessarily amount to an assertion of absolute moral purity. Yet taken in connection with the statement made earlier in this discourse (ver. 29), it is impossible to evade the conviction that Christ intended His words to bear the significance commonly attached to them, viz. that He stood among them as one whose outer walk and inner being were equally untainted by sin. 2. *The sufficient proof.* The challenge remained untaken up. To an unprejudiced reasoner the bare fact that such a claim was advanced by Christ, not once or twice merely, but frequently (vii. 18 ; viii. 29 ; xiv. 30 ; xv. 10 ; xvii. 4), and never under excitement, but always with deliberation and in perfect sobriety of reason, cannot fail to carry with itself an indirect testimony to its truth. The simple circumstance that no sane man would ever think of putting forward such a pretension before his fellows is the best evidence that either Christ was not sane (as the Jews at this time alleged, ver. 48), or that He spoke the truth in what He said concerning Himself. If additional demonstration be demanded in support of Christ's sinlessness, that also may be held as supplied by the fact that Christ's enemies declined to take up the gage which He had thrown down. They hurled at His head abusive epithets, called Him 'Samaritan' and 'devil,' but they did not mention one solitary act or word in which they considered it conclusively established that He had sinned. And to this day the sinless character of Jesus has never been successfully assailed.

II. **An Uncomfortable Question.** 1. *The undeniable hypothesis—* " If I say the truth." Not as if this were problematical, since it was directly involved in His claim to sinlessness. A morally perfect being could neither deceive nor be in error. Hence there was no doubt that what Christ said about His Father, about Himself, about them, was true. 2. *The resulting demand—* " Why do ye not believe Me ? " It is ever felt that unbelief is justified where either the character of the testifier is open to suspicion of deceitfulness, or the substance of what is testified is deficient in respect of evidence. But in Christ's case neither of these conditions was present. On the contrary, the opposites of both held good (1 John v. 9-12).

III. **A Condemnatory Explanation.** 1. *The true reason of unbelief.* Not intellectual, but moral ; not the want of evidence, but the lack of moral affinity with the witness. The spirit that is 'of God' in the sense ·of being morally upright, sincere, earnest, and truth-loving has no difficulty in recognizing God's words. Had the Jews been of this character they would have heard in Christ's utterances the tones of the Father's voice. Were men generally of this sort they would accord instantaneous reception to the gospel of the grace of God. The heart that is not 'of God,' that is whose moral affinities are on the side of evil, cannot and does not hear the words of God. As the eye sees what it brings the capacity of seeing and the ear hears what it brings the capacity of hearing, so the spirit of man discerns only that which it brings the capacity of discerning (iii. 19 ; Matt. v. 8 ; 1 Cor. ii. 14). 2. *The deep guilt of unbelief.* It is not merely a rejection of the Son, but it is also a dishonouring of the Father (ver. 49), who seeks to glorify the Son (ver. 50) by commending Him to the confidence and love of men. Faith sets its seal to this that God is true in so bearing witness of the Son (iii. 33) ; unbelief contests the accuracy of the Father's judgment concerning the Son, records concerning the Son a different verdict from that of the Father, and thus practically makes God a liar (1 John v. 10).

Learn 1. That the weightiest argument in support of Christianity is the holy personality of Christ. 2. That unbelief stands convicted at the bar of reason as wholly unjustifiable. 3. That a growing relish for the words of Christ is a sure sign that one is born of God. 4. That it is easier to hurl hard names at Christ's people and Christ religion than to demonstrate the insincerity of the one or the falsehood of the other. 5. That Christ's people, like their Master, when reviled, should revile not again. 6. That saints should leave the keeping of their honour to the care of God.

VER. 51-59.—ABRAHAM AND JESUS.

I. **The Greatness of Abraham.** 1. *The ancestor of the Jewish People.* "Our father," said the Jews (ver. 53) ; "your father" conceded Christ (ver. 56). It was unquestionably no small mark of distinction to be the natural progenitor of a people so renowned in the world's annals as the Jews. 2. *The father of the faithful.* Abraham believed in God's promise of a coming seed in whom all the families of the earth should be blessed (Gen. xv. 6 ; Rom. iv. 20), and as such became "the father of many nations," the head of a spiritual progeny of believers who will ultimately far outnumber those who shall have descended from his loins. 3. *A conqueror of death.* Christ had assured His hearers that the man who kept His word should never see death (ver. 52). Unintelligible to their carnal minds, it nevertheless signified that in the experience of His believing people, who were Abraham's children, and therefore of Abraham himself who had kept God's word (ver. 40), death in all its essential characteristics was abolished (cf. 2 Tim. i. 10). Though Abraham had died, tasted dissolution as an external phenomenon, as the prophets had done and as all mankind must in turn do (Heb. ix. 27), yet Abraham had not seen death in the sense of experiencing what death is, considered as the wages of sin (Rom. vi. 23), but had evaded it, passed by it, overcome it, surmounted it, and passed away beyond it into a realm of existence where he was then living as an undying personality (Matt. xxii. 32). 4. *A beholder of Christ's day.* Not merely did he exult in the thought that he should, and indulge the wish or hope that he might, see the day of Christ's appearing on the earth, but he actually beheld it—either in vision on Mount Moriah when his soul, looking forward through the dim vista of the future, saw, as if it were a present reality than his mind's eye, the birth of his greater seed than Isaac (cf. Job's vision of the Redeemer in the latter days on the other side of the grave ; xix. 25), or from Paradise, it being in some mysterious way permitted him to become cognizant of the transcendent event which took place in Bethlehem. (See Exposition.)

II. **The Superiority of Jesus.** 1. *Of loftier calling.* Abraham, a prophet ; Christ, a Saviour. Abraham, the ancestor of the promised seed ; Christ, the promised seed. Abraham, the progenitor of Christ (according to the flesh) ;

Christ, the Redeemer of Abraham (according to the Spirit). The Jews exulted in their physical connection with Abraham; Abraham exulted in his spiritual connection with Christ. 2. *Of nobler name.* Abraham, a servant; Christ, the Son. Abraham called the Divine Being 'God'; Christ addressed and spoke of Him as 'Father.' 3. *Of older existence.* Abraham was not before he came into this world; Christ was before Abraham was born. 4. *Of higher being.* Abraham began to be; Christ always was. Abraham was a creature. Christ was the Creator—the great I Am!

Lessons. 1. The supreme divinity of Christ. 2. The power of faith. 3. The certainty of existence after death. 4. The true secret of soul joy. 5. The one object of faith in all ages and for all peoples—Christ's day.

IV. AFTER THE FEAST. 1. THE HEALING OF A MAN BORN BLIND

Chap. IX. Ver. 1-41

Exposition

Chap. ix. ver. 1. **And**—not commencing the account of Christ's proceedings at the feast of dedication (Westcott), but continuing the record of what occurred in connection with the feast of tabernacles—**as He,** i.e. Jesus, **passed by**—lit., *and passing by,* or *in passing* (cf. Matt. ix. 9; Mark ii. 14) through the streets, either on the same day as that to which the preceding chapter relates (Tholuck, Lange), or on a subsequent day (Godet, Milligan and Moulton),—in any case on a Sabbath (ver. 14)—**He saw** observed with marked attention (v. 6) **a man** sitting begging (ver. 8), either by the wayside near one of the city gates (Matt. xx. 30), or at one of the temple doors (Acts iii. 2),—a well-known mendicant **blind from birth.** With this circumstance, which Christ did not require to learn from others (cf. i. 42, 48; ii. 24; v. 6), the disciples might have become acquainted from remarks of passers-by or of the man himself.

2. **And His disciples,** having probably observed the fixed and searching look with which Christ gazed upon the beggar, and perhaps moved with a feeling of pity,—hardly out of curiosity or dogmatic interest, **asked Him, saying, Rabbi** (see on iii. 2; iv. 31; and cf. iii. 26), **Who did sin?** In their belief all suffering had its cause in some antecedent sin—the mistake of Job's friends (Job iv. 17; viii. 4; xi. 6), and a popular notion in Christ's time seemingly favoured by passages of O. T. Scrip-

ture (Deut. xxxi. 17; 2 Sam. vii. 14; Ps. lxxxix. 30-32) and even by utterances of Christ Himself (Matt. ix. 2), but an idea against which Christ declares Himself now as on an earlier occasion (Luke xiii. 1-5). **this man, or his parents?** Not meaning "this man, or," since that is impossible, "his parents" (Lampe, Luthardt, and others), but setting forth, as the only alternatives that presented themselves to their minds, that the man's blindness must have resulted from some antecedent wickedness either of himself or of his parents. In the former case the notion, it is said, is that of sin committed in another body (Calvin, Beza, Grotius), or in a pre-existent state (Cyril, De Wette, Brückner), or in the womb (Lücke, Meyer, Lange, Milligan and Moulton), or of suffering inflicted by anticipation in punishment of after sins (Tholuck, Stier); in the latter case that the iniquities of the parent were visited upon the child according to the well-known law of heredity. The latter notion the disciples might have derived from Scripture (Exod. xx. 5; xxxiv. 7; Num. xiv. 18, 33; Jer. xxxii. 18) ; of the explanations offered of the former none is entirely satisfactory. It is hardly likely the disciples were thinking of such philosophic speculations as the doctrines of the transmigration of souls, and of a pre-existent state which might be known to the Rabbis of the day, but were little current among the common people, while the ideas of embryonic sin, though apparently countenanced by Scripture (Gen. xxv. 26), is extremely improbable, and that of anticipatory punishment of sin is as destitute of support from Scripture as from reason. Either therefore the disciples rejected both alternatives as explanations of the man's blindness and wanted Christ to furnish them with the true interpretation of the mystery (Chrysostom, Ebrard, Godet), or they placed the two alternatives before Christ without exactly understanding their respective bearings on the individual sufferer before them, in the hope that Christ would elucidate what to them was a dark enigma, the connection of this man's suffering with sin (Westcott, Trench). **that he should be, or,** *should have been* **born blind ?** *ἵνα*, expressing more than a mere retributive result, points significantly to a teleological end contemplated by the afflictive dispensation to which the man had been made subject.

3. **Jesus answered, Neither did this man sin nor his parents** (that he should be born blind) ; i.e. the divine purpose in ordaining that he should be born blind was not to requite any sin either of himself or of his parents ; **but it was that the works of God,** i.e. the works God had given Him (Jesus) to accomplish (v. 36),—in this particular instance a bodily healing (ver. 6, 7) and a spiritual illumination (ver. 35-37) —**should be made manifest in him,** not merely, 'symbolically set forth,' as if the physical miracle were not in itself a work of God, but only the picture of a work of God,—in this case the enlightenment of the world (Meyer) ; but 'brought to view,' so that what was previously in concealment and unrecognized is now disclosed and apprehended (cf. i. 31 ; iii. 21),—to wit, the gracious activity of God in behalf of men (v. 17), which had been in operation from the commencement of human history, but was now visibly exhibited in the beneficent mission and work of Christ Himself. Christ's answer supplies the only satisfactory theodicy, or vindication of the ways of God in the distribution of human suffering.

4. **We must work** Or, *it is necessary that we be working.* The pronoun 'we'

(א* B D L etc., Tischendorf, Meyer, Westcott and Hort), rather than 'I,' is employed not as an editorial 'we,' but either because Christ desires to include along with Himself His disciples "as helpers and continuers of His Messianic activity" (Meyer), or because He enunciates a principle applicable to men in general. **the works of Him that sent Me** The Father, who assigns to all men their tasks as He has done to the Son (v. 36). **while it is day** The day not of natural light (Paulus), or of grace (Olshausen), but of opportunity—the image resting on the thought that 'day' is the appointed season for labour (Ps. civ. 23) ; and *the* day referred to by Christ signifying the period of His continuance on earth. **the night cometh, when no man can work.** The 'night,' as the season of rest, will point to the swiftly approaching time of Christ's departure from the earth, when His present opportunity for doing the works of God will be over, and when, so far as these are concerned, He will have entered on an era of repose, though in another sense His activity will not have ceased, but only changed its form.

5. **When**—not 'as long as' (A.V.), *quamdiu* (Vulgate), or 'since,' *quandoquidem* (Lücke), but 'whensoever,' whether now, at any former period, or hereafter, the point, rather than the duration, of time being that on which stress is laid—**I am in the world,** of benighted, because sin-beclouded, men (see on i. 9, 10), the world that walketh in darkness (xii. 35, 46) and is 'darkness' (i. 5), I, the True Light (i. 4, 5, 9), **am the light of the world,** or, *am light of* (to) *the world,* am not merely the exclusive source of light for the world (τὸ φῶς, viii. 12 ; xii. 35), but am light itself to the world (φῶς, xii. 46), so that while I am in the world, it is day.

6. **When He had thus spoken,** lit., *having spoken these things,* **He spat** not on the blind man's eyes as in a former case of healing (Mark viii. 23), **but on the ground and made clay,** or *wet earth, mud,* γῇ ὑγρῷ φυραθεῖσα (Plato, Theæt. 147, c), **of the spittle, and anointed his eyes with the clay.** Not to defy the hierarchy by doing work upon the Sabbath (Ewald), the application of spittle to the eyes of the blind being

one of the healing acts forbidden on the Sabbath (Wetstein, Lightfoot) ; or to make use of the medicinal virtue supposed by the Greeks and Romans (Tacitus, Hist. iv. 8 ; Pliny, H. N. xxviii. 7) and even by the Jews (see Riehm, Handwörterbuch des Biblischen Altertums, art. *Speichel*) to reside in saliva ; or to employ the saliva as a material conductor of His healing power (Meyer, Tholuck, Olshausen) ; or to symbolize the truth that he who would see in reality must first become blind (Luthardt), which, though seeming to have a point of support in Christ's words (ver. 39), is nevertheless far-fetched ; but probably (1) to arrest the blind man's attention to the miracle about to be performed, (2) to test (Calvin), or awaken (Lücke), faith in the man himself, and (3) to enable him to connect the miracle with Christ's person (Godet)—if indeed it be not as safe to affirm that the precise motive of this part of our Saviour's action cannot be known (Westcott).

7. **And said unto him, Go, wash in,** lit., *into*, meaning either ' go *unto* and wash *in*,' or ' go and wash so that what is washed off shall fall *into*,' or as here rendered ' go and wash in' (see Winer's Grammar, § l. 4), or 'plunging bath' as in v. 2, **of Siloam.** Σιλωάμ, חַלֹשׁ, *a sending forth* (sc. of water)—called the waters of Shiloah (Is. viii. 6), situated near the king's gardens south of Jerusalem (Neh. iii. 15) ; described by Josephus (Wars v. 4, 2) as a fountain at the mouth of the valley of the cheesemongers, having sweet water in great plenty ; and mentioned by Jerome as "at the foot of Mount Moriah"—has by travellers, geographers, and archæologists generally, been identified as the modern ' *Ain Silwân*,' an artificial basin into which the water comes "through a subterraneous channel from the fountain of Mary, higher up in the Valley of Jehosaphat," and which with an older pool, constructed it has been supposed by King Hezekiah (2 Kings xx. 20), was probably intended to irrigate the royal gardens that lay below (Robinson, Biblical Researches, vol. i. p. 341 ; Wilson in Warren's Recovery of Jerusalem, p. 22 ; Riehm's Handwörterbuch, art. *Siloah*). The explanatory clause (**which is by interpretation, Sent.**)

shows that the Evangelist, taking חַלֹשׁ (Shiloach) as equivalent to חַילֹשׁ (Shaluach), sent, saw in the waters which were discharged from the fountain an emblem, not of the man who was sent (Bengel, De Wette, Ewald, Meyer), but of *Christ the Sent of God*, the true Siloam, who had come forth to cleanse men from the moral blindness of sin and error (Theophylact, Calvin, Ebrard, Luthardt, Godet, Brückner, Westcott, and others). **He, the blind man, went away therefore,**—under the direction of a guide whom he might easily have found (Godet), or without a guide, having been probably acquainted with the neighbourhood (Meyer), hardly because already he had begun to see (Lange)— **and washed,** thereby evincing his faith (iv. 50), **and came again** not to Jesus, but to his own home (ver. 8), **seeing,** as his faith expected and as Christ intended.

8. **The neighbours therefore, and they which saw him,** lit., *those having seen him*, which has here the force of an imperfect, *those who were seeing*, or *used to see*, *him*, **aforetime, that,** or *because* (Westcott), **he was a beggar, said,** amongst themselves, **Is not this he that sat and begged ?** lit., *this is not the* (one) *sitting and begging*, i.e. the man who was accustomed to sit and beg, *is it ?* meaning that the speakers thought it was (cf. vi. 42).

9. **Others**—if different persons from the foregoing speakers (Westcott) ; but if a section of the same (Godet, Luthardt, Paley), then—*Some* **said, It is he** ; agreeing with the former speakers, or replying in the affirmative to their inquiry : **others said,** deciding in the negative, **No, but he is like him. He said, I am** *he*, or *I am* (sc. the man who sat and begged).

10. **They said therefore unto him,** not as questioning his truthfulness or doubting his identity, but as anxious to hear about the marvellous occurrence — **How then were thine eyes opened?** not challenging the fact, but desiring to learn how the fact was brought about.

11. **He answered,** confining himself to a simple narration of facts, **The man that is called Jesus,** that well-known person of whom report speaks, *ille homo* (Vulgate)—of whom it need not be supposed the blind man knew nothing

John 9:11–18

but the name (Bengel)—**made clay** (see ver. 6), **and anointed mine eyes, and said unto me, Go to Siloam and wash: so I went away and washed, and I received sight**; or, *having then gone away and washed, I recovered sight* (Matt. xi. 5; Mark x. 51; Luke xviii. 41), rather than 'I looked up' (Mark xvi. 4), though the idea of one recovering what he never had appears unnatural, and the man's language requires for explanation the notion that sight as a natural gift belongs (in a sense) to even a blind man. *Nec male recipere quis dicitur, quod communiter tributum humanæ naturæ ipsi abfuit* (Grotius).

12. **And they said unto him, Where is he? He saith, I know not.** The dramatic liveliness of this conversation may be accounted for by supposing that John heard the story from the man's own lips.

13. **They**, the neighbours (ver. 8), or those of them disinclined to credit the man's story (ver. 9), **bring**, for the purpose of having the alleged miracle investigated and a judgment pronounced thereupon (Tholuck), rather than because it had been done upon the Sabbath (Meyer), **to the Pharisees**—not the Sanhedrim (Tholuck), for which in this Gospel the official designation is 'the chief priests and the Pharisees' (vii. 45); but one of the two smaller synagogal courts, mentioned in Matt. v. 21, 22 (Paulus, Lücke, Lange); or the Pharisees as a corporate body (Meyer), of which the persons here introduced were "its chosen representatives, its committee of management" (Godet)—**him that aforetime was blind**, lit., *the once blind man*.

14. **Now it was the Sabbath** (see v. 10) **on the day when Jesus made the clay, and opened his eyes.** The court of inquiry might be held, if not on the same, on the following day. The mention of 'making clay'. serves to call attention to the (so-called) violation of the Sabbath the miracle involved; though there is no ground in this for thinking that "the story is perhaps not authentic, but inserted to illustrate the oft-repeated charge of the Pharisees that Jesus was breaking the law of the Sabbath" (Paley).

15. **Again therefore the Pharisees also asked him**, or *again then they asked*

him, even the Pharisees*, i.e. the first time the neighbours (ver. 10), but this time the Pharisees (probably dissatisfied with the report of the neighbours) asked, **how he had received his sight. And he said unto them**, abbreviating the statement previously given, **He**, the man called Jesus (ver. 11), **put clay upon mine eyes, and I washed and do see**, or *I washed myself and I see*.

16. **Some therefore of the Pharisees**, belonging probably to the Shammaites or binders (cf. v. 18), **said**, *were saying*, or *began to say*, speaking from the strong legal standpoint occupied by them, **This man is not from God**, or, more emphatically, *this person is not from God* in the sense of being sent from Him (i. 6), *the man* you speak of; **because he keepeth not the Sabbath.** They meant by healing on that sacred day: see on v. 18. "A Rabbinical precept specially forbids the anointing of the eyes with spittle on the Sabbath: Maimonides, Schabbath 21" (Meyer). **But others said**, arguing with more conclusiveness, **How can a man that is a sinner do such signs?** Their contention was that if Christ wrought the miracle He could not be a sinner. **And there was a division** or *schism* **among them.** The same sort of split concerning Christ occurred previously among the multitude (viii. 43), and afterwards among the Jews (x. 19).

17. **They**—not the hostile section alone (Apollinaris), or the favourably disposed alone (Chrysostom), but both together—**say therefore unto the blind man again**, with the view doubtless of eliciting information that might enable them to come to a decision (Meyer), perhaps also of extorting from him some admission that might furnish a pretext for suspecting his truthfulness (Godet): **What sayest thou of him, in that**, or, with reference to the fact that (cf. ii. 18) **he opened thine eyes?** What impression did that so-called miracle leave upon thy mind, as to His personality? **And he, the man, said, He is a prophet.** See on i. 21.

18,19. **The Jews**, the hierarchical party among the Pharisees, **therefore**, either because of the unsatisfactory character of the man's answer, or because they suspected some collusion between the man and Christ, or because they could not reconcile breaking the Sabbath with the working of a real miracle, **did not believe concerning him that he had been blind, and had received his sight,** but were disposed to regard him as an impostor, until **they called,** summoned before them, **the parents of him that had received** (or that claimed to have received) **his sight, and asked them, saying, Is this your son, who ye say was born blind? how then doth he now see?** The questions were practically three : as to (1) the identity of their son ; (2) the alleged fact of his birth-blindness ; and (3) their knowledge of the manner in which his sight had been restored—the questioners assuming that the parents would answer the second affirmatively.

20, 21. **His parents answered, and said,** with frankness, so far as the first and second points were concerned, **We know that this is our son, and that he was born blind.** On these matters they were authorities. **But how he now seeth, we know not ; or who opened his eyes we know not.** On this point their information was second-hand ; hence they offered no personal testimony, but referred their inquisitors to their son himself, saying : **Ask him ; he is of age,** lit., *he has age,* he has attained to manhood ; **he shall speak for himself.** He shall tell his own story.

22, 23. **These things said his parents, because they feared the Jews ; for the Jews had agreed already,** if not formally decreed, at least come to an understanding with one another, **that if any man should confess him** Jesus *to be* **Christ, he should be put out of the synagogue.** The excommunication threatened was probably the first of the three degrees of ecclesiastical censure subsequently known to and practised by the Rabbis, which condemned to a thirty days' separation from all religious and social fellowship with other Jews (cf. xii. 42 ; xvi. 2 ; Luke vi. 22 ; see Keil, Handbuch des Biblischen Archäologie, § 72, 2). **Therefore,** i.e. because of this attitude of the rulers towards Jesus, **said his parents, He is of age ; ask him.** See on ver. 21.

24. **So they called a second time the man that was blind,** who had

probably been removed whilst his parents were under examination, **and said unto him, Give glory to God :**—*a formula of adjuration* (Bengel, Lücke, De Wette), by which the man was invited to render homage to the Divine Being as the supreme judge and omniscient searcher of hearts, by telling the truth (cf. Josh. vii. 19) ; or, simply *a pious exhortation* suggesting that the man should wipe out the dishonour done to God, in his ascription of the miracle to Jesus, and designation of Jesus as a prophet, by acknowledging that in both he had erred (Lampe, Luthardt, Godet) ; **we,** as the appointed guardians of the divine honour and authorized representatives of theological learning, **know,** without argument or evidence, by spiritual insight and religious discernment, **that this man is a sinner,** and therefore could not have performed such a miracle as you allege. By this intimation the authorities hoped to overawe the man, who, however, proved invincible.

25. **He therefore answered,** with prudence and simplicity, **Whether he be a sinner, I know not,** I presume not to offer judgment or opinion thereupon—though ver. 30 proves he did know that Christ was not a sinner ; **one thing I know,** as lying within the sphere of ·my ability to testify, **that, whereas I was blind,** lit., *being blind,* in my natural state or condition, **now I see.**

26. **They said therefore unto him,**—obviously because they had failed to shake his testimony—**What did he to thee? how opened he thine eyes ?**—repeating questions previously put and answered (ver. 15), in the hope that the man might contradict himself, by giving different versions of the story.

27. **He** (however) **answered them, I told you even now** (ver. 15), **and ye did not hear**—rather than 'and have you not heard ?' (Meyer) ; **Wherefore would ye hear it again?** or, *why do ye again wish to hear it?* or, 'What do ye again wish to hear ?' **Would ye also become His disciples?**—*surely ye also do not wish to become His disciples, do ye?*

28. **And they reviled him,** passionately railed at him, "abused him for making an impudent suggestion"

(Paley), **and said,** with contempt, **Thou art his** (or, *that* man's) **disciple ;** by the term 'that man' placing a moral gulf between him and them—*hoc vocabulo removent Jesum a sese* (Bengel); **but we are disciples of Moses.** See on i. 17 ; and cf. v. 45.

29. **We know that God hath spoken unto Moses,** i.e. did speak in the past, certainly, clearly, and emphatically (i. 17), so that his words remain with us unto this day (v. 47)—an assertion in both parts correct : **but as for this man, we know not whence he is,** i.e. as to his authority and commission, although we know well whence he is not—he is not from God (ver. 16). With the origin and descent of Christ the Jews professed to be perfectly acquainted (vii. 27).

30. **The man answered and said unto them, Why** γάρ, for ; meaning, 'ye ought to know,' for **herein** rather than 'with respect to this one' (Lange), **is the marvel**—better than 'this one thing is marvellous,' reading ἐν instead of ἐν (Masson, in Winer, § xxix. 3, note on p. 197, Engl. ed.)—**that ye know not** whence he is, **and** *yet*—not 'and how' as if πῶς had dropped out (Paley)—**he opened mine eyes.** This fact had left the *man* in no doubt as to whence Jesus was, as he proceeded to explain.

31. **We know**—a colloquial expression signifying, everybody recognizes it to be the case—**that God heareth not sinners,** or wicked persons, in the sense of favourably regarding their petitions (see Job xxvii. 9 ; Ps. lxvi. 18 ; Prov. xv. 29) ; **but if any man be a worshipper of God,** a God-fearing person (Ex. xviii. 21 ; Job i. 1, 8 ; cf. Acts x. 2), **and do His will** (cf. vii. 17), **him,** or *this man* He heareth (see Acts x. 35). The major premiss of the man's argument.

32. **Since the world began,** or *from all time,* **it was never heard that any one opened the eyes of a man born blind.** The minor premiss in the syllogism.

33. **If this man were not from God, he could do nothing.** In such a case as mine an ordinary person would be helpless : hence this man must be from God. The conclusion of the man's reasoning.

34. **They answered and said unto**

him, who had presumed to instruct them in logic and divinity, **Thou wast** altogether **born in sins,** or, *in sins wert thou wholly begotten,* i.e. thou hast been from thy birth a wretched creature cursed with physical and mental blindness because of thy wickedness ; **and dost thou,** a reprobate such as thou ! **teach us ?** And they **cast him out**—out of the audience chamber in the first instance (Meyer, Luthardt, Godet, Westcott), though this may have been, and probably was (see ver. 22) in due course followed by excommunication from the synagogue (Olshausen, Lücke, Ewald, Tholuck, and others).

35. **Jesus heard** probably soon after that they the Pharisees **had cast him out** as above explained ; **and finding,** or, *having found* him, scarcely by accident (Lücke), most likely after having sought him, **he said unto** him, **Dost thou,** whom I have healed and they have cast out ! **believe on the Son of God?** τοῦ θεοῦ (T. R., Meyer, Godet, Lücke, Brückner, Luthardt), rather than Son of man ? τοῦ ἀνθρώπου (ℵ B D, Tischendorf, Westcott and Hort, Paley), which is less suitable to the context, and was probably introduced into the text as the usual self-designation employed by Christ.

36. **He answered and said, And** (the conjunction καὶ increasing the liveliness of the question : cf. Mark x. 26 ; Luke x. 29) **who is he, Lord,** or Sir (iv. 11), **that I may believe on Him?** Cf. i. 22.

37. **Jesus said unto him, Thou hast both seen Him, and He it is that speaketh with thee,** or, *He speaking with thee, is that person :* or, *that person is* (sc. the Son of God), Johannine usage favouring the taking of ἐκεῖνος as subject : see i. 18, 33 ; v. 11 ; cf. iv. 26. On καὶ . . . καὶ, *both* . . . *and,* see vi. 36 ; vii. 28.

38. **And he said, Lord, I believe,** rather, *I believe, Lord.* 'Lord' now conveys more than mere respect. **And he,** the man, **worshipped Him.** The term 'worship' in John always signifies the payment of religious homage : cf. iv. 20 ; xii. 20.

39. **And Jesus said**—neither to the blind man nor to the bystanders (Luthardt, Meyer), but as a general reflection or soliloquy, in and with Himself (Godet, Westcott), recording the impression made upon His heart by the whole incident—**For judgment came I**

into this world Christ's coming into
the world had in view as its result, end,
purpose a judgment; which however
was not to be a judicial process (κρίσις)
exercised by Him personally (iii.
17), but a judicial decision, or sentence
(κρῖμα) indirectly pronounced upon
men's characters by His appearing
in their midst as the Light of the
world (iii. 19). **that they which see not
may see ; and that they which see may
become blind.** 'The not seeing' and
'the seeing,' symbolized by the blind
beggar and the Pharisees, manifestly
signify—(1) and specifically, 'the multitude who know not the law' (viii. 49),
and the rulers who 'know' everything;
then (2) and generally the ignorant and
unlearned, the 'babes' (Luke x. 21 ;
Matt. xi. 25), who have no superior
wisdom of their own to obstruct the
entrance of the light of truth into their
minds or prevent its reception by their
hearts, and 'the wise and prudent' who
believe themselves to be already in possession of the truth. Christ's object in
coming to the world was that the
former might receive the light of heavenly truth and see thereby, and that
the latter might, by closing their eyes
against its illuminating beams, relapse
into utter darkness. This aim becomes
a definitely fixed and settled judgment
(κρῖμα) in the case (3) of those on the
one hand who are conscious of their intellectual and moral darkness (Matt.
v. 3), and, on the other hand of those
who imagine they see but do not (Rev.
iii. 17). With the former the closed
spiritual organ is relieved of its dis-
ability, so that from being μὴ βλέποντες,
'not seeing,' they become βλέποντες,
'seeing'; while with the latter the
organ gradually deteriorates till they

become τυφλοί or wholly destitute of the
capacity of seeing.

40. Those of the Pharisees which
were with Him—hardly earlier disciples
who had fallen away (Chrysostom), or
Pharisees who still affected to be disciples while retaining their old Pharisaic spirit (Westcott, Lange), but more
probably hostilely disposed persons,
possibly spies from Jerusalem (Tholuck), who were present in the group
surrounding Jesus, in order to make
their observations (Meyer, Luthardt)—
**heard these things, and said unto Him,
Are we also blind?** *not also we are
blind, are we?* In the sense put
upon the word by Christ, they were
not : in the meaning they attached to
the expression, they were.

41. **Jesus** therefore **said unto them,
If ye were blind,** in the sense that I
mean, **ye would have no sin,** meaning
either (1) if ye were like the common
crowd ignorant, your present unbelief
in Me would not be sinful, inasmuch as
then it would be the result of 'not seeing,' not of 'seeing and hating' the
light (Meyer); or (2) if ye were humbly
conscious of your blindness ye would
have no sin, because ye would come to
me to have it cured (Calvin), yea, your
sin would be taken away and ye would
have it no more (Luthardt) ; **but now
ye say, We see: your sin** therefore
remaineth, either (1) because your unbelief is now no longer an error induced
by ignorance, but is a wanton offence
against knowledge—a sin against the
light ; or (2) because, through conceit
of your superior illumination rejecting
Me, your sin continues unremoved,
and, as a sin against the light, a sin
against the Holy Ghost, has a tendency
to become irremovable (Godet).

HOMILETICS

VER. 1-12.—THE OPENING OF A BLIND MAN'S EYES.
I. **The Subject of the Miracle.** 1. *A victim of distressing ills.* (1) Poverty.
The individual in question belonged to the order of beggars, always a numerous
class in Oriental countries. (2) Blindness. Whether a severer calamity to be
born blind or to be deprived of sight after having once possessed it, in either
case it is sad to have to mourn like Milton—
"Thus with the year
Seasons return, but not to me returns
Day, or the sweet approach of even or morn,

Or sight of vernal bloom, or summer's rose,
Or flocks or herds, or human face divine ;
But clouds instead, and ever-during dark
Surrounds me," etc.—(Paradise Lost, iii. 40-47.)

2. *An object of profound compassion.* (1) On the part of the Saviour whose searching glance comprehended his case in a moment (v. 6) and whose tender bosom, it may be certain, responded instantly to the mute appeal of his abject misery (Matt. viii. 17 ; ix. 36). (2) On the part of the disciples, who doubtless were not devoid of sympathy for a suffering fellow-creature—" One touch of nature makes the whole world kin " (Shakespeare, Troil. and Cres. act iii. sc. 3)-- and who might be wronged were this, though unrecorded, to be denied them. 3. *An occasion of perplexed inquiry.* According to then current notions of theology, all suffering had its deepest roots and generally its immediate cause in sin. Had the man on whom the disciples gazed been born seeing and afterwards deprived of vision, his case would have presented no insuperable difficulty—he would simply have been suffering for some secret transgression. But the man having been born blind, that solution would not suffice. If the man's parents had been sinners, that would have resolved the riddle, since the law of Moses taught that the guilt of parents should be visited upon the children to the third and fourth generations (Ex. xx. 5). But might not the man himself have been the true *origo mali,* the actual offender, by transgressing either in the womb or in a pre-existent state ? The disciples were at a loss to understand the mystery, and laid the problem before the Teacher :—" Rabbi, who did sin ?" etc. (ver. 2). 4. *A subject of divine dispensation.* The unhappy mendicant had been born blind for no special iniquity of himself or of his ancestors, immediate or remote, but for the glory of God—that the works of God might be made manifest in him, and through him to the world.

II. **The Worker of the Miracle.** "The man that is called Jesus." 1. *His relation to the Father;*--ambassador, plenipotentiary, commissioner, sent forth to execute the works connected with the Father's purpose of salvation (ver. 4). 2. *His relation to the world.* (1) A true inhabitant thereof—" I am *in* the world " ; (2) a temporary visitor thereto—" as long as I am in the world " ; (3) an illuminating sun therefor—" I am light of the world." 3. *His relation to His disciples*—that of teacher (ver. 2).

III. **The Motive of the Miracle.** I. *To relieve human misery.* Jesus never failed to be touched with a fellow feeling of the infirmities of those with whom He mingled, and with a strong impulse to mitigate their woes and ease their pains (v. 6 ; vi. 5 ; xi. 34 ; Matt. viii. 17 ; ix. 36 ; xiv. 14 ; Heb. iv. 15). 2. *To fulfil His Father's trust.* Fidelity to Him whose commission He bore required Him to put His hand to the work that lay before Him (iv. 34 ; vi. 38). 3. *To educate His disciples.* What He was about to do would illustrate the nature of His mission, which a Hebrew prophet (Is. lxi. 1) had described as "an opening of that which was bound," interpreted by a Christian evangelist (Luke iv. 18), perhaps also by Christ Himself, as "a recovering of sight to the blind." 4. *To improve the season of opportunity.* As the Father's workman, He had only a brief space in which to labour in His heavenly calling. The night was approaching when, even for Him, such work as now invited Him would be impossible (Eccles. ix. 10).

IV. **The Method of the Miracle.** 1. *The means used by Christ.* (1) Acts ;— spitting on the ground, making clay, anointing the beggar's eyes (cf. Mark vii. 33 ; viii. 23). (2) Words ;—" Go, wash in the pool of Siloam !" a test of the blind man's faith. Apart from this the use of means was unnecessary. 2. *The means employed by the man.* (1) Faith ;—else he would not have acted on the Saviour's instructions. (2) Obedience ;—he carried out Christ's prescription to the letter (ver. 7). Faith in this way evinces its reality.

V. **The Proof of the Miracle.** 1. *The success of the man's experiment.* When he had washed he 'looked up' and saw, he received his sight (ver. 11), and came to his home seeing (ver. 7). The man amongst his neighbours was proof that a miracle had been wrought. 2. *The astonishment of the man's friends.*

They could not deny his identity, or refuse to admit that he saw ; they were only puzzled to know how the closed eyes had been opened.

Learn 1. That the same object may strike different persons in different ways, as the blind beggar did Christ and His disciples. 2. That the woes and miseries, the sufferings and even the sins of men, only fit them the more for Christ's healing and salvation. 3. That no man has a right to spend the day of life in indolence, and far less in sin. 4. That the source of all the saving influence now exerted on the world is Jesus Christ. 5. That without faith and obedience there can be no recovering of sight to a blinded soul.

VER. 13-34.—THE INVESTIGATION OF THE MIRACLE.

I. **The First Examination of the Man** : ver. 13-18. 1. *An important admission.* The Pharisees recognized that the man saw (ver. 13). If therefore he had been previously blind there must have been a miracle. 2. *An irrelevant question.* They wished to know *how* the man had received his sight (ver. 15), when all they had to determine was whether he had received his sight. 3. *A straightforward answer.* The man, having nothing to conceal, gave a simple recitation of what had taken place (ver. 15). 4. *A palpable evasion.* One part of the Pharisees attempted to avoid giving judgment on the case before them—whether a miracle had been wrought—by pronouncing on another question not before them, viz., the character of Christ, whom they declared to be ' not from God ' because He kept not the Sabbath (ver. 16). 5. *A sound conclusion.* Another part amongst the Pharisees, reasoning that the miracle had been proved, decided that the worker of such a ' sign ' could not be a sinner, and therefore could not have really violated the Sabbath law (ver. 16). 6. *A safe deduction.* The healed man inferred, as Nicodemus had done (iii. 2), that the physician who had cured him was a prophet (ver. 17). 7. *A disingenuous procedure.* The matter seemed settled, and the miracle made out ; but the hostile party, unwilling to allow a verdict so favourable for Jesus to go forth into the public ear, determined to hold the man an impostor, or at least suspend their judgment, until they had ascertained the truth from the man's parents (ver. 18).

II. **The Testimony of the Man's Parents:** ver. 19-23. 1. *Joyful recognition.* They identified the healed man as their son. The neighbours could only say he was like the beggar they had known (ver. 9): the man's parents had no doubt as to who he was. 2. *Sorrowful concession.* Their son's report as to his blindness was correct. From birth onwards he had never beheld the light of day. 3. *Cautious negation.* They declared ignorance of how the miracle had been wrought,—so far at least as their own personal observation went. 4. *Prudent suggestion.* Their questioners might inquire at their son, who was both responsible, and able to answer, for himself.

III. **The Second Examination of the Man:** ver. 24-34. 1. *Intimidation.* The hostile section of the court sought to overbear the man's judgment by their superior knowledge and position. They, the heaven-appointed leaders of the people and guardians of morality, were satisfied the man spoken of was a sinner. Not only had he broken the Sabbath, but,—shocking profanity!—he had actually spit upon the ground, manufactured clay by kneading the moistened dust into a paste and spread it on a blind man's eyes as an artizan might have plastered it upon a wall ! Consequently there had, and could have, been no such thing as a miracle ; and he had better confess both himself a deceiver and Christ an impostor (ver. 24). To all this the man opposed the testimony of his own personal experience (ver. 25). 2. *Entanglement.* By a species of cross-examination, in which they invited him a second time to rehearse the details of the story, they hoped to make him contradict himself (ver. 26). But the man, too clever to be caught by such an artifice (Prov. i. 17), declined their invitation, reminding them he had already supplied all the information he possessed upon the subject, and inquiring with a fine touch of irony, if they desired to become Christ's disciples (ver. 27). 3. *Reproach.* They reviled him as the follower, not of Moses, the great commissioner and plenipotentiary of Jehovah, but of a nameless fellow concerning whom no one could say whence he was, or with whose authority he came (ver. 29). To this the man replied with crushing logic, setting forth with dialectic skill, which, if artless, was nevertheless perfect in form as well as resistless in force, how no honest mind could evade the conclusion that Christ must at least be a prophet sent from God no less than was Moses (ver. 30-33). 4. *Expulsion.* They could not answer the man's syllogism, but they could do what foiled controversialists commonly do to victorious opponents—they could hurl at him angry invective, call him a double-dyed reprobate, taunt him with what they had been labouring to deny, his birth-blindness, declaring it an evidence of his moral vileness and spiritual obtuseness ;—they could drive him from their chamber, they could take steps to have him expelled from the synagogue ; which also they did (ver. 34).

Lessons. 1. The danger of approaching religious questions with preconceived notions of our own;—exemplified in the Pharisees. 2. The power Christianity possesses to convince all sincere inquirers of its heavenly origin ;—illustrated in the case of the healed man. 3. The duty of standing true to Christ in the face of all opposition ;—again shown in the brave conduct of the man. 4. The certainty that Christ's witnesses will suffer persecution. 5. The helplessness of man's wisdom in opposing the truth.

VER. 35-41.—THE VERDICT OF CHRIST UPON THE WHOLE CASE.
I. **The Demand Christ makes upon the Human Heart :**—Faith (ver. 35). 1. *Personal.* It must be the trust of the individual soul. 2. *Immediate.* It must be exercised now, at the present moment, without delay. 3. *Intelligent.* It must be directed to the right object, the Son of God.
II. **The Homage Christ accepts from the Human Heart :**—Worship (ver. 38). 1. *Adoring.* It must be more than outward courtesy or formal obeisance—even the prostration in lowly reverence of the human spirit at His feet. 2. *Believing.* It must be rooted in, and proceed from, the soul's faith in Christ as the Son of God and Saviour of the world. 3. *Joyous.* It must be the utterance of a heart bounding forth to accord a welcome to the self-revealing Son of God.
III. **The Work Christ performs upon the Human Heart :**—Judgment. 1. *Indirect.* It follows as an inevitable result of His presenting Himself before men as ' The Light of the World.' 2. *Real.* It infallibly results in (1) separating men into two classes, ' the not seeing' and ' the seeing,' and (2) retributively acting upon them in accordance with their ascertained characters and dispositions. 3. *Progressive.* This work is still going on as truly and efficiently as when Christ was on the earth. 4. *Permanent.* The issues it records are irreversible. The eye opened by the 'light of life' can never again be closed: the soul that through wilful and persistent unbelief loses the capacity of ' seeing' can never again emerge into the light. (See Homiletics on iii. 17-21.)

Lessons. 1. The importance of ascertaining in which group one is placed by Christ's judicial work. 2. The necessity of faith corresponding in fulness to the revelation of Himself which Christ has given. 3. The propriety of making Christ the object as well as the ground and medium of our worship.

VER. 24, 25.—'We know' and 'I know.' I. *We know* (the Pharisees). The voice of 1. Official pride. 2. Dead traditionalism. 3. Religious error. II. *I know* (the healed man). The language of 1. Personal humility. 2. Experimental belief. 3. Spiritual discernment.

2. THE PARABLES OF THE GOOD SHEPHERD

CHAP. X. VER. 1-21

EXPOSITION

Chap. x. ver. 1. **Verily, verily I say unto you** The hostile attitude of the Pharisees (ix. 40) to Christ proved them to be false leaders of the people. This truth Christ sets before them in a series of parabolic utterances, based on familiar scenes of Oriental pastoral life. **He that entereth not by the door into**

the fold of the sheep The first picture may have been suggested by the sight of flocks resting in the fields, or being driven home to the city from neighbouring pastures (Neander, Godet), although the supposition is unnecessary. The 'fold' was commonly a circular enclosure of stone or brick, with low walls, open to the sky, and entered by a 'door' or 'gate' (Thomson, The Land and the Book, p. 201). **but climbeth up some other way** *Ascendeth from another quarter*, i.e., from another direction than that leading to the gate—the verb 'ascend' being peculiarly suitable, as folds were commonly constructed on the slopes of hills (Ewald). **the same, that man, is a thief and a robber.** The dominant idea in the first term is that of secrecy (cf. Matt. xxvii. 64 ; xviii. 13), in the second that of violence (xviii. 40 ; cf. Matt. xxi. 13 ; Mark xi. 17 ; Luke x. 30).

2. **But he that entereth in by the door,** in opposition to the foregoing intruder, **is the** (or a) **shepherd of the sheep,** i.e., corresponds with the conception of a shepherd, as the person climbing over the wall answers to that of a thief and robber.

3. **To him the porter openeth ;** the porter or gate keeper, ὁ θυρωρὸς (cf. xviii. 16, 17 ; Mark xiii. 34), *ostiarius* (Vulgate), being the slave to whose care the flocks are committed during night, who takes up his station inside of the fold, and whose duty it is to watch against thieves and robbers, whether wolves or men, and to open the gate at dawn when the shepherd returns to lead forth his flock (see Stapfer, Palestine in the Time of Christ, p. 226) ; **and the sheep hear his voice,** recognize it as that belonging to their shepherd ; **and he calleth his own sheep,** the sheep belonging to his own particular flock, **by name** (cf. Is. xliii. 1)—it being usual for Oriental shepherds to know the individual members of their flocks by name—**and leadeth them out,** to the pasture grounds (Ps. xxiii. 2).

4. **When he hath put forth all his own,** having for this purpose frequently to enter in amongst them, **he goeth before them, and the sheep follow him.** " This is true to the letter. They are so tame and so trained that they *follow* their keeper with the utmost docility " (Thomson, The Land

and the Book, p. 202); **for they know his voice,** having often heard it in wind and storm.

5. **And a stranger will they not follow, but will flee from him ; for they know not the voice of strangers.** "The shepherd calls them sharply from time to time to remind them of his presence. They know his voice and follow on ; but, if a stranger call, they stop short, lift up their heads in alarm, and, if it is repeated, they turn and flee, because they know not the voice of a stranger. This is not the fanciful costume of a parable ; it is simple fact" (ibid., p. 203).

6. **This parable spake Jesus unto them ;** the παροιμία signifying (1) a by-discourse (παρὰ οἶμος), or side piece, any species of composition deviating from the common path, (2) in classical Greek, a proverb, a rendering it also has in this Gospel (xvi. 25, 29) and in the second Petrine Epistle (ii. 22), and (3) a short, sententious parabolic utterance, equivalent to παραβολή never used by John, in which sense it is here employed ; **but they understood not what things they were which He spake unto them.** Those who boasted of their knowledge (ix. 29, 34) failed to grasp the spiritual significance of the picture Christ placed before them. Could better proof have been furnished that they were "blind"?

7. **Jesus therefore said unto them again,** varying somewhat the metaphor, and giving them a second picture —not an exposition of the preceding parable (Meyer), **Verily, verily, I say unto you, I am the door of the sheep.** As in the last similitude His hearers had not discerned its applicability to Him any more than to them, He now explicitly connects this with Himself, describing Himself as the door, not of the fold, i.e. to or into the sheep (Bengel, Brückner, Meyer, Luthardt, Paley), but of the sheep, i.e. through which the sheep pass into, and out from, the fold (Chrysostom, Lampe, Godet, Westcott, and others).

8. **All that came before Me,** lit., *all, as many as, came before Me ;* i.e. all who presented themselves to the people in the capacity of The True Shepherd for whom they were waiting, rather than as the Door (Godet)—who came, not *apart from* (Camerarius), or

in front of, instead of after me (Calovius), or without using Me as the door (Lampe), without being divinely authorized (Augustine), or receiving their title from Messiah (Luthardt), or instead of me (Lange), but *before me in time* (Godet, Meyer, Westcott);—all such before Me who came in the fulness of time (Gal. iv. 4), and who therefore am the legitimate shepherd and only door, in one, **are thieves and robbers ;** *and they tried to call the sheep* (Paley) but **the sheep did not hear them.** Such false shepherds awoke no genuine response in the national bosom. Those waiting for the consolation of Israel (Luke ii. 25) recognized them not.

9. **I am the door** of the fold (ver. 2), and of the flock (ver. 7), for the shepherds and for the sheep ; the one way of access to the Father (xiv. 6 ; Acts iv. 12 ; Eph. ii. 18), the one Mediator between God and man (1 Tim. ii. 5, 6), the one entrance into the Church of the Living God (1 Pet. ii. 5) ; **by Me, if any man enter in,** lit., *through Me, if any one has entered in*, to the fold of Jehovah's flock, as a shepherd (Lücke, Ewald, Meyer, and others), or, better, as a sheep (Godet, Brückner, Westcott, and others), by exercising faith in Him whom Jehovah sent and who came to be the shepherd of the sheep, **he shall be saved**—if a shepherd, set free from all dangers by the protecting door (Meyer) ; if a sheep, shall possess complete defence against all those perils which menace the spiritual life, symbolized by the thieves and robbers that invade the fold, and the wolves that devour the sheep—**and shall go in and out,** into the fold and out to the field, in the free exercise of his calling as a shepherd, or, better, in the fullest enjoyment of liberty as a sheep, **and shall find pasture,** the shepherd for his flocks, the sheep for himself—the former shall experience entire success, the latter obtain the amplest nourishment.

10. **The thief cometh not, but that he may steal, and kill, and destroy :** the habitual and universal practice of all who show themselves to be false shepherds by entering not in through Me the door : **I came** once for all **that they,** the sheep, **may have life,** ζωήν, the Messianic salvation, **and may have** *it* **abundantly,** lit., *have in abundance*,

either 'all they want' (Paley), or 'the Messianic life,' meaning 'the fulness of grace and truth' Christ possesses and communicates (i. 16) ; not something over and above, as the kingdom of heaven, or joy in the Holy Ghost,—which, besides, are not things in addition to, but essential parts of, the life Christ bestows.

11. **I am the good shepherd :** ὁ ποιμὴν ὁ καλὸς, not 'that good-looking shepherd,' 'represented familiarly in art, e.g. on gems and cameos' (Paley), but 'the shepherd, the excellent one,' the shepherd by pre-eminence, the one possessing all the qualities pertaining to a shepherd ; hence the ideal shepherd (equal to 'the true shepherd,' ὁ ἀληθινός) who corresponds to the essential conception of a shepherd set forth in O. T. Scripture (Ps. xxiii. 1 ; Is. xl. 11 ; Ezek. xxxiv. ; Jer. xxiii. ; Zech. xi. ; Mic. v. 3), exhibits that inward correspondence in all its outward and attractive loveliness : **the good shepherd layeth down his life for the sheep.** The phrase 'to lay down one's life,' τὴν ψυχήν τιθέναι, is Johannean (cf. ver. 15, 17 ; xiii. 37 ; xv. 13 ; 1 John iii. 16), and points (1) to the image of disrobing oneself of a garment, as in xiii. 4 (Brückner, Godet, Westcott), and, as this is done for the advantage of (ὑπέρ) the sheep, i.e. to turn away destruction from them, (2) to the idea of substitutionary suffering or vicarious dying, of paying down one's life for the benefit of others, as in Matt. xx. 28 (Meyer, Luthardt, Tholuck, and others).

12. **He that is a hireling,** lit., *the hireling,* a person taking charge of a flock for pay (μισθός), **and not a shepherd,** lit., *and not being a shepherd;* epexegetic of the former, meaning 'the hireling'—even he who is not a shepherd, **whose own the sheep are not,** and for whom consequently he has no love, **beholdeth the wolf coming, and leaveth the sheep, and fleeth**—in the true spirit of a hireling attending first to his own safety ; **and the wolf snatcheth them** *and* **scattereth** *them :* or seizeth the individual sheep and scattereth the flock.

13. *He fleeth,* or, without any supplement, understanding the preceding clause as a parenthesis, and connecting ὅτι with φεύγει (ver. 12)—**because he is**

an hireling, and careth not for the sheep, or, *and there is no concern to him* about the sheep.

14, 15. I am the good shepherd (see ver. 11); **and I know Mine own** *sheep* (ver. 2, 4), **and Mine own** *sheep* **know Me** (ver. 4), **even as the Father knoweth Me, and I know the Father:** cf. xiv. 20; xv. 10 ; xvii. 8, 21 ; **and I lay down My life for the sheep :** see on ver. 11.

16. And other sheep I have, which are not of this fold, not Jewish disciples of the Dispersion (Paulus), since these formed one fold with their Palestinian brethren (Lücke), but Gentile believers who are represented not as belonging to another fold, as if Christ meant to depict Himself as a Great Flockmaster with many folds (De Wette), but as not belonging to this fold, or to a fold at all (De Wette, Godet), rather as " scattered abroad " (xi. 52) : **them also I must,** δεί as usual pointing to a divine necessity : " the decree of His Father's love and of His own " (Lange), **bring,** not συναγαγεῖν εἰς ἕν, gather into one (xi. 52), which however will be the end of this leading, but simply ἀγαγεῖν, *lead,* as a shepherd (ver. 3), **and they shall hear My voice** (Acts xxviii. 28), thereby showing they are of the number of My sheep (ver. 4, 27); **and they shall become** or, *there shall be,* γενήσεται, **one flock, one shepherd.** Already in the divine purpose and idea constituting one flock presided over by one shepherd (Ezek. xxxiv. 23), they shall eventually *become* so in reality, through the breaking down of the middle wall of partition between Jew and Gentile and the conversion of the latter to the faith of Christ (Eph. ii. 11-22), a work which began under the Apostles (Acts x. 45), and will be completed at the coming in of the fulness of the Gentiles (Rom. x. 25). The use of ' flock ' (ποίμνη) for ' fold ' (αὐλή) shows that the unity of Christ's flock consists not in their visible organization into one ' corporate body,' 'church,' or ' fold,' but in their spiritual union with the One Shepherd (ποιμήν), the Church's Head (xvii. 22). The substitution in many later versions of ' fold ' for ' flock ' was probably due to Romanizing tendencies in the early Church, " and has served in no small degree to confirm and extend the false

claims of the Roman See " (Westcott). The notion that the last clause ' one flock, one shepherd ' was "a later addition at a time when the Petrine and Pauline, Jewish and Gentile, schools were at variance " (Paley) is without foundation.

17. Therefore, διὰ τοῦτο, referring back to ver. 15 (ver. 16 being parenthetical), and forward to the ὅτι, which resumes the thought of ver. 15 (cf. v. 16, 18), **doth the Father love Me** (cf. iii. 35 ; v. 20), **because I lay down My life** (see on ver. 11), **that I may take it again.** These words are not to be connected with the first clause thus :— ' Because I lay down my life, the Father loves me so greatly that I have power to take it again,' but with the second—"I lay down my life that I may take it again "—and express not the result (Calvin, De Wette), but the purpose of Christ's death— not the purpose of the Father (Tholuck), but of Christ Himself. In laying down His life it was Christ's purpose to resume it in order to make men partakers of it ; and for this double reason, Christ declared, the Father loved Him—(1) that He designed to lay down His life for the sheep to save them from death, and (2) to resume it in order to enrich them with life.

18. No one taketh it away from Me —not even God (Godet) takes (αἴρει) now in time, or in eternity took, ἦρεν (א B, Tischendorf, Westcott and Hort), it ; **but I lay** (or, *am laying*) **it down of Myself**—ἀπ’ ἐμαυτοῦ, in virtue of My own authority and power, i.e. without external constraint of any kind, of My own free will. **I have power** ἐξουσίαν, right, authority, leave, ability (see on i. 12) **to lay it down,** to dispose of it in a way no creature can do, surrender it as a sacrifice for others, **and I have power to take it again,** to recall it from death and replace it in its pristine power and condition. **This commandment** ἐντολὴν, or commission, the source of eternal life (xii. 50), viz. the mandate to lay down my life and to take it again (Meyer, Brückner, Luthardt, Westcott), or the mandate with which I came into the world, the power of being able to die or rise again at will (Godet), **have I received from My Father.** Christ meant that while possessed in virtue of His divine personality of power to die and rise again, yet His doing so was in execution of a commission with which He had been entrusted by the Father.

19-21. **There arose a division again among the Jews because of these words,** as previously on account of similar utterances there had arisen among the multitude (vii. 40) and among the Pharisees (ix. 16). **And many of them said,** or, *began to say,* **He hath a devil** or *demon* (cf. vii. 20; viii. 48), **and is mad,** raves under the evil spirit's influence : **why hear ye Him?** or, *why do ye still listen to Him?*

Of what use can it be to pay attention to the splutterings of a maniac? The question showed the anxiety of the speakers on account of the impression made by Christ's words. **Others said, These are not the sayings of,** or *these sayings are not of,* i.e. proceed not from, **one possessed with a devil** (demon). **Can a devil** (demon) **open the eyes of the blind?** The two arguments on which the unsophisticated among the Jews rested the claims of Christ were (1) the intrinsic excellence of His teaching, and (2) the unparalleled splendour of His miracles.

HOMILETICS

VER. 1-6.—THE FOLD AND THE SHEPHERD.
I. **The Fold of the Sheep.** 1. *The similitude set forth.* (1) A flock. An interesting spectacle, common in oriental countries. (2) A fold. A low walled enclosure in the middle of an open field, into which the flocks are driven at decline of day to secure them against attacks from wolves and thieves. (3) A porter. An under-shepherd, or slave, to whom the folded flocks are entrusted to guard them against the dangers incident to darkness, while the master-shepherd spends the evening at home with his family or in his tent close by. 2. *The similitude explained.* (1) The flock an emblem of (a) the Israelitish nation : Ps. lxx. 20 ; lxxviii. 52 ; lxxx. 1 ; Is. xl. 11 ; lxiii. 11 ; Jer. xiii. 17 ; Ezek. xxiv. 17 ; (β) Christian believers : xxi. 16, 17 ; Luke xii. 32 ; Heb. xiii. 20 ; (γ) the world of mankind : Ps. c. 3. (2) The fold a picture of (a) the Hebrew Church, in which through the long night of Judaism God's ancient people were kept like a flock until the breaking forth of gospel day, when their heaven-appointed shepherd should come to lead them forth to the green pastures and beside the still waters of N. T. grace and truth ; (β) the N. T. Church in which until the day dawns and the shadows (of time's night) flee away a similar service is performed for believers, who are kept by the power of God through faith unto salvation (1 Pet. i. 5), and kept for Jesus Christ (Jude 1) until He comes on the resurrection morning to claim them as His purchased possession (Eph. i. 14) ; (γ) the moral and spiritual environment in which mankind as a whole is now kept in order to be redeemed and emancipated by Jesus Christ. (3) The porter a symbol of the Holy Spirit, through whose gracious influence alone it was that Israel was not utterly corrupted and led astray during the years of her antecedent history, and that in particular hearts an entrance was obtained for Christ and His salvation. The same offices are still performed by this heavenly and efficient watchman in the N. T. Church and in the world.
II. **The Invaders of the Fold.** 1. *Their practices described.* (1) Negatively. They enter not by the door through which the lawful shepherd passes. (2) Positively. They ascend up from another quarter, they climb over the wall as unauthorized intruders. 2. *Their characters defined.* "Thieves and robbers" ; men who choose secret and stealthy ways and devise violent deeds. Those who invade their neighbour's rights or despoil their neighbour's goods mostly elect the night season for doing so (Job xxiv. 14 ; Prov. i. 11-19), resort to under-hand methods for carrying out their purpose, and scruple not at violence to accomplish their designs. 3. *Their persons identified.* The Pharisees, who were no true shepherds of the people, since they entered not upon the duties of their office by themselves exercising and endeavouring to excite in others faith in

Christ, but played the part of thieves and robbers towards both the shepherd and the sheep ; first robbing Christ, the True Shepherd, of those who had been given Him by the Father as His flock, through leading them and keeping them away from Him ; and second, robbing the sheep of that nourishment of grace and salvation Christ alone could give, as well as shepherding the sheep, i.e. ruling over the people, for their own glory and enrichment rather than for the people's good.

III. **The Shepherd of the Sheep.** 1. *His access to the fold.* He enters by the door, the legitimate mode of reaching the interior. So Christ, as distinguished from the Scribes and Pharisees, self-elected guides of the people, was appointed by God, and sent by the Father (Heb. v. 5). In opposition also to these, Christ sought an entrance into the fold of the Hebrew Church not in the way of self-seeking, but purely under His Father's leading (v. 30, 43 ; vi. 38 ; viii. 54). 2. *His attention from the porter.* Different from the thieves and robbers against whom the watchman guards, he is by the latter eagerly expected and waited for ; and lo ! the instant his step is heard upon the sward or his whistle on the morning air, to him the porter openeth. So the Spirit in the Hebrew Church (in the souls of the devout) was looking and waiting for the coming of the Great Shepherd long before promised (Is. xl. 11 ; Ezek. xxxiv. 23, 24 ; Zech. xi. 16) ; and when He came, that same Spirit (speaking through the Holy Scriptures) bore testimony in His favour, and opened men's hearts to receive Him. 3. *His relation to the flock.* (1) What the sheep receive from Him. Affection—they are "his own." Individualization—He 'calls them by name,' not merely deals with them in mass. Constraint—He putteth them out, that they might be taken to the green pastures and led by the still waters. Guidance—He goeth before and leadeth them. All these believers enjoy at the hands of Christ (Ps. xxiii. 2). (2) What He obtains from the sheep. Recognition—they 'hear' His voice, distinguish it from that of a stranger. Appreciation—they 'know' His voice, understand its sense as well as sound. Obedience—they follow where He leads ; docilely, trustfully, cheerfully. All these Christ obtains from His people.

Lessons. 1. Marks of being a true shepherd. 2. Signs of being a true sheep.

VER. 7-10.—THE DOOR AND THE SHEPHERDS.

I. **The Door of (or to) the Sheep.** 1. *Of the sheep,* i.e. the entrance through which a soul passes into the fold of God's redeemed flock. This Christ claims to be (1) Personally. *I* am the door : not My teaching, example, propitiation, but Myself. 2. Exclusively. I am *the* door. As a Saviour, Christ stands alone, shares His honours with no colleague, not even with a Moses and far less with a Zoroaster, a Confucius, a Mahomet—with neither angel nor virgin, neither priest nor pope. (3) Universally. If *any one* enter in ; Christ's services as a Saviour and Mediator are available for all (Heb. vii. 25). (4) Certainly. He *shall be* saved. Christ's ability to help is no peradventure, but a clearly ascertained, fully demonstrated, and amply confirmed fact. (5) Completely. Whosoever seeks through Him shall obtain salvation, the most desirable in quality, perfect freedom, the most abundant in quantity, ample satisfaction. 2. *To the sheep or of the shepherds ;* i.e. the entrance by which these find access to the sheep. This also Christ claims to be ; thereby teaching that no one is either entitled, or qualified, to perform towards his fellow men the functions of a religious shepherd or spiritual guide, who does not (1) derive his authority to assume such an office from Christ (Eph. iv. 11), (2) approach men through his own personal acquaintance with Christ (2 Cor. iv. 13), (3) seek to lead men to a believing recognition and acceptance of Christ (1 Cor. ii. 2), and (4) devote himself to the spiritual edification of those who have believed on Christ (Eph. iv. 12; 1 Tim. iv. 6 ; 2 Tim. iv. 2).

II. **The Shepherds of the Sheep.** 1. *The false shepherds.* (1) The time they appeared—"before Christ." (2) The characters they bore—"thieves and robbers." (3) The objects they pursued—they came to 'steal, kill, and destroy' the flock in order to advance their own enrichment (ver. 10). (4) The ex-

7

perience they met with—" the sheep did not hear them " (ver. 8). See preceding homily. 2. *The True Shepherd.* (1) Whence He came—from above, from heaven, from God. (2) When He appeared—in the fulness of the times. (3) What He sought—the welfare of God's flock; (1) that men (God's larger flock) might have life, and (2) that believers (God's special flock) might have it or all that they need in abundance (i. 16).

Lessons. 1. A voice of warning for the under-shepherds. 2. A note of comfort for the sheep.

VER. 11-18.—THE HIRELING AND THE GOOD SHEPHERD.

I. **The Hireling.** 1. *Mercenary.* He tends the flock simply for wages as Jacob did (Gen. xxix. 15, 18), though not with the love for the dumb animals that Jacob showed (Gen. xxxi. 38). An emblem of the Pharisees and Jewish rulers generally who served Jehovah in a purely legal spirit (Matt. xix. 16) and shepherded Jehovah's flock with an eye to the merit they might thereby acquire and the recompense they should therefor receive; of those who in Christ's day thrust themselves into the priest's office for a piece of bread (1 Sam. ii. 36); of all who at any time assume the ministerial office in the Christian church for filthy lucre's sake (Tit. i. 11). 2. *Selfish.* He pursues his calling with an eye to his own interest, seeks his own profit, and studies his own comfort. In this respect a type of the Jewish Leaders, the Pharisees, who exactly answered Ezekiel's description of the shepherds who fed themselves and not the flock, who ate the fat and clothed themselves with the wool and killed them that were fed (xxxiv. 2, 3); and of (so-called) Christian pastors who use their official position solely for the purpose of securing for themselves worldly emolument, social preferment, material benefit, or temporal renown (1 Tim. iii. 3, 8). 3. *Negligent.* Chiefly occupied with thoughts of his own happiness and comfort, he not only leaves the sheep to cater for themselves (Ezek. xxxiv. 4; Zech. xi. 16, 17), but, fleeing at the first approach of danger, permits the helpless creatures to be ravaged and the flock to be scattered by wolves and other beasts. Once more a representative of the corrupt hierarchy that presided over Israel, and of such (nominally) Christian teachers who, neglecting the highest interests of their people, leave them to fall a prey to the principalities and powers of evil.

II. **The Good Shepherd.** 1. *The owner of the flock.* Christ; the Proprietor of His believing people, (1) by right of creation (i. 3; Col. i. 16; cf. Ps. c. 3), (2) by his Father's donation (vi. 37, 39), (3) by purchase of His blood (Rev. xiv. 4; 2 Pet. ii. 1; 1 Cor. vi. 20; vii. 23). 2. *The friend of the flock.* As the shepherd and the sheep, so Christ and His people know one another; yea the mutual knowledge of the latter so far surpasses its earthly type, in inwardness, intelligence, sweetness, clearness, purity, strength, that its proper antitype exists only in the mutual knowledge which the Father and the Son possess of each other (ver. 15). 3. *The saviour of the flock.* As the good shepherd defends his flock at the peril, and sometimes at the expense, of his life, so Christ lays down His life for His people (ver. 11, 15, 17)—dies to preserve them from dying and rises to enrich them with life (ver. 10). 4. *The collector of the flock.* Like the good shepherd who seeks after his sheep when scattered (Ezek. xxxiv. 6; Matt. xviii. 12; Luke xv. 4, 6), Christ gathers into one community all who are His, out of every nation and kindred and people and tongue (xvii. 11, 21, 22, 23; Rom. xii. 4, 5; 1 Cor. xii. 12, 13; Eph. i. 10; ii. 15); constituting them a spiritual flock of which He is the chief (1 Pet. v. 4) and the great (Heb. xiii. 20) shepherd.

Lessons. 1. The love of Christ for His people. 2. The voluntariness of Christ's death. 3. The substitutionary character of His sufferings. 4. The world-wide aspect of the atonement. 5. The resurrection necessary to perfect Christ as a Saviour.

SECTION FOURTH.—CHRIST'S FOURTH PRESENTATION OF HIMSELF TO HIS
OWN (THE JEWISH PEOPLE); IN THE THIRD AND FOURTH
YEARS OF HIS MINISTRY

CHAP. X. 22—XII. 11

Beginning, like the others already considered, in Jerusalem on the occasion of a feast—that of Dedication—this fourth exhibition of the glory of the Incarnate Word, terminated after four months in Bethany, six days before the last Passover. Of the interval the greater portion was spent in Perœa, where He enjoyed indeed comparative seclusion from the now aroused and vigilant authorities, but no cessation from the active labours of His ministry. It seems probable that at the close of the preceding feast—that of Tabernacles—our Lord did not remain in Jerusalem (Meyer, Hengstenberg), but returned to Galilee (Godet, Andrews), from which He soon after took His final departure, in a public manner, travelling through Perœa towards the metropolis (Matt. xix. 1 ; Luke ix. 51). From Perœa He proceeds to the capital to attend the Feast of Dedication, returning almost immediately thereafter to the same quarter, which He does not leave, until summoned to Bethany. After the raising of Lazarus He seeks retirement for a brief period in Ephraim, a city near the Judæan wilderness. At Bethany a second time He arrives six days before the Passover. The contents of this section may be thus arranged :—

I. In Jerusalem ; at the Feast of Dedication: chap. x. 22-39.

II. In Perœa ; with the Mountaineers : ver. 40-42.

III. In Bethany ; among His friends :—

    1. The Raising of Lazarus : xi. 1-57.
    2. The Supper in Simon's House : xii. 1-11.

I. IN JERUSALEM; AT THE FEAST OF DEDICATION
CHAP. X. VER. 22-39

EXPOSITION

Chap. x. ver. 22, 23. **And it was the feast of the dedication**, lit., *but (then :* B L, Westcott and Hort) *there was taking place the Encaenia ;*—a feast instituted by the Maccabees in commemoration of the purification of the temple after its profanation by Antiochus Epiphanes (1 Macc. iv. 36 : Jos. Ant. xii. 7, 6); beginning on the 25th of Kislev (December) and lasting eight days—days of joy, during which lights were kindled at the doors of the houses in remembrance, say the Talmuds, of a vial of oil which the Greeks found not,

and which, though it contained only
oil enough for one day, through a
miracle lasted eight days ;—at Jerusalem (ii. 13): it was winter; mentioned probably to account for the
statement ensuing ; and Jesus was
walking in the temple (ii. 14), in
Solomon's porch. This cloister (Acts
iii. 11) ran along the eastern wall on
both sides of the gate of Susa ; had
three rows of columns 50 feet high,
and two walks 30 feet wide, the
columns each of one stone (white
marble), the walks paved with stones
of various colours, and the roofs
adorned with sculptures in wood ; was
a survival from the Solomonic temple ;
and stood over the valley of Jehosaphat
(Jos. Ant. xv. 11, 5 ; xx. 9, 7).

24. The Jews therefore came round
about Him, the piazza being a place
of public resort (ii. 14), and said, or,
kept saying, unto Him, How long dost
Thou hold us in suspense, lit., *raise our
soul*, i.e. excite it with conflicting emotions? If thou art the Christ, tell us
plainly : cf. vii. 13 ; xi. 14.

25, 26. Jesus answered them, I told
you, not indeed directly as to the
Samaritan woman (iv. 26) and the
healed man (ix. 37), but still indirectly
and frequently (v. 43 ; vi. 38 ; vii. 29 ;
viii. 23, 25), and ye believe not : ye
continue still in unbelief : the works
that I do in My Father's name, these
bear witness of Me. See on v. 36.
But ye believe not, because ye are not
of My sheep—or, *of the sheep that are
Mine*, ver. 14-16. The clause "as I
told you" (T. R., Tischendorf) here
omitted (אּ B L, Westcott and Hort),
must, if genuine, be connected with
ver. 26 (Meyer, Godet, etc.) rather than
with ver. 27 (Paley).

27, 28. My sheep hear My voice
(ver. 3, 16), and I know them (ver. 14),
and they follow Me (ver. 4): and I
give unto them eternal life (see on iii.
15) ; and they shall never perish (iii.
16), and no one shall snatch them out
of My hand, as the wolf snatches the
sheep (ver. 12). The clauses of these
verses are susceptible of a threefold
arrangement :—(1) three pairs of two
each (Bengel) ; (2) two groups of three
each (Luthardt) ; or (3) three divisions
of one, two, and three respectively.
The first seems the best.

29. My Father which hath given

them unto Me, is greater, not a greater
potence, μεῖζον (Meyer), but a greater
being, μεῖζων, than all, not merely than
all hostile powers (Lücke), but all outside of Himself, better than "what
My Father hath given Me," אּ* B L,
Tischendorf, Westcott and Hort), i.e.
the one body of My believing people
(vi. 37, 39), 'is stronger' or 'more precious than all' ; and no one is able to
snatch *them*, or *anything*, out of the
Father's hand : cf. Deut. xxxii. 39 ; Is.
xliii. 13.

30. I and the Father are one. Not
simply in ethical correspondence, in
mind, intention, will (Arius, Socinus,
Beyschlag, Paley), or in dynamical
fellowship, as being possessed of co-
ordinate power (Calvin, Luthardt,
Tholuck, Meyer), but also in metaphysical essence or oneness of being
(Augustine, Bengel, Godet, Westcott,
and others).

31. The Jews took up, perhaps
fetched from a distance, βαστάζω signifying 'to carry in the hands' as a
weight, stones to stone Him, as they
had done before (viii. 59), and for a
similar reason (ver. 33). This shows
the construction put upon the preceding declaration.

32. Jesus answered them, Many
good, καλὰ, not beneficent merely, but
morally beautiful, works have I
showed, or, *did I show*, you from the
Father (cf. v. 20 ; ix. 3); for which of
those works, lit., *for what sort of work*
of (or from among) *these* do ye stone
Me? Language of indignant irony—if
Christ ever employed such, which is
doubtful.

33. The Jews answered Him, For a
good work we stone thee not, but for
blasphemy (see Lev. xxiv. 10-16); and
(=even) because that thou, being a man,
makest thyself God, i.e. a divine being:
cf. 'equal with God' (v. 18).

34-36. Jesus answered them, Is it
not written in your law (viii. 17), I
said, Ye are gods? (Ps. lxxxii. 6). If
he called them, not *angels* (Bleek), or
heathen princes (De Wette), but Israelitish judges—who besides were unrighteous—gods, unto whom the Word
of God ὁ λόγος τοῦ θεοῦ, not 'divine revelations received by them ' (Olshausen), or 'divine enlightenment conferred upon them ' (Luther), or the
words of the Psalm addressed to them

(De Wette, Ewald), but the earlier word to which the Psalm refers, the word spoken to them at the period of their induction into office (Brückner, Hofmann, Meyer, Luthardt), with perhaps a glance at the pre-incarnate Word of God (Cyril), from whom such word came (**and the**) or, placing the clause under the government of ' if '— *and if* **the Scripture cannot be broken** loosened, or deprived of its validity (v. 18 ; vii. 23), **say ye of him whom the Father** surely greater than the word of God! **sanctified,** or consecrated (xvii. 17, 19 ; cf. Jer. i. 5 ; Eccles. xlv. 4 ; xlix. 7), **and sent into the world** (iii. 17), **Thou blasphemest ;** *because I said* (indirectly, ver. 29, 30) **I am** *the* **Son of God,** or *Son of God am I*—fixing attention on the dignity He claimed rather than on the fact that such dignity belonged to Him ? **37, 38. If I do not the works of My**

Father, believe me not. Cf. ver. 25, 32 ; v. 36 : xiv. 11. **But if I do them,** as ye cannot deny (vii. 31), **though,** or, *even if,* **ye believe not Me,** credit not my word as ye do not (ver. 26), **believe the works,** accept them as ' signs ' testifying on behalf of me ; **that ye may know and understand,** that ye may *learn to know* and may at length *acknowledge* (Godet), that ye may *attain to knowledge* and *may permanently know* (Meyer); although the reading ' may know and believe ' (A. V.) is not without support (Brückner, Hengstenberg, De Wette, and others : cf. Is. xliii. 10 ; 1 John iv. 16), **that the Father is in Me, and I in the Father.** See on xiv. 10.

39. **They sought again to take Him, and He went forth out of their hand.** How is not specified, but it is unnecessary to resort to the hypothesis of a miracle.

HOMILETICS

VER. 22-39.—CHRIST'S ACCOUNT OF HIMSELF.
I. **The Nature of His Credentials.** 1. *His sayings.* He had often told the Jews, who now interrogated Him, who He was (ver. 25). 2. *His miracles.* His works had been ' signs ' they should have understood (ver. 25, 38). 3. *His acceptance by the pious.* Jehovah's flock and His own sheep recognized Him ; an indirect testimony that He was no impostor (ver. 27). 4. *His ability to save.* He could and did bestow eternal life on them who believed and followed Him (ver. 28).
II. **The Dignity of His Person.** 1. *The Father's commissioner.* The Father had sent Him into the world (ver. 36). 2. *The Father's shepherd.* The Father had put His flock into Christ's hand (ver. 29). 3. *The Father's son.* He distinctly claimed to be the Son of God (ver. 36). 4. *The Father's equal.* He and the Father were one (ver. 30) ; while the Father was in Him and He in the Father (ver. 38). The Jews understood this (ver. 33).
III. **The Vindication of His Pretensions.** 1. *The charge preferred against Him.* Blasphemy, in making out Himself, a man, to be God (ver. 33). 2. *The punishment proposed for Him.* Stoning, the penalty prescribed by the law for such offenders. 3. *The answer returned by Him.* (1) Scriptural—drawn from their own holy writings. (2) Logical. If God's word called civic rulers ' gods,' it could not be blasphemy for God's Son to call Himself ' Son of God.' (3) Final. They could not reply to it except by violence ; and He withdrew Himself beyond the reach of their machinations.
Learn 1. The sufficiency of existing evidences for Christ and Christianity. 2. The irreconcileable antagonism between the unrenewed heart and Christ. 3. The ease with which objections and objectors to Christ can be answered. 4. The certainty that evil men can never achieve a final triumph over Christ.
VER. 27-29.—CHRIST'S SHEEP.
I. **Their Characters.** 1. They hear Christ's voice. 2. They know Christ's person. 3. They follow Christ's lead.
II. **Their Privileges.** 1. Recognition. " I know them." 2. Salvation. " I give unto them eternal life." 3. Protection. " They shall never perish."

II. IN PERŒA : WITH THE MOUNTAINEERS
Chap. X. Ver. 40-42

Exposition

Ver. 40. **And He went away** from Jerusalem **again** having probably come thence, beyond Jordan ; or, as He had done on a previous occasion (i. 28), **into the place where John was at the first baptizing** (see on i. 28) ; and there He abode, until summoned by the messengers from Bethany.

41. **And many** *people of the district,* perhaps the posthumous fruits of John's labours (Bengel), **came unto** Him ; and they said, or *began to say,* John indeed did no sign—a statement showing the people were not predisposed to ascribe miracles to their prophets, as is often alleged ; **but all things whatsoever John spake of this man were true.** A valuable testimony to both John and Jesus.

42. **And many believed on Him there.** In this respect the province was a striking contrast to the capital.

Homiletics

Ver. 40-42.—A Season of Retirement.
I. **Old Scenes revisited** : ver. 40. Bethany beyond Jordan : the scene 1. Of His *baptism* by the forerunner. 2. Of His *consecration* by the Father, through the voice and the dove. 3. Of His *showing unto Israel* as the Lamb of God. 4. Of His *first acquisition of adherents,* in Andrew and John, Peter and James, Philip and Nathanael.
II. **Accustomed Labours pursued** : ver. 41. 1. *With disinterested zeal.* Though Christ needed rest, He could not resist the silent invitation of the people who flocked towards Him. 2. *With unwearied diligence.* Christ neglected no opportunities that presented themselves for doing His Father's work. 3. *With practical beneficence.* It is obvious He performed miracles, most likely of healing.
III. **Fresh Testimonies gained** : ver. 41. 1. *That He was a greater prophet than the Baptist had been.* He did signs : John did not. 2. *That John's witness concerning Him had been true.* Christ had formerly appealed to John (v. 33-35).
IV. **New Disciples secured** : ver. 42. 1. *Numerous.* Many at this time adhered to Him. 2. *Intelligent.* They were actuated by conviction. 3. *True.* They believed on Him as Messiah.
Lessons. 1. Grateful remembrance of past experiences. 2. Diligent employment of present opportunities. 3. Hopeful expectation of future vindication.

III. AT BETHANY. 1. THE RAISING OF LAZARUS
Chap. XI. Ver. 1-57

Exposition

Chap. xi. ver. 1-16. The Departure from Perœa.

Ver. 1. **Now** but—the narrative proceeding to record an event which occasioned Christ's departure from Perœa—**a certain** *man,* indefinitely introduced because he has not yet been mentioned in this or the other Gospels, **was sick,** lying ill, in a weak state of health, **Lazarus,** a shortened form of Eleazarus, 'Helped of God,' employed in Luke (xvi. 20), Josephus (Wars, v. 13, 7), and the Talmud, **of** ἀπὸ, residing in, though more probably, deriving his birth from, **Bethany,** 'The House of Mourning' (Keim), 'The House of the Poor' (Luthardt), 'The House of Depression' (Simon); better, 'The House of Dates' (Lightfoot) from the abundance of palm trees in its environs (xii. 13)—now a small village (*El-Azarieh*, from El-Azir the Arabic form of Lazarus) of twenty houses occupied by Bedouin Arabs (Robinson, Biblical Researches, ii. 100)—of ἐκ, meaning also from **the village of Mary and her sister Martha**—neither a hint that this was Magdala (Hengstenberg), nor a differentiation of this from the other Bethany, i. 28 (Meyer), but a more exact description of the village as that to which the sisters, already well known (Luke x. 38-42) belonged, Mary being mentioned first not as the elder (Ewald), or more spiritual (Hengstenberg), but as the more important in the ensuing narrative (Brückner, Godet).

2. **And it was that Mary** (lit., *But the Mary* I refer to *was she*) **who anointed the Lord with ointment,** fragrant essence, a compound of olive oil with spice, described by Lucretius (ii. 547-53), **and wiped His feet with her hair** This incident, afterwards detailed (John xii. 1), is presupposed as well known—though not identical with that in Luke vii. 36, 50 (Hengstenberg)—and is now adverted to not to distinguish this Mary from some other, but to indicate the loving relationship in which this family stood towards Jesus (Tholuck). **whose brother Lazarus was sick.** See ver. 1.

3. **The sisters therefore sent unto Him** Their joint action refutes the fancy that "Lazarus stood nearer to Mary as an unmarried sister than to the married sister (Hengstenberg), and shows that Mary's brother was also Martha's and as dear to her as to Mary. **saying** Not formally preferring a request, though that may be due to the abbreviation of the writer (Tholuck), but simply making a communication, in which however lies concealed (Hengstenberg, Meyer, Luthardt), a desire that in some way He should interpose for their relief. **Lord** How much was included in this designation may be gathered from ver. 22, 27. **behold** Anticipating "the impression which could not fail to be made upon Him by the unexpected intelligence" (Godet). **he**

whom thou lovest "More modest than if they had said he who loves thee" (Bengel). **is sick** Dangerously ill, "since they would hardly have sent so far to Jesus, if there had not been danger of life" (Stier).

4. **But**—contrasting the sorrowful anticipations of the sisters with the hopeful declaration of the Saviour—**when Jesus heard it,** viz. that his friend was sick and that Martha and Mary feared the worst, **He said**—not directly to the messengers, in which case the text would probably have read "He answered and said," nor exclusively to the disciples, but indirectly to both—to the messengers that they might report to the sisters, and to the Apostles that they might be prepared for the approaching miracle :—**This sickness is not unto death,** i.e. as its permanent result. Whether it should be arrested by a process of healing or transformed into a resurrection is not yet announced, although from the first it was foreseen by Christ. Contrast the opposite expression with reference to Hezekiah's illness (2 Kings xx. 1). **but for the glory of God** (cf. John xix. 3), **that the Son of God might be glorified thereby.** This calm reassertion of His Sonship shows how fully Christ was possessed with a consciousness of His metaphysical oneness with the Father. The glory of God and the glory of the Son of God, one glory (Bengel). "In these words, and not in ver. 25 (Baur), the doctrinal design of the narrative is contained" (Meyer).

5. **Now Jesus loved Martha, and her sister, and Lazarus.** Neither an elucidation of ver. 3 (De Wette) which was not necessary, nor a preparation for ver. 6 (B. Crusius, Westcott), as if, without such, Christ's mysterious delay might render His affection doubtful; but an explanation of the comforting assurance of ver. 4, and of His subsequent behaviour in first delaying and then going, which was dictated by affection for the family at Bethany. For this affection the more dignified and spiritual expression ἀγαπᾶν is employed, rather than the more tender and sensuous term φιλεῖν, not because it is Christ's love for the sisters (Meyer) that is referred to, but because the former more fittingly describes the

tie by which Christ is bound to His people.

6. **When therefore He heard that he was sick, He abode at that time two days in the place where He was.** Not to allow Lazarus to die that He might effect a resurrection (Strauss, Baur), since Lazarus must have been dead before Christ was informed of his illness (cf. ver. 39); but because He either wished to complete His labours in Peroea before quitting that district (Lücke, Tholuck), or sought to exercise the faith of the sisters (Olshausen), or desired to go at the moment when He could do the most good (Westcott, Ebrard); or, perhaps best, because " He waited for the signal of the Father by which He always regulated His proceedings" (Godet, Meyer, Luthardt).

7. **Then after this He saith to the disciples** Not simply the delay, but likewise the return, was a consequence of the news (Tholuck). **Let us go into Judæa again.** Judæa rather than Bethany because of the hostility He had there encountered, and the danger he had so recently escaped.

8. **The disciples,** inferring (ver. 4) that the sickness of Lazarus was not to prove mortal, and remembering the peril in which their Master had so lately stood, **say unto Him, Rabbi, the Jews,** i.e. the hierarchical party, **were but now seeking to stone Thee** at the Feast of Dedication (x. 31) ; **and goest Thou thither again?** A question dictated by solicitude for Christ's safety ; meaning, Dost Thou expose Thyself again to such persecutions, and that so unnecessarily, seeing the sickness of Lazarus is not designed to prove fatal ?

9, 10. **Jesus answered,** with a view to calm their anxiety, **Are there not twelve hours in the day ?** in the working day : cf. ix. 4. **If a man walk—** under the image of a walk setting forth the entire round of a man's daily activity—**in the day,** the period appointed for walking, **he stumbleth not** striketh not against any obstacle or impediment with his feet : cf. Matt. iv. 6, **because he seeth the light of this world,** or the sun ; **but if a man walk in the night**—not the time for walking —**he stumbleth, because the light is not in him.** It being dark there is no light to enter into him and become vision.

The verses form a parable, the primary import of which admits of easy statement. Only the explication of its secondary sense occasions diversity of sentiment. According to one interpretation (De Wette), the day is to be understood of "upright, clear, innocent action," the twelve hours as " ways and means " of action, and the night as the "lack of prudence and single-mindedness " ; according to another (Calvin, Luthardt, Godet, Lange), the day means the sphere of one's calling, the sunlight the will of God, and walking in the night doing one's own pleasure ; according to a third (Chrysostom), the walking in the daylight signifies a blameless life, in the course of which one has no cause to be filled with alarm, because he is certain to enjoy the divine protection. It is however better to understand the day as symbolizing the period allotted to Christ for the performance of His life work (cf. ix. 4), a period in which were successive hours or seasons for executing certain works (cf. ii. 4 ; vii. 6, 30 ; viii. 20 ; cf. Luke xxii. 53), just as in the natural day were twelve hours, and to understand Christ as affirming that so long as the allotted period continued He was safe from hurt, as one who walked in the sunshine, because He enjoyed the sunlight of His Father's providence, while after that period, like one walking in the night, He would fall into the hands of His enemies (Bengel, Hengstenberg, Meyer, Westcott). The main objection to this interpretation is that the second member of the comparison scarcely applies either to Christ or to men in general, since no one can walk on the other side of his life-time. It must therefore be viewed as unimportant drapery belonging to the figure, "as a detail not intended for interpretation " (Meyer) ; or the idea of one's calling must be introduced into the notion of " day," since the life-time of men is also their calling-time, and the clause explained as meaning : " He who stands not in his calling wants the certainly guiding light, and will stumble, that is suffer damage " (Tholuck).

11. **These things spake He** to allay the anxieties of His disciples by showing He regarded His working-day as

not yet terminated, since this providential call had summoned Him into Judæa, and that no danger could befall Him so long as He adhered to the path of duty ; **and after this He saith unto them** in explication of the end contemplated in His journey : **Our friend** —a term of endearment, suggested by the words of the messengers (ver. 3) ; also an indication that Lazarus belonged to the circle of Christ's disciples ; perhaps also a proof of existence after death, and of the continuance of Christ's friendship in the land of spirits—**is fallen asleep :** cf. Luke viii. 52 ; Matt. ix. 24. The thought-germ here dropped by Christ is taken up by the Apostles and exalted into the permanent Christian conception of death (Matt. xxvii. 52 ; Acts vii. 60 ; xiii. 36 ; 1 Cor. xv. 6, 18, 20, 51 ; 1 Thess. iv. 13-15). **but I go that I may awake him out of sleep.** Though not so understood by the Apostles, the words meant that Christ was going to resuscitate his dead friend. It was thus an announcement beforehand that He intended to work a miracle ;—an important fact to be considered in estimating the historic credibility of this event.

12. **The disciples therefore** having misunderstood the announcement (ver. 3), **said unto Him, Lord, if he is fallen asleep, he will recover,** lit., *he will be saved;* hence, they imply, no urgent necessity can exist for undertaking this perilous journey.

13. **Now Jesus had spoken of his death ; but they thought that He spake of taking rest in sleep.** This misunderstanding has been pronounced improbable in order to argue against the authenticity of the record (Strauss, De Wette, Reuss), but is sufficiently explained on the above assumption.

14. **Then Jesus therefore said unto them plainly,** or without any figure, **Lazarus is dead.** The event, which had become known to Him not by a second embassy (Paulus, Neander), but by spiritual insight (Meyer), had taken place on the day of the arrival of the sorrowful intelligence.

15. **And I am glad for your sakes that I was not there** Christ meant not as Martha and Mary afterwards did (ver. 32), that His presence was necessary to effect a cure in Lazarus, or that

He could not have prevented Lazarus from dying though at a distance from Bethany (cf. iv. 50) ; but simply wished His disciples to understand that had He been at Bethany Lazarus would not have died, because He would have healed His friend, though for their sakes (and no doubt also for the sake of the sisters and Lazarus) He was better pleased He had been absent—the reason being subjoined in the words that follow. **to the intent ye may believe** Not as if they were not already believers, but " faith *is* as it were where it *grows* and not before " (Hengstenberg), and " every *new* flight of faith is in its degree a *progress* towards belief " (Meyer), and this new flight of faith would be much more certainly brought about by a miracle of resurrection than by one of healing. **nevertheless,** although not present while our friend was yet in life, **let us go unto him,** now that he lies in death.

16. **Thomas therefore,** not convinced of the prudence of Christ's proposed journey, **who is called Didymus**— "Twin," the Greek translation of Thomas (Hebrew) and of the same import ; probably the designation of this disciple among the early Greek Christians for whom John wrote ; the idea that Christ called him Didymus to suggest his double nature (Hengstenberg) being a fancy—**said unto his fellow-disciples,** who probably still evinced a degree of reluctance, **Let us also go, that we may die with Him.** Words of affection and courage !

Ver. 17-37. The Arrival at Bethany.

Ver. 17. **So when Jesus came, he** (lit. *having then come,* sc. to Bethany, *Jesus*) **found,** by inquiry (Meyer) or from information imparted to Him (Godet), what He must already have known (Stier), **that he** Lazarus **had been in the tomb four days already.** The distance of Peræa from Jerusalem, not more than 10 hours, might easily have been traversed in one day. Allowing one day for the journey of the messenger and another for that of Jesus, by adding two days of delay, we may suppose Christ reached Bethany on the morning of the fifth day. In this case, if Lazarus had died on the day of the departure of the messenger, and, according to Jewish custom, had been buried the same evening (Acts v.

6, 10), then at the moment of Christ's arrival he would have been in the grave four days (Godet, Luthardt, Tholuck, and others), though, if Lazarus did not die till the second day of waiting (Bengel, Meyer, Ewald), then Christ must have spent three days upon the road, which is scarcely probable.

18, 19. Now Bethany was nigh unto Jerusalem, on the eastern slope of the Mount of Olives, **about fifteen furlongs off** : properly, at a distance of about 15 furlongs, or 2 miles, the construction ὡς ἀπὸ σταδίων being peculiar (vide Winer's Grammar of the New Test. Diction, part iii. § lxi. 4 ; cf. xxi. 8 ; Rev. xiv. 20). The proximity of Bethany to Jerusalem is specified probably to account for what follows : **and many of the Jews** If "not Sanhedrists" (Tholuck), certainly belonging to the party hostile to Jesus, though it need not be supposed that they hoped through their sympathy to detach the family of Bethany from Jesus (Lampe, Lange). **had come to Martha and Mary** The reading "to those about Martha and Mary" (A, Tischendorf) is not simply a periphrasis for Martha and Mary (Stier, Olshausen), although οἱ περί with an accusative is sometimes used by Attic writers with reference to only one individual (vide Buttmann's Larger Greek Grammar, p. 441), but signifies Martha and Mary with their attendants (cf. Acts xiii. 13 ; xxviii. 7) who were not the mourning women from the village (Olshausen, Tholuck, Alford) but the female servants of the sisters (Meyer, Godet, Luthardt), who were thereby shown to be in comfortable circumstances. **to console them concerning their brother.** The period of mourning usually lasted seven days (cf. 1 Sam. xxxi. 13, the mourning for Saul ; Judith xvi. 24, for Judith), during which it was customary to receive visits of condolence from friends : cf. Job ʼii. 11 ; 2 Sam. x. 1, 2.

20. Martha therefore, who was probably attending to her domestic duties in the outer apartment, while Mary was detained by grief in the inner chamber : cf. the characters of the sisters as they appear in Luke x. 38 sq. **when she heard** Just as likely by Christ's having sent to inform her, as from a passing Jew who had overtaken

Jesus (Luthardt). The notion that Martha was called secretly because of the internal relations of the house at the time (Hengstenberg) is improbable. **that Jesus was coming** (lit., *that Jesus cometh*, probably the exact message delivered to Martha) **went,** without taking time to inform her sister, **and met Him,** with the view of acquainting Him with the death of Lazarus, **but Mary still sat,** or, *continued sitting,* the force of the imperfect, **in the house.** She may have done so because it was customary to receive visits of condolence sitting (Meyer, Luthardt), perhaps because of her deeper sorrow (Tholuck, Godet), or because such was her wont (Luke x. 38, Hengstenberg) ; certainly not because on account of her previous life she now desired to live in seclusion (ibid.). The characters of the two sisters as here sketched harmonize with those previously drawn by Luke, Martha being the active and Mary the contemplative.

21, 22. Martha therefore said unto Jesus on meeting with Him, **Lord, if Thou hadst been here, my brother had not died.** Not the language of complaint (Strauss, Lücke, B. Crusius), since she must have known Lazarus died before Christ could have received the tidings of his illness (Godet), but simply of regret that Christ had not been present during her brother's illness. She no doubt believed Christ would have healed Lazarus by praying unto God on his behalf, as the next verse implies. **And even now** καὶ νῦν (א B C X, Tischendorf, Westcott and Hort) *and now,* though the stronger ἀλλὰ καὶ νῦν (T. R.) is by some (Godet) preferred — "but *even now,*" i.e. in present circumstances, though, contrary to thy promise and our expectation, the illness of Lazarus has resulted in death. **I know** A strong expression of confidence (contrast the milder "I believe" of ver. 27), probably based upon her remembrance of Christ's words, which were doubtless reported to her. **that whatsoever** Indefinite, because that which she desired is too great to be expressed (Godet). **Thou shalt ask of God** Martha employs in connection with Christ a word (αἰτεῖσθαι, to solicit for oneself) Christ uses when speaking of men (cf. xiv. 13 ; xv. 16 ; xvi. 23), but never when referring to Himself (vide Luke xxii. 32, ἐδεήθη ; John xiv. 16, ἐρωτήσω). The word was probably due to the intensity of her emotion which led her to select the more human term (Meyer), and in any case "it fits the situation and is quite natural in Martha's mouth" (Luthardt), although it has been styled a less dignified word (Bengel) than should have been employed in addressing Christ. **God will give thee.** The position of "God" indicates that Martha was thinking of some miraculous interposition,—and as Lazarus was dead, a resurrection, the hope of which she might have derived from Christ's promise, or from the Galilean awakenings of which she must have heard.

23, 24. Jesus saith unto her, Thy brother shall rise again. Whether at the last day or in the immediate present Christ says not, although He means the latter —purposely shaping His language to exercise Martha's faith (Bengel), to try whether the subjective conditions for so great a miracle as He purposed when present in her (Hengstenberg, Tholuck, Godet), and "to lead her faith away from merely personal interest to the higher domain of the one thing needful" (Meyer). **Martha saith unto Him** mournfully (Luthardt), and resignedly (Meyer), as if sinking under a sense of inward disappointment, that she is referred only to the customary consolation of the bereaved (Tholuck), yet perhaps also hopefully and inquiringly (Calvin), as if desirous to know all our Lord's utterance contained, **I know that he shall rise again in the resurrection at the last day.** The doctrine of a future bodily resurrection was a popular as well as a Pharisaic article of faith in Apostolic times (Acts xxvi. 8 ; xxiii. 8) ; was tacitly acknowledged by the Sadducees in the testing question they proposed to Christ (Matt. xxii. 23, 28) ; was taught in the O. T. Scriptures (Job xiv. 12 ; xix. 26 ; Ps. xvii. 15 ; Is. xxvi. 19 ; Dan. xii. 2 ; Hos. xiii. 14); and was not unknown in patriarchal times (Matt. xxii. 29, 32). To her acquaintance with this tenet of the Hebrew religion Martha gives utterance not because required to declare her faith in the resurrection (Hengstenberg), but to indicate that that did not afford the immediate consolation she sought.

25, 26. Jesus said unto her desiring to lift her thoughts upward "from the momentary and the individual, to the higher general, constantly existing, essential part of believing certainty" (Luthardt)—in one sublime utterance at once meeting her difficulties, and imparting to her that spiritual illumination which was needful to prepare her for the miracle about to be wrought — **I am** ('the great *I am* of this, and at heart also of the other gospels' : Luthardt); not simply I proclaim, give, work, or create, but I, in my divine personality constitute **the resurrection and the life** : the absolute and inward essence of both : not merely the one who raises again and who makes alive " (Meyer). "As Christ is the life not merely because He makes alive (ζωοποιεῖ, John v. 21), but because He Himself as the source of life is the same, even so is He the resurrection, not simply because He awakes, but because He is the thing itself in actuality" (Olshausen). In one aspect the two terms may be said to be synonymous, since "the resurrection is nothing else than the life in conflict with death ; the life (ζωή) comprehends the existence without its antithesis (the death, θάνατος) which is to be overcome, but in the resurrection (ἀνάστασις) appears the life as overcoming death in itself and others " (ibid.) ; or perhaps the life should be viewed as the principle and ground, the origin and cause (Godet, Luthardt) rather than the positive result (Meyer) of the resurrection. **he that believeth on Me** Having explained the relation He Himself bore to the resurrection and the life, Christ proceeds to unfold the nature of their connection with the believer. **though he die** κἂν ἀποθάνῃ, *even if he should have died*, not spiritually (Calvin) but physically, as Lazarus has died, **yet shall he live,** spiritually, but of course also in the end physically, because through faith he has already received that life (ζωή) which contains in itself the resurrection ; it being impossible to restrict the verb 'live' which here stands contrasted with 'die' to the enjoyment of a spiritual existence beyond the grave : **and whosoever liveth,** again not spiritually, but physically, **and believeth on Me,** becoming thereby a

possessor of that life, spiritual and
eternal, which is in Me and is by Me
communicated to all who believe, **shall
never die** *shall not die, for ever;* either
shall not, at any time, now or in the
future, fall beneath the power of death
(Westcott), physical dissolution not
being death in the pregnant sense of
the expression; or shall never die eternally (Meyer), though he may die
physically, physical death not being
included in the true negation of eternal
life. In either case the sense is the
same that the believer is possessed of
a life which sets him eternally beyond
the reach of death. **Believest thou
this?** Intended not to ascertain the
correctness of Martha's views, but to
assist her faith to appropriate for herself that life which would deliver her
from the power as well as from the
fear of death and to perceive how the
same life might even now operate for
the resurrection of her brother.
27. She saith unto Him Not acknowledging she had not understood
the words of Christ (Stier), but declaring her assent to, and acceptance
of, the truth discovered to her (Luthardt, Godet, Meyer, Westcott). **Yea,
Lord, I have believed** "I have convinced myself and believe" (Meyer),
not now for the first time (Bengel),
but all along from the day I began to
repose trust in thee (Luthardt, Hengstenberg, and others). **that Thou art
the Christ.** The fore-announced and
fore-expected Messiah to whom Moses
and the prophets gave witness—"the
end of the theocratic revelations and
dispensations" (Godet). **the Son of
God** (see i. 49), *even* **He that cometh
into the world** Not He that has come
into the world (Luther) *venisti* (Vulgate), or He who will come, *qui ven-
turus erat* (Erasmus), but he who is,
ever was, and always will be, the one
coming into the world. The language
may be viewed as a third and separate
title applied to Jesus (Stier, Luthardt),
but should perhaps be considered as in
apposition to the two former (Godet),
and as intimating that in both of the
two preceding aspects He is ever
coming into the world, and, as it were,
fulfilling men's expectations. In her
confession she "sums up all that Jesus
is to her faith; the promised Messiah
who should come into the world, and

who actually is come as the Son of
God" (Besser).
28. And when she had said this The
confession of the preceding verse,
though of many parts, is yet one
(Westcott). **she went away** Not
because she lacked repose of mind for
further continuance in such high words
and things (Stier), or because "her
faith answering to the revelation left
nothing more to be said" (Westcott),
or because of the joyful expectation
which led her to desire her sister's
presence before the miracle was
wrought (Tholuck), but probably because Christ had directed her to call
her sister (Luthardt, Godet, Meyer,
Hengstenberg). **and called Mary, her
sister** In obedience to Christ's instructions, as the next words "and calleth
thee" appear to show; perhaps also
prompted by sisterly affection.
secretly, saying or, *saying secretly.*
The call may have been given secretly,
or, if openly, the communication may
have been delivered privately; in
either case the caution observed was
probably due to the presence of the
Jews (Bengel, Meyer, Tholuck, Hengstenberg), and may have been advised
by Christ Himself (Godet). **The
Master** ὁ διδάσκαλος, the Teacher (cf.
xiii. 13; xx. 16), probably the usual
designation of Jesus in the Bethany
circle (Bengel). **is here and calleth
thee.** Those who think Jesus said not,
"Where is thy sister?" interpret
Martha's language as signifying that
she regarded Christ's presence as equivalent to "an indirect calling."
29. And she, when she heard it, lit.,
as soon as she heard, Martha's communication, **arose** ἠγέρθη (אBC* LX,
etc.); ἐγείρεται (A., T. R.). **quickly**
Indicating the liveliness of Mary's
emotion at the reception of the news
(Godet): "the double fact that Jesus
was there, and had sent for her, gave
wings to Mary's haste" (Stier). **and
went unto Him.** ἤρχετο rather than
ἐγείρεται of the T. R., the respective
authorities being the same as above.
**30. Now Jesus was not yet come
into the village, but was still in the
place where Martha met Him.** Christ
remained on the outskirts of Bethany
probably at Martha's request that He
might not expose Himself to danger
from the presence of the Jews (Calvin)

or in accordance with His own desire to meet Mary in secret (Meyer, Luthardt, Godet, Westcott), rather than because of the proximity of the grave (Olshausen, Hengstenberg), of which fact He was not then aware (cf. ver. 34).

31. **The Jews then which were with her in the house, and were comforting her, when they saw Mary, that she rose up quickly and went out, followed her,** with a kindly desire to continue their consolatory offices, but with the result that Martha's attempt at secresy was defeated, **supposing** δόξαντες, thinking (אBC*DLXᶜ) rather than λέγοντες, saying (A) **that she was going,** lit., *that she goeth,* **unto the tomb,**—a custom common to the Jews (cf. Matt. xxvii. 61) and Greeks (Wetstein) — **to weep there.** κλαινείν, describing continuous, almost passionate, expression of sorrow (cf. xvi. 20; xx. 11 ff.), is used specially of wailing for the dead (cf. Matt. ii. 18; Mark v. 38; Luke vii. 13; viii. 52; Acts ix. 39), and must be carefully distinguished from δακρυείν, ver. 35 (Westcott). "A very characteristic description of what might be seen and heard at a Jewish grave is given by Lucian." (Lange's Life of Christ, vol. iii. p. 471 : Note by Editor).

32. **Mary, therefore, when she came where Jesus was, and saw Him, fell down at His feet,** which Martha had not done (Bengel)—an indication of the greater violence of her grief than that of Martha (Luthardt, Godet, Meyer) ; perhaps also an act of adoring homage, paid to Him as the Son of God (Calvin), though it need not be viewed as "appropriate to the forgiven sinner" (cf. Mark v. 22 ; vii. 25); whom by some she is supposed to have been (Hengstenberg) — **saying unto Him, Lord,** expressive of religious homage, **if Thou hadst been here, my brother had not died.** Employing Martha's words, without adding any apologetic reflection (Stier)—no doubt because they had been often used interchangeably in their common conversations on the subject. That Christ replied not to Mary's ejaculation is to be explained neither by an abbreviation on the part of the narrator, nor by the disturbance occasioned through the presence of the Jews (Meyer), but either by the intensity of

Christ's own emotion which prevented speech (Tholuck), or by a desire on His part to intimate thereby that the time for speaking was past and the moment for action come (Luthardt, Westcott).

33. **When Jesus therefore**—οὖν indicating a causal connection between the spectacle Christ beheld and the emotion He felt—**saw her weeping** or, *wailing* **and the Jews** *also* **weeping** or, *wailing*—the same verb depicting the tears of both—**who came with her,** to the grave, **as they supposed,** (ver. 31), **He groaned in spirit** ἐνεβριμήσατο τῷ πνεύματι, He was moved with indignation in the spirit, *infremuit spiritu* (Vulgate), *ergrimmte er im Geist* (Luther). ἐμβριμάομαι, from βρίμη, any expression of anger such as snorting, applied to the neighing of horses (Aesch. Theb., 461), and to the fretting of men (Luc. Nec., 20), occurs, besides here and in ver. 38, elsewhere only in Matt. ix. 30 ; Mark i. 43 ; and xiv. 5, each time with the notion of anger (cf. Trench on the Miracles, p. 408). In the present instance it points to a severe mental disturbance or agitation of spirit, excited not by intense sorrow or grief (Calvin, Olshausen, Tholuck), but by vehement indignation (Lampe, Kuinoel, Godet, Luthardt, Meyer, Westcott, and others). If "in the spirit," τῷ πνεύματι, mark the object of this angry emotion, as in the Synoptists, then it must be supposed that Christ was angry at Himself on account either of the emotion He displayed (Chrysostom), which is not likely, seeing He immediately thereafter yielded to it (Godet) ; or of the shrinking He felt from the conflict with death (Westcott) ; or of the forwardness His Spirit evinced to accomplish the miracle without first giving expression to His sympathy with those on whose behalf it was to be wrought (ibid.) ; neither of which however recommends itself as natural ; hardly on account of having been absent (Paley), since His presence was not necessary for a cure. If τῷ πνεύματι signify the instrument rather than the object of Christ's emotion, then possibly the Evangelist designs to say that Jesus by the power of His Spirit, i.e. of His higher divine nature, angrily controlled and subdued the emotion of His humanity (Cyril, Ammonius), an interpretation which fa-

vours the idea of a Docetic Christ, and on that account is adopted by the Newer Criticism (Köstlin, Hilgenfeld). But if the analogy of the Fourth Gospel (xiii. 21; xix. 30), as well as the parallel clause "in Himself" (ver. 38), may be regarded as authoritative guides, then τῷ πνεύματι will describe the sphere, or seat of Christ's emotion (cf. xii. 27), and will represent Christ as being inwardly angry, deeply agitated in His soul with indignant emotion. The exciting cause of this indignation has been variously explained; as the unbelief of the Jews and the sisters (Lampe, Kuinoel), to which however the context makes no allusion; as the hypocritical sorrow of the Jews as contrasted with the sincere grief of Mary (Meyer, Watkins), to which again the words do not point; as the reflection that He had not been able to avert the sorrowful event of Lazarus's death (De Wette); but was probably the contemplation of death's power over humanity on account of sin (Olshausen, Ebrard) and of death itself as the great foe of the human race, behind which was concealed the personal enemy, Satan (Hengstenberg, Westcott, Luthardt), combined perhaps with the thought that for vanquishing this death by the most glorious of His miracles He should Himself have to pay the penalty of death (Godet). The interpretation that supposes Christ merely exercised self-restraint in checking His tears by a more powerful emotion (Bengel) in order to be able to utter the question that follows (Alford) is insufficient. **and was troubled** lit., *and troubled Himself.* Not equivalent to was 'troubled' ἐταράχθη xiii. 21, *turbatus est* (Vulg.), and therefore not synonymous with the inward emotion expressed by the antecedent phrase, but indicative rather of the physical commotion or bodily trembling in which that inward emotion culminated and through which it revealed itself (Godet, Luthardt, Meyer, Hengstenberg, Tholuck, Westcott); the active voice of the verb signifying that this corporeal shuddering was not an involuntary, but a distinctly voluntary act of Christ, who thereby gave complete expression to the horror He felt (*Affectus Jesus non fuere passiones sed voluntariæ commotiones:* Bengel).

34. And said to Martha and Mary, where have ye laid him? The only instance in which Christ is represented as asking information; which He could hardly have done merely for effect, to prepare the way for the miracle (Hengstenberg, Stier), and yet it is difficult to hold that He did not know where Lazarus was buried (Meyer). *Scisti quia mortuus sit, et non ubi sit sepultus?* (Augustine). **They say unto Him, Lord, Come and see.** Κύριε reflecting "the impression of the dignity of His person which the deportment of Jesus had created in the mourners' minds" (Hengstenberg); and the words " Come and see " containing a reminiscence not only of Ps. xlvi. 8 ; lxvi. 5, but also of i. 46.

35. Jesus wept. ἐδάκρυσεν, *lacrimatus est* (Vulgate); not sobbed aloud as over Jerusalem, ἔκλαυσεν (Luke xix. 41), but shed silent tears, which were not insincere, theatrical (Baur), and unnatural (Keim), but a genuine expression of sympathy with the sisters and of sorrow for Lazarus ; a proof of our Lord's true and tender humanity, and an indirect demonstration of the authenticity of the narrative, since " a cold or stony-hearted raiser of the dead would belong to the region of fiction " (Hengstenberg).

36, 37. The Jews, i.e. some of them, **therefore,** at the spectacle of Christ weeping, **said, Behold how he loved him!**—arguing from the tears He shed above the grave of Lazarus how intensely He must have loved Lazarus alive. **But some of them,** i.e. others of the party, being of a more suspicious nature, **said,** not in good will, as if believing in, and appealing to, the miraculous power of Christ (Chrysostom, De Wette, Olshausen, Tholuck, Hengstenberg), but in enmity and illwill, scoffing at what they deemed the powerlessness of Christ's tears (Calvin, Bengel, Godet, Luthardt, and others): **Could not this man, which opened the eyes of him that was blind** An allusion to the miracle of healing (ix. 1, 12), and therefore an indirect authentication of the same. That this rather than the awakenings in Galilee is referred to does not demonstrate the fictitious character of these latter (Strauss), but shows either that the speakers naturally alluded to what was freshest in their memory (Tholuck, Hengstenberg), or did not anticipate a resurrection (Tholuck, Meyer), or were not acquainted with the Galilean raisings (Luthardt, Ebrard, Westcott), or, if acquainted with the rumours concerning them, were not believers in their reality (Alford). The circumstance that they do not refer to the Galilean awakenings which a 2nd century composer would almost certainly have done, demonstrates the historic credibility of this part of the narrative (cf. Neander, Life of Christ, § 232, note j; Trench on the Miracles, p. 412). **have caused that this man also,** Lazarus, *juvenis carus* (Bengel), **should not die?** They do not speak about a Resurrection, since that they regard as beyond Christ's power; but they reason either that Christ had not been able to prevent the death of Lazarus, otherwise He must have done so, if He really loved Lazarus as intensely as His tears appeared to say, or that, though He had been able He had not also been willing, and therefore His present weeping was insincere. On either hypothesis Christ, they desire it to be inferred, must stand discredited.

Ver. 38-44. The Miracle at the Grave.

38. **Jesus therefore,** moved by the remark of the unbelieving Jews (ver. 37), which no doubt had its secret origin in the diabolic activity of him (Satan) who had also been the true author of Lazarus's death, **again groaning in Himself** lit., *again moved with indignation in Himself* (see ver. 33); "another of those mighty shudderings that shook the frame of the Lord of Life" (Trench). "Christ comes not to the sepulchre as an idle spectator, but as a champion who prepares for a contest; and therefore we need not wonder that He again groans" (Calvin). **cometh to,** not into (cf. ver. 31), **the tomb,** which was, according to Oriental custom (Luke vii. 12), outside the town (ver. 30); cf. Jahn's Antiquities, § 206. **Now it was a cave** Sepulchral vaults were usually caves, either natural (Gen. xxiii. 9; Judith xvi. 23), or hollowed out of rocks (Is. xxii. 15, 19; Matt. xxvii. 60). Entered by perpendicular or horizontal passages, on either side of which were cut recesses or chambers for the dead bodies, they

were closed by a large stone or door. Such tombs abound in Palestine at the present day, and are of three kinds. "The first kind is the common excavation in the flat rock, covered by an oblong stone, of which very many are seen in the valley of Jehosaphat. The second is the more costly sepulchral grotto, consisting of excavated chambers, approached through galleries, or opening from a portico. The third is the isolated sepulchre, like the well-known tombs of Absalom and Zechariah in the valley of Jehosaphat. . . . The tombs of the second kind correspond in their main characteristic with the cave sepulchre spoken of in Scripture" (R. S. Poole, in Kitto's Cyclopædia, art. *Burial and Tombs*). The tomb of Lazarus, or what tradition points to as such,. "is a deep vault, partly excavated in the rock, and partly lined with masonry. The entrance is low, and opens on a long, winding, half-ruinous stair-case, leading down to a small chamber, and from this a few steps more lead down to another smaller vault, in which the body of Lazarus is supposed to have lain. The situation of the tomb in the centre of the village scarcely agrees with the Gospel narrative, and the masonry of the interior has no appearance of antiquity. But the real tomb could not have been far distant" (Porter, Handbook, i. 188). "By the dim light of a taper we descended very cautiously by twenty-five slippery steps to the reputed sepulchre of Lazarus, or El-Azariyeh, as both tomb and village are now called. . . . It is a wretched cavern, every way unsatisfactory, and almost disgusting" (Thomson, The Land and the Book, p. 697). Robinson affirms that the present sepulchre could not have been that of Lazarus (vol. ii. p. 101); cf. Keil, Handbuch der Biblischen Archæologie, § 15. **and a stone lay against it.** In this case the entrance must have been by a horizontal passage, as in the tomb of Christ (Mark xv. 46); if *upon it*, then the entrance was by a perpendicular descent, probably by means of a flight of stone steps. "This stone, blocking up the entrance, kept aloof the beasts of prey, above all the numerous jackals, which, else, might have found their way into these receptacles of the dead and torn the bodies" (Trench on the Miracles, p. 412).

39. Jesus saith to those present, Martha, Mary, and their attendants, **Take ye away the stone.** The stone was commonly of great size and weight (Mark xvi. 3, 4). "That Christ commands it to be taken rather than rolled away does not prove that the entrance to the vault was perpendicular: cf. xxi. 1, with Matt. xxviii. 2; Mark xvi. 4; Luke xxiv. 2. "He might indeed have Himself commanded the stone to roll itself away, as a mountain or a fig-tree; He might even have commanded Lazarus to come forth through the impediment of the stone. But the miracles of God avoid with the supremest propriety all that is superfluous" (Stier). **Martha, the sister of him that was dead** A delicate allusion to Martha's relationship to Lazarus, to account for her feeling of horror at the prospect of beholding the ravages death must already, in her estimation, have made of the corpse. **saith unto Him,** while Mary abides in silent resignation, **Lord! by this time he stinketh** Not necessarily a fact she perceived by the smell of putrefaction issuing from the tomb (Strauss, Stier, Godet, Hengstenberg, Alford), although, if it were, the miracle would not thereby be rendered either impossible (Schenkel), or *monstrous* (Olshausen, Trench), unless indeed the corpse were raised in a state of putrefaction; but probably only an inference she drew from the facts that already he had been four days buried (Meyer, Luthardt, Westcott), that probably he had not been embalmed (De Wette, Tholuck, Meyer), or embalmed only "after the manner of the Jews, who limited themselves to wrapping the body in perfumes, a process which could not prevent corruption" (Godet), and that putrefaction commonly commenced on the third day (Wetstein). **for he hath been** *dead* **four days,** lit., *he is a four-days-ago* (corpse). This seems to show that Martha's previous statement was only a deduction, natural enough perhaps, but still not necessarily correct, since the process of decay could easily have been suspended in the case of one whose death had been for the glory of God (Lange, Luthardt). As the object of Martha's observation was to hinder Christ from opening the tomb, the motive of her behaviour has been sought, and probably with truth, in a momentary failure or eclipse of her faith (Godet, Luthardt, Trench), rather than in a desire to set before Christ the greatness of the work He designed to accomplish (Hengstenberg). For a similar mode of speech τὸ τεταρταῖος, *quadriduanus* (Vulg.), see τριταῖος, *triduanus* (Vulg.), three days ago (1 Sam. ix. 20: xxx. 13). There is no reason to suppose that Martha alluded to the peculiar ideas of the Greeks that until the third day expired the spirit was within call and the apparently dead might be only in a trance (see Paley, The Gospel of St. John, p. 92).

40. Jesus saith unto her, for the purpose of reviving her faith, **Said I not unto thee**—alluding not so much to the message He had sent to Martha (Godet) as to the conversation with her which took place on the occasion of their first meeting—**that if thou wouldest believe** A reference to ver. 25, 26, in which Christ had demanded faith as the condition of attaining to the resurrection, or even of seeing, if not of receiving His miraculous interposition in the awakening of Lazarus. **thou shouldest see the glory of God.** These words prove that Christ from the first meant the sisters to expect a resurrection.

41. So, or *then,* after Christ's reasoning with Martha, **they took away the stone.** The addition "from the place *where the dead was laid* (T. R.) has the authority of E S H M, the so-called Byzantine-Recension MSS., but wants that of א B C¹ D L X; A K append "where it was," οὗ ἦν, which is probably also an interpolation. **And Jesus lifted up His eyes** to Heaven (xvii. 1), and to His Father, whose dwelling-place it was. "To man the visible heaven is the most eloquent witness of the invisible power of God" (Godet). **and said, Father,** (cf. xii. 27; xvii. 1, 24, 25; Matt. xi. 25; Luke xxiii. 34, 46, in which Christ directly addresses God as His Father), **I thank Thee that Thou heardest me.** Not equivalent to "I thank Thee that Thou wilt hear me"; the past tense indicating that Christ regarded the miracle as already effected and the prayer included in the words "Lazarus, come forth!" as already answered (Olshausen, Hengstenberg, Ewald, Godet);

or to "I thank Thee that Thou hast heard me!" as if petition and thanksgiving had been simultaneous, the former having been made by "a look into His Father's eyes" and instantly thereupon the other following (Merz, quoted with approbation by Tholuck); but constituting a formal public acknowledgment of the fact that His Father had heard the prayer for Lazarus's life or for the power to effect his restoration, which, though not recorded by the Evangelist, He had previously offered, either when He first heard of the sickness of Lazarus (Bengel, Alford, Westcott), or afterwards in the inarticulate yearnings of His heart (Meyer), or amidst the groanings uttered on the way to the tomb (Calvin). That Christ prays for the power to resuscitate Lazarus does not disprove the truth of His assertion that He is the Resurrection and the Life, but only demonstrates His economical subordination to the Father—"He does nothing more than acknowledge that He is the servant of the Father" (Calvin), or rather His perfect fellowship in working with the Father (cf. v. 19). "The miracle of Christ" (i.e. wrought by Christ) "took place through the coincidence of the soliciting will of the God-man, and of the creative omnipotence of God in nature, and in virtue of this co-working were also all Christ's prayers heard" (Tholuck).

42. **And I knew** at the time when I prayed **that Thou hearest me always.** "From this it follows that He never stood in need of separate answers (to separate prayers); His request was always heard. For this reason already in His impulse to pray lay the certainty of His being heard" (Gess, Christi Person und Werk, vol. i. p. 105). **but because of the multitude which standeth around I said it** On the ground that this is supposed to transform the preceding thanksgiving into a mere piece of acting, "a show" (Weisse) or "sham prayer" (Baur), a "prayer of cold accommodation" (Strauss), performed for the sake of the audience, the prayer itself has been explained as a fiction of the Evangelist put into Christ's mouth to supply an argument for the story (De Wette), or for the purpose of maintaining the apparent truthfulness of Christ's claim to be regarded as divine

(Strauss); but the simple circumstance that Christ now openly in the form of a solemn eucharist intimated that of which He had all along been conscious, viz., that the Father always heard Him, did not necessarily prove that He was insincere either in His private petition or in His public thanksgiving, any more than a Christian minister is aiming at stage effect because He prays aloud before the congregation (Tholuck). The opinion that ver. 42 is a reflection of the Evangelist (Lücke) is sufficiently disposed of by the observation that in this case "the Jews" would probably have been used rather than the multitude (Meyer). **that they may believe that Thou didst send Me.** In these words Christ explains the reason why He gave audible utterance to His thanks. He wished distinctly in the hearing of the people to connect the miracle He was about to work with God, so that when the event took place they might be led to recognize Him as the Son whom the Father had sent into the world. They had refused to accept the healing of the blind man as a work of divine Power; now before raising Lazarus He publicly claims that He is about to do so with the full consent and by the power of His Father. If therefore He fails, it will be an overwhelming refutation of His pretensions; if He succeeds, it will irrefragably demonstrate His claims. The incident recalls Elijah's appeal to Jehovah on Mount Carmel (1 Kings xviii. 21 sq.). See Lange on Christ's Prayer at the Tomb of Lazarus, The Life of Christ : vol. iii. p. 475.

43. **And when He had thus spoken, He cried with a loud voice** possibly to contrast Himself with the whispering necromancers of Is. viii. 19 ; xxix. 4 (Bengel, Grotius, Lampe, Stier, Westcott), but more probably to symbolize to the bystanders at once the greatness of the work He attempted, and the irresistibility of the power He wielded: **Lazarus !**—addressing him by name not because he was already awakened, the miracle of revivification having taken place before the thanksgiving (Origen, Lampe), but "as one would call a sleeping man" (Besser), and perhaps also as one would awake a friend— **come forth !** lit., *hither out ! δεῦρο ἔξω, huc foras !* not 'be raised,' *ἐγέρθητι*, as in the case of the young man at Nain

(Luke vii. 15), or 'Arise!' ἐγείρου, as in that of Jairus's daughter (Luke viii. 54), because Lazarus lay within the sepulchre, whereas the youth lay upon a bier and the maid upon a bed.

44. He that was dead came forth or, *came forth the dead man!* The solemnity of the statement is increased by the omission of the "and" of the Received Text ; and this solemnity almost guarantees that the re-animation of him who had been buried was effected by the call. **bound hand and foot with grave clothes** lit., *bandages*, or, *cuttings*, κειρίαις, elsewhere called ὀθόνιαις xix. 40 ; xx. 5-7), which may have been wrapped about his limbs separately as in the case of Egyptian mummies (Olshausen), or round both of them together (Hengstenberg) ; **and his face was bound about with a napkin** lit., *a sweat band*, σουδάριον, *sudarium* (Lat.), the last article in the death-dress ; cf. xx. 7 ; though it was also used for other purposes: see Luke xix. 20 ; Acts xix. 12. The mention of this detail betrays an eye-witness (Godet, Westcott). That Lazarus could come forth in this condition has been pronounced a new miracle (Basil, Augustine, Lightfoot, Lampe, Stier), but, without a miracle, may be explained either by the limbs having been separately swathed (Olshausen), or by the looseness of the shroud (Meyer, Luthardt, Tholuck, and others). **Jesus** having done His part of the work, **saith unto them** who were capable of doing what still remained to be performed, though they were in all probability so struck with astonishment that they required to be summoned to their duty—**Loose him and let him go !** i.e. to his home. Perhaps in so commanding the bystanders, Christ desired to afford them an opportunity of assuring themselves that Lazarus was not an apparition but a veritable flesh-and-blood human being like themselves.

Ver. 45-57.—The Results of the Miracle.

Ver. 45, 46. **Many therefore of the Jews** who had visited the sisters from Jerusalem (ver. 19), accompanied Mary to the tomb (ver. 33), and been spectators of the Saviour's miracle (ver. 36), **which came to Mary and beheld that** (or the things) **which He did** lit., *those having come...and seen,*—the participles

agreeing with the word 'many,' not with the term 'Jews' (A. V.)—**believed on Him** probably, some with genuine self-surrender, like the blind man (ix. 38), and others with a faith excited simply by the miracle, like the early witnesses of Christ's signs in Jerusalem (ii. 23). But δὲ : "Almost throughout this Gospel the great subject, the manifestation of the glory of Christ, is carried onward by οὖν, therefore, whereas δὲ, but, as generally prefaces the development of the antagonist manifestation of hatred and rejection of Him " (Alford). **some of them went away to the Pharisees** If these 'some' were of the many who had become believers (Origen, Meyer, Luthardt, Olshausen), then either their new-born faith must have speedily declined or their purpose in repairing to the enemies of Christ must have been good, either to bear witness to them concerning the miracle and to ask their faith in Christ's Messiahship (Meyer), or to ask their decision on the new wonder (Luthardt), or perhaps only to have the pleasure of relating a fresh novelty (Olshausen, Paley) ; but if, as the antithesis implied in the particle 'but' appears to demand, the narrative proceeds to indicate the outbreak of hostility on account of the miracle (*vide supra*), then the "some" must refer to other Jews than those who had come to Mary—not those who had come to Martha as distinguished from Mary (Hengstenberg) ; a distinction of which there is no trace in the record—but those belonging to the multitude (ver. 42) then present (Godet, Westcott, Stier, and others), or other Jews to whom these may have narrated the strange story, and their purpose in hastening to the Pharisees may have been of a hostile character (Godet, Lange) although this cannot certainly be determined, since they may have been actuated by sheer perplexity as to what to make of so remarkable an occurrence (Westcott). **and told them the things which Jesus had done.** The Evangelist abstains from saying whether Christ's actions were maliciously denounced or only indifferently reported by the informers, though the former hypothesis is not incredible.

47. **The chief priests** i.e. those mem-

bers of the sacerdotal order who had already filled the office of High Priest, which in the time of Herod had been reduced to almost an annual appointment, and who along with the High Priest for the year formed a third part of the Sanhedrim. **therefore** In consequence of what they heard. If the miracle at Bethany was not the cause of Christ's death, or even of the resolution to accomplish Christ's death, it was at least the occasion which led to the formal determination of the latter, and ultimately to the execution of the former. **and the Pharisees** Though the Pharisees appear as the instigators of the present movement against Christ, the chief priests from this time forward step into the place of its leaders. **gathered a council** not a regular diet of the Sanhedrim (Luthardt) but an informal meeting, the article being wanting before the word council, συνέδριον. **and said, What do we?** not ' What shall we do?' (Acts iv. 16, τί ποιήσομεν) as if ample leisure existed for deliberation, but *what are we doing now?* τί ποιοῦμεν, as if the time for deliberation had gone by and the moment for action had arrived. **for** indicating the reason why they should be doing something, viz. that Christ was not idle, or as they contemptuously name Him **this man** (cf. ix. 16) notwithstanding they had cut both Him and His followers off from the synagogue (ix. 22) **doeth many signs** which ought to have convinced them that their duty was to believe (Lange).

48. **If we let him thus alone,** without doing something to lay a permanent arrest upon His activity, **all men will believe on him,** and we will lose our religious dominion over the people—an indirect testimony to the popularity excited by the miracle at Bethany; **and the Romans will come** The growing progress of Christ's cause, they feared, might bring them into collision with the power of Cæsar, through the people, in an outburst of enthusiasm, resolving to put forward Christ as their Messianic king—by no means a groundless apprehension (cf. vi. 15); though their giving forth this as the reason of their action may have been only a cloak for their wickedness (Calvin, Luthardt, Stier, Hengsten-

berg). **and take away both our place and nation.** By our place (τόπος) they probably signify their city or capital as the seat and centre of their theocracy (Chrysostom, Meyer, Luthardt, Godet, Lange, and others) rather than their temple (Origen, Lücke, De Wette, Hengstenberg), or their country (Bengel, Luther, Olshausen); and by both the taking away of city and nation they mean that their Roman masters would be provoked to a war of extermination (Ebrard), or at least to deprive them of the last remnants of their political privileges and religious liberties—in short to make an end of the last fragments of their independence (Olshausen).

49, 50. **But a certain one of them,** lit., *but one,* in contrast to the wavering, perplexed, and irresolute many, proved himself a man of counsel and action, *a certain person of them;* but whether this person was the president of the meeting or not can scarcely be determined. If the phrase "one of them" suggests that he was not (Godet), on the other hand his occupancy of the high priestly office would appear to say that he was. **Caiaphas** Joseph Caiaphas was appointed to the high priestly office by Valerius Gratus, the Roman procurator in A.D. 25, in succession to Simon, son of Camithus, and Eleazar, the son of Ananus, who had each held the dignity for one year (Jos. Ant. xviii. 2, 2). Caiaphas continued in office till A.D. 36, when he was deposed. His subsequent history is not known. The name Caiaphas (Syriac for Cephas, which is Chaldee for Petros, which is Greek for Rock) was probably adopted on his assumption of the high priestly office. "It designated the high priesthood as the rock on which the edifice of the theocracy rested" (Hengstenberg). "Caiaphas should have been the right rock of the Church of God, but he was the caricature of the same, and Simon Peter stepped as the Rock of the True Church into his place" (Olshausen). **being high priest that year** an expression three times used by the Evangelist (see ver. 51; xviii. 13). Not an assertion that Caiaphas held office only for one year—and therefore a proof that the author was a pseudo-John (Baur, Strauss), who was unacquainted with the fact that Caiaphas's tenure of office continued eleven years ; but either an ironical allusion to the frequent changes in the high priestly office (Hengstenberg, Lange), since there may have been five living high priests and ex-high priests at this council—Annas, Ismail Ben Phabi, Eleazar Ben Hanan, Simon Ben Camith, and Caiaphas ;—or a solemn reference to that remarkable and fatal year (Meyer), in which Christ was crucified, that memorable year in which Christ was about to die (Bengel, Luthardt, Westcott), that unique and decisive year in which the perfect sacrifice terminated the typical sacrifices and the Levitical priesthood as exercised by Caiaphas (Godet, Tholuck, Ebrard, Stier). **said unto them, Ye know nothing at all, nor do ye take account** "A needless impertinence" since "he might have begun his answer without any such rough introduction, at the words ' It is expedient ' " (Hengstenberg) ; "a proud and discourteous style of address evincing passionate feeling" (Meyer). **that it is expedient** The high priest thinks only of public policy, not of the sacred demands of duty. **for you** Putting a sharp contrast between himself and the others — you, common people, stupid incapables !—he does not hesitate to make them feel how much farther he can see than all of them (Luthardt). **that one man should die for the people** *for*, ὑπέρ, in behalf of, for the advantage of, and *the people*, λαός, pointing to the nation as a community, in order to form a direct antithesis to the one, εἰς ; **and that the whole nation** The substitution of ἔθνος for λαός brings into prominence the oneness of the people as a Jewish nationality. **perish** not as above explained (ver. 48), by their complete subjection to the Roman power. " The opinion thus expressed was in its meaning and purpose a nefarious proposal founded on the principle that the end sanctifies the means. Under the plea that the welfare of the nation imperatively required it, Jesus was to be sacrificed to their vindictive hatred. This same sentence, however, admitted of being viewed in a higher sense, as an expression of that doctrine of salvation which teaches that the death

of one is deliverance for all " (Lange).

51, 52. Now *but*, introducing a reflection of the Evangelist, **this he said not of himself, but being high priest for that year he prophesied** John sees in the counsel of Caiaphas an involuntary prophecy. As the high priest of the nation, Caiaphas should have been the mouth-piece of God in making known to them the divine will. Though in ordinary circumstances God had ceased to speak through the high priest, John expressly affirms that in this instance He did. Leaving him to deliver his advice according to the impulses of his own bad heart, God yet so guides him in the selection of language to set forth his infamous proposal, that, unconsciously to himself, as the divine mouth-piece to the nation, he proclaimed the divine will and purpose in the death of Christ. "Thus Caiaphas was at this moment bilingual. He pointed out his impious and cruel purpose of rejecting Christ which he had conceived in his mind ; but God gave his tongue another turn, so that he should at the same time utter a prophecy in ambiguous words. It was God's will that a celestial oracle should issue from the pontifical seat" (Calvin). " Caiaphas and Pilate condemned Jesus ; each however gave a testimony foreign to his own meaning ; Caiaphas, in this place concerning the sacrificial death of Christ, Pilate concerning his kingly office, in the title on the cross " (Bengel). **that** better than *because* (Luthardt) or with reference to the fact that (Meyer), **Jesus should die for the nation** These words properly express the contents of the prophecy of Caiaphas, John using the term " nation " (ἔθνος) rather than people (λαός), because at the time when he wrote the Jews had ceased to be a people, and were only one among the many nations of the earth (Westcott). What follows is the amplification which John sees to be germinally included in the speaker's words (Godet). **and not for the nation only, but** for others also, e.g. the sheep belonging to another fold (x. 16), **that He might also gather together into one** i.e. into one undivided community, if not locally, at least spiritually, **the children of God that are scattered abroad.** That these are Gentile believers who along with the Jewish disciples should form the one people of God corresponding to the one Israel of the Hebrew theocracy is apparent ; the sole question is whether they are denominated "children of God" prior to their gathering into the general body of the faithful on the ground of their original relation to God (Westcott, Reuss, Hilgenfeld, Hengstenberg), or, as seems was to be the case, on the ground of a predisposing susceptibility which they manifest for the reception of the truth (Tholuck, Godet), or by prolepsis in anticipation of their entering upon the filial state through a believing reception of and reliance on the death of Christ (Bengel, Meyer, Luthardt).

53. So—the consequential particle indicating that Caiaphas's counsel was accepted—**from that day forth they** the members of the Sanhedrim **took counsel** deliberated and planned, ἐβουλεύσαντο, or if the less authorized reading συνεβουλεύσαντο be adopted, they consulted or held deliberations with one another (Matt. xxvi. 4), **that they might put Him to death.** The removal of Jesus had been resolved upon by the Pharisaic party almost from the first, certainly from the working of the Bethesda miracle (v. 18); now it was formally adopted by the Sanhedrim (xi. 57), whose meetings henceforth become "meetings for Messianic murder" (Lange), although not without the opposition of one or two dissenting voices, such as those of Joseph of Arimathea and Nicodemus (Luke xxiii. 50, 51). This deliberate organization of a standing conspiracy against Jesus formed the second direct result of the miracle at Bethany. Nor does this contradict the Synoptical accounts (Matt. xxi. 15 ff. ; Mark xi. 18; Luke xix. 47) which seem to say that the hostile action of the Sanhedrim was occasioned solely by the Temple Purification and the Teaching of the Passion Week (Schenkel), but which manifestly mean nothing more than that the already formed resolution and already published decree were by that work and these words confirmed.

54. **Jesus therefore** as a consequence of this conspiracy of which He knew without being told (Lampe), though He may have been informed of it by

Nicodemus or Joseph (Meyer); and therefore, as a third result of the raising of Lazarus, **walked no more openly** i.e. boldly, and unmindful of the perils to which He was exposed (cf. vii. 4), **among the Jews** i.e. He withdrew Himself from further public intercourse with His enemies. His testimony to them was finished. His attempts to gain them were at an end. **but departed thence,** from Bethany and the neighbourhood of the metropolis, **into the country** as distinguished from the capital **near to the wilderness** of Judea, **into a city called Ephraim** 8 miles N.E. of Jerusalem (Eusebius); 20 miles N.E. from Jerusalem (Jerome); in the vicinity of Bethel (Jos. Wars, 4, ix. 9) ; probably the Ephron mentioned in 2 Chron. xiii. 19 ; identified with the modern *Taiyibeh* situated about 20 Roman miles N.E. of Jerusalem, and 5 or 6 N.E. of Bethel, upon a lofty hill and overlooking all the valleys of the Jordan (Robinson, ii. p. 315);—an identification accepted by the best authorities (Ritter, Porter, Stanley, Conder), although by some it has been questioned as lying too far towards the west (Ebrard, Meyer). **and there He tarried with the disciples,** who may either have withdrawn along with Him, or, if He retired secretly, gathered themselves about Him as He lingered there.

55. **Now** but, introducing by way of contrast the aspect of affairs in the metropolis, **the Passover of the Jews** (cf. ii. 13 ; vi. 4) **was at hand** An indication of the time of year. "Supposing the Lord to have gone to Bethany beyond Jordan immediately after the feast of dedication or in the latter part of December, and remained there several weeks before He heard that Lazarus was sick, we may place His departure to Ephraim in the latter part of February or early in March. Here He continued till the Passover, which fell this year on the 7th of April. He was thus at Ephraim about six weeks" (Andrews, The Life of Our Lord upon the Earth, p. 336) : **and many went up to Jerusalem out of the country,** not out of the district about Ephraim merely (Bengel, Grotius, Olshausen), but out of the rural parts generally, **before the Passover to purify themselves.** Though not specially commanded by

Moses, ceremonial observances of self-purification were required of every Israelite before the celebration of the Paschal Feast, in accordance with the general statute that every member of the congregation should appear before God clean : see Gen. xxxv. 2 ; Exod. xix. 10, 11 ; Num. ix. 10 ; Josh. iii. 5 ; 2 Chron. xxx. 16, 20 ; and cf. xviii. 28 ; Acts xxi. 24.

56. **They** the pilgrims who had arrived from the country districts, **sought therefore for Jesus** either because they had been accustomed to see Jesus at the Passover (Luthardt), or because they remembered the incidents which had occurred at the last feast (Westcott), or because they were favourably impressed towards the person of Christ (Olshausen), some of them having conceivably been among those who had experienced His miraculous aid (Lange), or because they knew that Christ was in the vicinity of the capital (Bengel, Tholuck) ; **and spake one with another** forming little groups of eager questioners, **as they stood in the temple,** where previously they had seen and listened to the Saviour, **What think ye?** That He **will not come to the feast?** not one question —' What think you concerning the fact that He will not come to the feast ?' (Lücke), since that assumes the questioners had already concluded, from their not perceiving Christ amongst the crowds that thronged the temple, that He had determined not to appear ; but two questions—" What think you ?" What have you to say about the matter ? " Do you think that He will not come to the feast ? " The questions may have been prompted by curiosity (Westcott), but were more likely dictated by knowledge of the rulers' plans (Meyer, Godet).

57. **Now,** contrasting the conduct of the rulers with that of the common people, **the chief priests and the Pharisees** who were probably also apprehensive lest Christ, by His continued absence from the city, intended to withdraw altogether from public life, **had given commandment,** as the result of their formal decree to effect His murder (ver. 47-53), **that, if any man knew where He was, he should shew it** to them, the rulers, **that they might take Him,** i.e. that they the rulers might arrest Him.

HOMILETICS

VER. 1–16.—BAD NEWS FROM BETHANY.

I. **The Village Household.** 1. *Small :* consisting of three members. 2. *Loving :* united by ties of nature and grace. 3. *Pious :* all three, disciples of Jesus. 4. *Honoured :* with the friendship and love of the Son of God. 5. *Afflicted :* Lazarus was sick. 6. *Bereaved :* Lazarus died. 7. *Believing :* Martha and Mary sent to Jesus.

II. **The Sorrowful Message.** 1. *Reverently conceived.* The envoy of the sisters addressed Christ as Lord ! 2. *Delicately worded.* He emphasized Christ's love to Lazarus rather than the affection Lazarus had borne to Christ. 3. *Briefly told.* Preferring no request, he adhered to a simple statement of fact—Lazarus was ill ! 4. *Hopefully answered.* Lazarus's sickness should not finally terminate in death.

III. **The Mysterious Delay.** 1. *Strange :* when contrasted with the fervent love Christ bore to Lazarus and his sisters, and with the perilous condition of the former (Is. lv. 8). 2. *Wise :* when viewed in connection with the reasons Christ may have had for so acting (see Exposition). 3. *Kind :* when it is remembered who it was that did so delay (Ps. xxv. 10).

IV. **The Contemplated Journey.** 1. *Opposed by the disciples.* As (1) dangerous (ver. 8), (2) unnecessary (ver. 12, 13), hence (3) imprudent, if not also (4) wrong. 2. *Justified by Jesus.* As (1) imperative, being undertaken at the call of His Father, (2) safe, since He could not stumble in the path of duty, (3) merciful, inasmuch as He went to comfort the sisters, and waken Lazarus, and (4) profitable, even for them who were so strongly against it.

V. **The Courageous Disciple.** Of 1. *A moody mind.* Thomas, a person of melancholic temperament, prone to look upon the dark side of things—a frequent type of character in the church as well as in the world. 2. *A warm heart.* Thomas's affection for Jesus was hardly less ardent and impulsive than Peter's. Love's heart is often aglow even when faith's eye is dim. 3. *A courageous spirit.* Like Peter on a subsequent occasion (xiii. 37), Thomas was ready to die with and for his Master. Learn 1. That Christ's people will not escape from either sickness or death. 2. That they have a strong encouragement to seek His aid in seasons of affliction and bereavement. 3. That Christ has at every moment a perfect knowledge of the circumstances in which His people are placed. 4. That the supreme end contemplated by all life's afflictive dispensations is the glory of God. 5. That the delays of Jesus, though not always intelligible by, are never disadvantageous for, His friends. 6. That the saint's journeyings, like those of Jesus, should be regulated by the call of duty rather than by considerations of worldly prudence. 7. That he who walks in the path of duty may calculate on walking safely so long at least as God has a walk and a work for him to perform on earth. 8. That the Christian conception of death robs the grave of its terror and gives promise of a resurrection. 9. That Christ's teachings are often misunderstood by His disciples. 10. That love to Christ and willingness to suffer for His sake are truer tests of saintship than correct views of divine truth or joyous experiences in the Christian life.

Ver. 11.—The Christian in Life and in Death.

I. **In Life.** 1. *The friend of Jesus.* Expressing ideas of (1) acquaintance and (2) endearment. 2. *The friend of Jesus's friends.* Adding thoughts of (1) social intercourse and (2) loving brotherhood.

II. **In Death.** Asleep. 1. *Withdrawn from the ordinary activities of life,* as the mind is during the hours of slumber. 2. *Possessed of a real, though different, existence,* as the mind neither ceases to be, nor to be active, during the hours of repose. 3. *Certain to awake refreshed after the period of rest has terminated,* as mind and body both do when night is passed.

Ver. 17-27.—The Interview with Martha.

I. **Martha's Regretful Lamentation ;** or faith struggling with imperfect knowledge (ver. 21). The language neither of reproach nor of complaint, but 1. *of deep sorrow,* that Christ had not been present during Lazarus's illness or at least before the end came. 2. *Of sincere faith,* since she believed that had He been present, He would have laid His hands upon and healed her sick brother, or if, through the virulence of the malady, the case had been difficult, He would have entreated God in behalf of their dear patient. 3. *Of imperfect knowledge.* (1) Allied to superstition in thinking Christ's presence was needful to effect a cure (cf. iv. 47) ; and (2) akin to over-confidence in asserting that Lazarus would have lived had Christ not been absent.

II. **Martha's Confident Persuasion ;** or faith rising into ardent hope (ver. 22). 1. *Faith's firm assurance.* That Christ's access to the Father in behalf of men is (1) immediate, at any moment, (2) direct, by simply asking, (3) unlimited, extending to 'all things,' (4) efficacious, certain to prevail. 2. *Faith's joyous expectation.* That nothing will prove too great (1) for Christ's love to devise, or (2) for Christ's power to execute on behalf of his people (Eph. iii. 20, 21)—hence that a resurrection is neither impossible nor absurd.

III. **Martha's Desponding Admission ;** or, faith relapsing into doubt (ver. 24). 1. *Her disappointment.* She had expected Christ to speak about an immediate restoration of her dead brother, whereas He had only hinted, or seemed to hint, at a far away resurrection (ver. 23). 2. *Her concession.* She acknowledges, notwithstanding, her belief in the reality and certainty of such a resurrection, and also in what that implied, Lazarus's continued existence beyond the grave.

IV. **Martha's Sublime Confession ;** or, faith soaring into lofty adoration (ver. 27). That which lifted Martha beyond the atmosphere of doubt was the exposition Christ gave of the true doctrine of the resurrection (ver. 25, 26), in which were set forth—1. *That the resurrection is not an event to be thought of as distinct from the life ;* as something, e.g., ultimately leading to the life, but should be conceived of as a manifestation, phase, product, or result of the life.

2. *That the resurrection and the life, as thus explained, have their primal source and first cause in Himself*, Christ, in whom is life (i. 4) and from whom all true life in the soul proceeds. 3. *That the resurrection, and the life from which it springs, are secured to men by their union to Him through faith.* And 4. That in the spiritual experience of the believing soul, there is first *a resurrection of the soul* from the grave of sin, then a *living in the spirit* by faith in Jesus Christ, next a *transformation of death* so that the believer may be said to "never die," and finally a *complete abolition of death* by the resurrection of the body at the last day.

Lessons. 1. Christ's presence with the soul is the certain destruction of death. 2. Christ's intercession for His people, as magnificent a reality as in the days of Martha, is now better understood than it was then (Heb. vii. 25). 3. The doctrine of the resurrection as explained by Christ a perennial source of comfort for the sorrowing and the dying. 4. The only just verdict that can be pronounced upon Jesus Christ is that of 'Son of God.'

VER. 28-37.—THE MEETING WITH MARY.

I. **The Urgent Summons** (ver. 28). Christ's message to Mary was—1. *Lovingly sent.* This certain, since it issued from the lips of Incarnate Love. 2. *Secretly imparted.* Martha delivered her communication to Mary in private. There were present among the mourners those who belonged to the hostile party in Jerusalem, who were entirely out of sympathy with Christ, and to whom accordingly the intimation of His arrival would only have been a source of irritation, if not also a subject of derision. A hint that caution and discretion should be practised, and sometimes even secrecy observed, in publishing the news of salvation and calling sinful men to Christ (Matt. vii. 6). 3. *Tenderly expressed.* The mention of Christ by the familiar and beloved name of 'Teacher' would at once strike a chord in Mary's breast, recalling the precious opportunities she had enjoyed of sitting at His feet and listening to His word (Luke x. 39). 4. *Promptly obeyed.* "She arose quickly and went unto Him" (ver. 29); a proof of the simplicity of her faith and of the ardour of her love ; a pattern to Christ's followers, who have a standing invitation to come to Him, everywhere and always.

II. **The Mysterious Emotion** : ver. 34. 1. *Its occasion.* The arrival of Mary and her attendants upon the scene (ver. 33). 2. *Its nature.* A vehement inward disturbance in Christ's human soul, a violent agitation in His spirit, that expressed itself in a voluntary shudder of the bodily frame. 3. *Its object.* (1) The havoc sin had wrought upon the human family ; (2) the unseen enemy, Satan, who lay concealed behind death's mask ; perhaps also (3) the wickedness of man, that would find in the triumph over death He was about to achieve a ground and occasion for bringing Himself to the grave.

III. **The Tender Sympathy** : ver. 35. 1. *Genuine in character.* No sham tears, but sincere tokens of heartfelt sympathy for human sorrow. 2. *Subdued in expression.* Still waters run deep ; and that sorrow is seldom profound or long continued which is vociferous and demonstrative. 3. *Helpful in operation.* Not spending itself in tears, it hastened to proffer aid as well as comfort. 4. *Misconstrued in meaning.* If some of the spectators beheld in Christ's tears an evidence of the greatness of His love for Lazarus (ver. 36), "there were others who only sucked poison from His tears" (Besser), and drew inferences prejudicial to His claims.

Learn 1. That Jesus Christ is *par excellence* the Teacher of the soul. 2. That, as such, He summons all men to become His disciples. 3. That He adapts His teaching to the peculiar characters and dispositions of His pupils. 4. That as, and because He is, Teacher, Jesus Christ is also the Lord and Master of men. 5. That, as such, He accepts the homage of those who come to Him in faith. 6. That Christ, if the Teacher and Master, is also the Friend of man.

VER. 38.—THE RAISING OF LAZARUS.

I. **The Literary Record of the Miracle.** 1. *The preparatory order :* "Take ye away the stone" (ver. 39). Christ never sought to accomplish by supernatural means what could be done by the ordinary forces of nature. In the exercise of those powers which He possessed Christ always displayed a divine parsimony. Then, though He could have dispensed with the aid of others, He did not. In all His miracles, what little assistance others could render He never failed to accept (cf. ii. 7, 8 ; vi. 10, 11). 2. *The encouraging remonstrance :* "Said I not unto thee," etc. (ver. 40). In the distress occasioned by the prospect of once more beholding the buried corpse of her brother, Martha forgets all about the hope of a resurrection which a short while before she so vividly entertained. But Christ will not leave her thus to fall away from her lofty confidence at the moment when her fondest hopes are about to be realized. Not without rebuke indeed, reminding her of her failing faith, He administers to her the most encouraging consolation. 3. *The solemn thanksgiving :* "Father, I thank Thee," etc. (ver. 41). Expressive of (1) gratitude to the Father for having vouchsafed the assurance that He would be able to accomplish the miracle ; (2) confidence in Himself that, as the Father's Son, he always stood within the Father's favour ; and (3) care for the multitude that they might be prepared to believe when they beheld the stupendous sign. 4. *The awakening summons :* "Lazarus, hither out !" (ver. 43). (1) Affectionate, like that of one who calls upon a sleeping friend to awake. (2) Authoritative, like the mandate of one who is accustomed to be obeyed. (3) Efficacious, it being followed on the instant by the appearance of the reanimated man. 5. *The concluding charge :* "Loose him and let him go" (ver. 44). Issued (1) for the sake of Lazarus, to complete his restoration to the world of life and movement ; (2) for the sake of Martha and Mary, that they might be able to withdraw with and rejoice over their new-found brother ; but chiefly (3) for the sake of the spectators, to convince them of the reality of the miracle. Had the multitude dispersed in alarm on first beholding Lazarus, or had Lazarus himself been promptly hurried from the scene as he was, not only would the moral effect of the miracle have been impaired, but its reality would by-and-by have come to be questioned.

II.—**The Historic Credibility of the Miracle.** 1. *Objections to the authenticity of the Narrative.* (1) The silence of the Synoptists. Answer : a. This not more strange than their omission to report several other incidents that find a place in John's history, as e.g. the Wedding Feast at Cana (ii. 1-11), the first Cleansing of the Temple (ii. 13-22), the Curing of the Lame Man (v. 1-9), the Healing of the Blind Man (ix. 1-41), etc. β. This less strange than that Matthew and Mark should not record the Raising of the Young Man at Nain, which Luke alone preserves in his narrative (vii. 14), or the appearance of the Risen Christ to the five hundred, mentioned by Paul (1 Cor. xv. 6). γ. This not at all strange if a reasonable explanation can be given of its omission by the Synoptists ; and this can be done by assuming either that in the formation of the primitive evangelical tradition from which the first three Gospels were drawn, it was felt desirable that nothing should be placed on record which might tend to compromise the safety of the inmates of Bethany (Grotius, Herder, Ebrard, Olshausen, Lange, Godet, and others), who were probably then alive, although at the time when the Gospels were actually composed they were dead ; or that the Synoptists deliberately excluded the miracle at Bethany, as they did the earlier miracles in Jerusalem, on the ground that to record these formed no part of their design, which was to recite the history of the founding of the New Testament Church by our Lord's Galilean ministry (Meyer). δ. Then a glance into their narratives shows that exactly at the time and in the place where, according to the Fourth Evangelist, a great outburst of popular enthusiasm took place in consequence of the raising of Lazarus, they represent a similar demonstration as having been made in the interest of Christ (Matt. xxi. 8-11 ; Mark xi. 1-10 ; Luke xix. 29-40), who yet, so far at least as can be gathered from their histories, had not previously visited the capital, but rather constantly regarded it as the abode of His enemies, and His entrance thereinto as the signal for His death (Matt. xx. 18, 19 ; Mark x. 33, 34 ; Luke xiii. 33, 34). It would be treating them as very simple persons indeed to assume that they imagined all this excitement (connected with the triumphal entry) was, or could be generated without some powerfully determining cause ; and if we perceive that they were aware of that which John affirms was one of the results of the Bethany miracle, common sense should lead to the inference that they were not unacquainted with its cause, the miracle itself. (2) The so-called improbabilities of the narrative. *a.* That Christ should have represented the sickness of Lazarus as one that would not result in death, when He knew that at the moment when He said so Lazarus was dead and buried (ver. 4). *β.* That Christ should have delayed two days before setting out from Peroea to the sickbed of his friend (ver. 6). *γ.* That the disciples were not able to understand Christ's language about the sleep of Lazarus, although three of them at least had heard Him use the same metaphor for death in the house of Jairus (ver. 12, 13). *δ.* That Christ should have wept at the grave of one whom He was the moment after to recall to life (ver. 35). *ε.* That Christ should have resorted to so theatrical a device as to offer up a prayer purely for the sake of its impression upon others. For replies to these alleged difficulties, see Exposition. (3) The non-mention of the miracle at the trial of Jesus. But *a.* so far as Christ was concerned, that was not surprising, since He neither offered any form of defence against the accusations preferred against Him, nor cited witnesses to testify concerning either His character or His works; while *β.* that the Sanhedrim were equally silent on the subject of the miracle is sufficiently explained by the twofold circumstance that they were unable to deny its validity (xi. 47), and that to have credited their prisoner in the hearing of Pilate with so astounding a deed would have been to ensure the failure of their plot to have Him put to death for making Himself the Son of God (xix. 8). 2. *Considerations in support of the authenticity of the miracle.* (1) The circumstance that the narrative reporting it palpably proceeds from an eye and ear witness, as is proved both by what is recorded, as for instance, that a secret message was sent to Mary (ver. 28), that Mary prostrated herself at the feet of Jesus (ver. 32), that the Jews who followed Mary to the grave wept (ver. 33), that Christ groaned at different times (ver. 33-38), that the sepulchre was a cave (ver. 38), and that Lazarus on emerging from its dark recess wore his grave clothes (ver. 44); and by what is omitted, as e.g. the return of the messengers (ver. 4), the call addressed to Mary (ver. 28), Christ's answer to her address (ver. 32), the welcome to Lazarus (ver. 44)—all of which it is scarcely probable a second century romancist would have left undepicted. (2) The public manner in which the miracle was performed,—the presence not alone of friendly, but also of hostile observers at the grave of Lazarus amounting to an almost perfect guarantee of the truth of the Evangelist's narration. (3) The certainty that the miracle was believed to have taken place, which was evinced by the conduct of those Jews who reported the occurrence to the Pharisees (ver. 46), who again showed that they believed it by declaring that Christ should be put to death because of it (ver. 53). (4) The total insufficiency of all other offered explanations. These are of two kinds : such as proceed upon the assumption that nothing happened at Bethany, and such as concede that something took place, though not a resurrection. *a.* According to the former, the story of the Evangelist is a pure myth, invented to put Christ upon a level with the Old Testament prophets, who wrought miracles and even raised the dead (Strauss), or a fiction constructed to give a body to the metaphysical thesis concerning the resurrection (Baur), or a transformation of the parable of Lazarus in the Third Gospel (Schenkel, Keim), or a narrative based upon a misunderstood conversation between Christ and the sisters concerning the Resurrection (Weisse), or a reproduction of the account of the awakening of the (only apparently dead) young man at Nain (Gfrörer). *β.* According to the latter, Lazarus was only seemingly dead when he was laid in the grave, and, after four days of suspended animation, came to life again just at the moment when Jesus called (Paulus); or, *mirabile dictu,* Lazarus may have caused himself to be bandaged as one dead and carried forth to the sepulchre, and may have come forth on the removal of the stone in order to assist the cause of Christ by creating the appearance of a miracle (Renan).

    III. **The Doctrinal Significance of the Miracle.** Its bearing on 1. *The question of the divinity of Jesus.* The mere fact that Christ raised a dead man from the grave was no absolute proof that Christ was divine, since miracles of resurrection had been wrought by Elijah and Elisha; but Christ having beforehand claimed to be the Son of God, and appealed in vindication of that pretension to the miracle He was about to perform, it seems impossible to avoid the conclusion that the miracle amounts to a demonstration of our Lord's divinity. Accordingly, Spinoza is reported to have said to his friends that if only he could have persuaded himself of the truth of Lazarus's resurrection, he would have abandoned his own system of philosophy and embraced the Christian faith; and one feels that, while Christ might have been divine, even though He had not raised Lazarus, if He did, there can hardly be place for doubt. 2. *The doctrines of the non-materiality of the soul and of its separate existence after death.* Nothing can be clearer than that if Lazarus actually died and was afterwards restored to life, the soul of man must be something distinct from the material brain, while the dissolution of the physical organism cannot mean the extinction of personal and conscious existence. As to the manner of the soul's existence in the disembodied state, the miracle affords no information.

> "When Lazarus left his charnel-cave,
>   And home to Mary's house return'd,
>   Was this demanded—if he yearn'd
> To hear her weeping by his grave?" etc.
>
>   TENNYSON, *In Memoriam*, xxxi.

3. *The doctrine of a future resurrection.* It shows that such an event is by no means an impossibility. It is quite true that Lazarus was called back to the old terrestrial life he had previously enjoyed. Yet in this lay a promise that the higher form of the risen life would not prove beyond the power of Christ to confer. And what a difference there will be between the raising of the saints and the awakening of Lazarus! There will be the same loving call from the lips of their heavenly friend, the same authoritative summons, the same efficacious word; but, when the sleeping saints emerge from their tombs, it will not be like Lazarus who wore the bandages of death, but like Lazarus's Lord who left His grave clothes in the sepulchre and stepped forth to a life of glory, honour, and immortality (xx. 7; 1 Cor. xv. 42-44).

VER. 45-57.—RESULTS OF THE MIRACLE.

I. **The Conversion of Mary's Friends through beholding the Miracle**: ver. 45. At first hostilely disposed towards the Saviour (ver. 37), these were nevertheless not unmoved by the sympathetic tears Christ shed beside the grave of His friend,—perhaps also by the solemn appeal to the Father Christ made in His public thanksgiving. In any case the last barrier of their unbelief was swept away when they saw the dead man emerge from the rocky vault. Without exception, the entire company of Mary's friends were converted. The informers who carried tidings of the miracle to the Pharisees were either other Jews who were present at the working of the miracle, or such as had come to know of its performance from these. Perhaps the most remarkable result of a favourable sort that had been effected by any single miracle, it was a striking testimony to the power of the truth in overcoming the native hostility of the human heart. It naturally suggests how much greater influence should be exerted upon that carnal mind which is enmity against God by the larger wonder of Christ's own resurrection. It fills one with sorrow to reflect how many still withhold from Him their confidence, notwithstanding that He is risen from the dead.

II. **The Consternation of Christ's Enemies on hearing of the Miracle**: ver. 47. 1. *The cause of their apprehension.* The undeniable character of the miracle. Men like Caiaphas and the other ex-high priests in the council, not to speak of Nicodemus and Joseph of Arimathea, were too astute to be hoodwinked by any manufactured miracle such as modern criticism supposes the raising of Lazarus was. If the common people were superstitious and craved for portents, these leaders of the people had no interest in ascribing supernatural powers to the man whose death they were attempting to effect. On the contrary, they who would scarce believe the blind man when he told them that, and how, he had been cured (ix. 18), were not likely to lend a too credulous ear to the report of Lazarus's resurrection. It may be held as indisputable that if they could have denied it, or explained it away, they would have done so. But they could not, and because they could not, they were seized with a paralyzing fear, asking one another in pitiable impotence—"What are we to do"? 2. *The nature of their apprehension.* They were afraid that, unless a prompt and permanent arrest were laid on Christ's career, He would kindle such a fire of enthusiasm in the hearts of the populace that at any moment they might break forth into revolution, putting forward Christ as their Messianic king, as once before they had threatened to do in Galilee, and raising the standard of revolt against the power of Rome. In that case nothing would remain to be anticipated but stern retribution at the hands of their Roman masters, either complete extirpation of both place and people, i.e. their total destruction as a race, or their entire subjugation to the foreign yoke by being deprived of the last remnants of their independence (ver. 48). 3. *The allaying of their apprehension.* In the council was at least one resolute spirit who had courage equal to the occasion. Caiaphas, the high priest of that ever memorable year, a bold, bad man, haughty and defiant, as well as unprincipled and base, did not hesitate, while half rebuking and half sneering at his colleagues for their feeble outcries, to propose the Machiavelian policy of sacrificing one for the many. Simple in conception, and not needing to be difficult in execution, it was certain to be efficacious in its results. Besides, it had about it a show of reason and even of clemency. Better one die than many. That the one was better than the many, that the one was the wisest, noblest, best in all the land, wholly innocent, utterly undeserving of such cutting off, did not enter into Caiaphas's calculations. For him *salus populi*, not the intellectual and moral, but only the political and national, safety of the people was the supreme consideration, before which truth, justice, mercy, everything human and divine, must give way. For the higher import of the language of Caiaphas, see next homily. 4. *The dismissal of their apprehensions.* Whether any voice was raised against the Satanic counsel of Caiaphas is not recorded. Luke (xxiii. 51) tells us that one man at least in the meeting—Joseph of Arimathea—did not consent to the deed of the majority. Doubtless also Nicodemus dissented, though he may have deemed it futile to lift his voice against the powerful high priest. Be that however as it may, the advice of the crafty counsellor was taken. From that day forward their fears were dismissed, and their energies directed to the task of plotting how they might best give effect to their murderous decree. Without delay they issued against Christ what is known in modern times as a hue and cry : "They gave commandment that if any man knew where He was, they should shew it, that they might take Him" (ver. 57).

III. **The Concealment of Christ's Person after the publication of the Miracle.**
1. *The reason of Christ's retirement from Bethany.* The fresh outburst of hostility provoked by the raising of Lazarus. It was no longer safe to linger in the vicinity of His would-be murderers. Christ never ceased to exercise a holy watchfulness over His own personal safety. Not until His hour was come, and that would not be until His Father gave the signal, would He expose Himself to unnecessary peril. Nor was it longer worth while to continue testifying to a generation that had shut its eyes upon the clearest light, and resisted the most powerful appeals. Jerusalem's day of grace had closed, and He had withdrawn from her for ever. When He next appeared in her streets, it would be to fall a victim to her murderous hate, and thereby accomplish the counsel of heaven by dying for the salvation of a lost and ruined world. 2. *The place of Christ's seclusion in the country.* A city, called Ephraim, situated in the neighbourhood of Bethel, about 20 miles N.E. of Jerusalem, on the confines of the Judæan wilderness : see Exposition. It was a region full of great memories. In the neighbourhood had Abraham built an altar to Jehovah on entering the Land of Promise, and Jacob enjoyed a vision of the opened heaven and a ladder with the angels of God ascending and descending thereupon when he fled to Padan-aram, as well as set up his pillar of remembrance on returning to the home and country of his fathers (Gen. xii. 8 ; xxviii. 10-19 ; xxxv. 14). 3. *The*

occupation of Christ while at Ephraim. The time spent in this locality, which was probably about six weeks (see Exposition) was not consumed in listless indolence. Even if Christ did not attempt to prosecute further any public labours, He utilized the leisure, we cannot doubt, in instructing His disciples who still continued with Him, and in preparing Himself for the deadly conflict with the Jerusalem authorities which He now saw to be fast approaching.

IV. **The Commotion at Jerusalem on account of Christ's prolonged absence :** (ver. 56). 1. *The disappointed search.* The country people who had come to Jerusalem to attend the Passover hoped they might have found Christ in the Temple. Perhaps they had seen Him there on the occasion of earlier visits, at the Feast of Dedication, or at the Feast of Tabernacles. It was an unconscious testimony to Christ's regard for the House of God. It was equivalent to an intimation that the natural place in which to look for Christ is the Temple. As Christ revealed Himself to His ancient people within the precincts of that sacred edifice, so does he still discover Himself to His believing followers within the courts of the Christian sanctuary. Nor does it ever happen that any seek for Him in vain who look for Him in the latter place with their whole hearts. 2. *The animated conversation.* Not finding Christ, they formed themselves into eager groups to talk about Him. And certainly no better subject could they have found to talk about than He, provided they themselves had been actuated by a praiseworthy spirit. But there are different ways of talking about Christ. with affectionate reverence like the Emmaus travellers, or with ill-concealed malignity like the colleagues of Caiaphas, or with mere idle curiosity like the country people who had come to Jerusalem. 3. *The reduplicated question.* " What think ye? That He will not come to the feast?" They hardly anticipated that He would come, because of the action of the Sanhedrim, of which they probably were cognizant. But in this they were in error, showing how little capable is reason of understanding he movements of a God of grace. The speakers imagined Christ had every reason for absenting Himself from the feast. Christ on the contrary had every reason for being present. It was to be the last feast He should enjoy on earth, the feast at which His Father's work should be brought to a termination, the feast at which the world's Propitiation should be offered, the feast at which the new wine of the Kingdom should be formally put into the hands of His disciples.

Learn 1. That even in Christ's congregations there were disbelievers and doubters ; how much more then in man's? 2. That the best and noblest works of divine grace are apt to be spoken against, as was the miracle at Bethany. 3. That the occupation of a sacred office does not necessarily argue piety—witness Caiaphas and his colleagues ! 4. That God commonly disappoints the devices of the crafty. Caiaphas thought by removing Christ to save the nation ; he only thereby accelerated its ruin. 5. That God may sometimes employ a wicked man in publishing His will, as He once did with Balaam, and now does with Caiaphas.

VER. 50-52. THE COUNSEL OF CAIAPHAS.

I. **The Death of Christ as a Political Crime.** 1. *The real reason.* Caiaphas and his fellow councillors condemned Christ to die because He would not be for them another Maccabeus to achieve their political and national emancipation. 2. *The ostensible pretext.* They alleged that He was threatening to bring them into open conflict with the power of Rome, that He was dangerous to their liberties, that He was an enemy to their continued existence as a nation. In modern phraseology, they said that Jewish interests demanded his removal. 3. *The fatal blunder.* All political crimes are blunders and so was this. The murder of Jesus was the very thing which eventually brought about the destruction of the Jewish state.

II. **The Death of Christ as a Divine Sacrifice.** 1. *Its substitutionary character.* It was, and that according to the divine intention, the death of one man for the people. The Son of man gave His life a ransom for many. He died the just for the unjust. 2. *Its world-wide significance.* Christ died not for the Jews alone, but also for the Gentiles. He was the propitiation not for our sins only but for the sins of the whole world (1 John ii. 2). **3.** *Its ultimate design.* "That He should gather into one the children of God that were scattered abroad:" cf. **x. 16.**

2. THE SUPPER IN SIMON'S HOUSE
Chap. XII. Ver. 1-11
Exposition

Ver. 1. Jesus therefore Because the Passover (xi. 55) was at hand (Godet), or in order to confound the thoughts and machinations of the people and the priests mentioned in xi. 55-57 (Hengstenberg), or better because such was the time (xi. 55), and such were the general circumstances (xi. 56, 57) of the situation (Westcott), the particle being designed simply to connect the present with the preceding section (Meyer, Luthardt). **six days before the Passover** lit., *before six days from the Passover* (cf. xi. 18 ; and see Winer's Grammar, § lxi. 4) ; *i.e.*, on the 8th Nisan, a Friday, if the 14th, the first day of the feast (Lev. xxiii. 5), fell upon a Thursday, and be itself excluded from the reckoning (Tholuck, Lange, Hengstenberg, Luthardt, Westcott), but a Saturday if either the 14th fell upon a Friday (Meyer, Ewald) or it be taken as the first of the six days (Olshausen), or a Sunday if the 14th fell on a Friday, and be included in the calculation(Godet, De Wette). **came to Bethany** *via* Jericho, according to the Synoptists, Matt. xx. 29, xxi. 1 ; Mark x. 46; xi. 1 ; Luke xviii. 35 ; xix. 29 (Godet, Luthardt, Lange, Westcott, and others), although the possibility of harmonizing the statements of the Synoptists with the Johannine account has been disputed (Meyer)—unsuccessfully however —on the ground that the enthusiasm awakened by the healing of the blind men and the visit of Zaccheus are scarcely compatible with the statement in xi. 54. **where Lazarus was** The clause " who had been dead " (A. V.) must be rejected as a subsequent interpolation. **whom Jesus raised from the dead.** A solemn confirmation of the miracle reported in the preceding chapter.

2. So therefore ; being moved thereto doubtless by their love for Jesus and by the presence of Lazarus. **they** the people of the village generally (Bengel, Godet, Westcott, Luthardt) and in particular Simon the Leper (Matt. xxvi. 6 ; Mark xiv. 3), rather than the family of Bethany (Hengstenberg, Meyer),—which seems forbidden by the statement that Martha served while Lazarus was one of the guests. **made Him** in celebration of the resurrection of Lazarus, and in gratitude for the honour conferred upon their village by the performance of so great a miracle. **a supper** δεῖπνον, an evening entertainment as distinguished from a morning meal, ἄριστον, the phrase δεῖπνον ποιεῖν, to make a supper, pointing to a special banquet rather than to an ordinary repast (cf. Mark vi. 21 ; Luke xiv. 12 ; xvi. 17—which would seem also to require the supposition that the time when it was given was either on the Friday evening before Sabbath began, or on Saturday evening after it was ended. **there** i.e. in Bethany, where Lazarus was. **and Martha served** A proof that Martha was playing the part of hostess in her own house (cf. Matt. viii. 15 ; Mark i. 31), since "it would not have been becoming for an eminent woman to have discharged such a service in another house than her own " (Hengstenberg) ; but the most that can be inferred from Martha's position is that in all probability she was a friend of the host, Simon. **but Lazarus was one of them that sat at meat** lit., *of those reclining* (at table) **with Him.** It is not probable that Lazarus would have been thus introduced if Simon had been his father (Ewald), or his brother-in-law, being Martha's husband (Hengstenberg).

3. Mary therefore, moved by the common impulse to do the Saviour honour, as well as inspired by a special ardour arising from her own great love to Him at whose feet she had often sat, and who had so recently crowned His favours to her and Martha by restoring Lazarus, **took a pound of ointment of spikenard, very precious** lit., *took a pound* (The λίτρα, or weight of 12 ounces, was current among the Jews as a measure of quantity. The Synoptists—Matt. xxvi. 7 ; Mark xiv. 3—speak of an alabaster box or flask or cruise) *of ointment* (μύρον was the generic name for all kinds of liquid perfume), *of nard* (νάρδος, an aromatic oil taken from the stem of an Indian plant, and much used by wealthy Roman ladies as an unguent) *pure* (πιστικός, trustworthy, genuine, unadulterated, unless here it be regarded as a technical term and rendered *pistic*), *very costly* (πολυτίμου, for which Mark has πολυτελοῦς, which may refer to the nard (Luthardt), but more probably applies to the ointment (Meyer, Godet). The enormous quantity of this ointment which Mary had in her possession (about £8 10s. in value ; see below, ver. 5) has been explained by the supposition that she had purchased it in order to embalm Lazarus (Lange). **and anointed the feet of Jesus, and wiped his feet with her hair** The Synoptists omit this circumstance and insert what John omits, viz., that the ointment was poured upon the head of Christ (cf. Matt. xxvi. 7 ; Mark xiv. 3). The similarity of this incident with that recorded in Luke vii. 36 has led to the opinion that the two occurrences are the same, and that Mary of Bethany and the woman that was a sinner were one and the self-same individual (Hengstenberg) ; but the two acts of homage, while in several points resembling one another, are essentially distinct. 1. The *Place* is not the same ; in Luke's narrative a city in Galilee, in John's Bethany in Judaea. 2. The *Time* is different ; according to Luke, the one occurred during the earlier ministry of our Lord, according to John, the other happened within six days of the termination of our Lord's life. 3. The *Actions* are not identical. In John's narrative there is no account of the bathing of Christ's feet with tears. 4. The *Conversations* are dissimilar. On the one side Simon and the woman are addressed by the Saviour; on the other, no remark is offered to the woman, while Simon does not appear as a

speaker at all, the only interlocutors being first the disciples, in particular Judas, and then Christ. 5. In short, everything is different except the facts that an anointing took place, that it was followed by a rebuke (in the one case of Jesus by the Pharisee, in the other of Mary by the disciples), that the name in both cases was Simon, and that the feet of Jesus are wiped with hair. "But the one Simon was a Pharisee, while the other was a quiet follower of Christ ; and the wiping of the feet with the hair was a circumstance by no means unlikely to be repeated (cf. Ebrard, Gospel History, § 85, 1). **and the house was filled with the odour of the ointment.** Another of those incidental traits which bespeak the hand of an actual witness ; "the keen sense of the fragrance belongs to experience and not to imagination" (Westcott).

4. **But Judas Iscariot** (*vide* vi. 71), **one of His disciples** Not singled out thus, because the rest of the disciples did not agree with him (Meyer), which according to the Synoptists they did (Matt. xxvi. 8 ; Mark xiv. 4), but in order to emphasize the baseness of that act of treachery which he was about to commit. **which should betray Him** The traitorous design is represented as already formed, cf. vi. 71 ; and only waiting an opportunity for execution. **saith,** giving utterance to a thought which probably from the countenances of his companions he discerned was also in their minds. **Why was not this ointment sold for three hundred pence?** 300 denarii = about £10 in the time of the Roman emperors. The denarius, worth about 8½d. in English money, was the principal silver coin of the Romans, and took its name from being equal to 10 ases, or 10 pounds of brass. "A denarius was the day wage of a labourer in Palestine (Matt. xx. 2, 9, 13), and the daily pay of a Roman soldier was less (Tacit. Annals, i. 17). In the time of Christ the denarius bore the image of the emperor (Matt. xxii. 21 ; Mark xii. 16), but formerly it was impressed with the symbols of the republic" (Kitto's Cyclopædia of Biblical Instruction, art. *Denarius*). **and given** i.e. the sum realized by its sale, **to the poor,** lit., *to poor people.* Judas had forgotten seemingly that

Christ belonged to the very class among whom he thought the money should have been distributed (Luke ix. 58).

6. **Now** *But*, meaning that, whereas Judas affected to be moved by high philanthropical feelings, he was secretly impelled by a totally different motive. **this he said, not because he cared for the poor** Not that John or his fellow disciples knew this at the time, but the whole subsequent career of their guilty colleague abundantly revealed it. **but because he was a thief** A person of a theftuous disposition. **and having the bag** The word here translated bag, γλωσσόκομον, literally signifies a case for keeping the mouth-piece of a flute, and hence a box or chest for holding money (2 Chron. xxiv. 8). That Judas had been promoted to the office of apostolic treasurer shows he must have been regarded as a person of administrative talent. **took away** i.e. *purloined*, the verb βαστάζειν, to carry, as the context appears to require, having the sense of carrying away clandestinely, a meaning it also has in xx. 15, although the ordinary import of the word is not impossible, and by some (Bengel, Luthardt, Lücke) is preferred, notwithstanding its tautological aspect—"and having the bag, he carried **what was put therein** i.e. the contributions given by believing friends (Luke viii. 3) for the support of Jesus and His companions, rather than the earnings of the latter, or the gifts of the former, since the disciples did not follow their customary occupations after finally associating with Christ (Matt. iv. 20, 22 ; xix. 27), and Christ Himself was not possessed of property (Matt. xvii. 27). As to why Jesus, who must have known the deceitful and avaricious character of Judas, appointed him to an office which for him was so full of temptation, it may be replied that Judas may have been elected to the apostolic treasurership by his colleagues on account of his special fitness for its duties (Godet), and that it was no more incumbent on Jesus to remove Judas out of the temptations which arose from his providential surroundings than it was to keep Peter from entering Pilate's judgment hall. But even conceding that Judas did

hold his appointment directly from Christ, Judas was not thereby constrained or even tempted by Christ to indulge in pilfering. If Christ knew that the near proximity of money would tend to influence the cupidity of His disciple, on the other hand may He not have reasoned that there was more than enough to counterbalance that temptation in the signal mark of honour which had been conferred upon that disciple in electing him to fill the office ? Hence there is no need for supposing that Christ deliberately selected Judas for this situation of trust because he was a covetous man (Hengstenberg), and in order that his sin might break out (Lampe), or that Judas might be adequately tried and tempted, man's strongest temptations commonly coming to him through that for which he is naturally fitted (Westcott) : still less is there occasion for falling back on the divine destination (Meyer).

7. **Jesus therefore said** At once rebuking Judas and those of the disciples who sympathized with him, and casting the shield of His protecting love around Mary. **Suffer her to keep it**, or, *let her alone*—perhaps, lit., *dismiss her* i.e. from the charge or blame (Paley) : it was *that she might keep it.* According to the first reading, the meaning is, " Permit her to keep that portion of the ointment which she has not used against the day of my burying " (Meyer), which proceeds on the assumption that Mary had not expended all her ointment on the Saviour, but only a part, in which case Judas's remark about " waste " and " the sin of not having sold the ointment " must have been out of place ; or, better, " Permit her to have kept it " for this purpose and this day (Lange, Luthardt). According to the second the words ἄφες αὐτὴν are taken absolutely—" let her alone ! " and the force of ἵνα brought out by supplying the clause, " it was that " or " she acted as she did," i.e. she did not sell it and distribute the money among the poor " that she might keep it,"—which is practically equivalent to the sense of the T. R., " let her alone, because she hath kept it." **against the day of my burying** or, rather, *of my preparation for burial.* According to Jesus, Mary's

prescient love had foreseen the near approach of His death, and this had determined her to keep the ointment, instead of selling it, that she might therewith do honour to her Lord. Her act Christ interprets as an embalming of His body, in preparation for burial, and pleads that she might be suffered thus to express her love, even though the poor should in the meantime be the losers. **8. For the poor ye have always with you:** cf. Deut. xv. 11. Mark adds, "and whensoever ye will ye may do them good," which shows that Christ did not intend to discourage kindness and liberality to the poor, but only to justify the act which had been done to Himself. **but Me ye have not always.** Our Lord thus again announces the fact of His impending removal, and intimates that whatever kindness was meant for him must be offered without delay. **9. The common people** lit., *much people*, or a great multitude, ὄχλος πολὺς (T. R.). **therefore** because of the intelligence spread by the pilgrims that Christ was in the neighbourhood (Godet), because of Christ's continuance in Bethany (Meyer), but chiefly because of the report of the feast (Westcott). **of the Jews** Not simply of the inhabitants of Jerusalem (Hengstenberg), but of the members of the opposition party (Meyer, Tholuck), the rulers as distinguished from the people (Alford), the representatives of the ancient order of things (Godet). **learned that He was** (is) **there,** i.e. in the village of Bethany. **and**

they came, or went forth from Jerusalem. This was still on the day of the feast, either on Friday, Saturday or Sunday evening. **not for Jesus' sake only** The desire of meeting with Jesus was not excluded from their motives, from which it may be inferred that the miracle of Bethany had favourably disposed many who had previously been hostile. **but that they might see Lazarus also** Perhaps out of idle curiosity, but more likely in order to convince themselves of the reality of the miracle, and so establish themselves in the faith. **whom He had raised from the dead.** Another emphatic intimation of the credibility of the miracle. **10. But the chief priests,** i.e. the Sanhedristic party, who had not been favourably impressed by the miracle, **took counsel,** as they had already done with reference to Jesus (xi. 53), **that they might put Lazarus also to death** —an indirect but powerful corroboration of the truth of the miracle; **because that** (introducing the reason for the fresh conspiracy against Lazarus) **by reason of him,** i.e. in consequence of the miracle of which he had been the subject, **many of the Jews went away** not fell away (Lampe), or withdrew to a distance after which the lapsing ensued (Meyer), but went off probably to Bethany (Bengel), **and believed on Jesus.** Thus the Jerusalem authorities could not longer count on the apathy and unbelief of the inhabitants of the metropolis to counterbalance the increasing faith and enthusiasm of the country people.

HOMILETICS

VER. 1-9.—THE BETHANY SUPPER.

I. The Grateful Company. 1. *The sisters of Bethany:* Martha, who served, and Mary, who doubtless, as usual, sat at Jesus' feet (Luke x. 39).

> "Her eyes are homes of silent prayer;
> No other thought her mind admits,
> But he was dead, and there he sits,
> And He that brought him back is there."

TENNYSON, In Memoriam, xxxii.

2. *Lazarus.* Though not represented as taking active part in the preparations, there can be little doubt his heart heaved with the thankful emotions expressed by the banquet (ver. 2). 3. *Simon the leper.* From the Synoptists we gather that the entertainment was given in Simon's house. He was probably a friend of the sisters and Lazarus. 4. *The villagers.* This appears to be suggested by the peculiar phraseology of John—"They made Him a supper."

II. **The Honoured Guests.** 1. *Jesus.* The honour done to Him was occasioned by the feelings of gratitude and reverence which had been inspired in their breasts by the amazing miracle of Lazarus's resurrection. 2. *The disciples of Jesus.* These were honoured for the sake of Jesus, and because of their connection with Him.

III. **The Unexpected Homage.** 1. *By whom rendered.* By Mary, whose prescient love had enabled her to catch a glimpse ·of the dark shadow that was gathering round the person of her Lord. 2. *Of what it consisted.* The anointing of His feet with precious spikenard, and the wiping of them with her hair. A beautiful symbol of woman's homage to the Saviour. 3. *In what it resulted.* The house was filled with the fragrance of the ointment. So the Christian Church is to-day filled with the fragrance of her lovely deed.

IV. **The Censorious Criticism.** 1. *The matter of it.* That the ointment should rather have been sold and given to the poor! that, in fact, it was a sheer waste of good money to spend so much in an ostentatious action such as Mary performed. 2. *The author of it.* Judas Iscariot, Simon's son, who was already meditating his Master's betrayal. In his lips the observation was natural. The sad thing is that it seemed to chime in with the reflections of his fellow disciples (Mark xiv. 4). Had Judas already begun to infect them with his evil spirit? 3. *The reason of it.* It was not sympathy with the poor that led Judas to comment on the waste of the ointment, but love of money, the secret desire which arose within him to obtain the keeping of so large a sum—in which case he could have carried on his pilferings with ease. Had the money been devoted to the poor, it would have found its way into his bag (xiii. 29), and then !—as to how the money went out of that bag, why, no man knew except himself, Judas, the treasurer. He was a thief, and carrying the bag, bare what was put therein (ver. 6).

V. **The Indignant Rebuke.** 1. *In protection of Mary.* (1) They had no right to interfere with her in the homage she chose to offer Him, her Lord—"Let her alone !" (2) She had good reason for adopting this way rather than another to express her love—"against the day of my burying hath she kept this." 2. *In exposure of Judas.* He pretended to be anxious about the poor—the hypocrite ! He could find as many objects of his charity as he desired any day and every day, if he pleased (ver. 8).

Learn 1. The duty of showing gratitude to Jesus Christ. 2. The permissibility of Christian festivity. 3. The acceptability of love's offerings to Jesus. 4. The doubtfulness of utilitarianism as a test of right action. 5. The hypocrisy of much seemingly religious sentiment. 6. The possibility of hypocrisy amongst the nominal followers of Jesus. 7. The certainty that such hypocrisy is known to, and will eventually be exposed by, Christ.

Ver. 3.—Mary's ministry. I. Inspired by a loving heart. II. Prepared by a liberal hand. III. Criticised by a censorious tongue. IV. Defended by a noble word. V. Requited by a generous reward.

SECTION FIFTH.—THE LAST PRESENTATION OF CHRIST TO HIS OWN IN JERUSALEM, ON THE DAY OF THE TRIUMPHAL ENTRY INTO THE CITY

CHAP. XII. 12-50

Already rejected by His countrymen and condemned by the Sanhedrim (xi. 53-57), Our Lord had little more to do on earth but die. Yet, as if unwilling to abandon hope while the day of grace lasted, He resolves on one more appeal to the blinded understandings, obdurate hearts, and

insensate consciences of the rulers of the city. On four previous occasions
in connection with their great national feasts—the Passover, ii. 13-22;
the Passover, or the Feast of Purim, v. 1-47; the Feast of Tabernacles,
vii. 1, x. 21; the Feast of Dedication, x. 22-39—He had publicly solicited
their faith in Him as Messiah, but without success; this time He will
present Himself before them in the very guise in which one of their own
prophets had predicted He should come. Mayhap, ere it was too late,
they would resile from the position of hostility towards Him they had
assumed. He would appear amongst them in the very character of Zion's
King, surrounded by a crowd of grateful and adoring worshippers, receiving from these the homage which they denied.

The sub-sections into which this portion of the Narrative arranges itself
are as follow :—

1. The Entry into the City: xii. 12-19.
2. The Inquiring Greeks : ver. 20-28.
3. The Address to the Multitude: ver. 29-36.
4. The Final Departure: ver. 37-43.
5. The Last Words : ver. 44-50.

1. THE TRIUMPHAL ENTRY INTO JERUSALEM

Chap. XII. Ver. 12-19

Exposition

Ver. 12, 13. **On the morrow** i.e. after the arrival at Bethany and the banquet above described (Meyer, Luthardt, Hengstenberg, Westcott, and others), rather than after the consultations mentioned in ver. 10, 11 (Ebrard), and therefore on the Sunday (Meyer, Luthardt, Westcott), rather than on the Monday (Godet). **a great multitude that had come to the feast** The 'great multitude' of ver. 9 consisted of Jews who had fallen away from the Pharisaic party, and gone over to the side of Christ (ver. 11); this was composed of feast pilgrims from all parts of the country, but mainly from Galilee. **having heard** probably from those who had come from Jericho in Jesus' company, and had pushed on to the metropolis, while He lingered in Bethany, or from the Jews who had gone out to Bethany and returned with the intelligence that Christ was on the way to the city. **that Jesus was**

coming (lit., *cometh*, is on the way) **to Jerusalem** notwithstanding the edict which He must have known had been issued for His apprehension (xi. 57). **took the branches of the palm trees** lit. *the palm branches of the palm trees*, the mention of the trees as 'palms' indicating the minute touch of an eye-witness —the Synoptists speaking only generally of 'branches from the trees' (Matt. xxi. 8), or layers of 'leaves which they had cut from the fields' (Mark xi. 8); and the reduplication, palm branches of palm trees—φοινίκων being added lest the more technical term βαΐα should not be understood—points to the joyous nature of the act. Cf. the ceremony prescribed for the Feast of Tabernacles (Lev. xxxiii. 40), the triumphal entry of Simon into Jerusalem (Maccab. xiii. 51), and the palm bearing of the redeemed in the New Jerusalem (Rev. vii. 9). **and went forth to meet Him**, impelled to this by the impression made upon them by the report of Lazarus's resurrection (ver. 18). **and cried out, Hosanna** lit. *save, I beseech thee,* the Israelitish 'God save the King' (Godet), borrowed from Ps. cxviii. 25. **Blessed is he that cometh in the name of the Lord** Better so (cf. Matt. xxiii. 39) than "Blessed in the name of the Lord be he that cometh," which the order of the words in Luke appears to justify (Hengstenberg); also borrowed from Ps. cxviii. 26. **even the King of Israel.** The last mentioned writer thinks that "since the benediction should, as in Matt. (xxi. 9), consist of three clauses, we must add in thought, 'Blessed be,' or 'Hosanna to the King"; but this is not necessary. The import of such a salutation on the lips of the people was not difficult to understand. The Psalm from which it was taken was manifestly composed for some festal occasion, probably for the first celebration of the Feast of Tabernacles after the completion of the Second Temple, for that, namely, recorded in Neh. viii. 13-18 (Stier.   Cf. Perowne on the Psalms *in loco*). According to the Midrash, the words of ver. 26 were employed to welcome the caravans of pilgrims as they arrived in the Holy City to attend the Feast ; while numerous Rabbinic quotations render it at least possible that in Christ's time the Psalm had come to be regarded as Messianic. If so, it was the more significant an attestation on the part of the people that they regarded Jesus as their long-promised and ardently expected Messiah.

14, 15. **And Jesus having found** in the way described by the Synoptists (Matt. xxi. 2 ; Mark xi. 2 ; Luke xix. 30) **a young ass** "a colt, the foal of an ass," "whereon no man ever yet sat." The divine prohibition against the multiplication of horses by the future kings of Israel (Deut. xvii. 16) caused the ass to be held in higher estimation then than it is now. Solomon was the first to violate this injunction (1 Kings iv. 28 ; x. 25, 28), and from his day downward horses had formed a part in the equipage of Israel's kings. Hence the appearance of Christ on an ass was a token at once of His personal humility and of His adherence to the law of the king. **sat thereon** The Synoptists mention that He was set thereon by

his disciples (Matt. xxi. 7). **as it is written** in Zech. ix. 9, which is more fully quoted in Matthew, **Fear not, daughter of Zion ; behold thy King cometh sitting on an ass's colt.** This is not a literal citation of the original, but probably a reproduction from memory. Even Matthew does not furnish a complete quotation of the prophet's words. Both evangelists, however, substantially reproduce the prophet's thought ; and the correspondence of Christ's appearance with the Hebrew seer's prediction of the coming of Israel's Messianic King ought to have arrested the attention of all. But it did not.

16. **These things** i.e. the fulfilment of the prophecy by the history then being enacted before their eyes, **understood not His disciples at the first** and hence it need not be wondered that it was overlooked by both the multitude who cried Hosanna ! and the Pharisees who looked on with ill-concealed indignation ; **but when Jesus was glorified** i.e. after His resurrection and ascension (cf. vii. 39 ; xvii. 1-5), **then remembered they that these things were written of Him** (cf. ii. 17-22), **and that they had done these things unto Him.** An undesigned coincidence appears here between John's narrative and that of the Synoptists. Hitherto the former has not stated that the disciples had performed any prominent part in the incidents of the triumphal entry. That we learn from the Synoptists ; and what they say is now implied in the statement of John that the disciples had done those things unto Him.

17-18. **The multitude therefore that was with Him when He called Lazarus out of the tomb, and raised him from the dead, bare witness.** This explains the enthusiasm that had arisen amongst the feast pilgrims who had come to Jerusalem. From the spectators who had witnessed the miracle at Bethany (xi. 42) they had learnt of that amazing deed and of the impression it had left on those by whom it had been beheld. **For this cause also** i.e. because of the testimony they had received, **the multitude** spoken of in ver. 12, **went and met Him** This proves that the multitudes in ver. 17 and 18 were not the same, though the latter, that went out from Jerusalem, may have included the former which came in from Bethany. **for that they heard that He had done this sign**—the miracle at Bethany.

19. **The Pharisees therefore said among themselves,**—mutually blaming one another for the failure of their plans, as defeated conspirators commonly do—**Behold !** or, *ye behold,* the verb being capable of translation as a present indicative no less than an imperative, **how ye prevail nothing** against Him, by your edicts and proclamations. **Lo !**— as the present spectacle reveals — **the world is gone after Him.** Jerusalemites and Galileans, natives and strangers, have all alike gone over to the side of the man whom we in our wisdom have determined to remove.

Note.—The account of this Epiphany preserved by the Fourth Evangelist is briefer, but in all points accordant with that of the Three Synoptists. That these connect it immediately with Christ's departure from Jericho (Matt. xx. 29; Mark x. 46; Luke xix. 28) does not prevent it from being true that Christ spent the Sabbath before at Bethany. That John does not narrate the story of the sending for the ass, does not imply that he was ignorant of the same. Nor though he omits to mention the incident of Christ's weeping over the city, can it be legitimately inferred that nothing of the kind ever happened. The truth is that the Synoptists themselves do not give in all respects perfectly identical accounts, Matthew speaking of an ass and a colt, whereas Mark and Luke allude only to the latter, and Luke recording the displeasure of the Pharisees, about which the other two narrators are silent. Yet the three versions of this remarkable occurrence are in substantial accord, and enable us to form a complete picture of all that happened on the way from Bethany to Jerusalem. That the Synoptical traditions were already well known may explain the circumstance that John does not present a detailed statement of all that took place, but limits his attention to the three points that were needful for his design, viz. the royal progress of the Saviour towards Jerusalem in the character of Zion's King, the jubilant hosannas of the multitude, and the implacable hostility of the Pharisees.

HOMILETICS

VER. 12-19.—THE KING COMES TO HIS CAPITAL.

I. **The King's Person**—*Jesus* recently condemned by the Sanhedrim ; who from the first had tacitly claimed to be Zion's King—who had repeatedly proved His right to such a dignity—who had lately established it by the miracle at Bethany—and who now in the most open and unambiguous manner asserted it by riding in royal state into His capital.

II. **The King's Credentials.** 1. *Consisted in the fact that He was coming to His metropolis in the name of the Lord.* He was no usurper, but one to whom the throne belonged by divine appointment. In a more real sense than it had ever been true of any of Israel's kings, the crown and the kingdom pertained to Him. 2. *Were displayed in the manner of His coming.* He approached the Holy City exactly as it had been predicted Zion's King would come—sitting on an ass's colt. Had He come as the kings of the earth were accustomed to approach their capitals—nay, as Solomon and his successors had been wont to do—riding on fiery chargers, there would have been required no further demonstration that He was not God's Messiah. But He came clothed with humility and arrayed in righteousness ; and these were indisputable tokens of His claim to be accepted as Zion's King.

III. **The King's Welcome.** *The multitudes.* Accompanied by a train of rejoicing pilgrims from Galilee, who had joined Him at Jericho and Bethany ; He was met by a second crowd who came out from Jerusalem to give Him welcome. And the two crowds were enthusiastic in their demonstrations of joy at beholding Him. They waved before Him as they marched palm branches, they strewed leaves on His way to form a carpet for His charger's feet, they shouted their acclamations in words of welcome from an old Hebrew Psalm—" Hosanna ! Blessed is He that cometh in the name of the Lord !" For the moment at least, they were a believing multitude, who, through what they had learnt of Lazarus's resurrection, had been led to recognize Christ as Messiah.

IV. **The King's Attendants.** *The disciples,* who themselves had taken part in the joyous celebration, were as yet incapable of understanding its true significance. Not until after Christ was raised from the dead did they penetrate its real import. When they reverently lifted the Saviour on the back of the young colt, and assisted the shouting multitude to give expression to their joy, they imagined they were on the eve of seeing all their earthly hopes fulfilled in the setting up of a temporal kingdom that would restore again the glory to Israel. When they recalled the scene after Christ's departure from the earth they perceived how in all that He then did He was supplying them with evidence, had they been able to read it, that He was not one of earth's common potentates, but Israel's heaven-sent Prince of Peace, and Monarch of Salvation.

V. **The King's Enemies.** *The Pharisees.* The spectacle on which these gazed seemed for a moment to confound their plots and dash their hopes. It filled them with indignation, urged them to recrimination, impelled them to fiercer determination. The prophecy of Caiaphas appeared upon the eve of coming true. The nation was slipping from their hands. The whole world was running after the hated Teacher whom they wished to destroy.

Lessons. 1. The religious instincts of the multitudes. 2. The credibility of ancient Scripture. 3. The illumination Christ's glorification has cast on history. 4. The certainty that the world will ultimately be won by Christ.

2. THE INQUIRING GREEKS

Chap. XII. Ver. 20-26

Exposition

Ver. 20. **Now** The incident here reported happened (ver. 36) just before Our Lord's final departure from the temple (Matt. xxiv. 1 ; Mark xiii. 1), and probably on the Tuesday after the triumphal entry. The movements of Our Lord between the two occurrences are set forth in Mark's Gospel with seeming chronological accuracy. On Sunday evening, after looking round about the precincts of the temple, Our Lord withdraws to Bethany. On the following morning He repairs a second time to the city, cursing the fig tree on the way, and afterwards, on reaching the temple, casting out the traders, returning again at eventide to Bethany. The day after He proceeds as before_to the metropolis, and enters the temple. On the way to the capital He instructs His disciples as to the necessity of exercising faith in God, and the duty of practising forgiveness towards

men. Walking in the temple, He is soon confronted by the chief priests and the scribes and elders, who demand His authority for the action of the preceding day, to whom He replies by proposing a question about the baptism of John. Then He occupies His time in further teaching the people by parables, interrupting His conversation with them to repel the captious questions proposed to Him by the Pharisees and Herodians about the tribute money, by the Sadducees about the woman with seven husbands, by the lawyer about the great commandment. Just before He leaves the temple, He observes the widow casting in her mites into the treasury, after which He retires to the Mount of Olives with His disciples. The whole of Wednesday He spends in retirement. On Thursday He re-appears in Jerusalem at a pre-arranged paschal meal with his disciples. **there were certain Greeks**— neither Greek-speaking Jews, who are usually styled Hellenists (Calvin, Ewald), nor heathen Greeks who still adhered to their idolatries (Chrysostom, Theophylact, etc), but Gentile proselytes (Meyer, Godet, Luthardt), like the eunuch (Acts viii. 27) and the Roman centurion (Acts x. 1)—**among those who went up to worship at the feast.** The present participle ἀναβαινόντων indicates that they were in the habit of attending the Jerusalem solemnities (Bengel, Meyer, Luthardt), i.e. they were proselytes of the gate, who, though not accepting the Jewish rite of circumcision, yet adhered to the word and worship of Jehovah (Acts xiii. 43-50 ; xvi. 14 ; xvii. 4-17).

21. **These therefore** Probably they had witnessed the triumphal entry and the cleansing of the temple, and listened to Our Saviour's teaching as He instructed the people in parables, and repelled the insidious questions of the Pharisees, Herodians, and Sadducees. **came to Philip** — whom most likely they had previously known, and whom they now found in the forecourt of the temple ; or perhaps simply because they must address themselves to some one—**which was of Bethsaida of Galilee** If the Greeks belonged to Decapolis, this might account for their acquaintance with Philip, the region of the Ten Cities reaching as far north as Bethsaida. **and asked him, saying, Sir, we would see Jesus** lit. *we wish to see Jesus.* By this they meant not merely that they desired to obtain a sight of Him, like Zaccheus in Jericho (Luke xix. 3), which they might easily have done without the assistance of Philip, or any body else, but that they were anxious to secure an opportunity of conversing with Him,—it can hardly be thought as the emissaries of King Abganus of Edessa, who, according to tradition, had sent them to invite Christ to take refuge at his court from the persecution of His people, but rather in the spirit of Nicodemus, who wished to know more about the personal character and doctrine of one who was apparently a heaven-sent Teacher and Prophet.

22. **Philip** who from centre to circumference was of a hesitating and prudent nature (Luthardt : cf. vi. 5 ; xiv.

8, 9) **cometh** or, **goeth, and telleth Andrew,** being unwilling on his own responsibility to decide a question of so much difficulty as, whether these Greeks should be introduced to the Saviour who had so expressly assured them He was not come except for the lost sheep of the House of Israel (Matt. xv. 24), and who in sending them forth had so distinctly cautioned them to " go not into the way of the Gentiles " (Matt. x. 5). Philip appears to have selected Andrew as one with whom to take counsel, either because Andrew happened at the moment to be nearest, or, what is more likely, because they belonged to the same city ; or because Andrew and he were companions, and we find them more than once mentioned together (i. 44 ; vi. 7, 8) ; or because Andrew was one of those who much enjoyed the Saviour's confidence (Mark xiii. 3), and was possessed of a sound judgment and a cautious disposition. **Andrew cometh**—of a more robust character than Philip, the brother of Peter now takes the lead— **and Philip,** *cometh,* following after, and permitting Andrew to be the spokesman ; **and they tell Jesus** Philip obviously assenting to what his fellow-Apostle states.

23. **And Jesus answereth them** Manifestly first the two deputies who had approached him (Meyer, Hengstenberg, Westcott, and others), though the Greeks also may have been included (Ebrard),—directly, if these accompanied Andrew and Philip (Westcott), indirectly, if they did not (Godet). **saying** Whether Christ conceded the request of the Greeks (Tholuck, Godet), that they should be admitted to an interview with Him, or denied it (Hengstenberg, Ewald), cannot be inferred from the narrative. The supposition that Christ intended to receive them after replying to Andrew and Philip, but was prevented from doing so by the voice which interposed and changed the scene (Meyer), is extremely constrained. John's silence on this point may be explained on the ground that it was not Christ's reception or denial of these individual Greeks that constituted the importance of this event, but the coming of the Greeks and the thoughts which such an occurrence awakened in the mind of Christ. The reply of Jesus

has been pronounced inappropriate (De Wette), without the slightest justification. **the hour is come** or, "come is the hour !"—the *hora fatalis* (Meyer) which of late had been rapidly approaching, of which He had more than once spoken to them in Galilee (vi. 62), and in Jerusalem (vii. 33 ; viii, 14, 28). **that**—*ἵνα*, expressive of the divine purpose—**the Son of man** (cf. i. 51) Not without design Christ uses this designation when about to speak of His glorification. By means of it He recalls to the minds of His hearers that He stands before them as the representative of humanity (Godet, Westcott), as at Bethany He had styled Himself the Son of God (xi. 4), because there he appeared as the Father's representative. **should be glorified** not simply by the publication of His gospel and the extension of His kingdom among the Gentiles (Calvin, Reuss, Lücke), which would rather be a result of His glorification (xii. 32) than a constituent part of the same, but by His personal exaltation to the throne of His Father, which, however, could only be reached through death. Cf. vi. 62 ; xvii. 5 ; 1 Pet. i. 11. "This δόξα consists principally in that which the Lutheran dogma comprehends under the Exaltation, *exaltatio*, in the glorification of the Son by the Father, xiii. 32 ; xvii. 5. As the consequence of that is the communication of the Spirit to be thought of, and as the result of that the exalted activity of the exalted Son of Man in and upon humanity " (Tholuck). 24. **Verily, verily, I say unto you** The solemn repetition, Amen, Amen, is occasioned by the difficulty of getting His hearers to believe that the pathway to glory lay by the cross (Meyer). **Except a grain of wheat fall into the ground and die, it abideth alone** lit., *except the grain of wheat, falling into the ground, die* (not in the sense of absolutely perishing, becoming annihilated, ceasing to exist, but in that of decaying, shedding its outer husk, and so setting free the imprisoned life) *it abideth alone* (it continues a solitary grain); **but if it die** in the mode explained, viz., by the thrusting forth of the vital germ through the dissolution of the outer rind, **it bringeth forth much fruit.** So Christ by dying would give freedom to His life-possessing

spirit to develop and reproduce itself in the souls of men ; whereas until He died the spiritual germ of His divine humanity would remain alone—inoperative and inefficient among the Gentiles no less than among the Jews. 25. **He that loveth his life** his ψυχή, his immaterial, intellectual, soul-nature, (Meyer, Luthardt), *animam suam, id est, se ipsum*, his soul, that is, himself (Bengel), the breath of life with all the faculties with which it is endowed (Godet),—loves it in the sense of seeks to preserve it from what seems destruction, not however in obedience to the natural instinct of self-preservation, which is not only not contrary to the spirit of Christianity, but in perfect harmony with the behaviour of Christ Himself (x. 39 ; viii. 59), but in preference to walking in the path of duty, —that man **loseth it** not merely *shall lose it or destroy it*, at some future time, in the day of judgment, for example, ἀπολέσει, but *loseth* and *destroyeth* it now, ἀπολλύει, in the very act of attempting to keep it (cf. Matt. x. 39 ; xvi. 25 ; Luke ix. 24); **and he that hateth his life in this world** in the sense, again, of parting, even in a spirit of generous contempt (Godet), with all that seems to make life comfortable and desirable in this world, yea with life itself as one of the things of this world, rather than forsake the path of duty— that man who so acts **shall keep it unto life eternal.** The contrast between 'in this world' and 'unto life eternal' points to the immeasurable superiority of that life which arises out of every such devotement of the merely earthly existence. "A great and wonderful sentence, according to which a man loves his life in order to destroy it, and hates it that it may not perish : if thou hast badly loved then hast thou hated, and if thou hast hated well, then hast thou loved " (Augustine). 26. **If any man serve Me, let Him follow Me** In these words Christ applies the moral maxim just announced to His followers as well as to Himself. The law which holds good of men in general, that only by the sacrifice of the present life can the future glorious existence be secured, is equally valid concerning Him and His disciples. He can only reach His heavenly glory by giving up His life on the cross ; if they would prove themselves His servants they must evince the like spirit of self-sacrifice which He displayed. **and where I am after my glorification**—a present of anticipation—**there will also My servant be,** when the life which He has sacrificed has begun to bear its appropriate fruit, as it will do, immediately, but fully in the Parousia, when I shall have raised him from the dust of death : cf. xiv. 2-3 ; xvii. 24.

If any man serve Me, him will My Father honour. The future glorification of the self-sacrificing follower of Jesus Christ is here presented in the light of a recompense of honour,— τιμήσει, "a grand word, fitting well with glorified, δοξασθῇ " (Bengel)—bestowed by the Father for faithful service done to His Son. "The Father will as certainly honour the faithful servant, as He has glorified the Master " (Godet).

Homiletics

Ver. 24.—The Parable of the Corn of Wheat.
I. The Time when it was spoken. On the last Tuesday of Our Lord's life, in the last public discourse uttered in Jerusalem, the last exposition given of Himself and His mission ere He finally departed from the temple, shutting the door of mercy against the doomed city for evermore. As among the latest words that fell from Our Lord's lips on earth, they are worthy of respectful and even reverential attention ; as constituting Christ's farewell testimony concerning Himself, they may be reasonably expected to be pregnant with meaning. Their fitness to the occasion is apparent to every one who reflects. His hour was at hand, and He talks about His dying. The Greeks were desiring to see Him, and His thoughts turn to His glorification, which was at hand.
II. The Occasion by which it was prompted. The request of certain Greek proselytes, who desired to see Him. Whether they were admitted at this time to a private audience with Christ or not, it may be supposed they either themselves listened to, or heard from others, the lofty words Christ spoke on being informed of their request. If they did, they would perceive that He did not foreclose to them the possibility of reaching His presence and obtaining an interview with Him, but rather held up before them the prospect of being not only admitted to His audience chamber, but made partakers of His glory, and pointed out to them the way in which that prospect might be realized.
III. The Truth which it contained. If the corn of wheat is retained in the farmer's granary, it may conserve its form and symmetry, yea, and for a time at least, its life also ; but it will never multiply or increase, never germinate and bring forth other grains, never spring up into higher life, it will abide alone. If it drops into the soil, it will shed its outer integuments, in its external wrappings fall a prey to corruption and decay, but the inner germ of life it contains will not decay, but will forthwith leap into mysterious activity ; will begin to draw up nutriment from its own putrefying frame, will shoot up into fresh and increased activity, will bring forth, in some thirty, in some sixty, and in some an hundred fold. And in that, Christ designs to say, lies a parable, that death is the way to life, and self-sacrifice the path to self-preservation and self-multiplication.
IV. The Application which it received. 1. *Valid for men in general* (ver. 25). The Saviour aims not at discommending the practice of self-preservation, to which all are impelled by natural instinct, but at revealing the worthlessness and folly of a life of selfishness, and in contrast therewith, the complete success, in every true respect, of a life of lowly and cheerful self-surrender. The man who cannot at the call of duty yield up anything and everything that pertains to his natural existence, to his soulish being—who thinks to protect his soul in the enjoyment of all that constitutes its mundane felicity rather than advance upon the path of trial God in His providence may mark out for him—that man will not only never reap a moral and spiritual harvest, but, on the contrary, is losing and destroying the essential life principle that resides within his soul ; whereas he who at the call of heaven lets all go with a sort of generous and lofty

contempt, parting with his money, giving up his ease, surrendering his enjoyments, yea, yielding up his loves and loved ones, not even withholding health or life when demanded—that man will discover he has lost nothing but the mere external wrappings of his soul, that he has conserved all that is valuable and precious, yea, that he has sown the seed of an abundant harvest. 2. *Good for His disciples* (ver. 26). The path Christ was taking must be resolutely accepted and adhered to by those who claimed to be His servants. For them no more than for Him was it possible to enter into glory except by descending to the cross of self-humiliation and death. But as certainly as the cross with Him would be followed by the crown, so would it also with them. If, like Him, they renounced their all, like Him they would be recompensed with a full reward of honour at His Father's hand. "If any man serve Me, him will my Father honour."

Lessons. 1. The certainty of Christ's world-wide dominion in the future. 2. The importance of Christ's death as a means of converting men. 3. The glory of self-sacrifice.

3. THE VOICE FROM HEAVEN

Chap. XII. Ver. 27-33

Exposition

Ver. 27. **Now** *Magni momenti hoc* νῦν (Bengel) : of great moment this now, cf. ver. 31 ; *temporal*, pointing out the instant of seizure, and *consequential*, indicating the cause of Christ's sorrow. **is my soul** ψυχή, *anima* (Vulgate), the seat of the natural affections, rather than πνεῦμα, *spiritus* (Vulgate), that of the religious emotions—showing that Christ's agitation proceeded from the inward shrinking of His human nature at the prospect which lay before Him, not of death simply, in which case He had displayed less fortitude than many of His followers, but of what for Him death involved, the bearing of a world's sin and the enduring of His Father's anger on its account (Calvin, Hengstenberg, Steinmeyer). **troubled** τετάρακται, *turbata est* (Vulgate): *decora declaratio in qua concurrebat horror mortis et ardor obedientiae* (Bengel), a becoming declaration in which met together the horror of death and the ardour of obedience : cf. xi. 33. **and what shall I say?** Christ's perturbation of spirit was so great that He could scarcely tell in what words to speak to His Father concerning it, though as yet the consciousness of His Sonship was not, as afterwards, obscured (see Matt. xxvii. 46). **Father, save Me from this hour.** Either (1) an

interrogation, "Father, save Me," etc., *shall I say ?* (Chrysostom, Lampe, Tholuck, Ewald, Lange, Godet), as if mentioning the request to which His feeble humanity was prompting Him —in favour of which may be urged its resemblance to the prayer in Gethsemane (Matt. xxvi. 39), although against it stands the unlikelihood of a mind, so deeply moved as Christ's was at this moment, praying in the form of a reflective monologue ; or (2) and preferably, a direct *supplication*, either for protection against the impending sorrow in Gethsemane (Meyer, Hengstenberg, Alford), or for support under, and emergence out of, it (Luthardt, Westcott, Milligan and Moulton), with which harmonizes Heb. v. 7. **But for this cause came I unto this hour.** Expressive either (1) of *resignation*, like the 'nevertheless' in the Gethsemane prayer—meaning that for the very purpose of undergoing this sorrow and this death had He come to the hour of His approaching passion (Bengel, Godet, Luthardt); or (2) of *expectation*, signifying that in order to be supported under and delivered out of His sorrowful passion had He arrived at the impending hour (Westcott, Milligan and Moulton). Other renderings of διὰ τοῦτο, such as 'that I might redeem mankind' (Olshausen), 'that my soul might be troubled' (Hengstenberg), 'that the Father's name might be glorified' (Lücke, Meyer), though containing elements of truth, are not immediately embraced in the words themselves.

28. Father — corresponding to the filial affection out of which this petition springs—**glorify Thy Name** by causing it to be revealed to, and known by, all men, Greeks as well as Jews, through My death and resurrection. **There came therefore** in response to the Son's self-consecration and in correspondence with the subject matter of His prayer, **a voice out of heaven**—not a thunder clap—represented as a voice in O. T. Scripture (Job xxxvii. 4; Ps. xxix. 3)—which Jesus interpreted as an answer to His petition (De Wette, Lücke) in the same way as in classical antiquity (Odyss. xx. 99, 112; Eur., Iph. T., i. 1385; Virg. ii. 687) portents of the sky were understood; but a real objective voice, whose intelligibility, however, depended on the moral and spiritual susceptibility of the hearers —the same voice that had been heard at the baptism (Matt. iii. 17; Mark i. 11; Luke iii. 22) and at the transfiguration (Matt. xvii. 5; Mark ix. 7; Luke ix. 35)—*saying*, **I have both glorified it** by Thy life and ministry on earth, **and will glorify it again** through Thine approaching death and resurrection. That the voice is represented as having uttered audible and articulate words negatives the notion of a sudden subjective inspiration like the Jewish or Rabbinical *Bath Kol*—'the daughter of the voice.'

29. The multitude therefore, or *therefore*, i.e. because they lacked the susceptibility requisite for understanding the voice out of heaven, **the multitude that stood by** (cf. iii. 29; Matt. xxvi. 73) probably in the outer court of the temple, **and heard**, like Saul's companions (Acts ix. 7: xxii. 9; xxvi. 13, 14), not the words, but it, the sound of the voice, **said**, regarding the phenomenon as a purely natural occurrence, **that it had thundered**— the judgment of the least spiritually susceptible : **others**, either a portion of the bystanders as distinguished from the general body, or the disciples and believing followers of Jesus, **said**, show-

ing a higher degree of appreciation of the voice, **An angel hath spoken to him.** The voice, though a distinct and articulate utterance, sounded so strange that it was conjectured to belong to an angel. On the word 'angel,' see i. 51. The highest degree of appreciation the voice received was that evinced by Jesus and John, if not also by the disciples generally.

30. Jesus answered and said (1) to the disciples who had understood the voice, but also (2) to the bystanders who, though misinterpreting the voice, yet conceived it to be a supernatural utterance, a wonderful sound (Lange), which however they placed in no relation to themselves (Meyer): **This voice** which Christ may have explained to the multitude, **hath not come for My sake,** to assure me of the certain answer of My prayer, of which I was already conscious (cf. xi. 42), **but for your sakes,** to confirm and increase faith in you, where it exists, as well as awaken faith, where it is absent.

31. Now, at this moment—Christ speaks as if already He had conquered in the struggle (Calvin)—**is the judgment,** not the final judgment, except in so far as it prepares the way for, in a manner anticipates, and in kind exemplifies that event, but *a* preliminary *judgment* (cf. iii. 19), **of this world** (see on iii. 16) whose true character as hostile to God will by My death be fully revealed and judicially condemned : **now shall the prince of this world,** Satan (cf. xiv. 30; xvi. 11; 2 Cor. iv. 4; Eph. ii. 2; vi. 12), so styled because 'this world,' having lapsed into sin, has become subject to his sway (Luke iv. 6), **be cast out,** not from heaven (Olshausen), but from his dominion over the world, the prime cause of his ejection being the death of Christ (Col. ii. 15), and its instrument the spread of the gospel. According to the Rabbis "this world" signified all mankind except the Jews; in Johannean or Christian conception it means the non-Messianic kingdom.

32. And I, in opposition to the prince of this world, **if I be lifted up from** or *out of* **the earth,** to a sphere of super-terrestrial activity, though ὑψωθῆναι by itself appears to point rather to the manner of Christ's death (iii. 4; viii. 28) **will draw** not by mechanical force or physical constraint, but by moral suasion and spiritual influence (cf. Hos. xi. 4), as the Father draws (vi. 44)—not necessarily irresistibly so that those drawn shall come, since in point of fact many do not come, but still sufficiently so as to render without excuse—all men not all the children of God merely, all the elect (Calvin), or all who resist not My drawing (Luther), or all classes of men, Gentiles as well as Jews (Chrysostom, Lampe, De Wette, Olshausen), but all men, without restriction and without limitation unto Me —πρὸς ἐμαυτόν, unto Myself, defining both the direction in which the drawing should take place and the end in which it was designed to issue, viz. personal fellowship with Christ. The import of the clause seems to be that after Christ's

glorification through exaltation to His Father's throne, He would begin, through the outpouring of His Spirit, to exert an influence upon the hearts of all men with the view of drawing them into personal union and communion with Himself. The words involve the doctrine neither of universal salvation (Meyer), nor of irresistible grace (Calvin). 33. **But this He said, signifying by what manner of death He should die.** The Evangelist has not fallen into an error (Reuss), since the interpretation here put upon ὑψωθῆναι neither excludes nor contradicts that given in the preceding verse, Christ's lifting up on the cross being the way by and through which He was lifted up out of the earth. See on viii. 28.

HOMILETICS

VER. 27-33.—A FORETASTE OF GETHSEMANE.
I. **The Sorrow of the Saviour :** ver. 27. 1. *Its seat.* Christ's soul as distinguished from His spirit, His human rather than His divine nature. 2. *Its cause.* Not the prospect of death, even of a martyr's upon a cross, aggravated by the horrors of cruelty and marks of shame which in His case He foresaw should be heaped upon Him, but either (1) the anguish of Gethsemane which He beheld approaching Him, or (2) that which caused the anguish of Gethsemane, the prospect of dying such a death as should expiate a world's sin. 3. *Its significance.* (1) For the true humanity of Jesus. If Christ was possessed not alone of a 'body' that could 'die' (ver. 33), but of a 'soul' that could be 'troubled' (ver. 27), it is idle to contend He was not a *verus homo*, a genuine man, but merely a *simulacrum*, a Docetic Christ. (2) For the import of Christ's death. If Christ's soul was unusually perturbed in prospect of Gethsemane and Calvary, there must have been elements of horror in the cup of death He anticipated drinking, and eventually drank, that are not found in the cups put to the lips of common martyrs. (3) For the credibility of the Evangelist. On the ground that the fourth gospel contains no Gethsemane struggle the newer criticism (Baur, Keim) rears an argument against the authenticity of its narrative and for the purely imaginary character of its Christ. But the present incident renders this hypothesis untenable. The accounts furnished by the earlier Evangelists of what occurred in Gethsemane exhibit the same sort of soul experiences as are here recorded. In both there is (a) the same sudden seizure by a seemingly inexplicable trouble—in Gethsemane after the soul elevation experienced at supper table (Matt. xxvi. 36 ff. with parallels), here after enjoying a vision and foretaste of heavenly glory through the coming of the Greeks (ver. 23) ; (β) the same fervent turning to His Father in prayer—in Gethsemane three times, here twice, in close succession ; (γ) the same style of language, if not in form at least in meaning (cf. Matt. xxvi. 39, with ver. 27) ; and (δ) the same sort of answer—in Gethsemane an angel to strengthen Him, here a voice from heaven to comfort Him. Perhaps also the circumstance that John had already related this strange passage in our Saviour's history was part, if not the whole, of the reason why he deemed it unnecessary to rehearse again the similar story of Gethsemane.
II. **The Prayer to the Father :** ver. 27. 1. *Mental disturbance :*—" What shall I say ?" Though Christ in His sorrow betook Himself to prayer, thereby

offering His disciples an example to be followed in like circumstances of distress. (Matt. vii. 7-11 ; Phil. iv. 6), yet His inward agitation was so intense that He scarcely knew what words to utter or thoughts to express—a fact full of comfort for sad souls who cannot pray, because of the unrest and tumult of their hearts, whilst contending against "fightings without and fears within." 2. *Filial confidence:*—"Father !" Christ lost not hold of that endearing name, but clung to it as His best and truest support—again presenting a pattern to His people (Rom. viii. 15). 3. *Human weakness:*—"Save Me from this hour." Whatever explanation be adopted of these words, they reveal that Christ was conscious of a shrinking from the ordeal before Him, and spoke to His Father about it—once more teaching us, when called to face trials too alarming or duties too imposing for our feeble hearts, to speak concerning them to the Father who knoweth our frame (Ps. ciii. 14), and to Christ Himself who can be touched with a feeling of our infirmities (Heb. iv. 15). 4. *Sublime resignation:* —"But for this cause came I unto this hour." Thus, according to one interpretation, Christ expressed His acquiescence in His Father's will, as He afterwards did in Gethsemane (Matt. xxvi. 39), and as previously He had taught His disciples (Matt. vi. 10). 5. *Hopeful expectation.* According to another interpretation, Christ expressed the conviction that He would be supported in and borne through the hour of sorrow which had come upon Him ; and in this He was not disappointed, as neither will His disciples be disappointed of the Father's or of His gracious succour and support in the trials through which they are called to pass (Ps. xci. 14, 15 ; Is. xliii. 2 ; 2 Cor. xii. 9).

III. **The Voice from Heaven :** ver. 28. 1. *Grossly misunderstood*—by the bystanders ; (1) as a natural phenomenon, as thunder (ver. 29), and (2) as a supernatural utterance, the speech of an angel (ver. 29)—a significant proof of man's incapacity to understand the words of God (1 Cor. ii. 14). 2. *Lovingly recognized*—by Jesus ; as an old and familiar voice, the voice of His Father, which twice previously had addressed Him out of heaven (Matt. iii. 17 ; xvii. 5). It needs a child's heart to recognize a father's voice. 3. *Rightly interpreted*— again by Jesus (perhaps also by John and his co-apostles) ; to whom it spoke in the language of (1) approbation—" I have glorified My Name " (ver 28), and (2) consolation—" I will glorify it again."

IV. **The Address to the Bystanders.** 1. *The purpose of the voice :* (1) not for His sake had it been sent ; since He knew His Father always heard Him (xi. 42), but (2) for their sakes, to assure them He was the Father's Son and the heaven-sent Messiah of Israel. 2. *The purpose of His death :* ver. 31. (1) To discover the true character of ' this world ' as an organized confederacy of evil, presided or rather tyrannized over by the Prince of Darkness (Acts. ii. 23 ; 1 Cor. ii. 8 ; Eph. ii. 2). (2) To eject the Prince of Darkness from his usurped dominions (Col. ii. 15). 3. *The purpose of His exaltation :* to supply to the emancipated world a new centre of attraction (ver. 32 : cf. xi. 52).

Lessons. 1. The certainty that Christ's people will fall into seasons of soul trouble. 2. The propriety in such seasons of following Christ's example and turning to God in prayer. 3. The spirit in which supplication should be made to God, that of filial confidence. 4. The object to desire in prayer, not deliverance from, but support under and safe passage through affliction. 5. The duty of recognizing the divine appointment in every experience that befalls us on earth. 6. The necessity of making God's glory the chief end of all our words and deeds. 7. The superiority of faith to unbelief in the understanding of divine revelations. 8. The condescension of Christ in considering man's weakness and infirmity. 9. The light cast on human depravity by the Cross. 10. The unhappy state of those who belong to the ' world ' which Christ's Cross has condemned. 11. The indebtedness of mankind to Jesus for effecting their emancipation from the thraldom of Satan, and placing them beneath His own benignant sway. 12. The hope there is for the world in the fact that Christ is drawing all men to Himself.

Ver. 32. The Great Magnet :—I. **Who is He?** The glorified Jesus. II. **Whom draws He?** All men—the attractive influence of Jesus is exerted upon every member of the race, in a degree inversely proportioned to the individual's moral distance from Him. III. **How acts He?** 1. By the force of His character and example. 2. By the legal and moral virtue of His death as a sacrifice for sin. 3. By the quickening and saving influences of His Spirit. IV. **Whither leads He?** To Himself. 1. To believing discipleship. 2. To spiritual fellowship. 3. To moral correspondence. 4. To Heaven.

4. THE LAST WORDS OF JESUS

Chap. XII. Ver. 34-36

Exposition

Ver. 34. **The multitude** as distinguished from the disciples and the Greek strangers **therefore** — omitted (T. R.), added (א B L X etc.), implying that Our Lord's last spoken words had stirred them to reflection—**answered Him** setting forth two difficulties raised by His language, **We have heard** (Scripture being then known by hearing rather than by reading, cf. Gal. iv. 21) **out of the law** (cf. x. 34)—the passages alluded to being probably Ps. xvi. 10 ; xlv. 7 ; lxxii. 5 ; lxxxix. 29 ; Is. liii. 8 (Bengel), or Ps. cx. 4 ; lxxix. 29 ; Is. ix. 6 ; Dan. vii. 13-14 (Meyer, Godet), if not chiefly the last (Hengstenberg), though the continuous view of the O. T. concerning the permanence of Messiah's kingdom (Luthardt) need not be excluded—**that the Christ,** the Messianic King, **abideth for ever**— "According to the Jewish programme the Messianic kingdom was simply a glorified earth, and the Messiah the perpetual sovereign of this new Eden " (Godet) ; **and how sayest thou,** how canst thou reconcile with this thy language, **the Son of man must be lifted up?** Whether the multitude derived the expression ' Son of man ' from Dan. vii. 13-14 (Hengstenberg, Stier, Meyer), or from their knowledge that Christ was accustomed so to style Himself (Godet), or from ver. 23, in which the thought of the glorification (by lifting up) of the Son of man is substantially contained (Luthardt), it is impossible to concede that the evangelist has here been guilty of an inaccuracy (Tholuck). The first difficulty felt by the multitude was to understand how Christ could be the true Messiah, the ' Son of man ' of Daniel for instance, when He

was talking about removing from the earth. **Who is this Son of man ?** If Himself was the Son of man to whom He alluded, then, as by the hypothesis, He could not be the Messianic Son of man referred to by Daniel, they wanted to know, *who he really was ;* if He was the Messianic Son of man, then they desired to learn *who this other Son of man was.* Either alternative presented a difficulty. The question shows that, while the people understood Christ to call Himself 'The Son of man,' they did not necessarily regard the title as synonymous with 'The Christ.'

35. **Jesus therefore,** prompted by their interpellation to reply, but passing over in silence the difficulties they affected to feel, and the dilemma upon which they sought to impale Him, **said unto them,** delivered an independent utterance (εἶπεν ·rather than ἀπεκρίθη), **Yet a little while**—in contrast to "for ever" (ver 34): cf. vii. 33 ; xiii. 33 ; xiv. 19 ; xvi. 16—**is the light** (see i. 4; iii. 19 ; ix. 4) **among you** ἐν ἡμῖν, *in you,* in your midst, or μεθ' ὑμῶν, with you. So far from the Messiah setting up a permanent visible empire upon the earth, the brief period of His sojourn with and among you is fast drawing to a close. **Walk** (see on xi. 9) **while ye have the light,** or *as, since* ye have, etc., ὡς (A B D K L P II, etc.)—it being doubtful whether ὡς can be rendered 'while' ἕως (א, T. R.) which, however, better corresponds with the preceding words—**that darkness** the antithesis of light and the opposite of Messianic salvation (cf. iii. 9) **overtake you not,** fall upon and seize you not, as a hostile power (Meyer), or perhaps simply descend upon you and

so extinguish your opportunity of attaining to salvation : cf. i. 5 ; vi. 17 ; 1 Thess. v. 4 ; **and he that walketh in the darkness knoweth not whither he goeth** and as a consequence cannot hope to go in safety. See on xi. 10.

36. **While** or *since* (see above) **ye have the light, believe on the light—** εἰς with the accusative, rather than ἐν with the dative, because the light on whom they were invited to believe was *a person*, rather than a doctrine : cf. vi. 29, 40 ; vii. 38—**that ye may become** as the result of your believing (faith being the root and condition of all gracious development) **sons of light**, persons of whom the inner principle is light : cf. 'sons of the resurrection' (Luke xvi. 8), 'sons of the day' (1 Thess. v. 5) : contrast 'sons of disobedience' (Eph. ii. 2).

HOMILETICS

VER. 36.—THE SIMILITUDE OF THE LIGHT.
I. **A Gracious Privilege.** " While " or " as ye have the light." 1. *Great.* A day without light, a world without a sun, expressive but faint emblems of a soul without moral and spiritual illumination, of humanity without Christ. 2. *Present.* Indeed it may be questioned if there ever was a moment since the Fall in which the world was entirely destitute of this light ; though only since the Incarnation of the Son of God, or rather exaltation of the Son of Man, has it attained to meridian splendour. 3. *Temporary.* It is not permanent to us to-day any more than it was to the Jews or than is the natural light of day to any.
II. **A Solemn Duty.** " Believe in the light." 1. *Plain.* Christ's language is neither vague nor ambiguous. " He that runs may read." 2. *Easy.* It is not work or suffer for, but only believe, trust, and walk in the light. 3. *Continuous.* It is not one act of faith and all is done. The word 'walk' implies continuance, progress, and perseverance.
III. **A Glorious Result :** " that ye may become sons of light." 1. *Magnificent.* The light, for man, can illuminate his understanding, purify his heart, quicken his conscience, vitalize his spirit, direct his conduct, beautify and dignify his whole life. It can put him into direct contact with Him who is the light, assimilate his being to that of Him who dwells continually in the light, make him in his measure and degree luminous and light-giving as Christ is. 2. *Designed.* This it does, not unexpectedly and as it were by accident, but purposely and necessarily. 3. *Certain.* Not a peradventure in the case of any. He who walks in the light will as certainly be transfigured by it as the flower is transformed into a spectacle of beauty by the beams of the sun.
Lessons. 1. Thankfulness to Him who hath furnished the light. 2. Watchfulness lest the light should pass away unimproved. 3. Hopefulness with respect to the future of those who believe upon the Saviour. 4. Pitifulness for the fate of those who still walk in darkness.

CONCLUDING OBSERVATIONS

CHAP. XII. 36-50

In bringing his history of Christ's life to a close, the Evangelist appends a brief section in which he summarizes the contents and indicates the result of the whole. *First*, he pathetically sets forth the melancholy fact, that, notwithstanding the clear and repeated manifestation of His glory before the rulers of His people in the successive presentations of Himself recorded in the foregoing narrative, Christ was decisively and finally rejected by "His own" unto whom He had come (ver. 36-43); and then, *secondly*, he compendiously rehearses the character of that self-presentation Christ had made and they had so persistently despised (ver. 44-50).

Exposition

Ver. 36. These things, the topics touched upon in the preceding sermon (ver. 24-36), **spake Jesus** in the presence of His disciples and the Greek strangers but *to* the multitude as representing the Jewish nation, for whom they had formed a farewell address, **and He departed and hid Himself from them**: lit., *and having departed* from the temple (Matt. xxiv. 1; Mark xiii. 1) first to the slopes of Olivet where He sketched in the hearing of His disciples the programe of the last things, and afterwards at nightfall to Bethany, *He hid Himself*, or was hidden, *from them*—from their bodily sight (viii. 59) through remaining all next day in concealment (Meyer), but much more from their spiritual perception (Luthardt), since He no more unveiled His glory in their presence. His departure was thus an ominous prelude of the fate reserved for them (Bengel) when in the midst of their fast approaching desolation they should seek and not be able to find Him (vii. 34, 36); 'a prelude of the severest judgment of the hiding of the Lord which even Moses (Deut. xxxii. 20) had threatened' (Lampe).

37. But though He had done, lit., *He having done*, **so many**, rather than *so great* (De Wette, Lücke)—τοσαῦτα being in this gospel used of number rather than of importance (vi. 9; xiv. 9; xxi. 11)—**signs** (see on ii. 11) of which the Evangelist has up to this point related only seven (ii. 1-11; iv. 46-54; v. 2-9; vi. 1-14; 16-21; ix. 1-12; xi. 43-44), though he distinctly implies and even asserts (ii. 23; iii. 2; iv. 45; vii. 31; x. 32; xi. 47; xx. 30) that there were others done **before them** in their presence, so that they were wholly inexcusable; **yet they**, the Jewish people generally, but their

rulers principally, **believed not**, *were not believing*, or kept on disbelieving **on Him**, not 'so that' (Ebrard, Luthardt)—a sense it is doubtful if ἵνα ever has in the N. T. (Winer, § liii. 6)—but *in order* **that the word of Isaiah the prophet**, the prophecy fore-announced by him (see on i. 23), **might be fulfilled**—"The prophetic word had been spoken because the Lord had resolved to bring to pass the facts. And hence, in the fulness of time, the facts were brought to pass that the prophetic words might be fulfilled" (Morison on Matt. i. 22)—**which He spake** in liii. 1, lamenting over the unbelief of Israel, not in his own time (Meyer, Godet, Luthardt, Tholuck), but in that of the suffering servant of Jehovah (Delitzsch), to whom he was then looking forward as the Evangelist was now looking backward: **Lord!** κύριε, Jehovah, **who hath believed our report?**—either 'the report given by us,' the speaker being the prophet or his successors, the first publishers of the gospel (Godet) or Christ Himself (Meyer); or 'the report addressed to us,' i.e. to repentant Israel after it has come to believe in the risen and exalted servant of Jehovah, and to bewail its own impenitence and hardness of heart (Hofmann, Delitzsch, Luthardt, Milligan and Moulton). **And to whom hath the arm of the Lord been revealed?** As the 'report' referred to the preaching of Christ, so 'the arm of the Lord' (cf. Luke i. 51; Acts xiii. 17) points to His miracles which were wrought by the finger of God (Matt. xii. 28; Luke xi. 20), although this the unbelieving Jews perceived not.

39. For this cause διὰ τοῦτο (cf. v. 16, 18; vi. 65; vii. 22; viii. 47; ix. 23; x. 17; xiii. 11; xv. 19; xvi. 15; xix. 11) **they could not believe**, not 'were unwilling' (Chrysostom), but were unable to believe—faith to them was a moral impossibility—because of the divine necessity that the words of prophetic Scripture should receive fulfilment ; which again resolved itself into a deeper cause introduced by ὅτι ; for that or *because* Isaiah (vi. 9, 10) said again—though the words are not exactly cited from either the Hebrew or the LXX.—

40. He, not Christ (Grotius, Hofmann, Lange, Ebrard), or the devil (Hilgenfeld), but God, though in the original it is the prophet to whom the action is ascribed—in which however lies no contradiction, since *qui facit per alium facit per se*—hath blinded their eyes, and he hardened or *hath hardened their heart* since this moral blindness and spiritual hardening was the result of Jehovah's message to them through His Son—though the case of Pharaoh, with regard to whom it is six times said 'he hardened himself,' and as many times that 'God hardened him,' shows that this judicial action on the part of God does not exempt the individual from responsibility for the same (Tholuck)—lest they should see, lit., *in order that they might not see with their eyes*—the dimming of the spiritual vision which results from every separate act of unbelief being viewed as the direct effect of a divine law which deliberately intends that such should be the consequence of want of fidelity to the truth—and perceive with their heart as they would were they sincerely receptive of the truth, and should turn as again they would did they honestly believe—that they do not turn is sufficiently accounted for by the loss of spiritual susceptibility and the moral hardening which ensue upon deliberate and wilful unbelief—and I should heal them. The moral and spiritual depravity under which they labour is now represented as a sickness or malady requiring a physician (cf. Is. i. 5, 6 ; Matt. ix. 12 ; 1 Pet. ii. 24) who accordingly introduces himself in the first person, *I* referring (1) to the divine personage who spoke to and through Isaiah (vi. 1), and (2) to Christ, as the Evangelist next explains.

41. These things, the just cited prophecy, said Isaiah not 'when' (A. V.), but because—setting forth not the time when the above words were spoken, but the occasion by which they were prompted—he saw His Christ's glory, the μορφὴ θεοῦ (Phil. ii. 6) of His pre-existent state ; which shows that the Evangelist understood and believed the divine personage, Jehovah, or the Angel of Jehovah, who appeared to the prophets in the O. T. theophanies to be the pre-existent Jesus (see the Theological Library—'How is the Divinity of Jesus depicted ?' p. 19) ; and he spake of Him, not of it, the glory (Luthardt). Co-ordinate with 'these things said Isaiah' (Godet, Alford), the clause may with equal grammatical authority be made dependent on 'because' (Meyer, Westcott).

42. Nevertheless, but still, for all that, notwithstanding that such was the general condition of Israel, and the general ill-success of Christ in consequence, even, or also of the rulers—implying that Christ was not entirely without adherents among the common people—"The people of the covenant could never sink so low as to rise up as one man against the most glorious manifestation of their God" (Hengstenberg)—many, including probably Nicodemus and Joseph of Arimathea, if not also Gamaliel (Acts. v. 34), believed on Him with a faith which, if as yet defective, not being followed by confession (Rom. x. 10), was nevertheless sincere and true so far as it went, a remarkable change having come upon their attitude towards Christ since the Feast of Tabernacles (vii. 48) and the miracle at Bethany (xi. 53) ; but because of the Pharisees, the most powerful party in the Sanhedrim, and the most bitterly opposed to Jesus (cf. vii. 13 ; ix. 22 ; and see on i. 24), they did not confess it or Him (the verb being used absolutely), so that they fell short of being disciples in the full sense of the expression ; lest they should be put out of, or *that they should not become persons cut off from* the synagogue, this having already been decreed by the Sanhedrim as the fate of those who should acknowledge Christ's Messiahship (ix. 22) ; for they loved the glory of men, the honour (δόξα) which came from men, which Christ declared to be a fatal barrier to the existence of true faith, more than the glory of God, i.e.

the glory derived from God, cf. v. 44, to which the language of this verse has an obvious allusion.

44. **And** or *but*, the Evangelist now turning to the second part of his concluding observations, to indicate the character of the message the despisers of the Son of God had rejected, **Jesus cried**—neither in the act of departing from the temple (Bengel, Lampe, Hengstenberg), since Christ's last words have already been recorded (ver. 36); nor afterwards in presence of His disciples (Besser, Jacobus), since of this is no hint in the context, while ἔκραξε would scarcely be used of a private conversation with the disciples; but in the course of His public teaching, of which the Evangelist presents a summary—**and said**, if in a tone to arrest attention, also with such simplicity, directness, and lucidity, as to leave His hearers in no uncertainty as to His meaning ; **He that believeth on Me, believeth not on Me but on Him that sent Me ;** i.e. not 'believeth not on Me only, but believeth also on Him that sent Me' (Bengel), but 'believeth not on Me at all as a private person (since in that capacity Christ solicited no man's faith), but believeth on Me as the Father's representative, and hence believeth on Him, the Father, who sent Me.' If Christ never employed this form of expression in any of His discourses reported in this Gospel, He frequently uttered the thought it contains : see vii. 28 : viii. 16, 19, 42 ; x. 38 ; and cf. Matt. x. 40 ; Mark ix. 37 ; Luke ix. 48.

45. **And he that beholdeth Me,** with that intent spiritual contemplation (θεωρεῖν) which pierces through the vail of My humanity and discerns the sender in the sent (cf. i. 14 : vi. 40 ; xiv. 9), **beholdeth Him that sent Me,** the Father (viii. 17), and therefore seeth the Father in the Son (viii. 19 ; xiv. 7, 9).

46. **I am** or *have* **come** ἐλήλυθα—a distinct allusion to His pre-existence (cf. v. 43 ; vii. 28 ; viii. 42), and to the permanence of His mission, in contradistinction to ἦλθον (vii. 14 ; ix. 39 ; x. 10 ; xii. 27) which looks merely to the past historical event—**a light** or, *light* (cf. ix. 5), absolutely and essentially possessing and dispensing it,—the true light (i. 9), **into the world,** and therefore from a supra-mundane sphere, **that**

whosoever believeth on Me may not abide in the darkness which enwraps the world and in which he naturally dwells : cf. for the thought iii. 19 ; viii. 12 ; ix. 5 ; xii. 35, 36 ; and for the phrase "abiding in the darkness," which occurs only here, 1 John ii. 9-11; iii. 14.

47. **And if any man hear My sayings** in the sense, not of believing (Lücke) but simply of learning or becoming acquainted with them through hearing (v. 24 ; vi. 60 ; viii. 47 ; ix. 27 ; x. 3 ; xiv. 24)—though the language has perhaps a more direct echo of Matt. vii. 24 ; Luke vi. 49—**and keep them not** rather than ' believe them not ' (A.V.) —φυλάξῃ expressing the ideas of laying hold of by faith and guarding from violation by personal obedience (cf. Matt. vii. 26 ; Luke xi. 28 ; xviii. 21 ; Rom. ii. 26)—**judge him not** (cf. iii. 17, 18 ; v. 45 ; viii. 15) ; **for I came not to judge the world, but to save the world.** This involves not a denial of the doctrine of a future judgment by Jesus (Reuss, Hilgenfeld), but simply announces that such was not the prime object of His coming. *Hoc limitatur tripliciter : ego, solus; et in praesenti, non judico; et causaliter, non judico ego, sed qui non credit, ipse in judicium incurrit, verbo non credens* (Bengel).

48. **He that rejecteth Me** lit., *he rejecting Me,* making nothing of Me, disesteeming and despising Me, *qui spernit Me* (Vulg.), **and receiveth not My sayings** (the opposite of hearing and keeping them : ver. 47) **hath** not 'will have' but 'has' one that judgeth him, he stands already under trial (cf. v. 45); **the word that I spake,** the witness I have given during My ministry, the revelation of truth I have presented, the one great message, ὁ λόγος, I, the Incarnate Logos have announced to men, the same, that, ἐκεῖνος, **shall judge him in the last day.** See on vi. 39, 40, 44, 54 ; xi. 24; and cf. 'the last hour,' 1 John ii. 18, 'the last trumpet,' 1 Cor. xv. 52. This clause taken along with vi. 39 shows that the Resurrection and the Judgment will be simultaneous and not separated by an interval (say) of 1000 years; *uno die erit resurrectio et judicium* (Bengel).

49. **For**—giving the reason why such power would attach to His word —**I spake not from Myself** (see on v.

30; vii. 17, 28; viii. 28, 41), **but the Father who sent Me** (cf. iv. 34; v. 23; vi. 44; vii. 16; ix. 4; x. 36; xi. 42). **He**, Himself (αὐτός), **hath given Me** not 'gave' in a byegone past, but 'hath given,' so that up to the present moment I feel the constraint of His authority, **a commandment**, a specific commission (see on x. 18), **what I should say and what I should speak.** If 'say' designates the doctrine according to its *contents*, 'speak' alludes to its *publication* through oral speech (Meyer).

50. **And I know** with the certitude of personal experience, **that His commandment** when its result is realized in them who hear My word and keep My sayings, **is life eternal**—the ultimate goal of Christ's mission and ministry: see on iii. 15: **the things therefore which I speak**, the messages and doctrines I proclaim, **even as the Father hath said unto Me, so I speak**; otherwise it were impossible that any efficacy could attach to My words: cf. viii. 38; xiv. 10.

HOMILETICS

VER. 36-43.—THE REJECTED MESSENGER.

I. **The Closed Ministry :**—" These things spake Jesus and departed " (ver. 36). It had been a ministry of—1. *Manifested glory.* The term "glory" one of the keynotes of this gospel (i. 14; ii. 11; v. 41, 44; vii. 39; viii. 54; xi. 4; xii. 41). The Divine Being looked upon by Isaiah in the first temple 800 years before was the same who had now been rejected by Israel in the second temple. For three years and a half He had unfolded before Israel's gaze the same glory which had been witnessed by the Hebrew prophet and in a manner of which that Hebrew prophet had no conception (Is. lxiv. 4). The 'glory' revealed to them was (1) of a higher order than that which had been seen by him. What he beheld was the visible symbol of that uncreated glory in which the Son of God had dwelt from eternity (xvii. 5); what they gazed upon was the reflection of that glory in the mirror of a human nature like their own. And (2) of more frequent exhibition, since the prophet had obtained only one glimpse of this resplendent spectacle, whereas they had enjoyed repeated manifestations of the same. 2. *Offered grace.* So far as it had related to them, the ministry now terminated had been distinguished by the most persistent efforts to effect their personal and social redemption. 3. *Attesting power.* Not alone the revelations of His glory but the proclamations of His grace had been supported and confirmed by many "signs" (ver. 37), every one of which had been a mirror of the first and a symbol of the second.

II. **The Forsaken People :**—" And did hide Himself from them," (ver. 36). 1. *The unbelieving majority:* ver. 37. The completest evidence of Christ's Messiahship and Divinity had been laid before them. And yet they had voluntarily closed their eyes against the light. One would have expected the opposite to have been the case, and for a moment it looked as if it would eventually prove so, when the palm branches waved in the streets of Jerusalem and an excited populace shouted "Hosanna" to "the King of Israel" (ver. 13). But Christ was not deceived by the popular applause of which He was the centre. If the Evangelist was, he also was soon *un*deceived. Notwithstanding appearances, the mass of the community believed not on Christ. 2. *The believing minority* (1) Considerable. Though a minority in respect of the whole, yet in itself it was by no means insignificant, embracing as it did, besides numbers of the common people, many of the rulers. (2) Sincere. Though defective their faith was still true in kind—they recognized that Christ was Messiah. (3) Timid. Though convinced in their judgments, they were lacking in courage—afraid of excommunication from the synagogue. (4) Reprehensible. Governed by fear of man rather than by fear of God, they preferred the approbation of their fellows to the commendation of their consciences and the favour of heaven.

III. **The Fulfilled Prediction :**—" That the word of Isaiah the prophet might be fulfilled," ver. 38. 1. *The prediction.* (1) That the report concerning Jehovah's suffering servant would not be believed by those to whom it should be spoken ; (2) that the ' signs ' which should be performed in attestation thereof would not be understood by those who beheld them. 2. *The fulfilment.* This, according to the Evangelist, came to pass when the Jewish nation with its rulers misinterpreted the ' signs,' disbelieved the ' message,' and rejected the ' person ' of Christ. 3. *The connection :* the fulfilment necessary because of the prediction. (1) Not that compulsion was laid upon the Jewish people to constrain them to reject Christ in order to save the credit of a Hebrew prophet. But (2) the issue of Christ's ministry was so far from being a surprise to Jehovah who had sent Him that eight centuries before it happened it was foreseen, and, having been fore-announced as something the divine mind had foreseen, it could not fail in attaining fulfilment. Hence the necessity which required the rejection of Christ was a necessity that the fore-announced divine programme of human history should come to pass. Unless it be maintained that the eye of omniscience could mistake in forecasting the course of events— an impossible supposition—it must be held that, so far as the divine plan was concerned, the rejection of Jesus was inevitable. Still that did not exempt from guilt those by whom He was rejected.

IV. **The Accomplished Design :**—" For this cause they could not believe," etc., ver. 39. 1. *The law of moral hardening.* That truth rejected always results in a diminution of the soul's susceptibility for receiving truth. 2. *The author of this law.* God. It being a part of the moral order imposed upon His universe that men who deliberately shut their eyes against the light of truth shall gradually lose the power of seeing, that they who resist impressions for good shall by and by cease to feel any such impressions, and that this process shall go on until conversion and recovery become impossible, until in fact the soul becomes past feeling (Eph. iv. 19), whatever issues are produced by the operation of this law may be properly ascribed to God as their author. Nor does God shrink from the responsibility this involves. It would in fact be contrary to divine holiness, righteousness, wisdom, love, were the law otherwise. 3. *The working out of this law.* It was God's intention that this law should remain valid for Israel as for other peoples. Consequently they could not do other than reject the Saviour, because they hated the light which in Him shined upon them, and shunned it so persistently that they at last failed to see it ; they despised the truth so constantly that at last they could not understand the truth they were despising.

Lessons. 1. The day of grace may terminate before the day of life. 2. Unbelief seldom springs from lack of evidence. 3. No prediction of God will ever fail to reach fulfilment. 4. The divine foreknowledge exempts no man from responsibility 5. It is perilous to shut one's eyes against the light of truth. 6. Unbelief is a disease for which Christ is the only physician. 7. Christ the healer of souls is the supreme Jehovah of the Old Testament. 8. It is not enough to believe on Christ with the heart, confession of Him must also be made with the mouth. 9. They who follow Christ must expect to suffer persecution. 10. Who love the praise of men more than the glory of God cannot be saved.

VER. 44-50.—THE REJECTED MESSAGE.

I. **A Message of Love from the Father :** ver. 49. 1. *The substance of the message*—a revelation of the Father (ver. 45) ; of his name, Father ; of His character, love ; of His gift, the Son ; of His purpose, salvation (ver. 47). 2. *The medium of its transmission*—through Christ, the Father's Son (ver. 50), representative (ver. 44), and commissioner (ver. 44, 49). 3. *The heinousness of its rejection*—to reject Christ and His message the same thing as to reject the Father and the Father's message (ver. 44).

II. **A Message of Salvation for the World :** ver. 46, 47. 1. *Of salvation from the darkness*—of intellectual error, moral unholiness, legal condemnation, eternal death. 2. *Of salvation through faith*—through hearing, believing, keeping

Christ's words. 3. *Of salvation for ever*—through escaping the final judgment and entering at the last day upon eternal life.

III. **A Message of Judgment for the Unbelieving** : ver. 48. 1. *Its time*—the last day. 2. Its *author*—the word of Christ. 3. Its *ground*—unbelief and disobedience.

IV. **A Message of Eternal Life for the Faithful** : ver. 50. 1. *The object of the Father's commission :* Eternal life ! 2. *The burden of the Son's ministry :* Eternal life ! 3. *The issue of the individual's faith :* Eternal life !

Lessons. 1. Thankfulness for the gospel message. 2. Watchfulness against the sin of unbelief. 3. Prayerfulness that the news of salvation may be propagated through the earth. 4. Trustfulness that we may escape the judgment of the last day. 5. Earnestness to lay hold upon eternal life.

PART II.—THE HISTORY OF CHRIST'S PASSION

(XIII. 1—XX. 31.)

Subject :—The Glory of Christ unveiled before His own (the spiritually born who had received Him, and who were now represented by the disciples)—"But as many as received Him, to them gave He the right to become children of God, *even* to them that believe on His name" (i. 12).

Having completed his account of Our Lord's ministry, in so far as that was necessary to illustrate the theme he had undertaken, viz., to show how the Incarnate Son of the Father had manifested His glory to the Jewish nation, how that nation as represented by its rulers had rejected the revelation of grace and truth with which in His person they had been furnished, and how, notwithstanding the prevailing unbelief, a small minority of spiritually susceptible souls had been able to discern the heavenly light which shone around and radiated forth from the Son of Man and to consciously rejoice therein, the Evangelist proceeds in the second portion of his history to unfold the manner in which the Divine Word made flesh conferred upon the spiritually born who had received Him at once the right and the power to become children of God, by disclosing to them—henceforth 'His own' in a loftier sense than had ever been true of Israel—aspects of His glory which had hitherto been unrevealed. Up to this time such discoveries of the glory of the Incarnate Word or Son as had been furnished to men had been of a nature fitted to arrest attention, excite admiration, and generate faith in the breasts of those by whom they were beheld, unless indeed, like the Pharisees, these should wilfully shut their eyes against the light. From this moment onward the revelation of the Saviour's glory was to be of such a character, at least generally, as to be discernible only by the eye and appreciable only by the heart of faith—a revelation of self-sacrificing love, of love humbling itself, enduring persecution, experiencing sorrow, submitting to death in behalf of those who had believed upon His name. "Hereby know we love, because He laid down His life for us" (1 John iii. 16).

The main divisions of this portion of Christ's history are three: first, that in which are unveiled the riches of Christ's love for 'His own,' now His believing people (xiii. 1—xvii. 26); second, that in which the Incarnate Son is exhibited as stooping on their behalf to the lowest depths of self-abasement, or, in Pauline phraseology, as becoming obedient unto death, even the death of the cross (xviii., xix.); and third, that in which the glory of the Incarnate Son is beheld rising into meridian splendour through the resurrection, and thereby conferring on believers the right as well as endowing them with the power to become children of God (xx.). Each section is composed of several scenes as the appended analysis shows.

I. The Glory of Christ unveiled to His own (the disciples) through the discovery before them and to them of the riches of His love: xiii.-xviii.

    1. The Feet Washing: xiii. 1-17.
    2. The Revelation of the Traitor: ver. 18-30.
    3. The Arrival of His Hour: ver. 31-38.
    4. The Farewell Discourses: xiv.-xvi.
    5. The High-Priestly Prayer: xvii.

II. The Glory of Christ unveiled to His own (the disciples) through His stooping unto death in their behalf: xviii., xix.

    1. The Garden of Gethsemane: xviii. 1-12.
    2. The Palace of the High Priest—The Denial of Peter: ver. 13-27.
    3. The Trial before Pilate: ver. 28—xix. 16.
    4. The Place called Golgotha: ver. 17-37.
    5. The Tomb in a Garden: ver. 38-42.

III. The Glory of Christ unveiled to His own (the disciples) in full and undimmed splendour, in and through the resurrection, by which He was declared (Rom. i. 4) to be the Son of God with power: xx. 1-29.

    1. The Empty Tomb: xx. 1-10.
    2. The Threefold Manifestation—
        (1) To Mary: xx. 11-18.
        (2) To the Disciples: ver. 19-23.
        (3) To Thomas: ver. 24-29.
    3. Concluding Remarks: ver. 30-31.

SECTION FIRST—THE GLORY OF CHRIST UNVEILED TO HIS OWN (THE
DISCIPLES) AT THE LAST SUPPER

CHAP. XIII. 1—XVII. 26

I. THE FEET-WASHING

CHAP. XIII. VER. 1-17

EXPOSITION

Chap. xiii. ver. 1. Now δὲ, *autem*
(Vulgate), *but;* probably designed to
set the ensuing narration in contrast to
the preceding account of Christ's hiding
Himself from the Jews (xii. 36). **before
the feast of the passover** A note of time
marking the point of departure for the
incidents that follow; to be connected
not with 'riseth,' ver. 4 (Bleek, Ebrard,
Ewald, Brückner), 'knowing,' ver. 1
(Luthardt), or 'having loved' (Tholuck),
but with 'loved' (Godet, Meyer, Westcott, and others); and signifying not
necessarily the day before, since the
phrase is indefinite (cf. xi. 55; xii. 1),
but simply some time before, which
may have been (cf. v. 7; Luke xi. 38;
πρὸ τοῦ ἀρίστου), and probably was immediately before, *i.e.* just at the commencement of the feast. To indicate
this it was not required to write 'before
the passover,' or 'before the supper of
the passover' (Godet), for although in
O.T. Scriptures (Exod. xii. 11, 21;
xxxiv. 18; Lev. xxiii. 5, 6; Num.
xxviii. 16, 17; 2 Chron. xxx. 18-21)
and in Josephus (Ant. iii. 10, 5)
a distinction is sometimes made
between the passover and the feast it
inaugurated, yet this distinction is not
always maintained by either (Ex. xii.
14; Ezek. xlv. 21; Ant. ii. 14, 6; xvi.
2, 1; xvii. 9, 3), as certainly it is not by
the Evangelist (vi. 4). **Jesus, knowing
that His hour was come** Of this hour
it had been twice stated that it was 'not
yet come' (vii. 30; viii. 20), and the
mention of its arrival at this juncture
indicated the gravity of the situation,
—it was the hour fore-appointed for
the purpose to be stated. **that** ἵνα
(in order that) setting forth the end
contemplated by its fore-appointment.
He should depart μεταβῇ, *transeat*

(Vulg.), occurring in this sense only
here, conveys the idea of passing over
from one place to another. **out of this
world** Already described by Christ as
the native home of men and the source
whence they derive their moral as well
as physical being (viii. 23), as a territory
usurped and ruled over by the prince of
darkness (xii. 31; cf. Eph. ii. 2), as a
realm into which He, Christ, had come
from supernal regions (viii. 23; ix. 39),
as a community inwardly alienated
from and deeply embittered against
(vii. 7), but also as already judged
by Him (xii. 31). **unto the Father**
Having come forth from the Father
(vi. 46, 57; viii. 16, 18; xvi. 28) to the
Father he returned (viii. 33; xvi. 28).
The words assert Christ's post-incarnate
existence. **having loved His own** Not
as formerly 'The Jewish Nation,' but
(1) the Apostles and (2) the universal
body of believers (xvii. 20). **which
were in the world** lit., *those in the
world;* in contrast to Himself departing
out of it. **He loved them unto the end.**
εἰς τέλος, *in finem* (Vulg.); either *at last,
finally* (cf. Luke xviii. 5) as if Christ
now furnished His disciples with the
last proof of His love before His death
(Meyer, Luthardt); or *completely,* in the
highest degree, to the uttermost (cf.
1 Thess. ii. 16), as if Christ at His
closing meal carried His affection for
His own to the highest pitch of tenderness (Ewald, Godet, Westcott, Paley);
or *unto the end* (cf. Matt. x. 22), as if
Christ's tender care of His own only
terminated with His life (Brückner,
Hengstenberg, Stier).

2. And during supper δείπνου γινομένου
(א B L X, Tischendorf, Westcott and
Hort), 'and *a supper going on,*'
rather than δείπνου γενομένου (T. R.,

Godet), 'a supper having taken place.' That this was not an ordinary evening repast (Ewald, Meyer, Godet, Westcott) but the paschal meal with which the feast of the passover commenced seems a natural deduction from the context, and is not contradicted by the absence of the article, which may be omitted before appellatives "when from the connection the particular object meant is obvious" (see Winer, § xix. 1). That it was the same meal as that described by the Synoptists (Matt. xxvi. 17-20 ; Mark xiv. 12-17 ; Luke xxii. 7-14) can scarcely be questioned, since at both feasts the same incidents happened, as e.g. the revelation of the Traitor (cf. ver. 21 with Matt. xxvi. 21 ; Mark xiv. 18 ; Luke xxii. 21) and the prediction of Peter's fall (cf. ver. 38 with Luke xxii. 34). Hence, if what the Synoptists described was the paschal supper (Matt. xxvi. 19 ; Mark xiv. 16 ; Luke xxii. 13), then that of which John speaks was the same. On the question as to whether it was observed on the legal day, the evening after the 14th Nisan or on that after the 13th, see note at the end of this exposition. **the devil having already put into the heart of Judas Iscariot, Simon's son, to betray Him** lit., *the devil* or accuser (cf. vi. 70 ; viii. 44) *having already* (cf. Matt. xxvi. 14) *cast into the heart* (cf. Jos. Ant. vi. 13, 4 ; Hom. Odys. i. 201), not of himself, the devil (Vulgate, Meyer), who is never represented in Scripture as possessed of a heart, but of Judas, *that* (ἵνα, i.e. having as its purpose or design that) *Judas, Simon's son, the man of Kerioth,*—Iscariot being in this case an appellation of Judas, whereas in vi. 71 it is of Simon—*should betray Him.* The Evangelist's motive in thus alluding to the traitor has been explained as a desire to set forth the long-suffering love of Jesus in condescending to wash the feet of such an one as Judas (Chrysostom, Calvin, Luthardt), to show the undisturbed serenity of Christ's mind while contemplating the near approach of His doom (Meyer), to account for the frequent allusions about to be made to the traitor at the supper table (Godet), to mark out Judas as the chief author of the dispute about their ranks which arose amongst the disciples on this occasion (Lange)—a

contention, however (Luke xxii. 24-27) concerning which John is silent. Probably John's intention was to indicate that Christ recognized in the fully projected design of His disciple a significant hint that His end was near and that He must act with promptitude if in the brief space that remained He would discover to His disciples all the love that was in His heart towards them and for them. 3. *Jesus* **knowing**, i.e. *because* or *since* rather than although (Meyer, Tholuck, Hengstenberg), He knew, **that the Father had given** lit., *gave*, i.e. in eternity ἔδωκεν (אBKL) pointing to the indefinite past, **all things**, i.e. all things absolutely, or 'the universe' and not merely all things necessary for the accomplishment of His work and the establishment of His kingdom (Schweitzer), **into His hands** to be subject to His authority and rule : see on iii. 35 ; and cf. Matt. xi. 27 ; 1 Cor. xv. 25 ; Eph. ii. 22 ; Phil. ii. 9-11 ; **and that He came forth from God and goeth unto God**, or, *that from God He came forth* (see on viii. 42) *and to God goeth* (vii. 33), the mention of His heavenly and divine origin and end emphasizing "that oneness of Jesus with the Father of which at this moment His consciousness was full" (Brückner) ; **riseth from supper** at which already He had taken His place, **and layeth aside His garments**, i.e. divested Himself of his outer robe which would probably have impeded Him in the service He designed to render—"retaining only the tunic which was the vesture of slaves" (Godet) ; **and He took a towel and girded Himself** lit., *and having taken a towel, λέντιον, a* linen apron (cf. Luke xvii. 8), *He girded Himself*, so as to leave both hands free for carrying the bason. *Nihil ministerii omittit* (Grotius). That Christ with His own hand prepared himself for His work vividly depicted the depth of his humiliation. *Quid mirum si praecinxit se linteo qui, formam servi accipiens, habitu inventus est ut homo!* (Augustine). 5. **Then** εἶτα, *after that, next* (cf. xix. 27 ; xx. 27)—the detailed narration of every incident in this transaction setting forth not merely its own intrinsic importance, but also the excitement with which it was beheld by the dis-

-ciples (Luthardt, Tholuck)—-**He poureth water into the bason** or washing vessel ⟨τὸν νιπτῆρα⟩ which stood ready in the chamber for such purposes, **and began** ἤρξατο—"*rarum Johanni verbum*" (Bengel), though common enough with the Synoptists; probably here used to indicate that Christ's action was intended to be performed over a wide circle (Henstenberg), or, that the act was only then commenced but not finished (Meyer), or that it was an uncommon and specially exciting occurrence (Luthardt)—**to wash the disciples' feet** ("Among men," said the Rabbis, "the slave washes his master; but with God it is not so," Lightfoot, quoted by Westcott) **and to wipe them with the towel wherewith He was girded.** *Non sic angelus Petro fecit*, Acts xii. 8 (Bengel). The occasion of this action, pronounced incompatible with the institution of the Last Supper and therefore performed, if at all, at an earlier moment (Schenkel, Strauss, Keim), has been sought in the contention about rank of which Luke (xxii. 24) speaks (Ebrard, Luthardt, Godet); or in the supposed omission of the disciples to perform for Christ the act of feet-washing customary at the commencement of a meal (Lange, Hengstenberg)—a service not commanded by the law, and not generally practised at banquets (Luke vii. 44); or, and with equal probability, in Christ's desire to furnish His disciples with a symbolic representation of that self-denying love which was about to receive its highest exemplification in Himself, and which was necessary to be reproduced in them if they would be His followers and servants (Meyer, Tholuck, Westcott). That the paragraph is only a historically formed exposition of Matt. xx. 26 and Luke xxii. 26 (Baur, Strauss, Keim, Schenkel, Hilgenfeld) requires no refutation.

6. **So,** *accordingly* or *then*, **He cometh to Simon Peter** not first (Augustine, Ewald, Hengstenberg, Alford, Westcott), but after He had washed the feet of others (Bengel, Luthardt, Godet, Meyer). Whether He began with Judas and ended with Peter (Chrysostom) cannot be ascertained. **He,** Peter, with characteristic impetuosity, yet with mingled reverence and astonishment, **saith unto Him,** Christ, **Lord, doth**

Thou wash my feet? or, *Thou of me dost wash*, or propose to wash, *the feet?* the present tense, νίπτεις, being used for an action about to take place : cf. x. 32. See Winer, § xl. 2. To the Apostle it seemed too great a condescension that One so exalted should wash the *feet* of one so lowly and obscure as he : cf. the language of the Baptist (Matt. iii. 14).

7. **Jesus answered and said unto him,** mildly furnishing a reason which should have removed his objections to the proposed service, **What I do** or, *am doing*, **thou knowest not now, but thou shalt understand hereafter,** lit., *after these things* (cf. iii. 22 ; v. 1, 14 ; vi. 1 ; vii. 1 ; xix. 38 ; xxi. 1), not in eternity (Luther), but first in the explanation to be forthwith given (Meyer, Luthardt, Godet), and afterwards more fully in the apostolic enlightenment which would ensue at Pentecost (Chrysostom). The antithesis between οἶδας and γνώσῃ is observable : thou knowest not by intuitive discernment, but thou shalt know from experience or come to learn by being taught : cf. iii. 10, 11.

8. **Peter saith unto Him,** with increasing impressiveness and self-will, **Thou shalt never wash my feet,** or, *Thou shalt not* (a double negative for emphasis) *wash the feet of me for ever*, while the world lasts, for all time, into eternity : cf. iv. 14 ; viii. 51, 52 ; x. 28 ; xi. 26. For the exhibition of a similar spirit by this apostle see Matt. xvi. 22. **Jesus answered him** with calmness and decision, in words of solemn warning, **If I wash thee not thou hast no part with Me.** That Christ referred first to His proposed washing of Peter's feet is apparent, since otherwise His words would not have been a direct response to Peter's objection : that they went beyond this is obvious from the result declared as certain to follow Peter's continued refusal. That Christ's washing of Peter's feet could not in itself have entitled him to a share in the lot of Jesus must be conceded, as then Judas must have been equally a partaker with Peter ; but Peter's refusal to accept such a service at the hands of Christ, more especially if persisted in after Christ's explanation, would be an indication that the higher spiritual cleansing of which the material ablution was but a symbol had not taken place ; and in that case Peter could have no

part with Christ—not merely no part in the lowly spirit exhibited by Christ (Bengel, De Wette, Brückner) : " Jesus recognizes, in short, that a spirit leads Peter which has nothing in common with the mind and spirit of the Master" (Schweitzer) ; or no part in Christ's friendship (Maldonatus) ; but also and chiefly no part in Christ's salvation and eternal life (Meyer, Tholuck, Luthardt), in Christ's kingdom and glory (Lange, Westcott), in the Messianic good things of the future which Christ will bring (Ewald). Cf. Matt. xxiv. 51 ; Luke xii. 46 ; Josh. xxii. 24, 25 ; 2 Sam. xx. 1 ; 1 Kings xii. 16.

9. **Simon Peter saith unto him,** repeating his old fault of dictating to His Lord, only in an opposite direction, **Lord, not my feet only** do thou wash, **but also my hands and my head.** Though Peter had manifestly not got beyond the idea of external purification, his words evinced the intensity both of his affection for, and of his horror at the bare thought of separation from, Christ.

10. **Jesus saith to him,** and to the rest of the disciples as well (cf. iii. 11), **He that is bathed** ὁ λελουμένος, λούω being used of the washing of the whole body, whereas νίπτω refers always to a partial ablution, **needeth not save to wash his feet,** the words 'save his feet' being omitted by some authorities (ℵ Tischendorf), probably because of the difficulty of reconciling them with the next clause—**but is clean every whit,** i.e. with the exception, just mentioned, of the feet, which have become soiled through stepping out of the bath ; **and ye are clean** because ye have been already bathed—it is not necessary to suppose the apostles had already bathed before their meal (Lücke)—the allusion being not so much, if at all, to their baptism (Augustine, Erasmus, Olshausen, Ewald, Hengstenberg, Godet), as to their regeneration (cf. Tit. iii. 5), the inward renewal of their natures which had taken place through their fellowship with Christ and belief in His word, xv. 3 (Meyer, Luthardt, Tholuck, Westcott) ;—**but not all.** The Saviour speaks of His disciples collectively as a body whose extremities were defiled, though its main trunk was clean. The impure member referred to was Judas.

11. **For He knew him that should betray Him,** lit., *him betraying Him,* already in the act of carrying out his treacherous designs. The expressions used by the Evangelist with reference to the traitor show the development and progress of the treasonable thought : 1. he that was about to betray (vi. 71) ; 2. he that should betray (vi. 64) ; 3. he that is betraying (xiii. 11) ; 4. he that betrayed (xviii. 2: cf. Matt. xxvi. 48). **therefore said He, Ye are not all clean,** or, *Not all of you are clean.* The 'therefore' indicates that in the judgment of the Evangelist, reflecting on the scene, which at the time he had not understood, Christ had important reasons for making this announcement. These were probably (1) to give one more revelation of Himself as the Searcher of hearts ; (2) to obviate the possibility of objection against His Messiahship arising out of the approaching betrayal ; and (3) to pierce the heart of Judas. The latter half of this verse is omitted by the Beza text (D).

12. **So, when,** or *when then,* **He had washed their feet**—not excepting Judas —**and taken His garments, and sat down again,** lit. *and reclined again* (at the table), **He said unto them,** explaining His action, **Know ye what I have done unto you?** have you come to perceive and understand (γινώσκετε) the import and design of My surprising behaviour? —asking not so much with a view to elicit an answer as to fix attention on His forthcoming explanation.

13. **Ye call me Master and Lord** or the *Teacher* (xi. 28 ; cf. Matt. viii. 19) and the *Ruler* (vi. 68 ; cf. Matt. viii. 25), the former term referring to Christ's doctrine, the latter to His authority over the life. So the Rabbis were addressed by their scholars, their pupils on the other hand being known as disciples and servants. **and ye say well** in addressing Me by these names ; **for so I am,** or *for I am* (The Teacher and the Ruler). Christ more than once acknowledged the fitness of these titles as applied to Himself. See Matt. xxiii. 8-10 ; Luke vi. 46.

14. **If I then, the Lord and the Master, have washed your feet,** lit., *if then I washed your feet*—I, the Lord and the Teacher* (the emphasis lying not upon the time of the action, but upon the

action itself as having been performed by one so exalted), **ye also ought to wash one another's feet.** The argument has three stages : 1. If *I*, then *ye also ;* if the Teacher, then the scholar ; if the Master, then the servant. 2. If *I yours*, then *ye one another's ;* if the Teacher washed the scholar's feet, then the scholars might wash one another's feet ; if the Master the servant's feet, then the servants each other's. 3. If I did this *freely* to you, then this free service of mine to you should render yours to each other a necessity, an obligation of love. The Beza reads, 'how much more are ye also bound,' etc.

15. **For I have given you an example** ὑπόδειγμα: cf. Heb. iv. 11 ; viii. 5 ; ix. 23 ; Jas. v. 10 ; 2 Pet. ii. 6 ; other words for ' example ' being τύπος, a type or model, 1 Cor. x. 6 ; 1 Tim. iv. 12 ; ὑπογραμμός, a copy or underwriting, 1 Pet. ii. 21 ; and δεῖγμα, a sample or exhibition, Jude 7. **that ye also should do as I have done to you,** lit., *that as I did to you ye also should do* (to one another). The language refers not to the external act of feet washing, and least of all to the institution of such a rite as arose in the Christian church in the 14th century, and at the present day is practised by the Pope on Maunday Thursday, but to the internal spirit which was manifested in the action.

16. **Verily, verily I say unto you** This customary formula (see on i. 51) was probably here employed because the self-denying love Christ sought to impress upon them was something which had never before entered into men's conceptions of human duty. **a servant,** a slave, δοῦλος, **is not greater than his lord,** master or owner: cf. xv. 10 ; Matt. x. 24 ; Luke vi. 40 ; **neither one that is sent,** an apostle, ἀπόστολος, or envoy, **greater than he that sent him,** from whom he holds his commission and whom therefore he represents.

17. **If,** or since, **ye know these things,** the lessons conveyed by the feet-washing, **happy are ye** as being possessed of the blessedness which belongs to the subject of Messiah's kingdom (cf. Matt. v. 3), **if ye do them.** Action arising out of, and in complete conformity to, the truth proclaimed by Christ, and not simply knowledge divorced from con-duct, is invariably represented in Scripture as the source of true spiritual felicity : Matt. vii. 21 ; Luke xi. 28 ; Jas. i. 25 ; Rev. xvi. 15 ; xxii. 14.

Note.—*Concerning the date of the Last Supper.*

That Christ was crucified on Friday, and on the Thursday evening previous along with His disciples partook of a repast, called by the Synoptists ' the passover,' and by John ' a supper,' is attested by all the four Evangelists. The question to be determined is, whether the Jewish festival that year fell upon the Thursday or the Friday evening.

I. *In favour of the latter view* (Bengel, Lampe, Kuinoel, Grotius, Meyer, Godet, Ewald, Brückner, Beyschlag, Schenkel, and others), the evidence adduced is of two sorts : direct and indirect.

A. Alleged *direct* evidence that Thursday evening was the night before the passover, the night after the 13th Nisan.

1. xiii. 1. The note of time ' before the passover.' But this phrase does not necessarily and exclusively mean ' the day before ': it may also signify *immediately* before. See Exposition.

2. xiii. 29. The belief of the disciples that Judas left the chamber to buy what things were needful for the feast or to give something to the poor. But (1) the term 'feast,' though occasionally signifying the eating of the paschal lamb (Exod. xii. 14), yet commonly denotes the entire festival of which the eating of the passover was the introduction (Exod. xxiii. 15 ; xxxiv. 18 ; Lev. xxiii. 6 ; Deut. xvi. 16 ; Ezra vi. 22 ; Ezek. xlv. 21 ; Matt. xxvi. 5 ; Mark xv. 6 ; Luke xxii. 1 ; John iv. 45) ; hence (2) the things needful for the feast may have been the offerings for next morning's celebrations ; while (3) if the paschal supper did not begin till the following evening, there was no need for haste on the part of Judas or Jesus either to purchase offerings or to present gifts, since both of these could have been done on the ensuing day. See Exposition.

3. xviii. 28. The reason given by the Jews for declining to enter Pilate's palace. Here again, however, (1) If the passover was not due till after sunset on Friday, there was no reason why the Jews, although they had become

unclean through entering a heathen prince's house, should have troubled themselves, since such defilement might be removed by a bath at the end of the day (Lev. xxii. 5-7 ; Maimmi, Hilchoth, Korban, Pesach, vi. 1 ; Stapfer, Palestine in the Time of Christ, p. 377). (2) If the passover was already passed and the first day of the feast commenced, then the Jews might naturally dread contamination, since that would exclude them from the further solemnities of the first day of the feast, and in particular would prevent them from "eating the holy things," i.e., the thank-offerings on that day sacrificed and eaten (Lev. xxii. 6 ; Num. xxviii. 17-25). (3) The phrase 'to eat the passover' does not signify exclusively to eat the paschal lamb, but may also mean to partake of the offerings of the other days. At least the term 'passover' is employed in the O.T. (Deut. xvi. 2, 3 ; 2 Chron. xxxv. 7 ; Ezek. xlv.21),in the N.T. (Matt. xxvi.2; Mark xiv. 1 ; Luke xxii. 1 ; John ii. 23 ; vi. 4; xi. 35; xviii. 39), and in Josephus (Antiq. xiv. 2, 1), to denote the entire festival, and the similar phrase 'to eat the feast,' as applied to the other days, is not unknown (2 Chron. xxx. 22). Should it be urged that to 'eat the passover' cannot be used of eating *only* the holy things of the first day (for which the customary phrase was 'to eat the feast') without also partaking of the paschal lamb, the common-sense reply is that the Jews, if already they had done this, were 'eating the passover' in the sense defined, and might naturally shrink from such defilement as would hinder them from continuing what already they had begun. (4) It is even supposable that though the general body of the people had already partaken of the passover, their leaders, the chief priests, had not done so, having been engaged till a late hour in the temple slaughtering lambs, and afterwards interrupted by the appearance of Judas before they had finished or even begun their own ceremonial repast.

4. xix. 14, 31, 42. The statement that the day of our Lord's crucifixion was 'the preparation of the passover.' But if grammatically viewed, ' the preparation of the passover' may mean the preparation for the passover; it is no less certain (1) that the term 'preparation'

as employed by the Synoptists (Matt. xxvii. 62 ; Mark xv. 42 ; Luke xxiii. 54) signifies the day before the Sabbath, and (2) that nothing hinders it from having this sense in John, in which it is directly connected with the Sabbath (xix. 31), and even designated 'the Jews' preparation' (xix. 42), i.e. the day known to the Jews as 'the preparation,' to wit for the Sabbath. If the Sabbath in question is described as a *high* day, this may have been because it had a doubly sabbatic character as the first day of the feast and the seventh day of the week ; but the epithet would have been equally appropriate without assuming that the Sabbath was also the first day of the feast, since as a Sabbath falling in the middle of the passover week it would be invested with a peculiar sanctity. For a like reason 'the preparation' in question, as a 'preparation' occurring during the passover and on a day (the first day of the feast) which was itself possessed of a sabbatic character, would be doubly sacred ; and this circumstance might account for the phraseology employed by John—'the preparation of the passover,' i.e. the preparation day falling in the paschal week.

5. xix. 36. The identification by the evangelist of Christ as the antitypical paschal Lamb. But the ground given for this identification by John is not (the supposed) fact that Christ died at the moment when the paschal lambs were being slain, but the *actual* fact that, as in the case of the passover victims, "not a bone of Him was broken."

B. Alleged *indirect* evidence for Thursday being the day before the legal passover.

1. The withdrawal of Judas from the chamber during the supper (xiii. 30) and the departure of Jesus with His disciples from the same at the close of the feast (xiv. 31), as also their leaving the precincts of the city (xviii. 1) ; all of which were forbidden on the passover night (Exod. xii. 22). But the original prescription to eat the passover standing, with loins girt and staves in hand (Exod. xii. 11) had in Christ's time been modified ; and hence it is at least possible that then also the injunction against going out was not strictly enforced.

2. The illegality of making purchases on the passover night. This however is by no means established (see Exod. xii. 16 ; Luke xxiii. 56). If the first day of the feast was a Sabbath, it is still doubtful whether it was observed with the same strictness as the seventh day, and whether purchases were not permitted where no money was exchanged (see Tholuck on xiii. 29).

3. The impossibility of carrying out the process against the Saviour on the first day of the feast on account of its sabbatic character, since on a day so holy neither could the Sanhedrim have held a regular court, nor could the Pharisees have so far violated their traditional reverence for a feast Sabbath as to request Pilate to send out an armed band, nor could an execution have then taken place. But (1) the Sanhedrim, some think, had no scruples in holding a sederunt upon a regular Sabbath (v. 10 ; ix. 13), and were not likely to shrink from meeting on a feast Sabbath, as indeed they had already done (vii. 30, 45). (2) As for apprehending Jesus on a feast Sabbath, this, according to the Synoptists (Matt xxvi. 4 ; Mark xiv. 2 ; Luke xxii. 2), they had distinctly contemplated, but did not propose to carry out—not, however, because of its illegality, but for fear of exciting a tumult among the people. (3) Though forbidden by the Talmudists to hold a court of justice on the Sabbath or on feast days (Mischna *Jom tob* v. 2), the Sanhedrists got over this by assembling on these days in a building (called by Maimonides 'the school house') near the fore court of the women, instead of in the stone judgment hall, and by holding their sessions after morning instead of at the time of evening sacrifice (Gemara, Sanhedr. x. fol. 88, 1). It is not clear that executions were in all cases prohibited at feasts (2 Sam xxi. 9 ; Acts xii. 3). At least Maimonides (Rebels iii. 8), speaking of the infliction of the capital sentence upon the man who hearkens not to priest or judge, says, "They put him not to death in the judgment hall that is in his city, but carry him up to the high Synedrion in Jerusalem and keep him until the feast, and strangle him at the feast, as it is said, 'And all the people shall

hear and fear" (see Ainsworth on Deut. xvii. 13).

4. The certainty that Joseph of Arimathea could not have conducted the burial of Jesus on the first day of the feast (xx. 38). But if the Talmud prohibited interment on the Sabbath (Yoma viii. 7), it cannot be established that this restriction extended to the day before the Sabbath, even though it were a feast day ; and in any case the law of Moses (Deut. xxi. 23) commanded that the body of one who had been hanged should not remain all night upon the tree, but should be buried the same day (cf. Josh. viii. 29).

5. The facts mentioned by the Synoptists (1) that Simon the Cyrenian was coming from the country (from his work, it is said) on Friday morning (Mark xv. 21 ; Luke xxiii. 26), and (2) that the women purchased spices on the same afternoon or evening (Luke xxiii. 56)—neither of which could have happened on that day, had it been the first day of the feast. But, with reference to the *first* (*a*), it is hardly likely that Simon was coming from his work at so early an hour in the morning, while (β) if " the immediate neighbourhood of Jerusalem, at least as far away as Bethphage, had the right to eat the Easter lamb outside the city " (Keim), he may have been returning with the dawn to the metropolis, after having observed the passover in its outskirts and (γ) to come from the country into the city on a feast Sabbath was no violation of the law. As regards the *second*, that falls under the same category as the supposed purchases of Judas.

6. The Talmud states that Jesus died in the afternoon of the 14th Nisan (Sanh. fol. 43, 1). But the same tractate affirms that Christ's condemnation was publicly proclaimed by the Sanhedrim for forty days, that He was not crucified, but first stoned and then hanged, that His accusers never brought Him before Pilate as an offender against the state, and that His trial was wholly religious. In short, it is impossible to stand upon the historical validity of this document, which probably was " drawn up by people eager to justify themselves, because they felt the awful responsibility cast upon them by the account of the passion given in the Gospels "

(Stapfer, Palestine in the Time of Christ, p. 108).

7. In the Easter controversies of the second century the churches of the West contended for the right to celebrate the Lord's Supper without observing the passover, on the ground that, according to John, Jesus had not partaken of the passover in His last year, when He Himself was slain as the true paschal lamb (Clemens Alex. in the Chron. Pasch. i. 12); but against this stands the fact that the churches of Asia Minor kept the passover (along with the Lord's Supper) on the evening after the 14th Nisan, pleading as their authority for so doing that such had been the practice with John and the other apostles of the Lord (Irenæus in Eusebius v. 24). The force of this reply would no doubt be considerably modified by the supposition (Weitzel, Ebrard, Meyer, and others) that the Quartodecimans celebrated the 14th Nisan, not because Christ observed the passover on that day, but because He died on that day ; only it is doubtful if this is more than a happy conjecture.

II. *In favour of the view that Thursday evening was the night of the legal passover*, the evening after the 14th Nisan (Lücke, Luthardt, Tholuck, Keim, Lange, Hengstenberg, Milligan and Moulton, Andrews and others), cogent arguments exist.

1. On the assumption that the passover fell upon the Friday, it is difficult to explain (1) how *all the three* Synoptists should have erred in placing it upon the Thursday ; (2) how the first three gospels should have found acceptance in the early church if they did not represent the prevalent Christian tradition ; and (3) how the tradition which the three Synoptists follow could have arisen, if it was not the case that Christ ate the legal passover on the Thursday evening.

2. Even had Christ intended to celebrate the passover on an earlier day than usual, it is scarcely likely that such a thought would have occurred to his disciples (Matt. xxvi. 19), or to the owner of the room (Mark xiv. 15), unless indeed they had both been forewarned—which is not the impression given by the narratives.

3. It is unlikely that the priests in the temple would (or could) have slain a paschal lamb on any except the legal day. It has been asserted that in consequence of the enormous number of lambs slaughtered at the passover—Josephus (Wars ii. 14, 3 ; vi. 9, 3) says 600,000—it was allowable to keep the passover on the 13th or 14th; but this opinion is devoid of historical support.

4. If not inconceivable that Christ should have observed a meal with His disciples on the 13th of Nisan (Thursday), because he knew He would not be able to partake with them of the national passover on the following day, it is inexplicable that Christ should have called it not *a* passover, but 'the passover' (Matt. xxvi. 18), when He must have been aware it was not.

5. It is fair to argue that if John had intended to correct the Synoptists with regard to the date of the passover, he would have done so by a statement more definite and explicit than any that have been above considered.

6. The conclusion which seems most warranted by the facts of the case is that no discrepancy exists between John and the Synoptists, but that he agrees with them in saying the meal Christ observed with His disciples on the Thursday evening before His death was the legal passover of the Jews, which in His case was followed by the institution of the Lord's Supper. (For a full discussion of this question, see Andrews, The Life of Our Lord upon the Earth, pp. 367 ff. ; Bleek's Introduction to the N.T. vol. 1, §§ 72, 73, 74 ; Beyschlag, Zur Johanneischen Frage, pp. 94-98 ; Ebrard's Gospel History, § 92 ; Keim's Jesus von Nazara, vol. vi. pp. 195 ff.).

HOMILETICS

VER. 1-17.—A THREEFOLD MARVEL.

I. **A Marvellous Love** :—that of Christ for His own : ver. 1. Marvellous in respect of 1. *Its time.* (1) Before the feast of the passover, when His thoughts might have been occupied with the memories suggested by that sacred season. (2) Before His departure from the world, when he might have been absorbed in contemplation, if not of the death which lay before Him, at least of the realm into which, and of the Father unto whom he was returning. (3) Before His exaltation and enthronement beside the Father as supreme Lord and Governor of the universe, when the vision of the 'glory that should follow' might have fixed His spirit's eye. Yet none of these could detach His affections from those He was about to leave behind Him on the earth. 2. *Its intensity.* "He loved them unto the end." (1) To the uttermost, or in the highest possible degree, with a love passing knowledge (Eph. iii. 19), which many waters (of affliction) could not quench, nor floods (of sorrow) drown (Song. viii. 7). (2) Unto the end, or to the latest moment of His life, with a love which, as it had been without beginning, so also would it be without end (Jer. xxxi. 3). (3) At the last, or with a love which surpassed every previous demonstration of affection He had given, a love that stooped even unto death for those it loved (xv. 13 ; 1 John iii. 16 ; Rom. v. 8). 3. *Its reason.* While He was departing from the world, they were remaining in it, exposed to that relentless enmity and burdened with those oppressive ills, from which He was escaping. The very thought of their feeble and defenceless position as well as of their suffering and imperfect condition added fuel to the fire of His affection. "Not being untutored in suffering" said a heathen poet (Virgil), "I learn to pity those in affliction." Christ had Himself encountered the sharp blast of adversity while in the world and could feel for those who were soon to be exposed to its pitiless severity (Heb. iv. 15).

II. **A Marvellous Deed :**—Christ washes His disciples' feet : ver. 5. An act of 1. *Amazing condescension.* Considering (1) the nature of the act itself—such a service as was commonly performed by a menial or slave (cf. 1 Sam. xxv. 41) ; (2) the dignity of Him by whom it was performed—the Incarnate Son, who at the moment was conscious of His heavenly origin and destiny (ver. 3), whom the Father had appointed heir of all things (Heb. i. 2), and who was then upon the eve of grasping the sceptre of the universe (Matt. xxviii. 18); and (3) the character of those to whom it was rendered—not sinless and obedient, but frail and erring men, who had followed Him indeed sincerely but with much stumbling and numerous imperfections, yea among whom was a traitor and a devil into whose heart had already been cast the Satanic project of selling Him, the incarnate Son of God, into the hands of His foes. When one reads that Jesus actually washed the feet of Judas, one wonders at the kind of heart Judas must have had, that could have suffered him to sit through the ceremony, obviously unmoved, without a pang of remorse shooting through his conscience, a blush of shame mantling his brow, or a tear of pity filling his stony eye ; and at the unspeakable yearning which must have resided in the bosom of Jesus for that unhappy man whom the devil was so certainly impelling towards his fate ! Had Jesus been only a man He would have loathed and spurned Judas from His presence like a human reptile : being God incarnate, He loved him and even washed his feet. One does not wonder that a Claudius should have cried aloud that 'anything so sublime had never come into a human heart,' or that Christians should at times feel disposed to say—'Such self-humiliation is beyond the power of man.' 2. *Sublime significance.* Symbolic (1) of the self-abasement of Christ who in order to effect the moral and spiritual cleansing of His people laid aside the form of God, clothed Himself in the garment of humanity, and poured forth His blood upon the cross (Phil. ii. 7, 8 ; 1 John i. 7). (2) Of the washing of regeneration through which sin's defilement is removed from the soul (Eph. v. 26 ; Tit. iii. 5). (3) Of that daily cleansing which even the renewed need in the fountain of atoning blood as well as in the laver of regeneration (Ps. li. 7 ; 1 John i. 9).

III. **A Marvellous Obligation :**—to wash one another's feet : ver. 14, 15. Christ's example called (and still calls) His disciples to the cultivation of 1. *Personal humility.* If Christ, the Lord and the Master, could stoop from the throne of deity so far as to wash the feet of a Judas, then it ill became them, the servants and the scholars, to be puffed up with thoughts of their own greatness (Rom. xii. 3). If he could say, "Behold I am among you as one that serveth!" (Luke xxii. 27), then the chief among them should be the servant of all. If He was 'meek and lowly in heart' (Matt. xi. 29), they should be clothed with humility (1 Pet. v. 5). 2. *Loving service.* If He washed their feet, they should wash one another's feet—not literally as if Christ had in so speaking instituted a new religious ordinance (Ambrose), that of foot-washing, at the present day practised every Maunday Thursday upon twelve poor men by the Pope, who however thereby shows himself to be rather Christ's ape than Christ's imitator (Calvin); but metaphorically and spiritually—a much harder task—by ministering to each other's necessities and practising towards one another Christian kindness (xv. 17; Matt. xxv. 34-40; Rom. xii. 9, 10; xiii. 8; Gal. v. 13, 14, 22; vi. 2; Eph. v. 2; 1 Tim. v. 10). "The *essence* of the rite is preserved, where the *love* from which the practice flowed abides" (Meyer). 2. *Brotherly forgiveness.* If the feet-washing symbolized to Christ's apostles the daily cleansing they required and Christ bestowed, so ought Christians to exemplify towards one another that charity which covers a multitude of sins. (Matt. vi. 12; Mark xi. 25; Luke xvii. 3, 4; Eph. iv. 32; Col. iii. 13).

Learn 1. The supreme divinity of Christ. 2. The diabolical depravity of the fallen heart. 3. The imperfections of even Christ's followers. 4. The absolute necessity of Christ as a Saviour. 5. Christ's perfect knowledge of the human heart. 6. The duty of taking Christ as our example. 7. Obedience the royal road to happiness.

Ver. 7. Now and Hereafter. I. With reference to **Christ's Working.** 1. *Now* veiled in mystery; as to (1) manner, (2) time, (3) purpose: cf. Job ix. 11; xxiii. 8, 9; Is. xlv. 15; 1 Cor. xiii. 12. 2. *Hereafter*—set forth in light: Job xxviii. 11; 1 Cor. iv. 5; Col. i. 12; Rev. xxi. 23; xxii. 5. II. With reference to **Man's understanding** of the same. 1. Now—(1) always inadequate, and (2) often erroneous: Job xxxvii. 21; 1 Cor. xiii. 12. 2. *Hereafter*—(1) complete and (2) true: 1 Cor. xiii. 12; 1 John iii. 2.

Ver. 8. Partnership with Christ. I. Its *condition*—Being washed by Christ. 1. In His blood—pardon; 2. By His Spirit—renewal; 3. Through His word—sanctification. II. Its *character*—A partnership. 1. In legal acceptance before God. 2. In moral likeness to God. 3. In heavenly glory with God. III. Its *consequence*—leading to 1. perfect trust in, 2. lowly obedience to, 3. and patient imitation of Christ.

2. THE REVELATION OF THE TRAITOR

Chap. XIII. Ver. 18-30

Exposition

Chap. xiii ver. 18. **I speak not of you all** the words immediately preceding (Meyer, Godet, Luthardt), rather than those of ver. 10 (Lampe, Tholuck). One among them would never attain to the felicity Christ promised because he would never do what Christ enjoined : and this again he would fail to perform because he had never in reality been bathed in the cleansing laver of regeneration, so that in his case the foot-washing had entirely lost its significance. In this way the language may have a backward look to ver. 10. I, for my part, **know** intuitively discern and perfectly understand the personalities and characters of those **whom I have chosen** or *chose;* not to salvation (Augustine) or the grace of perseverance (Calvin), but apostleship—Christ's meaning being that though He had elected Judas equally with the others (vi. 70), He had not done so in ignorance of his character. but 'I chose whom I chose' (Olshausen, Meyer, Hengstenberg); or 'this happened' as in xix. 36; Matt. xxvi. 56; Mark xiv. 49; 1 Cor. ii. 9 (Grotius, Tholuck, Lange, Godet, Lücke, Westcott, and others), the 'this' being 'that Christ had chosen Judas' (Godet), or, 'that Christ could not apply ver. 17 to all' (Meyer); or, without any supplement (Calvin, Kuinoel, Milligan and Moulton), but, **that the Scripture may be fulfilled.** According to the first construction Christ's selection of Judas, according to the second the declension of Judas, according to the third the actual treason of Judas, had taken place in accordance with a divine determination that the Scripture prophecy concerning Himself should be accomplished. **He that eateth my bread lifteth up his heel against me.** Freely cited from the Hebrew or the LXX. (Ps. xli. 10), with neither of which it entirely agrees, the clause depicts the treachery of one who "has made great his heel" against his benefactor and friend, by either lifting it on high so as to trample on the object of his attack, or by striking out against it with a violent and hard blow (Perowne). In the conduct of such a traitor—either Ahithophel (2 Sam. xv. 12 ; xvi. 20, 21), or, less probably, Mephibosheth (2 Sam ix. 17 ; xvi. 3)—Christ beholds a typical anticipation of the behaviour towards Himself of Judas who had sat at His table, not corporeally alone but also spiritually, having received from Him in offer at least, and seemingly also in enjoyment, the bread of life. Significantly Christ omits the words "Mine own familiar friend whom I trusted," because Judas having been known from the beginning, had not been trusted.

19. From henceforth ἀπ' ἄρτι, *a modo* (Vulgate), signifying not *now*, but from *this time onward*, in contrast to the time past, during which Christ had maintained silence regarding the traitor: cf. xiv. 7 ; Rev. xiv. 13 ; Matt. xxiii. 39 ; xxvi. 29, 64. **I tell you before it,** the fulfilment of that O. T. Scripture, **come to pass that,** in order that, **when it is come to pass,** as it will, since the Scripture must needs be fulfilled (Luke xxii. 37), **ye may believe that I am** *He*, or all that I have ever claimed to be, the self-existent Son of God and Saviour of the world as well as Israel's Messiah : see on viii. 24. Had Christ not made known beforehand His perfect acquaintance both with the fact and the agent of His betrayal, the faith of His disciples might have afterwards been shaken.

20. Verily, verily I say unto you (see on i. 51), **He that receiveth whomsoever I send receiveth Me, and he that receiveth Me, receiveth Him that sent Me.** Neither a gloss out of Matt. x. 40 ; Luke ix. 48 (Kuinoel), nor to be connected with ver. 16 (Lampe), the intervening verses being regarded as parenthetical, but purposely introduced either (1) to restrain the disciples from following the bad example of Judas by reminding them of the dignity of their office (Calvin, Grotius, Lücke, Ewald, Meyer, Westcott), or (2) to confirm the declaration just made concerning Himself (Ebrard). Other explanations are less satisfactory, as, e.g., that this verse was spoken to contrast the treason of Judas with the dignity of the apostolic office (Hilgenfield), to remind Judas of the grace from which he had fallen, and the other apostles of the grace they had received (Tholuck, Alford), to set forth the dignity of their office, notwithstanding the injunction laid upon them to cultivate humility (Hengstenberg), to illustrate the happiness which would await them if they faithfully adhered to Christ (Godet).

21. When Jesus had thus said, He, or *These things* (ver. 18-20) *having spoken*, as it were, to protect them beforehand from the probable consequences of His communication, *Jesus* **was troubled in the spirit** as at the grave of Lazarus (xi. 33), and for a similar reason, viz. the presence of the Satanic adversary who revealed himself in Judas, **and testified,** or *bore witness* to what was then present to His consciousness—the choice of this word indicating the elevated state of the speaker's mind (cf. i. 15 ; iv. 44 ; vii. 7)—**and said, Verily, verily I say unto you,** employing the well-known formula, with which He had just introduced the allusion to His own personal and official dignity (ver. 20), in order to mark the solemn character of what He was about to communicate, viz. **that one of you shall betray Me,** the traitor being not yet personally mentioned, perhaps to prevent premature excitement, perhaps to put the apostles on a course of self-examination.

22. The disciples, struck with astonishment at the scarcely credible atrocity of the thing (Grotius), **looked one on another** obviously silent and perplexed, though Judas may have been unmoved (Calvin) or dissembled (Meyer), **doubting of whom He spake,** watching if they could detect each on the other's face a sign of conscious guilt (Brugensis), or of suspicion of himself (Hengstenberg). At this point they began to say, 'Lord ! is it I ?' (Matt. xxvi. 22 ; Mark xiv. 19).

23 **There was at the table reclining in Jesus' bosom one of the disciples ;** or *there was reclining* (cf. vi. 11) at the table *one of His disciples in the bosom of Jesus ;* or *there was one of His disciples leaning back on the bosom of Jesus* (Paley). The Oriental custom was to lie with the left arm on the cushion and the right free to partake of the banquet, so that the head of one guest would frequently reach back to the girdle of the other (see Keil, Handbuch der Biblischen Archäologie, § 100). The disciple here named lay so close to the person of the Saviour that his head appeared to rest upon the Saviour's bosom (κόλπος, or bosom-like fold of the garment). The disciple is identified as he **whom Jesus loved.** That this was John the son of Zebedee was the unanimous tradition of the primitive church and may even be conclusively inferred from the gospel itself : see on xxi. 24 ; and cf. xix. 26 ; xx. 2 ; xxi. 7, 20.

24. **Simon Peter therefore,** manifesting his characteristic impulsiveness, **beckoneth** or *noddeth* **to him,** probably behind Christ's back, himself reclining, it is supposed, on the other side of Jesus (Bengel). They were clearly so close to one another that a whisper might be exchanged between them, since it is added, **and saith unto him, Tell** *us,* or, *say,* 'ask' being an altogether unsuitable rendering of εἰπὲ, **who is it of whom He speaketh.** Peter obviously thought that John was in the secret, in which, however, he was mistaken as John's action at once showed. The reading 'that he should ask, etc.' (T. R.), appears to have been suggested by John's action. ℵ has both readings.

25. **He,** the disciple whom Jesus loved, or John, **leaning back,** ἀναπεσών (ℵᵉ B C* K L X Π*, Lachmann, Meyer, Westcott and Hort), lying back with the head propped up (Paley), cf. vi. 10, rather than ἐπιπεσών (ℵ A D etc., Tischendorf, Godet), throwing himself, cf. Acts xx. 10, **as he was** (cf. iv. 6) **on Jesus' breast,** upon the actual body (στῆθος) as distinguished from the ' bosom' (κόλπος, ver. 23), **saith unto Him,** doubtless in a whisper, **Lord !**—not forgetting reverence in his familiarity and affection—**who is it ?** That John so interrogated Christ does not render it either impossible or untrue that the disciples generally asked Christ, Lord ! is it I ? (Matt. xxvi. 23 : Mark xiv. 19).

26. **Jesus therefore,** because He had been asked, and disclosure need no longer be avoided, **answered,** in a whisper, audible and intelligible only to Peter and John, or perhaps only to John, **He it is for whom I shall dip the sop** (cf. Ruth ii. 14) **and give it him**—referring to a custom in accordance with which the father of the family was wont at the paschal feast to give to his children or guests pieces of bread (ψωμίον, a bit or morsel) dipped into the dish of bitter herbs (cf. Matt. xxvi. 23 ; see Stapfer, Palestine in the Time of Christ, p. 445). **So when He had dipped the sop, He taketh and giveth it to Judas, the son of Simon Iscariot** (see on vi. 71). Outwardly a mark of favour to Judas, the gift was probably understood as such by the other disciples. Perhaps also it was designed as a last appeal to the traitor's heart. The answer Christ gave to the disciples generally (Matt. xxvi. 23) may have preceded this which He gave to John ; the response of Judas (Matt. xxvi. 25) may have followed it.

27. **And after the sop,** not *with* the sop, as if some magical influence proceeded from the bread, but *after* it, i.e. after Jesus had bestowed upon him this mark of distinction, **then,** at that instant, when his soul was inflamed with mingled hatred and shame, **entered Satan into him,** or *entered into him* (cf. Luke xxii. 3, with reference to Judas, and Matt. xii. 45 ; Mark v. 12, 13 ; Luke viii. 30, of demoniacal possession), *Satan* ὁ Σατανᾶς שָׂטָן, the lier in wait, the adversary (1 Chron. xxi. 1 ; Job i. 6 ; Ps. cix. 6 ; Zech. iii. 1), the personal principle of evil, the devil, ὁ διάβολος (vi. 70 ; viii. 44). As applied to Judas the clause signifies that he had now become completely overmastered and possessed by

the enemy, who used him as a willing instrument or tool (cf. 2 Tim. ii. 26). "As David strengthened himself in God, so Judas strengthened himself in Satan" (Hengstenberg). "The pronoun ἐκεῖνος here and in ver. 30 isolates the traitor, and as it were sets him outside of the company" (Westcott). **Jesus therefore,** not because the traitor was an annoyance to Him (Lücke), but because the traitor had now decided his fate, and compelled divine mercy to give him up, **saith unto him,** not 'pushing him over the precipice,' or ordering him away (Keim), or desiring to be rid of his hateful presence (Lücke), or addressing to him words which contained a bitter reproach (Renan), but commanding rather than merely permitting him (Grotius) to complete his diabolic work as speedily as possible, **That thou doest,** or *What thou purposest to do, wilt do, art for doing,*—the present tense here, as in ver. 6, conveying the idea of a work already determined, fixed, about to be entered upon, and therefore to that extent begun (cf. Matt. xxvi. 2 ; Luke xii. 54 ; John xiv. 3; and see Winer's Grammar, § xl. 2)— **do quickly,** lit., *more quickly,* the comparative suggesting the notion of haste —more quickly than you appear disposed to do, i.e. hasten the execution (Winer, § xxxv. 4).

28. **Now no man at the table,** lit., *of those reclining,* **knew for what intent** πρὸς τί, *with reference to what,* hence with what design, *quo consilio* (cf. Matt. vi. 1 ; 1 Cor. x. 11), **He spake this unto him.** That the other disciples should have failed to comprehend the significance of Christ's words to Judas is intelligible on the assumption that they had not overheard the conversation carried on by Christ first with John (ver. 26) and next with Judas (ver. 26 : cf. Matt. xxvi. 25)— that John did not apprehend their meaning (Lücke, Meyer, Luthardt, Brückner, Westcott), though John is believed by some to have excepted himself (Bengel, Kuinoel, Lange, Hengstenberg, Godet) can only be explained by supposing that either he did not imagine the accomplishment of the treason was so near, or did not at the moment connect the two announcements together.

29. **For some thought,** putting one construction on the Saviour's language, **that because Judas had the bag,** or box (see on xii. 6), **that Jesus said unto him, Buy what things we have need of for the feast,** not for the passover proper at which they were then seated, but for the next day's offerings ; **or,** taking another view of Christ's words, **that he should give something to the poor** to enable them to purchase festive offerings (Deut. xvi. 14). For the bearing of this verse on the date of the Last Supper, see note on xiii. 2, at the end of the preceding Exposition.

30. **He then having received the sop went out straightway.** Though not mentioned by the Synoptists, Judas's withdrawal from the chamber is by them implied, since, on going forth from the table to Gethsemane, Christ is represented as meeting Judas at the head of "a great multitude" (Matt. xxvi. 46, 47 ; Mark xiv. 42, 43 ; Luke xxii. 39-47). *At what time the traitor left the upper room, whether before, during, or after the institution of the Supper,* cannot be conclusively determined, though a careful examination of the records points to the inference that it was before "Jesus took bread and blessed and brake it." I. Though John does not mention the institution of the Lord's Supper—probably because (1) it had already been sufficiently described in the earlier accounts, and was when he wrote a well-known Christian ordinance, (2) it lay apart from his design in composing this part of his gospel, which was to exhibit the glory of Christ's love for His own, (3) he had previously set forth (vi. 52-57) the fundamental spiritual transaction which the Supper embodied, and (4) he had indirectly implied its institution by designating the Thursday evening meal 'a supper' instead of 'the passover';—yet it is certain that *John's narrative is not inconsistent with the hypothesis that the Supper was observed.* And that this took place after Judas had left the company three considerations seem to show. 1. No break in the proceedings of the evening occurs, according to this Evangelist, from their commencement till after the traitor's departure (see xiii. 1-30) ; 2. The institution of the Supper appears to harmonize better

with Christ's mood after the removal of the traitor than with His state of mind before it (contrast ver. 31 with ver. 21); (3) Judas left the room immediately after receiving the sop, which is generally admitted to have formed part of the paschal celebration. II. Of the Synoptists, Luke (xxii. 21) indeed seems to state that Judas was at the Supper, and Mark (xiv. 23) after mentioning the cup, writes, 'And they all drank of it.' But 1. Mark's language does not necessarily imply that Judas was present. 2. Luke's narrative can with difficulty be regarded as strictly chronological. 3. Matthew (xxvi. 26) expressly places the Supper after Christ had revealed to Judas that he was the traitor—at which instant John says he went out. Hence 4. There is a strong presumption that *Judas did not partake of the Lord's Supper* (Calvin, Olshausen, Tholuck, Luthardt, Keim, Lücke, Lange, Oosterzee, Milligan and Moulton, and others)—which accordingly should be inserted in John's narrative not before ver. 30, as e.g. between ver. 22-23 (Stier), or between ver. 19-21 (Bäumlein), but after ver. 30, before either ver. 31 (Paulus), or ver. 33 (Neander, Ebrard), or ver. 34 (Lücke, Lange), or ver. 36 (Milligan and Moulton), after ver. 38 (Olshausen, Luthardt), or after xiv. 31 (Keim). The notion that the bread was given before ver. 18 and the cup after ver. 30 is not without advocates (Beyschlag, Godet). **And it was night.** Not chronological, but suggestive of the unfitness of the time for making purchases (Lange) as well as of its suitability for the work of treason Judas had in hand (Lücke). Perhaps also symbolic of the spiritual condition of the traitor, within whom, as well as round whom, it was night.

Homiletics

Ver. 18-30.—A Last Appeal.
I. **A Solemn Announcement**: ver. 21. 1. *The reason of it.* (1) To indicate Christ's knowledge of the human heart, and to show He had not been mistaken in Judas, ver. 18. Had Christ not in any way beforehand alluded to the fate which eventually overtook Him, or signified He knew the 'traitor,' the thought might have afterwards arisen in the minds of His followers that after all their Master had been deceived or at least was not omniscient. But Christ's clear intimation on this occasion precluded the possibility of any such subsequent reflections. (2) To direct His disciples' minds to an impressive fulfilment of Scripture : ver. 18. All the ways of reading this verse (see Exposition) come to the same end, that Jesus chose Judas in obedience to a divine pre-arrangement which had been foreshadowed in ancient Scripture. It was in the plan of heaven that Jesus and Judas should meet as Master and disciple, and finally as Victim and betrayer. (3) To confirm the faith of His disciples in Himself : ver. 19. Had Christ never spoken of the treachery of Judas, it might have been difficult for His friends to reconcile such silence with the claims He had put forward to Messiahship and Divine sonship. But the remembrance of what He now said (ver. 20) would enable them to maintain their trust in Him unshaken when the dark day of trial came for them, when they should see Him die at the hands of a traitor from among themselves. (4) To arrest and, if yet possible, rescue the soul of Judas. If the appalling declaration now made was meant to put the disciples generally upon a work of self-examination, there can be little question it was designed as well to startle and recover, ere it was too late, the unhappy wretch who was then standing on the brink of infamy and perdition. 2. The *certainty* of it. Indicated by the formula 'Amen, Amen!' ver. 21. Had such an announcement been made by any other than Christ, the disciples would assuredly have repelled it with scorn, but this they could not do with a statement from lips that spake as never man spake, a statement vouched for by the faithful and true witness (Rev. iii. 14). 3. The *effect* of it. (1) It filled the Saviour with inward horror : ver. 21. It visibly perturbed His spirit as before it had been perturbed at Lazarus's grave (xi. 33). See Exposition. (2) It plunged the disciples into consternation and dismay : ver. 22.

II. **An Anxious Question**: ver. 25. 1. *Moved by Peter.* With characteristic impetuosity Simon was the first to break silence. Whether or not at this stage he inquired of Jesus—Lord, is it I? (Matt. xxvi. 22), he signalled to John who lay upon the Saviour's bosom to lean behind Christ's back. When John had done so, Peter, believing him to be in the secret, asked who it was to whom Christ referred. John, however, was equally ignorant with himself, and accordingly carried Peter's question to the Lord. 2. *Proposed by John.* (1) With affection—leaning back till his head rested on the Saviour's breast; (2) with reverence—Lord! who is it?; (3) with pity—for Christ who should suffer, and for the unknown disciple who should inflict, so sad a fate; (4) with humility and self-examination—as if he almost dreaded it should be himself; and yet surely (5) with conscious innocence—though Judas had the brazen-faced effrontery to ask—Lord, is it I?

III. **An Explicit Answer**: ver. 26. 1. *Clearly given.* There could be no mistaking the import of Christ's action. It pointed out the traitor to John who had received the whispered reply, and to Judas who understood the meaning of the 'sop.' 2. *Defiantly accepted.* Not necessary to suppose Judas had overheard the answer Christ gave to John. The simple presentation of such a mark of favour to Judas in his then mood was equivalent to an intimation that his treachery was detected. It could not be that he, Judas, conscious as he was of harbouring designs against his Master's life, was regarded by that Master as the chief object of His love. Was it possible that Christ showed him such attention because He had secretly begun to fear Him? Or could it be that Christ intended to reveal thereby that He was perfectly aware of the dark transaction already negotiated with the rulers? Perhaps Judas saw and realized what the giving of the sop speechlessly proclaimed, that notwithstanding his meditated treason Christ regarded him with pitying love. In any case he interpreted aright the Saviour's action. Christ had detected him, and even then would love and save him if he would. Had the heart of Judas at that late moment melted, who can doubt that the arms of infinite love would have embraced him? But instead, his heart incased itself in triple brass. With shameless effrontery, looking up into the face of his intended victim he asks, ' Is it I?' and when Christ answers, 'Thou hast said!' he neither breaks forth into indignant denial nor falls upon his knees, bemoaning his guilt with tears, but coolly, moodily, defiantly assents to the correctness of Christ's answer, confirms it and seals it by dark-browed silence—inwardly betaking himself to the devil, as Saul betook himself to the witch of Endor when left by God (1 Sam. xxviii. 8), flinging himself into the arms of Satan, and eventually hastening from the hated presence of incarnate love to set his hellish plot in motion. 3. *Strangely misunderstood,* ver. 28. Whether the words whispered to John were heard by all may be doubtful: the sop was conferred in the sight of all; and the words, ' What thou doest, do quickly,' were audible to all. Judas understood them: perhaps John did: the rest understood them not, but imagined they were instructions relating to the feast. (See Exposition.)

Lessons. 1. Christ in His Church a searcher of hearts. 2. It is possible to sit at Christ's table without being a true disciple, to enjoy religious ordinances without possessing grace, to fall from Christ's society so far as to lift up the heel against Him. 3. Declensions and apostasies of insincere professors, though they do not affect Christ's position in the Church, are nevertheless to Him occasions of pain. 4. As all disciples are not equally dear to the Saviour, so they whom Jesus loves, the John-like spirits, are most likely to obtain from Him revelations of His grace and truth. 5. Christ loves even those who hate Him; but he who will not permit himself to be won by that love must eventually fall into the devil's grasp. 6. They who wish to harm Christ or hinder His cause cannot escape from acting even in their malice, under His orders. 7. Christ's people often misconstrue Christ's words and acts. 8. The soul which goes out from Christ's presence goes out into the night.

Ver. 30. **Memorable Nights.** I. The Night of *Andrew and John's meeting with Christ* (i. 39)—a night of notable discovery: finding the Messiah. II. The

Night of *Nicodemus's visit to Christ* (iii. 1)—an evening talk about earthly and heavenly things. III. The Night of *Christ's walking on the sea* (vi. 17)—-a night of fears allayed, of dangers escaped, of wonders seen, of surprises experienced. IV. The Night of *Christ's Supper with the Twelve* (xiii. 30)—a night distinguished by amazing revelations of Divine love (the feet-washing), of celestial truth (the farewell discourses), and of human wickedness (the betrayal). V. The Night of *the first Easter day* (xx. 19)—an evening visit from the risen One.

3. THE ARRIVAL OF CHRIST'S HOUR

CHAP. XIII. VER. 31-38

EXPOSITION

Chap. xiii. ver. 31. **When therefore he** i.e. Judas **was gone out**—to be connected with the clause following (אBCDL, Tischendorf, Meyer, Westcott and Hort), rather than with that preceding omitting 'therefore' (Chrysostom, Griesbach), as thus :—"it was night when he went out"—**Jesus saith**, the departure of the traitor having removed a weight from His soul, **Now is** or, *was* **the Son of man glorified, and God is** or, *was* **glorified in Him**—the past tense ἐδοξάσθη, *clarificatus est* (Vulgate), indicating either that Christ was alluding to the glory which He, the Son of man, had obtained by the lowly act of foot-washing and the voluntary retirement of the traitor (Godet), or rather, was contemplating as already won the moral and spiritual glory of His completed life work, "the glory of His death, the splendour of His *it is finished*" (Meyer), and with that was looking forward to the heavenly exaltation which would result therefrom (Luthardt). The use of 'Son of man' instead of 'Son of God' (xi. 4) points to the fact that Christ referred not to the pre-existent glory which belonged to Him as the eternal Son, but to that which had been conferred on Him as the incarnate Son through whom the glory of God had been manifested to the world. 32. **And God shall glorify Him in Himself**—God, not Christ (Ewald)—**and straightway shall He glorify Him**, the clause prefixed in the T. R. 'if God was glorified in Him' (אᶜ A C** L etc., Tischendorf, Meyer, Godet and others), being omitted in accordance with superior authority (א* B C* D L X II

etc., Griesbach, Scholz, Luthardt, Westcott and Hort). If the glory (δόξα) of the preceding verse referred chiefly to the 'glory' which culminated in the death of self-sacrificing love upon the cross, that of this verse alludes more especially to the glory of His heavenly exaltation. The glory of the Son of man attains its meridian splendour in the cross and the exaltation : in the glory of the Son of man God is also glorified : hence, in thus glorifying Himself through the Son of man, God, will glorify the Son of man 'in Himself,' by showing that the glory of the Son of man is one with the glory of the eternal God. 33. **Little children** τεκνία, a word occurring here only in this gospel (cf. xxi. 5, παιδία) though used frequently in the Epistles (1 John ii. 1, 12, 18, 28; iii. 7, 18; iv. 4 ; v. 21), its employment at this time being an index of tender feeling. **yet a little while am I with you.** What for Christ would be glorification for the disciples should prove bereavement and separation : cf. vii. 33. **Ye shall seek Me** without the addition 'and shall not find Me' (vii. 34), meaning, in the days of trial that shall befall after My departure ye shall long with *faith* and *love* to rejoin Me : cf. vii. 34 ; Luke xvii. 22 ; **and as I said to the Jews** (vii. 34 ; viii. 21), **Whither I go, ye cannot come, so now I say unto you** or, *also to you I say now*, ἄρτι for the present. Like the Jews as to the fact, the disciples were unlike as to the cause and the continuance of this inability to accompany Christ. The Jews were hindered by moral and spiritual antagonism to Christ, which was gradually growing worse; the disciples were prevented merely by a state of moral unripeness or spiritual imperfection which was daily becoming less. Hence with those the separation was permanent; with these it was temporary.

34. A new commandment ἐντολή, not = διαθήκη (Luke xxii. 20), and therefore signifying the institution of the Lord's Supper (Lange), but a precept or instruction for the regulation of the life (xv. 12 ; cf. 1 John ii. 8). **I give unto you,** as those about to depart are accustomed to give instructions to their dependents (Grotius) : cf. Mark xiii. 34. The Lord claims to be the lawgiver for His people (cf. 1 Cor. xiv. 37). **that** in order that, having as its end, aim, purpose that, **ye** My disciples **love one another.** Already prescribed in the O. T. (Lev. xix. 18), this commandment is designated *new* not because it is *another*, additional to that of the foot-washing (Gerhard), a commandment *excellent* (Wolf), *most recent* (Nonnus), *always new* (Olshausen), *renewed* (Irenæus, Calvin), *renewing* (Augustine), *unexpected* (Semler), or *latest* (Heumann), but because it enjoins an altogether new love as the next clause explains. **even as I have loved you, that ye also love one another—** which shows that the love commanded by Christ springs from a new principle, that of a consciousness of Christ's love (De Wette, Brückner, Meyer), moves within a new sphere, the household of faith (Grotius), directs itself to new objects, the brethren of Christ, whether Gentiles or Jews (Clericus), rises to a new measure or degree, and in fact shapes itself after a new model, that of Christ's love to His own (Cyril, Theophylact, Kuinoel, Lücke, Tholuck, Ewald, and others).

35. By this exhibition of brotherly love, **shall all men know,** come to learn, **that ye are my disciples,** disciples belonging to me, sharing my spirit, illustrating my teaching, following my example, and therefore recognized and acknowledged by me, **if ye have love one to another :** cf. 1 John iii. 10.

36. Simon Peter saith unto Him, recalling Christ's words concerning His departure (ver. 33), **Lord, whither goest Thou?** Peter had failed to grasp the idea of Christ's leaving the earth. **Jesus answered,** replying to the thought latent in Peter's mind that if he only knew whither Christ was really going he would follow, **Whither I go thou canst not follow Me now,** the impossibility being not objective (Meyer, Westcott) but moral (Luthardt, Tholuck, Hengstenberg) ; **but thou shalt follow afterwards,** i.e., when thou hast attained to that moral fitness for rejoining me which is still wanting to thee : cf. xxi. 18, 19.

37. Peter saith unto Him, evincing even in so saying that unreadiness to follow Christ, to which allusion has been made, **Lord, why cannot I follow Thee even now?** Peter begins to perceive that the way of following of which Christ speaks will involve self-sacrifice and peril, but he imagines that already he is perfectly prepared for these. **I will lay down my life for Thee.** Chivalrous, affectionate, sincere, but still over-confident language on the part of Peter.

38. Jesus answereth, giving no reply to Peter's 'Why?' perhaps because that could not then be fully disclosed, perhaps because it would be better learnt from experience, **Wilt thou lay down thy life for me ?** Afterwards thou wilt ; meantime not thou for Me, but I for thee. **Verily, verily I say unto thee, The** (or a) **cock shall not crow till thou hast denied Me thrice.** Between this account and that of the Synoptists seeming discrepancies occur. (1) *As to the time.* Matthew (xxvi. 31) and Mark (xiv. 27) place this warning on the way to Gethsemane ; John, with whom Luke (xxii. 34) agrees, represents it as having been given at the Supper table. There is, however, nothing improbable in the conjecture (Meyer, Luthardt, Westcott, and others) that the warning may have been uttered more than once, or that Matthew and Mark may simply have desired to finish their account of the Supper before introducing it. (2) *As to the words.* Mark speaks of two crowings of the cock ; Matthew, Luke, and John of only one. The account of Mark is probably the more accurate, as being derived, it is commonly supposed, from Peter himself ; but the accounts of the other writers are not therefore wrong, and may be satisfactorily explained by supposing either (1) that Christ gave two versions of His warning ; or (2) that the second cock - crowing was usually regarded as the more important, the first being usually heard by few (Alford) ; or (3) that the statements were intentionally compendized (Morison on Matt. xxvi. 34).

HOMILETICS

VER. 31-38.—A LOOK INTO THE FUTURE.
I. A Glorious Future described : ver. 31, 32. 1. *The glory of God in the glory of the Son of man.* With the exit of Judas from the supper chamber, the soul of Jesus burst into transports of joyous exultation. He beheld immediately before Him the hour of His highest glorification. To be sure it could only be reached through the cross. But that instrument of shame and death would itself be a symbol of the glory to which He would thereby attain—the glory of sacrificing self for the sake of others, for the salvation of lost sinners of the human race,—the glory of triumphing over principalities and powers at the moment when appearing to experience defeat (Col. ii. 15),—the glory of finishing His Father's work and completing man's redemption by His death and resurrection—the glory of being thereby proved to be the Son of God with power (Rom. i. 4). And what imparted to the soul of Jesus a sweeter joy was this, that in this glory to which he looked forward, not He Himself alone, but also His Father was glorified 2. *The glory of the Son of man in the glory of God.* Behind the glory of the cross Christ beheld the glory of God, into which He, the Son of man, should pass on departing out of this world—the glory which He had had with the Father before the world was (xvii. 5), out of which He had descended when He became incarnate, and into which, as a reward for His completed work, He was, as the Son of man, to be raised. That glory was certain—"God shall glorify Him " (twice repeated) : it was near—" straightway " : it was divine—it was the glory of God Himself : it would be essential, in Him as in God, His because of His oneness with God—" In Himself " God would glorify Him. Hence also it would be eternal.

II. A Sorrowful Bereavement foretold : ver. 33. 1. *With tenderness*—"little children !" 2. *As impending*—"a little while am I with you." 3. *As sure*—as He had spoken to the Jews, so now did He speak to them. 4. *As real*—they would seek Him, but would not be able to come to Him. 5. *As temporary*—the separation would only be for the present.

III. A New Commandment enjoined : ver. 34. 1. *The persons upon whom imposed.* Not men in general, but the followers of Christ—though, of course, all men lie under a primary obligation to become Christ's followers. 2. *The nature of the duty prescribed*—love to one another in Christ's spirit, after Christ's example, to Christ's measure, among Christ's people, and for Christ's sake ;—in all of which respects the injunction is substantially new. 3. *The blessed result experienced.* It would be a striking and incontestable evidence of the reality of their discipleship : ver. 35. "They do not love who do not show their love " (Shakespeare). The spirit of love they could not have imbibed, if they lived in contention, wrangling with one another for precedence, as perhaps they had been doing (Luke xxii. 24). Nor would the world believe they were disciples of His if love were absent—whereas were this always conspicuous in their behaviour, the world would be constrained to cry as did the heathen in the early days of Christianity —" Behold how these Christians love one another !" (Tertullian, Apol. 39).

IV. A Friendly Warning given : ver. 38. 1. *The time.* According to Matthew (xxvi. 34) and Mark (xiv. 30), on the way to Gethsemane ; according to Luke (xxii. 34) and John, during supper. (For the reconciliation see Exposition). 2. *The occasion.* The exhibition of an inquisitive and over-confident spirit on the part of Peter, who not only was not satisfied to accept Christ's statement of his (Peter's) inability at present to follow Him (Christ), but somewhat presumptuously demanded to know the reason ' why ' ; and who, when assured that he would by and by be able to follow in the steps of his Master, expressed himself as confident that he could do it then, even though it should involve the laying down

,of life in the attempt. 3. *The manner.* With reproof, no doubt, but also with tenderness, with admiration of his courage and appreciation of his affection—all of which resound in the tones of His reply, ' Wilt thou lay down thy life for Me ?' 4. *The import.* That he, Peter, should so far lapse as to become not a traitor, indeed, like Judas, but a denier of his Master, and that, too, three times over before the morning dawned. 5. *The certainty.* Vouched for by the formula ' Amen, Amen !' Peter had never known that to fail. 7. *The effect.* Peter never again spoke at the supper table.

Learn 1. That the time will eventually arrive when even Christ will rejoice in the removal of the wicked from His presence. 2. That the chief end of man is to glorify God on earth, and the highest recompense of man is to be glorified with God in heaven. 3. That the bodily separation of Christ from His people is not intended to continue for ever. 4. That Christ is the supreme lawgiver in His church. 5. That love is the best proof of discipleship. 6. That confidence in self is no sign of grace, but the almost certain precursor of a fall. 7. That even Christians are prone to imagine themselves better than they are. 8. That Christ knows His people better than they do themselves.

4. THE FAREWELL DISCOURSES

Chap. XIV. 1—XVI. 33

That these tender and pathetic utterances, so replete with consolation, instruction, and warning, were breathed forth from the inmost heart of Jesus in connection with the Last Supper, a cursory examination shows. That chap. xvi. was spoken on the way to Gethsemane may be inferred from the correspondence of its closing words (ver. 32) with those recorded by Matthew (xxvi. 31) and Mark (xiv. 27) as having fallen from the Saviour's lips after He had gone forth from the supper room " unto the Mount of Olives " and before He had arrived at " the place which was named Gethsemane." That chap. xv. began after Christ had risen from the table is the natural inference from xiv. 31, though whether He continued standing in the same place, or proceeded forth from the chamber cannot be determined. That chap. xiv. was delivered while yet Our Lord was seated at the table in the midst of His disciples is apparent from its close connection with the preceding context. Indeed it is doubtful if the farewell discourses should not be held as beginning at xii. 31 (Godet, Gess, Ewald, Luthardt, Westcott, and others), the entire passage from that point on to xiv. 31 being perfectly homogeneous, consisting, after a prefatory ejaculation concerning His own approaching departure (xiii. 31), from ver. 32 onwards, of a series of exhortations addressed to the disciples generally, which are in turn interrupted by interjections first from Peter (xiii. 36), next from Thomas (xiv. 5), then from Philip (xiv. 8), and finally from Judas (xiv. 22). As, however, sentiment is divided about the precise place in the narrative at which the supper should be inserted (see on xiii. 30, note), and as there is complete unanimity in holding that it was at latest before the words in chap. xiv. were uttered, it is better to adhere to the customary practice of commencing with these the farewell discourses of Our Lord.

Though not admitting of strictly logical subdivision, these discourses are yet possessed of distinctively marked features. The first—at the table—partakes more of a *consolatory* character and is designed to cheer the hearts of His disciples who were saddened by the prospect of His departure. The second—after leaving the upper room—assumes the form of *didactic* exposition, although still with the view of administering comfort to His followers, exhibiting their vital oneness with Himself, though He should be absent, and the certainty of their sharing a like experience with Him in the world. The third—before crossing the Cedron—becomes *predictive* in its style, directing them to anticipate tribulation while they lingered on the earth, yet not without the hope that their sorrows would eventually be turned into joy. Or, briefly, the theme of the first may be said to be Faith ; of the second, Love ; of the third, Hope (Stier).

(1.) THE DISCOURSE AT THE TABLE

Chap. XIV. Ver. 1-31

In this discourse are unfolded the *consolations* Christ administered to His sorrowing disciples to support them in prospect of, and subsequent to His departure.

1. The prospect of a final re-union with Himself in His Father's House : ver. 1-3.

2. The revelation of the way by which the Father's House might be reached : ver. 4-11.

3. The guarantee that miraculous works should not cease after His departure from the earth : ver. 12-14.

4. The promise of a Comforter to be with them during the entire period of His separation from them : ver. 15-17.

5. The assurance that, although no longer corporeally present in their midst, He would nevertheless manifest Himself to them more fully and efficaciously than before : ver. 18-24.

6. The assistance of the Paraclete in remembering and understanding His (Christ's) words : ver. 25-26.

7. The legacy of peace to sustain them in the midst of life's calamities : ver. 27.

8. Concluding observations—A right view of Christ's departure would fill them with joy instead of sorrow : ver. 28, 29. The separation He had spoken of was at hand : ver. 30. Himself was ready to execute His Father's commandment : ver. 31.

EXPOSITION

Chap. xiv. ver. 1-3. *First consola-tion :* Reunion in the Father's house.

1. **Let not your heart be troubled** on account of My departure (Bengel), rather than in consequence of My prediction of Peter's denial (Chrysostom), or even of Judas's betrayal. On the import of the verb see xi. 33 ; xii. 27 ; xiii. 21. In the present instance the seat of emotion is represented as the *heart, καρδία*—though *soul, χυχή,* whose middle point the heart is, but not *spirit, πνεῦμα,* might have been used—because the discourse here is of pure human personal feeling. **Ye believe in God, believe also in Me.** Four constructions possible. (1) Believe in God and (in so doing) ye believe in Me (Ebrard). But this is not necessarily true. (2) Ye believe in God, therefore, or also, believe in Me (Vulgate, Erasmus, Beza, Calvin, Grotius, and others). Against this only stands the fact that the two verbs are rendered differently. (3) Ye believe in God, and ye believe in Me (Luther : *translation*). The second half of this assertion is perhaps stronger than the circumstances of the disciples at the moment warranted. (4) Believe in God and believe in Me (Bengel, Lücke, Brückner, Meyer, Luthardt, Godet, and most moderns). The two exhortations appear to suit more exactly their despondent condition. N.B.—A mere man (if a good man) would never have connected his name with God's as Christ here does. Moses never said, "Believe in God and believe in me."

2. **In My Father's house,** *i.e.* the house to which the children are admitted, the house where the Father dwells (Bengel), meaning heaven, the abode of the divine "glory" (Ps. ii. 4 ; xxxiii. 13, 14 ; Is. lxiii. 15), the spiritual and eternal antitype of the earthly and temporal habitation which the temple formed ; hence probably embracing the notion of the kingdom of God as realized in heaven (Luthardt), though that of the universe (Lange) is too vague, while it is fanciful as well as incorrect to suppose Christ at this moment pointed to the starry firma-ment (Lange). **are many mansions** *μοναί,* occurring in the N. T. only here and in verse 23 (though frequent in the classics and appearing in 1 Macc. vii. 38), signifies places of permanent rest —the word " many " pointing not so much to their variety in the sense of suggesting different degrees of glory (Augustine, Bengel, Stier, Lange) as to their plurality. The image, it has been thought, was derived from "those Oriental palaces in which there is an abode not only for the sovereign and the heir to the throne, but also for all the sons of the king, however numerous these may be " (Godet) ; but probably the basis of the language was found by Our Lord in the many chambers that opened out from the sides of the temple court : 1 Kings vi. 5, 6, 10; Ezek. xli. 6. Cf. Homer's description of Priam's palace : Iliad vi. 224 ff. **If it were not so, I would have told you ;** for *ὅτι* omitted (T. R.), retained (אABCDKLX etc.) ; meaning not 'I would have told you that' (Erasmus, Luther, Bengel, Hofmann, Ebrard, Paley), or 'would I have told you that ?' (Ernesti, Lange, Ewald), as if Christ were alluding to some previous saying of which no account has been preserved ; but ' I would have told you, *for,*' either assigning a reason for the assurance concerning the many mansions, taking ' If it were not so, I would have told you ' as a parenthesis (Meyer), or explaining the reason why He would not have left them in uncertainty (Luthardt, Westcott, Milligan and Moulton), viz., because **I go** as your forerunner (Heb. vi. 20) **to prepare a place for you** in those mansions ; which shows that they exist ; which again explains why I did not tell you it was not so. Christ distinctly represents His departure from the world and to heaven by death and resurrection as the indispensable condition of, and presupposition for, His people's following.

3. **And if I go and prepare a place for you, I come,** not will come (A. V.), but *am coming* (indicating the imminence of His return) **again,** not at Pentecost (Lücke, Neander, Godet, Olshausen), or after Christ's resurrection

(Ebrard), but first at the death of the believer (Grotius, Reuss, Tholuck, Lange, Hengstenberg) and finally at the last day (Lampe, Calvin, Luthardt, Meyer), though it has been questioned whether any of these comings should be excluded (Westcott), Christ's return to His disciples being in this Gospel represented in all these different ways: see xiv. 19 ; xxi. 22, 23 ; xvi. 22. **And will receive you unto Myself,** not spiritually by imparting to you the spirit at Pentecost (Godet), but locally, by welcoming you into heaven, **that where I am,** after I shall have gone from you, **there ye may be also** as co-partners of My glory : cf. xvii. 24.

Ver. 4-11. *Second consolation :* The way to the Father's house revealed.

4. **And whither I go, ye know the way** (ℵ B C L Q X ; Tischendorf, Meyer, Westcott and Hort), i.e. the way by which you, not I (Grotius, Luther) may reach the region to which I am departing, though the reading 'Whither I go ye know and the way ye know ' (T. R.) is by some authorities (Olshausen, Hengstenberg, Godet) preferred. The difference of meaning is not material. If they knew the way they could scarcely be in entire ignorance as to the terminus to which it led.

5. **Thomas** (see on xi. 16) **saith unto Him,** perhaps as the mouth-piece of the others (Hengstenberg) since his usual cognomen is wanting ; though the circumstance that none of the greater apostles (Peter, John, James) appear as interlocutors at the table has been thought to warrant the inference that Thomas, along with Philip and Jude, represented only the feebler among the disciples (Olshausen). Possibly both suppositions are correct. That Thomas uttered the language of sober, hesitating intelligence (Meyer) is not so evident as that he spoke in doubt and melancholy (Godet). **Lord ! we know not whither Thou goest ; how know we the way ?** That Thomas here appears to contradict Christ is sufficiently explained by assuming either that Christ meant His disciples ought to have understood the way, or that Thomas meant he and his companions had as yet only confused and indistinct notions of the unseen realm into which He was departing,

and accordingly could only have dim perceptions of the way. *Quod si ignoretur, quae sit meta, non potest via sub ratione viae concipi* (Grotius). Or it may be said that Jesus knew, although the disciples themselves did not, that they understood the way (Luthardt) : *isti sciebant, et scire se nesciebant* (Augustine).

6. **Jesus saith unto him,** personally, if Thomas spoke for himself, though the plurals (ver. 5, 7) countenance the idea that Thomas represented his brethren as well as himself, and that they, as well as he, were intended to profit by the answer he received—an answer which went considerably beyond the interrogation—**I am the way, and the truth, and the life.** Neither *one complex conception,* as e.g. *vera via vitæ,* the true way of life (Augustine), *via vera, non curva, fallax, aut seductrix, et vivifica, sive ducens ad vitam,* the way, true, not crooked, fallacious, or misleading, and vivifying or leading to life (Brugensis), or *via per quam itur ad veram vitam,* the way by which the true life may be reached (Gerhard) ; nor *three co-ordinate conceptions* setting forth three stages of the way, the beginning, middle, and end (Luther, Calvin, Stier), three aspects of faith, *via, rudimenta fidei,* the way, the rudiments of faith ; *veritas, fidei perfectio,* the truth, the perfection of faith ; *vita, beatitudo,* the life, heavenly blessedness (Calvin), or three parts of doctrine, the first answering the question, What is the way ? the second replying to the inquiry, What is truth ? and the third responding to the interrogation, Whither ? (Bengel) ; nor the first term the means by which the second and third may be attained (Olshausen, Reuss) ; but the second and third epexegetic of the first, as thus Christ is the way because He is the truth and the life (Godet, Luthardt, Brückner, Tholuck, and others)—not simply the teacher of the truth, but the absolute personal manifestation thereof, and not merely the giver of the life, but the essential principle of the same. **No one cometh unto the Father but by Me,** or, *through Me,* i.e. by accepting Me as the truth and the life. Christ here advances a claim to exclusive mediatorship between God and man : cf. x. 9 ; Acts iv. 10 ; Eph. iii. 13.

**7. If ye had known Me, ye would
have known My Father also:** cf.
Christ's language to the Jews (viii. 19).
Christ designed not to place His
apostles on the same platform with the
unbelieving Jews, in respect of knowledge of Himself and the Father. Yet
both had failed—the Jews utterly, the
apostles partially—to apprehend the
manifestation presented to them
by Jesus; and to that extent they
had likewise failed to know the
Father. **From henceforth** or *and*
(א A D N etc., Tischendorf) *from henceforth* **ye know Him and have seen Him**
—not corporeally (i. 18) but spiritually.
The phrase ἀπ᾽ ἄρτι (xiii. 19) *from now
on* has been taken as covering the entire historical appearance of Jesus
(Hengstenberg) which is too general;
as proleptically pointing to the time of
the Spirit's communication (Chrysostom, Lücke, Ewald), against which
stands the fact that Philip is immediately reproved for not knowing Christ
(ver. 9); as referring to the fast
approaching hour of his glorification
(Stier); as alluding to the declarations
just made in ver. 6 (Meyer, Westcott);
but should probably be viewed as
including all His last instructions and
self-revelations (Godet). From this
moment onward it would be impossible
for the disciples to say they had not
known, or did not know the Father.
This marked an important difference
between them and the unbelieving
Jews.

8. Philip (i. 43; vi. 7; xii. 21), as if
to show that Christ in His last words
had taken too favourable an estimate of
the effect of His communications upon
the hearts of His disciples, and certainly
discovering that one of them had failed
to apprehend their spiritual significance, **saith unto Him,** speaking probably for himself, **Lord, shew us the
Father**—thinking of a visible theophany of the invisible Deity similar to
that which had been granted to Moses
(Exod. xxiv. 9, 10; cf. xxxiii. 18) or
promised by the O. T. prophets (Is. xl.
5; Mal. iii. 1); perhaps also of a sign
as much more resplendent than these
as the new dispensation was superior
to the old;—**and it sufficeth us;** i.e.
such a manifestation will satisfy our
deepest longings after God (De Wette,
Brückner, Lücke, Stier, Godet, Heng-

stenberg), content us as an adequate
revelation of the Father until the last
glorious appearance (Meyer), set at
rest all our fears as well as give us
perfect confidence (Alford), and certify
Thyself to us as the absolute revelation
of God (Luthardt).

9. Jesus saith unto him, with mingled
sadness and love, **Have I been,** or *am I,*
so long time with you, i.e. manifesting
Myself to you, **and dost thou not know,**
or, *and thou hast not known* **Me, Philip?**
That Christ addresses Philip by name
is an index of both His surprise and
affection: cf. xx. 16; xxi. 15; Matt.
xvi. 17; xvii. 25; Mark xiv. 37; Luke
x. 41; xxii. 31. **He that hath seen,**
not believingly only (Luther, Lücke,
De Wette), but also corporeally, **Me
hath seen the Father,** as revealed in
Me. In these words our Lord discloses the exact import of ver. 7. Both
utterances teach that Christ was an
incarnation of the Father. Neither
utterance could Christ have used had
He been only a creature, though
existing in perfect moral union with
God. **How sayest thou then, Shew us
the Father?** Since God had fully revealed Himself in Christ, Christ was
such a visible theophany as Philip
desired and of any further showing of
the Father there could be no need.

**10. Believest thou not that I am in the
Father and the Father in Me?** So
Christ had already declared (x. 38):
now He inquires whether Philip hesitated to accept that declaration. The
mutual indwelling of the Father and
Christ is not to be reduced to a mere
moral union, whether of power (Calvin,
Meyer) or of love (Beyschlag), as certainly it cannot signify that the Father
and the Son are the same person
(Swedenborg), but points to a oneness
of essence between both (Olshausen,
Tholuck, Hengstenberg, Godet, Gess,
and others) and of personal fellowship
grounded thereupon (Luthardt). The
two phrases "I and the Father are
one" (x. 30) and "I in the Father and
the Father in Me" explain one another
(Bengel). Cf. Weiss *der Johanneische
Lehrbegriff,* p. 205, and Bib. Theol. of
the N. T., vol. ii. § 143. **The words,** special
utterances (ῥήματα), **that I say unto you,
I speak not from Myself:** cf. vii. 16,
17; xii. 49. A first proof of the
mutual indwelling of the Father and

Christ, Philip should have found in
Christ's teaching ; a second in His
works, as the next clause shows : **but
the Father abiding in Me doeth His
works,** ἔργα, not = ῥήματα, the words
(Nosselt), but the whole Messianic
activity of Christ, in particular his
σημεῖα, His miracles or supernatural
deeds, which were pre-eminently the
Father's works as done by Him (v. 19,
20), through the Son (x. 37).
11. Believe me, i.e. credit my assertion, that not because (Bengel) **I am in
the Father and the Father in Me,** in a
unity of essence ; **or else,** if my words
be not such as to command faith,
believe Me for the very works' sake,
on account of (διὰ) the works themselves, i.e. irrespective of My person ;
or, according to different readings
' believe (that I am in the Father, etc.)
on account of the works themselves '
(א D L, Tischendorf, Godet, Westcott
and Hort) ; 'believe the works themselves' (א); or 'believe on account of
His (the Father's) works' (B).
Ver. 12-14. *Third consolation :*—The
continuance of miraculous works.
**12. Verily, verily, I say unto
you :** introducing a new consolation.
To meet the reflection, perhaps excited
by the mention of ' works ' in the preceding verse, that after His departure
these works would cease, Christ assures
them that, so far from terminating,
His beneficial activity would become
more extended, only passing into
different forms and employing a new
agency. **he that believeth on Me** Not
to be limited to the disciples (Grotius,
Meyer) but extended to all Christ's
followers. The phrase ' believing on
me ' should be distinguished from
' believing me ' (ver. 11), of which it is
the result. *Qui Christo de se loquenti
credit, in Christum credit; qui Petro de se
loquenti credit, non in Petrum, sed in
Christum credit* (Bengel). **the works that
I do shall he do also** Not simply works
equally great with those I do (Bengel)
but the works themselves that I do,
the same in kind, referring primarily to
miracles : cf. Mark xvi. 17 (Godet,
Meyer), though not to be restricted to
those in the case of Christ's people any
more than of Himself (v. 20). **and greater
works than these** which I do **shall he
do** Not ' more astounding miracles,'
such as the healing of the sick by means

of Peter's shadow, Acts v. 15, and Paul's
handkerchief, Acts xix. 12 (Bengel),
but ' those higher kinds of activity '
upon which believers should enter after
Christ's glorification, those 'greater
spiritual wonders' which subsequent
to that event would be effected by the
ministry of the church, as e.g. the
larger success which would attend the
preaching of the Apostles, an instance
of which was furnished in the effect of
Peter's sermon on the day of Pentecost,
Acts ii. 41. **because I go unto the
Father.** Here Christ gives an explanation of the startling assertion
just made. The higher and greater
activity of His people would not begin
till after His ascension. Nor could it
commence at all unless that were
accomplished. The moment however
that was effected it would be set in
operation. The obvious deduction was
that Christ's exaltation would be the
power which would cause it to move ;
so that after all, His people's working
would be His no less, but even more,
than theirs—His working through their
instrumentality. How He is to reach
them subsequent to His departure is
by and by related. His next words
declare how they may reach Him.
Hence it appears immaterial whether
after this verse a period (Chrysostom,
Erasmus, Kuinoel, Ebrard, Luthardt,
B. Crusius, Westcott, Alford, and others)
or a comma (Grotius, Lücke, Meyer,
Godet, Tischendorf, Lange, Stier,
Ewald, Paley, and others) should stand.
In the first case the thought following
is new, but not disconnected with the
preceding ; in the second case, it continues the explanation in this verse
begun.
**13. And whatsoever ye shall ask in
My name, that will I do.** 1. Christ
confirms the impression which perhaps
His language had made upon the
hearts of His listeners, that in the
higher activity of which He had spoken
He Himself was to be the chief worker
—" that will *I* do." 2. He reveals the
way in which they were to reach Him
for the purpose of setting His power
in motion, viz., by prayer :—" ye shall
ask." 3. He defines the character of
this ' asking ' by adding 'in My name'
(cf. xvi. 23, 26) ; which must be held
to signify more than ' with the in-
vocation of My name,' as in Acts iii. 6,

invocato meo nomine (Chrysostom), or 'recognizing Me as mediator,' *me agnoscentes mediatorem* (Melanchthon), or 'pleading my merits,' *per meritum meum* (A' Lapide). The name of God or of Christ pointing to the historically manifested personality of either, to ask in the *name* of Christ means to ask (1) as one who has believed in Christ's manifested personality—*respicitur illud, qui credit in Me* (Bengel); (2) as one who when he asks is *in Christ* (Luthardt); consequently (3) as one whose asking, as to its mind and spirit, object and contents, is determined by the whole revelation of Christ (Olshausen, Tholuck, Hengstenberg, Meyer); and (4) as one who, in virtue of his union with Christ, may be said to represent Christ (Alford, Godet, Westcott): cf. ver. 26, in which the Spirit is said to be sent in Christ's name, i.e. as His representative. Distinguish the similar phrases—'in the name' (xiv. 13, 14), 'into the name' (Matt. xxviii. 19), 'upon the name' (Luke xxiv. 47), 'on account of the name' (xv. 21). **that will I** (not the Father) **do.** Thereby Christ shows (1) that prayer addressed to the Father is the same as prayer addressed to Himself and prayer answered by Himself the same as prayer answered by the Father (cf. xv. 16; xvi. 23),—which could only arise out of His essential oneness with the Father; and (2) that in all the activity of His believing people upon the earth He would be the prime worker,—which again could only spring from their essential union with Him. It has been suggested (Paley) that the old reading may have been "τοῦτο ποιήσετε," this will ye do, i.e. work miracles in my name. **that the Father may be glorified in the Son.** The clause assigns the reason why the glorified Christ should hear His people's prayers, and proceed to manifest through them the power of His glorified personality. By so doing He would reflect glory on the Father, in whose name He should act (v. 43), as they would have previously glorified the Father by asking in His, Christ's, name (v. 23). The end of all the Son's activity in His exalted, no less than in His humiliated, condition is the advancement of the Father's glory: vii. 18; xi. 4; xii. 28; xvii. 1.

14. If ye shall ask Me anything in My name, that will I do. The insertion of Me (ℵ B E H U Δ etc., Tischendorf, Wescott and Hort (?), Milligan and Moulton, and others), may suggest a new thought that prayer is to be directed to Christ as its object as well as offered in His name; but it wears the aspect of having been a device invented to explain the preceding thought of Christ answering a prayer presented to the Father. On the other hand, the exclusion of Me (A D, Luthardt, Meyer, Godet, Alford, and others) gives a smoother reading, while it renders the thought no more singular or difficult. The repetition of τοῦτο ποιήσω (A B L, Meyer, Westcott and Hort) —Paley thinks the original reading may have been τοῦτο δώσω—is decidedly inferior to ἐγὼ ποιήσω (T. R., ℵ, Tischendorf, Godet, Alford). In either case the emphasis must lie on "I." *Hoc jam indicat gloriam* (Bengel).

Ver. 15-17. *Fourth consolation:*—The promise of another Comforter.

15. If ye love Me The moral condition here hypothetically assumed, though objectively real and undoubted, yet depended for its realization on the result expressed in the next clause, as the use of ἐάν with the subjunctive shows: see Winer, § xli. 2, 6. Though substantially a new consolation is at this point introduced (Meyer), it is closely connected with what precedes. The mode in which the believer should afterwards reach the glorified Christ having been declared to be by prayer, and the condition of success in prayer explained to be asking in Christ's name, the Saviour proceeds to show how He, the glorified Son of man, should be able to reach them, viz., by His Spirit,—first, however, setting forth the condition needful for its reception, viz., the existence of a love verified and revealed in and through obedience. **ye will keep** τηρήσετε (B L, Tischendorf, Westcott and Hort, Ewald), τηρήσητε (ℵ) or *keep* τηρήσατε (D, Godet, Meyer), **My commandments,** lit., *the commandments that are mine* (cf. vii. 16; viii. 31, 37, 43, 51); referring to the "orders He had given, and especially the instructions of this last evening" (Godet), but not excluding the various 'commandments,' ἐντολαί, of the O. T. law, νόμος, which had equally proceeded from and been republished by Him (Matt. v. 19). Christ's use of ‘My commandments’ implies oneness of nature between Christ and the Supreme Lawgiver (Hengstenberg).

16. And I will pray the Father, i.e. *I, on my part,* when you shall have done your part as above defined, *will ask the Father*, ἐρωτᾶν being the usual word put by the Evangelist into Christ's mouth when addressing the Father : see xvi. 26 ; xvii. 9, 15, 20. The promise here made does not contradict, and is not contradicted by the statement of xvi. 26, 27. **and He shall give you** not simply send (ver. 26) but give or bestow in such a manner that what is given shall be your possession. Though the Spirit proceeds from the Father (xv. 26) He ever does so at the request of the glorified Christ, who, moreover, supplicates His Father, not as a servant, but as a Son (Hengstenberg). **another Comforter** παράκλητον, *Paraclete, Helper, Advocate* (Tertullian, Augustine, Bengel, Calvin, Lampe, Meyer, Luthardt, Godet, Westcott, Alford, and others), the verbal adjective signifying *one who is called towards*, hence one who undertakes the cause of another, *defensor, patronus, qui pro aliquo dicit et ei dicenda suggerit* (Bengel), *Fürsprecher, Beistand, Berather* (Brückner) — the image of the *Fürsprecher* or advocate forming the antithesis to Satan the accuser, the *Verkläger* (Ewald) ; the translation *Comforter* (Origen, Chrysostom, Jerome, Erasmus, Luther : *translation*, and others), as if παράκλητος were equivalent to παρακλήτωρ, though not entirely destitute of arguments in its support, being decidedly inferior ; and that of *Teacher* (Theodore of Mopsuestia, Ernesti), certainly erroneous. The term occurs in John's writings only ; four times in the gospel (xiv. 16, 26 ; xv. 26; xvi. 7), each time referring to the Holy Spirit, and once in the First Epistle (ii. 1) where Christ is so designated. The use of ἄλλος, *another*, shows both that Christ appropriated to Himself the title ‘paraclete,’ and that the Holy Spirit was to be something more than an influence, or Christ Himself glorified to Spirit (Tholuck), was in fact to be a personal agent resembling, but yet distinct from, Himself, Christ : cf. Weiss. Bib. Theol. vol. ii. p. 406 ;

Schmid. Bib. Theol. of the N. T. § 24. **that He may be with you** μεθ' ὑμῶν denoting the relation of fellowship (xiv. 7 ; xv. 27) ; while παρ' ὑμῖν (xiv. 17) conveys the idea of a contiguity or neighbourhood (cf. viii. 38 ; xiv. 23 ; xvii. 5) ; and ἐν ὑμῖν (ver. 17) points to the notion of indwelling (xiv. 10). **for ever** not merely until the age to come, or until the consummation of the ages (Matt. xxviii. 20), but throughout time and into eternity : see vi. 51, 58 ; viii. 35 ; xii. 34; and cf. 1 John ii. 17; 2 John 2.

17. *Even* **the Spirit of truth** τὸ πνεῦμα τῆς ἀληθείας, the Holy Spirit, who is so called (xv. 26 ; xvi. 13 ; 1 John iv. 6) because He is the absolute possessor (1 John v. 7), and the perfect revealer (xvi. 13) of the truth of God in Christ, and as such is distinguished from the spirit of error (1 John iv. 6). **whom** rather *which*, ὅ, the Spirit being here viewed as a gift. **the world cannot receive** however willingly God might bestow it, *quamvis Deus omnibus dare velit* (Bengel), because of the want of those moral and spiritual conditions to be stated which are indispensable to its reception. **for it beholdeth Him** (it, αὐτό) **not, neither knoweth Him** (it). This of course does not signify that the world (ὁ κόσμος : see on i. 9) of the unbelieving and unregenerate may not be subjects of the Spirit's manifestations, since like the wind the Spirit bloweth where it listeth (iii. 8), but that the inward character of the world is such that it neither sees, looks into, or beholds with appreciative discernment (θεωρεῖ : see on vi. 40 ; xii. 45) ; nor knows in such a way as experience teaches the true nature of that Spirit ; and as a consequence cannot be made a permanent depositary of the same : cf. 1 Cor. ii. 14. **ye know Him** (or, *it*) not *ye will know Him* (Vulgate, Kuinoel), i.e. after He has come—the present being taken as a future ; since the disciples even then possessed some degree of acquaintance with the Spirit (see iii. 5, 6, 8 ; iv. 23, 24 ; vi. 63 ; vii. 39 ; and cf. Matt. iii. 16 ; x. 20 ; Mark i. 12 ; Luke ii. 27 ; iv. 18 ; xi. 13), and some measure of appreciation of His nature and excellence ; the reason for which is next stated. **for He abideth with you** As Christ is now present with His Church in the person of the Spirit, so then was the Spirit present with (παρά) the disciples in the person of Christ. Hence even before the Pentecostal outpouring it could be said that the disciples possessed a true acquaintance with the Spirit. Not only had they been instructed concerning His person and work (Luke xi. 13), but they had witnessed His operations in Christ's miracles (Matt. xii. 18 ; Luke xi. 20), and experienced His influences in their own illumination and regeneration (iii. 5 ; vi. 63). They were therefore, unlike the world, in a moral and spiritual condition for receiving the higher gift of the Spirit as a permanent endowment or abiding paraclete. To this the next clause probably alludes. **and shall be in you.** The future ἔσται (א A L, Tischendorf, Godet) points to the fact that the permanent endowment of the Holy Spirit was still in the future; if the present ἐστί (B D, Lachmann, Luthardt, Lücke, Westcott and Hort) be adopted, the meaning is that even then the indwelling of the Holy Spirit was begun, though only in its preparatory and inchoative measure and form.

Ver. 18-24. *Fifth consolation :*—The assurance that He Himself would return to them.

18. **I will not leave you,** let you go or dismiss you as desolate, ὀρφανούς, *orphans* (cf. Jas. i. 27 ; Lament. v. 3), i.e. bereft of your natural guardian, and therefore without one to take your part, without *a paraclete.* Christ had already addressed them as a father, calling them "little children," τεκνία (xiii. 32). **I come unto you.** The intensity of Christ's emotion is indicated (1) by the absence of any connecting particle, (2) by the use of the present 'I am coming,' rather than the future 'I will come,' (3) by saying 'I come' instead of 'I return' as if their fellowship were scarcely to suffer interruption, and (4) by setting forth His future advent to them as a personal coming. The 'coming' referred to was of course not that of His final *parousia* (Augustine, Beda, Hofmann) which will be a coming to the world as well as to the disciples ; or of His reappearing after the resurrection (Origen, Chrysostom, Theophylact, Erasmus, Grotius, Hilgenfield, Weiss), or even of this along with the 'coming' in the spirit (Bengel,

Lampe, Ebrard, Hengstenberg, Brückner, Westcott), since the 'coming' here spoken of is represented as taking place after Christ has gone to the Father, whereas Christ's post-resurrection visits were prior to that, and as being permanent, whereas these were only temporary ; but pointed solely to His return in the person of the Spirit (Calvin, Olshausen, Lücke, Luthardt, Godet, Meyer, Alford, and others)—which, however, does not prove that the Spirit is only the person of Jesus spiritualized (Tholuck), or the continued activity of the glorified Christ (Schenkel), or that Christ only came and comes representatively, but that Christ and the Spirit, though different hypostases or persons, are yet one in essence and divinity.

19. **Yet a little while and the world beholdeth Me no more,** i.e. corporeally, as even now, it does not recognize Me spiritually : cf. vii. 33 (to the Jews), and xiii. 33 ; xvi. 16 (to the disciples) ; **but ye,** My disciples who have believed upon Me, in contradistinction from the world who have remained in unbelief, **behold Me,** not corporeally and externally, any more than the world does, but spiritually and internally through the organ of faith. To the Evangelist the space of 40 days, during which the Risen Christ appeared to His disciples (Acts i. 3), is blotted out, and both the 'coming' of the preceding verse and the 'seeing' of this are conceived as occurring after the Ascension. **because I live, ye shall live also.** The words ὅτι ἐγὼ ζῶ, καὶ ὑμεῖς ζήσεσθε may be differently construed. 1. (*Ye behold Me*) *because I live and ye shall live* (Meyer, Luthardt, Milligan and Moulton) ; i.e. because Christ lives absolutely (Rev. i. 18), and believers shall live relatively (vi. 57), after His ascension being partakers of His risen life (xi. 25, 26 ; cf. Eph. ii. 5, 6 ; Col. iii. 1), He and they shall meet and behold one another— *the living behold the Living one* (Meyer). 2. (Ye behold Me) *because I live and* (as a consequence of that sight) *ye shall live,* meaning that faith's life would be awakened, perpetuated, and glorified by and through its vision of a glorified Saviour. 3. *Because I live, ye also shall live,* as an independent clause, stating that in addition to their vision of the glorified Saviour, their spiritual life

would be guaranteed by the fact that it was a living Saviour they beheld (Beza, Godet, Hengstenberg, Lange, Westcott, and others). All three express the same underlying thought that even now faith beholds a living Saviour and lives thereby.

20. **In that day**—not of the Parousia or of the Resurrection, but of the spiritual Return, which was to begin on the day of Pentecost—**ye shall know** in ever deepening experience through the teaching of the Spirit what is now completely hid from the world and only imperfectly apprehended by yourselves, **that I am in**, not merely with or beside (παρὰ, xvii. 5), but in personal, essential, and metaphysical oneness with **My Father**—the converse truth "and My Father in Me' being either purposely omitted because "the thought is predominantly that of the consummation of life in the divine order, and not that of the divine working in the present order" (Westcott), or tacitly implied : *Subaudi; et Pater in Me* (Bengel)—**and ye in Me and I in you.** The relation in which Christ stood to the Father and the Father to Him they would understand from the experience they should then have of the union subsisting between Him and them. They would then realize that they were in Christ as members of His glorified body, while He was in them the source and principle of their life (cf. vi. 56).

21. **He that hath My commandments, and keepeth them** The first verb points to actual possession by and through the reception of faith, as in v. 38 (Meyer, Luthardt, Westcott) rather than to mere notional retention in the memory,—*qui habet in memoria*(Augustine) ; and the second to actual fulfilment in practical life as in xii. 47—*qui servat in vita* (Augustine). **he it is that loveth Me,** that man (ἐκεῖνος) and no other ; **and he that loveth Me will be loved of My Father, and I will love him.** The Father loves him who loves the Son ; and the Son loves him who loves the Father. In both cases the love is not general like that cherished for the world by both the Father (iii. 16) and the Son (1 John iii. 16), but special and tender like that a parent bestows upon his child or one member of a family upon another. **and will manifest Myself unto him,** i.e.

will reveal My gracious presence to him, not externally as at My final *parousia*, but internally by making My indwelling known to him through the spirit :—than which "promise has nothing higher or greater for man" (Stier). Cf. Exod. xxxiii. 13—" If then I have found grace in Thy sight, manifest Thyself to me " (Bengel).

22. **Judas** ·The son or brother of James (Luke vi. 16 ; Acts i. 13), the writer of the epistle of Jude (ver. 1), not the brother of our Lord (Matt. xiii. 55), from whom he is distinguished by Luke (Acts i. 13) ; called also in the lists of the Apostles (Matt. x. 3 ; Mark iii. 18) Thaddeus or Lebbæus, i.e. *the strong, the hearty, the beloved.* **not Iscariot** Added to mark him off from the traitor, perhaps also to mark him out as the lesser of the two Judes, or even to express the horror of the Evangelist at having to write the ill-omened name. **saith unto Him** The only recorded utterance of this apostle, who probably on this occasion spoke for himself, although his difficulty may have been shared in by the others. **What is come to pass** τί γέγονεν = מָה הָיָה what has happened? Jude obviously conjectured that something had occurred to lead Christ to depart from the idea of a public manifestation of His Messianic glory and to determine upon granting only a private theophany. **that Thou wilt manifest Thyself unto us and not unto the world.** No more than Philip (ver. 8) or the unbelieving brethren of Christ (vii. 4) had Jude been able to emancipate himself from the notion that Christ should establish His kingdom by "showing Himself unto the world." Accordingly the thought that Christ intended (as he imagines) to restrict His self-revelation to the extremely limited circle of the apostles fills him with surprise, if not with disappointment.

23. **Jesus answered and said unto** him, not directly meeting his question, but removing the double misconception under which he laboured (1) as to the nature of that self-manifestation which Christ designed to give, and (2) as to the conditions under which it should be extended to any : **If a man,** any one, not of you merely, but of mankind in general, **love Me, he will keep my**

word, including and consisting of My 'commandments' (ver. 21)—the moral and spiritual qualification *love* being placed first and its evidence *obedience* second, to suggest perhaps that the promised manifestation was to be in accordance with that, such as would satisfy a loving and obedient spirit, and not of a character to dazzle the external senses or gratify an unbelieving world ; **and My Father will love him** because of his love and obedience towards Me, **and we will come unto him and make our abode with him.** The use of 'we' implies a distinct consciousness on the part of Christ of essential oneness with the Father (cf. x. 30), and is equivalent to an assertion of His divinity. " We will come " and " we will make " is the language of Jehovah's fellow (Zech. xiii. 7). The last clause recalls the O. T. conception of Jehovah's dwelling in the midst of His people, by means of His symbolic presence in the tabernacle and the temple, and of the spiritual fellowship therein realized (Exod. xxv. 8 ; xxix. 45 ; Lev. xxvi. 11, 12 ; Ezek. xxxvii. 26). Cf. Rev. iii. 20 ; and contrast the idea of man's dwelling with God, as set forth in the opening of this chapter (ver. 2).

24. **He that loveth Me not keepeth not My words**, the individual parts of the word (ver. 23), as the 'commandments' (ver. 21) are the preceptive parts of the same ; **and the word which ye hear** now for instance while I speak with you (Bengel), or, taken unemphatically, which ye hear because it is addressed to you (Westcott), **is not Mine** (cf. vii. 16), of my own devising or commanding, in which case it might have been rejected with impunity, but **the Father's who sent Me** (xii. 49), so that in rejecting My word ye practically reject His.

Ver. 25, 26. *Sixth consolation :*— The assistance of the Paraclete in remembering and understanding His (Christ's) words.

25. **These things**, the consolations previously uttered, **have I spoken unto you**,—a suggestion that the discourse was now closing—**while yet abiding with you**—a hint that His earthly ministry was also about to terminate—a hint which might almost justify the reference of " these things " to all that

He had spoken during the period of His earthly sojourn.

26. **But**—introducing a contrast. In what had been already said much had been left unspoken, as not a little would be passed without allusion in what remained of His farewell discourse (xvi. 12 ; cf. Mark iv. 33), while of what he had unfolded before them a large part was as yet incomprehensible to, or at least not perfectly understood by them (ii. 22 ; viii. 27 ; xii. 16 ; cf. Matt. xvi. 12), and of what had fallen or might yet fall upon their ears a great deal would pass away altogether from their recollection; but after His separation from them these defects would be removed. **the Comforter** the Paraclete or Advocate (see on ver. 16) already mentioned as about to come *even* **the Holy Spirit** τὸ Πνεῦμα τὸ "Αγιον, the full and emphatic name of the promised *paraclete*, occurring only here in this gospel, though employed frequently in the Synoptists (Matt. i. 18, 20 ; iii. 11 ; xii. 31, 32 ; xxviii. 29 ; Mark xii. 36 ; xiii. 11 ; Luke i. 15 ; ii. 25 ; iii. 22 ; iv. 1 ; xii. 12) ; probably selected by Christ on this occasion to indicate not only that the Spirit was the author of their moral and spiritual sanctification just referred to (ver. 21, 23), but that in Him was the ideal of their renewed life absolutely realized. **whom the Father will send in My name** Not at My request simply as in ver. 16 (Grotius, De Wette, Alford), or on account of Me, i.e. on account of the Father's love of Jesus and of him who loves Jesus (Godet), but either in My stead, as my representative (Tholuck, Ewald, Weiss), or, with specific reference to the great salvation which in Me has been brought nigh to and set before you (Meyer, Luthardt, Hengstenberg, Westcott). As Christ had come in the Father's name (v. 43), so was the Spirit to come in Christ's name. **He** ἐκεῖνος. If taken by itself this pronoun is not absolutely conclusive as to the personality of the Spirit, it is yet more easily explained on that hypothesis. **shall teach you** not orally and verbally as I have done, but inwardly and spiritually by imparting illumination to your minds. **all things**, not all things absolutely, but all things connected with 'the Truth' I have come to reveal. **and bring to your remembrance** not

merely indicating the method and manner of the Spirit's teaching (Luthardt), but pointing to a distinct operation, the recalling of Christ's words and the interpretation of their meaning. **all that I said unto you,** but which at the time you did not comprehend.

Ver. 27. *Seventh consolation:*—The heavenly legacy of Peace.

27. Peace I leave with you As our Lord was on the eve of his departure from the world, the word ἀφίημι, 'I send away,' 'dismiss,' hence 'I let go from myself,' 'I leave' (see iv. 28; xii. 48; xii. 7; xiv. 18), has been supposed to contain an allusion to the oriental custom of wishing peace (Heb. שָׁלוֹם) in taking farewell: cf. 1 Sam. i. 17; xx. 42; xxix. 5; Mark v. 34; Luke vii. 50; viii. 48; Acts xvi. 36; James ii. 16; 1 Pet. v. 14; 3 John 15 (Luther, Calvin, Bengel, and most moderns); but the precise force of ἀφίημι will be better preserved if the departing Saviour be thought of as 'sending down' or 'letting go' Peace from heaven as one might let a bird fly out of the hand, rather than as leaving it behind or bequeathing it before He goes. Cf. Milton in the "Ode to the Nativity"—"But he, her fears to cease, sent down the meek-eyed Peace," etc. (See Paley: The Gospel of St. John, p. 118 note). In any case 'Peace' must not be watered down to mean merely 'outward prosperity,' but taken in its highest acceptation as that absolute serenity of soul which one enjoys who is reconciled to God, to himself, to his fellows, to his entire environment — *pax reconciliationis* (Bengel). **My peace I give unto you** 'The peace which is mine' (cf 'the joy which is mine' : xv. 11 ; xvii. 13) ; so called either because in Christ it received its highest exemplification, being the peace He Himself possessed (Bengel and others); or because He was its immediate and exclusive source —it proceeded forth from Him (Tholuck, Meyer, Hengstenberg); or to distinguish it from such false peace as the world confers upon its votaries. **not as the world giveth, give I unto you,** in respect either of what, how, or on what conditions I give. **Let not your heart be troubled, neither let it be fearful.** With the first clause Our Lord returns to the starting point of His consolatory address; with the second He adds a caution against fear. Though δειλιάω occurs here only in the N. T., the adjective δειλός, fearful, is found more than once (Matt. viii. 26; Mark iv. 40; Rev. xxi. 8), and the noun δειλιά, fear, at least once (2 Tim. i. 7).

Ver. 28-31. Conclusion of address.

28. Ye heard how or that **I said unto you, I go away, and I come unto you** See on ver. 3, 19. **If ye loved Me, ye would have rejoiced because I go unto the Father** Our Lord does not thereby challenge the sincerity or deny the fact of their affection for Him, but merely suggests that if it had been pure, ideal, and not mixed with worldly elements, it would have led them to rejoice in His departure unto the Father, which in reality meant for Him not extinction or suppression, but exaltation and promotion. **for the Father is greater than I.** That Christ here compares Himself with the Father is an indirect proof that He was at the moment conscious of being a partaker of the divine nature. "The creature who should say, 'God is greater than I,' would blaspheme no less than one who should say, 'I am equal with God'" (Godet). Hence the superiority Christ ascribed to the Father over Himself was based not upon the *supposed* fact that Christ was only a man (Socinus), or only a creature (Arius), or upon the *actual* fact that as Son of God he was officially and economically subordinate to the Father, as his servant, commissioner, agent, representative (Grotius, Meyer), or was at the moment existing in a state or condition of temporary humiliation (Cyril, Augustine, Luther, Calvin, Bengel, De Wette, Brückner, Luthardt, and others), but upon the *revealed* fact of the essential and metaphysical subordination of His personality to that of the Father (Athanasius and the Nicene Fathers, Olshausen, Reuss, Godet, Westcott, and others). See 'How' is the divinity of Jesus depicted?' by the author, pp. 88, 89. Accordingly, the return of Christ to the Father would be for Him an exaltation, not alone as a 'return to the glory which He had with the Father before the world was, but as the return of a son to the bosom of a father : and the right apprehension of this should and would have led the disciples rather to rejoice than to weep and mourn.

29. **And now I have told you** of My departure **before it come to pass, that when it is come to pass** through My death **ye may believe** not merely that I have gone to the Father (Meyer), but that I am *He*, as in xiii. 19 (Brückner, Luthardt, Godet).

30. **I will no more speak much with you,** or *No longer many things will I speak with you;* **for the prince of the world,** not the Roman power (Paley), but Satan (see on xii. 31) **cometh—** Christ having by this time a present iment not merely of the approach of Judas, but also of the conflict with Satan in Gethsemane, and regarding all His human adversaries as the organs and instruments of that chief foe (xiii. 2, 27; vi. 70; Luke iv. 13); **and he hath nothing in Me,** lit., *and in Me he hath not anything,* et in Me non habet quicquam (Vulgate). It is not necessary to supply εὑρεῖν, to find (D), or ποιεῖν, to do, as in Luke xii. 4 (Kuinoel), or μέρος, part (Nonnus), 'of which he can accuse Me before God' (Ewald); or to read εὑρίσκει, finds, or εὑρήσει (K II etc.) will find. The phrase means 'he hath nothing (i.e. no possession, nothing that belongs to him) in Me,' and therefore nothing over which he has any power or dominion, claim or right—consequently he has no title to inflict upon Me that death of which he has the power (Lücke, Brückner, Meyer, Luthardt, Godet, Westcott, and others). The sinlessness of Jesus, though not directly expressed (Augustine, Cyril, A' Lapide, Olshausen, and others), is certainly here implied.

31. **But,** although the devil hath no claim, right, or power to put Me to death, nevertheless, **that the world may know** (cf. xvii. 21, 23) **that I love the Father—**the first and only time Christ spoke of His love for the Father, though He frequently alluded to the Father's love for Him (x. 17; xv. 9; xvii. 23, 26)—**and as the Father gave Me com-mandment** to lay down My life (x. 18),

even so I do (cf. xii. 50); i.e. I go to death, freely surrender myself to him who hath no power over Me, because he hath nothing in Me. **Arise, let us go hence.** The construction which makes the preceding clauses dependent on this as thus—" But that the world may know that I love the Father, and that as the Father gave Me com-mandment so I do, arise, let us go hence," i.e. to meet the prince of the world who is approaching (Meyer, Luthardt, Godet), seems artificial (Westcott), and is synoptical (Matt. ix. 6) rather than Johannine, while after the ejaculation "Arise, etc.," not further discourses are what one would expect, but an immediate conflict with the advancing foe (Milligan and Moulton). That which regards the clause begin-ning 'that the world . .' as dependent on a substituted phrase, 'it happens that' (Tischendorf), or 'he cometh' (Milligan and Moulton), or 'that cometh to pass, which will come to pass' (Westcott), is not necessary to render the words intelligible. The adopted reading does so. (1) The two clauses, 'that the world may know' and 'as the Father gave Me,' are under the regimen of 'so I do'; the first expressive of the end contemplated and the second emphasizing the rule observed in Christ's free surrender of Himself to death. (2) The last words form an independent sentence and are a summons to leave the chamber and be moving forward towards the impend-ing denouement. Cf. Matt. xxvi. 46, where the words are again repeated after the Gethsemane sorrow. That Christ and His disciples at this stage left the room seems the obvious deduc-tion (Grotius, Lampe, Luther, Rosen-müller, Lange, Gess, Godet, Westcott, and others); though others hold He still continued standing where He was, and only left the chamber after the high-priestly prayer (Bleck, Brück-ner, Lücke, Luthardt, Ewald, Meyer, Alford, Milligan and Moulton, and others).

HOMILETICS

VER. 1-3. THE FATHER'S HOUSE; OR, THE HEAVENLY HOME.

I. **Its Reality** :—" If it were not so I would have told you " (ver. 2). The conviction that such a Father's house exists rests on faith. 1. *Faith in God:*

ver. 1. (1) In the existence of God. If God is not, or is only an abstraction, then heaven is not or is also only an abstraction. (2) In the personality of God. If God be merely a force, there may be a substance in which that force inheres and a centre from which it operates; there cannot be a home. (3) In the fatherhood of God. If God be exclusively a Sovereign, a Lawgiver, a Judge, there may be a palace in which He resides, a habitation in which His glory reposes, a throne on which His imperial greatness sits, a court from which His regal mandates issue, but there cannot be a Father's house. But inasmuch as God is personal in His nature and paternal in His character, being not alone the absolute Father (ver. 6), or the Father of Jesus Christ (ver. 2), but the Father of the spirits of all flesh (Num. xvi. 22; xxvii. 16; Heb. xii. 9), and in particular the Father of believers (xx. 17; Gal. iv. 6; Rom. viii. 15), the presumption, if not the certainty, is that there is a Father's house beyond the skies. (4) In the revelations of God concerning the future life. Had God never intimated that such a home existed, it might have been unsafe to repose unlimited credence in *a priori* speculations concerning a hereafter, but God having at sundry times and in divers manners spoken unto the fathers in the prophets about both the fact and the nature of the future life (Ps. xvi. 11; lxxiii. 24; Prov. iii. 35; Is. xxv. 8; xxxiii. 17; li. 11; Dan. xii. 3; Mal. iii. 17), and having in addition brought life and immortality to light through the gospel (xii. 26; xvii. 24; Matt. v. 8, 12; viii. 11; xxv. 34; Luke xxiii. 43; 2 Cor. v. 1-4; Col. iii. 4; 2 Tim. i. 10; Heb. iv. 9; Rev. ii. 7, 17; iii. 4, 5, 12), man's reasonings in favour of existence on the farther side of the tomb are thereby strengthened and confirmed. (5) In the instincts of, and aspirations after such a Father's house which have been planted by God in the human breast. Not only has the soul been originally endowed with an intuition of immortality—

> "O listen, man !
> A voice within thee speaks the startling words,
> Man—thou shalt never die !" etc. (Dana);

and not only have heathen nations of antiquity generally cherished this belief, the Egyptians and Assyrians no less than the Greeks and Romans; but within the spirits of good men have been awakened true and sometimes passionate yearnings after fellowship with God (cf. lxiii. 1) which it is inconceivable that God should have excited only to disappoint. 2. *Faith in Christ:* ver. 1. (1) In Christ's heavenly origin and divine Sonship. If Christ was God's Son who came forth from the Father's bosom, then the doctrine of a Father's house is established. (2) In Christ's present announcements and revelations. If Christ, having come from above, declared or even did not disillusionize men whom he found possessed of the idea that such a Father's house existed, not for Himself alone but also for man, then the possibility of doubt on the part at least of Christ's followers is reduced to a minimum, if not entirely destroyed. (3) In Christ's impending return to the Father's bosom and glory. If Christ with His human nature is presently ascended up where He was before, there is no room for question whether a Father's house exists.

II. Its Locality :—"I go to prepare a place for you" (ver. 2, 3). Though Christ's language requires not that heaven should be pictured as a magnificent palatial residence, gleaming in celestial light and enriched with untold material splendours, it as little warrants the etherealization of the future life into pure subjectivity, an inward consciousness of felicity, a state of beatific feeling without any external environment. On the contrary it suggests what other Scriptures confirm that heaven is a definite locality, as well as a specific condition. 1. *Where the Father Himself dwells*, the habitation of His holiness, the abode of His glory, the seat and centre of His regal authority, the place where His throne is established : Deut. xxvi. 15; 1 Kings viii. 30; xxii. 19; Ps. xi. 4; Is. lvii. 15; lxiii. 15; lxvi. 1. 2. *Whither the Son has ascended*, the region into which Christ passed when He was taken up, the realm where He now abides with His risen body until the times of the restitution of all things : vi. 62; vii. 33; xx. 17; Matt. xvi. 19; Luke xxiv. 50, 51; Acts i. 9; iii. 21; vii. 55, 56; 1 Pet. iii. 22. 3. *Where the angels reside*, who serve as God's attendants and ministers: i. 51; Ps. lxviii. 17; civ. 4; Is. vi. 2; Matt. xviii. 10; Luke xv. 10; Heb. xii. 22; 1 Pet. i. 12; Rev. v. 11.   4. *Whither the spirits of the just have departed:* Heb. xii. 23; Luke xxiii. 43; Col. i. 12.

III. **Its Felicity :**—"Let not your heart be troubled" (ver. 1). That the palace of the Great King should be incomparably splendid, and the habitation of the blessed God (1 Tim. i. 11) a scene of unmixed happiness, is what the mind naturally judges.   That heaven shall prove an abode of pure joy, a realm of sincere delight for its inmates is what Christ's language implies. There the Father's children will obtain everything that goes to constitute home. 1. *Rest.* After the journeyings, labours, conflicts of life, they shall find repose. In the fullest and sweetest sense of the word they shall rest—from the charges of the law on account of sin (Rom. viii. 1, 33), these being for ever cancelled and silenced (Col. ii. 14),—from struggles against indwelling corruption, since they will then be blameless and unreprovable (1 Cor. i. 8), without spot or wrinkle or any such thing (Eph. v. 27), and into the holy city nothing shall ever enter that defileth (Rev. xxi. 27),—from conflicts with the world and with Satan, the Father's house being a new heaven and a new earth wherein dwelleth righteousness (2 Pet. iii. 13),—from labours and sufferings in behalf of Christ and His kingdom on earth (Rev. xiv. 13). 2. *Love.* Without this heaven might be a vast assemblage, a resplendent city, a glittering palace, but it could not be a home. But the Father's house is a home,

"Where hate is not,—where envy cannot soar,
And nought save unimaginable love,
And tenderest peace (a white and winged dove)
And beauty and perennial bloom are seen."—CORNWALL.

3. *Society.* A home is not created by mere contiguity in space, unless along with this go interchange of thought and feeling as between them that know, love, and trust each other. Hence in the very idea of heaven it is involved that departed saints shall recognize and communicate with one another and with Jesus Christ.

IV. **Its Immensity :**—"Many mansions" (ver. 2). That the Father's house will be a narrow and contracted dwelling, capable of accommodating only the few who shall at last escape from the ruins of a falling universe, has always been a notion dear to Pharisees, whether Jewish or Christian, the few being ever those who entertain this opinion. It has even been supposed to be countenanced by Scripture (Matt. vii. 14; xxii. 14), and to be in accord with the best biological science of the day, that the higher the type of being the smaller the number of individuals by which it is represented (Natural Law in the Spiritual World, pp. 410-412). Happily this is not the opinion of Jesus, who speaking of His Father's house not only described it as composed of many mansions, but afterwards directed the Apocalyptic seer to depict its inmates as "a great multitude which no man can number" (Rev. vii. 9). That the vast preponderance of the race will ultimately be recovered and made partakers of the inheritance of the saints in light is not only more pleasing to the heart than the opposite belief, but it seems to be required by the teaching not of this gospel merely (xii. 32), but of Scripture generally which declares that Christ came to destroy the works of the devil (1 John iii. 8), that the Father promised He should be satisfied with the number of His spiritual posterity (Is. liii. 11), and that in the end the kingdoms of this world should become the kingdom of our Lord and of His Christ (Rev. xi. 15).

V. **Its Perpetuity :**—"In My Father's house are mansions" (ver. 2). The word 'mansion' conveys the idea of permanence. Mutation, which most distinguishes earth, will be absent from the heavenly life. "We have not here an abiding city, but we seek after *the city* which is to come"—"the city which hath the foundations, whose maker and builder is God" (Heb. xi. 10; xiii. 14).

Learn 1. What Christ *is* to the believer—an elder brother, a consoler, a teacher, a forerunner, a friend. 2. What life *should be* to the believer—a land of exile, a place of pilgrimage, a wilderness of passage, a scene of preparation.

3. What death *will be* to the believer—a departing from a foreign shore, a going home, a meeting with the elder brother, an entering into the Father's house.

VER. 4-11.--THE WAY TO THE FATHER'S HOUSE.

I. **Understood**— "And whither I go, ye know the way" (ver. 4). 1. *Not through intuitive discernment.* No man naturally possesses insight into the way of life. This wisdom is hid from the eyes of all living (Job xxviii. 21). Such knowledge is too wonderful for a creature who through sin has become ignorant and brutish (Job xi. 12 ; Ps. x. 5 ; lxxiii. 22). 2. *Not by individual discovery.* No one has ever by unaided effort either devised or lighted on the road to heaven. "The world by wisdom knew not God" (1 Cor. i. 21). "No man can find out the work that God maketh from the beginning to the end" (Eccles. iii. 11). 3. *But from divine revelation.* "Thou wilt show me the path of life," exclaimed David (Ps. xvi. 11), after which he prayed, "Show me thy ways, O Lord : teach me thy paths" (Ps. xxv. 4). Christ came to impart such knowledge to the world in general (iii. 2) and to believing souls in particular (xiii. 13)

II. **Personal.** "*I* am the Way" (ver. 6). The way to the Father's house is, 1. *Not a doctrine to be believed.* Not that the way can be either set forth or apprehended without doctrine or regularly formulated truth. Only intellectual propositions do not constitute, though they show the way. "The letter killeth, but the spirit giveth life" (2 Cor. iii. 6). 2. *Not a work to be performed.* It is certain the way cannot be discerned and far less entered on without the most complex and sustained activity of body, soul, and spirit, since religion means the energizing of man's nature in all its departments through the propelling power of an indwelling life. Only this activity is not the way, though it may prove one is on the way. "By the works of the law shall no flesh be justified" (Gal. ii. 16). Salvation is "not of works, lest any man should boast" (Eph. ii. 9). 3. *But a person to be trusted.* That person Christ affirmed was Himself. "I am the door: by Me, if any man enter in, he shall be saved" (x. 9). So said the Evangelist, "He that hath the Son hath the life" (1 John v. 12) ; and the Baptist (iii. 36).

III. **Sufficient.** "I am the Way, the Truth, and the Life" (ver. 6). The sufficiency of Christ as a way springs from two facts. 1. *Christ is the Truth.* Not *a* or *the* possessor of the truth, but the Truth itself. In Him is exhibited a perfect revelation of the Father. Any soul seeking the Father may find the object of its search in Him. As the Truth He is the Father's image. (1) Really. Not figuratively or metaphorically, but actually and personally ; nor representatively only, but identically also ; since 'the Father is in Him and He is in the Father' (ver. 10, 11),—the Father in Him with the fulness of the godhead (Col. i. 19 ; ii. 9), and He in the Father as in the fount of His eternal being. Hence he who looks upon, or knows the Son by that act also looks upon and knows the Father (ver. 7). (2) Completely. Not in part but in totality does Christ image forth the Father, embodying before men His ineffable nature because of the unity of essence and personal fellowship above described (ver. 10, 11), declaring His character as a God of love in the words of ' grace and truth,' spoken not of Himself but from the Father (ver. 10), and unfolding the manner as well as the purpose of His (the Father's) activity in works done by the Father, through Him, the Son (ver. 10) ; so that Christ could declare to Philip—" He that hath seen Me hath seen the Father" (ver. 9). (3) Adequately. So commensurate was Christ's image of the Father both with the nature of God and the needs of man that henceforth there is no room for either Philip's request, "Shew us the Father" (ver. 9), or for Job's cry, "Oh, that I knew where I might find Him !" (Job xxiii. 3). 2. *Christ is the Life.* Not the possessor merely but the personal embodiment, the original fountain and essential principal of that life, without which no one can reach the Father's presence or enter the Father's house. The Father's children alone, that is, they alone who share the life of the Father's Son, can be admitted to the Father's home. Hence, as Christ, the Son, can impart that life which the soul needs to secure its entrance into heaven—nay, as it is Christ dwelling in the heart by faith (Eph. iii. 17 ; Col. i. 27) which con--

stitutes that life, it is obvious that Christ as a way to the Father's house is sufficient.

IV. **Exclusive.** "No man cometh unto the Father, but by Me" (ver. 6). 1. *Of momentous significance.* Not one of many ways but the only way is Christ,—not one of many mediators but the one mediator between God and man (1 Tim. ii. 5),—not one Saviour out of many equally gifted and powerful, but the absolutely peerless one, beside whom is no other (Acts iv. 12 ; 1 Cor. iii. 11). He who would attain to heavenly felicity must call in the services of Jesus. He who would see God beyond the veil and be found of Him in peace must first approach Him here in the name and through the merits of His Son. If a man will reject the mediation of Christ, he must be satisfied with perpetual exclusion from the Father's presence. 2. *Of extreme unpleasantness.* That is, to the natural heart, which ordinarily pronounces it an hard saying. "Many ways paved by divinity lead to happiness" is the world's maxim, and because Christ's is different the world is offended. 3. *Of absolute truth.* This cannot be disputed if what has been advanced be not denied, that, before a man can come to the Father, he must understand the truth concerning that Father, and be possessed of that life which renders communion with the Father possible.

Learn 1. That Christ sometimes takes a more favourable view of the character and attainments of His people than they do of themselves. 2. That Christ claims to be the highest conceivable or possible revelation of the Father. 3. That true moral and spiritual life is impossible to those who do not seek God in the person of Christ. 4. That if the religion of Christ is true, no other is or can be. 5. That a high responsibility rests on those who possess the knowledge of God Christ gives to diffuse it amongst their fellow-men.

VER. 12–14. THE ACTIVITY OF THE GLORIFIED CHRIST.

I. **Its Reality and Certainty.** It may seem as if Christ's language pointed rather to the activity His believing followers should exercise when He had departed from the earth (ver. 12); closer attention shows that Christ regarded Himself as the real worker and His followers only as His agents (ver. 13, 14).

II. **Its Organ and Instrument.** The phrase "he that believeth on Me" (ver. 12) cannot be restricted to the Apostles, but must be extended to embrace Christ's followers, collectively and individually, in every age and generation from that night of the Betrayal to the end of time. 1. Our Saviour's language *does not mean that after leaving earth, He will work in no other way than through the collective church which is His body* (Eph. i. 23) *and the individual believer who is a member of the same* (Eph. v. 30) ; because in point of fact He does. As the glorified Son, exalted to a share in the world-governing dominion of the Father (Rev. iii. 21), He is to-day, has been since the Ascension, and will be till the close of this dispensation, presiding over the affairs of the universe, which as the pre-incarnate Word He summoned into being (xiii. 3 ; Matt. xxvii. 18 ; Eph. i. 21, 22 ; 1 Pet. iii. 22 ; Heb. i. 3). 2. *Nor does it imply that everything done by the church collective or by the individual believer is a manifestation of His activity.* To maintain this would be to open a wide door to fanaticism ; and indeed it is chiefly the failure to observe this that has led to the multitudinous vagaries into which both religious sects and private Christians have fallen. 3. What Christ's language signifies is *that He makes use of His church, collectively and individually, to operate upon the earth ;* and that not merely in the sense of commissioning her to act as His representative, ambassador, plenipotentiary, but in that of employing her as His body, pervaded by his life and swayed by His will. Already He had pointed to His own works as indications of His essential unity with the Father (ver. 11); now He points to the works of believers as evidence that He and they are one (ver. 12), He in them and they in Him (ver. 20), He the Head and they the members of one mystical body. They derive their life from Him ; He makes use of them to execute His works upon the earth.

III. **Its Nature and Extent.** 1. *Its nature*—"The same works that I do shall he do also," ver. 12. Believers, acting independently of Him, would not be able to work miracles when, where, and how they pleased ; but miracles would be done by them similar to those which had been done by Him, when, where, and as He, the prime worker, who used them as His instruments, might determine. This prediction and promise were fulfilled in the miracles wrought by the disciples after Pentecost, as e.g. by Peter on the lame man in the temple (Acts iii. 6, 7, 8) and on Dorcas at Joppa (Acts ix. 40), by Paul on the sorcerer in Cyprus (Acts xiii. 11), on the young man at Troas (Acts xx. 12), and on the demoniac girl in Philippi (Acts xvi. 18), and by the early Christians in Corinth, many of whom possessed supernatural endowments, as ' gifts of healing,' ' workings of miracles,' ' discernings of spirits,' ' interpretations of tongues ' (1 Cor. xii. 4-11). But that neither Peter nor Paul could perform supernatural deeds except as they were employed for that purpose by Christ, was revealed by the circumstance that Paul wrought no miracle to cure either Epaphroditus (Phil. ii. 26, 27) or Trophimus (2 Tim. iv. 20). That no early Christian had in himself the power of working miracles was evidenced by the fact that he could not perform marvels indiscriminately, but only of the kind for which he had the gift, and only when and as he was moved thereto by the Spirit. 2. *Its extent*—" And greater *works* than these shall he do." Christ's people in general and Christ's apostles in particular would not perform more startling miracles than had been done by Christ. At least (1) it is certain that they have not done so. The cases adduced, —the healings by Peter's shadow (Acts v. 15) and by Paul's handkerchiefs (Acts xix. 12) are in no sense greater or more wonderful, if indeed they are not less wonderful than Christ's curing by a word at a distance (iv. 50), not to speak of recalling to life a four days' corpse (xi. 44). Then (2) where all miracles are equally incompetent to any power less than omnipotence, it is simply an abuse of speech to say that one miracle is or can be greater than another. The meaning was that Christ's followers should do works greater in their kind than those physical miracles just alluded to, would after Christ's ascension enter upon forms of activity which in grandeur and importance as well as in the quality and permanence of their results would transcend anything that had been done during the period of Christ's humiliation. Witness Peter's sermon on the day of Pentecost (Acts ii. 41), Philip the deacon's visit to Samaria (Acts viii. 5), and Paul's missionary travels in Asia Minor and Europe. Nor have marvels of this sort ceased. Because of the exaltation of Jesus Christ and the descent of the Holy Spirit wonders can be wrought by the followers of Jesus that would have been impossible during the period of His sojourn upon the earth.

IV. **Its Mode and Condition.** If the glorified Christ is the prime worker, and the individual believer the instrument, connection must be established between both. Christ must be able to reach the believer, and the believer must be able to communicate with Christ. 1. *The former Christ effects by the impartation of His Spirit* (ver. 16, 17 : see next homily), to which He gradually leads up their thoughts by mentioning the fact of His exaltation—" because I go unto the Father " (ver. 12). 2. *The latter the believer accomplishes by means of prayer* (ver. 13, 14). Nothing could be simpler—it would only be needful that they should ask (Matt. xxi. 21, 22 ; Mark xi. 23, 24). Nothing could be ampler—all things whatsoever they might ask and all things should be done (Matt. vii. 7 ; xviii. 19). Nothing could be surer—Christ would do what they asked, not merely issue orders that it should be done, but should Himself do it, not for their sakes alone, but also and principally for the Father's sake, " that the Father might be glorified in the Son." Nothing could be freer—the only stipulation was that they should ask in Christ's name (see Exposition).

Lessons. 1. The supreme divinity of Jesus Christ involved in all Christ here says about Himself. 2. The essential dignity of the Christian—a fellow-worker with Christ. 3. The true doctrine of prayer—asking in the name of Christ. 4. The reason why miracles have ceased in the Christian Church—the Holy Ghost does not consider them necessary.

VER. 15-17.—ANOTHER COMFORTER.

I. **The Being spoken of.** 1. *Spiritual.* " He," the Father, " shall give you the Spirit of Truth " (ver. 36). Whereas Christ had been found in fashion as a man, the being that should succeed Him on earth would be spirit. 2. *Personal.* Yet would He not be merely an influence or energy, as has been imagined (Monarchians, Patripassians, Sabellians, Unitarians, Swedenborgians), but a person, as Christ was. That Christ taught the doctrine of the Spirit's personality is apparent, (1) from the use of the personal pronoun when alluding to Him (ver 26 ; xv. 26), (2) from the names given to Him, ' The Comforter, Helper or Advocate' (ver. 26 ; xv. 26), and ' Another Comforter ' (ver. 16), resembling Christ who had hitherto served in that capacity, (3) from the offices assigned to Him, as e.g. comforting or helping and teaching the disciples, and (4) from the manner in which He is associated with the Father and the Son (ver. 26). 3. *Divine.* Not directly stated in the present paragraph, it may yet be inferred. It is inconceivable that Christ, who was Himself divine, could have been adequately represented by a being who was only a creature ; it is doubtful if the interests of Christ's people could have been managed by a being less exalted than Christ Himself. 4. *Distinct.* Though equally divine with the Father and the Son, He is not simply the Father or the Son in a different aspect, but is personally distinct from both. He is another comforter than Christ, and a separate person from the Father.

II. **The Relations in which He stands.** 1. *To the Father.* (1) Ontologically or metaphysically, one with the Father, equal in being, wisdom, power, and glory (see above), and yet proceeding forth from Him, in the sense of deriving His divine essence from the Father (xv. 26). (2) Economically or historically, He is sent (ver. 26) and given (ver. 16) by the Father. 2. *To the Son.* (1) Essentially the Son's as the Father's equal, He is nevertheless (2) historically exhibited as sent forth by the Father at His, the Son's, intercession. 3. *To the truth.* This is defined by the phrase 'the Spirit of truth' (ver. 17 ; xv. 26 ; xvi. 13), which may signify the Spirit whose essence is the truth, or whose manifestations and operations concern the truth—the Spirit who is the absolute possessor and perfect revealer of the truth, whose office it is to testify of Him who is the truth (xv. 26), and to guide into all the truth (xvi. 13). 4. *To the disciples.* A presence (1) inward, not *with* and *by*, but *in*, not accompanying or residing near, but actually dwelling in them (1 Cor. iii. 16) ; (2) permanent, not temporary as Christ's had been—' he should abide with them for ever ' ; and (3) helpful—He should be to them a Paraclete, an advocate pleading their cause before the bar of God, and at the courts of men (Matt. x. 20). 5. *To the world.* More fully opened afterwards (xvi. 8). Meantime attention is called to the fact that the Holy Spirit can enter into no permanent living relations with the unbelieving world because of its complete insensibility to the Spirit's manifestations (ver. 17).

III. **The Conditions of receiving Him.** 1. *Loving obedience to Christ*—"If ye love Me ye will keep My commandments, and I will ask the Father, etc.," ver. 15. Not upon the world does the Father bestow the gift of the Spirit, but upon the ' body' of Christ ; and vital union with the exalted Redeemer can be maintained and manifested only by a faith which works by love and brings forth the fruits of obedience. 2. *Believing recognition of the Spirit.* Implied in the reason given for the world's non-reception of the same—" It beholdeth Him not, neither knoweth Him," and directly expressed concerning those who receive Him—"ye know Him," ver. 17. The world had closed its eyes and steeled its heart against the Spirit's manifestations of Himself in Christ ; and accordingly became incapable of either apprehending His higher revelations or experiencing His higher operations. The apostles had known and believed in the Spirit as revealed to them in and through Christ, and hence were in a state of readiness to receive the gift of the Holy Ghost. The same condition must be implemented by all who would receive the Spirit.

Learn 1. That love to Christ is an indispensable mark of true discipleship. (Cf. xxi. 17), and a preliminary requisite to the communion of the Holy Ghost (cf. xiv. 23, with 1 John iii. 24). 2. That the only reliable evidence of love to Christ is obedience to His commandments (ver. 21, 23 ; 1 John v. 3 ; 2 John 6). 3. That all a saint obtains on earth, whether of a temporal or spiritual character, he owes to the Saviour's intercession (Rom. viii. 34 ; Heb. vii. 25). 4. That the highest gift a human spirit can receive is the indwelling of the Holy Ghost—as a divine being, an all-sufficient helper, a heavenly teacher, an unchanging friend. 5. That the world's unbelief in the Holy Ghost is no proof that the Holy Ghost does not exist. 6. That the most convincing demonstration of the reality of Christ's salvation is the soul's experience of the same (Ps. xxxiv. 8).

VER. 18-24.—THE RETURN OF THE GLORIFIED CHRIST.

I. **Spiritual**:—"I am coming to you," ver. 18. 1. *Not His final coming* or second glorious advent, which will be to all and at the world's end, while this would be soon and only to the disciples. 2. *Not His post-resurrection appearances*, since these were temporary, whereas this should be permanent. 3. *But His return in the person of the Spirit*, of whom He had just spoken (ver. 16).

II. **Personal**:—"*I* am coming," ver. 18 ; "*I* will manifest *Myself*," ver. 21 ; "*we* will come unto Him," ver. 23. Christ intended not to say that the coming of the Spirit would be equivalent to a coming of Himself, representatively and instrumentally ; but that in the coming of the Paraclete there would take place a veritable coming of His own glorified person. As during His sojourn on the earth the Spirit had been personally present in Him, so after His departure would He be personally present in the Spirit. N.B. The way in which Christ in this passage associates with Himself both the Father and the Spirit, points by no means obscurely to the doctrine of the Trinity.

III. **Consolatory**:—"I will not leave you desolate," ver. 18. A fourfold consolation His coming to them would bring. 1. *A believing realization of His presence:*—"Yet a little while and the world beholdeth Me no more ; but ye behold Me," ver. 19. After His corporeal presence should have been withdrawn, the disciples would still be able to see Him with the eye of faith. 2. *A personal participation in His life:*—"Because I live, ye shall live also," ver. 19. His continued existence would be a guarantee that they should not relapse into spiritual death, but derive from Him a principle of spiritual life which would ultimately conduct them to His presence. 3. *An experimental knowledge of His divinity :*— "In that day ye shall know that I am in My Father," ver. 20. During the period of His earthly sojourn, His disciples had been privileged at intervals to behold forth flashings of His indwelling deity which left upon their minds the (perhaps momentary) impression of His godhead (see Matt. xiv. 33 ; xvii. 5 ; Luke v. 8). It is doubtful if, prior to the Resurrection, the conviction of His essential oneness with the Father was either permanently or clearly fixed in their minds. It is certain that after Pentecost that mysterious relationship became fully illumined. What assisted them to apprehend His oneness with the Father was the experience they then possessed of their oneness with Him—"ye in Me and I in you." 4. *A perfect revelation of His person :*—"I will manifest Myself unto him," ver. 21. This, however, would be conditional on the existence of certain moral and spiritual qualifications in him to whom such manifestation should be given. (1) It would presuppose on the part of the believer a sincere and well-attested love to the Saviour, evidenced by a life of earnest and active obedience to His commandments. (2) Such love to Christ on the part of the disciple would draw towards him the love of the Father, who regards with affection all who honour and obey the Son. (3) The contemplation of the Father's love towards the loving and obedient soul would again awaken in the heart of Christ a special love for him who was the object of the Father's love. (4) Moved by this love, He, Christ, would unfold His gracious person to the loving and obedient one—"I will manifest myself unto him"—not simply as a divine friend and helper standing by, yet outside of, but entering into him, not alone but accompanied by the Father and the Spirit, who along with Me, will make permanent abode with him, extending to him love, imparting to him grace, granting to him house-and-table fellowship with ourselves (cf. Rev. iii. 20).

IV. **Conditional** : "If a man love Me, he will keep My word" (ver. 23). Unlike Christ's first and second comings, His immediate return, though not limited in respect of place or time like His post-resurrection visits to the disciples, is nevertheless restricted to persons of a certain moral and spiritual character. So it was with Jehovah's visits under the O. T. dispensation (Is. lvii. 15 ; lxvi. 2). The requirements for Christ's self-manifestations to and in the soul are two—1. *Love to His person:*—"He that loveth Me, . . . I will manifest Myself unto him" (ver. 21), and "If a man love Me, . . . We will come unto him" (ver. 23); and 2. *Obedience to His word:*—"If a man keep My words" (ver. 23). And the two are inseparable—"He that loveth Me not keepeth not My words" (ver. 24); though the converse is perhaps hardly correct—"He that keepeth not My words, loveth Me not,' since some who love Christ often fail to remember His words.

Lessons. 1. The mystery of the believer's inner life—Christ in him! "I live, yet not I, but Christ liveth in Me" (Gal. ii. 20). 2. The supreme importance of love to Christ—it brings all into the soul (ver. 21), and it sends all out of the soul (2 Cor. v. 14). 3. The necessity of holy living—since without holiness no man can see the Lord either here or hereafter (Heb. xii. 14).

VER. 25, 26.—THE MISSION OF THE HOLY SPIRIT.

I. **Its Distinction from that of Jesus Christ.** In respect of two points, the mission of the Paraclete was to resemble that of the Son :—(1) in being sent by the Father, and (2) in being designed to impart instruction to the minds of men. Outside of these correspondences the two were separated by important differences. 1. *In respect of character.* Christ had been sent in the Father's name, as the Father's representative and vicegerent ; the Spirit was to come in Christ's name, as His representative and vicegerent. 2. *In respect of purpose.* Christ had been sent to furnish men with an objective image of God, or external presentation of divine truth ; the Spirit was to come to give men an inward apprehension of the same. 3. *In respect of duration.* Christ had been sent to continue on the earth for a season ; the Spirit was to make a permanent abode with believers. 4. *In respect of results.* Christ's mission was but imperfectly realized, so far as it related to the enlightenment of men ; that of the Holy Spirit would attain to complete success in instructing the understandings and sanctifying the hearts of believers.

II. **Its Fulfilment in the case of Christ's Apostles.** 1. *Scripture illumination.* A wonderful light began to shine upon the O. T. which enabled them to perceive in it references to Christ which had previously been hidden from their sight (cf. Ps. xvi. 8-11 with Acts ii. 25-28 ; xiii. 35 ; Ps. cx. 1 with Acts ii. 34 ; Ps. ii. 1, 2 with Acts iv. 25 ; Ps. ii. 7 with Acts xiii. 33 ; Amos ix. 11 with Acts xv. 16 ; Zech. ix. 9 with John xii. 16). 2. *Quickened recollection.* A lively remembrance of forgotten words of Jesus began to show itself in their experience. Examples—ii. 22 ; Luke xxiv. 8 ; Acts xi. 16 ; xx. 35. In particular Christ's utterances concerning His relation to the Father, which had often been dark to the disciples no less than to the Pharisees, then recurred to their memories and became clear to their understandings (viii. 28). 3. *Further revelation.* A gradual disclosure to their minds of truths which had lain concealed in the teaching of Christ, but which by Him had not been developed, as e.g. the doctrines of (1) His divinity (Acts i. 36), (2) His atoning death (Acts iii. 19), (3) His exclusive Mediatorship (Acts iv. 12), the doctrines of (4) justification by faith (Acts xiii. 39 ; Rom. i. 16, 17 ; iii. 21-26 ; v. 1, etc.), and (6) the catholicity of the N. T. Church (Acts xi. 17 ; Rom. i. 16 ; ii. 11 ; Gal. vi. 15 ; Eph. ii. 14-16). In short out of this flowed the New Testament.

III. **Its Relation to the General Body of Believers.** 1. *Negatively.* It does not warrant the expectation that *new* revelations will be imparted to either the church or the individual—a pretension advanced by the Church of Rome, which places the traditions of the fathers on an equal platform with the writings of the apostles. 2. *Positively.* Christ's language implies that the church and the individual have to-day, as the apostles had, a teacher qualified to lead them into all truth (1 John ii. 20)—not all sorts of truth, as e.g. scientific and philosophic, but the whole circle of religious truth.

Learn 1. The high esteem in which the Holy Spirit should be held, as the Father's commissioner, the Saviour's expositor, the Apostle's remembrancer, the Church's teacher, the Saint's comforter. 2. The great confidence which in the Holy Spirit should be placed, possessing as he does the twofold stamp and seal of the Father and the Son. 3. The sincere gratitude with which the Holy

Spirit should be welcomed, since without His assistance the revealed Christ cannot be understood.

VER. 27. THE SAVIOUR'S PARTING BEQUEST.

I. The Nature of the Gift—"Peace, My Peace." Not merely such peace as He only could impart and they could experience only in union with Him, but such peace as He Himself possessed,—the peace 1. *Of perfect agreement with God.* To peace of this sort the world is a stranger, though it sometimes fashions for itself an inward quietness which it mistakes for peace, saying, 'Peace, Peace,' when there is no peace. On the other hand, no one can peruse the history of Christ without perceiving that at every moment within His bosom dwelt the blessed calm of a soul that existed in conscious enjoyment of the divine favour. And the like peace He bestows on His believing people—the peace of reconciliation (Eph. ii. 14-17). 2. *Of complete harmony with oneself.* That the world has no acquaintance with this kind of peace apart from Christ and His religion must be obvious. "The wicked are like the troubled sea when it cannot rest" (Is. lvii. 20). Nor can the world by any stratagem produce such a peace as Christ here describes, in which the entire nature of man shall be at rest, the lower parts and principles thereof acting in subordination to the higher, and both sweetly co-operating towards the production of a perfect life. The most the world can do is to create a desolation and call it peace. But not of that sort was the peace which reigned in the bosom of the Saviour and which He bequeathed to His believing followers —the peace not of spiritual death but of eternal life, the calm not of a soul out of which good has been driven, but of one in which evil will ultimately have no place, and holiness alone shall reign (Is. xlviii. 18). 3. *Of absolute concord with men.* So little characteristic of the world is this that a celebrated English philosopher (Hobbes) affirmed selfishness to be the first principle of human action, man's natural condition to be one of mutual warfare, and the seemingly peaceful order of society to be only an armed truce. This, however, was not the conception of good will amongst men entertained by the angels when they chanted their Christmas carol above Bethlehem's plains (Luke ii. 14), or by Christ when He bequeathed His peace to the disciples ere He went forth to meet His death on Calvary (cf. xiii. 12-15 ; 34). 4. *Of entire satisfaction with one's lot.* Of this the world had never learnt the secret. The weariness and unrest of the human soul has been a fruitful theme of poesy from the days of Horace to those of Burns, a constant subject for the moralist from the time of Cicero to that of Carlyle. Only one Being has appeared on earth who has left behind the impression of having no acquaintance in Himself with this disquietude, who never needed like the founder of Buddhism to go in search of peace, because from the opening of His career to its close He possessed it, and never required like Marcus Antoninus to learn the secret of inward calm by means of study, because He knew it from the first. The spirit of Jesus Christ was never ruffled or fretted by the external circumstances of His lot, by the privations he endured, the labours He performed, the reproaches He encountered, the sufferings He experienced, the death He died. In the midst of all He was "in perfect peace"; and the like peace He offers to His believing people.

II. The Manner of its Bestowment—"Not as the world giveth, give I unto you." 1. *Not scantily but largely.* The world doles out its benefits in crumbs and morsels : Christ in handfuls and basketfuls. 2. *Not exceptionally but universally.* The world gives to its favourites, who are mostly few : Christ proffers His gift of peace to all. 3. *Not conditionally, but freely.* The world exacts terms from those it proposes to enrich : Christ bestows blessings without money and without price. 4. *Not seemingly but really.* The world often deceives those whom it pretends to succour : Christ's gifts are always genuine and sincere. 5. *Not temporarily but permanently.* The world can only lend for a season : Christ can impart for ever. "The gifts and calling of God are without repentance."

Conclusion 1. Have we felt our need of this peace? 2. Have we obtained it? Have we asked it?

VER. 28. CHRIST'S GOING TO THE FATHER AN INCREASE OF JOY.

I. The Reason Why—"The Father is greater than I." 1. *An indirect proof of*

Christ's essential equality with God. Had Christ been a mere man He would not have required to tell His disciples that the Father was greater than He.   Had He desired to dissuade His disciples from ascribing to Him the honours of divinity, to which He was not entitled, His language was below what was demanded by the occasion, was not equal in respect of holy indignation and vehement remonstrance to that of the angel who restrained John from falling down to worship at his feet (Rev. xxii. 9) or of Paul and Barnabas when the Lystrans would have done them sacrifice (Acts xiv 15).   Hence Christ's assertion that His Father was greater than He can be redeemed from a charge of presumption, only by supposing that Christ was conscious of essential equality with God and that notwithstanding there was a sense in which the Father was greater than He.   2. *A direct statement of Christ's personal subordination to the Father.* However baffling to the human understanding to explain or conceive, the notion that in the mysterious interrelations of the adorable Godhead the Father occupies the place of preeminence, and the Son a position of dependence, appears to be what our Saviour here designs to express.   This notion too, besides being to human reason involved in the relationship expressed by the term Son, is corroborated by Christ's testimony concerning the Son's dependence on the Father for being (viii. 42) and for life (v. 26), and was probably here introduced to correct the impression which perhaps the disciples had received from His utterances about His divine Sonship, that a being so exalted as He could scarcely be capable of any increase of felicity.   (See ' How is the divinity of Jesus depicted ?' by the Author, pp. 89, 90.)

II. **The Sense in which.**   It was 1. *A termination of His state of humiliation.* If Christ was the Son of God then His earthly sojourn must have partaken of the nature of humiliation (Phil. ii. 6, 7).   With Christ's return to the Father that state or condition would end.   2. *A completion of His God-appointed work.* At least that part of it which was to be accomplished on the earth was finished —the revelation of the Father (ver. 9), the atoning for sin (iii. 14, 15), the exemplification of holiness (xiii. 13), the establishment of a kingdom of truth (xviii. 36, 37).   3. *The beginning of His mediatorial reward.*   Besides returning to the heavenly life out of which He had descended, He would enter on that glory of which He had been assured in reward for His work on earth (Is. liii. 10, 11 ; Phil. ii. 8).   4. *The attainment of the highest personal felicity.*   If by the expression " My Father is greater than I " Christ referred, as above explained, to the relationship of authority on the one hand and dependence on the other, which subsists between the first and second persons of the Godhead, then the happiness to which he alluded as arising to Him in consequence of His departure from the earth would be the happiness which He as the divine Son should experience in returning to the bosom of the Father.

Learn 1. The short-sightedness of man—highest blessings he frequently bemoans as calamities. 2. The glory of discipleship—to rejoice more in Christ's felicity than in one's own. 3. The mystery of the Godhead—" Touching the Almighty who can find Him out ? "

VER. 30, 31. THE COMING STRUGGLE.

I. **The Enemy**—The prince of the world.   1. *Of large dominions*—" all the kingdoms of this world " (Matt. iv. 8).   2. *Of many subjects*—" the children of disobedience " (Eph. ii. 2).   3. *Of great power*—" the prince of the power of the air, the ruler of the principalities and powers of darkness " (Eph. ii. 2 ; vi. 12). 4. *Of subtle craft*—" the destroyer of man " (Gen. iii. 1), " the deceiver of the whole world " (Rev. xii. 9).   5. *Of evil mind*—essentially " the wicked one " (1 John ii. 13), who " sinneth from the beginning " (1 John iii. 8), " a murderer from the beginning who abode not in the truth," and " a liar " (viii. 44), and " an accuser of Christ's brethren " (Rev. xii. 10).

II. **The Onset**—The prince of the world cometh.   1. *Its proximity.*   Judas was at hand, and in him Satan was drawing near.   2. *Its violence.*   Quite an army had the devil put in force against the Saviour.   3. *Its aim.*   It was directed against heaven's purpose of redemption.   It was meant by destroying Christ to confound the counsel of salvation.   4. *Its skill.*   The campaign had on

Satan's side been planned with ingenuity. Judas, an apostle, had been persuaded to become a traitor. The ecclesiastical authorities of the day had been turned against God's Son. The Roman power had been secured to lend assistance in effecting His arrest. All signs augured well for the success of his infernal scheme. III. **The Defeat**—The prince of the world hath nothing in Me. 1. *The seeming victory.* Outwardly Satan was to triumph. Christ was about to be arrested and put to death. Yet that was not to be because of any power which Satan possessed over Him. It was to be because of Christ's free will. Christ was to lay down His life out of love to His Father and in accordance with His Father's commission (x. 18). 2. *The actual overthrow.* In so doing Christ was to accomplish the very work which Satan supposed he was effectually hindering by putting Christ to death. Through death He was to conquer death and him that hath the power of death (Heb. ii. 14). By putting off from Himself His body He was to make a show of the principalities and powers, triumphing over them in His cross (Col. ii. 15). Learn 1. That Christ is wiser than Satan, and 2. That as He conquered, so shall His people.

(2) THE DISCOURSE AFTER LEAVING THE ROOM

CHAP. XV. 1-27

It is probable that Christ purposed closing His observations with the words, "Arise, let us go hence" (xiv. 31), had not the depth and tenderness of His emotion rendered silence impossible. His disciples He has consoled with the assurance that they will rejoin Him in His Father's House, and that till then He will Himself be with them in the person of the Paraclete ; but He cannot ponder their situation in the world when He shall have left them, without perceiving that they stand in need of further counsel. This accordingly He gives them, setting forth first, under the parable or similitude of the Vine and its Branches, the relation in which they shall stand to Himself when He is corporeally absent but spiritually present with them, a relation of union and communion (ver. 1-11); next,the relation they must bear to one another, a relation of mutual love and goodwill (ver. 12-17); and finally, the relation in which the world will continue to them, a relation of hatred and persecution (ver. 18-27). Whether the contents of this chapter were spoken on the way to Gethsemane or in the upper room, cannot be determined. 1. In favour of the former supposition (Luther, Zwingli, Bengel, Lampe, Lange, Hengstenberg, Ebrard, Godet, Gess, Westcott) are the words, " Arise, let us go hence !" (xiv. 31), which suggest a withdrawal from the supper chamber ; while against it lies the statement (xviii. 1) that when Christ had finished His high-priestly prayer " He went forth with His disciples over the brook Kidron," not to speak of the psychological difficulty of delivering the thoughts here recorded while travelling through the city or even among the vineyards in its outskirts. 2. In favour of the latter hypothesis (Lücke, Tholuck, Olshausen,

Luthardt, Meyer, Milligan and Moulton) stands the fact that no distinct indication of a change of place is furnished by the Evangelist, and that the two chapters are as closely and directly connected as if they had been spoken in immediate succession; against it must be reckoned the correspondence of the words, " Arise, let us go hence!" with those afterwards used in Gethsemane, "Arise, let us be going!" (Matt. xxvi. 46), which were immediately followed by a change of place, or an onward movement, —more especially when taken in connection with the fact that John offers no explanation for delay in leaving the upper chamber. Between such conflicting views a certain decision is impossible.

EXPOSITION

Chap. xv. ver. 1-11. The relation of the disciples to Christ.

Ver. 1. **I am the true Vine** The point of view from which Christ speaks is that of His post-resurrection glory. The true vine is Himself, not as He then appeared in humiliation, but as He would be subsequent to His exaltation. ἡ ἄμπελος ἡ ἀληθινή is not the true, as opposed to the false or degenerate vine, which Israel then was, but the *actual* or *real* vine of which the earthly plant was an emblem : cf. τὸ φῶς τὸ ἀληθινόν, the true light (i. 9), and τὸν ἄρτον τὸν ἀληθινόν, the true bread (vi. 32). "Two currents of thought are united by the Lord when He speaks of Himself as 'the true, the ideal vine.' Israel failed to satisfy the spiritual truths symbolized in the natural vine ; the natural vine only imperfectly realizes the idea which it expresses. In both respects Christ is the ideal vine as contrasted with these defective embodiments" (Westcott). **and my Father** i.e. God **is the husbandman.** The vinedresser or vine cultivator, ὁ γεωργός (cf. Matt. xxi. 33), is in the parable of the Barren Fig-tree styled ἀμπελουργός (Luke xiii. 7, 9). In Matthew's parable the husbandmen are the leaders of the Jewish people, Israel being the vine ; in Luke's parable the husbandman is Christ ; in John's, God, who is also the owner and planter of the vine. The external occasion for this image has been variously conjectured. Those who believe the discourse to have been spoken in the room think the figure

may have been suggested by a vine whose tendrils had crept thereinto (Tholuck), by the vine foliage with which the chamber was adorned (Olshausen), by the vineyards which were seen through the window in the moonlight (Storr), by the wine which had been used in the celebration of the supper (Meyer, Besser), or by the sight of the disciples standing round Him like clusters on a vine (Tholuck, Stier, Luthardt) ; those who hold it to have been uttered on the way to Gethsemane have recourse for the inspiring object to the golden vine which decorated one of the temple gates, near which Christ may have passed in His progress through the city (Jerome, Lampe), or to a branch-laden vine beneath which Christ may have paused as He moved through the vineyards in the suburbs of the metropolis (Godet). But whatever its objective occasion it had a subjective basis in "the fulness of Old Testament thought which dwelt in the mind of Jesus" (Milligan and Moulton); cf. Ps. lxxx. 9 ; Is. v. 7 ; Ezek. xvii. 6; xix. 10 ; Jer. ii. 21 ; Hoz. x. 1 ; and this perhaps suggested the similitude to Christ's mind without any external occasion at all.

2. **Every branch in Me that beareth not fruit** This, better than "Every branch which beareth not fruit in Me," does not necessarily imply either that a branch may be vitally connected with the trunk without bearing fruit, or that an unfruitful branch may nevertheless be vitally united to the trunk. But a branch or twig may

maintain its external connection with the trunk after it has ceased to derive from the latter vital sap ; and in the same way a person may possess a nominal connection with the body of Christ (the Church) without partaking of the inner life of the same. In this case he is unfruitful ; and his unfruitfulness is that which reveals the true character of his connection with the vine, shows it to be rather outward and material than inward and spiritual. The assertion that " a man may be a branch in Christ even though unfruitful " (Luthardt), or that " even the unfruitful branches are true branches " (Westcott), can be regarded as correct only on the assumption that "in Christ" refers solely to outward and visible fellowship. **He taketh it away** The preceding clause being put in the nominative absolute for the sake of emphasis, the pronoun " it " is inserted in this. The removal of the fruitless and therefore lifeless branch is effected by the husbandman. Barren and unproductive professors of the faith are eventually separated from the fellowship of Christ, if not in time by the exposure of their true character, at least at death by the pruning knife of divine retribution. **and every** *branch* **that beareth fruit** i.e. every soul that shows the reality of its vital union with Me by the manifestation of spiritual life in such acts and deeds of holiness as are the proper outcome thereof, **He cleanseth it** καθαίρει, clears, dresses, e.g. by taking away "superfluous leaves and side shoots" (Paley). The correspondence in sound between αἴρει and καθαίρει has been deemed intentional : *suavis rhythmus* (Bengel). The καθαρισμός here applied to the fruitful branches, which consists in removing from them whatever might drain away the sap and so hinder their productivity, the husbandman effects by the pruning knife—either temptations or afflictions, the design of which is to render gracious souls fruitful in every good work and word : cf. Deut. viii. 5 ; Job v. 17 ; xxiii. 10 ; xxxiii. 17 ; Ps. xciv. 12 ; Acts xiv. 22 ; Rom. v. 3 ; viii. 17 ; 2 Cor. iv. 17. **that it may bear more fruit,** more abundant in quantity and richer in quality. It is not enough that a vine produce some fruit : the fruit must be sufficient to

repay the labour of the husbandman, and so justify the right of the tree to a place in the vineyard.

3. **Already ye are clean** "like well-pruned trees" (Paley). In the hearts of the disciples the cleansing process had begun. Essentially and fundamentally the moral purification of their natures had been effected, although, as had been taught them by the feet-washing (xiii. 10), they might require to be cleansed from subsequent defilement. **because of** not *through* (Paley), but *on account of,* **the word** meaning that while the word in itself could effect no change upon the heart, the change effected was nevertheless brought about on account of the word, i.e. not for the sake of the word, in order to correspond to Christ's commission (B. Crusius), or because the word is the purifying power, xvii. 17 (Brückner), but on account of its having been received in faith : cf. 1 Thess. ii. 13. **which I have spoken unto you.** Our Lord refers not simply to His present communications at the supper table, or to the special announcement in xiii. 10 (Hilgenfeld), but to the entire doctrine He had delivered to them : cf. viii. 43.

4. **Abide in Me** not merely *on* Me (Meyer), which an unfruitful branch might do, but *in* Me, i.e. in vital connection with Me, who am the vine. The maintenance of this connection is exhibited as depending on the voluntary action of the believer. This, however, must not be so understood as to contradict the truth contained in ver. 5. **and I in you.** *Facite, ut maneatis in Me, et ut ego maneam in vobis,* Act so that ye may abide in Me, and I may abide in you (Bengel, Grotius, Augustine, Tholuck, Stier, Alford, Westcott); which is harsh. Better, 'And I will abide in you,' the indwelling of Christ in the believer being represented as the necessary result of the believer's abiding in Christ (Meyer, Luthardt, Godet), although this only represents one aspect of the case, other texts declaring the latter to be the cause of the former (ver. 5, 16 ; vi. 56, 57). Best to interpret 'and' as equivalent to 'in which case,' so making both clauses parallel and co-ordinate, as thus: "Abide in Me, in which case I abide in you," both as effect and cause of your abiding in Me. Thus both sides

of the union are exhibited, without condescending upon which is cause and which is effect. In the same fashion Christ represents the mutual indwelling of the Father and the Son. The one is not the cause or the consequence of the other ; but both are cause and both are consequence. "This is a great mystery"—the mystery of absolute and unconditioned existence. **As the branch cannot bear fruit of itself** not simply 'in' or 'by,' but 'from' itself, ἀφ' ἑαυτοῦ, finding in itself the source of its vitality, and deriving from itself its power of productivity, **except it abide in the vine** A further definition of 'not of itself,' to be conjoined with the preceding words, as thus : ' As the branch cannot bear fruit from itself,' or 'as the branch cannot bear fruit except it abide in the vine' : cf. v. 19 (Meyer, Godet, Westcott, and others). **so neither can ye** bring forth the fruits of the spiritual life in, by, or from yourselves, or in any way, measure, or degree at all, **except ye abide in Me.** Though the subject treated of is not the natural impotence of human nature, yet that doctrine is involved in the words. *His locus egregie declarat discrimen naturae et gratiae* (Bengel). *Qui a semetipso se fructum existimat ferre, in vite non est ; qui in vite non est in Christo non est; qui in Christo non est, Christianus non est* (Augustine).

5. **I am the Vine, ye are the branches.** Not an idle repetition, but a specific declaration of the relation which not only they, the disciples, but believers generally, held to Himself the Saviour. He was the Vine, life possessing and life giving : they were only branches, possessing no vitality they did not draw from Him. Hence what He had affirmed about the natural vine and its branches was pre-eminently true of Him and them. **He that abideth in Me and I in him** (see on ver. 4), **the same** lit., *this one,* and no other, **beareth** The verb φέρειν points to the passivity, rather than the personal activity, ποιεῖν, of the Christian. The life the believing soul derives from Christ causes it to bear the fruits of righteousness, as the vine-sap pervading the branches causes them to produce grapes. **much fruit** Though the emphasis lies rather on οὗτος, this man and no other, than on

πολύν, much, the introduction of this qualifying term was probably not without a purpose, viz., to heighten the contrast between the spiritual fertility of the living Christian and the utter barrenness of the soul when severed from the Saviour, which is set forth in the next words. **for apart from Me** not necessarily removed (as yet) from external connection with Me, a thought which follows (ver. 6), but severed from Me inwardly, in the sense that no living union with Me exists, χωρισθέντες ἀπ' ἐμοῦ, out of living fellowship with Me (Meyer). **ye can do** The verb ποιεῖν brings into prominence the Christian's personal activity in fruit bearing, which personal activity becomes an impossibility (οὐ δύνασθε, ye are not able) when the soul lives or tries to exist apart from Christ. The amount it can perform or do in that condition is **nothing.** This word, which cannot be restricted to the Christlike and Apostolic activity of the disciples (Tholuck), distinctly implies, if it does not directly assert, the total inability of the soul, apart from and out of vital connection with Christ, to produce one single fruit of the Christian life. The distinction taken between a higher moral activity and a lower natural moral volition and ability, which cannot attain to Christian morality (Meyer), even if sound, is little serviceable, since Christ regards this lower moral ability as insufficient to avert ultimate excision from the Vine.

6. **If a man abide not in Me** lit., *if any one,* seemingly in union with Me, *abide not*—better than 'has not abode,' μένῃ (ℵ A B D)—*in Me.* The words teach not that falling from grace is possible (Alford, Stier, Luthardt, Meyer, and others) but merely that one who has seemed to be in union with Christ may ultimately give evidence of never having had real connection with Christ at all (see on ver. 2). **he is cast forth as a branch and is withered** lit., *he has been cast out* (sc. of the vineyard, i.e. out of the Christian community) *and has been withered ;* the aorists being employed not as futures (Kuinoel, Baumgarten Crusius), but either because our Lord speaks from the standpoint of the day of judgment (Meyer, Godet, Alford), or because He desires to set forth what must inevitably

happen (Tholuck, Luthardt, Hengstenberg, Westcott, Weiss and others)—cf. Winer : Grammar of the N. T. Diction, part iii. § xl. 6. **and they** i.e. the vineyard labourers, in this case the angels (cf. Matt. xiii. 41), **gather them and cast them into the fire** τὸ πῦρ, *the* fire prepared for them, i.e. Gehenna (Matt. xiii. 42 ; xxv. 41), **and they are burned** lit., *and it,* the withered branch, *burns!* The present tense suggests the idea of duration ; the thought corresponds with that of the unquenchable fire of the Synoptists. *Simplex verbum magna vi positum, eximia cum majestate* (Bengel).

7. If ye abide in Me The Saviour turns from depicting the doom of the unfruitful branches to set forth the privileges and encouragements of such as are fruitful. **and My words abide in you** This clause may express the necessary consequence (Meyer, Luthardt, Weiss), condition (De Wette, Godet), or import (Stier) of the former ; or it may be taken as explanatory of the words " and I in you " of ver. 5 (Westcott), the indwelling of Christ's words rather than of Christ Himself being referred to, because " the thought now is of the communion of prayer " (ibid.). **ask whatsoever ye will** in Christ's name (cf. xiv. 13) **and it shall be done unto you** lit., *and it shall come to pass to you.* The success which attends believing prayer results from the fact that the prayer springs from the indwelling of Christ's words.

8. Herein is My Father glorified that ye bear much fruit lit., *in this My Father was glorified, in order that,* or to the end that *ye bear much fruit ;* ἐν τούτῳ referring not to what follows, the bearing of much fruit (Luthardt, Godet, Alford), but to what precedes, the granting of prayer to the believer who abides in Christ (Meyer, Westcott); ἐδοξάσθη not equivalent to *statuit se glorificari* (Bengel), or to be translated as a future, or as an aorist of anticipation like ἐβλήθη in ver. 6 (Winer, Tholuck), but to be rendered either *has been glorified,* meaning that when prayer has been answered (Meyer) or the believer's union with Christ has been realized (Westcott), the Father has been glorified ; ἵνα, not the same as ὅτι, *because,* but preserving its telic force ' in order that,' ' to the end that,'

the bearing of much fruit being represented as the end contemplated by the Father's answering the believer's prayer (Westcott),—consequently, since this arrangement redounds to, as it was originally framed for, the glory of the Father, as the end contemplated also by the Father's glory (Meyer). The thought becomes clear by regarding the clause "Herein has my Father been glorified" as parenthetical (though this is contrary to John's style), or as parallel to what precedes, as thus :— " It shall be done unto you . . . . that ye may bear much fruit "; and this arrangement is one that has redounded to the glory of my Father who in making it aimed at showing forth His glory. **and so shall ye be My disciples.** γενήσεσθε (א A E G, Tischendorf, Westcott and Hort); but if γένησθε (B D L) be read, then the clause will be dependent on ἵνα and require to be translated "and that ye may be My disciples."

9. Even as the Father hath loved Me, I also have loved you lit., *As the Father loved Me, I also loved you :* the aorist being employed either because the thought is lifted out of the sphere of time into that of eternity, or because Christ speaks from the standpoint of His finished earthly life (Meyer, Luthardt, Westcott). The words "I also," κἀγώ, are not dependent on καθὼς, in which case "abide," μείνατε, would be the principal verb, but introduce the apodosis or correlative clause to that prefaced by "Even as." **Abide ye in My love.** Not in your love of Me (Kuinoel), but in My love of you (Augustine, Calvin, Lücke, Ewald, Meyer, and others). Cf. "My peace" (xiv. 27), and "My joy" (xv. 11), "My commandments" (xiv. 10). The Sinaitic (א), omitting the first clause of the next verse, continues, "Even as I kept My Father's commandments and abide in His love."

10. If ye keep or, *shall have kept,* **My commandments** (cf. xiv. 15, 21, 23, 24 ; xii. 47, 48), **ye shall abide in My love.** Though Christ's love in one aspect is unchangeable and unconditioned, in another it is changeable and conditioned. **even as I have kept My Father's commandments.** Another testimony on the part of Christ to His personal sinlessness ! At the close of

His earthly career, He hesitates not to claim that He had rendered perfect obedience to all the instructions of His Divine Father. **and abide in His love.** "The prominent position of αὐτοῦ corresponds to the consciousness of the happiness and dignity of abiding in the love which His Father bears to Him, x. 17; xvii. 24" (Meyer).

11. **These things** i.e. these words just uttered, not in ver. 9 only (De Wette), but in ver. 1-10, **have I spoken unto you that my joy** ἡ χαρὰ ἡ ἐμή, not the joy produced by (Calvin), or derived from Me (De Wette); or the joy which you feel on My account (Euthymius) or I on your account (Augustine, Lampe, Hengstenberg); or the joy opened up to you by Me (Tholuck), but the joy I experience in the conscious possession of the Father's love (Godet, Luthardt, Hofmann, Meyer, Westcott), **may be in you** i.e. that the joy you experience may be the same in kind as that I feel, **and that your joy**, the joy which is yours, which you will experience through abiding in My love, **may be full** filled up to the measure of perfection, i.e. "that we both may rejoice in the confidence of mutual love" (Paley).

Ver. 12-17. The relation of the disciples to each other.

12. **This is My commandment**, the commandment which is Mine; the sum of those commandments of Mine, τὰς ἐντολάς μου (ver. 10), already referred to; the commandment that corresponds to My nature and mission (Westcott), **that** ἵνα, in order that,— expressing not merely the contents but also the design of Christ's commanding (cf. vi. 29, 40; xiii. 34; 1 John iii. 11, 23; see Winer, § xliv. 8). **ye love** lit., *may*, or *should love* **one another** (cf. Rom. xiii. 8; Gal. v. 14; vi. 2), **even as I have loved** or *loved* **you** (cf. ver. 9).

13. **Greater love hath no man than this** which I have manifested and am still manifesting towards you, a love which has for its end and aim, **that a man lay** or, *may* or *should lay* **down his life** On τιθέναι τὴν ψυχήν, see x. 11. **for his friends.** This conflicts not with Rom. vi. 6-8, since the φίλοι of the present passage are included among the ἀσεβοι of the latter. "Love is con-

templated here from the side of Him who feels it, so that the objects of it are spoken of as "friends," that is, as persons "loved by Him." In Rom. v. 8 the sacrifice of Christ is regarded from the side of those for whom it was offered, and men are described as being in themselves "sinners" (Westcott).

14. **Ye are My friends, if ye do the things which I command you.** The relation of 'friendship' in which the disciples stood to Christ had its reciprocal obligations, responsibilities, and duties; in particular demanded cheerful and loving obedience to Christ's commandment.

15. **No longer** (as before, xii. 26; xiii. 13 ff.) **do I call you servants** Though Christ ceased to call them, they did not cease to call themselves, servants or *slaves*: cf. Rom. i. 1; Jude 1. **but friends** This contradicts neither Luke xii. 4, in which (earlier) Christ had designated His disciples "friends," nor xv. 20, in which He (afterwards) names them "servants." In the former the expression "my friends" is used in the manner of familiar address; the latter simply recalls a former saying. Or the contrast in οὐκέτι may point to the relative positions of believers under the law before Christ had fully revealed Himself, and under the gospel when Christ's love was perfectly disclosed. **for the servant** or *slave* **knoweth not what his lord doeth.** Not what his Lord intends to do (Grotius, Kuinoel), but what the meaning is of that he sees his lord doing (Meyer, Luthardt, and others); he comprehends not either the inner spirit or the ultimate purpose of his lord's working, because he has not been taken into his lord's confidence and is treated simply as an instrument: *servus tractatur ut organon* (Bengel). **but I have called you friends** or, *but you* (first the eleven, and afterwards believers) *I have called* (I have just now addressed as and designated) *friends.* **for all things** not absolutely (see xvi. 12), but relatively; i.e. all things designed for you (Lücke, Olshausen, Stier), or the whole counsel of salvation (Luthardt), or all things necessary for you to know (Calvin), or all things laid upon Him by the Father to do (Meyer), which the con-

text seems most to favour. **that I heard from My Father** not exclusively in time, and from time to time, as they were requisite to be made known for the salvation of the world (Beyschlag), but also, and rather, in the pre-existent state when He undertook the work of redemption and became man (Meyer. Luthardt). **I have made known unto you.** Spoken proleptically. Christ's revelation of the Father's will was not then complete, though it now is.

16. **Ye did not choose Me, but I chose you** The relationship into which they had been taken did not originate with them but with Him. It was not they who had selected Him as their friend, but He who had selected them as His friends. Christ alludes to their election to the apostleship, here as in vi. 70; xiii. 18. A proof that God's grace precedes man's will. **and appointed you** ἔθηκα, *posui* (Vulg.); not ἐφύτευσα, *planted*, whether as a vine or fruit tree generally (Chrysostom, Theophylact, Bengel, Stier, Olshausen); but either established you in this loving relation (Luthardt) or assigned you this special task (Meyer, Westcott). The idea of endowing with spiritual light and power (Godet) seems to go beyond the exact import of the word. **that ye should go** Perhaps containing an allusion to the execution of their apostleship, in which they should afterwards 'go away' into all the world (Meyer), but probably only pointing to the fact that they, the disciples, were henceforth to maintain an independent activity (De Wette, Lücke, Luthardt, Godet, and others), or that the spiritual life was to be one of continuous movement (Hengstenberg). **and bear fruit** i.e. bring forth the productions of the spiritual life, **and that your fruit should abide** The results they should achieve should not be transient but permanent. "In this lies the promise of the foundation and perpetuity of the church" (Westcott). **that** ἵνα, either subordinate to (Luthardt, Olshausen) or parallel and co-ordinate with (Meyer, Godet) the preceding 'that.' If subordinate, then the clause expresses the result and purpose of their fruit bearing, as in ver. 7: which see; if co-ordinate then, it points to the means by which the fruit should be brought forth. Both thoughts are true; "the

consummation of faith grows out of fruitful obedience; and on the other hand fruitful obedience coincides with the fulfilment of prayer" (Westcott). **whatsoever ye shall ask the Father in My name** (see on xiv. 13) **He may give it you.** In the preceding passage it is Christ who answers the believer's prayer: here it is the Father. This points to the truth: "I and My Father are one" (x. 38). Perhaps the solution lies in xvi. 26. Christ asks the Father for His people, and the Father gives.

17. **These things** above spoken I **command you** The believer is thus under law to Christ: 1 Cor. ix. 21. **that** see above, ver. 12. **ye may love one another.** By some regarded as the commencement of a new section (Luthardt, Westcott), this verse is better taken as rounding off our Lord's instructions to His disciples concerning their relation to one another.

Ver. 18-27. The relation of the disciples to the world.

18. **If the world hateth you** The present tense, μισεῖ, shows this is no mere hypothetical conjecture on the part of Christ, but the statement of a fact which would in due course come to realization. Though as brethren His followers should love one another, in obedience to His command, yet from the world without they would as surely encounter hate. **ye know** or, better, reading γινώσκετε as an imperative, like μνημονεύετε in ver. 20, know ye, for your consolation; **that it hated Me before** it **hated you:** literally, *first of you*, not merely before you, in point of time as one entirely separated from you, *priorem vobis* (Vulgate), but the first and the earliest of that body of which you are the members and I am the head. Here, as throughout these discourses, the Saviour never loses sight of, but keeps in the foreground, the thought of His oneness with His followers, and their oneness with Him. Cf. for the world's hatred of Christ i. 15, and for the consolation derived therefrom 1 Pet. iv. 12, 14. The ground or reason of the world's hatred is next declared.

19. **If ye were of the world** i.e. were the offspring of the world, having in the world the source and spring of your moral natures; (cf. iii. 31; vii. 7; viii. 2, 3), **the world would love its**

own, i.e. its own creature, offspring, production, as a something wearing its likeness and animated by its spirit; **but because ye are not of the world and do not represent the world's principles, as I am not of the world** (cf. viii. 23), **but I chose you out of the world** Christ intends not to distinguish His disciples, from others who have not been chosen, but only to contrast them with the world out of which they have been chosen. The doctrine of a divine predestination to eternal life, though true, is not here alluded to by Christ. **therefore,** or *on this account,* διὰ τοῦτο. This separation from the world is the deepest cause of the world's antagonism to the followers of Christ: cf. 1 Pet. iv. 4. **the world** The fivefold repetition of the term "world" lends a peculiar solemnity to Christ's language. **hateth you** "Here they all agree together— Pilate, Herod, Caiaphas and all devils —against Christ and His people, however otherwise at enmity amongst themselves. Towards each other, apart from Christ, they are such friends as dogs and cats; but in all that concerns Christ, they are quite unanimous" (Luther).

20. **Remember the word that I said unto you** alluding to either Matt. x. 24, or John xiii. 16. The form of the proverb corresponds with that given in the latter; the application of it resembles that made in the former. In the former, as here, Christ uses it to recommend patience; in the latter to enjoin humility. **A servant** or *slave* **is not greater than his lord.** Accordingly a servant need not expect to fare better than his lord. Hence our Lord advises His followers of the treatment they might anticipate at the hands of men when they went forth upon their apostolic mission. **If they persecuted Me** as you know they have done— Christ speaks of his career as finished, and for this reason uses the aorist—**they will also persecute you** who are, and because you are, My servants; **if they kept My word, they will keep yours also.** Best understood as setting forth another item in which their experience should resemble His. While the world as a whole had rejected Him, some spiritually susceptible souls had kept—not maliciously or hostilely observed (Bengel), such a use of τηρεῖν

being non-Johannine, but sincerely received and obeyed, as in viii. 52; xiv. 23; xvii. 6 (Olshausen, Godet, Alford, Westcott), His Word; so they, while meeting in their own persons persecution from the world, would find that their message would obtain a welcome wherever His had. The suggestion that John either uses irony in speaking about the world as keeping Christ's word (Lange, Stier, Lücke, Hengstenberg) or states the two alternative receptions the disciples might expect, leaving them to find out from experience which should be theirs (Meyer, Luthardt, Tholuck), does not appear so suitable.

21. **But all these things will they do unto you** Notwithstanding the favourable reception which their message should here and there obtain, their chief experience would be persecution. The "all these things" are the hostile activities the world's hatred would set in motion against them; and it was well they should clearly know what they had to expect. **for My name's sake** cf. Acts v. 41; ix. 17; 1 Peter iv. 14. In such a thought they would find their highest consolation. It would show they suffered persecution because of their connection with Christ, either because of their resemblance to Christ in character (cf. ver. 19) or on account of their testimony concerning Christ (cf. ver. 27), or both. Yet in such a thought they might read the world's guilt and condemnation, since it would not be they that would suffer persecution so much as Christ in them. And the underlying reason of the world's hatred of Christ even more signally proclaimed their depravity: **because they know not Him that sent Me.** Had they not been incurably alienated from God, they would have recognized and received Christ. But because in their hearts they hated God, they turned away from Him who was God's image. This contradicts not, but reveals the other side of Christ's doctrine. "If ye had known Me, ye would have known My Father also" (viii. 19).

22. **If I had not come** Christ refers to His having appeared before the Jews in the character and capacity of the Messiah—as the ambassador and representative of God who had sent Him.

In this capacity and character He had revealed to them the name and nature of the Father; so that their rejection of Him could not have proceeded from an innocent ignorance of the Father. **and spoken unto them** The allusion is to Christ's teaching throughout His entire ministry. This was the first of the two ways in which Christ had revealed the Father. His words had been such that they ought to have known God who had sent Him : cf. vi. 63 ; xii. 47, 48, 49 ; xiv. 10. **they had not had sin** Not in disbelieving Christ simply (Lücke, Stier, Hengstenberg, Luthardt) but either in being thus ignorant of God (Ebrard, Ewald, Godet), or in hating and rejecting Christ and with Christ His followers (Bengel, Meyer, Alford, Westcott). The meaning cannot be that they would have been entirely blameless, if Christ had not come,—that in that case they would not have been guilty and liable to condemnation, even though they had been ignorant of God or hostilely disposed towards good men. Christ however having revealed to them the Father, their culpability was great. The phrase 'to have sin' is peculiar to John : cf. ix. 41 ; xv. 24 ; xix. 11. **but now they have no excuse for their sin.** πρόφασιν ἔχειν, to have a pretext for anything, occurs only here in the N.T. Unbelief in Christ, ignorance of Christ's Father, and hatred of Christ's Church are absolutely indefensible ; the revelation of the Father given to men in Christ's teaching renders them without excuse, as the revelation of the Supreme Deity written on the page of nature puts even the heathen in the same condition : Rom. i. 20.

23. **He that hateth Me hateth My Father also** As to see Christ was to see the Father (xiv. 9), and to honour Christ was to honour the Father (v. 23), so to hate Christ was to hate the Father. In so speaking Christ disclosed the infinite criminality of the world's rejection of Himself, and the utterly indefensible character of their persecution of His followers. Christ's language implies not only that He and His Father were one (x. 30), but that His teaching had been such as to convince candid minds and sincere hearts of this essential oneness between Him and the Father; hence the rejection of

Him was not merely the same thing as, but the direct result of, a previous rejection of God. Their hatred of Jesus, the manifested Son, showed that they hated the invisible Father.

24. **If I had not done among them the works** The second form of Christ's Messianic activity, viz., His miracles, is here referred to as confirming Israel's guilt ; and is introduced in a manner exactly parallel to that used in speaking of the first form, viz., His words. **which none other did** Christ claims that His miracles were superior to any that had been performed by other heaven-sent prophets ; and this they were not only in respect of number, beneficence, and grandeur, but also in the ease and majesty with which they were performed, as well as in the power and authority He wielded—a power and authority residing in and belonging to Himself: cf. vii. 31 ; ix. 32 ; Matt. ix. 33. That Christ adds no similar comparison between His words and those of other messengers may be accounted for by the fact that "never man spake like this man" (vii. 47). **they had not had sin** Christ frequently alluded to His works as affording sufficient ground for the exercise of faith (v. 36 ; x. 38 ; xiv. 10, 11) ; so that while the absence of those works might have justified unbelief, the presence of them rendered that unbelief without excuse. **but now,** in consequence of My having come, spoken and worked, **have they both seen and hated both Me and My Father.** The object to the verb "seen" is not "the works" (Bengel, Lücke), but "Me" and "My Father" (Meyer, Alford, Westcott, and others).

25. **But** (sc. *this cometh to pass:* cf. i. 8 ; ix. 3 ; xi. 4 ; xiii. 18 ; xiv. 31) **that the word may be fulfilled** The rejection of Christ was not only inexcusable in itself, but it was from the standpoint of God inevitable. In hating Christ the world was unconsciously glorifying God by carrying out His divinely-made and fore-announced programme. **that is written in their law** which they assiduously use and of which they boast, *quam assidue terunt et jactant* (Bengel) : cf. viii. 17. There is no need to discover irony in these words as if Christ designed to suggest that they complied faithfully with

what was written in their law (De
Wette), or even to hint that the law in
which they trusted condemned them
(Westcott). **They hated Me without a
cause** δωρεάν, not to no purpose, but
undeservedly, *immerito* (Vulgate), without pretext. The citation occurs in Ps.
xxxv. 19 and Ps. lxix. 4, and was probably taken from one or other of these
places, though a similar expression
may be found in Ps. cix. 3. All the
three sacred poems depict the sufferings of an ideally righteous man ;
which sufferings were intended to
typify and foreshadow those of Christ.
Ps. lxix. is frequently alluded to in
N. T. Scripture : see John ii. 17 ; Rom.
xv. 3 ; Acts i. 20 ; Rom. xi. 9.

26. **But when the Comforter** the
Paraclete, Advocate, or Helper, **is
come** (see on xiv. 16), **whom I will
send unto you** Cf. xiv. 26, in which
the Father is represented as the sender
of the Spirit. The two passages together imply the essential oneness of
the Father and the Son. **from** παρά,
from the side or presence of, not ἐξ, out of,
as proceeding from, **the Father,** *even* **the
Spirit of truth** (cf. xiv. 17) **which proceedeth from the Father** ὁ παρὰ τοῦ
πατρὸς ἐκπορεύεται. Had this expression
been intended to describe the metaphysical derivation of the Spirit from
the Father (Olshausen, Lücke, Stier,
Godet, and others), it is probable the
preposition ἐκ would have been employed. It is better therefore to un-

derstand it as pointing to the
economical relation of the Spirit to
the Father, to the temporal mission
or historical coming forth from the
Father's presence, rather than to the
ontological relation known in church
doctrine as the eternal procession
(Hengstenberg, Meyer, Luthardt,
Westcott). Cf. the Theological Library : How is the divinity of Jesus
depicted ? pp. 96-98. **He shall bear
witness of Me,** and thus demonstrate
the sinfulness of the world's rejection
of Me. The Spirit's witness is not
borne merely through the disciples
(Matt. x. 19, 20), but was first given
through the miracle of Pentecost, and
is continuously given through the influence of Christ upon the world : cf. 1
John v. 7, 8.

27. **And ye also bear witness** rather
than 'and bear ye also witness' (Hofmann, B. Crusius), since Christ is not
enjoining duties, so much as indicating
that twofold testimony by which His
name shall in future be vindicated—
the witness of the Spirit and the witness of His disciples : cf. Acts v. 32 ;
because ye have been lit., *because* or,
that (Paley), *ye are,* Christ regarding
the relationship as continuous. and unbroken. **with Me** enjoying My fellowship. **from the beginning** viz. of My
Messianic activity. Their fellowship
with Christ began then, but did not
terminate with the close of Christ's
earthly career : cf. 1 John i. 3.

HOMILETICS

VER. 1-3.—THE SIMILITUDE OF THE VINE.
I. **The Vine** :—" I am the true Vine," ver. 1. **1.** *The point of view.* That of
the exaltation. It is the glorified Christ who constitutes the tree of which
believers are the branches. **2.** *The exact sense.* The term 'vine' had been
frequently employed by the Hebrew prophets and poets to designate Israel (Ps.
lxxx. 8 ; Is. v. 2 ; Jer. ii. 21 ; Hos. x. 1). But Israel had not proved a true
vine in the sense of perfectly embodying the divine thought. The spiritual
truths of which the vine and its branches were the emblems had their highest
expression in the interrelations henceforth to subsist between the glorified
Saviour and His people.
II. **The Branches** :—" Every branch in Me," etc., ver. 2, and again, " Ye are
the branches," ver. 5. **1.** *Not exclusively genuine believers.* If " in Me " be held
to signify 'participation in Christ's risen life,' then these unscriptural positions
follow :—(1) that a soul may be graciously renewed and yet bring forth no
fruit, which contradicts both Paul (Rom. viii. 5) and Jesus (x. 27); and (2) that
a soul may be in Christ and yet be cast away, which also opposes Christ's
declaration (x. 28) and the doctrine of the N. T. generally (Rom. viii. 30 ; Phil.

i. 6). **2. But also professed believers.** Christ speaks of all who claim to be in visible fellowship with Himself, and teaches these truths :—(1) that the object for which a branch exists is to bear fruit (Matt. iii. 10 ; Luke xiii. 6-9), (2) that a branch may seem to be in the vine and yet not produce fruit (Matt. xxi. 19), (3) that the fruitless branch thereby shows itself to have no vital connection with the vine (Hos. xiii. 8), and (4) that the fruitless branch will be eventually removed (Matt. xxv. 30). III. **The Husbandman** :—"My Father," ver. 1. 1. *His relation to the vine.* (1) The planter (Jer. ii. 21 ; xi. 17 ; Matt. xxi. 33. (2) The owner (Is. v. 1-7 ; Matt. xxi. 28 ; Luke xiii. 6). (3) The cultivator (ver. 2). 2. *His relation to the branches.* (1) Judicial, towards those which are unproductive—for their removal (Ps. i. 5). (2) Purgative, towards such as are fruitful—for their cleansing.

Lessons. 1. A vital and permanent connection subsists between the Saviour and His people. 2. The visible church may contain a large degree of impurity and imperfection. 3. Nominal professors will eventually be separated from the visible fellowship of the saints. 4. Even in Christ's true followers sin may remain. 5. The strongest assurance of salvation is a large growth of the fruits of righteousness. 6. The chief means of soul purification is the word of Christ. 7. Afflictions are to God's children blessings in disguise.

VER. 4-8. CHRISTIAN FRUIT-BEARING.

I. **Impossible without vital connection with Christ**—"Apart from Me ye can do nothing," ver. 5. The Spirit's fruits can only be produced by those in whom the Spirit dwells. The Spirit dwells in such only as are "in Christ."

II. **Indispensable to continued connection with Christ**—"If a man abide not in Me," and so become unfruitful, "he is cast forth as a branch," ver. 6 : cf. ver. 2.

III. **Requisite as a precondition of successful prayer**—"If ye abide in Me . . . ask whatsoever ye will," etc., ver. 7. The reason is that prayer is the Spirit's voice in the believer's soul (Rom. viii. 16, 26 ; cf. Zech. xii. 10), and fruitfulness a necessary condition of the Spirit's continuance therein.

IV. **Redounds to the glory of Christ's Father**—"Herein is My Father glorified," ver. 8. Since the Father is the husbandman, and believers are the branches, their productivity proclaims His skill (1) in selecting the plant, (2) preparing the soil, (3) pruning the branches, and (4) generally in tending the tree.

V. **Affords the surest evidence of Christian discipleship**—"So shall ye be My disciples," ver. 8. It shows that the individual is (1) following Christ's example, (2) obeying Christ's precepts, and (3) exhibiting Christ's spirit.

Lessons. 1. The entire dependence of the believer on Christ. 2. The utter helplessness of man apart from Christ. 3. The certain destruction of those who apostatize from Christ. 4. The great encouragement a Christian has to abide in Christ. 5. The high responsibility which rests upon the followers of Christ.

VER. 9-11. THE FATHER'S LOVE TO CHRIST, AND CHRIST'S LOVE TO THE BELIEVERS.

I. **Compared.** In respect of 1. *Their dateless beginning.* (1) Before the world was the Father loved Christ—"The Father loved the Son," ver. 9 : cf. xvii. 24. (2) Christ carries His love for His people back to the same source—"As the Father loved Me, I loved you" : cf. Jer. xxxi. 3 ; Prov. viii. 31. 2. *Their illimitable measure.* (1) As existing between infinite beings, the Father's love to Christ could not be less than infinite in fulness, tenderness, sweetness. This love evinced itself by the greatness of its 'giving' (iii. 35), and the universality of its 'showing' (v. 20) to the Son. (2) Christ's love to His people is also unsearchable —it "passeth knowledge" (Eph. iii. 19) ; and like the Father's love to Him, it discovers itself by 'giving' (Rev. ii. 7, 17, 28 ; iii. 21), and by 'showing' (xiv. 21). 3. *Their unchanging continuance.* (1) As the Father's love had no beginning, so likewise has it no end : Matt. iii. 17 ; John viii. 29 ; xvii. 5. (2) Christ's love for His people is also the same, yesterday, to-day and for ever: xiii. 1 ; Rom. viii. 35. 4. *Their indispensable conditions.* (1) On the part of Christ, obedience to the Father's commandments (ver. 10). (2) On the part of Christ's people, obedience to His commandments (ver. 10). 5. *Their blessed effects.* (1) In the case of Christ, joy. (2) In the case of His disciples, also joy (ver 11). II. **Contrasted.** In respect of 1. *Their essential natures.* (1) The Father's love to Christ that of one divine person to another, of a divine Father to a divine Son, who had never departed by a hairsbreadth from His commandments (viii. 29), who had always rejoiced in and reciprocated His affection, and who had ever proved Himself worthy of His Father's delight. (2) The love of Christ to His people that of a divine, human person to those who are His creatures, and not only creatures but sinners, renewed indeed, but still far removed from perfection, and certainly not worthy of such affection as His. 2. *Their realized fulness.* (1) The Father's love was always perfectly experienced by Christ : hence His joy was ever full. (2) Christ's love to His people is not yet completely realized by them : hence their joy is 'becoming' full. Learn 1. The gratitude the believer owes to Christ for His love. 2. The believers' duty to reciprocate Christ's love by keeping His commandments. 3. The desire Christ has for the perfect happiness of His people.

VER. 12-17. THE BELIEVER'S LOVE TO HIS BRETHREN.

I. **The Ground on which it rests**—The commandment of Christ : ver. 12, 17 : cf. xiii. 34. The Christian, though free from the law as a condemning judge (Rom. viii. 2), is not delivered from the law as a commanding king (Jas. ii. 8). Only to him the law is summarily comprehended in two precepts—Love God and love man (Matt. xxii. 37), or even in one, love (Rom. xiii. 8, 9 ; Gal. v. 14 ; Jas. ii. 8).

II. **The Pattern after which it is formed**—The love of Christ to His people : ver. 12. The love of believers to one another should resemble this in freeness and spontaneousness, in tenderness and sympathy, in intensity and endurance (Eph. v. 2 ; 1 John ii. 21 ; iv. 11).

III. **The Motive by which it is inspired**—The friendship of Christ : ver. 14. Christ asks and expects His people to exhibit such love to one another on account of 1. *The love He had manifested towards them*—He had laid down His life for them (ver. 13, 14). 2. *The confidence He had reposed in them*—He had named them and treated them rather as friends than as servants (ver. 15). 3. *The calling He had assigned them*—a call of grace, a call to work, a call to fruit-bearing, a call to permanent results (ver. 16). 4. *The privilege He had conferred upon them*—that of always offering successful prayers (ver. 16).

Lessons. 1. The permanence of moral obligation. 2. The greatness of Christian duty. 3. The encouragement to Christian fidelity.

VER. 18-27. THE HATRED OF THE WORLD.

I. **Its Certainty**—'If the world hateth you,' ver. 18. This was no possible contingency merely, but a positive reality : cf. xvi. 1, 3 ; xvii. 14. What Christ said the Apostles afterwards confirmed (2 Tim. iii. 12 ; 1 John iii. 13).

II. **Its Intensity**—'They will persecute you,' ver. 20. The world's hostility does not confine itself to cherishing angry and malignant feelings, but breaks out into open acts of violence and oppression. Exemplified in the after history of the apostles, most of whom appear to have sealed their testimony with their blood. See on xvi. 1-4 (Homiletics).

III. **Its Reason**—1. *The character of Christ's followers.* 'Ye are not of the world' : if ye were, the world would love you (ver. 19). 2. *The world's hatred* of Christ. 'It hath hated Me before it hated you' (ver. 18). The world discerns in Christ's people His representatives and ambassadors, observes in them the same principles of action as it beheld in Him ; and because of the deep-seated enmity it cherishes against Him it fumes and fulminates against them.

IV. **Its Guiltiness**—1. *It originated not in ignorance* (ver. 22). Had Christ not appeared among them in the character of Messiah, speaking and acting as He did, they would not have been chargeable with sin in cherishing hatred against the Church of God ; but Christ having furnished them with the twofold testimony of His words and works, they were wholly without excuse. 2. *It sprang from antipathy against God* (ver. 23). The world's antagonism to the Church then was the outcome of moral dislike of God. So it is still.

V. Its Consolations—1. *In such hatred they would only be having fellowship with Him.* " If the world hateth you, ye know that it hated Me, before it hated you," ver. 18. 2. *In such hatred they would find a sure proof of their inward separation from the world.* Were they of the world, the world would love its own (ver. 19). 3. *Notwithstanding such hatred they would not be left without encouraging tokens of success* in their mission. As Christ had gathered round them a few who docilely accepted His word, so would they—" If they have kept My word, they will keep yours also," ver. 20. 4. *The world's hatred in their case as in His would be without real pretext* (ver. 22). If they suffered it would be not for their wickedness but for their goodness ; it would be not as evil doers but as Christians (1 Pet. iv. 16). 5. *The world's hatred would not come upon them without the Father's permission.* The world might imagine it was setting the Father's will at defiance ; in reality it would only be carrying out a pre-arranged pro-gramme (ver. 25). As the world by hating and crucifying Christ only revealed its own depravity, advanced the Father's purpose of salvation, and exalted Christ Himself to a throne of glory, so will it by the same policy of persecuting Christ's followers disclose its unchanged wickedness, promote heaven's plans concerning the saints, and further their highest interests. 6. *They would not lack the aids of Christ's Spirit* in meekly bearing the world's hate. The Comforter would bear witness of Him in them and through them to the world (ver. 26). 7. *The world's hate would not prevent them from accomplishing their mission* (ver. 27). They would be co-workers with the Holy Spirit in bearing witness of Him.

Learn 1. The true character of a Christian—separated from the world, com-missioned by the Saviour to the world. 2. The serious criminality of unbelief—the advent of Christ has rendered it without excuse. 3. The complete power lessness of the world to injure the Church or the Christian.

(3) THE DISCOURSE UPON THE WAY TO GETHSEMANE

CHAP. XVI. VER. 1-33

Though not naturally dividing itself into formal sections, the present chapter may be conveniently arranged into the following paragraphs—

1. The relation of the Church to the Synagogue as a part of the un-believing world : ver. 1-4.

2. The mission of the Paraclete : ver. 5-15.

3. The return of Christ to His Church : ver. 16-24.

4. The communion of the Church with the Father : ver. 25-28.

5. The closing conversation : ver. 29-33.

EXPOSITION

Chap. xvi. ver. 1-4. The relation of the Church to the synagogue.

1. **These things,** the statements made in the preceding section, xv. 18-27 (Meyer, Tholuck, Lücke, Heng-stenberg), or the entire contents of the former chapter (Westcott), **have I spoken unto you, that ye should not be made to stumble,** " either at the seeming triumph of the world's power, or at the seeming subjection of Christ's kingdom " (Besser) ; by think-ing either that some strange thing has happened to you, or that that cannot be the true religion which evokes such hostility from the world ; and as a

consequence drifting into unbelief and sin. The metaphor of ' stumbling over an obstacle,' though frequently employed by the Synoptists (Matt. xi. 6 ; xiii. 21 ; xxiv. 10 ; Mark vi. 3 ; ix. 42 ; xiv. 27 ; Luke vii. 23 ; xvii. 2), occurs only twice in this gospel—here and in vi. 61.

2. **They,** the children of this world, of whom in Christ's day, the Scribes and Pharisees, chief priests and rulers of the synagogue, were the representatives, **shall put you out of the synagogues,** lit., *shall make you* (persons) *outside of the synagogue ;* i.e. shall excommunicate you ;— as they did the blind man whom Christ cured (ix. 34), and as they had already resolved to do to any who should confess Christ (ix. 22 ; xii. 42). **Yea** ἀλλ', but, *sed,* (Vulgate), used elliptically, to introduce a gradation of thought—"Not only will they ... *but* —" ; hence equivalent to *immo* (Bengel, Tholuck), or, nay further (Meyer): cf. Acts xix. 2 ; 1 Cor. vi. 6 ; 2 Cor. vii. 11. **the hour cometh** Always in John denoting the moment at which some particular point or part in the divine programme is developed : cf. iv. 23; v. 25; xii. 23; xiii. 1 ; xvi. 32 ; xvii. 1). **that** ἵνα, indicates the purpose for which the hour was coming. **whosoever killeth you** lit., *every one having killed you,* the act of killing being contemplated as accomplished. **shall think** lit., *may think,* the aorist never being employed as a future—may, reflecting on your murder, think (cf. Acts vii. 58 ; xxvi. 9, 10). **that he offereth service unto God.** Not simply does a good work, performs an acceptable deed, but offers a sacrificial service. The phrase λατρείαν προσφέρειν always conveys the idea of presenting a sacrifice, as the highest expression of the O. T. worship : cf. Rom. ix. 4 ; xii. 1 ; Heb. v. 1 ; viii. 3 ; ix. 7. Of the spirit here described the Jewish maxim, *Quisquis effundit sanguinem impii, idem facit, ac si sacrificium offerat,* i.e. whosoever sheds the blood of a wicked person does the same thing as if he offered a sacrifice, may be taken as a fitting explanation. In the estimation of the Jewish adherents of the synagogue, the early Christians were the offscourings of the earth's population (1 Cor. iv. 13). **3. And these things will they do**

This repetition leaves the disciples in no doubt as to the certainty of Christ's prediction. **because they have not known the Father, nor Me.** With pathetic iteration Christ again traces the wickedness of the world as represented in and by the leaders of the synagogue to its true cause, a complete lack of moral sympathy between Him and them (xv. 21). On this occasion He uses a milder term than He had employed in the close of the preceding chapter (xv. 24), but by ' lack of knowledge ' He signifies the same thing. The Jewish leaders had failed to recognize the revelation of the Father given by Christ. In this they had not been guiltless, though Christ calls attention merely to the fact of their unbelief.

4. **But these things have I spoken unto you** The force of " but " has been explained as equivalent to "Although it is not otherwise to be expected" (Lücke, De Wette), "But so little would I terrify you hereby, that I have only said these things to you" (Tholuck, Lange), "But, to go no further into details " (Meyer, Westcott). Perhaps, however, it should be understood as introducing a contrast to the preceding clause (Hengstenberg), as thus : "These things will they do... but, though such be the future awaiting you, I have spoken these things unto you" with a special eye towards that future, viz., to prepare you beforehand for its coming. **that when their hour,** i.e. the hour of these excommunications and murders, the hour appointed for their accomplishment, **is come,** and ye are exposed to their violence, **ye may remember them,** i.e. these persecutions or the words I have now uttered, **how that I told you,** of them, saying, that such persecutions would overtake you, and may find consolation in the thought that they were all foreseen. **And these things I said not unto you from the beginning** To harmonize this statement with the earlier announcements of the Synoptists (Matt. v. 10 ; x. 16 ; xxiv. 9 ; Luke vi. 22), it has been supposed Christ meant (1) that He had never before spoken to His disciples of the Holy Spirit as their comforter in affliction (Augustine); or (2) that He had previously spoken *minus aperte et*

parcius, less openly and more sparingly than now (Bengel), had not urged them beyond their strength, *ultra vires* (Calvin), whereas now He explicitly discovers the persecutions awaiting them because they were soon to be strengthened by the Spirit (Tholuck) —*Jam contra odium istud per promissionem Spiriti Sancti munitis apertius ea de re loquitur* (Bengel); or (3) that He now makes the impending persecutions the more exclusive subject of His conversation (Hofmann, Luthardt); or (4) that He had never before spoken so affectingly of these coming sorrows as He now does (Hengstenberg). Perhaps, however, it is better (5) to admit the literal accuracy of John's assertion and to say that the earlier recorded utterances have been brought together out of later discourses, according to a well-known practice specially exemplified by Matthew, of grouping Christ's sayings and doings rather according to subject than chronology (Godet, Olshausen, Meyer); unless it be maintained that Christ intended (6) that whereas formerly He had occasionally and slightly referred to their future sufferings He had never before connected these as He now does with their condition, His departure, with their source, the world's hatred, or with their consolation, the coming of the Paraclete (Westcott, Milligan and Moulton). **because I was with you.** These words give the reason for Christ's earlier reticence upon the subject of the sufferings of His disciples. So long as Christ was with His disciples, the world's hatred would concentrate itself upon Him; when He departed it would descend upon them. Hence it was not necessary for Him to speak earlier than He had done, though the near approach of His departure rendered it indispensable that He should no longer remain silent.

Ver. 5-15. The mission of the Paraclete.

5. **But now I go unto Him that sent Me,** i.e. the Father, whose mission to the world I have accomplished and whose message to you I have delivered; **and none of you asketh Me, Whither goest Thou?** Either Christ meant that on former occasions (xiii. 36, or xiv. 5) they had not asked out of a regard to His glory (Westcott), but simply with a view to their own consolation (Godet), or that they had inquired not into the nature of His departure but merely concerning the place and the way (Luther, Lücke, Alford); or, He signified that then they had not received so full an answer to their interrogations as might have been returned, and that, His departure being so obviously at hand, they should have pressed Him to tell more about that heavenly life into which He was on the eve of withdrawing (Bengel, Meyer, and others). There is no need to set a period after 'Him that sent Me' (Kuinoel, Olshausen), as if Christ had momentarily paused in expectation of some inquiry. **But because I have spoken these things unto you,** concerning My removal and your tribulation, **sorrow hath filled your heart** so that, being absorbed in your own grief, you have not been able to interest yourselves in My future (cf. xiv. 28), or question Me about the unseen realm into which I am departing.

7. **Nevertheless,** i.e. notwithstanding your apprehensions that My going will entail upon you loss, I who am the Truth as well as the Way and the Life (xiv. 6), **tell you the truth** concerning this matter: **It is expedient for you,** it will turn out for your advantage (cf. xi. 50; in which, though for a different reason Caiaphas declared that Christ's death would benefit the nation), **that I go away,** or remove My bodily presence from you; **for if I go not away,** but continue on the earth, either deferring My departure till the end of time, or dying and remaining on the earth after My resurrection, **the Comforter** (see on xiv. 16) **will not come unto you**—the Paraclete's coming, like Christ's going, being personal and voluntary; **but, if I go, I will send Him unto you.** The pronouns "I" and "Him" applied in these verses to Christ and the Spirit show that the personality of the one is distinct from the personality of the other. That Christ speaks of sending the Spirit, does not contradict the previous statements that the Spirit is the Father's gift (xiv. 16), and that the Father sends Him in Christ's name (xiv. 26); since the Father hath committed all things—the dispensation of the Spirit not excepted—into the hands

of the Son (xiii. 3). The verbs employed by Christ in this verse and verse 5 to describe His departure are worthy of remark :—(1) ὑπάγω, to withdraw from a place ; (2) ἀπέρχομαι, to set out from a particular point; (3) πορεύομαι, to move towards a goal.

8. And He, when He is come lit., *and having come* (sc. into your hearts), *He* viz. that Paraclete, whom I will send, **will convict,** using you as His instruments, through the testimony He shall give concerning Me (xv. 26). The verb ἐλέγχω, as used in the N. T. and more particularly in John, signifies to set forth in clear and convincing light by means of searching examination and judicial proof the true character of any thing or person (iii. 20 ; viii. 9, 46 ; cf. 1 Cor. xiv. 24 ; Eph. v. 13 ; Jas. ii. 9). "It involves the conceptions of authoritative examination, of unquestionable proof, of decisive judgment, of punitive power" (Westcott). It implies the furnishing to him who is the subject of it of such a demonstration as may result either in conviction and conversion or in rejection and condemnation (Calvin, Lampe, Meyer, Luthardt, Tholuck and others). "In ἐλέγχειν is always implied the refutation, the overcoming of an error, a wrong,—by the truth and the right. And when by means of the ἔλεγχος, the truth detects the error, and the right the wrong, so that a man becomes conscious of them—then arises the feeling of guilt which is ever painful" (Alford). "Ἐλέγχειν ist nie bloss lehren, sondern immer das polemische Belehren, Ueberführen" (Lücke). **the world** Not the already condemned and lost world, but the unbelieving and sinful world, as such, in which are yet many who shall afterwards become believers. **in respect of sin, and of righteousness, and of judgment.** The three subjects concerning which the Spirit will carry on His work of convicting. In each case the article is wanting to show that the subject is intended to be taken in its widest and most general conception. The absence of any genitive of the person shows that the supplement was designed to be made from the clauses which follow (Lücke). Thus that of which the Spirit convicts is the sin of the world, the righteousness of

Christ, the judgment of the prince of this world.

9. Of sin, not of this or that particular transgression, but of sin in general, of being in a sinful condition. **because they believe not on Me.** Not "*In that* they believe not on Me," as if the point of which the world required to be convicted was that unbelief was a sin (Bengel, Meyer, Hengstenberg, Luthardt and others), but "*because* they believe not on Me," in the sense that unbelief in Christ was the crowning evidence that the world was sinful (Calvin, Lücke, Godet). The world denied the fact and misunderstood the nature of its own sinful condition. When the Spirit came He would carry on a legal process against the world which would issue in convicting it of both. The proof of both would be found in the fact of its rejection of Christ.

10. Of righteousness As the "sin" pertained to the persons who "believed not," it is most natural to understand the "righteousness" as belonging to the subject of "go," i.e. to Christ (Lücke, Godet, Luthardt, Meyer, etc.). The world believed itself to be righteous and Christ to be sinful or unrighteous. As the Spirit would reverse the first judgment, so would He disprove the second by convincing the world that Christ was possessed of that very righteousness which they denied Him. The explanation which regards δικαιοσύνη as the righteousness Christ has provided for the believer or the believer finds in Him (Augustine, Luther, Calvin, Hengstenberg, and others), though naturally following from the truth it expresses, is nevertheless not that truth itself. That truth is that righteousness would be shown to have had both an ideal and an actual existence in the person of Christ, whom the world had condemned as sinful. **because** not in so far as (Meyer), but by the fact that (Godet, Luthardt), **I go to the Father, and ye behold Me no more.** The language conveys the thought of an abiding residence beside the Father. This—His resurrection from the dead with His ascension to Heaven and His permanent acceptance by the Father—would constitute the proof to which the Holy Spirit would point, that there was a ιighteousness for men before God. It would show that Christ was not a ἁμαρτώλος, as men supposed, but ὁ δίκαιος—not a sinner but the Righteous One. Then in Christ men would see what righteousness signified, as to both its inward moral character and its outward legal results—would see that it meant sinless perfection and complete enjoyment of divine favour. They would discern that only in vital union with Christ could such righteousness be enjoyed by themselves.

11. Of judgment i.e. following the analogy of the preceding clauses, of the judgment that belongs to sin or to the sinful world (Stier), though not as inflicted on the world, which may yet be saved through the righteousness of Christ, but as exemplified in that which was inflicted upon the world's head (Luthardt, Meyer, Godet). because This again introduces the proof that there is for sin a judgment, and shows what sort of a judgment it is. the prince of this world (see on xiv. 30) is judged. The perfect tense shows that for Satan judgment is already an accomplished fact. From this flows the inference that all who adhere to him will eventually share in his doom, as all who by faith are united to Christ will be made partakers of His righteousness.

12. I have yet many things to say unto you, not concerning future events merely, but concerning that body of truth which Christ had communicated to them (xv. 15); not new truth (Meyer, Godet), but further developments of such doctrines as had already, in principle and essence, been imparted (Luther, De Wette, Lücke, Brückner, Westcott, and others); but ye cannot bear them, or carry them as a load (βαστάζειν : see on x. 31 ; xii. 6 ; xx. 15), owing to the immaturity of your spiritual strength, now ἄρτι at the present moment (as in xiii. 33), though afterwards (subsequent to My resurrection) ye will be able to sustain their pressure. "The entire, full truth is a heavy burden for him who is not yet ripe and strong enough for it" (Luthardt).

13. Howbeit when He, that one (ἐκεῖνος) just spoken of (ver. 7, 8), the Spirit of truth (see on xiv. 17), is come, He shall guide you into all the truth, εἰς

πᾶσαν τὴν ἀλήθειαν (T. R.), better εἰς τήν ἀλήθειαν πᾶσαν (A B Y etc., Lachmann, Meyer, Westcott and Hort); the reading ἐν τῇ ἀληθείᾳ πάσῃ (ℵ D L, Tischendorf) having probably originated from the LXX.'s translation of Ps. lxxxvi. 10, ὁδήγησόν με ἐν τῇ ὁδῷ σου ; for He shall not speak from Himself (see on v. 19 ; and cf. xii. 49); but what things soever lit., *as many things as* He shall hear from the Father, ver. 15 (Lücke, Brückner, Meyer, and others); from the Son, ver. 14 (Olshausen, B. Crusius); probably from both (Luthardt, Godet, Westcott), *these* shall He speak (cf. iii. 32, of Christ), and He shall declare unto you, He shall show unto you (A. V.), He will bring you the tidings of (Paley) the things that are to come, i.e. the future development of the kingdom of God. The promise includes the gift of prophetic discernment, but only so far as it relates to the history of the Church. If xiv. 26 accounts for the Gospels, the present verse explains the production of the Epistles and the Apocalypse. *Maxime huc spectat apocalypsis, scripta per Johannem* (Bengel).

14. He, that divine person (ἐκεῖνος) of whose advent I am speaking, shall glorify Me, as I have glorified the Father (xvii. 4), will fully manifest My name as I have manifested that of the Father (xvii. 6); for He shall take of mine, and shall declare *it* unto you, or bring it as a message to you (Paley).

15. All things whatsoever the Father hath are mine (cf. xiii. 3 ; Col. ii. 3, 9): therefore said I, that he taketh λαμβάνει (B D E G L M etc., Lachmann, Griesbach, Tischendorf, Westcott and Hort), a present for a future, rather than λήψεται (A K Π etc., T. R.) will take of mine, and shall declare *it* unto you. See above.

Ver. 16-24. Christ's return to His Church.

16. A little while, and ye behold Me no more, corporeally ; and again a little while, and ye shall see Me, spiritually : see on xiv. 19.

17. *Some* of His disciples (cf. vii. 40) therefore, because of failing to grasp the true sense of His words, said one to another, doubtless in a whisper, What is this that He saith unto us, A

little while, and ye behold Me not; and again a little while, and ye shall see Me; and, because, ὅτι, stating the reason why they should see Him (Luthardt, Godet, Westcott); better than 'that' introducing the citation (Paley), **I go to the Father?** See on ver. 10.

18. **They said therefore,** or, *kept on saying,* **What is this that He saith, A little while?** lit., *What is this which He speaks of—the little while?* **We know not what He saith.** B omits the last words, 'What He saith.'

19. **Jesus perceived,** perhaps from their anxious whisperings, though he knew what was in man (see ii. 25), that **they were desirous**—'intended' (א,— **to ask Him** what was the purport of His words; **and He said unto them,** affording one more proof of His superior knowledge, **Do ye inquire among yourselves**—μετ' ἀλλήλων, to be distinguished from πρὸς ἀλλήλους (ver. 17)—**concerning this, that,** or, *because,* **I said, A little while, and ye behold Me not; and again a little while, and ye shall see Me?**

20. **Verily, verily, I say unto you** (see on i. 51) **that ye shall weep and lament,** or, preserving the order of the original, *that weep and lament shall ye,* as those mourning for the dead, on account of My departure—a prediction which was literally fulfilled (see xx. 11; Mark xvi. 10; Luke xxiii. 27); **but the world shall rejoice** "as having been freed from one who was a dangerous innovator as well as a condemner of its ways" (Westcott): **ye shall be sorrowful, but your sorrow shall be turned into joy** when you once more behold Me: cf. Ps. xvi. 9-11; Is. li. 11; 1 Pet. i. 6.

21. **A woman,** lit. *the woman* (of the family), i.e. the wife (Paley), or, *the woman as such* and not any particular woman (Westcott) **when she is in travail,** or, *when she beareth,* **hath sorrow** (cf. Gen. iii. 16), **because her hour of** distress and danger **is come; but when she is delivered of,** or, *has given birth to,* **the child, she remembereth no more the** anguish of parturition, for, or *on account of,* **the joy that a man,** not a man as distinguished from a woman, but one who is a man (ὁ ἄνθρωπος : א), a being endowed with the attributes of a man, a human being **is born into the world**· cf. xviii. 37, in which the ideas

here combined are resolved into separate expressions.

22. **And ye therefore now have sorrow:** the pronoun 'ye' making it evident that the parable was designed by Christ to find its application *not in Himself,* as if in His death were intended to be seen the painful birth act of humanity (Olshausen, Stier, Westcott, Milligan and Moulton), or, in His resurrection, the birth of the church (Ebrard), or, in His passage through death to life, the birth hour of inward fellowship for the disciples (Brückner); *but in His disciples,* yet not as if these were meant to be regarded as in some sense occupying the position of a mother, whose office it was "to realize the Christ of the resurrection and present Him to the world" (Westcott), but merely as experiencing a transition from sorrow to joy like that of the travailing woman (Luthardt, Meyer, Hengstenberg, and others); but **I will see you again,** not at the parousia (Paley), or after the resurrection only (Kuinoel), but first at the resurrection and afterwards at the pentecostal return—Christ saying, 'I will see you,' not to express any radically different idea from that contained in, 'ye shall see Me' (ver. 17), but solely to bring out the other side of that loving intercourse which would begin with His resurrection; **and your heart,** which is now troubled (xiv. 1), **shall rejoice** (cf. Is. lxvi. 14), **and your joy no one taketh away from you.** The present tense αἴρει is employed rather than ἀρεῖ, will take (B, Westcott, Paley), either because Christ in speaking transports Himself into the standpoint of the future (Godet), or desires to represent the certainty (Meyer), or permanence (Luthardt) of that joy which He depicts.

23. **And in that day** of your seeing Me (ver. 17) and of My seeing you (ver. 22), not any particular day, but the entire period commencing with His spiritual return at Pentecost (Meyer, Luthardt, Godet, Westcott, and others), rather than with their inward reception of Him (De Wette, Lange, Ebrard, Brückner): cf. xiv. 20, **ye shall ask,** not 'beg,' 'pray,' 'entreat' (Chrysostom, Grotius, Weiss), **Me nothing,** or, *Me ye shall ask no question,* as you have just been proposing to do (ver. 19).

Either that would then be unnecessary (ver. 30), because of the higher spiritual illumination they would enjoy (ver. 13), or their questions would then be addressed not to Him, but to the Father through Him (xiv. 13). **Verily, verily, I say unto you,** as usual introducing a new thought ; the thought, viz., of that which would enable them to dispense with such questioning of Himself as hitherto they had practised (xiii. 36 ; xiv. 5, 8, 22). **If ye shall ask anything of the Father** (see on xiv. 13) **He will give it you in My name**—not in My stead (Weiss), but in virtue of My name, as the medium and motive (see on xiv. 26). The reading which places 'in My name' after 'Father' (T. R.), though not objectionable in sense and seemingly the more natural (Godet), probably arose out of this, that Christ had already spoken of 'asking in His name' (xiv. 13), and recurs to it again in the ensuing verse.

24. **Hitherto have ye asked nothing in My name**—for the reason that the revelation of Christ's name was not yet complete (Hofmann, Luthardt, Westcott), rather than because they lacked the right desire (B. Crusius), or the necessary faith and union with Himself (Lücke, Godet), or the requisite illumination (Meyer), or because they were not yet purged from their old Messianic hopes (Lange) : **ask and ye shall receive** (xiv. 13, 14 ; xv. 7 ; cf. Matt. vii. 7), **that your joy may be fulfilled.** See on xv. 11.

Ver. 25-27. The church's communion with the Father.

25. **These things**—not exclusively the thoughts immediately preceding (Meyer, Luthardt, Brückner), but all that Christ had uttered at the table (Godet, Lange, Tholuck, Westcott)— **have I spoken unto you in proverbs,** parables, or short sayings (see on x. 6). Of these He had that night offered several examples ; the vine (xv. 1), the travailing woman (xvi. 21), His return (xiv. 19), and their seeing one another again (xiv. 19 ; xvi. 22). **The hour cometh** (see on iv. 23), from the day of Pentecost onward, **when I shall no more speak unto you in proverbs, but shall tell you,** or *report to you* (ἀπαγγελῶ) i.e. send a message to you from heaven, speaking through the Holy Spirit, **plainly,** boldly, openly,

without reserve or concealment. (see on vii. 13 ; xi. 14), **of the Father,** whom it is My office to declare : cf. i. 18.

26, 27. **In that day ye shall ask in My name,** which will then be fully made known ; **and I say not unto you that I will pray** or *make request of* **the Father for you,**—meaning not that it did not require saying that He would intercede for them (Grotius, Hengstenberg, Rosenmüller, Kuinoel), but that such intercession would not be necessary (Meyer, Godet, Luthardt, Brückner); and contradicting neither xiv. 16, which speaks of Christ's praying for the Spirit here viewed as come, nor with 1 John ii. 1, which alludes to Christ's intercession for believers when they sin ; **for the Father Himself loveth** with the love which He bestows on Me, the Son (v. 20), **you,** who are also His sons (Rom. viii. 15), **because ye have loved Me** (see on xiv. 21, 23) **and have believed** (see on vi. 69) **that I came forth from the Father :** παρὰ τοῦ πατρὸς (א° B C* D L X etc., Westcott and Hort), i.e. *from beside* the Father : cf. xv. 26 : rather than παρὰ τοῦ θεοῦ (א* Λ etc., Tischendorf).

28. **I came out from the Father,** ἐκ τοῦ πατρὸς (B C* L X etc., Tischendorf), i.e. *out from* the Father as the source of My being (cf. viii. 42), an emphatic assertion of His pre-existence ; **and am,** or have, **come into the world**—an equally clear declaration of His incarnation ; **again I leave the world**—an impressive announcement of His death ; **and go unto the Father**—a solemn intimation of His impending exaltation.

Ver. 29-33. The closing conversation.

29. **His disciples say, Lo !**—giving expression to their astonishment—**now** (and not merely in the future) **speakest thou plainly, and speakest no proverb,** or *parable.* Christ's utterance in ver. 28 seemed to them so clear that they fancied the fulfilment of Christ's promise (ver. 25) was already begun.

30. **Now know we that thou knowest all things** They had inferred this from His reading of their thoughts (ver. 19) ; cf. the case of Nathanael i. 49. **and needest not that any man should ask thee.** On χρείαν...ἵνα see ii. 25. **By this,** lit., *in this,* herein (Paley); cf. 1 John ii. 3, 5 ; iii. 16, 19, 24 ; iv. 9, 10, 13, 17 ; v. 2 ; rather than *on account*

of this, propter hoc (Meyer, Brückner). "The proof is rather vital than instrumental" (Westcott). Supported by thé inward conviction of Christ's omniscience, to which they had just attained, they could say : **we believe** not because (Lange), but **that thou camest forth from God.** The use of ἀπό instead of ἐκ has been thought to show that the disciples had scarcely got beyond the position of Nicodemus (iii. 2), who recognized in Christ only the bearer of a divine mission (Westcott, Milligan and Moulton), but this seems irreconcileable with Christ's statement in ver. 27 (Meyer), and perhaps the two ideas of divine mission and divine origin should be viewed as combined in the use of ἀπό and ἐξῆλθες (Godet).

31, 32. Jesus answered them, Do ye now believe? questioning not the reality, but the permanence of their faith (Calvin, Kuinoel, Olshausen, De Wette, Brückner, Ewald, and others) ; or, *Ye believe now,* the contrast in *now* being with their subsequent behaviour (Meyer, Luthardt) ; or *now at last ye believe,* though before ye were not fully convinced, the antithesis lying between their present and their former faith (Godet, Paley). **Behold, the hour cometh, yea is come**—instead of 'and now is' (iv. 23 ; v. 25), perhaps because designed to express the idea of 'the fulfilment of condition rather than of the beginning of a period' (Westcott). **that ye shall be scattered,** lit., *that ye may be scattered,* or, for you to be scattered,—this being the force of ἵνα (see on ver. 2, and compare xii. 23)—as the flock is scattered by the wolf (x.

13). According to the Synoptists (Matt. xxvi. 31 ; Mark xiv. 27) this saying was derived directly from Zech. xiii. 7 : the Synoptists also record its fulfilment (Matt. xxvi. 56 ; Mark xiv. 50). **every man to his own** τὰ ἴδια, his own things, his own house (xix. 27), or, better, his own pursuits (Luke xviii. 28). **and shall leave Me alone,** lit., *and that ye may leave Me a'one,* or, and (for you) to leave Me alone in the hands of My enemies (xviii. 8) ; **and yet I am not alone, because the Father is with Me :** see on viii. 29. The momentary feeling of forsakenness which the Father which Christ experienced on the cross (Matt. xxvii. 46) must be explained in harmony with this.

33. These things, all the foregoing utterances at the table, after leaving the room and on the way, **have I spoken unto you,** My believing followers, that **in Me,** the sphere of the inner life, i.e. in living and loving fellowship with Me **ye may have peace** (see on xiv. 27). The formula here employed 'These things,' etc., occurs five times in the farewell discourses (xiv. 25 ; xv. 11 ; xvi. 1, 25, 33). **In the world,** the sphere of the outer life, i.e. in your intercourse with the unbelieving, **ye have tribulation** (see on xv. 18 ; xvi. 21) : **but be of good cheer** (cf. Matt. ix. 2 ; xiv. 27 ; Mark x. 49) ; **I**—rendered more emphatic by the absence of the pronoun in the preceding clause—**I,** in My own person, **have overcome the world :** cf. xiv. 30. Christ speaks by anticipation the language of a conqueror. The Christian conquers through faith in Him (1 John v. 4).

HOMILETICS

VER. 1-4. CHRIST'S FLOCK AMONG WOLVES ; OR TRIBULATION IMPENDING.
I. **The Tribulation predicted:**—'These things have I spoken unto you,' ver. 1; 'these things will they do,' ver. 2 ; 'these things I said not unto you from the beginning,' ver. 4. 1. *The communication.* Christ leaves His disciples in no doubt as to the sorrowful career upon which they were soon to enter. In His sermon on the Mount (Matt. v. 11), in His instructions to the Twelve (Matt. x. 17), in His great eschatological discourse (Matt. xxiv. 9), He had already advertised them of the approach of tribulation, hatred and death. These, however, were isolated statements of fact, and gave no proper indication of the real cause of the world's hostility against the church, of the exact time when it should break forth, of the form it should assume, or of the support by which it should be met. Now He expressly makes these the theme of His conversation. 2. *The reason.* That which constrained Him to do so was the circumstance that the

tribulation was at hand, since He was on the eve of departure. So long as He had been with His disciples the world's hostility had concentrated itself upon Him ; when He should leave, it would fall on them. In case therefore they should think themselves exceptionally dealt with when the storm burst upon their heads, or begin to question whether that could be the true religion which involved its adherents in such sufferings, or whether He could be the Son of God who was unable to defend His followers against the world's power, Christ deemed it indispensable that they should be acquainted beforehand with the evil times that lay before them.

II. **The Tribulation described :**—'They shall put you out of the synagogues, etc.,' ver. 2. 1. *Excommunication.* In the Hebrew Church synagogues were what congregations are in the Christian Church. To be excluded from the synagogue was to be cut off from the congregation of the Lord, to be deprived of all participation in the hope of Israel, to be denuded of all rights in the kingdom of Messiah, to be adjudged to misery in the future life. As yet the disciples had not been separated from the synagogues. After Christ's departure their continuance therein would be impossible. The deepening hostility of the corrupt synagogue against the rising church of the N. T. would inevitably lead to a separation between the two. Moreover, this separation would most likely be effected by violence on the part of the synagogue. This began to be experienced by the disciples in the days of Paul (Acts xix. 9). 2. *Murder.* In so far as Christ's language implied that the disciples would seal their testimony with their blood, it was in due course fulfilled—at least if ecclesiastical tradition may be relied on. "Matthew suffered martyrdom (by the sword) in Ethiopia. Mark died at Alexandria after being dragged through the streets of that city. Luke was hanged on an olive tree in Greece. Peter was crucified at Rome with his head downward. James was beheaded at Jerusalem. James the Less was thrown from a pinacle of the temple, and beaten to death below. Philip was hanged against a pillar in Phrygia. Bartholomew was flayed alive. Andrew was bound to a cross, whence he preached to his persecutors till he died. Thomas was run through the body at Coromandel in India. Jude was shot to death with arrows. Matthias was first stoned and then beheaded. Barnabas was stoned to death by Jews at Salonica. Paul 'in deaths oft' was beheaded at Rome by Nero" (Angus's Bible Handbook, p. 91). But Christ's words contained the further thought that not only would the world aim at the destruction of His disciples,—the very synagogue out of which they should be cast, would add to its spiritual decisions temporal inflictions, would regard the assassination and martyrdom of His followers as the highest form of sacrificial service they could offer to God. It was the first beginnings of religious persecution to which He pointed them. What a pity His own followers so soon learnt the fatal lesson !

III. **The Tribulation explained :**—'These things will they do, etc.' ver. 3. 1. *Traced to its cause.* This was ignorance. It is strange how differently Christ and man may view the same action. The Jews imagined they above all men were acquainted with the Father and knew better than all the world besides what kind of service to present upon His altar. That was not the judgment of Christ. 2. *Condemned in its character.* Though Christ ascribed their behaviour to ignorance, He does not say that for this they were not responsible. If they did not know the Father or Him, they might have known (xv. 22). 3. *Commiserated in its actors.* One cannot help thinking Christ designed His words to awaken pity in the breasts of His persecuted followers, like that afterwards found in His own, when, hanging on the cross, He prayed for His murderers—" Father, forgive them, for they know not what they do" (Luke xxiii. 34).

IV. **The Tribulation mitigated :**—' These things have I spoken unto you, etc.' ver. 4. The impending tribulation was 1. *Foreknown.* To be forewarned is to be forearmed ; and this advantage at least Christ had given His disciples. 2. *Controlled.* Like all other events in time, these approaching calamities were under the direction of Christ's own omnipotent and gracious hand—they had

their appointed hour when they should fall and bear sway. 3. *Shortened.*
The period during which they were to rage was not to be of long duration
—not a term of years like that allotted to disobedient Israel in Babylon (Jer. xxv.
11), or even of days like that defined for the Two Witnesses (Rev. xi. 3), but an
hour, a brief space of sixty minutes. It is at least suggestive of the thought
that the saints' sufferings on earth shall be transient.

Learn 1. Even the most advanced of Christ's followers are in danger of
stumbling. 2. They who claim to be the best of people often turn out the worst.
3. A soul may become so debased and blind as to lose all sense of moral distinctions. 4. There is no depth of depravity to which one may not sink who rejects
the revelation of God in Christ. 5. Christ watches with a loving eye over the
pathway of His followers on earth.

Ver. 7. The Expediency of Christ's Departure.
I. **His Presence nearer.** Had Christ continued on the earth and in the flesh,
His presence would have been confined to one particular locality at a time :
having gone to the skies, He is removed beyond the boundaries of time and
sense, so that at one and the same moment He can fill all things with His fulness
(Eph. i. 23 ; iv. 10).

II. **His Godhead clearer.** When Christ tabernacled here below, men found it
difficult to believe that He was ' God manifest in the flesh.' Had He remained
on the earth as before, after rising from the dead, it is doubtful if men would
not sooner or later have relapsed into the old condition of scepticism—as the
ages rolled on questioning whether Christ had ever died at all and risen as He
said, and in any case finding it hard to credit that one in human likeness was
indeed ' The Son of God.' But as the truth of Christ's divinity was for Christ's
contemporaries established beyond controversy by the firmly established fact of
His resurrection (Rom. i. 4), so for all subsequent generations was it placed in
the clearest light by His exaltation to the right hand of the Majesty on high
(viii. 28 ; Phil. ii. 9 ; 1 Pet. i. 21).

III. **His Salvation surer.** Had Christ remained upon the earth after having
finished the work His Father had given Him to do, there would always have
lingered about men's minds a suspicion either that the work was in some respects
incomplete, or that Christ, the worker, had not been accepted by the Father ;
and that, as a consequence, the grounds on which the hopes of their salvation
rested were insecure. But Christ, having passed through the heavens, there to
appear in the presence of God for us, the evidence is perfect that His redemption
is complete and His salvation sure (Heb. x. 12-14).

IV. **His Church richer.** Had Christ not departed from the world, His church
would still have been rich in the possession of Him who was ' The Father's
image,' as well as the Way, the Truth, and the Life ; but His departure, while
not robbing the church of His real presence (see above), has enriched her, in
addition, with the presence and indwelling of the Spirit, who is the Father's and
the Son's highest gift to believing men (xx. 22 ; Acts ii. 38 ; 1 Cor. iii. 16).

V. **His Heaven dearer.** Had Christ lingered among men after rising from
the dead, the Father's house might have none the less been a certainty ; but it
would have wanted its chief attraction. "There is nothing but perfect garden-
flowers in heaven, and the best plenishing that is there is Christ." . . . "He
graceth heaven and all His Father's house with His presence. He is a rose that
beautifieth all the upper garden of God" (Rutherford's Letters, p. 106). "I
would be in heaven, suppose I had not another errand but to see that dainty
golden ark, and God inhabiting a body such as we sinners have, that I might
adore Him for evermore" (ibid. p. 320).

> "His presence fills each heart with joy,
>   Tunes every mouth to sing ;
> By day, by night, the sacred courts
>   With glad hosannas ring." (Watts).

Ver. 8-15. The Functions of the Spirit.
I. **Towards the World.** Conviction. 1. *In respect of Sin :* ver. 9. (1) The
charge. That the world was not merely guilty of particular acts of trans-

gression, but inherently and essentially sinful. This the world did not believe, but, on the contrary, imagined itself to be righteous and holy (Rev. iii. 17). Nor had Christ succeeded in awakening either the mind, heart, or conscience of the world to a just perception of the essential character of sin, or even of the fact that itself was sinful. But when the Spirit came He would deal so effectively that all that would be remedied. The sin which adhered to the world, the fact of it, the wickedness of it, the guilt of it, would be set in clear light before the mind, pressed home upon the heart, and thrust in upon the conscience, with such power that the world would be constrained to recognize and admit the truth of Christ's allegation, that it was a sinful world. (2) The proof. The Spirit would convince the world that no further evidence was needed in support of the indictment brought against it than the fact that it had not believed on Christ. Had it been a pure and holy world, it would at once have recognizèd and accepted Him who was the Father's image and the sinless One : that it declined to welcome and believe in Him—much more, that it despised and rejected Him, was irrefragable witness of its radical depravity. 2. *In respect of righteousness:* ver. 10. (1) The assertion. If the world was unrighteous, as above proved, then the question rose, whether righteousness such as God's law demanded could anywhere be found or existed at all. To this the world answered ' No ! if we are not righteous, then no one is,—nay, righteousness itself is not.' But Christ replied ' Yes ! righteousness does exist, and righteousness may be found as well as seen in Me, for I am the righteous One.' Of this, however, Christ had failed to convince the world, which, so far from regarding Christ as the righteous One, was on the eve of crucifying Him as the worst of malefactors. But this, too, the Spirit when He came would rectify. He would so operate upon the understandings and consciences of men as to convince them both that righteousness existed, and that righteousness was provided for them in Christ. (2) The demonstration. That to which the Spirit would appeal would be the fact of Christ's ascension. He would assist the world to perceive that nothing could be more self-evident than that, if Christ was and is at the right hand of the Majesty on high, He must have been personally righteous (Ps. xv. 1, 2 ; Hab. i. 13 ; Rev. xxi. 27),—and being personally righteous, must have been and must still be the Son of God (Rom. i. 4),—and being the Son of God must also, as man's representative, be possessed of a righteousness available for man (Is. xlv. 24 ; Jer. xxiii. 6 ; Rom. i. 22 ; 1 Cor. i. 30),—and having such a righteousness must be able to impart it to all who by faith are united to His glorified person (2 Cor. v. 21 ; Phil. iii. 9). 3. *In respect of judgment:* ver. 11. (1) The allegation. That the world as sinful and unrighteous was also lying under condemnation Christ had declared (iii. 18). The world, however, did not credit this. To the Spirit Christ left the task of bringing home to the world's mind a conviction of its truth. (2) The evidence. The Spirit would point the world to the fact that its head had been judged,—that Christ's death, resurrection, and exaltation, were equivalent to a sentence of condemnation against the world's prince (Col. ii. 15), and would of necessity involve in the end the irremediable destruction, not alone of Satan, the world's ruler, but of all who belonged to his house or acknowledged his sway.

II. **Towards the Church.** Hearing and teaching. 1. *Glorifying the Church's Head.* (1) Indirectly, by listening to and speaking only what things he hears from the Father, ver. 13. As the Father is glorified in the Son (v. 23 ; xiii. 32 ; xiv. 13), so is the Son glorified in the Father. (2) Directly, by revealing to the minds of Christ's people the things that are Christ's, the truth that belongs to, and concerns, Him : ver. 14. 2. *Edifying the Church's members.* By declaring Christ's truth to them (1) fully—leading them into all the truth, (2) clearly—enabling them to understand the import of what He sets before them, (3) authoritatively—since He speaks not from Himself, but as He hears from the Father and the Son.

Learn 1. Man's natural condition is one of sin. 2. The discovery of this truth by the individual in every instance results from the Spirit's teaching. 3. The Holy Spirit never discovers the soul's disease without at the same time directing to the remedy. 4. Like Christ, the Spirit delights to speak of mercy rather than and before judgment. 5. Nevertheless, in mercy, too, He commonly follows this by revealing the certainty and severity of divine judgment against sin. 6. For the sin of man righteousness and judgment are the only alternative issues.

VER. 13. THE HEAVENLY TEACHER.

I. **The Name He bears.** The Spirit of truth. Descriptive of 1. His *nature*—spirit. In this respect different from Christ, who was God in human form. 2. His *character*—true. Implied in His designation Spirit of truth. 3. His *intelligence*—involved in the fact that He is the possessor of truth. 4. His *divinity*—if the possessor of truth He must be divine.

II. **The Scholars He instructs.** The disciples of Christ. 1. The *apostles* of the Lord—Peter, James, John, Paul, etc. 2. The *pastors* of the Christian Church—the able ministers of the New Testament being ministers of the Spirit (2 Cor. iii. 6), furnished by Him with gifts and graces for the prosecution of their work (2 Tim. i. 6, 14). 3. The universal company of *believers*—the Spirit dwelling in them (1 Cor. iii. 16), helping their infirmities (Rom. viii. 26), and leading them into all the truth.

III. **The Lessons He imparts.** All the truth. Not ordinary, scientific, or philosophic truth, but 1. truth *heard from the Father*—therefore divine ; and 2. truth *relating to Christ*—hence specifically Christian.

IV. **The Aim He pursues.** The glory of Christ. For this end He exhibits Christ : 1. *As the possessor of the truth*—He shall take of Mine (ver. 14). 2. *As the substance of the truth*—'I am the truth' (xiv. 6). 3. *As the end of the truth*—persuading and enabling men to accept and rest on Christ.

VER. 16-24. THE LITTLE WHILE : AN OLD DIFFICULTY REVIVED.

I. **The Difficulty stated.** 1. Its *nature.* The disciples failed to understand two things :—(1) What Christ meant by saying that after one 'little while' they would not behold Him ; and again, after another 'little while,' they would behold Him ; and (2) how it was that their seeing Him was to spring from His 'going to the Father.' 2. Its *effect.* (1) It produced perplexity—they said to one another, What is this which He saith ? (ver. 17). (2) It provoked confession —they acknowledged it was beyond them to solve the enigma ; they could not tell what He said (ver. 18). (3) It awakened desire—they felt an inward longing to unbosom themselves upon the subject before their Master (ver. 19). (4) It engendered humility—it kept them dumb, as if in presence of a mystery.

II. **The Difficulty explained.** 1. *His departure.* This Christ assured them was (1) certain—'Verily, verily, I say unto you' (ver. 20) ; (2) near—His hour was come ; He was on the eve of going away ; (3) sorrowful—for them, if not for Him (ver. 20) ; (4) necessary—again for them as for Him ; the sorrow it inflicted upon them would be the prelude of higher joys (ver. 21) ; and (5) temporary—it would only be for 'a little while,' and would be followed by a swift return. 2. *His return.* This also was (1) certain—their sorrow would be turned into joy (ver 20). It would likewise be (2) real—He would see them again(ver. 22), and they too would behold Him (xiv. 19). It would be (3) joyful—for them as for Him. It would fill them with a gladness which would be deep : their heart would rejoice (ver. 22) ; sweet—like the joy of a mother exulting over her new born babe ; abiding (ver. 21)—no one would be able to filch their joy from them (ver. 22). And it would be (4) permanent—the relationship then established between them would not be broken up.

Learn 1. Christ's utterances are not always understood by His people. 2. Christ's separations from His people are only for a little while. 3. The joy of Christ's return to His people will cause all previous anguish to be forgotten. 4. The hour approaches when Christ and His people will meet never again to separate. 5. The joy of a true Christian is indestructible by any but himself.

VER. 23-27. CHARACTERISTICS OF THE CHRISTIAN AGE.

I. **Complete Revelation.** 1. The *Subject*, the Father ; His nature, God ; His character, love ; His purpose, salvation. 2. The *Medium*, Christ ; the Father's Son, ambassador, revealer.

II. **Adequate Illumination.** 1. *Clear.* No longer in proverbs, parables, or veiled forms is the truth presented by the Spirit, but in plain and easy-to-be-understood propositions (ver. 25). 2. *Sufficient.* Enjoying the Spirit's teaching, the Christian needs not to ask of any external authority (ver. 23 ; cf. Heb. viii. 11).

III. **Perfect Communion.** 1. *On the part of the Christian.* (1) Liberty in prayer. He may ask of the Father anything (ver. 23, 26) ; (2) Success in prayer —guaranteed by three things—the Christian's plea, Christ's name (ver. 24, 26); the Saviour's intercession (ver. 26) ; the Father's love (ver. 27). 2. *On the part of the Father.* (1) Loving Christ's people (ver. 27) ; (2) granting their requests (ver. 23).

IV. **Augmenting Exultation.** 1. The *nature* of it. The joy of a Christian is always (1) inward, (2) spiritual, (3) progressive, and (4) permanent. 2. The *cause* of it. (1) The Spirit's indwelling. (2) The soul's beholding of Christ (ver. 22). (3) The Father's giving (ver. 23).

Lessons. 1. The superiority of the Christian age to all that have preceded. 2. The increased responsibility of all who live in it.

VER. 28. THE FUNDAMENTAL FACTS OF CHRISTIANITY.

I. The **Pre-existence** of Christ—"I came out from the Father." II. The **Incarnation** of Christ—"I am come into the world." III. The **Death** of Christ —"Again, I leave the world." IV. The **Exaltation** of Christ—"I go unto the Father."

VER. 30. FAITH'S CONFESSION OF CHRIST.

I. The **Substance** of it—that Christ came forth from God. II. The **Ground** of it--the realization of Christ's omniscience. III. The **Spontaneity** of it--the disciples were not on this, as on a former occasion, asked to give it. IV. The **Unanimity** of it—it was the testimony not of one apostle but of all the eleven.

VER. 31-33. LOVE'S FAREWELL.

I. **A Kind Inquiry**—Do ye now believe? (ver. 31). A question. 1. *Authoritative.* Put by Him who alone has right to do so. 2. *Necessary.* The existence of faith (ix. 35 ; Mark iv. 40) was the one thing needful (Luke xviii. 8 ; Heb. xi. 6). 3. *Urgent.* Then the time was short—Christ was on the eve of departure : now the time is short (1 Cor. vii. 29)—the Lord is at hand (Phil. iv. 5 ; Jas. v. 8). 4. *Personal.* The question was addressed to the disciples individually. So must each soul consider and reply for himself.

II. **A Gentle Admonition**—Behold, the hour cometh, etc. (ver. 32). A warning. 1. *Startling.* Otherwise it would have been worthless. 2. *Painful.* It intimated the fact of their impending desertion. Hence it suggested the propriety of examining whether their faith, though real, was capable of enduring the strain that was soon to be put upon it. 3. *Softened.* Their dispersion would leave Him alone in the hands of His enemies, i.e. so far as they, His friends, were concerned ; yet, as if to mitigate the blow His allusion to their criminal apostasy must have inflicted on them, He adds that even then He would not be alone, because the Father would be with Him.

III. **A Cheering Prediction**—That in Him they would have peace (ver. 33). 1. The *blessing.* Christ desired they might have peace. It was His dying legacy or parting bequest (xiv. 27). It was the purpose at which He was aiming in all His conversations with and labour for them. 2. *The sphere.* Such peace as He desired could only be secured in vital union with Himself (Rom. viii. 6 ; xiv. 17 ; Eph. ii. 14 ; Phil. iv. 7).

IV. **A Comforting Consolation**—That Christ had overcome the world (ver. 33). 1. *For Himself.* Hence they need not doubt that He was the Father's Son and the Saviour of men, or question His ability to support and succour them. 2. *For them.* If they continued one with Him, they also in Him and through Him would prove victorious over all the tribulation they might suffer in the world (Rom. viii. 37 ; Rev. vii. 14).

Lessons. 1. The gentleness of Christ. 2. The weakness of man. 3. The blessedness of faith.

VER. 32. ALONE, YET NOT ALONE.

I. **The Loneliness of Jesus.** 1. In the mystery of His person. 2. In the elevation of His spirit. 3. In the intensity of His sufferings. 4. In the-character of His work. 5. In the extent of His influence. II. **The Society of Jesus.** The Father was with Christ. 1. In personal union with his Godhead. 2. In active co-operation with His divine manhood. 3. In the exercise of spiritual communion. 4. In the manifestation of paternal sympathy. VER. 33. 'THESE THINGS'; OR CHRIST'S SECRETS. I. The secret of communion :—xiv. 25. II. The secret of joy:—xv. 11. III. The secret of steadfastness :—xvi. 1. IV. The secret of prayer :—xvi. 25. V. The secret of peace and victory :—xvi. 33.

5. THE HIGH PRIESTLY PRAYER

CHAP. XVII. VER. 1-26

1. If the predictions of the preceding chapter were spoken by our Lord to His disciples on the way to Gethsemane, the prayer contained in this was probably out-breathed on the margin of the Kidron ere He passed into the scene of His last conflict, though the opinion has been entertained that Christ had not yet left the upper room (Meyer), or, if he had, at the moment was standing in the temple court (Grotius, Westcott). The only recorded prayer of the many which proceeded from the lips of Christ, this perhaps, rather than the " Our Father " which He taught to His disciples (Matt. vi. 9), should be designated " The Lord's Prayer." The closest parallel it finds in the Synoptists is the brief thanksgiving to which He gave utterance in Galilee when rejected by the cities on the sea (Matt. xi. 25). Like that earlier also, this later thanksgiving was spoken in the hearing of those who were present, i.e. the disciples, for whose sakes, as much as for His own, it was offered. From the circumstance, that it partook of the nature partly of a prayer of consecration, in which Christ prepared Himself for and devoted Himself to the offering of death (ver. 19), and partly of a prayer of intercession, in which He pled with His Father in behalf of His Own (ver. 20), it has been styled *oratio sacerdotalis*, the sacerdotal or high priestly prayer. And, indeed, in listening to its solemn tones or reading in silence its sacred thoughts, one feels as if standing beside the world's High Priest in the Holy of Holies, as if overhearing the Incarnate Son pouring out his heart before the Father in dedication of Himself to His great work of dying, and in supplication of grace for His believing followers. For simplicity of language and loftiness of thought, for religious fervour and spiritual power, this prayer has won the admiration of Christians in every age. One or two discordant voices (Strauss, Bretschneider), it is true, have pronounced it a pure invention of the pseudo-John, to whom by them this gospel is assigned, and have characterized its devout strains as "frigid, dogmatical, and metaphysical"; but they have done so in flagrant opposition to the almost unanimous testimony of capable critics. " This

chapter is in words most easy, but in sense most profound" (Bengel).
"It is verily beyond measure an earnest hearty prayer, in which Christ opens
out and completely empties the abyss of His heart towards both us and
His Father" (Luther). "A more noble, sacred, fruitful, or pathetic voice
had never before been heard in heaven or on earth" (Melanchthon).
"There is nothing either in the Scriptures or in the literatures of the
nations that can be compared with this prayer for simplicity and depth,
majesty and fervour" (Luthardt). "To every believer in the invisible
world, this prayer must seem the loftiest effort of the human spirit to rise
to it. It seems like the steady soaring of the eagle into the eternal light"
(Pressensé). "So high is its strain that none has ever approached it since,
and yet the words are so childlike that children find their instruction,
edification, and comfort in them" (Stier).

2. The historic credibility of this prayer has been assailed on the ground
that the lofty calm and victorious joyfulness it reveals, as having prevailed
in Christ's soul at the moment of its utterance, is incompatible with the
intense perturbation of spirit which followed immediately on crossing into
Gethsemane. But similar transitions are represented as having taken
place in the inner consciousness of Christ, and that not merely by John
(cf. xii. 27 with xii. 23), but by the Synoptists (cf. Matt. xxvi. 64 with
xxvii. 46). The truth is that such psychological objections are of little
moment, since no man's mental history can be accepted as a universal
standard by which to try the inward experiences of others; and to deny
the possibility of such alternations of feeling on the part of Jesus is simply
to impeach the doctrine of His true humanity.

3. With almost perfect unanimity the prayer is recognized as falling
into a threefold division; according to which Christ prays, first, for Himself (ver. 1-5); secondly, for His immediate disciples (ver. 6-19); and,
thirdly, for His future followers (ver. 20-26), the subject of the first
petition being His own approaching glorification; that of the second, the
preservation of His disciples in and through whom Christ's glory was to
be manifested to the world; that of the third, the unification and perfection of His church universal, to whom already a foretaste of Christ's glory
has been imparted, and by whom it will be ultimately enjoyed in everlasting fulness.

EXPOSITION

Chap. xvii. ver. 1-5. Christ's prayer for Himself.

1. **These things** or *words*, the exhortations contained in the preceding
discourses **spake Jesus** audibly, pray-
ing as much for the edification of His disciples as for the consolation of Himself. That John here reports the
ipsissima verba of the Saviour, and
does not merely put into His mouth
language of his own invention, scarcely
stands in need of proof. It is easier to

explain the recollection of such a prayer by John on the supposition that he heard it, than, on the assumption that it was never uttered, its fabrication by either the son of Zebedee, or a second century composer. The mind that conceived a prayer so exquisitely adapted to the situation, both internal and external, of Jesus Christ at this moment, must have been little short of divine ; the heart that remembered it after upwards of half a century needs only have been one susceptible of lively impressions. **and lifting up His eyes** lit., *having lifted up*, ἐπάρας, as in vi. 5 (אBCDL) rather than ἐπῆρε, lifted up (A), although the construction καὶ ἐπῆρε . . . καὶ εἶπεν would be equally Johannine: cf. xi. 41. **to heaven** Though not necessarily implying that Christ was out of doors (Grotius, Ebrard, Hengstenberg, Lange, and others), it is more than probable He was on the edge of the Kidron ; see above. **He said** praying to His Father and teaching His disciples, *Orat patrem simulque discipulos docet* (Bengel) ; perhaps also expressing by His attitude the uncommon ardour and vehemence of His affections (Calvin). **Father** אבא *abba*, commonly employed by Christ in expressing His relation to the Deity. This word is the key-note of the prayer. It implies the whole doctrine of Christ's divinity. The Being who could address God not simply as ' Our Father,' or as " The Living Father," but as Father in the fullest sense, could be none other than divine. " In the entire prayer there are six invocations ; twice with this word in its bare simplicity, twice with σὺ πάτερ corresponding to the adjoined " I " ; once πάτερ ἅγιε, and once finally πάτερ δίκαιε " (Stier). **the hour is come** sc. that the Son of man should be glorified : xii. 23 ; cf. vii. 30 ; viii. 20 ; xiii. 1. **glorify Thy Son** not simply by extending His moral and spiritual influence among men (Reuss), but by exalting Him to that divine form which He laid aside on becoming man, restoring Him to that heavenly glory of which He emptied Himself (Phil. ii. 7) when in the fulness of the times He became incarnate (Lücke, Meyer, Luthardt, Godet, Westcott, and others) that as Thy Son He might do Thy will and accomplish the redemption of

man. **that the Son** The omission of ' Thy ' (אBCD) emphasizes the fact of Christ's essential relation to the Father as the fundamental reason of the Son's glorification of the Father, as of the Father's glorification of the Son. **may glorify Thee** by the moral and spiritual sway which, in consequence of Thy glorification of Him, He will be able to exercise among men.

2. **Even as Thou gavest Him,** by Thy decree when sending Him forth as Thy Son, **authority over all flesh** i.e. sovereign rule (see v. 27 ; x. 18 ; and cf. xiii. 3) over the entire world of humanity, in its weakness and transitoriness. Christ alludes to the fact that the Father in the councils of eternity had appointed Him, the Son, to be a new Head for the race : cf. Eph. i. 10. **that whatsoever thou hast given Him** i.e. put into His hand in time by leading, through grace, to believe upon His name : cf. vi. 37. The expression ' whatsoever,' πᾶν ὁ, contemplates the Church as a whole ; the next clause regards it in its individual members. **to them He should give eternal life.** The language implies (1) that the world of humanity—" all flesh "—is destitute of eternal life ; (2) that Christ has been constituted Head over all, in order that eternal life may be imparted to that spiritually dead world ; and (3) that for the communication of this life on the part of Christ, there must be a divine influence exerted on the world, that men may be led to believe on His name ; for in no other way can eternal life be bestowed on a soul save through bringing it into contact with God as revealed in Christ.

3. **And** δέ introducing an enlargement of the foregoing idea—a specific definition of that eternal life Christ imparts. **this is life eternal** lit., *the life eternal* : αὕτη δέ ἐστιν ἡ αἰώνιος ζωή, a construction characteristic of John : cf. xv. 12 ; 1 John iii. 11, 23 ; v. 3 ; 2 John 6. **that** (ἵνα as in vi. 29, 39 ; xv. 8) **they should know Thee the only true God** Eternal life leads to and expresses itself in the knowledge of God, not as one deity among many, but as the only true God ; i.e. as the only God corresponding to the idea of a divine being (ἀληθινός as in i. 9 ; iv. 23 ; vi. 32 ; xv. 1) ; nor yet as the Father to the

exclusion of the Son and the Spirit, but as the Father, whom the Son has revealed. **and Him whom Thou didst send,** *even* **Jesus Christ.** Not Jesus *as the Christ* (Kuinoel, Ewald, Meyer), but Jesus Christ, as a proper name (Lücke, De Wette, Luthardt, Godet, Brückner, and others). It has indeed been argued (Bretschneider) that since Jesus was not in the habit of calling Himself "The Christ," but "The Son of man," and even forbade His disciples to make known that He was the Christ (Matt. xvi. 20), this employment by the Saviour of the word "Christ" as a proper name must be regarded as spurious ; but why should not our Lord once at least before He died have authorized that peculiar appellation by which He was hereafter to be known when He should go forth upon His conquering mission through the earth? (Godet). It has likewise been contended that the application of the words "the only true God" to the Father by Christ shows that Christ did not really claim for Himself the rank of supreme divinity (Arians and Socinians); but one who was merely a creature would never have in this way ranked himself alongside of the Supreme. As has been remarked, "Not Moses or any other prophet could have been named in such co-ordination along with God, but only He who could say of Himself : 'Who sees me sees the Father'" (Tholuck).

4. I glorified Thee upon the earth A retrospect upon His world-historical life (now approaching its termination) which in its essential character had been a glorification of the Father. **having accomplished the work which Thou hast given Me to do.** That work, specified (ver. 6) as the manifestation of the Father's name, must not be restricted to the promulgation of gospel truth, or the exemplification in actual life of the Father's character, but interpreted as embracing the sacrificial death upon the cross, its culminating act.

5. And now, since that work is finished, **O Father** — revealing the intensity of Christ's feeling—**glorify Thou Me** (see on ver. 1) **with Thine own self** παρὰ σεαυτῷ, beside Thine own self, in heavenly fellowship with Thee (Meyer), in participation of Thy Godlike essence (Brückner), **with the glory**

which I had with Thee before the world was. See i. 1. Not simply in ideal pre-existence (Beyschlag), or in the divine predestination (Socinians, Grotius), but in actual personal enjoyment.

Ver. 6-19. Christ's prayer for His disciples.

6. I manifested while on the earth (ver. 4), the aorist being employed because Christ contemplates His mundane work as accomplished (ver. 4). **Thy name** The name of God, not equivalent to 'Glory,' 'Word of God,' 'God,' or 'Jehovah,' signifies the essential character of God so far as that can be revealed or made known unto men. It is "the reflection of the divine essence in the consciousness of the Being who knows it perfectly, in that of Jesus Himself" (Godet). "It is God as the God of the saving revelation" (Luthardt). "It is the essence and fatherly relation of God to the world first rightly opened through the doctrine of Christ" (Lücke). It is *nomen tuum paternum* (Bengel). Christ revealed the name of God not in the sense of making it for the first time known, but in that of fully and clearly disclosing it. **unto the men** Besides looking back to "upon the earth " (ver. 4), the introduction of 'to men' before 'whom thou hast given Me' may have been intended "to mark a certain correspondence between the revelation and the recipients of it " (Westcott). Still not without limitations could Christ claim to have made known the father-name of God to men ; since up to that time that name had been revealed only to those more particularly defined in the words that follow. **whom Thou gavest Me** by the drawing of thy grace (cf. vi. 37 ; x. 29 ; xviii. 9 ; xvii. 2, 24). **out of the world.** The addition of this clause indicates that Christ is thinking not of the eternally predestinating act of election, but of the gracious influences by which in time believers are separated from the mass of the ungodly. **Thine they were** Christ means either that the apostles belonged to God as men, i.e. as creatures, in virtue of their creation by Him (Hengstenberg), or as O. T. believers in consequence of God's covenant with the nation, *per fidem V. T.* (Bengel, Meyer, Luthardt) ; or

352 *John 17:6–10*

that in moral and religious character and disposition they were of God, taking the phrase as equivalent to ἐκ τοῦ θεοῦ in viii. 47 (Godet, Westcott). **and Thou gavest them to Me** in the eternal act of predestination (Calvin), in the operations of Thy grace in time (Godet), *ut sint fideles N. T.* that they might be N. T. believers (Bengel), *ut in me crederent, me Dominum suum agnoscerent* (Grotius). **and they have kept Thy word.** See on viii. 51 ; xiv. 23. This describes the result of Christ's work upon those the Father had given Him. The disciples had not simply received the Father's word revealed to them by Christ, but had continued to rest upon and live in it. **7, 8. Now they,** as My disciples, in their Christian consciousness, **know** in the sense of spiritually understanding, **that all things whatsoever thou hast given Me are from Thee** The 'all things' in this clause must not be limited to Christ's words (De Wette), but regarded as including the totality of Christ's saving activity : cf. v. 19, 36 (Luthardt, Meyer), although special emphasis was no doubt designed by Christ to be laid upon His doctrine received from the Father : vii. 16 ; viii. 26 ; xii. 49 ; xiv. 10. **for the words which Thou gavest Me** Not simply in time (v. 30) but in eternity (xii. 49) when as Son Christ lay in the Father's bosom, these words—τὰ ῥήματα, the constituent parts and elements of the Father's λόγος—were communicated to Him. **I have given unto them** in My teaching to which they have listened, **and they,** i.e. the disciples, on their part **received** *them.* The first act of faith on hearing Christ's doctrine. To that doctrine faith ever accords a willing and docile reception, admitting it to the understanding, welcoming it to the heart, subjecting to it the will. **and knew of a truth** The second stage in faith's education. The apostles came to apprehend with clear moral discernment all that was contained in Christ's verbal communications to them. The inner contents of Christ's words is next stated. **that I came forth from Thee** (cf. viii. 42 ; xvi. 28), **and they believed** as a consequence of recognizing My heavenly origin, **that Thou didst send Me** with a word of salvation from Thyself—

which word (as above stated) they have kept. **9, 10. I pray for them** lit., *I,* for my part, *on behalf of them,* My disciples *make request*—"I, who have so long laboured to bring them to this point, for them the fruit of my labours" (Godet) ; "I, thy Son, for those who have been faithful to Thee" (Westcott) make entreaty ; ἐρωτῶν, as in iv. 40, 47 ; xiv. 16. **I pray not for the world** Not to be understood as if Christ meant that the world had no interest in His intercessions or in the sacrifice He was about to offer (Lampe, Calvin), or that it was not in accordance with God's will to intercede for the world which, as such, was shut out from grace (Hengstenberg) ; but to be taken as declaring that Christ did not now make request for it, since neither the blessings for which, nor the grounds on which, He prayed were appropriate to it (Bengel, Meyer, Lücke, Godet, Luthardt, Tholuck, Westcott, Alford, etc.). In this prayer, Christ practically does intercede for the world (ver. 20) ; on the cross He pled for His enemies (Luke xxiii. 34) ; in His sermon on the mount (Matt. v. 44) He commanded His disciples to do the same. Stephen prayed for his executioners (Acts vii. 59). Paul directs that prayers should be made for all men (1 Tim. ii. 1). **but for those whom Thou hast given Me :** cf. ver. 2. 6. The blessings He was about to supplicate were such as were applicable only to them. "What must be asked for the world is that it may be converted, not that it may be sanctified and kept" (Luther). **for they are Thine** Christ's disciples had belonged to God before they had been given to Christ—they were God's property ; this was the first argument by which the prayer was supported : cf. on ver. 6. **and all things that are Mine are Thine and Thine are Mine** The clauses point to the community of interest between the Father and the Son. The disciples as belonging to Christ were the property of the Father ; as belonging to the Father they were the property of Christ. "It were not so much to say, All mine is Thine, for every man may declare that whatever he has is God's ; but it is much greater when he can invert it and say, All Thine is mine, for no creature can say that of God" (Luther). **and I am glorified** lit., *I have been glorified;* Christ speaking with prophetic anticipation, as if what was begun He knew would attain complete realization. The verb, not ἐδοξάσθην as in xiii. 31, but δεδόξασμαι, describes not a past occurrence, but a present and abiding result. **in them** not *by them*, through their faith and truth (Lucke), or "in so far as they are bearers and furtherers of My glory on the earth" (Meyer), but *in them*, in their believing recognition of My glory, as one whom Thou didst send (ver. 8), discerning it even through the veil of My humiliation (Godet, Brückner, Luthardt, Hengstenberg, Westcott, Alford).

11. And I am no more in the world An additional argument derived from the situation in which Christ's disciples were soon to find themselves. Christ, who had been their comforter and friend, was about to leave them. **and these are in the world** While He would be in glory they would be exposed to the merciless hatred and persecution of the world. **and I come to thee.** He should pass for ever beyond the reach of that hostility from which, after His departure, they would continue to suffer. Hence, with tender entreaty, He commends them to His Father's care. **Holy Father.** The epithet ' Holy '—*appositissima appellatio* (Bengel)—was probably selected with special reference to the contents of the prayer (Tholuck). The designation " Holy Father " characterizes God as Him who has traced the line of separation between the disciples and the world (Godet). The holiness of God is not so much " His absolute supremacy over all things created and temporal " (Hengstenberg) as that on which this supremacy rests, the absolute purity of nature which not only renders God of purer eyes than to look upon iniquity, but constrains Him to seek the reproduction of the same moral quality in His intelligent creatures. The essential idea in the term " Holy " is not that of God's exaltation above the world (Luthardt), or of "the penetration of all His attributes by love " (Alford), or of His absolute power to grant what was prayed for (Hengstenberg), but that of the absolute antithesis of His nature to that of the profane world (Meyer). **keep them** Because God is holy it is His interest to keep Christ's people ; because He is a Father that interest is intensified ; because He is the Holy Father it is implied that He has the power to preserve and protect His children. **in Thy name** The sphere in which this preservation should be realized was to be the name of God as Christ had revealed it. Christ desires that His disciples may be kept in and through the continued believing reception of that name. **which thou hast given Me** The reading (ᾧ) adopted by the more important MSS. (Lachmann, Griesbach, Tischendorf, Westcott and Hort) can only signify the name which Thou hast given Me to reveal (Lücke, Brückner, Meyer), " the essential revelation of the Father " (Luthardt, Westcott, Tholuck), which name also belonged to Christ as the revealer of the Father (Hengstenberg, Alford). The reading οὕς (D, T.R., Kuinoel) must be set aside. By some exegetes ᾧ—by attraction for ὅ, which—is understood to be equivalent to οὕς (cf. ver. 24), and to refer not to the name, but to the disciples (Bengel, Ewald, Godet, Tholuck, and others). **that** (the purpose of the keeping) **they may be one even as we** *are* **one** in life, love, and spiritual fellowship. The unity of Father and Son implies equality of nature between God and Christ, therefore involves the supreme divinity of the latter. The oneness subsisting between the Father and the Son is the model after which the unity prayed for among believers is fashioned. *Illa unitas est ex natura ; haec ex gratia. Igitur illi haec similis est, non aequalis* (Bengel). "As the divine unity consists with a variety of persons, so the final unity of men does not exclude, but perfectly harmonizes the separate being of each in the whole " (Westcott).

12. While I was with them The best codices omit " in the world." The past tense is employed because Christ contemplates His earthly ministry as accomplished : cf. ver. 11. **I kept them in Thy name which Thou hast given Me.** The repetition of ᾧ δέδωκάς μοι (א B C L, etc., Tischendorf, Westcott and Hort), as applied to the name of God, is not inappropriate to John's style of composition (Luthardt), although οὓς δέδωκάς μοι (A D) is by some preferred (Meyer, Lücke, Godet). **and I guarded them** If καί should be omitted (T. R.) then probably the reading οὓς should be adopted instead of ᾧ; if καί must be inserted (א B C L), then the above translation will be the more correct. The action denoted by φυλάσσειν marks the means employed in the τηρεῖν : cf. x. 28-30. **and not one of them perished,** ἀπώλετο, fell away into perdition, **but the son of perdition,** ὁ υἱὸς τῆς ἀπωλείας : cf. 2 Thess. ii. 3. Either "he who belongs to, i.e. is destined to destruction" (Meyer, Tholuck, Hengstenberg, Olshausen) ; or, "he who has fallen away under the power of destruction" (Luthardt), he whose moral life was not the ζωή Christ imparts, but its antithesis ἀπώλεια, or death (Godet). The εἰ μή, 'but,' does not require the son of perdition to be viewed as having been given to Christ (Alford) ; rather this seems forbidden by the circumstance that Christ says not οὐδένα . . . ἀπώλεσα, εἰ μὴ τὸν υἱὸν τῆς ἀπωλείας, but εἰ μὴ ὁ υἱὸς τῆς ἀπώλειας, i.e. not "None but the son of perdition have I lost" ; but "I have lost none of them, but the son of perdition is lost," i.e. he has lost himself, never having been really given to Me. That the son of perdition means Judas Iscariot, although Christ names him not, is obvious. His perdition was in one sense the inevitable outcome of his own wicked choice, the necessary result of the principle of sin and death by which he was dominated ; yet Christ recurs to the thought that it had also been brought about in accordance with Scripture prediction. **that** (see on xiii. 18) **the Scripture might be fulfilled.** Not the general tenor of O. T. prophecy concerning Christ's death (Kuinoel), but the passage (Ps. xli. 10) quoted in xiii. 18 (Lücke, Meyer, etc.), rather than Ps. cix. 8 fulfilled in Acts i. 20 (Grotius), or Is. lvii. 12, 13 (Lange). Although the fall of Judas was in Scripture foretold, the responsibility of Judas was not thereby impaired. What was foreknown and foreannounced was the free act of one whose moral nature lay under sin's dominion. In asserting that Judas went to his own place that the Scripture might be fulfilled, Christ simply intimated that in acting as he did the

son of perdition did not take God by surprise, but only carried out the counsel God beforehand had determined should be done : cf. Acts iv. 28.

13. **But now I come to Thee** (see on ver. 11) ; **and,** since I can no longer keep them, **these things** the words of this prayer on their behalf **I speak** audibly, λαλῶ, that they may hear and be comforted thereby **in the world on** the eve of my departure, *jam ante discessum meum* (Bengel), **that they may have My joy fulfilled in themselves.** Cf. xv. 11. What should give them joy was the circumstance that Christ had prayed for them and the thought that in consequence they would not be forsaken by the Father.

14. **I have given them Thy word** i.e. the word concerning Thyself which I, Thy Son and servant, have received from Thee (cf. xiv. 24 ; xvii. 6); **and the world hated them** (Christ speaks of the world's hostility as a concentrated act, which from His lofty standpoint He regards as already past, in contrast with the permanent endowment He had conferred upon them) **because they are not of the world** in character or disposition, in essential nature or moral life (see ver. 6 ; cf. xv. 19), **even as I am not of the world.** See on ver. 8, and cf. viii. 23.

15. **I pray not that Thou shouldest take them from** or, *out of* **the world** This might have seemed the natural request to prefer on their behalf. As in the inner spirit of their lives they had been already separated from the world, it would not have been surprising had Christ asked that, like Himself, they should be withdrawn from it. The reason however why Christ did not urge this petition was that He had work for them to do in the world. **but that Thou shouldest keep them from the evil** one. ἐκ τοῦ πονηροῦ ; either from the evil *thing*, regarding the adjective as neuter (Luther, Calvin, Olshausen, Ewald, Hengstenberg, Godet, and others), or, from the evil *one*, taking it as masculine (Lücke, Meyer, Luthardt, Brückner, Tholuck, Westcott, and others). In favour of the former is urged that ἐκ, *out of*, points to a realm out of which one is taken rather than to an individual, and that, had Satan been intended, the more appropriate designation would have been 'the

prince of this world,' ἄρχων τοῦ κόσμου (Olshausen) ; in support of the latter is contended that both John's Gospel (xiv. 30 ; xiii. 27 ; xii. 31) ; and Epistles (1 John ii. 13, 14 ; iii. 12 ; v. 18) represent Satan as the enemy of Christ and His disciples and as the sphere in which the world lives and moves and has its being.

16. They are not of the world, do not belong to it, **even as I,** who am about to leave it, **am not of the world,** but by the whole diameter of My being am separated from it. This verse, though repeating the sentiment of ver. 14, cannot be regarded as an instance of tautology. In ver. 14 introduced as an explanation of the world's hatred (cf. John xv. 18, 19 ; 1 John iii. 13), it is here repeated as the ground or basis of the ensuing prayer.

17. Sanctify them As the *first* petition aimed at their protection from the power of evil without, so this, the *second* seeks the perfection of the principle of grace within. To sanctify, ἁγιάζω, is to separate from common and consecrate to holy uses (cf. x. 36 ; Matt. xxiii. 19) ; hence to make pure and holy (Eph. v. 26 ; 1 Thess. v. 23 ; Heb. ii. 11). In these two senses separately the word is employed in ver. 19 ; in this verse both senses are conjoined. The sanctification of the disciples for which Christ prayed was not merely their entire devotement to their official calling (Theophylact, Lampe,) and their complete equipment for the same by the gift of the Holy Spirit (Lücke), by bestowing on them "divine illumination, power, joyfulness. love, inspiration for their official activity which should ensue and did ensue through means of the Holy Spirit" (Meyer) ; but likewise their whole-hearted self-surrender and consecration to God (Godet, Luthardt, Hengstenberg, Westcott), which consecration however was specially to manifest itself in their apostolic mission. **in the truth** Not equivalent to *truly*, ἀληθῶς (Luther, Hengstenberg), or through the truth, διὰ τῆς ἀληθής (De Wette, Godet, Tholuck), but pointing to the sphere (or condition) in which alone such sanctification is possible, viz., while abiding in the truth (Meyer, Brückner, Luthardt, Alford, Westcott): cf. ver. 11. This latter sense however

implies that the truth in which they abide becomes the instrument or agency through which their personal and official consecration is reached. The pronoun σοῦ (T. R.), ' Thy ' (A.V.), is omitted by the best codices. John often speaks of the truth, but never of the truth of God (Bengel). **Thy word** lit., *the word that is Thine,* which I have received from Thee and given unto them (ver. 8), **is truth,** hence only by abiding in Thy word can they be sanctified.

18. As Thou didst send Me into the world See on ver. 3, 8, 21, 23, 25 ; and compare iii. 34 ; v. 38 ; vi. 57 ; vii. 29 ; viii. 42 ; x. 36; xx. 21 ; from first to last Christ claimed to have been sent into the world by the Father, and therefore to have been in possession of a premundane and pretemporal existence. **even so sent I them into the world.** Either Christ refers to His first commission to the twelve, which was already an accomplished fact (Matt. x. 5 ; Mark vi. 7 ; Luke ix. 2) and which He regarded as involving every subsequent instruction (Westcott), or He speaks proleptically, viewing the commission they were afterwards to receive (xx. 21) as already given (Meyer). In either case He represents them as sent into the world in a manner analogous to Himself, because through grace they had been raised to a condition of being above the world. He also puts forth their apostolic mission as the first of two motives for their sanctification. As Christ had been sanctified and sent into the world, His mission being based upon and finding its justification in, His perfect consecration to the Father's will, so their mission required as its support and vindication a similar sanctification of their persons in and through a whole-hearted dedication to Christ from whom it was received. The second motive Christ adduces for their sanctification is the fact that nothing less than that was the object of His death.

19. And for their sakes or, for their advantage ὑπέρ), **I sanctify Myself** i.e. consecrate Myself to the will of God ; which, however, must not be limited to the death He was about to endure, as if He meant only to say, for their sakes I now devote Myself to death as a sacrificial offering (Chrysostom, Bengel,

Meyer, Ewald, Brückner, Reuss), though this of course cannot be excluded ; but must be extended so as to embrace Christ's entire career (Calvin, Hengstenberg, Godet, Luthardt, Westcott, and others), which throughout had been one of self-consecration to the will of God, which self-consecration was about to culminate in the devotement of Himself to death. **that they themselves also may be sanctified** i.e. consecrated and devoted to God in a life of self-surrender and willing obedience, consequently in a life of purity and love. **in truth.** *ἐν ἀληθείᾳ* ; either *truly*, as in 1 John iii. 18 ; 2 John 1 ; 3 John 1 (Chrysostom, Calvin, Bengel, Meyer, Godet, Westcott, and others), or, as in ver. 17, *in truth* as the sphere of such sanctification (Lücke, Ewald, Brückner, Luthardt, and others).

Ver. 20-26. Christ's prayer for His church.

20. **Neither for these only do I pray** (or *make request*). Christ restricted not His preceding supplications, for keeping (ver. 11) and for sanctifying (ver. 17), to the apostles, but included in them all subsequent adherents of the faith. **but for them also that believe on Me** lit., *the believing;* the present tense being employed—rather than the future ' shall believe ' (T. R.)—because, although no one has yet been won to the faith of Christ by means of the apostles, Christ already, by anticipation, had the final result of their labours present before His mental vision. **through their word.** The specific instrumentality by which (διά) this result should be accomplished was the word (λόγος) of the apostles (cf. Rom. x. 14); understanding by this not the bare recital of historical facts, or narration of the doctrines they had received from Christ, the testimony (μαρτυρία) as distinguished from the explanation (ἐξήγησις) of those facts and doctrines ; in other words not the oral apostolic tradition merely, but also the written Gospels and Epistles. " All faith in the Church is dependent on the word of the Apostles, the oral or the written" (Hengstenberg). "There is no real coming to Christ at any time but by this means" (Godet).

21. **That** This, the first of the three ἵνα occurring in the present verse, points out not the contents of the

Saviour's prayer (Grotius), but the reason why our Lord includes all subsequent believers in His intercession (Meyer), the final aim towards which His supplication is directed (Tholuck, Alford). **they may all be one** Generally that purpose or aim is the unification or gathering into one of all believers in respect of life and love, of faith and obedience : cf. Acts iv. 32; Rom. xv. 5, 6 ; Ephes. iv. 3, 6. **even as Thou, Father, *art* in Me and I in Thee** The unity Christ prays for amongst His followers is a unity corresponding to that subsisting between Himself, the Son, and the Father (cf. x. 38 ; xiv. 10, 20) ; a union not of affection merely, or of will, or of power, but also of nature. So the union of believers prayed for by Christ is more than a community of sentiment and affection, or of power and activity, it is also a unity of nature and life. **that** This second ἵνα, in a manner co-ordinate with and explicative of the first, defines more particularly the purpose of Christ's prayer as the bringing about of a unity among believers modelled after the original pattern or type of the divine unity existing between the Father and the Son. **they also may be in us** The unity of believers is only possible through their being in the Father and in the Son (1 John i. 3), which they only can be through the Spirit's dwelling in them collectively and individually as believers (1 John iv. 13). Abiding in the Father and the Son believers find in Them the principle and bond of their unity. ἕν (T.R.), dropped (B C* D, Tischendorf, Meyer, Luthardt, Westcott and Hort)—probably by the corrector (Brückner); retained (א A L), required by the context (Godet). **that the world may believe that Thou didst send Me.** The third ἵνα, subordinate to the two former, expresses the ultimate design of Christ's prayer. The sight of a united church would awaken in the minds of those who beheld it the conviction that its centre and support must be in one who was Himself divine ; in other words that Christ around whom and in whom all believers are united could be no other than The Sent of God.

22. **And the glory which Thou hast given Me, I have given them** The glory (δόξα) Christ had received of the

Father, and imparted to His disciples, has been explained as the glory (1) of the apostolic office and miraculous gifts as in ii. 11 and xi. 40 (Chrysostom, Grotius), (2) of the inner life (Olshausen), (3) of the oneness of believers through Christ living in them (Hengstenberg), (4) of that grace and truth (i. 14) which was manifested in the incarnate Son, and passed over from Him to His disciples (Tholuck, Brückner, Stier), (5) of Sonship (Bengel, Godet), (6) of manifesting the Father's purpose (Westcott), (7) of self-sacrificing love which, when displayed by Jesus was owned by the Father as the only true glory (Milligan and Moulton), (8) of heaven to which Christ was Himself proceeding, to which He desired His people ultimately to be brought, and of which He had already imparted to them the foretaste (Meyer, Luthardt, Alford, and others), (9) of possessing God's image, which was communicated to Christ's human nature, and is formed anew in believers (Calvin). Perhaps, however, it should be said 1. that the glory Christ received from the Father was the glory (1) of having life in Himself (v. 26), (2) of being in His incarnate condition the Son of God (i. 14), (3) of manifesting the Father's name to mankind (i. 14 ; xvii. 6), (4) of imparting eternal life to believers (xvii. 4); and 2. that this glory Christ had already imparted to His apostles (as He still communicates it to His believing followers) in order that through it they may be able to realize that perfected unity which He sets before them as their aim and for which He prays. (1) He bestows upon them the life eternal He has received from the Father (x. 28 ; xvii. 3), (2) He constitutes them along with Himself sons of God (i. 12 ; 1 John iii. 1, 2), (3) He confers upon them the honour of revealing to the world the Father's name, by acting as Christ's ambassadors and representatives (xvii. 18), and (4) He entrusts them with the power of imparting eternal life to others, in so far as they are His appointed ministers and agents for the dissemination of the word of truth and life (xvii. 20). **that they may be one even as we** *are* **one** : cf. on ver. 21. Believers, interpenetrated each one with the life that is in the Father and

the Son, realizing that each and all are the objects of a common Father's love, conscious also of wearing that Father's image and of reflecting its moral radiance upon the world around, besides rejoicing in the lofty life-task assigned them of imparting the knowledge of the truth to others, and anticipating the uninterrupted fellowship of life and love which awaits them in heaven, of necessity feel drawn to one another and gradually grow together into a oneness of life and love, of nature and activity resembling the oneness existing between the Father and the Son.

23. **I in them and Thou in Me** This explains the nature of that unity for which Christ prays. It is a unity not merely of believers amongst themselves, but also of believers with the Father and the Son ; with the Son through His indwelling in them by His Spirit—" I in them " ; and with the Father through the indwelling of the Father in the Son—" Thou in Me." **that they may be perfected into one** The thought advances. Only through their union with the Father and the Son can their oneness, as a body of believers, be brought to complete realization. The phrase ' perfected into one,' τετελειωμένοι εἰς ἕν, *consummati in unum* (Vulgate), suggests that on earth the unity of the saints is incomplete, imperfect, as it were inchoative, and immature, but that in heaven, when the state or condition of τελείωσις has been attained it will be full-orbed and absolute. Unity is thus not a means to, but the goal of, perfection. **that the world may know that Thou didst send Me !** The threefold ἵνα, ' in order that,' of ver. 21 is again repeated. As Christ prayed for the keeping and sanctifying of believers (1) that they might all be one ; (2) that they might be in the Father and the Son ; and (3) that the world might believe ; so now He declares that He has given His glory to believers (1) that they may be one, (2) that they may be perfected into one, and (3) that the world may know that the Father had sent Him. The distinction between may believe (ver. 21) and may know (ver. 23) is that between assurance founded on faith, and conviction based on experience.

The world begins by believing in the divine mission of Jesus Christ in consequence of observing the growing unity of the church ; when that unity shall have been perfected the world's faith will also have ripened into knowledge. The use of γινώσκῃ rather than γνῷ points to a gradual growth in knowledge, to a learning by slow degrees. If the knowledge spoken of is that of grateful recognition (Westcott, Luthardt, Alford, Meyer), then care must be taken not to found upon the term *κόσμος*, a doctrine of universal salvation (Luthardt), since Christ may mean nothing more than that then the world generally will have come to recognize the saving mission of the Son ; if the notion of the forced conviction of unbelievers is introduced (Godet, Milligan and Moulton), then the term 'world' may be understood in its widest acceptation. **and lovedst them,** i.e. believers, or the church of the faithful, **as Thou hast loved Me.** The love of the Father to Christ the Son is the model after which the Father's love to Christ's people is framed. After the same pattern also was Christ's love for them fashioned : xv. 9.

24. Father, that which Thou hast given Me ὁ δέδωκας μοι (א B D) as in ver. 11 (cf. vi. 39) instead of οὕς (A C L): Christ contemplating the collective body of His church rather than the individual members of which it is composed. **I will,** not I ask or pray, ἐρωτῶ (Kuinoel), but I *will*, θέλω, which is not the language of desire simply (Calvin, B. Crusius, Tholuck, Ewald), or only the last wish of a dying man (Godet), or merely the voice of one conscious of His divine Sonship (Bengel, Luthardt, Hengstenberg), or solely the utterance of one to whom absolute power and authority in the realm of grace and salvation has been deputed (Meyer), but is all of these together. On Christ's use of θέλω, I will, see xxi. 22, 23 ; Matt. viii. 3 ; xxiii. 37 ; xxvi. 39. In Gethsemane pleading for Himself Christ employs the language of submission and assumes the attitude of a servant—"Not my will, but thine, O Lord, be done !" here He speaks as if from the standpoint of His throne in the heavens, and uses the style not of a subject but of a sovereign

—"I will!" **that** ἵνα, not merely defining the contents of the "I will" previously spoken, but indicating the purpose for which it was spoken. The power latent in the "I will" was deliberately put forth *in order that* the ultimate glorification of Christ's people might be attained. **where I am** in the heavenly world, into which Christ pictures Himself as having already gone (cf. ver. 11 ; vii. 34 ; xiv. 3). **they may also be with Me** as partakers of the same heavenly form of existence. The full realization of this destiny would only be experienced at the parousia or second coming ; yet the thought is not excluded, but rather included, that His people on leaving earth should be admitted into His presence : cf. 2 Cor. v. 8 ; Phil. i. 23. **that they may behold My glory** ἵνα, pointing out a second part of the purpose contemplated by Christ's "I will." Christ's unified church was not merely to be translated into His presence, they were also to have a beatific vision of His glory, in the sense of seeing, enjoying, and partaking of it. **which Thou hast given Me** The glory believers shall contemplate in heaven will be the glory the Father had imparted to His incarnate Son (*vide* on ver. 22), the glory i.e. of being the Saviour of His church. What that glory was in its fulness could not be seen, known, realized, till Christ had His ransomed, unified, sanctified, glorified church around Him in Heaven. Then would His people understand the glory which had been given to the Son in sending Him forth on a mission of salvation to sinful men. In ver. 5 Christ speaks of this glory as having been His before the foundation of the world. So it was in destination and in the existence of that which alone could make it possible. **for** ὅτι, *because:* this goes back to the primal source whence the Saviour's mediatorial glory originated, viz., the Father's love. **Thou lovedst Me** And in that love lay the glory which the Eternal Son received from the Father. Because of that love the Father conferred upon the Son the glory of being the Head and Saviour of His church. **before the foundation of the world.** Cf. Eph. i. 4 ; 1 Pet. i. 20. Language like this cannot be explained as implying merely an ideal pre-existence (Beyschlag), but must be regarded as the putting forward on the part of Christ of a distinct claim to personal existence in a pre-incarnate state or condition.

25. **O righteous Father** δίκαιε, instead of ἅγιε, holy, as in verse 11, because Christ now appeals to the righteous character of God as the ultimate reason justifying the separation of Himself and His disciples from the world. Δίκαιε, not equivalent to *benignissime* (Semler), or ἅγιε (Neander), signifies that attribute of Deity which requires all God's actions to be in absolute harmony with what is right, and in particular which necessitates His rendering to every man according to his works; Ps. lxii. 13. **the world knew Thee not** The precise import of the καί (which the R. V. has not attempted to render into English, and which has been left out by the Vulgate and some other authorities), has been explained—(1) as forming an antithesis with what precedes, as if Christ had said, 'Father, Thou art righteous, and yet the world hath not known Thee' (Meyer, Hengstenberg, Luthardt), (2) as contrasting with the subsequent δέ, thus :—'Although the world knew Thee not, yet I knew Thee' (Lücke, Tholuck, Alford), but is perhaps best interpreted (3) as constituting with the καί which follows a parallel in

which two opposing thoughts are ranged over against one another, on the one side the world's unbelief and ignorance of God, on the other side the faith and knowledge of the followers of Christ (Godet, Westcott, Milligan and Moulton). **but I knew Thee** This clause explains how and why the above contrast was possible. Because Christ had known the Father Christ's people had become distinguished from the world. Thus the mention of Christ's knowledge prepares the way for and leads up to the second member of the parallel—the knowledge possessed by His disciples. **and these** καὶ οὗτοι ; on the other hand these, My disciples, **knew that Thou didst send Me** recognized by faith and so came to understand the truth of My heavenly mission.

26. **And I made known unto them Thy name** (cf. ver. 6) **and I will make it known** by the teaching of the Holy Spirit, **that the love wherewith Thou lovedst Me may be in them and I in them.** The design, ἵνα, of this manifestation of the name of God by Christ to His people was that they might experience in themselves the love the Father had for the Son, which again could only be in the manner indicated in the last clause, i.e. by Christ abiding in them.

HOMILETICS

VER. 1-5. CHRIST'S PRAYER FOR HIMSELF.
I. The Circumstances. 1. *The place.* The western bank of the Kidron ; but see Exposition. To a devout soul as to the praying Son of God any spot serves as an oratory (iv. 21 ; 1 Tim. ii. 8). 2. *The time.* The last night of His life. Not surprising that sinful men should at such a season resort to prayer, it is comforting to know that the sinless One found solace in communing with His Father when the hour of His departure was at hand. 3. *The audience.* Not in solitude as oftentimes before He had prayed (vi. 15 ; Matt. xiv. 23 ; Luke ix. 28), or in the company of strangers, as on two former occasions He had addressed the Father (xi. 41 ; Matt. xi. 25), but in the hearing of His disciples was this supplication presented. He desired not merely to benefit by His intercessions, but also to comfort and instruct by His words. This may suggest a distinction between private and public devotion, the former aiming chiefly at the profit of the individual who prays, the latter contemplating in addition the advantage of them that hear.
II. The Spirit. 1. *Reverential.* Indicated by Christ's attitude—"lifting up His eyes to heaven" (ver. 1). It becomes those who approach the throne of grace to remember whose throne it is (Ps. xi. 4 ; xlv. 6), to cherish exalted thoughts of the majesty of Him who sits thereupon (Ps. xxxi. 8 ; lxxxix. 7),

and to manifest the awe they feel by the outward posture of their bodies as well as by the inward disposition of their souls (Ex. iii. 5 ; Heb. xii. 28). If the incarnate Son exhibited reverence in drawing near His Father's presence, much more should sinful men in entering the audience chamber of the High and Holy One (Gen. xviii. 27 ; Is. vi. 5 ; Job xl. 3). 2. *Filial.* Expressed by the twice repeated 'Father.' As a son to a father so Christ stood related to God before the incarnation (i. 18 ; iii. 16), throughout the course of His earthly ministry (vi. 40 ; viii. 19), and at its close (Luke xxiii. 46). In the spirit of a son He maintained communion with the Father. And for us, as for Him, a spirit of adoption is the true spirit of devotion (Rom. viii. 15). The burden of the gospel is that God is a father to them that trust Him and believe upon His Son (Is. lxiii. 16 ; Jer. xxxi. 9 ; Matt. vii. 11 ; John i. 12 ; Rom. viii. 14) ; the response that gospel should awaken is a feeling of sonship (Gal. iv. 6). 3. *Believing.* Shown by the appeal Christ makes to the arrival of His hour as a reason why His prayer should be heard. The hour, prearranged by the Father and waited for by Him, when He should depart out of this world having come (xiii. 1), He intercedes for the fulfilment of the promise which in the councils of eternity had with that hour been bound up. Christ believed in the promise, and knowing that the hour had struck for its bestowment prayed. So does true prayer spring from faith in the Father's promise (Ps. cxix. 49 ; Heb. xi. 6). 4. *Urgent.* Revealed by the action above described (ver. 1), and by the twofold recurrence of the main petition (ver. 1, 5). Fervent importunity a characteristic of right prayer.

III. **The Petition.** 'Father, glorify Thy Son.' 1. *What it implied.* (1) That the praying Son had been in existence before the world was (ver. 5) ; (2) that, though still the Son, He was not in that 'glory' in which He had then been ; and (3) that He had laid aside that 'glory' in order to become the Father's servant and do the Father's work (Phil. ii. 6, 7). 2. *What it desired.* (1) Not that a brighter lustre should surround His name after His death, through the increased influence His gospel should exercise upon men—a sort of enlarged posthumous fame, which should certainly accrue to Him throughout all subsequent generations (Ps. lxxii. 17), but which in no intelligible sense could He speak of as having had with the Father before the world was. (2) That having finished His Father's work He might resume that glory He had had with the Father before the world was,—that He, the incarnate Son, not putting off His humanity, but carrying it up with Him into the heavenly sphere, might be restored to that divine form out of which for a season He had stooped in order to effect the redemption of a lost world.

IV. **The Pleas.** 1. *The honour of the Father.* Christ perceived that the cause the Father had at heart (Is. liii. 10) would be more successfully carried forward by Him the Son seated on the throne of the universe, invested with power and authority over angels, men, and things, than by Him still residing on the earth, encompassed by human frailty, and enfeebled by mortal weakness, or, even if exempt from these, still subject to limitations of time and sense (see Homily on xvi. 7). Accordingly He prayed, 'Father, glorify Thy Son, that Thy Son also may glorify Thee' (ver. 1). 2. *The salvation of the Church.* This was the cause the Father had at heart. Christ desired that whatsoever had been given Him should by Him be brought to eternal life. For this purpose the Father had deputed to Him authority over all flesh, to give eternal life to as many as He (the Father) should conduct to Him by the gracious drawings of the Spirit (ver. 2). Hence, He argued, it would be better that He should be glorified. The work of bestowing eternal life on dead souls would proceed more efficaciously were He in heaven. This necessarily so, because eternal life in a soul could begin only in the believing recognition of the Father as the only true God, and of Himself Jesus Christ as the Father's messenger and son—as in the perfect knowledge of the Father and the Son it would find its consummation (ver. 3). Accordingly again the Saviour prayed—"Father, glorify thy Son ! " 3. *The recompense of Himself.* As in all Christ did and suffered He had an eye to the "joy that was set before Him" (Heb. xii. 2), as Moses "looked unto the recompense of the reward" (Heb. xi. 26), so here He craves the bestowment of that premium on the ground that He had earned it by finishing the task His Father had assigned Him to do (ver. 4). Yet Christ employs this argument not in the first but in the third place. As He had taught His disciples (Matt. vi. 9), so prays He Himself—first for the Father's honour, so hallowing the divine name,—then for the salvation of the church, in that advancing the divine kingdom,—and only after these for Himself, craving the reward He had won.

Learn 1. The fatherhood of God is the best refuge for dying men. 2. The chief end of man is to glorify God. 3. Eternal life is impossible apart from the grace of God and the revelation of Jesus Christ. 4. The best preparation for heaven is the faithful execution of God's will upon earth.

VER. 3.—ETERNAL LIFE.

I. *In what it consists*—the knowledge of God as revealed in Jesus Christ. II. *From whom it is obtained*—Jesus Christ, whom the Father has constituted its sole depositary. III. *On whom it is bestowed*—on them the Father by His grace gives to Christ, i.e. on believers. IV. *On what terms it is dispensed* —without money and without price, it partaking ever of the nature of a gift (Rom. vi. 23). V. *With what aim it is conferred*—the glory of the Father through the Son, who bestows it, and in the saints who receive it (2 Thess. i. 10).

VER. 6-8.—CHRIST'S WORK UPON THE EARTH.

I. **Its Nature.** The manifestation of the name of God (ver. 6). In Himself invisible and incomprehensible (i. 18 ; vi. 46 ; Job xi. 7 ; xxxvii. 23 ; 1 Tim. vi. 16), who and what He is must have remained a secret (Gen. xxxii. 29 ; Judg. xiii. 18), had God not been pleased to make some disclosure thereof to His creatures. This he did in the material creation (Ps. viii. 1 ; xix. 1, 2, 3 ; Rom. i. 20), and still does in His providential government of the world (Dan. iv. 34, 35 ; Rom. xi. 36 ; Eph. i. 11). A further revelation of His name and character He furnished to the Jews in the words of the law He gave them, and the covenant of love into which He took them, at Sinai—a revelation whose import He also declared through Moses (Exod. xxxiv. 5, 6, 7) ; but never until Christ came who was the image of the invisible God (Col. i. 15 ; Heb. i. 2) and who could say 'He that hath seen Me hath seen the Father' (xiv. 9), was God's name completely manifested. Besides publishing to men the fact of the divine existence, Christ unfolded 1. *The nearness of God* to man, and conversely man's nearness to God—a thought so little understood by the human mind that even the Hebrews with the 139th Psalm to guide them had no proper conception of God as of a heavenly friend with whom they might hold daily, hourly, close and loving fellowship. It required God's Son to robe Himself in flesh and taber-nacle amongst men, before they could perceive that the supreme Deity was not a God afar off simply, but also a God at hand. 2. *The holiness of God*—which, though dimly apprehended and vaguely believed in by men before the advent of Christ, was never adequately comprehended until it was beheld embodied in the person and character, life and death of Him who was holy, harmless, undefiled, and separate from sinners (Heb. vii. 26). 3. *The graciousness of God*, the mercifulness, pitifulness, fatherly kindness of Him who was Creator, Sovereign, Judge of man—which, though referred to by poets (Ps. ciii. 13) and prophets (Mal. ii. 10) in the Hebrew Church, was but imperfectly realized until Christ taught men to say 'Our Father.' Unquestionably this was the great addition to human thought on the subject of the Deity made by Jesus Christ. 4. *The helpfulness of God*—which signified that God not only possessed such emotions as have been described, but was as able as willing to succour men in their feebleness and misery. No one who looked on Christ as He walked this earth, healing the sick, casting out devils, raising the dead, pardoning the guilty, cleansing the unholy, could doubt that, if He was God's image, God of whom He was the image could also relieve the poor and needy when they cried to Him in their distresses. 5. *The blessedness of God*—or, more correctly, the eternal life which was and is in God (1 John i. 1). In Christ men beheld that

eternal life for them signified participation in a life like Christ's, a life of knowledge and communion with the Father (ver. 3, 21, 24).

II. Its Subjects. 1. *The world.* Although throughout this prayer a distinction is drawn between the world and the Church (ver. 6), and the Saviour's
intercession is for the latter rather than the former (ver. 9), it is yet true that
Christ's manifestation of the Father's name had an outlook to the race of mankind no less than to the select circle of believers. Of this perhaps a hint is
furnished by the word 'men' (ver. 6). 2. *The church.* Christ describes those
in whom His work took effect as a company of persons who had been (1)
separated from the race—"the men whom Thou hast given Me out of the
world" (ver. 6), i.e. separated in their characters as believers while the world
remained and remains in unbelief (ver. 25 ; vii. 7 ; 1 John v. 19), separated by
the hand of grace which alone made them to differ (1 Cor. iv. 7 ; xv. 10), and
separated unto the ends and purposes of the gospel (Rom. i. 1 ; Gal. i. 15) ; (2)
owned by the Father—"thine they were," i.e. they had belonged to the Father
in the more fundamental sense of being His creatures (Ezek. xviii. 4), as well as
in the more special sense of being born of God (i. 13) and so inwardly disposed
to hear and obey God's voice (viii. 47 ; xviii. 37) ; and (3) given to Christ—
"Thou gavest them to Me," in eternity by a gracious act of predestinating love
(Eph. i. 4, 5), in time by the drawings of the Spirit and the truth (vi. 45).

III. Its Results. 1. *The reception of Christ's words.* "The words which Thou
gavest Me, I have given unto them, and they received *them*" (ver. 8). The
world had rejected Christ's words (xii. 48) ; the disciples had believed them
(xvi. 27). A gracious soul desirous of learning the Father's name does not begin
by subjecting Christ's teaching to a process of criticism, does not assume the
right or the capacity to sit in judgment on it, but in a spirit of meek docility
receives it into his understanding and admits it to his heart (1 Sam. iii. 9 ; Ps.
lxxxv. 8 ; 1 Pet. ii. 2 ; James i. 29). 2. *The recognition of Christ's words as the
Father's.* "Now they know that all things whatsoever Thou hast given Me are
from Thee" (ver. 7). Christ had promised that if any man received and did
His teaching he would know that it was not from Himself but from God (vii.
17). The apostles had attained to this discovery. The Thessalonians afterwards
did (1 Thess. ii. 13). All who follow their example will. 3. *The preservation of
the Father's words.* "They have kept Thy word" (ver. 6). To keep God's word,
more than to remember it, signifies to enshrine it in the inner sanctuary of the
spirit, to accord it the chief place in the affections, to subject to it the entire
being, intellect, heart, conscience, will (see xiv. 23, 24).

Lessons. 1. Who would know God must study Him as revealed in Christ. 2.
Who would be wise unto salvation must learn at Christ's feet. 3. Who would
reach eternal glory must keep the Father's words.

VER. 9-16. THE KEEPING OF THE SAINTS.

I. The Persons. 'Those whom thou hast given Me' (ver. 9, 11) ; i.e. the
disciples ; in contrast 1. *With the world*—"I pray for them : I pray not for the
world" (ver. 9). Christ meant not that men as men were excluded from His
intercessions, but that they were not then the object of His pleadings (see Exposition). He was then acting as the Church's High Priest, preparing to sanctify
or set Himself apart as a sacrifice for His believing people ; hence the unbelieving world had no direct interest in the blessings He was asking. 2. *With
the son of perdition.* Judas had by this time been formally excluded from the
apostolic circle (xiii. 30). As distinguished from the latter Christ designates
him 'a son of destruction' and as good as intimates that he had perished and
was already past praying for (ver. 12).

II. The Blessing. Preservation 1. In *unity* :—'Holy Father, keep them in
Thy name, that they may be one even as we are one' (ver. 11). Extended
illustration of this point may here be deferred till a later stage (ver. 21).
Suffice it at present to observe that Christian unity ;—such as expresses itself in
one faith, one love, one body, one life (Eph. iv. 3-6),—is not only the subject of
Christ's intercession with the Father, but the object of the Father's keeping of
the saints. He keeps them, not by forcible compulsion, but by spiritual per-

suasion, bringing home the truth about God to their minds, helping them to understand the oneness of life, love, and power subsisting between the Father and the Son, in such a fashion that they earnestly desire and labour after such oneness among themselves, in this showing themselves to be followers of God as dear children. 2. In *safety.* 'I pray not that Thou shouldst take them from the world, but that Thou shouldst keep them from the evil *one*' (ver. 15). One can imagine reasons why Christ might have prayed that the disciples by His side should be taken from the world along with Himself—reasons having a value for Himself, reasons bearing specially on them, and reasons applicable mainly to the world. He might have argued for instance that for Himself as He was going from this mundane sphere, He would rather be accompanied by those who had loved Him and whom He had loved on earth than be separated from them even for a brief interval; that for them it would be better to be taken home to His Father's house than to be left lingering here below, exposed to the temptations and cruelties of a sinful and persecuting world (Phil. i. 23); for the world that it would in no way disadvantage them to have no further opportunity of augmenting their guilt and filling up the measure of their iniquities by evil entreating His feeble followers. But Christ does not so reason or pray. Rather He discerns grounds why it would be better that when He went His disciples should be left behind. (1) For themselves, it would be better not to be taken out of the world so soon, when as it were the work of grace was little more than commenced in their hearts; when as yet they were so imperfectly sanctified. (2) For Christ, for the vindication of His honour, for the propagation of His truth, for the extension of His cause, it would be more advantageous that they should not be so suddenly withdrawn from the gaze of men. (3) For the world, it would be more beneficial that they should remain as a salt to preserve it (Matt. v. 13), as a light to illumine it (Matt. v. 14), as a leaven to work in it (Matt. xiii. 33). Hence Christ only prayed that they might be kept in safety, shielded from evil in all its forms and manifestations, from hurtful things (Mark xvi. 18; Luke x. 19; Acts xviii. 10), from wicked men (2 Thess. iii. 2), from the evil one (1 John v. 8). 3. In *felicity.* 'These things I speak in the world that they may have My joy fulfilled in themselves' (ver. 13). Christ leaves them with this prayer that in the days of tribulation coming they might be sustained by the reflection that the Father would not desert them but would in answer to His supplication protect and preserve them.

III. **The Arguments.** 1. *They belonged to Him, the Father.* 'They are Thine' (ver. 9). Believers are God's (1) by nature as His creatures, (2) by grace as His children, (3) by community of interest with Christ (ver. 10). 2. *Christ's glory was involved in their preservation.* 'I am glorified in them' (ver. 10). In them the world would behold at once the proof of His glorification beside the Father and the character of His religion. By them the fact of His glorification should be proclaimed, and the glory of His cause and kingdom advanced (Acts ii. 33; iii. 13). 3. *They were about to be deprived of His presence.* 'And now I am no more in the world, but these are in the world, and I come to Thee' (ver. 11). Up till then Christ had shielded them and done so with success, not one of them having been lost (though Judas had). Henceforth He would not be able by His bodily presence to protect them. Accordingly like a dying parent He commends them (His children) to their heavenly Father's care.

Lessons. 1. That Christ's believing people are specially dear to His heart. 2. That they are sure of salvation, being prayed for by Christ and kept by the Father. 3. That they ought to be a happy people, since though hated by the world they have the friendship of the Father and the Son.

Ver. 10.—CHRIST GLORIFIED IN HIS SAINTS (2 Thess. i. 10).

I. *As the purchase of His blood.* As the fruit of His soul-travail they indicate the success of His redeeming and mediatorial work. II. *As the trophies of His power.* Having been rescued from the thraldom of sin and brought into His kingdom they attest the all-conquering might of His love. III. *As the creations of His grace.* Being renewed in the spirit of their minds and recreated after His image they reveal in their moral likeness to Him the beauty of holiness.

that is in Him. IV. *As the subjects of His empire.* In their willing subjection to His throne they proclaim the gentle character of His rule. V. *As the preachers of His gospel.* In the testimony they afford by their lips and lives that Christ is exalted they show forth His glory before men.

Ver. 11. Kept for Jesus Christ (Jude 1). I. **Who?** The saints, those given by the Father to Christ. II. **What?** Keep them. As it were Christ having obtained them from the Father for safe keeping for Him, replaces them in the Father's hand for safe keeping for Himself. III. **How?** In Thy name ; i.e. by graciously revealing in them Thy name which I have outwardly manifested to them. IV. **Why?** Because Christ was returning to the Father. The Keeper of God's spiritual Israel is not now Christ but the Father (1 Peter i. 5). V. **Wherefore?** That they might be one. Unless the Father keeps the saints they never will be or become one.

VER. 17-19. THE SANCTIFICATION OF THE SAINTS.

I. **An Object dear to Christ.** 1. *He prayed for this on earth :* ver. 17. Always a sign of earnest desire for another's good as well as of a firm and determined purpose to accomplish that desire when one is driven to speak of it to God, the fact here recorded that Christ, ere He bade farewell to His followers, lifted up His eyes to heaven and interceded for their perfecting in grace, for their complete devotement to God in voluntary self-surrender, was no mean indication of the strength and fervency of the emotion of which He was conscious. The time, place, and circumstances of His supplication likewise show that His soul must have been profoundly moved, since that can have been no transient or superficial feeling which was able for the moment to bid back the onrush of sorrow from Gethsemane and Golgotha. 2. *He died for this upon the cross :* ver. 19. Nothing can be more incorrect than the notion that the purpose aimed at by Christ's mission as a whole, and by His death upon the cross in particular, was only the erasure from heaven's statute book of the penalty due to man for his transgressions. Far beyond that Christ had His eye fixed upon the recovery of men's souls to purity and truth, their entire consecration, soul, body, and spirit, to the will of His Father, as the ultimate end and issue of His obedience unto death (Gal. i. 4 ; Eph. v. 26 ; Tit. ii. 14). 3. *He pleads for this in heaven.* Within the veil He intercedes for them for whom without the veil He shed His blood ; and the object of His intercession is that the gracious work commenced within their souls may be carried forward to a glorious consummation (Heb. vii. 25).

II. **A Gift sought from the Father.** 1. *The reason of this.* (1) Every good and perfect gift is from above and cometh down from the Father of Lights (James i. 17); hence from Him the sanctification of the soul. (2) The work of making holy belongs essentially the realm of the supernatural (Exod. xxxi. 13 ; Lev. xxi. 23 ; Ezek. xxxvii. 28 ; Zech. iv. 6 ; Acts xx. 32 ; Jude 1). (3) The grace of purity God distinctly desires to see reproduced in the souls of men (1 Thess. iv. 3). (4) The gift of holiness He has expressly included in the promise (Is. i. 25 ; Jer. xxxi. 33 ; Hos. xiv. 5 ; Zech. x. 12). 2. *The comfort of this.* If God be the author and giver of sanctification, then must it be (1) freely begun (Jas. i. 5), (2) faithfully pursued (1 Thess. v. 24), and (3) successfully accomplished (Phil. i. 6).

III. **A Work effected in the Truth.** 1. *The knowledge of it.* Hence an apostle represents growth in grace as keeping pace with growth in the knowledge of Christ (2 Peter iii. 18), while Christ Himself identifies that knowledge with eternal life (ver. 2). 2. *The belief of it.* Paul connects the sanctification of the spirit with belief of the truth in such a way as to show that the two are at least co-ordinate—if the former does not spring from the latter (2 Thess. ii. 13), since he also depicts the word of God as effectually working, i.e. producing its appropriate results, in them that believe (1 Thess. ii. 13). 3. *The love of it.* Before truth can exercise its rightful sway over the life, it must be enshrined in the affections. Hence an indispensable prerequisite to salvation in its highest sense is the love of the truth (Ps. cxix. 47), as the absence of this is the cause of judgment in them that perish (2 Thess. ii. 10). 4. *The obedience of it.* One apostle speaks of purifying the heart in obeying the truth (1 Peter i. 22), and another of obeying from the heart that form of doctrine which has been delivered to one (Rom. vi. 17). The new life of grace ever moves within the sphere of the truth. 1V. **A Qualification requisite for Christian Work.** As Christ had a mission to the world, so also have the saints ; a mission—1. *Resting on similar authority.* As the Father had sent Christ so also did Christ send His apostles (xx. 21 ; Matt. x. 16), and so does He still send His believing followers (Matt. v. 16 ; xxviii. 18 ; Phil. ii. 15). 2. *Possessing a similar object.* As Christ's mission aimed at the salvation of the world, so did, and so still does, theirs. As Christ revealed the Father's name to mankind, so under and after Him are they intended to bear Christ's name (and in that the Father's) unto the world (Acts. ix. 15 ; 2 Cor. iii. 3). 3. *Demanding a similar consecration.* As Christ was sanctified by the Father and sent into the world (x. 36), so does Christ sanctify by His own blood (Heb. ix. 14 ; x. 10 ; xiii. 12) those He commissions to be His ambassadors. As Christ sanctified Himself in the sense of entirely consecrating Himself to the Father's will, that He might be sent into the world (Ps. xl. 6-8 ; Heb. x. 5-7), so can Christ's servants only successfully discharge their mission in proportion as they are consecrated to the will of their Leader.

Lessons. 1. Is the sanctification of our souls a matter of interest to ourselves ? 2. Are we asking God to begin, carry on, and complete it ? 3. Are we bringing our souls into close and frequent contact with the truth ? 4. Are we remembering the mission for which our sanctification is indispensable ?

VER. 20-23.—THE UNITY OF THE CHURCH.

I. **For whom it is desired.** 1. *Not for men as men,* i.e. as members of social communities, citizens of states, subjects of empires ; it is not that of persons voluntarily allied for the prosecution of some common object in trade, commerce, politics, or science. 2. *But for men as believers ;* for the apostles and all who might afterwards believe on Christ through their word : ver. 20. Christ begins His enumeration with the apostles, laying them as it were at the foundation of the spiritual temple of His church ; but He takes into the grand total every individual believer who in after ages shall arise, and in His divinely prophetic vision contemplates a unity, a one body, a temple in which each of these shall find a place and bear a part. Cf. Paul's vision of a unified church (Eph. i. 10 ; ii. 21), and Peter's picture of the spiritual house (1 Pet. ii. 4, 5).

II. **In what it consists.** Generally in a oneness resembling and corresponding to that between the Father and the Son (ver. 21, 22) : particularly in 1. *A oneness of life,* or community of nature. As Christ and the Father were one in essence, not only when the former, as Son, lay in the bosom of the latter (i. 18), but after He had become incarnate (v. 26 ; x. 30), so believers are one with each other through the possession of a common life or new nature received from Christ (1 Cor. xii. 13 ; Eph. iv. 4, 6). 2. *A oneness of love,* or community of affection. This also has its antitype in the mutual affection of Father and Son. As the Father loveth the Son (iii. 35 ; v. 20) and the Son loveth the Father (xiv. 31), so the unity Christ desired for His people was one in which they should love as brethren (xiii. 34 ; xv. 12, 17). Cf. Eph. iii. 15 ; iv. 16. 3. *A oneness of faith,* or community of sentiment. Again the archetypal unity is that of the Father and the Son. As a perfect correspondence of thought and feeling prevailed between the Father and the Son—as the words the Son spake were not His but the Father's (iii. 34 ; vii. 16 ; viii. 26, 28, 38 ; xii. 49, 50 ; xiv. 10) —as the Father had no other organ of communicating His mind to the world than the Son, and the Son had no other message to impart to mankind than that heard and learnt of the Father ; so should the union of the saints reveal itself in a steadfast adherence to the Father's word given them by Christ (xiv. 23 ; xv. 10 ; xvii. 6). Cf. Paul's 'one faith' (Eph. iv. 5, 13). Of course neither Christ's words nor Paul's imply that never should believers diverge from one another in their modes of conceiving or presenting the truth, but that they should ever strive to be of the same mind (2 Cor. xiii. 11 ; Phil. iii. 15, 16), and that when the state of unity for which Christ prayed and to which Paul looked forward was realized, they would be of the same mind with reference to the main body of truth which had been made known to them. 4. *A oneness of action*, or community of labour. Once more the pattern of this union is found in that between the Father and the Son. As the Son can do nothing of Himself but what He seeth the Father do (v. 19), and the Father abiding in Him doeth the works (xiv. 10), so should Christians harmoniously co-operate with one another, striving together for the hope of the gospel (Phil. i. 27), being helpers of one another's faith and joy (2 Cor. i. 24; 3 John 8), and considering one another to provoke unto love and good works (Heb. x. 24).

III. **By what means it may be realized.** By believers doing three things. 1. *Remaining in union with the Father and the Son.* It is only by being "in us," Christ tells His Father, that the oneness of the saints can be realized (ver. 21). 2. *Participating in the glory Christ has received from the Father.* "The glory which Thou hast given Me I have given them, that they may be one" (ver. 22). See Exposition. 3. *Pressing forwards towards moral and spiritual perfection.* Christ asks that they may be "perfected into one" (ver. 23); i.e. He expects that their oneness will be the outcome and issue, the flower and fruit, of their 'perfection' as individuals and as a whole. Cf. Eph. iv. 13.

IV. **To what result it should lead.** It should awaken in the world 1. *Faith in the divine mission of Jesus*—"That the world may know that Thou didst send Me" (ver. 21). The spectacle of a united church, Christ anticipated, would beget in the world first a feeling of surprise, then a secret conviction, and finally a firm belief that Christ, upon whom that church was based and by whom it was inspired, could have been no other than the sent of God, and therefore His Son. 2. *Knowledge that that divine mission of Jesus was a fact*—"That the world may know," etc., (ver. 23). From inward experience of that which it signified, viz. that the Father loved them (believers) as He had loved Christ, the world, now believing, would come to realize that the heavenly and saving embassy of God's Son was a stupendous fact.

Learn 1. The mission assigned to the church—that of gathering a people out of the world and unto Christ by the preaching of the word. 2. The aim Christ has in thus collecting a people from the world—that they all may be perfected into one body in Him. 3. The certainty that this aim will be realized—since Christ has both empowered His church to do the work and prayed for its successful execution. 4. The obstruction offered to the realization of this aim by the disunited condition and imperfect character of the church. 5. The means of hastening the world's conversion to Christ—the church striving to attain to complete sanctification and unity. 6. The destiny awaiting the world when the Church shall have reached its proper manhood—that of being brought to a saving knowledge of the truth.

VER. 24-26. THE GLORIFICATION OF THE CHURCH.

I. **Its Significance explained** : ver. 24. 1. *Coexistence with Christ.* "That they may be with Me where I am." Now Christ coexists with the Church (Matt. xviii. 20; xxviii. 20) : then the Church will coexist with Christ (xii. 26; 1 Thess. iv. 17)—an important difference. Now Christ comes down to be with His Church : then the Church will be taken up to be with Christ. The place where they are together now is the wilderness, the scene of the Church's sufferings and trials, the arena of the Church's labours and conflicts, the school of the Church's discipline, the workshop in which the Church's unification is being brought about : the realm in which they shall then be together is the Father's house of many mansions, the place of Christ's exaltation, the scene of His glory. 2. *Communion with Christ.* Here Christ and His Church have communion and fellowship with one another (John i. 3)—He sees them (xvi. 22), and they see Him (xiv. 19) – only on their part it is not an open vision (1 Cor. xiii. 12). Then the vision will be direct, unveiled and full (1 Cor. xiii. 12; 1 John iii. 2; Rev. xxii. 4)—they shall "behold His glory," not that alone which is its outward emblem and symbol—the throne on which He sits, the sceptre He wields, the angels that attend Him, the trumpets that resound before Him, the clouds that support Him as He moves throughout His universe; but that also of which these are the tokens—the love the Father had for the Son, a love dateless in its origin, supreme in its measure and degree, unspeakable in its character and eternal in its duration,—and the glory which, moved by that love, the Father put upon the Son, when He constituted Him the Crown of redeemed humanity, Head of the Church and Head over all for the Church's sake (Eph. i. 22 ; Phil. ii. 9, 10 ; 1 Peter iii. 22). **3.** *Conformity to Christ.* On this side the vail the Church, collectively and individually, is being conformed to Christ's image (2 Cor. iv. 18) ; on that side the correspondence will be complete (Rom. viii. 29). " We shall be like Him, for we shall see Him as He is " (1 John iii. 2) :—i.e. since otherwise we should not and indeed could not see Him (Matt. v. 8), and because we shall see Him—it being impossible to behold without being assimilated to Him. **4.** *Copartnership with Christ.* In the meanwhile Christ is a copartner with His people in their sufferings and sorrows (Heb. iv. 15) ; by and by they shall participate with Him in His glory (ver. 22 ; Rev. iii. 21 ; 2 Tim. ii. 12). Gathered out of every nation, country, and tribe, owing their salvation to Him, each bearing on the countenance His image, all ascribing to Him their life, their joy, their all, they may fitly be conceived as singing while they cross the threshold of the Father's House—

" Glory to God that here we come,
And glory to the glorious Lamb :
Our light, our life, our joy, our all
Is in our arms and ever shall.
Our Lord is ours, and we are His,
Yea, now we see Him as He is ;
And hence we like unto Him are,
And full His glorious image share.
No darkness now, no dismal night,
No vapour intercepts the light ;
We see for ever face to face
The highest Prince in highest place.
This, this does heaven enough afford :
We are for ever with the Lord.
We want no more, for all is given ;
His presence is the heart of heaven."

(Ralph Erskine's Gospel Sonnets, p. 294).

II. Its Certainty guaranteed : ver. 24. **1.** *By the ' I will' of the divine Servant.* Having accomplished the work God had entrusted to His hands (ver. 4), Christ was entitled to claim the stipulated reward—to say not merely ' I ask,' ' I wish ' (though either of these would have been enough), but ' I will ' ; and, as failure is impossible with reference to either God's promise (Heb. v. 18) or Christ's reward (Is. liii. 11), so certainly Christ's believing people will eventually be glorified beside Him in heaven. **2.** *By the ' I will ' of the divine Son.* As the Father's Son Christ had been invested with full power and authority to bestow eternal life (ver. 2). Hence as possessed of such authority He could say—' In virtue of that power and prerogative conferred upon Me, I will.' And just because an ' I will ' of the glorified Christ cannot fail, the ultimate glorification of the Church is sure.

III. Its Justice vindicated : ver. 25, 26. **1.** *If the world is not glorified, that is because it cannot really be otherwise.* Eternal righteousness forbids the glorification of such as know not the Father. **2.** *If the Church is glorified, that is because glory is the necessary outcome of grace.* The Church being led here by Christ ever more into the knowledge of the Father and experience of His love is to that extent already made a partaker of eternal life. Eternal life in consummation is just the perfection of such knowledge and such experience. As certainly as Christ's glorification was involved in His knowledge of the Father, so certainly is the glorification of the Church the necessary outcome of its knowledge of the Father and the Son.

Lessons. **1.** The blessedness of heaven. **2.** The certainty of salvation. **3.** The necessity of growing in knowledge. **4.** The righteousness of the unbelieving world's doom. **5.** Grace the song of the glorified.

Ver. 22. The knowledge of the Father. I. The *want* of such knowledge, the world's sin. II. The *possession* of such knowledge, the prerogative of the Son. III. The *communication* of such knowledge, the purpose of the Incarnation. IV. The *reception* of such knowledge, the duty of faith. V. The *fruit* of such knowledge, the essence of eternal life.

SECTION SECOND.—THE GLORY OF CHRIST UNVEILED TO HIS OWN THROUGH HIS VOLUNTARY SELF-ABASEMENT AS FAR AS TO DEATH ON THEIR BEHALF

CHAP. XVIII—XIX

Having completed the necessary preparations for dying that " His Own " might go free, our Lord begins the steep descent. The way He travels is a *via dolorosa* indeed. The Evangelist exhibits Him in five successive scenes—in the garden of Gethsemane (xviii. 1-11), in the palace of the high-priest (xviii. 12-27), in the praetorium of Pilate (xviii. 28—xix. 16), in the place called Golgotha (xix. 17-37), and in the tomb in a garden (xix. 38-42)—each scene leading on and down to that beneath, till the lowest deep of self-humiliation is reached, and the crucified Son of God is beheld lying in the sinner's grave. Only a glance at these impressive tableaux is required to show that while some incidents are narrated which the Synoptists have omitted, as e.g. the falling of the band to the ground (xviii. 6), the examination before Annas (xviii. 13-24), Pilate's first conference with the Jews (xviii. 28-32), and first interview with Christ (xviii. 33-37), the words from the cross (xix. 25-30), the piercing of the side (xix. 34), and the part played by Nicodemus in the burial (xix. 39); on the other hand matters are related that might have been supposed to be sufficiently detailed by them, as e.g. the arrest (xviii. 1-11), the fall of Peter (xviii. 15-18, 25-27), the examination before Pilate (xviii. 33), the crucifixion (xix. 17-22),—from which it is evident that John was guided in the composition of his narrative, not to any appreciable extent at least, by a desire to supplement pre-existent accounts, but by an independent purpose, viz., to set forth the glory of Jesus in giving up His life for His Own, This will become apparent as the different subsections are examined.

1. THE GARDEN OF GETHSEMANE

CHAP. XVIII. VER. 1-11

EXPOSITION

Chap. xviii. ver. 1. **When Jesus had spoken**, lit., *Jesus having spoken* these **words**, the farewell discourses and the high-priestly prayer, **He went forth** from the city (Bengel, Godet, Meyer, etc.), or from the Jerusalem side of the

Kidron (Hengstenberg), rather than from the upper room (De Wette), in which sense however ἐξῆλθεν is used by the Synoptists (Matt. xxvi. 30 ; Mark xiv. 26 ; Luke xxii. 39), **with His disciples,** the *eleven,* Judas having before this separated from His company (xiii. 30), **over the brook,** χείμαρρος (cf. 2 Sam. xv. 23 (LXX.), 1 Kings xv. 13 (LXX.) ; Jos. Ant. viii. 1, 5 ; ix. 7, 3), or *winter torrent,* which flows in the rainy season and dries up in summer. **Kidron** τῶν Κεδρῶν (א Bᶜ L X. etc. Griesbach, Lachmann, Westcott and Hort), 'of the Cedars'; so called because of the cedars which grew upon the Mount of Olives—a fact usually denied by expositors (Godet), or at least hitherto unknown to them, but affirmed by the Talmud (Taanith iv. 8) which mentions that in the last days of the Temple two cedars stood upon the Mount of Olives (see Westcott and Hort, The N. T. in Greek, vol. ii. 90). If τοῦ Κεδρών (A S Λ, Bengel, Lücke, Meyer, Godet, etc.) be preferred, then the plural τῶν where it occurs will require to be ascribed to the ignorance of copyists, and the name explained as an allusion to the darkness of the water (Meyer, Hengstenberg) קדרין. (Job vi. 16) signifying 'turbid or 'troubled,' or of the thickly woodeu valley through which it flowed (Lücke, Olshausen),—the valley of Jehosaphat, a deeply cut ravine beginning about ½ hour N. of Jerusalem, surrounding it on the N. and E. sides, and separating it from the Mount of Olives. From the connection of the brook with David's history, as well as from the epithet χείμαρρος, in the O. T. employed as a symbol of sorrow (Ps. xviii. 4 ; cx. 7 ; cxxiv. 4 ; Jer. xlvii. 2), it has been surmised that John, according to his wonted practice (cf. x. 22 ; xiii. 30), designed to suggest that the Kidron was for Jesus a veritable brook of tribulation, and that in passing over it into Gethsemane He was fulfilling the type of His sufferings which had been prepared beforehand in the experience of the Israelitish king (Hengstenberg, Westcott, Milligan and Moulton). **where was a garden** a κῆπος or place planted with herbs and trees (ver. 26 ; xix. 41 ; Luke xiii. 19)—in this case attached to a χωρίον or enclosed piece of ground, a country manor or estate

called Gethsemane or 'Oil-Press' (Matt. xxvi. 36 ; Mark xiv. 32), situated on the Mount of Olives (Luke xxii. 39), near Bethany (Matt. xxi. 17 ; Mark xi. 11) in which, it would seem, Christ had other friends besides Martha, Mary, and Lazarus. **into the which He entered, Himself and His disciples.** From this the inference is natural that the owner of the estate and garden was friendly to Jesus. " The matter thus mentioned clearly implies that such gardens were during feast times left open for all who needed them" (Thomson, The Land and the Book, p. 694).

2. **Now Judas also** (as well as the other disciples) **which betrayed Him** (see ver. 5 and cf. xii. 4 ; xiii. 11) **knew the place,** having been at the farm and in the garden ; **for Jesus ofttimes** (see viii. 1, if authentic) **resorted thither,** or *assembled* (συνήχθη) there, **with His disciples,** probably for purposes of instruction, though this time for resting. The incident recorded by Mark (xiv. 51) has led to the conjecture that the young man who left his linen garment in his captor's hands and fled was a member of the farmer's family, who, having been roused from sleep by the uproar in the garden, had ventured out in his night clothes to ascertain the cause of the disturbance (Hengstenberg).

3. **Judas then** or *therefore,* knowing from the advanced hour of the night that Christ must have left the city and would likely be discovered at His usual place of resort, **having received the band** *of soldiers,* the well-known body of men-at-arms (τὴν σπεῖραν) serving as a garrison in the fort of Antonia, on the N.E. corner of the Temple hill, the soldiers of the governor (Matt. xxvii. 27), usually a full cohort of Roman infantry with a tribune or chiliarch (Acts xxi. 31), though it is not necessary to assume that the whole cohort of 600 men (Hengstenberg)—"half an army " one sarcastically observes (Keim)—or even a third part of it, a maniple, *manipulus* (Tholuck), escorted the traitor, but only a detachment which would sufficiently represent the whole, since its chiliarch, or presiding officer, attended (ver. 12). That the Synoptists do not include Roman military in the "great multitude"

that came with Judas does not prove either that they were not aware of that fact, or that it was not a fact. The message of Pilate's wife (Matt. xxvii. 19) shows that the Roman authorities must have been communicated with upon the subject of Christ's apprehension (Godet), while, as indications that Caesar's troops had to do with His capture, appeal has been taken (Hengstenberg) to the double style of arms borne by the crowd, partly swords and partly staves (Matt. xxvi. 47 : Mark xiv. 43), to Our Lord's language concerning the twelve legions (Matt. xxvi. 53), to the young men who arrested the youth in the garden, the Roman military being usually designated *juvenes, juniores, juventus* (Mark xiv. 51—T. R.), to the commandants of the temple who accompanied the chief priests and elders (Luke xxii. 4, 52), one of whom must have been a Roman officer (cf. Jos. Ant. xx. 6, 2 ; Wars ii. 17, 2 ; with Ant. xx. 8, 11). **and officers from the chief priests and the Pharisees,** i.e. members of the temple watch, ὑπηρέται (see on vii. 32, 45). **cometh thither** That the armed force did not enter the garden (Tholuck, Meyer, Godet), ver. 26 renders doubtful. **with lanterns and torches and weapons.** The torches blazing on the end of poles (φανοί) and oil lamps enclosed in lanterns (λαμπάδες)—a distinction which is far from certain—were obviously taken, though the moon was full, because Christ was not expected to be captured under the free heaven, but either within doors or in some dark recess of the garden or of the valley ; the weapons—ὅπλων, a heavy-armed force (Paley), or simply 'arms,'—the 'swords and staves' of the earlier narrators (Matt. xxvi. 47 ; Mark xiv. 43 ; Luke xxii. 52), because it was anticipated violence would be needed to secure Him. The mention of the 'lights,' omitted by the Synoptists, belongs to the greater accuracy of detail supplied by an eye-witness.

4. **Jesus therefore,** in consequence of the approach of Judas, of which He became aware either by His quick ear detecting the noise of the advancing multitude, or because He knew that His hour was at hand, **knowing all the things that were coming upon Him,**

and therefore without surprise or fear, **went forth**—not out of the garden (Lampe, Meyer, Godet), but out of its interior (Tholuck), the garden house (Brückner), the chamber (Ewald), the more retired place in which He was (Luthardt), or may have sought concealment (Westcott), out of the shadow of the trees (Alford)—hardly out of the circle of His disciples (Schweitzer, Hengstenberg, Lange) ;—or, without reference to locality, advanced towards the fulfilment of the divine purpose (Milligan and Moulton), **and saith unto them,** Himself taking the initiative, **Whom seek ye ?** The kiss of Judas (Matt. xxvi. 49 ; Mark xiv. 45 ; Luke xxii. 47, 48), omitted by John, was probably given before this question was addressed to the multitude (Lücke, Ewald, Meyer, Godet, etc. , though some (Lange, Stier) place it later.

5. **They,** the chiliarch, the soldiers, the temple watch, **answered Him, Jesus of Nazareth.** Either they had not observed the kiss of Judas (Besser), or they avoided saying 'Thee,' because already they had begun to be afraid. **Jesus saith unto them, I am** *He.* With calm majesty He deigns not to flee, but challenges them to do their worst against Him, if they can. The same expression had more than once before fallen from Christ's lips (cf. iv. 26 ; vi. 20 ; viii. 24, 28, 58 ; xiii. 19), and could not fail to startle Judas. **And Judas also who betrayed Him** See on ver. 2. This constantly recurring appellation, like a melancholy refrain, serves to emphasize the atrocious criminality of the traitor, to brand him like another Cain, to impale him on the pillory of everlasting infamy. **was standing with them.** After the kiss he had, it may be assumed, fallen back into their ranks, glad to escape his late Master's eye.

6. **When therefore He said unto them, I am** *He,* **they** not the disciples (Paulus), but the soldiers and police, **went backwards, and fell to the ground**—though not necessarily backward. The incident was natural (Lücke, Tholuck, De Wette, Ewald, Brückner, and others), in so far as it resulted from inward terror or awe in the presence of Christ's majesty : cf.

the instances cited from profane history of murderers shrinking before and from their intended victims, as e.g. of the slave sent to murder Marius, who flung down his sword, and fled from the aged hero's presence, exclaiming, 'I cannot slay Marius.' For other examples, see Farrar's Life of Christ, chap. lvii. At the same time, the incident cannot be excluded from the category of the supernatural (Lampe, Meyer, Luthardt, Godet, and others), but must be classified with similar occurrences in the Saviour's earlier history, as e.g. vii. 44, 46; viii. 59; x. 39; Luke iv. 30. It is idle to inquire whether the miracle consisted in the power exerted by Christ's word, or in the influence that streamed from Christ's presence. Doubtless both concurred to produce the effect witnessed, which was probably intended to demonstrate the inability of Judas and his myrmidons to carry out their programme, as well as the absolute voluntariness of Christ in surrendering Himself into their hands.

7. **Again therefore,** because they could not take Him unless He would and because He of His own free will desired to be taken, **He asked them, Whom seek ye?** Christ's purpose in repeating this question may have been to fix attention on Himself and so secure the preservation of His disciples. **And they said, Jesus of Nazareth.** That they did not now say 'Thee' is an almost certain indication that they were under the constraint, if not of a higher power, of their own fears.

8. **Jesus answered, I told you that I am** *He.* This second reply had the effect of restoring a degree of tranquility to the soldiers and watchmen. Bengel thinks that if Christ had repeated His declaration a third time they would not have taken Him. Its third repetition occurred before the high priest (Mark xiv. 62). **If therefore ye seek Me, let these go their way.** The disciples seemingly had rallied round their Master (Westcott). If John does not state that their subsequent departure was a flight, that had already been implied in Christ's farewell discourse (xvi. 32). What John remembers is that not even the flight of which all were guilty would have been possible, had Christ not previously secured their safety.

9. **That the word might be fulfilled which He spake** (xvii. 12), **Of those whom Thou hast given Me I lost not one.** Of these words, used by Christ with reference to the spiritual preservation of His disciples, the application by John to the bodily protection of the eleven, has been pronounced "in clear contradiction with the ingenious and ideal tone of this gospel" (De Wette), and ascribed to the pen of a later and less elevated writer than the author of its other parts (Schweitzer); but it harmonizes exactly with the prevailing symbolism of this book to see in the external phenomenon an emblem of a higher spiritual fact (cf. iv. 10; xiii. 30), while the external fact in this case was part of the means by which Christ preserved His disciples from ultimate apostasy, and so accomplished the spiritual result of which it was the symbol (Luthardt).

10. **Simon Peter therefore,** attempting to defend his Master, **having a sword,** or, *long knife in a sheath* (Paley), **drew it and struck the high priest's,** i.e. Caiaphas's (see xi. 49), **servant,** or slave, **and cut off his right** (cf. Luke xxii. 50) **ear,** perhaps lobe of the ear, *auriculam* (Paley), ὠτάριον (א B C* L X etc., Tischendorf, Westcott and Hort), rather than ὠτίον (T. R.) 'as in the Synoptists (Matt. xxvi. 51; Mark xiv. 47). **Now the servant's name was Malchus.** John preserves the name both of the violent disciple and of the object of his assault. That John knows the name of the high priest's slave confirms, and is in turn confirmed by, the statement in ver. 15.

11. **Jesus therefore,** because disapproving of His disciple's action, **said unto Peter, Put up the sword into the sheath,** the pronoun 'thy' before sword (A. V.), as in Matt. xxvi. 52, being here ungenuine: **the cup** τὸ ποτήριον, a drinking vessel, hence the contents of a cup, and therefore the portion or lot which God presents to be drunk, either for evil (Ps. xi. 6; lxxv. 8) or for good (Ps. xvi. 5; xxiii. 5)—here the cup of sorrow and death which awaited Christ (Matt. xx. 22, 23; xxvi. 39, 42; Mark x. 38, 39; xiv. 36)—**which the Father hath given Me,** put into My hands by

the approach of this My hour, **shall I not drink it?** The language of Christ here employed, an echo of His words in Gethsemane (Matt. xxvi. 39, 42), shows that the evangelist was not unacquainted with the soul-struggle in the garden. That he omitted it from his narrative was not because it was inconsistent with his idea of a Christ, in fact beneath the dignity of a Christ, who was not a human but a divine person (Origen, Baur, Keim, Strauss, Schenkel), or because it does not harmonize with the farewell discourses (Meyer), or because John himself was not in a mood of mind for recording the Gethsemane prayer (Neander), but either because he deemed it already sufficiently known from the earliest accounts (Olshausen) or from universal tradition (Lücke, Tholuck), or most likely because it did not exactly fall in with the leading purpose he had in view. He may have felt that he could leave it out with safety inasmuch as he had previously recorded a similar sorrow to that of Gethsemane (xii. 27), and because his language in the present instance distinctly implied it.

HOMILETICS

VER. 1-11.—THE ARREST OF JESUS.

I. **The Approach of Judas:** ver. 1-3. 1. *To what place?* The garden of Gethsemane, whither Christ had retired after leaving the city with His disciples. 2. *At what time?* Towards or after midnight. Since withdrawing from the upper room, the traitor had occupied the interval in mustering his regiment. 3. *By whom attended?* By a company of guardsmen with their chiliarch from the castle of Antonia and a body of policemen with the temple watch, the former with their swords, the latter with their batons, and both with lanterns and torches. 4. *For what purpose?* To apprehend Jesus. This 'half army' to take a solitary prisoner from eleven men has been cited as an indication of the fictitious character of the narrative, whose truth it rather confirms. It would have been ridiculous to organize such an expedition to capture Jesus, had He been only a man—a Jewish Socrates and nothing more : the only rational explanation of the 'band' is that Judas knew, while the Sanhedrists feared, He was also a God.

II. **The Surrender of Jesus:** ver. 4-11. That Christ was not forcibly taken so much as freely self-delivered four things attest. 1. *The impotence of His assailants.* Neither Judas with his bailiffs nor the chiliarch with his guards could do anything against Jesus until He wished. When He asked whom they sought, they could not answer 'Thee,' but only in a far-off way 'Jesus of Nazareth,' though it is probable Judas's kiss had already pointed Him out ; and, when He told them 'I am He,' they could not lift a finger against Him. As if a hand from the invisible world had given them *a push,* they recoiled from His presence, reeled and staggered to the ground, overawed by the majesty of the feeble and defenceless man who stepped forth to meet them with the composure and dignity of a God? 'Thus conscience does make cowards of us all!' 2. *The submission of Himself.* Having repeated His former question and received the old reply, He a second time announced who He was, adding, 'If ye seek Me, let these go their way,' meaning—'Lo! I am ready ; take and bind Me whose majesty ye have just now recognized and whose power ye have involuntarily owned ; behold, Myself, whom ye cannot capture, I now place into your hands!" Christ's arrest was due to Himself, not to them, to a willing acquiescence on His part to be bound, not to any ability on their part to bind : cf. Matt. xxvi. 53. 3. *The command given to Peter.* 'Put up the sword into the sheath!" It was not much Peter could have done with his blade : but little or much Christ declined to accept it. His words meant that He discouraged all attempts at rescue, whether rash or prudent, whether likely to succeed or calculated only to fail. 4. *The recognition of His Father's will.* The death He beheld impending was the 'cup' the

Father had given Him to drink ; and that was enough to make it His will : cf. vi. 38 ; Mark xiv. 36 ; Heb. x. 7.

III. **The Safety of the Disciples** : ver. 8, 9. 1. *A command issued.* 'Let these go their way.' Not a wish but an order. (1) Merciful—with compassionate regard for the situation of His followers. (2) Powerful—with the authority of a king, with a force that even Cæsar's legions could not resist. (3) Successful. The soldiers could not have hindered the disciples though they would. The hand that had hurled them to the sward when they sought to take Himself now restrained them whilst His followers escaped. 2. *A prophecy fulfilled.* 'Of those whom thou hast given Me, I lost not one.' John beheld in the preservation of himself and co-apostles on that eventful night an emblem of what had been in a far loftier sense the purpose of his Master's arrest, viz., the freedom and safety of 'His Own.'

Lessons. 1. The wickedness of the fallen heart—exemplified in Judas. 2. The love of the divine heart—pictured in Jesus. 3. The imperfection of the renewed heart—illustrated in Peter.

VER. 1.—THE SCENE IN GETHSEMANE.

I. *Sorrow experienced.* The agony and bloody sweat (Matt. xxvi. 36 ; Luke xxii. 44). II. *Indignity suffered.* The traitor's kiss (Matt. xxvi. 49) and the soldiers' assault (ver. 3, 12). III. *Majesty displayed.* Christ's advance towards the band (ver. 4) and announcement of Himself (ver. 5, 6). IV. *Power exerted.* The hurling of the band to the ground (ver. 6) and the restraining of them while the disciples escaped (ver. 8). V. *Love manifested.* Christ's care for His Own. 'Let these go their way' (ver. 8). VI. *Mercy extende l.* The healing of the servant's ear (Luke xxii. 51). VII. *Submission rendered* The drinking of the Father's cup (ver. 11).

VER. 2.—THE SON OF PERDITION ; OR, THE STORY OF JUDAS.

I. **His Personal History.** 1. His *name.* Judas—'renowned.' A providence in the naming of children. The traitor's cognomen ominously significant. 2. His *parentage.* The son of Simon of whom nothing is known 3. His *birthplace.* Kerioth, whence his designation 'Iscariot'—'man of Kerioth.' See on vi. 71 (Exposition). 4. His *talents.* That Judas was a person of ability may be inferred from the distinction he subsequently enjoyed as an apostle. 5. His *privileges.* Besides the religious training which as a Jewish boy he would of necessity obtain, he enjoyed for two years at least the friendship, confidence, teaching, example, and love of Jesus of Nazareth.

II. **His Recorded Character.** 1. *A son of perdition.* A true child of the devil, the proper outcome and fruit of those principles of 'corruption' and 'moral decay' that prevail in and dominate over the world—a radically bad man, a man 'fit for treasons, stratagems, and spoils.' 2. *An insincere disciple.* How he came to be an adherent of Jesus Christ is difficult to understand. Most likely, along with other restless spirits at the time, Judas had his Messianic hopes and expectations—not religious and spiritual, but carnal, worldly, social, and political ; and having witnessed Christ's miracles, perhaps at Jerusalem (ii. 23), may have conceived that at last his eye rested on the coming Deliverer who should restore the kingdom to Israel. Anyhow the impulse which led him to associate with Christ as a disciple was neither piety nor patriotism, but personal aggrandizement, if not paltry pelf. The new times that were dawning opened up 'visions' which inflamed his depraved heart and corrupt mind ; in the ferment of social revolution which he beheld approaching, it would go hard with him if he could not improve his fortunes. 3. *A false apostle.* It is even harder to explain why Jesus who knew what was in man, and in particular who discerned from the first that Judas was a devil, chose him to be an apostle (see p. 172). But He did ; and Judas accepted the office, though inwardly its duties (with one exception) must have been repugnant to his base and diabolic spirit. 4. *A secret thief.* Purse-bearer to the twelve, he pilfered the moneys, mostly contributions of the pious, that were entrusted to his care for the necessities of Christ and His disciples as well as for their ministrations to the poor.

III. **His Infamous Transgression.** 1. *The first inception.* Doubtless the word of Jesus in Galilee (vi. 64, 70) came to Judas as a revelation, showing that his inward hypocrisy was known ; but the horrible idea of 'treason' probably did not cross the threshold of his spirit until he suffered the rebuke at Bethany. 2. *The swift maturation.* Once admitted to the chamber of his soul, the dark thought began to germinate. The clouds that were gathering round Christ's path would assist the process. The hozannas of the multitude were silent. The emissaries of the Sanhedrim were abroad. The cause of the Nazarene was on the wane. He (Judas) would covenant with the leaders to arrest his Master. And he did (Matt. xxvi. 14 ; Mark xiv. 10 ; Luke xxii. 3). 3. *The final decision.* This was reached at the supper table (xiii. 7). Up to this point Judas might have retraced his steps : after this *nulla vestigia retrorsum*, there was no drawing back. Satan then entered into and took possession of him. Henceforth he was Satan's instrument and tool. 4. *The ultimate execution.* This was done without delay. When Judas left the upper room, it was night : before morning had fully dawned Jesus was condemned to die. 5. *The underlying motive.* (1) Avarice has been thought of (Steinmeyer, Strauss, Renan, Farrar) as the secret passion that hurried on the traitor to his fatal deed. But against this stand the smallness of the price—thirty pieces of silver, the compensation for a slave gored by an ox (Ex. xxi. 32), not a high reward for so valuable a prize as Jesus !—the returning of the blood-money (Matt. xxvii. 4, 5), and the fact that Christ had allowed, perhaps appointed, him to act as treasurer to the apostolic college. (2) Enthusiasm, mistaken zeal, a desire to force Christ's hand, to compel him to declare Himself and stand forth as Messiah, has been suggested (Paulus, De Quincey) as the cause of Judas's deed—his remorse and suicide resulting from the unexpected failure of his plan. This, however, shatters itself against the fact that all through the farewell discourses Christ speaks of the traitor not as 'a misguided enthusiast' but as 'a lost man,' 'a son of perdition.' (3) Prudence, a regard to his own personal safety, a wish to stand well with the authorities when the collapse came, as he now saw it coming, was enough, it is said (Schenkel), to inspire the treachery. But Judas could have saved himself by flight ; and in any case this does not appear a force powerful enough to account for the diabolic project. (4) Revenge, springing from disappointment and apostasy, was probably the deepest motive. Judas was offended at the character of Christ's Messiahship when it began to unfold itself before his eyes, hated the doctrines of self-denial and humility which it preached, turned from it in disgust when he beheld the total wreck of all his hopes and avenged himself upon the Master who had betrayed him (Neander, Keim, Weiss, Fairbairn). (5) Inasmuch as this problem roots itself in the dark depths of the sinful possibilities that are in man, a satisfactory solution of the same is impossible (Beyschlag).

IV. **His Melancholy End.** 1. *Remorse.* When he saw that Christ was condemned he repented (Matt. xxvii. 3), not sincerely, humbly, inwardly, as Peter afterwards did, but only outwardly, proudly, remorsefully. He regretted having done the fatal deed, not because of its deplorable wickedness, so much as because of its fatal issue. 2. *Suicide.* Despairing of heaven's mercy, he felt the burden of life too intolerable to be longer borne. Having purchased a field with the reward of his iniquity, or the Sanhedrim having done so—a field to bury strangers in, he hanged himself upon a tree therein (Matt. xxvii. 5 ; Acts i. 18). The sorrow of the world worketh death (2 Cor. vii. 10).

VER. 11.—'PUT UP THE SWORD' ; OR THE USE OF FORCE IN RELIGION.
I. **Unavailing.** The Church's feeble instruments can do as little against the world's battalions as Peter's sword could have done against the guardsmen of Caesar. II. **Unnecessary.** He who could have commanded twelve legions of angels had no need of Peter's rapier : the cause which is supported by 'all power in heaven and earth' requires not to be furthered by carnal weapons. III. **Unchristian.** The recourse of Peter to a knife in order to repel the attack upon his Master was in flagrant opposition to the precept that Master had taught (Matt. v. 39) ; that of the Church to force for the purpose of ad-

vancing its interests is in total contradiction to the character of Christ's kingdom (ver. 36). IV. **Unreasonable.** Had Peter been able to rescue Christ that would not have proved either that he was right or that Christ's assailants were wrong. 'Force is no remedy' and 'no argument.' So Christ told the menial who slapped Him when He stood before the high priest (ver. 23). Instead of resorting to magisterial authority, the Church should labour to convince and convert its opponents. V. **Unwise.** Could Peter have delivered Christ, he would only have hindered the Father's purpose. The Church when she unsheathes the sword rather retards than advances the triumph of the truth. VI. **Unsafe.** Peter's sword practice in the garden led to his identification in the palace, to the suspicions and cross-examinations that brought about his fall, to his own ultimate martyrdom (Matt. xxvi. 52). So when the Church resorts to violence she may anticipate danger to herself.

VER. 11. **The Father's Cup** (affliction). I. Prepared by the Father's wisdom. II. Appointed in the Father's love. III. Designed for the Father's child. IV. Accepted for the Father's sake.

2. THE PALACE OF THE HIGH PRIEST

CHAP. XVIII. VER. 12-32

EXPOSITION

Ver. 12, 13. **So the band,** the soldiers of the cohort **and the chief captain,** chiliarch or captain of a thousand, **and the officers of the Jews,** the temple police (see on ver. 3), **seized Jesus and bound Him.** The three parties combine to apprehend a prisoner who had freely put Himself into their hands, making Him as fast as possible, as if they considered Him a dangerous criminal. "They thought they could only be sure of Him, if all helped" (Luthardt). **and led Him to Annas** Annas, "Gracious"—Hanan, Ananias, Ananus —high priest from A.D. 7-14, was succeeded by Ismael the son of Phabi, who was within a year followed by Eleazar the son of Annas, who in turn was displaced at the end of a twelvemonth in favour of Simon the son of Camithus, who after an equally brief tenure was deprived of his dignity, when Joseph Caiaphas was installed, and continued in the office till A.D. 35-6. Caiaphas was followed by two sons of Annas in succession, and again by another after one interregnum, and later by a fourth, Ananus, a bold and insolent Sadducee, who put to death the brother of Our Lord. In consequence of this long enjoyment of the high-priestly office, Annas was popularly regarded as a

most fortunate man (Jos. Ant. xviii. 2, 1 ; xx. 9, 1). **first** John was aware of another trial, before Caiaphas (ver. 24). As to why Christ was conducted first to Annas, it has been supposed, that the house of Annas lay in the way of those leading Jesus (Lücke, Tholuck), or that Annas, though deposed, was still regarded as the legitimate high priest (Lange), or that he was president of the Sanhedrim (Wieseler); but a sufficient reason was, the fact next mentioned, that he stood in close family relationship to the acting high priest and was therefore one whom it was desirable to treat with respect (Meyer, Godet, Luthardt, and others). **for he was father in law to Caiaphas who was high priest that year.** See on xi. 51.

14. **Now Caiaphas was he which gave counsel to the Jews that it was expedient that one man should die for the people.** See on xi. 51, 52. Repeated here perhaps to suggest the unlikelihood of Jesus obtaining justice in a court whose president had already sentenced him to die.

15. **And** *but*,—introducing an antithesis to the action of the band— **Simon Peter** who along with his fellow disciples had fled immediately on Christ's arrest (Matt. xxvi. 56 ;

Mark xiv. 50), **followed**, lit. *was follow-ing* (the imperfect representing an action in progress) 'afar off' (Matt. xxvi. 58 ; Mark xiv. 54 ; Luke xxii. 54), i.e. at a considerable distance in the rear of, not the soldiers and con-stables, but **Jesus** whom he had avowed he would follow to death (xiii. 37)—his object in following being not to attempt a rescue, but " to see the end"; **and so did another disciple,** ἄλλος μαθητής, not a citizen of Jerusalem (Grotius), or Judas (Heumann), or some unknown disciple (Augustine, Calvin), perhaps James his brother (Godet), but himself, John (Meyer, Keim, Luthardt, Westcott and others), the article being omitted before 'other' because this is the first use of this particular ex-pression, and the customary peri-phrasis not employed, because if too often obtruded it might become dis-tasteful. **Now** or *but*, giving a fresh turn to the thought, **that disciple** not *this*,—John thinking of himself as the more remote—**was** not related to (Ewald) but **known unto the high priest**—presumably Caiaphas, the only high priest as yet mentioned and as such distinguished from Annas (see ver. 13, 24), though Annas had been high priest and was sometimes so styled (Luke iii. 2 ; Acts iv. 6). See on ver. 19. John's acquaintance with the high priest has been traced to *religious necessities* on the part of John, who at an earlier stage in his spiritual development may have sought to discover in the high priest what he ultimately found in Christ (Hengstenberg), to *business transactions* between the two, the Gali-lean fisherman having furnished the high priest's table with fish (Luthardt), to the fact of John's possessing a resid-ence in Jerusalem (?), which xix. 27 renders probable (Tholuck, Lange), but just as likely it was to none of these that it owed its rise. **and entered in with Jesus** (meeting with no opposition probably as one who had often been observed about the house) **into the court of the high priest.** "An oriental house is usually built around a quad-rangular interior court, into which there is a passage (sometimes arched) through the front part of the house, closed next the street, by a heavy folding gate, with a smaller wicket for single persons, kept by a porter"

(Robinson). This quadrangular court, usually open to the sky, was the court (αὐλή) into which John entered.

16. **But Peter**, who had not been beside John when he entered, **was standing at the door without** at the wicket gate above referred to, through which he may have been observed by John at a moment when the gate was opened. **So**, *then*, in consequence of having noticed his companion, **the other disciple**, already alluded to, ver. 15—hence the art., **was known to the high priest**, and therefore in a manner possessed of a right of entrance, **went out** from the court, **and spake unto her that kept the door**—the Jews making use of women for this purpose (cf. Acts xii. 13 ; Jos. Ant. vii. 2, 1), while the Greeks and Romans employed men **—and brought in Peter.** How much better had it been for Peter to stay without !

17. **The maid therefore that kept the door,** sauntering into 'the court where Peter was and either observing some-thing in his manner to arouse suspicion or simply judging from his acquain-tanceship with John, **saith**—in a teas-ing tone (Luthardt) and in the hope of embarrassing Peter before the other servants (Hengstenberg), though there is no reason to suppose she purposed to endanger Peter's safety (Lange),— **unto Peter**, having first looked (Mark xiv. 67) and steadfastly fixed her eyes upon him (Luke xxii. 56), **Art thou also** —μὴ suggesting that she expects a negative answer (cf. vi. 67 ; xii. 47 ; ix. 40), while καὶ hints that she knows of John's relationship to Jesus—**one of this man's disciples ?** Expressive more of contempt than of compassion (Chrys-ostom). **He saith, I am not.** There was no reason, so far as personal safety was concerned, for Peter hesitating to avow his connection with Jesus, since John, though known to be a follower of the Nazarene, appears to have remained unmolested. That John was not assaul-ted as Peter was, has been ascribed to his greater boldness (Tholuck) ; the truth rather seems to be that Peter's manner and state of mind naturally drew towards him temptations from which John escaped.

18. **Now the servants,** the domestic slaves or private attendants, of the high priest, **and the officers** (see on ver.

3) **were standing** *there*, the soldiers having by this time withdrawn, **having made a fire of coals** lit., *a heap of charcoal;* i.e. having prepared a fire by heaping up charcoal, which did not emit a bright flame but afforded sufficient light to see the features of any one turned towards it (Westcott). **for it was cold** "About the time of the passover the nights in Palestine are cold" (Lücke). "There are occasionally outbreaks of winter down to May. We sat in the evening trembling with the frost, wrapped up in mantles" (Tobler : quoted by Hengstenberg). **and they were warming themselves; and Peter also was with them— standing and warming himself.** It is not necessary to conclude that John intended to blame Peter for attending to his own comfort while his Master was suffering (Milligan and Moulton).

19. The high priest see on ver. 15. Either 1. *Caiaphas*, ver. 10, 13 ; xi. 49 (Calvin, Luther, Bengel, Lücke, De Wette, Tholuck, and others : cf. Andrews, The Life of our Lord, p. 420); in which case the verses following report a trial before Caiaphas, while nothing is recorded of what occurred before Annas (Geikie); against which only stands ver. 24, while in its favour may be cited (1) the fact that Caiaphas is the only high priest hitherto mentioned by the evangelist (ver. 13 ; xi. 49), (2) the intention of the evangelist to distinguish Caiaphas as high priest from Annas who simply acted as a relation (ver. 13, 24), and (3) the statement of the Synoptists that Peter's denials all happened in the court of Caiaphas (Matt. xxvi. 69; Mark xiv. 66; Luke xxii. 54); or 2. *Annas* (Godet, Luthardt, Meyer, Brückner, Westcott, and others : cf. Farrar's Life of Christ, chap. lviii); in which case the paragraph relates to an examination held before Annas, John passing over in silence the hearing before Caiaphas, perhaps as already well known (Grotius, Paulus, Ebrard, Olshausen, etc.), or because it had a foregone conclusion which already had been stated (xi. 50); in favour of which speaks ver. 24, which appears to record the conclusion arrived at in the previous examination, but against which may be urged all that is above stated in behalf of

Caiaphas. The best solution probably regards Caiaphas as the high priest throughout, and as the acting prosecutor in this first preliminary examination, or *precognition*, over which, as a compliment to his dignity, age, relationship, and perhaps ability, Annas was invited to preside. The main objection to this hypothesis is that it assumes Annas and Caiaphas to have had official residences in the same building (since the court in which Peter's denials took place was one) : if this be too violent an assumption, then the high priest must be held to have been Caiaphas, and the trial that recorded in the Synoptists—"sent" in ver. 24 being read as a pluperfect (cf. ix. 18 : xiii. 12 ; xxi. 9 ; and see Winer, § xl. 5 a), or the entire verse being viewed as displaced from its true sequence after ver. 14. **therefore** because (if Annas) invited to precognosce the prisoner, or because (if Caiaphas) he was the chief authority in the court. **asked Jesus** with a view to obtain materials to bring against Him at His trial. **of His disciples** in the hope of incriminating them, or of showing that Christ was placing Himself at the head of a revolutionary movement. **and of His teaching,** expecting that Christ would entangle Himself in the attempt to explain and defend His doctrine.

20. Jesus answered him, passing over the first question entirely as irrelevant, or because He wished to shelter His disciples, concerning whom, as they were not at the bar, He was under no obligation to be communicative. **I have spoken openly to the world** : cf. vii. 4 ; xi. 54. With perfect frankness had Christ made known His views of truth and duty to His countrymen— the idea in 'openly' being that of complete absence of reserve, that in 'to the world' perfect publicity. **I ever taught in synagogues,** lit. *in synagogues,* or synagogal assemblies, **or in the temple** (cf. Matt. xxvi. 55 ; Luke xxi. 37, 38). Not that Christ confined His teaching to these places, but that whenever He could He resorted to them (see vi. 59 ; vii. 14 ; viii. 20). **where all the Jews come together** as the Athenians were wont to congregate in the Agora or market-place : Acts xvii. 17 ; **and in secret spake I nothing.**

The statement implies not that Christ did not instruct His disciples apart from the multitude (Matt. xiii. 36; Mark ix. 28), but merely that He had no private doctrines which on account of their dangerous character could be imparted only in obscure places and to sworn followers.

21. Why askest thou Me? It is not usual to require suspected criminals to impeach themselves. **Ask them that have heard** *Me* **what I spake unto them.** Christ could fearlessly ask to be tried at the bar of public opinion, to be condemned or acquitted as the conscience of His countrymen might decide. **Behold, these know the things which I said.** No need to conjecture that Christ here alluded to Peter and John whom He saw present (Ewald), or even to others in the court who were aware of His teaching (Westcott). His reply meant that as His doctrines were widely known, the necessary witnesses could be easily procured.

22. And when He had said this, one of the officers or constables (ver. 3), **standing by struck Jesus with his hand,** lit., *gave Jesus a stroke* or blow (ῥάπισμα, *anglice* rap); but whether a slap on the face (Paley), a box on the ear (Lampe, Meyer, Luthardt), or a stroke with a rod (Bengel, Godet) cannot be determined: cf. Matt. xxvi. 67; Acts xxiii. 2—though its reality need not be questioned (Keim). **saying,** with a view to court the favour of his master, **Answerest thou the high priest so?** It may be assumed that there was nothing in either the tone or the manner of Christ's reply to provoke this outrage.

23. Jesus answered him, without heat, with perfect serenity, with calm dignity: contrast the behaviour of Paul in similar circumstances (Acts xxiii. 3)—one requires not to ask which is the servant? and which the master? which the man? and which the God? **If I have spoken,** lit., *if I spoke* evil in My doctrine, as you insinuate, **bear witness of the evil :—** that will be a better vindication of the charge preferred against Me than personal abuse ; **but, if well,** if My doctrine is not evil but good, **why smitest thou Me?** δέρειν, to *skin*, to flay, hence to cudgel, to thrash, may signify that Christ was struck with a

rod ; but the verb is also used of a slap in the face, see 2 Cor. xi. 20.

24. Annas therefore sent Him bound, the fetters having probably been removed during the progress of the trial, **unto Caiaphas the high priest,** who by this time had perhaps left the court in order to convene the Sanhedrim (Andrews). See on ver. 17. If οὖν (B C* L X Δ etc., Tischendorf, Lachmann, Westcott and Hort) be correct, then the preceding trial must have been conducted by or at least before Annas ; if δὲ be accepted and 'sent' read as a pluperfect (Vulgate, Calvin, etc.), then the judge will have been Caiaphas. A and D omit the connective particle altogether.

25. Now Simon Peter was standing and warming himself at the fire in the court. According to Matthew and Mark, the second denial occurred in the porch ; according to Luke, the place is indefinite. **They,** the persons about, the officers and servants,—"another maid" (Matt.) ; "the maid" (Mark), i.e. the same as before ; another *man* (Luke). **said therefore unto him,** probably all putting the same question in different words, which would account for the variations in the gospel reports, **Art not thou also** *one* **of His disciples?** "This man also was with Jesus the Nazarene" (Matt) ; "This is *one* of them" (Mark) ; "Thou also art *one* of them" (Luke). John's question, the same as in ver. 17, suggests that the speaker was the same. He denied, with an oath (Matt.), a second time (Mark), **and said, I am not** ; "I know not the man" (Matt.) ; "Man, I am not" (Luke).

26. One of the servants of the high priest (see on ver. 10), **being a kinsman of him whose ear Peter cut off,** i.e. of Malchus ; they that stood by (Matt., Mark) ; another (Luke), **saith,** after a little while (Matt.), a little after (Mark), about the space of an hour after (Luke), **Did not I see thee in the garden with Him?** "Of a truth thou also art *one* of them, for thy speech betrayeth thee" (Matt.) ; "Of a truth thou art *one* of them, for thou art a Galilean" (Mark) ; "Of a truth this man also was with Him, for he is a Galilean" (Luke).

27. Peter therefore, because, having become entangled in deception, he had not courage to break through the net, **denied again,** with cursing and swearing, saying, " I know not the man " (Matt.), " I know not the man of whom you speak " (Mark), " Man, I know not what thou sayest" (Luke) ; **and straightway the cock crew.** The second crowing, the first having taken place after the first denial (Mark xiv. 72). Mark (xiv. 68, 72) the only evangelist who mentions the two crowings, though Matt. (xxvi. 34) joins him in predicting two. Luke (xxii. 34) and

John (xiii. 38) refer indefinitely to the crowing of a cock, without indicating whether it should happen once or twice. See on xiii. 38. The look Christ cast on Peter (Luke xxii. 61) and the bitter weeping that followed (Matt. xxvi. 75 ; Mark xiv. 72 ; Luke xxii. 62) are not recorded by John, since these were not needful to advance his purpose, which was to trace not the upward steps of Peter, but the downward steps of self-humiliation trod by Christ.

HOMILETICS

VER. 12-14 ; 19-24.—THE ECCLESIASTICAL TRIAL OF JESUS.
I. **The Prisoner.** Jesus. 1. The *dignity* pertaining to Him. (1) An innocent man, (2) A religious teacher, (3) A philanthropic citizen, (4) A patient sufferer, (5) An incarnate God. 2. The *indignity* put upon Him. (1) Seized by those He had befriended, (2) Bound by those He desired to liberate, (3) Led away as a criminal by those who were themselves transgressors, (4) Placed at the bar of one who should have been His advocate rather than His judge.

" See, they lay hold on Me, not with the hands
Of faith but fury ; yet at their commands
I suffer binding, who have loosed their bands ;
Was ever grief like Mine ?
Then from one ruler to another bound
They lead Me."—Herbert's Poems, ' The Sacrifice.'

II. **The Judge.** Annas or Caiaphas. See ver. 17 (Exposition). 1. *Head of the state,* he (the high priest) ought to have protected the interests of Jesus as a member thereof ; and, above all, ought to have dispensed justice and right judgment. 2. *Holder of a sacred office,* he ought to have been incapable of violating the claims of either truth or right. 3. *Vicegerent of Jehovah,* he ought to have stood forth as the champion of God's Son.

III. **The Examination.** 1. Its *character.* Preliminary, followed by a second (ver. 24 ; Mark xxvi. 57 ; Mark xiv. 53), and a third (Luke xxii. 66). " The first was the practical, the second the potential, the third the actual and formal decision that sentence of death should be passed judicially upon Him." "That of Annas was the authoritative *praejudicium,* that of Caiaphas the real determination, that of the entire Sanhedrim at daybreak the final ratification" (Farrar, The Life of Christ, chap. lvii.). 2. Its *object.* To entrap Christ into admissions that might be afterwards used against Him. 3. Its *course.* (1) The crafty question (ver. 19). Caiaphas required information concerning neither the disciples nor the teaching of Jesus, but hoped and expected Christ would commit Himself to some dubious utterance. (2) The prudent answer (ver. 20, 21). For His disciples who were not offenders replying nothing ; for Himself appealing to the boldness and publicity of His teaching as well as to the good faith and conscientious convictions of His hearers ; in both cases exemplifying the highest wisdom (Prov. xxvi. 4, 5). (3) The undeserved blow (ver. 22). A terrible indignity for a guilty creature, even though he had been a king, much more when he was a menial and a slave, to put upon the Son of God ; but " man, proud man, dressed in a little brief authority," etc. (Measure for Measure, act ii. sc. 2). (4) The gentle response (ver. 23). Persecution proves nothing and effects nothing in the determination of truth and right,—merely shows the weakness and sinfulness of those who resort to it ; the ' more excellent way ' is persuasion.

IV. The Verdict. 1. *Symbolized.* By replacing upon Christ's wrists the fetters which had probably been removed during the progress of the trial. **2.** *Interpreted.* Equivalent to an intimation that Annas regarded Jesus as a dangerous character, an uncomfortable person for unscrupulous schemers like him and his son-in-law to have in their path, and therefore as one who had better be removed : it was so understood by Caiaphas. **3.** *Pronounced.* Afterwards in the court of Caiaphas, and again in a full meeting of the Sanhedrim.

Lessons. **1.** The unspeakable condescension of Christ. **2.** The infinite meekness of Christ. **3.** The unflinching boldness of Christ.

VER. 15-18 ; 25-27.—THE FALL OF PETER.

I. Foreannounced : xiii. 38. Three surprises. **1.** *The person concerned.* Peter, the man of rock, whose faith had appeared the brightest (vi. 68 ; Matt. xvi. 16), whose zeal had seemed the greatest (xiii. 37), and whose courage had been counted the boldest (Matt. xiv. 28). Had it been Thomas the despondent (xi. 16), the wonder would have been less ; had it been John the beloved it could scarcely have been more. Let it teach (1) that no man knows himself or his fellows as Christ does, (2) that they who seem the least assailable are often the soonest overcome, and (3) that no saint, however large his capacities or high his attainments, is beyond the possibility of a fall. **2.** *The time indicated.* That night, on which Peter had been observing with his Master the paschal feast and the holy supper—when he would have said his faith in that Master was clearer and firmer, and his love towards that Master purer and more intense than it had ever been. Another time, more distant say, would have been less astonishing. This, too, has lessons (1) that times of highest spiritual excitement are often seasons of greatest danger, and (2) that these are the moments when Christ's followers have special need to be on their guard. **3.** *The sin predicted.* Desertion would have caused a shock : it staggers one to read of denial. It discloses (1) how near the best of saints are to abysses of sin, (2) how suddenly and swiftly one may be hurled from what seems a pinnacle of moral goodness to the lowest deep of guilt and shame, (3) how close even in renewed hearts lie the extremes of godliness and wickedness, and (4) how needful it is for him who thinketh he standeth to take heed lest he fall.

II. Accomplished : ver. 15-18, 25, 27. **1.** *The first denial :* ver 17. (1) The place—the court of the high priest, beside a fire kindled by the servants and officers. (2) The time—shortly after Peter had been admitted. (3) The questioner—the maid who kept the door. (4) The question—variously reported because variously given, first to Peter and then to the bystanders, but every time insisting on the fact that Peter was one of Christ's disciples. (5) The denial—spluttered forth in a variety of forms because of the uneasiness Peter felt, in all forms repudiating his discipleship, in all forms telling a direct lie—"I am not." (6) The result—Restless and unhappy, Peter withdrew from the fire and sauntered out into the porch (Matt. xxvi. 71 ; Mark xiv. 68). While there, a cock crew. If Peter's ears heard the chanticleer, Peter's conscience did not. **2.** *The second denial :* ver. 25. (1) The place—first in the porch and afterwards beside the fire. (2) The time—after a while. (3) The questioner— in the porch the maid who was perhaps joined by another female domestic, by the fire the maid and the officers. (4) The question—still insisting on the fact of his discipleship. (5) The denial—to the maids in the porch with an oath he denies all knowledge of Christ, to the officers beside the fire he says curtly he is not a disciple, adding to one more prominent than the rest, ' Man, I am not ! ' **3.** *The third denial :* ver. 27. (1) The place—the court (probably). (2) The time—a little after, about the space of an hour after, when Christ's trial before Caiaphas was drawing to a close. (3) The questioner—the bystanders among whom was a servant of the high priest, a kinsman of Malchus. (4) The question— first the bystanders remark that he speaks like a Galilean, and must be a disciple ; then one in particular maintains with vehemence that he is a Galilean, and therefore must belong to Christ's party ; and finally Malchus's kinsman identifies him as one whom he had noticed in the garden. (5) The denial—with cursing and swearing he declares again that he neither understands what they say nor knows the man of whom they speak. Oh! Peter. How are the mighty fallen! III. **Explained.** By three things. 1. *Peter's over-confidence in the upper room* (xiii. 37 ; Matt. xxvi. 33). Pride goeth before destruction (Prov. xvi. 18), and any coward can be brave before the hour of danger arrives. 2. *Peter's over-rashness in the garden* (ver. 10). Peter's lawlessness upon the sward made him timid in the palace. His foolish sword practice wrought less damage to Malchus than it did to himself. 3. *Peter's over-forgetfulness in the palace.* If Peter forgot his own sin in boasting as he had done, he should not have forgotten Christ's words. A good memory would probably have averted Peter's fall. IV. **Bewailed :** Matt. xxvi. 75. The tears of Peter. 1. Their *occasion.* (1) The crowing of the cock. The most trifling incident may be used by Providence to arrest the sinner and arouse the conscience. "The cock proved a preacher to Peter. Despise not the minister though never so mean ; it is the foolishness of preaching that must bring men to heaven" (Trapp). (2) The recollection of Christ's words. The warning uttered in the upper room had been quickly forgotten : now it was as suddenly recalled. As Peter's forgetfulness of Christ's words had laid him open to a fall, so now his recollection of them became the occasion of his rise. " A serious reflection upon the words of the Lord Jesus will be a powerful inducement to repentance, and will help to break the heart of sin" (Henry). (3) The glance of Christ's eye. The Lord looked on Peter, and "that one sweet look melted him, as God's kindness did the Israelites at the meet of Mizpeh " (Trapp). 2. Their *intensity.* Peter wept bitterly. Christ's glance enabled him to understand the wickedness of which he had been guilty, the love he had wounded, the holiness he had insulted, the truth he had trampled in the mire. All true piety springs from Christ's looking on the soul in pity and the soul's looking out to Christ in penitence (Zech. xii. 10). 3. Their *efficacy.* Peter's sorrow was secret, serious, and sincere. Peter never again denied Christ, but confessed Him often in the face of danger and death. " So far from saying, I know not the man, he made all the house of Israel know assuredly that this same Jesus was both Lord and Christ " (Henry). Learn 1. That Christ accurately gauges the characters and foresees the histories of His people. 2. That divine foreknowledge destroys not human responsibility, while divine foreannouncement increases it. 3. That overweening confidence in one's self is no mark of grace or stability, but rather of the opposite. 4. That it requires little to lead a good man, left to himself, into sin, and once started on the downward path none can predict where he will stop. 5. That Christ knows, if the world does not, when Christians deny Him, and that no greater indignity can be put upon Him than to be disowned by such as bear His name. 6. That if a child of God sins He must and will be brought to repentance, perhaps suddenly and painfully, but always with tears. 7. That "those who have truly sorrowed for sin will sorrow upon every remembrance of it ; yet not so as to hinder but rather increase their joy in God and in His mercy and grace" (Henry).

VER. 26.—IN THE GARDEN WITH CHRIST.

I. **A great privilege.** To be with Christ. 1. *In the garden of the heart,* enjoying His love (xiv. 23 ; Rev. iii. 20). 2. *In the garden of Gethsemane,* having fellowship with Him in His sufferings (Phil. iii. 10 ; 1 Peter iv. 13). 3. *In the garden of the Church,* communing with Him in the ordinances of religion (Matt. xviii. 20 ; Song i. 4). II. **A high responsibility.** 1. Upon the believer in this situation *the world's eye rests with minute observation*—it sees the individual in the garden (Acts iv. 13). 2. Concerning the believer in this situation *the world's mind cherishes enlarged expectations*—it anticipates that a Christian will neither be ashamed of nor deny his Lord (xiii. 35). 3. To the believer in this situation *the world's tongue often puts troublesome questions*—it asks him to give a reason for the hope that is in him (1 Peter iii. 15), and to tell the truth at all risks concerning himself and his Master.

VER. 27. STRAIGHTWAY THE COCK CREW.
I. A Witness for God. Proclaiming—1. His *creative power* in endowing so
humble a creature with so valuable an instinct. 2. His *providential wisdom*
in ordering this particular 'crowing' just at the moment when it was required
to awaken Peter's conscience. **II. A Testimony for Christ.** Declaring—1.
His *foreknowledge*, both of the events of time and of the acts of men. 2. His
divinity, since He who could beforehand read the thoughts of Peter and regulate
the habits of a fowl could only be the Maker of both. **III. A Preacher for
Peter.** Setting forth—1. His *sin* in denying Christ, its shame and its aggrava-
tions. 2. His *duty* to repent and return with tears and confessions. **IV. A
Sermon for All.** Concerning—1. *The danger of spiritual slumber.* Peter's conscience was not awake when he was in the palace. 2. *The duty of constant
watchfulness.* Peter was not upon his guard when among the soldiers. 3. *The
importance of avoiding temptation.* Had Peter remained without he would probably have been safe. 4. *The power of littles.* The crowing of the cock led to
the recovery of Peter's soul.

3. THE PRÆTORIUM OF PILATE

CHAP. XVIII. 28—XIX. 16

1. Condemned by the high priests Annas and Caiaphas as well as by the
Sanhedrim in a regularly constituted assembly (Luke xxii. 66), in ordinary
circumstances Jesus would, in all probability, have at once been subjected
to stoning, the punishment assigned by the law to blasphemers (Lev. xxiv.
16 ; cf. John viii. 59 ; x. 31)—which punishment also was subsequently
inflicted upon Stephen (Acts vii. 59). But about this time (see Exposition)
the power of inflicting capital sentences was taken from the Jews. It was
therefore necessary that the decision come to by Caiaphas and his associates
in the Sanhedrim should be passed on to the Roman governor for ratification and permission to carry it into execution. This accordingly was done
at an early hour on Friday morning, probably between the hours of 6 and
7 a.m. The Roman governor at this time was Pilate, whose palace was the
Prætorium or official residence of the Roman procurators (see Exposition).
The procedure before this representative of Roman law and majesty consisted of a cross game of manœuvring between him and the Jews for the
possession of Christ,—on the one hand Pilate endeavouring to rescue Jesus
from the hands of His would-be assassins, but failing chiefly through moral
cowardice ; on the other hand, the chief priests and the elders, trembling
lest their victim should escape from their grasp, resorting to stratagem after
stratagem to concuss the weak and vacillating governor, and finally securing
the triumph of their cause in the condemnation of Christ, and the formal
handing of Him over into their hands to be crucified.

2. The scene sub-divides itself into a series of minor acts or tableaux,
the local background shifting alternately from the outside to the inside of
the palace.

1. Outside the palace—Pilate and the Jews : the judge and the accusers : xviii. 28-32.

2. Inside the palace—Pilate and Jesus : the judge and his prisoner : first examination : ver. 33-38.

3. Outside the palace—Pilate and the Jews : Christ acquitted by the former ; Barabbas preferred by the latter : ver. 38-40.

4. Inside the palace—Pilate and Jesus : scourging and mockery : xix. 1-4.

5. Outside the palace—Pilate and the Jews : Ecce Homo ! Christ twice declared innocent by the former ; accused by the latter of calling Himself the Son of God : ver. 5-7.

6. Inside the palace—Pilate and Jesus : second examination : Christ declares to Pilate the source of his authority and the measure of his guilt : ver. 8-11.

7. Outside the palace—Pilate and the Jews : last attempt to rescue Christ : Pilate's courage and conviction overborne : Christ delivered into the hands of His foes : ver. 12-16.

3. The incidents of Pilate's sending Christ to Herod, the Galilean tetrarch (Luke xxiii. 7-12), and of the message sent to Pilate by his wife (Matt. xxvii. 19), are not referred to by John, obviously because they contributed nothing to the elucidation of the problem he had set before his mind in the composition of his gospel ; but a comparison of the two narratives shows that both probably occurred at the close of scene 2.

EXPOSITION

1. Chap. xviii. ver. 28-32. Outside the palace—Pilate and the Jews.

Ver. 28. **They,** i.e. the Jews, the members of the Sanhedrim ; not personally, but by means of their servants, **lead,** having first bound, " probably both hand and foot" (Keim), as one sentenced (Matt. xxvii. 2 ; Mark xv. 1), **Jesus,** whom previously they had buffeted and spit upon (Matt. xxvi. 67; Mark xiv. 65 ; Luke xxii. 63), **therefore,** because having condemned him, they had no power to proceed farther (see ver. 31), **from Caiaphas,** rather from the court of the Sanhedrim, over which Caiaphas presided (Luke xxii. 66), **into the palace,** lit., *the prætorium* where the procurator dwelt, either the spacious and magnificent palace built by Herod (Jos. Ant. xv. 9, 3) and subsequently used by Roman governors (Olshausen, Hengstenberg, Keim, Luthardt, etc.),

or more probably a building in the Tower of Antonia at the N.W. corner of the Temple (Godet, Ewald, Weiss, Westcott, etc.). The ordinary residence of the governor was at Cæsarea (Acts xxv. 1), but during the Passover his habit was to visit the metropolis, partly to preserve order in the city, and partly to uphold the prestige of the Roman power. **and it was early** Not before the morning twilight (Tholuck) but when morning was come (Matt. xxvii. 1), "in the morning" (Mark xv. 1), a phrase usually denoting the fourth watch (Mark xiii. 35) ; hence between 3 and 6 a.m. (Tholuck, Ewald), about 7 a.m. (Keim), about 6 or 7 (Weiss). Pilate had been visited the night before, knew what was afoot, and was doubtless prepared for their appearance at this early hour. Whether it was the custom for Roman procurators to be at business by 6 a.m. or earlier (Tholuck, Ewald) or not before 9 a.m. (Friedlieb), cannot be decided. **and they themselves,** i.e. the hierarchical leaders, **entered not into the palace,** which, as the house of a Gentile, had not been purged of leaven, **that they might not be defiled** by violating the Mosaic ordinance to put away leaven from their houses (Ex. xii. 19). Lange supposes they also feared to lose the aid of the populace, upon which they could securely count outside the palace. While declining to go in themselves they sent in the Lord. **but might eat the passover,** or, the 'holy things' of the first day of the feast (see note on xiii. 2).

29.   **Pilate** Introduced without further characterization as a well known personage, the name Pontius Pilate perhaps showing that he was connected with the *gens Pontia,* and that one of his ancestors or himself had received the cognomen *Pilatus,* adorned or furnished with a *pilum* or javelin (Virgil, Æn. xii. 121) on account of meritorious services. Called 'the governor' (Matt. xxvii. 2 ; Tacit. Ann. xv. 44), he was the fifth (Schürer), not the third (Pressensé), or the sixth (Keim)Roman procurator of Judæa, his predecessors having been (1) Coponius, (2) Marcus Ambivius, (3) Annius Rufus, and (4) Valerius Gratus. Pilate held the office for ten years during the reign of Tiberius. His arbitrary conduct in introducing Cæsar's ensigns into Jerusalem, and in bringing water into the city for which he paid with money belonging to the temple, led to successive risings amongst his subjects (Jos. Ant. xviii. iii. 1, 2 ; cf. Wars ii. 9, 2). Philo (Legat. ad Cajum 38) accuses him of " bribery, violence, robbery, cruelty, insult, continual executions without sentence of judgment, endless and unendurable atrocities." If this perhaps, as the testimony of an enemy, is too strong, it is still certain that Pilate was a Roman governor of the regulation type, who acted without the slightest regard for the peculiarities (especially religious) of the provinces over which he ruled, and punished every opposition to his arbitrary conduct with the greatest severity and cruelty (cf. Schürer, in Riehm's Handwörterbuch, art. *Pilatus*). " It would not be easy

to find another man so well fitted to drive the Jewish nation to desperation" (Luthardt). Accused before Vitellius the preses of Syria, he was deposed and sent to Rome to answer for his administration (Jos. Ant. xviii. 4, 2). **therefore** because of the religious scruples of the Jews, which in the circumstances he chose to respect. **went out unto them** ἔξω (א B C* L X etc.), without, indicates that Pilate not merely left the hall of judgment but went entirely outside the palace. **and saith,What accusation bring ye against this man ?** Although Pilate generally knew the case (Matt. xxvii. 18), Roman law and justice required that he should be furnished with a specific charge against the prisoner : see Acts xxv. 16 ; and cf. Adam's Roman Antiquities, p. 211.

30.   **They answered and said unto him,** indicating that the only service they desired of him was to carry out the sentence they had pronounced, **If this man were not an evil doer** i.e. one actively engaged in doing, not one who had done evil, **we should not have delivered Him up unto thee.** If Christ had only been a minor offender they could have punished Him themselves : the fact that they had delivered Him up into Pilate's hand was in their estimation proof sufficient that he was an extraordinary criminal.

31.   **Pilate therefore** perceiving they designed to use him as an instrument for carrying out their verdicts, **said unto them** with obvious reluctance to gratify their malevolence, out of either contempt for them whom he despised, or pity for Jesus whom he discerned to be a harmless person, or respect for himself as being too proud to stoop in the manner wished by the hierarchs : **Take Him yourselves, and judge Him according to your law.** If unwilling to produce an accusation, you must complete the case at your own tribunal —the Sanhedrim. Pilate, as yet unaware that Christ had been before that court, does not say they should put Him to death if they could or dared (De Wette, Lücke, Lange), speaking with a touch of irony or contempt ; but merely they should retain the case in their own hands and deal with it within the limits of their own jurisdiction. **The Jews** whose designs this did not satisfy **said unto him,** probably

informing him that already they had 'judged' the case and proceeded with it as far as they could, **It is not lawful for us to put any man to death**—thus acknowledging they had been deprived of the power of the sword. That at this time the Jews had been deprived of the *jus gladii* even in religious trials is asserted in the Talmud: *quadraginta annis ante vastatum templum ablata sunt judicia capitalia ab Israele* (Sanh. 24, 2), is confirmed by the statement of Josephus (Ant. xx. 9, 1) that it was not lawful for a high priest to convene a Sanhedrim, and far less to execute a criminal without the pro-curator's consent, and is not contra-dicted by the murder of Stephen (Acts vii. 58), since Pilate was then absent from Jerusalem, or by the fact (Ant. xiv. 10, 2) that Cæsar in the time of Hyrcanus the high priest (B.C. 135-105) granted to the Sanhedrim the power of determining any questions about Jewish customs (cf. Keil, Handbuch des Biblischen Archäologie, p. 717).

32. That the word of Jesus might be fulfilled, which He spake (xii. 32), **signifying by what manner of death He should die.** The Evangelist perceived a divine foreordination in the loss by the Jews just at this point in their history of the *jus gladii*. It was part of the divine plan that Gentile and Jew should unite in the condemnation of Jesus, as also that the specific form of death should be crucifixion ; both of which designs would have been frustrated had the Jews been able to carry out their own sentence. Christ would not then have required to be brought before the Gentile court at all, and instead of being crucified would like Stephen have been slain by stoning.

2. Ver. 33-38. Inside the palace. Pilate and Jesus.

33. Pilate therefore because of the urgency of the Jews which constrained him to make further examination (Westcott), "because he perceived they had set their minds on the punishment of death" (Meyer), or because they eventually complied with his demand for an accusation (Tholuck, Godet, Luthardt, and Brückner). Though not recorded by John it is by Luke (xxiii. 2) that the whole company of the Sanhedrim and people, when they had brought Christ before Pilate,

began to accuse Him, saying "We found this man perverting our nation, and forbidding to give tribute to Cæsar, and saying that He Himself is Christ a king." **entered again into the palace** or, *prætorium* (see on ver. 28) **and called Jesus** to his immediate presence, since Christ was already in the palace, **and said unto Him** with the view of ascertaining whether any ground existed for the accusation just preferred against Him—**Art thou the King of the Jews ?** "Thou art the King of the Jews, art Thou ?" (cf. Matt. xxvii. 11 ; Mark xv. 2 ; Luke xxiii. 3). If not spoken in a well-meant and friendly spirit (Stier) or from a holy awe of Jesus (Lampe), it can as little be proved to have been contemptuous (Meyer) or mocking (Luthardt), and was probably expressive of the surprise felt by Pilate that one so abject should be accused of aspiring to be a king (Hengstenberg, Westcott, Milligan and Moulton).

34. Jesus answered, Sayest thou this of thyself, or did others (those without, Mine accusers) **tell it thee** concerning **Me ?** The design of this return question has been thought to be a desire on Christ's part to know the author of the accusation, whether Pilate himself or the chief priests and rulers without (Meyer) ; that He might be able to fix the guilt upon the proper party (Milligan and Moulton), direct an appeal to Pilate's conscience (Hengstenberg, Westcott), or point out the suspicious character of the accusation as coming from the Jews (Lampe, Bengel, Luthardt, Brückner, Tholuck) ; most likely it was that he might understand exactly the sense in which Pilate used the words (whether political or theocratical) and know how to reply (Olshausen, Neander, Ewald, Godet).

35. Pilate answered, with mingled haughtiness and disdain, as well as with an obvious sense of irritation, **Am I a Jew ?** meaning, Do you suppose I would ever dream of trying you as a Jew ? (Meyer) ; better, Not being a Jew, how can I comprehend your subtleties and word distinctions ? (Godet), or What should I care about these things ? (Westcott), e.g. about how the Jews hope for a Messiah, (Brückner), and imagine you that I would ever hold you for one ? (ibid.).

Thine own nation and the chief priests delivered Thee unto me (cf. Matt. xxvii. 1). That, Pilate signified, was enough for him, and ought to be enough for Christ. The simple fact that Christ was handed over to him was constructive evidence that some crime had been committed. Pilate now demands that Christ should inform him what that crime was. **What hast Thou done?** what wickedness hast thou perpetrated? of what offence hast thou been guilty?

36. **Jesus answered** responding not to this but to the former question (ver. 33), **My kingdom is not of this world.** Christ avowed Himself a king : only not in an earthly or political, but in a religious or theocratic sense. His kingdom, like Himself (viii. 23), neither sprang from, nor belonged to, though necessarily it existed in this world ; hence it could never come into rivalry with, or antagonism to (at least directly and forcibly), the temporal monarchies of earth. Then having defined, negatively, the nature of His kingdom, He showed that His statement and definition were correct. **If My kingdom were of this world, then would My servants fight, that I should not be delivered to the Jews.** The servants (officers as in ver. 3) were not the angels (Bengel, Stier, Lampe), a sense too remote from Pilate's understanding; but either the soldiers Christ in the case supposed would have had (De Wette, Brückner, Lücke, Tholuck, Luthardt, Milligan and Moulton, and others), or the disciples and followers He then possessed (Meyer, Godet, Westcott, etc.). The fact that these had offered no resistance to his apprehension was proof that He did not aspire to be a king in the ordinary acceptation of the term. **But now is My kingdom not from hence,** and therefore they, My servants, will not prevent by armed opposition My deliverance into the hands of the Jews, if so it must be—and as eventually it was (xix. 16). Or, the words may be conversely interpreted : Now, i.e. since it is so that My servants do not fight for me (νῦν δέ expressing a logical rather than a temporal relation), it is evident that My kingdom is not from hence.

37. Pilate therefore, because of this declaration, **said unto Him, Art thou a king then ?** If οὐκοῦν be the accentua-

tion (Tischendorf, Westcott and Hort), the term signifies ' therefore,' ' thus,' ' consequently,' ' nevertheless,' ' after all ' ; if οὔκουν, thee opposite, ' not then,' ' therefore not.' In the latter case Pilate would say, ' Then thou art not a king, as these allege?' which seems the contrary of what Christ affirmed both before and after the question, and would imply defective intelligence on the part of the governor ; in the former case Pilate understands Christ to assert that He is a king, and expresses surprise at the announcement —" After all then thou art a king ? I am to hold thee as claiming to be a king ? " On οὐκοῦν, which occurs only here in the N. T., see Winer, § lviii. 3. **Jesus answered, Thou sayest that I am a king.** Not denying the accuracy of Pilate's interpretation of His words, and disclaiming the kingship imputed to Him (Reuss), or leaving Pilate's interpretation as he had put it forward and proceeding to explain the sense in which it should be taken (Westcott, Milligan and Moulton), but affirming in the most solemn manner (cf. Matt. xxvi. 25) that Pilate's interpretation is correct—that He is a king (Meyer, Godet, Lange, Luthardt, Hengstenberg, Tholuck, etc.). ὅτι might be rendered "for," assigning the reason why Christ declared Pilate to have spoken right in calling Him a king, viz., because that I am every inch a king (Lucke, Meyer, Luthardt, Lange, Tholuck, etc.). In this however there is too much of heroics to comport well with the character of Christ ; hence it is better to regard ὅτι as ' that,' introducing the subject matter of the previous λέγεις (Godet, Hengstenberg, Westcott, and others). **To this end have I been born, and to this end am I come into the world.** The two verbs express the birth and official appearance of Christ (Grotius, Lucke, De Wette, Godet) ; both designate the birth, the first in its human aspect, the second in relation to the higher nature of Him who was born (Meyer, Brückner) ; more simply, the first indicates the commencement of Christ's temporal and world historical appearance, the second carries the thought back to His pre-existence with the Father. The first εἰς τοῦτο may be connected with what precedes, ' To this end of being a king was I born' (Westcott, Alford) ; or both may be conjoined with what follows (Godet, Meyer, Luthardt)—"To this end was I born, and to this end did I come into the world," the reduplication adding emphasis to the thought expressed. **that I should bear witness unto the truth**— not this or that particular truth, but truth absolute and divine, which He had heard with the Father (iii. 11 ; xii. 49, 50), and of which He Himself was the highest embodiment and illustration (xiv. 6) : cf. Rev. iii. 14. Thus Christ indicated the weapon or instrumentality by which His kingdom shculd be established, maintained, and propagated : cf. 2 Cor. x. 4. **Every one that is of the truth heareth My voice.** To hear Christ's voice is to believingly accept and lovingly obey the truth He proclaims. It is thus to be a subject of His kingdom, which no one ever is except he is of the truth, i.e. has his inner life originated, inspired, and controlled by the truth : cf. iii. 21 ; vii. 17 ; viii. 47 ; x. 16, etc. This inward moral affinity towards or susceptibility for the truth is a fundamental and indispensable presupposition in the case of every one who hears Christ's voice. "Where belief is not reached, this presupposition is lacking. Belief always has moral roots" (Luthardt). Compare this " confession " before Pilate with that before the high priest (Matt. xxvi. 64). "The one addressed to Jews is framed in the language of prophecy, the other addressed to a Roman appeals to the universal testimony of conscience. The one speaks of a future manifestation of glory, the other of a present manifestation of truth. The one looks forward to the return, the other backward to the incarnation" (Westcott). 38. **Pilate saith unto Him, What is truth?** Scarcely a proof that Pilate had become sincerely desirous of ascertaining the truth (Chrysostom) or despaired of finding it (Olshausen) ; rather an evidence that Pilate as a man of the world, half cynically, half contemptuously, regarded truth as a *non ens*, a phantom, a something unattainable by man (Meyer, Luthardt, Godet, Westcott). "It was not the language of a theoretical sceptic,—the historical character of Pilate contra-

dicts that—but of a worldling who, entirely given up to the real interests of life, or to his passions, had lost the sense for truth, and had taught himself to regard it as a mere chimera" (Hengstenberg) 3. Ver. 38-40. Outside the palace— Pilate and the Jews. 38. **And when he** (Pilate) **had said this,** "What is truth?" **he went out again** from the prætorium **unto the Jews** still standing outside **and saith unto them, I find no crime in Him,** lit., *no ground of blame,* nothing to justify proceedings against Him at this tribunal. A testimony not to Christ's inherent sinlessness, but only to His freedom from political offence. 39. **But** At this point Pilate began to temporize. Had he been faithful to personal convictions or official obligations he ought at once to have dismissed the case and liberated Christ ; but Pilate was afraid of the Jews, although he hated them. Hence he sought to compromise matters by proposing to acquit Christ *ex gratia,* as a matter of favour, instead of setting Him free by law—thus seeming to favour the Jews whilst attaining his own end, the rescue of Christ. **ye have a custom** Cf. Matt. xxvii. 15 ; Mark xv. 6 ; Luke xxii. 17. This custom, if of Roman origin (De Wette, Brückner), had at least an analogy in the liberation of prisoners during the Roman festival of Lectisternium, *vinctis quoque dempta in eos dies vincula* (Livy, v. 13), and was probably introduced by the Romans for the gratification of the Jews (Grotius) when these were deprived of the power of executing capital sentences (Stapfer, Palestine in the Time of Christ, p. 446) ; if of Jewish origin (Olshausen, Luthardt, Godet, Lange)—which seems favoured by ὑμῖν—then it may have been intended to symbolize, as its connection with the passover appears to suggest, the deliverance of Israel from Egypt (Godet, Luthardt, Lange) or the reconciliation with Jehovah which that feast exemplified (Tholuck),— rather than the rescue of Jonathan from his father by the people. **that I should release unto you one at the passover** ἐν τῷ πάσχα : in or during the passover. Nothing can be inferred from this phrase as to whether the paschal feast was begun or not. **will ye there-**

fore (Mark ascribes the initiative to the people) **that I release unto you the King of the Jews ?** Pilate offered them a choice between Jesus and Barabbas (Matt. xxvii. 17). "King of the Jews," as addressed to the chief priests and elders, was ironical and contemptuous. 40. **They,** the multitude as well as the chief priests and rulers (Mark xv. 11), **cried out,** with a loud shout, **therefore,** when they perceived that Pilate wished to favour Jesus, **again,** having done so before, although not stated by the Evangelist (Luthardt), or having previously raised a clamour in general but this time a shout (Meyer), conjoining it with a specific cry, **saying,** gathering up their vociferations into one vehement demand : **Not this man,** whom in scorn and loathing they will not name, **but Barabbas,** τὸν Βαραββᾶν,

i.e., Bar-Abbas, 'Son of the Father' (God or Rabbi), or Bar-Rabbas, 'Son of the Rabbin.' The notion that Barabbas was also called Jesus, favoured by some cursive MSS. and approved by some interpreters (Origen, Fritzsche, Michaelis, Meyer, Lange, and others), does not appear to be well founded (Griesbach, Lachmann, Tischendorf, Westcott and Hort). **Now Barabbas was a robber.** One of those lawless characters who not unfrequently cover their deeds of violence under a cloak of patriotism (cf. Acts xxi. 38),—a kind of Jewish Rob Roy (Morison), a dangerous bandit (Paley), rather than a false prophet (De Wette)—Barabbas had been apprehended while engaged in a riot which ended in bloodshed and murder (Matt. xxvii. 16 ; Mark xv. 7 ; Luke xxiii. 19).

HOMILETICS

VER. 28-32. CHRIST BEFORE PILATE—THE TRIAL OPENED. I. **The Situation.** 1. The *place.* The prætorium or palace of Pilate. 2. The *time.* Friday morning after daybreak. 3. The *prisoner.* Jesus, sentenced and bound. 4. The *prosecutors.* (1) Their personal dignity—the Jews, members of the Sanhedrim, through their servants and the soldiers. (2) Their religious scruples —afraid to enter the prætorium in case of contracting defilement (ver. 28). See next homily. (3) Their murderous zeal—hurrying before the governor with their victim at the first approach of dawn (Prov. i. 16). 5. The *judge.* Pilate. (1) His office—procurator or governor of Judæa. (2) His character—unjust, tyrannical and cruel (see Exposition). II. **The Procedure.** 1. *An indictment demanded :* ver. 29. Pilate's motive may have been (1) contempt for the Jews, (2) pity for Jesus, or (3) respect for Roman law (cf. Acts xxv. 16). 2. *An evasion attempted:* ver. 30. A formal indictment was (1) not convenient for the Jewish leaders. To have asserted they had condemned Jesus as a blasphemer for calling Himself God's Son, to a heathen like Pilate, familiar with the notion of gods appearing on the earth, might not have sounded so profane, and would probably have led to Christ's liberation as a harmless enthusiast or religious fanatic, as well as to their expulsion from the judgment seat (cf. Acts xviii. 16). Hence they urged that it was (2) not necessary for the governor. The circumstance that they had come to him was proof enough that Christ was no mere every-day offender, but a notorious criminal, a person guilty not of one or two peccadilloes, but of many, a habitual malefactor. 3. *A concession offered :* ver. 31. Pilate was unwilling to accede to their suggestion that he should simply record and carry out the death penalty they had decreed. Not to speak of its illegality, its insolence was too much for the governor. If Pilate was to be the executioner, he must also be the judge : if they were to be the judges they could be their own headsmen. They might, if they pleased, withdraw the case from Roman jurisdiction altogether, and finish it up at their own tribunals, since already they had gone so far as to pronounce upon the question of life and death. Pilate saw that the Jewish hierarchs intended murder, for which he was not inclined, and, with exquisite irony, knowing well their impotence to inflict the death penalty, he tells them

to go as far as their law will allow. 4. *An admission made:* ver. 31. Brought
to bay the human sleuth-hounds were obliged to divulge their secret, to confess
they intended to take the life of their victim, but could not do so without his
assistance, their Roman masters having deprived them of the power of the
sword. III. **The Issue.** 1. *The purpose of Pilate fixed.* He would not stir without
an accusation. 2. *The design of the Jews frustrated.* They had purposed to cut
their prisoner off without troubling the world with any explanation of his
offences. In this, however, they were thwarted. 3. *The counsel of God fulfilled:*
ver. 32. It was in the divine programme that Christ should die by crucifixion.
Had Pilate yielded this would have been defeated. See Exposition.
Lessons. 1. The debasement of conscience,—seen in the Jewish hierarchs. 2.
The instincts of justice, operating even in a bad man,—exemplified in Pilate. 3.
The impossibility of defeating God's counsel,—observed in the actions of both.
VER. 28. SCRUPLES AND NO SCRUPLES.
I. **Scruples.** The Jewish hierarchs were afraid of 1. *Ceremonial defilement.*
Good! they had not otherwise been faithful Jews. 2. *Exclusion from the feast.*
Good again! it was a mark of true religion to observe the ordinances. II. **No
Scruples.** The rulers were not afraid 1. *To send in Christ to Pilate's house.* They
could not risk contamination, but He might—if indeed He could be more defiled
than He already was. The Pharisees had no acquaintance with the golden rule
(Matt. vii. 12). 2. *To plot the murder of the Son of God.* Yet they were the
leaders of religious society in their day! heaven's favourites if any were! Who-
ever were cast into Gehenna, they were sure to lie at last in Abraham's bosom.
Lesson: Beware of the leaven of the Pharisees, which is hypocrisy.
VER. 33-38. PILATE'S FIRST EXAMINATION OF CHRIST.
I. **An Important Question**: ver. 33. 1. *Its occasion.* Pilate having demanded
an accusation, the whole company began to accuse Christ of perverting the nation
from its allegiance, forbidding to give tribute to Cæsar, and saying that He
Himself is Christ a king (Luke xxiii. 1). This, of course, was a lie, having not
even the semblance of truth to give it countenance; but the Jewish leaders,
probably surmizing that Pilate would ask an indictment, had pre-arranged to
say nothing about the blasphemy, but to trump up a charge of treason. 2. *Its
motive.* Pilate wished to ascertain if any truth or reality lay behind the clamour
which now assailed him. 3. *Its reception.* Instead of answering, Christ inquired
at Pilate who had prompted the question (ver. 34). The reason of this request
on Christ's part was probably to know how to reply. If Pilate had asked
spontaneously, then Christ would understand him to have used the term King
in a political sense; if the Jews had suggested the question, then the word was
probably employed with a theocratic import. On the former hypothesis Christ's
answer would be No! on the latter, Yes! 4. *Its vindication.* Pilate had not
put the question of his own accord. Not being a Jew, he would never have
dreamt of troubling his head about either Christ or His pretensions. Christ's
own nation, people and leaders, had placed Him at the bar (ver. 35)—constructive
evidence that He had done something wrong. 5. *Its repetition.* If He had not
committed treason by aspiring to be a king, what other wickedness had He been
guilty of to so rouse the ire of His countrymen? (ver. 35).
II. **A Sublime Declaration.** Concerning 1. *His kingdom:* ver. 36. Setting
forth (1) its origin, heavenly—'from above,' (2) its nature, spiritual—'not of
this world,' (3) its character, peaceful—neither propagating nor defending itself
by the sword (see ver. 11, Homily), (4) its members, 'His servants,' 'sons of
the truth' (ver. 37). 2. *His kingship.* Announcing (1) His pretemporal existence—He had 'come into the world' (cf. vi. 28), (2) His supernatural birth—
He who had been before all time had been 'born,' (3) His divine mission— to
bear witness to the truth, (4) His loyal subjects—the sons of the truth who are
obedient to His voice. "Truth, absolute reality is the realm of Christ; and
every one who has a vital connection with the truth recognizes His sway"
(Westcott).
III. **An Unworthy Reply.** 1. *Astonishment.* Thou art a king then, art Thou?

ver. 37. Surprise (1) that one so abject should think himself a king, (2) that one so forlorn should speak of servants, (3) that one so defenceless should even entertain the idea of 'fighting.' 2. *Scepticism.* What is truth? ver. 38. The language of (1) insincere inquiry, (2) contemptuous indifference, (3) open infidelity. Truth in Pilate's judgment was a phantom. 3. *Rejection.* For Pilate it was such a day of grace as he had never before enjoyed, an hour of merciful visitation which never again returned, when divine love in the person of Christ stood before him and said, 'Every one that is of the truth heareth My voice.' It was tantamount to an invitation to listen to the wooing of Christ's words, and so become a member of His kingdom : but the gay, sceptical man of the world turned upon his heel, and went out—leaving the presence of the one Being on earth that could have answered his inquiry, who could have said, 'I am the Truth.'

Learn 1. The grace of our Lord, who, though a king, yea, the King of kings, stooped to be treated like a criminal and a slave. 2. The majesty of Christ, which even in His lowliest humiliation, Pilate did not fail to recognize. 3. The divinity of Jesus who, while a prisoner at Cæsar's bar, could talk of a pre-existent being and a heavenly mission.

Ver. 38. What is Truth? A question. I. *Important.* Nothing more necessary for the mind to know. II. *Old.* Men in all ages have been inquiring in this direction. III. *Intricate.* Not to ascertain what is truth relative and ephemeral, but what is truth absolute and eternal. IV. *Answered.* Jesus has replied to it for all time –'I am the Truth.'

VER. 38-40.—PILATE'S FIRST ATTEMPT TO RESCUE CHRIST.

I. **The Secret Motive**—a conviction of the innocence of Christ : ver. 38. A valuable testimony, 1. *directly to the blamelessness of Christ.* Whatever faults or sins his prisoner might be guilty of, whatever violations of ecclesiastical law or of social custom might be laid to His charge, Pilate saw He was no plotter of sedition, political incendiary, or fiery revolutionist—a religious enthusiast possibly, a crack-brained fanatic, a utopian transcendentalist, a philosophic visionary who thought himself appointed of heaven to found an empire of seekers after the truth ; but certainly no rival to Cæsar. Accordingly, he told the ruffians outside his palace, who like hungry wolves were sharpening their teeth in anticipation of their prey, that their case had broken down, that *primâ facie* there was no evidence against their prisoner—'I find no crime in Him.' A visionary or lunatic he may be ; but men cannot be put to death (you know) for being philosophers or fools. 2. *Indirectly to the sinlessness of Christ.* That the charge of treason was the strongest the Jewish hierarchs could prefer against Christ—not the strongest in the sense of the gravest *per se*, but the one they could most easily establish—may be assumed. If therefore this failed, it is more than likely every other would have proved abortive.

II. **The Ostensible Pretext**—a desire to honour Jewish customs : ver. 39. 1. *The custom was dubious.* (1) On the one hand, it might be argued that whatever its origin, it was praiseworthy—to signalize a season of universal rejoicing with an act of public clemency ; and instructive—being fitted to remind the Jews of that divine act of favour to their nation of which the feast was a memorial ; or (2) on the other hand, contended that its observance "involved a base and heinous crime" (Calvin), since "He who acquitteth the guilty is abomination in the sight of God" (Prov. xvii. 15), "a bloody man shall flee to the pit, and no man may stay him" (Prov. xxviii. 17), and the liberation of a prisoner like Barabbas could have been no boon to the people. 2. *The pretext was bad.* In this case was no room for pretext. Christ required not to be liberated *ex gratia*, but ought to have been dismissed from the bar as one in whom the judge could detect 'no crime.'

III. **The Formal Proposal**—to release Jesus : ver. 39. Pilate committed three mistakes. 1. *In not immediately discharging Christ.* Justice demanded and conscience impelled to this. Had he done so, the Jews would have scorned, perhaps impeached Him at Cæsar's bar, as one who connived at treason. At least he would have acted courageously and right. But for reasons known to himself, he acted differently. He hesitated, and was lost. 2. *In proposing to release Christ as a matter of grace instead of justice.* There are times when compromises are permissible, when of two courses both are legitimate, and have mutually balancing recommendations ; but where one course alone is right and the other is sinful, there is no room for compromise. 3. *In putting Christ in competition with Barabbas.* To do so was (1) a moral wrong, knowing as he did that Barabbas was a tumultuary and a murderer, while Jesus was an inoffensive subject of Cæsar ; and (2) a tactical mistake, for though intended (of which there can be small doubt) to eventuate in Christ's interest, believing that between the two people would never hesitate, it had exactly the contrary result.

IV. **The Utter Defeat**—by the preference of Barabbas: ver. 40. 1. *With unexpected eagerness.* It must have startled the governor to hear the people's response, to see his hopes so quickly blighted, and his project so completely given to the winds. But the hope of the wicked is usually shortlived (Job viii. 13) and his counsel carried headlong (Job v. 13). 2. *With prompt decision.* The balance did not hang long in suspense between the robber and the Redeemer. If Christ had any friends at all in the crowd, they either remained mute or their voices were drowned in the general outcry. 3. *With deafening clamour.* The shout of the people rose into the morning air, poured from throats hoarse with excitement and mad with rage.

Learn 1. The danger of trifling with conscience. 2. The doubtfulness of compromises. 3. The madness of sin.

Ver. 40. The Choice of Barabbas. I. *Popular.* Popular election wrong for once ! *Vox populi non semper vox Dei.* II. *Frenzied.* When passion rules, judgment reels. III. *Criminal.* They desired a murderer to be granted to them, and killed the Prince of life (Acts iii. 14). IV. *Foolish.* They chose an enemy and rejected a Friend, and such a friend ! V. *Fatal.* It sealed their destruction as a people. VI. *Predicted.* "He is despised and rejected of men !" (Is. liii. 3). VII. *Overruled.* It brought salvation to the world, even to the Jews. God makes the wrath of men to praise Him (Ps. lxxvi. 10), turns the shadow of death into the morning (Amos v. 8), makes crooked things straight (Is. xl. 4), and evolves good out of evil (Rom. viii. 28).

3. THE PRÆTORIUM OF PILATE (Continued)

Chap. XIX. Ver. 1-16

Exposition

4. Chap. xix. ver. 1-3. Inside the palace—Pilate and Jesus.

1. **Then,** immediately after Christ's rejection by the people, **Pilate,** by this time powerless to stem the torrent of passion the Pharisaic party had excited in the crowd, yet unwilling to abandon his prisoner to their rage, **therefore,** because his former attempt to rescue Christ had been a failure (xviii. 40), because he still remained persuaded Christ was innocent (ver. 4 : cf. Matt. xxvii. 24), and during the incident of Barabbas may have received his wife's message (Matt. xxvii. 19)—Pilate's hand washing, which appears (Matt. xxvii. 24) to be placed before Barabbas's release (Strauss, Hengstenberg) having probably occurred at a later stage, viz., before the final sentence of condemnation, i.e. before ver. 16 (Godet),—**took Jesus** inside the prætorium (Matt. xxvii. 27; Mark xv. 6), having previously caused Him to be brought forth before the people to assist their choice, **and scourged Him,** καὶ ἐμαστίγωσε, and flogged Him,—Matthew and Mark using φλαγελλόω = Lat. *flagellare,* whence *horribile flagellum* (Hor. Sat. i. 3, 119), and Luke παιδεύω, to discipline, to chastise, to punish—in accordance

with his own proposal (Luke xxiii. 16, 22), when the people first demanded crucifixion, and with the manifest intention (ver. 4) of setting Him before the people in the hope of thereby moving them to pity, and in the expectation that, as he had granted them the life of Barabbas, they would be satisfied with something less than a capital sentence for Jesus. This was Pilate's *second* attempt to effect Christ's rescue, or the *third* if xviii. 31 be regarded as the first. The scourging here mentioned—not to be distinguished from that inflicted later (Matt. xxvii. 26; Mark xv. 15) as a preliminary to execution (Jos. Ant. ii. 14, 9; v. 11, 1), and probably in the absence of Pilate (Brückner)—was commonly commanded by some such phrase as 'Go, lictor, bind his hands: he shall be scourged with rods': *I, lictor, conliga manus* (Livy i. 26), and carried out conformably to Roman, which was much more severe than Jewish practice. The Jews bared only the upper part of the body; the Romans exposed it entirely. The Jews numbered the lashes (Deut. xxv. 2; 2 Cor. xi. 24); the Romans laid them on without number or mercy. Those who were scourged were usually tied hands behind back to a pillar, or bound in a stooping posture over a low block, so that the skin, being stretched tight, drew blood at every stroke of the lash, which was sometimes an elm rod (cf. Acts xvi. 22, *ῥαβδίζειν*), sometimes a leathern thong in the end of which was lead or bones. Under this fearful punishment victims often fainted and sometimes died: cf. Cic. Verr. 3, 29: *virgis ad necem caesi;* Hor. Sat. i. 2, 41, *flagellis ad mortem caesus,* and see Riehm's Handwörterbuch des Biblischen Altertums: Art. *Leibesstrafen;* Keil's Handbuch der Biblischen Archäologie, p. 725; Keim, Jesus von Nazara, vol. vi. p. 117; Stäpfer, Palestine in the Time of Christ, p. 111. In a subterranean chamber on the supposed site of Pilate's prætorium stands "a truncated column, no part of the construction, for the chamber is vaulted above the pillar, but just such a pillar as criminals would be tied to to to be scourged" (Ferguson, The Temples of the Jews, p. 176; quoted by Westcott).

2. **And the soldiers** of the governor, the representatives of the lictors, by whom this infliction was carried out, **plaited a crown of thorns,** *ἐξ ἀκανθῶν,* probably of the *licium spinosum,* a thorny plant abounding near Jerusalem, whose flexible stalks could be easily twisted (Hug, Godet, Luthardt, and others), though other thorns have been suggested, as the hedge thorn (Paulus), the acacia (Lange),—perhaps the *Zizyphus spina Christi* or Nubk tree, very common in all the warmer parts of Palestine, which grows 20 or 30 feet high, and whose subangular branches are studded with long pointed and rather reflex thorns, very strong (Tristram, The Land of Israel, p. 202), which also the soldiers may have found in the quadrangle of the prætorium or at least in the vicinity ; **and put it,** lit., *having plaited, they put it* **on His head,** not so much to cause pain,—though "no doubt the savages would see to it that the thorns should be prickly enough" (Morison),—as in mockery of His regal claims, **and arrayed Him in a purple garment,** having first stripped off His outer robe (Matt. xxvii. 28)— also as a caricature of His royalty ; the purple garment *ἱμάτιον πορφυροῦν* (Mark xv. 17), or scarlet robe *χλαμύς κοκκίνη* (Matt.) being most likely a soldier's scarlet mantle, *sagum* or *paludamentum,* fastened with a buckle on the right shoulder, rather than a royal robe (Hengstenberg).

3. **And they,** the soldiers, **came unto Him,** or *kept coming up to Him* (Paley), as if to render homage, perhaps bowing down or bending the knee before Him in mock humility (Matt. xxvii. 29), **and said,** or *kept saying,* in tones of ironical derision, **Hail, king of the Jews !**—the usual salutation of an eastern monarch ; **and they struck Him with their hands,** lit., *were giving Him slaps,* probably on rising from their pretended obeisance, and in the face as some codices add. "It is difficult to understand how Roman dignity could stoop to acts so shameful. It is true that Pilate, in the capacity of procurator, had under his command scarcely any but auxiliary troops (Inscript. Rom. of Algeria, No. 5, fragm. B). Roman citizens, as the legionaries were, would not have degraded themselves by such conduct" (Renan). The

mockery here directed against Jesus exhibits a remarkable similarity to that afterwards (A.D. 38) inflicted by proxy on Agrippa I., by the people of Alexandria, who having laid hold of a well known city fool, named Carabas, "exhibited him in an elevated position in the gymnasium, wrapped him in a carpet, placed a paper crown upon his head, gave him a reed sceptre in his hand, and three attendants with staves by his side," after which they greeted him in Aramaic as Mari, Lord! (see Keim, Jesus von Nazara, vol. vi. p. 121).

5. Ver. 4-7. Outside the palace— Pilate and the Jews.

4. **And Pilate went out again** from the interior, **and saith unto them,** the Jews, who stood without, but had probably witnessed the scourging by gazing through the porch into the court : **Behold, I bring,** or *am bringing,* **him out to you**—"The scene here becomes dramatic, not to say theatrical " (Strauss)—**that ye may know,** learn or be made aware, **that I find no crime in him,** although He has been subjected to scourging (cf. Acts xxii. 24). That fierce ordeal had elicited from Him nothing worthy of condemnation. Keim thinks "it would have been contrary to all Roman gravity, strictness, and dignity for a governor to make himself a veritable peripatetic going between the parties " (Jesus von Nazara, vol. vi. 110), and accordingly pronounces the scene unhistorical ; but the reason of this back and forthgoing, this "*ambulatorisch-peripatetische Geschäftsbehandlung,*" the Evangelist has explained, xviii. 29 (see Beyschlag, *zur Johanneischen Frage,* p. 112).

5. **Jesus therefore,** in consequence of this determination of the governor, and in obedience to his will, **came out** from the prætorium, for the first time (Westcott), if He had not, previous to the scourging, been brought forth and, along with Barabbas, set before them for choice, **wearing the crown of thorns and the purple garment.** See on ver. 2. **And** *Pilate* **said unto them** in tones of scorn and pity—scorn for them, pity for Jesus : **Behold, the man!** Ἴδε ὁ ἄνθρωπος (B omits the article), *Ecce homo!*—since become a watchword of Christians. The verb forms an ejaculation by itself. Behold, see! 'the

man' standing in the nominative, as if Pilate meant to say—'See, this is the man ye wish me to put to death!' or 'This is the man of whom you are afraid ! and whom ye accuse of being Cæsar's rival !'—rather than, ' This is the man whom I said I was going to bring out to you' (Paley). It was an appeal to their common sense and compassion in one. If pity did not move them, the absurdity of the situation might shame them. The deep interest taken by the Roman governor in Jesus has been pronounced improbable (Schenkel), contrary to everything known of Pilate's character (Keim), borrowed from the Christian consciousness of the evangelist (Strauss), in the spirit of post-apostolic Christianity which turned its hopes from the Jewish synagogue to the heathen world (Baur). But Pilate's interest in Jesus appears in exactly the same light in Matthew, the most ' Jewish' of the earlier evangelists, and so far from the church of the second century being an object of favour to the heathen world-power, it was subjected by that power to numerous and fierce persecutions (cf. Beyschlag, p. 111).

6. **When therefore the chief priests** (see xviii. 35) **and the officers** (see xviii. 12) **saw Him** standing on the raised platform crowned with thorns and robed in purple, **they cried out,** *raised a yell,* themselves shouting and stirring up the crowd (Matt. xxvii. 20 ; Mark xv. 11), **saying, Crucify** *Him*, **crucify** *Him* —the second time the ominous words had escaped their lips! **Pilate,** startled by their vehement malignity and still struggling to resist their demand, **saith unto them,** with combined irony and determination, **Take Him yourselves and crucify Him.** This Pilate knew they could not do, as neither had the Jews the power of executing capital sentences (see xviii. 31), nor was crucifixion a Jewish punishment (see on ver. 16). **for I find no crime in Him.** See on xviii. 38 ; xix. 4. The frequency with which Pilate recurs to the innocence of his prisoner demonstrates the strong impression made upon him by Christ and the struggle going on within his conscience.

7. **The Jews answered him,** bringing forward the ecclesiastical verdict at which they had arrived in the court of

Caiaphas (xviii. 28 ; cf. Matt. xxvi.
66), but which up to that moment they
had suppressed, **We**—since you refer
the matter to us, *we*, ἡμεῖς, answering to
the ὑμεῖς of ver. 6 and contrasting with
Pilate's 'I' in ver. 4, 6—we, the
ecclesiastical rulers, as opposed to *you*
the political governor, **have a law**—the
Roman governors had been accustomed
to respect Jewish institutions and to
recognize within limits the validity of
Jewish laws (Jos. Ant. xvi. 2, 3)—in fact
had accorded to the Jews *Home Rule*.
Accordingly the chief priests and rulers
now expect Pilate in compliance with
this practice to order the instant
execution of their intended victim.
and by that law recorded against
blasphemers (Lev. xxiv. 16) **He ought to
die** as a blasphemer,—in which case He
would have suffered lapidation. The
Jewish leaders seem at this point to
have been prepared to abandon the
idea of crucifixion, if only Pilate would
yield to them so far as to pronounce
sentence of death—**because He made
Himself the Son of God.** This was
true (see v. 18 ; viii. 19, 42 ; x. 33,
37 ; cf. Matt. xxvi. 63, 64 ; Luke xxii.
70) ; and the advancement of this as a
ground of condemnation shows that the
Jews did not understand the phrase
'Son of God' as synonymous with
Messiah.

6. Ver. 8-11. Inside the palace—
Pilate and Jesus.

8. **When Pilate therefore heard that
saying**, not that the Jews had a law
which he as a Roman governor was
bound to respect, but that Christ had
made Himself the Son of God, **he was
the more afraid**—more than he had
previously been, not lest the outcry
against Jesus should lead to a riot or
an accusation against himself at Rome
(Paley), but lest Jesus should indeed
be the Son of God, or, *the Son of a
God*, a supernatural being who had
come to earth after the manner of
pagan divinities (cf. Matt. xxvii. 54 ;
Acts xiv. 11).

9. **And he entered into the palace** or
prætorium **again**, for the third time
(see xviii. 33; xix. 1), taking with him
Jesus, **and saith unto Jesus**, clearly in
a state of trepidation as the vagueness
of his question reveals, **Whence art
thou?** Not 'From what place do you
come?' (Paley) as if hoping to find in

this a pretext for declaring his inability
to adjudicate (Renan), since Pilate
knew Christ was a Galilean and had
already sent Him to Herod (Luke xxiii.
6, 7), but 'Of what race art Thou?
divine or human?' **But Jesus gave
him no answer.** As Christ had been
silent before Caiaphas (Matt. xxiv. 63;
Mark xiv. 60), before Herod (Luke
xxiii. 9), before the accusations of the
priests (Matt. xxvii. 12 ; Mark xv. 5),
so now was He dumb before Pilate (cf.
Is. liii. 7). Why? Because "there
was some danger lest Pilate should
accuse Christ as one of the pretended
gods" (Calvin) ; because " it was proper
that He should be condemned when He
appeared in our room " (ibid.) ; because
"He would not prevent that from
taking place which He knew was to
take place" (Luthardt) ; because the
question of His origin did not lie within Pilate's jurisdiction (Ebrard) ; and
for a heathen like Pilate an adequate
reply to it would have been meaningless and fruitless (Lücke, Meyer, Westcott) ; because, foreseeing that Pilate
would not be able to carry through the
struggle in which he was involved,
Christ would not lead him into greater
temptation (Olshausen); because already
He had testified enough to indicate His
heavenly origin, and no further testimony could avail him who had turned
his back upon the King of truth
(Tholuck) ; because all Pilate's previous
words had shown him to be incapable
of understanding higher and godlike
things (Ewald); because Pilate already
knew sufficient to enable him to decide
the question before him, knowing as
he did that Christ was innocent
(Godet) ; because Pilate was insincere
and unworthy of an answer (Alford) ;
perhaps because the answer was involved in His silence and required no
words to render it more eloquent or
intelligible (Hengstenberg). " It is
certain that He in whose mouth was
no guile, had He been a mere man,
would at this moment have honestly
explained He was a man (cf. Acts xiv.
15 ; Rev. xxii. 9). Hence even the
silence of Jesus attests His godlike
origin " (Lücke). This silence of Jesus
before Pilate—not inconsistent with the
earlier 'long confessions' (Keim)—has
been well pronounced "the worthiest
behaviour that Jesus could have

chosen—as lowly as self-conscious" (Schenkel).

10. **Pilate therefore**, in consequence of Christ's silence, **saith unto Him**, as much with affected as with real dignity, the form of Pilate's question betraying the uneasiness he can scarcely conceal, **Speakest thou not unto me?** or, *To me dost thou not speak?* which shows Pilate had remarked His silence before the accusations of the priests (cf. Matt. xxvii. 14). **Knowest thou not that I have power**, ἐξουσίαν, authority and ability, **to release thee, and have power**, authority and ability, **to crucify thee?** The order of the verbs, 'release' before 'crucify' (א A B E etc., Lachmann, Tischendorf, Westcott and Hort), is defended as presenting the alternatives with most impressive distinctness (Westcott), as well as being psychologically correct and skilful to place the motive of hope before that of fear (Luthardt); although the order which places 'crucify' before 'release' (T. R.) is vindicated on the ground that it corresponds better to the state of the procedure (Meyer), that the beam in the balance decidedly vibrated towards crucifixion (Hengstenberg), and that the idea of imminent death is that which prevails in the conversation (Godet).

11. **Jesus answered** him, not keeping silence longer, since Pilate laboured under a delusion concerning himself, which it behoved Christ to correct, but replying to the official pride of the governor with the sublimer dignity of a god. **Thou wouldest have** Not 'Thou hast' ἔχεις (א A D L, Tischendorf), or 'Thou hadst' on account of the absence of ἄν before εἶχες (Buttmann)—οὐκ ἄν εἶχες was probably the true reading (Paley); but Thou wouldest or couldest have (Meyer, Godet, Luthardt, and others), the imperfect without ἄν being used as the strongest form of assertion, as e.g. Acts xxvi. 32 (see Winer, § xlii. 2, b, c). **no power against Me** κατὰ with the genitive denoting hostile movement against something or some one (cf. Matt. x. 35 ; xxvii. 1 ; Acts vi. 13 ; 1 Cor. iv. 6 ; xv. 15 ; Rom. viii. 33), the opposite idea being expressed by ὑπέρ also with the genitive (cf. x. 11, 16 ; xvii. 19). **except it were given thee from above** ἄνωθεν : not from the Roman emperor (Usteri), or the Sanhedrin

(Semler), but from God, as in iii. 31—a statement which even a heathen such as Pilate could understand (Meyer), which may have been intended to humble his pride by placing him beneath a higher power (Chrysostom), and to suggest the true reply to his unanswered question, Whence art Thou? *inde scilicet unde ortus sum* (Grotius), since He spoke of that of which He knew (Westcott), but which certainly admonished him on account of the responsibility that fact implied to think well what he was about to do (Ewald). **therefore** διὰ τοῦτο ; because of this, not that thou dost not know Me (Grotius, Bengel, Stier), or that such power has not been given to the Jews (Lampe), or that they constrain a divinely appointed government to comply with their lawless desires (Calvin), or are contemplating the murder of God's Son, but thou only that of an innocent man (Olshausen, Ebrard), or because of their greater knowledge of My innocence (Ewald), but because the power thou wieldest has been put into thy hand at this particular crisis in human history, so that thou canst not avoid acting, whereas that exercised by the chief priests over Me was not assigned them by God, but has by them been usurped (Godet, Luthardt, Meyer, and others). **he that delivered Me unto thee** Not Judas (Daub), but either the Jews collectively, the Sanhedrin and the nation in whose name that body acted (Godet), or better, Caiaphas as the representative of both (Bengel, Stier, Meyer, Westcott, and others). **hath greater sin.** Not greater *because* of employing thy magisterial authority than he would have otherwise contracted (Calvin, Baur, Godet), but greater *than* thou. Pilate's sin was less than that of Caiaphas, not because it proceeded from weakness rather than wickedness (Euthymius), but either because he exercised his authority by divine appointment (Rom. xiii. 1), whereas Christ was not subject to the Sanhedrim (Lücke, Meyer, Luthardt, and others), or because Pilate possessed less knowledge of who Christ was than Caiaphas (Bengel, Olshausen, Lange, Milligan and Moulton).

7. Ver. 12-16. Outside the palace—Pilate and the Jews.

12. **Upon this**, ἐκ τούτου : not from

this time onward (De Wette, Lücke, Hengstenberg), but from this cause, for this reason: cf. vi. 66. "'Eκ is specially employed to express the mental state, the thought or feeling out of which something springs, 1 Tim. i. 5, . . . the reason (ratio), Rev. viii. 13; the grounds of a judgment, the evidence and considerations out of which a judgment is deduced, Matt. xii. (33), 37" (Winer, § xlvii. 5, a). **Pilate sought**, ἐζήτει; not simply was more disposed (De Wette, Brückner, but more actively exerted himself. The verb denotes energy and determination : cf. v. 18; vii. 19; viii. 37; x. 39; Luke v. 18; xiii. 24; xix. 3; Acts xxvii. 30. In comparison with this, his previous attempts were as nothing—which may account for the omission of 'more,' μᾶλλον, which, however, is implied. **to release Him**, with the concurrence of the Jews. This was the weak point in all Pilate's action. Instead of *seeking* to release Christ he ought to have *released* Him, —as he was on the point of doing (Lange)—and braved the consequences. How he *did* seek, what arguments, persuasions, entreaties he employed, is not recorded; but, whatever these were they availed not,—**the Jews**, instigated by their rulers, **cried out**, ἔκραζον (א^c), better ἐκραύγαζον (A I L M Y etc., Tischendorf), or ἐκραύγασαν (B D etc., Westcott and Hort) raised an outcry, a simultaneous yell, rather than repeated exclamations, **saying, If thou release this man** They clearly suspected Pilate of being on the eve of liberating Christ, as a little before he had suggested (Luke xxiii. 22), and so "they play their last card" (Strauss). **thou art not Cæsar's friend.** The phrase 'Cæsar's friend' was a title of honour bestowed by the emperor and others upon prefects, legates, and allies (Jos. Ant. xiv. 2), in which sense it may be here employed (Tholuck, Hengstenberg, Lange), although the more general meaning of loyal, well-disposed towards the emperor (De Wette, Lücke, Meyer, and others) is equally admissible and correct. **every one that maketh**, lit., *making* himself a **king**, by pretending to be a royal person as this man has done, **speaketh against Cæsar**, i.e. controverts the emperor's authority, and thereby

practically raises a standard of rebellion.

13. When Pilate therefore heard these words, i.e. those just spoken, which struck the governor's most vulnerable part, and filled him with alarm. It was the aim of Pilate (as of all in similar positions) to stand well with Tiberius. This, however, was extremely difficult to do, on account both of Tiberius's cruel character,—he enforced the laws against high treason in the most cruel manner, *atrocissime exercuit* (Suet. Tib. 58), and regarded the crime of lese-majesty as including in it all other offences, *majestatis crimen omnium accusationum complementum erat* (Tacit. An. iii. 38)—and of his own (Pilate's) arbitrary and tyrannical behaviour (see on xviii. 29). **he brought Jesus out** The final judgment required to be pronounced not inside the prætorium, but outside in the open air (Jos. Wars, ii. 9, 3; 14, 8). This leading forth of Jesus was the signal of Pilate's submission. "His playing with the situation was at an end; the situation now plays with him" (Lange). **and sat down on the** (or, a) **judgment seat**, or raised platform. The βῆμα, *suggestus* (Lat.)—any elevated seat ascended by steps: cf. Neh. viii. 4 (LXX.); Esdr. ix. 42; Acts xii. 21; Jos. Ant. xix. 8, 2—was a judge's chair (cf. Acts xviii. 12, 16, 17; xxv. 6, 10, 17), which was probably fetched from the inside and placed in front of the palace, though during the procurator's stay in Jerusalem it may have been permanently fixed there. When the procurator departed from the metropolis, the judge's chair was removed. **at a place called the pavement**, λιθόστρωτον, a place covered with stones, a Mosaic floor, or tesselated pavement. **but in Hebrew or Aramaic Gabbatha**, 'elevation,' not from גַּבְעָה, hill (Hengstenberg), but from גַּבְּבְּיְתָא, the ridge or humph (i.e. back) of the house, i.e. of the temple (Meyer, Tholuck, Luthardt, Westcott, and others). The derivation from גְּבַע which in Aramaic signifies to insert (Ewald), is not so probable.

14. Now it was the preparation of the passover, i.e. the preparation of the Sabbath in the passover week (see on xiii. 2 note): **it was about the sixth hour**, i.e. about noon, which is difficult to harmonize with the statement of the Synoptists that Christ was crucified about the third hour, i.e. 9 A.M. (Mark xv. 25 : cf. Matt. xxvii. 45). Perhaps the simplest solution is (1) that John speaks of the time of the actual nailing to the cross, about 12 A.M., while Mark gives the time when Christ was delivered up to the soldiers for scourging, the usual preliminary to crucifixion, and forming as it were the first part thereof, though in this instance, as John explains, separated by an interval which Mark overlooks (Godet, Lange : cf. Andrew's Life of Christ, pp. 457 ff.). Other explanations are :—(2) that a mistake has occurred in the copying of John's gospel, the sixth being inserted for the third (Eusebius, Beza, Bengel, Luthardt, Alford) ; (3) that the day is divided into quarters, and that the second quarter from 9 to 12 A.M. is mentioned in Mark by its beginning, the third hour, in John by its ending, the sixth hour (Grotius, Calvin, Hengstenberg), against which may be urged that neither Mark (xv. 33) nor John (i. 40) follows this practice throughout ; (4) that Mark has made an error, and John furnished the correct time (Lücke, Meyer, Beyschlag, Renan) ; but Mark's statement is too precise to admit of the suggestion that he has fallen into accidental inaccuracy ; (5) that Mark is correct and John mistaken (Schenkel, Keim), but it is still harder to conceive how John, an eyewitness of the whole melancholy transaction, could be at fault as to the hour when it happened ; (6) that John follows the (supposed) Roman method of dividing the day from midnight to midnight, according to which the sixth hour would be 6 A.M. (Rettig, Hug, Tholuck, Ebrard, Olshausen, Ewald, Westcott, Milligan and Moulton)— against which may be urged (a) that the Romans had no such method of reckoning the hours as is here assumed (see Adams' Rom. Ant. p. 269), (β) that even if they had, 6 A.M. would be too early for the close of the stormy trial before Pilate (De Wette), which did not commence till after morning had dawned (xviii. 28 ; Mark xv. 1 ; Luke xxii. 66), and (γ) that on this hypothesis the interval between the condemnation and the crucifixion is as wide as that between the scourging and the crucifixion on the hypothesis adopted ;—(7) that the discrepancy is quite insoluble (Weiss). **And he** (Pilate) **saith unto the Jews,** "with a flash of genuine conviction" (Farrar), **Behold your king !** Not a final effort to release Christ (Baur, De Wette, Brückner, and others), or a word of mockery directed against Jesus (Grotius), but savage rony concerning the Jews. Whether Pilate intended to remind them of the welcome Jesus had lately received from the people (Westcott), or to convey a threat that first their king and then themselves should be crucified (Lange), or to suggest that he regarded Jesus as assuredly a representative of the Messianic hope of the nation (Hengstenberg), or to hint that if there was a man by whom the Jewish people could carry out any great mission, that man was Jesus (Godet), it is impossible to say.

15. **They,** the people including the chief priests, **therefore,** because of the stinging sarcasm of Pilate's words, **cried out** with one loud simultaneous shout (ἐκραύγασαν) **Away with** *him !* **away with** *him !* **crucify** *him !* The three imperatives reveal the fierceness of their impatience to be done with the business. Contrast the Hozanna of triumphal entry : xii. 13 ; Matt. xxi. 9. **Pilate saith unto them,** venting the rage and soreness of his heart upon the frantic rioters before him (Farrar), **Shall I crucify your king ?** Had Pilate a secret conviction that notwithstanding His rejection by the Jewish leaders, Christ was their Messianic King? **The chief priests answered,** though scarcely aware of what their answer implied, **We have no king but Cæsar.** It was a clear renunciation of their Messianic hope, a virtual abolition of the Theocracy—a deliberate abandonment of their place and purpose as a nation. "When they despised Christ, their true king, and delivered Him up to death they ceased to be God's people and kingdom and sank entirely under the power of this world" (Hengstenberg). "The Kingdom of God, in the confession of its rulers, has become the kingdom of the world. In the place of the Christ, they have found the emperor" (Westcott). "After this, they can say no more. Israel has denied herself ; this is the price at which she attains

the delivery of Jesus to her" (Godet).

16. Then therefore, having probably at this stage washed his hands (Matt. xxvii. 24), **he,** Pilate, the representative of Cæsar, who alone could inflict the death penalty, **delivered Him unto them** No contradiction to the Synoptists (Matt. xxvii. 26 ; Mark xv. 15) who simply say that Christ was delivered to be scourged ; and not implying that the Jews were the executioners rather than the Romans to whom the work primarily and usually belonged, though not always—under Claudius a tribune Celer was given up to the Jews as an enemy of theirs to suffer death at their hands (Keim, Jesus von Nazara, vol. vi. p. 115)—but merely that the Jews were the prime agents, while the Romans acted as their instruments (cf. Acts ii. 23). **to be crucified.** See on

ver. 18. This was commonly done by exclaiming, "Go, soldier, get ready the cross !" *I miles expedi crucem.* Whether the crucifixion was preceded by a second scourging cannot be determined. On the one hand it is asserted that scourging before crucifixion was never omitted (Keim) and that either Christ was twice scourged (Brückner) or John has set the scourging in the wrong place (Keim, Strauss) ; on the other hand it is urged that the physical weakness of Jesus could not have sustained another scourging (Farrar), that the scourging already inflicted had been intended as a preliminary to execution (Ewald, Stier, Hengstenberg, and others), and that even if it was not, Pilate out of pure humanity omitted a second infliction.

HOMILETICS

VER. 1-7. PILATE'S SECOND ATTEMPT TO RESCUE CHRIST.

I. **A Shameful Infliction**—on Jesus. Scourging and mockery : ver. 1-3. 1. *The character of it.* (1) Severe. Stripped to the skin, strapped to a pillar, or tied down upon a low block, with a rod or more probably a leathern thong weighted in the ends with bones or lead, Christ was flogged by the soldiers of the governor. (2) Insulting. Upraised from His recumbent position, wounded and bleeding, He was first arrayed in a worn-out purple *sagum* of some Roman soldier, while a thorn crown was pressed upon His quivering temples, and a reed set between His fettered palms (Matt. xxvii. 29 ; Mark xv. 19). Next the soldiers affected to do him courtly obeisance, coming towards Him with mock attitudes of loyalty, bending the knee before His so-called majesty, saluting Him with acclamations of pretended honour—'Hail, King of the Jews!' and, as they rise from their affected homage, striking Him upon the face with their hands, or upon the head with the reed which they snatch from His unresisting grasp. Finally, they spit upon Him, as the menials had done in the high priest's palace (Matt. xxvi. 67). Appropriately does Herbert make Him say—

> " Behold, they spit on Me in scornful wise ;
> Who with My spittle gave the blind man eyes,
> Leaving his blindness to Mine enemies :
> Was ever grief like Mine ?"

(3) Illegal. Hardly excusable, had Christ been a criminal, such inhumanity was indefensible when Christ had just been pronounced innocent (xviii. 38). 2. *The object of it.* (1) As a preliminary to execution. Barabbas having been preferred by the people, Pilate was in a manner committed to inflict the last penalty on Jesus, and with this in view may have handed over Jesus to what Horace called " the horrid whip," *horribile flagellum* (Sat. i. 3, 119), and Cicero described as a middle death *media mors* (Verr. v. 6). (2) As a method of examination. Pilate may have hoped this fierce ordeal would elicit something from the lips of Christ which would either secure His release or justify His crucifixion. (3) As a means of appeasing the Jews. Pilate seems to have cherished the expectation that these would be satisfied with something less than a capital sentence when they beheld the piteous aspect of their victim.

II. **An Earnest Appeal**—to the Jews : ver. 4, 5. Setting Christ before them, clothed in purple, crowned with thorns,—a mockery king of woe—he appeals to— 1. *Their sense of justice.* Was it right that one should be put to death whom already he had declared and once again was ready to declare innocent,—the appalling ordeal of scourging having elicited nothing from His lips ? 2. *Their feelings of compassion.* Could they gaze on Him unmoved ? "Behold, the man ! " 'Have you no pity for a fellow-creature reduced to such exquisite misery ? Have ye yourselves ceased to be human and become panthers, hyenas, leopards, tigers, that ye can gloat upon a picture that might draw tears from eyes of marble and sighs from hearts of brass ?' Ah ! Pilate—

> " I pray you, think you question with the Jew ?
> You may as well go stand upon the beach
> And bid the main flood bate his usual height ;
> You may as well hold question with the wolf
> Why he hath made the ewe bleat for the lamb," etc.
> —Merchant of Venice, act iv. sc. 1.

3. *Their perception of truth.* Was it reasonable to suppose that the meek prisoner before them was a dangerous revolutionary, a rival to Cæsar ? To Pilate the bare imagination of it seemed grotesque, the very inversion and caricature of common sense.

III. **A Hopeful Decision**—by Pilate : ver. 6. 1. *The fierce demand.* Crucify Him ! crucify Him ! This was the answer of the people and their rulers to Pilate's appeal. "Oh heaven ! that one might read the book of fate, and see the revolution of the times !" (King Henry IV. pt. 2, act iii. sc. 2). Yesterday they cried "Hozanna !" to-day they yell "Crucify !" Then they shouted "Blessed be He that cometh ! " now they shriek "Away with Him ! " In six short days they have become insensate, past feeling, given up to remorseless hate, incapable of responding to any breath from heaven, only susceptible of being played upon by blasts from hell. 2. *The firm reply.* ' Take Him yourselves and crucify Him.' Pilate again refuses to incarnadine his hands in their prisoner's blood. Only, Pilate, having put thy foot down, pray heaven for strength to keep it fast. Thy prisoner and thyself will then be safe. 3. *The forceful reason.* 'I find no crime in Him.' Pilate could not escape from the thought of Christ's innocence. Clearly " some certain dregs of conscience " were within him, even " at his elbow persuading him not to kill " his prisoner. Besides this prisoner of his he seems to feel—

> " Hath borne his faculties so meek, hath been
> So clear in his great office, that his virtues
> Plead like angels, trumpet-tongued, against
> The deep damnation of his taking off "
> —Macbeth, act i. sc. 7.

And so he puts his foot down. If those bloodthirsty ruffians will have Him crucified, they must do it themselves.

Learn 1. The certainty that Christ's words will be fulfilled. Six months before He had predicted this scourging (Matt. xx. 19). 2. The depth of humiliation to which Christ stooped for men. The Holy One of God was flogged, insulted, spit upon like a common slave. 3. The difficulty felt by even wicked men in doing crimes. Conscience "makes a man a coward . . . fills one full of obstacles . . . beggars any (wicked) man that keeps it" (King Richard III., act i. sc. 4). 4. The moral insensibility which men professing religion may at times exhibit. The spectacle of the thorn-crowned Saviour excited no pity in the bosoms of the Jews.

Ver. 5 Ecce Homo ! Behold the Man ! See I. His *humanity* attested—His flesh was lacerated, His body bruised. II. His *innocence* confirmed—Scourging had elicited no secret crime. III. His *majesty* revealed—He endured without a murmur of complaint. IV. His *love* proclaimed—He suffered stripes that sinners might be healed. V. His *divinity* suggested—Only a Son of God indeed could have borne himself as Jesus did in that appalling ordeal.

Ver. 7-11. Pilate's Second Interview with Christ.
I. Startled Inquiry—on the part of Pilate. "Whence art Thou?" ver. 9.   1.
Its occasion. (1) Not the outcry of the Jews for Christ's death. Pilate had
already twice resisted that. (2) Not the reminder that he, as governor, ought
to respect their laws. The Jews clearly thought this would end the controversy
between him and them. (3) But the intimation that Christ had called Himself
'The Son of God.' 2. *Its motive.* (1) Not idle curiosity or angry impatience.
The situation was too solemn for the former, too critical for the latter. (2) Not
horror at the supposed blasphemy with which his prisoner was charged. This
were to ascribe to Pilate a too high religious consciousness. (3) Not alarm lest
he should be delated to Tiberius. It had not yet come to that with Pilate—
though it was coming. (4) But fear (semi-superstitious) lest Jesus, whose preter-
human greatness had impressed Pilate, should after all be the offspring of some
divinity, or some divinity himself in human form—in which case it would be far
from comfortable for Pilate to be found fighting against the gods. 3. *Its import.*
(1) Not to what country dost thou belong? Pilate knew that Jesus was a
Galilean. (2) But of what race art Thou? human or divine? Next to 'Is there
a God?' the greatest question of the day.
II. Mysterious Silence—on the part of Christ. "But Jesus gave him no
answer," ver. 9. 1. *Predicted.* As a lamb before its shearers is dumb, so He
openeth not His mouth (Is. liii. 7). 2. *Becoming.* The question was (1) irrelevant.
The problem Pilate had to solve was that of Christ's guilt or innocence, not of
His origin. (2) Unnecessary. Pilate had evidence enough to enable him to
arrive at a decision. Pilate had already decided—Jesus was without crime. (3)
Insincere. Pilate was not prepared to accept the answer Christ might give.
He had not done so on a former occasion (xviii. 38). (4) Too late. Pilate was
not likely to be able now to extricate himself from the net in which he had been
taken. 3. *Eloquent.* Christ's silence more significantly than His speech could
have done proclaimed His heavenly and divine origin. 4. *Perplexing.* Pilate
could not understand his prisoner.
III. Angry Remonstrance—on the part of Pilate. "Speakest thou not unto
me?" etc., ver. 10. The language of 1. *Offended dignity.* Pilate had marvelled
greatly at his prisoner's taciturnity when the mob first gnashed their teeth, and
hurled their accusations against Him (Matt. xxvii. 14); but was not he the
governor, the representative of Tiberius, the visible embodiment of imperial
authority? "To *me* dost Thou not speak?" exclaims he, putting ruffled pride
and mortified vanity into his tones, as men whose causes are bad and arguments
weak, are accustomed to take shelter behind their self-importance. Men
commonly stand upon their dignity when they have nothing else to stand upon.
2. *Mean intimidation.* This vicegerent of imperial authority could not resist
telling the meek and gentle prisoner by his side that life and death for him, the
prisoner, was in his hands—"Knowest thou not that I have power to release thee
and have power to crucify thee?" Yes! despicable in the extreme it was to
attempt to intimidate Christ by reminding Him that he, Pilate, could send Him
to the cross or could set Him free. It was the speech of a small dignitary who was
a great coward. 3. *Mistaken assumption.* Pilate imagined he held the life of
Jesus in his hands, as unjust judges and fiery persecutors have often since
supposed they held the life of Christ's followers and of Christ's cause; but in
this Pilate erred as his imitators have always done.
IV. Dignified Correction—on the part of Christ. "Thou couldest have no
power," etc., ver. 11. 1. *Pride rebuked.* Pilate conceived of himself as a sort of
mundane divinity, a *deus minor*, invested with at least a delegated omnipotence
—in his bearing towards Jesus had just been trying to 'assume the god'; Christ
tells him—with calm majesty, quiet earnestness, clear certainty, lofty sublimity,
fearlessly, peacefully, solemnly—that both he and Cæsar, the procurator and the
emperor, were simply puppets in the hands of Providence, instruments by which
God worked, and were scarcely worthy of being taken into account at all,—in
particular that he, Pilate, had no power over Him, Christ, one way or another,
except as the temporary holder of the magisterial office; that it was owing to that

circumstance entirely and solely that he had anything to do with the problem then being worked out in his person, that otherwise not even his opinion and far less his authority would have been required for its determination. 2. *Error corrected.* Whatever part Pilate had to play in the momentous drama going forward, and whatever authority he might be called upon to wield, he held not from Cæsar, who himself was a vassal of the King of kings, but from above (cf. Rom. xiii. 1), from Him who is higher than the highest and by whose authority alone 'kings reign and princes decree justice' (Prov. viii. 15). Hence the way in which that power should be exercised was not to be determined by such an accident as the answer that might be extracted from Him, Christ, by means of threatenings or allurements, but by the responsibility under which he, Pilate, lay to the God of heaven, by whom it was bestowed. A great and illuminating thought it must have been to the Roman governor if only it had kindled a permanent light in his heathen soul. 3. *Sin qualified.* Pilate and his prisoner have changed places. Pilate's sin was great,—great even when judged by the light he possessed ; a sin against evidence, against conscience, against heaven's warning, and Christ could say nothing to underestimate these. Only He closes not the door of hope against the governor as one fears He did against the traitor (Matt. xxvi. 24). Rather with gentle mercifulness He suggests forgiveness (or at least the possibility thereof) in the same breath with which He utters condemnation ! In the transaction then speeding to a close there had been a greater sinner than he—not Judas, but (either the Sanhedrim or) Caiaphas. In comparison with the guilt that stained his soul that which the high priest had incurred was as a mountain to a feather, as an ocean to a tributary stream. See Exposition.

Lessons. 1. The judicial blindness into which an unbelieving soul may fall (2 Cor. iii. 14)—exemplified in the Jewish nation and priests. 2. The paralyzing fear which ever clings to a guilty conscience (Job xviii. 11)—illustrated by the case of Pilate. 3. The real reason why the Jews rejected Christ—He was not the sort of Messiah they wanted (1 Cor. i. 23). 4. The dignified reticence with which heaven treats men's demands for more evidence—enough having been provided to enable all in earnest to decide the attitude they shall assume towards Jesus Christ (Luke xvi. 29, 31). 5. The insufferable vanity which official dignity not unfrequently inspires in small souls—Pilate talks with large self-importance about his power to crucify and his power to release. 6. The extreme necessity of remembering that the source of all power and authority is God—to whom therefore all must eventually render account (cf. Rom. xiv. 12). 7. The different degrees of culpability attaching to different sins—all are not equally heinous in God's sight (Matt. xi. 22, 24 ; Luke xii. 47). 8. The Christian duty of keeping silence when not required by faithfulness to God or the interests of others to speak—there are times when, though speech may be silvern, silence is golden (Jas. i. 19).

Ver. 9. The Silences of Jesus. 1. *Before Caiaphas and the false witnesses* (Matt. xxvi. 63 ; Mark xiv. 61)—The Faithful and True Witness before liars and hypocrites. II. *Before Herod* (Luke xxiii. 9)—The Holy One of God before the idle curiosity of a flagitious prince. III. *Before the accusations of the chief priests* at Pilate's bar (Matt. xxvii. 14)—The Sinless One before charges the speakers knew were lies. IV. *Before Pilate* (John xix. 9)—The King of Truth before an insincere inquirer. V. *Before the Syrophenician Woman* (Matt. xv. 23) —Incarnate Love before a humble and earnest petitioner.

Ver. 12-16. Pilate's Last Attempt to rescue Christ.

I. **Despairing Struggles by a Feeble Soul.** "Upon this Pilate sought to release Him " (Christ): ver. 12. I. *The earnestness of this attempt.* Already two, or three, distinct efforts had been made by the governor to rescue Christ, (1) by refusing to proceed without an accusation (xviii. 29) ; (2) by offering the Jews a choice between Barabbas and Jesus (xviii. 39 ; cf. Matt. xxvii. 17) ; and (3) by delivering Christ to be scourged and afterwards appealing to their sympathy (xix. 5). One after another however these successive stratagems had been defeated —perhaps largely because Pilate had not been in earnest. Now he bends himself with energy and determination to accomplish the task of liberating his mysterious prisoner—becomes so absorbed and resolute in his purpose that his previous exertions were as nothing. 2. *The mode of this attempt.* Though not recorded it may be conjectured. Recurring to the arguments previously used—the failure of their witnesses to establish against Christ any crime, the manifest contradiction to their charges Christ's meek and unresisting behaviour gave, the inward conviction he (Pilate) had of Christ's innocence, the exquisite torture Christ had already suffered, the palpable absurdity of supposing Christ could be a dangerous seditionary—he urged them afresh with redoubled energy, perhaps announcing at the close his determination to set Christ free. 3. *The reason of this attempt.* Pilate was induced to this by (1) the inward conviction (or fear) that Christ was a supernatural being, (2) the deepening impression made upon his soul by Christ's person and character, (3) the secret apprehension that it would not be safe to proceed farther against Christ, and (4) the gentleness Christ had displayed towards him in palliating (though not overlooking) his offence, and suggesting hopes of its forgiveness.

II. **Dexterous Manœuvring by a Crafty Foe.**—" But the Jews cried out, saying," etc., ver. 12. The last arrow the Jews had in their quiver was—1. *Sharply pointed.* It was a return to the original indictment of political sedition. An hour before Pilate had waived that aside as absurd and destitute of evidence. The Jews then advanced the charge of blasphemy. This however had issued differently from what they had intended and anticipated. It had so staggered Pilate that Christ appeared to be on the eve of escaping. Hence they revert to the former political accusation, and show Pilate how adroitly it may be turned against himself. What did it matter that their prisoner had never raised a standard of rebellion ? He had claimed to be a king, and Pilate, the representative of Cæsar and vicegerent of the imperial authority, had not only refused to proceed against Him but actually proposed to set Him free. It was barely likely that Tiberius would regard this as the action of one friendly to his throne. And so the crafty assassins, discerning their advantage, shouted, " If thou let this man go, thou art not Cæsar's friend." 2. *Correctly aimed.* The shaft found the open joint in Pilate's harness and went straight to his heart. There was nothing Pilate dreaded more than delation to the emperor. His own infamous misdeeds, his tyrannical oppressions and heartless cruelties, had so roused the ire of his Jewish subjects that any day he might hear of a formal complaint against himself being forwarded to Rome. And if now in the ear of Tiberius it should be whispered in addition that he (Pilate) had been unfaithful to his master, not only would there be for him an end of promotion, but he might at once prepare for the headsman's axe or the poisoner's cup. All this the Jews knew as well as Pilate when they launched their last arrow. 3. *Powerfully driven home.* Like men bent on having their way they cried out with one simultaneous yell. And they had it ! The procurator reeled as one shot upon the field of war.

III. **Ignominious Surrender by an Unjust Judge.** " When Pilate therefore heard these words he brought Jesus out," ver. 13. The capitulation was—1. *Cowardly.* That which he feared was about to come upon him. Those wildly raging but inwardly determined men he saw before him would accuse him before the emperor, unless he yielded. The moment he perceived that he felt he was checkmated. Those accursed hierarchs had proved better players than himself for Jesus' life. With truth, justice, conscience, heaven, Christ, and God upon his side he had lost the game—because he was a coward. The one thing he could not contemplate without a shudder was being reported to the emperor. 2. *Complete.* The struggle so long, at one time so gallantly and to appearance so hopefully maintained, was ended. There was no mistaking the import of Pilate's next actions, the fetching out of Jesus, the sitting down upon the judge's chair, and perhaps the washing of his hands. They meant that Christ was now to be formally handed over to execution. 3. *Contemptuous.* Pilate gave Him up reluctantly, it may well be believed ; but deliberately—not even for Christ was he willing to risk his neck ; and scornfully, with fierce disdain and stinging mockery of the people who had conquered him, saying, as he handed them their victim, " Behold, your king !" as if intimating that after all he believed the thorn crowned and purple-clothed prisoner whose life they were about to take was indeed their king. 4. *Conclusive.* The deed was irrevocable. "Then therefore delivered he Him unto them to be crucified." If for a moment there was hesitation while for the last time he asked 'Shall I crucify your King?' it was only a moment—it was swept away before the awful shout--"We have no king but Cæsar!"

Lessons. 1. The difficulty of doing right when self-interest stands in the way. "If self the wavering balance shake, it's rarely right adjusted" (Burns: Epistle to a Young Friend). 2. The feebleness of every soul that hesitates to follow conscience. Had Pilate listened only to the still small voice within his breast he had been invincible. 3. The guilt incurred by openly defying conscience. Christ palliated Pilate's sin before the preceding interview : it is not clear He would have done so after that interview closed. 4. The degeneracy into which a soul may fall by turning away from Jesus Christ. Caiaphas, the rulers, and the people elected Cæsar for their king rather than have God's Son for their Messiah!

Ver. 12. Cæsar or Christ. I. *Cæsar's friend.* 1. An enemy of Christ. 2. A lover of self. 3. A slave of men. Such Pilate was! II. *Christ's friend.* 1. A lover of the truth. 2. A doer of the right. 3. A champion of the wronged. 4. A sympathizer with the suffering. 5. A servant of conscience. 6. A denier of self. Such Pilate might have been!

Ver. 13. The character of Pilate. I. **Its Excellences.** 1. *Intellectual discernment.* Pilate saw from the first that the Jews had no case against Christ. 2. *Sense of justice.* Pilate shrank from putting a stain upon the escutcheon of Roman equity. 3. *Natural sympathy.* Pilate's heart was touched if those of the Jews were not by the spectacle of the thorn-crowned king. 4. *Moral sensibility.* Pilate recognized more clearly and quickly than the Jews the moral majesty of Jesus. 5. *Desire to do right.* Pilate both heard and wished to follow the inward voice of conscience. II. **Its Defects.** 1. *Sceptical indifference.* Revealed in the question, What is truth? 2. *Superstitious fear.* Shown by the effect upon him of Christ's claim to be the Son of God. 3. *Moral cowardice.* Pilate heard the inner voice and wished to obey but he obeyed not. Like the heathen poet he might have said, 'I see and approve of better things : I follow worse" (Ov. M. 7, 20). 4. *Self-love.* Pilate could have done the right, and probably would have done the right, had the interest of self not intervened.

4. THE PLACE CALLED GOLGOTHA

CHAP. XIX. 17-37

The trial before Pilate having resulted in the handing over of Jesus to the chief priests to be crucified, the story of the Evangelist passes on to describe the execution of this appalling sentence at a place called Golgotha, nigh to the city. This was the fourth downward step in our Lord's self-humiliation. To evince His love for His own, He became obedient as far as to death, even the death of the cross. The account furnished by John has three divisions : —

1. The Crucifixion : xix. 17-25.
2. The Sayings from the Cross : ver. 26-30.
3. The Dead Christ : ver. 31-37.

EXPOSITION

Ver. 17-25. The crucifixion.

Ver. 17. **They,** the Jews, in particular the chief priests and rulers, whom John regarded as the principal actors in the tragedy about to be related (Meyer, Luthardt, Godet, Westcott), rather than the soldiers (De Wette, B. Crusius, Hengstenberg), their instruments and agents, **took,** lit., *received* (παρέλαβον) for death from the governor who for that purpose (ver. 16; Matt. xxvii. 26; Mark xv. 15) had delivered (παρέδωκεν) Him unto them, though they had not received Him (cf. i. 11) for salvation and eternal life, when delivered to them by the Father through the teaching of their prophets). **Jesus** already scourged (Mark xv. 15), whether now (cf. Matt. xxvii. 27) or earlier (ver. 1-3). **therefore,** because Pilate had at length yielded and delivered Him into their hands. **and He went out** ἐξῆλθεν, answering to the 'coming in' ἔρχεται εἰς of xii. 12. The words "and they led Him away" (T. R.), are better omitted (B D L X, etc.), as an addition out of Matt. xxvii. 31 ; and Luke xxiii. 26. It harmonizes more with the elevated thought of the gospel to represent the action as a free going forth on the part of Jesus in solemn self-surrender to His death. **bearing the cross for Himself.** Convicts were usually compelled to bear the instrument of their execution to the place of doom. According to Matt. (xxvii. 32), Mark (xv. 21), and Luke (xxiii. 26), Christ's cross was borne by "Simon, the Cyrenian." The statements are not inconsistent—Christ may have carried His cross from the Prætorium to the city gate, and Simon from the city gate to Golgotha. **unto the place called the place of a skull** Not because of the unburied skulls which lay about (Jerome, Luther), since the Jews would not have permitted skulls to remain uncovered, and "skulls" rather than "skull" would have been employed in its designation; or because it was "a place of execution" (Steinmeyer), since it is doubtful if fixed 'places of execution' were customary in the East, and in any case a pious Jew like Joseph would hardly have had a garden so near an execution

ground (Beyschlag) ; but because of the form of the locality, which had the shape of a skull (Lücke, Tholuck, and others). **which is called in Hebrew Golgotha,** Γολγοθᾶ ; Aramaic, גֻּלְגַּלְתָּא *Gulgolta* : Hebrew גֻּלְגֹּלֶת *Gulgoleth,* translated "skull" (Judges ix. 53 ; 2 Kings ix. 35); Latin *calvaria,* from which comes Calvary. The site of Golgotha has been identified with that of the Church of the Holy Sepulchre within the walls and in the N.W. quarter of the modern city (Raumer, Schubert, Krafft, Williams, Tischendorf) ; but against this (Robinson, Wilson, Tobler, Ewald, Thomson, and others) Heb. xiii. 12 appears decisive, although the ancient wall may have had a less extensive circuit than the modern. The exact locality is as yet a problem ; a spot on the S.W. of the city near the ancient Gennath Gate (Keim), a site farther south, towards the west, at the corner of the present-day wall, or on the mounds overlooking the valley of Hinnon (Renan) ; the place of stoning, N. of the Damascus gate and outside the ancient city (Conder), having been severally suggested as probable solutions.

18. **Where they crucified Him** Crucifixion *crudelissimum teterrimumque supplicium,* Cicero, Ver. v. 64—a form of punishment never inflicted on Roman citizens, its horrors and agonies being reserved for slaves, highway robbers, rebels, and prisoners of war (Jos. Wars, v. 11, 1)—appears to have been introduced into Palestine by Romans —" In Judæa the Roman rule began and ended with crosses (with salutary examples) without number" (Keim)—although the practice of hanging or impaling was not unknown amongst several ancient nations besides the Greeks (Odyss. xxii. 462) and Romans (Livy, xxxviii. 48), as e.g. the Egyptians (Gen. xl. 19), the Assyrians (see Layard's Nineveh, p. 355), the Persians (Num. xxv. 4 ; Ezra vi. 11 ; Esther ii. 23 ; vii. 9 ; Herod. i. 128 ; iii. 159), the Phœnicians, Carthaginians, and Numidians (Keim, vol. vi. p. 139). The cross commonly consisted of an upright and a transverse beam in the form of a

letter T, the upright occasionally extending beyond the transverse. That the former (⊤) was the shape of Christ's cross (Keim) has been argued on the grounds (1) that the Church Fathers liked to find an image of the cross in the Greek letter T (Τ), and (2) that in the catacombs of Rome the figure ⊤ appears as the early Christian art form of the cross ; but the latter (†) seems favoured by preponderating evidence (Beyschlag), as e.g. (1) that on it more easily than on the other could the title be fixed so as to be visible, (2) that the Church Fathers compare the cross to a mast, to a man with outstretched arms, to the praying Moses, to the Roman standard, (3) that they apply to it Eph. iii. 18, (4) that Iraeneus mentions 5 ends of the cross, counting the saddle pin, and (5) that though not the only it was the usual form in the time of Christ. In the middle of the upright beam was a piece of wood on which the crucified sat. The hands were usually nailed to the crossbar, and the feet to the upright beam. The height of the cross was not great, and the feet of the criminal were seldom more than two feet from the ground. Sometimes the nailing took place before and sometimes after the elevation of the cross. (See Keil, Handbuch des Biblischen Archäologie, p. 721 ; Riehm, Handwörterbuch des Biblischen Altertums : art. *Kreuzigung ;* Kitto, Bib. Cycl., arts. *Cross* and *Crucifixion*). **and with Him two others,** robbers, like Barabbas, λησταί (Matt. xxvii. 38 ; Mark xv. 27) ; evil doers, κακοῦργοι (Luke xxiii. 32); whom either Pilate had handed over or the Jews had demanded for execution along with Jesus, to place His alleged offence on a level with theirs. **one on either side** ἐντεῦθεν καὶ ἐντεῦθεν : on the one side and on the other ; cf. ἐντεῦθεν καὶ ἐκεῖθεν, on this side and on that (Rev. xxii. 2), **and Jesus in the midst** as the greatest criminal of the three ; an arrangement of Pilate's to insult the Jews, as in 1 Kings xxii. 19 (B. Crusius, De Wette, Lange, Westcott) ; or, more probably, of the Jews to dishonour Jesus (Meyer, Luthardt, Hengstenberg) ; an arrangement of God's that the Scripture might be fulfilled : Mark xv. 28 (T. R.).

19. And Pilate wrote while the execution was going on (Meyer, Lu-

thardt, Brückner, Westcott), or, rather immediately after the condemnation (De Wette, Tholuck): although the emphasis lies upon not the time but the fact. Pilate, besides delivering up Christ to be crucified, wrote **a title also** *a τίτλος, titulus,* ἐπιγραφὴ, or writing, on an official white tablet, proclaiming the offence for which the person about to be crucified was to suffer. This tablet was usually borne by the criminal himself or carried before him by another to the place of execution ; and afterwards affixed to the cross. See Adam's Roman Ant. p. 221. **and put it on the cross** in accordance with the custom just specified, and by the hands of others, Pilate not having been himself present at the crucifixion (cf. Mark xv. 43, 44). **And there was written** or, *and the writing was* **Jesus of Nazareth, the King of the Jews.** "This is Jesus, the King of the Jews " (Matt. xxvii. 37); "The King of the Jews " (Mark xv. 26) ; "This is the King of the Jews " (Luke xxiii. 38). So far as Pilate was concerned an ironical mocking of the Jews (De Wette, Lücke, Luthardt, Meyer) ; yet done in obedience to a certain singular prompting of God, *singulari quodam dei instinctu* (Lampe). John probably gives the exact words of the title (Bengel), the other evangelists reporting its substance ; although the honour of originality has been claimed for Mark's title as the shortest (Keim, Schenkel, Weiss), and for a combination of Matthew's and John's as the fullest—"This is Jesus of Nazareth, the King of the Jews " (Steinmeyer). Whether John's title was the Greek (Westcott) or the Hebrew (Langen), and Mark's the Roman (Langen) form is uncertain.

20. This title therefore read many of the Jews, not merely those present at the execution, but others afterwards upon the scene ; **for,** accounting for the multitude of readers, **the place where Jesus was crucified** (cf. Rev. xi. 8) **was nigh to the city** (cf. Heb. xiii. 12), **and** (another reason why many read the title) **it was written in Hebrew** *and* **in Latin** *and* **in Greek,** i.e. in the national, the official, and the common dialect, the language of religion, of the state, and of culture. It is absurd to characterize the three languages as "useless verbiage " (Volkmar). On the grave of Gordian the soldiers placed a title in Greek, Latin, Persian, Judæan, Egyptian.

21. **The chief priests of the Jews** An expression occurring nowhere else ; employed to contrast the faithless priests with the true King (Westcott), as the two powers who had been striving together for dominion (Hengstenberg) ; or simply to indicate that the chief priests acted, or supposed they were acting, as defenders of the theocratic people (Godet), who desired not to see the ancient designation of Messiah profaned (Meyer). **therefore,** because the title, which in its terms stung them, could be read by many of the Jews. **said to Pilate,** probably sending a deputation to him for that purpose, since he was not present at the crucifixion : see above on ver. 19. **Write not the King of the Jews** The present expresses the idea they conveyed to Pilate (Godet), rather than suggests that the title was not yet finished (De Wette), because still capable of alteration (Meyer). **but that he said, I am King of the Jews.** Thus they repeat and desire to perpetuate their calumny, that Christ was a Messianic pretender.

22. **Pilate answered,** with characteristic obstinacy (Philo), which had no difficulty in maintaining its ground when the element of personal danger was awanting ; although perhaps sight should not be lost of the overruling providence of God in arranging that Pilate should decline to give way on a point so important as this. **What I have written, I have written,** i.e. it cannot and will not be altered. Thus in the three principal languages of the world the Messianic dignity of Jesus was proclaimed even in His death and from His cross.

23. **The soldiers,** whom John now mentions as having taken part in the crucifixion. The work was commonly assigned to a quaternion or company of four (cf. Acts xii. 4). **therefore,** because they had acted as the executioners. **when they had crucified Jesus,** i.e. when, their horrible labour having been accomplished, they were at leisure to survey their handiwork and enjoy their ease. **took,** as their perquisites, in accordance with established practice. **His garments,** His upper robe,

cap, girdle, and other articles of apparel, all included in His *ἱμάτια.* **and made four parts, to every soldier a part** This proves that not more than four soldiers were engaged in the work of crucifixion ; though four may have been told off to each cross. **and also the coat,** ὁ χιτών, the inner tunic or vestment, worn next the body. **Now the coat was without seam, woven from the top throughout.** It resembled the tunic or vestment of the high priest: Jos. Ant. iii. 7, 4.

24. **They said therefore one to another**—the thought perhaps striking them simultaneously, though first uttered by one to his fellow : **Let us not rend it**—being of one piece, it could not well be divided—**but cast lots for it whose it shall be,** which they did, perhaps in a brazen helmet. Mark (xv. 24) says they distributed the other articles also by lot, so settling who should take what, τίς τί ἄρῃ ; which is not inconsistent with the lotting of the seamless coat ; **that the Scripture** (Ps. xxii. 18), in which David describes the sufferings of Jehovah's anointed servant, **might be fulfilled which saith, They parted My garments among them, and upon My vesture did they cast lots.** The distinction here the same as that insisted on by John, namely, between ' the over-clothing ' or ' garments ' and the ' vesture ' or ' body-dress.' Even were the terms synonymous (De Wette, Lücke), the place would be typical of Christ (Tholuck) ; but Hebrew parallelism justifies the inference that the Psalmist, using in the former member the plural, and in the latter the singular, designed to mark the distinction to which John alludes (Godet, Westcott, Luthardt, and others). **These things therefore the soldiers did.** The Evangelist emphasizes this heartless conduct of the soldiers in parting Christ's garments and casting lots for His coat under His very eyes, in contrast with the tender behaviour of the women next related, whose feelings he rather suggests by silence than records in words.

25. **But** in contrast to the soldiers **there were standing by the cross of Jesus** inside the circle of spectators, and so close to the Saviour as to be addressed by Him (ver. 26). Matthew

(xxvii. 56) and Mark (xv. 40) say 'afar off.' This apparent contradiction invalidates (?) the whole matter (Strauss); but the women, though afar off at first, may have gradually approached, till they found themselves, when the soldiers' work was done, in the immediate vicinity of Jesus (Olshausen, Lücke). Or, they may have been at first near the cross and afterwards withdrawn to a distance when John, with Jesus's mother, had departed (Meyer), and this may explain why the Synoptists do not mention the presence of the mother of Jesus (Godet). This nearer position John specifies because of what follows (ver. 26); the more distant the Synoptists, when detailing the effects of the crucifixion scene upon different groups of spectators. **His mother** Mary, whose husband Joseph, it may be supposed, was by this time dead, **and His mother's sister, Mary the wife of Clopas** Two women, the first Salome, the mother of John, stated by the Synoptists to have been in the group (Wieseler, Lücke, Meyer, Luthardt, Westcott, Milligan and Moulton, Alford, and others); one woman (De Wette, Godet, Hengstenberg, Ebrard, Olshausen, and others). In favour of the first is urged that (1) otherwise two sisters had the same name—an unlikely supposition, (2) it accords with John's style to describe groups of persons in pairs, and (3) to indicate his own presence by means of a periphrasis, (4) Salome was in the group (the Synoptists), and (5) John's reason for introducing four women may have been to complete the antithesis to the quaternion. In favour of the second is contended that (1) the Christian church has from the beginning regarded the women as three, (2) had John meant to distinguish Mary's sister from the wife of Clopas, he would have inserted the conjunction "and," (3) elsewhere is no trace of this relationship between John and Jesus, and (4) if John's mother had been in the group spoken of by the evangelist, Christ would scarcely have addressed John as He did a moment after without an explanation. Clopas was probably the Alphæus in the list of apostles (Matt. x. 3), since his wife is characterized as "the mother of James the less and of Joses" (Matt. xxvii. 56 ; Mark xv. 40.) There is no

reason for identifying him with the Emmaus traveller (Luke xxiv. 18). **and Mary Magdalene.** Introduced as well known (Luke viii. 2) though the first time named in this gospel. The presence of the Galilean women at the cross has been doubted (Volkmar), but without ground (Schenkel), and "with senseless fanaticism" (Keim) ; but equally baseless is the assertion that, while the Galilean women were not absent, the mother of Jesus was not present (Schenkel, Keim).

Ver. 26-30. The sayings from the cross.

26. **When Jesus therefore** because of the contiguity of the women, who had approached nearer when the soldiers had concluded their work **saw His mother** whose sorrow must have deeply affected Him **and the disciple standing by whom He loved** i.e. the evangelist (cf. xiii. 23), whose allusion to himself in this now familiar way has been set down as "the basest self-laudation" (Weisse), or something approaching thereto (Keim, Hilgenfeld), but was obviously intended as an explanation of, and motive for, the word and action of Christ about to be recorded (Luthardt), and was perfectly compatible with the 'truest humility' on the writer's part (Meyer, Westcott), **He saith unto His mother,** not to show that He was reconciled to (Schenkel), since He had never been estranged from, her, but to console her, on the eve of being bereaved of her Son, **Woman, behold thy Son.** He says not Mother! because henceforth for Him—as indeed already had been the case in all matters connected with His divine calling—earthly relationships were at an end (see ii. 4 ; Matt. xii. 48); He bids her henceforth regard As her son, not for his sake, but for hers, directing her not to give John maternal love, but to look to him for filial duty, and not because Mary had no other children of her own from whom to expect support and consolation (Lücke, Olshausen, Hengstenberg), or only sons of her deceased husband by a former marriage (Westcott), or because these were in less easy circumstances than John (Lampe), but either because these sons, whether her own or Joseph's, by another, were as yet unbelieving (Tholuck, Alford), though Christ must have foreseen their early

conversion to the faith (Meyer), which occurred after the resurrection and before Pentecost (Acts i. 14), or because John's womanly tenderness fitted him to be a son to her who had been the mother of our Lord (Tholuck, Lange, Meyer, and others).

27. **Then**, after comforting His mother, for whom the words were principally spoken, **saith He to the disciple** laying on him the necessary commandment, which his relation to Christ as a disciple and friend would constrain him to fulfil (xiii. 34-35 ; xiv. 21 ; xv. 10, 14), **Behold thy mother!** Omitting 'Friend or son'! because John's relationship to Jesus was not to be changed by either the trust about to be received or bereavement suffered, He enjoins John to regard Mary henceforth as a mother, to treat her as such, and in turn to anticipate being treated by her as a son. This injunction was not incompatible with John's duty to his own mother then beside him. **And, from that hour**—not necessarily from that moment (Stier, Alford, Bengel), although this is not impossible, but after Christ's death, **the disciple took her unto his own home.** It cannot be inferred from this that John had a house in Jerusalem (Stier, Tholuck) ; but merely, during the feast, a lodging into which he received Mary, when the feast was ended taking her with him into Galilee, xxi. 2 (Godet, Luthardt, Meyer, Westcott, Alford, Hengstenberg, Lange, Lücke) ; it weakens the phrase to refer it only to the commencement of such dutiful relationship between John and Mary without implying that Mary became an inmate of John's household (De Wette). The last notice of Mary is in Acts i. 14. One tradition says she lived with John eleven years in Jerusalem, and died there ; another that she accompanied him to Ephesus, and was buried there.

28. **After this**, not immediately after, for the next voice related to His sense of forsakenness (Matt. xxvii. 46), and in the meantime the three hours of darkness had intervened ; but after the above scene with Mary and John (Meyer), after, in respect of moral order. After having closed His ministry to others, He turns to Himself (Westcott). **Jesus knowing that all**

things are now finished The "all things" were not the prophecies relating to His death (Beza, Baur), but the work of salvation entrusted to Him by the Father (Calvin, Grotius, Godet, Meyer, Tholuck, De Wette). **that the Scripture might be accomplished,** or *finished*, the same verb as in the antecedent clause. Whether this should be connected with the preceding (Bengel, Michaelis, Tholuck, Meyer, Luthardt, Lange) or the succeeding clause (Chrysostom, De Wette, Lücke, Godet, Hengstenberg, Alford) is not important. In either case the result is the same. In the former, Jesus knew that all things had been accomplished that the Scriptures might be accomplished. There was no prophecy remaining unfulfilled. Hence the "I thirst" was not regarded by Him as a fulfilment of Scripture. In the latter, Christ understood "all things" to be accomplished except this one detail, and in order to bring it also to accomplishment, proceeded to speak as next reported. In support of connection with the preceding clause, it is argued that (1) it is John's practice to call attention to Scripture fulfilment, not before, but after mentioning that which fulfils it (Meyer) ; (2) the fulfilments of Scripture pointed out by John are commonly things done to, rather than by, Christ ; (3) when John speaks of any Scripture fulfilment it is his custom to cite the particular passage of Scripture fulfilled (Meyer, Luthardt) ; (4) the word "now" appears to indicate that no further Scripture remained behind unfulfilled (Meyer) ; and (5) had Christ intended in His next utterance to fulfil Scripture, He would have used the verb 'fulfilled'—πληρωθῇ, rather than 'accomplished'—τελειωθῇ (Luthardt). In favour of connection with what follows it is contended that (1) xiv. 31 shows John sometimes places "in order that," ἵνα, before that to which it refers (Lücke, Alford); (2) the construction "finished that" is unnatural (Godet) ; (3) John, though not citing the passage (Ps. lxix. 21), yet regards it as receiving fulfilment in the drink offered to Christ in answer to His cry (Godet, Hengstenberg, Milligan and Moulton) ; (4) John uses "finished" rather than "fulfilled" because the subject in question is not the fulfilment of this or that particular prophecy, but the finishing up of Scripture prediction as a whole (Godet); and (5) if unnatural and strained to say Christ uttered *one voice* " that Scripture might be finished," it is hardly less so to maintain that *all things* were done with this end in view. The truth is, both views are correct. The programme of Christ's earthly life, including His passion in all its details, was pre-arranged in O. T. Scripture; hence in finishing the last Scripture Christ was ending His work and passion, in closing His passion He was accomplishing Scripture. **saith, I thirst.** The thirst produced by the extreme pain to which the sufferer was subjected, the nervous exhaustion which his agonies induced, and (in Christ's case) the burning sun to which he was exposed, was one of the most cruel tortures of crucifixion. At the beginning Christ rejected the stupefying draught—wine mingled with myrrh—offered Him with the merciful purpose of deadening His sensibilities (Matt. xxvii. 34 ; Mark xv. 23), because He would enter upon the appointed path of suffering in full possession of consciousness ; He now asks refreshment to revive His drooping energies that in full possession of consciousness He may freely die.

29. **There was set there a vessel full of vinegar** sour wine (*posca, vinum acidum*) prepared for the soldiers, not the stupefying draught above referred to. Luke (xxiii. 36) speaks of an intermediate occasion on which the soldiers offered Christ vinegar to drink, viz. between the first and second voices, and simultaneous with the mockery of the priests and the people. This was probably a repetition of the draught offered Him at the first to allay His pains (Godet), if not rather a mocking proffer of the sour wine the soldiers were then drinking as a part of their mid-day meal (Alford, Westcott, Oosterzee), which He refused then, but now desired, and they now extend to Him in answer to His cry. **So they,** doubtless the soldiers, though not named, **put a sponge full of the vinegar upon hyssop** The hyssop plant, to be identified with "the reed" spoken of in Matt. xxvii. 48 (Meyer, Godet, Lange, Lücke), though some distinguish the two (De Wette, Milligan and Moulton, Westcott), grows stalks from 1 to 1½ feet

high. **and brought it to His mouth.** If the hyssop stalk sufficed to reach Christ's parched lips, the cross must have been of no great height ; if it was placed upon the end of a reed, the altitude of the cross cannot be ascertained.

30. **When Jesus therefore had received the vinegar,** by which His declining vitality was for a moment arrested and His spirit revived, **He said, It is finished** τετέλεσται, a word " in Christ's heart before, but now brought forth with the lips " (Bengel), signified that the programme of Scripture and the work of the Father were alike completed. **and He bowed His head,** having previously cried with a loud voice (Matt. xxvii. 50) as well as uttered a seventh saying (Luke xxiii. 46), and having up to this moment sustained His head erect, **and gave up His spirit.** Not a periphrasis for " expired," but a description of the free, spontaneous, and deliberate character of Christ's death, as a voluntary surrender of His human spirit into the hands of God. The death of Christ was at once a *passion* and an *action*, a suffering and a doing.

Ver. 31-37. The dead Christ.

31. **The Jews** the Jewish authorities, who, by this time, had returned to the city to attend to the temple duties (Matt. xxvii. 51 ; Mark xv. 38), **therefore** not because Jesus was already dead (Meyer), a fact of which they were not yet aware (see ver. 33), but because the crucifixion having been accomplished, they were now anxious to observe the law with regard to the approaching Sabbath : *Magnifici honoratores Dei, cum in conscientia mala reposuissent sanguinem justi* (Ruperti.) **because it was the Preparation** not the preparation of the Passover, but the preparation of the Sabbath ; see on xiii. 2 note. **that the bodies should not remain upon the cross upon the Sabbath** The law required the corpses of criminals who had died by hanging to be taken down from the gallows before night, and indeed before sundown : Deut. xxi. 23 ; Josh. viii. 29 ; x. 26. The practice was in vogue in Christ's time among the Jews (Jos. Wars iv. 5, 2). The Romans left the bodies of the crucified to putrefy upon the cross, *sublime putrescere* (Cic. Tusc.

i. 43), or to be devoured by birds of prey, *pascere corvos* (Hor. Ep. i. 16, 48), although friends were at liberty to purchase for them the right of sepulture (see Adam's Rom. Ant. p. 220). **for the day of that Sabbath was an high day** not as being the fifteenth of Nisan, or the first day of the feast, but as being a Sabbath day to which unusual solemnity attached through its occurring in the paschal week ; see above on xiii. 2 note. **asked of Pilate that their legs might be broken** The *crurifragium*, or 'breaking of the legs' of a criminal, a usual accompaniment of crucifixion, although sometimes employed as an independent punishment (Lactantius, Instit. iv. 26 ; Lipsius, de Cruce ii. 14), is commonly regarded as having been designed to accelerate death (Meyer, De Wette, Lange, Luthardt, Westcott, and others). It has also been viewed as intended to protract the sufferings of the crucified, and to render recovery impossible, although taken down from the cross (Tholuck). There is no reason to suppose an additional *coup de grace* was added to occasion death (Michaelis, Kuinoel). **and that they might be taken away** i.e. removed from the cross for burial which Jewish humanity denied neither to executed criminals nor to fallen foes (Jos. Ant. iv. 8, 24 ; Wars iv. 5, 2).

32. The soldiers A special company despatched by Pilate to see to the crurifragium (Kuinoel, Olshausen, De Wette, Lücke), since the soldiers who crucified Christ must have already noticed He was dead (Mark xxvii. 54 ; Mark xv. 39); but the language of the Synoptists does not necessarily imply that the soldiers were as yet satisfied Christ's life was extinct. **therefore,** doubtless because of orders forwarded by Pilate, **came** advanced towards the cross from the spot where they were stationed, **and brake the legs of the first, and of the other which was crucified with him.** The work was probably done simultaneously by two soldiers on each side of the three crosses, although from the use of "other" instead of "second" it has been inferred that the crurifragium began with the penitent robber. *Ex quo colligi posse videtur, primum, qui celerius a doloribus sit liberatus, con-*

versum illum dici (Bengel.) **but when they came to Jesus, and saw that He was dead already** as they had suspected, and for that reason did not begin with Him (Hengstenberg) ; or, with equal probability, as the fact of Christ's death had, up till this moment, been unobserved by them, in consequence of their indifference (Meyer). **they brake not His legs.** The extinction of life had rendered this unnecessary. "So speedy a death was certainly a seldom occurrence." When violence was not used, "the crucified often lived 24 or 36 hours, sometimes three days and nights." Yet "it is quite conceivable that," after all Christ had passed through, "His strength should suddenly break down" (Keim).

34. Howbeit, to make assurance doubly sure, **one of the soldiers with a spear** the ordinary long lance of a Roman horseman **pierced His side,** the left (De Wette, Lücke, Lange, Meyer, Luthardt) : the stab not a slight scratch (Paulus), but a violent thrust (Meyer, Luthardt, etc.), though ἔνυξεν is applied to a light touch (Ecclus. xxii. 19), as well as a deep gash (Jos. Wars iii. 7, 35). **and straightway there came out water and blood.** Not a hendiadys for a reddish or bloody lymph (Paulus); or the flowing forth of decomposed blood in the form of *serum*, or bloody water and *placenta*, or clots of blood (Hase, Ebrard, De Wette), since it is not certain that such an outflow of the constituent parts of blood on the wounding of a dead body by a spear thrust can be anatomically established (Meyer), and since, according to Scripture, Christ's body saw no corruption ; or the complete bleeding away of Christ's body, till at last not blood but water followed (Hofmann), of which total draining of the blood the text supplies no hint (Meyer), while the physiological fact that such a bleeding closes with water was not so well known as to be assumed by the writer without offering a word of explanation (Luthardt); or the discharge of water first from the pericardium, which was first reached by the spear, and next of blood from the heart, when it was touched (Lücke, Tholuck) ; but a miraculous occurrence (Origen, Meyer, Luthardt, Godet, and others). N.B.—The theory that the physical cause of Christ's death was a broken heart (Ewald, Stroud, Hanna) is, though not impossible, at least doubtful (Keim); whether the suggestions that death was due to paralysis of the heart (Keim), or rupture of a blood vessel in the region of the heart (Renan), or simply exhaustion (Langen), are any nearer the truth, it is impossible to say. **35. And he that hath seen** i.e. John (Meyer, Luthardt, Godet, and others), who speaks of himself as having been an eye-witness of the event. The notion that the Evangelist is a late writer who here distinguishes himself from John (Weisse, Schweitzer, and others) shatters itself on the statement, "and he knoweth that he saith true" (De Wette). **hath borne witness** to the fact above stated. **and his witness is true,** or, *and true is his witness,* the most emphatic place in the sentence being occupied by the adjective and the next by the pronoun ; the word ἀληθινή implying not merely the veracious character of the testimony, but its correspondence with the true idea of a testimony or μαρτυρία (Meyer) —"a testimony which really deserves the name " (Godet), and this again resting on the fact that it was the testimony of one who had been a personal spectator of the occurrence he reports. **and he knoweth that he saith true.** The Evangelist claims not merely to be verbally accurate in reporting what he believes he saw, but to be also true in the sense of reporting true things, or things that actually happened. This disposes of the theory that John here manufactures history to suit the conception he had formed of the death of Christ as the source of moral and spiritual cleansing for the world (Baur); while it equally confirms the impression that John believed himself to be recording not a usual phenomenon but an extraordinary incident, if not a supernatural rather than a natural occurrence, certainly an event which was unique. **that ye also may believe.** What ? First, the testimony that blood and water flowed from the pierced side of the dead Christ; and second, what that

signified, which was not merely the reality of Christ's death (Beza, Grotius, De Wette, Lücke), or the genuine corporeity of Christ as opposed to the very old Docetic heresy (Paulus, Olshausen, and others), but also that Jesus was indeed the Christ, the Son of God (Bengel, Meyer, Luthardt, Godet, Hengstenberg; etc.). How it did so John does not explain ; but probably the key to his thought is furnished in 1 John v. 6. **36. For,** introducing a confirmatory proof that Jesus was indeed the Christ and therefore the Son of God, **these things,** the piercing of the side instead of the breaking of the legs, **came to pass,** in the overruling providence of God, **that the Scripture,** i.e. the passage of Scripture, as in xiii. 18, **might be fulfilled,** by the type finding its realization, **A bone of Him shall not be broken.** See Exod. xii. 46 ; Num. ix. 12 ; in which the allusion is to the paschal lamb which John regards as having been a type of Christ (Luthardt, Meyer, Hengstenberg, and others), though out of this idea it is absurd to maintain (Baur) he has fashioned his history. Ps. xxxiv. 20 (Grotius, Bäumlein, Brückner) seems to be a promise rather of preservation from, than of protection in, death. **37. And again another Scripture** (Zech. xii. 10) **saith,** predicting what should be afterwards fulfilled in Christ. **They shall look on Him whom they pierced.** The citation here and in Rev. i. 7 is freely made from the Hebrew which the LXX. has weakened by translating—" ἐπιβλέψονται πρός με, ἀνθ᾽ ὧν κατωρχήσαντο "— *they shall look towards Me, because they have insulted Me.* The subject of both verbs is the Jews ; and the Evangelist's meaning is that the passage was fulfilled first in the actual piercing of the side of Jesus, the act of the Jews, though done by a soldier's spear, and second in that which followed as the result of the crucifixion, when the repentant Jews, beholding their handiwork turned towards Christ a look of faith and contrition (Acts ii. 37).

HOMILETICS

VER. 17-25.—THE CROSS OF CHRIST.
I. Under the Cross : the procession towards Golgotha : *the Via dolorosa :* ver.
17.   1. *The wearied pilgrim.* Jesus. (1) Exhausted by the holy emotion of
the upper room, the mysterious sorrow and bloody sweat in Gethsemane, the
excitement attending the arrest, the trials, and the condemnation, not to speak
of the want of sleep. (2) Suffering through the scourging which doubtless had
loaded every nerve in His exquisitely sensitive frame with pain. (3) Burdened beneath the weight of the cross—two massive beams in the form of a T
or †, the upright lying along His back, and the transverse fastened in His
fettered hands, or the two clasped around His neck in the form of a V. (4)
Degraded by a white tablet borne aloft before Him or suspended from His
neck, proclaiming His alleged crime. 2. *The varied attendants.* (1) The robbers,
who accompanied Him, whom Pilate had fetched, or the people had asked, from
their dungeons to lend a touch of sensation to the exciting spectacle, to put a
deeper mark of degradation on their despised victim. (2) The soldiers who led
Him by a halter round His neck. (3) The people who mocked Him. (4) Simon
who assisted Him. (5) The daughters of Jerusalem who lamented Him (Luke
xxiii. 27). 3. *The sorrowful way.* Out from Pilate's palace on the temple hill,
through the city streets, now thronged with eager multitudes who "climb to
walls and battlements, to towers and windows, yea, to chimney tops," to see the
strange procession of the felons, the Nazarene and the robbers ; if not along the
so-called *Via dolorosa* with its fourteen stations invented by Roman Catholic
tradition, since the Jerusalem of Our Lord's day lies many feet beneath the
surface of the ground on which the so-called way is traced—yet away towards a
well-known spot outside the city, from its resemblance to a human head named
Golgotha.
II. Upon the Cross : Jesus in the midst : numbered with transgressors :
ver. 18. Arrived at Golgotha, the cross was—1. *Furnished with its victim.* As
it lay upon the sward, with nails driven through His hands and feet (Ps. xxii.
16 ; Luke xxiv. 40), our Lord was impaled thereupon, praying as the executioners did their work, and the rough bolts went tearing through His quivering
flesh—" Father, forgive them, for they know not what they do" (Luke xxiii.
34)—*the first saying from the cross.* 2. *Upraised to its position.* Suspended by
His hands and feet, His body resting on an upright peg in the middle of the
main beam, our Lord was exhibited to angels and to men as a 'spectacle of
woe,' the priests and the people who looked on, mocking His misery, wagging
their heads, and crying, 'Thou that savest others, save Thyself !' 'If Thou be
the Son of God, come down from the cross,' 'Come down from the cross, and
we will believe Thee,' 'This man delighted in God, let God deliver Him, if He
will have Him' (Matt. xxvii. 39 ; Mark xv. 29 ; Luke xxiii. 35). 3. *Set in the
midst.* On either side a crucified robber proclaimed Him the worst of the
three. Verily, He was numbered with the transgressors ! *The second saying,*
"To-day shalt thou be with Me in paradise" (Luke xxiii. 43), probably fell from
Christ's lips soon after the crosses had been set up.
III. Above the Cross : the trilingual title : Jesus of Nazareth, the King of
the Jews : v. 19. 1. *Its conspicuous position.* Above Christ's head, to be seen
by all. 2. *Its threefold language.* Hebrew, Roman, Greek, to be read by all.
3. *Its immediate design.* An accusation, setting forth the (alleged) crime for
which Christ died. 4. *Its providential use.* To attest (1) Christ's true humanity
—Jesus of Nazareth, (2) His Messianic dignity—King of the Jews, (3) Israel's
sin—they had crucified their Sovereign, (4) The World's hope—Israel's rejected
Messiah was the Saviour of men.
IV. Beneath the Cross : gambling for the Saviour's clothes : the soldiers
fulfilling prophecy : ver. 23, 24. 1. *Heartless cruelty.* "These things therefore

the soldiers did," sadly writes John. They gambled for the Saviour's seamless coat (perhaps also for His other articles of raiment), in His very presence, at the foot of the cross, in full view of his dying agonies. Could brutal inhumanity further go? 2. *Moral insensibility*. The men who did so were soldiers, inured to the horrors of war, to the groans of the wounded and dying, to the perpetration of unmentionable cruelties upon the weak and the defenceless, no less than upon assailants and foes. And they had just been acting as executioners, and their own nerves had never quivered. Why, then, should it ruffle their composure, as they coolly sit down to watch the dying struggles of the crucified, to cast the dice a time or two to ascertain who should take what—who should have His tunic, who should have His girdle, who should have His cap, who should have His seamless coat? 3. *Appalling criminality*. To cast the lot into the lap for such a purpose, to practically ask God to divide among them the clothes of their victim, was surely the height of defiant godlessness. 4. *Unconscious instrumentality*. Though they dreamt not of it, these military ruffians were fulfilling an ancient oracle of Scripture, and so indirectly giving testimony to Christ as Israel's Messiah and God's Son.

V. **Near the Cross** : the Galilean women : the post of love : ver. 25. 1. *Their names*. (1) Mary, the mother of Jesus, upon whose bosom He had lain when an infant, from whose breast He had drawn sweet sustenance, *consolationes lactis humani* (Augustine), by whose love His opening manhood had been cherished, in whose heart He had lived during the years of His ministry. True to her motherhood, Mary was there to look the last (as she supposed) upon her Son, the sword of which Simeon had spoken three and thirty years before (Luke ii. 35) piercing her through with unutterable anguish. 2. Mary's sister, Salome, the wife of Zebedee, and mother of the Evangelist (see Exposition). The Evangelist and Jesus were thus cousins ; which may largely account for the mental and spiritual affinity between them. (3) Mary, the wife of Clopas or Alphæus, the mother of James the less and Joses. (4) Mary Magdalene, or Mary of Magdala. 2. *Their position*. By the cross. Marking (1) their courage —not afraid of the crowd or of the soldiers ; (2) their fidelity—Christ's male disciples had deserted, these faithful women had adhered to Him ; (3) their affection—drawn to the awful spectacle by the fervour of their attachment to Jesus ; (4) their sympathy—intending their tears in some degree to console Him, as doubtless they did ; (5) their privilege—a gracious opportunity of hearing His last words from the cross.

Lessons. 1. The completeness of Christ's obedience—" as far as to death, even the death of the cross " (Phil. ii. 8). 2. The depth of His humiliation—"numbered with transgressors" (Is. liii. 12). 3. The reality of His atoning work— "made sin for us " (2 Cor. v. 21). 4. The certainty of His Messiaship—proved by the title. 5. The moral insensibility to which depraved natures may sink— exemplified in the soldiers ; " past feeling " (Eph. iv. 19). 5. The heroism of feeble women when inspired by faith and drawn by love—"they that know the Lord, etc." (Dan. xi. 32). 7. The startling contrasts of life—illustrated by the soldiers and the women. 8. The power which still lies in the cross to reveal human hearts.

Ver. 17. The Lonely Cross-bearer. I. *Bearing the cross for Himself.* "Of the people there was none with Him" (Is. lxiii. 3). 1. An aggravation of His misery. 2. An intensifying of their sin. 3. A heightening of His love. 4. An enlargement of their hope. II. *Bearing the cross for us.* 1. As an expiation of our guilt (Col. i. 20 ; ii. 14.) 2. As a pattern for our life (1 Pet. ii. 21). (See Thomas à Kempis : The Imitation of Christ, bk. ii. ch. xii.)

Ver. 17. The place called Golgotha. I. A scene of human wickedness. II. A theatre of divine love. III. An arena of splendid victory.

Ver. 18. Light from the Cross. On—I. The infatuation of the priests. II. The regret of Pilate. III. The brutality of the soldiers. IV. The pity of the women. V. The patience of Christ. VI. The love of God. VII. The salvation of the world.

Ver. 18. The Three Crosses. I. That of Jesus ; *dying for sin*—redemption.

II. That of the impenitent robber; *dying in sin*—perdition.   III. That of the penitent robber; *dying out of sin*—salvation.

Ver. 18. Jesus in the midst.   I. *Of the Trinity.*   Father, Son, and Holy Ghost.   II. *Of Creation.* "By Him or in Him all things consist."   III. *Of Humanity.* "The Word became flesh, and dwelt among us."   IV. *Of the Church.* "Where two or three are met together, there am I in the midst of them."   V. *Of the Bible.* "These are they that testify of Me."   VI. *Of Providence.* Christ the central thought of history.   VII. *Of Heaven.* "His presence fills each heart with joy."

Ver. 26–30.   Voices from the Cross; or, The Last Words of Jesus.

I. **The Voice of the Church's Head.**—'Woman, behold thy Son!' (Son,) 'behold, thy mother!' ver. 26-27.   *The third saying*, uttered soon after the elevation of the cross, and before the darkness at noon.   In the first saying, the Advocate of sinners; in the second, the Saviour of believers; in the third, Christ reveals Himself as the Church's Head.   1. *Approving Himself perfect in His human relations*, since without this He could not have been the Church's Head.   (1) Perfect as a Son.   Self-forgetful—in the hour of death noticing and thinking of His mother; sympathetic—in the midst of His own anguish feeling for her sorrow; considerate—Himself in extremest need, yet caring for her comfort when He should have breathed His last; tender—commending her to the care of His loved disciple.   (2) Perfect as a friend.   Forgiving—when He looks on John, saying nothing about the shameful desertion; trusting—though John, like the rest of His disciples, had failed Him, not withholding from him confidence; honouring—committing to his care the dearest earthly friend He possessed.   2. *Disentangling Himself from all earthly relations*, the more efficiently to be the Church's Head.   (1) In His boyhood Christ perceived that this must be (Luke ii. 49).   (2) Throughout His ministry He ruled His action by this consideration, as e.g. at the Cana wedding (Matt. ii. 4), and in the Capernaum synagogue (Matt. xii. 49).   (3) On the cross He announces that this disentanglement must be permanent.   Instead of calling Mary mother, He addresses her as woman. Henceforth the relations He will hold to men will be those of a Saviour to sinners, of a Firstborn among brethren, of a Lawgiver to His people, of a Head to the Church His body.   Mary will be to Him no more than other members in His Father's family, other sisters and brothers in His Father's house, other disciples who have followed Him in faith, other sinners who have been saved by His grace; and He will be to Mary no more than He is to them—a Redeemer, a Saviour, a High Priest, a Lord, a Forerunner.   The same truth He emphasizes by omitting 'Friend' or 'Son' in directing His speech to John.   His dying charge He lays not on John, the son of Zebedee, but on John the disciple.   (3) *Creating new relationships among His people*, by giving John to Mary as a son, Mary to John as a mother, in the sense not simply of commending, but also of commanding. If Christ declared the mission of Himself and of His gospel on earth and in the world to be what it still is, disruptive, disintegrating, volcanic, revolutionary (Matt. x. 34, 36), He also said it should be within the sphere of the Christian Church, combining and consolidating, binding up the fragments broken off from the mass of the ungodly into a higher unity, "setting the solitary in families," establishing between them relationships (Matt. xix. 29; Mark x. 30)—(1) more exalted in character, being based upon spiritual affinity, as between Paul and Timothy (1 Tim. i. 2), Titus (i. 4), or Onesimus (Phil. 10), and as between believers in general (Acts ix. 30; Rom. xii. 10; 1 Thess. v. 26, 27); (2) more beneficial in results, being framed for mutual helpfulness (Rom. xvi. 1), as was that between John and Mary (ver. 27); and (3) more permanent in duration, being such as would survive the lapse of time, and continue in a realm beyond the grave.   Find examples—1. In Christ, of filial piety; 2. in Mary, of holy resignation; 3. in John, of Christian affection.

II. **The Voice of the Human Sufferer.**—"I thirst"; ver. 28.   *The fifth saying*, spoken as the darkness began to clear away, shortly before 3 P.M. (*the fourth saying*, 'My God!' etc., having been uttered when that darkness was at its deepest); a witness to—1. *The reality of Christ's human nature.*   This is important, since,

when John wrote, persons had arisen in the church who denied that Christ had
come in the flesh, or in possession of a *bonâ fide* human nature (1 John iv. 1-3).
2. *The greatness of Christ's sufferings.* The solitary instance in which language
expressive of pain escaped Christ's lips. What must have been the physical
distress that extorted it from Him who had been silent in the desert about His
hunger (Matt. iv. 2), on His journeyings about His fatigue (iv. 6), in the palace
of the high priest when they insulted Him (Matt. xxvi. 67), in Pilate's
prætorium when they scourged Him (xix. 1-4), on Golgotha when they nailed
Him to the tree! The pain occasioned by extreme thirst, one of the most
excruciating forms of agony human nature can endure. For want of water the
Israelites were ready to stone Moses (Exod. xvii. 4; Num. xx. 3); Samson
(Judg. xv. 18) and David (2 Sam. xxiii. 15; 1 Chron. xi. 17) were like to
perish notwithstanding their victories. To slake their burning thirst men have
been known like Darius to drink of filthy pools, or like shipwrecked mariners
to taste each other's blood. That Christ should have experienced such extreme
thirst will not surprise those who remember that not a drop of liquid had
passed His lips for nearly eighteen hours, and that during these hours much
had occurred to turn His moisture into summer's drought. 3. *The completeness
of Christ's obedience.* Suggested by what precedes. However connected the
clause intimates that the programme of Scripture as to Christ's work, and consequently Christ's work itself, was completed, or nearly so. 4. *The nearness of
Christ's victory.* A warrior begins to feel his wounds when he knows that his
triumph is secure. During the foregoing contest with the principalities and
powers of darkness, Christ had not been conscious of His thirst. Now that He
knows Himself to have so far prevailed as to render the issue certain, He calls
for a draught that, His Spirit being refreshed, He may deliver upon His
adversary a final blow. 5. *The ardour of Christ's spiritual desire.* The thirst
which consumed His body emblematic of another thirst which burned within
His soul, and which perhaps more than the agonies of crucifixion "dried up
His strength like a potsherd," the thirst for not alone the successful
termination of His labours, and sufferings, but the prosperous realization of
their fruit in the ingathering of redeemed and renewed souls into the kingdom
of His grace.

Lessons. 1. Christ's fellowship with us in community of nature (Heb. ii. 14)
and suffering (Matt. viii. 17). 2. Our fellowship with Him also in nature (2
Pet. i. 4) and suffering (Phil. iii. 10).

III. **The Voice of the Father's Servant**—'It is finished': ver. 30. *The sixth
saying,* followed by a *seventh,* 'Father, into thy hands,' etc. 1. *The Saviour's
earthly life was ended.* The noblest, wisest, purest, most active, loving, beneficent, beautiful, but sorrowful—in short, the only perfect life that ever had (or
has) been here below was closed. One mourns when a great and good life is withdrawn from the earth, feeling one's self to be poorer in consequence of its
departure (Ps. xii. 1), and the faster flows sorrow if the circumstances attending
its removal have been specially distressful, if e.g. like that of the Baptist
(Matt. xiv. 10), or Stephen (Acts vii. 59), or James (Acts xii. 2), or in modern
times of Williams or Hannington, it has been cut off by violence, or like that of
a Xavier and a Howard, it has fallen a victim to its own zeal in mercy's cause, or
like that of a Livingstone, it has expired far from home in weakness and
weariness, in poverty and pain, or like that of the Nain youth it has suddenly
terminated in middle course, its sun going down while yet noon;—and doubtless there were those like the daughters of Jerusalem (Luke xxiii. 28) and
the Emmaus travellers (Luke xxiv. 17), who lamented Jesus's death as one
in which all these affecting circumstances met and many more besides. But
the world!—at the moment when God's incarnate Son was dying, and it
ought to have been sitting penitent beneath the cross's foot,—the world
was laughing!—laughing at its own diabolic handiwork! No wonder that
the earth trembled and the sun wrapt its lustrous face in a mantle of cloud
at the unnatural and hideous sight! 2. *The programme of Scripture was exhausted.* If it be true that every man's life is prearranged by God no less

than was that of Cyrus (Is. xliv. 28 ; xlv. 1-4 : cf. Hamlet, act v. sc. 2; 'There's a divinity,' etc., and Julius Cæsar, act ii. sc. 2, ' What can be avoided,' etc.), much more was that the case with Jesus. The broad outline of His career was traced in O. T. Scripture,—all that He should be, the woman's seed (Gen. iii. 15), Abraham's descendant (Gen. xii. 3 ; xiii. 15 ; xvii. 8 ; xxii. 18), David's son (2 Sam. vii. 13), Jehovah's servant (Is. xlii. 1), a virgin's child (Is. vii. 14), a man of sorrows (Is. liii. 3) ; all that He should do, open up God's counsel of redemption (Is. ix. 6), publish salvation to men (Is. lxiii. 1), atone for sin (Is. liii. 6), bring in an everlasting righteousness (Dan. ix. 24) ; and much that He should suffer, that His own brethren and mother's children should reproach Him (Ps. lxix. 8), that a friend and disciple should betray Him Ps. xli. 9), that He should die upon a cross (Ps. xxii. 16), that His clothes should be gambled for (Ps. xxii. 17), that He should suffer the pains of thirst and that His enemies should give Him vinegar to drink (Ps. lxix. 21). And now that programme was exhausted. 3. *The Father's work was accomplished.* (1) Patiently. As far as to death He had been obedient. (2) Cheerfully. All through it had been His meat to do the will of Him that sent Him, and to finish His work (iv. 34). (3) Bravely. He had not been deterred by the prospect of a cross (Heb. xii. 2). (4) Perfectly. He had left no part unaccomplished (xvii. 4). He had revealed the Father's name (xvii. 6), atoned for human sin (xvii. 19), exemplified holiness (xiii. 15), founded an empire of righteousness and truth (xviii. 37). 4. *The world's redemption was completed.* Everything needful to enable men to find salvation had been done. The law had been magnified and made honourable (Is. xlii. 21). The penalty due to man's transgression had been endured (Is. liii. 4-6). The blood of atonement had been shed (Job xxxiii. 24; Rom. v. 11). The requisite propitiation had been offered (Rom. iii. 25).

Learn 1. The certainty that every one's life on earth will one day be finished (Heb. ix. 27). 2. The importance of having one's life work completed before one dies (2 Tim. iv. 7). 3. The necessity of resting on the finished work of Christ if one would live well and die happily. 4. The glory of the gospel in proclaiming a finished atonement, a finished righteousness, a finished redemption, a finished and therefore a free salvation.

Ver. 31-37.—The Dead Christ.

I. **The Sights John beheld** : ver. 32-35. 1. *The breaking of the robbers' legs.* How and why this came to pass the Evangelist explains ; also how and why the operation was omitted in the case of Christ. 2. *The piercing of the Saviour's side.* Not a slight scratch, but a strong thrust from a soldier's lance, given to render assurance of Christ's death doubly sure. 3. *The streaming of blood and water from the wound.* For explanations see Exposition. John regarded it as unusual, if not directly miraculous. It has been accounted for (Lange) in a way which recognizes its supernatural, yet does not set aside its natural character. As Christ's body saw no corruption, the change upon it which should culminate in the glory of a resurrection had begun. The water and the blood pouring forth in pure and separate streams was an indication of the presence of that new life which was to issue in the transformation of what was earthly and corporeal into that which is heavenly and spiritual. Perhaps it was ; only that it was can never be more than "a pious opinion," a beautiful fancy of the devout heart.

II. **The Reflections John made** : ver. 36, 37 ; 1 John v. 6. 1. *That Christ was the true paschal lamb.* John arrived at this conclusion by observing the co-incidence between the not breaking of Christ's legs and the ancient paschal ordinance, "A bone of it (the lamb) shall not be broken" (Exod. xii. 46). At the time perhaps it escaped his notice ; but reflecting on it afterwards he saw in that seemingly accidental but really providentially brought about circum-stance that Jesus was the antitype of that ancient sacrifice—was 'the lamb of God that taketh away the sins of the world' (i. 29). 2. *That Israel would one day be converted to Christ.* John remembered another Scripture about Israel piercing their Messiah, and repenting of their hideous work when they gazed upon His bleeding wounds (Zech. xii. 10), and as John believed no Scripture could go without fulfilment, he felt assured that what was here predicted of his countrymen would come to pass. That the first part of the prophecy had been fulfilled it was impossible to deny. Though Roman soldiers had nailed Christ to the cross, the Jews were the agents heaven held responsible for the crucifixion. The piercing of the Saviour's side was to all intents and purposes their work. Hence John expected the other part of the prediction would come true. If this thought occurred to him beside the cross, he had not long to wait for its realization. Within two months after that tragic and woeful day, the men that cried 'Away with him!' 'Crucify him!' 'His blood be on us and on our children' shrieked in terror, 'Men and brethren, what shall we do?' (Acts ii. 37). And the day will come when, looking back to that mournful event on Golgotha, Israel will recognize in Him whom their fathers crucified the long expected Messiah of their nation, and with tears of heartfelt sorrow will repent and turn to the Lord (Rom. xi. 25, 26 ; 2 Cor. iii. 16). 3. *That Christ crucified was an all-sufficient Saviour for men.* This was suggested if not then, afterwards, by the streaming forth of blood and water from Christ's pierced side. John perceived that Israel (and indeed mankind at large) wanted more for purification than mere external reformation symbolized in John's water baptism —wanted such an inward cleansing of heart and conscience, as could be effected only by the blood of propitiation and the bath of regeneration ; and John beholding emblems of these in the blood and water, knew that the world's redeemer and regenerator had arrived—setting it down so in his epistle : "This is he that came by water and by blood" (1 John v. 6).

Learn 1. The light cast by O. T. Scripture on the person and work of Christ. 2. The spring of evangelical repentance—looking on the crucified Christ. 3. The hope of Israel's conversion.

Ver. 31. The Great Sabbath. A day of—I. Godless festivity—for Israel. II. Blessed repose—for Jesus. III. Gracious opportunity—for 'the spirits in prison' (1 Pet. iii. 19). IV. Momentous waiting—for the world.

5. THE TOMB IN A GARDEN

CHAP. XIX. VER. 38-42

EXPOSITION

Ver. 38. **And after these things,** μετὰ δὲ ταῦτα, or, omitting the δὲ (ℵ A B), no where else thrust between the preposition and the pronoun, μετὰ ταῦτα, indicating a less close connection with the preceding than "after this," μετὰ τοῦτο, ver. 28 ; consequently not requiring Joseph's application to Pilate to be placed after the crurifragium and spear thrust. **Joseph of Arimathæa** "A rich man, who also himself was Jesus' disciple" (Matt. xxvii. 57), " a good man and a righteous, a councillor who had not consented to the deed of the Sanhedrim" (Luke xxiii. 50), "a councillor of honourable estate who also himself was looking for the kingdom of God" (Mark xv. 43). Arimathæa, the city from (ἀπὸ) which Joseph hailed, and of which he was probably a native, has been identified with

Ramleh, between Joppa and Jerusalem (Raumer, Hengstenberg), with *Rama* in Benjamin (Luthardt), but was probably *Ramathaim* in Ephraim, or more fully, *Haramathaim-Zophim,* with the remnant of the Hebrew article prefixed, i.e. the double height of Zophim (1 Sam. i. 1), the birthplace of Samuel, and usually written by the LXX. Armathâim (Stanley), if indeed it should not be regarded as still unidentified (Robinson, Conder). **being a disciple of Jesus, but secretly for fear of the Jews,** i.e. of the Sanhedrim to which he belonged, and which had decreed (ix. 22) that whoever confessed Jesus should be put out of the synagogue, and therefore out of the Sanhedrim. This detail of character corresponds with the earlier witness of the Evangelists (xii. 42). **asked of Pilate**

Mark says that "even was now come,"
—it was therefore approaching 6 p.m.—
when this request was made to Pilate.
**that he might take away the body of
Jesus,** not merely bear it away after
the soldiers had taken it down from
the cross (Lücke), but himself both
take it down and bear it away. It
accorded with Roman custom to grant
friends the privilege of disposing by
burial of the dead bodies of criminals :
see Adam's Roman Antiquities, p. 220.
Sometimes, especially on occasion of a
feast, the corpse of the capitally
punished was given up to the relations
(Philo, In Flacc. § 10 : quoted by
Bäumlein). In like manner the Christian martyrs of Rome were afterwards
interred by friends in the catacombs.
and Pilate gave *him* **leave.** "A great
and hitherto unobserved difficulty"
has been detected in this incident (De
Wette)—how Pilate could extend such
permission to Joseph after having previously commissioned soldiers to break
the legs of the crucified and bear them
away. But (1) Pilate's order was to
break the legs of the crucified with a
view to hastening their death for the
purpose of removal. (2) That was done
about 3 p.m. or soon after, at which
time the crosses were not relieved of
their burdens, as the robbers were not
then dead. (3) Whilst the soldiers were
waiting on the extinction of life in the
robbers, Joseph repaired to Pilate to
solicit Christ's corpse. (4) Pilate
wished to be assured of the reality of
Christ's death before disposing of His
body. (5) Accordingly having called the
centurion who had presided at the execution, he learned that the Saviour had
expired about 3 p.m. (6) Pilate then
accorded Joseph permission to take
down the lifeless corpse, if still suspended, or to bear it away if already
unfastened from the wood when he
arrived upon the scene. (7) The previous commission to the soldiers remained unaltered in respect of the
robbers. Thus stated, the facts present no difficulty. **He came therefore,**
in consequence of having obtained permission, and doubtless furnished with
a writing the soldiers would recognize
as the procurator's sign manual (cf.
Matt. xxvii. 58). **and took away His
body.** Matthew says the body was
given up i.e. by the soldiers, Mark

(xv. 46) and Luke (xxiii. 53) add that
Joseph took it down with either his
own hands or those of others, probably
his own servants, for he was rich, or
with the help of Nicodemus, John, and
the Galilean women.

39. And there came also to assist in
removing the dead body from the
cross, if that had not been done by his
brother councillor, whose courageous
behaviour now inspired him with fortitude. **Nicodemus** (cf. iii. 1), not 'a
fictitious duplicate of Joseph' (Keim),
but **he who at the first came to him**
(Jesus) **by night** τὸ πρῶτον, "at the
first," may point to subsequent visits
after the first made by Nicodemus to
Christ, though this is not likely, such
visits being nowhere recorded, or contrast his present coming to the Saviour
dead with his earliest interview, while
Jesus lived (Meyer), but was more
probably designed as a note of time,
equivalent to in the beginning of
Christ's ministry, as at x. 40 (De
Wette, Godet, Westcott). The contrast between the boldness of the
present and the timidity of the former
visit is suggested in the clause "by
night." **bringing a mixture of myrrh
and aloes** The myrrh, frequently
mentioned in Old and New Testaments, was an odoriferous gum, the
aloes a sweet-scented wood (Ps. xlv. 9)
which, in a pulverized condition, were
placed between the bandages in which
the corpse was wrapt. **about a hundred
pound** *weight.* Though surprising, the
quantity, 1200 Roman ounces (cf. xii.
3), is not incredible, as Nicodemus may
have purposed completely covering the
body with the aromatic dust. Besides,
it was not too much for either the
devotion of Nicodemus or the worthiness of Jesus. "Even Gamaliel, the
elder, the leader of the Pharisees, is
said to have had 80 lbs. of balsam
burned at his death" (Keim).

40. So they, the two councillors,
took the body of Jesus, lowered from
the cross, **and bound it in linen cloths,**
bandages of fine linen (ὀθόνια : xx. 6, 7 ;
Luke xxiv. 12) in which the members
of the body were swathed—probably
the κειρίαι mentioned in connection
with the burial of Lazarus, xi. 44 ; but
to be distinguished from the linen
cloth (σινδών, Matt. xxvii. 59), in
which the body when so swathed was

wrapped (see Keil's Biblische Archäologie, § 115) — with the spices
the aromatics (ver. 39), which were
placed inside the bandages, and probably in this case inside the outer
covering ; as the custom of the Jews is
to bury, or to prepare for burying.
This they commonly did by anointing
the body with oil (cf. xii. 7), and
wrapping it about as here indicated
with aromatic powder. Mark (xvi. 1)
reports that the women who came to
the sepulchre purposed to add the
anointing here omitted. The Egyptian
process of embalming, with which perhaps it is intended to contrast the
Jewish mode of interment (Godet,
Lücke, Lange, Meyer, Westcott, and
others), consisted of removing the
brain and intestines from the corpse,
filling the cavity thus made with
myrrh, cassia, etc., and steeping the
body for seventy days in natron ; after
which it was washed and swathed in
linen bandages gummed on the inside
until every part was covered (see Herodotus ii. 86 ff.; Wilkinson's Manners
and Customs of the Ancient Egyptians,
vol. iii. p. 471, ed. 1878 ; Rawlinson's
Herodotus, vol. ii. pp. 118-123).

41. Now in the place, or district,
τόπος, where He was crucified, as in
the place where He passed through
the agony, and was afterwards arrested
(xviii. 1), was a garden, belonging to
Joseph (Matt. xxvii. 60); and in the
garden a new tomb, "his own, which
he had hewn out of the rock" (Matt.
xxvii. 60) ; "a tomb which had been
hewn out of a rock," or "out of stone"
(Mark xv. 46). 'Such rock or cave
sepulchres were very common, and at
the present day Jerusalem is surrounded by them' (Keim). wherein
was never man yet laid : cf. Luke
xxiii. 53. Only such a grave was worthy
of such an occupant. Christ entered
Jerusalem riding on an ass whereon
man had never sat : Luke xix. 30.

42. There then, in Joseph's tomb,
not 'under the cross' (Volkmar), because of the Jews' preparation (see on
xiii. 2 note), for the tomb was nigh at
hand,—This note of locality along with
the preceding, a note of time, explains
why the tomb of Joseph was selected
as the place of Christ's interment.
O. T. prediction was thereby fulfilled :
see Is. liii. 9—they laid Jesus. Cf. the
burials of John Baptist (Matt. xiv. 12),
of Stephen (Acts viii. 2), and of Herod
the Great (Jos. Ant. xvii. 8, 3).

HOMILETICS

VER. 38-42.—THE BURIAL OF JESUS.
I. The Descent from the Cross : ver. 38. 1. *By whom effected.* Joseph of
Arimathæa (assisted by Nicodemus, John, and the Galilean women). (1) A
native of Arimathæa or Ramathaim in Ephraim, the birthplace of Samuel. (2)
A rich man, which rendered his coming forward to pay the last rites of sepulture to one who had been crucified, a signal display of courage, and a true token
of inherent nobility ; while that coming forward itself was a striking companion
picture to the approach of the Magi at Christ's birth (Matt. ii. 4), and a beginning
at least of fulfilment for Isaiah's oracle concerning His death (liii. 9). (3) A
member of the Sanhedrim, though (there is ground for believing) not present
at the morning sederunt in the high priests' palace when all pronounced Christ
guilty of death (cf. Luke xxiii. 50, with Matt. xxvi. 66 ; Mark xiv. 64). (4) A
good man, one among the few pious Israelites like Simeon and Anna (Luke ii.
24), Elizabeth and Zacharias (Luke i. 6), who kept God's commandments, and
waited for the consolation of Israel. (5) A secret disciple—like others of the
rulers (xii. 42), e.g. Nicodemus—whose faith waxed stronger as Christ's cause
grew darker, till at length, when Christ had reached the lowest depth of
humiliation, he could no longer forbear avowing his discipleship—which he did
by going in boldly to Pilate and requesting permission to take down and bear
away the body of Jesus for burial. 2. *When attempted.* Not necessarily after
the breaking of the robbers' legs, but after Christ's death, which happened
about 3 P.M., did Joseph repair to Pilate's prætorium on his sacred mission.
Obtaining leave from the governor, he would then proceed to concert measures
with Nicodemus, and to make the requisite purchase of linen cloth. It would

thus be approaching "even" when the sad and sorrowful work was begun. **3.**
How carried out. The evangelist is silent: but if Nicodemus, John, and the
women were Joseph's helpers, it may be safely concluded it was done with
reverence, with tenderness, and with tears.

II. The Embalmment of the Corpse: ver. 39-40. In this, though all the
above-named were present, Nicodemus steps into the foreground. 1. *His
person identified.* The same Nicodemus—like Joseph, a ruler of the Jews—
who in the opening years of Christ's ministry came to Him by night (iii. 1).
2. *His courage emphasized.* In contrast with that first timid interview, his present
espousal of Christ's cause was a mark of bravery—more conspicuous even than
his championing the same six months before at the Feast of Tabernacles, when
his colleagues sneeringly inquired—"Have any of the rulers or of the Pharisees
believed on him?" (vii. 48). 3. *His love proclaimed.* Not content with taking
part in the solemn obsequies contemplated by his colleague, he determines for
himself to do something to express the depth and tenderness of his affection:
If Joseph is to purchase and carry out with him to Golgotha a large linen
sheet, white and clean, in which to wrap the body before it is interred : he will
procure a quantity of linen cloths also, smaller and divided into strips, with the
requisite assortment of spicery to embalm the corpse. And John observes
when Nicodemus appears upon the scene that with no straitened hand has he
carried out his heart's design. 4. *His reverence recorded.* Along with Joseph,
John, and the women, he proceeds to embalm the corpse. First they lay the
body out upon the sward, the large white winding sheet underneath. Next the
women (it may be supposed) take the smaller cloths from Nicodemus, and
filling them with aromatic powder, wrap them around its members. After
this Joseph folds around it his large white sheet, and the work of embalming
is done.

III. The Interment of the Body : ver. 41-42. 1. *The place of sepulture.* (1)
A garden grave. In a garden (Eden) centuries before, death achieved its first
victory (Gen. iii. 1); it was fitting that in a garden that victory should be
reversed. (2) A strange grave. Joseph's tomb. "What need had He for a
grave of His own who was only to remain three days in the grave? In
another grave is laid He who died for another's guilt" (Gerhard). (3) An
honourable grave. He who died between malefactors on the cross is laid to
sleep in a just man's tomb. (4) A new grave. It was congruous that He who
was a new man (sinless), born in a new way (of a virgin), who had come to
Israel on a new beast (a colt whereon man had never sat), who had died a new
death (for sin, but not his own), and who was in three days to rise to a new life
(of glory and immortality)—it was congruous that He should rest in a new
sepulchre. (5) A near grave. It was nigh to the place of execution (ver. 42), and
the place of execution was nigh to the city (ver. 20). "The grave of Joseph
was nigh unto Jerusalem : ours is close to the heavenly city" (Oosterzee). 2.
The funeral procession. When a great man dies, the world's custom is to lavish
on his obsequies splendour and magnificence, sometimes doing larger honour to
the lifeless corpse than was ever paid to the living spirit of the deceased. Even
wicked men are often carried to their tombs with pomp that arrests and dazzles
beholders (cf. the burial of Herod the Great, described by Josephus). How
wide the contrast between that funeral procession from Jericho to Herodium,.
and the dead march from Golgotha to Joseph's tomb. Amid the falling
shadows of approaching night, with no bier on which to bear the dead, with no
train of mourners except two or three women, three men uplift the corpse, now
swathed in the cerements of the tomb, perhaps Nicodemus supporting the body,
while Joseph takes the feet, and the head lies in the bosom of John. With
slow and reverend step they carry it across the sward till they reach the garden
with its rock-hewn grave, when, with tearful eyes and sorrow-laden hearts, they
perform the last service they can do for Him they have loved and lost. Rolling
up a massive stone in front of its aperture, "the so-called *Golal* or roll stone"
(Keim), to serve as a protection against evil men and wild beasts, they take
their departure, leaving behind the anguish-stricken women who cannot tear

themselves from the spot, but continue in their grief sitting over against the sepulchre. So ended the funeral of the incarnate Son of God.

> " At length the worst is o'er, and Thou art laid
> Deep in Thy darksome bed," etc.—Keble, Christian Year.

Lessons. 1. The overruling providence of God in bringing about Christ's burial in Joseph's tomb, and so fulfilling Scripture. 2. The guarantee afforded by Christ's burial that the sinner's debt has been paid. 3. The certainty that the grave can never be to a believer what it was to Christ when He entered it.

SECTION THIRD—THE GLORY OF THE SON OF GOD COMPLETELY UNVEILED BY HIS RESURRECTION FROM THE GRAVE:—"DECLARED TO BE THE SON OF GOD WITH POWER" (Rom. i. 4)

CHAP. XX

The importance of the Resurrection history has been recognized alike by friends and foes of Christianity. With the standing or falling of this one article, it is admitted, the whole superstructure of the Christian system is established or overthrown. If Jesus of Nazareth did not rise from Joseph's tomb, then not only was He not the Son of God, He was not even a true prophet, since during His lifetime He frequently predicted He would (Matt. xii. 40 ; xvi. 21 ; xx. 19 ; xxvi. 32; xxvii. 63; Mark ix. 9, 10 ; xiv. 28 ; Luke ix. 22 ; xxiv. 7 ; John ii. 19, 21, 22), and if a false prophet, then not a good man or a real Saviour. If, however, He did rise from the garden sepulchre, then not only was His previous testimony concerning Himself guaranteed, but all it implied was confirmed—Himself was declared to be the Son of God with power, His work attested as a propitiation for the world's sin, life and immortality brought to light, and the future resurrection of the saints placed beyond the reach of doubt. Hence with reference to the person of Jesus, the resurrection was the culmination of His glory, the mounting as it were into meridian splendour of that divine effulgence which during the period of His humiliation had been veiled, and in the last days of His terrestrial career, more especially in His crucifixion, had appeared to be extinguished, but which eventually broke forth into undimmed and never to be diminished lustre. It is noticeable that the fourth Evangelist no more than the other three attempts a description of the resurrection, doubtless because all beginnings lie beyond the cognizance of the creature ; and yet scarcely anything is more certain than that, if the gospel histories had been the production of second century romance, some delineation of an event so stupendous, even in its miraculousness, would have been attempted. That the New Testament writers have not ventured upon this fascinating enterprise, but have preserved throughout a well-balanced moderation—nowhere more conspicuous than in their treatment of the resurrection history—is one of the most convincing proofs that can be desired or attained of their credibility. Nor should it be overlooked that an account of the actual rising, on the assumption that it could have been given, was not required for the purpose of either historian or theologian. For either it was sufficient to demonstrate that Christ, having died and been buried, was afterwards seen alive by those who, having beheld Him before death, were competent to identify Him after His return from the grave. Accordingly, all John contemplates is to furnish evidence that Christ whom he helped to bury in the tomb of Joseph became alive, and was recognized by His disciples. The section subdivides itself as under :—

1. The Empty Sepulchre : xx. 1-10.
2. The Manifestations of the Risen Christ :—

    (1) To Mary Magdalene : ver. 11-18.
    (2) To the disciples (without Thomas) : ver. 19-23.
    (3) To the disciples (with Thomas) : ver. 24-29.

3. Concluding words : ver. 30, 31.

1. THE EMPTY SEPULCHRE

Chap. XX. Ver. 1-10

Exposition

Chap. xx. ver. 1. **Now** The incidents that took place between the burial and the resurrection of Jesus, though passed over by the evangelist, may be collected from the earlier accounts, which record (1) the preparations made by the women for completing the embalmment of Christ's body when the Sabbath was past (Luke xxiii. 56), and (2) the setting of a watch at the tomb by the chief priests with Pilate's permission (Matt. xxviii. 66). **on the first day of the week** lit., *on the one of the Sabbaths* (cf. Luke xxiv. 1), i.e. on the first day of 'the Sabbaths,' the plural τὰ σάββατα, a *pluralis excellentiae* after the Hebrew, being employed like τὸ σάββατον (Luke xviii. 12) to designate the entire week. See Winer, § xxvii. 3. The time is described in Matt. (xxviii. 1) as "late on the Sabbath day as it began to

dawn towards the first day of the week," and in Mark (xvi. 1) as "the Sabbath being past." **cometh Mary Magdalene** See on xix. 25. Mentioned prior to the passion history only by Luke (vii. 2). The visit here recorded is not different from that alluded to by Matthew (xxviii. 1), which took place not before 6 P.M. on Saturday (Westcott), but before dawn on Sunday morning. Mary Magdalene was accompanied by the other Mary, i.e. the mother of James and Joses (Matt. xxviii. 1 ; cf. xxvii. 56), by Salome (Mark xvi. 1), and by Joanna, the wife of Chuza (Luke xxiv. 10). **early** after the Saturday night had passed ; very early (Mark xvi. 1). **while it was yet dark** therefore before actual sunrise ; though "the sun had risen " (Mark xvi. 2) "it was early dawn" (Luke xxiv. 1), "it began to dawn" (Matt. xxviii. 1) when the women came to the sepulchre. The company left the city before sunrise (while yet dark, though beginning to dawn), and reached the sepulchre as the sun rose above the horizon. **unto the tomb** " to see it " (Matthew); " to anoint Him" (Mark, Luke); John not condescending on the object of Mary's visit, though not contradicting either of the above. It may also have been "to weep there": cf. xi. 31. **and seeth the stone taken away from the tomb.** The Sinaitic (א) adds "away from the door." On the way the women had been perplexed about the difficulty of effecting ingress to the tomb in consequence of the size and weight of the stone (Mark xvi. 3); before their arrival the difficulty had been anticipated, and the stone rolled back by the angel of the Lord (Matt. xxviii. 2).

2. **She** Mary, apparently alone, having in all probability moved on in advance of her companions (perhaps burdened with the spices), and arrived earlier than they at the sepulchre (Luthardt, Lange, Ewald, Stier)–although this hypothesis is not necessary, since she and they may have all arrived together, she turning back the instant she beheld the opened sepulchre, they going on and perceiving the angels (Lücke, Godet). **runneth,** in her eagerness and excitement, **therefore**, because of her discovery and of what it appeared to imply, that the body had been removed, or at least that the tomb was empty. **and cometh to Simon Peter and to the other disciple** How does the precedence here accorded to Peter harmonize with the notion that the gospel was written for the purpose of exalting John—"the once more artfully introduced rival of Peter" (Keim)—to a position of equality with, if not superiority over, Peter? (Hilgenfeld, Weizsäcker, Baur, Renan). On "the other disciple" see xviii. 15. From the repetition of "to" it has been inferred that the two disciples did not live together, *non una fuisse utrumque discipulum* (Bengel), which is probable (Luthardt), and perhaps natural, if John lived with his own mother and the mother of Jesus (Godet), although not necessary (Luthardt, Meyer, Lange), and ver. 3 may seem to hint the opposite. **whom**

Jesus loved The use of ἐφίλει instead of ἠγάπα to devote Christ's affection for John (xiii. 23; xix. 26; xxi. 7, 20) indicates greater familiarity : cf. Christ's love for Lazarus (xi. 3) and Peter's love to Christ (xxi. 17). **and saith unto them** As Mary was not "weeping", it has been conjectured that she must already have begun to think of a resurrection as at least possible—"already she must have experienced something which did not paralyze her feet but gave them wings. Further, if Mary had nothing further to report, she would have come *weeping* to the apostles" (Hengstenberg) ; but see ver. 11. **They,** obviously the enemies, "the Jews," though Joseph and Nicodemus may have been intended (Westcott), **have taken away the Lord** Though lifeless still for her 'the Lord.' **out of the tomb** So far as Mary was concerned, purely a surmise—not an incorrect one (Keim)—as she had not yet looked into the vault. **and we know not** "We" an indirect acknowledgment on Mary's part that she had not visited the sepulchre alone (Luthardt, De Wette, Tholuck, Godet, Westcott, and others); though it may have been spoken out of the consciousness of the friends of Jesus generally in contrast to the enemies above alluded to (Brückner, Meyer, Ebrard). **where they have laid Him.** Mary was not yet thinking of a resurrection.

3. **Peter therefore,** in consequence of Mary's communication, **went forth,** out of the house, and out of the city, **and the other disciple,** John, whom Luke (xxiv. 12) does not specify as having accompanied Peter, although afterwards he introduces Clopas as stating (xxiv. 24) that the sepulchre was visited by "some of them which were with us" ; **and they went,** lit., *were going*, a lively picture of their journey: cf. iv. 30, **toward the tomb,** which lay some distance off. א omits this clause.

4. **And they ran both together,** lit., *but they began to run, the two together;* probably starting off with a rapid walk, then breaking out into a run, at first and for some distance keeping pace with, but eventually separating from each other. **and the other disciple,** younger and more agile than his

companion (Bengel, Godet, Tholuck, Westcott, Meyer); without ascribing John's fleetness of foot to the fact "that he was the disciple whom Jesus loved" (Hengstenberg), or Peter's laggard steps to the circumstance that his conscience was still burdened with the sin of having denied his Lord (Lampe, Luthardt), against which may be urged the incident recorded in xxi. 7 (Brückner); **outran Peter**, lit., *ran on before, more quickly than Peter*,—a characteristic trait "which vouches for the genuineness of the gospel to even the most doubtfully inclined" (Lücke), though Tübingen critics discover in it only a desire to exalt John above Peter (Strauss, Baur)—with which ver. 6 does not well agree—**and came first to the tomb**, from which the rest of the women had by this time departed (Matt. xxviii. 8) to carry to the apostles tidings of the resurrection (Luke xxiv. 23).

5. **And stooping and looking in**— παρακύπτω (cf. ver. 11 ; Luke xxiv. 12), signifying to bend forward the head so as to peep into any place or thing (cf. 1 Pet. i. 12 ; Jas. i. 25)—**he seeth the linen cloths**, ὀθόνια, the bandages with which the limbs had been wrapped in the process of embalming (xix. 40), **lying** about the tomb ; **yet entered he not in**—withheld by the depth and tenderness of his emotion (Godet, Hengstenberg), by constitutional timidity or reluctance (Lücke, Luthardt, Tholuck), or by a feeling of awe (Lange, Westcott), rather than by either natural dread (Meyer) or apprehension of pollution (Wetstein, Ammon).

6, 7. **Simon Peter therefore also cometh, following him**, and making up on him because of his lingering outside the sepulchre, **and**, not merely stooped and looked in as John had done (Luke xxiv. 12), but also **entered into the tomb**, at once, without reluctance, hesitation, timidity, or fear (This does not look like setting John before Peter !); **and he beholdeth the linen cloths lying**, θεωρεῖ, indicating a closer inspection than that made by John who only observed them (βλέπει) from the outside, **and the napkin**, or sweat band, *sudarium* (see on xi. 44), **that was about His head**—the pronoun instead of the personal name of

Christ being used according to the well-known manner of the Evangelist, whose mind and heart were so full of His Lord that further designation of Him was unnecessary : see the Johannine epistles *passim*—**not lying with the linen cloths, but rolled up in a separate place by itself.** Whether "into one place" is to be connected with 'lying' (Luthardt, Lange, Brückner), or as is the more probable from the use of εἰς with the accusative with 'rolled up' (Meyer), the disposition of the clothes was a sign that Christ had not been hastily removed, but had departed from the sepulchre as one who, awaking from sleep, divests himself of his night garments, and leisurely folding them up, sets them carefully aside.

8. **Then entered in therefore**, unconsciously drawn to do so by Peter's example, **the other disciple also** (see on ver. 2)—**which came first to the tomb** —added for more particular designation, not out of vain glory—**and he saw**, what Peter had beheld, **and believed**, not merely the report of Mary that the tomb was empty (Augustine, Grotius, Bengel, Luther, Ebrard, Stier, and others), a circumstance not affected one way or another by the careful disposition of the clothes, but that Christ had risen (Chrysostom, Lampe, Lücke, Luthardt, Godet, and others).

9. **For as yet they knew not the Scripture** The ground of John's conviction, and perhaps also of Peter's, was the evidence supplied by what they had seen—the stone rolled away, the tomb empty, and the grave clothes arranged—not any O. T. prediction, such as Ps. ii. 7 which Paul applied to (Acts xiii. 33), or Ps. xv. 9 which Peter interpreted of (Acts ii. 24-27), the resurrection. That John refers not to any prediction of Our Lord that He would rise again, although surprising, may be explained from the circumstance that Christ's words on that theme were to be explained by His resurrection (ii. 22), not His resurrection by His words. **that He must rise again from the dead.** 'Must' the imperative of a divine necessity (δεῖ) such as had controlled the Saviour's entire career (see iii. 14 ; iv. 4 ; ix. 4 ; x. 16 ; xii. 34 ; and cf. Matt.

xvi. 21 ; Mark viii. 31 ; Luke ii. 49 ;
iv. 43 ; ix. 22 ; xiii. 33 ; xvii. 25 ; xix.
5 ; xxiv. 7).
10. **So the disciples,** John and Peter,
went away again, from the sepulchre,
without having seen the risen Lord,

and as if nothing more could be done
by them in the matter (Bengel), **unto
their own home,** πρὸς ἑαυτούς : cf. Luke
xxiv. 12, πρὸς ἑαυτὸν, and Acts xxviii.
16, καθ' ἑαυτόν.

Homiletics

VER. 1-10.—"HE IS NOT HERE : HE IS RISEN."
I. **The First Witness**—Mary of Magdala : ver. 1-3. 1. *Her qualifications.*
A Galilean woman who had (1) enjoyed a rich experience of Christ's healing
power (Luke viii. 2 ; Mark xvi. 2), (2) spent many months in His society
(Matt. xxvii. 55), (3) witnessed His crucifixion, taken part in His burial, and
passed some time the night of His interment sitting over against the sepulchre
(Matt. xxvii. 56, 61 ; Mark xv. 40, 47), and (4) was thus not likely to be mistaken as to either the locality or appearance of the tomb on the one hand, or as
to the person and aspect of the Saviour on the other. 2. *Her deposition.* (1)
That she undertook a journey to the sepulchre on the morning of the first day
of the week,—not alone (see ver. 2), but accompanied by Mary, the mother of
James and Joses, Salome, the mother of Zebedee's children, and Joanna, the
wife of Chuza (Matt. xxviii. 1 ; Mark xvi. 1 ; Luke xxiv. 10)—leaving the city
while it was yet dark, and arriving at the tomb with the first rays of the
morning sun. On the way she and her companions had talked about the
difficulty they would have in rolling away the stone from the door. Their
purpose was to complete the work of embalming imperfectly done on the
Friday afternoon. (2) That on approaching the tomb she observed the stone was
rolled away from the mouth of the vault in which she had seen Christ
deposited ; but on perceiving the state of matters with reference to the
sepulchre did not proceed farther—did not, as her companions, enter the vault,
so that she saw neither the angel on the stone without (Matt. xxviii. 2) nor the
young man in white within (Mark xvi. 5), the two in shining garments (Luke
xxiv. 4) whom her companions beheld. (3) That the instant she noticed the stone
away she believed the tomb to be empty. It is evident she thought the
body had been removed, whether by friends or by foes ; it is not evident she
as yet believed Christ was risen. (4) That having arrived at this conclusion
she paused and, wheeling round, fled with hind's feet to the house or houses of
Simon and John with the startling intelligence.
II. **The Second Witness**—Simon Peter. 1. *His recommendations.* (1) A man
and therefore less likely than Mary to be the sport of ardent feelings, the
victim of a lively imagination. (2) Of mature judgment, probably about forty
years of age—the mercurial temperament of his youth being by this time
sobered. (3) A disciple who had enjoyed Christ's friendship for at least two
years. 2. *His declaration.* (1) That on learning Mary's news, he along with
John started for the sepulchre—running as became the important mission they
were about—" the king's business required haste" (1 Sam. xxi. 8) ; that John
as the younger and fleeter arrived at the cave before him, but that he not long
after came up, when he found John standing by the door without, too timid to
enter in ; that he at once without fear or hesitation stepped into the vault and
surveyed the situation. (2) That he perceived the grave clothes had been
carefully disposed—the bandages and winding sheet together, the napkin or
sweat band carefully rolled up and set in a place by itself. As Peter had not
seen "a vision of angels" there is no reason to suppose that his faculties had
been disturbed, or he had not been able to note things with exactitude. (3)
That he reached the conclusion that whatever had come of the body, it had not
been removed by violence, but in an orderly manner. It is doubtful whether
he got beyond this.
III. **The Third Witness**—"The other disciple" : ver. 8. 1. *His excellences.*

(1) If younger than Peter, less forward in disposition, and therefore more likely to be calm in judgment. (2) Of finer sensibilities than Peter, and therefore better fitted to discern what related to the Lord. (3) A disciple who had specially enjoyed Christ's friendship and love, and therefore one who had the highest interest in ascertaining the truth. (4) A spectator of the crucifixion, and perhaps also a helper in the burial of Jesus, so that he at least could have no doubt of the reality of Christ's death. 2. *His testimony.* (1) That before Peter's arrival he had stooped down and looked into the sepulchre and observed the linen cloths lying about. (2) That after Peter's arrival, emboldened and unconsciously influenced by Peter's example, he also entered and examined the interior of the cave. (3) That in this examination he perceived what Peter had, but he in his first glance from the outside had not noticed, the carefully-folded up napkin laid in a place by itself. (4) That in consequence of what he then saw, he believed that Christ was risen.

Lessons. 1. The devotion of woman to Jesus Christ—exemplified in Mary. 2. The mourning of a saintly heart over a dead Christ—again exhibited in the Magdalene. 3. The unconscious influence of one soul upon another—illustrated in Peter's over John. 4. The varieties of temperament that may exist among the followers of Christ—seen in the two disciples. 5. The different degrees of evidence that in different souls are required to produce faith—again witnessed in John and Peter. 6. The frequency with which in Christ's kingdom this saying is fulfilled—'The last first and the first last.' 7. The illumination cast on O. T. Scripture by Christ's resurrection.

2. THE MANIFESTATIONS OF THE RISEN CHRIST

CHAP. XX. VER. 10-29

Having established that the sepulchre was empty, and indicated the incipience of his own faith in Christ's resurrection, the Evangelist completes his demonstration of the stupendous fact thus announced, by narrating certain appearances of Christ, or manifestations of Himself to three competent and reliable witnesses,—Mary Magdalene, the ten disciples, and the eleven. Besides these there were other discoveries of Himself not related by the author of this gospel. Indeed, no single Scripture writer furnishes a perfect list of the interviews which Christ held with His disciples during the forty days prior to His ascension. Matthew mentions only the appearances to the women (xxviii. 9, 10) on the morning of the resurrection day, and to the eleven on a Galilean mountain (xxviii. 16-20). Mark reports those to Mary Magdalene, distinctly notifying this as the first (xvi. 9), to the Emmaus travellers (xvi. 12), and to the eleven as they sat at meat (xvi. 14). If the last two verses of Mark be disconnected from those which precede, then a fourth appearance will be implied though not expressed. Luke records the appearances to the Emmaus travellers (xxiv. 13-35), to the eleven in the upper room (xxiv. 36-49), and, if ver. 50-53 be detached from the antecedent narrative, to the disciples at Bethany on the occasion of the ascension. John enumerates the three above specified, to Mary Magdalene (xx. 10-18), to the disciples without Thomas (xx. 19-23), and to the disciples including Thomas (xx. 26-29), and a fourth at the Galilean lake to seven (xxi. 1-14), which however is added for another purpose than to attest the resurrection, as will afterwards appear. Even Paul whose list (1 Cor. xv. 4-8) is fuller than that of any of the Evangelists makes no mention of Christ's appearances to Mary Magdalene, to the Galilean women, to the Emmaus travellers, to the seven at the lake, but confines his narrative to those made to Cephas, to the twelve, to 500 disciples, to James, to all the apostles, to himself. Doubtless each writer had his reasons for incorporating some and omitting others of Our Lord's visits to His followers during the forty days. The instances selected by Paul, for example, appear to have been those most likely to weigh with the Corinthians, i.e. such as had been made to the pillars and representatives of the Church. For an opposite reason Luke, writing for a wider circle of readers than Jewish Christians, avoids giving prominence to either James or Peter, and only introduces the eleven once, while the larger portion of his narrative is taken up with the account of Christ's appearance to two who stood outside the apostolic circle altogether. Perhaps it is permissible to detect in Mark's list the instances regarded by Peter as most important— the first of all the manifestations made, that to Mary; the first that really awakened the expectation of the Christian community when reported to them, that to the travellers; and the first that fixed in the Church's mind the conviction that Christ was indeed risen, the visit on that same evening to the eleven in the upper room. It is more difficult to explain the somewhat scanty narrative of Matthew, who however may have deemed it sufficient, after stating the occurrences at the grave, the arrival of the women and the tidings of the angels, simply to rehearse how the angel's story was corroborated by the Lord's appearance to the women, and how the disappearance of the Lord from the earth was not to be accounted for in the way suggested by the Jewish rulers, but by the event alluded to, the interview in Galilee with the eleven. John's selection was clearly guided by a consideration of what would best contribute to the óbject he had in view, viz. to establish the certainty that He who had died and been buried was actually risen and alive.

I. THE APPEARANCE TO MARY MAGDALENE
Chap. XX. Ver. 11-18
Exposition

Ver. 11. **But**, in contrast to the disciples who went away again unto their own home, **Mary,** who had set out a second time towards the sepulchre, and arrived thither after (or before) John and Peter had departed,

was standing, or, *continued standing*
(which may imply that she had reached
the tomb before the disciples left it),
without at, in, ἐν (א) **the tomb,** lit.,
beside or near the tomb, from which in
her grief she felt unable to tear herself
away, but *without,* equally unable
through feminine timidity and religious awe to enter its gloomy precincts. **weeping,** giving vent to her
distress in tears and audible sobs : cf.
xi. 31, 33, and Luke xix. 41, in which
as here the stronger term (κλαίειν) denoting violent lamentation is employed, the milder expression, to shed
tears (δακρύειν), being used in xi. 35.
So, as she wept, lit., *as, then, she wept,*
i.e. whilst she was weeping, **she
stooped and looked into the tomb,** as
John had done (ver. 5), **and she beholdeth,** with earnest contemplation,
(θεωρεῖ), as Peter had examined the
linen clothes (ver. 7), **two angels,**
whom she at first recognized not as
angels but considered to be men, as the
women had done (Luke xxiv. 4). This
explains why she was neither alarmed
at their appearance nor surprised at
their interrogation. That neither
John nor Peter perceived any ' men '
or ' angels ' does not prove that Mary
did not, or that this whole passage
describes an ' ecstatic vision ' of the
Magdalene (Schweitzer). Nor does it
affect the credibility of this report
that according to Matt. xxviii. 2, the
women saw one angel sitting on the
stone outside the sepulchre—this was
doubtless what they first beheld ; or
that according to Mark xvi. 5, they
saw a young man within the tomb
clothed in a long white garment, and
sitting on the right side of the now
deserted bier—-this might easily have
been the same angel (spoken of by
Matthew) who, though sitting on the
stone when first observed, as the
women approached may have entered
the grave, and taken up the posture in
which he was found when they entered the vault ; while, according to
Luke (xxiv. 4), there were two angels
instead of one—which might easily
have been the case if this occurred
when they emerged from the sepulchre, or if the angel first perceived
was joined by a companion ere they
made their exit. But as Mary's visit
happened after that of the women

John's narrative would not be affected
even should an irreconcilable discrepancy be found to obtain amongst
the others. John more than likely
gives the story as heard from Mary's
lips. **in white,** sc. *garments.* Similar
elisions of substantives easily supplied
are common in Scripture : cf. Matt. xi.
8 ; Rev. xviii. 12, 16 ; see Winer,
§ lxiv. 5. The garments were white
because those who wore them belonged
to the world of light. **sitting,** not inconsistent with the fact that when the
women saw them (if they were the
same (?)) they were stan iing (Luke
xxiv. 4). " Angels are not immove-
able after the fashion of stone statues "
(Godet). **one at the head, and one at
the feet where the body of Jesus had
lain.** "There are two in contrast with
the two men crucified on each side of
Jesus. They sit, for they need not
strive, having guarded Jesus' body
in peace. One sits at the head and the
other at the feet, where Jesus had
lain ; for from head to foot Jesus' body
had been under the care of the Father
and His servants " (Luthardt); though
beautiful, this is rather "arbitrary invention and poetry " (Meyer) than
exegesis.

13. **And they say unto her, Woman,
why weepest thou ?** A natural interrogation considering that her tears
were profuse and accompanied with
lamentation. **She saith unto them,** not
regarding it as strange that they
should speak to her—**Because they**
alluding to the Jews, **have taken away
my Lord.** She speaks of Jesus more
endearingly to those she considers
strangers than she had done to Peter
and John. To these she said "the
Lord," because Christ was Peter's and
John's Lord as well as hers ; to those
she says " my Lord " as if to express
the ardour of her affection : cf. ver. 28.
**and I know not where they have laid
Him.** Even if John had imparted to
Mary a knowledge of his awakening
hope of a resurrection she had not been
able as yet to share it.

14. **When she had thus said, she
turned herself back,** not half (B.
Crusius) but wholly ; as not willing to
continue a conversation which promised no help (Westcott) or caring to
hear what one within the sepulchre
might say, *non attendit quis quid in*

sepulchro loqueretur (Bengel), but as urged on by love to prosecute her search for the Lord (Luthardt, Godet, Hengstenberg), rather than as attracted by a noise behind her back (De Wette, Brückner, Lücke),—"the Risen One makes no rustling when he appears" (Luthardt), or because the angels had in some way signed that one was coming (Chrysostom, Theophylact, Westcott), or because she still looked for some one to appear and furnish her with the desired information (Lange);—**and beholdeth** (see on ver. 12) **Jesus standing,** beside her in full view, **and knew not that it was Jesus.** Not because His features had been disfigured by death, or He had borrowed the clothes of the gardener (Paulus, Lücke), or because she did not look with sufficient care and steadiness (B. Crusius, Stier), but either because she was so absorbed in her grief that only one thought filled her mind (Brückner, Westcott), or Christ appeared to her as He afterwards did to the Emmaus travellers, "in another form," ἐν ἑτέρᾳ μορφῇ: Mark xvi. 12 (Godet, Luthardt), or Christ's corporeity had already begun to change (Meyer), or because of all of these together (Lange, Hengstenberg).

15. **Jesus saith unto her,** for the purpose not of eliciting information, but of arresting attention, **Woman! why weepest thou?** This repetition of the angel's question might have startled her. **whom seekest thou?** Her surprise ought by this to have been increased. This stranger had not only heard the inquiry of the angels who spoke from within the tomb, but He also knew the nature of her reply. **She, supposing Him to be the gardener** because the most likely person to be about at so early an hour in the morning (Meyer, Luthardt, Westcott); hardly because He had borrowed the gardener's clothes as above stated (Paulus, Olshausen), or had around Him the white linen band or loin-strip in which He was crucified (Hug, Tholuck), an article also worn by gardeners and field labourers. Is it asked 'Where did Christ get His clothes?' The answer is, "Where the angels got theirs" (Luthardt). **saith unto Him, Sir,** κύριε, a form of address which "in its respectfulness goes be-

yond the position of the gardener" (Hengstenberg), and is to be explained by her feeling of dependence on Him for what was her dearest treasure (Hengstenberg), or by a sense of her helplessness which impelled her to seek aid even from Him. **if thou hast borne Him hence** Still she mentions not of whom she speaks, but, as before, assuming He understands the occasion and quality of her grief, appeals to Him, saying, 'If thou,' the servant of Joseph, and therefore a friend—not His enemies—hast removed Him, **tell me where thou hast laid Him, and I will take Him away.** Through intensity of love she overlooks the weakness of her strength. "She forgets everything, her feminine habits and person" (Luther), and proposes with her own hand to remove Christ's body to another and a safer tomb for burial.

16. **Jesus saith unto her, Mary.** The familiar name Μαρία, uttered with well remembered tones, breaks through the barrier of her grief : cf. Luke xxiv. 35. "Since the voice of every human being in a healthy condition is the expression of the man within him, we can infer the impressiveness of Jesus' voice" (Lange). **She turneth herself, and saith** lit., *she, having turned, saith ;* the participial clause showing that, after replying to Christ's question, there had intervened a pause, during which in her anguish she had once more directed her gaze to the tomb. **unto Him,** whom she now recognized, **in Hebrew,** in which tongue Christ had probably addressed her, **Rabboni,** 'Ραββουνί, a dialectical variety of *Rabban,* occurring only here and in Mark x. 51 ; and signifying ' My Teacher !' as the Evangelist explains. **which is to say, Master,** Διδάσκαλε, Teacher.

17. **Jesus saith to her** Mary, according to some copies, had cast herself at Christ's feet, with the view of detaining Him, and offering to Him worship. **Touch Me not,** or, *take not hold on Me,* Μή μου ἅπτου : other proposed readings—σύ μου ἅπτου (Schulthess), ἅπτου μου (Gersdorf), as if Christ invited Mary, as afterwards the disciples (ver. 27 ; Luke xxiv. 37 ff.), to assure herself by touching that He was not a spirit ; and μή οὐ

πτόου (Vogel), 'be not afraid,' as if Christ wished to calm her apprehensions, μὴ οὐ being an un-Johannine combination—are to be rejected. Christ desired that Mary should not touch Him,— she probably by gestures had signified her intention to do so. As to the reason of this prohibition it has been urged that (1) Christ was unwilling she should come in contact with one still levitically unclean (Ammon), (2) His wounds still pained Him (Paulus), (3) He was as yet pure spirit, a bodiless apparition (Weisse), (4) His new life, still delicate, was sensitive to the touch of a mortal (Schleiermacher, Olshausen), (5) He wished from her a greater and higher honour than the ordinary touching of feet, since His body had now become divine (Chrysostom, Erasmus), (6) He meant her to defer touching till a later period, till for example she had carried her message to His brethren (Beza, Bengel, Lampe), (7) He recognized it might be indecorous to permit Mary's touch in the midst of overflowing excitement (Meyer), or (8) He was on the eve of ascending, and did not want to be delayed (Baur). But these may all be set aside as incorrect. The touching Christ forbade was not the simple contact of another, which He afterwards invited in the case of Thomas (ver. 27). The verb ἅπτεσθαι signifies *to fasten oneself to another*, so as to detain, retain, and enjoy. Mary sought to embrace Christ with her human love as she had done before the crucifixion ; to resume again the relations of endearing fellowship which had been broken off by the terrible tragedy of the cross. Christ had indeed promised that after He had gone away He

would come again (Mary seemingly imagined this was the coming spoken of) ; but the 'coming' Christ referred to was a coming in the spirit after His resurrection. Then, but not till then, would Mary be able to resume the fellowship which the cross had interrupted (Calvin, Grotius, Tholuck, Luthardt, Godet, Westcott, De Wette, Brückner, Hengstenberg, Lange, and others). **for I am not**, lit. *have not*, **yet ascended unto the Father**, as I must do before I can return to resume permanent fellowship with My friends (xiv. 3, 19 ; xvi. 5, 7, 17). **but go unto My brethren and say to them**—a different commission from that given to the women (Matt. xxviii. 10—I ascend or, *am ascending*. The ascension was now imminent, if not already begun by His having entered into a superterrestrial form of existence. **unto My Father and your Father** He does not say 'Our,' because His Sonship was different from theirs. His Father on the ground of an eternal relationship, God was their Father on account of their relationship to Him (Rom. viii. 14 ; Gal. iii. 26). **and my God and your God**—Mine by nature, yours by grace ; Mine from eternity, yours in time ; Mine that He might be yours, yours because He is mine. "His consciousness of God was specifically unique and the source of theirs" (Lange).

18. **Mary Magdalene cometh and telleth**, or, *goeth, brings tidings to*, **the disciples, I have seen**, lit., (saying) *that I have seen*, or, that she has seen (T. R.) **the Lord ; and** *how that* **He had said these things unto her**, the things just mentioned (ver. 17).

HOMILETICS

VER. 11-18.—LOVE IN TEARS ; OR, MARY AT THE SEPULCHRE.
I. **Mary's Mourning**, or, love's grief expressed : ver. 11. 1. *Standing beside the vacant tomb.* The first hopeful circumstance in Mary's situation. How much worse had her condition been had the tomb been occupied by the lifeless body of her Lord ! And how much would her anguish have been lightened had she realized that her Lord had for ever left the grave. No Christian requires now to mourn as Mary did, since He knows Christ is risen as He said. 2. *Lamenting in mistaken sorrow.* Most sorrow perhaps of this sort ; Mary's certainly, since Christ was no longer dead but alive for evermore. • With the like mistake of grieving when they ought to be rejoicing, mourning when they

should be exulting, sighing when they might be singing, Christ's people are sometimes chargeable, as e.g. when they repair to the graves of departed friends to weep there with noisy lamentation, forgetting that those they seek are not really there, having in spirit ascended to be with Christ (Phil. i. 23), and that even now their tombs are as good as vacant, for it is written 'the dead in Christ shall rise' (1 Thess. iv. 16). 3. *Continuing dejected without.* Had Mary gone within, as the women did, she would have discovered that the tomb was no more what she imagined it to be, a place of dead men's bones, a charnel house, an abode of corruption, but a habitation of angels and a gateway to heaven.

> " No more a charnel house to fence,
> The relics of lost innocence," etc.—Keble.

II. **Mary's Vision**, or, love's attention arrested : ver. 12-14. 1. *The advanced guards of the king.* (1) Their nature—angels (Ps. lxviii. 17 ; ciii. 20 ; cxlviii. 2 ; Matt. xiii. 41 ; xxv. 31 ; Heb. i. 14). (2) Their number—two, perhaps to correspond with the two 'robbers' betwixt whom Christ was crucified. (3) Their appearance—in white, or shining, garments. 'Light' the clothing of God (Ps. civ. 2 ; Dan. vii. 9 ; 1 Tim. vi. 16), of the angels (Dan. x. 6 ; Rev. x. 1), of glorified saints (Luke ix. 29, 30 ; Rev. iii. 4), and of the exalted Christ (Matt. xvii. 2 ; Mark ix. 3 ; Rev. i. 13-16). (4) Their situation—one at the head and one at the feet where the body of Jesus had lain ; to mark it out, to guard it as a hallowed spot from profanation, to suggest the explanation of its unexpected desertion. (5) Their question—Woman, why weepest thou? Put not for information or from idle curiosity, but to arrest attention, convey sympathy, and ultimately impart instruction. (6) Their success. Seemingly she recognized them not as 'angels,' at least at first (though perhaps she should have done so), but supposing them to be men (probably assistants of the gardener) replied to their interrogation—" Because," etc. (ver. 13).

> " With myrrh and with aloes
> We balmed and we bathed Him,
> Loyally, lovingly,
> Tenderly swathed Him :
> With cerecloth and band
> For the grave we arrayed Him ;
> But oh, He is gone
> From the place where we laid Him."
> —Goethe's Faust (Martin), p. 40.

2. *The person of the Risen Lord.* (1) Near her, as the risen Lord always is to His people (Matt. xviii. 20), especially in times of sadness (Luke xxiv. 15) ; (2) speaking to her, as the angels had done, like them inquiring into the cause of her sorrow,—as the risen Lord still notes the tears of His people (Luke xxiv. 17 ; Heb. iv. 15), and invites the confidence of His people as to their cause (xiv. 18) ; yet (3) unrecognized by her, as He often is still by His sorrowing disciples (Luke xxiv. 16).

III. **Mary's Mistake**, or, love's blindness discovered : ver. 15. 1. *Great.* Already Mary had committed several blunders. She had sought the living among the dead, sorrowed when she ought to have rejoiced, imagined Christ to be carried off by enemies when He was returned to His friends, regarded as common men the couriers of her Lord, "angels of Jesus, angels of light," remained without the sepulchre when she ought to have gone in ; but none of all these was equal to this of mistaking the risen Christ for Joseph's gardener. 2. *Natural.* The likeliest person to be about at early morn was the gardener. Then as to the Emmaus travellers afterwards, so now to her He may have showed Himself 'in another form.' (For other explanations see Exposition). 3. *Persistent.* Though addressed by Christ in the same terms as the angels had employed, she persevered in her mistaken belief. Conceiving the Saviour's body to have been removed by Joseph's orders rather than by the malice of the Jews, she desires to be informed of its whereabouts that she might bear it off to some appropriate and secure place of rest. 4. *Beautiful.* It revealed the intensity of Mary's love, if nothing else. Love knows of no impossibilities; and no passion is so omnipotent as that of a renewed heart for Jesus Christ. Mary's proposal 'I will take Him away' shows what love for Him could attempt while as yet His glory was veiled : the lives of millions since proclaim what love for Him can accomplish still.

> "It makes the coward spirit brave,
> And nerves the feeble arm for fight."

"At this hour millions of men would die for Him" (Napoleon).

IV. **Mary's Awakening,** or, love's darkness dispelled : ver. 16. 1. *The familiar voice.* Mary! What a wealth of pitying love would be infused into the utterance of that one word! Cf. the occasions on which Christ addressed Himself to individuals by name, as e.g. to Simon (xxi. 15), to Judas (Luke xxii. 48), to Saul (Acts ix. 4), to Ananias (Acts ix. 10). 2. *The spell broken.* The human voice an instrument more delicate than the finest organ or harp, capable of expressing emotions more manifold and spiritual than these ; the human soul within a player of marvellous subtlety that can so handle this divine instrument as to translate into articulate sounds (of talk or music), and sometimes into a word the thousand and one emotions of which the spirit is susceptible. Only one other phenomenon rivals these in respect of strangeness, the capacity which belongs to the intelligence that sits behind the ear of interpreting, with a speed surpassing thought and an accuracy excluding mistake, the thoughts and feelings that another has impressed upon those waves of sound. When Mary, wrapt in sorrow, heard the old voice speak, caught the undefinable 'something' that made that voice stand out from all others as pre-eminently dear to her heart, she comprehended the situation without further remark. No voice but One could sound like that! (vii. 47.) No voice but One could call her Mary like that! It was the voice of her old Teacher, her heavenly Friend, her beloved Master, returned, come back again from the dead, risen as He said. 3. *The heart relieved.* With a quick gesture turning round, she exclaimed, Rabboni! My Master! and (probably) made as if she would clasp and detain Him. Mary did not think of her returned Lord as a bloodless and bodiless apparition ; she clearly regarded Him as a veritable flesh and blood form.

V. **Mary's Prohibition,** or, love's ardour restrained : ver. 17. 1. *The restriction.* 'Touch Me not.' Christ meant that He could not now be retained in the old familiar fellowship which had existed between them before His crucifixion, and that therefore she was not to expect it or lay hold of Him for any such purpose. (See Exposition.) 2. *The reason.* 'I have not yet ascended.' Only after His exaltation could He return to institute permanent relations of fellowship between Himself and His disciples. 3. *The consolation.* Christ's language implied that this restriction would be only temporary.

VI. **Mary's Commission,** or, love's service claimed : ver. 17. 1. *To whom sent.* Christ's brethren—Peter, John, James, Andrew, and the rest. (1) The condescension in it—God's Son calls them brethren ; (2) The honour in it—He calls brethren them who are Adam's children, creatures of a day, worms of the dust, ignorant, polluted, and condemned ; (3) The love in it—He does this though they all had deserted Him, and Peter had denied Him. 2. *With what charged.* A message, (1) concerning Himself—"Say to them I." That will let them know I am risen. (2) Concerning His ascension—"Say, I am ascending." That will help them to understand that when I spoke of going to the Father (xiv. 28 ; xvi. 10), I did not simply mean departing from the world by death, or passing into a superterrestrial life—I have done both, and yet I am not ascended—but ascending to where I was before (vi. 62), to the Father's house (xiv. 2), the Father's bosom (i. 18), the Father's glory (xvii. 5). (3) Concerning the Father—"Say I am ascending to My Father and your Father, and My God and your God." That will teach them that while there must ever remain a distinction between My relationship to God and yours, yours will resemble Mine in that (through grace) God will be to you a Father and all you will be brethren.

VII. **Mary's Obedience,** or, love's willingness expressed : ver. 18. 1. *With cheerful resignation.* Mary possibly would have liked to touch Him just to assure herself she again possessed Him, to talk with Him about the unseen world into which He had journeyed and from which He had returned, to hear Him once more discourse about the heavenly things of which He used to speak, to linger in His presence a little longer, were it only to gaze upon His semi-glorified countenance (cf. Luke ix. 33). Nevertheless Mary without a murmur resigned these gratifications (cf. Matt. vi. 10 ; Acts xxi. 14). 2. *With prompt execution.* Immediately she hastened on the joyous mission entrusted to her (xv. 14). For the second time she fled with nimble footsteps to the city, called at the lodging of John and Peter, sought out the quarters of the rest, and communicated the glad news—" I have seen the Lord." 3. *With faithful repetition.* All she had heard from the risen Lord she rehearsed minutely and fully to their wondering ears (Num. xxiv. 31 ; Ps. cxix. 13 ; Acts iv. 20).

Learn 1. " Blessed are they that mourn ; for they shall be comforted " (Matt. v. 4). 2. " The angel of the Lord encampeth round them that fear Him and delivereth them " (Ps. xxxiv. 7). 3. The eyes of Christ's people are sometimes "holden" that they cannot see Him (Luke xxiv. 16). 4. " My sheep hear My voice, and I know them, and they follow Me " (x. 27). 5. " Truly our fellowship is with the Father and with His Son Jesus Christ " (1 John i. 3). 6. " When He ascended on high He led captivity captive, and gave gifts unto men " (Ps. lxviii. 18 ; Eph. iv. 8). 7. The exalted Christ is not "ashamed to call His people brethren " (Heb. ii. 11).

2. THE APPEARANCE TO THE DISCIPLES—WITHOUT THOMAS

CHAP. XX. VER. 19-23

EXPOSITION

Ver. 19. **When therefore it was evening** The day having been far spent when Christ showed Himself to the travellers at Emmaus, between seven and eight miles distant from the metropolis (Luke xxiv. 29), it might easily be somewhat advanced into the evening, perhaps 8 p.m., when these reached the upper room ; it was after their entrance that Christ appeared (Luke xxiv. 36). **on that day,** on which He had discovered Himself to Mary Magdalene, " that memorable day, the birthday of the Christian Church" (Westcott). **the first day of the week** lit., *on the first of the Sabbaths :* see on ver. 1. **and when the doors were shut** lit., *the doors being shut,* so that their opening was impossible except from the interior of the room—a precaution rendered necessary by what is after related. **where the disciples were,** i.e. in Jerusalem (Luke xxiv. 33), probably in the upper room where they were found abiding after the ascension (Acts i. 13), most likely in the supper chamber to which Christ had led them

before His death (Matt. xxvi. 18 ; Mark xiv. 15 ; Luke xxii. 12), in any case a place of rendezvous well known in the circle of disciples. **for fear of the Jews** Apprehensive that the rumours, getting abroad and coming to the ears of the authorities, might lead to their arrest on suspicion of being the propagators, if not the authors of those rumours. **Jesus came and stood in the midst** Neither by entering as the Emmaus travellers had done, through the door way, which had been opened to them from within (Schleiermacher), nor by the doors suddenly and miraculously opening of themselves (Calvin, Pressensé, Baumgarten Crusius, Beza, and others), *creatura cedenti Creatori* (Jerome), nor by simply appearing in a sudden and unexpected manner (Lücke), nor by passing through the closed doors (Theophylact, and Lutherans), which would have required διὰ τῶν θυρῶν, but by mysteriously and supernaturally, it is not said how, making His appearance amongst them (Tholuck, Brückner,

Meyer, Godet, Luthardt, and others). Cf. ἐφανέρωσεν ἑαυτὸν, showed Himself (xxi. 1); and contrast ἄφαντος ἐγένετο, became invisible (Luke xxiv. 31). **and saith unto them,** not upbraiding them because of their unbelief (Mark xvi. 14),—this was obviously after the salutation with which He addressed them on entering (Luke, John),—but saying, **Peace be unto you.** The usual salutation formula (Gen. xliii. 23; Judges vi. 23; xix. 20; 1 Sam. xxv. 6; 2 Sam. xviii. 28; Luke x. 5; Gal. vi. 16; Eph. vi. 23; 1 Pet. v. 14; 3 John 14), employed by the risen Lord to express an entirely new thought (Godet), *usitata formula, singulari virtute* (Bengel)—the peace of reconciliation already bequeathed to them as a dying legacy (xiv. 27), and now announced to them after the victory of His resurrection (Tholuck), brought to them as the fruit of His redeeming work (Godet), and conferred upon them as a qualification for the mission on which they were soon to enter. In connection with their appointment to this it is repeated (ver. 21); which it would scarcely have been had it only been a wishing instead of a bestowing peace.

20. **And when He had said this He showed unto them His hands and His side.** Luke connects this action of the risen Lord not with the salutation of peace, but with what followed. The utterance of this familiar benediction did not at once carry conviction to the hearts of the doubters. "They were terrified and affrighted, and supposed that they had seen a spirit," as on a former occasion, when He had come to them walking on the sea (Matt. xiv. 26; Mark vi. 49). At this point the note of Mark may be inserted—"He upbraided them for their unbelief." Luke (xxiv. 37-40) permits us to hear the upbraiding. "And when He had thus spoken He showed them His hands and his feet:" John says "His hands and His side." Doubtless He exhibited all the three—hands, feet, and side. **The disciples therefore** (i.e. because of what Christ said and what they beheld) **were glad when they saw the Lord.** So overjoyed were they that they rebounded to the opposite extreme of "believing not for joy"—it was too good to be true. This caused

the Lord to reassure them by eating in their presence a piece of a broiled fish and of an honeycomb (Luke xxiv. 42-43).

21. **Jesus therefore** because of the faith to which they had now attained, **said to them,** not to the "apostles" as distinguished from the "disciples" (Hengstenberg), but to the "disciples" generally, though with special reference to "the eleven." **again** The repetition of the salutation was not intended as a leave-taking or farewell (Kuinoel, and others), or occasioned by the fact that the disciples had not yet clearly apprehended its meaning, *vim prioris salutationis nondum plane ceperant,* (Bengel), or meant to secure for what the Lord was about to say greater attention (Calvin), or to emphasize the greeting already given (Meyer), but aimed at preparing and empowering them for their future mission (Tholuck, Godet, Luthardt, Westcott, and others): it was *fundamentum missionis ministrorum evangelii* (Bengel). **Peace be unto you,** see ver. 19: **as the Father hath sent Me** not to you out of the kingdom of resurrection and reconciliation (Lange), but unto the world out of my pre-existent state: cf. v. 57; vii. 29; viii. 42; xi. 42; xvii. 18, 23, 25. Christ regards His mission not in its historical commencement in time, but in its permanent continuance throughout all time. **even so send I you.** Christ grounds the mission of His disciples on His own higher mission as its basis and pattern (xvii. 18). As Christ had been and was the apostle of the Father (Heb. iii. 1), so were they to be the apostles, ambassadors, or messengers of Christ; the word πέμπω being used of them instead of ἀποστέλλω of Christ Himself, "to avoid placing the mission of the apostles on a level with that of their Master" (Hengstenberg).

22. **And when He had said this** endowed them with His peace and assigned them their commission (ver. 21), **He breathed:** cf. Gen. ii. 7. That the breathing was symbolic of the impartation of the Holy Spirit, and Christ's action designed to mark out his personality as the source of that spiritual communication (Brückner), may be conceded; but that the action of afflation only was symbolic (Chrysostom, Grotius, Tholuck, De Wette, and others),

cannot be maintained in face of the accompanying words Christ employed on the occasion. **on them** Not on the apostles only, but also on the disciples; hence no reason to suppose that Thomas was not included with the rest, or that, when he arrived at the point of believing, a special afflation for him would be necessary. **and said, Receive ye** not *ye will receive*, translating λάβετε as a future (Chrysostom, Kuinoel, Grotius, Lampe, Tholuck, and others), but *receive ye*, as a present endowment (Olshausen, Godet, Meyer, Luthardt, Westcott, and others). **the Holy Ghost** lit., *Holy Spirit* (without the art.), which may signify " an effusion of the Spirit " (Godet), but cannot point to a different spirit from that Christ imparted on the day of Pentecost (Hofmann, Luthardt), and still less be interpreted as identical with the effusion at Pentecost (Baur). The Holy Spirit now communicated was not the *gratia ministerialis* as distinguished from the *gratia sanctificationis* enjoyed before Christ's appearing, and from the *gratia χαρισματική* afterwards imparted at Pentecost (Theophylact, Maldonatus, A' Lapide, Weiss, and others), but was a fuller measure of that spirit they already possessed as subjects of the new life, and an earnest of the larger effusion they should experience at Pentecost (Origen, Calvin,

Neander, Brückner, Tholuck, Meyer, Godet, Westcott, and others).
23. Whosoever sins ye forgive Not conferring the power of absolution in the strict sense of remitting the penalty due to transgression, since that can be done only by God, but bestowing through the Holy Spirit the capacity of spirit discernment (1 John iv. 1) in such measure and degree that they could infallibly discern those to whom the blessing of forgiveness belonged by the gospel, as well as the authority requisite to publicly and officially declare such forgiveness. The power here conferred upon the Church by the risen Lord—not to be limited to the exercise of church discipline—belonged preeminently to the apostles (Acts v. 3; xiii. 9), but is also in a lesser measure and degree enjoyed by all believers (1 Cor. vi. 2; 1 John ii. 20). **they are forgiven unto them** i.e. Your spiritual judgments being the fruit of the indwelling and inworking of My spirit will be endorsed by the Father of whose Spirit in you they are the utterance. **whosoever sins ye retain, they are retained.** As the former clause cannot be restricted to the idea of ecclesiastical fellowship, so neither can this. N.B.—This the only verse in this gospel which speaks directly of the forgiveness of sins.

HOMILETICS

VER. 19-23. DOUBT DISPELLED, OR, THE LORD AMONG HIS BRETHREN.
I. **The Manifestation**—"Jesus came," etc. (ver. 19). 1. *The place.* Jerusalem, probably the upper room, in any case a well-known rendezvous. Christ always knows where to find His people (Acts ix. 11). 2. *The time.* The evening of the resurrection day, that memorable day on which Christ as conqueror of death had appeared to Mary, the first day of the week, the birthday of the Christian church. 3. *The company.* The disciples—the "eleven" without Thomas, but with the Emmaus travellers (Luke xxiv. 33-36). 4. *The situation.* Mary's startling intelligence in the morning had brought them together to talk over the amazing news. When they meet Peter tells them how the Lord had that forenoon appeared to him. While the words are in his mouth the Emmaus travellers burst in with the tidings that they too have seen Him. 5. *The appearance.* While rehearsing the things that had happened on the way, and how He was known of them in the breaking of bread (Luke xxiv. 35)—perhaps depicting how immediately thereafter and instantaneously "He vanished out of their sight" (Luke xxiv. 31), lo! suddenly the veil of the invisible world is withdrawn, and "He Himself stands in the midst of them." That the phenomenon was supernatural is indicated by the statement that "the doors were shut where the disciples were for fear of the Jews" (ver. 19), so that Christ's coming into their midst, however brought about, was not effected through the ordinary mode of ingress. (For explanations, see Exposition).

II. **The Salutation**—"Peace be unto you" (ver. 19). 1. *An old voice repeated.*
The customary greeting which had doubtless often fallen from His lips when
He was with them. As with Mary (ver. 16) so now with them, He employs
well-known and familiar accents, repeating them again during the course of the
interview (ver. 21). 2. *A promised legacy paid.* The gift He bequeathed them,
departing (xiv. 27); now having purchased it by dying, He returns on the
resurrection morning to put them in possession. 3. *A needed blessing conferred.*
The specific blessing of the covenant, it included every kind of peace the soul
could want—peace with God, peace of conscience, peace with one's fellows, and
peace in the midst of life's trials (see homily on xiv. 27). A blessing urgently
required by the agitated and doubting disciples (but no less by Christ's followers
to-day), it was also efficaciously bestowed on them as it ever is on hearts to
which Christ speaks. The voice that calmed the Galilean lake by saying 'Peace,
be still!' (Mark iv. 39) can also by the same word soothe the tumult of the
human breast (Mark v. 15); and "when He giveth quietness who can cause
trouble?" (Job xxxiv. 29).
III. **The Revelation**—Himself (ver. 20). 1. *The reality of it.* Vouched for
by (1) Christ's position in the midst of the company,—which showed He desired
not to evade publicity, but courted the fullest and closest inspection ; (2) the
discovery of His hands and His side—also of His feet (Luke xxiv. 39-40),—which
proved the body on which they gazed at least resembled the body which had
been impaled upon the cross ; (3) the invitation to handle Him with which they
did not need to comply ; (4) by the act of eating in their presence (Luke xxiv.
43); and (5) the exhortation He afterwards addressed to them (Luke xxiv. 44-
49),—all of which demonstrated He was no bloodless apparition. 2. *The effect
of it.* First fear (Luke xxiv. 37), afterwards joy (ver. 29 : cf. Luke xxiv. 41).
The sight of the risen Christ attested (1) that Christ was the Son of God (Rom.
1-4), (2) that fellowship with Him was henceforth to be for them more than a
possibility, a sublime reality (xvi. 22 : cf. Luke xxiv. 45), (3) that the power of
the grave was broken (2 Tim i. 10), and (4) that their future resurrection was
secured (1 Cor. xv. 20).
IV. **The Delegation**—Message-bearing (ver. 21). 1. *Conditioned by a prior
gift of peace.* The Saviour's *pax vobiscum* designed not as a farewell, but as an
authoritative confirmation of their gracious standing ; Christ commissions as
His ambassadors none who are not themselves possessed of His peace. Those
He selects as for this office and entrusts with the ministry of reconciliation must
be themselves reconciled (Is. vi. 7). 2. *Based upon Christ's personal authority.*
As He had been sent forth out of His pre-existent state and condition by the
Father, so forth from the new state and condition of peace into which they were
entered they should go as His representatives empowered with His authority
(Matt. xxviii. 18, 19). To that authority alone were they henceforth to appeal
as the highest ground of their right to address men. This what is signified
by the sole Headship of Jesus Christ. The Church has no king, lawgiver,
leader, or commander but Him, and requires no authority or power but His
to entitle or equip it for doing its work upon the earth. 3. *Fashioned after
Christ's own commission.* As the Father had sent Him, so did He send them
(xvii. 18). As He had been sent and had come for 'salvation' (iii. 17) and for
'judgment' (ix. 39), so they should go upon an errand in which the same issues
would appear. With them, as with Him, the mission would result in forgiveness of sins to some—"Whose soever ye forgive they shall be forgiven," in
retention of sins to others—"Whose soever sins ye retain, they are retained"
(ver. 23 : cf. Matt. xviii. 18).
V. **The Dotation**—the Holy Spirit (ver. 22). 1. *Real.* Not a promise merely
but a present endowment; nor a different Spirit from that received at Pentecost,
but the same, only not in full measure—an earnest of what was coming. 2.
Necessary. Without the Spirit the apostles' mission could not have been
accomplished. Neither can that of the Church to the world to-day (1 Cor.
xii. 11). In its congregations and councils, in its office-bearers and members,
the first and greatest requirement is the indwelling of the Holy Spirit (Zech. iv.

6). 3. *Sufficient.* Not perhaps for urgencies and exigencies, duties and trials not yet come upon them, but for present necessities. Between the Resurrection and Ascension they had a preliminary work to do, viz., to testify about the risen Lord to the church itself, and for that they had received a preliminary grant of gracious aid in the shape of an effusion of 'Holy Spirit.' When the more arduous task arrived of bearing witness of the resurrection to the world they would receive the larger endowment required. As their day, so their strength would be (Deut. xxxiii. 25); as their work, their equipment (1 Cor. xii. 7); as their duty, His grace (2 Cor. xii. 9).

Learn 1. The Christian duty of assembling together for mutual comfort and edification (Heb. x. 25). 2. The authority for observing the first day of the week as the Christian sabbath (Rev. i. 10). 3. The certainty that Christ will visit the assemblies of His people (Matt. xviii. 20). 4. The possibility of Christ's approaches to His people causing trouble and alarm instead of peace and joy (vi. 20). 5. The difficulty of overcoming unbelief even in the hearts of Christians (Matt. xxviii. 17). 6. The urgency of praying for the Holy Spirit (Eph. iii. 16). 7. The solemnity of the ministerial office (2 Cor. ii. 15 ; iv. 3).

3. THE APPEARANCE TO THE DISCIPLES—WITH THOMAS

Chap. XX. Ver. 24-29

Exposition

Ver. 24. **But Thomas,** whose character may be deciphered from the notices already furnished in this gospel (xi. 16 ; xiv. 5. See homily on ver. 24). **one of the twelve** His apostolic call mentioned by all the synoptists : Matt. x., Mark iii., Luke vi. **called Didymus,** i.e. twin : see on xi. 16. **was not with them** As the reason is not mentioned charity should suggest that it was perfectly sufficient. Only the conjecture is probable that "his melancholy might prefer to live undisturbed in his grief" (Luthardt). **when Jesus came** i.e. on the occasion just mentioned, when He shewed unto them His hands and His side. Either Thomas had not been present at all ; or, what is less probable, he had been present at an earlier hour, but had left before Jesus came.

25. **The other disciples therefore said unto Him,** in the hope doubtless of imparting to him the joy they felt themselves, **We have seen the Lord.** The emphasis lies upon the verb. The disciples attached no weight to the circumstance that they had been the witnesses ; the point of importance was that Christ had been seen. **But he said unto them,** tenaciously adhering to a pre-formed judgment of his own,

and presumptuously waiving aside the united testimony of his brethren, **Except I shall see in His hands the print of the nails, and put my finger into the print of the nails, and put my hand into His side** For the second 'print' some MSS. read ' place,' τόπον (Lachmann, Tischendorf, Meyer, etc.), on the ground chiefly that it is more appropriate to speak of putting one's hand into a place than into a print,—τύπος *videtur*, τόπος *impletur*—a print is seen, a place is filled (Grotius). But just on this account the substitution of 'place' for 'print' is explicable, while the repetition of the same word serves to mark both the tenacity of Thomas's purpose as well as the intensity of his conviction that it was impossible to reconcile that evidence of death with a resurrection. A similar observation applies to the repetition of the verb 'put,' for which, in the second instance, the A. V. less happily substitutes 'thrust.' **I will not believe.** Instead of saying 'I also will believe if I see,' which would at least have admitted his readiness to be convinced, he says 'unless I see I will not believe,' defiantly laying down conditions upon which alone he will yield assent to the fact or even possibility of a resurrection. *Neque dicit : si videro* *credam ; sed solummodo, nisi videro, non credam. Neque existimat, se visurum esse, etiamsi ceteri se vidisse dicant* (Bengel). **26. And after eight days** i.e. on the first day of the following week, the weekly return of the Resurrection day, which from this time forward was known to the church as 'The Lord's Day' (Rev. i. 10), and eventually came to supplant the Jewish sabbath. **again** Pointing to the fact that even thus early the followers of Jesus recognized the first day of the week as the most appropriate season for their religious gatherings. **His disciples** Not necessarily the apostles by themselves, but these along with other adherents of the faith, as in the previous instance. **were within** Not in Galilee (Olshausen), but in Jerusalem, and in the same upper room as before (see on ver. 19), **and Thomas with them.** Perhaps an indication that Thomas was returning to a better state of mind, was secretly hoping a vision of the Risen Lord might be granted to him ; at all events a proof that the other disciples did not shun him, or exclude him from their society, because of his hesitation and doubt. **Jesus cometh,** honouring His own day, implementing His own promise, and rewarding the faith and expectation of His own people. **the doors being shut,** from the same cause as before (ver. 19), though the clause may be introduced only to indicate, as before, the manner of His coming. **and stood in the midst** as He had formerly done, **and said, Peace be unto you** (see on ver. 19-21).

27. Then saith He to Thomas Not because the disciples had spoken to Him about Thomas (Schleiermacher, Lücke), but because of His higher insight into Thomas's character and thoughts (Meyer, Luthardt, Lange, Brückner), or because He was actually present, though unseen, when Thomas uttered his doubts and difficulties concerning the Resurrection (Westcott). **Reach hither thy finger, and see My hands** Thomas had spoken of the nail prints in the hands, mentioning that he should require to see them : Christ invites him to examine His opened palm with his finger and his eye. **and reach hither thy hand and put it into My side** That neither Thomas nor

Christ alludes to the feet has led to the opinion that Christ's feet had not been nailed, but only bound (De Wette, Lücke) ; this opinion, however, is rejected alike by believing and unbelieving critics (Meyer, Luthardt, Tholuck, Hug, Bähr, Strauss, Keim). **and be not faithless** lit., *become not faithless.* Thomas was on the way to, but had not yet arrived at, the terminus of unbelief. **but believing.** The opposite pole to "faithless." The contrast in the original—ἄπιστος, πιστός— is lost in the English translation.

28. Thomas answered and said unto Him Satisfied with the sight without requiring to touch the prints, to which state of mind he was doubtless assisted by perceiving that Christ had repeated the very words himself had used. **My Lord and My God.** Not an exclamation of wonder (Theodore of Mopsuestia, Socinians, Paulus, Fritzsche), against which stands the fact that Thomas addressed himself to Christ (εἶπεν αὐτῷ), as well as the consideration that in a Jew such a use of the divine name would have been regarded as sinful ; but an adoring confession of Jesus as the divine Son of God. It was the culminating point towards which John was leading up his Gospel, the acknowledgment by the disciples of Christ as the Son of God.

29. Jesus saith unto him, Because thou hast seen Me thou hast believed, or, *hast thou believed ?* In the former case, a gracious acknowledgement and acceptance on the part of Christ of the late offered faith of His disciple ; in the latter, suggestive of a doubt as to its sincerity, and, therefore, not to be preferred. **blessed** as possessing the secret and the principle of true felicity (see xiii. 17). **are they that have not seen and yet have believed,** οἱ μὴ ἰδόντες, those (by the supposition) not seeing— not the disciples because they had seen, but those who after Christ's ascension should believe.

Note on the **Vision Theory** of the resurrection of Jesus Christ. The various appearances made by Christ to His disciples have been explained (Strauss, Keim, Renan, and others) as subjective impressions, visionary deceptions, rather than as objective, literal, matter-of-fact realities. I. *In support of this view* appeal has been taken to 1. The character of those appearances which were always sudden, momentary, intermittent, and without speech. This, however, is hardly correct. 2. The time when they occurred which was commonly at night. This again is contradicted by the appearances to Mary, Simon, and the Emmaus travellers, which took place in the daytime. 3. The persons to whom they were granted —always believers, and of these generally the most impressionable. The reply is that Christ's appearances were designed principally for the confirmation of already existing faith, though the case of Paul shows that Christ could also appear to an unbeliever. If Mary and Peter were impressionable, it can hardly be maintained that Thomas and Paul were. 4. The appearance to Paul, which, it is alleged, was not an objective presentation of the glorified Jesus, but a purely subjective vision. It is certain, however, that Paul himself regarded it as an objective reality (Acts xxii. 6-11 ; xxvi. 12-18), and that Luke distinguishes between the Lord's appearance to Saul and His appearance to Ananias, calling the latter a vision (Acts ix. 10). 5. The certainty that visions were characteristic of the apostolic times—the cases e.g. of Stephen (Acts vii. 36) and of John (Rev. i. 9), of Ananias (Acts ix. 10) and of Cornelius (Acts x. 30), as well as of the Jewish-Christian opponents of Paul who "boast of their visions and revelations of the Lord." But the last example is imaginary, and

the others must be *proved* to have been purely subjective before they can be called in to support a vision theory of the resurrection. 6. The difficulty of conceiving a corporeal resurrection.— "Resurrections, dead men appearing upon the earth are to be found only in mythical stories" (Keim). To offer this as a barrier in the way of believing in Christ's resurrection is to be guilty of a *petitio principii.* II. *Against this hypothesis* it is argued (Schenkel) 1. The limitation of the appearances of the Risen One to a few instances (in all not more than 10), to a short time (40 days), and to a narrow circle (the immediate followers of Christ). 2. The clear distinction between these appearances and the ecstasies and vanishments peculiar to the apostolic age. 3. The complete absence of any trace of nervous excitement in the apostles in their ordinary labours. 4. The certainty that a large stock of soundness of mind and body is required for the founding of a new religion. 5. The exceptional character of 'visionary' experiences in the apostolic age, and the inability of 'miraculous gifts' to spread themselves beyond the limits of the Christian Church. 6. The absurdity of supposing that a world historical religion such as Christianity could be the product of a diseased nervous system. 7. The difficulty of understanding why, if diseased nerves in the case of the first disciples' led to the highest inspiration, they should not do so still.

HOMILETICS

VER. 24-29.—UNBELIEF CONVINCED ; OR, THOMAS WITH HIS LORD.

I. **Thomas's Mistake**—"He was not with them (the disciples) when Jesus came" : ver. 24. 1. *Perhaps justifiable.* Thomas may have been either (1) unwell and confined to his own abode, the intensity of his sorrow having preyed so heavily on his mind as to endanger his body's health ; or (2) uninvited to the meeting, which, however, if advised concerning it, he ought to have attended without an invitation ; or (3) unaware of the startling intelligence which had prompted them to come together—hardly a likely supposition ; or (4) unsatisfied with the grounds upon which that intelligence was based, and employed at the moment in sifting out the truth ; or (5) unwilling to be idle when there was good news to spread abroad, and therefore unable to assemble with his former colleagues—which is putting the best construction on Thomas's behaviour, as the following hypothesis is assuredly the worst ; (6) that Thomas had been present at the beginning of the evening in the upper room, and had listened to 'the idle tales' of the women, the story of Peter, and the narration of the Emmaus travellers, but had afterwards retired, being unable to accept the testimony even of so many witnesses, every one of whom besides he knew ; (7) the likeliest assumption is that he had not been there at all, and that he was detained not by any of the above reasons, but by his own morose and melancholy disposition which felt unequal to the task of crediting the amazing rumour that Christ was risen. 2. *Decidedly wrong.* (1) If grief was the cause of his detention, it was wrong for him to become selfish in his sorrow, to be so wrapt up in his own mental trouble and anxiety as to forget the similar sadness of his brethren who no less than himself stood in need of comfort and consolation. (2) If absent because waiting for further evidence, more light on this sublime and mysterious subject, he ought to have remembered that the likeliest place to look for such was the company of the disciples, since Christ before His departure had said, ' If I go, I will come again,' yea, ' I will see you again, and your heart shall rejoice.' (3) Had he been where he should have been on that first Lord's day evening, in the upper room with his brethren, he would have found what he was seeking, obtained such a sight of Christ as would have instantly put to flight his doubts and difficulties, anticipated the scene which followed eight days later, and so saved himself at least a week of unspeakable sorrow and perhaps misery.

II. **Thomas's Declaration**—" Except I shall see," etc. : ver. 25. 1. *The occasion of it.* The communication made to him by the ten,—" We have seen the Lord." A testimony (1) clear and unambiguous. They had seen *the Lord*— not an apparition, ' a spirit,' which they believed to be that of their departed Master, but the Master Himself, in the body, alive, standing amongst them and conversing with them ; and they had *seen* Him—not dreamt about Him, or beheld Him in vision merely, or looked upon Him with the mind's eye, or imagined they had done so, but in plain and sober reality, in honest and unvarnished literality, with the eye of the body, had seen Him, as they then saw Thomas himself. (2) Unanimous and decided. Not the unsupported assertion of Peter who was always ' enthusiastic ' and might easily persuade himself that he had ' seen ' what he only fancied ; but backed up and confirmed by the evidence of John and James, the other two of Christ's confidential associates, of Matthew the publican, a man accustomed to look into matters, of Andrew and Philip, both persons of sagacity, not to speak of the others. Nor was there the least hesitation on the part of any. With one accord they testified, ' We have seen the Lord.' (3) Ample and sufficient. Ample as to both the number of witnesses and the details of evidence supplied, it was sufficient for the requirements of historic credibility, and ought to have been for the faith of Thomas. 2. *The good in it.* Thomas did not (1) assume that a resurrection was in any case impossible, or (2) deny that in Christ's case a resurrection was actual, or (3) assert that no amount of evidence would secure his belief in a phenomenon so unusual, or (4) allege that no weight of testimony would render credible any such phenomenon to one who had not himself been a spectator of it, or (5) bargain for ' conditions of believing ' which in themselves were impossible. 3. *The evil in it.* (1) Unreason, in rejecting the testimony of ten brethren, supported as it was by that of the women, of Mary, of Simon, of the travellers, all of whom declared they had seen Christ. (2) Presumption, in dict...ng the amount of evidence upon which alone he would accord faith, as if he had either the right or the ability to fix the line beyond which responsibility ceased, as if it fell to him rather than to God to determine how much of proof to offer faith before asking its assent. (3) Pride, in demanding more satisfaction than was either offered to or desired by the ten. Though Christ had invited them to ' handle Him and see,' they were content to see without handling. But Thomas's critical spirit must have the nail prints tested with his finger and the spear wound with his hand. That Thomas thought would be a scientific examination of the question. If this phantom which they all ' saw ' would stand an investigation as searching as that, Thomas would give in !—but not unless. (4) Folly, in calling for demonstration which, as the event showed, was not required. When Christ came Thomas did not need to put his finger into the nail prints or his hand into the side, but for him as for his brethren a sight sufficed.

III. **Thomas's Invitation**—"Reach hither thy finger," etc. : ver. 27. 1. *Gracious.* Certainly Thomas did not deserve it; but He who had just been declared the Son of God with power by His resurrection from the dead, overlooked the ill desert of His follower, and invited him to believe upon his own terms. 2. *Startling.* Thomas must have felt this the moment it was uttered. How had Christ come to know he had used these words? He could hardly suppose his brethren had informed Christ, since, according to his hypothesis, there was no Christ to inform. It would doubtless flash upon his mind as an instance of that higher knowledge his Master had frequently exhibited on earth (i. 47, 48; ii. 25; iv. 17, 18). If so, it probably contributed to his awakening. 3. *Admonitory.* It warned Thomas he was on dangerous ground, at the commencement of a downward path. 'Become not faithless!' Not yet definitely committed to the side of unbelief, he was at the junction of the ways, and on the step then taken would depend the course of after years. 4. *Urgent.* In earnest about this hesitating follower, the risen Lord would condescend, would accept him on his own terms; though He well knew what the issue would be, that He would get Thomas not upon his, Thomas's, terms, but upon His own, Christ's.

IV. **Thomas's Confession**—"My Lord and my God": ver. 28. 1. *A declaration of faith in Christ's resurrection.* He no longer doubted that his Master was risen, and this he adoringly expressed by saying—'My Lord!' 2. *A recognition of Christ's supreme divinity.* If Peter had been the first to confess this before the crucifixion (vi. 69; Matt. xvi. 16), to Thomas belongs the honour of having been the first to make public avowal of it after the resurrection. 3. *An appropriation of Christ as Lord and as God.* To the risen One in both of these aspects he made a joyful surrender—to serve Him as Lord, to adore Him as God.

V. **Thomas's Rebuke**—"Because thou hast seen Me," etc. : ver. 29. 1. *Graciously prefaced.* His faith, though late offered, was recognized and accepted. Thomas, thou hast believed. 2. *Tenderly expressed.* Rather suggested than uttered. Christ does not remind His disciple that he ought to have believed without seeing; only tells him that by not doing so he has missed the opportunity of rising to a higher blessedness than will henceforth,for him be possible. He might have reached the felicity of those who without sight believe, whereas he can only now have the satisfaction of such as believe because they see. 3. *Really conveyed.* That Thomas understood Christ's words to be language of rebuke there can be little doubt.

Learn 1. How much a Christian may lose by absence from the house of God! 2. How foolishly one acts in laying down beforehand conditions upon which he will believe! 3. How faithfully Christ keeps His promise to His people! 4. How tenderly Christ deals with the errors of His own! 5. How dangerous it is to cherish doubt! 6. How graciously Christ accepts the homage of repenting and believing souls! 7. How high is the felicity of those who now believ·: in the Risen Lord!

Ver. 24. Thomas called Didymus. I. **His history.** 1. *Parentage.* Unknown, though from the circumstance that in the lists of the apostles (Matt. x., Mark iii., Luke v.) he is always conjoined with Matthew, who, according to Mark (ii. 14), was a son of Alphæus, and the two are always followed by James, also the son of Alphæus, it has been supposed that he was Matthew's twin brother —all the three, Matthew, Thomas, and James, being sons of the same father (see Beyschlag in Riehm's Handwörterbuch, art. *Thomas*). 2. *Apostleship.* Belonging originally to the circle of John's disciples, he appears, like Andrew and Simon, James and John, to have gone early over to the following of Christ. In the second year of Christ's ministry he was called to serve as an apostle. 3. *Appearances.* On three occasions he steps to the front : (1) in Peræa, when he says to his fellow disciples—'Let us go (to Jerusalem) that we may die with Him' (xi. 16); (2) at the supper table, when he interjects—'Lord, we know not whither Thou goest, and how can we know the way ?' (xiv. 5); and (3) after the resurrection, as here recorded. 4. *Disappearance.* After this he vanishes from the page of history, being only once again mentioned in Scripture (Acts i. 13). According to the 'Fathers,' he preached in Parthia and was buried in Edessa. A later tradition says he carried the Gospel into India, where afterwards an old colony of Syrian Christians on the coast of Malabar, calling them selves 'Thomas Christians,' claimed him as the founder of their church community. II. **His character.** Of 1. *A melancholy disposition.* Constitutionally and habitually looking on the dark side of things, Thomas preferred to walk (as men say) on the shady side of the street (see xi. 16). 2. *A slow judgment.* Thomas never travelled faster than his understanding or reason would permit, and these were never hasty in forming or announcing decisions (see xiv. 5). 3. *A critical mind.* Thomas liked to search things to the bottom, to ▸ee before he believed. This comes out in his words after Christ's resurrection (xx. 25). 4. *A courageous spirit.* Thomas was not afraid to encounter danger and death with and for his Master (xi. 16), although, taken with a panic in the garden, like the rest of his brethren, he forsook Christ and fled. 5. *A true heart.* His judgment once convinced, his heart never hesitated. The moment he perceived Christ stood before him he exclaimed in adoring contrition, My Lord and my God.

Ver. 25. A sight of the Lord—what it produces. I. An ever-deepening sense of sin : see Isaiah (vi. 5), Job (xlii. 5, 6), Peter (Luke v. 8). II. An ever-enlarging measure of joy : cf. David (Ps. iv. 6, 7 ; xvi. 11 ; xxi. 6), the disciples (ver. 20), the eunuch (Acts viii. 39), the Philippian jailer (Acts xvi. 34). III. An ever-advancing degree of holiness (2 Cor. iii. 18 ; 1 John iii. 2, 3). IV. An ever-strengthening resolution to endure : like Moses (Heb. xi. 27), like Paul (2 Tim. iii. 11), like Christ (Heb. xii. 2, 3). V. An ever-growing determination to speak for Christ : like the Apostles (Acts iv. 20). VI. An ever-kindling desire to be with Christ : as was manifest in the case of Paul (Phil. i. 23).

Ver. 29. Faith and sight. I. *Sight without faith*—Sin. 1. Ancient, the sin of the Jewish people. 2. Common, the sin of many at the present day. 3. Great, since that which in Christ is presented to the eye of sense and reason ought to lead to heart acceptance of Christ. II. *Faith after sight*— Salvation. Exemplified 1. In the disciples (if John should not be excepted) who believed in Christ risen after they had seen Him. 2. In those who (to-day) believe in Christ only after all their intellectual difficulties as to Christianity have been solved. III. *Faith without sight*—Blessedness. 1. It implies a larger measure of divine grace. 2. It exhibits a higher degree of Christian virtue. 3. It secures a richer experience of inward felicity. 4. It wins a readier commendation from the lips of Christ.

CONCLUDING WORDS

Chap. XX. Ver. 30-31

Exposition

Ver. 30, 31. **Many other signs** σημεῖα (see on ii. 11), not proofs of the resurrection, τεκμήρια (Acts i. 3), *documenta resurrectionis* (Chrysostom, Luther, Kuinoel, Lücke, Ewald, and others), but miraculous deeds generally (Lampe, Bengel, De Wette, Brückner, Tholuck, Luthardt, and others), therefore as might naturally be expected from perusing the foregoing narrative, **did Jesus in the presence of His disciples** not as distinguished from the people (cf. xii. 37), but because the disciples alone (i.e. those who believed) were able to interpret the full significance of those 'signs' which Christ performed before all the people, **which are not written in this book** ; though

John, as an eye-witness, could have recorded them ; **but these are written** those recorded in this book, **that ye,** for whom it has been composed, i.e. not any definite circle of readers (Lücke, Luthardt), but any one who reads (Schweitzer, Brückner), **may believe**—faith the end aimed at by the author,—**that Jesus is the Christ** (see on i. 17 ; iv. 25), **the Son of God** (see on i. 18; v. 19, etc.) ; **and that believing** (see on iii. 15, 16, 36) **ye may have life in His name,** i.e. in fellowship with Him as the Christ and as the Son of God. Baur regards these verses as spurious, because (in his judgment) the previously-related appearances close the book in such a manner that other manifestations are not to be thought of ; but this, however valuable as an 'opinion,' cannot be regarded as 'conclusive demonstration.'

HOMILETICS

VER. 30-31. THE PLAN AND PURPOSE OF THE BOOK.
I. **Its Plan**—Selection. 1. *From a large stock of literary material :* " Many other signs," &c. 2. *By a competent eye-witness*—since these signs were done " in presence of His disciples."
II. **Its Purpose**—Faith. 1. In Christ's name. 2. Unto eternal life.
Lessons. 1. The value, 2. The sufficiency, 3. The aim of Scripture.

THE EPILOGUE

CHAP. XXI

The Evangelist's design in this concluding chapter, assuming it to have proceeded from his pen (see note at end of ver. 25), will be understood by recalling the main purpose of the gospel of which it forms a part. That purpose was to exhibit the glory of Jesus as the Word of God. In *pre-incarnate* form that glory had revealed itself in the creation and preservation of the universe, but more especially in the enlightenment of men ; and of this the Evangelist had spoken in the prologue (i. 1-18). From the birth of Christ till His ascension it had been unfolded in *incarnate* form, of which, also, the Evangelist had treated in the main body of his work, in the history of Christ's life and in the history of Christ's passion. Now, finally, after the resurrection, but more fully at and after the exaltation, that glory passed into its ultimate and highest form, which throughout the Christian dispensation it was to assume and attain, and which it still displays within the sphere of the Christian Church, viz., the *post-incarnate* or spiritual form ; and of this the author writes in the so-called epilogue with which his treatise terminates. That the additional manifestation it furnishes was not introduced simply as another item in our Saviour's post resurrection history is apparent from the circumstance that the author does not mention the appearance (also Galilean) to five hundred brethren at once ; while that it was not intended as a further proof of Christ's resurrection may be inferred from the fact that on this point the writer has already closed his evidence. That it was inserted for some specific purpose the remark that Christ "manifested Himself on this wise" appears to indicate. A study of the chapter suggests that its object was to teach 1. that the earthly theatre within which Christ's glory is now to be beheld is the Christian Church ; 2. that the organ by which alone that glory can be apprehended is the spirit of love ; and 3. that the things in which Christ's glory is now displayed are (1) the work of saving souls through the preaching of the gospel, symbolized by the letting down of the net into the sea ; (2) the rewarding of His faithful servants by providing for them, even here, though chiefly and perfectly in heaven, a feast of joy, of which the banquet on the shore was an emblem ; and (3) the appointing and directing of the Church's ministers, assigning to them their respective spheres, marking out for them their different experiences, and generally guiding them till the consummation of His glory, at His final *parousia*. In connection with this last the Evangelist corrects a foolish rumour in the Christian community concerning himself (ver. 23).

The chapter divides itself into three sections—

1. The Manifestation to the Seven : ver. 1-14.
2. The Conversation with Peter : ver. 15-23.
3. The concluding Attestation : 24-25.

SECTION I.—THE MANIFESTATION TO THE SEVEN

CHAP. XXI. VER. 1-14

EXPOSITION

Chap. xxi. ver. 1. **After these things** μετὰ ταῦτα, a frequent Johannine phrase (v. 1 ; vi. 1 ; vii. 1), the things referred to being the appearances recorded in the preceding chapter. **Jesus manifested Himself** Also a genuine Johannine expression (cf. vii. 4 ; and contr. Mark xvi. 12, 14, ἐφανερώθη), pointing to a state not of purely spiritual existence (De Wette), but of concealment or invisibility out of which. Christ emerged by free self-determination. **again** Presupposing and confirming the earlier manifestations. **to the disciples** As in xx. 25, 26, including others besides the apostles ; see on ver. 2. **at the sea of Tiberias** ἐπὶ τῆς θαλάσσης, *upon the sea* not upon its surface as in vi. 19 (cf. Matt. xxi. 19 ; Luke xxii. 30), but upon its margin or coast as in vi. 21, ἐπὶ τῆς γῆς, upon the land, i.e. at the water's edge. The usual Johannine expression for 'upon' is ἐπὶ with the

dative : cf. iv. 6 ; v. 2. The clause belongs to 'manifested' and not to 'the disciples,' as if the sense were that Christ showed Himself to them when they were on the sea. The 'sea of Tiberias' is Johannine (vi. 1); the Synoptists read 'the sea of Galilee' (Matt. iv. 18) or 'the lake of Gennesaret' (Luke v. 1). **and He manifested** not His glory (Hengstenberg) but *Himself*, though the Evangelist omits ἑαυτόν because he wishes to lay stress on the manner in which Christ revealed Himself, rather than on the fact that it was Himself He revealed. **on this wise.** Not mere prolixity purposely introduced as a set-off against traditional misrepresentation (Meyer), but solemn iteration marking the importance of that about to be related (Godet).

2. **There were together Simon Peter** (see on i. 42) **and Thomas called**

Didymus (see xi. 16; xx. 24) **and Nathanael** (see i. 45, 46) **of Cana of Galilee** (see on ii. 1). The birthplace of the last is mentioned to repair an omission in the earlier passage (Godet), and to throw light upon the connection between i. 45ff and ii. 1 (Westcott), or just as likely without any particular design (Meyer)—the notion that the clause was meant to set forth Nathanael as the representative of the first miracle (Hengstenberg) being far-fetched and fanciful. **and the sons of Zebedee** John and James : usually so styled in the Synoptists (Matt. iv. 21; x. 2; xx. 20, with parallels), but never in the Fourth Gospel. That in this enumeration of apostles John and James occupy the last place, whereas in the synoptical tables they always stand immediately after Peter, should perhaps be regarded as an indirect hint of Johannine authorship. **and two other of His disciples.** If apostles (Hengstenberg) then possibly Andrew, Simon's brother, and Philip, Nathanael's friend, though in this case one fails to see why their names should have been omitted. But the term 'disciples' does not necessarily and exclusively mean 'persons belonging to the apostolic circle.' Hence the unnamed on this occasion cannot be identified, though a claim has been put forward (Godet) in behalf of Aristion and Presbyter John, whom Papias mentions as old disciples of the Lord living at Ephesus when John wrote, and having almost the rank of apostles.

3. **Simon Peter saith unto them, I go a-fishing.** The apostles had not returned to Galilee to resume their old occupations (Calvin, Keim), which would have been in flagrant disobedience to instructions received (Luke xxiv. 49; Acts i. 4); but Christ had distinctly required their presence in Galilee (Matt. xxvi. 32; xxviii. 7), and Peter's language points to rather an exceptional proposal than a regular employment. Besides, it is doubtful if Thomas and Nathanael were fishermen, though both they and the unnamed may have been acquainted with the art. **They say unto him, We also come with thee.** ἐρχόμεθα, instead of ἀκολούθεθα or ἄγωμεν καὶ ἡμεῖς (xi. 16) has been pronounced non-Johannine; but the spokesman on this occasion was not bound to express

himself as John would have done. **They went forth,** most likely out of the house of Peter or of Peter's wife's mother, where they were accustomed to stay when in Capernaum (Matt. viii. 14), or out of the town towards the sea, **and entered into the boat,** i.e. the boat necessary for fishing, perhaps the boat Peter had renounced when he left all to follow Christ (Luke v. 11). The omission of 'straightway' (T. R.), to which objection has been taken (Lücke) as un-Johannine (cf. v. 9 : vi. 21), is in accordance with the best authorities (א B C D L X etc., Lachmann, Tischendorf, Westcott and Hort). **and that night though night** was the most favourable time for fishing and the sea of Galilee abounded in fish (see on vi. 1), **they took nothing.** Cf. Luke v. 5. πιάζειν elsewhere in this gospel six times, not once in the Synoptists.

4. **But when day was now breaking** (contrast vi. 16) **Jesus stood on the beach** εἰς τὸν αἰγιαλόν (cf. xx. 19, 26)— the sense being *Jesus having come to the beach, stood there.* The substitution of ἐπί for εἰς (א, Lachmann, Tischendorf) is an interpretation. In vi. 19 Jesus goes to His disciples on the water : here He waits for them upon the shore. **Howbeit the disciples knew not that it was Jesus.** Either the light was insufficient, or He appeared in another form (Mark xvi. 12), or their eyes were holden (Luke xxiv. 31). Cf. xx. 14.

5. **Jesus therefore saith unto them,** in a voice which sounded strange, **Children,** παιδία boys, young people, marking a distinction in respect of age or position (cf. 1 John ii. 13, 18)—perhaps purposely avoiding the familiar τεκνία, little children (a relationship of affection), in order not to be prematurely recognized, **have ye aught to eat ?** i.e. with other food, in this instance 'fish : μή, expected a negative reply. It is not necessary to hold that Christ spoke like an intending purchaser, i.e. like a fish merchant (Chrysostom, Lampe), or desired to obtain food for Himself, since already He was provided with a fish and bread (ver. 9 : cf. Ps. l. 12). His purpose was to breakfast with His disciples (ver. 12). **They answered Him, No.** This furnished Him with occasion to

offer them the counsel which follows.

6. And He said unto them, Cast the net on the right side of the boat They appear to have been fishing on the left side. Why Christ directed them to try the right cannot have been that that was the fortunate side (Brückner, Keim), but that His divine power had drawn the fish thither, *eo pisces coegit virtus Domini* (Bengel). **and ye shall find.** An ordinary person would have said, ' Perhaps ye shall find.' Christ knew that they would find. **They cast therefore,** not confident of success, or already recognizing Christ, but probably believing the supposed stranger had observed what had escaped their notice, the presence of a shoal of fish (Lampe) ; **and now they were not able to draw it** *the net* up into the boat—ἑλκύσαι; σύρειν (ver. 8), meaning to draw after—**for the multitude of the fishes.** Cf. Luke v. 6.

7. That disciple therefore whom Jesus loved (see on ver. 24 ; and cf. xiii. 23), i.e. John, the first to recognize the stranger, possibly through his speech and action, but chiefly through the miracle which recalled the earlier incident upon the lake, **saith unto Peter,** who ought to have been the first to detect Christ's presence, considering what had on that former occasion occurred (Luke v. 4) : **It is the Lord !** 'Ο κύριος, the usual designation of Christ after the resurrection (cf. Matt. xxviii. 6 ; Mark xvi. 19, 20 ; Luke xxiv. 34; Acts i. 6). **So when Simon Peter heard that it was the Lord,** with characteristic impetuosity (cf. Matt. xiv. 28), **he girt** or fastened by binding, **his coat** ἐπενδύτης, an upper garment of linen, a workman's frock or blouse, used by fishermen and artizans in general (Theophylact, Meyer, Godet, Brückner, and others) —not the same as χιτών (Kuinoel), which was strictly a woollen shirt or smock worn next the body (see Odys. xv. 60 ; Herod. i. 155), and probably different also from the ἱμάτιον (Godet), outer garment, cloak, or mantle, which usually completed the civilian's dress (Herod. ii. 47)—**about him** (cf. xiii. 4) ; **for he was naked,** whether destitute of all clothing, except the *subligaculum* demanded by decency (Theophylact,

Godet, and others), or only stripped to his χιτών, as in Xen. An. i. 10, 3 (Meyer, Tholuck, Luthardt, and others), in his shirt sleeves, or ' in his jersey ' as we say (Paley), cannot be determined, though the former may well have been the case if Peter had already been in the water lending assistance to lift the net, **and cast himself into the sea** (possibly, as just surmized, a second time) to be the first to reach the Lord.

8. But the other disciples who must not be blamed because they did not, like Peter, abandon the net and allow the fish to escape, **came in the little boat** more slowly, yet as surely—it may be also more usefully and dutifully—eventually reaching the same goal as he, the Saviour's presence ; **for they were not far from the land** (and therefore did not think of deserting the vessel and the net), **but about** (on ὡς ἀπὸ, see xi. 18) **two hundred cubits off** i.e. about 100 yards ; **dragging the net full of fishes** doubtless prizing their large take all the more because of its having been given them by the Lord.

9. So when they the other disciples, **got out upon the land,** or went out from the boat to the beach, **they see a fire of coals there** lit., *a heap of charcoal* (cf. xviii. 18) *lying* in a kindled state, and fish, ὀψάριον being taken collectively as in ver. 13 (Meyer, Brückner, Luthardt, Lange), or *a fish, ὀψάριον* being interpreted, as in vi. 9, of a single fish (Beza, Bengel, Lampe, De Wette, Godet, Westcott, and others), **laid thereon, and bread** or *a loaf.* As to whence Christ obtained these provisions different answers have been given. They were—(1) created out of nothing (Chrysostom, Theophylact, Grotius), against which stands the fact that creation ceased on the seventh day (Gen. ii. 2), and the circumstance that not so did Christ act in turning the water into wine at Cana (ii. 7, 8), or in multiplying the loaves at Bethsaida (vi. 11). (2) Prepared by the ministry of angels (Luthardt), but of this the narrative affords no trace. (3) Purchased by Christ from some fisherman in the vicinity, or in some way procured beforehand by Christ Himself (Meyer); but the risen Christ cannot be thought of, in accordance with this gospel at least, as resuming everyday relations with men in general, such as this hypothesis assumes. (4) Obtained from one of His believing friends, some of whom were to be found almost everywhere along the lake (Lange). There is, however, no reason to suppose Christ appeared to any of His Galilean followers before the present interview with the disciples. (5) Fetched from the boat by Peter, who also assisted the Saviour to gather wood for the fire (Lücke)—a notion requiring no refutation. (6) Supernaturally provided by the same power that had suddenly collected 153 fishes into the disciples' net (Godet, Hengstenberg, Westcott, and others)—which manifestly most accords with the situation.

10. Jesus saith unto them, Bring of the fish which ye have now taken. The reason of this command can hardly have been that the fish upon the coals, whether one or more, was too small a provision for seven men, and required to be supplemented (Lücke, Meyer), or that His disciples might satisfy themselves that what He had provided was genuine fish (Bengel), or that Peter might be reminded of his mistake in totally overlooking through his haste to reach the shore, the blessing Christ had prepared for him and his companions (Lisco), or that Christ's gifts might be marked out as intended for use (Westcott), but that the meal was designed to be symbolical,—not of the Lord's Supper (Augustine), or of the mode in which the wants of the disciples were henceforth to be supplied, partly by the divine blessing and aid, partly through their own faithful labour (Godet), or of the duty of devoting that to Christ which had been acquired rather through His grace than through personal effort (Jacobus), but —either of the spiritual fellowship Christ and His disciples should have in the success of their ministry (Hengstenberg), or, perhaps best, of the blessed reward awaiting His faithful followers in the heavenly world (Olshausen, Stier).

11. Simon Peter, therefore, went up into the boat (cf. Mark vi. 51), it may be supposed to release the net which

was fastened to it, **and drew the net to land,** not by himself alone (Meyer), but with the help of the others, **full of great fishes.** The adjective "heightens the miraculous effect" (Meyer), and contains an additional blessing (Lisco). **—an hundred and fifty three.** The number is recorded not because it was symbolic of the conversion of the Gentiles, the heathen being represented by 100, the Jews by 50, and the Trinity by 3 (Cyril of Alexandria, Theophylact), or of all who shall be saved by grace (7) in harmony with law (10), the sum of 1, 2, 3... up to 17 (the unity of law and grace) being 173 (Augustine), or of the name Shimeon bar Iona Kepha (Volkmar, Keim) ; but because it was according to fact—the Evangelist probably saw the fish counted. The symbolism lay in the numbering not in the number (Lange). The notion that this was designed to teach that men of every kind should be drawn out of the sea of the world to salvation (Bengel) was based on the ancient belief that there were exactly 153 different sorts of fish in the sea (Jerome). **and for all there were so many, the net was not rent,** as in the former miracle : Luke v. 6 :—"a sign of the indestructibility of the universal church" (Keim).

12. Jesus saith unto them, acting the part of house-father, **Come** *and* **break your fast.** The ἄριστον was the morning (Matt. xxii. 4), as distinguished from δεῖπνον (xiii. 2 ; Luke xiv. 12 , the afternoon meal. **And none of the disciples durst inquire of Him, Who art Thou?** cf. iv. 27. The verbs τολμᾶν, to dare, to venture (Matt. xxii. 46 ; Mark xii. 34 ; Luke xx. 40), and ἐξετάζειν, to inquire by careful investigation (Matt. ii. 8 ; x. 11), though unusual in John, are by no means unsuitable. **knowing that it was the Lord.** The conviction they had of Christ's identity rendered all additional interrogation as unnecessary as it was unbecoming.

13. Jesus cometh towards the fire of coal, having already invited the disciples to approach, **and taketh the bread,** mentioned in ver. 9, **and giveth them, and the fish likewise.** Not the fish alone which He Himself had provided (Westcott), the 153 being only "looked at" (Keim), but the fish generally. It is not stated that Christ gave thanks before the meal, and His silence has been explained on the ground that Christ desired to omit what was purely human, τά ἀνθρώπινα (Euthymius), that Christ's table communion with His people in this æon is a silent one (Luthardt), that Christ did not as yet wish to make Himself known (Lange), that Christ appeared as the giver only of the food which He brought (Westcott), that the repast was not a 'regular meal' but only a 'breakfast' or morning meal partaken of standing (!) (Meyer), but is perhaps best accounted for by saying that as "the meal represented benefits not to be imparted until a future state, the benediction and thanksgiving would have been out of place" (Hengstenberg). It is not however certain that He did not offer thanks (see Luke xxiv. 30; and cf. vi. 11). It is not probable that He partook of the meal (Strauss).

14. **This is now** (ἤδη, see xix. 28) **the** (or, *a*) **third time** (cf. 2 Cor. xiii. 1) **that Jesus was manifested** (cf. Mark xvi. 12) **to the disciples after that He was risen**, lit., *being raised*, **from the dead.** Ἐγερθείς ἐκ νεκρῶν is said to be non-Johannine (Lücke, Brückner), but cf. ii. 22. For the construction cf. iv. 54. The appearance thus referred to was not the third in reality (Lücke), or in John's enumeration (Milligan and Moulton), or in the writer's belief, he not being aware of any except those described in xx. 19, 26 (Brückner), but the third made to the disciples as a body or to more of them than one (Godet, Tholuck, Luthardt, Meyer, and others). It has been suggested (Westcott) that 'the third time' may describe 'groups' or 'days' of appearance. That John's enumeration conflicts with Paul's (Meyer) cannot be maintained since they proceed upon different principles : John as explained reckoning only those made to the disciples, Paul counting up the various classes of witnesses—first Peter the chief witness, then the apostles (including xx. 19, 26 in one), after that the church, next James the Lord's brother, the president of the Jerusalem Church, once more the twelve, probably on the occasion of the ascen-

sion, when they received their final commission, and lastly Paul himself (Luthardt). The precise number of manifestations made by the risen Lord was 11 or 12 :—To (1) Mary Magdalene (xx. 14), (2) the women (Matt. xxviii. 5), (3) Peter (Luke xxiv. 34), (4) the Emmaus travellers (Luke xxiv. 13-31), (5) the disciples without Thomas (xx. 19), (6) the disciples with Thomas (xx. 26), (7) the seven in Galilee (xxi. 1), (8) the 500 brethren (1 Cor. xv. 6), (9) James (1 Cor. xv. 7), (10) the apostles at Bethany (1 Cor. xv. 7 : cf. Luke xxiv. 50), (11) Stephen (Acts vii. 56), (12) Paul (1 Cor. xv. 8).

Note. *On the miraculous draught.* 1. Between the miracle here recorded and that reported in Luke (v. 1-11), certain resemblances have suggested that the later account is only a revised version of the earlier modified by the introduction of a scene from Matthew (xiv. 28) in accordance with the subjective purpose of the redactor, e.g. (1) the scene of the miracle, (2) the presence of the sons of Zebedee with Peter at the fishing, (3) the unsuccessful night toil, (4) the miraculous draught, (5) the singular behaviour of Peter—in the earlier account walking on the sea, in the later plunging into it and swimming ashore. But no reason exists in the nature of things why two occurrences should not present as many and as great correspondences as those above named. 2. The differences observable in the two narratives are too numerous and important to admit of their being explained as varying reports of the same event. (1) The time in Luke is at the commencement of the Galilean ministry ; in John, after the resurrection. (2) The company in Luke numbers four ; in John, seven. (3) The situation of Jesus in the former is in the boat, in the latter on the beach. (4) The command is not the same ; in the one case, 'Launch out and let down'; in the other, 'Cast on the right side.' (5) The draught is there 'a great multitude'; here a specific number. (6) In the earlier miracle the net breaks ; in the later it holds. (7) What ensued upon the miracle is in each case different.

HOMILETICS

VER. 1-14.—THE APPEARANCE AT THE LAKE.
I. **The Unsuccessful Fishing** : ver. 1-3. 1. *The scene of operation.* The Galilean sea. (1) Endeared by early associations. Many a time had Simon and Andrew, with the sons of Zebedee, plied their craft upon its waters (Matt. iv. 18-22). (2) Hallowed by sacred memories. Across that lake had the disciples often sailed with their Master in the days of His flesh (vi. 16 ; Matt. vii. 18-23). On that lake had they thrice at least witnessed a display of His all-commanding power, when He gave them a miraculous draught of fish (Luke v. 1-11), when He calmed the stormy billows (Matt. viii. 26), and when He came to them walking upon its snowy crests (vi. 16 ; Matt. xiv. 22-33). From that lake they had frequently heard Him discourse to assembled crowds upon its margin (Luke v. 3 ; Matt. xiii. 2). Around that lake they had travelled with Him in His wanderings. (3) Recommended by past experience. Besides having once been a scene of miraculous display in giving them an unexpected draught, it was well known to them as a water famed for the multitude, variety, and excellence of its fish. 2. *The company of fishermen.* (1) Their number. Seven, the perfect number, the symbol of completeness. The group of disciples thus representative of the infant church of Jesus. (2) Their names. Simon Peter, the man of rock, the symbol of energy, strength, steadfastness, and zeal. Thomas, called Didymus, the man of doubt, typical of prudence, caution, timidity, reason. Nathanael of Cana, in Galilee, the man of no guile, emblematic of transparent sincerity and sweet simplicity. The sons of Zebedee, once sons of thunder, now men of love and self-sacrifice. Two others of His disciples, representative of the great army of unknown, undistinguished, unrenowned, to be found in every age and country in the train of Christ. Together let them shadow forth the varieties of character and endowment of which the church of the resurrection was and still is composed. 3. *The proposed expedition.* (1) Its proposer—Peter. The church no less than the world needs men of action to lead the way—pioneers to open up new paths—persons of imagination and enthusiasm to devise and impress others with the practicability of what they suggest. (2) Its accepters. Started by Peter, the notion was taken up by his companions. The mass of mankind in religion as in politics not only require to be led but are ready to follow. The capable man never wants instruments to carry out his projects. He who has the gift of ruling is certain to find subjects to rule. (3) Its commencement. It began well. Everything augured hopefully for its success. The reputation of the lake was high ; the time the best possible for fishing. The company were manifestly ardent ; most of them besides experienced boatmen who knew the art. They lost no time in launching out upon the deep ; spared no pains to make their work a success ; seemingly were not soon disheartened. The day was breaking ere they thought of giving up their fruitless toil. Whatever Christ's people do in common life, and much more in matters of religion, they should act so as to deserve, if they cannot command success. (4) Its result. Nothing, at least to appearance. They caught no fish. Their toils were in vain. Something—yea, everything in one. They met with Christ, found what they expected not, returned with what they had not gone to seek. So Christ defeats His people's schemes that He may the better carry out His own, disappoints His people's hopes that He may give them immediate fruition, and leaves them to themselves that they may the more readily welcome and enjoy Himself when He comes.
II. **The Miraculous Draught** : ver. 4-8. 1. *The Stranger on the beach.* (1) The time of His appearing—morning. The angel of Jehovah came to Jacob during night and left him at daybreak (Gen. xxxiii. 26) ; Christ in the days of His flesh visited His disciples about the fourth watch of the night (Matt. xiv.

25); the risen Lord goes to them with the breaking of dawn. So Christ still appears to His people in the morning, because in every soul it is morning when He appears.

> "'Tis midnight in my soul till He,
> Bright morning star, makes darkness flee."

(2) The circumstance of His non-recognition. They knew not that it was Jesus, as Mary and the Emmaus travellers had failed to recognize Him, and perhaps for similar reasons. Anyhow they did not know Him—which suggests that Christ may be beside His people when they are not aware, and that they do not always discern when their heavenly friend is at hand. (3) The unexpected question. Cheerily put and with friendly solicitude—Children,' better 'lads,' 'young men have ye aught to eat?' i.e. anything to eat with bread, any fish? has your cast been successful? Put also not for information but to arrest attention and excite expectation. (4) The disappointed reply. No! They had toiled all night and caught nothing, as three of them at least had once done before (Luke v. 5); they had spent their strength for nought and in vain (Is. xlix. 4), as gospel fishers often seem to do (Gal. iv. 11 ; 1 Thess. iii. 5). (5) The proffered counsel. 'Cast the net upon the right side of the ship.' The *right* side always the side Christ appoints. He who follows not where Christ leads or goes not where Christ directs or does not what Christ bids is like one who fishes on the *wrong* side. (6) The prompt obedience. 'They cast therefore.' It is wise never to be above taking advice, especially from such as are likely to be better informed than ourselves—much more when the advice comes from the lips of Him in whom are hid all the treasures of wisdom and knowledge (Col. ii. 3). (7) The marvellous success. 'Ye shall find,' said Christ, 'and they found.' The royal road to success in religion is obedience to Christ's instructions. Christ keeps His promises to them that do His commandments—nay does for them far beyond their askings or thinkings (Eph. iii. 20);—"They were not able to draw for the multitude of fishes." 2. *The recognition from the boat.* (1) By whom made. By "that disciple whom Jesus loved," and in whose heart glowed a pure flame of love for Jesus. The heart rather than the intellect the organ of spiritual apprehension. John had been the first to perceive Christ was risen (xx. 8); now is He the first to recognize His person. (2) How expressed. "It is the Lord!' concentrating in the brief exclamation, love, joy, adoration, desire—a world of thought, an ocean of holy feeling, a heaven of spiritual aspiration. (3) With what followed. Instantaneous recognition by Peter to whom John secretly whispered his discovery, and startling activity on Peter's part similar to that once before displayed (Matt. xiv. 28). Having girt his fisher's coat about him, he forthwith plunged into the sea, and struck out with his strong arms for the shore. A second century romancist would have portrayed Peter's meeting with his Lord : John does not, because probably in the grey morning it was not distinctly visible from the boat. 3. *The landing of the net.* (1) The labour of it. Having come slowly after with the boat, John and his companions reached the margin of the lake, and assisted by Peter, hauled the net upon the beach, with its 'harvest of the sea.' (2) The success of it. 153 fishes lay upon the land, every one great and counted. So will all the gospel net drags to heaven's shore be 'great,' ripe, and rich in grace, as well as numbered and known. (3) The wonder of it. 'For all there were so many the net was not rent.' Neither will the gospel net fail till it has landed all Christ's believing people on the shores of eternity.

III. **The Mysterious Banquet** : ver. 12-14. 1. *The heavenly provision.* 'The fire of coals upon the beach, with fish thereupon and bread' (ver. 9). Emblematic of the reward Christ's servants will enjoy upon the coast of bliss, of the marriage supper of the Lamb to which within the veil they shall be welcomed (Rev. xix. 9). 2. *The earthly contribution.* 'Bring of the fish which ye have now taken.' A large part of the future satisfaction and reward of Christ's servants will consist in beholding the fruit of their labours in souls through their instrumentality guided to eternal life (1 Thess. ii. 19, 20). 3. *The royal* *invitation.* 'Come and break your fast.' So will they be welcomed when they reach the heavenly land (Matt. xxv. 34). Not until they stand within that King's banquet hall will they realize what it is to eat the 'bread of God' and drink the 'wine of heaven.' 4. *The solemn distribution.* 'Jesus cometh and taketh the bread, and giveth them and the fish likewise.' A picture of the higher and better entertainment Christ is preparing for His people in His Father's kingdom (Matt. xxvi. 29), of which He here gives them happy fore-tastes in the Lord's Supper.

Lessons. 1. The fruitlessness of labour even in the church apart from the presence and power of the glorified Redeemer (xv. 5). 2. The certain and abundant success of those who work in the way and along the lines suggested by Jesus Christ. 3. The blessed recompense awaiting faithful labourers in Christ's service.

Ver. 3. 'I go a fishing.' 1. A sudden inspiration. 2. A prompt resolution. 3. A hopeful expedition. 4. A laborious occupation. 5. A fruitless speculation. 6. A happy termination.

Ver. 3. Leaders and followers. I. **Leaders.** In church or state these like Peter should be men of 1. prompt resolution, 2. self-reliant action, 3. cheery expectation, 4. contagious inspiration. II. **Followers.** Like Peter's com-panions, these should be 1. unbroken in their ranks—"We"; 2. hearty in their co-operation—"also"; 3. simultaneous in their movement—"come"; 4. unen-vious in their dispositions—"with thee."

Ver. 3. Catching nothing: I. *A common experience.* Not the first time this had happened in the history of three at least of the seven (Luke v. 5). Nor were these the first as they have not been the last who have spent their strength for nought and in vain (Is. xlix. 4). II. *A sore disappointment.* Con-sidering (1) the high expectations with which men usually start upon their enterprises, and (2) the great labour they often expend upon them. III. *An excellent discipline.* (1) Teaching personal humility. (2) Suggesting the need of heavenly assistance. (3) Preparing for ultimate success.

Ver. 4. Morning beside the lake. I. *Realized failure.* The disciples had toiled all night and caught nothing. II. *Imperfect knowledge.* The disciples knew not Jesus on the beach. III. *Unexpected assistance.* The risen Lord directs them to cast on the right side of the ship. IV. *Divine manifestation.* The great draught discovers to John who the stranger is. V. *Heavenly com-munion.* They breakfast with the Lord upon the shore.

Ver. 5. "Children, have ye aught to eat?"—Suggestive of 1. *Affection*—'Children.' 2. *Sympathy*—'Have ye aught to eat?' Christ knew they had not and felt for their disappointment; also saw they required refreshment, and grieved at their non-success. 3. *Hope.* The mere putting of the question fitted to inspire hope. 4. *Help.* When once they had made known their need, Christ gave them a rich supply.

Ver. 7. Love's recognition of the Lord. 1. Sudden. 2. Ardent. 3. Com-municative. 4. Self-restrained.

Ver. 9 with xviii. 18. The two fires—a contrast. I. The fire in the palace-court (xviii. 18). I. *A scene of sorrow*—the Saviour's trial. 2. *A place of temptation*—in the company of Christ's enemies. 3. *A witness of sin*—the denials of Peter. II. The fire upon the sea-shore (ver. 9). 1. *A scene of glory*—the presence of the risen Lord. 2. *A place of safety*—the society of Jesus and His friends. 3. *A witness of grace*—the restoration of Peter.

Ver. 12. The morning banquet of the saints. I. *The place*—on the further shore. II. *The hour*—when time's night is passed. III. *The host*—the glorified Jesus. IV. *The company*—the multitude of the redeemed from among men. V. *The feast*—gifts of heaven's grace and fruits of earth's toil.

Section II —THE CONVERSATION WITH PETER

Chap. XXI. Ver. 15-23

Exposition

Ver. 15. So when they had broken their fast Not before, since Christ by this manifestation of grace and goodness towards His disciples would prepare for the scene to follow, in which Peter should first be reminded of his fall as well as humbled on its account, and next reinstated in office as leader among the apostles and guardian of the flock. **Jesus saith to Simon Peter** The preceding meal had probably been partaken of in silence (Bengel), the notion that during its course Christ had carried on a conversation with the other disciples, and only at its close turned to Peter (Tholuck) being unlikely. **Simon, *son* of John:** cf. i. 42. That Christ says not "Peter" has been interpreted as pointing to the confidence Peter had lost through his fall (De Wette, Brückner), which is perhaps asserting too much ; or as only indicating Christ's usual mode of addressing His disciple (Lücke, Westcott), with the deep solemnity of feeling under which Christ spoke (Meyer, Tholuck), which on the other hand is affirming too little ; but was probably designed to remind Peter of his natural state, out of which he had been called into the apostolate, and into which again he had relapsed by his fall (Lange, Godet), or, omitting any reference to his fall, to set forth the human presupposition of the apostolical calling (Luthardt, Alford), as it were to remand the apostle into his original condition that he might be exalted out of it into a new dignity (Hengstenberg). **Lovest thou Me more than these?** Not more than thou lovest these fish or these things pertaining to a fisher's occupation (Bolten), or these thy brethren, but more than these love Me? The question was intended to remind Peter not of the pre-eminent love he had just exhibited in casting himself into the sea (Hengstenberg), or had manifested before his fall—a love which besides was henceforth to be expected of him (Meyer), but of the presumptuous superiority he had once claimed (Godet, Lücke, Lange, Tholuck, Luthardt, and others). Against this has been urged that Peter's boastful saying (Matt. xxvi. 33 ; Mark xiv. 29) is not recorded in this gospel—an argument against the Johannine authorship of the words (De Wette); but this merely proves that the Evangelist presupposed the existence of, as well as the acquaintance of his readers with, the synoptical tradition (Brückner). **He saith unto Him, yea, Lord, Thou knowest that I love Thee!** Contrast the "love" Christ demands with that Peter claims to have ; the former (ἀγαπᾶν) a love full of reverence, commensurate with the worthiness of the object loved,—in this case such as formed the basis and spring of the Christian life ; the latter (φιλεῖν) a love containing more of personal attachment ;—the former more a matter of the will ; the latter more a matter of passion (Luthardt). **He saith unto him, Feed My lambs,** ἀρνία, *little lambs*, signifying not immature Christians or children (Euthymius), or the laity as distinguished from the clergy (Catholic interpreters), but the whole flock of believers characterized as objects of Christ's tender love and solicitude (Godet, Luthardt, Meyer, and others) ; corresponding to which the word employed to depict the apostolic office (βόσκειν) conveys the motion of tenderly nurturing.

16. He saith to him again a second time, πάλιν δεύτερον : cf. πάλιν ἐκ δευτέρου (Matt. xxvi. 42), **Simon, *son* of John, lovest thou Me?** Still retaining ἀγαπᾶν, but dropping out 'more than these,' which Peter in his reply had studiously omitted, probably because he understood and felt the rebuke they conveyed. **He saith unto Him, Yea, Lord, Thou knowest that I love Thee.** As before adhering to the milder, more human and emotional term for love, and appealing for confirmation of his truthfulness to the Lord's knowledge of his heart. **He saith unto him, Feed My sheep.** πρόβατα or προβάτια, *little sheep* (B C, Tischendorf, Godet, Luthardt), again designates the flock, as a whole, consisting of individuals all requiring common guidance, to which allusion is made in ποίμανε, the term commonly employed to describe the whole, but more particularly the guiding, office of a shepherd.

17. He saith unto him the third time, Simon, *son* **of John, Lovest thou Me?** —this time adopting Peter's φιλεῖν. **Peter was grieved because He said unto him the third time, Lovest thou Me?** The thrice repeated question could not fail to remind Peter that Christ had not forgotten the threefold denial; its recurrence for a third time after Peter's strong protestations of affection and appeals to Christ's knowledge might suggest that Christ was still not satisfied as to his (Peter's) sincerity; the substitution of Peter's word (φιλεῖν) for Christ's (ἀγαπᾶν) was calculated to show that not even the lower sort of attachment claimed by Peter was beyond suspicion. **And He said unto Him, Lord Thou knowest all things, Thou knowest that I love Thee.** Explained according to xvi. 30, the first clause in Peter's answer must not be restricted to an acknowledgment of Christ's unlimited and intuitive knowledge of the human heart (Meyer, Luthardt), but extended to signify a confession and recognition of Christ's absolute omniscience (Bengel, Godet, Tholuck, Hengstenberg, Lange, Alford, Westcott); the second is an admission of Christ's immediate observation of the state of Peter's heart. On both of these Peter now casts himself for witness to his sincerity. **Jesus saith unto him, Feed My sheep,** or *little sheep,* the word in this case being πρόβατια (A B C, Tischendorf, Luthardt, Meyer, Lange, Brückner, Alford, Westcott and Hort); yet the reading sheep, πρόβατα, is not without support (א D, Godet).

18. Verily, verily, I say unto Thee A strictly Johannine mode of expression, *gravissima formula* (Bengel)

which the risen Christ uses (exactly as in the days of His humiliation) to introduce a solemn communication relative to Peter's future. **when thou wast young,** lit., *younger,* sc. than now. Peter had been for some time married (Matt. viii. 14), and was probably in middle life. The period embraced under 'younger' need not be limited to the time when he was not yet in Christ's service (Luthardt), or the youthful stage of his discipleship (Lange); but may legitimately include his whole previous life up to the then present or even to the borders of old age (Bengel, Godet, Brückner, Hengstenberg), the point of contrast being found in the succeeding clause— "When thou shalt be old." **thou girdest thyself and walkedst whither thon wouldest** Descriptive of complete personal freedom, such as pertains to opening youth or mature manhood before the powers of mind and body have begun to decay; there is no ground for discovering in the language an allusion to the arbitrariness and self-willedness of Peter's earlier religious life (Bleek, Hengstenberg, Lange). **but when thou shalt be old** An indirect promise that Peter should attain to an advanced age: cf. 2 Peter i. 14. Tradition places his martyrdom at A.D. 64. **thou shalt stretch forth thy hands,** in the helplessness of age (Gurlitt, Olshausen), in meek passivity of suffering (Luthardt, Westcott), in humble submission to the power of another (Lange, Meyer), or to external constraints generally (Stier), in preparation for being girded by another (Godet, Meyer); or, what seems best, in suffering death by crucifixion (Bengel, Brückner, Lücke, Tholuck, Hengstenberg). **and another shall gird thee** If the former clause refer to the extending of the arms in crucifixion, this will contain an allusion either to the fastening of the criminal to the cross—*Tunc Petrus ab altero vincitur, cum cruci adstringitur* (Tertullian, Scorp. c. 15). The Gospel of Nicodemus relates (c. 10) that before Christ was crucified He was bound with a linen cloth round the loins;—or to the binding of the hands and feet in order to facilitate nailing. If the former clause be explained only as a preparation for this, then the girding by another will point to the binding of one who has been condemned to death. **and carry thee whither thou wouldest not,** viz., to the place of execution. The idea of a violent death is generally recognized as lying in the third clause ; the only uncertainty is as to whether the stretching out of the hands refers to crucifixion. Against this is urged— (1) That by separating this clause from that which speaks of girding the completeness of the parallel between the two members of the verse is broken,—" When thou shalt be old," forming an antithesis to "when thou wast younger" ; "thou shalt stretch forth thy hands and another shall gird thee," contrasting with "thou girdedst thyself" ; and "another shall carry thee," etc., standing over against "thou walkedst," etc. (2) That by viewing the stretching forth of the hands as an allusion to crucifixion, the order of events appears to be inversely narrated, the natural succession being to carry away to the place of execution, to bind to the cross, and to stretch out the hands upon the transverse beam. But in favour of regarding the stretching forth of the hands as an allusion to crucifixion may be stated : (1) That the mere fact that a person must lift up his arms before being bound seems too insignificant to be recorded in a narrative so full of solemnity. (2) That crucifixion is mentioned first because on that Christ designed to lay emphasis, the girding and leading away coming in with perfect propriety and naturalness afterwards to complete the description by depicting the usual preliminaries to that mode of execution. (3) That John, who wrote after Peter's death, seemed to see in its manner, which tradition says was by crucifixion (Euseb. H. E. ii. 25 ; iii. 1), a fulfilment of our Lord's words. (4) That if the stretching forth of the hands do not refer to crucifixion, then no indication is given of the particular kind of death by which Peter should glorify God, but only a general hint that he should die by violence.

19. **Now this He spake, signifying by what manner of death he should glorify God.** Cf. xii. 33 ; xviii. 32, in the first of which death by crucifixion, and in the second of which death by violence generally is pointed out. In the language of subsequent martyrology, probably suggested by this verse, "to glorify God" became the current expression for dying as a martyr. John's statement as to the import of Christ's language does not imply that it was comprehended by him or even by Peter at the time ; to the Evangelist it became luminous after Peter's death. **And when He had said this, He saith unto him, Follow Me.** This command previously given by Christ to him and others (i. 43 ; Matt. viii. 22 ; ix. 9 ; xix. 21 : cf. Matt. iv. 19, 20), and now solemnly repeated, can only have meant that Peter should henceforth follow Christ, in the exercise of his apostolic office, as far as to a death of martyrdom (Ewald, Luthardt, Meyer), and even of crucifixion (Chrysostom, Euthymius, Theophylact) : cf. xiii. 36. At the same time Christ may have given it a symbolical expression by withdrawing from the group and calling Peter to follow (Hengstenberg, Godet), or, if Christ was now preparing to depart, Peter seeing this may have interpreted the command literally and supposed Christ desired him to come aside. This, while explaining Peter's action next related, will harmonize the Lord's utterance in this verse with its repetition in ver. 22.

20. **Peter,** undaunted by the communication just received, which he perfectly understood to foreshadow a life of patient endurance terminating in a violent death, **turning about,** with his customary vivacity, and (as the clause presupposes) rendering a literal obedience to Christ's call, i.e. going after Him, **seeth the disciple whom Jesus loved** (cf. xiii. 23 ; xix. 26) **following,** because of the intimacy which had previously existed between him and Jesus (Bengel, Godet, Luthardt), an intimacy referred to in the ensuing clause ; or, more probably attracted by the same force that impelled Peter, viz., love to the risen Lord ; **which also leaned back on his breast at the supper, and said, Lord, who is he that betrayeth Thee ?** Cf. xiii. 23 ff. Added to show how since the time to which this incident refers Peter and John had changed places in respect of boldness, John then asking

Christ for Peter, Peter now inquiring at Christ concerning John (Chrysostom, Theophylact, Olshausen) ; rather to explain the motive of Peter's question, which was not jealousy (Meyer), but perhaps curiosity (Tholuck), based upon a reasonable expectation that one so beloved as the Evangelist should also have a career marked out for him ; or to account for John's following Christ unrequested (Bengel, Godet, Luthardt, Lange, Westcott).

21. Peter therefore, probably interpreting John's following as a silent question (Luthardt, Westcott), **seeing him**, and the sight prompting the question, **saith to Jesus**, with reverence towards his Lord, and with love for John, but also with characteristic forwardness, not unmingled with boldness, **Lord, and what shall this man do?** lit., *Lord, but this man, what?* i.e. of him, What shall he do or suffer, *Domine, hic autem quid* (Vulgate).

22. Jesus saith unto him, with a tone and in words that must have told Peter he had been indiscreet with his hasty and over bold interrogation, **If I will that he tarry till I come**, not till I return from this walk and conversation with thee (Paulus) ; or till I come to lead him out into apostolic activity (Theophylact) ; or till I come at the destruction of Jerusalem (Theophylact, Bengel, Luthardt), or at the beginning of the conflict between Christ and Rome which began under Domitian (Hengstenberg) ; or in the Apocalyptic visions I shall bestow upon him (Ebrard, Stier) ; or at death to give him a peaceful departure (Lampe, Olshausen, Grotius, Lange, Ewald) ; but till I come in my glorious parousia (Kuinoel, Meyer, Tholuck, Weiss, Godet, Brückner, Westcott). John outlived all the comings alluded to except the last two. As death is a coming of the Lord, Peter survived till the Lord's advent no less than

John. Hence the second coming at the end of time can alone be intended. The emphasis lies on "abiding" rather than on "coming." That John should "abide" instead of "following" in the sense assigned to Peter, though hypothetically expressed, was indirectly implied. How long that "abiding" should continue Christ did not assert. He only suggested it should be long— if till the parousia was not a matter that concerned Peter, as the next words declared. **what *is that* to thee?** That comes not within the scope of thy duty or even interest to know. Thy task lies in yielding obedience to the call I have given. **follow thou Me**, or, preserving the order of emphasis, *thou*, as distinguished from him and others, *follow Me*.

23. This saying, word, or legend, to be after mentioned, **therefore went abroad among the brethren**, or, went out to the brethren (cf. Matt. ix. 26), not from the Apocalypse (Baur, Hilgenfeld), but from Christ's statement in ver. 22, **that that disciple should not die**. Tradition mentions that John, though seemingly dead and buried only slumbered in his grave at Ephesus, and moved the dust with his breathing (see Augustine, *in loco*) ; but whether that tradition arose directly out of Christ's words or was a farther development of the legend here referred to cannot be ascertained. **yet Jesus said not unto him that he should not die ; but, if I will that he tarry till I come, what is that to thee?** The Evangelist disposes of the foolish story in the simplest way by calling attention to the exact words used by Christ on the occasion. The circumstance that the story needed correction, because it had not been refuted by fact, shows that this chapter was written before John's death, and therefore most likely by himself.

HOMILETICS

VER. 15-17.—THE RESTORATION OF PETER.
I. **The Time :** ver. 15. 1. *After the resurrection.* This delay, if (1) seemingly inevitable, since when Peter fell Christ was in the grasp of His enemies, was yet (2) not absolutely necessary, since Christ might have absolved Peter from the cross as He prayed for His murderers, or sent a message of forgiveness to him by the lips of John, while (3) it was extremely appropriate as giving time

for Peter to bewail his guilt and for the true enormity of his sin to be set in clear light by the resurrection which declared Christ to be the Son of God with power (Rom. i. 4). 2. *After the miracle.* By this Christ proclaimed Himself the sole Creator and only Lord of the Christian Church ; and not until this had been made apparent was the repentant apostle reponed. 3. *After the banquet.* This had lessons for the whole company (see previous Homilies), and it was well that these should be learnt by the seven collectively and singly before Christ proceeded to restore His servant.

II. **The Manner** : ver. 15-17. 1. *A pointed address*—Simon, son of John ! Either (1) Christ's usual mode of speaking to His disciple (Matt. xvii.25 ; Mark xiv. 37 ; Luke xxii. 31), whom He appears to have only once called Peter (Luke xxii. 34) ; or (2) designed to remind Peter of the original ground of natural condition out of which he had been raised by grace, but into which he had temporarily lapsed through his fall—and that his present restoration no less than his former election was a matter of grace on Christ's part, not of merit or works on his. 2. *A threefold question*—Lovest thou Me ? (1) Personal. The question concerned Peter. Not that love was not demanded equally of his companions, but meantime the inquiry was directed to him. Christ deals with His followers as individuals—accepts, commands, guides, comforts, searches, rebukes, and rewards them one by one (Is. xxvii. 12). (2) Lofty. It related not to Peter's knowledge, activity, service, capability, humility, courage, hope, or even faith, but solely to his love for the risen Lord. This the essence of religion. Without personal devotion to Jesus other qualities are destitute of value. Nor is it superficial, transient, and sentimental affection Christ solicits from the hearts of His disciples, but love, pure, exalted, spiritual, in some degree commensurate with the dignity of Him upon whom it is bestowed (xvii. 26 ; 1 Pet. i. 8). (3) Urgent. This evident from its threefold repetition, which must have made it plain to Peter and those who listened to the conversation that of all Christian graces this was the least dispensable (1 Cor. xvi. 22). (4) Searching. Intended to put Peter on a course of self-examination as it doubtless put his companions and ought also to put us. The process may be painful at the first to us as it was to Peter (ver. 17), but where faithfully conducted it is salutary. Happy they in whom it issues as it did with Peter : " Lord ! Thou knowest all things : Thou knowest that I love Thee ! " (5) Tender. Though at first the love demanded was high and spiritual, yet, considerate of His servant's weakness, Christ closed His interrogation by graciously accepting the lower and more human affection of which that servant was conscious—not as a substitute for, but as a preparation leading up to, that more exalted emotion in which the renewed soul's love to Christ will ultimately culminate, bloom, and shine. 1. *A threefold commission*—Feed My lambs ; tend My sheep ; feed My little sheep. (1) The affection Christ has for His people. They are His lambkins whom He carries in His bosom (Is. xl. 11), His sheep for whom He laid down His life (x. 15), His little sheep, His younglings for whose nurture He now provides (Ezek. xxxiv. 23). (2) The duty Christ's under-shepherds owe them. To feed them carefully, with food convenient for them, the elder (sheep) with wholesome words, even the words of Our Lord Jesus Christ (1 Tim. vi. 3), that they may be nourished up in the words of faith and of the good doctrine (1 Tim. iv. 6), the younger (lambkins) with the sincere milk of the word, that they may grow thereby (1 Pet. ii. 2) ;—lovingly, as those that belong to their Master, and are regarded by Him with affection ;—tenderly, as requiring gentle treatment ;—regularly, as those needing to have their portions in due season. To tend them, doing towards them all the offices of a faithful and skilful shepherd—not only feeding them in the fold, but leading them out into the rich pastures of divine truth and beside the still waters of heavenly grace, guarding them in times of danger, cherishing them in seasons of affliction, and generally watching over them as those who must one day render an account to Him who is the chief and the great Shepherd of the sheep (Heb. xiii. 17).

III. **The Extent** : ver. 15-17. To what was Peter restored ! To what he held before. Hence 1. *Not to primacy over the church.* This erroneously supposed by Romanists to have been conferred on Peter by Christ when He said, "Thou art Peter, and upon this rock (*petra*) will I build My church" (Matt. xvi. 18). But the scene at the lake shows Peter was not entrusted with any primacy over his brethren, or lordship over the church; and Peter himself certainly never understood that he was (see 1 Pet. v. 1-4). 2. *But to apostleship within the church.* The duties of the office as above explained were not such as only he was expected to perform. Nor can it be argued that he alone was entrusted with them. At least the qualification declared requisite for their performance, love, was possessed not by him alone (see ver. 15). On what ground then can it be reasoned that they who shared Peter's love to Christ did not also share his commission? Does it not rather seem as if, so far from Peter being exalted over his brethren, he was only now for the first time since his fall replaced on a platform of equality with them?

Learn 1. No follower of Christ need expect to be employed in his Master's service, so long as he allows himself in sin. 2. If a follower of Christ does lapse into great transgression, he will certainly be brought to repentance and confession before he is restored to his Lord's favour. 3. The recovery and restoration of a backslider may sometimes be preceded by rebukes and humiliations. 4. Under these rebukes, however painful, the follower of Christ should not faint, but like Peter should accept them with meekness and humility. 5. The grand qualification for service in Christ's church is love to Christ's person. 6. Christ's people serve a Master from whom nothing can be hid. 7. The chief shepherd of the Christian flock is Christ, and from Him alone undershepherds hold their commissions.

Ver. 17. Love to the risen Lord. I. The innermost essence of personal religion. II. The only reparation a pardoned soul can make for sin. III. The indispensable prerequisite for communion with Him. IV. The most needful qualification for engaging in His service. V. The certain highway to promotion in His church and kingdom.

VER. 18-23.—LIGHT UPON PETER'S WAY.

I. Peter's Future Destiny disclosed: ver. 18, 19. 1. *The manner of this disclosure.* (1) Solemnly—"Verily, verily, I say unto you" (ver. 18). (2) Authoritatively—"I," the faithful and true witness, whom thyself hast just acknowledged to know all things—"say unto you." (3) Feelingly. If Peter was not deeply affected at hearing, there can be small question Christ was not unmoved at making the communication. 2. *The form of this disclosure.* Not in literal but in veiled speech. Peter had once been young (even then was not extremely old), and had been able to gird himself as well as shape his goings out and comings in in accordance with his own sweet will. And so for years it might continue. But the time would arrive when old and feeble he should not be able to exercise the same free and independent activity, when, as an aged person stretched forth his hands in helplessness and relied on the services of others for girding and going, he also would stretch forth his hands and another would gird him and carry him whither he would not. 3. *The import of this disclosure.* (1) Indirectly a promise that Peter would attain to a ripe old age, after having passed through a life of honoured usefulness as a shepherd of the flock of Christ—a promise literally fulfilled, tradition placing Peter's martyrdom at A.D. 64. (2) Directly, a prediction that Peter's glorious career would terminate in martyrdom, probably in crucifixion, though this is not absolutely certain from the language (see Exposition). 4. *The reason of this disclosure.* Why did Christ unveil the future to Peter alone of all the apostles? Perhaps (1) to indicate to him the necessity of maintaining in a state of liveliness and ardour the love he had just professed; (2) to furnish him with an opportunity of wiping out the inglorious disgrace of his denial by doing what he had once boastfully declared his willingness, but quickly shown his inability, to do (xiii. 37); (3) to set before him the highest honour it was possible for a follower of Christ to win, that of having fellowship with Him, not merely in publishing, but also in dying for the truth (Matt. v. 10-12; Luke vi. 22,

23 ; Acts v. 41 ; Rom. viii. 17 ; Phil. i. 29 ; 2 Tim. ii. 12 ; Heb. xiii. 13 ; 1 Pet. iii. 14).

II. **Peter's Present Duty declared :** ver. 19. 1. *The symbolical action.* Having announced to the apostle the character of the end awaiting him Our Lord further said to him, Follow Me ! at the moment (it may be) suiting action to the word by turning and making as if about to depart. 2. *The spiritual significance.* If this suggestion be correct, it is still true that Christ intended more than to invite Peter aside from the company. His summons was a call to follow Him (1) in official service, (2) by personal imitation, (3) as far as to death, (4) through the agonies of martyrdom, and (5) into the world of glory that lay beyond.

III. **Peter's Characteristic Impetuosity restrained :** ver. 20-23. 1. *Peter's question*—"Lord, and this man ! what of him ?" (ver. 21.) (1) The occasion of it—seeing John following, attracted no doubt by Christ's love for him ("the disciple whom Jesus loved") and impelled by his love for Christ ("who also leaned," etc.). (2) The motive of it. Not jealousy—a suggestion unworthy of the situation. Perhaps curiosity—from which the best of saints are not always free. As likely, friendly interest in John. ·(2) The wrong of it. Not irreverent towards Christ whom he addressed as Lord ! or unkind towards John though he did say ' this man,' or sinful in itself, seeing Christ had once said, 'If ye shall ask Me anything in My name that will I do ' (xiv. 13), it was irrelevant, having no bearing on the subject in hand, Peter's duty, not John's destiny, and inquisitive, manifesting a concern in the affairs of others not required by brotherly love, if not bordering on the presumptuous, as seeking to be informed of secret things which belong to God (Deut. xxix. 29). 2. *Jesus's reply*—"If I will that he tarry till I come, what *is that* to thee ?" (ver. 22). (1) What it meant to Peter—rebuke. It did not belong to him, Peter, to arrange, nor ought it to concern him to know (Acts i. 7) the future destinies of those who might labour by his side within the church ; these were understood by the Master they served, and would be disclosed at the times and in the ways which to that Master might appear best ; meantime his present duty should suffice for him without intermeddling with high problems of mortal destiny ; and that duty was summed up in the two words—"Follow Me !" (2) What it signified for John. Not that he should not die ; merely that it might be Christ's will that he, John, should tarry long upon the field of labour, even till Christ came again—Christ did not say that *was* but only that *might be* His will with regard to John ; and that if it was, that was a matter which exclusively concerned John.

Learn 1. To Christ alone pertains the prerogative of appointing to His servants their respective spheres and experiences in the church. 2. The future destinies of Christ's servants no less than their present duties are known to Him, having been prearranged and prescribed by Him. 3. For the happiness of Christ's servants it is enough to apprehend present duty without ascertaining beforehand future destiny. 4. Secret things belong unto God, to men only things that are revealed. 5. While Christ's people may exercise boldness in making known unto Him their requests, there are limits beyond which they must not pass in asking. 6. The strongest propelling force that can act upon the Christian heart is love to Christ. 7. Christ's people are not exempt from mistakes in interpreting His words. 8. When Christ's words are partly dark, it is wise to adhere to that in them which is plain and to wait for further light.

Ver. 19. The saint's calling. I. High—proceeding from the risen Lord (Phil. iii. 14). II. Holy—to follow in the footsteps of Christ (2 Tim. i. 9 ; 1 Pet. ii. 21). III. Hard—as far as to death (Matt. xvi. 24 ; Rev. ii. 10). IV. Heavenly—conducting to glory (Heb. iii. 1 ; 1 Thess. ii. 12).

Ver. 20. Followers of Jesus. 1. The *spontaneous* and *inquiring* follower—Andrew (i. 38). 2. The *prompt* and *obedient* follower—Philip (i. 43). 3. The *guileless* and *sincere* follower—Nathanael (i. 47). 4. The *doubting* and *despondent* follower—Thomas (xi. 15 ; xx. 25). 5. The *self-seeking* and *temporary* follower

—the Galileans (vi. 66). 6. The *deceitful* and *treacherous* follower—Judas (vi. 70, 71). 7. The *impetuous* and *brave* follower—Peter (xiii. 37 ; xviii. 10). 8. The *close* and *loving* follower—John (xviii. 15).

SECTION III.—THE CONCLUDING ATTESTATION

CHAP. XXI. VER. 24, 25

EXPOSITION

Ver. 24. **This,** the disciple whom Jesus loved (ver. 20-23), **is the disciple who beareth witness,** lit., *bearing witness* — because still living (Meyer, Godet), though this is not necessarily implied (cf. i. 15)—**of these things,** not the appendix alone (Meyer, Tholuck, Lange), or the gospel alone without the appendix (Ebrard), but the two together (Lücke, Brückner, Godet), **and wrote these things,** not necessarily by his own hand (cf. Rom. xvi. 22 ; 1 Cor. xvi. 21): **and we know,** οἴδαμεν not οἶδα μέν (Chrysostom, Theophylact); the 'we' being not the Evangelist who speaks out of conscious fellowship with his readers at the time (Meyer, Hengstenberg) — he would probably have written as in xix. 35, κἀκεῖνος οἶδεν, but the friends of the author, the Ephesian elders, at whose suggestion probably the gospel was written and with whom it was deposited for publication (Godet, Lange, Luthardt, Westcott, and others), and who perhaps in sending it forth to the churches deemed it proper to accompany it with an official certification : **that his witness is true,** ἀληθής i.e. true in point of fact, i.e. honest and veracious (cf. v. 31, 32 : viii. 14, and contr. xix. 35).—Note. *Who was the disciple whom Jesus loved ?* 1. One of the twelve (ver. 20). Hence probably he was neither of the unnamed disciples (ver. 2). 2. One of the seven (ver. 2). Therefore, either Thomas, Nathanael, or one of the sons of Zebedee, since he cannot be Peter, from whom he is distinguished (ver. 20). 3. Not James, who died too early to have been the author of this gospel (Acts xii. 2). 4. Hardly Thomas, since (1) the disciple whom Jesus loved frequently appears in company with Peter (xiii. 23 ; xviii. 15 ;

xx. 2 ; xxi. 7 ; cf. Acts iii. 1 ; iv. 13), Thomas never ; (2) the disciple whom Jesus loved had been at the sepulchre (xx. 2), whereas Thomas apparently had not ; (3) it is little likely Christ would have commended His mother to one who was to prove himself so slow to believe ; (4) Thomas would in this case be distinguished by two appellatives, a thing unusual in this gospel. 4. The choice lies between Nathanael and John. But Nathanael also is distinguished by a second name (i. 47), and by a clause descriptive of his birthplace—both rendering it unlikely that he should have a third designation. 5. Whence the natural deduction is that John was the disciple whom Jesus loved. 6. This conclusion is confirmed by the impression made on impartial minds by other passages in which this disciple is named. 7. It is borne out by the almost unanimous witness of ecclesiastical tradition.

Ver. 25. **And there are also many other things which,** ἃ as to matter of fact ; if ὅσα, as to quantity, **Jesus did, the which if they should be written** every one, or *one by one* (cf. Acts xxi. 19), **I suppose**—not placed in John's mouth by the unknown composer of this verse (Meyer), but a colloquialism used either by John himself, from whom the verse proceeds (Bengel, Lange, Hengstenberg, Alford), or by the Ephesian elders who added ver. 24 (Luthardt, Paley), or by the person who acted as their scribe or depositary, perhaps Papias (Godet)—**that even the world itself would not contain the books that should be written,** lit., *the books written.* A bold hyperbole, not to be set down as a too emphasized (Godet), or inharmonious and unspiritual (Meyer) exaggeration, not corresponding to the simplicity of

John (Lücke, Brückner); since we make use of a hundred similar expressions without their hyperbolism being called in question (Lange), and this hyperbole in particular answers to a deep truth, viz., the utter impossibility of exhausting the significance of Christ's human life (Westcott, Milligan, and Moulton), while it may also have been designed to vindicate the comparatively fragmentary character of the gospel against early objectors (Alford).

Note :—1. *The genuineness of this chapter has been assailed* (Grotius, Paulus, Lücke, De Wette, Bleek, Baur, Keim, and others) on the following grounds—(1.) The closing verses in chapter xx. seem the natural termination of the evangelist's work. But the Evangelist may have purposed by their insertion to indicate merely that the main body of his writing was finished, viz., that which had been occupied in tracing the earthly history of Jesus ; and even if at first he regarded his task as concluded that would not prove he did not afterwards append the present supplement. (2.) The admission of the non-Johannine origin of verses 24, 25 appears to carry with it that of the spuriousness of the entire chapter. This, however, is not self-evident. Although few doubt the former, the latter is denied by many (Lampe, Kuinoel, Tholuck, Olshausen, Ebrard, Godet, Luthardt, Hengstenberg, Meyer, Alford, Westcott, Milligan, and Moulton), which shows that the two portions of the chapter are not so connected that the fortunes of the larger must infallibly be determined by those of the smaller. (3.) The scene of the Manifestation it records, viz., Galilee, is out of harmony with that of those related in the preceding chapter, all of which happened in Jerusalem or its vicinity, and accords badly with the instruction given to the apostles by our Lord on His first appearing in the upper room, that they should "tarry in the city" (Luke xxiv. 49). But Christ before His death promised that after rising He would meet them in Galilee (Matt. xxvi. 32), and the angels at the sepulchre directed the women to tell the disciples generally, and Peter in particular, that Christ went before them thither, and would meet them

there (Matt. xxvii. 7 ; Mark xvi. 7). (4.) The self-characterization which occurs in ver. 20 is regarded as unbecoming, and therefore not likely to have proceeded from John. But the same designation of himself is ascribed to John at the supper-table (xiii. 23), while its supposed want of modesty and humility depends entirely on the spirit in which it was written. (5.) The chapter wears the aspect of having been written after John's death (ver. 23) as well as Peter's (ver. 19). But while at the date when this gospel was composed Peter was dead, it is doubtful if any hint that Peter was no longer alive can be extracted from ver. 19, and it is scarcely doubtful that ver. 23 presupposes John still lived. (6.) The reference to the second advent of Christ (ver. 23) is pronounced foreign to John's doctrinal system, which it is said, makes no mention of the *parousia*. This, however, is not correct : see xiv. 3, and cf. v. 28. (7.) A want of clearness in some parts (ver. 5, 9, 10, 11, 12, 18, 20, 21), combined with a trifling circumstantiality in other parts (ver. 3, 4, 8, 11), has been adduced in evidence of non-Johannine authorship. But the same darkness, arising from a love of symbolism (xiii. 27, 29, 30), and the same attention to small details (cf. iv. 6 ; vi. 23) characterize the preceding gospel, while it should not be forgotten that judgments on an author's obscurity of thought or non-perspicuity of style are largely dependent on the subjective qualifications of the reader. (8.) Words and phrases in this chapter are distinctly non-Johannine, as *e.g.* ἐπὶ τῆς θαλάσσης (ver. 1), instead of ἐπὶ τῇ θαλασσῇ, ἔρχεσθαι σύν (ver. 3), instead of ἀκολουθεῖν, πρωΐα (ver. 4) instead of πρωΐ; ἐξετάζειν (ver. 12) instead of εἰπεῖν, as in iv. 27. But over against these are words and phrases as decidedly Johannine, as e.g. μετὰ ταῦτα (ver. 1): cf. iii. 12 ; οὐδέν after the verb (ver. 3): cf. iii. 27 ; v. 19 ; οὐ μέντοι (ver. 4) : cf. iv. 27 ; while the whole passage bears a Johannean stamp. 2. *There are not wanting considerations which vouch for its genuineness* : (1) The chapter appears in all existing MSS. of this gospel. (2.) The Evangelist's designation of himself without using his name is quite in accordance with the style of the author of the preceding gospel. (3.) The contents of the chapter form a fitting termination to the book (see Exposition and Homiletics). (4.) It is not difficult to find a motive for its being appended probably at a later period than that at

which the earlier portions were composed (see Exposition). (5.) The later time of writing may sufficiently explain its slightly altered style.

HOMILETICS

Ver. 24, 25. The Gospel of St. John.
I. **Its Transcendent Theme.** "The things which Jesus did." 1. Their *number.* "Many." 2. Their *variety.* "Other." 3. Their *importance.* So deep had been the impression made by them that they were even then remembered and could have been written down. 4. Their *significance.* The world would not contain the books that might and should be written about them.

II. **Its Unnamed Author.** The disciple whom Jesus loved. That this was John.—1. *The gospel indirectly attests*—cf. ver. 24 note, and see Introduction ; and 2, *ecclesiastical tradition confirms* (see Introduction).

III. **Its Veracious Character.** The author's witness is true. 1. *The testimony of the author's own consciousness*—if ver. 24 be authentic. 2. *The testimony of his contemporaries,* probably the Ephesian elders—if ver. 24 be non-Johannine.

Lesson. Gratitude. 1. To God for His Son, Jesus Christ. 2. To Jesus Christ for the things which He did. 3. To the Holy Spirit for this sublime gospel.

HOMILETICAL INDEX